The International Guide to
Securities Market Indices

The International Guide to
Securities Market Indices

HENRY SHILLING

International Publishing
Chicago

Fitzroy Dearborn Publishers
Chicago, London

TABLE OF CONTENTS

ABOUT THE AUTHOR XI

ACKNOWLEDGMENTS XIII

1 INTRODUCTION 1

OVERVIEW.. 1
THE UNIVERSE OF INDICES 2
SELECTION CRITERIA 3

2 USES AND APPLICATIONS 5

MARKET PERFORMANCE... 5
PERFORMANCE BENCHMARK/STANDARD... 5
PORTFOLIO STRUCTURE, RISK AND STYLE ANALYSIS.................................... 5
DERIVATIVE INSTRUMENTS.. 6
PASSIVE INSTEMENT STRATEGIES/INDEXING 7
REGULATORY REPORTING AND DISCLOSURE 7
ASSET ALLOCATION 8
INCENTIVE COMPENSATION ARRAGEMENTS... 8
TECHNICAL ANALYSIS.. 8
AUDIT, SURVEILLANCE AND CONTROL.. 8

3 REASONS FOR GROWTH OF INDICES 11

MEASURES FOR MANAGER SELECTION AND EVALUATION 11
GROWTH OF MUTUAL FUNDS 12
GROWTH OF INDEXATION 12

New Markets, Investment Styles and Security Types..............................13
New Stock Exchanges 13
Computer Technology 14
Promotional Considerations, Enhancement to Reputation and Revenue Source.. 14

4 Index Construction and Maintenance.................................15

Index Composition 15
Selection Criteria 16
    Markets 16
    Market Coverage 16
    Security Type 16
    Economic Sector/Industry Representation 17
    Credit Quality 17
    Size 17
    Trading Activity 17
    Financial and Operating Characteristics 17
    Data Quality 17
    Factors Unique to the Institutional Marketplace 17
        Float/Cross Ownership 17
        Liquidity...18
Selection Methods/Techniques 18
    Rank-Order Method 18
    Opmimization Technique 18
Index Maintenance...18
    Pricing/Foreign Exchange 19
    Other Considerations...19
Methods of Weighting 20
    Market Value and Price-Weighted Methods.....................................20
    Equal-Weighted Method 21
Methods of Averaging 22
Index Formulas...22
    Simple Aggregative of Actual Prices Index Formula 22
    The Goemetric mean index Formula 23
    An Agggregate of Prices Times Quantities Index Formula or Weighted
        Aggregative Compite Index Formula 23
Total Rate of Return Computation 24
Selection of Base Date 25
Chain-Linking 25

5 Characteristics of Preferred Indices 27

6 Historial Highlights..29

7 GUIDE TO INDEX PROFILES: 35

DEFINITION OF TERMS 35
INDEX NAME 35
PERFORMANCE GRAPH 35
PERFORMANCE RECORD 35
INDEX VALUE 36
PRICE RETURN (%) 36
TOTAL RETURN (%) 36
CUMULATIVE (%) 36
MAXIMUM VALUE 36
MINIMUM VALUE 36
DATE 36
AVERAGE ANNUAL RATE OF RETURN (%) 36
COMPOUND ANNUAL RATE OF RETURN (%) 36
STANDARD DEVIATION (%) 36
SYNOPSIS 37
NUMBER OF ISSUES 37
MARKET VALUE 37
SECTION CRITERIA 37
BACKGROUND 37
BASE DATE 37
COMPUTATION METHODOLOGY 37
DERIVATIVE INSTRUMENTS 37
SUBINDICES 37
RELATED INDICES 38
REMARKS 38
PUBLISHER 38

8 INDEX PROFILES — STOCKS 39

NORTH AMERICA 39
BERMUDA 40
CANADA 42
MEXICO 54
UNITED STATES (U.S.) 58
ASIA/PACIFIC 261
AUSTRALIA 262
BANGLADESH 272
CHINA 274
HONG KONG 282
INDIA 290
INDONESIA 298
JAPAN 300
KOREA 322
MALAYSIA 332
NEPAL 338
NEW ZEALAND 340
PAKISTAN 348
PHILIPPINES 350
SINGAPORE 352
SRI LANKA 360

TAIWAN	362
THAILAND	368
ASIA/PACIFIC REGIONAL	**371**
ASIA	372
ASIA/PACIFIC	374
EAST ASIA/PACIFIC	376
EUROPE	**379**
AUSTRIA	380
BELGIUM	386
CYPRUS	396
CZECH REPUBLIC	398
DENMARK	400
FINLAND	404
FRANCE	408
GERMANY	416
GREECE	426
HUNGARY	428
ICELAND	430
IRELAND	432
ITALY	434
LUXEMBOURG	440
NETHERLANDS	442
NORWAY	450
POLAND	454
PORTUGAL	458
RUSSIA	466
SLOVAKIA	470
SPAIN	472
SWEDEN	476
SWITZERLAND	484
TURKEY	488
UNITED KINGDOM (UK)	490
EUROPE REGIONAL	**509**
EUROPE	510
NORDIC REGION	522
CENTRAL/ LATIN AMERICA	**525**
ARGENTINA	526
BARBADOS	530
BRAZIL	532
CHILE	538
COLOMBIA	542
COSTA RICA	544
ECUADOR	546
JAMAICA	548
PANAMA	550
PERU	552
TRINIDAD AND TOBAGO	556
VENEZUELA	558
CENTRAL/LATIN AMERICA REGIONAL	**561**
AFRICA/MIDDLE EAST	**565**
BOTSWANA	566
COTE D'IVIORE	568
GHANA	570
ISRAEL	572

JORDAN...576
KENYA...578
KUWAIT...580
MAURITIUS...582
MOROCCO...584
NAMBIA..586
NIGERIA...588
OMAN..590
SOUTH AFRICA..592
SWAZILAND...602
ZIMBABWE..604
WORLD 607

9 INDEX PROFILES — BONDS 643

NORTH AMERICA 643
    UNITED STATES..644
WORLD 689

10 INDEX PROFILES — MONEY MARKET INSTRUMENTS 723

NORTH AMERICA 723
    UNITED STATES..724
WORLD 737

11 INDEX PROFILES — COMMODITIES...743

NORTH AMERICA 743
    UNITED STATES..744

12 INDEX PROFILES — CONVERTIBLE SECURITIES 757

NORTH AMERICA 757
    UNITED STATES..758
WORLD 771

13 INDEX PROFILES — GUARANTEED INVESTMENT CONTRACTS 779

NORTH AMERICA 779
    UNITED STATES..780

14 INDEX PROFILES — MUTUAL FUNDS..789

NORTH AMERICA 789
    UNITED STATES..790

15 INDEX PROFILES — CLOSED-END FUNDS.................................821

NORTH AMERICA... 821
    UNITED STATES...822

16 INDEX PROFILES — REAL ESTATE..825

NORTH AMERICA... 825
    UNITED STATES...826
WORLD 835

17 INDEX PROFILES — MISCELLANEOUS 839

APPENDIX 1 ILLUSTRATIONS OF INDEX CALCULATIONS 843

APPENDIX 2 SUPPLEMENTAL SECURITIES MARKET INDICES.....849

APPENDIX 3 ADDITIONAL PERFORMANCE DATA 921

APPENDIX 4 GLOSSARY 939

APPENDIX 5 COMPREHENSIVE DIRECTORY OF INDICES 947

APPENDIX 6 INDICES BY ASSET CLASS/COUNTRY...................967

APPENDIX 7 DIRECTORY OF INDEX PUBLISHERS 985

APPENDIX 8 GLOBAL MARKET CAPITALIZATIONS 1003

APPENDIX 9 YEAR-END 1995 CURRENCY EXCHANGE RATES PER THE U.S. DOLLAR 1011

APPENDIX 10 INDEX-BASED DERIVATIVE INSTRUMENTS.........1013

APPENDIX 11 1994-1995 PERFORMANCE TABLES 1021

ABOUT THE AUTHOR

Henry Shilling is a Vice President/Senior Analyst with Moody's Investors Service[1] where he is responsible for analyzing and rating money market and bond mutual funds, other pooled investment vehicles and money management companies.

A graduate of Lehman College, CUNY, with a B.A. degree in Economics, he developed an interest in the subject of securities market indices in the course of evaluating alternative methodologies used for computing total rates of return on popular benchmarks and their impact on long-term performance results.

---

[1] The opinions expressed herein are those of the author and may not represent the views of Moody's Investors Service.

ACKNOWLEDGMENTS

A large number of persons and organizations provided information and assistance in the research and preparation of *The Guide to Securities Market Indices*, without whose help it would have been difficult, if not impossible, to complete the project in its present form. I am grateful to each and every one of them for responding to my inquiries and, at times, tight deadlines.

In particular, I'd like to personally thank the following individuals and organizations for their generosity, cooperation and valuable guidance.

American Stock Exchange-Michele Rirotolo
Amman Financial Market
Amsterdam EOE-Opteibeurs-Berney Van Stelten
Amsterdam Stock Exchange
Athens Stock Exchange-Ismini Chinou
Australian Stock Exchange-David Peacock and
    John Douglas
Banca Commerciale Italiana-Remo Antonielli
Banco Totta & Acores
Bankers Trust
Barcelona Stock Exchange
Bermuda Stock Exchange-Greg Wojciechowski
Bloomberg Financial Services
Bogota Stock Exchange-Oscar Camargo Nino
Bombay Stock Exchange-Dr. B.D. Ghonasgi and
    K.G. Kerekar
Bond Buyer
Bratislava Stock Exchange-Maria Kunikova
Bratislava Stock Exchange-Olga Porubska and   Maria Kunikova
Brussels Stock Exchange-D. Maertens
Budapest Stock Exchange-Veronika Ujvari and
    Agnes Halasz
Buenos Aires Stock Exchange-Osvaldo Luis Mignini
Business Times-Julie Wee
Capital Nepal-Sanjesh Koirala
Central Bureau of Statistics (Netherlands)
Chicago Board of Trade
Commerzbank AG-Peter Pietsch
Copenhagen Stock Exchange-Rolf Allen
Costa Rica Stock Exchange-Gretty Clausen G.

CS First Boston-Grace Kennedy
CS First Boston-Julia Baeva
Cyprus Investment and Securities Corporation
    Ltd. (CISCO)
Cyprus Stock Exchange-Constantinos N. Tymvios
Davy Stockbrokers
DBS Investment Research-Mano Sabnani
Delhi Stock Exchange Association Ltd-R.K.
    Pandey and S.K. Bajpai
Deutsche Borse AG -Magnus Olsson
Dhaka Stock Exchange-Sarker Ali Ashgar
Dow Jones-Humphrey Chang
Economic Daily News-W. P. Teng
Financial Times-Anthony Cloke
Frank Russell Co.-Tricia O'Connell and Christy Kitsu
FT-SE International-Maryann Boland
Goldman Sachs & Co.
Helsinki Stock Exchange-Mika Hayry
Hoare Govett-Andy Yeo
HSBC James Capel & Co. Limited-Adrian Tupper
HSI Services Ltd.-Tony Chiu
Iceland Stock Exchange
IDC
ING Baring Securities Limited-Nic Corry
International Finance Corp.-Stephanie Hughes
International Financial Review
International Organization of Securities Commissions
    (IOSCO)
Irish Stock Exchange-Colum Ring
Istanbul Stock Exchange-Hikmet Turlin and
    Gursel Akpinar

Jakarta Stock Exchange-Hetty Sual-Rumambi
Jamaica Stock Exchange-Errol C. Greene
Jeffries & Company, Inc.-Gregory S. Oberholtzer
    and Tim Osby
Johannesburg Stock Exchange-Michael Davidow, Debbie
Humphris, Darrell Till
JP Morgan Securities
Karachi Stock Exchange (Guaranteed) Ltd.-
    Mohammed Yacoob Memon
Knight-Ridder Financial-Bob Hafer
Korea Stock Exchange-Jae Doo Cho
Kuala Lumpur Stock Exchange-Winnie Choong
Kuwait Stock Exchange-Wafa Al Rasheed
Lehman Brothers-Steve Berkley
Lima Stock Exchange-Rafael Gomez de la Torre P.
Lipper Analytical Services, Inc.-Julie Friedlander
    and Joanne Jaeger
Lisbon Stock Exchange-M. Irene Carvalho
Lombard Odier and Cie-Ilana Regly
Lucas, Douglas
Lusaka Stock Exchange-C. Mate
Luxembourg Stock Exchange-Johan Thiriart
Madrid Stock Exchange-Domingo Garcia
MEFF Renta Variable-Juan Pizcueta
Merrill Lynch & Co.-Phil Galdi and Lorraine Gringer
Mexico Stock Exchange
Milan Stock Exchange-Luigi Ruggerone and
    Claudio Zanoli
Montreal Stock Exchange-Concetta Savoia
Morgan Stanley & Co.
Morley Capital Management-Peter L. Journey
Moscow Times-Liena Bereezanskaia
Muscat Securities Market-Ashraf Al Nabhany
Nagoya Stock Exchange-Mizuyo Sasaki
Namibia Stock Exchange-Tony Minney
Nasdaq-Kate Mitchell
National Association of Real Estate Investment Fiduciaries
National Association of Real Estate Investment Trusts
Nepal Stock Exchange Ltd.-Pant Shambhu Prasad
New York Stock Exchange-Joe Kendrick
New Zealand Stock Exchange-Frank Aldridge
    and Kim Bird
Nigerian Stock Exchange-Rasaki Oladejo
Nihon Keizai Shimbun, Inc.
Nomura Equity Research (London)-Reza
    Ghassemieh
OCBC Investment Research-Lew Chee Wei
OMLX, The London Securities & Derivatives
    Exchange-Jeremy Stanyer
Osaka Stock Exchange-Yoshinori Shima

Oslo Stock Exchange-Aud Ebba Lie
Osterreichische Termin-Und Optionenborse
    (OTOB)-Gunther Shiendl
Pacific Stock Exchange- Scott Stark and Brad Zigler
Panama Stock Exchange-Ivan A. Diaz
Paris Stock Exchange-Veronique Bosselin
Peregrine Brokerage Ltd.-Gopi Krishna Maliwal
Philadelphia Stock Exchange-Richard Angelosi and
    Bill Pizzuto
Philippine Stock Exchange-Sergio S. Marquez
Pimbley, Joe
Prague Stock Exchange-Tomas Jursik
Quito Stock Exchange-Patricia Guerrero A.
Randall, Jean
Rio de Janeiro Stock Exchange-Marcelo Salgado
Ryan Labs, Inc.
Salomon Brothers-Carol Sabia
Salomon Brothers-Marc Deluise
Santiago Stock Exchange-Natalie Tabensky and
    Juan Pablo Schiappacasse
Sao Paulo Stock Exchange-Moema Unis
Schmidt Management Company-Ned W. Schmidt
Schoepke, Stephen
Securities Exchange of Barbados-Beverly
    Cheltenham-Corbin
Shanghai Stock Exchange-Hoe Yan
Siebel, Rudulph
Smith Barney, Inc.-Mark Hunt
Standard & Poor's Corp.-Mary Oshea and Elliot Shurgin
Stock Exchange of Hong Kong-Iris Cheung
Stock Exchange of Singapore Ltd.-Grace Ooi
Stock Exchange of Taiwan-Ju Fu-Chen
Stock Exchange of Thailand-Busaba Lertbunnaphongs
Stockbrokers Botswana Ltd.-Andrew Ashton
Stockholm Stock Exchange-Anna-Lisa Stockel
Swaziland Stockbrokers Ltd.-A. Mc Guire
Swiss Stock Exchange-Marc Berthoud
Tel Aviv Stock Exchange-Etti Tutnauer
The Economic Times-Shankar P.
The Federation of International Bourses de Valores
    (F.I.B.V.)
Tokyo Stock Exchange-Hitoshi Izumi
Toronto Stock Exchange-Sayuri Childs
Trinidad & Tobago Stock Exchange-Dexter Webb
UOB Investment Research-Tan Joo San
Vancouver Stock Exchange-Wade J. Murray
Vienna Stock Exchange
Warsaw Stock Exchange-Leonard Furga
Wilshire Associates
Zimbabwe Stock Exchange-N. Brown

I am also indebted to my wife Susan, for her support, encouragement, and time, and to Joshua and
Alex for enduring years of exposure to securities market index facts and figures.

1

INTRODUCTION

OVERVIEW

A securities market index is a statistical indicator, benchmark or measure of movements in the general level and direction of prices of financial instruments or securities such as stocks, bonds, money market instruments, commodities, convertible securities, currencies, Guaranteed Investment Contracts (GICs), mutual funds and real estate.

Securities market indices are alike in that they are ordinarily calculated based on standard forms of simple and composite index formulas expressed in relation to a "base" value that is established at the time of their inception and thereafter, on movements that are derived from a series of observations. Otherwise, just about every index, whether calculated continuously throughout the trading day, once daily, monthly or on a quarterly frequency, is constructed diferently in terms of its constituent universe and selection procedures, maintenance practices and computational methodologies.

An index may be based on the prices of all, or only a sample, of the securities whose value it represents. Approaches to sample selections are numerous and range from strictly objective methodologies to subjective guidelines that take into account common factors such as markets, market coverage, security type, economic sector/industry representation, size, trading volume, liquidity, company performance and the availability and quality of prices.

Indices are generally subject to periodic reconstitution, at which time securities may be added to the index or dropped from the index due to mergers, liquidations, declining capitalization and in the event a particular security is no longer thought to represent the type of security covered by the index. In any case, applicable guidelines, frequency and timing of additions and deletions vary from one index to the next.

To maintain continuity of an index and ensure that changes in the index level are attributed entirely to price movements during the trading day, indices must be adjusted from time to time to reflect various corporate actions, such as share issuances, share repurchases, special cash dividends, rights offerings and spin-offs. Here too, differences in methods and variations as to frequency and timing of implementation are in evidence. In addition, varying pricing sources and currency exchange rates, where applicable, and the treatment of dividends and interest in connection with total rate of return calculations, also contribute to variations among indices.

Securities market indices also differ from each other in the way constituents are weighted. Often, prices of constituent securities in the index are market value-weighted. That is, in calculating the index value, the market price of each security is multiplied by the number of shares outstanding or, in the case of bond indices, the amount of bonds outstanding. Pursuant to this method of calculation, changes in the prices of larger companies or companies with more shares or bonds outstanding will generally have a greater influence on the level of a market value-weighted index than price changes affecting smaller corporations. Examples of leading stock indices that weight members on a market value basis include the Standard & Poor's 500 Composite Stock Price Index (S&P 500), the FT-SE Actuaries All-Share Index in the United Kingdom (UK), and the Nikkei Stock Index in Japan. A few leading bond indices that weight members on the basis of market value include the Lehman Brothers Aggregate Bond Index, Merrill Lynch Global Bond Index and Salomon Brothers Broad Investment Grade Bond Index.

Index components may also be equally-weighted so that each index member has an equal influence on the results, or they may be unweighted, such that securities are combined strictly on the basis of quoted prices. This latter method of weighting characterizes the Dow Jones Industrial Average (DJIA), the oldest surviving and most widely recognized securities market benchmark in the world, as well as the Nikkei 225 Stock Average that was fashioned after the Dow. It is worth noting that indices, though typically based on averages, are not quite the same as averages. The difference consists of the fact that an index is constructed by setting its initial value equal to some arbitrary but generally rounded number at some point in time in order to facilitate comparison of the value of the index in subsequent periods. An average, on the other hand, does not involve the selection of an arbitrary value for some base period. It is simply an average. The Dow Jones Industrial Average and its companions are not indices technically. They are simply the arithmetic mean of the prices of the stocks included at each point in time adjusted for stock splits and other capital changes. Nevertheless, the two tend to be used interchangeably.

Finally, regardless of weighting methodology, index components are combined in one of two ways to arrive at an index value. The most common approach relies on arithmetic averaging, but geometric averaging is still in use both in the United States as well as overseas.

THE UNIVERSE OF INDICIES

Worldwide, it is estimated that upwards of 600 securities market indices are compiled and published by not less than 250 stock exchanges and publishing enterprises, including newspapers, investment banking concerns and investment management organizations. There may be nearly 10,000 in number when subindices, or strictly constructed narrower segments of indices, are taken into consideration.

New indices and subindices are frequently being introduced due to increased usage. For example, between January 1, 1994 and June 30, 1996, at least 118 new indices were launched throughout the world. Of these, 48 were launched in 1995, up from 38 that were introduced in 1994.[1] The pace of new index introductions continues, with at least 32 new indices (excluding subindices) making their debut by mid-1996.

While usage varies, whether for the purpose of performance evaluation, creation of derivative instruments, passive management, or the establishment of incentive fee arrangements, differences in construction, maintenance and calculation methodologies will affect how an index measures the relevant market. They can produce differences in the level and movements of indices over time and, in turn, the portrayal of the marketplace.

For example, the cumulative 10-year price only return to December 31, 1995 for broad equity indices such as the New York Stock Exchange (NYSE) Composite Index, the S&P 500 Index, Wilshire 5000 Equity Index and the Russell 3000 Index, which gained 171.02%, 191.52%, 179.82% and 183.38% respectively, varies by as much as 20.5%. During the same time period, annual price only returns have diverged by a maximum of 3% in a given year.

---

[1]Excluding subindices. Also, indices designed to track market capitalization segments, such as large, medium and small companies, or stock characteristics, such as growth or value stocks, are each treated as one index.

The Guide to Securities Market Indices is designed to assist professionals as well as individual investors in the selection of an appropriate securities market index, on a worldwide basis. *The Guide's* purposes are to:

1. Identify and catalogue available performance indicators along with their publishers;

2. Describe their relevant characteristics; and

3. Provide a perspective on their historical price and total return performance.

The Guide to Securities Market Indices contains descriptive profiles along with historical performance data on 400 of the world's leading global, regional and local securities market indices and subindices covering 10 asset classes. In addition, over 200 indices are referenced in abbreviated form.

SELECTION CRITERIA

In addition to usage, indices for which descriptive profiles are provided were selected on the basis of the following considerations:

1. Asset class coverage.

2. Market coverage, including individual countries and regions and the world.

3. Coverage by market capitalization and style of management.

4. Availability of exchange-traded derivative instruments.

5. Perceived areas of interest.

6. Availability of adequate and reliable information.

Index descriptions, computation methodologies and historical performance data were, for the most part, obtained directly from their publishers in the form of written specifications and accompanying explanatory materials. Supplemental research was also conducted along with follow-up discussions, as appropriate, with index publishers. In some instances, historical performance data was obtained and/or verified using Bloomberg Financial and Interactive Data Services data bases.

The quality of descriptive materials in general and specifications relating to index calculation methodologies and maintenance procedures in particular, both in the U.S. and overseas, vary considerably. Except for documentation associated with indices of leading publishers and, in particular, index purveyors whose express goal is to ensure transparency in terms of component securities and construction methodologies, publishers in general offer limited disclosure and related documentation lacks precision. Often, index documentation may refer to the use of a standard formula, such as the Paasche index formula, without expanding upon factors such as the frequency and timing of constituent additions and deletions, adjustments for shares outstanding as well as corporate actions or pricing sources that could have meaningful price and total return implications over time. The profiles of indices that fall into this category have been prepared on a best effort basis using all available information. Future editions of *The Guide* will attempt to expand upon these considerations in a more methodical fashion.

2

USES AND APPLICATIONS

MARKET PERFORMANCE

In their most basic form, securities market indices are designed to answer the fundamental question: "how did the market do today, yesterday or over any other chosen period of time?" This was the intent behind the creation of the Dow Jones Industrial Average (DJIA) in 1884, an early proxy for the performance of the stock market in the United States, as well as the predecessor to the S&P 500 that was introduced 39 years later. While relying on an entirely different and more complex computational methodology, the Standard & Poor's Index nevertheless expanded upon the popular and easy to understand DJIA by providing a broader market indicator that measured the changes in the value of a market portfolio.

PERFORMANCE BENCHMARK/STANDARD

Equally important, securities market indices are used to gauge or measure how well individual securities, an investment manager or a portfolio of securities, including separate accounts, pooled accounts as well as mutual funds, have performed. In this context, securities market indices facilitate performance comparison in that they provide a systematic basis for evaluating, monitoring and comparing the performance of individual securities as well as managed portfolios.

According to a quarterly survey of corporate and public pension fund sponsors conducted by *Institutional Investor* in 1995, 90.3% of respondents use a securities index, market index or style index to measure the performance of pension funds.[2] Also, securities market indices are now more frequently used by individual investors to measure the relative performance of their portfolios, Individual Retirement Accounts, 401(k) plan accounts as well as their mutual funds and their use of a benchmark is increasing over time.

PORTFOLIO STRUCTURE, RISK AND STYLE ANALYSIS

Beyond their application as a performance benchmark, securities market indices are used to describe the relationship between the return on a security or a portfolio of securities and the overall market, as represented by a broad based index, for purposes of establishing the trade-off between risk and expected returns.

---

[2] "Measure for Measure," *Institutional Investor Magazine*, 1995, p. 195.

They also serve as a diagnostic tool to assess a portfolio's overall posture relative to the market and analyze its risk/reward profile. This is accomplished by comparing and contrasting such factors as security holdings, levels of exposure, and industry diversification, maturity and credit quality of an actively managed portfolio with the characteristics of an appropriate securities market index.

Lastly, indices are used to conduct return-based style analysis where manager styles are analyzed without evaluating portfolio holdings. Proposed by William Sharpe in 1988, style analysis evaluates whether an investment manager's marketed investment style conforms with its investment results. This is accomplished, using a factor model, by comparing historical investment performance results with that of selected benchmark indices. In effect, style analysis tries to find the portfolio of indices that best explains a manager's returns.

DERIVATIVE INSTRUMENTS

Indices are used as underlying vehicles for derivative products. In recent years, there has been a proliferation of exchange-traded as well as Over-the-Counter (OTC)-traded financial instruments such as futures, options and swap contracts that have been created using stock market indices and, to a lesser extent, bond market indices. As many as 112 stock, bond, commodity and real estate indices and subindices served as underlying vehicles for exchange-traded derivative products throughout the world at year end 1995.[3] Of these indices, 31 were introduced between 1994 and 1995. During the first six months of 1996, six stock and bonds indices along with 15 subindices were created to serve as underlying vehicles for exchange-traded derivative products.

This development has been in response to a variety of increasingly popular strategies involving futures, options, options on futures as well as other forms of structured instruments, which are intended to achieve various portfolio objectives, adjust the risk/reward characteristics of a portfolio and facilitate portfolio management activities. Some of these portfolio applications are as follows:

- To hedge or protect current investment or portfolio positions by writing index options or selling index futures to obtain protection against market swings and reduce volatility of the underlying returns. They may also be used for trading purposes and to enhance returns by taking advantage of risk arbitrage opportunities, such as when a futures contract is priced more attractively than the underlying stock index. Or, they may be used for speculation purposes on the anticipated direction of stocks, interest rates and commodity prices.

- To gain exposure to an asset class, a variety of markets, both domestically and overseas, as well as narrower, industry segments. Stock index options and futures, for example, offer investors as well as traders the opportunity to gain foreign equity exposure without actually buying foreign stocks with their attendant transaction costs along with custodial fees, and in some cases, exposure to difficult settlement periods. In international investing, for example, futures on the Tokyo Stock Exchange Price Index (TOPIX), which tracks the performance of all domestic common stocks listed on the First Section of the Tokyo Stock Exchange (TSE), can be used by investors as a cash equity substitute. In some cases, investors can gain easier access to an otherwise hard to penetrate market and often at less cost than by buying underlying securities, or where there are restrictions against foreign ownership. Also, they offer a way to implement Tactical Asset Allocation

---

[3]Country Basket Index Fund, Inc. and World Equity Benchmark Shares Foreign Fund, Inc. (WEBS), consisting of 26 and 22 markets, respectively, have been treated as two indices.

strategies to supplement or reduce portfolio exposure to a particular market due to short-term departures from long-term portfolio policies without effecting the underlying assets.

- To facilitate index fund management by allowing index funds to replicate the returns of stock indices. This is possible through the use of futures, options, swaps and other derivatives to maintain cash reserves while remaining fully invested, to rebalance without incurring excess transaction costs and to promptly redeploy new money in anticipation of individual security purchases. In index fund management, futures and options can be used to equitize cash due to cash inflows and dividend payments in order to minimize tracking error or the difference between the total return of the portfolio and the index.

PASSIVE INVESTMENT STRATEGIES/INDEXING

Securities market indices make it possible to manage portfolio assets through a strategy known as indexation. Indexation, or passive investing, is an investment strategy devoted to duplicating or matching the performance of a selected stock index, bond index or other financial index while minimizing management fees and transaction costs. The investment results of the target index are replicated by holding all, or in the case of very broad indexes that may also include illiquid securities, a representative sample of the securities in the index in the appropriate proportions based on relative total market value. Such a strategy does not rely on traditional methods of active portfolio management that typically involve frequent changes in the make up of a portfolio of securities on the basis of economic, financial and market analysis. Instead, the only purchases and sales that are made are those necessary to create and maintain a portfolio that substantially replicates the selected index.

REGULATORY REPORTING AND DISCLOSURE

The Securities and Exchange Commission (SEC) in the United States has adopted the following revisions and amendments to disclosure documents that are designed to give investors more information in order to evaluate corporate performance as well as the performance of mutual funds. The SEC requires corporations and mutual funds to compare their performance against a broad market index and a more narrowly constructed index consisting of peer group companies.

- In October 1992, the Securities and Exchange Commission adopted revisions to its rules governing disclosure of executive compensation in proxy and information statements as well as other Commission filings. In addition to consolidating requisite disclosure information in a series of tables and requiring a report on compensation decisions, the SEC also mandated the use of a line graph comparing total shareholder returns of the company against those of a broad market index and a narrower group of peers. The SEC is even more prescriptive concerning S&P 500 member companies in that they are required to use the S&P 500 as their broad market indicator.

- In April 1993, the SEC adopted rule and form amendments under the Securities Act of 1933 and Investment Company Act of 1940. The rule requires every equity, fixed income, balanced and hybrid mutual fund to compare its performance to that of an appropriate broad based securities market index, and to publish a graph of this relationship in its prospectus or annual report to shareholders.

ASSET ALLOCATION

Securities market indices are an integral part of the asset allocation process by which the amount of assets to be allocated among various investment alternatives is determined. Asset allocation has been the subject of increased attention largely due to a growing acceptance on the part of professional managers that the asset mix of a portfolio, more so even that the selection of specific stocks, is the single most important determinant of performance.

A number of approaches are currently being used to assess asset mix, but certain basic inputs are common to all. One of these involves forecasts of risks and returns for each asset class and the examination of historic relationships between them. An investor using this approach begins by examining a series of historic returns and these are typically in the form of generally accepted securities market indices. For common stocks, this includes such indices as the S&P 500 or the Wilshire 5000 Equity Index while the Morgan Stanley Capital International Europe, Australia and Far East Index (MSCI/EAFE) may be used as a proxy for the performance of international equities.

In addition, asset mix studies incorporate all assets in which an investor may have an opportunity to invest. Traditionally, these have been limited to domestic common stocks, bonds and money market instruments. In recent years, the number of investment class options has expanded to include foreign stocks of developed and emerging markets, real estate and synthetic Guaranteed Investment Contracts (GICs), to mention just a few. In response, additional securities market indices have been created to accommodate these areas of interest.

INCENTIVE COMPENSATION ARRANGEMENTS

In late 1985, the SEC liberalized the use of performance based incentive management fees. Subsequently, pension and endowment fund administrators turned to performance based fees as a means of directly tying manager compensation to portfolio results. Mutual funds and closed-end investment companies also employ incentive fee arrangements, though their use is more limited.

In each instance, performance-based fee arrangements reward a manager for investment performance above a specified benchmark or penalize a manager for below benchmark results. Typically, broad based securities market indices are used for this purpose, although a limited number of peer group universes are also in use. Whether in connection with pension fund portfolios or mutual funds, the most common benchmark remains the Standard & Poor's 500 Composite Stock Price Index.

TECHNICAL ANALYSIS

Securities market indices assist the technical analyst in the attempt to study, observe and record the daily performance of individual securities and the market as a whole in order to predict future market trends. Interestingly, the first theory of technical analysis was formulated by Charles H. Dow, creator of the Dow Jones Industrial Average. Known as the Dow Theory, its basic proposition of identifying market trends relies on both the Dow Jones Industrial Average and the Dow Jones Transportation Average to determine the market's direction.

AUDIT, SURVEILLANCE AND CONTROL

Securities market indices are useful devices for auditing and validating portfolio prices, particularly the net asset value (NAV) of mutual funds and other actively managed collective funds that must be valued on a regular basis within a restricted time period. In this context, benchmarks are used to confirm the prices of various domestic and foreign securities to ensure their accuracy before releasing data to the general public.

Also, the Dow Jones Industrial Average is used by the SEC as a mechanism for tracking and implementing so-called "circuit breakers" that are imposed on share trading on the New York Stock Exchange to avoid steep declines in share prices during the course of a single day.

3

REASONS FOR GROWTH OF INDICES

In addition to growth that is directly attributable to new uses and applications, as outlined in the preceding Chapter, the following important developments have contributed to the expansion in the number and type of indices in recent years.

MEASURES FOR MANAGER SELECTION AND EVALUATION

Increased emphasis on manager evaluation, in general, and performance measurement in particular by institutional investors, such as corporate and public pension funds, endowments and foundations, have contributed significantly to the development and growth of indices over the last 25 years or so. Several factors in particular have been responsible for the increased reliance on numeric measures, including the passage of The Employee Retirement Income Security Act of 1974 (ERISA), changes to portfolio composition, competition for money management business as well as emphasis on pension cost reduction.

- The passage of the ERISA in September 1974 brought about at least two significant changes to traditional investment practices. First, ERISA adopted a "prudent man" standard for persons engaged in the administration, supervision and management of pension moneys according to which they assumed a fiduciary responsibility to ensure that all investment related decisions were subject to the ". . . care, skill, prudence and diligence that a prudent man familiar with such matters would use."[4] The second change mandated the requirement that investments be diversified so as to minimize the risk of large losses. The passage of ERISA ushered in the era of multi-manager arrangements in which several independent counseling firms were selected to manage pension fund assets on the basis of asset class management expertise, investment style and performance

---

[4] Section 404(a)(1) of the Employee Retirement Income Security Act of 1974.

results over three- and five-year time horizons. Whereas banks and, to a lesser extent, insurance companies, dominated the defined pension fund asset management market, their share of market experienced a long and sharp decline following the recession of 1972 and shortly thereafter, the passage of ERISA. The rise of independent investment counseling firms and with them, the arrival of pension consultants to evaluate and monitor these new managers, placed greater emphasis on relative performance measurement and reliance on benchmarks.

- The growth in the number of investment managers during this period served to intensify competition among managers, with performance evaluations becoming an increasingly important role in the screening and selection process.

- Portfolio composition has been expanded beyond traditional asset classes, to include emerging markets, real estate, commodities, and oil and gas, to mention just a few, and these have been followed by the introduction of new benchmarks to evaluate their performance.

- In recent years, a new emphasis by corporate pension funds on investment performance and a demand for greater accountability from their managers. As defined benefit plans grew in size and importance during the seventies and eighties, corporations realized that their levels of contributions and consequently, corporate performance, could be substantially impacted through more effective management of pension assets. Thus, greater emphasis was placed on the quality and frequency of investment manager evaluations through the use of performance benchmarks.

GROWTH OF MUTUAL FUNDS

Along a similar vein, the widespread acceptance over the last 10 years of mutual funds by individual investors as an investment vehicle of choice, either directly or through defined contribution plans, including 401(k) plans, has also increased emphasis on performance and performance measurement. The mutual fund industry now serves more than 38 million individual shareholders, represents about 31% of U.S. households, with over 7,000 stock, bond and money market mutual funds, at least 21 different investment objectives, and total net assets of approximately $3.0 trillion.

Diversity in fund types within the open end and closed-end funds universe has been accompanied by the introduction of new benchmarks. Also, widespread ownership of funds has made investors more sensitive to investment performance. In fact, investor purchase decisions are most heavily influenced by fund performance, which is evaluated and promoted on an absolute basis and in relation to a securities market index or peer group universe.

GROWTH OF INDEXATION

The expansion of indexation in the U.S. and, to a lesser extent, overseas has also been a factor in the growth and development of securities market indices. According to *Pensions and Investments*, the amount of indexed U.S. tax-exempt assets, including both separate accounts and mutual funds, reached about $730.3 billion at May 31, 1996.[5] This represents a market-adjusted increase of about 3.6% in six months when indexed assets stood at $676.5 billion.

---

[5] Schramm, Sabine, "International Stock Index Funds Surge," *Pension and Investments*, August 5, 1996, p 1.

Reliance on indexing as part of a total investment strategy has gained acceptance among corporate pension fund sponsors and more recently, individual investors. The Efficient Market Hypothesis (EMH), which prescribes that, in efficient markets, all stocks are fully discounted for expected future events so that profit opportunities for active portfolio managers are severely restricted if not eliminated, along with corporate downsizing and low cost, have been important factors in indexation. In addition, manager underperformance has had an equally profound influence on the receptivity of indexation. According to data on the performance of general equity mutual funds in the United States during the 25-year period between 1971 and 1995, the S&P 500 Index rarely outperforms less than 30% of actively managed funds and often outperforms 70% of managed funds. In 1995, the S&P 500 Index outperformed 85% of actively managed general equity mutual funds.[6]

While most of the focus on index investing to date has been on the Standard & Poor's 500 Composite Stock Price Index, the use of indexing is growing steadily and is being applied to different categories of stock, both domestic and international, and fixed income investment. In recent years, the concept of indexing has been extended to encompass more narrowly defined market capitalization segments, i.e., small-, medium- and large-capitalization as well as styles of management, such as value and growth investing. As a result, new indices have been created to measure these segments.

NEW MARKETS, INVESTMENT STYLES AND SECURITY TYPES

Manager underperformance and the appeal of indexation, however, have not diminished investor appetite for various active management strategies that are designed to beat the market and/or avoid the risk of large losses through diversification. In response, investing has branched out to embrace additional asset classes such as real estate and commodities, new markets such as foreign and emerging markets, new industries consisting of the Internet and telecommunications, as well as new investment styles with their emphasis on growth and value investing within or across large-, medium- and small-sized company segments. These developments have been followed by the creation of indices designed to track these areas.

The creation of new security types, such as mortgage-backed securities, asset-backed securities and Brady bonds, has also generally been followed by the introduction of indices designed to quantify and track their performance.

NEW STOCK EXCHANGES

Growth in the number of new stock markets in recent years has contributed to the proliferation of new indices as benchmarks are created to track the performance of listed stocks and serve as hedging vehicles. Privatization of state owned enterprises has been the primary reason for the expansion in the number of stock exchanges, each of which provides a place to trade and value shares in privatized companies, and to attract foreign capital. This has been particularly pronounced in Eastern Europe where nations have been shifting from centrally controlled command economies to free markets.

---

[6] Vanguard Index Trust 1995 Annual Report, pp 4-5.

Simultaneously, the proliferation of futures and options exchanges and the increased competition among them has also been a factor in the creation of new indices and subindices to track the local market and to serve as underlying vehicles for derivative products, both for portfolio management purposes and to build transaction volume.

COMPUTER TECHNOLOGY

Computer technology has made it easier to build new, more accurate indices, that can be computed on a more timely basis and with greater frequency, including intraday, minute by minute index calculations. When combined with the greater availability and access to underlying data, such as prices, dividends, shares outstanding, and share cross-ownership, the cost of building and maintaining indices is dropping.

PROMOTIONAL CONSIDERATIONS, ENHANCEMENT TO REPUTATION AND REVENUE SOURCE

The creation and regular publication of an index generates publicity for index publishers and therefore, serves as a useful device for promoting the firm before the public. The brand name recognition of firms like Standard and Poor's, Morgan Stanley and more recently, J.P. Morgan for its global government bond index, is both valuable and difficult to quantify. More important, it serves to establish the firm as an authority in the particular segment of the market and creates opportunities for revenue production, either directly or indirectly. The cost of developing and maintaining an index varies in relation to its complexity. At the low end, creation of an index requires an investment of about $35,000 to $45,000 while maintenance can run about $1,000 a month. Some entrants, however, reportedly invested in excess of US$2.0 million.[7] Nevertheless, the financial rewards can be substantial for the more widely accepted and used benchmarks. Revenue generating opportunities are available through licensing fees associated with indices used for passive products such as the S&P 500 and MSCI/EAFE, exchange-traded options and futures contracts, the creation of customized derivative products and related securities trading commissions, and the production and sale of financial data.

---

[7] Ioannou, Lori. "Constructing Indexes," *Global Finance*, August 1991, pp 46-48.

4

INDEX CONSTRUCTION AND MAINTENANCE

INDEX COMPOSITION

Indices are based on an entire population of homogeneous securities or a sample intended to represent the universe under consideration. In either case, the objective is to properly describe the market or population of securities that is relevant to investors and portray the behavior of the financial asset that is being studied. The population may be broadly defined to incorporate an entire class of securities, such as stocks, bonds, convertible securities or real estate assets. It may be expressed on a global, regional, national or local level. It may consist of a particular market segment or sector, such as an economic sector, industrial group, investment objective or investable universe of securities. It may be limited by issuer or security size, such as large-, medium-, or small-capitalization stocks, large- or small-sized bonds or mutual funds investing in large- or small-capitalization stocks. Or, the population may be defined by the character of a security, such as growth or value stocks that are, in turn, isolated using price-to-book ratios, price-earnings ratios and divident yields, credit quality and/or maturity.

When indices were first constructed, before the advent of calculators or computers, the number of securities in an index had to be restricted to a few stocks. Otherwise, it would have been too difficult, time consuming and expensive to calculate an index on a timely basis. The Dow Jones Industrial Average for example, consisted of only 11 stocks when it was first published on July 3, 1884. Since then, developments in computer technology have made it possible to construct indices with a large number of securities that can be computed and disseminated quickly and less expensively. Standard & Poor's, which in 1923 introduced a broad market indicator consisting of 233 stocks, created a 90-stock subset that was published daily starting in 1928 and later on an hourly basis. Twenty-nine years later in 1957, the availability of computers enabled Standard & Poor's to calculate and disseminate the S&P 500 Index at one minute intervals. Today, computer technology enables Wilshire Associates to generate daily index values for its 6,972 stock Wilshire 5000 Equity

Index and Merrill Lynch along with Lehman Brothers to compute daily index values for broad based bond indices with 8,472 and 5,343 constituents, respectively.[8] Because of advances in computer technology, the selection of index constituents and any restrictions that may be applied to them is generally influenced by factors that are not strictly related to computational considerations.

SELECTION CRITERIA

Stock market indices that rely on a selection rather than the entire population of securities generally operate pursuant to a set of rules or guidelines governing the inclusion of markets, market segments and the individual securities. These rules not only apply to the initial selection process, but they also serve as the framework for ongoing maintenance that determines new entrants and deletions to the index. Often, markets, market segments and securities selection are based on qualitative and quantitative considerations that are predicated on usage, and may consider a combination of some or all of a number of factors, including markets, market coverage, security type, economic sector/industry representation, credit quality, size, trading activity, financial and operating characteristics, data quality, float/cross ownership, and liquidity.

MARKETS

Markets can be variously defined. For example, the International Finance Corp. (IFC), in constructing its IFC Global Index, defines an emerging stock market as any stock market located in a developing country as established by the World Bank's Gross National Product (GNP) per capita criteria. J.P. Morgan, for purposes of its Emerging Markets Bond Index (EMBI), defines emerging market countries based on their ability to repay external-currency denominated debt, using a Standard & Poor's and Moody's Investors Service rating ceiling of BBB+/Baa1.

MARKET COVERAGE

Some indices pursue a strategy of capturing a minimum percentage of cumulative available market capitalization. For example, the Dow Jones Global Stock Index aims to achieve 80% market coverage in each country based on market capitalization. To that end, all eligible stock issues are ranked by market capitalization and constituent stocks are selected from the highest capitalization within each industry in the market until the 80% level has been reached. Morgan Stanley Capital International, on the other hand, aims to capture a 60% level from a universe of available stocks in each market for its World Index.

SECURITY TYPE

Stock indices typically consist of common stocks and preferred stocks. Participation certificates and other securities, without regard to their voting status, may also be eligible. On the other hand, investment trusts, unit trusts, mutual funds and closed-end funds are typically excluded, but this is not always the case. Broad based bond indices generally include fixed-rate, publicly placed, dollar-denominated and non-convertible, investment grade debt issues with at least one year to final maturity. Non-fixed rate securities or stripped securities or securities with esoteric or one of a kind feature such as structured notes or range notes with coupons that depend on market indices and private placement securities are generally deemed ineligible for inclusion.

---

[8] New Merrill Lynch Bond Index selection criteria, effective as of April 30, 1996, will drop about 2,500 issues from the index.

ECONOMIC SECTOR/INDUSTRY REPRESENTATION

Securities are selected to reflect the economic and industry characteristics of the overall market or market segments.

CREDIT QUALITY

Long-term ratings assigned by one or more of the leading rating agencies. These include Moody's Investors Service and Standard & Poor's Corp.

SIZE

Market capitalization, amount outstanding, contract size or, in mutual funds, total net assets.

TRADING ACTIVITY

Stocks, bonds or other securities are selected based on trading activity in terms of number of transactions, value or volume of shares traded during a specified period of time.

FINANCIAL AND OPERATING CHARACTERISTICS

Securities may be selected from such measures as sales, net income and industrial output. The Singapore Straits Times Industrial Index, for example, selects index constituents from a company's record of profitability for the three years before inclusion in the index. Additions to the S&P 500 are, in part, screened based on their financial and operating condition with a view toward minimizing company turnover and maintaining stability in the constituent universe.

DATA QUALITY

Availability of accurate, reliable and timely data concerning prices, interest and dividends and capital changes, which are essential to ensure reliable index values, may influence the selection of securities, particularly in emerging markets.

SELECTION FACTORS UNIQUE TO THE INSTITUTIONAL MARKETPLACE

The increased institutionalization of investing, interest in international investing generally and emerging markets in particular, combined with the growing acceptance of indexation, have served to emphasize the following two additional selection factors:

FLOAT/CROSS OWNERSHIP

Available float, or the percentage of shares freely tradable. This is difficult to determine, however, as good sources for information may not be available, it may not be made public or information may be subject to errors and time delays. Most important, float is often defined differently by different index publishers.

Liquidity

This may be variously defined, but generally assessed based on trading value over a specified period of time, trading volume, market capitalization or face amount outstanding, bid/asked spreads, number of brokers making a market in a particular security, and the ability to affect settlement through a recognized settlement facility.

Selection Methods/Techniques

Within this broad framework of selection criteria, indices generally employ the rank order method or the optimization technique or some combination of these two approaches to actually identify individual issues for inclusion in the index.

Rank-Order Method

The universe of eligible securities is determined through a process of elimination and index constituents are selected strictly based on their aggregate market value. Stocks are added to the index until a predetermined level of coverage has been achieved. This may include a specified number of securities, e.g., 30, 100, 300 or 500, or market coverage defined as a percent of market capitalization.

Optimization Technique

A process by which a number of selection variables are optimized to achieve the desired index or portfolio profile, including a predetermined number of securities or percent of market capitalization.

Index Maintenance

The procedures applicable to the maintenance of an index are just as important as the criteria applied to the selection of its constituents.

Index maintenance involves the process of monitoring and, where appropriate, adjusting indices for company additions and deletions, and various corporate actions such as stock splits, rights offerings, share issuance, special cash dividends, stock dividends, spinoffs and corporate mergers.

Company additions and deletions are required periodically to maintain the character of the index, as with indices that track a specific number of constituents selected on market value. Such indices are typically reconstituted on a quarterly or annual basis. Constituent additions and deletions, however, may also be required in connection with mergers, acquisitions, spinoffs, and bankruptcies. Despite the reason, such changes have an effect on the market value of the index.

Similarly, issuer-related developments affect the market value of the index in a way that requires adjustments to the index divisor to prevent the value of the index from changing for reasons other than market related actions. The quality and timeliness of information regarding such adjustments, however, can vary from one market to the next. On the other hand, some corporate actions, such as stock splits, require simple changes to the index to reflect the revised number of shares outstanding.

The policies and practices that govern the implementation of corporate actions are equally important, if not more so. While shares outstanding and available share capital change constantly, daily updates and adjustments may not only serve to distort the integrity of the index but also make it difficult, if not possible, to establish indexed portfolios. Thus, index publishers face the challenge of maintaining a balance between the mathematical properties of the index and its long term validity as an indicator of market activity.

While detailed disclosure in this area is limited, in general, maintenance adjustments are implemented on a weekly or monthly basis, or with less frequency, on a quarterly or annual basis. The world's leading indices monitor and implement maintenance adjustments on a more frequent basis. For example, the Standard & Poor's 500 Index, is monitored on a daily basis and share changes of less than 5% are implemented quarterly. Share changes in excess of 5% are reviewed and, if appropriate, implemented after the close of trading on the following Wednesday of the week. At the other end of the spectrum, some indices are reviewed and adjusted once a year.

Due to changing market conditions, markets and country selections tracked by world and regional indices are subject to periodic review that is also likely to require maintenance adjustments on these levels. Such reviews typically take place on a quarterly or annual basis.

Pricing/Foreign Exchange

Index results are influenced by choices made regarding what prices to use. Intraday as well as closing prices applicable to actively-traded common stocks are generally obtained from third party pricing sources that track transaction activity in local markets on the primary stock exchanges. Even in the United States, subtle differences in index results are introduced by the selection of one pricing source over another, such as the use of New York Stock Exchange closing prices versus composite closing prices. These differences are likely magnified concerning smaller and less actively traded stocks and especially in pricing fixed income securities, where prices, either trader quotes or matrix generated, can vary considerably, or may not be available at all.

Likewise, sources for financial exchange rates, the time of day that these rates are taken and methods of averaging, if any, can influence index results. In this regard, a number of world index publishers adopted in October 1994 the WM/Reuters Spot Rates as of 4 PM London Time as a convention for exchange rates.

Other Considerations

Particularly concerning indices that track a large number of securities, both domestically and across national borders, or emerging market indices, there are potential sources for error that can serve to distort index results with compounding effects over time. These consist of errors in prices, errors as well as delays associated with the receipt of information on corporate changes, various operations errors as well as transmission errors.

While errors are inevitable, the long-term validity of index results rests largely with the practices and procedures used by index publishers to monitor, identify and correct errors. This is no small task, requiring a significant commitment of resources, such that actual practices vary considerably. In fact, a limited number of index publishers actually disclose their practices in this area. The FT/S&P World Index is one benchmark that does employ a variety of validation and error checking mechanisms, duplicate processing and third party confirmation, combined with published recalculation guidelines in case of errors that distort a country index by more than 25 basis points or 10 basis points for the World Index.

Methods of Weighting

The prices of each stock, bond or other security included in an index must be combined to determine the value of the index. For that purpose it is necessary each time the index is computed to determine the relative importance of each included security. The reason for weighting is to insure that the index reflects the relative importance of each stock in a way suited for that index. The most common ways of weighting stocks are by market value, price value and by assigning equal weights to relative price changes. In addition, a limited number of indices employ a variety of hybrid weightings, such as modified dollar weightings, or weightings based on characteristics that are unique to the particular asset class, as is the case with commodity indices that rely on production figures or traded value. Finally, a limited number of indices rely on some combination of market-value, trading volume and/or value of shares traded. This approach is similar to the market capitalization weighted method, except that weights are based on the number or value of shares traded, and is mostly in evidence in Latin America, including Argentina, Brazil and Colombia.

Market Value and Price-Weighted Methods

The market value and price value methods are appropriate for indicating changes in the aggregate market value of stocks represented in the index. The equal weight method is more appropriate for showing the movement in the prices in the typical or average stock.

The market-value or capitalization-weighted method aggregates security prices by the number of shares outstanding. While not the first publisher to employ this technique, the market-value weighted method was adopted by Standard & Poor's in the construction of its U.S. stock indices in 1923. The Index addresses the needs of the professional investor to compare directly the performance of their stock portfolios to a stock market indicator that measures the changes in the value of a market portfolio.

The market value-weighted index approach is based on the theory that a company's economic impact in the marketplace is directly proportional to its market value. A given percentage change in the market value of a large firm has a much greater economic impact on the market than a similar percentage change in the market value of a small firm. Accordingly, the best way for an index to provide an undistorted view of the market is to represent the constituent companies at their capitalization weight.

The market value-weighted index approach was reinforced by the advancement of Modern Portfolio Theory (MPT) and the development of the Capital Market Asset Pricing Model (CAPM). According to this model, developed by William Sharpe, a major characteristic of the market portfolio is that each asset in the portfolio is held in exact proportion to its market value.

The aggregate current market value of constituent shares is calculated, in stock indices, based on total or available share capital, or free float. Because corporate ownership ranges from totally private to totally public companies, or due to foreign investor restrictions that limits share ownership possibilities, use of total share capital rather than available share capital can introduce some distortion between the performance of the index and the experience of the underlying market. Put another way, the use of total share capital may not be a good representation of the investment opportunities available to investors. Some companies, for example, are controlled by one or more individuals, corporations or government entities and few, if any, of their shares ever trade in the open market. Overseas, and more recently in emerging markets, a large and often defined proportion of a market or companies' share capital is not available to foreign investors. Sometimes, the restrictions can represent in excess of 70% of the market. For example, Korea maintains total market restrictions that place 78% of their market capitalizations off-limits to foreign investors while the Philippines have investment restrictions on specific classes of shares.

Weighting by available share capital rather than total capital is a method that helps ensure that only the liquid subset of equity capital is included in the calculation of stock indices. Determinations regarding available share capital can be difficult to make, however, and ultimately these rely on both objective and subjective judgments that can contribute to variations in the performance of indices from one period to the next. This is because float capital can be difficult to define, determine and monitor. In some markets, good sources of information are generally not available while in other markets, information on smaller and less prominent issues can be subject to error and time delays.

These considerations have influenced some index publishers to calculate indices, both in the U.S. and overseas, based on full market capitalization, or float capitalization, or both. For example. Morgan Stanley Capital International and the International Finance Corporation publish indices based on full and partial market capitalization. Frank Russell and Standard & Poor's in the United States as well as HSBC James Capel overseas, on the other hand, calculate indices based entirely on available capitalization.

In contrast, the unweighted method is one in which the prices of constituent stocks are aggregated strictly based on quoted prices. This approach characterizes the weighting method employed in the computation of the Dow Jones Industrial Average, its companion Utilities, Transportation and Composite averages, as well as the Nikkei 225 Stock Average in Japan. The term unweighted, however, is somewhat of a misnomer in that securities that are combined in this manner influence the index in proportion to the magnitude of their price per share. Consequently, unweighted indices are also referred to as price weighted indices.

For example, a 1% change in the price of IBM (priced at $108.50 at 1/31/96) has nearly seven times the impact of a 1% change in the price of Bethlehem Steel ($15.13 at 1/31/96). Nevertheless, the long term performance of the DJIA tends to be similar to that of the S&P 500, because the thirty stocks of the Dow are among the largest companies in the United States.

EQUAL-WEIGHTED METHOD

A third weighting method is one in which security prices are equally-weighted to give as much weight to a 1% fluctuation in the price of a stock that sells for US$108.50 as to a 1% move in the price of a stock that sells for US$15.13, regardless of market capitalization. This approach exemplifies the weighting method used in the calculation of the Value Line Composite Average as well as a number of indices published by the American Stock Exchange (AMEX), Philadelphia Stock Exchange (PSE) and the Chicago Board Options Exchange (CBOE) for use with stock and bond index-based futures and options products.

The AMEX Biotechnology Index, for example, is an equal dollar-weighted index. It was created by designating the number of shares of each constituent security that represented approximately US$10,000.0 in market value based on closing prices on October 18, 1991. Under this approach, a stock that closed at US$20.0 per share would be represented in the Biotechnology index by 500 shares, for a total market value of US$10,000.0.

A variation of this weighting method is one in which dollar amounts invested in each stock are modified somewhat to achieve a particular result.

METHODS OF AVERAGING

A collection of prices attributable to stocks, bonds or other securities, either weighted or unweighted, have to be combined in some form into a single number to create a descriptive measure. This is accomplished through the process of averaging. While statistics books list and discuss several kinds of averages or measures of central tendency and although throughout the history of securities market indices various averaging methods have been employed, research indicates that, at present, only two methods of averaging security prices are used throughout the world in the construction of indices. These are the arithmetic mean and the geometric mean. The most widely used and recognized indices, such as the S&P 500, Dow Jones Industrial Average, MSCI/EAFE Index and FT-SE Actuaries All-Share Index are based on arithmetic means of prices or average price changes. Only 12 indices and 18 subindices in *The Guide* are calculated based on the geometric mean. Of these, the Value Line Composite Index, the FT 30 Share Index and the Knight-Ridder Commodity Research Bureau's Futures Price Index are the most widely known.

TABLE 4.1: MOST COMMON AVERAGING AND WEIGHTING METHODS

	MARKET VALUE-WEIGHTED	UNWEIGHTED/PRICE- WEIGHTED	EQUAL- WEIGHTED
Arithmetic Average	x	x	x
Geometric Average			x

INDEX FORMULAS

Index formulas combine various methods of weighting and averaging, as illustrated in Table 4.1 above, to arrive at the index value. The purpose of this section is not to delve into the complexities of index formulas, but to describe the basic forms of index formulas applicable to stocks, bonds, money market securities and other financial instruments, used today.

THE SIMPLE AGGREGATIVE OF ACTUAL PRICES INDEX FORMULA

The closing prices of index constituents are aggregated and the result is divided by the number of securities in the index. The influence of each issue upon the average is thus proportional to the magnitude of its price per share.

The index formula is expressed, as follows:

$\Sigma p_1 / \Sigma p_0$ = Index value, or $\Sigma p_1 / n$

where p_1= the current day's price
   p_0= the previous day's price
   n = the number of constituents

A variation of this index formula is used in the computation of the Dow Jones Industrial Average. To preserve its continuity for comparative purposes, adjustments are made to the index by reducing its divisor to reflect constituent changes as well as corporate actions. This produces the following divisor adjusted arithmetic mean index formula:

$$\Sigma p_1 / d_1 = \text{Index value}$$

where p_1 = the current day's price
d_1 = the current divisor

The formula is illustrated in Appendix 1.

THE GEOMETRIC MEAN INDEX FORMULA

Regardless of weighting, constituent prices are geometrically averaged. When combined with an equal weighting scheme, the closing stock price of each index constituent is divided by the prior day's close and aggregated. The result is divided by the number of constituents and geometrically averaged, as follows:

$$\sqrt{\sum (p_1 / p_0)} = \text{Index value}$$

where p_1 = the current day's price
p_0 = the prior day's price
n = the number of constituents

This form of index formula gives as much weight to the same percentage increase in the price of a stock regardless of market capitalization, and equal consideration to stocks despite selling price. The result reflects the changes in the price of a typical stock. A characteristic of the geometric mean is that, to some extent, it reduces the effect of very large or very small numbers. This gives an index calculated on this basis a downward bias such that its results will generally lag behind a comparably weighted arithmetic average.
The formula is illustrated in Appendix 1.

AN AGGREGATE OF PRICES TIMES QUANTITIES INDEX FORMULA, OR WEIGHTED AGGREGATIVE COMPOSITE INDEX FORMULA

The initial development of weighted indices was proposed by two German economists, Etienne Laspeyres and Hermann Paasche, in 1864 and 1874, respectively, for use in comparing the relative changes in the prices of various commodities. Both formulas establish a ratio between the current market value and the market value of the constituent securities at the base date, but differ slightly in their approach to calculating the current value of the market portfolio.
In the Laspeyres index formula, the current value of the market portfolio is calculated using current prices and the number of shares outstanding as of the base period.

$$\Sigma p_1 q_0 / \Sigma p_0 q_0 \, (100) = \text{Index value}$$

where p_1 = the current price
p_0 = the price of a constituent at the base date
q_0 = the number of shares outstanding at the base date

The Paasche index formula, on the other hand, uses current prices and the number of shares outstanding in the current period to establish the current value of the market portfolio.

$$\Sigma p_1 q_1 / \Sigma p_0 q_0 \, (100) = \text{Index value}$$

where p_1 = the current price
p_0 = the price of a constituent at the base date
q_1 = the number of shares outstanding in the current period
q_0 = the number of shares outstanding at the base date

The formula is illustrated in Appendix 1.

Both the Laspeyres and the Paasche Index formulas produce "fair" results. The application of the Laspayers and Paasche index formulas to a static market portfolio from one time period to the next, in which $q_1 = q_0$, produces identical results. Over time, very similar, but not identical results, would be produced by each index formula following the implementation of periodic maintenance adjustments due to security additions and deletions, changes to the number of shares outstanding and various corporate actions. Variations in index maintenance practices and procedures employed by index publishers throughout the world concerning the type, frequency and timing of index adjustments, however, seems to mitigate any differences that might arise between these two formulas. Indeed, research suggests that these formulas are used interchangeably.

The complexity of the aggregate of prices times quantities index formula is magnified when it is applied to the calculation of global and total return indices. In addition to accounting for the share value of individual securities and local market weightings, the formula must be expanded to reflect the impact of foreign exchange and dividend income.

While the same basic form of index formula has been adopted for the calculation of leading domestic and global bond indices, factors unique to fixed income securities further add to its complexity. These include settlement conventions, gains or losses on the repayment of principal, accrued interest as well as interest received.

TOTAL RATE OF RETURN COMPUTATION

Total rate of return is widely used and generally accepted as the best single measurement of performance. Total return performance calculations, unlike results that are strictly limited to price behavior, take into consideration the impact of stock dividends and interest income by adding to the ending price index value a factor that represents dividends and/or interest, including both accrued interest and coupon payments, applicable to all index constituents during the measurement period under consideration. Actual calculation and procedural methodologies differ concerning the timing, frequency and allocation of dividends and interest income. Regardless of the approach, index levels calculated with the reinvestment of all dividends and interest as compared to index levels assuming no reinvestment can vary substantially over extended time periods, depending on the securities involved. This is due to the compounding effect of reinvesting dividends and interest income which produces geometric growth in the index. For example, the S&P 500 produced an average annual price only return of 12.01% for the 10-year period ended December 31, 1995 versus an average annual total rate of return of 15.60%. The impact on bond performance is more dramatic. For example, the Lehman Brothers Aggregate Bond Index produced an average annual price only return of 1.25% for the 10-year period ended December 31, 1995 versus an average annual total rate of return of 9.81%.

The importance associated with the calculation of indices on a total return basis has been reinforced in recent years by the SEC and more recently by the Association for Investment Management and Research (AIMR). AIMR, which adopted standardized performance reporting guidelines for the investment management industry in the U.S., effective January 1, 1993, acknowledged that total return is the only valid benchmark for relative performance evaluation and mandated its use.[9]

Besides publishers of leading domestic and global indices that have calculated on this basis for some time, an increasing number of index publishers have begun to expand index calculations to include total rates of return.

SELECTION OF BASE DATE

The selection of the base period can be extremely important in the portrayal of a market over time. On the one hand, a base period that relies on security prices which have experienced a sharp increase may contribute to the understatement of performance achieved during the ensuing period. On the other hand, a base period that relies on security prices which have experienced a sharp decline may serve to overstate the performance results recorded by the index during the following period of recovery. To avoid such distortions, as far as possible, the base date or period should represent a fairly normal or typical period.

CHAIN-LINKING

This is the process by which sub-period returns are combined through compounding to produce a rate of return for the entire time period. Technically, linking involves multiplying one plus the sub-period return for each sub-period and subtracting one from the product, as follows:

$$R = (1 + r_1)(1 + r_2)...(1 + r_n) - 1$$

where R = the cumulative rate of return
r = the periodic rate of return
n = number of sub periods

The formula is illustrated in Appendix 1.

[9]Report of the Performance Presentation Standards Implementation Committee. Association for Investment Management and Research, December 1991.

5

CHARACTERISTICS OF
PREFERRED INDICES

Indices should be constructed, maintained and calculated according to a set of published objectives, including rules and guidelines. These should offer interested parties an opportunity to properly assess a benchmark in terms of how it measures the relevant market and its application to their own particular situation.

While investor requirements and actual usage are likely to differ, indices should be evaluated against the following attributes that are associated with well constructed indices:

- The index should be relevant and appropriate. That is, the index should track the relevant markets, market segments, instruments, individual securities and investment style.

- The index should be comprehensive, or broad based, incorporating to the extent appropriate, the markets, security types and individual securities that reflect the investment opportunities available to investors.

- The index should be investable and market participants should be able to replicate it. A useful index consists of securities that can be purchased by investors, local and foreign, retail and institutional investors. To ensure investability, an appropriate benchmark should qualify based on float capitalization, liquidity, and the absence of ownership restrictions.

- The index should be transparent. In addition to information regarding security selection and maintenance policies involving the addition and deletion of companies, calculation methodologies and related practices should be disclosed by the index publisher. Actual changes, if any, should be announced prior to implementation. In some cases, securities eligible for inclusion in the index at a future date due to maintenance adjustments will be identified in advance.

- The index should be constructed so that each security's return is weighted according to its market value at the beginning of the period the return is measured. Also, the performance of component stocks, bonds or other securities should be arithmetically averaged.

- The index should be maintained accuratly and reliably, with a stated corrections policy regarding prices, capital changes, dividends, exchange rates, etc., to reflect the actual changes in the value of the portfolio instead of the influence of other factors.

- In addition to price only returns, the index should also measure total rates of return. The latter includes cash dividends recorded in the period received and reinvested at the earliest date in the market. With bonds, total rates of return should include the reinvestment of interest income received or accrued, as may be appropriate, and principal payments, if applicable.

- Index results should be published frequently, be disseminated on a timely basis and be readily available to investors.

6

HISTORICAL HIGHLIGHTS

1834

The earliest dated stock price index in the United States, one in a series of railroad stock price indices published by Cole and Frickey, includes one series consisting of eight railroad stocks calculated back to 1834, using an unweighted geometric average of stock prices. By the turn of the century, at least 14 U.S. index publishers and two firms in Europe–the Statistique Générale de la France and the London and Cambridge Economic Service in the UK–were offering stock market indices with historical data prior to the year 1900.

1864-1874

German economists Etienne Laspeyres and Hermann Paasche advocate the use of a formula in which the price of each index constituent is weighted by the number of shares outstanding and the product is divided by the product of the prices of each index constituent weighted by the shares outstanding as of the base date. This general method, widely used today, was first proposed for use in comparing the relative changes in the prices of various commodities.

JULY 3, 1884

The Dow Jones Industrial Average made its debut in a two-page financial bulletin entitled "Customer's Afternoon Letter" which was the forerunner to *The Wall Street Journal*. It consisted of a list of 11 stocks, nine railroads and two industrial companies, that was calculated by adding up the closing prices of these stocks and dividing the total by 11. The index was one of the three or four indices available at the time and the oldest surviving proxy for the performance of the U.S. stock market. It was compiled by Charles Henry Dow, the first editor of *The Wall Street Journal* and co-founder, in 1882, of Dow Jones & Co., in response to a need for a market barometer to reflect the general movement of stocks in the United States.

Over the next 12 years, Charles Dow experimented with different lists of stocks in an effort to develop an index consisting entirely of industrial stocks. On May 26, 1886, the first industrial stock average consisting of 12 industrial issues was published. Like its predecessor, this average was computed in the same manner by adding up closing prices and dividing the total by 12. At the same time, Dow also created a 20 stock railroad average (later becoming the Transportation Average) and publication of the two averages began October 7, 1896 on a continuous basis. The list of 12 companies was expanded to 20 in 1916 and to 30 in 1928.

1923

The predecessor of today's Standard & Poor's Corporation pioneered the Standard & Poor's Composite Index. Standard & Poor's, which is today owned by McGraw Hill, was formed in 1941 with the merger of Poor & Co. (founded by Henry Varnum Poor) and the Standard Statistics Bureau (founded by Luther Blake).

The S&P Index was created to address the needs of the professional investor to compare directly the performance of their stock portfolios to a stock market indicator that measured the changes in the value of a market portfolio. The index was computed using a "base-weighted aggregative" technique derived from the Paasche index formula. (The current index is expressed in relatives with the base market value represented by an average of the 1941-1943 period set equal to 10.)

The Standard & Poor's Composite Index tracked 233 stock issues and covered 26 industry groups for which individual indexes were also calculated. Index values were computed weekly but in response to a need to disseminate its market indicator information more frequently, a 90-stock composite, featuring daily calculations, was begun in 1926. The 90-stock composite index, which was calculated in addition to the 233 stock index, consisted of 50 industrials, 20 rails and 20 utilities. Daily publication of the 90-stock composite index was initiated in 1928.

DECEMBER 25, 1929

On this date, Dow Jones introduced a utility average. Then, on November 11, 1933, the Dow Jones Composite Average was introduced. This index was calculated by combining the three Dow Averages, including the Dow Jones Industrial Average, Transportation and Utility Averages.

1930'S

Alfred Cowles developed a stock index that partially satisfied the broad criteria for a well constructed index. His index, for New York Stock Exchange stocks, was the first to measure total returns and to weight these returns correctly for as large a population of stocks. However, the index used the average value of the market price each month, rather than a stock's end of month value, so that returns, over a given period, can only be approximated. Nevertheless, the Cowles index provided valuable data.

1935

The Financial News, a London publishing company which was later absorbed by the *Financial Times,* introduced the Financial Times Index. At the time of its introduction, it was known as the 30 Share Index in recognition of the number of constituent shares making up the index. Calculated once a day, this geometric index is one of the nine or so stock indices in the world still calculated on this basis. The Financial Times Index was followed up in 1962 with the introduction of the Financial Times-Actuaries Share Index covering over 700 constituent shares.

1948

The National Quotation Bureau introduced the Over-The-Counter Industrial Index. This index included 35 companies all having a market value of over $10 million and a large group of shareholders.

SEPTEMBER 5, 1950

Nihon Keizai Shimbun, Inc. introduced the Nikkei 225 Stock Average. The index was fashioned after the Dow Jones Industrial Average in terms of its simple arithmetic average calculation methodology.

1955

The New York Stock Exchange (NYSE) began producing a broad measure of stock price movements. Called the Stock Price Profile, this indicator provided a frequency distribution of percentage price changes over a given span of time. It was limited to 300 issues, usually representing slightly less than three quarters of the total market value of all the NYSE-listed stocks. As it fell short of representing a succinct figure describing what happened to the market, the Exchange, which benefited from its new computerized Market Data System, advanced to a point where it could produce, efficiently and economically, a stock price index that would be useful to the investing public. Thus, on July 14, 1966, the NYSE began to publish the new NYSE Composite Index and subindices.

1957

The S&P Composite Index was expanded to include 500 stocks, with 83 individual industry groups, which formed three main sector groups: The industrials with 425 stocks, utilities with 60 stocks and rails with 15 stocks.

1968

Capital International, S.A., the Swiss subsidiary of the Capital Group, Inc., created the first international performance benchmark designed to track the world's developed markets. The right to the index was acquired in 1986 by Morgan Stanley.

JANUARY 1973

Lehman Brothers introduced the Lehman Government/Corporate Bond Index, which was expanded to include mortgage-backed, Yankee securities and the Aggregate Bond Index in January 1986.

MID-1981

International Finance Corporation, a subsidiary of the World Bank, initiated a series of indices based on the 10 to 20 most active stocks in each of 10 emerging markets.

MARCH 1, 1983

The Chicago Board Options Exchange developed the CBOE 100 Index (subsequently renamed the S&P 100 Index) and options on the index commenced trading on this date.

JULY 1983

The Federation of International Bourses de Valores (F.I.B.V.) adopted voluntary common computation guidelines for the production of a stock return index, pursuant to "FIBV Standards." These specify a weighted index composed of all domestic shares listed on the individual stock exchange, the addition of paid dividends as of the ex-dividend date for total rate of return results and a computation method derived from the Paasche index formula

1987

Frank Russell Co. introduced the Russell series of equity indices, including the Russell 2000 Index of small capitalization stocks.

JANUARY 1, 1988

Standard & Poor's began daily calculation of a total rate of return version of the S&P 500 Index. Previously, total return performance was calculated with dividends reinvested either monthly or quarterly.

DECEMBER 1989

J.P. Morgan introduced the J.P. Morgan Government Bond Index, a family of indices consisting of regularly traded government bonds of 11 countries.

JUNE 5, 1991

Standard & Poor's launched the MidCap 400 Index, consisting of an investable universe of middle capitalization stocks.

DECEMBER 1991

The Association of Investment Management and Research (AIMR) published standard methodology guidelines for investment managers to use in presenting their performance records to the public. These became effective on January 1, 1993.

MAY 1992

Standard & Poor's and BARRA introduced the S&P/BARRA Growth and Value indices.

AUGUST 1992

J. P. Morgan introduced the Emerging Market Bond Index, a total return index that tracks emerging market debt instruments.

DECEMBER 1995

Frank Russell Company and Nomura Research Institute introduced a Japanese total market index and an equity style index series designed to track large-, middle-, and small-capitalization stocks. The index series is further delineated by growth and value orientation.

JULY 1, 1996

Dow Jones renames its Dow Jones World Stock Index to Dow Jones Global Index and is the first index publisher to calculate an entire global index on a "real-time" basis.

7

GUIDE TO INDEX PROFILES

DEFINITION OF TERMS

INDEX NAME

The name of the index or subindex. The abbreviated name assigned to indices that serve as underlying vehicles for exchange-traded derivative instruments in the U.S. generally corresponds to the instrument's trading symbol.

PERFORMANCE GRAPH

The chart displays calendar year price or total return performance along with cumulative performance results for a period up to the last 10 calendar years through December 31, 1995. Unless otherwise indicated, performance results are expressed in *local currency terms*.

PERFORMANCE RECORD

The table displays year-end index values, annual price only performance and total rates of return, cumulative performance results, and yearly maximum and minimum index values along with their corresponding dates, for a period up to the last 10 calendar years through December 31, 1995. Unless otherwise indicated, index values and performance results are expressed in *local currency terms*. The Performance Record places emphasis on total rates of return. The periodic returns associated with stock and to a lesser extent, commoditiesindices, are typically reported by the financial media and, to a lesser degree, financial data vendors, on a price only basis such that the index values corresponding to these performance results are familiar to investors. For this reason, the Performance Record applicable to stock indices displays the year-end price only index values along with the maximum and minimum values pertaining to the price only performance results. Some exceptions apply. To the extent available, a separate additional column displays calendar year total rates of return. This is not generally the case for indices that track bonds, money market instruments, convertible securities, Guaranteed Investment Contracts, mutual funds and real estate. The more common practice concerning these asset classes is to emphasize and publish total rate of return results. Accordingly, the first three columns display index values based on total rates of return, and cumulative performance. A companion fourth column offers calendar year price only returns. Here too, some exceptions apply.

INDEX VALUE

The calendar year-end price only index value or total rate of return index value, as indicated, since its inception or for each of the last 10 years, whichever is longer. Values are generally displayed to two decimal places.

PRICE RETURN (%)

Annual rate of return expressed in percent terms, calculated on a price only basis.

TOTAL RETURN (%)

Annual total rate of return, with reinvestment of dividends, interest income and accrued interest, expressed in percent terms.

CUMULATIVE (%)

The final compounded price only or total rate of return performance for the 10-year period starting December 31, 1985 to December 31, 1995 and intervening years. In the absence of a 10 year performance record or data availability, the cumulative returns cover an abbreviated time period.

MAXIMUM VALUE

The highest *closing* index value recorded during the calendar year. For stock indices, this is generally the highest closing daily value, but, in some cases, the value may represent the highest intraday value. For all other indices, the maximum index value is generally as of month-end, regardless of frequency of calculation. This is noted as such, except for indices whose values are calculated on a less frequent monthly or quarterly basis.

MINIMUM VALUE

The lowest *closing* index value recorded during the calendar year. For stock indices, this is generally the lowest closing daily value, but, in some cases, the value may represent the lowest intraday value. For all other indices, the minimum value is generally as of month-end, regardless of frequency of calculation. This is noted as such, except for indices whose values are calculated on a less frequent monthly or quarterly basis.

DATE

The actual or month-end date on which the maximum or minimum value was recorded.

AVERAGE ANNUAL RATE OF RETURN (%)

The arithmetic average of the annual rates of return.

COMPOUND ANNUAL RATE OF RETURN (%)

The annual rate of return which, when compounded (reinvested) for the number of periods over which performance is available, results in the cumulative rate of return at December 31, 1995. It is calculated on a price only and total rate of return basis, subject to the availability of data.

STANDARD DEVIATION (%)

A statistical measure that describes the range or variability in the annual price only and total rates of return around the average annual rate of return. The standard deviation is calculated for a sample population using available annual data.

SYNOPSIS

A brief description of the index or subindex, its coverage, frequency of calculation and method of constituent weighting and averaging.

NUMBER OF ISSUES

The number of stocks, bonds or other instruments that constitute the index at December 31, 1995. In some cases, the number of companies rather than issues may be reported.

MARKET VALUE

The aggregate market value of the stocks, bonds or other instruments that are tracked by the index, expressed in U.S. dollars, as of December 31, 1995. In some cases, adjusted market values or float capitalization are reported. Refer to Appendix 9 for foreign currency exchange rates used to compute market values.

SELECTION CRITERIA

A description of the guidelines, practices and procedures used to qualify, select, monitor and replace index constituents.

BACKGROUND

Relevant historical information regarding the index, its launch date, modifications and the availability of historical data.

BASE DATE

The initial or starting value assigned to the index and its corresponding date. Indices may be launched with backdated or simulated historical data, in which case index values are available for periods of time that precede the base date.

COMPUTATION METHODOLOGY

In addition to the general form or specific index formula used in the calculation of the index, this section cites additional pertinent policies and/or factors relating to the calculation of the index. These include weighting of index constituents, frequency and timing of reconstitution, frequency and timing of divisor adjustments due to capital changes and constituent additions and deletions, treatment of stock dividends and/or interest, securities pricing, exchange rates, reinvestment of cash flows and any other available pertinent information.

DERIVATIVE INSTRUMENTS

This section identifies the availability of *exchange-traded* stock index futures and options, and other derivative securities, along with all the exchanges where traded. *Please note:* Investment banks offer a variety of non-exchange listed customized financial products that are based on entire indices or segments of indices, such as forwards, options, swaps, index notes and index linked bonds. Such proprietary products, however, are beyond the scope of this section.

SUBINDICES

This section cites the availability of subindices calculated by the publisher. In some cases, publishers offer the flexibility to customize subindices on the basis of user defined criteria such as security type, geographic subdivision, industry segments, economic sectors, quality, and maturity. The availability of this feature is also noted, based on available information.

RELATED INDICES

A full or partial listing of any other securities market indices offered by the publisher. Related indices are identified for cross reference purposes. In the event related indices are too numerous to list, the reader is referred to *Appendix 5: Comprehensive Directory of Indices* for a comprehensive list. Related indices are generally profiled elsewhere in *The Guide,* or described in abbreviated form in *Appendix 2: Supplemental Securities Market Indices.*

REMARKS

Additional relevant information relating to the index, its composition, construction and computation methodology.

PUBLISHER

The name of the stock exchange, publisher, money management organization, investment bank or other entity that publishes the index. Some indices, which have been created and published by independent publishers, but adopted by an exchange for purposes of trading derivative instruments, are generally attributed to the publisher. For example, the S&P 100 Index, published by Standard & Poor's Corp., has also been adopted by the Chicago Board Options Exchange (CBOE) as a vehicle for stock index options. The index is listed under the Standard & Poor's name. The BioTechnology Index, on the other hand, has been created and maintained by the CBOE. This index, therefore, is attributed to the CBOE.

8

INDEX PROFILES — STOCKS
NORTH AMERICA

BERMUDA STOCK EXCHANGE INDEX

PRICE PERFORMANCE

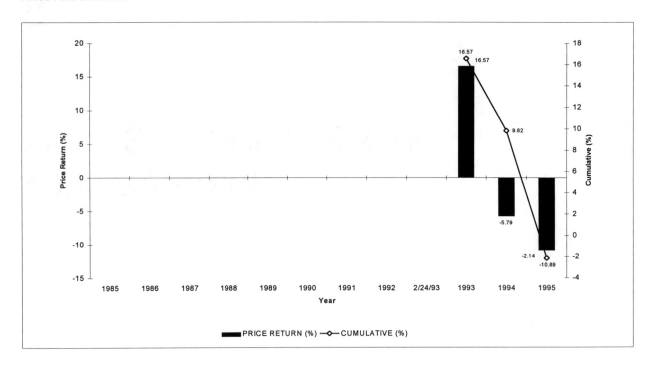

PRICE PERFORMANCE

YEAR	VALUE	PRICE RETURN (%)	CUMULATIVE (%)	MAXIMUM VALUE	DATE	MINIMUM VALUE	DATE
1995	978.58	-10.89	-2.14	1,113.92	11-Jan	976.92	27-Dec
1994	1,098.17	-5.79	9.82	1,221.36	20-Jul	944.71	14-May
1993	1,165.65	16.57	16.57	NA	NA	NA	NA
2/24/93	1,000.00						
1992							
1991							
1990							
1989							
1988							
1987							
1986							
1985							
Average Annual (%)		-0.04					
Compound Annual (%)		-0.76					
Standard Deviation (%)		NM					

SYNOPSIS
The Bermuda Stock Exchange Index is a market value-weighted index that tracks the daily stock price performance of the most widely held and actively traded domestic stocks traded on the Bermuda Stock Exchange.

NUMBER OF STOCKS—DECEMBER 31, 1995
20

MARKET VALUE—DECEMBER 31, 1995
US$877.0 million

SELECTION CRITERIA
Constituents are limited to domestic companies whose stocks are widely held and actively traded.

BACKGROUND
The index was rebased in 1993, concurrent with the commencement of trading on a daily basis.

BASE DATE
February 24, 1993=1000.00

COMPUTATION METHODOLOGY
(1) An aggregative of prices times quantities index formula. Maintenance adjustments to the divisor are made for capitalization changes, new listings and delistings. (2) The index, including number of shares issued and outstanding, is reviewed every six months. Modifications may be implemented on a more frequent basis as may be dictated by the development of significant events.

DERIVATIVE INSTRUMENTS
None

SUBINDICES
None

RELATED INDICES
None

REMARKS
Top three stocks, including Bank of Bermuda, Bank of N.T. Butterfield and Belco Holdings account for 74% of the index.

PUBLISHER
Bermuda Stock Exchange.

THE CANADIAN MARKET PORTFOLIO (XXM) INDEX

PRICE PERFORMANCE

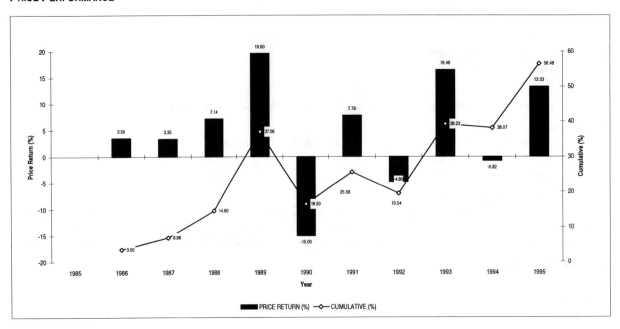

PRICE AND TOTAL RETURN PERFORMANCE

YEAR	VALUE	PRICE RETURN (%)	CUMULATIVE (%)	TOTAL RETURN (%)	MAXIMUM VALUE	DATE	MINIMUM VALUE	DATE
1995	2,318.55	13.33	56.48	17.00	2,344.31	11-Dec	1,954.50	30-Jan
1994	2,045.79	-0.82	38.07	2.78	2,182.69	1-Feb	1,868.48	28-Jun
1993	2,062.71	16.46	39.22	20.50	2,071.43	30-Dec	1,720.97	21-Jan
1992	1,771.12	-4.80	19.54	-0.58	1,942.25	16-Jan	1,627.37	5-Oct
1991	1,860.43	7.78	25.56	11.89	1,907.74	12-Nov	1,682.58	14-Jan
1990	1,726.13	-15.00	16.50	-11.42	2,066.98	3-Jan	1,606.45	16-Oct
1989	2,030.83	19.60	37.06	25.25	2,069.68	10-Oct	1,677.48	3-Jan
1988	1,698.00	7.14	14.60	11.26	1,723.71	7-May	1,489.95	8-Feb
1987	1,584.77	3.35	6.96	6.72	2,063.92	13-Aug	1,435.94	26-Oct
1986	1,533.46	3.50	3.50	7.27	1,623.33	16-Apr	1,386.60	22-Jan
1985	1,481.66							
Average Annual (%)		5.05		9.03				
Compound Annual (%)		4.58		8.54				
Standard Deviation (%)		10.34		10.66				

SYNOPSIS

The Canadian Market Portfolio (XXM) Index is an equal-weighted index that tracks the continuous price only and daily total return performance of the 25 most widely held "blue chip" Canadian common stocks listed on at least two Canadian exchanges. These shares account for about 47% of the Canadian equities traded on the Montreal Stock Exchange (MSE).

NUMBER OF STOCKS—DECEMBER 31, 1995

25

MARKET VALUE—DECEMBER 31, 1995

US$143,015.0 million

SELECTION CRITERIA

Eligible constituent stocks must be listed on the Montreal Stock Exchange (MSE), be issued by a company incorporated in Canada or held by a majority of Canadian investors, be a common share, be listed for at least two years, have had a market capitalization of at least $10 million during the last two years, have had trading volume of at least 100,000 shares and a value of at least $4 million (total Canadian trading) over the last completed year, have a minimum 3.6 million shares outstanding, and have traded at a price over $5.00 during a period of 12 conservative months.

BACKGROUND

None

BASE DATE

January 4, 1983=1000.00

COMPUTATION METHODOLOGY

(1) A simple aggregative of actual prices index formula. (2) Prices used are based on the most recent sales, regardless of which exchange the sale occurred. (3) Component stocks are revised annually to assure proper representation of Canadian companies in their respective economic sectors and that their proportionate weighting in the index reflect the companies' importance.

DERIVATIVE INSTRUMENTS

None

SUBINDICES

Six subindices: Canadian banks, Canadian forest products, Canadian industrial products, Canadian mining and minerals, Canadian oil and gas, and Canadian utilities.

RELATED INDICES

None

REMARKS

None

PUBLISHER

The Montreal Stock Exchange (MSE).

TORONTO STOCK EXCHANGE 35 (TSE 35) INDEX

PRICE PERFORMANCE

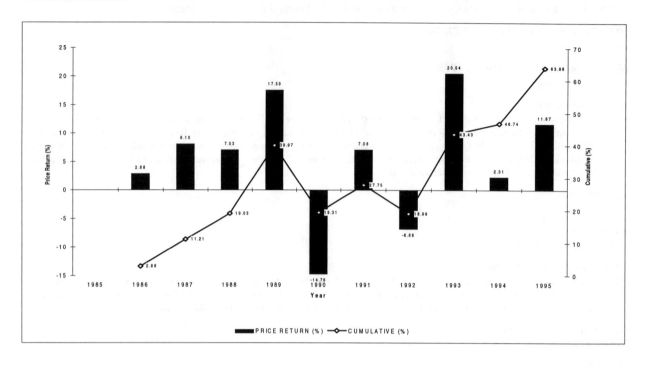

PRICE PERFORMANCE

YEAR	VALUE	PRICE RETURN (%)	CUMULATIVE (%)	TOTAL RETURN (%)	MAXIMUM VALUE	DATE	MINIMUM VALUE	DATE
1995	248.49	11.67	63.86	14.72	250.86	11-Dec	210.63	30-Jan
1994	222.53	2.31	46.74	5.52	233.53	23-Mar	200.89	24-Jun
1993	217.51	20.54	43.43	24.34	218.61	30-Dec	174.68	22-Jan
1992	180.45	-6.86	18.99	-3.58	201.03	16-Jan	172.46	14-Oct
1991	193.74	7.08	27.75	11.01	198.66	12-Nov	176.03	9-Jan
1990	180.93	-14.76	19.31	-11.65	215.54	NA	168.18	NA
1989	212.27	17.59	39.97	21.89	215.83	6-Oct	178.01	3-Jan
1988	180.51	7.03	19.03	11.32	184.66	NA	155.55	NA
1987	168.65	8.10	11.21	11.29	216.92	NA	148.04	NA
1986	156.01	2.88	2.88	6.34	161.08	NA	143.12	NA
1985	151.65							
Average Annual (%)		5.56		9.12				
Compound Annual (%)		5.06		8.62				
Standard Deviation (%)		10.55		10.81				

Synopsis

The Toronto Stock Exchange 35 (TSE 35) Index is a market value-weighted index that tracks the continuous price only and daily total return performance of the largest and most heavily traded Canadian common stocks listed on the Toronto Stock Exchange (TSE). These stocks, attributable to companies that must be incorporated in Canada, account for about 35% of the Toronto Canadian market capitalization.

Number of Stocks—December 31, 1995

35

Market Value—December 31, 1995

US$127,451.0 million

Selection Criteria

Criteria for inclusion are as follows:

(1) Constituent companies must be incorporated in Canada and tracked in the Toronto Stock Exchange 300 (TSE 300) Composite Index. (2) TSE 300 major industry groups with a weighting of 5% or more must be represented in the TSE 35 Index. (3) All shares added to the index must be options eligible, including compliance with the rule that the stock must not close below $5.00 for the majority of business days of the preceding nine month period. (4) The trade-weighted average float quoted market value (QMV) from the previous year is used to rank the stocks in the Toronto 35 stock pool, thereafter, liquidity is the first consideration employed in the selection of new stock additions to the index. (QMV is defined as the one-year trade weighted average price of the stock for the preceding 12-month period, or total value traded divided by the total volume of the shares traded for the preceding 12-month period, multiplied by its float outstanding at the end of this period). (5) Any stock added to the index must rank in the top 150 in terms of volume traded, value traded and total transactions executed, based on a composite of the stock's trading activity on the Toronto Stock Exchange (TSE). (6) Trading value for the stock for the year immediately preceding its consideration as a candidate for inclusion in the index must have been at least C$100 million, and the company's float QMV must exceed C$200 million at the time of inclusion.

When a company has more than one class of common stock or equivalent shares outstanding, only one class of shares is eligible for inclusion in the index. With some exceptions, preferred shares are excluded from consideration as index constituents.

Background

The TSE 35 was developed in 1987 for the purpose of providing a liquid vehicle that reasonably tracks the Toronto Stock Exchange 300 Composite Index and to establish trading derivative products. It was launched on May 25, 1987.

Base Date

January 1, 1982=100.00

Computation Methodology

(1) An aggregate of prices times quantities index formula. Maintenance adjustments to the divisor are made for capitalization changes, new listings and delistings, and loss of Canadian incorporation. (2) Market capitalization is computed based on quoted market value (QMV). A ceiling of 10% has been placed on any one stock to ensure that no one stock or industry dominates the index. (3) The composition of the index is reviewed and adjusted annually, in February, and, unless special circumstances dictate otherwise, revisions become effective once a year at the opening of the first day following the expiration of the February options and futures contracts. This usually falls on the third Friday of the month. Special circumstances include suspensions, delistings, a decline in the QMV to a level below $100 million over a period that extends to 51% of the trading days for three consecutive months, based on its daily close, mergers, bankruptcies, etc. (4) Prices used are based on the most recent sales, regardless of which exchange the sale occurred. (5) Dividends are reinvested as of the ex-dividend date.

Derivative Instruments

TSE 35 stock index options and futures contracts trade on the Toronto Stock Exchange (TSE).
Toronto Index Participation Units (TIPS) and TIPS options contracts trade on the Toronto Stock Exchange (TSE).

Subindices

None

Related Indices

TSE 300 Index
TSE 100 Index
TSE 200 Index

Remarks

(1) Control block is defined as any individual or group of related individuals who control 15% or more of a company's outstanding shares. (2) Percent of market capitalization calculated on the basis of quoted market value.

Publisher

The Toronto Stock Exchange (TSE).

TORONTO STOCK EXCHANGE 100 (TSE 100) COMPOSITE INDEX

PRICE PERFORMANCE

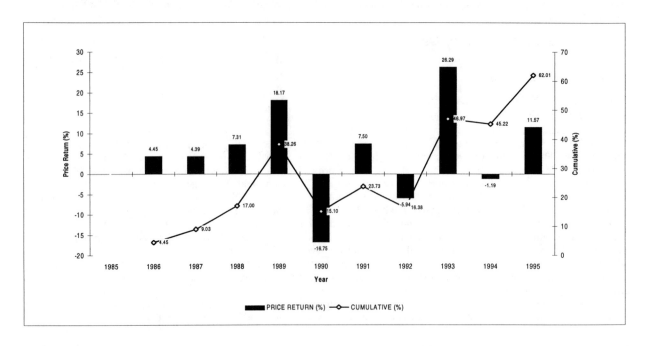

PRICE AND TOTAL RETURN PERFORMANCE

YEAR	VALUE	PRICE RETURN (%)	CUMULATIVE (%)	TOTAL RETURN (%)	MAXIMUM VALUE	DATE	MINIMUM VALUE	DATE
1995	286.31	11.57	62.01	14.47	289.57	6-Dec	242.50	30-Jan
1994	256.63	-1.19	45.22	1.36	277.38	NA	237.89	NA
1993	259.72	26.29	46.97	30.04	260.71	NA	200.43	NA
1992	205.66	-5.94	16.38	-2.60	227.97	NA	196.58	NA
1991	218.65	7.50	23.73	11.73	224.03	NA	197.69	NA
1990	203.40	-16.75	15.10	-13.44	247.25	NA	186.63	NA
1989	244.33	18.17	38.26	22.66	247.41	NA	204.40	NA
1988	206.76	7.31	17.00	11.30	210.93	NA	180.83	NA
1987	192.68	4.39	9.03	7.40	247.37	NA	172.09	NA
1986	184.58	4.45	4.45	7.84	189.95	NA	166.56	NA
1985	176.72							
Average Annual (%)		5.58		9.08				
Compound Annual (%)		4.94		8.43				
Standard Deviation (%)		12.06		12.35				

SYNOPSIS

The Toronto Stock Exchange 100 (TSE 100) Composite Index is a market value-weighted index that tracks the price and total return performance of the largest and most actively traded Canadian common stocks listed on the Toronto Stock Exchange (TSE). These stocks account for about 43% of the Toronto Canadian market capitalization.

NUMBER OF STOCKS—DECEMBER 31, 1995

100

MARKET VALUE—DECEMBER 31, 1995

US$156,540.0 million

SELECTION CRITERIA

To be eligible for inclusion in the index, a constituent company must be a member of the Toronto Stock Exchange 300 (TSE 300) Composite Index.

Stocks are ranked and selected on the basis of one-year average float quoted market value (QMV). QMV is defined as the one-year trade-weighted average price multiplied by its float outstanding at the end of this period of the stock for the preceding 12-month period (total value traded divided by the total volume of the shares traded).

Any TSE 300 Index constituent is eligible for inclusion in the index if the stock's aggregate dollar value of shares traded for the previous 12 months ranks within the top 150 of the TSE 300 Index on the month-end prior to the annual review meeting, or the stock ranks within the top 50 of the 300 stocks of the existing TSE 300 Index on the basis of float QMV. Stocks that rank between 1 and 50 of the TSE 300 Index on the basis of float QMV at the end of each month are added to the index at the open of the following month's options and futures contracts expiration date.

Refer to the TSE 300 Index for additional information regarding selection criteria.

BACKGROUND

Introduced on October 1, 1993, the index was created to better reflect the investing universe of large domestic institutional investors in light of the view that the TSE 300 Composite Index contained stocks judged to be "not investable" due to their small size and illiquidity.

Index values have been backdated to December 31, 1981.

BASE DATE

August 31, 1993=250.00

COMPUTATION METHODOLOGY

(1) An aggregate of prices times quantities index formula. Maintenance adjustments to the divisor are made for capitalization changes, new listings and delistings and loss of Canadian incorporation. (2) Market capitalization is computed based on quoted market value. QMV is the total number of a company's shares outstanding less any shares that are controlled by an individual or group of related individuals who control 15% or more of the company's outstanding shares, multiplied by the last trade price for a board lot of shares. Excepting share capitalization changes or series of share capitalization changes having an index weight impact estimated to be 0.05 or greater which are implemented at the first practical date, shares outstanding are reviewed and updated once every calendar quarter. (3) The composition of the index is reviewed and adjusted annually, in February, and, unless special circumstances dictate otherwise, revisions become effective once a year at the opening of the first day following the expiration of the February options and futures contracts. This usually falls on the third Friday of the month. Special circumstances include suspensions, delistings, a decline in the QMV to a level below $100 million over a period that extends to 51% of the trading days for three consecutive months, based on its daily close, mergers, bankruptcies, etc. (4) Prices used are based on the most recent sales, regardless of which exchange the sale occurred. (5) Dividends are reinvested as of the ex-dividend date.

DERIVATIVE INSTRUMENTS

None

SUBINDICES

Four economic sector subindices (price only performance): Resources, consumer, industrial and interest sensitive sectors.
Fourteen industry group subindices (price only performance): Metals and minerals, gold and precious metals, oil and gas, paper and forest products, consumer products, industrial products, real estate, transportation/environmental services, pipelines, utilities, communications and media, merchandising, financial services and conglomerates.

RELATED INDICES

TSE 300 Composite Index
TSE 200 Composite Index
TSE 35 Index

REMARKS

(1) Control block is defined as any individual or group of related individuals who control 15% or more of a company's outstanding shares. (2) Trading activity is based on combined transactions on The Toronto Stock Exchange (TSE) and Montreal Stock Exchange (MSE). (3) Percent of market capitalization calculated on the basis of quoted market value.

PUBLISHER

The Toronto Stock Exchange (TSE).

TORONTO STOCK EXCHANGE 200 (TSE 200) COMPOSITE INDEX

PRICE PERFORMANCE

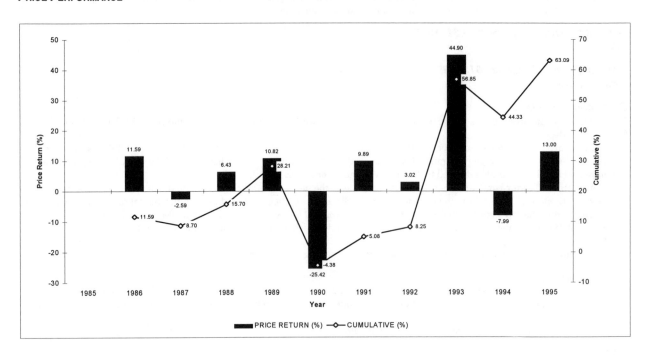

PRICE AND TOTAL RETURN PERFORMANCE

YEAR	VALUE	PRICE RETURN (%)	CUMULATIVE (%)	TOTAL RETURN (%)	MAXIMUM VALUE	DATE	MINIMUM VALUE	DATE
1995	282.93	13.00	63.09	14.62	282.93	29-Dec	239.22	16-Feb
1994	250.38	-7.99	44.33	-6.59	288.84	NA	236.49	NA
1993	272.11	44.90	56.85	47.50	272.53	NA	186.44	NA
1992	187.79	3.02	8.25	5.19	198.70	NA	176.67	NA
1991	182.29	9.89	5.08	13.59	190.62	NA	159.56	NA
1990	165.89	-25.42	-4.38	-23.05	222.68	NA	160.69	NA
1989	222.42	10.82	28.21	13.95	232.56	NA	199.35	NA
1988	200.71	6.43	15.70	9.67	208.85	NA	180.63	NA
1987	188.58	-2.59	8.70	-0.45	260.81	NA	172.93	NA
1986	193.59	11.59	11.59	14.02	195.06	NA	170.38	NA
1985	173.48							
Average Annual (%)		6.37		8.85				
Compound Annual (%)		5.01		7.49				
Standard Deviation (%)		17.94		18.13				

SYNOPSIS

The Toronto Stock Exchange 200 (TSE 200) Composite Index is a market value-weighted index that tracks the continuous price and daily total return performance of the smaller and less actively traded Canadian common stocks listed on the Toronto Stock Exchange (TSE) which are represented in the Toronto Stock Exchange 300 (TSE 300) Composite Index, excluding shares that constitute the Toronto Stock Exchange 100 (TSE 100) Composite Index. These stocks account for about 20% of the Toronto Canadian market capitalization.

NUMBER OF STOCKS—DECEMBER 31, 1995

200

MARKET VALUE—DECEMBER 31, 1995

US$71,821.0 million

SELECTION CRITERIA

Eligible common stocks which are limited to companies incorporated in Canada and listed on the Toronto Stock Exchange (TSE), include TSE 300 Index constituents that are not members of the TSE 100 Index. The latter includes the largest and most actively traded Canadian common stocks.

Refer to the TSE 100 Index and TSE 300 Index for additional information regarding selection criteria.

BACKGROUND

The index was introduced on October 1, 1993 and index values were backdated to December 31, 1981.

BASE DATE

August 31, 1993=250.00

COMPUTATION METHODOLOGY

(1) An aggregate of prices times quantities index formula. Maintenance adjustments to the divisor are made for capitalization changes, new listings and delistings and loss of Canadian incorporation. (2) Market capitalization is computed based on quoted market value (QMV) which is the total number of a company's shares outstanding less any shares that are controlled by an individual or group of related individuals who control 15% or more of the company's outstanding shares, multiplied by the last trade price for a board lot of shares. Excepting share capitalization changes or series of share capitalization changes having an index weight impact estimated to be 0.05 or greater which are implemented at the first practical date, shares outstanding are reviewed and updated once every calendar quarter. (3) The composition of the index is reviewed and adjusted annually, in February, and, unless special circumstances dictate otherwise, revisions become effective once a year at the opening of the first day following the expiration of the February options and futures contracts. This usually falls on the third Friday of the month. Special circumstances include suspensions, delistings, a decline in the QMV to a level below $100 million over a period that extends to 51% of the trading days for three consecutive months, based on its daily close, mergers, bankruptcies, etc. (4) Prices used are based on the most recent sales, regardless of which exchange the sale occurred. (5) Dividends are reinvested as of the ex-dividend date.

DERIVATIVE INSTRUMENTS

None

SUBINDICES

Four economic sector subindices (price only performance): Resources, consumer, industrial and interest sensitive sectors.
Fourteen industry group subindices (price only performance): Metals and minerals, gold and precious metals, oil and gas, paper and forest products, consumer products, industrial products, real estate, transportation/environmental services, pipelines, utilities, communications and media, merchandising, financial services and conglomerates.

RELATED INDICES

TSE 100 Composite Index
TSE 300 Composite Index
TSE 35 Index

REMARKS

Percent of market capitalization calculated on the basis of quoted market value.

PUBLISHER

The Toronto Stock Exchange (TSE).

TORONTO STOCK EXCHANGE 300 (TSE 300) COMPOSITE INDEX

PRICE PERFORMANCE

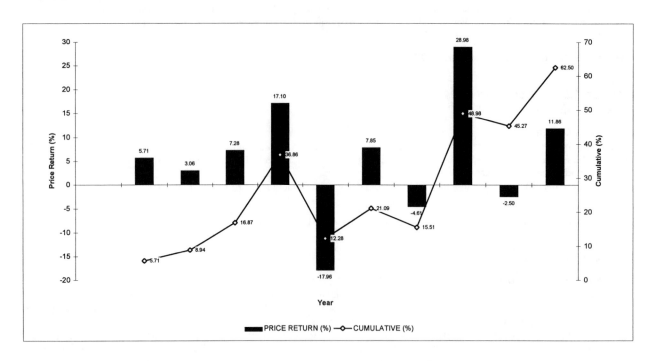

PRICE AND TOTAL RETURN PERFORMANCE

YEAR	VALUE	PRICE RETURN (%)	CUMULATIVE (%)	TOTAL RETURN (%)	MAXIMUM VALUE	DATE	MINIMUM VALUE	DATE
1995	4,713.54	11.86	62.50	14.53	4,745.10	6-Dec	3,991.41	30-Jan
1994	4,213.61	-2.50	45.27	-0.18	4,609.93	23-Mar	3,935.66	27-Jun
1993	4,321.43	28.98	48.98	32.55	4,330.01	30-Dec	3,263.19	21-Jan
1992	3,350.44	-4.61	15.51	-1.43	3,672.58	16-Jan	3,149.97	5-Oct
1991	3,512.36	7.85	21.09	12.02	3,604.09	12-Nov	3,150.88	16-Jan
1990	3,256.75	-17.96	12.28	-14.80	4,020.86	3-Jan	3,007.80	16-Oct
1989	3,969.79	17.10	36.86	21.37	4,042.28	6-Oct	3,348.47	3-Jan
1988	3,389.99	7.28	16.87	11.08	3,478.94	6-Jul	2,976.32	8-Feb
1987	3,160.05	3.06	8.94	5.88	4,118.94	13-Aug	2,783.25	28-Oct
1986	3,066.18	5.71	5.71	8.95	3,134.49	29-Apr	2,743.97	23-Jan
1985	2,900.60							
Average Annual (%)		5.68		9.00				
Compound Annual (%)		4.98		8.29				
Standard Deviation (%)		12.73		13.00				

SYNOPSIS

The Toronto Stock Exchange 300 (TSE 300) Composite Index is a market value-weighted index that tracks the continuous price and daily total return performance of the largest and most actively traded 300 Canadian common stocks listed on the Toronto Stock Exchange (TSE). These stocks account for about 85% of the Toronto Canadian market capitalization.

NUMBER OF STOCKS—DECEMBER 31, 1995
300

MARKET VALUE—DECEMBER 31, 1995
US$310,150.0 million

SELECTION CRITERIA

To be eligible for inclusion in the index, a company must be incorporated in Canada and listed on the Toronto Stock Exchange (TSE). Only one class of shares is eligible for inclusion in the index. With some exceptions, preferred shares are excluded from consideration as index constituents. The stock must also meet the following criteria:

(1) It must have been listed on the TSE for twelve consecutive months prior to consideration, unless a stock has been listed on the TSE for at least six months and it ranks between 1-150 on a quoted market value (QMV)-basis on the month-end prior to the annual stock replacement review meeting. (2) Trading volume of the stock for the year immediately preceding its consideration must be at least 100,000 shares and at least 100 transactions. (3) Trading value of the stock for the year immediately preceding its consideration must have been at least C$1 million.

Stocks are ranked and selected on the basis of one-year average float quoted market value (QMV). QMV is defined as the one-year trade weighted average price multiplied by its float outstanding at the end of this period of the stock for the preceding 12-month period (total value traded divided by the total volume of the shares traded).

During this process, constituent stocks that have fallen lower than 325 in the average float QMV ranking are replaced by a stock which has taken its place within the largest 300. Similarly, if a stock which was not in the TSE 300 ranked higher than 275 in the eligible pool, then it replaces whichever TSE 300 stock ranked lowest from the largest 300.

BACKGROUND

Introduced in January 1977, the index replaced a simple, mathematical average index that had tracked the Canadian stock market from 1934 to 1963 when a 108 stock index was implemented.

BASE DATE

December 31, 1976=1000.00

COMPUTATION METHODOLOGY

(1) An aggregate of prices times quantities index formula. Maintenance adjustments to the divisor are made for capitalization changes, new listings and delistings and loss of Canadian incorporation. (2) Market capitalization is computed based on quoted market value (QMV). QMV is the total number of a company's shares outstanding less any shares that are controlled by an individual or group of related individuals who control 15% or more of the company's outstanding shares, multiplied by the last trade price for a board lot of shares. Excepting share capitalization changes or series of share capitalization changes having an index weight impact estimated to be 0.05 or greater which are implemented at the first practical date, shares outstanding are reviewed and updated once every calendar quarter. (3) The composition of the index is reviewed and adjusted annually, in February, and, unless special circumstances dictate otherwise, revisions become effective once a year at the opening of the first day following the expiration of the February options and futures contracts. This usually falls on the third Friday of the month. Special circumstances include suspensions, delistings, a decline in the QMV to a level below $100 million over a period that extends to 51% of the trading days for three consecutive months, based on its daily close, mergers, bankruptcies, etc. (4) Prices used are based on the most recent sales, regardless of which exchange the sale occurred. (5) Dividends are reinvested as of the ex-dividend date.

DERIVATIVE INSTRUMENTS

None

SUBINDICES

Four economic sector subindices (price only performance): Resources, consumer, industrial and interest sensitive sectors.
Fourteen industry group subindices (price only performance): Metals and minerals, gold and precious metals, oil and gas, paper and forest products, consumer products, industrial products, real estate, transportation/environmental services, pipelines, utilities, communications and media, merchandising, financial services and conglomerates.
Forty-three industry subgroups subindices (price only performance).

RELATED INDICES

TSE 100 Composite Index
TSE 200 Composite Index
TSE 35 Index

REMARKS

(1) Control block is defined as any individual or group of related individuals who control 15% or more of a company's outstanding shares. (2) Trading activity based on transactions on The Toronto Stock Exchange (TSE). (3) Percent of market capitalization calculated on the basis of quoted market value.

PUBLISHER

The Toronto Stock Exchange (TSE).

VANCOUVER STOCK EXCHANGE (VSE) INDEX

PRICE PERFORMANCE

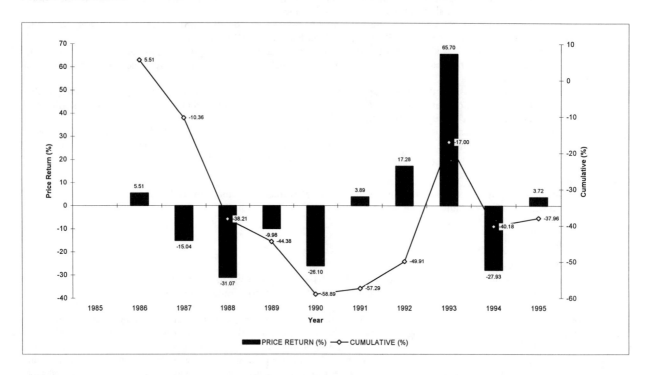

PRICE PERFORMANCE

YEAR	VALUE	PRICE RETURN (%)	CUMULATIVE (%)	MAXIMUM VALUE	DATE	MINIMUM VALUE	DATE
1995	795.93	3.72	-37.96	872.79	15-Sep	692.23	8-Mar
1994	767.40	-27.93	-40.18	1,169.55	3-Feb	722.53	20-Dec
1993	1,064.80	65.70	-17.00	642.44	5-Jan	1,064.80	31-Dec
1992	642.59	17.28	-49.91	544.62	27-Oct	642.59	31-Dec
1991	547.90	3.89	-57.29	493.95	23-Jan	547.90	31-Dec
1990	527.37	-26.10	-58.89	505.84	10-Dec	527.37	31-Dec
1989	713.63	-9.98	-44.38	850.88	8-Sep	676.31	16-Oct
1988	792.72	-31.07	-38.21	1,197.41	8-Jan	759.85	20-Dec
1987	1,150.02	-15.04	-10.36	2,024.45	19-May	1,101.51	22-Dec
1986	1,353.63	5.51	5.51	1,472.47	8-Sep	1,282.95	2-Jan
1985	1,282.95						
Average Annual (%)		-1.40					
Compound Annual (%)		-4.66					
Standard Deviation (%)		28.69					

Synopsis

The Vancouver Stock Exchange (VSE) Index is a market value-weighted index that tracks the continuous price only performance of stocks traded in meaningful levels on the Vancouver Stock Exchange (VSE).

Number of Stocks—December 31, 1995

1,225

Market Value—December 31, 1995

US$5,342.6 million

Selection Criteria

Eligible stocks must be listed on the VSE and trade at meaningful levels. In addition, the following selection criteria apply:
(1) Newly listed companies are not tracked in the index until 30 days after listing. (2) In the event a company is already inter-listed on another Canadian Stock Exchange, or NASDAQ in the United States, its stock is included in the index if at least 50% of trading on the issue, by volume, takes place on the VSE for a 90 day period. (3) A stock is removed from the index in the event it becomes inter-listed and trading on the VSE falls below 30% of all trading in any 30-day period. The stock will not be included again unless trading on the VSE increases to at least 50% of all trading volume for a 90-day period.

Background

The VSE formally launched its first equally-weighted share price index in January 1982 at an initial value of 1,000. It suffered from several drawbacks, however, and was reformulated to become market value-weighted. The reformulated VSE Index was formally introduced on January 2, 1986 at a value of 1,300.46.

In September 1989, as part of a major upgrade of its listing regulations, the VSE launched an entirely revised classification system for its listed companies. It was designed to recognize companies as they mature and develop and, at the same time, acknowledge differences between resource and non-resource companies. Thus, companies were classified as venture class, resource or commercial/industrial.

On June 1, 1990, the VSE introduced three subindices to track the performance of the three classification sections.

Base Date

January 2, 1986=1300.46

Computation Methodology

(1) An aggregate of prices times quantities index formula. Maintenance adjustments to the divisor are made for capitalization changes, new listings and delistings. (2) Market capitalization is computed based the total number of a company's shares outstanding, which is updated on a daily basis. (3) Companies are classified into one of three subindex classification sections on the basis of certain assets, market value and shareholder distribution tests. (4) All stocks are reviewed monthly for index eligibility requirements.

Derivative Instruments

None

Subindices

Three subindices: Commercial/Industrial, resource companies, and venture companies.

Related Indices

None

Remarks

In May 1995, the VSE established an Asian Board trading section designed exclusively for companies with substantial interests in Asia. Eleven companies make up the Asian Board as of September 1995 and account for 25% of the total market capitalization of the VSE Commercial/Industrial subindex. The VSE intends to launch an Asian Board index in the near future.

Publisher

The Vancouver Stock Exchange (VSE).

BOLSA MEXICANA DE VALORES INDICE DE PRECIOS Y COTIZACIONES (IPC) INDEX

TOTAL RETURN PERFORMANCE

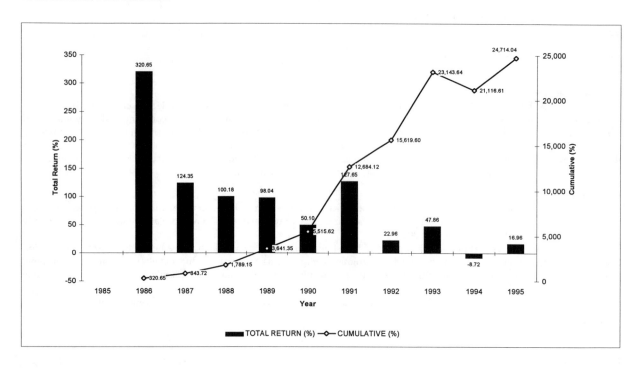

TOTAL RETURN PERFORMANCE

YEAR	VALUE	TOTAL RETURN (%)	CUMULATIVE (%)	MAXIMUM VALUE	DATE	MINIMUM VALUE	DATE
1995	2,778.47	16.96	24,714.04	2,834.39	21-Dec	1,447.52	27-Feb
1994	2,375.66	-8.72	21,116.61	2,881.17	8-Feb	1,957.33	20-Apr
1993	2,602.63	47.86	23,143.64	2,602.63	30-Dec	1,504.15	25-Feb
1992	1,760.15	22.96	15,619.60	1,907.38	1-Jun	1,252.10	25-Sep
1991	1,431.46	127.65	12,684.12	1,459.28	14-Nov	567.09	14-Jan
1990	628.79	50.10	5,515.62	683.64	25-Jul	417.43	2-Jan
1989	418.93	98.04	3,641.35	443.03	21-Sep	203.72	11-Jan
1988	211.53	100.18	1,789.15	230.09	25-Nov	86.61	7-Jan
1987	105.67	124.35	843.72	373.22	6-Oct	47.22	2-Jan
1986	47.10	320.65	320.65	47.10	30-Dec	10.83	6-Jan
1985	11.20						
Average Annual (%)		90.00					
Compound Annual(%)		73.57					
Standard Deviation (%)		93.64					

SYNOPSIS
The Bolsa Mexicana de Valores Indice de Precios y Cotizaciones (IPC) Index is a market capitalization weighted index that tracks the continuous total return performance of the largest and most actively traded stocks on the Mexican Stock Exchange. These shares account for about 52% of the domestic stock market capitalization.

NUMBER OF STOCKS—DECEMBER 31, 1995
35

MARKET VALUE—DECEMBER 31, 1995
US$47,039.1 million

SELECTION CRITERIA
IPC Index constituents, which vary between 30 and 40 companies, are selected on the basis of market capitalization, volume, and value of shares traded over a period of six months. Also taken into consideration is the number of days during which a company's shares are traded.

Index constituents are reviewed every two months.

BACKGROUND
In May 1991 the index value was divided by 1,000.

BASE DATE
October 30, 1978=781.62

COMPUTATION METHODOLOGY
Aggregate market value-weighted arithmetic average of the price ratios index formula is used. Maintenance adjustments to the divisor are made for capitalization changes, new listings and delistings.

DERIVATIVE INSTRUMENTS
None

SUBINDICES
Seven sectoral subindices: Mining, construction, commercial, transportation and communications, services, manufacturing and others.

RELATED INDICES
Inflation adjusted IPC Index

REMARKS
None

PUBLISHER
Bolsa Mexicana de Valores.

INMEX INDEX

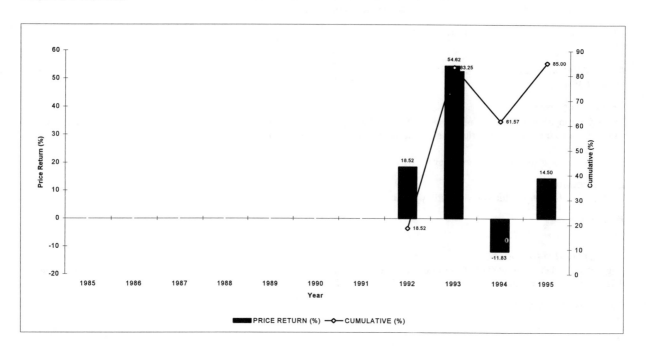

PRICE PERFORMANCE

YEAR	VALUE	PRICE RETURN (%)	CUMULATIVE (%)	MAXIMUM VALUE	DATE	MINIMUM VALUE	DATE
1995	185.00	14.50	85.00	186.02	27-Dec	92.72	27-Feb
1994	161.57	-11.83	61.57	203.96	23-Sep	136.87	20-Apr
1993	183.25	54.62	83.25	183.37	29-Dec	102.45	25-Feb
1992	118.52	18.52	18.52	132.36	3-Mar	82.51	25-Sep
1991	100.00						
1990							
1989							
1988							
1987							
1986							
1985							
Average Annual (%)		18.95					
Compound Annual (%)		16.63					
Standard Deviation (%)		27.32					

SYNOPSIS

The INMEX Index is a market capitalization weighted index that tracks the continuous stock price only performance of the largest and most actively traded stocks on the Mexican Stock Exchange.

NUMBER OF STOCKS—DECEMBER 31, 1995

20

MARKET VALUE—DECEMBER 31, 1995

US$38,090.8 million

SELECTION CRITERIA

Index constituents, which are reviewed every six months, are selected on the basis of market capitalization, volume, and value of shares traded over a period of six months. Minimum market capitalization requirement of 100 million pesos is required for eligibility.

BACKGROUND

The index was created to serve as an underlying vehicle for derivative products.

BASE DATE

December 31, 1991=100.00

COMPUTATION METHODOLOGY

(1) Aggregate market value weighted arithmetic average of the price ratios index formula is used. Maintenance adjustments to the divisor are made or capitalization changes, new listings and delistings.
(2) Capitalization weights are maximized at 10% of the index.
(3) Index constituents are reviewed and revised every six months, following one month's notice.

DERIVATIVE INSTRUMENTS

None

SUBINDICES

None

RELATED INDICES

IPC Index

REMARKS

None

PUBLISHER

Bolsa Mexicana de Valores.

AMERICAN STOCK EXCHANGE MARKET VALUE INDEX (AMVI)

TOTAL RETURN PERFORMANCE

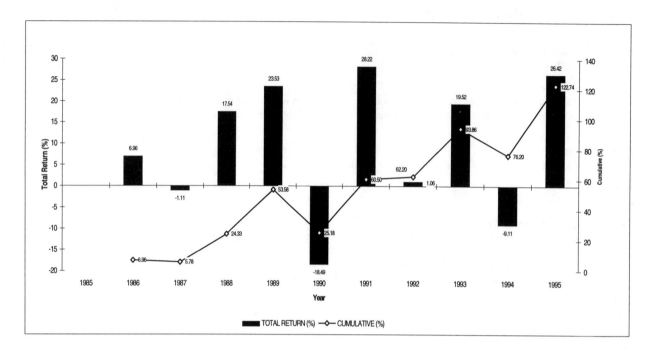

TOTAL RETURN PERFORMANCE

YEAR	VALUE	TOTAL RETURN (%)	CUMULATIVE (%)	MAXIMUM VALUE	DATE	MINIMUM VALUE	DATE
1995	548.23	26.42	122.74	553.58	12-Sep	433.12	6-Jan
1994	433.67	-9.11	76.20	487.89	2-Feb	420.23	13-Dec
1993	477.15	19.52	93.86	484.28	2-Nov	395.84	8-Jan
1992	399.23	1.06	62.20	418.99	12-Feb	364.85	9-Oct
1991	395.05	28.22	60.50	395.05	31-Dec	296.72	14-Jan
1990	308.11	-18.49	25.18	382.45	5-Jan	287.79	31-Oct
1989	378.00	23.53	53.58	397.03	10-Oct	305.24	3-Jan
1988	306.01	17.54	24.33	309.59	5-Jul	262.76	12-Jan
1987	260.35	-1.11	5.78	365.01	13-Aug	231.90	4-Dec
1986	263.27	6.96	6.96	285.19	25-Jun	240.30	4-Feb
1985	246.13						
Average Annual (%)		9.45					
Compound Annual (%)		8.34					
Standard Deviation (%)		16.05					

SYNOPSIS
The American Stock Exchange Market Value Index (AMVI) is a broad based market value-weighted index that tracks the continuous total return performance of all domestic and foreign common shares and various other securities traded on the American Stock Exchange (AMEX).

NUMBER OF STOCKS—DECEMBER 31, 1995
936

MARKET VALUE—DECEMBER 31, 1995
US$137,272.1 million

SELECTION CRITERIA
The index includes all common domestic as well as foreign shares, American Depositary Receipts (ADRs) and warrants traded on the AMEX. Rights, preferred stock and "when issued stock" are excluded from consideration.

BACKGROUND
Effective as of September 4, 1973, the American Stock Exchange introduced the Market Value Index (AMVI) along with 16 subindices which replaced its Price Change Index in effect since April 1966. Because the Price Change Index was an unweighted indicator, it was concluded that this form of index tended to understate price movement and was no longer the most suitable format for reflecting the movement of listed securities. The aim of the American Stock Exchange was to "provide investors with an improved perspective on current market performance" with an index that aligned itself more closely with other market value indicators in the securities industry, such as the New York Stock Exchange, NASDAQ and Standard & Poor's.

On July 5, 1983, the AMVI was adjusted to one half its previous level in order to make options on the AMVI attractive to institutional and individual investors. As a result, changes in the index and subindices are now measured against a base level of 50.00.

Daily values are available to January 2, 1969.

BASE DATE
August 31, 1973=100.00

COMPUTATION METHODOLOGY
(1) An aggregate of prices times quantities index formula. Maintenance adjustments to the divisor are made for capitalization changes, new listings and delistings. (2) Cash dividends are reflected in the index as of the ex-dividend date.

DERIVATIVE INSTRUMENTS
None

SUBINDICES
Industrial subindices: High technology, capital goods, consumer goods, service, retail, financial, natural resources, housing, construction and land development.
Geographic subindices: New England, Middle Atlantic, North Central, South Atlantic, South Central, Mountain, Pacific and Foreign.

RELATED INDICES
AMEX Airline Index
AMEX Biotechnology Index
AMEX Computer Technology Index
AMEX Institutional Index
AMEX International Market Index
AMEX Major Market Index
AMEX Mexico Index
AMEX Natural Gas Index
AMEX North American Telecommunications Index
AMEX Oil Index
AMEX/Oscar Gruss Israel Index
AMEX Pharmaceutical Index
AMEX Retail Index
AMEX Securities Broker/Dealer Index

REMARKS
The total return performance of the index is influenced by listed Canadian and foreign issues. Forty-eight Canadian issues with a market capitalization of US$26,292.6 million and 21 other foreign issues with a market capitalization of US$34,036.4 million, for a combined total of US$60,328.9 million, as of February 29, 1996, were listed on the exchange and included in the index.

PUBLISHER
The American Stock Exchange (AMEX).

AMEX AIRLINE (XAL) INDEX

PRICE PERFORMANCE

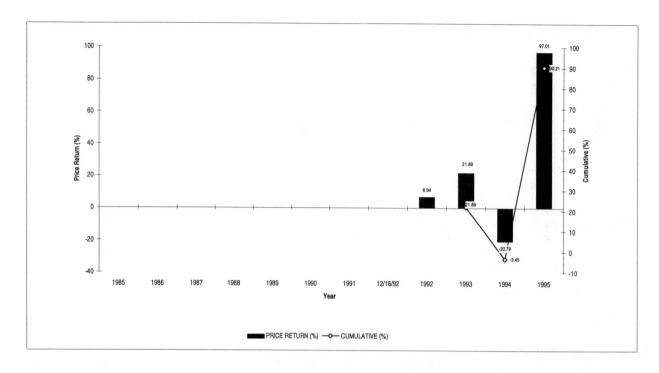

PRICE PERFORMANCE[1]

YEAR	VALUE	PRICE RETURN (%)	CUMULATIVE (%)	MAXIMUM VALUE	DATE	MINIMUM VALUE	DATE
1995	348.14	97.01	90.21	366.18	5-Dec	182.54	4-Jan
1994	176.71	-20.79	-3.45	252.89	3-Feb	169.31	21-Dec
1993	223.09	21.89	21.89	236.10	2-Dec	176.53	19-Feb
1992	183.03	6.94					
12/16/92	171.15						
1991							
1990							
1989							
1988							
1987							
1986							
1985							
Average Annual (%)		24.53					
Compound Annual (%)		23.90					
Standard Deviation (%)		59.64					

[1]Statistical measures applicable to the three-year period 1993-1995.

SYNOPSIS

The AMEX Airline (XAL) Index is an equally-weighted stock price index that measures the price only performance of 10 highly capitalized companies in the United States (U.S.) and overseas airline industry.

NUMBER OF STOCKS—DECEMBER 31, 1995

10

MARKET VALUE—DECEMBER 31, 1995

US$30,987.1 million

SELECTION CRITERIA

Constituents consist of highly capitalized companies in the U.S. and overseas airline industry, including shares in the form of American Depositary Receipts (ADRs).

BACKGROUND

The index was established to serve as an underlying vehicle for stock index options traded on the American Stock Exchange (AMEX). Options were introduced on January 6, 1995, but the index was backdated to October 16, 1992.

BASE DATE

October 21, 1994=200.00

COMPUTATION METHODOLOGY

(1) An equal dollar-weighting index formula. Equal dollar-weighting was established by designating the number of shares of each component stock that represented approximately $10,000 in market value, based on closing prices on October 21, 1994. (2) Adjustments to the index are made quarterly after the close of trading on the third Friday of March, June, September, and December so as to maintain the approximate equal dollar value of each constituent stock.

DERIVATIVE INSTRUMENTS

Airline Index options trade on the American Stock Exchange (AMEX).

SUBINDICES

None

RELATED INDICES

AMEX Biotechnology Index
AMEX Computer Technology Index
AMEX Institutional Index
AMEX International Market Index
AMEX Major Market Index
AMEX Market Value Index
AMEX Mexico Index
AMEX Natural Gas Index
AMEX North American Telecommunications Index
AMEX Oil Index
AMEX Pharmaceutical Index
AMEX Retail Index
AMEX Securities Broker/Dealer Index
AMEX/Oscar Gruss Israel Index

REMARKS

None

PUBLISHER

The American Stock Exchange (AMEX).

AMEX BioTechnology (BTK) Index

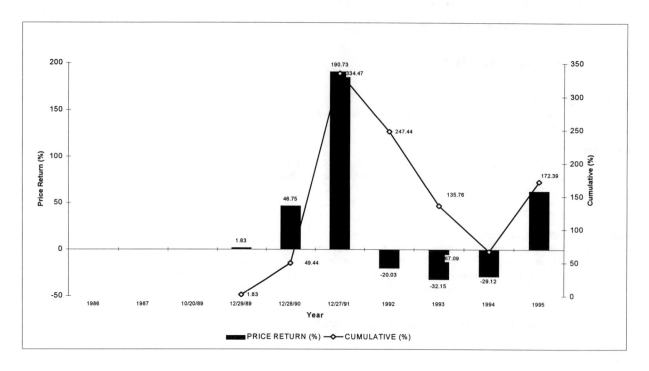

PRICE PERFORMANCE

YEAR	VALUE	PRICE RETURN (%)	CUMULATIVE (%)	MAXIMUM VALUE[1]	DATE	MINIMUM VALUE[1]	DATE
1995	133.77	63.01	172.39	133.77	29-Dec	73.76	20-Jan
1994	82.06	-29.12	67.09	126.03	24-Jan	73.18	25-Jul
1993	115.78	-32.15	135.76	173.52	11-Jan	103.02	20-Sep
1992	170.63	-20.03	247.44	256.6	14-Jan	130.60	9-Oct
12/27/91	213.37	190.73	334.47	221.87	8-Nov	70.22	11-Jan
12/28/90	73.39	46.75	49.44	73.39	28-Dec	47.85	2-Feb
12/29/89	50.01	1.83	1.83	51.41	1-Dec	47.68	27-Oct
10/20/89	49.11						
1987							
1986							
Average Annual (%)		36.53					
Compound Annual (%)		18.18					
Standard Deviation (%)		85.80					

[1]Maximum/minimum index values applicable to the period 10/20/89-12/27/91 are based on weekly values.

SYNOPSIS
The AMEX Biotechnology (BTK) Index is an equal dollar-weighted stock price index that is designed to measure the price only performance of companies in the biotechnology industry.

NUMBER OF STOCKS—DECEMBER 31, 1995
15

MARKET VALUE—DECEMBER 31, 1995
US$29,140.96 million

SELECTION CRITERIA
A cross section of companies in the biotechnology industry that are primarily involved in the use of biological processes, the development of products or providing services.

BACKGROUND
The index was created to serve as an underlying vehicle for derivative instruments. Options were introduced on October 9, 1992 whereas computation of the index commenced as of October 20, 1989 through back-dating. The index is currently calculated on a daily basis and daily closing values are available since January 1, 1992. Weekly closing prices are available for the prior period.

BASE DATE
October 18, 1991=200.00

COMPUTATION METHODOLOGY
(1) An equal dollar-weighting index formula. Equal dollar-weighting was established by designating the number of shares of each component stock that represented approximately $10,000 in market value based on closing prices on October 18, 1991. (2) Adjustments to the index are made quarterly after the close of trading on the third Friday of March, June, September, and December so as to maintain the approximate equal dollar value of each constituent stock.

DERIVATIVE INSTRUMENTS
Biotechnology Index options and Long-Term Index Options trade on the American Stock Exchange (AMEX).

SUBINDICES
None

RELATED INDICES
AMEX Airline Index
AMEX Computer Technology Index
AMEX Institutional Index
AMEX International Market Index
AMEX Major Market Index
AMEX Market Value Index
AMEX Mexico Index
AMEX Natural Gas Index
AMEX North American Telecommunications Index
AMEX Oil Index
AMEX Pharmaceutical Index
AMEX Retail Index
AMEX Securities Broker/Dealer Index
AMEX/Oscar Gruss Israel Index

REMARKS
None

PUBLISHER
The American Stock Exchange (AMEX).

AMEX COMPUTER TECHNOLOGY (XCI) INDEX

PRICE PERFORMANCE

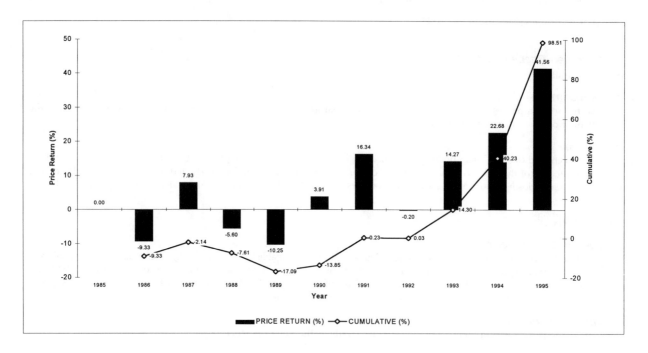

PRICE PERFORMANCE

YEAR	VALUE	PRICE RETURN (%)	CUMULATIVE (%)	MAXIMUM VALUE	DATE	MINIMUM VALUE	DATE
1995	228.62	41.56	98.51	263.72	3-Nov	160.21	3-Jan
1994	161.50	22.68	40.23	164.10	18-Nov	127.15	20-Apr
1993	131.64	14.27	14.30	135.10	2-Jun	114.25	4-Jan
1992	115.20	-0.20	0.03	130.62	12-Feb	109.58	24-Aug
1991	115.43	16.34	0.23	127.04	7-Mar	95.39	9-Jan
1990	99.22	3.91	-13.85	119.66	15-Jul	82.20	16-Oct
1989	95.49	-10.25	-17.09	114.73	7-Feb	92.57	18-Dec
1988	106.40	-5.60	-7.61	119.51	7-Jan	98.57	16-Nov
1987	112.71	7.93	-2.14	160.91	21-Aug	98.03	26-Oct
1986	104.43	-9.33	-9.33	125.92	28-Apr	100.62	14-Oct
1985	115.17						
Average Annual (%)		8.13					
Compound Annual (%)		7.10					
Standard Deviation (%)		16.17					

SYNOPSIS
The AMEX Computer Technology (XCI) Index is a market value-weighted index that measures the price only performance of the largest, most actively traded United States (U.S.) corporations involved in various phases of the computer industry.

NUMBER OF STOCKS—DECEMBER 31, 1995
26

MARKET VALUE—DECEMBER 31, 1995
US$389,208.8 million

SELECTION CRITERIA
Constituents include the largest, most actively traded and widely held U.S. corporations involved in various phases of the computer industry.

BACKGROUND
Specifically designed by the American Stock Exchange (AMEX) as an industry indicator for investors who follow this market segment and the creation of derivative products, the index was introduced on July 29, 1983 with 29 issues. It was expanded to 30 issues about six years later and, following the close of trading on April 21, 1995, the index was adjusted to include the largest and most actively traded 26 companies that make up the index at the present time.

Computation of the index commenced as of December 31, 1980 through backdating.

BASE DATE
July 29, 1983=100.00

COMPUTATION METHODOLOGY
An aggregate of prices times quantities index formula. Maintenance adjustments to the divisor are made for capitalization changes, new listings and delistings.

DERIVATIVE INSTRUMENTS
Computer Technology Index options trade on the American Stock Exchange (AMEX).

SUBINDICES
None

RELATED INDICES
AMEX Airline Index
AMEX Biotechnology Index
AMEX Institutional Index
AMEX International Market Index
AMEX Major Market Index
AMEX Market Value Index
AMEX Mexico Index
AMEX Natural Gas Index
AMEX North American Telecommunications Index
AMEX Oil Index
AMEX Pharmaceutical Index
AMEX Retail Index
AMEX Securities Broker/Dealer Index
AMEX/Oscar Gruss Israel Index

REMARKS
None

PUBLISHER
The American Stock Exchange (AMEX).

AMEX INSTITUTIONAL (XII) INDEX

PRICE PERFORMANCE

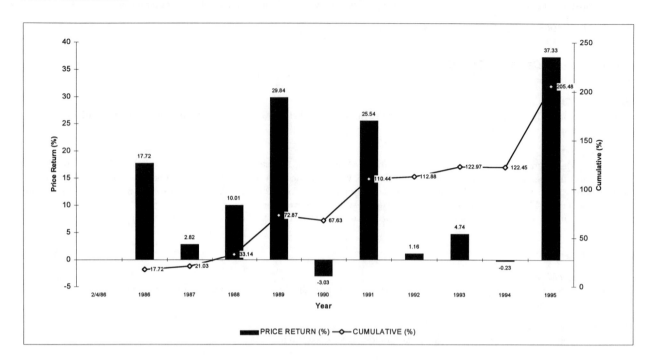

PRICE PERFORMANCE

YEAR	VALUE	PRICE RETURN (%)	CUMULATIVE (%)	MAXIMUM VALUE	DATE	MINIMUM VALUE	DATE
1995	636.72	37.33	205.48	647.13	13-Dec	462.03	12-Jan
1994	463.65	-0.23	122.45	480.57	2-Feb	435.11	4-Apr
1993	464.74	4.74	122.97	471.52	29-Dec	431.06	18-Feb
1992	443.70	1.16	112.88	454.56	22-Dec	407.56	8-Apr
1991	438.63	25.54	110.44	438.63	31-Dec	328.07	19-Jan
1990	349.40	-3.03	67.63	385.01	16-Jul	317.53	11-Oct
1989	360.32	29.84	72.87	362.39	13-Dec	273.28	3-Jan
1988	277.51	10.01	33.14	282.61	20-Dec	244.55	12-Jan
1987	252.27	2.82	21.03	345.97	25-Aug	231.27	4-Dec
1986	245.36	17.72	17.72	257.19	4-Sep	208.42	5-Feb
2/4/86	208.43						
Average Annual (%)		12.59					
Compound Annual (%)		11.81					
Standard Deviation (%)		14.17					

SYNOPSIS
The AMEX Institutional (XII) Index is a market value-weighted index that tracks the continuous price only performance of the core stock portfolio holdings of the largest institutional investors in the United States (U.S.) as well as the Standard & Poor's 500 (S&P 500) Composite Price Index.

NUMBER OF STOCKS—DECEMBER 31, 1995
75

MARKET VALUE—DECEMBER 31, 1995
US$2,522,562.2 million

SELECTION CRITERIA
The index is composed of the 75 major stocks currently held in the highest dollar amounts in institutional portfolios that have a market value of more than $100 million in investment funds. Components of the index are selected based on stock positions declared in Securities and Exchange Commission (SEC) 13(f) reports which must be filed quarterly with the SEC on behalf of all institutions with portfolios in excess of $100 million in market value. To qualify for inclusion in the index, stocks must be held by a minimum of 200 of the reporting institutions and must have traded at least seven million shares in each of the two preceding calendar quarters.

BACKGROUND
The Institutional Index was created to serve as an underlying vehicle for index options that are traded on the American Stock Exchange (AMEX). It was introduced by AMEX on June 24, 1986 and options on the index commenced trading on October 3, 1986. The index was backdated to February 4, 1986.

BASE DATE
June 24, 1986=250.00

COMPUTATION METHODOLOGY
(1) An aggregate of prices times quantities index formula. Maintenance adjustments to the divisor are made for capitalization changes. (2) The composition of the index is reviewed quarterly, on the third Friday in March, June, September and December. It is updated, with as many as four changes, on average, to ensure its continued reflection of the most current institutional holdings.

DERIVATIVE INSTRUMENTS
Institutional Index options and Long-term Equity Anticipation Securities (LEAPS) trade on the American Stock Exchange (AMEX).

SUBINDICES
None

RELATED INDICES
AMEX Airline Index
AMEX Biotechnology Index
AMEX Computer Technology Index
AMEX International Market Index
AMEX Major Market Index
AMEX Market Value Index
AMEX Mexico Index
AMEX Natural Gas Index
AMEX North American Telecommunications Index
AMEX Oil Index
AMEX Pharmaceutical Index
AMEX Retail Index
AMEX Securities Broker/Dealer Index
AMEX/Oscar Gruss Israel Index

REMARKS
The index is intended to closely track the price performance of the S&P 500.

PUBLISHER
The American Stock Exchange (AMEX).

AMEX INTERNATIONAL MARKET (IMI) INDEX

PRICE PERFORMANCE

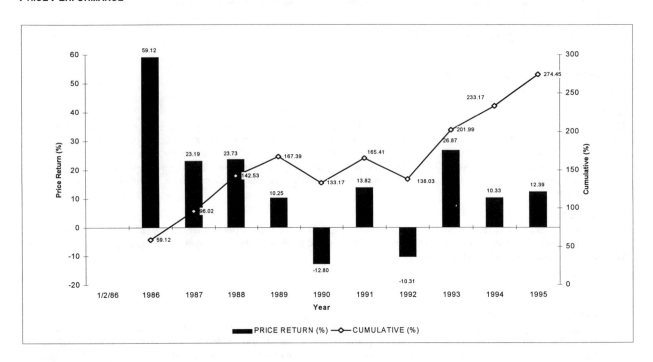

PRICE PERFORMANCE

YEAR	VALUE	PRICE RETURN (%)	CUMULATIVE (%)	MAXIMUM VALUE	DATE	MINIMUM VALUE	DATE
1995	466.75	12.39	274.45	466.75	29-Dec	388.78	27-Feb
1994	415.30	10.33	233.17	433.36	31-Oct	375.59	3-Jan
1993	376.43	26.87	201.99	388.64	25-Oct	288.49	13-Jan
1992	296.71	-10.31	138.03	336.61	6-Jan	278.50	17-Nov
1991	330.83	13.82	165.41	333.62	12-Nov	280.13	16-Jan
1990	290.65	-12.80	133.17	338.69	4-Jan	273.20	28-Sep
1989	333.30	10.25	167.39	NA	NA	NA	NA
1988	302.31	23.73	142.53	NA	NA	NA	NA
1987	244.34	23.19	96.02	294.52	8-Oct	198.84	8-Jan
1986	198.34	59.12	59.12	199.57	26-Dec	121.46	14-Jan
1/2/86	124.65						
Average Annual (%)		15.66					
Compound Annual (%)		14.11					
Standard Deviation (%)		20.25					

SYNOPSIS

The AMEX International Market (IMI) Index is a market value-weighted index that measures the price only performance of 50 leading, blue chip foreign stocks which actively trade in the United States (U.S.) either directly in the form of common stock or in the form of American Depositary Receipts (ADRs) on the New York Stock Exchange (NYSE), the American Stock Exchange (AMEX) or the Nasdaq/NMS.

NUMBER OF STOCKS—DECEMBER 31, 1995

50

MARKET VALUE—DECEMBER 31, 1995

US$972,351.9 million

SELECTION CRITERIA

Constituent shares include the leading companies in the European Economic Community, Australia, Japan and other Far Eastern countries that were selected on the basis of their capitalization and trading activity with best efforts made to ensure that country and industry group representations are reflective of current world market conditions. The total worldwide capitalization of the component stocks determines the weighting of the various countries.

To qualify for inclusion in the index:

(1) Stocks must be issued by a foreign issuer and registered under Section 12 of the Securities Exchange Act of 1934. (2) must be actively traded in the U.S. and have a minimum worldwide market value in U.S. dollars of $100 million. At least 75% of the component stocks must have had an average monthly trading volume of not less than 50,000 ADRs (or shares) for the preceding six months while all of the stocks must have averaged not less than 20,000 ADRs (or shares) for the six-month period. Each stock traded through NASDAQ must have a minimum of eight market makers regularly making markets in the stock. Composition of the index is reviewed quarterly and updated to assure that all component stocks meet the qualifying criteria. Selection of suitable alternatives is considered by AMEX in the event a stock should fail to meet the foregoing criteria.

U.S. and Canadian companies are not eligible for inclusion in the index.

BACKGROUND

The IMI, which is highly correlated to leading foreign indexes, was created to serve as an underlying international market vehicle for trading of stock index futures and options on the American Stock Exchange and the Coffee, Sugar & Cocoa Exchange (CSCE). It was initiated on January 2, 1987. The index is still maintained by the American Stock Exchange even though stock index futures and options trading have been discontinued.

BASE DATE

January 2, 1986=200.00

COMPUTATION METHODOLOGY

(1) An aggregate of prices times quantities index formula. Maintenance adjustments to the divisor are made for capitalization changes, new listings and delistings. (2) The constituent weights of the index reflect the total capitalization of the component securities worldwide.

DERIVATIVE INSTRUMENTS

None

SUBINDICES

None

RELATED INDICES

AMEX Airline Index
AMEX Biotechnology Index
AMEX Computer Technology Index
AMEX Institutional Index
AMEX Major Market Index
AMEX Market Value Index
AMEX Mexico Index
AMEX Natural Gas Index
AMEX North American Telecommunications Index
AMEX Oil Index
AMEX Pharmaceutical Index
AMEX Retail Index
AMEX Securities Broker/Dealer Index
AMEX/Oscar Gruss Israel Index

REMARKS

None

PUBLISHER

American Stock Exchange (AMEX).

AMEX Major Market (XMI) Index

Price Performance

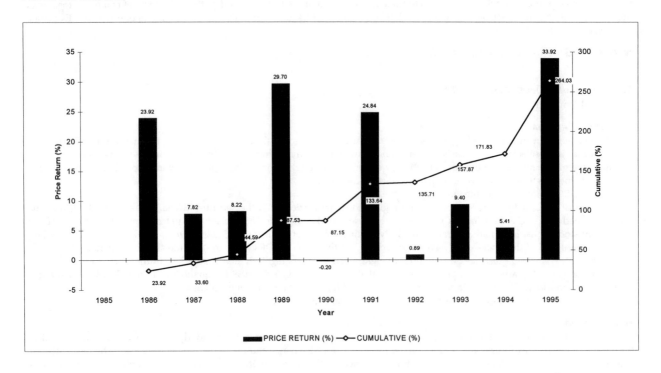

Price Performance[1]

YEAR	VALUE	PRICE RETURN (%)	CUMULATIVE (%)	MAXIMUM VALUE	DATE	MINIMUM VALUE	DATE
1995	535.60	33.92	264.03	548.69	13-Dec	399.23	12-Jan
1994	399.95	5.41	171.83	409.40	19-Oct	358.99	4-Apr
1993	379.41	9.40	157.87	385.02	29-Dec	337.81	8-Jan
1992	346.80	0.89	135.71	361.20	2-Jun	329.69	5-Oct
1991	343.75	24.84	133.64	346.83	31-Dec	257.55	14-Jan
1990	275.35	-0.20	87.15	302.75	20-Jul	246.12	12-Oct
1989	275.91	29.70	87.53	277.73	13-Dec	209.16	3-Jan
1988	212.73	8.22	44.59	215.37	20-Dec	185.14	22-Jan
1987	196.57	7.82	33.60	270.78	25-Aug	177.83	4-Dec
1986	182.32	23.92	23.92	188.67	3-Dec	139.55	23-Jan
1985	147.13						
Average Annual (%)		14.39					
Compound Annual (%)		13.79					
Standard Deviation (%)		12.46					

[1]Index rebased by halving index values as of November 30, 1989. Prior values have been adjusted.

SYNOPSIS

The AMEX Major Market (XMI) Index is a price-weighted index that tracks the continuous price only performance of United States (U.S.) blue chip stocks. The index is designed to follow the movement of the Dow Jones Industrial Average (DJIA).

NUMBER OF STOCKS—DECEMBER 31, 1995

20

MARKET VALUE—DECEMBER 31, 1995

US$1,025,113.97 million

SELECTION CRITERIA

The index was initially constructed to serve as a reliable and responsive counterpart to the Dow Jones Industrial Average (DJIA). Twenty companies that make up the index were selected to represent a broad spectrum of the leading industrial corporations in the U.S. Subsequently, the index was reconstituted to reflect the growing importance of the service and entertainment industries. Changes to the composition of the index might occur due to mergers, acquisitions or fundamental changes in the market. Replacement stocks are to be selected with a view toward preserving the original character of the index. The following companies, 17 of which are also in the DJIA, make up the index: American Express; AT&T; Chevron Corp.; Coca-Cola Co.; Walt Disney; Dow Chemical; Dupont E.I. DeNemours; Eastman Kodak; Exxon; General Electric; General Motors; IBM; International Paper; Johnson & Johnson; McDonalds Corp.; Merck & Co.; Minnesota Mining & Mfg.; Philip Morris; Procter & Gamble; and Sears Roebuck & Co.

BACKGROUND

The index was created to serve as an underlying vehicle for options trading. Options were introduced on April 29, 1983. The index was initiated with a base value of 100.00 as of March 1983 and subsequently rebased to 200.00 as of July 24, 1984. The index value was halved as of November 30, 1989.

Effective December 23, 1991, Walt Disney Co. replaced Mobil Corp. as an index constituent.

BASE DATE

July 24, 1984=200.00 (as rebased)

COMPUTATION METHODOLOGY

(1) A simple aggregative of actual prices index formula. Adjustments to the divisor for the addition of new index members, deletion of members, stock splits, stock dividends and distributions of assets, are made after the close of trading on the night before prior to substitution or on the day prior to the ex-dividend date. (2) New York Stock Exchange (NYSE) last sale prices are used in the calculation of the index.

DERIVATIVE INSTRUMENTS

XMI Index options trade on the American Stock Exchange (AMEX) and the European Options Exchange (EOE).

XMI Index Long-term Equity Anticipation Securities (LEAPS) and Long-Term Index Options trade on the American Stock Exchange.

XMI Index futures and options on futures traded by the Chicago Board of Trade (CBOT).

SUBINDICES

None

RELATED INDICES

AMEX Airline Index
AMEX Biotechnology Index
AMEX Computer Technology Index
AMEX Institutional Index
AMEX International Market Index
AMEX Market Value Index
AMEX Mexico Index
AMEX Natural Gas Index
AMEX North American Telecommunications Index
AMEX Oil Index
AMEX Pharmaceutical Index
AMEX Retail Index
AMEX Securities Broker/Dealer Index
AMEX/Oscar Gruss Israel Index

REMARKS

None

PUBLISHER

The American Stock Exchange (AMEX).

AMEX MEXICO (MXY) INDEX

PRICE PERFORMANCE

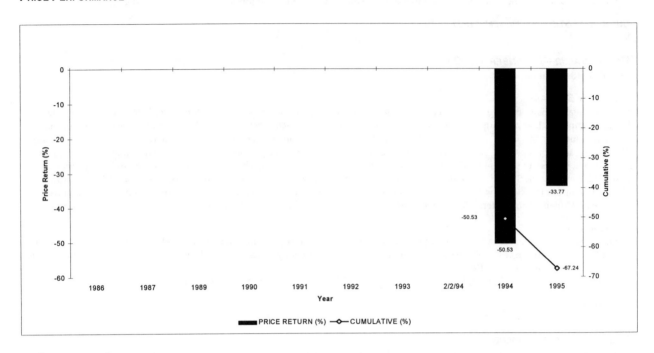

PRICE PERFORMANCE

YEAR	VALUE	PRICE RETURN (%)	CUMULATIVE (%)	MAXIMUM VALUE	DATE	MINIMUM VALUE	DATE
1995	83.62	-33.77	-67.24	118.07	3-Jan	58.32	8-Mar
1994	126.26	-50.53	-50.53	258.46	3-Feb	118.00	27-Dec
2/2/94	255.22						
1993							
1992							
1991							
1990							
1989							
1987							
1986							
Average Annual (%)		-42.15					
Compound Annual (%)		NM					
Standard Deviation (%)		NM					

SYNOPSIS

The AMEX Mexico (MXY) Index is a modified equal dollar-weighted index that measures the daily price only performance of the Mexican stock market based on the movement of highly capitalized companies with major business interests in Mexico whose shares are listed on the American Stock Exchange (AMEX).

NUMBER OF STOCKS—DECEMBER 31, 1995

10

MARKET VALUE—DECEMBER 31, 1995

US$28,173.17 million

SELECTION CRITERIA

Constituent stocks include highly capitalized companies with major business interests in Mexico that are selected from a variety of industries so as to reflect the diversity of the Mexican market. Shares are listed on the AMEX in the form of American Depositary Receipts (ADRs), American Depositary Shares (ADSs) or United States (U.S.) shares.

BACKGROUND

The index was designed by the American Stock Exchange as a vehicle for stock index options, which began trading along with LEAPS on August 8, 1994. A substitution following the close of trading on April 21, 1995 resulted in the index accounting for over 90% of the weight of the securities that make up Mexico's BMV Index.

BASE DATE

June 17, 1994=179.84

COMPUTATION METHODOLOGY

(1) A modified equal dollar-weighting index formula. Each component's weight in the Mexico Stock Market is approximated in the index by designating the number of shares representing an investment with 24% in the highest capitalized stock in the index, 12% in the second highest and 8% in the remaining index components. (2) Adjustments to the index are made quarterly, if necessary, after the close of trading on the third Friday of March, June, September, and December so that the modified dollar weighting relationships are maintained.

DERIVATIVE INSTRUMENTS

Mexico Index options and Long-term Equity Anticipation Securities (LEAPS) trade on the American Stock Exchange (AMEX).

SUBINDICES

None

RELATED INDICES

AMEX Airline Index
AMEX Biotechnology Index
AMEX Computer Technology Index
AMEX Institutional Index
AMEX International Market Index
AMEX Major Market Index
AMEX Market Value Index
AMEX Natural Gas Index
AMEX North American Telecommunications Index
AMEX Oil Index
AMEX Pharmaceutical Index
AMEX Retail Index
AMEX Securities Broker/Dealer Index
AMEX/Oscar Gruss Israel Index

REMARKS

None

PUBLISHER

The American Stock Exchange (AMEX).

AMEX NATURAL GAS (XNG) INDEX

PRICE PERFORMANCE

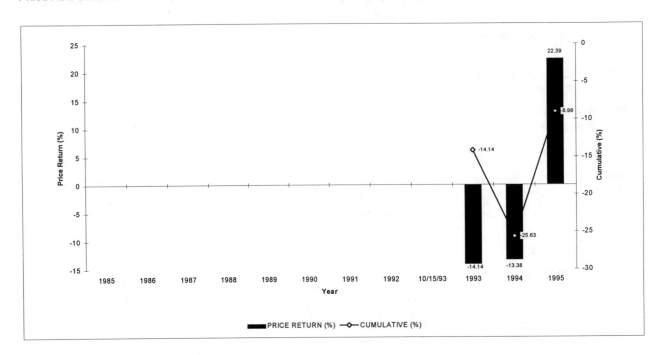

PRICE PPERFORMANCE[1]

YEAR	VALUE	PRICE RETURN (%)	CUMULATIVE (%)	MAXIMUM VALUE	DATE	MINIMUM VALUE	DATE
1995	273.07	22.39	-8.98	273.07	29-Dec	207.14	1-Feb
1994	223.12	-13.38	-25.63	223.12	31-Dec	219.54	NA
1993	257.58	-14.14	-14.14				
10/15/93	300.00						
1992							
1991							
1990							
1989							
1988							
1987							
1986							
1985							
Average Annual (%)		4.50					
Compound Annual (%)		2.96					
Standard Deviation (%)		25.29					

[1]Statistical measures applicable to the two-year period 1994-1995.

SYNOPSIS

The AMEX Natural Gas (XNG) Index is an equal dollar-weighted index that measures the continuous price only performance of highly capitalized companies primarily involved in natural gas industry .

NUMBER OF STOCKS—DECEMBER 31, 1995

15

MARKET VALUE—DECEMBER 31, 1995

US$30,053.3 million

SELECTION CRITERIA

Constituents are selected to represent a cross section of highly capitalized companies in the natural gas industry primarily involved in the exploration and production, and natural gas pipeline transportation and transmission whose prices are most sensitive to natural gas prices.

BACKGROUND

The index was designed by the American Stock Exchange (AMEX) as a vehicle for stock index options, which commenced trading on May 12, 1994.

BASE DATE

October 15, 1993=300.00

COMPUTATION METHODOLOGY

(1) An equal dollar-weighting index formula. Equal dollar-weighting was established by designating the number of shares of each component stock that represented approximately $10,000 in market value, based on closing prices on October 15, 1993. (2) Adjustments to the index are made quarterly after the close of trading on the third Friday of January, April, July, and October so as to maintain the approximate equal dollar value of each constituent stock.

DERIVATIVE INSTRUMENTS

Natural Gas Index options trade on the American Stock Exchange (AMEX).

SUBINDICES

None

RELATED INDICES

AMEX Airline Index
AMEX Biotechnology Index
AMEX Computer Technology Index
AMEX Institutional Index
AMEX International Market Index
AMEX Major Market Index
AMEX Market Value Index
AMEX Mexico Index
AMEX North American Telecommunications Index
AMEX Oil Index
AMEX Pharmaceutical Index
AMEX Retail Index
AMEX Securities Broker/Dealer Index
AMEX/Oscar Gruss Israel Index

REMARKS

None

PUBLISHER

The American Stock Exchange (AMEX).

AMEX NORTH AMERICAN TELECOMMUNICATIONS (XTC) INDEX

PRICE PERFORMANCE

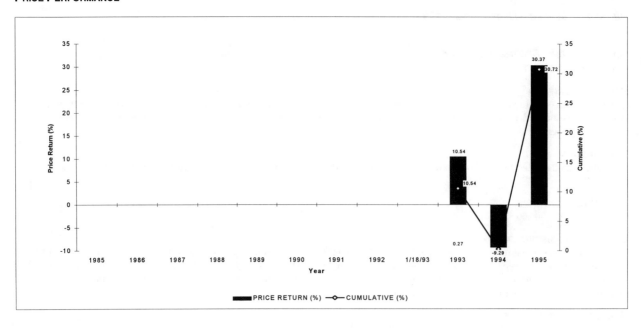

PRICE PERFORMANCE[1]

YEAR	VALUE	PRICE RETURN (%)	CUMULATIVE (%)	MAXIMUM VALUE	DATE	MINIMUM VALUE	DATE
1995	392.17	30.37	30.72	392.17	29-Dec	295.62	12-Jan
1994	300.81	-9.29	0.27	340.74	31-Jan	300.80	8-Dec
1993	331.62	10.54	10.54	343.08	15-Oct	293.59	29-Jan
1/18/93	300.00						
1992							
1991							
1990							
1989							
1988							
1987							
1986							
1985							
Average Annual (%)		10.54					
Compound Annual (%)		9.34					
Standard Deviation (%)		19.83					

[1]Statistical measures applicable to three-year period 1983-1995.

Synopsis

The AMEX North American Telecommunications (XTC) Index is an equal dollar-weighted index that measures the continuous price only performance of highly capitalized companies engaged in the telecommunications industry in North America.

Number of Stocks—December 31, 1995

15

Market Value—December 31, 1995

US$425,263.4 million

Selection Criteria

Constituents consist of highly capitalized United States (U.S.), Canadian and Mexican companies that are active in the telephone, long distance, cellular telephone and paging market, or in telecommunications-related services or manufacturing.

Background

The index was designed by the American Stock Exchange (AMEX) as a vehicle for stock index options, which commenced trading on November 23, 1993. It was originally created with 16 companies.

Base Date

January 18, 1993=300.00

Computation Methodology

(1) An equal dollar-weighting index formula. Equal dollar-weighting was established by designating the number of shares of each component stock that represented approximately $66,666 in market value, based on closing prices on January 18, 1993. (2) Adjustments to the index are made quarterly after the close of trading on the third Friday of January, April, July, and October so as to maintain the approximate equal dollar value of each constituent stock.

Derivative instruments

North American Telecommunications Index options trade on the American Stock Exchange (AMEX).

Subindices

None

Related Indices

AMEX Airline Index
AMEX Biotechnology Index
AMEX Computer Technology Index
AMEX Institutional Index
AMEX International Market Index
AMEX Major Market Index
AMEX Market Value Index
AMEX Mexico Index
AMEX Natural Gas Index
AMEX Oil Index
AMEX Pharmaceutical Index
AMEX Retail Index
AMEX Securities Broker/Dealer Index
AMEX/Oscar Gruss Israel Index

Remarks

None

Publisher

The American Stock Exchange (AMEX).

AMEX Oil (XOI) Index

PRICE PERFORMANCE

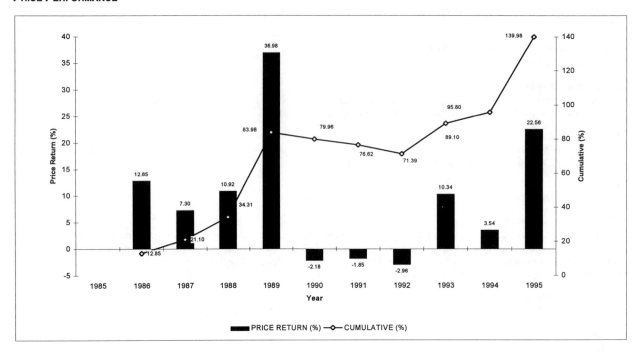

PRICE PERFORMANCE

YEAR	VALUE	PRICE RETURN (%)	CUMULATIVE (%)	MAXIMUM VALUE	DATE	MINIMUM VALUE	DATE
1995	320.80	22.56	139.98	322.24	28-Dec	258.24	11-Jan
1994	261.75	3.54	95.80	279.94	31-Oct	240.21	4-Apr
1993	252.79	10.34	89.10	271.54	1-Oct	220.95	22-Jan
1992	229.11	-2.96	71.39	248.19	26-May	209.92	2-Apr
1991	236.11	-1.85	76.62	259.86	17-Apr	220.16	11-Dec
1990	240.57	-2.18	79.96	273.48	6-Aug	231.95	22-Jan
1989	245.94	36.98	83.98	247.74	12-Dec	178.43	3-Jan
1988	179.55	10.92	34.31	191.30	12-Apr	158.76	20-Jan
1987	161.88	7.30	21.10	220.42	3-Aug	146.85	3-Dec
1986	150.86	12.85	12.85	153.91	22-Dec	118.10	5-Feb
1985	133.68						
Average Annual (%)		9.75					
Compound Annual (%)		9.15					
Standard Deviation (%)		12.47					

SYNOPSIS

The AMEX Oil (XOI) Index is an equally-weighted stock price index that is designed to measure the continuous price only performance of leading companies in the oil industry.

NUMBER OF STOCKS—DECEMBER 31, 1995

16

MARKET VALUE—DECEMBER 31, 1995

US$448,111.83 million

SELECTION CRITERIA

Constituents are selected to represent a universe of widely held and actively traded stocks representing a cross section of corporations involved in various phases of the oil industry.

BACKGROUND

Created to serve as an underlying vehicle for stock index options, the index was originally introduced as the Oil and Gas Index on September 9, 1983. It was revised and renamed on October 22, 1984. Computation of the reconstituted index commenced as of December 31, 1980.

BASE DATE

August 24, 1984=125.00

COMPUTATION METHODOLOGY

A simple aggregative of actual prices index formula. Adjustments are made over the years to reflect stock splits and other capital changes by reducing the value of the divisor accordingly.

DERIVATIVE INSTRUMENTS

Oil Index options trade on the American Stock Exchange (AMEX).

SUBINDICES

None

RELATED INDICES

AMEX Airline Index
AMEX Biotechnology Index
AMEX Computer Technology Index
AMEX Institutional Index
AMEX International Market Index
AMEX Major Market Index
AMEX Market Value Index
AMEX Mexico Index
AMEX Natural Gas
AMEX North American Telecommunications Index
AMEX Pharmaceutical Index
AMEX Retail Index
AMEX Securities Broker/Dealer Index
AMEX/Oscar Gruss Israel Index

REMARKS

None

PUBLISHER

The American Stock Exchange (AMEX).

AMEX/Oscar Gruss Israel (XIS) Index

PRICE PERFORMANCE

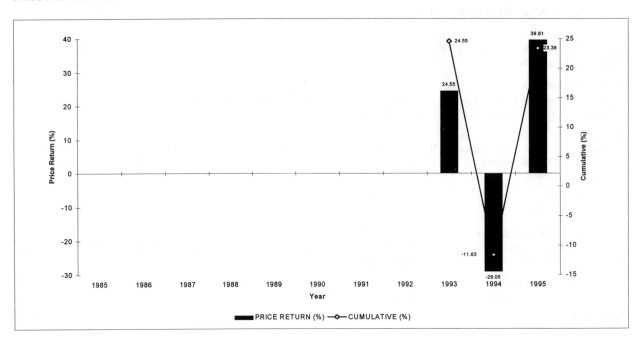

PRICE PERFORMANCE[1]

YEAR	VALUE	PRICE RETURN (%)	CUMULATIVE (%)	MAXIMUM VALUE	DATE	MINIMUM VALUE	DATE
1995	158.71	39.61	23.38	167.07	20-Sep	108.06	11-Jan
1994	113.68	-29.05	-11.63	159.68	3-Feb	98.00	30-Jun
1993	160.22	24.55	24.55	178.35	10-Nov	126.48	22-Jul
1992	128.64						
1991							
1990							
1989							
1988							
1987							
1986							
1985							
Average Annual (%)		11.70					
Compound Annual (%)		7.25					
Standard Deviation (%)		36.09					

[1]Statistical measures applicable to three-year period 1983-1995.

SYNOPSIS
The AMEX/Oscar Gruss Israel (XIS) Index is a modified equal dollar-weighted stock price index that tracks the continuous price only performance of highly capitalized United States (U.S.) listed companies with major business interests in Israel.

NUMBER OF STOCKS—DECEMBER 31, 1995
11

MARKET VALUE—DECEMBER 31, 1995
US$8,540.8 million

SELECTION CRITERIA
Constituents are selected on the basis of market capitalization and trading liquidity to represent a universe of highly capitalized U.S. listed companies, either in the form of American Depositary Receipts (ADRs) or U.S. shares, with major business interests in Israel.

BACKGROUND
The index was created to serve as an underlying vehicle for stock index options traded on the American Stock Exchange (AMEX).

BASE DATE
June 17, 1994=106.50

COMPUTATION METHODOLOGY
(1) A modified equal dollar-weighting index formula. The equal dollar-weighting was established by designating the number of shares representing an investment with 12% in each of the five highest capitalized securities in the index, for a combined total of 60%. Each of the remaining six securities were assigned weights of 6.67%, for a total of 40%. Shares were rounded to the nearest whole shares, based on closing prices on June 17, 1994. (2) Adjustments to the index are made quarterly after the close of trading on the third Friday of March, June, September, and December so as to maintain the 60/40% relationship between the five highest capitalization stocks and the remaining six securities.

DERIVATIVE INSTRUMENTS
Oscar Gruss Israel Index options trade on the American Stock Exchange (AMEX).

SUBINDICES
None

RELATED INDICES
AMEX Airline Index
AMEX Biotechnology Index
AMEX Computer Technology Index
AMEX Institutional Index
AMEX International Market Index
AMEX Major Market Index
AMEX Market Value Index
AMEX Mexico Index
AMEX Natural Gas Index
AMEX North American Telecommunications Index
AMEX Oil Index
AMEX Pharmaceutical Index
AMEX Retail Index
AMEX Securities Broker/Dealer Index

REMARKS
None

PUBLISHER
American Stock Exchange (AMEX).

AMEX PHARMACEUTICAL (DRG) INDEX

PRICE PERFORMANCE

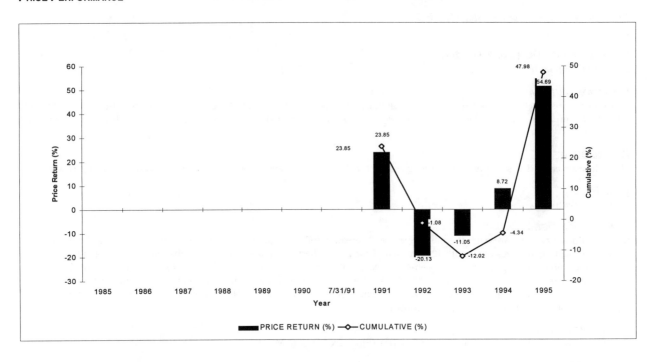

PRICE PERFORMANCE[1]

YEAR	VALUE	PRICE RETURN (%)	CUMULATIVE (%)	MAXIMUM VALUE	DATE	MINIMUM VALUE	DATE
1995	295.95	54.69	47.98	297.21	14-Dec	189.14	12-Jan
1994	191.32	8.72	-4.34	195.17	21-Dec	149.45	4-Apr
1993	175.97	-11.05	-12.02	197.61	4-Jan	148.18	12-Aug
1992	197.84	-20.13	-1.08	200.67	NA	197.84	NA
1991	247.70	23.85	23.85				
7/31/91	200.00						
1990							
1989							
1988							
1987							
1986							
1985							
Average Annual (%)		8.06					
Compound Annual (%)		4.55					
Standard Deviation (%)		33.34					

[1] Statiistical measures applicable to the four-year period 1992-1995.

SYNOPSIS
The AMEX Pharmaceutical (DRG) Index is a market vlaue-weighted index that measures the continuous price only performance of highly capitalized United States (U.S.) and European companies involved in various phases of the pharmaceutical industry.

NUMBER OF STOCKS—DECEMBER 31, 1995
15

MARKET VALUE—DECEMBER 31, 1995
US$464,243.42 million

SELECTION CRITERIA
Constituent shares are selected to represent a cross section of widely held, highly capitalized companies in the U.S and Europe that are actively involved in the development, manufacturing, and marketing of prescription, non-prescription, ethical and proprietary drugs and other related health products.

BACKGROUND
The index was designed to service as an underlying vehicle for stock index options, which commenced trading on June 22, 1992. LEAPS were introduced on April 12, 1993.

BASE DATE
July 31, 1991=200.00

COMPUTATION METHODOLOGY
An aggregate of prices times quantities index formula. Maintenance adjustments to the divisor are made for capitalization changes, new listings and delistings.

DERIVATIVE INSTRUMENTS
Pharmaceutical Index options and Long-Term Index Options trade on the American Stock Exchange (AMEX).

SUBINDICES
None

RELATED INDICES
AMEX Airline Index
AMEX Biotechnology Index
AMEX Computer Technology Index
AMEX Institutional Index
AMEX International Market Index
AMEX Major Market Index
AMEX Market Value Index
AMEX Mexico Index
AMEX Natural Gas
AMEX North American Telecommunications Index
AMEX Oil Index
AMEX Retail Index
AMEX Securities Broker/Dealer Index
AMEX/Oscar Gruss Israel Index

REMARKS
None

PUBLISHER
The American Stock Exchange (AMEX).

AMEX RETAIL INDEX

PRICE PERFORMANCE

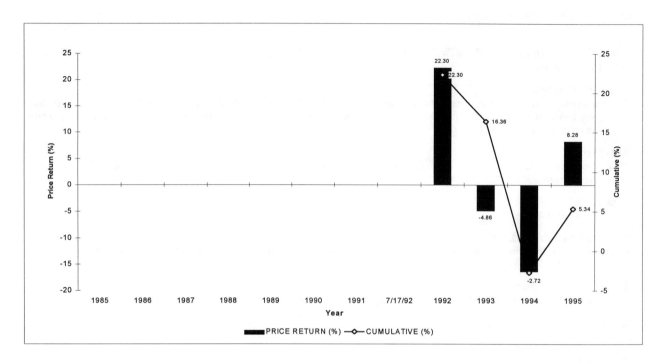

PRICE PERFORMANCE[1]

YEAR	VALUE	PRICE RETURN (%)	CUMULATIVE (%)	MAXIMUM VALUE	DATE	MINIMUM VALUE	DATE
1995	210.68	8.28	5.34	225.01	20-Jul	190.92	9-Mar
1994	194.57	-16.39	-2.72	234.97	24-Mar	190.62	28-Dec
1993	232.71	-4.86	16.36	234.20	NA	231.87	NA
1992	244.60	22.30	22.30				
7/17/92	200.00						
1991							
1990							
1989							
1988							
1987							
1986							
1985							
Average Annual (%)		-4.32					
Compound Annual (%)		-4.85					
Standard Deviation (%)		12.34					

[1] Statistical measures applicable to the three-year period 1993-1995.

SYNOPSIS

The AMEX Retail Index is an equally-weighted stock price index that measures the price only performance of 15 companies involved in the retail sector.

NUMBER OF STOCKS—DECEMBER 31, 1995

15

MARKET VALUE—DECEMBER 31, 1995

US$153,736.1 million

SELECTION CRITERIA

Constituents consist of highly capitalized companies that are primarily engaged in merchandising activities in the United States (U.S.) and overseas.

BACKGROUND

The index was established to serve as an underlying vehicle for stock index options traded on the American Stock Exchange (AMEX).

BASE DATE

July 17, 1992=200.00

COMPUTATION METHODOLOGY

(1) An equal dollar-weighting index formula. Equal dollar-weighting was established by designating the number of shares of each component stock that represented approximately $10,000 in market value based on closing prices on October 21, 1994. (2) Adjustments to the index are made quarterly after the close of trading on the third Friday of March, June, September, and December so as to maintain the approximate equal dollar value of each constituent stock.

DERIVATIVE INSTRUMENTS

None at this time.

SUBINDICES

None

RELATED INDICES

AMEX Airline Index
AMEX Biotechnology Index
AMEX Computer Technology Index
AMEX Institutional Index
AMEX International Market Index
AMEX Major Market Index
AMEX Market Value Index
AMEX Mexico Index
AMEX Natural Gas
AMEX North American Telecommunications Index
AMEX Oil Index
AMEX Pharmaceutical Index
AMEX Securities Broker/Dealer Index
AMEX/Oscar Gruss Israel Index

REMARKS

None

PUBLISHER

The American Stock Exchange (AMEX).

AMEX SECURITIES BROKER/DEALER (XBD) INDEX

PRICE PERFORMANCE

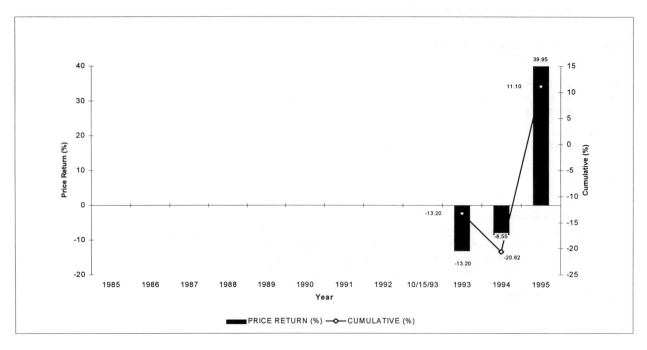

PRICE PERFORMANCE[1]

YEAR	VALUE	PRICE RETURN (%)	CUMULATIVE (%)	MAXIMUM VALUE	DATE	MINIMUM VALUE	DATE
1995	333.30	39.95	11.10	398.81	13-Oct	236.76	3-Jan
1994	238.15	-8.55	-20.62	239.07	NA	238.15	NA
1993	260.41	-13.20	-13.20				
10/15/93	300.00						
1992							
1991							
1990							
1989							
1988							
1987							
1986							
1985							
Average Annual (%)		15.70					
Compound Annual (%)		13.13					
Standard Deviation (%)		34.30					

[1]Statistical measures applicable to the 2-year period 1994-1995.

SYNOPSIS

The AMEX Securities Broker/Dealer (XBD) Index is an equal dollar-weighted index that measures the continuous price only performance of highly capitalized companies in the United States (U.S.) securities broker/dealer industry.

NUMBER OF STOCKS—DECEMBER 31, 1995

11

MARKET VALUE—DECEMBER 31, 1995

US$39,703.6 million

SELECTION CRITERIA

Constituents are selected to represent a universe of companies in the U.S. which provide securities brokerage service, market making, U.S. Treasury Primary Dealer functions and other functions dealing with U.S. and international securities.

BACKGROUND

The index was designed by the American Stock Exchange (AMEX) as a vehicle for stock index options, which began trading on May 12, 1994.

BASE DATE

October 15, 1993=300.00

COMPUTATION METHODOLOGY

(1) An equal dollar-weighting index formula. Equal dollar-weighting was established by designating the number of shares of each component stock that represented approximately $10,000 in market value based on closing prices on October 15, 1993. (2) Adjustments to the index are made quarterly after the close of trading on the third Friday of January, April, July, and October so as to maintain the approximate equal dollar value of each constituent stock.

DERIVATIVE INSTRUMENTS

Securities Broker/Dealer Index options trade on the American Stock Exchange (AMEX).

SUBINDICES

None

RELATED INDICES

AMEX Airline Index
AMEX Biotechnology Index
AMEX Computer Technology Index
AMEX Institutional Index
AMEX International Market Index
AMEX Major Market Index
AMEX Market Value Index
AMEX Mexico Index
AMEX Natural Gas
AMEX North American Telecommunications Index
AMEX Oil Index
AMEX Pharmaceutical Index
AMEX Retail Index
AMEX/Oscar Gruss Israel Index

REMARKS

None

PUBLISHER

The American Stock Exchange (AMEX).

CHICAGO BOARD OPTIONS EXCHANGE AUTOMOTIVE (CAUX) INDEX

PRICE PERFORMANCE

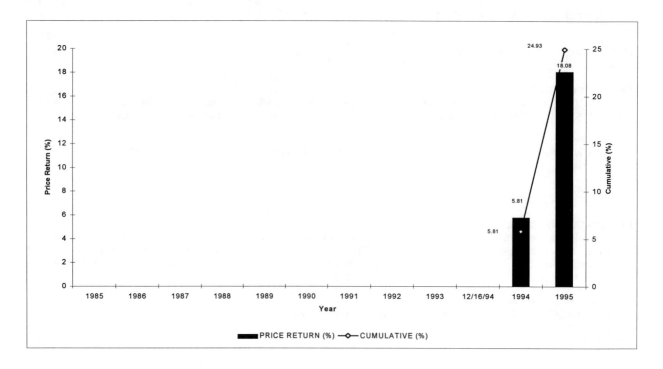

PRICE PERFORMANCE

YEAR	VALUE	PRICE RETURN (%)	CUMULATIVE (%)	MAXIMUM VALUE	DATE	MINIMUM VALUE	DATE
1995	187.40	18.08	24.93	191.09	10-Jul	149.29	30-Jan
1994	158.71	5.81	5.81	200.76	3-Feb	146.09	12-Dec
12/16/94	150.00						
1993							
1992							
1991							
1990							
1989							
1988							
1987							
1986							
1985							
Average Annual (%)		2.39					
Compound Annual (%)		2.25					
Standard Deviation (%)		8.68					

SYNOPSIS

The The Chicago Board Options Exchange Automotive (CAUX) Index Automotive Index is a modified equal dollar-weighted index that tracks the stock price only performance of companies involved in the design and manufacturing of automobiles and automotive parts.

NUMBER OF STOCKS—DECEMBER 31, 1995

10

MARKET VALUE—DECEMBER 31, 1995

Not Available

SELECTION CRITERIA

Constituents include the following companies: General Motors, Ford Motor Co., Chrysler Corp., Goodyear Tire, TRW Inc., Eaton Corp., Genuine Parts Co., Dana Corp., Echlin Corp., and Magna International A-Shares.

BACKGROUND

The Automotive Index was created in 1995 to serve as an underlying vehicle for index options traded on The Chicago Board Options Exchange (CBOE).

BASE DATE

December 16, 1994=150.00

COMPUTATION METHODOLOGY

(1) A modified equal dollar-weighting index formula. The number of shares (rounded to the nearest whole share) of each constituent stock varies in proportion to its designated weighting in a US$10,000 market value investment. The weightings are, as follows: General Motors, 20.0%; Ford Motor Corp., 17.49%; Chrysler Corp., 12.52%; Goodyear Tire and Rubber Corp., 9.99%; Genuine Parts Co., 8.35%; Eaton Corp., 8.33%; TRW, 8.32%; Dana Corp., 5.01%; Magna International Inc., 5.0%; and Echlin Corp., 4.99%. (2) Adjustments to the index are made quarterly after the close of trading on the third Friday of March, June, September, and December so as to maintain these relationships among the ten constituent stocks.

DERIVATIVE INSTRUMENTS

Automotive index options trade on The Chicago Board Options Exchange (CBOE).

SUBINDICES

None

RELATED INDICES

CBOE BioTechnology Index
CBOE Computer Software Index
CBOE Environmental Index
CBOE Gaming Index
CBOE Global Telecommunications Index
CBOE Internet Index
CBOE Israel Index
CBOE Latin 15 Index
CBOE Mexico Index
CBOE REIT Index
CBOE Technology Index
CBOE U.S. Telecommunications Index

REMARKS

None

PUBLISHER

The Chicago Board Options Exchange (CBOE).

CHICAGO BOARD OPTIONS EXCHANGE BIOTECHNOLOGY (BGX) INDEX

PRICE PERFORMANCE

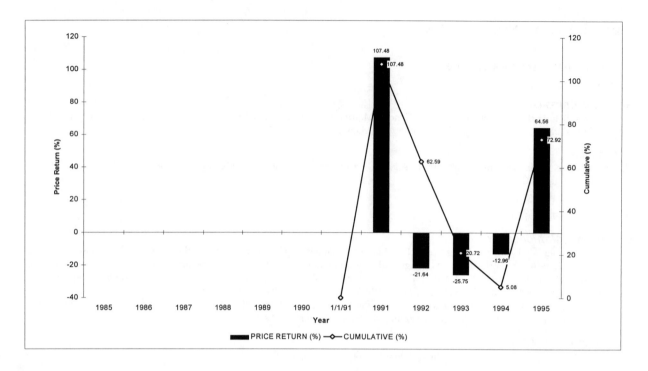

PRICE PERFORMANCE

YEAR	VALUE	PRICE RETURN (%)	CUMULATIVE (%)	MAXIMUM VALUE	DATE	MINIMUM VALUE	DATE
1995	172.92	64.56	72.92	172.92	29-Dec	100.31	12-Jan
1994	105.08	-12.96	5.08	132.84	31-Jan	85.10	25-Jul
1993	120.72	-25.75	20.72	161.58	4-Jan	96.15	8-Apr
1992	162.59	-21.64	62.59	184.94	2-Mar	122.92	9-Oct
1991	207.48	107.48	107.48	207.48	31-Dec	92.23	9-Jan
1/1/91	100.00						
1990							
1989							
1988							
1987							
1986							
1985							
Average Annual (%)		22.34					
Compound Annual (%)		1.42					
Standard Deviation (%)		60.26					

SYNOPSIS

The BioTechnology Index is a price-weighted index that tracks the price only performance of domestic small and medium capitalization common stocks in the biotechnology sector.

NUMBER OF STOCKS—DECEMBER 31, 1995

19

MARKET VALUE—DECEMBER 31, 1995

Not Available

SELECTION CRITERIA

Constituent shares are representative of small and medium capitalization stocks in the biotechnology sector.

BACKGROUND

The index was created to serve as an underlying vehicle for derivative instruments.

BASE DATE

January 1, 1991=100.00

COMPUTATION METHODOLOGY

A simple aggregative of actual prices index formula.

DERIVATIVE INSTRUMENTS

BioTechnology index options trade on The Chicago Board Options Exchange (CBOE).
BioTechnology Long-term Equity Anticipation Securities (LEAPS) trade on The Chicago Board Options Exchange (CBOE).

SUBINDICES

None

RELATED INDICES

CBOE Automotive Index
CBOE Computer Software Index
CBOE Environmental Index
CBOE Gaming Index
CBOE Global Telecommunications Index
CBOE Internet Index
CBOE Israel Index
CBOE Latin 15 Index
CBOE Mexico Index
CBOE REIT Index
CBOE Technology Index
CBOE U.S. Telecommunications Index

REMARKS

None

PUBLISHER

The Chicago Board Options Exchange (CBOE).

CHICAGO BOARD OPTIONS EXCHANGE COMPUTER SOFTWARE (CWX) INDEX

PRICE PERFORMANCE

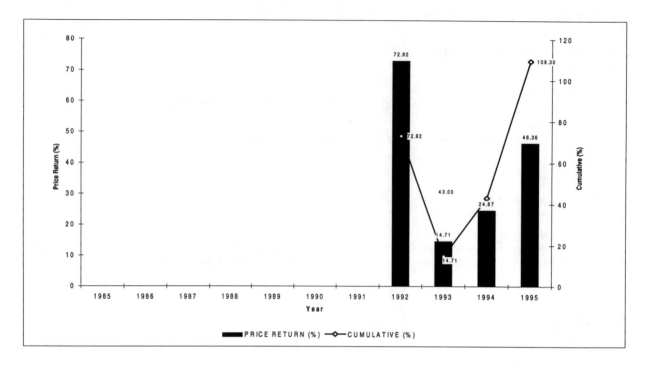

PRICE PERFORMANCE

YEAR	VALUE	PRICE RETURN (%)	CUMULATIVE (%)	MAXIMUM VALUE	DATE	MINIMUM VALUE	DATE
1995	361.92	46.36	109.30	389.59	10-Nov	239.86	5-Jan
1994	247.28	24.67	43.00	247.45	29-Dec	186.24	23-Jun
1993	198.35	14.71	14.71	208.14	12-Nov	159.37	26-Apr
1992	172.92	72.92	72.92	213.26	15-Jan	135.67	24-Aug
1991	100.00						
1990							
1989							
1988							
1987							
1986							
1985							
Average Annual (%)		39.66					
Compound Annual (%)		20.28					
Standard Deviation (%)		25.81					

SYNOPSIS

The Chicago Board Options Exchange Computer Software (CWX) Index is a price-weighted index that tracks the price only performance of domestic common stocks of companies in the computer software sector that are traded on the New York Stock Exchange (NYSE) and Nasdaq.

NUMBER OF STOCKS—DECEMBER 31, 1995

15

MARKET VALUE—DECEMBER 31, 1995

Not Available

SELECTION CRITERIA

Constituent shares are selected from the leading computer software companies traded on the New York and Nasdaq exchanges.

BACKGROUND

The index was created to serve as an underlying vehicle for derivative instruments.

BASE DATE

January 1, 1992=200.00

COMPUTATION METHODOLOGY

A simple aggregative of actual prices index formula.

DERIVATIVE INSTRUMENTS

Computer Software index options trade on The Chicago Board Options Exchange (CBOE).

SUBINDICES

None

RELATED INDICES

CBOE Automotive Index
CBOE BioTechnology Index
CBOE Environmental Index
CBOE Gaming Index
CBOE Global Telecommunications Index
CBOE Internet Index
CBOE Israel Index
CBOE Latin 15 Index
CBOE Mexico Index
CBOE REIT Index
CBOE Technology Index
CBOE U.S. Telecommunications Index

REMARKS

None

PUBLISHER

The Chicago Board Options Exchange (CBOE).

CHICAGO BOARD OPTIONS EXCHANGE ENVIRONMENTAL (EVX) INDEX

PRICE PERFORMANCE

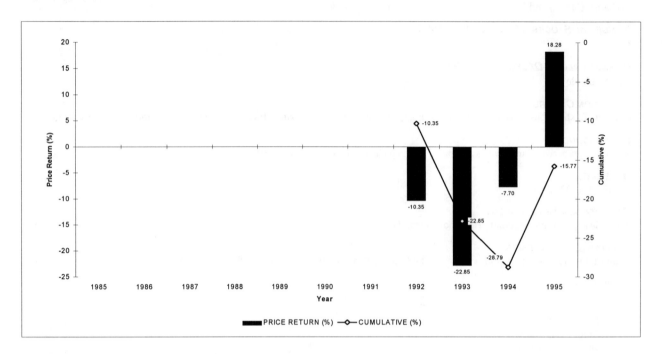

PRICE PERFORMACE

YEAR	VALUE	PRICE RETURN (%)	CUMULATIVE (%)	MAXIMUM VALUE	DATE	MINIMUM VALUE	DATE
1995	151.02	18.28	-15.77	158.69	31-Jul	126.99	4-Jan
1994	127.68	-7.70	-28.79	151.76	2-Feb	123.32	8-Dec
1993	138.33	-22.85	-22.85	181.77	3-Feb	118.27	8-Nov
1992	179.30	-10.35	-10.35	220.98	17-Jan	158.44	25-Aug
1991	200.00						
1990							
1989							
1988							
1987							
1986							
1985							
Average Annual (%)		-5.65					
Compound Annual (%)		-4.20					
Standard Deviation (%)		17.27					

SYNOPSIS
The Chicago Board Options Exchange Environmental (EVX) Index is a price-weighted index that tracks the price only performance of domestic common stocks of companies involved in the business of environmental control that are traded on the New York Stock Exchange (NYSE), American Stock Exchange (AMEX) and Nasdaq.

NUMBER OF STOCKS—DECEMBER 31, 1995
15

MARKET VALUE—DECEMBER 31, 1995
Not Available

SELECTION CRITERIA
Constituent shares are selected from the leading environmental control companies traded on the New York, AMEX and Nasdaq exchanges.

BACKGROUND
The index was created to serve as an underlying vehicle for derivative instruments.

BASE DATE
January 1, 1992=200.00

COMPUTATION METHODOLOGY
A simple aggregative of actual prices index formula.

DERIVATIVE INSTRUMENTS
Environmental index options trade on The Chicago Board Options Exchange (CBOE).

SUBINDICES
None

RELATED INDICES
CBOE Automotive Index
CBOE BioTechnology Index
CBOE Computer Software Index
CBOE Gaming Index
CBOE Global Telecommunications Index
CBOE Internet Index
CBOE Israel Index
CBOE Latin 15 Index
CBOE Mexico Index
CBOE REIT Index
CBOE Technology Index
CBOE U.S. Telecommunications Index

REMARKS
None

PUBLISHER
The Chicago Board Options Exchange (CBOE).

CHICAGO BOARD OPTIONS EXCHANGE GAMING (GAX) INDEX

PRICE PERFORMANCE

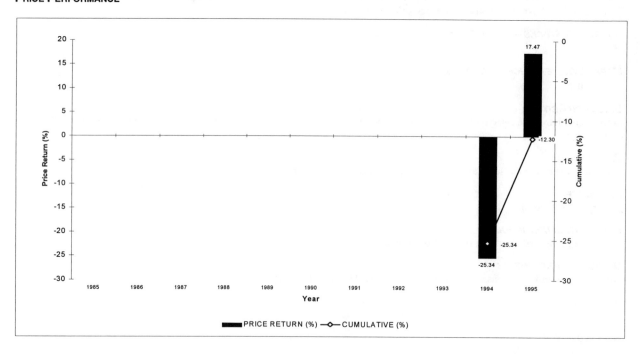

PRICE PERFORMANCE

YEAR	VALUE	PRICE RETURN (%)	CUMULATIVE (%)	MAXIMUM VALUE	DATE	MINIMUM VALUE	DATE
1995	217.95	17.47	-12.30	253.15	6-Sep	183.01	27-Jan
1994	185.54	-25.34	-25.34	269.24	18-Jan	153.26	13-Dec
1993	248.52	NA	NA	287.98	5-Oct	159.22	23-Feb
1992	NA	NA	NA	NA	NA	NA	NA
1991	100.00						
1990							
1989							
1988							
1987							
1986							
1985							
Average Annual (%)		-3.94					
Compound Annual (%)		-0.62					
Standard Deviation (%)		NM					

SYNOPSIS
The Chicago Board Options Exchange Gaming (GAX) Index is a price-weighted index that tracks the price only performance of domestic common stocks of companies involved in the gaming sector traded on the New York Stock Exchange (NYSE), American Stock Exchange (AMEX), and Nasdaq exchanges.

NUMBER OF STOCKS—DECEMBER 31, 1995
15

MARKET VALUE—DECEMBER 31, 1995
Not Available

SELECTION CRITERIA
Constituent shares are selected from the leading gaming sector companies traded on the New York, AMEX and Nasdaq exchanges.

BACKGROUND
The index was created to serve as an underlying vehicle for derivative instruments.

BASE DATE
January 2, 1992=100.00

COMPUTATION METHODOLOGY
A simple aggregative of actual prices index formula.

DERIVATIVE INSTRUMENTS
Gaming Index options trade on The Chicago Board Options Exchange (CBOE).

SUBINDICES
None

RELATED INDICES
CBOE Automotive Index
CBOE BioTechnology Index
CBOE Computer Software Index
CBOE Environmental Index
CBOE Global Telecommunications Index
CBOE Internet Index
CBOE Israel Index
CBOE Latin 15 Index
CBOE Mexico Index
CBOE REIT Index
CBOE Technology Index
CBOE U.S. Telecommunications Index

REMARKS
None

PUBLISHER
The Chicago Board Options Exchange (CBOE).

Chicago Board Options Exchange Global Telecommunications (GTX) Index

Price Performance

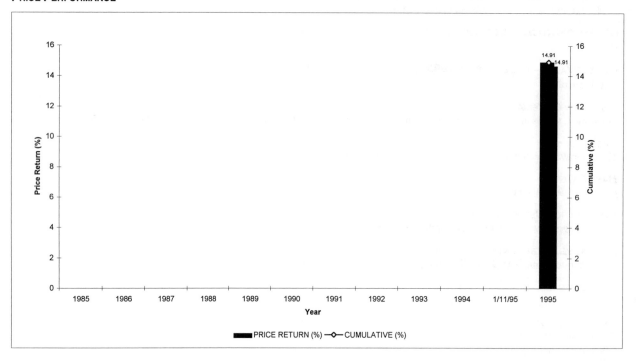

Price Performance

YEAR	VALUE	PRICE RETURN (%)	CUMULATIVE (%)	MAXIMUM VALUE	DATE	MINIMUM VALUE	DATE
1995	148.94	14.91	14.91	151.02	12-Jul	121.54	8-Mar
1/11/95	129.61						
1994							
1993							
1992							
1991							
1990							
1989							
1988							
1987							
1986							
1985							
Average Annual (%)		NM					
Compound Annual (%)		NM					
Standard Deviation (%)		NM					

SYNOPSIS
The Chicago Board Options Exchange Global Telecommunications (GTX) Index is a price-weighted index that tracks the price only performance of common stocks, of companies involved in the world telecommunications industry whose shares trade on the New York Stock Exchange (NYSE), American Stock Exchange (AMEX) and Nasdaq.

NUMBER OF STOCKS—DECEMBER 31, 1995
20

MARKET VALUE—DECEMBER 31, 1995
Not Available

SELECTION CRITERIA
Constituent shares include common stocks and American Depositary Receipts (ADRs) that are involved in the telecommunications industry around the world and are traded on the New York, AMEX and Nasdaq exchanges.

BACKGROUND
The index was created to serve as an underlying vehicle for derivative instruments.

BASE DATE
January 2, 1992=100.00

COMPUTATION METHODOLOGY
A simple aggregative of actual prices index formula.

DERIVATIVE INSTRUMENTS
Global Telecommunications Index options trade on The Chicago Board Options Exchange (CBOE).

SUBINDICES
None

RELATED INDICES
CBOE Automotive Index
CBOE BioTechnology Index
CBOE Computer Software Index
CBOE Environmental Index
CBOE Gaming Index
CBOE Internet Index
CBOE Israel Index
CBOE Latin 15 Index
CBOE Mexico Index
CBOE REIT Index
CBOE Technology Index
CBOE U.S. Telecommunications Index

REMARKS
None

PUBLISHER
The Chicago Board Options Exchange (CBOE).

CHICAGO BOARD OPTIONS EXCHANGE INTERNET (CINX) INDEX

PRICE PERFORMANCE

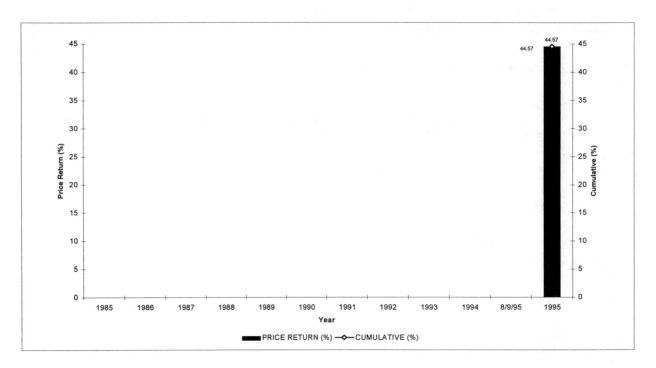

PRICE PERFORMANCE

YEAR	VALUE	PRICE RETURN (%)	CUMULATIVE (%)	MAXIMUM VALUE	DATE	MINIMUM VALUE	DATE
1995	144.57	44.57	44.57	169.78	5-Dec	98.42	11-Aug
8/9/95	100.00						
1994							
1993							
1992							
1991							
1990							
1989							
1988							
1987							
1986							
1985							
Average Annual (%)		NA					
Compound Annual (%)		NA					
Standard Deviation (%)		NA					

SYNOPSIS
The Chicago Board Options Exchange Internet (CINX) Index is an equal dollar-weighted index that tracks the stock price only performance of companies involved in the business of software and hardware that facilitates access to the Internet.

NUMBER OF STOCKS—DECEMBER 31, 1995
15

MARKET VALUE—DECEMBER 31, 1995
Not Available

SELECTION CRITERIA
Constituents include the following companies: McAfee Associates; Micron Inc.; Cisco Inc.; America Online; Oracle Corp.; Sun Microsystems; H&R Block; Silicon Graphics; Netscape Communications; Quarterdeck Corp.; Netmanage Inc.; Uunet Technology; Netcom Online; Spyglass Inc.; and Psinet Inc.

BACKGROUND
The CINX was created in 1995 to serve as an underlying vehicle for index options traded on The Chicago Board Options Exchange (CBOE).

BASE DATE
August 9, 1995=100.00

COMPUTATION METHODOLOGY
(1) An equal dollar-weighting index formula. Equal dollar weighting was established by designating the number of shares (rounded to the nearest whole share) of each component stock that represented 1/15th of approximately US$10,000 in market value. (2) Adjustments to the index are made quarterly after the close of trading on the third Friday of March, June, September, and December so as to maintain the approximate equal dollar value of each constituent stock.

DERIVATIVE INSTRUMENTS
Internet index options and Long-term Equity Anticipation Securities (LEAPS) trade on The Chicago Board Options Exchange (CBOE).

SUBINDICES
None

RELATED INDICES
CBOE Automotive Index
CBOE BioTechnology Index
CBOE Computer Software Index
CBOE Environmental Index
CBOE Gaming Index
CBOE Global Telecommunications Index
CBOE Israel Index
CBOE Latin 15 Index
CBOE Mexico Index
CBOE REIT Index
CBOE Technology Index
CBOE U.S. Telecommunications Index

REMARKS
None

PUBLISHER
The Chicago Board Options Exchange (CBOE).

CHICAGO BOARD OPTIONS EXCHANGE ISRAEL (ISX) INDEX

PRICE PERFORMANCE

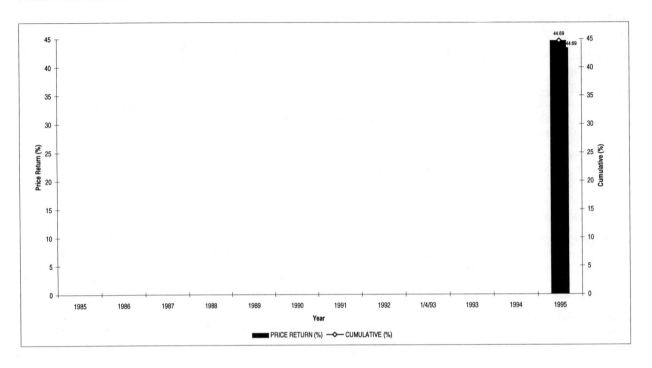

PRICE PERFORMANCE

YEAR	VALUE	PRICE RETURN (%)	CUMULATIVE (%)	MAXIMUM VALUE	DATE	MINIMUM VALUE	DATE
1995	166.63	44.69	44.69	175.49	9-Nov	109.44	4-Jan
1994	115.16	NA	NA	NA	NA	NA	NA
1993	NA	NA	NA	NA	NA	NA	NA
1/4/93	100.00						
1992							
1991							
1990							
1989							
1988							
1987							
1986							
1985							
Average Annual (%)		44.69					
Compound Annual (%)		NA					
Standard Deviation (%)		NM					

SYNOPSIS
The Chicago Board Options Exchange Israel (ISX) Index is a price-weighted index that tracks the stock price performance of United States (U.S.) traded Israeli stocks that are listed on the New York Stock Exchange (NYSE), American Stock Exchange (AMEX), and Nasdaq/NMS.

NUMBER OF STOCKS—DECEMBER 31, 1995
15

MARKET VALUE—DECEMBER 31, 1995
Not Available

SELECTION CRITERIA
Constituents include U.S. traded companies domiciled in Israel or U.S.-based companies having operations in Israel.

BACKGROUND
The ISX was created to serve as an underlying vehicle for index options traded on The Chicago Board Options Exchange (CBOE).

BASE DATE
January 4, 1993=200.00

COMPUTATION METHODOLOGY
A simple aggregative of actual prices index formula.

DERIVATIVE INSTRUMENTS
Israel index options trade on The Chicago Board Options Exchange (CBOE).

SUBINDICES
None

RELATED INDICES
CBOE Automotive Index
CBOE BioTechnology Index
CBOE Computer Software Index
CBOE Environmental Index
CBOE Gaming Index
CBOE Global Telecommunications Index
CBOE Internet Index
CBOE Latin 15 Index
CBOE Mexico Index
CBOE REIT Index
CBOE Technology Index
CBOE U.S. Telecommunications Index

REMARKS
The index is somewhat concentrated with one company, Electronics for Imaging, Inc., accounting for 21.4% and four companies accounting for 53.3% of the ISX Index.

PUBLISHER
The Chicago Board Options Exchange (CBOE).

CHICAGO BOARD OPTIONS EXCHANGE LATIN 15 (LTX) INDEX

PRICE PERFORMANCE

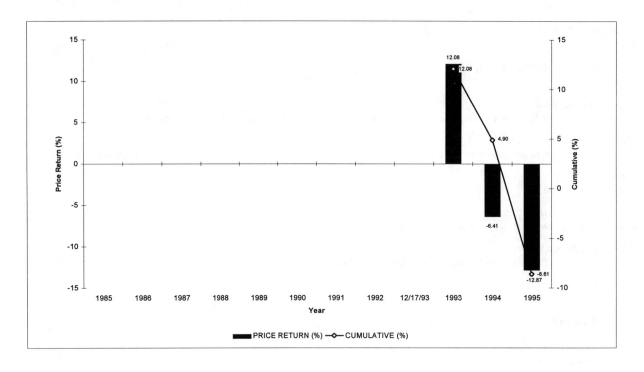

PRICE PERFORMANCE

YEAR	VALUE	PRICE RETURN (%)	CUMULATIVE (%)	MAXIMUM VALUE	DATE	MINIMUM VALUE	DATE
1995	125.01	-12.87	-8.61	149.57	13-Jul	89.09	8-Mar
1994	143.48	-6.41	4.90	189.78	26-Feb	134.05	20-Apr
1993	153.30	12.08	12.08	153.30	31-Dec	136.78	17-Dec
12/17/93	136.78						
1992							
1991							
1990							
1989							
1988							
1987							
1986							
1985							
Average Annual (%)		-2.40					
Compound Annual (%)		-2.95					
Standard Deviation (%)		12.95					

SYNOPSIS
The Chicago Board Options Exchange Latin 15 (LTX) Index is a modified dollar-weighted index that tracks the price performance of four Latin American markets, including Argentina, Brazil, Chile and Mexico with American Depositary Receipts (ADRs), American Depositary Shares (ADSs) and closed-end investment companies which trade on the New York Stock Exchange (NYSE).

NUMBER OF STOCKS—DECEMBER 31, 1995
15

MARKET VALUE—DECEMBER 31, 1995
Not Available

SELECTION CRITERIA
The following constituent stocks make up the index: Argentina Fund; Telefonica de Argentina SA; YPF Sociedad Anonima; Aracruz Celulose; Brazil Fund Inc.; Brazilian Equity Fund Inc.; Banco; Osorno Y La Union; Compania de Telefonos de Chile; Empresa Nacional Electricidad Chile; Empresas La Moderna SA de CV; Grupo Tribasa SA de CV; Coca Cola Femsa SA de CV; Grupo Televisa SA Global; and Virtro Sociedad Anonima.

BACKGROUND
The LTX Index was created to serve as an underlying vehicle for stock index options and was introduced by the Chicago Board of Trade (CBOT) on Monday, July 24, 1995.

BASE DATE
December 3, 1994=150.00

COMPUTATION METHODOLOGY
(1) A modified equal dollar-weighting index formula. The component securities within each country are equally weighted. However, the weights assigned to Argentina, Brazil, Chile, and Mexico are set at 17.5%, 35%, 17.5%, and 30%, respectively. (2) The index is rebalanced quarterly after the close on the third Friday of March, June, September, and December.

DERIVATIVE INSTRUMENTS
Latin 15 index options trade on The Chicago Board Options Exchange (CBOE).

SUBINDICES
None

RELATED INDICES
CBOE Automotive Index
CBOE BioTechnology Index
CBOE Computer Software Index
CBOE Environmental Index
CBOE Gaming Index
CBOE Global Telecommunications Index
CBOE Internet Index
CBOE Israel Index
CBOE Mexico Index
CBOE REIT Index
CBOE Technology Index
CBOE U.S. Telecommunications Index

REMARKS
The relative weightings assigned to both Chile and Mexico are consistent with their relative market capitalizations as of year-end 1994. But the assigned weights to Argentina and Brazil contrast with their relative market capitalizations which stood at 8.7% and 44.5%, respectively as of year-end 1994.

PUBLISHER
The Chicago Board Options Exchange (CBOE).

CHICAGO BOARD OPTIONS EXCHANGE MEXICO (MEX) INDEX

PRICE PERFORMANCE

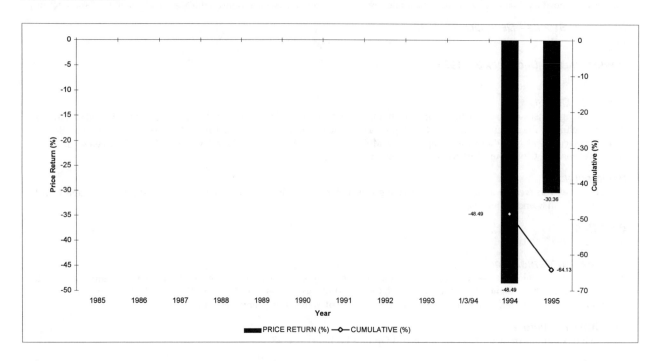

PRICE PERFORMANCE

YEAR	VALUE	PRICE RETURN (%)	CUMULATIVE (%)	MAXIMUM VALUE	DATE	MINIMUM VALUE	DATE
1995	71.74	-30.36	-64.13	95.80	3-Jan	44.43	8-Mar
1994	103.02	-48.49	-48.49	216.53	21-Jan	95.78	27-Dec
1/3/94	200.00						
1993							
1992							
1991							
1990							
1989							
1988							
1987							
1986							
1985							
Average Annual (%)		-39.43					
Compound Annual (%)		-40.11					
Standard Deviation (%)		12.82					

SYNOPSIS
The Chicago Board Options Exchange Mexico (MEX) Index is a price-weighted index that tracks the price performance of ten United States (U.S.) traded Mexican American Depositary Receipts (ADRs), American Depositary Shares (ADSs) as well as one closed-end investment company.

NUMBER OF STOCKS—DECEMBER 31, 1995
10

MARKET VALUE—DECEMBER 31, 1995
Not Available

SELECTION CRITERIA
The 10 constituent securities include: Empresas La Moderna SA de CV ADS; Grupo Mexicano de Desarrollo ADR; Grupo Tribasa SA de CV ADR; Empresas ICA Sociedad Controladora ADR; Coca-Cola FEMSA; SA de CV ADS; Mexico Fund Inc.; Transportacion Maritima Mexicana AD; Telefonos de Mexico; SA de CV ADS; Grupo Televisa SA ADS; and Vitro Sociedad Anomina ADR.

BACKGROUND
The index was created to serve as an underlying vehicle for index options traded on The Chicago Board Options Exchange (CBOE).

BASE DATE
January 3, 1994=200.00

COMPUTATION METHODOLOGY
A simple aggregative of actual prices index formula.

DERIVATIVE INSTRUMENTS
Mexico Index options and Long-term Equity Anticipation Securities (LEAPS) trade on The Chicago Board Options Exchange (CBOE).

SUBINDICES
None

RELATED INDICES
CBOE Automotive Index
CBOE BioTechnology Index
CBOE Computer Software Index
CBOE Environmental Index
CBOE Gaming Index
CBOE Global Telecommunications Index
CBOE Internet Index
CBOE Israel Index
CBOE Latin 15 Index
CBOE REIT Index
CBOE Technology Index
CBOE U.S. Telecommunications Index

REMARKS
None

PUBLISHER
The Chicago Board Options Exchange (CBOE).

CHICAGO BOARD OPTIONS EXCHANGE TECHNOLOGY (TXX) INDEX

PRICE PERFORMANCE

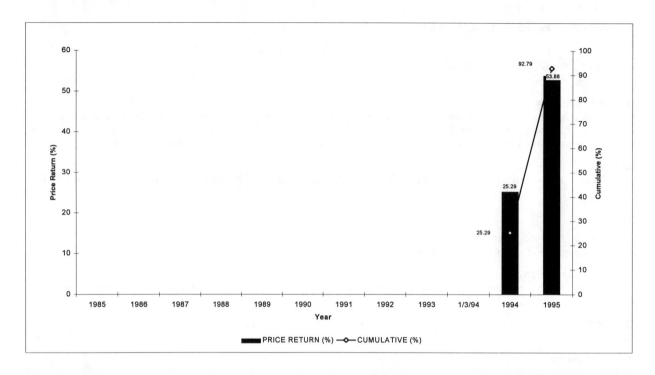

PRICE PERFORMANCE

YEAR	VALUE	PRICE RETURN (%)	CUMULATIVE (%)	MAXIMUM VALUE	DATE	MINIMUM VALUE	DATE
1995	156.53	53.88	92.79	175.99	3-Nov	99.98	30-Jan
1994	101.72	25.29	25.29	102.45	29-Dec	74.25	24-Jun
1/3/94	81.19						
1993							
1992							
1991							
1990							
1989							
1988							
1987							
1986							
1985							
Average Annual (%)		39.58					
Compound Annual (%)		38.85					
Standard Deviation (%)		20.22					

SYNOPSIS
The Chicago Board Options Exchange Technology (TXX) Index is a price-weighted index that tracks the price only performance of high technology common stocks traded on the New York Stock Exchange (NYSE) and Nasdaq.

NUMBER OF STOCKS—DECEMBER 31, 1995
30

MARKET VALUE—DECEMBER 31, 1995
Not Available

SELECTION CRITERIA
Constituent shares include the common stocks of high technology companies that are traded on the New York and Nasdaq exchanges.

BACKGROUND
The index was created to serve as an underlying vehicle for derivative instruments.

BASE DATE
January 3, 1995=100.00

COMPUTATION METHODOLOGY
A simple aggregative of actual prices index formula.

DERIVATIVE INSTRUMENTS
Technology index options and Long-term Equity Participation Securities (LEAP) trade on The Chicago Board Options Exchange (CBOE).

SUBINDICES
None

RELATED INDICES
CBOE Automotive Index
CBOE BioTechnology Index
CBOE Computer Software Index
CBOE Environmental Index
CBOE Gaming Index
CBOE Global Telecommunications Index
CBOE Internet Index
CBOE Israel Index
CBOE Latin 15 Index
CBOE Mexico Index
CBOE REIT Index
CBOE U.S. Telecommunications Index

REMARKS
None

PUBLISHER
The Chicago Board Options Exchange (CBOE).

CHICAGO BOARD OPTIONS EXCHANGE U.S. TELECOMMUNICATIONS (TCX) INDEX

PRICE PERFORMANCE

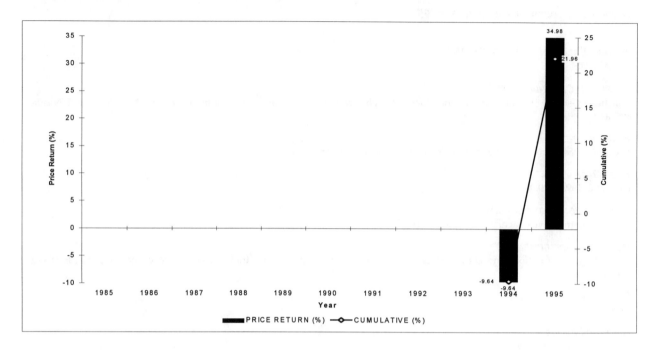

PRICE PERFORMANCE

YEAR	VALUE	PRICE RETURN (%)	CUMULATIVE (%)	MAXIMUM VALUE	DATE	MINIMUM VALUE	DATE
1995	187.32	34.98	21.96	191.67	20-Sep	138.45	6-Jan
1994	138.78	-9.64	-9.64	153.65	31-Jan	133.36	4-Apr
1993	153.59	NA	NA	180.11	15-Oct	116.23	4-Jan
1992	NA	NA	NA	NA	NA	NA	NA
1991	100.00						
1990							
1989							
1988							
1987							
1986							
1985							
Average Annual (%)		12.67					
Compound Annual (%)		10.44					
Standard Deviation (%)		NM					

SYNOPSIS
The Chicago Board Options Exchange U.S. Telecommunications (TCX) Index is a price-weighted index that tracks the price only performance of stocks of United States (U.S.) firms participating in the telecommunications industry whose shares trade on the New York Stock Exchange (NYSE), American Stock Exchange (AMEX), and Nasdaq exchanges.

NUMBER OF STOCKS—DECEMBER 31, 1995
24

MARKET VALUE—DECEMBER 31, 1995
Not Available

SELECTION CRITERIA
Constituent shares include the common stocks of U.S. companies involved in the telecommunications industry that are traded on the NYSE, AMEX and Nasdaq exchanges.

BACKGROUND
The index was created to serve as an underlying vehicle for derivative instruments.

BASE DATE
January 2, 1992=100.00

COMPUTATION METHODOLOGY
A simple aggregative of actual prices index formula.

DERIVATIVE INSTRUMENTS
U.S. Telecommunications index options trade on The Chicago Board Options Exchange (CBOE).

SUBINDICES
None

RELATED INDICES
CBOE Automotive Index
CBOE BioTechnology Index
CBOE Computer Software Business Index
CBOE Environmental Index
CBOE Gaming Index
CBOE Global Telecommunications Index
CBOE Internet Index
CBOE Israel Index
CBOE Latin 15 Index
CBOE Mexico Index
CBOE REIT Index
CBOE Technology Index

REMARKS
None

PUBLISHER
The Chicago Board Options Exchange (CBOE).

DOW JONES COMPOSITE AVERAGE

PRICE PERFORMANCE

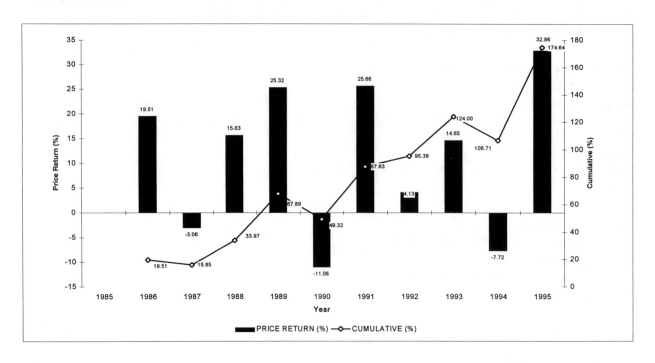

PRICE AND TOTAL RETURN PERFORMANCE

YEAR	VALUE	PRICE RETURN (%)	CUMULATIVE (%)	TOTAL RETURN (%)	MAXIMUM VALUE	DATE	MINIMUM VALUE	DATE
1995	1,693.21	32.86	174.64	35.21	1,735.81	13-Dec	1,281.46	3-Jan
1994	1,274.41	-7.72	106.71	-4.88	1,447.06	31-Jan	1,224.18	8-Dec
1993	1,381.03	14.65	124.00	17.76	1,394.05	29-Dec	1,201.66	13-Jan
1992	1,204.55	4.13	95.38	7.73	1,211.16	30-Dec	1,107.47	9-Oct
1991	1,156.82	25.66	87.63	29.88	1,156.82	31-Dec	880.82	9-Jan
1990	920.61	-11.06	49.32	-7.63	1,063.92	4-Jun	839.00	11-Oct
1989	1,035.10	25.32	67.89	29.18	115.15	9-Oct	816.95	3-Jan
1988	825.94	15.63	33.97	20.25	830.24	29-Dec	700.70	21-Jan
1987	714.27	-3.06	15.85	NA	992.21	25-Aug	653.76	4-Dec
1986	736.83	19.51	19.51	NA	767.89	2-Dec	602.83	10-Jan
1985	616.53							
Average Annual (%)		11.59		12.75				
Compound Annual (%)		10.63		11.76				
Standard Deviation (%)		15.22		16.12				

SYNOPSIS

The Dow Jones Composite Average is a price-weighted benchmark that tracks the continuous price only and daily total return performance of the 65 stocks that make up the Dow Jones Industrial Average (DJIA), the Dow Jones Transportation Average, and the Dow Jones Utilities Average. These consist of large capitalization, widely held stocks that are listed on the New York Stock Exchange (NYSE) and Nasdaq, including 30 industrial and financial companies, 20 transportation companies and 15 corporations involved in various phases of the utilities industry in the United States which, together, account for 27% of the domestic market capitalization.

NUMBER OF STOCKS—DECEMBER 31, 1995

65

MARKET VALUE—DECEMBER 31, 1995

US$1,965,666.3 million

SELECTION CRITERIA

Constituent stocks are actively traded, large capitalization stocks that are widely held. Refer to the Dow Jones Industrial Average, Dow Jones Transportation Average and the Dow Jones Utilities Average for additional information regarding selection criteria.

BACKGROUND

The Dow Jones Composite Average was introduced in the morning edition of *The Wall Street Journal* on November 30, 1933. It was computed on the basis of the closing prices of the 70 stocks that made up the three Dow Jones averages. The number of issues declined to 65 as of June 2, 1938 when the Dow Jones Utilities Average was reconstituted to include 15 rather than 20 stocks.

Starting in 1993, Dow Jones began to compute total return performance. Total returns have been backdated to September 30, 1987.

For additional information, refer to the Dow Jones Industrial Average.

BASE DATE

November 9, 1933=38.90

COMPUTATION METHODOLOGY

(1) A simple aggregative of actual prices index formula. Adjustments are made to the divisor in connection with constituent changes, stock splits and other corporate actions. (2) New York Stock Exchange closing prices are used in the calculation of the index. (3) Dividends, for total return performance calculations, are assumed to be reinvested at the beginning of the ex-dividend date.

DERIVATIVE INSTRUMENTS

None

SUBINDICES

None

RELATED INDICES

Dow Jones Industrial Average
Dow Jones Transportation Average
Dow Jones Utilities Average
Dow Jones Equity Market Index
Dow Jones World Stock Index
Refer to Appendix 5 for additional indices.

REMARKS

Yellow Corp., a member of the Dow Jones Transportation Average, is the only non-NYSE-listed company.

PUBLISHER

Dow Jones & Company, Inc.

DOW JONES EQUITY MARKET INDEX

PRICE PERFORMANCE

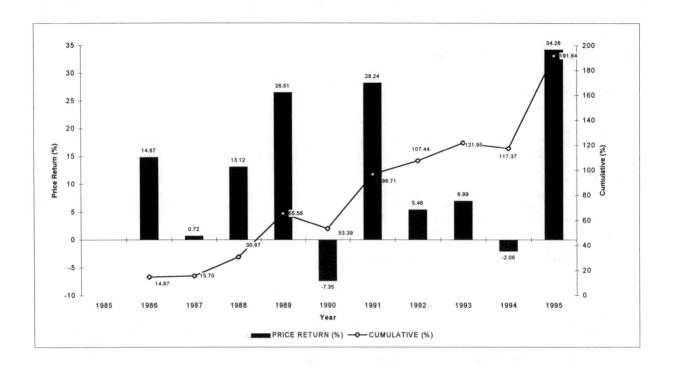

PRICE PERFORMANCE

YEAR	VALUE	PRICE RETURN (%)	CUMULATIVE (%)	TOTAL RETURN (%)	MAXIMUM VALUE	DATE	MINIMUM VALUE	DATE
1995	581.43	34.26	191.84	37.85	586.69	13-Dec	432.87	3-Jan
1994	433.07	-2.06	117.37	0.39	456.27	2-Feb	416.31	4-Apr
1993	442.19	6.99	121.95	-0.99	445.86	28-Dec	406.94	8-Jan
1992	413.29	5.46	107.44	8.57	417.43	18-Dec	371.37	8-Apr
1991	391.90	28.24	96.71	32.44	391.90	31-Dec	288.96	9-Jan
1990	305.59	-7.35	53.39	-3.93	342.67	16-Jul	272.91	11-Oct
1989	329.85	26.51	65.56	30.40	337.63	9-Oct	258.45	3-Jan
1988	260.74	13.12	30.87	17.42	266.13	21-Oct	227.68	20-Jan
1987	230.50	0.72	15.70	NA	313.73	25-Aug	209.24	4-Dec
1986	228.86	14.87	14.87	NA	241.56	4-Sep	193.18	22-Jan
1985	199.23							
Average Annual (%)		12.07		12.22				
Compound Annual (%)		11.30		11.23				
Standard Deviation (%)		13.93		16.64				

SYNOPSIS

The Dow Jones Equity Market Index is a market value-weighted index that measures the continuous price only and daily total return performance of U.S. common stocks listed on The New York Stock Exchange (NYSE), the American Stock Exchange and Nasdaq/NMS. These companies account for 67% of the total United States (U.S.) market capitalization.

NUMBER OF STOCKS—DECEMBER 31, 1995

713

MARKET VALUE—DECEMBER 31, 1995

US$4,679,169.2 million

SELECTION CRITERIA

Constituents must represent readily marketable, common or ordinary shares, with the usual participation rights, including dividends and are selected on the basis of objective and subjective criteria:

(1) Eligible companies consist of those whose primary market is the United Stated and, within this group, companies whose stock is 52% controlled by another corporation are excluded. Also, companies controlled by a government, a family, an individual or another corporation are reviewed before accepted into the index. (2) The companies comprising the index represent about 80% of the total U.S. market capitalization. All eligible stock issues are ranked by market capitalization and constituent stocks are selected on the basis of the highest capitalizations within each industry group. Constituent stocks are aligned into 95 or so industry groups. Exceptions may be made for certain well known corporations with long track records that may not qualify on the basis of the strict application of these guidelines. Such exceptions do not exceed 0.2% of the market's total capitalization.

Preferred stock, mutual fund shares and closed-end funds are not eligible for inclusion in the index.

BACKGROUND

The index, along with a scheme consisting of nine economic sectors and industry groups, was introduced in late 1988 for the purpose of monitoring the performance of stock groups and establishing whether individual issues have outperformed or underperformed their peers. It was subsequently incorporated into the Dow Jones World Stock Index as its U.S. component. Assistance in the development of the groups was provided by the Leuthold Group, Wilshire Associates and Shearson Lehman Hutton.

The index was backdated to June 30, 1982. Originally, the index consisted of 693 companies in each of 79 basic industries. One economic sector, consisting of conglomerates, has since been consolidated into the basic materials economic sector.

Starting in 1993, Dow Jones began to compute total return performance. Total returns have been backdated to September 30, 1987.

BASE DATE

June 30, 1982=100.00

COMPUTATION METHODOLOGY

(1) An aggregate of prices times quantities index formula. Maintenance adjustments to the divisor are made periodically for capitalization changes, new listings and delistings. (2) Dividends, for total return performance calculations, are assumed to be reinvested at the beginning of the ex-dividend date. (3) The index is reviewed on a periodic basis.

DERIVATIVE INSTRUMENTS

None

SUBINDICES

(1) An equal weighted version of the index is calculated once a week. (2) Nine economic sector subindices: Basic materials, consumer cyclical, consumer non-cyclical, energy, financial, industrial, technology, utilities, and independent companies or multi-industry companies which are very large and whose activities cut across industries and other economic sectors. (3) One hundred and twenty-four industry group subindices.

RELATED INDICES

Dow Jones Industrial Average
Dow Jones Transportation Average
Dow Jones Utilities Average
Dow Jones Composite Average
Dow Jones World Stock Index
Refer to Appendix 5 for additional indices.

REMARKS

(1) Market capitalization of index constituents is determined on the basis of index eligible companies. (2) Dow Jones World Stock Index was renamed the Dow Jones Global Index, effective as of June 30, 1996.

PUBLISHER

Dow Jones & Company, Inc.

Dow Jones Industrial Average (DJIA)

PRICE PERFORMANCE

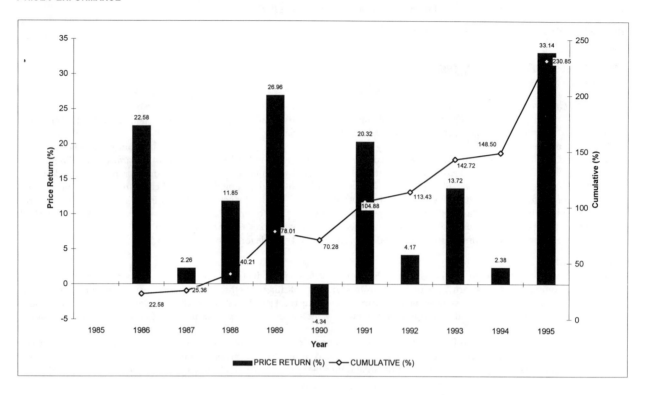

PRICE AND TOTAL RETURN PERFORMANCE

YEAR	VALUE	PRICE RETURN (%)	CUMULATIVE (%)	TOTAL RETURN (%)[1]	MAXIMUM VALUE	DATE	MINIMUM VALUE	DATE
1995	5,117.12	33.14	230.85	36.11	5,216.47	13-Dec	3,832.08	30-Jan
1994	3,843.44	2.38	148.50	5.03	3,978.36	31-Jan	3,593.35	4-Apr
1993	3,754.09	13.72	142.72	16.95	3,794.33	29-Dec	3,241.95	20-Jan
1992	3,301.11	4.17	113.43	7.03	3,413.21	1-Jun	3,136.58	9-Oct
1991	3,168.83	20.32	104.88	24.33	3,168.83	31-Dec	2,470.30	9-Jan
1990	2,633.66	-4.34	70.28	-0.58	2,999.75	16-Jul	2,365.10	11-Oct
1989	2,753.20	26.96	78.01	30.83	2,791.41	9-Oct	2,144.64	3-Jan
1988	2,168.57	11.85	40.21	16.12	2,183.50	21-Oct	1,879.14	20-Jan
1987	1,938.83	2.26	25.36	5.55	2,722.42	25-Aug	1,738.74	19-Oct
1986	1,895.95	22.58	22.58	27.25	1,955.57	2-Dec	1,502.29	22-Jan
1985	1,546.67							
Average Annual (%)		13.30		16.86				
Compound Annual (%)		12.71		16.26				
Standard Deviation (%)		12.26		12.47				

[1] Total returns for 1986 and 1987 calculated based on the quarterly reinvestment of dividends accumulated as of the ex-dividend dates.

SYNOPSIS

Probably the best known market barometer in the world, the Dow Jones Industrial Average (DJIA) is a price-weighed benchmark, that tracks the continuous price only and daily total return performance of 30 large, widely owned, stocks of corporations listed on the New York Stock Exchange (NYSE). These shares account for 17% of the total United States (U.S) market capitalization.

NUMBER OF STOCKS—DECEMBER 31, 1995

30

MARKET VALUE—DECEMBER 31, 1995

US$1,177,870.5 million

SELECTION CRITERIA

The DJIA was originally limited to industrial companies. In recent years, however, the composition of the index has been broadened to include a greater weighting from such sectors as the services, health care, and advanced technology so as to reflect the long-run changes in the economy and the stock market. Constituent stocks are actively traded, large capitalization stocks, that are widely held. Changes in the composition of the Average are infrequent. The last substitution was effective March 12, 1987 when both Coca-Cola Co. and Boeing Co. replaced Owens-Illinois and Inco Ltd. The removal of Owens-Illinois, one of the Dow 30 since 1950, was attributable to its going private. Inco Ltd., one of the Dow stocks added when the index was expanded to thirty stocks in 1928, was dropped in order to make the index more representative of the market.

The following 30 stocks make up the DJIA: Alcoa, Allied Signal, American Express, AT&T, Bethlehem Steel, Boeing, Caterpillar, Chevron, Coca-Cola, Walt Disney, DuPont, Exxon, General Electric, General Motors, Goodyear, IBM, International Paper, Kodak, McDonalds, Merck, Minnesota Mining and Manufacturing, JP Morgan, Phillip Morris, Proctor & Gamble, Sears, Texaco, Union Carbide, United Technologies, Westinghouse and Woolworth.

BACKGROUND

The oldest surviving proxies for the performance of the stock market in history, the DJIA was compiled by Charles Henry Dow, first editor of *The Wall Street Journal* and co-founder in 1882 of Dow Jones & Co., in response to a need for a market barometer to reflect the general movement of stocks in the United States at a time when trading volume of U.S. stocks approximated 250,000 shares daily and the number of actively traded issues exceeded 35. When it made its debut in a two page financial bulletin entitled *Customer's Afternoon Letter* (forerunner to *The Wall Street Journal*) on July 3, 1884, the Average consisted of a list of 11 stocks, including nine railroads and only two industrial companies. It was constructed by adding up the closing prices of these stocks and dividing the total by 11.

Over the next 12 years, Charles Dow experimented with different lists of stocks in an effort to develop an index consisting entirely of industrial stocks. On May 26, 1886, the first industrial stock average consisting of 12 industrial issues was published. Like its predecessor, this average was computed in the same manner. At the same time, Dow also created a 20 stock railroad average (later becoming the transportation average) and publication of the two averages was begun October 7, 1986 on a continuous basis. The list of 12 companies was expanded to 20 in 1916 and to 30 on October 1, 1928. Publication of the Utility Average was begun in January 1929.

Daily prices are available to 1896, except for 1914 when the NYSE was closed due to World War I. Starting in 1993, Dow Jones began to compute total return performance for the DJIA. Total returns have been backdated to September 30, 1987.

The DJIA's historical continuity, consistency and availability of information are its most popular features. Of all the benchmarks pertaining to the performance of the stock market, none receive as much attention in the financial news as the Dow Jones Industrial Average. Indeed, to people all over the world, the Dow Jones Industrial Average has come to represent the New York Stock Exchange, if not the entire United States stock market.

BASE DATE

May 26, 1986=40.94

COMPUTATION METHODOLOGY

(1) A simple aggregative of actual prices index formula. Adjustments are made to the divisor in connection with constituent changes, stock splits and other corporate actions. (2) New York Stock Exchange closing prices are used in the calculation of the index. (3) Dividends, for total return performance calculations, are assumed to be reinvested at the beginning of the ex-dividend date.

DERIVATIVE INSTRUMENTS

None

SUBINDICES

None

RELATED INDICES

Dow Jones Composite Average
Dow Jones Equity Market Index
Dow Jones World Stock Index
Dow Jones Utilities Average
Dow Jones Transportation Average
Refer to Appendix 5 for additional indices.

REMARKS

The DJIA is frequently referred to as an "unweighted" benchmark in which the prices of included stocks are added up and divided by the number of stocks that make up the index. But as with any arithmetic mean calculation methodology, the higher-priced stocks within the DJIA have a greater effect on the average than lower priced stocks. This is due to the fact that the arithmetic mean gives equal weight to absolute dollar changes. For example, a 1% change in the price of IBM (priced at $108.50 at 1/31/96) has nearly seven times the impact of a 1% in the price of Bethlehem Steel ($15.13 at 1/31/96).

PUBLISHER

Dow Jones & Company, Inc.

DOW JONES TRANSPORTATION AVERAGE

PRICE PERFORMANCE

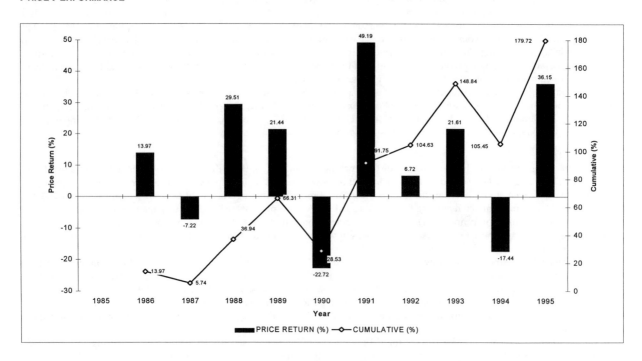

PRICE AND TOTAL RETURN PERFORMANCE

YEAR	VALUE	PRICE RETURN (%)	CUMULATIVE (%)	TOTAL RETURN (%)	MAXIMUM VALUE	DATE	MINIMUM VALUE	DATE
1995	1,981.00	36.15	179.72	36.10	2,092.11	5-Dec	1,473.19	3-Jan
1994	1,455.03	-17.44	105.45	-15.86	1,862.29	2-Feb	1,377.48	8-Dec
1993	1,762.32	21.61	148.84	22.98	1,775.61	28-Dec	1,453.83	4-Jan
1992	1,449.21	6.72	104.63	9.62	1,467.68	20-Feb	1,204.40	26-Aug
1991	1,358.00	49.19	91.75	51.68	1,358.00	31-Dec	894.30	7-Jan
1990	910.23	-22.72	28.53	-21.24	1,212.77	6-Jun	821.93	17-Oct
1989	1,177.81	21.44	66.31	22.89	1,532.01	5-Sep	959.95	3-Jan
1988	969.84	29.51	36.94	31.99	973.61	29-Dec	737.57	21-Jan
1987	748.86	-7.22	5.74	NA	1,101.16	14-Aug	674.92	26-Oct
1986	807.17	13.97	13.97	NA	866.74	4-Dec	686.97	10-Jan
1985	708.21							
Average Annual (%)		13.12		13.82				
Compound Annual (%)		10.83		11.58				
Standard Deviation (%)		23.37		25.24				

SYNOPSIS

The Dow Jones Transportation Average is a price-weighted benchmark, that tracks the continuous price only and daily total return performance of 20 actively traded transportation stocks listed on the New York Stock Exchange (NYSE) and the Nasdaq/NMS market.

NUMBER OF STOCKS—DECEMBER 31, 1995

20

MARKET VALUE—DECEMBER 31, 1995

US$809,243.1 million

SELECTION CRITERIA

Constituent stocks are actively traded, large capitalization stocks that are widely held. They are selected to represent a cross section of corporations involved in various phases of the transportation industry in the United States. The following 20 companies make up the Average: AMR Corp., Airborne Freight, Alaska Air, American President, Burlington Northern S.F., Caliber Systems Inc. (formerly Roadway Services, Inc.), CSX, Consolidated Rail, Consolidated Freightways, Delta Air, Federal Express, Illinois Central, Northfolk Southern, Ryder System, Southwest Airlines, UAL Corp., Union Pacific, USAir Group, XTRA and Yellow Corp. (Nasdaq/NMS-listed).

BACKGROUND

First known as the Railroad Average, this measure made its debut on October 7, 1896 in *The Wall Street Journal* along with daily values extending back to September 8, 1896. The average consisted of 20 stocks, including two industrial companies that were removed on October 26, 1896. This date marked the first time the average was computed entirely on the basis of railroad stocks. *The Wall Street Journal* reconstituted the Average on January 2, 1970 by introducing a transportation measure that reflected the drastically altered pattern of commercial transportation in the United States. While the number of stocks in the Dow Jones Transportation Average remained at 20, nine railroad stocks were deleted and replaced by nine other transportation securities, including six airlines and three trucking companies. Transition to the revised average was affected smoothly through adjustments to the divisor.

Daily prices are available to September 8, 1896, except for 1914 when the New York Stock Exchange (NYSE) was closed due to World War I. Starting in 1993, Dow Jones began to compute total return performance. Total returns have been backdated to September 30, 1987.

For additional information, refer to the Dow Jones Industrial Average (DJIA).

BASE DATE

September 8, 1896=48.55

COMPUTATION METHODOLOGY

(1) A simple aggregative of actual prices index formula. Adjustments are made to the divisor in connection with constituent changes, stock splits and other corporate actions. (2) New York Stock Exchange closing prices are used in the calculation of the index. (3) Dividends, for total return performance calculations, are assumed to be reinvested at the beginning of the ex-dividend date.

DERIVATIVE INSTRUMENTS

None

SUBINDICES

None

RELATED INDICES

Dow Jones Industrial Average
Dow Jones Utilities Average
Dow Jones Composite Average
Dow Jones Equity Market Index
Dow Jones World Stock Index
Refer to Appendix 5 for additional indices.

REMARKS

None

PUBLISHER

Dow Jones & Company, Inc.

DOW JONES UTILITIES AVERAGE

PRICE PERFORMANCE

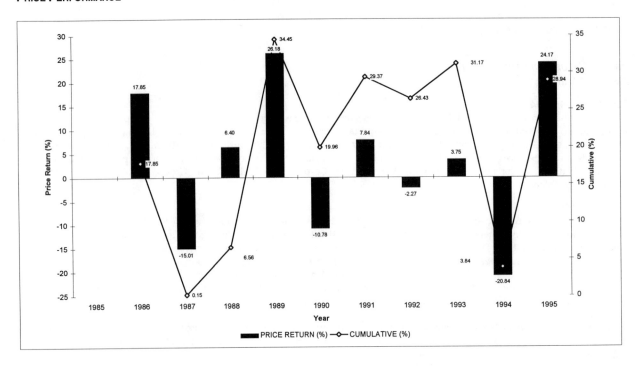

PRICE AND TOTAL RETURN PERFORMANCE

YEAR	VALUE	PRICE RETURN (%)	CUMULATIVE (%)	TOTAL RETURN (%)	MAXIMUM VALUE	DATE	MINIMUM VALUE	DATE
1995	225.40	24.17	28.94	30.04	225.40	29-Dec	183.03	3-Jan
1994	181.52	-20.84	3.84	-15.29	227.06	3-Jan	173.94	22-Nov
1993	229.30	3.75	31.17	9.63	256.46	31-Aug	217.14	5-Jan
1992	221.02	-2.27	26.43	4.86	225.59	3-Jan	200.74	8-Apr
1991	226.15	7.84	29.37	15.25	226.15	31-Dec	195.17	10-Jul
1990	209.70	-10.78	19.96	-4.56	236.23	2-Jan	190.96	24-Aug
1989	235.04	26.18	34.45	35.24	235.98	15-Dec	181.84	24-Feb
1988	186.28	6.40	6.56	15.80	190.02	29-Jan	167.08	18-May
1987	175.08	-15.01	0.15	NA	227.83	22-Jan	160.98	19-Oct
1986	206.01	17.85	17.85	NA	219.15	20-Aug	169.47	22-Jan
1985	174.81							
Average Annual (%)		3.73		9.10				
Compound Annual (%)		2.57		8.11				
Standard Deviation (%)		16.15		16.75				

SYNOPSIS

The Dow Jones Utilities Average is a price-weighted benchmark that tracks the continuous price only and daily total return performance of 15 actively traded stocks representing a cross-section of corporations involved in various phases of the utility industry listed on the New York Stock Exchange (NYSE).

NUMBER OF STOCKS—DECEMBER 31, 1995

15

MARKET VALUE—DECEMBER 31, 1995

US$75,266.9 million

SELECTION CRITERIA

Constituent stocks are actively traded, large capitalization stocks that are widely held. They are selected to represent a cross section of corporations involved in various phases of the utilities industry in the United States. The following 15 companies make up the Average: American Electric Power, Centerior Energy, Consolidated Edison, Consolidated Natural Gas, DTE Energy (formerly Detroit Edison Co.), Edison International, Houston Industries, Niagara Mohawk Power, NorAm Energy, PECO Energy, Pacific Gas & Electric, Panhandle Eastern, People Energy, Public Service Enterprise, and Unicom Corp.

BACKGROUND

The Dow Jones Utilities Average, consisting of 20 stocks, made its debut in the morning edition of *The Wall Street Journal* on December 25, 1929, with back data to July 1, 1929. The addition of this measure to the complement of Dow Jones benchmarks was made at the culmination of a year that recorded developments of unusual range and depth, marking it as probably the most exceptional year in the utility history to 1929. These include major consolidations, record earnings, widespread interest in utility equity issues and tremendous buying power by investment trusts which, in turn, brought about a scarcity of utility stocks.

Effective June 2, 1938, the Utility Average was reconstructed without interruption in the historical data stream to include 15 instead of 20 stocks. Starting in 1993, Dow Jones began to compute total return performance. Total returns have been backdated to September 30, 1987.

For additional information, refer to the Dow Jones Industrial Average (DJIA).

BASE DATE

January 1, 1928=

COMPUTATION METHODOLOGY

(1) A simple aggregative of actual prices index formula. Adjustments are made to the divisor in connection with constituent changes, stock splits and other corporate actions. (2) New York Stock Exchange closing prices are used in the calculation of the index. (3) Dividends, for total return performance calculations, are assumed to be reinvested at the beginning of the ex-dividend date.

DERIVATIVE INSTRUMENTS

None

SUBINDICES

None

RELATED INDICES

Dow Jones Composite Average
Dow Jones Equity Market Index
Dow Jones Industrial Average
Dow Jones Transportation Average
Dow Jones World Stock Index
Refer to Appendix 5 for additional indices.

REMARKS

None

PUBLISHER

Dow Jones & Company, Inc.

HAMBRECHT & QUIST (H&Q) TECHNOLOGY INDEX

PRICE PERFORMANCE

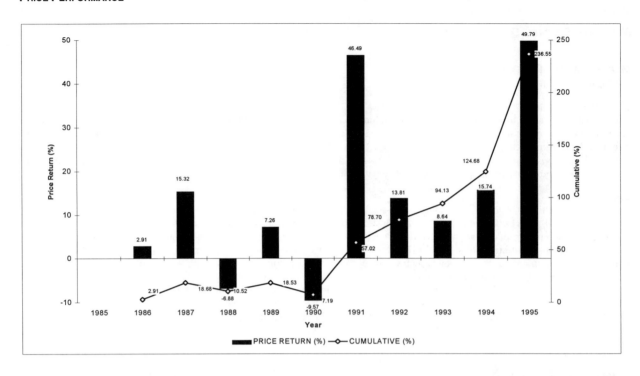

PRICE AND TOTAL RETURN PERFORMANCE

YEAR	VALUE	PRICE RETURN (%)	CUMULATIVE (%)	TOTAL RETURN (%)	MAXIMUM VALUE[1]	DATE	MINIMUM VALUE[1]	DATE
1995	728.67	49.79	236.55	50.15	783.97	3-Nov	478.27	3-Jan
1994	486.45	15.74	124.68	16.07	490.17	29-Dec	380.01	24-Jun
1993	420.31	8.64	94.13	9.13	424.49	3-Dec	345.65	26-Apr
1992	386.90	13.81	78.70	15.02	386.90	31-Dec	310.26	25-Jun
1991	339.96	46.49	57.02	47.83	339.96	31-Dec	222.03	14-Jan
1990	232.07	-9.57	7.19	-8.58	293.37	4-Jun	190.09	11-Oct
1989	256.64	7.26	18.53	8.47	278.34	2-Jun	235.14	22-Mar
1988	239.28	-6.88	10.52	-5.95	271.50	30-Jun	224.07	30-Nov
1987	256.95	15.32	18.68	NA	344.40	31-Aug	220.27	30-Nov
1986	222.81	2.91	2.91	NA	248.72	31-May	213.89	30-Sep
1985	216.51							
Average Annual (%)		14.35		16.52				
Compound Annual (%)		12.90		11.67				
Standard Deviation (%)		19.80		21.94				

[1]Maximum/minimum index values for the period 1986-1988 are as of month-end.

SYNOPSIS

The Hambrecht & Quist (H&Q) Technology Index is a market value-weighted index that measures the daily price only and monthly total return performance of publicly traded stocks in the technology sector, including companies in the electronics, medical and related technology industries.

NUMBER OF STOCKS—DECEMBER 31, 1995

201

MARKET VALUE—DECEMBER 31, 1995

US$413,600.0 million

SELECTION CRITERIA

Based upon an annual review, index constituents are selected to represent the technology universe as a whole as well as particular industry sectors and are not intended to represent the universe of stocks covered by Hambrecht & Quist Research Department. Five major industry sectors are covered: Computer hardware, computer software, communications, semiconductors, and health care. Market capitalization, revenue growth, earnings growth, liquidity and company fundamentals are taken into consideration in the selection of companies for inclusion in the index.

Stocks of large diversified technology companies whose operations span several subsectors, are excluded from the index.

BACKGROUND

The index was originally conceived in the mid-1970s as a price-weighted index with a fixed number of constituents. In February 1985, the index, with its 175 constituent stocks, was reconstituted as a market value index. Index values based on the revised weighting methodology were backdated to 1970. The number of index constituents had been expanded to 200 as of year-end 1995 and 250 stocks starting in 1996.

The index had been calculated on a price only basis to December 31, 1992. Total rates of return calculations commenced in 1993, with backdata available to December 31, 1987. At the same time, a market capitalization ceiling was introduced.

BASE DATE

December 31, 1978=100.00

COMPUTATION METHODOLOGY

(1) An aggregate of prices times quantities index formula. Maintenance adjustments to the divisor are made for capitalization changes, new listings and delistings. (2) The market capitalization of individual companies is limited to a maximum value of US$10 billion. (3) While index substitutions are made only once a year, companies that cease to trade due to mergers, acquisitions, and other developments are removed from the index without being replaced. (4) Total rates of return are calculated at the end of each month.

DERIVATIVE INSTRUMENTS

None

SUBINDICES

H&Q Growth Index
H&Q Biotechnology Index
H&Q Communications Index
H&Q Computer Hardware Index
H&Q Health Care Index
H&Q Internet Index
H&Q Semiconductor Index
H&Q Computer Software Index

RELATED INDICES

None

REMARKS

None

PUBLISHER

Hambrecht & Quist LLC.

MORGAN STANLEY CONSUMER (CMR) INDEX

PRICE PERFORMANCE

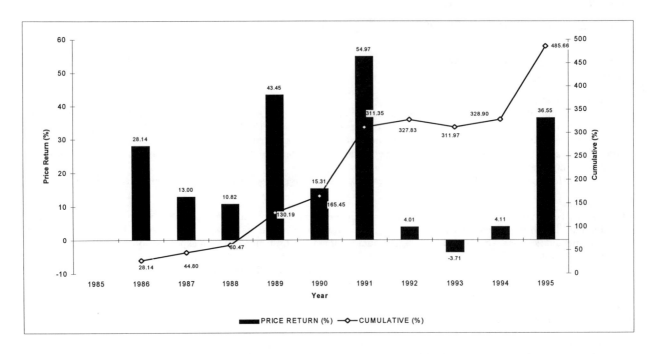

PRICE PERFORMANCE[1]

YEAR	VALUE	PRICE RETURN (%)	CUMULATIVE (%)	MAXIMUM VALUE	DATE	MINIMUM VALUE	DATE
1995	284.75	36.55	485.66	289.49	13-Dec	206.48	9-Jan
1994	208.53	4.11	328.90	209.56	16-Dec	186.46	4-Apr
1993	200.30	-3.71	311.97	207.55	4-Jan	181.94	12-Aug
1992	208.01	4.01	327.83	214.16	18-Dec	179.88	17-Jun
1991	200.00	54.97	311.35	200.00	31-Dec	120.18	9-Jan
1990	129.06	15.31	165.45	133.79	17-Jul	101.35	23-Feb
1989	111.92	43.45	130.19	111.91	29-Dec	77.26	3-Jan
1988	78.02	10.82	60.47	79.73	21-Oct	68.81	18-May
1987	70.40	13.00	44.80	90.01	25-Aug	61.85	19-Oct
1986	62.30	28.14	28.14	67.47	2-Jul	47.15	9-Jan
1985	48.62						
Average Annual (%)		20.67					
Compound Annual (%)		19.33					
Standard Deviation (%)		19.25					

[1] Index values and performance data prior to 1991 are as a result of back-testing.

SYNOPSIS
The Morgan Stanley Consumer (CMR) Index is an equal-weighted index that tracks the continuous price only performance of large capitalization, consumer-oriented, stable growth stocks.

NUMBER OF STOCKS—DECEMBER 31, 1995
30

MARKET VALUE—DECEMBER 31, 1995
US$825,033.2 million

SELECTION CRITERIA
Component stocks are selected from a universe of companies that make up the S&P 500 Index, with a market capitalization in excess of US$1 billion. There is an emphasis on companies whose stocks participate in other securities market indices. Consumer oriented stocks, which are not expected to be significantly impacted by economic cycles, are selected to represent particular industries that in turn, are chosen for their lack of sensitivity to economic factors. The following stocks make up the index: Allied-Signal Inc.; Aluminum Company of America; Bethlehem Steel Corporation; Caterpillar, Inc.; Citicorp; CSX Corp.; Dana Corp.; The Dow Chemical Company; Eaton Corp.; Ford Motor Co.; Georgia-Pacific Corp.; The Goodyear Tire & Rubber Co.; Hewlett-Pakcard Company; Honeywell Inc.; Ingersoll-Rand Company; International Paper Company; Kmart Corp.; Knight-Ridder Corp., Inc.; Masco Corp.; Maytag Corp.; The Mead Corp.; Motorola, Inc.; Parker-Hannifin Corp.; Phelps Dodge Corp.; PPG Industries, Inc.; Roadway Services, Inc.; Rohm & Haas Company; Ryder-System, Inc.; Tenneco Inc.; and United Technologies Corp.

BACKGROUND
The index was developed by Morgan Stanley & Co., Inc. in 1992 and back tested to January 3, 1978 with a portfolio of securities that would have been available for inclusion in the index had it been created 15 years earlier. Stock index options were introduced on September 21, 1993.

BASE DATE
December 31, 1991=200.00

COMPUTATION METHODOLOGY
(1) An equal dollar-weighting index formula. The weighting of constituents is rebalanced annually to reestablish equal dollar amounts. (2) The composition of the index is reviewed annually based on the closing prices on the third Friday in December.

DERIVATIVE INSTRUMENTS
Morgan Stanley Consumer Index options trade on the American Stock Exchange (AMEX).

SUBINDICES
None

RELATED INDICES
Morgan Stanley Capital International World Index
Morgan Stanley Consumer Index
Morgan Stanley High-Technology 35 Index
Refer to Appendix 5 for additional indices.

REMARKS
None

PUBLISHER
Morgan Stanley & Co.

MORGAN STANLEY CYCLICAL (CYC) INDEX

PRICE PERFORMANCE

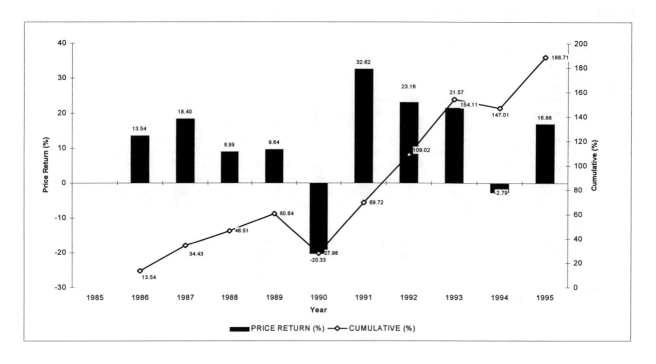

PRICE PERFORMANCE[1]

YEAR	VALUE	PRICE RETURN (%)	CUMULATIVE (%)	MAXIMUM VALUE	DATE	MINIMUM VALUE	DATE
1995	340.22	16.88	188.71	360.45	12-Jul	285.51	30-Jan
1994	291.08	-2.79	147.01	321.53	2-Feb	273.02	23-Nov
1993	299.44	21.57	154.11	296.62	22-Dec	246.21	13-Jan
1992	246.31	23.16	109.02	252.43	11-May	200.42	2-Jan
1991	200.00	32.62	69.72	199.18	4-Jun	143.90	14-Jan
1990	150.81	-20.33	27.98	196.35	4-Jun	129.79	17-Oct
1989	189.30	9.64	60.64	210.57	4-Sep	171.56	3-Jan
1988	172.65	8.99	46.51	182.39	5-Jul	150.49	20-Jan
1987	158.41	18.40	34.43	210.41	2-Oct	121.14	26-Oct
1986	133.79	13.54	13.54	143.48	28-Mar	116.04	9-Jan
1985	117.84						
Average Annual (%)		12.17					
Compound Annual (%)		11.19					
Standard Deviation (%)		14.86					

[1]Index values and performance data prior to 1991 are as a result of back-testing.

SYNOPSIS

The Morgan Stanley Cyclical (CYC) Index is an equal-weighted index that tracks the continuous price only performance of large capitalization stocks that are highly sensitive to movements in the economy and levels of consumer confidence.

NUMBER OF STOCKS—DECEMBER 31, 1995

30

MARKET VALUE—DECEMBER 31, 1995

US$324,493.5 million

SELECTION CRITERIA

Component stocks are selected from a universe of companies that make up the S&P 500 Index, with a market capitalization in excess of US$1 billion. There is an emphasis on companies whose stocks participate in other securities market indices. Cyclical stocks, which are expected to show particular strengths during periods of economic expansion and somewhat less strength during other phases of the economic cycle, are selected to represent particular industries that, in turn, are chosen for their lack of sensitivity to economic factors. The following stocks, representing 20 industries, make up the index: Abbott Laboratories; Albertson's, Inc.; American Home Products Corp.; Anheuser-Busch Companies, Inc.; Automatic Data Processing, Inc.; Banc One Corp.; Baxter International Inc.; The Coca-Cola Company; Colgate-Palmolive Co.; ConAgra, Inc.; Crown Cork & Seal Company, Inc.; Emerson Electric Company; General Mill, Inc.; The Gillette Company; Grainger (W.W.) Inc.; International Flavors & Fragrances, Inc.; Johnson & Johnson; Kimberly-Clark Corp.; McDonald's Corp.; Medtronic, Inc.; Merck & Company, Inc.; PepsiCo, Inc.; Philip Morris Companies, Inc.; The Proctor & Gamble Company; Rubbermaid Inc.; Schering-Plough Corp.; Sysco Corp.; UST Inc.; Walgreen Company; Wal-Mart Stores Inc.

BACKGROUND

The index was developed by Morgan Stanley & Co., Inc. in 1992 and back-tested to January 3, 1978 with a portfolio of securities that would have been available for inclusion in the index had it been created 15 years earlier. Stock index options were introduced on September 21, 1993.

BASE DATE

December 31, 1991=200.00

COMPUTATION METHODOLOGY

(1) An equal dollar-weighting index formula. The weighting of constituents is rebalanced annually to reestablish equal dollar amounts. (2) The composition of the index is reviewed annually based on the closing prices on the third Friday in December.

DERIVATIVE INSTRUMENTS

Morgan Stanley Cyclical Index options trade on the American Stock Exchange (AMEX).

SUBINDICES

None

RELATED INDICES

Morgan Stanley Capital International World Index
Morgan Stanley Consumer Index
Morgan Stanley High-Technology 35 Index
Refer to Appendix 5 for additional indices.

REMARKS

None

PUBLISHER

Morgan Stanley & Co.

THE MORGAN STANLEY HIGH-TECHNOLOGY 35 (TECH 35) INDEX

PRICE PERFORMANCE

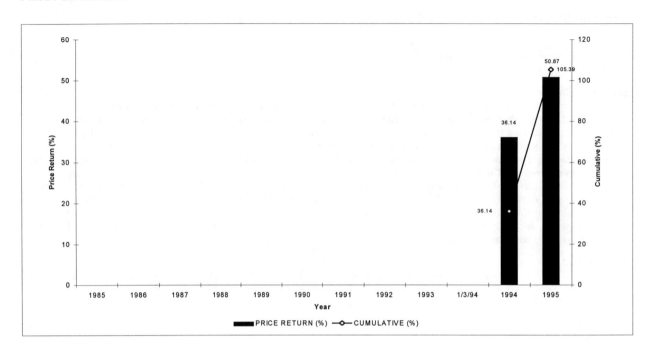

PRICE PERFORMANCE

YEAR	VALUE	PRICE RETURN (%)	CUMULATIVE (%)	MAXIMUM VALUE	DATE	MINIMUM VALUE	DATE
1995	315.77	50.87	105.39	361.21	3-Nov	202.70	30-Jan
1994	209.30	36.14	36.14	209.45	27-Dec	149.03	23-Jun
1/3/94	153.74						
1993							
1992							
1991							
1990							
1989							
1988							
1987							
1986							
1985							
Average Annual (%)		43.50					
Compound Annual (%)		43.32					
Standard Deviation (%)		NM					

SYNOPSIS

The Morgan Stanley High-Technology 35 (Tech 35) Index is an equal dollar-weighted index that measures the daily price only performance of 35 stocks from nine technology subsectors.

NUMBER OF STOCKS—DECEMBER 31, 1995

35

MARKET VALUE—DECEMBER 31, 1995

Not Available

SELECTION CRITERIA

Constituent stocks represent a cross-section of highly capitalized Unites States (U.S.) companies that are active in each of the nine technology subsectors. These include: Computer services, design software, server software, personal computer software and new media, networking and telecommunications equipment, server hardware, personal computer hardware and peripherals, specialized systems and semiconductors.

BACKGROUND

The index was established at the end of 1994 and daily index values were backdated to January 3, 1994. It was subsequently adopted by the American Stock Exchange (AMEX) for use as an underlying vehicle for stock index options which commenced trading in September 1995.

BASE DATE

December 16, 1994=200.00

COMPUTATION METHODOLOGY

(1) An equal dollar-weighting index formula. Equal dollar-weighting was established by designating the number of shares of each component stock that represented a market value of approximately $300,000 based on closing prices on December 16, 1994. (2) The index is rebalanced annually, after the close of trading on the third Friday of December, if necessary, to reestablish equal dollar amounts.

DERIVATIVE INSTRUMENTS

Tech 35 Index options trade on the American Stock Exchange (AMEX).

SUBINDICES

None

RELATED INDICES

Morgan Stanley Capital International World Index
Morgan Stanley Consumer Index
Morgan Stanley Cyclical Index
Refer to Appendix 5 for additional indices.

REMARKS

None

PUBLISHER

Morgan Stanley & Co.

NASDAQ 100 INDEX

PRICE PERFORMANCE

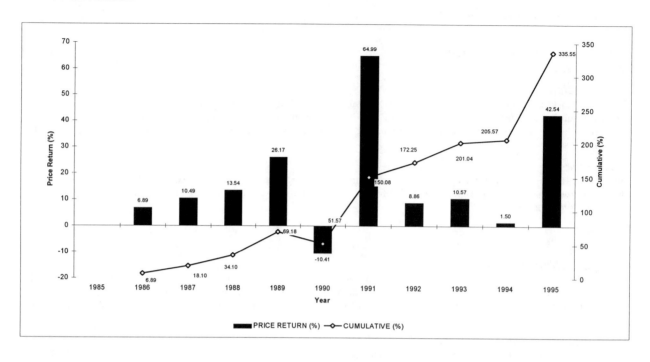

PRICE PERFORMANCE[1]

YEAR	VALUE	PRICE RETURN (%)	CUMULATIVE (%)	MAXIMUM VALUE[2]	DATE	MINIMUM VALUE[2]	DATE
1995	576.23	42.54	335.55	621.71	3-Nov	398.00	3-Jan
1994	404.27	1.50	205.57	418.45	17-Mar	351.76	24-Jun
1993	398.28	10.57	201.04	401.77	3-Dec	327.28	26-Apr
1992	360.19	8.86	172.25	361.83	7-Dec	290.03	26-Jun
1991	330.86	64.99	150.08	330.85	31-Dec	191.69	9-Jan
1990	200.53	-10.41	51.57	246.18	16-Jul	165.19	11-Oct
1989	223.83	26.17	69.18	236.79	9-Oct	174.63	3-Jan
1988	177.41	13.54	34.10	177.41	30-Dec	171.11	12-Dec
1987	156.25	10.49	18.10	209.58	31-Aug	137.13	30-Nov
1986	141.41	6.89	6.89	163.16	31-May	132.93	31-Jan
1985	132.30						
Average Annual (%)		17.52					
Compound Annual (%)		15.85					
Standard Deviation (%)		21.84					

[1]Index values have been adjusted to reflect 1994 split.
[2]Maximum/minimum values for the period 1986-1987 are based on month-end index values.

SYNOPSIS

The Nasdaq-100 Index is a market value-weighted index that tracks the continuous stock price only performance of the 100 largest non-financial, domestic only common stocks traded on the Nasdaq National Market (Nasdaq/NMS). These shares account for 34.6% of the Nasdaq market.

NUMBER OF STOCKS—DECEMBER 31, 1995

100

MARKET VALUE—DECEMBER 31, 1995

US$ 405,472.4 million

SELECTION CRITERIA

Constituent stocks are selected on the basis of market capitalization from the universe of domestic, non-financial companies that are traded on the Nasdaq/NMS. These include transportation, utilities and all other industrial companies.

BACKGROUND

At the beginning of trading on Monday, January 3, 1994, the value of the index was halved, from 795.45 to 397.725 in order to accommodate the creation and trading of derivative instruments. Up to year-end 1989, the index was calculated on a price only and total return basis. The total return computation was discontinued in 1990.

BASE DATE

February 1, 1985=250.00

COMPUTATION METHODOLOGY

(1) An aggregate of prices times quantities index formula. Maintenance adjustments to the divisor are made for capitalization changes, new listings and delistings. (2) Market capitalization of foreign issues is computed on the basis of Nasdaq-listed shares and not worldwide shares outstanding. (3) Last sale price is used.

DERIVATIVE INSTRUMENTS

Nasdaq 100 Index options trade on The Chicago Board Options Exchange (CBOE).

SUBINDICES

None

RELATED INDICES

Nasdaq Composite Index

REMARKS

(1) The top 10 listed companies have a combined market capitalization of US$201.1 billion and account for 50% of the index. (2) Eight of the top 10 companies, with a combined market capitalization of US$174.2 billion, or 48% of the index, are technology oriented companies involved in computer, telephone communications, electronics and cable or other pay-for-television activities.

PUBLISHER

The National Association of Securities Dealers, Inc. (NASD)/The Nasdaq Stock Market Inc.

NASDAQ AMERICAN DEPOSITARY RECEIPTS (ADRs) INDEX

PRICE PERFORMANCE

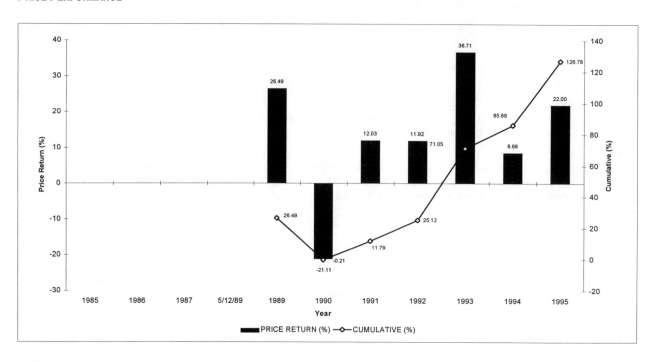

PRICE PERFORMANCE[1]

YEAR	VALUE	PRICE RETURN (%)	CUMULATIVE (%)	MAXIMUM VALUE	DATE	MINIMUM VALUE	DATE
1995	245.58	22.00	126.78	257.12	27-Nov	188.01	30-Jan
1994	201.30	8.68	85.89	222.10	20-Oct	176.60	4-Apr
1993	185.23	36.71	71.05	186.62	18-Oct	129.37	24-Feb
1992	135.49	11.92	25.12	139.43	16-Jul	116.10	30-Oct
1991	121.06	12.03	11.79	128.13	8-Mar	96.23	3-Jul
1990	108.06	-21.11	-0.21	172.84	16-Jul	99.09	29-Nov
1989	136.98	26.49	26.49	141.50	13-Dec	101.59	15-Jun
5/12/89	108.29						
1987							
1986							
1985							
Average Annual (%)		11.70					
Compound Annual (%)		6.01					
Standard Deviation (%)		19.07					

[1]Statistical measures applicable to the six year period 1990-1995.

SYNOPSIS

The Nasdaq American Depositary Receipts (ADRs) Index is a market value-weighted index that tracks the daily stock price only performance of all American Depositary Receipts (ADRs) traded on the Nasdaq National Market System (Nasdaq/NMS).

NUMBER OF STOCKS—DECEMBER 31, 1995

115

MARKET VALUE—DECEMBER 31, 1995

US$24,702.1 million

SELECTION CRITERIA

All American Depositary Receipts (ADRs) traded on the Nasdaq National Market System.

BACKGROUND

None

BASE DATE

May 1989=100.00

COMPUTATION METHODOLOGY

(1) An aggregate of prices times quantities index formula. Maintenance adjustments to the divisor are made for capitalization changes, new listings and delistings. (2) Market capitalization is computed on the basis of Nasdaq-listed ADRs and not worldwide shares outstanding. (3) Last sale price is used.

DERIVATIVE INSTRUMENTS

None

SUBINDICES

None

RELATED INDICES

Nasdaq Composite Index

REMARKS

The performance of the index is largely influenced by four companies that account for 52.5% of the index. These include LM Ericsson Telephone Company (21.3%), Reuters Holdings PLC (15.6%), Teva Pharmaceutical (8.0%) and NYNEX Cable Communications Group (7.6%).

PUBLISHER

The National Association of Securities Dealers, Inc. (NASD)/The Nasdaq Stock Market Inc.

NASDAQ BANK INDEX

PRICE PERFORMANCE

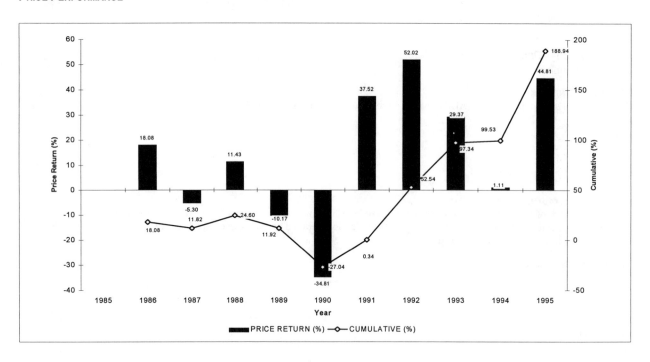

PRICE PERFORMANCE

YEAR	VALUE	PRICE RETURN (%)	CUMULATIVE (%)	MAXIMUM VALUE	DATE	MINIMUM VALUE	DATE
1995	1,009.44	44.81	188.94	1,009.44	29-Dec	702.95	3-Jan
1994	697.07	1.11	99.53	787.92	16-Sep	662.57	4-Jan
1993	689.43	29.37	97.34	725.65	15-Oct	530.03	5-Jan
1992	532.93	52.02	52.54	532.93	21-Dec	352.81	2-Jan
1991	350.56	37.52	0.34	350.56	31-Dec	355.75	15-Jan
1990	254.91	-34.81	-27.04	400.19	8-Jan	235.25	1-Nov
1989	391.02	-10.17	11.92	491.16	25-Aug	375.38	19-Dec
1988	435.31	11.43	24.60	464.91	5-Aug	396.44	4-Jan
1987	390.66	-5.30	11.82	526.64	20-Mar	365.63	28-Oct
1986	412.53	18.08	18.08	457.59	3-Jul	346.35	9-Jan
1985	349.36						
Average Annual (%)		14.41					
Compound Annual (%)		11.19					
Standard Deviation (%)		27.31					

SYNOPSIS
The Nasdaq Bank Index is a market value-weighted index that tracks the price only performance of domestic and foreign common stocks of banks that are traded on the Nasdaq National Market System (Nasdaq/NMS) as well as the SmallCap Market.

NUMBER OF STOCKS—DECEMBER 31, 1995
356

MARKET VALUE—DECEMBER 31, 1995
US$31,539.0 million

SELECTION CRITERIA
All stocks traded on Nasdaq, including the National Market and SmallCap Market, which are classified as banks based upon Standard Industrial Classification (SIC) Codes relative to a company's major source of revenue are included in the index. Coverage extents to all types of banks, including trust companies not engaged in deposit banking and establishments performing functions closely related to banking, such as check cashing agencies, currency exchanges, safe deposit companies and corporations for banking abroad.

BACKGROUND
None

BASE DATE
February 5,1971=100.00

COMPUTATION METHODOLOGY
(1) An aggregate of prices times quantities index formula. Maintenance adjustments to the divisor are made for capitalization changes, new listings and delistings. (2) Market capitalization of foreign issues is computed on the basis of Nasdaq-listed shares and not worldwide shares outstanding. (3) Last sale price is used.

DERIVATIVE INSTRUMENTS
None

SUBINDICES
None

RELATED INDICES
Nasdaq Composite Index

REMARKS
None

PUBLISHER
The National Association of Securities Dealers, Inc. (NASD)/The Nasdaq Stock Market, Inc.

NASDAQ BIOTECHNOLOGY INDEX

PRICE PERFORMANCE

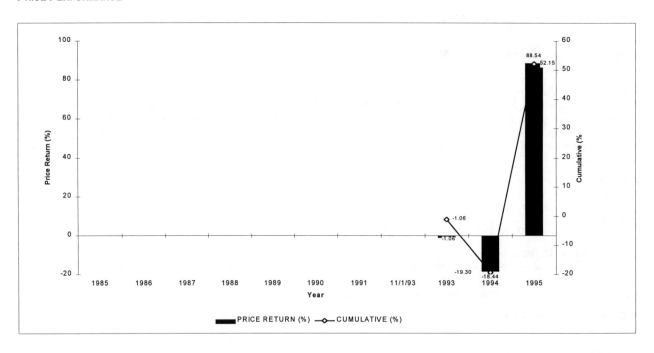

PRICE PERFORMANCE[1]

YEAR	VALUE	PRICE RETURN (%)	CUMULATIVE (%)	MAXIMUM VALUE	DATE	MINIMUM VALUE	DATE
1995	304.30	88.54	52.15	304.30	29-Dec	153.84	12-Jan
1994	161.40	-18.44	-19.30	209.70	28-Jan	143.13	20-Apr
1993	197.88	-1.06	-1.06	203.11	11-Nov	186.21	14-Dec
11/1/93	200.00						
1991							
1990							
1989							
1988							
1987							
1986							
1985							
Average Annual (%)		35.05					
Compound Annual (%)		4.40					
Standard Deviation (%)		NM					

[1]Statistical measures applicable to the two year period 1994-1995.

Synopsis
The Nasdaq Biotechnology Index is a market value-weighted index that tracks the price only performance of domestic and foreign biotechnology common stocks traded on the Nasdaq National Market System (Nasdaq/NMS) and SmallCap Market.

Number of Stocks—December 31, 1995
98

Market Value—December 31, 1995
US$46,965.0 million

Selection Criteria
Biotechnology companies listed on Nasdaq with a market capitalization greater than US$50 million, including the National Market System and SmallCap Market, are eligible for inclusion in the index. Constituents are selected based upon Standard Industrial Classification (SIC) Codes relative to a company's major source of revenue. These include companies primarily engaged in using biomedical research for the development of novel treatments and cures for human disease.

Background
None

Base Date
November 1, 1993=200.00

Computation Methodology
(1) An aggregate of prices times quantities index formula. Maintenance adjustments to the divisor are made for capitalization changes, new listings and delistings. (2) Market capitalization of foreign issues is computed on the basis of Nasdaq-listed shares and not worldwide shares outstanding. (3) Last sale price is used.

Derivative Instruments
None

Subindices
None

Related Indices
Nasdaq Composite Index

Remarks
None

Publisher
The National Association of Securities Dealers, Inc. (NASD)/The Nasdaq Stock Market, Inc.

NASDAQ COMPOSITE INDEX

PRICE PERFORMANCE

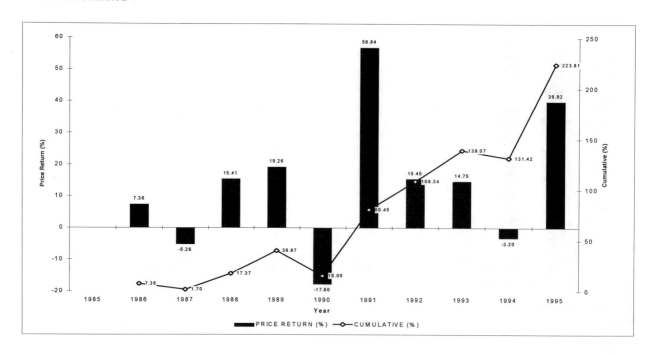

PRICE PERFORMANCE

YEAR	VALUE	PRICE RETURN (%)	CUMULATIVE (%)	MAXIMUM VALUE	DATE	MINIMUM VALUE	DATE
1995	1,052.14	39.92	223.81	1,069.79	4-Dec	743.58	3-Jan
1994	751.96	-3.20	131.42	803.93	18-Mar	693.79	24-Jun
1993	776.80	14.75	139.07	787.42	15-Oct	645.87	26-Apr
1992	676.95	15.45	108.34	676.95	30-Dec	547.84	26-Jun
1991	586.34	56.84	80.45	586.34	31-Dec	355.75	14-Jan
1990	373.84	-17.80	15.05	469.60	16-Jul	325.44	16-Oct
1989	454.82	19.26	39.97	486.73	9-Oct	378.56	3-Jan
1988	381.38	15.41	17.37	396.11	5-Jul	331.97	12-Jan
1987	330.47	-5.26	1.70	455.26	26-Aug	291.88	28-Oct
1986	348.83	7.36	7.36	411.16	3-Jul	323.01	9-Jan
1985	324.93						
Average Annual (%)		14.27					
Compound Annual (%)		12.47					
Standard Deviation (%)		21.76					

SYNOPSIS
The Nasdaq Composite Index is a broad based market value-weighted index that tracks the daily stock price only performance of domestic common stocks and foreign issues, including American Depositary Receipts (ADRs), traded on the Nasdaq National Market System (Nasdaq/NMS) as well as Nasdaq SmallCap Market.

NUMBER OF STOCKS—DECEMBER 31, 1995
5,957

MARKET VALUE—DECEMBER 31, 1995
US$1,170,705.0 million

SELECTION CRITERIA
All listed domestic common stocks traded on the Nasdaq National Market as well as Nasdaq SmallCap Market are included in the index. Rights, warrants, units, preferred stock, shares of beneficial interest and debentures are excluded from the index.

BACKGROUND
The Nasdaq market includes the National Market System (NMS) with its 4,027-listed issues and a market capitalization of US$1,133 billion while the smaller, SmallCap Market lists 1,930 issues with a market capitalization of US$37.4 billion, for a combined total of 5,957 listed companies with a market value of US$1,171 billion as of December 31, 1995.

BASE DATE
February 5,1971=100.00

COMPUTATION METHODOLOGY
(1) An aggregate of prices times quantities index formula. Maintenance adjustments to the divisor are made for capitalization changes, new listings and delistings.
(2) Market capitalization of foreign issues is computed on the basis of Nasdaq-listed shares and not worldwide shares outstanding.
(3) Last sale price is used.

DERIVATIVE INSTRUMENTS
None

SUBINDICES
Nasdaq/NMS Composite Index
Nasdaq-100 Index
Nasdaq ADR Index
Nasdaq Bank Index
Nasdaq Biotechnology Index
Nasdaq Computer Index
Nasdaq Financial Index
Nasdaq Industrial Index
Nasdaq Insurance Index
Nasdaq Other Finance Index
Nasdaq Telecommunications Index
Nasdaq Transportation Index
Seven regional subindices by company headquarters: San Francisco, Los Angeles, Seattle, New Orleans, Chicago, Washington D.C. and New York.
Various subindices based on market value ranges of listed companies, calculated using price-weighted, market value-weighted and equal- weighted methodologies.

RELATED INDICES
None

REMARKS
None

PUBLISHER
The National Association of Securities Dealers, Inc. (NASD)/The Nasdaq Stock Market Inc.

NASDAQ COMPUTER INDEX

PRICE PERFORMANCE

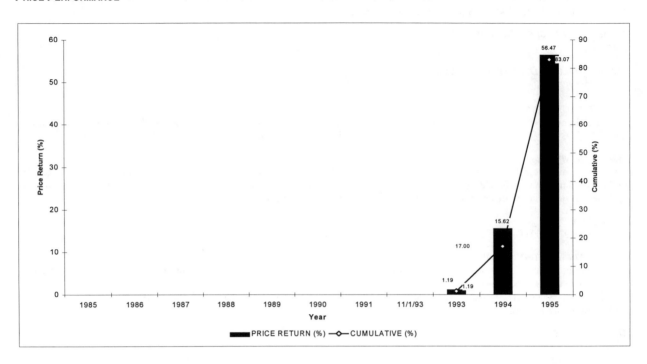

PRICE PERFORMANCE[1]

YEAR	VALUE	PRICE RETURN (%)	CUMULATIVE (%)	MAXIMUM VALUE	DATE	MINIMUM VALUE	DATE
1995	366.13	56.47	83.07	403.92	3-Nov	229.99	3-Jan
1994	233.99	15.62	17.00	235.62	29-Dec	182.82	23-Jun
1993	202.38	1.19	1.19	207.81	3-Dec	191.32	22-Nov
11/1/93	200.00						
1991							
1990							
1989							
1988							
1987							
1986							
1985							
Average Annual (%)		36.05					
Compound Annual (%)		6.11					
Standard Deviation (%)		NM					

[1]Statistical measures applicable to the two year period 1994-1995.

Synopsis

The Nasdaq Computer Index is a market value-weighted index that tracks the price only performance of domestic and foreign common stocks of computer companies traded on the Nasdaq National Market System (Nasdaq/NMS) and SmallCap Market.

Number of Stocks—December 31, 1995

554

Market Value—December 31, 1995

US$328,289.0 million

Selection Criteria

Constituent companies traded on Nasdaq, including the National Market System and SmallCap Market, are selected based upon Standard Industrial Classification (SIC) Codes relative to a company's major source of revenue. These include companies engaged in the manufacture of computer hardware, programming, electronic components/accessories (provided more than 50% of their business is computer related) and computer related services.

Background

None

Base Year

November 1, 1993=200.00

Computation Methodology

(1) An aggregate of prices times quantities index formula. Maintenance adjustments to the divisor are made for capitalization changes, new listings and delistings. (2) Market capitalization of foreign issues is computed on the basis of Nasdaq-listed shares and not worldwide shares outstanding. (3) Last sale price is used.

Derivative Instruments

None

Subindices

None

Related Indices

Nasdaq Composite Index

Remarks

None

Publisher

The National Association of Securities Dealers, Inc. (NASD)/The Nasdaq Stock Market, Inc.

NASDAQ FINANCIAL INDEX 100

PRICE PERFORMANCE

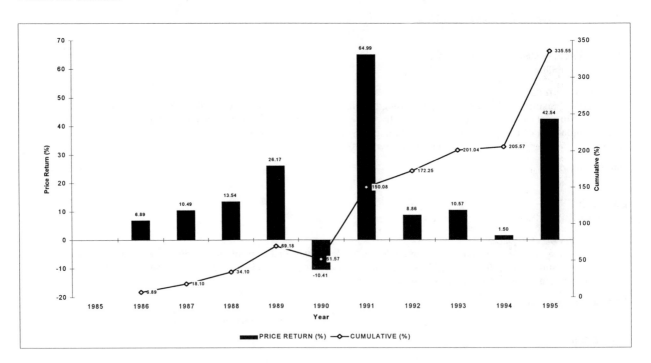

PRICE PERFORMANCE

YEAR	VALUE[1]	PRICE RETURN (%)	CUMULATIVE (%)	MAXIMUM VALUE[2]	DATE	MINIMUM VALUE[2]	DATE
1995	576.23	42.54	335.55	621.71	3-Nov	398.00	3-Jan
1994	404.27	1.50	205.57	418.45	17-Mar	351.76	24-Jun
1993	398.28	10.57	201.04	401.77	3-Dec	327.28	26-Apr
1992	360.19	8.86	172.25	361.83	7-Dec	290.03	26-Jun
1991	330.86	64.99	150.08	330.85	31-Dec	191.69	9-Jan
1990	200.53	-10.41	51.57	246.18	16-Jul	165.19	11-Oct
1989	223.83	26.17	69.18	236.79	9-Oct	174.63	3-Jan
1988	177.41	13.54	34.10	177.41	30-Dec	171.11	12-Dec
1987	156.25	10.49	18.10	209.58	31-Aug	137.13	30-Nov
1986	141.41	6.89	6.89	163.16	31-May	132.93	31-Jan
1985	132.30						
Average Annual (%)		17.52					
Compound Annual (%)		15.85					
Standard Deviation (%)		21.84					

[1]Index values have been adjusted to reflect 1994 split.
[2]Maximum/minimum values for the period 1986-1987 are based on month-end index values.

SYNOPSIS

The Nasdaq Financial Index 100 is a market value-weighted index that tracks the daily price only performance of common stocks of the 100 largest financial companies, as well as foreign issues, including American Depositary Receipts (ADRs), traded on the Nasdaq National Market System (Nasdaq/NMS) and SmallCap Market.

NUMBER OF STOCKS—DECEMBER 31, 1995

100

MARKET VALUE—DECEMBER 31, 1995

US$115,739.4 million

SELECTION CRITERIA

Constituent shares listed on Nasdaq, including the National Market System and SmallCap Market, are classified as banks and other finance companies, including credit agencies other than banks, savings and loan associations, security and commodity brokers, exchanges and dealers and related services, real estate and holding and investment companies (other than closed-end investment companies) under the Securities Industry Classification (SIC) scheme.

Rights, warrants, units, preferred stock, shares of beneficial interest and debentures are excluded from the index.

BACKGROUND

None

BASE YEAR

December 31, 1984=250.00

COMPUTATION METHODOLOGY

(1) An aggregate of prices times quantities index formula. Maintenance adjustments to the divisor are made for capitalization changes, new listings and delistings. (2) Market capitalization of foreign issues is computed on the basis of Nasdaq-listed shares and not worldwide shares outstanding. (3) Last sale price is used.

DERIVATIVE INSTRUMENTS

None

SUBINDICES

None

RELATED INDICES

Nasdaq Composite Index

REMARKS

None

PUBLISHER

The National Association of Securities Dealers, Inc. (NASD)/The Nasdaq Stock Market, Inc.

NASDAQ INDUSTRIAL INDEX

PRICE PERFORMANCE

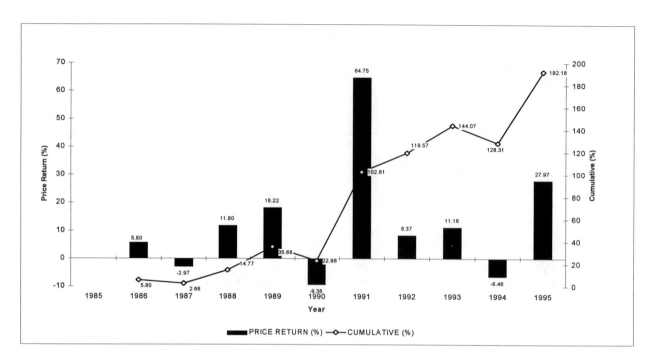

PRICE PERFORMACE

YEAR	VALUE	PRICE RETURN (%)	CUMULATIVE (%)	MAXIMUM VALUE	DATE	MINIMUM VALUE	DATE
1995	964.68	27.97	192.18	1,003.31	20-Sep	743.47	3-Jan
1994	753.81	-6.46	128.31	851.80	17-Mar	703.27	24-Jun
1993	805.84	11.16	144.07	809.72	12-Nov	660.17	26-Apr
1992	724.94	8.37	119.57	741.92	12-Feb	581.60	26-Jun
1991	668.95	64.75	102.61	668.95	31-Dec	387.47	14-Jan
1990	406.05	-9.36	22.98	510.61	16-Jul	344.11	16-Oct
1989	447.99	18.22	35.68	472.42	9-Oct	374.93	3-Jan
1988	378.95	11.80	14.77	413.09	5-Jul	334.85	20-Jan
1987	338.94	-2.97	2.66	488.92	5-Oct	288.30	28-Oct
1986	349.33	5.80	5.80	414.45	3-Jul	326.56	9-Jan
1985	330.17						
Average Annual (%)		12.93					
Compound Annual (%)		11.32					
Standard Deviation (%)		21.45					

SYNOPSIS

The Nasdaq Industrial Index is a market value-weighted index that tracks the daily price only performance of domestic and foreign industrial common stocks traded on the Nasdaq National Market System (Nasdaq/NMS) and SmallCap Market.

NUMBER OF STOCKS—DECEMBER 31, 1995

3,146

MARKET VALUE—DECEMBER 31, 1995

US$464,680.0 million

SELECTION CRITERIA

Constituent shares include all companies listed on Nasdaq National Market System and SmallCap Market that are classified as industrial companies based on Standard Industrial Classification (SIC) Codes relative to a company's major source of revenue.

BACKGROUND

None

BASE DATE

February 5,1971=100.00

COMPUTATION METHODOLOGY

(1) An aggregate of prices times quantities index formula. Maintenance adjustments to the divisor are made for capitalization changes, new listings and delistings. (2) Market capitalization of foreign issues is computed on the basis of Nasdaq-listed shares and not worldwide shares outstanding. (3) Last sale price is used.

DERIVATIVE INSTRUMENTS

None

SUBINDICES

None

RELATED INDICES

Nasdaq Composite Index

REMARKS

None

PUBLISHER

The National Association of Securities Dealers, Inc. (NASD)/The Nasdaq Stock Market, Inc.

NASDAQ INSURANCE INDEX

PRICE PERFORMANCE

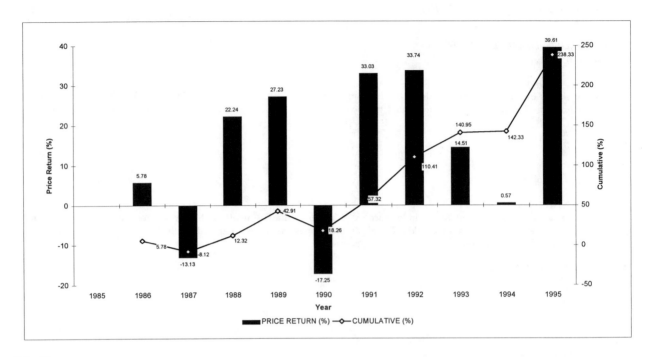

PRICE PERFORMANCE

YEAR	VALUE	PRICE RETURN (%)	CUMULATIVE (%)	MAXIMUM VALUE	DATE	MINIMUM VALUE	DATE
1995	1,292.64	39.61	238.33	1,292.64	29-Dec	921.12	3-Jan
1994	925.87	0.57	142.33	949.10	16-Sep	858.96	20-Apr
1993	920.59	14.51	140.95	956.91	12-Oct	787.80	8-Jan
1992	803.91	33.74	110.41	803.91	31-Dec	589.03	8-Apr
1991	601.09	33.03	57.32	601.09	31-Dec	434.23	14-Jan
1990	451.84	-17.25	18.26	554.21	4-Jan	379.36	17-Oct
1989	546.01	27.23	42.91	561.34	5-Dec	424.74	3-Jan
1988	429.14	22.24	12.32	435.80	10-Oct	339.41	26-Jan
1987	351.06	-13.13	-8.12	475.78	21-Aug	333.66	28-Oct
1986	404.14	5.78	5.78	467.05	19-Mar	381.59	9-Jan
1985	382.07						
Average Annual (%)		14.63					
Compound Annual (%)		12.96					
Standard Deviation (%)		20.02					

SYNOPSIS

The Nasdaq Insurance Index is a market value-weighted index that tracks the price only performance of common stocks of insurance companies traded on the Nasdaq National Market System (Nasdaq/NMS) and SmallCap Market.

NUMBER OF STOCKS—DECEMBER 31, 1995

110

MARKET VALUE—DECEMBER 31, 1995

US$33,030.0 million

SELECTION CRITERIA

Constituent shares consist of companies listed on Nasdaq, including the National Market System and SmallCap Market, which are selected based on Standard Industrial Classification (SIC) Codes relative to a company's major source of revenue. These include all types of insurance companies, including brokers, agents and related services.

BACKGROUND

None

BASE DATE

February 5,1971=100.00

COMPUTATION METHODOLOGY

(1) An aggregate of prices times quantities index formula. Maintenance adjustments to the divisor are made for capitalization changes, new listings and delistings. (2) Market capitalization of foreign issues is computed on the basis of Nasdaq-listed shares and not worldwide shares outstanding. (3) Last sale price is used.

DERIVATIVE INSTRUMENTS

None

SUBINDICES

None

RELATED INDICES

Nasdaq Composite Index

REMARKS

None

PUBLISHER

The National Association of Securities Dealers, Inc. (NASD)/The Nasdaq Stock Market, Inc.

NASDAQ/NATIONAL MARKET SYSTEM (NMS) COMPOSITE INDEX

PRICE PERFORMANCE

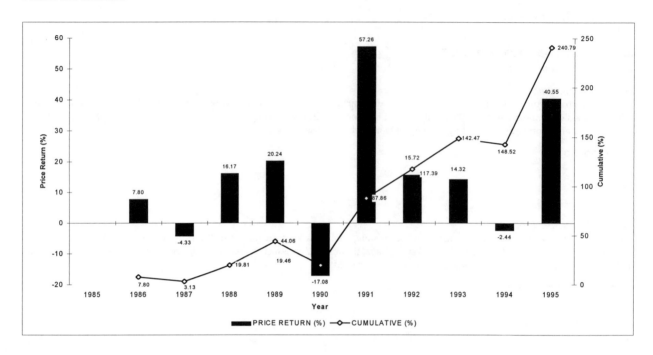

PRICE PERFORMANCE

YEAR	VALUE	PRICE RETURN (%)	CUMULATIVE (%)	MAXIMUM VALUE	DATE	MINIMUM VALUE	DATE
1995	471.17	40.55	240.79	479.55	6-Dec	331.27	3-Jan
1994	335.24	-2.44	142.47	356.61	18-Mar	307.65	24-Jun
1993	343.61	14.32	148.52	343.61	31-Dec	285.44	26-Apr
1992	300.56	15.72	117.39	300.56	31-Dec	242.25	26-Jun
1991	259.74	57.26	87.86	259.74	31-Dec	157.16	14-Jan
1990	165.17	-17.08	19.46	206.17	16-Jul	142.41	11-Oct
1989	199.18	20.24	44.06	212.43	9-Oct	164.40	3-Jan
1988	165.65	16.17	19.81	171.39	5-Jul	143.16	12-Jan
1987	142.59	-4.33	3.13	195.36	26-Aug	124.98	28-Oct
1986	149.04	7.80	7.80	174.84	3-Jul	137.20	9-Jan
1985	138.26						
Average Annual (%)		14.82					
Compound Annual (%)		13.04					
Standard Deviation (%)		21.67					

SYNOPSIS

The Nasdaq/National Market System (NMS) Composite Index is a market value-weighted index that tracks the daily stock price only performance of domestic common stocks and foreign issues, including American Depositary Receipts (ADRs), traded on the Nasdaq National Market System (Nasdaq/NMS).

NUMBER OF STOCKS—DECEMBER 31, 1995

4,027

MARKET VALUE—DECEMBER 31, 1995

US$1,133,328.0 million

SELECTION CRITERIA

All listed domestic common stocks traded on the regular Nasdaq National Market System are included in the index. Rights, warrants, units, preferred stock, shares of beneficial interest and debentures are excluded from the index.

BACKGROUND

The Nasdaq National Market System is the largest and most prominent part of the Nasdaq market, providing continuous, real time, last sale and volume information throughout the trading day. Introduced in April 1982, it now encompasses approximately 68% of all Nasdaq securities, accounts for about 88% of Nasdaq's share volume and 97% of Nasdaq's aggregate market value as of December 31, 1995.

BASE DATE

July 10, 1984=100.00

COMPUTATION METHODOLOGY

(1) An aggregate of prices times quantities index formula. Maintenance adjustments to the divisor are made for capitalization changes, new listings and delistings. (2) Market capitalization of foreign issues is computed on the basis of Nasdaq-listed shares and not worldwide shares outstanding. (3) Last sale price is used.

DERIVATIVE INSTRUMENTS

None

SUBINDICES

Nasdaq/NMS Industrial Index

RELATED INDICES

Nasdaq Composite Index

REMARKS

None

PUBLISHER

The National Association of Securities Dealers, Inc. (NASD)/The Nasdaq Stock Market Inc.

NASDAQ/NATIONAL MARKET SYSTEM (NMS) INDUSTRIAL INDEX

PRICE PERFORMANCE

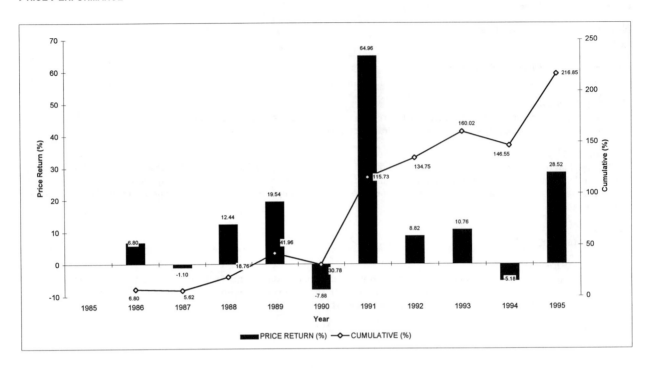

PRICE PERFORMANCE

YEAR	VALUE	PRICE RETURN (%)	CUMULATIVE (%)	MAXIMUM VALUE	DATE	MINIMUM VALUE	DATE
1995	393.31	28.52	216.85	409.28	20-Sep	301.56	3-Jan
1994	306.04	-5.18	146.55	342.72	17-Mar	282.87	24-Jun
1993	322.76	10.76	160.02	323.59	12-Nov	263.79	26-Apr
1992	291.40	8.82	134.75	296.32	12-Feb	232.48	26-Jun
1991	267.79	64.96	115.73	267.79	31-Dec	154.97	14-Jan
1990	162.34	-7.88	30.78	202.30	16-Jul	135.93	16-Oct
1989	176.22	19.54	41.96	185.00	9-Oct	145.82	3-Jan
1988	147.42	12.44	18.76	160.10	5-Jul	129.10	20-Jan
1987	131.11	-1.10	5.62	187.94	5-Oct	110.21	28-Oct
1986	132.57	6.80	6.80	155.55	3-Jul	122.51	9-Jan
1985	124.13						
Average Annual (%)		13.77					
Compound Annual (%)		12.22					
Standard Deviation (%)		21.09					

SYNOPSIS

The Nasdaq/National Market System (Nasdaq/NMS) Industrial Index is a market value-weighted index that tracks the daily price only performance of domestic and foreign industrial common stocks and foreign issues, including American Depositary Receipts (ADRs), traded on the Nasdaq National Market System (Nasdaq/NMS).

NUMBER OF STOCKS—DECEMBER 31, 1995

2,225

MARKET VALUE—DECEMBER 31, 1995

US$443,508.0 million

SELECTION CRITERIA

Constituent shares consist of companies listed on the Nasdaq National Market System that are classified as industrial and other companies under the Securities Industry Classification (SIC) scheme. Warrants, units, preferred stocks, shares of beneficial interest and debentures are excluded from the index.

BACKGROUND

None

BASE DATE

July 10, 1984=100.00

COMPUTATION METHODOLOGY

(1) An aggregate of prices times quantities index formula. Maintenance adjustments to the divisor are made for capitalization changes, new listings and delistings. (2) Market capitalization of foreign issues is computed on the basis of Nasdaq-listed shares and not worldwide shares outstanding. (3) Last sale price is used.

DERIVATIVE INSTRUMENTS

None

SUBINDICES

None

RELATED INDICES

Nasdaq Composite index

REMARKS

None

PUBLISHER

The National Association of Securities Dealers, Inc. (NASD)/The Nasdaq Stock Market, Inc.

NASDAQ OTHER FINANCE INDEX

PRICE PERFORMANCE

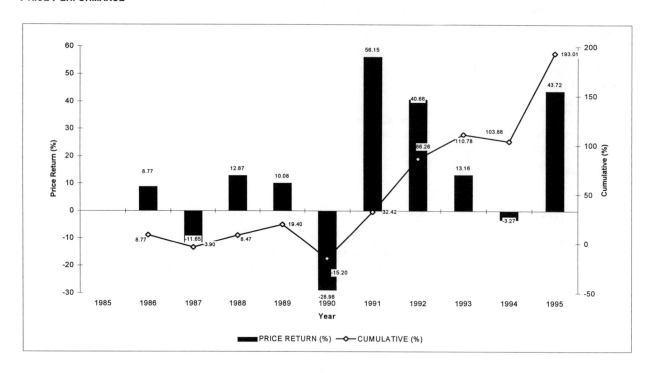

PRICE PERFORMANCE

YEAR	VALUE	PRICE RETURN (%)	CUMULATIVE (%)	MAXIMUM VALUE	DATE	MINIMUM VALUE	DATE
1995	1,240.87	43.72	193.01	1,240.87	29-Dec	861.99	3-Jan
1994	863.42	-3.27	103.88	966.19	16-Sep	831.79	9-Dec
1993	892.64	13.16	110.78	921.28	13-Oct	775.76	8-Jan
1992	788.81	40.66	86.26	788.81	31-Dec	558.38	2-Jan
1991	560.79	56.15	32.42	560.79	31-Dec	340.72	14-Jan
1990	359.13	-28.98	-15.20	512.55	3-Jan	323.14	30-Oct
1989	505.64	10.08	19.40	567.23	9-Oct	457.79	3-Jan
1988	459.34	12.87	8.47	477.88	10-Oct	410.75	13-Jan
1987	406.96	-11.65	-3.90	542.04	20-Mar	382.43	7-Dec
1986	460.64	8.77	8.77	553.42	3-Jul	424.52	2-Jan
1985	423.49						
Average Annual (%)		14.15					
Compound Annual (%)		11.35					
Standard Deviation (%)		26.29					

SYNOPSIS
The Nasdaq Other Finance Index is a market value-weighted index that tracks the price only performance of common stocks of other financial companies traded on the Nasdaq National Market System (Nasdaq/NMS) and SmallCap Market.

NUMBER OF STOCKS—DECEMBER 31, 1995
639

MARKET VALUE—DECEMBER 31, 1995
US$143,809.0 million

SELECTION CRITERIA
Constituent shares consist of companies listed on Nasdaq, including the National Market System and SmallCap Market that are selected based on Standard Industrial Classification (SIC) Codes relative to a company's major source of revenue. These include credit agencies other than banks, savings and loan associations, security and commodity brokers, exchanges and dealer related services, real estate and holding and investment companies (other than those subject to regulation under the Investment Company Act of 1940).

BACKGROUND
None

BASE DATE
February 5,1971=100.00

COMPUTATION METHODOLOGY
(1) An aggregate of prices times quantities index formula. Maintenance adjustments to the divisor are made for capitalization changes, new listings and delistings. (2) Market capitalization of foreign issues is computed on the basis of Nasdaq-listed shares and not worldwide shares outstanding. (3) Last sale price is used.

DERIVATIVE INSTRUMENTS
None

SUBINDICES
None

RELATED INDICES
Nasdaq Composite Index

REMARKS
None

PUBLISHER
The National Association of Securities Dealers, Inc. (NASD)/The Nasdaq Stock Market, Inc.

NASDAQ TELECOMMUNICATIONS INDEX

PRICE PERFORMANCE

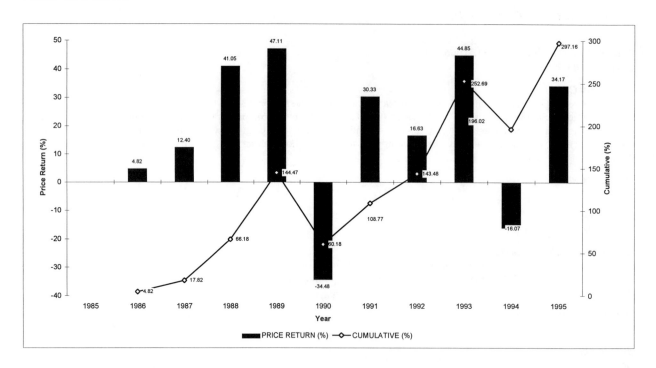

PRICE PERFORMANCE[1]

YEAR	VALUE	PRICE RETURN (%)	CUMULATIVE (%)	MAXIMUM VALUE	DATE	MINIMUM VALUE	DATE
1995	208.35	34.17	297.16	214.02	21-Sep	154.17	3-Jan
1994	155.29	-16.07	196.02	184.37	20-Jan	149.51	12-Dec
1993	185.02	44.85	252.69	205.94	14-Oct	126.05	4-Jan
1992	127.73	16.63	143.48	127.73	31-Dec	106.14	5-Oct
1991	109.52	30.33	108.77	109.52	31-Dec	77.85	14-Jan
1990	84.03	-34.48	60.18	128.66	2-Jan	76.95	17-Oct
1989	128.25	47.11	144.47	137.18	9-Oct	87.13	3-Jan
1988	87.18	41.05	66.18	87.18	30-Dec	60.83	12-Jan
1987	61.81	12.40	17.82	76.83	21-Aug	52.45	28-Oct
1986	54.99	4.82	4.82	63.13	3-Jul	51.49	9-Jan
1985	52.46						
Average Annual (%)		18.08					
Compound Annual (%)		14.79					
Standard Deviation (%)		27.15					

[1]Index values prior to November 1, 1993 have been adjusted using a factor of 5.74805.

SYNOPSIS

The Nasdaq Telecommunications Index is a market value-weighted index that tracks the price only performance of domestic and foreign common stocks of telecommunication companies traded on the Nasdaq National Market System (Nasdaq/NMS) and SmallCap Market.

NUMBER OF STOCKS—DECEMBER 31, 1995

150

MARKET VALUE—DECEMBER 31, 1995

US$89,116.0 million

SELECTION CRITERIA

Constituent shares consist of companies listed on Nasdaq, including the National Market System and SmallCap Market that are selected based on the Standard Industrial Classification (SIC) Codes relative to a to a company's major source of revenue. These include all types of telecommunications companies, including point-to-point communications services and radio and television broadcast companies.

BACKGROUND

The index was renamed and reconstituted on November 1, 1993. Up to that date, the index, known as the Utility Index, tracked natural gas pipeline companies, excluding railroads and buses. It became increasingly dominated by telecommunications issues, which made up 90% of the Index at the end of 1992. The Index was reset to a base value of 200.00 using a factor of 5.74805.

BASE DATE

November 1, 1993=200.00

COMPUTATION METHODOLOGY

(1) An aggregate of prices times quantities index formula. Maintenance adjustments to the divisor are made for capitalization changes, new listings and delistings. (2) Market capitalization of foreign issues is computed on the basis of Nasdaq-listed shares and not worldwide shares outstanding. (3) Last sale price is used.

DERIVATIVE INSTRUMENTS

None

SUBINDICES

None

RELATED INDICES

Nasdaq Composite Index

REMARKS

The index was originally established with a base date of February 5, 1971=100.00

PUBLISHER

The National Association of Securities Dealers, Inc. (NASD)/The Nasdaq Stock Market, Inc.

NASDAQ TRANSPORTATION INDEX

PRICE PERFORMANCE

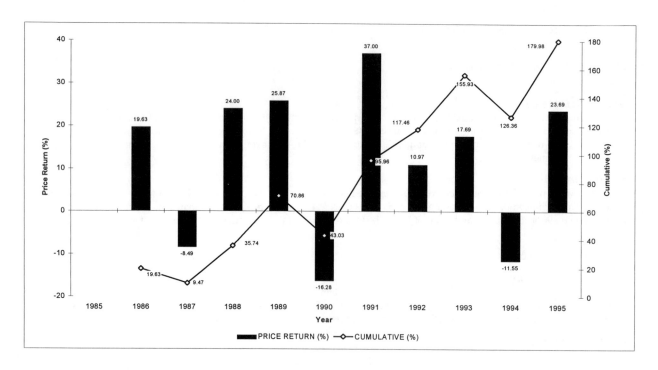

PRICE PERFORMANCE

YEAR	VALUE	PRICE RETURN (%)	CUMULATIVE (%)	MAXIMUM VALUE	DATE	MINIMUM VALUE	DATE
1995	816.39	23.69	179.98	843.66	30-Nov	652.46	9-Jan
1994	660.03	-11.55	126.36	808.09	17-Mar	621.31	12-Dec
1993	746.26	17.69	155.93	746.26	31-Dec	624.44	23-Feb
1992	634.10	10.97	117.46	634.10	31-Dec	530.66	20-Jul
1991	571.39	37.00	95.96	571.39	31-Dec	405.00	15-Jan
1990	417.07	-16.28	43.03	509.93	3-Jan	360.34	16-Oct
1989	498.20	25.87	70.86	498.20	29-Dec	394.62	3-Jan
1988	395.81	24.00	35.74	403.68	2-Nov	320.91	9-Feb
1987	319.21	-8.49	9.47	436.53	21-Aug	276.03	28-Oct
1986	348.84	19.63	19.63	365.81	20-Jun	288.13	9-Jan
1985	291.59						
Average Annual (%)		12.25					
Compound Annual (%)		10.84					
Standard Deviation (%)		18.15					

SYNOPSIS

The Nasdaq Transportation Index is a market value-weighted index that tracks the price only performance of domestic and foreign common stocks of transportation companies traded on the Nasdaq National Market System (Nasdaq/NMS) and SmallCap Market.

NUMBER OF STOCKS—DECEMBER 31, 1995

94

MARKET VALUE—DECEMBER 31, 1995

US$21,660.0 million

SELECTION CRITERIA

Constituent shares consist of companies listed on Nasdaq, including the National Market System and SmallCap Market that are selected based on Standard Industrial Classification (SIC) Codes relative to a company's major source of revenue. These include all types of transportation companies, including pipelines (except natural gas pipelines) and services incidental to transportation, such as warehousing, travel arrangements and packing.

BACKGROUND

None

DATE DATE

February 5,1971=100.00

COMPUTATION METHODOLOGY

(1) An aggregate of prices times quantities index formula. Maintenance adjustments to the divisor are made for capitalization changes, new listings and delistings. (2) Market capitalization of foreign issues is computed on the basis of Nasdaq-listed shares and not worldwide shares outstanding. (3) Last sale price is used.

DERIVATIVE INSTRUMENTS

None

SUBINDICES

None

RELATED INDICES

Nasdaq Composite Index

REMARKS

None

PUBLISHER

The National Association of Securities Dealers, Inc. (NASD)/The Nasdaq Stock Market, Inc.

THE NEW YORK STOCK EXCHANGE (NYSE) COMPOSITE INDEX

PRICE PERFORMANCE

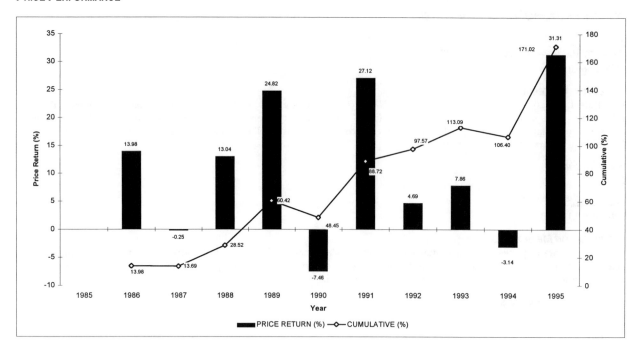

PRICE PERFORMANCE

YEAR	VALUE	PRICE RETURN (%)	CUMULATIVE (%)	MAXIMUM VALUE	DATE	MINIMUM VALUE	DATE
1995	329.51	31.31	171.02	331.17	13-Dec	250.73	3-Jan
1994	250.94	-3.14	106.40	267.71	2-Feb	243.80	8-Dec
1993	259.08	7.86	113.09	260.87	29-Dec	237.26	7-Jan
1992	240.21	4.69	97.57	242.08	18-Dec	217.92	8-Apr
1991	229.44	27.12	88.72	229.44	31-Dec	170.97	9-Jan
1990	180.49	-7.46	48.45	201.13	16-Jul	162.20	11-Oct
1989	195.04	24.82	60.42	199.34	9-Oct	154.98	3-Jan
1988	156.26	13.04	28.52	159.44	21-Oct	136.72	20-Jan
1987	138.23	-0.25	13.69	187.99	25-Aug	125.91	4-Dec
1986	138.58	13.98	13.98	145.75	4-Sep	117.75	22-Jan
1985	121.58						
Average Annual (%)		11.20					
Compound Annual (%)		10.48					
Standard Deviation (%)		13.30					

SYNOPSIS

The New York Stock Exchange (NYSE) Composite Index is a market value-weighted index that tracks the continuous stock price performance of all New York Stock Exchange (NYSE)-listed common stocks. These shares account for 85% of the domestic market capitalization.

NUMBER OF STOCKS—DECEMBER 31, 1995

2,637

MARKET VALUE—DECEMBER 31, 1995

US$5,915,329.3 million

SELECTION CRITERIA

The index is composed of all common stocks listed on the New York Stock Exchange, including foreign issues, ADRs and New York Stock Exchange-listed foreign shares, trusts and closed-end investment companies. Excluded from the index are warrants, rights and other securities.

BACKGROUND

From 1955 to mid-1966, the Exchange has been producing a broad measure of stock price movements called the "Stock Price Profile." This indicator provided a frequent distribution of percentage price changes over a given span of time. It was limited to 300 issues, usually representing slightly less than three quarters of the total market value of all NYSE-listed stocks. As it fell short of representing a succinct figure describing what happened to the market, the Exchange, which benefited from advances in its new computerized Market Data System, advanced to a point where it could produce, efficiently and economically, a stock price index that would be useful to the investing public. Thus, on July 14, 1966, the Exchange began to publish its new NYSE Composite Index and subindices. The index along with its companion subgroup indices was set at 50.00 so that the index level for all issues as of the base date would start reasonably close to their actual average price. On that date, the actual average price of all common stocks listed on the NYSE was 53.33. Effective with the start of trading on April 27, 1993, the value of the index was doubled from 112.37 to 224.74. The doubling of the index value was intended to facilitate the introduction and trading of options and futures on the index.

Index values have been recomputed back to December 31, 1965 on a daily basis and, starting July 14, 1966, appeared on the ticker tape every hour.

BASE DATE

December 31, 1965=50.00

COMPUTATION METHODOLOGY

(1) An aggregate of prices times quantities index formula. Maintenance adjustments to the divisor are made for capitalization changes, new listings and delistings. (2) Market capitalization is determined on the basis of shares trading and available on the NYSE. The capitalization of foreign issues is limited to the number of ADRs listed on the NYSE or NYSE listed foreign shares.

DERIVATIVE INSTRUMENTS

NYSE Composite Index futures and options trade on the New York Futures Exchange (NYFE) and NYSE, respectively.

SUBINDICES

NYSE Finance Sub-Group Index
NYSE Industrial Sub-Group Index
NYSE Transportation Sub-Group Index
NYSE Utilities Sub-Group Index

RELATED INDICES

None

REMARKS

(1) For purposes of computing market capitalization of listed shares, the number of shares trading and available on the New York Stock Exchange are used. The capitalization of foreign companies whose shares are listed in the form of ADRs is computed on the basis of the number of ADRs listed on the NYSE rather than the total capitalization of the company. This methodology, which is unlike the one used in the computation of the Standard & Poor's 500 (S&P 500) Composite Stock Price Index, can have an impact on the performance of the NYSE Composite Index and sub-group indices. (2) The index also includes 47 equity-linked derivative securities.

PUBLISHER

New York Stock Exchange (NYSE).

THE NEW YORK STOCK EXCHANGE (NYSE) FINANCE SUB-GROUP INDEX

PRICE PERFORMANCE

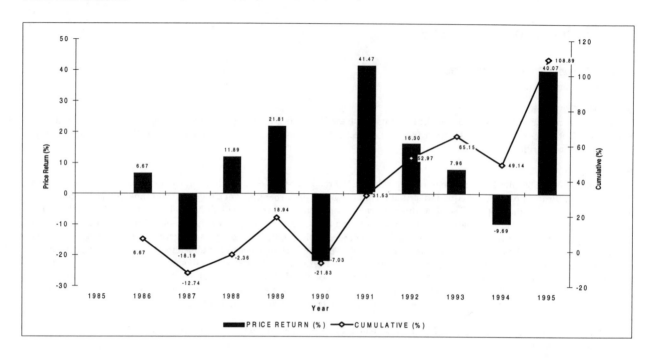

PRICE PERFORMANCE

YEAR	VALUE	PRICE RETURN (%)	CUMULATIVE (%)	MAXIMUM VALUE	DATE	MINIMUM VALUE	DATE
1995	274.25	40.07	108.89	279.07	6-Dec	196.62	3-Jan
1994	195.80	-9.69	49.14	224.90	31-Jan	190.17	22-Nov
1993	216.82	7.96	65.15	233.33	13-Oct	197.63	7-Jan
1992	200.83	16.30	52.97	200.96	30-Dec	165.40	18-Apr
1991	172.68	41.47	31.53	172.71	30-Dec	116.11	15-Jan
1990	122.06	-21.83	-7.03	158.71	3-Jan	103.26	29-Oct
1989	156.15	21.81	18.94	173.29	9-Oct	127.46	3-Jan
1988	128.19	11.89	-2.36	136.16	21-Oct	115.75	8-Jan
1987	114.57	-18.19	-12.74	165.36	17-Aug	107.39	7-Dec
1986	140.05	6.67	6.67	159.45	21-Apr	129.78	22-Jan
1985	131.29						
Average Annual (%)		9.65					
Compound Annual (%)		7.64					
Standard Deviation (%)		21.83					

SYNOPSIS

The New York Stock Exchange (NYSE) Finance Sub-Group Index is a market value-weighted index that tracks the continuous stock price performance of all New York Stock Exchange (NYSE)-listed common stocks that are classified as financial and real estate companies.

NUMBER OF STOCKS—DECEMBER 31, 1995

885

MARKET VALUE—DECEMBER 31, 1995

US$985,652.0 million

SELECTION CRITERIA

The index is composed of common stocks listed on the NYSE, including foreign issues, if any, both ADRs and NYSE-listed foreign shares, but excludes warrants, rights and other securities. The following industry groups are classified as financial companies: Banks, brokerage services, closed-end investment companies, finance companies, insurance, trusts, real estate and diversified financial services.

BACKGROUND

Initially calculated on a daily basis, the index began its appearance on the ticker tape every hour as of July 14, 1966.

For additional information, refer to the New York Stock Exchange (NYSE) Composite Index.

BASE DATE

December 31, 1965=50.00

COMPUTATION METHODOLOGY

(1) An aggregate of prices times quantities index formula. Maintenance adjustments to the divisor are made for capitalization changes, new listings and delistings. (2) Market capitalization is determined on the basis of shares trading and available on the NYSE. The capitalization of foreign issues is limited to the number of ADRs listed on the NYSE or NYSE-listed foreign shares.

DERIVATIVE INSTRUMENTS

None

SUBINDICES

None

RELATED INDICES

NYSE Composite Index

REMARKS

(1) For purposes of computing market capitalization of listed shares, the number of shares trading and available on the New York Stock Exchange are used. The capitalization of foreign companies whose shares are listed in the form of ADRs is computed on the basis of the number of ADRs listed on the NYSE rather than the total capitalization of the company. This methodology, which is unlike the one used in the computation of the Standard & Poor's 500 (S&P 500) Composite Stock Price Index, can have an impact on the performance of the NYSE Composite Index and subgroup indices. (2) The index may also include equity linked derivative securities.

PUBLISHER

New York Stock Exchange (NYSE).

THE NEW YORK STOCK EXCHANGE (NYSE) INDUSTRIAL SUB-GROUP INDEX

PRICE PERFORMANCE

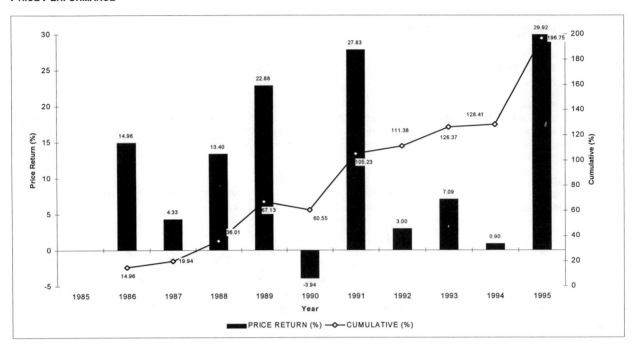

PRICE PERFORMANCE

YEAR	VALUE	PRICE RETURN (%)	CUMULATIVE (%)	MAXIMUM VALUE	DATE	MINIMUM VALUE	DATE
1995	413.29	29.92	196.75	417.46	13-Dec	317.29	3-Jan
1994	318.10	0.90	128.41	327.93	2-Feb	298.30	20-Apr
1993	315.26	7.09	126.37	316.95	29-Dec	287.65	22-Feb
1992	294.39	3.00	111.38	298.18	18-Dec	273.18	9-Oct
1991	285.82	27.83	105.23	285.82	31-Dec	210.80	9-Jan
1990	223.60	-3.94	60.55	252.24	16-Jul	200.80	11-Oct
1989	232.76	22.88	67.13	237.76	9-Oct	187.87	3-Jan
1988	189.42	13.40	36.01	192.81	21-Oct	163.02	20-Jan
1987	167.04	4.33	19.94	231.05	25-Aug	149.43	4-Dec
1986	160.11	14.96	14.96	167.50	2-Jul	134.22	22-Jan
1985	139.27						
Average Annual (%)		12.04					
Compound Annual (%)		11.49					
Standard Deviation (%)		11.75					

SYNOPSIS

The New York Stock Exchange (NYSE) Industrial Sub-Group Index is a market value-weighted index that tracks the continuous stock price performance of all New York Stock Exchange (NYSE)-listed common stocks that are classified as industrial companies.

NUMBER OF STOCKS—DECEMBER 31, 1995

1,455

MARKET VALUE—DECEMBER 31, 1995

US$4,127,828.9 million

SELECTION CRITERIA

The index is composed of common stocks listed on the NYSE, including foreign issues, if any, both ADRs and NYSE-listed foreign shares, but excludes warrants, rights and other securities. The following industry groups are included: Aerospace, business supplies and services, chemicals, computers, data processing, construction, electrical equipment, electronics, environmental control, foods and beverages, health and beauty products, health care services, household goods, industrial, machinery and equipment, lodging and restaurants, mining, refining and fabricating, motor vehicles, oil and gas, packaging, paper production, pharmaceuticals, publishing, recreation services and products, retail trade, textiles and apparel, tires and rubber, tobacco, wholesale distributors, multi-industry and other industries, including manufacturing and services.

BACKGROUND

Starting July 14, 1966, the index appeared on the ticker tape every hour.

For additional information, refer to the New York Stock Exchange (NYSE) Composite Index.

BASE DATE

December 31, 1965=50.00

COMPUTATION METHODOLOGY

(1) An aggregate of prices times quantities index formula. Maintenance adjustments to the divisor are made for capitalization changes, new listings and delistings. (2) Market capitalization is determined on the basis of shares trading and available on the NYSE. The capitalization of foreign issues is limited to the number of ADRs listed on the NYSE or NYSE-listed foreign shares.

DERIVATIVE INSTRUMENTS

None

SUBINDICES

None

RELATED INDICES

NYSE Composite Index

REMARKS

(1) For purposes of computing market capitalization of listed shares, the number of shares trading and available on the New York Stock Exchange are used. The capitalization of foreign companies whose shares are listed in the form of ADRs is computed on the basis of the number of ADRs listed on the NYSE rather than the total capitalization of the company. This methodology, which is unlike the one used in the computation of the Standard & Poor's 500 (S&P 500) Composite Stock Price Index, can have an impact on the performance of the NYSE Composite Index and subgroup indices. (2) The index may also include equity-linked derivative securities.

PUBLISHER

New York Stock Exchange (NYSE).

THE NEW YORK STOCK EXCHANGE (NYSE) TRANSPORTATION SUB-GROUP INDEX

PRICE PERFORMANCE

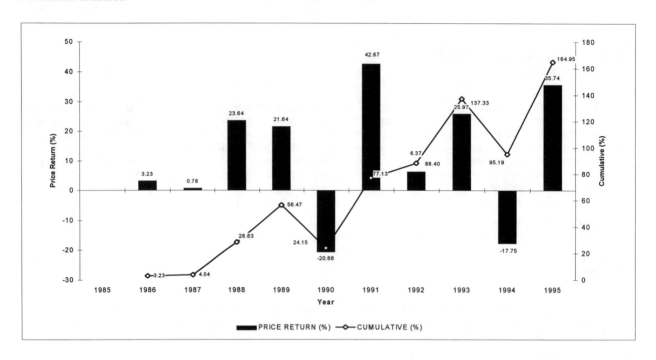

PRICE PERFORMANCE

YEAR	VALUE	PRICE RETURN (%)	CUMULATIVE (%)	MAXIMUM VALUE	DATE	MINIMUM VALUE	DATE
1995	301.96	35.74	164.95	310.47	5-Dec	224.68	3-Jan
1994	222.46	-17.75	95.19	285.03	2-Feb	212.94	13-Dec
1993	270.48	25.97	137.33	271.59	29-Dec	216.42	4-Jan
1992	214.72	6.37	88.40	216.46	30-Dec	182.66	9-Oct
1991	201.87	42.67	77.13	201.87	31-Dec	137.54	9-Jan
1990	141.49	-20.66	24.15	182.55	6-Jun	127.25	31-Oct
1989	178.33	21.64	56.47	212.37	30-Aug	145.54	3-Jan
1988	146.60	23.64	28.63	146.93	29-Dec	118.10	8-Jan
1987	118.57	0.78	4.04	168.20	14-Aug	104.76	4-Dec
1986	117.65	3.23	3.23	132.54	27-Mar	105.58	4-Aug
1985	113.97						
Average Annual (%)		12.16					
Compound Annual (%)		10.23					
Standard Deviation (%)		21.38					

SYNOPSIS

The New York Stock Exchange (NYSE) Transportation Sub-Group Index is a market value-weighted index that tracks the continuous stock Price Performance of all New York Stock Exchange (NYSE)-listed common stocks that are classified as transportation companies.

NUMBER OF STOCKS—DECEMBER 31, 1995

51

MARKET VALUE—DECEMBER 31, 1995

US$111,447.3 million

SELECTION CRITERIA

The index is composed of common stocks listed on the NYSE, including foreign issues, if any, both ADRs and NYSE-listed foreign shares, but excludes warrants, rights and other securities. The following industry groups are classified as transportation companies: Air, rail, trucking and other transportation services.

BACKGROUND

Starting July 14, 1966, the index appeared on the ticker tape every hour.

For additional information, refer to the New York Stock Exchange (NYSE) Composite Index.

BASE DATE

December 31, 1965=50.00

COMPUTATION METHODOLOGY

(1) An aggregate of prices times quantities index formula. Maintenance adjustments to the divisor are made for capitalization changes, new listings and delistings. (2) Market capitalization is determined on the basis of shares trading and available on the NYSE. The capitalization of foreign issues is limited to the number of ADRs listed on the NYSE or NYSE- listed foreign shares.

DERIVATIVE INSTRUMENTS

None

SUBINDICES

None

RELATED INDICES

NYSE Composite Index

REMARKS

(1) For purposes of computing market capitalization of listed shares, the number of shares trading and available on the New York Stock Exchange are used. The capitalization of foreign companies whose shares are listed in the form of ADRs is computed on the basis of the number of ADRs listed on the NYSE rather than the total capitalization of the company. This methodology, which is unlike the one used in the computation of the Standard & Poor's 500 (S&P 500) Composite Stock Price Index, can have an impact on the performance of the NYSE Composite Index and subgroup indices. (2) The index may also includes equity linked derivative securities.

PUBLISHER

New York Stock Exchange (NYSE).

THE NEW YORK STOCK EXCHANGE (NYSE) UTILITIES SUB-GROUP INDEX

PRICE PERFORMANCE

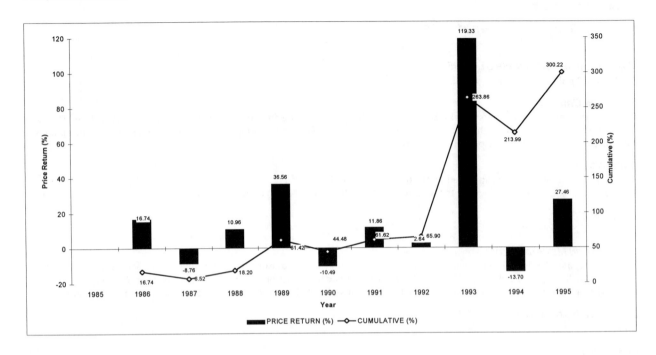

PRICE PERFORMANCE

YEAR	VALUE	PRICE RETURN (%)	CUMULATIVE (%)	MAXIMUM VALUE	DATE	MINIMUM VALUE	DATE
1995	252.90	27.46	300.22	252.90	29-Dec	197.75	11-Jan
1994	198.41	-13.70	213.99	230.70	31-Jan	197.30	22-Nov
1993	229.92	119.33	263.86	246.95	13-Sep	103.46	7-Jan
1992	104.83	2.64	65.90	106.55	23-Dec	91.57	18-Apr
1991	102.13	11.86	61.62	102.13	31-Dec	86.77	15-Jan
1990	91.30	-10.49	44.48	102.92	2-Jan	80.96	29-Oct
1989	102.00	36.56	61.42	102.00	29-Dec	73.91	3-Jan
1988	74.69	10.96	18.20	75.22	3-Nov	67.74	8-Jan
1987	67.31	-8.76	6.52	80.42	28-Jan	61.63	7-Dec
1986	73.77	16.74	16.74	80.85	29-Aug	61.35	22-Jan
1985	63.19						
Average Annual (%)		19.26					
Compound Annual (%)		14.88					
Standard Deviation (%)		38.79					

SYNOPSIS

The New York Stock Exchange (NYSE) Utilities Sub-Group Index is a market value-weighted index that tracks the continuous stock Price Performance of all New York Stock Exchange (NYSE)-listed common stocks that are classified as utilities companies.

NUMBER OF STOCKS—DECEMBER 31, 1995

246

MARKET VALUE—DECEMBER 31, 1995

US$690,040.1 million

SELECTION CRITERIA

The index is composed of common stocks listed on the NYSE, including foreign issues, if any, both ADRs and NYSE-listed foreign shares, but excludes warrants, rights and other securities. The following industry groups are classified as utilities companies: Electric services, gas services, telecommunications, water supply companies, and multi-service companies.

BACKGROUND

Initially calculated on a daily basis, the index began its appearance on the ticker tape every hour starting July 14, 1966.
For additional information, refer to the New York Stock Exchange (NYSE) Composite Index.

BASE DATE

December 31, 1965=50.00

COMPUTATION METHODOLOGY

(1) An aggregate of prices times quantities index formula. Maintenance adjustments to the divisor are made for capitalization changes, new listings and delistings. (2) Market capitalization is determined on the basis of shares trading and available on the NYSE. The capitalization of foreign issues is limited to the number of ADRs shares listed on the NYSE or NYSE-listed foreign shares.

DERIVATIVE INSTRUMENTS

NYSE Utility index futures and options trade on the New York Futures Exchange (NYFE) and the NYSE, respectively.

SUBINDICES

None

RELATED INDICES

NYSE Composite Index

REMARKS

(1) For purposes of computing market capitalization of listed shares, the number of shares trading and available on the New York Stock Exchange are used. The capitalization of foreign companies whose shares are listed in the form of ADRs is computed on the basis of the number of ADRs listed on the NYSE rather than the total capitalization of the company. This methodology, which is unlike the one used in the computation of the Standard & Poor's 500 (S&P 500) Composite Stock Price Index, can have an impact on the performance of the NYSE Composite Index and subgroup indices. (2) The index may also includes equity-linked derivative securities.

PUBLISHER

New York Stock Exchange (NYSE).

PACIFIC STOCK EXCHANGE TECH 100 (PSE TECH 100) INDEX

PRICE PERFORMANCE

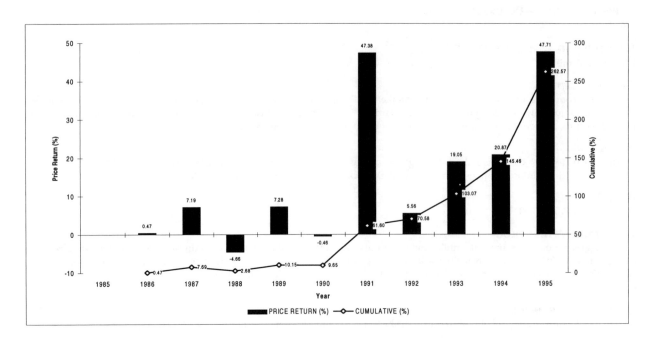

PRICE PERFORMANCE

YEAR	VALUE	PRICE RETURN (%)	CUMULATIVE (%)	MAXIMUM VALUE	DATE	MINIMUM VALUE	DATE
1995	201.77	47.71	262.57	212.10	3-Nov	134.10	30-Jan
1994	136.60	20.87	145.46	136.96	29-Dec	108.15	24-Jun
1993	113.01	19.05	103.07	113.01	31-Dec	88.99	26-Apr
1992	94.93	5.56	70.58	98.56	12-Feb	77.60	24-Aug
1991	89.93	47.38	61.60	89.93	31-Dec	58.01	14-Jan
1990	61.02	-0.46	9.65	74.64	16-Jul	49.25	16-Oct
1989	61.30	7.28	10.15	65.78	9-Oct	56.09	22-Mar
1988	57.14	-4.66	2.68	67.75	5-Jul	52.66	21-Nov
1987	59.93	7.19	7.69	86.64	5-Oct	48.22	26-Oct
1986	55.91	0.47	0.47	64.87	28-Apr	52.89	9-Oct
1985	55.65						
Average Annual (%)		15.04					
Compound Annual (%)		13.75					
Standard Deviation (%)		18.90					

SYNOPSIS

The Pacific Stock Exchange Tech 100 (PSE Tech 100) Index is a price-weighted index that measures the continuous price only performance of 100 technology oriented companies representing 15 industries that trade on the New York Stock Exchange (NYSE), American Stock Exchange (AMEX) and Nasdaq/NMS.

NUMBER OF STOCKS—DECEMBER 31, 1995

100

MARKET VALUE—DECEMBER 31, 1995

US$554,985.2 million

SELECTION CRITERIA

Constituent stocks are drawn from 15 industry groups which include: Data communications, semiconductor manufacturing, test, analysis and instrument equipment, computer software products medical technology, semiconductor capital equipment and manufacturing, biotechnology, information processing services, mini and mainframe computer manufacturing, micro computer manufacturing, very large diversified computer manufacturing, data storage and processing equipment, computer-aided design, computer-aided manufacturing and electronic equipment.

BACKGROUND

The index was created specifically as an underlying vehicle for derivative instruments. Originally conceived as a narrow based technology index, the PSE Tech 100 Index was dissolved in 1985 due to lack of interest. It was redefined and relaunched in 1991. As of September 12, 1995, the index value was decreased by 50%.

BASE DATE

December 31, 1982=100.00

COMPUTATION METHODOLOGY

(1) A simple aggregative of actual prices index formula. Adjustments are made to the divisor in connection with constituent changes, stock splits and other corporate actions equal to or in excess of 10% of market value. (2) Stock replacements have been limited due to corporate mergers, acquisitions and/or bankruptcy filings. Substitutions have been confined to the same industry group.

DERIVATIVE INSTRUMENTS

PSE Tech 100 Index futures and options on futures trade on the New York Futures Exchange (NYFE).
PSE Tech 100 options trade on the Pacific Stock Exchange (PSE).

SUBINDICES

None

RELATED INDICES

None

REMARKS

None

PUBLISHER

Pacific Stock Exchange (PSE).

PHILADELPHIA STOCK EXCHANGE AIRLINE SECTOR (PLN) INDEX

PRICE PERFORMANCE

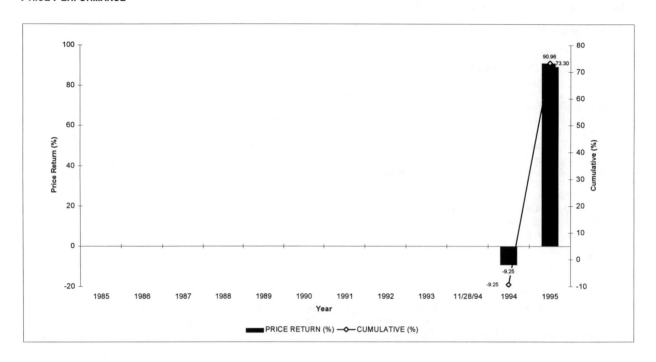

PRICE PERFORMANCE[1]

YEAR	VALUE	PRICE RETURN (%)	CUMULATIVE (%)	MAXIMUM VALUE	DATE	MINIMUM VALUE	DATE
1995	346.59	90.96	73.30	377.03	6-Dec	181.74	12-Jan
1994	181.50	-9.25	-9.25				
11/28/94	200.00						
1993							
1992							
1991							
1990							
1989							
1988							
1987							
1986							
1985							
Average Annual (%)		40.85					
Compound Annual (%)		NM					
Standard Deviation (%)		NM					

[1]December index value based on the index value for the week of December 26, 1994.

Synopsis
The Philadelphia Stock Exchange Airline Sector (PLN) Index is an equal dollar-weighted index that tracks the continuous price only performance of the airline industry in the United States (U.S.).

Number of Stocks—December 31, 1995
12

Market Value—February 6, 1996
US$53,275.0 million

Selection Criteria
Major domestic airlines, including long established carriers as well as progressive new companies that are representative of the airline industry in the United States.

Background
The index was created to serve as an underlying vehicle for stock index options which began trading on January 12, 1995.

Base Date
November 28, 1994=200.00

Computation Methodology
An equal dollar-weighting index formula, with quarterly rebalancing to reestablish equal dollar amounts. Rebalancing is implemented after the close on the third Friday of March, June, September and December.

Derivative Instruments
Airline index options trade on the Philadelphia Stock Exchange (PHLX).

Subindices
None

Related Indices
PHLX Forest & Paper Products Sector Index
PHLX Gold/Silver Sector Index
PHLX Keefe, Bruyette & Woods, Inc. Bank Sector Index
PHLX National Over-the-Counter Index
PHLX Phone Sector Index
PHLX Semiconductor Sector Index
PHLX Supercap Index
PHLX U.S. Top 100 Index
PHLX Utility Sector Index

Remarks
None

Publisher
The Philadelphia Stock Exchange (PHLX).

PHILADELPHIA STOCK EXCHANGE FOREST & PAPER PRODUCTS SECTOR (FPP) INDEX

PRICE PERFORMANCE

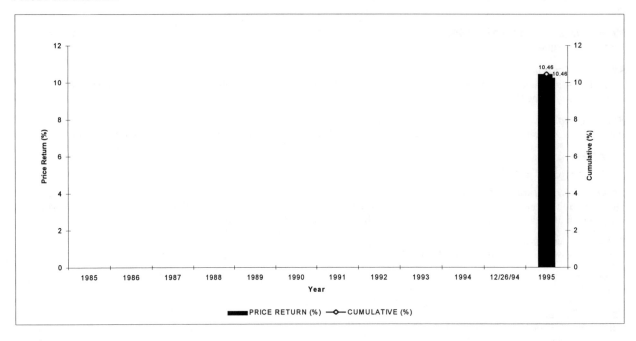

PRICE PERFORMANCE

YEAR	VALUE	PRICE RETURN (%)	CUMULATIVE (%)	MAXIMUM VALUE	DATE	MINIMUM VALUE	DATE
1995	249.56	10.46	10.46	307.21	12-Sep	231.15	23-Jan
12/26/94	225.93						
1994							
1993							
1992							
1991							
1990							
1989							
1988							
1987							
1986							
1985							
Average Annual (%)		10.46					
Compound Annual (%)		10.46					
Standard Deviation (%)		NM					

SYNOPSIS

The Philadelphia Stock Exchange Forest & Paper Products Sector (FPP) Index is a price-weighted index that tracks the continuous price only performance of the forest and paper products industry in the United States (U.S.).

NUMBER OF STOCKS—DECEMBER 31, 1995

14

MARKET VALUE—FEBRUARY 6, 1996

US$57,850.0 million

SELECTION CRITERIA

Constituent shares are selected to represent the forest and paper products industry, including companies that focus on the growth, harvest, and transformation of timber into building and paper products.

BACKGROUND

The index was created to serve as an underlying vehicle for stock index options which began trading on October 30, 1995.

BASE DATE

January 31, 1995=250.00

COMPUTATION METHODOLOGY

A simple aggregative of actual prices index formula.

DERIVATIVE INSTRUMENTS

Forest and Paper Products Sector index options trade on the Philadelphia Stock Exchange (PHLX).

SUBINDICES

None

RELATED INDICES

PHLX Airline Sector Index
PHLX Gold/Silver Sector Index
PHLX Keefe, Bruyette & Woods, Inc. Bank Sector Index
PHLX National Over-the-Counter Index
PHLX Phone Sector Index
PHLX Semiconductor Sector Index
PHLX Supercap Index
PHLX U.S. Top 100 Index
PHLX Utility Sector Index

REMARKS

None

PUBLISHER

The Philadelphia Stock Exchange (PHLX).

PHILADELPHIA STOCK EXCHANGE GOLD/SILVER SECTOR (XAU) INDEX

PRICE PERFORMANCE

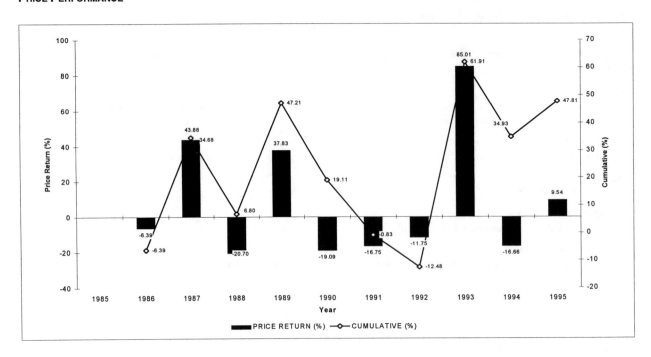

PRICE PERFORMANCE

YEAR	VALUE	PRICE RETURN (%)	CUMULATIVE (%)	MAXIMUM VALUE	DATE	MINIMUM VALUE	DATE
1995	120.42	9.54	47.81	131.00	12-Jul	97.38	31-Jan
1994	109.93	-16.66	34.93	145.57	17-Jan	100.13	5-Dec
1993	131.91	85.01	61.91	135.14	13-Dec	66.53	18-Jan
1992	71.30	-11.75	-12.48	87.09	17-Jul	65.00	27-Nov
1991	80.79	-16.75	-0.83	96.83	7-Jan	73.61	26-Dec
1990	97.04	-19.09	19.11	136.96	30-Jan	80.43	5-Dec
1989	119.93	37.83	47.21	128.02	12-Dec	85.58	23-May
1988	87.01	-20.70	6.80	111.83	21-Jun	84.71	3-Feb
1987	109.72	43.88	34.68	155.74	18-Sep	76.67	5-Jan
1986	76.26	-6.39	-6.39	94.66	16-Jan	59.13	25-Jul
1985	81.47						
Average Annual (%)		8.49					
Compound Annual (%)		3.98					
Standard Deviation (%)		35.72					

Synopsis

The Philadelphia Stock Exchange Gold/Silver Sector (XAU) Index is a market value-weighted index designed to measure the continuous price only performance of gold and silver mining companies operating across the globe.

Number of Stocks—December 31, 1995

9

Market Value—February 6, 1996

US$31,270.3 million

Selection Criteria

The index is composed of nine large capitalization, well known, gold and silver mining company stocks that are traded on the New York Stock Exchange and the American Stock Exchange. These include ASA Ltd., American Berrick Resources Corp., Battle Mountain Gold Company, Echo Bay Mines Ltd., Hecla Mining Company, Homestake Mining Company, Newmont Mining Corp., Pagasus Gold, Inc., and Placer Dome.

Background

Developed by the Philadelphia Stock Exchange (PHLX) to serve as an underlying vehicle for stock index options contracts traded on the Philadelphia Stock Exchange. The contract commenced trading on December 19, 1983.

Base Date

June 1979=100.00

Computation Methodology

An aggregate of prices times quantities index formula. Maintenance adjustments to the divisor are made for capitalization changes, new listings and delistings.

Derivative Instruments

Gold/Silver Sector index options and Long-term Equity Anticipation Securities (LEAPS) trade on the Philadelphia Stock Exchange (PHLX).

Subindices

None

Related Indices

PHLX Airline Sector Index
PHLX Forest & Paper Products Sector Index
PHLX Keefe, Bruyette & Woods, Inc. Bank Sector Index
PHLX National Over-the-Counter Index
PHLX Phone Sector Index
PHLX Semiconductor Sector Index
PHLX Supercap Index
PHLX U.S. Top 100 Index
PHLX Utility Sector Index

Remarks

None

Publisher

The Philadelphia Stock Exchange (PHLX).

PHILADELPHIA STOCK EXCHANGE KEEFE, BRUYETTE & WOODS, INC. BANK SECTOR (BKK) INDEX

PRICE PERFORMANCE

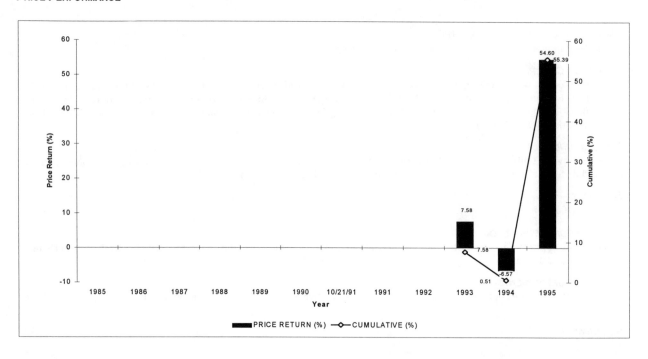

PRICE PERFORMANCE

YEAR	VALUE	PRICE RETURN (%)	CUMULATIVE (%)	MAXIMUM VALUE	DATE	MINIMUM VALUE	DATE
1995	393.85	54.60	55.39	411.97	6-Dec	257.40	3-Jan
1994	254.75	-6.57	0.51	298.64	13-Jun	249.61	22-Nov
1993	272.67	7.58	7.58	296.65	13-Apr	245.35	8-Jan
1992	253.46	NA	NA	NA	NA	NA	NA
1991	NA						
10/21/91	195.00						
1990							
1989							
1988							
1987							
1986							
1985							
Average Annual (%)		18.54					
Compound Annual (%)		15.83					
Standard Deviation (%)		32.03					

SYNOPSIS

The Philadelphia Stock Exchange Keefe, Bruyette & Woods, Inc. Bank Sector (BKK) Index is a market value-weighted index that tracks the continuous price only performance of major United States (U.S.) banking companies.

NUMBER OF STOCKS—DECEMBER 31, 1995

20

MARKET VALUE—FEBRUARY 6, 1996

US$278,662.6 million

SELECTION CRITERIA

Constituent shares represent the largest banking companies, including money center banks as well as leading regional banks, based on assets.

BACKGROUND

The BKK Bank Index was created as an equal-weighted index and published by Keefe, Bruyette & Woods, Inc. (KBW) in 1962 and calculated retroactively to 1947. A modified market value-weighted version of the index was adopted by the Philadelphia Stock Exchange (PHLX) to serve as an underlying vehicle for stock index options contracts traded on the PHLX. Options trading on the BKK Index commenced on September 21, 1992.

BASE DATE

October 21, 1992=250.00

COMPUTATION METHODOLOGY

An aggregate of prices times quantities index formula (versus an equal-weighted formula used by KBW). Maintenance adjustments are made periodically to eliminate the effect of all types of capitalization changes, new listings and delistings.

DERIVATIVE INSTRUMENTS

BKK Sector index options trade on the Philadelphia Stock Exchange (PHLX).

SUBINDICES

None

RELATED INDICES

PHLX Airline Sector Index
PHLX Forest & Paper Products Sector Index
PHLX Gold/Silver Sector Index
PHLX National Over-the-Counter Index
PHLX Phone Sector Index
PHLX Semiconductor Sector Index
PHLX Supercap Index
PHLX U.S. Top 100 Index
PHLX Utility Sector Index

REMARKS

None

PUBLISHER

The Philadelphia Stock Exchange (PHLX).

PHILADELPHIA STOCK EXCHANGE NATIONAL OVER-THE-COUNTER (XOC) INDEX

PRICE PERFORMANCE

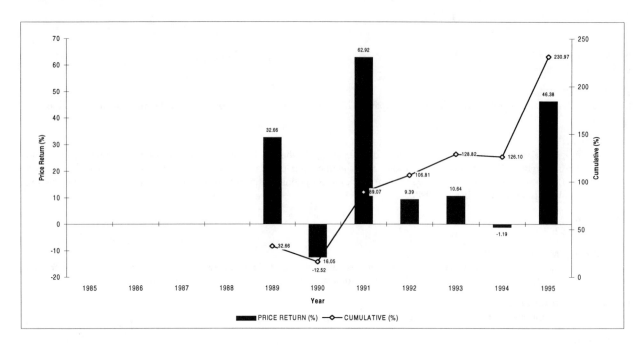

PRICE PERFORMANCE

YEAR	VALUE	PRICE RETURN (%)	CUMULATIVE (%)	MAXIMUM VALUE	DATE	MINIMUM VALUE	DATE
1995	424.70	46.38	230.97	451.92	3-Nov	286.35	3-Jan
1994	290.13	-1.19	126.10	303.77	18-Mar	264.86	24-Jun
1993	293.62	10.64	128.82	297.46	14-Oct	247.13	26-Apr
1992	265.38	9.39	106.81	265.38	31-Dec	217.07	26-Jun
1991	242.61	62.92	89.07	242.61	31-Dec	141.40	9-Jan
1990	148.91	-12.52	16.05	176.46	16-Jul	120.13	11-Oct
1989	170.23	32.66	32.66	180.88	10-Oct	127.75	3-Jan
1988	128.32	NA	NA	NA	NA	NA	NA
1987	NA	NA	NA	NA	NA	NA	NA
1986	NA	NA	NA	NA	NA	NA	NA
1985	NA	NA	NA	NA	NA	NA	NA
Average Annual (%)		21.18					
Compound Annual (%)		18.65					
Standard Deviation (%)		27.07					

Synopsis

The Philadelphia Stock Exchange National Over-the-Counter (XOC) Index is a market value-weighted index that tracks the continuous price only performance of the 100 most highly capitalized corporations whose common stocks are traded on the Nasdaq National Market System (Nasdaq/NMS).

Number of Stocks—December 31, 1995

100

Market Value—February 6, 1996

US$507,321.7 million

Selection Criteria

Constituent shares include the 100 most highly capitalized United States companies whose shares are traded on Nasdaq/NMS.

Background

Developed by the Philadelphia Stock Exchange (PHLX) to serve as an underlying vehicle for stock index options contracts traded on the Philadelphia Stock Exchange, the contract commenced trading on May 17, 1985.

Base Date

September 20, 1984=150.00

Computation Methodology

(1) An aggregate of prices times quantities index formula. Maintenance adjustments to the divisor are made for capitalization changes, new listings and delistings. (2) The index is re-compiled semi-annually, usually in February and August of each year, based on market capitalization.

Derivative Instruments

National Over-the-Counter index options and Long-term Equity Participation Securities (LEAPS) trade on the Philadelphia Stock Exchange (PHLX).

Subindices

None

Related Indices

PHLX Airline Sector Index
PHLX Big Cap Sector Index
PHLX Forest & Paper Products Sector Index
PHLX Gold/Silver Sector Index
PHLX Keefe, Bruyette & Woods, Inc. Bank Sector Index
PHLX Phone Sector Index
PHLX Semiconductor Sector Index
PHLX Supercap Index
PHLX Utility Sector Index

Remarks

The index differs from the Nasdaq-100 Index in that it is not limited to non-financial companies.

Publisher

The Philadelphia Stock Exchange (PHLX).

PHILADELPHIA STOCK EXCHANGE PHONE SECTOR (PNX) INDEX

PRICE PERFORMANCE

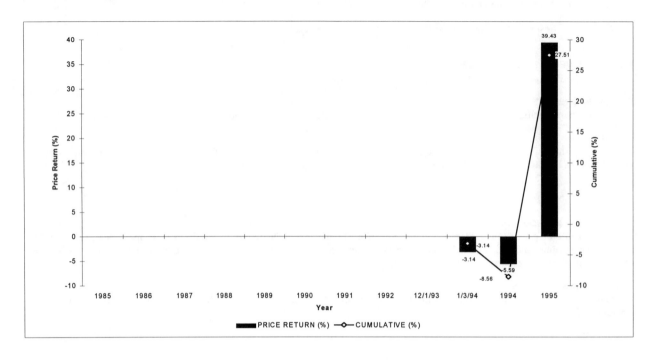

PRICE RETURN (%) ──◇── CUMULATIVE (%)

PRICE PERFORMANCE

YEAR	VALUE	PRICE RETURN (%)	CUMULATIVE (%)	MAXIMUM VALUE[1]	DATE	MINIMUM VALUE[1]	DATE
1995	255.01	39.43	27.51	256.78	15-Dec	179.79	12-Jan
1994	182.89	-5.59	-8.56	202.70	16-Jun	178.16	7-Dec
1/3/94	193.72	-3.14	-3.14	NA	NA	NA	NA
12/1/93	200.00						
1992							
1991							
1990							
1989							
1988							
1987							
1986							
1985							
Average Annual (%)		10.23					
Compound Annual (%)		8.44					
Standard Deviation (%)		25.32					

[1] 1994 maximum/minimum values based on weekly data for the period 1/3/94-5/9/94.

SYNOPSIS
The Philadelphia Stock Exchange Phone Sector (PNX) Index is a market value-weighted index that tracks the continuous price only performance of AT&T Corp. and the seven companies created after the 1983 divestiture of AT&T's regional operating units.

NUMBER OF STOCKS—DECEMBER 31, 1995
8

MARKET VALUE—FEBRUARY 6, 1996
US$41,925.0 million

SELECTION CRITERIA
In addition to AT&T Corp., constituents include Ameritech Corp., Bell Atlantic Corp., Bell South Corp., NYNEX Corp., Pacific Telesis Corp., Southwestern Bell Corp. and U.S. West, Inc.

BACKGROUND
Developed by the Philadelphia Stock Exchange to serve as an underlying vehicle for stock index options contracts traded on the Philadelphia Stock Exchange. The contract commenced trading on August 24, 1994.

BASE DATE
December 1, 1993=200.00

COMPUTATION METHODOLOGY
An aggregate of prices times quantities index formula. Maintenance adjustments to the divisor are made for capitalization changes, if any, new listings and delistings.

DERIVATIVE INSTRUMENTS
Phone Sector index options trade on the Philadelphia Stock Exchange (PHLX).

SUBINDICES
None

RELATED INDICES
PHLX Airline Sector Index
PHLX Forest & Paper Products Sector Index
PHLX Gold/Silver Sector Index
PHLX Keefe, Bruyette & Woods, Inc. Bank Sector Index
PHLX National Over-the-Counter Index
PHLX Semiconductor Sector Index
PHLX Supercap Index
PHLX U.S. Top 100 Index
PHLX Utility Sector Index

REMARKS
None

PUBLISHER
The Philadelphia Stock Exchange (PHLX).

PHILADELPHIA STOCK EXCHANGE SEMICONDUCTOR SECTOR (SOX) INDEX

PRICE PERFORMANCE

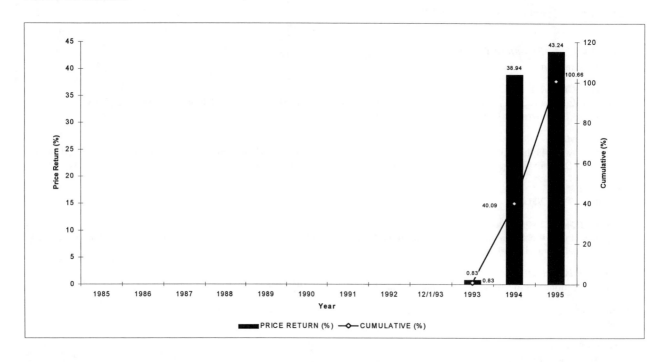

PRICE PERFORMANCE

YEAR	VALUE	PRICE RETURN (%)	CUMULATIVE (%)	MAXIMUM VALUE	DATE	MINIMUM VALUE[1]	DATE
1995	200.66	43.24	100.66	301.65	11-Sep	136.52	4-Jan
1994	140.09	38.94	40.09	143.30	2-Nov	103.57	3-Jan
1993	100.83	0.83	0.83	NA	NA	NA	NA
12/1/93	100.00						
1992							
1991							
1990							
1989							
1988							
1987							
1986							
1985							
Average Annual (%)		8.30					
Compound Annual (%)		7.21					
Standard Deviation (%)		23.34					

[1]1994 minimum index value based on weekly data for the week of January 3, 1994.

Synopsis

The Philadelphia Stock Exchange Semiconductor Sector (SOX) Index is a price-weighted index that tracks the continuous price only performance of United States (U.S.) companies involved in the design, manufacture, sale and distribution of semiconductors used in computer electronic device manufacturing.

Number of Stocks—December 31, 1995

16

Market Value—February 6, 1996

US$53,563.0 million

Selection Criteria

The largest and most widely-held U.S. semiconductor stocks are selected for inclusion in the index.

Background

Developed by the Philadelphia Stock Exchange (PHLX) to serve as an underlying vehicle for stock index options contracts traded on the Philadelphia Stock Exchange. The contract commenced trading on August 1, 1994.

Base Date

December 1, 1993=200.00

Computation Methodology

A simple aggregative of actual prices index formula.

Derivative Instruments

Semiconductor Sector index options trade on the Philadelphia Stock Exchange (PHLX).

Subindices

None

Related Indices

PHLX Airline Sector Index
PHLX Forest & Paper Products Sector Index
PHLX Gold/Silver Sector Index
PHLX Keefe, Bruyette & Woods, Inc. Bank Sector Index
PHLX National Over-the-Counter Index
PHLX Phone Sector Index
PHLX Supercap Index
PHLX U.S. Top 100 Index
PHLX Utility Sector Index

Remarks

None

Publisher

The Philadelphia Stock Exchange (PHLX).

PHILADELPHIA STOCK EXCHANGE SUPERCAP (HFX) INDEX

PRICE PERFORMANCE

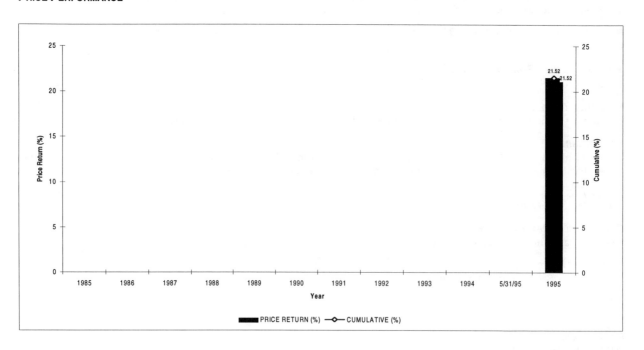

PRICE RETURN (%) —○— CUMULATIVE (%)

PRICE PERFORMANCE

YEAR	VALUE	PRICE RETURN (%)	CUMULATIVE (%)	MAXIMUM VALUE	DATE	MINIMUM VALUE	DATE
1995	425.32	21.52	21.52	443.53	13-Dec	341.72	9-Jun
5/31/95	350.00						
1994							
1993							
1992							
1991							
1990							
1989							
1988							
1987							
1986							
1985							
Average Annual (%)		NM					
Compound Annual (%)		NM					
Standard Deviation (%)		NM					

SYNOPSIS

The Philadelphia Stock Exchange Supercap (HFX) Index is a market value-weighted index that tracks the continuous price only performance of the five largest United States (U.S.) companies by market value.

NUMBER OF STOCKS—DECEMBER 31, 1995

5

MARKET VALUE—FEBRUARY 6, 1996

US$510,077.7 million

SELECTION CRITERIA

Constituent shares represent the five largest companies in the U.S, based on market value. These include AT&T Corp., Coca-Cola Co., Exxon Corp., General Electric Co., and Philip Morris Co.

BACKGROUND

The index was developed by the Philadelphia Stock Exchange (PHLX) to serve as an underlying vehicle for stock index options contracts which commenced trading on November 10, 1995

BASE DATE

May 31, 1995=350.00

COMPUTATION METHODOLOGY

(1) An aggregate of prices times quantities index formula. Maintenance adjustments are made periodically for capitalization changes, new listings and delistings. (2) Adjustments to the index are twice a year, on the last business day in May and November. Adjustments to the constituent shares, if any, are made after the close of trading following the January and July option expirations.

DERIVATIVE INSTRUMENTS

Supercap index options trade on the Philadelphia Stock Exchange (PHLX).

SUBINDICES

None

RELATED INDICES

PHLX Airline Sector Index
PHLX Forest & Paper Products Sector Index
PHLX Gold/Silver Sector Index
PHLX Keefe, Bruyette & Woods, Inc. Bank Sector Index
PHLX National Over-the-Counter Index
PHLX Phone Sector Index
PHLX Semiconductor Sector Index
PHLX U.S Top 100 Index
PHLX Utility Sector Index

REMARKS

None

PUBLISHER

The Philadelphia Stock Exchange (PHLX).

PHILADELPHIA STOCK EXCHANGE U.S. TOP 100 (TPX) INDEX

PRICE PERFORMANCE

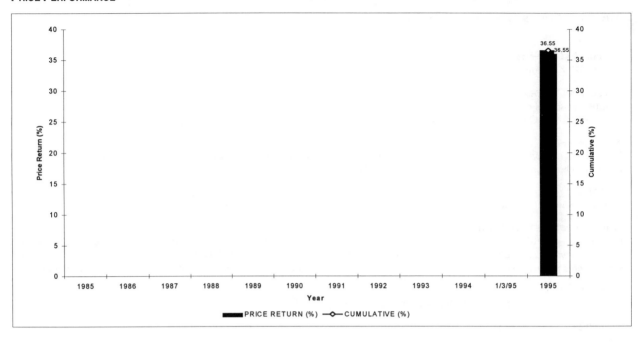

PRICE PERFORMANCE

YEAR	VALUE	PRICE RETURN (%)	CUMULATIVE (%)	MAXIMUM VALUE	DATE	MINIMUM VALUE	DATE
1995	553.02	36.55	36.55	560.66	13-Dec	405.00	3-Jan
1/3/95	405.00						
1994							
1993							
1992							
1991							
1990							
1989							
1988							
1987							
1986							
1985							
Average Annual (%)		36.55					
Compound Annual (%)		NM					
Standard Deviation (%)		NM					

SYNOPSIS
The Philadelphia Stock Exchange U.S. Top 100 (TPX) Index is a market value-weighted index that tracks the continuous price only performance of the 100 most highly capitalized and widely held United States (U.S.) common stock, including both listed and Over-the-Counter (OTC) issues. These companies represent about 43% of the U.S. market capitalization.

NUMBER OF STOCKS—DECEMBER 31, 1995
100

MARKET VALUE—FEBRUARY 12, 1996
US$3,023,361.0 million

SELECTION CRITERIA
Constituent shares include the 100 most highly capitalized U.S companies in the consumer product, automobile, technology, financial, industrial, petrochemical and pharmaceutical industries.

BACKGROUND
Developed by the Philadelphia Stock Exchange (PHLX) to serve as an underlying vehicle for stock index options contracts traded on the Philadelphia Stock Exchange, the contract commenced trading on May 8, 1995.

The index and the related stock index options replaced the Big Cap Sector Index which was composed of 50 of the most high capitalized U.S. companies.

BASE DATE
January 3, 1995=405.00

COMPUTATION METHODOLOGY
(1) An aggregate of prices times quantities index formula. Maintenance adjustments to the divisor are made for capitalization changes, new listings and delistings. (2) The index is re-compiled annually based on market capitalization.

DERIVATIVE INSTRUMENTS
Top 100 index options and Long-term Equity Anticipation Securities (LEAPS) trade on the Philadelphia Stock Exchange (PHLX).

SUBINDICES
None

RELATED INDICES
PHLX Airline Sector Index
PHLX Forest & Paper Products Sector Index
PHLX Gold/Silver Sector Index
PHLX Keefe, Bruyette & Woods, Inc. Bank Sector Index
PHLX National Over-the-Counter Index
PHLX Phone Sector Index
PHLX Semiconductor Sector Index
PHLX Supercap Index
PHLX Utility Sector Index

REMARKS
None

PUBLISHER
The Philadelphia Stock Exchange (PHLX).

PHILADELPHIA STOCK EXCHANGE UTILITY SECTOR (UTY) INDEX

PRICE PERFORMANCE

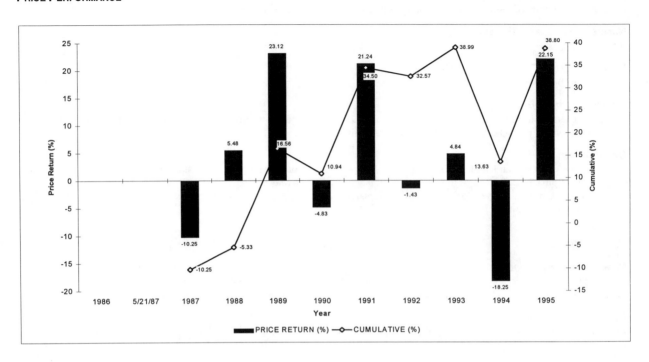

PRICE PERFORMANCE

YEAR	VALUE	PRICE RETURN (%)	CUMULATIVE (%)	MAXIMUM VALUE[1]	DATE	MINIMUM VALUE[1]	DATE
1995	277.60	22.15	38.80	277.60	29-Dec	228.34	3-Jan
1994	227.26	-18.25	13.63	275.86	3-Jan	209.41	20-Sep
1993	277.98	4.84	38.99	304.75	13-Sep	259.98	8-Jan
1992	265.14	-1.43	32.57	269.51	23-Dec	241.23	8-Apr
1991	268.99	21.24	34.50	268.99	31-Dec	213.96	16-Jan
1990	221.87	-4.83	10.94	234.86	2-Jan	193.84	24-Aug
1989	233.12	23.12	16.56	234.22	15-Dec	186.42	1-Mar
1988	189.34	5.48	-5.33	198.78	29-Jan	173.26	20-Apr
1987	179.51	-10.25	-10.25	200.48	13-Oct	164.17	19-Oct
5/21/87	200.00						
1986							
Average Annual (%)		4.21					
Compound Annual (%)		3.33					
Standard Deviation (%)		14.98					

[1]Maximum/minimum index values for 1987 based on data limited to the third quarter 1987.

SYNOPSIS
The Philadelphia Stock Exchange Utility Sector (UTY) Index is a market value-weighted index designed to track the continuous price only performance of public utility stocks listed on the New York Stock Exchange (NYSE).

NUMBER OF STOCKS—DECEMBER 31, 1995
20

MARKET VALUE—FEBRUARY 6, 1996
US$136,037.7 million

SELECTION CRITERIA
Constituent shares represent 20 geographically diverse, large capitalization United States (U.S.) electric utility companies.

BACKGROUND
The index was developed by the Philadelphia Stock Exchange (PHLX) to mirror the Dow Jones Utility Average without actually tracking the same 20 companies, and to serve as an underlying vehicle for stock index options contracts traded on the PHLX. The stock index options commenced trading on September 22, 1987.

BASE DATE
May 1, 1987=200.00

COMPUTATION METHODOLOGY
An aggregate of prices times quantities index formula. Maintenance adjustments to the divisor are made for capitalization changes, new listings and delistings.

DERIVATIVE INSTRUMENTS
Utility Sector index options trade on the Philadelphia Stock Exchange (PHLX).

SUBINDICES
None

RELATED INDICES
PHLX Airline Sector Index
PHLX Forest & Paper Products Sector Index
PHLX Gold/Silver Sector Index
PHLX Keefe, Bruyette & Woods, Inc. Bank Sector Index
PHLX National Over-the-Counter Index
PHLX Phone Sector Index
PHLX Semiconductor Sector Index
PHLX Supercap Index
PHLX U.S Top 100 Index

REMARKS
None

PUBLISHER
The Philadelphia Stock Exchange (PHLX).

RUSSELL 1000 INDEX

PRICE PERFORMANCE

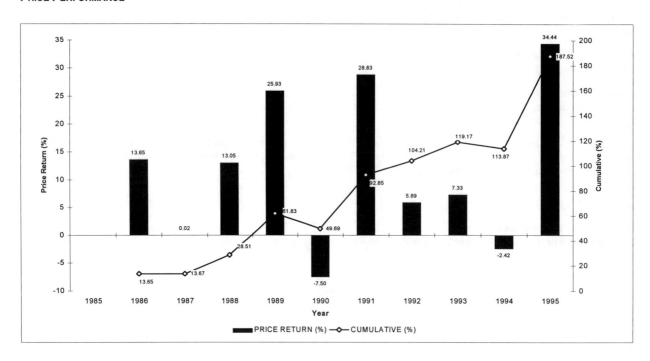

PRICE AND TOTAL RETURN PERFORMANCE

YEAR	VALUE	PRICE RETURN (%)	CUMULATIVE (%)	TOTAL RETURN (%)	MAXIMUM VALUE	DATE	MINIMUM VALUE	DATE
1995	328.89	34.44	187.52	37.77	331.18	13-Dec	244.41	3-Jan
1994	244.64	-2.42	113.87	0.38	258.31	2-Feb	235.50	4-Apr
1993	250.71	7.33	119.17	10.15	252.77	15-Oct	229.91	8-Jan
1992	233.59	5.89	104.21	9.04	235.06	18-Dec	208.87	8-Apr
1991	220.60	28.83	92.85	33.03	220.60	31-Dec	161.94	9-Jan
1990	171.23	-7.50	49.69	-4.16	191.56	16-Jul	152.36	11-Oct
1989	185.11	25.93	61.83	30.42	189.93	9-Oct	145.78	3-Jan
1988	146.99	13.05	28.51	17.23	149.94	21-Oct	128.35	20-Jan
1987	130.02	0.02	13.67	2.94	176.22	25-Aug	117.65	4-Dec
1986	130.00	13.65	13.65	17.87	137.87	2-Jul	111.14	22-Jan
1985								
Average Annual (%)		11.92		15.47				
Compound Annual (%)		11.14		14.66				
Standard Deviation (%)		14.05		14.44				

SYNOPSIS
The Russell 1000 Index is a market value-weighted index that tracks the continuous price only and daily total return performance of 1,000 investable common stocks belonging to the largest United States (U.S.)-domiciled corporations whose shares are publicly traded. These shares account for about 72% of the U.S. market capitalization.

NUMBER OF STOCKS—DECEMBER 31, 1995
1,000

MARKET VALUE—DECEMBER 31, 1995
US$5,033,656.0 million

SELECTION CRITERIA
Constituent stocks are primarily selected on the basis total market capitalization using prices and total shares outstanding as reported by Muller Data Services. Once a year, securities are ranked by descending total market value as of May 31st. Stocks traded in the U.S. but domiciled in other countries are excluded from consideration. Also excluded are: Preferred stock, convertible preferred stock, participating preferred stock, paired shares, warrants and rights, Trust Receipts, Royalty Trusts, limited liability companies, OTC Bulletin Board companies, pink sheet-listed companies, closed-end investment companies, and limited partnerships. In the event of a merger, acquisition, bankruptcy, liquidation, or other similar corporate change causes a stock to be dropped from the index, a replacement stock is selected from a list of eligible securities.

Real Estate Investment Trusts (REITs) and Beneficial Trusts are eligible for inclusion in the index. With some exceptions (i.e., General Motors and Pittston share classes), only one class of a security is permitted into the index.

Effective as of June 30, 1991, a minimum price rule was introduced which requires that companies must be trading at or above $1.00 as of May 31 of each year to be eligible for inclusion in the Russell indices.

BACKGROUND
The index was introduced in 1987. Daily index values are available, on an historical basis, starting at December 31, 1978. Total rates of return are calculated daily after the end of each month.

BASE DATE
December 31, 1986=130.00

COMPUTATION METHODOLOGY
(1) An aggregate of prices times quantities index formula. Maintenance adjustments to the divisor are made daily for capitalization changes, new listings and delistings after the close on the day that the stock starts trading with prices reflecting the change. (2) Market capitalization is computed by adjusting, on a continuous basis, shares outstanding for cross ownership so as not to overstate the overall market value of constituent companies. This is accomplished by reducing the total shares outstanding by the number of shares owned by other companies, including companies outside the index, stocks owned by foreign companies and other non-corporate entities. (3) Effective June 30, 1992, if a company is relegated to pink sheet status between reconstitution periods, it is dropped from the index at the time it is removed from the stock exchange. (4) The index is reconstituted annually on June 30th based on May 31 market capitalizations. (5) Closing price from the primary exchange for each stock is used.

DERIVATIVE INSTRUMENTS
Russell 1000 Index options trade on the Chicago Board Options Exchange (CBOE).

SUBINDICES
Russell Top 200 Index

RELATED INDICES
Russell 1000 Growth Index, Russell 1000 Value Index
Russell 2000 Index–Russell 2000 Growth Index, Russell 2000 Value Index
Russell 2500 Index
Russell 3000 Index
Russell Midcap Index–Russell Midcap Growth Index, Russell Midcap Value Index
Refer to Appendix 5 for additional indices.

REMARKS
(1) The market capitalization of constituent companies ranges from a low of US$75.5 million to a high of US$120,260 million as of December 31, 1995. (2) Market value reflects adjustments for cross ownership. Percent of U.S. market capitalization figure is unadjusted for cross ownership.

PUBLISHER
Frank Russell Company.

RUSSELL 1000 GROWTH INDEX

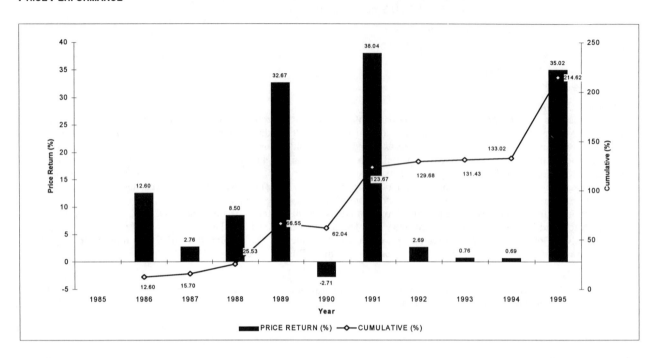

PRICE AND TOTAL RETURN PERFORMANCE

YEAR	VALUE	PRICE RETURN (%)	CUMULATIVE (%)	TOTAL RETURN (%)	MAXIMUM VALUE	DATE	MINIMUM VALUE	DATE
1995	194.17	35.02	214.62	37.19	197.11	13-Dec	142.95	6-Jan
1994	143.81	0.69	133.02	2.66	147.14	28-Oct	132.36	20-Apr
1993	142.83	0.76	131.43	2.90	143.26	29-Dec	131.71	26-Apr
1992	141.75	2.69	129.68	5.00	143.56	21-Dec	125.28	18-Jun
1991	138.04	38.04	123.67	41.16	138.04	31-Dec	93.74	9-Jan
1990	100.00	-2.71	62.04	-0.26	107.72	30-Jun	90.77	30-Sep
1989	102.79	32.67	66.55	35.92	102.79	31-Dec	80.65	28-Feb
1988	77.47	8.50	25.53	11.27	77.47	31-Dec	72.18	31-Jan
1987	71.41	2.76	15.70	5.31	96.59	31-Aug	65.56	30-Nov
1986	69.49	12.60	12.60	15.36	76.35	30-Jun	62.16	31-Jan
1985	61.72							
Average Annual (%)		13.10		15.65				
Compound Annual (%)		12.14		14.69				
Standard Deviation (%)		15.91		16.16				

SYNOPSIS

The Russell 1000 Growth Index is a market value-weighted index that tracks the daily price only and total return performance of growth oriented investable common stocks belonging to the largest United States (U.S.)-domiciled corporations whose shares are publicly traded. These securities represent a subset of the stocks that make up the Russell 1000 Index with a greater-than-average growth orientation. Securities in this index tend to exhibit higher price-to-book and price-earnings ratios, lower dividend yields and higher forecasted growth values than the more value oriented securities in the Russell 1000 Value Index.

NUMBER OF STOCKS—DECEMBER 31, 1995
629

MARKET VALUE—DECEMBER 31, 1995
US$2,553,633.5 million

SELECTION CRITERIA

Eligible securities consist of members of the Russell 1000 Index, and are selected on the basis of the following guidelines: (1) The 1,000 securities that make up the Russell 1000 Index are ranked by their adjusted book-to-price ratio as well as their Institutional Brokers' Estimate System (I/B/E/S) forecasted long-term growth mean. (2) Companies are ranked in ascending price-to-book value order and in descending I/B/E/S long-term growth mean value. A composite rank is determined on the basis of these two variables by converting them to standardized units which are combined to create a composite score. (3) The constituents are ranked by their composite value score and breakpoints are determined by cumulative available market capitalization to create three ranges of securities. (4) Using a probability algorithm, companies in the Russell 1000 Index are assigned a probability of being a growth or value stock. Roughly 70% are classified as either all growth or all value. The remaining 30% are assigned a probability of both value and growth. (5) Companies with probabilities of 100% growth or 100% value are placed entirely in the growth or value index. (6) Companies with a hybrid probability of part growth, part value are held in both the growth and value indices with a weight corresponding to their probability, based on market capitalization. Accordingly, the sum of the securities in the Russell Growth and Value indices will not be equal to the Russell 1000, but the sum of the available market capitalization will correspond to the Russell 1000 Equity Index.

For additional information, refer to the Russell 1000 Index.

BACKGROUND

(1) The index was known as the Russell Earnings Growth Index until its name change to the Russell 1000 Growth Index on April 1, 1993. (2) The probability methodology used in the assignment of companies to the growth and value indices was adopted in 1995. Prior to 1995, the index employed an all or nothing approach and stocks were categorized as either 100% growth or 100% value. Index history is based upon the old methodology. (3) I/B/E/S forecasted long-term growth mean factors have been employed since 1994. (4) A peer group analysis was introduced in 1993 for the purpose of making style determinations with regard to securities for which missing data is not available or style data is negative. (5) Monthly values are available to December 31, 1978. Daily values are available from January 2, 1991.

BASE DATE

December 31, 1990=100.00

COMPUTATION METHODOLOGY

(1) An aggregate of prices times quantities index formula. Maintenance adjustments to the divisor for capitalization changes, new listings and delistings are made daily after the close on the day that the stock starts trading with prices reflecting the change. (2) Market capitalization is computed by adjusting, on a continuous basis, shares outstanding for cross ownership so as not to overstate the overall market value of constituent companies. This is accomplished by reducing the total shares outstanding by the number of shares owned by other companies, including companies outside the index, stocks owned by foreign companies and other non-corporate entities. (3) Effective June 30, 1992, if a company is relegated to pink sheet status between reconstitution periods, it is dropped from the index at the time it is removed from the stock exchange. (4) The index is reconstituted annually, on June 30th based on May 31 market capitalizations. (5) Closing prices from the primary exchange for each stock is used.

DERIVATIVE INSTRUMENTS

None

SUBINDICES

Russell Top 200 Growth Index

RELATED INDICES

Russell 1000 Index, Russell 1000 Value Index
Russell 2000 Index–Russell 2000 Growth Index, Russell 2000 Value Index
Russell 2500 Index
Russell 3000 Index
Russell Midcap Index–Russell Midcap Growth Index, Russell Midcap Value Index
Refer to Appendix 5 for additional indices.

REMARKS

(1) A companys' reported price-to-book ratios are adjusted to reflect write-offs stemming from FAS 106, by assuming that each company amortized the FAS 106 transition obligation over a 20-year period beginning with the year of adoption. The unamortized portion of the write-off is then added back to the reported book value. (2) The market capitalization of constituent companies ranges from a low of US$20,465.0 million to a high of US$120,260.0 million as of December 31, 1995. (3) Market value reflects adjustments for cross ownership.

PUBLISHER

Frank Russell Company.

RUSSELL 1000 VALUE INDEX

PRICE PERFORMANCE

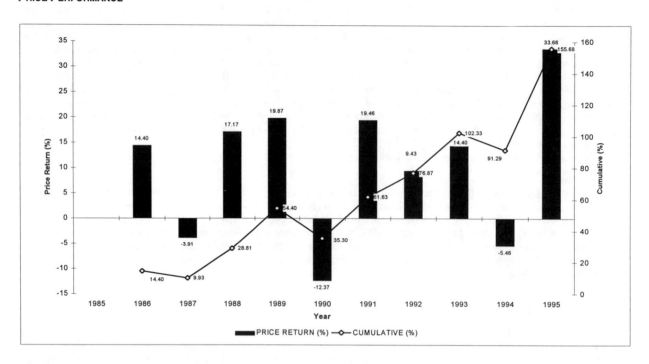

PRICE AND TOTAL RETURN PERFORMANCE

YEAR	VALUE	PRICE RETURN (%)	CUMULATIVE (%)	TOTAL RETURN (%)	MAXIMUM VALUE	DATE	MINIMUM VALUE	DATE
1995	188.97	33.66	155.68	38.35	188.97	29-Dec	141.83	3-Jan
1994	141.38	-5.46	91.29	-1.99	154.89	31-Jan	138.01	8-Dec
1993	149.54	14.40	102.33	18.12	152.17	13-Sep	129.43	8-Jan
1992	130.72	9.43	76.87	13.81	130.94	30-Dec	116.37	8-Apr
1991	119.46	19.46	61.63	24.61	119.46	31-Dec	95.20	14-Jan
1990	100.00	-12.37	35.30	-8.08	113.12	31-May	92.11	31-Oct
1989	114.12	19.87	54.40	25.19	117.09	31-Aug	99.30	28-Feb
1988	95.20	17.17	28.81	23.16	96.09	31-Oct	87.34	31-Jan
1987	81.25	-3.91	9.93	0.50	107.16	31-Aug	77.26	30-Nov
1986	84.56	14.40	14.40	19.98	88.74	31-Aug	74.67	31-Jan
1985	73.91							
Average Annual (%)		10.67		15.36				
Compound Annual (%)		9.84		14.52				
Standard Deviation (%)		14.01		14.43				

SYNOPSIS

The Russell 1000 Value Index is a market value-weighted index that tracks the daily price only and total return performance of value oriented investable common stocks belonging to the largest United States (U.S.)-domiciled corporations whose shares are publicly traded. These securities represent a subset of the stocks that make up the Russell 1000 Index with a less-than-average growth orientation. Securities in this index generally have low price-to-book and price-earnings ratios, higher dividend yields, and lower forecasted growth values than the more growth oriented securities in the Russell 1000 Growth Index.

NUMBER OF STOCKS—DECEMBER 31, 1995
639

MARKET VALUE—DECEMBER 31, 1995
US$2,480,023.4 million

SELECTION CRITERIA

Eligible securities consist of member of the Russell 1000 Index, and are selected on the basis of the following guidelines:
(1) The 1,000 securities that make up the Russell 1000 Equity Index are ranked by their adjusted book-to-price ratio as well as their Institutional Brokers' Estimate System (I/B/E/S) forecasted long-term growth mean. (2) Companies are ranked in ascending price-to-book value order and in descending I/B/E/S long-term growth mean value. A composite rank is determined on the basis of these two variables by converting them to standardized units which are combined to create a composite score. (3) The constituents are ranked by their composite value score and breakpoints are determined by cumulative available market capitalization to create three ranges of securities. (4) Using a probability algorithm, companies in the Russell 1000 Index are assigned a probability of being a growth or value stock. Roughly 70% are classified as either all growth or all value. The remaining 30% are assigned a probability of both value and growth. (5) Companies with probabilities of 100% growth or 100% value are placed entirely in the growth or value index. (6) Companies with a hybrid probability of part growth part value are held in both indices with a weight corresponding to their probability, based on market capitalization. Accordingly, the sum of the securities in the Russell Growth and Value indices will not be equal to the Russell 1000, but the sum of the available market capitalization will correspond to the Russell 1000 Index.

For additional information, refer to the Russell 1000 Index.

BACKGROUND

(1) The index was known as the Russell Price Driven Index until its name change to the Russell 1000 Value Index on April 1, 1993. (2) The probability methodology used in the assignment of companies to the growth and value indices was adopted in 1995. Prior to 1995, the index employed an all or nothing approach and stocks were categorized as either 100% growth or 100% value. Index history is based upon the old methodology. (3) I/B/E/S forecasted long-term growth mean factors have been employed since 1994. (4) A peer group analysis was introduced in 1993 for the purpose of making style determinations with regard to securities for which missing data is not available or style data is negative. (5) Monthly values are available to December 31, 1978. Daily values are available from January 2, 1991.

BASE DATE

December 31, 1990=100.00

COMPUTATION METHODOLOGY

(1) An aggregate of prices times quantities index formula. Maintenance adjustments to the divisor for capitalization changes, new listings and delistings.are made daily after the close on the day that the stock starts trading with prices reflecting the change. (2) Market capitalization is computed by adjusting, on a continuous basis, shares outstanding for cross ownership so as not to overstate the overall market value of constituent companies. This is accomplished by reducing the total shares outstanding by the number of shares owned by other companies, including companies outside the index, and stocks owned by foreign companies and other non-corporate entities. (3) Effective June 30, 1992, if a company is relegated to pink sheet status between reconstitution periods, it is dropped from the index at the time it is removed from the stock exchange. (4) The index is reconstituted annually, on June 30th based on May 31 market capitalizations. (5) Closing prices from the primary exchange for each stock is used.

DERIVATIVE INSTRUMENTS

None

SUBINDICES

Russell Top 200 Value Index

RELATED INDICES

Russell 1000 Index–Russell 1000 Growth Index
Russell 2000 Index–Russell 2000 Growth Index, Russell 2000 Value Index
Russell 2500 Index
Russell 3000 Index
Russell Midcap Index–Russell Midcap Growth Index, Russell Midcap Value Index
Refer to Appendix 5 for additional indices.

REMARKS

(1) Reported price-to-book ratios are adjusted to reflect write-offs stemming from FAS 106, by assuming that each company amortized the FAS 106 transition obligation over a 20-year period beginning with the year of adoption. The unamortized portion of the write-off is then added back to the reported book value. (2) The market capitalization of constituent companies ranges from a low of US$22.2 million to a high of US$100,731.0 million as of December 31, 1995. (3) Market value reflects adjustments for cross ownership.

PUBLISHER

Frank Russell Company.

RUSSELL 2000 INDEX

PRICE PERFORMANCE

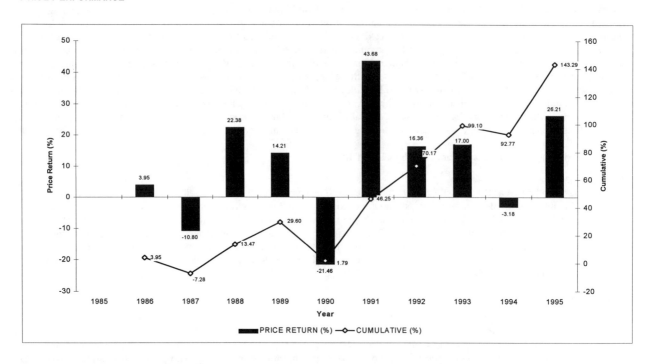

PRICE AND TOTAL RETURN PERFORMANCE

YEAR	VALUE	PRICE RETURN (%)	CUMULATIVE (%)	TOTAL RETURN (%)	MAXIMUM VALUE	DATE	MINIMUM VALUE	DATE
1995	315.97	26.21	143.29	28.44	316.12	14-Sep	246.56	30-Jan
1994	250.36	-3.18	92.77	-1.82	271.08	18-Mar	235.16	9-Dec
1993	258.58	17.00	99.10	18.91	260.17	2-Nov	217.55	23-Feb
1992	221.01	16.36	70.17	18.41	218.42	30-Dec	185.81	8-Jul
1991	189.94	43.68	46.25	46.05	189.94	31-Dec	125.25	15-Jan
1990	132.19	-21.46	1.79	-19.51	170.90	15-Jun	118.82	30-Oct
1989	168.31	14.21	29.60	16.24	180.78	9-Oct	146.79	3-Jan
1988	147.37	22.38	13.47	24.89	151.42	18-Jul	121.23	12-Jan
1987	120.42	-10.80	-7.28	-8.77	174.44	25-Aug	106.07	28-Oct
1986	135.00	3.95	3.95	5.68	155.30	3-Jul	128.23	9-Jan
1985								
Average Annual (%)		10.83		12.85				
Compound Annual (%)		9.30		11.32				
Standard Deviation (%)		19.10		19.29				

Synopsis

The Russell 2000 Index is a market value-weighted index that tracks the continuous price only and daily total return performance of 2,000 investable common stocks belonging to the smallest 2,000 United States (U.S.)-domiciled corporations in the Russell 3000 Index whose shares are publicly traded. These shares account for 8% of the U.S. market capitalization.

Number of Stocks—December 31, 1995

2,000

Market Value—December 31, 1995

US$555,480.0 million

Selection Criteria

Constituent stocks are primarily selected on the basis of total market capitalization using prices and total shares outstanding as reported by Muller Data Services. Once a year, securities are ranked by descending total market value as of May 31st. Stocks traded in the U.S. but domiciled in other countries are excluded from consideration. Also excluded from consideration are: Preferred stock, convertible preferred stock, participating preferred stock, paired shares, warrants and rights, Trust Receipts, Royalty Trusts, limited liability companies, OTC Bulletin Board companies, pink sheet-listed companies, closed-end investment companies, and limited partnerships. In the event of a merger, acquisition, bankruptcy, liquidation, or other similar corporate change causes a stock to be dropped from the index, a replacement stock is selected from a list of eligible securities.

Real Estate Investment Trusts (REITs) and Beneficial Trusts are eligible for inclusion in the index. With some exceptions (i.e., General Motors and Pittston share classes), only one class of a security is permitted into the index.

Effective as of June 30, 1991, a minimum price rule was introduced which requires that companies must be trading at or above $1.00 as of May 31 of each year to be eligible for inclusion in the Russell indices.

Background

The index was introduced in 1987. Daily index values are available on a historical basis starting at December 31, 1978. Total rates of return are calculated daily after the end of each month.

Until June 1991, stocks selected for the Russell 2000 Index were required to have a minimum of five years of financial data available through Compustat. This caused an underweighting in the financial sector due to Compustat's data limitations. Starting in June 1991 and continuing into June 1992, this requirement was phased out. Securities that comprised the Russell 1000 Index were not required to meet the five-year minimum.

Base Date

December 31, 1986=135.00

Computation Methodology

(1) An aggregate of prices times quantities index formula. Maintenance adjustments to the divisor for capitalization changes, new listings and delistings are made daily after the close on the day that the stock starts trading with prices reflecting the change. (2) Market capitalization is computed by adjusting, on a continuous basis, shares outstanding for cross ownership so as not to overstate the overall market value of constituent companies. This is accomplished by reducing the total shares outstanding by the number of shares owned by other companies, including companies outside the index, and stocks owned by foreign companies and other non-corporate entities. (3) Effective June 30, 1992, if a company is relegated to pink sheet status between reconstitution periods, it is dropped from the index at the time it is removed from the stock exchange. (4) The index is reconstituted annually, on June 30th based on May 31 market capitalizations. (5) Closing prices from the primary exchange for each stock is used.

Derivative Instruments

(1) Merrill Lynch Index Call Warrants trade on the American Stock Exchange (AMEX). (2) Russell 2000 index options, Long-Term Index options, Long-term Equity Participation Securities (LEAPS) and Flex Options trade on the Chicago Board Options Exchange (CBOE). (3) Russell 2000 index futures and futures options trade on the Chicago Mercantile Exchange (CME).

Subindices

None

Related Indices

Russell 1000 Index–Russell 1000 Growth Index, Russell 1000 Value Index
Russell 2000 Growth Index–Russell 2000 Value Index
Russell 2500 Index
Russell 3000 Index
Russell Midcap Index–Russell Midcap Growth Index, Russell Midcap Value Index
Refer to Appendix 5 for additional indices.

Remarks

(1) The market capitalization of constituent companies ranges from a low of US$8.8 million to a high of US$2,014.0 million as of December 31, 1995. (2) Market value reflects adjustments for cross ownership. Percent of U.S. market capitalization figure is unadjusted for cross ownership.

Publisher

Frank Russell Company.

RUSSELL 2000 GROWTH INDEX

PRICE PERFORMANCE

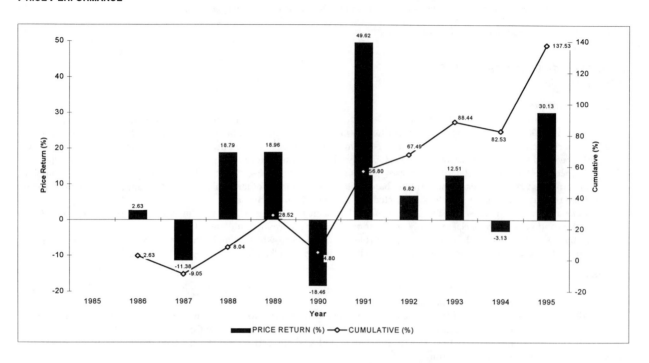

PRICE AND TOTAL RETURN PERFORMANCE

YEAR	VALUE	PRICE RETURN (%)	CUMULATIVE (%)	TOTAL RETURN (%)	MAXIMUM VALUE	DATE	MINIMUM VALUE	DATE
1995	1,411.65	30.13	137.53	31.04	1,427.72	14-Sep	1,060.91	30-Jan
1994	1,084.81	-3.13	82.53	-2.43	1,174.71	18-Mar	995.17	24-Jun
1993	1,119.91	12.51	88.44	13.36	1,134.40	15-Oct	944.20	30-Apr
1992	995.42	6.82	67.49	7.77	1,014.45	28-Feb	830.60	31-Aug
1991	931.85	49.62	56.80	51.19	931.85	31-Dec	680.74	31-Jan
1990	622.83	-18.46	4.80	-17.41	786.40	30-Jun	546.66	31-Oct
1989	763.81	18.96	28.52	20.17	794.00	30-Sep	669.04	31-Jan
1988	642.10	18.79	8.04	20.37	670.04	30-Jun	549.81	31-Jan
1987	540.53	-11.38	-9.05	-10.48	800.43	31-Aug	490.24	30-Nov
1986	609.96	2.63	2.63	3.58	723.84	30-Jun	604.84	30-Sep
1985	594.31							
Average Annual (%)		10.65		11.72				
Compound Annual (%)		9.04		10.09				
Standard Deviation (%)		20.11		20.29				

SYNOPSIS

The Russell 2000 Growth Index is a market value-weighted index that tracks the daily price only and total return performance of growth oriented investable common stocks belonging to the largest United States (U.S.)-domiciled corporations whose shares are publicly traded. These securities represent a subset of the stocks that make up the Russell 2000 Index with a greater-than-average growth orientation. Securities in this index tend to exhibit higher price-to-book and price-earnings ratios, lower dividend yields, and higher forecasted growth values than the more value oriented securities in the Russell 2000 Value Index.

NUMBER OF STOCKS—DECEMBER 31, 1995

1,255

MARKET VALUE—DECEMBER 31, 1995

US$287,725.1 million

SELECTION CRITERIA

Eligible securities consist of members of the Russell 2000 Index, and are selected on the basis of the following guidelines:

(1) The 2,000 securities that make up the Russell 2000 Index are ranked by their adjusted book-to-price ratio as well as their Institutional Brokers' Estimate System (I/B/E/S) forecasted long term growth mean. (2) Companies are ranked in ascending price-to-book value order and in descending I/B/E/S long-term growth mean value. A composite rank is determined on the basis of these two variables by converting them to standardized units which are combined to create a composite score. (3) The constituents are ranked by their composite value score and breakpoints are determined by cumulative available market capitalization to create three ranges of securities. (4) Using a probability algorithm, companies in the Russell 2000 Index are assigned a probability of being a growth or value stock. Roughly 70% are classified as either all growth or all value. The remaining 30% are assigned a probability of both value and growth. (5) Companies with probabilities of 100% growth or 100% value are placed entirely in the growth or value index. (6) Companies with a hybrid probability of part growth, part value are held in both indices with a weight corresponding to their probability, based on market capitalization. Accordingly, the sum of the securities in the Russell Growth and Value indices will not be equal to the Russell 2000, but the sum of the available market capitalization will correspond to the Russell 2000 Index.

For additional information, refer to the Russell 2000 Index.

BACKGROUND

(1) I/B/E/S forecasted long-term growth mean factors have been employed since 1994. (2) A peer group analysis was introduced in 1993 for the purpose of making style determinations with regard to securities for which missing data is not available or style data is negative. (3) Monthly index values are available to December 31, 1978. Daily index values are available starting June 1, 1993.

BASE DATE

May 31, 1993=1000.00

COMPUTATION METHODOLOGY

(1) An aggregate of prices times quantities index formula. Maintenance adjustments to the divisor for capitalization changes, new listings and delistings are made daily after the close on the day that the stock starts trading with prices reflecting the change. (2) Market capitalization is computed by adjusting, on a continuous basis, shares outstanding for cross ownership so as not to overstate the overall market value of constituent companies. This is accomplished by reducing the total shares outstanding by the number of shares owned by other companies, including companies outside the index, stocks owned by foreign companies and other non-corporate entities. (3) Effective June 30, 1992, if a company is relegated to pink sheet status between reconstitution periods, it is dropped from the index at the time it is removed from the stock exchange. (4) The index is reconstituted annually, on June 30th based on May 31 market capitalizations. (5) Closing prices from the primary exchange for each stock is used.

DERIVATIVE INSTRUMENTS

None

SUBINDICES

None

RELATED INDICES

Russell 1000 Index–Russell 1000 Growth Index, Russell 1000 Value Index
Russell 2000 Index–Russell 2000 Value Index
Russell 2500 Index
Russell 3000 Index
Russell Midcap Index–Russell Midcap Growth Index, Russell Midcap Value Index
Refer to Appendix 5 for additional indices.

REMARKS

(1) Reported price-to-book ratios are adjusted to reflect write-offs stemming from FAS 106, by assuming that each company amortized the FAS 106 transition obligation over a 20-year period beginning with the year of adoption. The unamortized portion of the write-off is then added back to the reported book value. (2) The market capitalization of constituent companies ranges from a low of US$2.5 million to a high of US$2,015.0 million as of December 31, 1995. (3) Market value reflects adjustments for cross ownership.

PUBLISHER

Frank Russell Company.

RUSSELL 2000 VALUE INDEX

PRICE PERFORMANCE

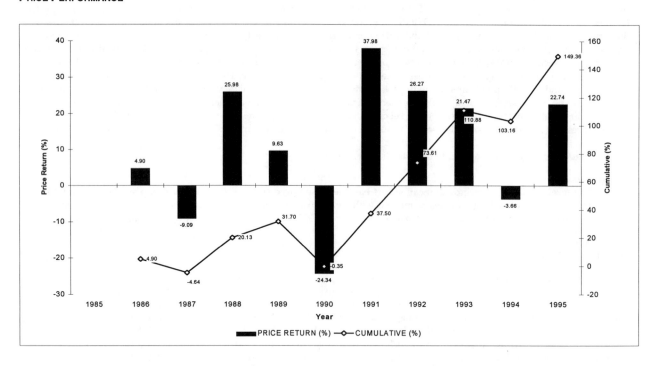

PRICE AND TOTAL RETURN PERFORMANCE[1]

YEAR	VALUE	PRICE RETURN (%)	CUMULATIVE (%)	TOTAL RETURN (%)	MAXIMUM VALUE	DATE	MINIMUM VALUE	DATE
1995	1,310.41	22.74	149.36	25.75	1,310.41	29-Dec	1,058.16	3-Jan
1994	1,067.64	-3.66	103.16	-1.55	1,159.55	23-Mar	1,009.24	9-Dec
1993	1,108.22	21.47	110.88	23.84	1,109.17	29-Oct	959.67	31-Jan
1992	912.36	26.27	73.61	29.14	912.36	31-Dec	782.03	31-Jan
1991	722.56	37.98	37.50	41.70	722.56	31-Dec	567.78	31-Jan
1990	523.68	-24.34	-0.35	-21.78	681.32	31-May	483.14	31-Oct
1989	692.11	9.63	31.70	12.43	749.91	31-Aug	659.69	31-Jan
1988	631.32	25.98	20.13	29.47	638.87	30-Sep	534.32	31-Jan
1987	501.11	-9.09	-4.64	-7.11	706.44	31-Aug	474.52	30-Nov
1986	551.25	4.90	4.90	7.41	612.91	31-May	529.32	31-Jan
1985	525.52							
Average Annual (%)		11.19		13.93				
Compound Annual (%)		9.57		12.29				
Standard Deviation (%)		19.26		19.68				

[1]1985-1993 performance numbers are simulated, based on backtesting.

SYNOPSIS

The Russell 2000 Value Index is a market value-weighted index that tracks the daily price only and total return performance of value oriented investable common stocks belonging to the largest United States (U.S.)-domiciled corporations whose shares are publicly traded. These securities represent a subset of the stocks that make up the Russell 2000 Index with a less-than-average growth orientation. Securities in this index generally have low price-to-book and price-earnings ratios, higher dividend yields, and lower forecasted growth values than the more growth oriented securities in the Russell 2000 Growth Index.

NUMBER OF STOCKS—DECEMBER 31, 1995

1,196

MARKET VALUE—DECEMBER 31, 1995

US$267,754.5 million

SELECTION CRITERIA

Eligible securities consist of members of the Russell 2000 Index which are selected on the basis of the following guidelines:
(1) The 2,000 securities that make up the Russell 2000 Equity Index are ranked by their adjusted book-to-price ratio as well as their Institutional Brokers' Estimate System (I/B/E/S) forecasted long term growth mean. (2) Companies are ranked in ascending price-to-book value order and in descending I/B/E/S long-term growth mean value. A composite rank is determined on the basis of these two variables by converting them to standardized units which are combined to create a composite score. (3) The constituents are ranked by their composite value score and breakpoints are determined by cumulative available market capitalization to create the three ranges of securities. (4) Using a probability algorithm, companies in the Russell 2000 Index are assigned a probability of being a growth or value stock. Roughly 70% are classified as either all growth or all value. The remaining 30% are assigned a probability of both value and growth. (5) Companies with probabilities of 100% growth or 100% value are placed entirely in the growth or value index. (6) Companies with a hybrid probability of part growth, part value are held in both indices with a weight corresponding to their probability, based on market capitalization. Accordingly, the sum of the securities in the Russell Growth and Value indices will not be equal to the Russell 2000, but the sum of the available market capitalization will correspond to the Russell 2000 Equity Index.

For additional information, refer to the Russell 2000 Index.

BACKGROUND

(1) I/B/E/S forecasted long-term growth mean factors have been employed since 1994. (2) A peer group analysis was introduced in 1993 for the purpose of making style determinations with regard to securities for which missing data is not available or style data is negative. (3) Monthly index values are available to December 31, 1978. Daily index values are available starting June 1, 1993.

BASE DATE

May 31, 1993=1000.00

COMPUTATION METHODOLOGY

(1) An aggregate of prices times quantities index formula. Maintenance adjustments to the divisor for capitalization changes, new listings and delistings are made daily after the close on the day that the stock starts trading with prices reflecting the change. (2) Market capitalization is computed by adjusting, on a continuous basis, shares outstanding for cross ownership so as not to overstate the overall market value of constituent companies. This is accomplished by reducing the total shares outstanding by the number of shares owned by other companies, including companies outside the index, and stocks owned by foreign companies and other non-corporate entities. (3) Effective June 30, 1992, if a company is relegated to pink sheet status between reconstitution periods, it is dropped from the index at the time it is removed from the stock exchange. (4) The index is reconstituted annually, on June 30th based on May 31 market capitalizations. (5) Closing prices from the primary exchange for each stock is used.

DERIVATIVE INSTRUMENTS

None

SUBINDICES

None

RELATED INDICES

Russell 1000 Index–Russell 1000 Growth Index, Russell 1000 Value Index
Russell 2000 Index–Russell 2000 Growth Index
Russell 2500 Index
Russell 3000 Index
Russell Midcap Index–Russell Midcap Growth Index, Russell Midcap Value Index
Refer to Appendix 5 for additional indices.

REMARKS

(1) Reported price-to-book ratios are adjusted to reflect write-offs stemming from FAS 106, by assuming that each company amortized the FAS 106 transition obligation over a 20-year period beginning with the year of adoption. The unamortized portion of the write-off is then added back to the reported book value. (2) The market capitalization of constituent companies ranges from a low of US$1.7 million to a high of US$1,375.0 million as of December 31, 1995. (3) Market value reflects adjustments for cross ownership.

PUBLISHER

Frank Russell Company.

RUSSELL 3000 INDEX

PRICE PERFORMANCE

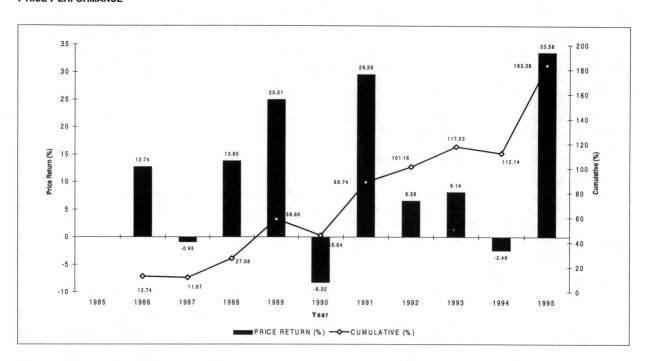

PRICE AND TOTAL RETURN PERFORMANCE

YEAR	VALUE	PRICE RETURN (%)	CUMULATIVE (%)	TOTAL RETURN (%)	MAXIMUM VALUE	DATE	MINIMUM VALUE	DATE
1995	351.91	33.58	183.38	36.81	353.74	13-Dec	262.87	3-Jan
1994	263.44	-2.48	112.14	0.18	278.44	2-Feb	254.01	24-Jun
1993	270.13	8.14	117.53	10.87	272.29	15-Oct	246.09	8-Jan
1992	249.80	6.58	101.16	9.68	250.78	18-Dec	222.86	8-Apr
1991	234.37	29.59	88.74	33.66	234.36	31-Dec	171.17	9-Jan
1990	180.86	-8.32	45.64	-5.06	203.85	16-Jul	161.10	11-Oct
1989	197.28	25.01	58.86	29.32	203.10	9-Oct	156.56	3-Jan
1988	157.81	13.80	27.08	17.82	160.86	21-Oct	137.16	20-Jan
1987	138.67	-0.95	11.67	1.94	188.97	25-Aug	125.26	4-Dec
1986	140.00	12.74	12.74	16.71	149.57	2-Jul	120.95	22-Jan
1985								
Average Annual (%)		11.77		15.19				
Compound Annual (%)		10.98		14.38				
Standard Deviation (%)		14.07		14.44				

SYNOPSIS

The Russell 3000 Index is a market value-weighted index that tracks the continuous price only and daily total return performance of 3,000 investable common stocks belonging to the largest United States (U.S.) domiciled corporations whose shares are publicly traded. These shares account for 80% of the U.S. market capitalization.

NUMBER OF STOCKS—DECEMBER 31, 1995
3,000

MARKET VALUE—DECEMBER 31, 1995
US$5,589,136.0 million

SELECTION CRITERIA

Constituent stocks are primarily selected on the basis of total market capitalization, using prices and total shares outstanding as reported by Muller Data Services. Once a year, securities are ranked by descending total market value as of May 31st. Stocks traded in the U.S. but domiciled in other countries are excluded from consideration. Also excluded from consideration are: Preferred stock, convertible preferred stock, participating preferred stock, paired shares, warrants and rights, Trust Receipts, Royalty Trusts, limited liability companies, OTC Bulletin Board companies, pink sheet-listed companies, closed-end investment companies, and limited partnerships. In the event of a merger, acquisition, bankruptcy, liquidation, or other similar corporate change causes a stock to be dropped from the index, a replacement stock is selected from a list of eligible securities.

Real Estate Investment Trusts (REITs) and Beneficial Trusts are eligible for inclusion in the index. With some exceptions (i.e., General Motors and Pittston share classes), only one class of a security is permitted into the index.

Effective as of June 30, 1991, a minimum price rule was introduced which requires that companies must be trading at or above $1.00 as of May 31 of each year to be eligible for inclusion in the index.

BACKGROUND

The index, which combines the common stocks that make up the Russell 1000 Index and Russell 2000 Index, was introduced in 1987. Daily index values are available on a historical basis starting at December 31, 1978. Total rates of return are calculated daily after the end of each month.

Until June 1991, stocks selected for the Russell 2000 Index were required to have a minimum of five years of financial data available through Compustat. This caused an underweighting in the financial sector due to Compustat's data limitations. Starting in June 1991 and continuing into June 1992, this requirement was phased out. Securities that comprised the Russell 1000 Index were not required to meet the five-year minimum.

BASE DATE

December 31, 1986=140.00

COMPUTATION METHODOLOGY

(1) An aggregate of prices times quantities index formula. Maintenance adjustments to the divisor for capitalization changes, new listings and delistings are made daily after the close on the day that the stock starts trading with prices reflecting the change. (2) Market capitalization is computed by adjusting, on a continuous basis, shares outstanding for cross ownership so as not to overstate the overall market value of constituent companies. This is accomplished by reducing the total shares outstanding by the number of shares owned by other companies, including companies outside the index, and stocks owned by foreign companies and other non-corporate entities. (3) Effective June 30, 1992, if a company is relegated to pink sheet status between reconstitution periods, it is dropped from the index at the time it is removed from the stock exchange. (4) The index is reconstituted annually, on June 30th based on May 31 market capitalizations. (5) Closing prices from the primary exchange for each stock is used.

DERIVATIVE INSTRUMENTS

None

SUBINDICES

Russell 1000 Index
Russell 2000 Index

RELATED INDICES

Russell 1000 Index–Russell 1000 Growth Index, Russell 1000 Value Index
Russell 2000 Index–Russell 2000 Growth Index, Russell 2000 Value Index
Russell 2500 Index
Russell Midcap Index–Russell Midcap Growth Index, Russell Midcap Value Index
Refer to Appendix 5 for additional indices.

REMARKS

(1) The market capitalization of constituent companies ranges from a low of US$8.8 million to a high of US$2,014.0 million as of December 31, 1995. (2) Market value reflects adjustments for cross ownership. Percent of U.S. market capitalization figure is unadjusted for cross ownership.

PUBLISHER

Frank Russell Company.

RUSSELL MIDCAP INDEX

PRICE PERFORMANCE

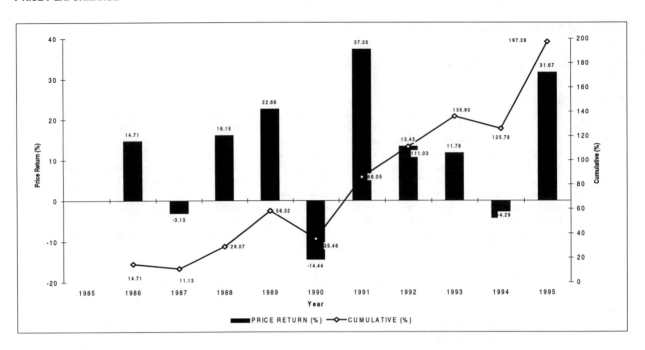

PRICE AND TOTAL RETURN PERFORMANCE

YEAR	VALUE	PRICE RETURN (%)	CUMULATIVE (%)	TOTAL RETURN (%)	MAXIMUM VALUE[1]	DATE	MINIMUM VALUE[1]	DATE
1995	805.94	31.67	197.28	34.45	811.04	5-Dec	623.82	31-Jan
1994	612.10	-4.29	125.78	-2.09	656.45	31-Jan	600.55	30-Jun
1993	639.53	11.78	135.90	14.30	639.53	31-Dec	582.17	28-Feb
1992	572.12	13.43	111.03	16.34	572.12	31-Dec	604.65	30-Jun
1991	504.40	37.35	86.05	41.70	504.40	31-Dec	391.33	31-Jan
1990	367.23	-14.44	35.46	-11.50	425.20	31-May	323.48	31-Oct
1989	429.22	22.66	58.32	26.27	445.02	31-Aug	368.16	28-Feb
1988	349.92	16.15	29.07	19.80	357.25	30-Jun	314.78	31-Jan
1987	301.27	-3.13	11.13	0.23	402.07	31-Aug	278.16	30-Nov
1986	311.00	14.71	14.71	18.20	330.17	30-Jun	276.69	31-Jan
1985	271.11							
Average Annual (%)		12.59		15.77				
Compound Annual (%)		11.51		14.68				
Standard Deviation (%)		16.19		16.53				

[1]Maximum/minimum index values are as of month-end through June 1, 1995.

SYNOPSIS
The Russell Midcap Index is a market value-weighted index that tracks the continuous price only and daily total return performance of medium sized common stocks belonging to United States (U.S.)-domiciled corporations whose shares are publicly traded. These securities, which fall within the market capitalization range of approximately US$75.6 million and US$10.0 billion, consist of the smallest 800 companies in the Russell 1000 Equity Index.

NUMBER OF STOCKS—DECEMBER 31, 1995
800

MARKET VALUE—DECEMBER 31, 1995
US$1,580,582.4 million

SELECTION CRITERIA
Constituent stocks are primarily selected on the basis total market capitalization using prices and total shares outstanding as reported by Muller Data Services. Once a year, securities are ranked by descending total market value as of May 31st. Stocks traded in the U.S. but domiciled in other countries are excluded from consideration. Also excluded from consideration are: Preferred stock; convertible preferred stock; participating preferred stock; paired shares; warrants and rights; Trust Receipts; Royalty Trusts; limited liability companies; OTC Bulletin Board companies; pink sheet-listed companies; closed-end investment companies; and limited partnerships. In the event of a merger, acquisition, bankruptcy, liquidation, or other similar corporate change causes a stock to be dropped from the index, a replacement stock is selected from a list of eligible securities.

Real Estate Investment Trusts (REITs) and Beneficial Trusts are eligible for inclusion in the index. With some exceptions (i.e., General Motors and Pittston share classes), only one class of a security is permitted into the index.

Effective as of June 30, 1991, a minimum price rule was introduced such that companies must be trading at or above $1.00 as of May 31 of each year to be eligible for inclusion in the Russell indices.

BACKGROUND
The index was introduced in 1991. Monthly index values are available on a historical basis starting December 31, 1978 and daily index values begin from June 1, 1995. Total rates of return are calculated daily after the end of each month.

BASE DATE
December 31, 1978=100.00

COMPUTATION METHODOLOGY
(1) An aggregate of prices times quantities index formula. Maintenance adjustments to the divisor for capitalization changes, new listings and delistings are made daily after the close on the day that the stock starts trading with prices reflecting the change. (2) Market capitalization is computed by adjusting on a continuous basis shares outstanding for cross ownership so as not to overstate the overall market value of constituent companies. This is accomplished by reducing the total shares outstanding by the number of shares owned by other companies, including companies outside the index, and stocks owned by foreign companies and other non-corporate entities. (3) Effective June 30, 1992, if a company is relegated to pink sheet status between reconstitution periods, it is dropped from the index at the time it is removed from the stock exchange. (4) The index is reconstituted annually, on June 30th based on May 31 market capitalizations. (5) Closing prices from the primary exchange for each stock is used.

DERIVATIVE INSTRUMENTS
None

SUBINDICES
None

RELATED INDICES
Russell 1000 Index–Russell 1000 Growth Index, Russell 1000 Value Index
Russell 2000 Index–Russell 2000 Growth Index, Russell 2000 Value Index
Russell 2500 Index,
Russell 3000 Index
Russell Midcap Growth Index, Russell Midcap Value Index
Refer to Appendix 5 for additional indices.

REMARKS
Market value reflects adjustments for cross ownership.

PUBLISHER
Frank Russell Company.

RUSSELL MIDCAP GROWTH INDEX

TOTAL RETURN PERFORMANCE

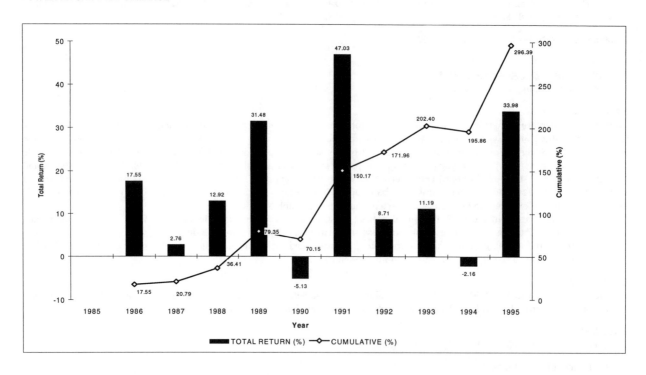

TOTAL RETURN PERFORMANCE[1]

YEAR	VALUE	TOTAL RETURN (%)	CUMULATIVE (%)	MAXIMUM VALUE	DATE	MINIMUM VALUE	DATE
1995	396.39	33.98	296.39	NA	NA	NA	NA
1994	295.86	-2.16	195.86	NA	NA	NA	NA
1993	302.40	11.19	202.40	NA	NA	NA	NA
1992	271.96	8.71	171.96	NA	NA	NA	NA
1991	250.17	47.03	150.17	NA	NA	NA	NA
1990	170.15	-5.13	70.15	NA	NA	NA	NA
1989	179.35	31.48	79.35	NA	NA	NA	NA
1988	136.41	12.92	36.41	NA	NA	NA	NA
1987	120.79	2.76	20.79	NA	NA	NA	NA
1986	117.55	17.55	17.55	NA	NA	NA	NA
1985	100.00						
Average Annual (%)		15.83					
Compound Annual (%)		14.77					
Standard Deviation (%)		16.88					

[1]Price return index value calculations commenced May, 31, 1995.

SYNOPSIS
The Russell Midcap Growth Index is a market value-weighted index that tracks the continuous price only and daily total return performance of growth oriented investable common stocks of medium sized United States (U.S.)-domiciled corporations whose shares are publicly traded. These securities represent a subset of the stocks that make up the Russell Midcap Index with a greater-than-average growth orientation. Securities in this index tend to exhibit higher price-to-book and price-earnings ratios, lower dividend yields and higher forecasted growth values than the more value oriented securities in the Russell Midcap Value Index.

NUMBER OF STOCKS—DECEMBER 31, 1995
509

MARKET VALUE—DECEMBER 31, 1995
US$774,742.2 million

SELECTION CRITERIA
Eligible securities consist of members of the Russell Midcap Index which are selected on the basis of the following guidelines:
(1) The 800 securities that make up the Russell Midcap Index are ranked by their adjusted book-to-price ratio as well as their Institutional Brokers' Estimate System (I/B/E/S) forecasted long-term growth mean. (2) Companies are ranked in ascending price-to-book value order and in descending I/B/E/S long-term growth mean value. A composite rank is determined on the basis of these two variables by converting them to standardized units which are combined to create a composite score. (3) The constituents are ranked by their composite value score and breakpoints are determined by cumulative available market capitalization to create the three ranges of securities. (4) Using a probability algorithm, companies in the Russell Midcap Index are assigned a probability of being a growth or value stock. Roughly 70% are classified as either all growth or all value. The remaining 30% are assigned a probability of both value and growth. (5) Companies with probabilities of 100% growth or 100% value are placed entirely in the growth or value index. (6) Companies with a hybrid probability of part growth, part value are held in both indices with a weight corresponding to their probability, based on market capitalization. Accordingly, the sum of the securities in the Russell Midcap Growth and Midcap Value indices will not be equal to the Russell Midcap Index, but the sum of the available market capitalization will correspond to the Russell Midcap Index.

For additional information, refer to the Russell Midcap Index.

BACKGROUND
The Russell Midcap Index was introduced in 1991 and calculations of the price only growth and value subindices commenced on a daily basis as of May 31, 1995. Total rates of return are available as of December 31, 1985.

BASE DATE
May 31, 1995=300.00

COMPUTATION METHODOLOGY
(1) An aggregate of prices times quantities index formula. Maintenance adjustments to the divisor for capitalization changes, new listings and delistings are made daily after the close on the day that the stock starts trading with prices reflecting the change. (2) Market capitalization is computed by adjusting, on a continuous basis, shares outstanding for cross ownership so as not to overstate the overall market value of constituent companies. This is accomplished by reducing the total shares outstanding by the number of shares owned by other companies, including companies outside the index, and stocks owned by foreign companies and other non-corporate entities. (3) Effective June 30, 1992, if a company is relegated to pink sheet status between reconstitution periods, it is dropped from the index at the time it is removed from the stock exchange. (4) The index is reconstituted annually, on June 30th based on May 31 market capitalizations. (5) Closing prices from the primary exchange for each stock is used.

DERIVATIVE INSTRUMENTS
None

SUBINDICES
None

RELATED INDICES
Russell 1000 Index–Russell 1000 Growth Index, Russell 1000 Value Index
Russell 2000 Index–Russell 2000 Growth Index, Russell 2000 Value Index
Russell 2500 Index
Russell 3000 Index
Russell Midcap Index, Russell Midcap Value Index
Refer to Appendix 5 for additional indices.

REMARKS
Market value reflects adjustments for cross ownership.

PUBLISHER
Frank Russell Company.

RUSSELL MIDCAP VALUE INDEX

TOTAL RETURN PERFORMANCE

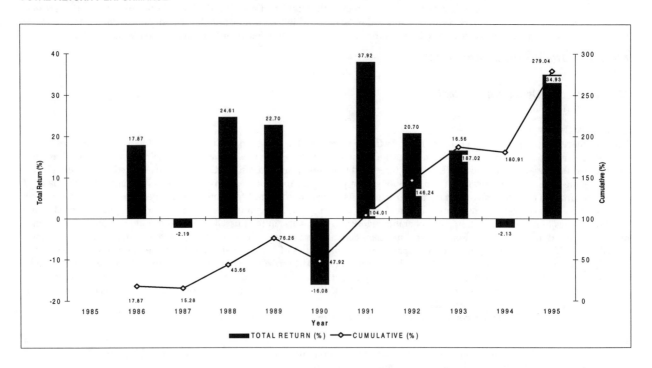

TOTAL RETURN PERFORMANCE[1]

YEAR	VALUE	TOTAL RETURN (%)	CUMULATIVE (%)	MAXIMUM VALUE	DATE	MINIMUM VALUE	DATE
1995	379.04	34.93	279.04	NA	NA	NA	NA
1994	280.91	-2.13	180.91	NA	NA	NA	NA
1993	287.02	16.56	187.02	NA	NA	NA	NA
1992	246.24	20.70	146.24	NA	NA	NA	NA
1991	204.01	37.92	104.01	NA	NA	NA	NA
1990	147.92	-16.08	47.92	NA	NA	NA	NA
1989	176.26	22.70	76.26	NA	NA	NA	NA
1988	143.66	24.61	43.66	NA	NA	NA	NA
1987	115.28	-2.19	15.28	NA	NA	NA	NA
1986	117.87	17.87	17.87	NA	NA	NA	NA
1985	100.00						
Average Annual (%)		15.49					
Compound Annual (%)		14.25					
Standard Deviation (%)		17.23					

[1]Price return index value calculations commenced May 31, 1995.

SYNOPSIS

The Russell Midcap Value Index is a market value-weighted index that tracks the continuous price only and daily total return performance of value oriented investable common stocks of United States (U.S.)-domiciled corporations whose shares are publicly traded. These securities represent a subset of the stocks that make up the Russell Midcap Index with a less-than-average growth orientation. Securities in this index generally have low price-to-book and price-earnings ratios, higher dividend yields, and lower forecasted growth values than the more growth oriented securities in the Russell Midcap Growth Index.

NUMBER OF STOCKS—DECEMBER 31, 1995

497

MARKET VALUE—DECEMBER 31, 1995

US$805,840 million

SELECTION CRITERIA

Eligible securities consist of members of the Russell Midcap Index which are selected on the basis of the following guidelines:
(1) The 800 securities that make up the Russell Midcap Index are ranked by their adjusted book-to-price ratio as well as their Institutional Brokers' Estimate System (I/B/E/S) forecasted long-term growth mean. (2) Companies are ranked in ascending price-to-book value order and in descending I/B/E/S long-term growth mean value. A composite rank is determined on the basis of these two variables by converting them to standardized units which are combined to create a composite score. (3) The constituents are ranked by their composite value score and breakpoints are determined by cumulative available market capitalization to create three ranges of securities. (4) Using a probability algorithm, companies in the Russell Midcap Index are assigned a probability of being a growth or value stock. Roughly 70% are classified as either all growth or all value. The remaining 30% are assigned a probability of both value and growth. (5) Companies with probabilities of 100% growth or 100% value are placed entirely in the growth or value index. (6) Companies with a hybrid probability of part growth part value are held in both indices with a weight corresponding to their probability, based on market capitalization. Accordingly, the sum of the securities in the Russell Midcap Growth and Midcap Value indices will not be equal to the Russell Midcap Index, but the sum of the available market capitalization will correspond to the Russell Midcap Index.

For additional information, refer to the Russell Midcap Index.

BACKGROUND

The Russell Midcap Index was introduced in 1991 and calculations of the price only growth and value subindices commenced on a daily basis as of May 31, 1995. Total rates of return are available as of December 31, 1985.

BASE DATE

May 31, 1995=300.00

COMPUTATION METHODOLOGY

(1) An aggregate of prices times quantities index formula. Maintenance adjustments to the divisor for capitalization changes, new listings and delistings are made daily after the close on the day that the stock starts trading with prices reflecting the change. (2) Market capitalization is computed by adjusting on a continuous basis shares outstanding for cross ownership so as not to overstate the overall market value of constituent companies. This is accomplished by reducing the total shares outstanding by the number of shares owned by other companies, including companies outside the index, and stocks owned by foreign companies and other non-corporate entities. (3) Effective June 30, 1992, if a company is relegated to pink sheet status between reconstitution periods, it is dropped from the index at the time it is removed from the stock exchange. (4) The index is reconstituted annually, on June 30th based on May 31 market capitalizations. (5) Closing prices from the primary exchange for each stock is used.

DERIVATIVE INSTRUMENTS

None

SUBINDICES

None

RELATED INDICES

Russell Top 200 Index–Russell Top 200 Growth Index, Russell Top 200 Value Index
Russell 1000 Index–Russell 1000 Growth Index, Russell 1000 Value Index
Russell 2000 Index–Russell 2000 Growth Index, Russell 2000 Value Index
Russell 2500 Index
Russell 3000 Index
Russell Midcap Index, Russell Midcap Growth Index
Refer to Appendix 5 for additional indices.

REMARKS

Market value reflects adjustments for cross ownership.

PUBLISHER

Frank Russell Company.

STANDARD & POOR'S 100 (S&P 100) INDEX (OEX)

PRICE PERFORMANCE

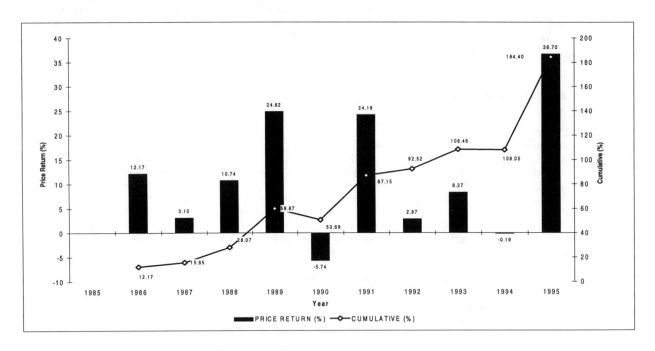

PRICE AND TOTAL RETURN PERFORMANCE

YEAR	VALUE	PRICE RETURN (%)	CUMULATIVE (%)	TOTAL RETURN (%)	MAXIMUM VALUE	DATE	MINIMUM VALUE	DATE
1995	585.92	36.70	184.40	40.09	597.24	13-Dec	428.40	3-Jan
1994	428.63	-0.19	108.05	2.60	446.67	2-Feb	406.90	4-Apr
1993	429.46	8.27	108.46	11.19	434.73	28-Dec	389.93	8-Jan
1992	396.64	2.87	92.52	5.93	403.40	18-Dec	368.57	9-Oct
1991	385.56	24.19	87.15	28.17	385.56	31-Dec	292.11	9-Jan
1990	310.45	-5.74	50.69	-2.26	350.81	16-Jul	280.12	11-Oct
1989	329.36	24.82	59.87	29.20	334.65	9-Oct	261.02	3-Jan
1988	263.86	10.74	28.07	14.77	267.21	25-Oct	232.45	20-Jan
1987	238.26	3.10	15.65	6.15	332.27	25-Aug	216.12	19-Oct
1986	231.09	12.17	12.17	15.99	241.00	3-Dec	196.71	22-Jan
1985	206.02							
Average Annual (%)		11.69		15.18				
Compound Annual (%)		11.02		14.50				
Standard Deviation (%)		13.18		13.47				

Synopsis

The Standard & Poor's 100 (S&P 100) Index (OEX) is a market value-weighted index that tracks the continuous price only and daily total return performance of the 100 largest constituent stocks that make up the broader Standard & Poor's 500 (S&P 500) Composite Stock Price Index. The shares account for 28% of the United States (U.S.) market capitalization and about 42% of the market value of the S&P 500 Index.

Number of Stocks—December 31, 1995

100

Market Value—December 31, 1995

US$1,926,110.0 million

Selection Criteria

Index members consist of the 100 largest constituent stocks that make up the broader S&P 500 Index. For additional information, refer to the S&P 500 Composite Stock Price Index.

Background

The Chicago Board Options Exchange (CBOE) developed the CBOE 100 Index in early 1983 and options on the index commenced trading on March 1, 1983. At its inception, the index consisted of the 100 largest capitalization stocks on which options were written on the floor of the CBOE. On July 1, 1983, through mutual agreement with Standard & Poor's Corp., the index was officially renamed the S&P 100 Index. Today, an Index Committee at Standard & Poor's Corp. has responsibility for determining the overall policy and objectives of the index and establishing the criteria for adding and deleting member companies.

Daily index values were computed until March 1, 1985, and hourly thereafter.

Base Date

January 2, 1976=100.00

Computation Methodology

(1) An aggregate of prices times quantities index formula. Maintenance adjustment to the S&P 500 Index also affect each of the major industry group subindices as well as the individual industry groups. Maintenance adjustments to the divisor are made for capitalization changes, namely share issuance, share repurchases, special cash dividends, rights offerings and spin-offs, new listings and delistings. All stock splits and stock dividend adjustments are made on the day before the ex-dividend date. These and all adjustments are made after the close of trading and after the calculation of the closing value of the index. Whenever possible, additions and deletions of constituent companies may be announced up to five business days in advance of their implementation, in accordance with a preannouncement policy announced by Standard & Poor's in 1989. (2) The number of common shares outstanding, for purposes of calculating market capitalization, is updated quarterly. Daily monitoring and weekly reviews, however, are conducted to screen out a 5% increase or decrease in shares outstanding relative to the prior week. Once verified, a maintenance adjustment to the index may be implemented in the event of a difference of 5% or more, if appropriate, after the close of trading on Wednesday of the following week. Otherwise, adjustments to shares outstanding are implemented on a quarterly basis. (3) The final S&P 100 closing value is calculated on the basis of last-trade prices on the New York Stock Exchange (NYSE), the American Stock Exchange (AMEX) and the Nasdaq/National Market System (Nasdaq/NMS). (4) Total return calculations assume the reinvestment of dividends on a daily basis. Monthly, quarterly and annual total rates of return are calculated on the basis of daily compounding of reinvested dividends.

Derivative Instruments

(1) S&P 100 Index options trade on the Chicago Board Options Exchange (CBOE). (2) Long-term Equity Anticipation Securities (LEAPS) and Long Term Index Options trade on the Chicago Board Options Exchange (CBOE). (3) Caps for retail investors and SPX Caps for institutional investors trade on the Chicago Board Options Exchange (CBOE). (4) FLEX Options trade on the Chicago Board Options Exchange (CBOE).

Subindices

None

Related Indices

S&P 500 Composite Stock Price Index
S&P 1500 Supercomposite Index
S&P SmallCap 600 Index
S&P MidCap 400 Index
S&P/BARRA Growth Index
S&P/BARRA Value Index
FT/S&P Actuaries World Index
Refer to Appendix 5 for additional indices.

Remarks

None

Publisher

Standard & Poor's Corporation (S&P Corp.).

STANDARD & POOR'S 500 (S&P 500) COMPOSITE STOCK PRICE INDEX

PRICE PERFORMANCE

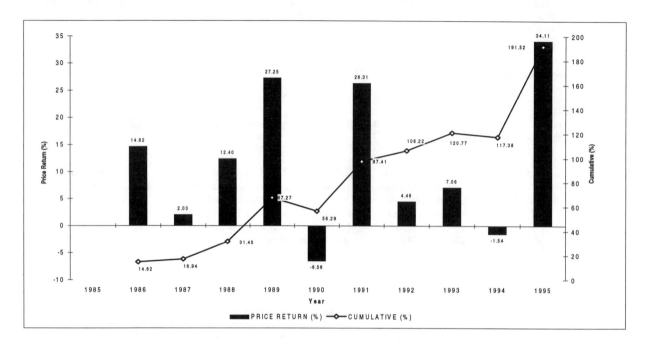

PRICE AND TOTAL RETURN PERFORMANCE

YEAR	VALUE	PRICE RETURN (%)	CUMULATIVE (%)	TOTAL RETURN (%)	MAXIMUM VALUE	DATE	MINIMUM VALUE	DATE
1995	615.93	34.11	191.52	37.62	621.69	13-Dec	459.11	3-Jan
1994	459.27	-1.54	117.38	1.32	482.00	2-Feb	438.92	4-Apr
1993	466.45	7.06	120.77	10.08	470.94	28-Dec	429.05	8-Jan
1992	435.71	4.46	106.22	7.62	441.28	18-Dec	394.50	8-Apr
1991	417.09	26.31	97.41	30.47	417.09	31-Dec	311.49	9-Jan
1990	330.22	-6.56	56.29	-3.10	368.95	16-Jul	295.46	11-Oct
1989	353.40	27.25	67.27	31.69	359.80	9-Oct	275.31	3-Jan
1988	277.72	12.40	31.45	16.61	283.66	21-Oct	242.63	20-Jan
1987	247.08	2.03	16.94	5.10	336.77	25-Aug	223.92	4-Dec
1986	242.17	14.62	14.62	18.56	254.00	2-Dec	205.96	10-Jan
1985	211.28							
Average Annual (%)		12.01		15.60				
Compound Annual (%)		11.29		14.86				
Standard Deviation (%)		13.51		13.88				

Synopsis

The S&P 500 Index is a market capitalization-weighted index that tracks the continuous price only and daily total return performance of 500 common stocks of leading domestic and foreign companies in leading industries within the United States (U.S.) that are listed on the New York Stock Exchange (NYSE), the American Stock Exchange (AMEX) and the Nasdaq National Market System (Nasdaq/NMS). The S&P 500, a measure of large-capitalization stocks, accounts for about 64% of the market value of shares listed on the three exchanges.

Number of Stocks—December 31, 1995

500

Market Value—December 31, 1995

US$4,588,269.5 million

Selection Criteria

The index matches, as closely as practicable, the economic sector distribution of securities drawn from the NYSE, the AMEX, and Nasdaq/NMS. Stocks added must represent a viable enterprise, be representative of the industry group it is assigned and its market price movements must, in general, be responsive to changes in industry affairs.The aggregate market value of the stock and its trading activity are also considered in the selection process. Index members consist of common share classes, including "A," "B" and "C" classes used in the calculation of primary earnings and dividends per share for the company's income statement. Excluded are special classes of common stock not used in the calculation of primary earnings and dividends per share for the company's income statement, preferred stock, convertible stock, foreign companies whose stocks trade as American Depositary Receipts (ADRs) or as American Depositary Shares (ADSs), mutual funds, limited partnerships, Royalty Trusts and Real Estate Investment Trusts (REITs) Equity Participation Units, warrants, rights, stock options and treasury stock.

Eligible common stocks are first ranked by their market value within their respective industry sectors, then the S&P Index Committee, which is responsible for the overall management of the index, policy guidelines and the establishment of criteria for adding or deleting a company, conducts quantitative screening and detailed fundamental analysis, using market statistics, financial statements and company operations, in the process of adding or withdrawing from the index. Companies selected must: (1) Generally have the largest market value within their industry. (2) Represent important industry segments within the U.S. economy. (Companies in emerging or new industries that are not currently representedrare not precluded from consideration, provided they satisfy all other guidelines.). (3) Have outstanding common stock ownership which is widely held (holdings are screened to avoid closely-held companies). (4) Have common stock which evidences ample liquidity and efficient share pricing. (Public float and liquidity/turnover ratios are examined, however, low turnover does not preclude eligibility. Companies with low turnover ratios due to large institutional holdings and significant long term holdings have been accepted.). (5) Be relatively stable, to minimize index turnover.

The capitalization activities of index components are monitored and developments involving mergers, acquisitions, and restructurings are analyzed and the most appropriate action is taken. Constituents are removed due to mergers, acquisitions, bankruptcies or lack of industry group representation or criteria for inclusion. Companies undergoing a restructuring are analyzed for possible withdrawal.

Background

The index was created in 1923 to provide professional investors a basis for comparing the performance of their stock portfolios to that of a market indicator (the only existing stock market indicator, the Dow Jones Industrial Average (DJIA), did not address this need.). At its inception, the index covered 233 stocks representing 26 industry subgroups selected from NYSE-listed common stocks. Separate indices were created for each industry group, with historical information dating back to 1918. In 1926, in response to the need for more frequent computation of its market indicator, S&P Corp. created the 90 Stock Composite Index which was calculated on an hourly and daily basis and consisted of 50 industrials, 20 rails, and 20 utilities from the universe of 233 stocks. The industry group indices along with the 233 composite index continued to be calculated weekly.

Continued on next page.

By 1941 there were 416 companies concentrated within 72 industry groups. In 1957, the index was expanded to include 500 stocks, with 83 industry groups which formed three main sector groups: 425 industrials, 60 utilities, and 15 rails.In July 1976, issues listed on the AMEX and the Over-the Counter (OTC) market became eligible and the number of main sector groups was expanded to four, including 400 industrials, 40 utilities, 20 transportation, and 40 financial companies. Bank and insurance stocks, both NYSE- and OTC-traded issues, which had been excluded for technical reasons, were added. As a result, the sectors became more representative and the overall index had more strength and breadth. Greater flexibility in the construction of the index was introduced as of April 6, 1988–a fixed number of companies within the four broad S&P sector groups was eliminated, and selection of new companies when openings arose and in switching between sectors as the nature of the business of companies changed. During 1988, S&P Corp. also began daily calculations on a total rate of return basis. As of December 31, 1995, the index included 371 industrials, 15 transportation, 49 utilities, and 65 financials.

S&P 500 index values are calculated as frequently as every second each day during trading hours; official values are disseminated at 15-second intervals. Daily closing price only values are calculated by 4:30 PM or later. Daily prices for the S&P 500, first published on March 1, 1957, have been extended back to 1918 by linking the S&P 500 to the 90 Stock Composite, using the 1941-1943 base period value.

BASE DATE
Base period of 1941-1943=10.00

COMPUTATION METHODOLOGY
(1) Aggregate market value-weighted arithmetic average of the price ratios index formula, expressed in relatives to the average weekly values. Maintenance adjustments to the divisor are made for capitalization changes, namely share issuance, share repurchases, special cash dividends, rights offerings and spin-offs, new listings and delistings. All stock splits and stock dividend adjustments are made on the day before the ex-dividend date after the close of trading and after the calculation of the closing value of the index. Additions and deletions may be announced up to five business days in advance of their implementation, by policy announced in 1989. (2) The number of common shares outstanding, for purposes of calculating market capitalization, is updated quarterly. Daily monitoring and weekly reviews, however, are conducted to screen out a 5% increase or decrease in shares outstanding relative to the prior week. Once a difference of 5% or more is verified, a maintenance adjustment may be implemented, if appropriate, after the close of trading on Wednesday of the following week. (3) The final S&P 500 closing value is calculated on the basis of last-trade prices on the NYSE, the AMEX and the Nasdaq/NMS. (4) Monthly, quarterly and annual total rates of return are calculated on the basis of daily compounding of reinvested dividends.

DERIVATIVE INSTRUMENTS
(1) S&P 500 options contracts trade on the Chicago Board Options Exchange (CBOE). (2) S&P 500 futures and futures options trade on the Chicago Mercantile Exchange. (3) S&P 500 CAPS trade on the CBOE. (4) S&P 500 Index-Long-Term Options trade on the CBOE. (5) S&P 500 End-of-Quarter Options trade on the CBOE. (6) Flexible Exchange Options (FLEX) trade on the CBOE. (7) SPX Long-term Equity Anticipation Securities (LEAPS) trade on the CBOE. (8) Indexed debt and indexed Certificate of Deposit. (9) Index Participations are offered by the American Stock Exchange and the Philadelphia Stock Exchange (PHLX). (10) S&P Depository Receipts (SPDRs) and Equity Index Participations (EIP) trade on the American Stock Exchange. (11) Cash Index Participation Products trade on the Philadelphia Stock Exchange. (12) Exchange Stock Portfolios (ESP) trade on the New York Stock Exchange.

SUBINDICES
Four broad sector subindices: S&P Industrial Index, S&P Transportation Index, S&P Utilities Index and S&P Financial Index. Eighty-nine industry group subindices. Refer to the four broad sector subindices for a complete list.

RELATED INDICES
S&P 1500 Supercomposite Index
S&P SmallCap 600 Index
S&P MidCap 400 Index
S&P 100 Index
S&P/BARRA Growth Index
S&P/BARRA Value Index
FT/S&P Actuaries World Index
Refer to Appendix 5 for additional indices.

(1) The index is widely recognized and serves as a common yardstick against which all U.S. stock performance is measured. It is especially used to compare and evaluate the performance of institutional portfolios and has become one of the U.S. Department of Commerce's 12 Leading Economic Indicators. (2) Index constituents include 12 foreign-based companies and their regular shares that trade on U.S. exchanges are used in the calculation of the index. (3) Three total return series are calculated: (A) The 1936 total return index, calculated quarterly with dividends reinvested during the period 1937-1988 and daily thereafter; (B) The 1970 total return index, calculated monthly with dividends reinvested since 1988 and daily thereafter; (C) The 1988 total return index, calculated daily with dividends reinvested since its January 1, 1988 base date.

PUBLISHER
Standard & Poor's Corporation (S&P Corp.).

STANDARD & POOR'S (S&P) FINANCIAL PRICE INDEX

PRICE PERFORMANCE

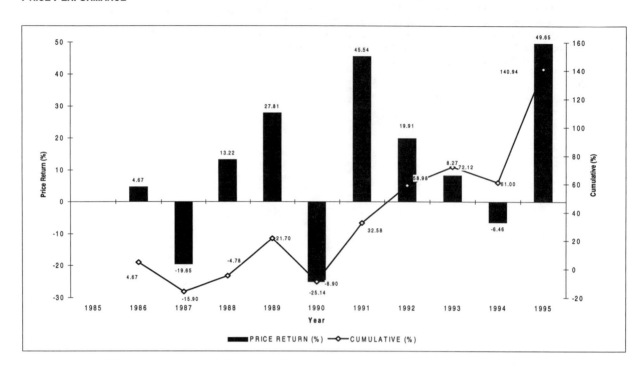

PRICE AND TOTAL RETURN PERFORMANCE

YEAR	VALUE	PRICE RETURN (%)	CUMULATIVE (%)	TOTAL RETURN (%)	MAXIMUM VALUE	DATE	MINIMUM VALUE	DATE
1995	61.97	49.65	140.94	54.02	63.66	6-Dec	41.64	3-Jan
1994	41.41	-6.46	61.00	-3.54	46.94	14-Jun	39.87	22-Nov
1993	44.27	8.27	72.12	11.10	48.40	28-Sep	39.89	8-Jan
1992	40.89	19.91	58.98	23.37	41.07	30-Dec	32.40	8-Apr
1991	34.10	45.54	32.58	50.74	34.27	30-Dec	21.97	9-Jan
1990	23.43	-25.14	-8.90	-21.43	31.87	3-Jan	18.80	29-Oct
1989	31.30	27.81	21.70	32.65	35.24	9-Oct	24.30	3-Jan
1988	24.49	13.22	-4.78	18.36	24.68	21-Oct	21.51	8-Jan
1987	21.63	-19.65	-15.90	-16.77	32.56	17-Aug	20.39	7-Dec
1986	26.92	4.67	4.67	8.00	31.13	14-Mar	25.19	22-Jan
1985	25.72							
Average Annual (%)		11.78		15.65				
Compound Annual (%)		9.19		13.03				
Standard Deviation (%)		25.05		25.68				

SYNOPSIS

The Standard & Poor's (S&P) Financial Price Index is a market value-weighted subindex that tracks the continuous price only and monthly total return performance of stocks in the financial sector of the Standard & Poor's 500 (S&P 500) Composite Stock Price Index. The index includes various banks, savings and loans, life insurance, property and casualty insurance, and other miscellaneous financial companies.

NUMBER OF STOCKS—DECEMBER 31, 1995
65

MARKET VALUE—DECEMBER 31, 1995
US$602,747.0 million

SELECTION CRITERIA
Constituents must qualify for inclusion in the S&P 500 Index on the basis of guidelines established by the Standard & Poor's Index Committee are selected from a universe of domestic and foreign companies with "A," "B" and "C" share classes that are used in the calculation of primary earnings and dividends per share for the company's income statement and are traded on the New York Stock Exchange (NYSE), the American Stock Exchange (AMEX) and the Nasdaq National Market System (Nasdaq/NMS). Excluded from consideration are special classes of common stock that are not used in the calculation of primary earnings and dividends per share for the company's income statement, preferred stock, convertible stock, foreign companies whose stocks trade as American Depositary Receipts (ADRs) or as American Depositary Shares (ADSs), mutual funds, limited partnerships, Royalty Trusts and Real Estate Investment Trusts (REITs) Equity Participation Units, warrants, rights, stock options and treasury stock.

For additional information, refer to the Standard & Poor's 500 Composite Stock Price Index.

BACKGROUND
The subindex has been modified and expanded over time. In July 1976 issues listed on the AMEX and the Over-the Counter (OTC) market became eligible for inclusion in the index and the number of main sector groups was expanded to four, including 400 industrials, 40 utilities, 20 transportation, and 40 financial companies. Moreover, bank and insurance stocks, both NYSE and OTC-traded issues, which had been excluded from the index for technical reasons, were added to the index.

Greater flexibility was introduced into the construction of the index as of April 6, 1988 with the elimination of a fixed number of companies within the four broad S&P sector groups, including the financial sector, in choosing new companies for the index when openings arose and in switching companies between sectors as the nature of the business of individual companies changes.

For additional information, refer to the Standard & Poor's 500 Composite Stock Price Index.

BASE DATE
1970=10.00

COMPUTATION METHODOLOGY
(1) An aggregate of prices times quantities index formula. Maintenance adjustment to the S&P 500 Index also affect each of the major industry group subindices as well as the individual industry groups. Maintenance adjustments to the divisor are made for capitalization changes, namely share issuance, share repurchases, special cash dividends, rights offerings and spin-offs, new listings and delistings. All stock splits and stock dividend adjustments are made on the day before the ex-dividend date. These and all adjustments are made after the close of trading and after the calculation of the closing value of the index. Whenever possible, additions and deletions of constituent companies may be announced up to five business days in advance of their implementation, in accordance with a preannouncement policy set by Standard & Poor's in 1989. (2) The number of common shares outstanding, for purposes of calculating market capitalization, is updated quarterly. Daily monitoring and weekly reviews, however, are conducted to screen out a 5% increase or decrease in shares outstanding relative to the prior week. Once verified, a maintenance adjustment to the index may be implemented in the event of a difference of 5% or more, if appropriate, after the close of trading on Wednesday of the following week. Otherwise, adjustments to shares outstanding are implemented on a quarterly basis. (3) The final closing value is calculated on the basis of last-trade prices on the NYSE, AMEX and Nasdaq/NMS. (4) Total return calculations assume the reinvestment of dividends on a daily basis. Quarterly and annual total rates of return are calculated on the basis of monthly compounding of reinvested dividends.

DERIVATIVE INSTRUMENTS
S&P Banks Index options (BIX) trade on The Chicago Board Options Exchange (CBOE).
S&P Insurance Index options (IUX) trade on The Chicago Board Options Exchange (CBOE).

SUBINDICES
Nine financial industry group subindices: Financial miscellaneous, life insurance, major regional banks, money center banks, multi-line insurance, other major banks, personal loans, property-casualty insurance, and savings and loan companies.

RELATED INDICES
S&P 1500 Supercomposite Index
S&P SmallCap 600 Index
S&P MidCap 400 Index
S&P 100 Index
S&P/BARRA Growth Index
S&P/BARRA Value Index
FT/S&P Actuaries World Index
Refer to Appendix 5 for additional indices.

REMARKS
None

PUBLISHER
Standard & Poor's Corporation (S&P Corp.).

STANDARD & POOR'S (S&P) INDUSTRIALS PRICE INDEX

PRICE PERFORMANCE

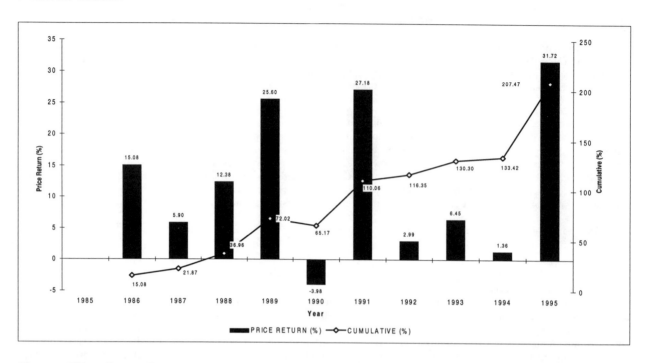

PRICE AND TOTAL RETURN PERFORMANCE

YEAR	VALUE	PRICE RETURN (%)	CUMULATIVE (%)	TOTAL RETURN (%)	MAXIMUM VALUE	DATE	MINIMUM VALUE	DATE
1995	721.19	31.72	207.47	34.59	731.65	13-Dec	546.27	3-Jan
1994	547.51	1.36	133.42	3.82	562.99	28-Oct	510.04	20-Apr
1993	540.19	6.45	130.30	9.03	453.86	28-Dec	496.48	26-Apr
1992	507.46	2.99	116.35	5.70	515.75	18-Dec	470.91	8-Apr
1991	492.72	27.18	110.06	30.76	492.72	31-Dec	364.90	9-Jan
1990	387.42	-3.98	65.17	-0.89	437.37	16-Jul	346.86	11-Oct
1989	403.49	25.60	72.02	29.41	410.49	9-Oct	318.66	3-Jan
1988	321.26	12.38	36.96	16.00	358.12	6-Jan	278.41	20-Jan
1987	285.86	5.90	21.87	8.68	326.84	21-Oct	278.41	20-Jan
1986	269.93	15.08	15.08	18.63	393.17	25-Aug	255.43	4-Dec
1985	234.56							
Average Annual (%)		12.47		15.57				
Compound Annual (%)		11.89		14.98				
Standard Deviation (%)		12.15		12.43				

SYNOPSIS

The Standard & Poor's (S&P) Industrials Price Index is a market value-weighted subindex that tracks the continuous price only and monthly total return performance of stocks in the industrial sector of the Standard & Poor's 500 (S&P 500) Composite Stock Price Index.

NUMBER OF STOCKS—DECEMBER 31, 1995
371

MARKET VALUE—DECEMBER 31, 1995
US$3,456,523.0 million

SELECTION CRITERIA

Constituents must qualify for inclusion in the S&P 500 Index on the basis of guidelines established by the Standard & Poor's Index Committee are selected from a universe of domestic and foreign companies with "A," "B" and "C" share classes, that are used in the calculation of primary earnings and dividends per share for the company's income statement, and are traded on the New York Stock Exchange (NYSE), the American Stock Exchange (AMEX) and the Nasdaq National Market System (Nasdaq/nms). Excluded from consideration are special classes of common stock that are not used in the calculation of primary earnings and dividends per share for the company's income statement, preferred stock, convertible stock, foreign companies whose stocks trade as American

Depositary Receipts (ADRs) or as American Depositary Shares (ADSs), mutual funds, limited partnerships, Royalty Trusts and Real Estate Investment Trusts (REITs) Equity Participation Units, warrants, rights, stock options and treasury stock.

For additional information, refer to the Standard & Poor's 500 Composite Stock Price Index.

BACKGROUND

The subindex, with its origins dating back to the formation of the S&P 500 in 1923, has been modified and expanded over time. In 1957, the fixed number of constituent stocks was expanded to 425 industrial companies.

Other significant changes were introduced in July 1976 when issues listed on the American Stock Exchange and the Over-the Counter (OTC) market became eligible for inclusion in the index and the number of main sector groups was expanded to four, including 400 industrials, 40 utilities, 20 transportation, and 40 financial companies. Greater flexibility was introduced into the construction of the index as of April 6, 1988 with the elimination of a fixed number of companies within the four broad S&P sector groups, including the industrials sector, in choosing new companies for the index when openings arose and in switching companies between sectors as the nature of the business of individual companies changes.

For additional information, refer to the Standard & Poor's 500 Composite Stock Price Index.

BASE DATE

1941-1943=10.00

COMPUTATION METHODOLOGY

(1) An aggregate of prices times quantities index formula, expressed in relatives to the average weekly value established during the based period 1941-1943. Maintenance adjustment to the S&P 500 Index also affect each of the major industry group subindices as well as the individual industry groups. Maintenance adjustments to the divisor are made for capitalization changes, namely share issuance, share repurchases, special cash dividends, rights offerings and spin-offs, new listings and delistings. All stock splits and stock dividend adjustments are made on the day before the ex-dividend date. These and all adjustments are made after the close of trading and after the calculation of the closing value of the index. Whenever possible, additions and deletions of constituent companies may be announced up to five business days in advance of their implementation, in accordance with a preannouncement policy set by Standard & Poor's in 1989. (2) The number of common shares outstanding, for purposes of calculating market capitalization, is updated quarterly. Daily monitoring and weekly reviews, however, are conducted to screen out a 5% increase or decrease in shares outstanding relative to the prior week. Once verified, a maintenance adjustment to the index may be implemented in the event of a difference of 5% or more, if appropriate, after the close of trading on Wednesday of the following week. Otherwise, adjustments to shares outstanding are implemented on a quarterly basis. (3) The final closing value is calculated on the basis of last-trade prices on the NYSE, AMEX and Nasdaq/NMS. (4) Total return calculations assume the reinvestment of dividends on a daily basis. Quarterly and annual total rates of return are calculated on the basis of monthly compounding of reinvested dividends.

DERIVATIVE INSTRUMENTS

S&P Health Care Index options (HCX) trade on the Chicago Board Options Exchange (CBOE).
S&P Chemical Index options (CEX) trade on the Chicago Board Options Exchange (CBOE).
S&P Retail Index options (RLX) trade on the Chicago Board Options Exchange (CBOE).

SUBINDICES

Seventy-two industrial group subindices: Aerospace/Defense, Aluminum, Auto Parts (After Market), Automobile, Beverages (Alcoholic), Beverages (Soft Drinks), Broadcast Media, Building Materials, Chemicals, Chemicals (Diversified), Chemicals (Specialty), Coal, Commercial Services, Communications Equipment/Manufacturers, Computer Software and Services, Computer Systems, Conglomerates, Containers (Metal and Glass), Containers (Paper), Cosmetics, Electrical Equipment, Electronics (Defense), Electronics (Instrumentation), Electronics (Semiconductors), Engineering and Construction, Entertainment, Foods, Food Wholesalers, Gold Mining, Hardware and Tools, Health Care (Diversified), Health Care (Drugs), Health Care (Miscellaneous), Heavy Duty Trucks and Parts, Home-building, Hospital Management, Hotel/Motel, Household Furniture and Appliances, Household Products, Housewares, Insurance Brokers, Leisure Time, Machine Tools, Machinery (Diversified), Manufactured Housing, Manufacturing (Diversified), Medical Products and Supplies, Metals (Miscellaneous), Miscellaneous, Office Equipment and Supplies, Oil Gas and Drilling, Oil (Domestic Integrated), Oil (Exploration and Production), Oil (International Integrated), Oil Well Equipment and Services, Paper and Forest Products, Pollution Control, Publishing, Publishing (Newspapers), Restaurants, Retail (Department Stores), Retail (Drug Stores), Retail (Food Chains), Retail (General Merchandise), Retail (Specialty), Retail (Specialty-Apparel), Shoes, Steel, Telecommunications (Long Distance), Textile (Apparel Manufacturers), Tobacco and Toys.

RELATED INDICES

S&P 1500 Supercomposite Index
S&P SmallCap 600 Index
S&P MidCap 400 Index
S&P 100 Index
S&P/BARRA Growth Index
S&P/BARRA Value Index
FT/S&P Actuaries World Index
Refer to Appendix 5 for additional indices.

PUBLISHER

Standard & Poor's Corporation (S&P Corp.).

STANDARD & POOR'S (S&P) MIDCAP 400 INDEX

PRICE PERFORMANCE

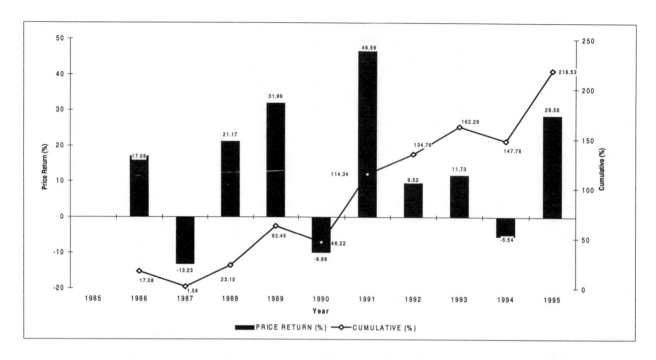

PRICE AND TOTAL RETURN PERFORMANCE[1]

YEAR	VALUE	PRICE RETURN (%)	CUMULATIVE (%)	TOTAL RETURN (%)	MAXIMUM VALUE[2]	DATE	MINIMUM VALUE[2]	DATE
1995	217.84	28.56	218.53	30.95	219.80	4-Dec	168.04	3-Jan
1994	169.44	-5.54	147.76	-3.58	184.79	18-Mar	162.44	24-Jun
1993	179.38	11.73	162.29	13.96	179.38	31-Dec	155.71	22-Feb
1992	160.55	9.52	134.76	11.91	160.56	31-Dec	136.02	25-Jun
1991	146.59	46.59	114.34	50.10	146.59	31-Dec	95.16	14-Jan
1990	100.00	-9.99	46.22	-5.12	115.89	31-Jul	91.48	30-Nov
1989	111.10	31.96	62.45	35.54	113.97	31-Oct	87.31	31-Jan
1988	84.19	21.17	23.10	20.87	87.60	31-Jul	74.67	31-Dec
1987	69.48	-13.23	1.59	-2.03	96.33	31-Oct	69.48	31-Dec
1986	80.07	17.08	17.08	16.21	86.72	31-Jul	71.60	31-Jan
1985	68.39							
Average Annual (%)		13.79		16.88				
Compound Annual (%)		12.28		15.64				
Standard Deviation (%)		19.38		18.13				

[1]Price-only index values for the period 1986-1990 are estimated based on monthly price-only performance data.
[2]Maximum/minimum values for the period 1986-1990 are based on month-end index values.

SYNOPSIS
The Standard & Poor's (S&P) MidCap 400 Index is a market value-weighted index that tracks the continuous stock price and daily total return performance of an investable universe of domestic, middle-capitalization range stocks, listed on the New York Stock Exchange (NYSE).

NUMBER OF STOCKS—DECEMBER 31, 1995
400

MARKET VALUE—DECEMBER 31, 1995
US$578,607.7 million

SELECTION CRITERIA
The middle capitalization range was defined by Standard & Poor's (S&P) to include companies with a market capitalization range between US$200.0 and US$5.0 billion as of December 31, 1990, with future adjustments to account for changes in the overall level of the equities market. As of February 2, 1994, market capitalization range shifted to between US$81.0 million and US$7.2 billion

To create the index, S&P narrowed the universe of stocks in the S&P database of equity securities to include a population of about 1,700 securities ranging from US$200.0 million to US$5.0 billion, excluding the constituents of the S&P 500 Index, resulted in a universe of 1,200 stocks. The following stocks were also eliminated: Foreign companies that trade as American Depositary

Receipts (ADRs) and American Depositary Shares (ADSs), except for certain Canadian industrial companies that met the guidelines for selection, Canadian bank and utility stocks, closed-end funds, Real Estate Investment Trusts (REITs), and limited partnerships.

From this population, the 400 companies were qualified on the following basis:
(1) Liquidity level. At its inception, companies with a liquidity ratio below 0.20 were excluded. For this purpose, liquidity is defined as trading volume for the previous 12 months divided by the average number of total common shares outstanding. (2) Float. A company with 50% or more of its common shares outstanding owned by another company or companies with 60% or more of their shares owned by insiders or in combination with other corporation's holdings are not eligible. (3) Industry group representation. Companies were ultimately selected based on the economic and industry characteristics of the overall equity markets and, in particular, the middle capitalization portion of the United States (U.S.) equities market, using four major industry groups: Industrials, transportation, utilities and financial. S&P applied the same screening process that it uses for these industries in the S&P 500. Thus, some otherwise acceptable, relatively large market value companies were eliminated. Although these MidCap 400 industry segments may still be over-weighted relative to the S&P 500, when the two indices are combined, the weightings for the four major industry groups accurately reflect the population of stocks covered by both indices.

BACKGROUND
The index is intended as a benchmark of the middle capitalization portion of the U.S. equities market, to provide an investable universe for passive portfolios and for creation of futures and options contracts. It was launched on June 5, 1991. Performance was backdated to January 1981 and index values were computed on a month-end basis from January 1, 1981 to December 31, 1990.

BASE DATE
December 31, 1990=100.00

COMPUTATION METHODOLOGY
(1) An aggregate of prices times quantities index formula. Maintenance adjustments to the divisor are made for capitalization changes, namely share issuance, share repurchases, special cash dividends, rights offerings and spin-offs, new listings and delistings. All stock splits and stock dividend adjustments are made on the day before the ex-dividend date. All adjustments are made after the close of trading and after the calculation of the closing value of the index. (2) Market capitalization is determined on the basis of shares outstanding, which are reviewed four times a year. Total changes of less than 5% are updated, on a Friday close to the end of each calendar quarter. Total changes in excess of 5% are reviewed weekly and updated, if appropriate, after the close of trading on the following Wednesday. In some cases, an immediate adjustment may be made. (3) The total rate of return is calculated using daily dividends that are reinvested daily as of the ex-dividend date. Monthly, quarterly and annual total rate of return calculations are calculated by daily compounding of the reinvested dividends. Industry group total rates of return are calculated monthly. The quarterly and annual total rates of return are calculated by compounding the monthly total returns.

DERIVATIVE INSTRUMENTS
S&P MidCap 400 Index options trade on The Chicago Board Options Exchange (CBOE).
S&P MidCap 400 options and futures options trade on the Chicago Mercantile Exchange (CME).
Long-term Equity Anticipation Securities (LEAPS), Long-Term Options, FLEX Options and Depositary Receipts (SPDRs) trade on the American Stock Exchange (AMEX).
Stock Index Return Securities, issued by PaineWebber Group., Inc., trade on the AMEX.

SUBINDICES
Four broad sector subindices: MidCap Industrial Index, MidCap Transportation Index, MidCap Utilities Index and the MidCap Financial Index.
Sixty-six industry group subindices: Aerospace/defense, agriculture products, auto Parts and equipment, biotechnology, broadcast media, building materials, cellular telecommunications, chemicals and materials, commercial services-advertising, commercial services-specialized, commercial services-uniform rentals, communications equipment, computer software, computer specialized services, consumer products, consumer services, electronic components and accessories-distributors, electronic components and other equipment, food and beverages, gold and other precious metals, health care products-distributors, health care services, home-building, uron and steel, leisure time-products, leisure time-services, manufacturing-transaction systems, manufacturing-diversified industries, manufacturing-specialized industries, medical products and supplies, metals-specialty, miscellaneous, office supplies-furniture and equipment, oil and gas, oil and gas drilling equipment and services, paper/forest products/containers, pharmaceuticals, pollution control, publishing-books, publishing-newspapers, restaurants, retail/specialty, telecommunications-long distance, textiles-apparel/footwear, textiles-specialty, waste management, air freight, airlines, railroads, shipping, miscellaneous transportation, electric utilities, utilities, local telephone companies, banks, brokerage, miscellaneous financial, insurance, investment banking and investment management.

RELATED INDICES
S&P 1500 Supercomposite Index
S&P 500 Composite Stock Price Index
S&P SmallCap 600 Index

S&P 100 Index
S&P/BARRA Growth Index
S&P/BARRA Value Index

FT/S&P Actuaries World Index
Refer to Appendix 5 for additional indices.

REMARKS
As noted above, backdated performance was calculated by taking the stocks in the index as of December 31, 1990 and tracking them backwards in time as long as there were prices reported to January 1981. When a stock price was not available, the stock was dropped from the earlier year's index calculations. Pursuant to this methodology, there were only 247 stocks out of the original 400 that were publicly traded. This approach is subject to an upward survivor bias in the historical results due to the fact that only companies that survived were tracked in the index, rather than the firms that were actually in business during this period.

PUBLISHER
Standard & Poor's Corporation (S&P Corp.).

STANDARD & POOR'S SMALLCAP 600 INDEX

PRICE PERFORMANCE

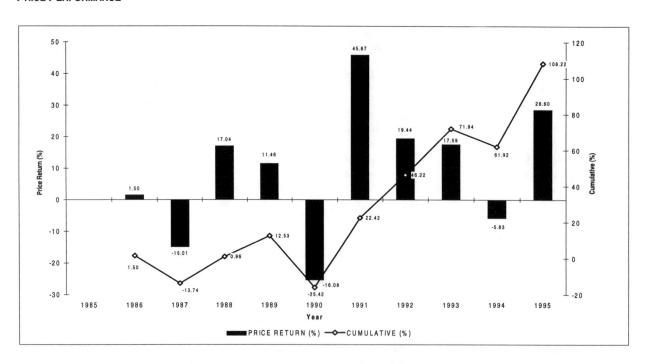

PRICE AND TOTAL RETURN PERFORMANCE

YEAR	VALUE	PRICE RETURN (%)	CUMULATIVE (%)	TOTAL RETURN (%)	MAXIMUM VALUE	DATE	MINIMUM VALUE	DATE
1995	121.10	28.60	108.22	29.96	122.61	13-Sep	92.68	30-Jan
1994	94.17	-5.83	61.92	-4.77	104.45	18-Mar	88.14	12-Dec
1993	100.00	17.59	71.94	18.79	101.35	15-Oct	82.28	23-Feb
1992	85.04	19.44	46.22	21.04	85.04	31-Dec	68.60	25-Jun
1991	71.20	45.87	22.42	48.49	71.20	31-Dec	45.91	15-Jan
1990	48.81	-25.42	-16.08	-23.69	66.00	3-Jan	44.24	31-Oct
1989	65.45	11.46	12.53	13.89	69.89	9-Oct	57.76	3-Jan
1988	58.72	17.04	0.96	19.49	NA	NA	NA	NA
1987	50.17	-15.01	-13.74	-13.50	NA	NA	NA	NA
1986	59.03	1.50	1.50	3.23	NA	NA	NA	NA
1985	58.16							
Average Annual (%)		9.52		11.29				
Compound Annual (%)		7.61		9.37				
Standard Deviation (%)		21.17		21.39				

SYNOPSIS

The S&P SmallCap 600 Index is a market capitalization-weighted index that tracks the daily stock price and total return performance of an investable universe of domestic, small capitalization stocks, listed on the New York Stock Exchange (NYSE), the American Stock Exchange (AMEX) and Nasdaq National Market System (Nasdaq/NMS).

NUMBER OF STOCKS—DECEMBER 31, 1995

600

MARKET VALUE—DECEMBER 31, 1995

US$239,000.0 million

SELECTION CRITERIA

Based on extensive surveys, Standard & Poor's (S&P) established a consensus definition of small capitalization companies to include those with an average market value range of US$80 million to US$600 million at market levels at year-end 1993. This market value range was converted into percentiles that were applied to the entire domestic market. The upper bound converted into the 50th percentile while the lower bound translated into the 83rd percentile. This percentile range was used to calculate the index's back-history and is also used to select future constituents.

S&P started with a universe of 7,000 stocks in the S&P database of equity securities. The following stocks, were ineligible for inclusion: Foreign companies that trade as American Depositary Receipts (ADRs), closed-end funds, limited partnerships, Royalty Trusts, Real Estate Investment Trusts (REITs) as well as securities representing other asset classes. Stocks that made up the S&P 500 Index and the S&P MidCap 400 Index were also excluded. After applying the definition of a small company, the resulting 4,700 companies were further narrowed to about 1,850 as well as 10 economic sectors. From this population, 600 companies qualified on the basis of the following criteria:

(1) A company must trade on the NYSE, AMEX or Nasdaq stock exchanges and have a stock price above US$1.00. (2) A company must have a trading history of at least six months, with share turnover in excess of 20% on an annualized basis. Share turnover is the annual trading volume as a percent of the total common shares outstanding. (3) A stock must be continuously traded. A stock that does not trade on any three days during a 12-month period is ineligible, including a company with a trading historyof less than 12-months. (4) A company with 50% or more of its common shares outstanding owned by another company is ineligible. Also ineligible are companies with 60% or more of their shares owned by insiders or in combination with other corporation's holdings. (5) Companies in bankruptcy or in severe financial distress, such that their continuance as a going concern is in doubt, are eliminated from consideration. (6) A company must trade on the basis of a bid/asked spread of 5% or less. These are calculated as a percentage of the last sale price for an average of 30 days trading activity.

After qualifying on the basis of the foregoing criteria, companies were ultimately selected on the need to balance sector weightings relative to the weightings of the broader population of small companies based on economic and industry characteristics using the following 10 macroeconomic sectors: Basic materials, capital goods, consumer cyclical, consumer staples, energy, financial services, services, technology, transportation and utilities. Only those companies that have the tightest bid-ask spreads within an underweighted sector are selected.

BACKGROUND

The index was created to offer an investable universe of small capitalization stocks, to permit creation of futures and options contracts and as an additional small cap benchmark.

Development of the index began in 1991 and was released in October 1994. S&P has created a simulation of how the index might have performed if it had been created 10 years earlier. The same criteria was applied to the small cap population over a 10-year period starting January 1984. Index values were computed on a month-end basis from 1984 to 1988 and on a daily basis from 1989-1993.

BASE DATE

December 31, 1993=100.00

COMPUTATION METHODOLOGY

(1) Aggregate market value-weighted arithmetic average of the price ratios index formula is used. Maintenance adjustments to the divisor are made for capitalization changes, namely share issuance, share repurchases, special cash dividends, rights offerings and spin-offs, new listings and delistings. All stock splits and stock dividend adjustments are made on the day before the ex-dividend date. These and all adjustments are made after the close of trading and after the calculation of the closing value of the index. (2) The total rate of return is calculated using daily dividends that are reinvested daily as of the ex-dividend date. Monthly, quarterly and annual total rate of return calculations are calculated by daily compounding of the reinvested dividends. Industry group total rates of return are calculated monthly. The quarterly and annual total rates of return are calculated by compounding the monthly total returns. (3) Market capitalization is determined on the basis of shares outstanding, which are reviewed four times a year. Share total changes of less than 5% are updated, on a Friday, close to the end of each calendar quarter. Changes in share totals in excess of 5% are reviewed weekly and updated, if appropriate, after the close of trading on the following Wednesday. In some cases, an immediate adjustment may be made to the number of shares outstanding.

DERIVATIVE INSTRUMENTS

S&P SmallCap 600 Index options trade on The Chicago Board Options Exchange (CBOE).

SUBINDICES

Four broad sector subindices: Industrials, utilities, financials and transportation.

RELATED INDICES

S&P 1500 Supercomposite Index
S&P 500 Composite Stock Price Index
S&P MidCap 400 Index
S&P 100 Index
S&P/BARRA Growth Index
S&P/BARRA Value Index
FT/S&P Actuaries World Index
Refer to Appendix 5 for additional indices.

REMARKS

None

PUBLISHER

Standard & Poor's Corporation. (S&P Corp.).

STANDARD & POOR'S (S&P) SUPERCOMPOSITE STOCK PRICE INDEX

PRICE PERFORMANCE

PRICE AND TOTAL RETURN PERFORMANCE

YEAR	VALUE	PRICE RETURN (%)	CUMULATIVE (%)	TOTAL RETURN (%)	MAXIMUM VALUE	DATE	MINIMUM VALUE	DATE
1995	133.23	33.23	33.23	36.53	134.18	13-Dec	99.81	3-Jan
1994	100.00							
1993								
1992								
1991								
1990								
1989								
1988								
1987								
1986								
1985								
Average Annual (%)		33.23		36.53				
Compound Annual (%)		NM		NM				
Standard Deviation (%)		NM		NM				

SYNOPSIS

The Standard & Poor's (S&P) Supercomposite Stock Price Index is a market value-weighted index that tracks the continuous price only and daily total return performance of the combined stocks that comprise the S&P 500, S&P MidCap 400 and S&P SmallCap 600 stock price indices, including shares of companies listed on the New York Stock Exchange (NYSE), the American Stock Exchange (AMEX) and the Nasdaq National Market System (Nasdaq/NMS). These shares account for 78% of the market value of shares listed on the three exchanges.

NUMBER OF STOCKS—DECEMBER 31, 1995

1,500

MARKET VALUE—DECEMBER 31, 1995

US$5,405,877.2 million

SELECTION CRITERIA

Index members consist of domestic and foreign companies that make up the S&P 500, S&P MidCap 400 and S&P SmallCap 600 stock price indices.

For additional information, refer to the S&P 500 Composite Stock Price Index, the S&P MidCap 400 Index and the S&P SmallCap 600 Index.

BACKGROUND

The index was introduced in 1995.

BASE DATE

December 31, 1994=100.00

COMPUTATION METHODOLOGY

(1) An aggregate of prices times quantities index formula. Maintenance adjustments to the divisor are made for capitalization changes, namely share issuance, share repurchases, special cash dividends, rights offerings and spin-offs, new listings and delistings. All stock splits and stock dividend adjustments are made on the day before the ex-dividend date. These and all adjustments are made after the close of trading and after the calculation of the closing value of the index. Whenever possible, additions and deletions of constituent companies may be announced up to five business days in advance of their implementation, in accordance with a policy announced by Standard & Poor's in 1989. (2) The number of common shares outstanding, for purposes of calculating market capitalization, is updated quarterly. Daily monitoring and weekly reviews, however, are conducted to screen out a 5% increase or decrease in shares outstanding relative to the prior week. Once verified, a maintenance adjustment to the index may be implemented in the event of a difference of 5% or more, if appropriate, after the close of trading on Wednesday of the following week. (3) Total return calculations assume the reinvestment of dividends on a daily basis. Monthly, quarterly and annual total rates of return are calculated on the basis of daily compounding of reinvested dividends.

DERIVATIVE INSTRUMENTS

None

SUBINDICES

None

RELATED INDICES

S&P 500 Composite Stock Price Index
S&P SmallCap 600 Index
S&P MidCap 400 Index
S&P 100 Index
S&P/BARRA Growth Index
S&P/BARRA Value Index
FT/S&P Actuaries World Index
Refer to Appendix 5 for additional indices.

REMARKS

None

PUBLISHER

Standard & Poor's Corporation (S&P Corp.).

STANDARD & POOR'S (S&P) TRANSPORTATION PRICE INDEX (TRX)

PRICE PERFORMANCE

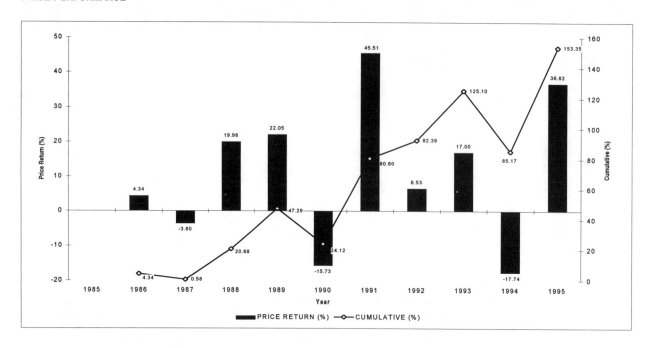

PRICE AND TOTAL RETURN PERFORMANCE

YEAR	VALUE	PRICE RETURN (%)	CUMULATIVE (%)	TOTAL RETURN (%)	MAXIMUM VALUE	DATE	MINIMUM VALUE	DATE
1995	479.01	36.82	153.35	39.34	491.95	5-Dec	356.53	3-Jan
1994	350.11	-17.74	85.17	-16.16	453.63	31-Jan	334.65	13-Dec
1993	425.60	17.00	125.10	19.03	429.71	28-Dec	364.15	1-Mar
1992	363.75	6.53	92.39	8.66	375.42	24-Feb	307.94	9-Oct
1991	341.46	45.51	80.60	48.80	341.46	31-Dec	223.62	14-Jan
1990	234.67	-15.73	24.12	-13.64	291.30	6-Jun	208.77	31-Oct
1989	278.48	22.05	47.29	24.74	331.07	30-Aug	226.42	3-Jan
1988	228.17	19.98	20.68	22.89	246.39	28-Nov	187.37	21-Jan
1987	190.17	-3.60	0.58	-1.49	274.20	14-Aug	167.59	4-Dec
1986	197.27	4.34	4.34	7.08	217.28	27-Mar	176.16	4-Aug
1985	189.07							
Average Annual (%)		11.52		13.93				
Compound Annual (%)		9.74		12.12				
Standard Deviation (%)		20.85		21.25				

SYNOPSIS

The Standard & Poor's (S&P) Transportation Price Index (TRX) is a market value-weighted subindex that tracks the continuous price only and monthly total return performance of stocks in the transportation sector of the Standard & Poor's 500 (S&P 500) Composite Stock Price Index. The index includes various airlines, railroads, trucking as well as miscellaneous companies.

NUMBER OF STOCKS—DECEMBER 31, 1995

15

MARKET VALUE—DECEMBER 31, 1995

US$74,500.0 million

SELECTION CRITERIA

Eligible constituents, which must qualify for inclusion in the S&P 500 Index on the basis of guidelines established by the Standard & Poor's Index Committee are selected from a universe of domestic and foreign companies with "A," "B" and "C" share classes that are used in the calculation of primary earnings and dividends per share for the company's income statement, that are traded on the New York Stock Exchange (NYSE), the American Stock Exchange (AMEX) and the Nasdaq National Market System (Nasdaq/NMS). Excluded from consideration are special classes of common stock that are not used in the calculation of primary earnings and dividends per share for the company's income statement, preferred stock, convertible stock, foreign companies whose stocks trade as American Depositary Receipts (ADRs) or as American Depositary Shares (ADSs), mutual funds, limited partnerships, Royalty Trusts and Real Estate Investment Trusts (REITs), Equity Participation Units, warrants, rights, stock options and treasury stock.

For additional information, refer to the Standard & Poor's 500 Composite Stock Price Index.

BACKGROUND

At its inception, the index consisted of 15 rail stocks. This fixed number was expanded in July 1976 to include 20 transportation companies. Greater flexibility was introduced into the construction of the index starting as of April 6, 1988 with the elimination of a fixed number of companies within the four broad S&P sector groups, including the transportation sector, in choosing new companies for the index when openings arose and in switching companies between sectors as the nature of the business of individual companies changes.

For additional information, refer to the Standard & Poor's 500 Composite Stock Price Index.

BASE DATE

1982=100.00

COMPUTATION METHODOLOGY

(1) An aggregate of prices times quantities index formula. Maintenance adjustment to the S&P 500 Index also affect each of the major industry group subindices as well as the individual industry groups. Maintenance adjustments to the divisor are made for capitalization changes, namely share issuance, share repurchases, special cash dividends, rights offerings and spin-offs, new listings and delistings. All stock splits and stock dividend adjustments are made on the day before the ex-dividend date. These and all adjustments are made after the close of trading and after the calculation of the closing value of the index. Whenever possible, additions and deletions of constituent companies may be announced up to five business days in advance of their implementation, in accordance with a policy announced by Standard & Poor's in 1989. (2) The number of common shares outstanding, for purposes of calculating market capitalization, is updated quarterly. Daily monitoring and weekly reviews, however, are conducted to screen out a 5% increase or decrease in shares outstanding relative to the prior week. Once verified, a maintenance adjustment to the index may be implemented in the event of a difference of 5% or more, if appropriate, after the close of trading on Wednesday of the following week. (3) The final closing value is calculated on the basis of last-trade prices on the NYSE, AMEX and Nasdaq/NMS. (4) Total return calculations assume the reinvestment of dividends on a daily basis. Quarterly and annual total rates of return are calculated on the basis of monthly compounding of reinvested dividends.

DERIVATIVE INSTRUMENTS

S&P Transportation Index options trade on the Chicago Board Options Exchange (CBOE).

SUBINDICES

Four transportation industry group subindices: Airlines, railroads, truckers and miscellaneous transportation companies.

RELATED INDICES

S&P 1500 Supercomposite Index
S&P SmallCap 600 Index
S&P MidCap 400 Index
S&P 100 Index
S&P/BARRA Growth Index
S&P/BARRA Value Index
FT/S&P Actuaries World Index
Refer to Appendix 5 for additional indices.

PUBLISHER

Standard & Poor's Corporation (S&P Corp.).

STANDARD & POOR'S (S&P) UTILITIES PRICE INDEX

PRICE PERFORMANCE

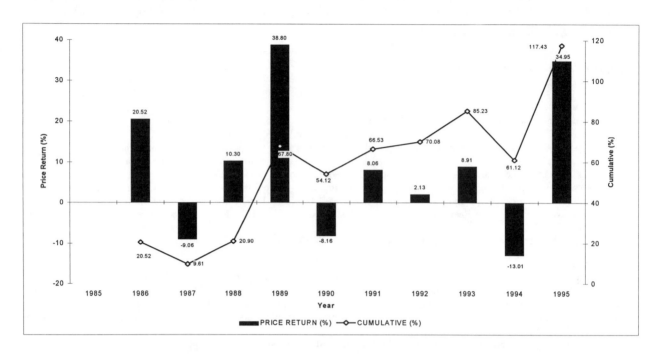

PRICE AND TOTAL RETURN PERFORMANCE

YEAR	VALUE	PRICE RETURN (%)	CUMULATIVE (%)	TOTAL RETURN (%)	MAXIMUM VALUE	DATE	MINIMUM VALUE	DATE
1995	202.58	34.95	117.43	42.03	202.58	29-Dec	150.32	11-Jan
1994	150.12	-13.01	61.12	-9.95	173.10	31-Jan	147.85	18-Nov
1993	172.58	8.91	85.23	14.44	189.49	13-Sep	156.50	8-Jan
1992	158.46	2.13	70.08	8.09	161.98	23-Dec	135.59	8-Apr
1991	155.16	8.06	66.53	14.62	155.16	31-Dec	133.52	24-Jun
1990	143.59	-8.16	54.12	-2.56	157.86	2-Jan	124.60	24-Aug
1989	156.34	38.80	67.80	47.22	156.04	29-Dec	111.15	3-Jan
1988	112.64	10.30	20.90	18.04	114.57	21-Oct	101.21	20-Apr
1987	102.12	-9.06	9.61	-2.90	124.04	28-Jan	91.80	19-Oct
1986	112.29	20.52	20.52	28.44	123.74	29-Aug	90.33	9-Aug
1985	93.17							
Average Annual (%)		9.34		15.75				
Compound Annual (%)		8.08		14.37				
Standard Deviation (%)		17.79		19.01				

SYNOPSIS

The Standard & Poor's (S&P) Utilities Price Index is a market value-weighted subindex that tracks the continuous price only and monthly total return performance of stocks in the utilities sector of the Standard & Poor's 500 (S&P 500) Composite Stock Price Index. The index includes electric, natural gas and telephone companies.

NUMBER OF STOCKS—DECEMBER 31, 1995

49

MARKET VALUE—DECEMBER 31, 1995

US$454,500.0 million

SELECTION CRITERIA

Eligible constituents, which must qualify for inclusion in the S&P 500 Index on the basis of guidelines established by the Standard & Poor's Index Committee are selected from a universe of domestic and foreign companies with "A," "B" and "C" share classes, that are used in the calculation of primary earnings and dividends per share for the company's income statement, that are traded on the New York Stock Exchange (NYSE), the American Stock Exchange (AMEX) and the Nasdaq National Market System (Nasdaq/NMS). Excluded from consideration are special classes of common stock that are not used in the calculation of primary earnings and dividends per share for the company's income statement, preferred stock, convertible stock, foreign companies whose stocks trade as American Depositary Receipts (ADRs) or as American Depositary Shares (ADSs), mutual funds, limited partnerships, Royalty Trusts and Real Estate Investment Trusts (REITs), Equity Participation Units, warrants, rights, stock options and treasury stock.

For additional information, refer to the Standard & Poor's 500 Composite Stock Price Index.

BACKGROUND

The subindex dates back to the formation of the S&P 500 in 1923 and has been modified and expanded over time. In 1957, the number of constituent stocks was expanded to 60 utility companies and fixed at that number. Greater flexibility was introduced into the construction of the index as of April 6, 1988 with the elimination of a fixed number of companies within the four broad S&P sector groups, including the utilities sector, in choosing new companies for the index when openings arose and in switching companies between sectors as the nature of the business of individual companies changes.

For additional information, refer to the Standard & Poor's 500 Composite Stock Price Index.

BASE DATE

1941-1943=10.00

COMPUTATION METHODOLOGY

(1) An aggregate of prices times quantities index formula, expressed in relatives to the average weekly value established during the based period 1941-1943. Maintenance adjustment to the S&P 500 Index also affect each of the major industry group subindices as well as the individual industry groups. Maintenance adjustments to the divisor are made for capitalization changes, namely share issuance, share repurchases, special cash dividends, rights offerings and spin-offs, new listings and delistings. All stock splits and stock dividend adjustments are made on the day before the ex-dividend date. All adjustments are made after the close of trading and after the calculation of the closing value of the index. Whenever possible, additions and deletions of constituent companies may be announced up to five business days in advance of their implementation, in accordance with a policy announced by Standard & Poor's in 1989. (2) The number of common shares outstanding, for purposes of calculating market capitalization, is updated quarterly. Daily monitoring and weekly reviews, however, are conducted to screen out a 5% increase or decrease in shares outstanding relative to the prior week. Once verified, a maintenance adjustment to the index may be implemented in the event of a difference of 5% or more, if appropriate, after the close of trading on Wednesday of the following week. (3) The final closing value is calculated on the basis of last-trade prices on the NYSE, AMEX and Nasdaq/NMS. (4) Total return calculations assume the reinvestment of dividends on a daily basis. Quarterly and annual total rates of return are calculated on the basis of monthly compounding of reinvested dividends.

DERIVATIVE INSTRUMENTS

None

SUBINDICES

Three utility industry group subindices: Electric, natural gas and telephone companies.

RELATED INDICES

S&P 1500 Supercomposite Index
S&P SmallCap 600 Index
S&P MidCap 400 Index
S&P 100 Index
S&P/BARRA Growth Index
S&P/BARRA Value Index
FT/S&P Actuaries World Index
Refer to Appendix 5 for additional indices.

REMARKS

None

PUBLISHER

Standard & Poor's Corporation (S&P Corp.).

STANDARD & POOR'S (S&P)/BARRA GROWTH INDEX

PRICE PERFORMANCE

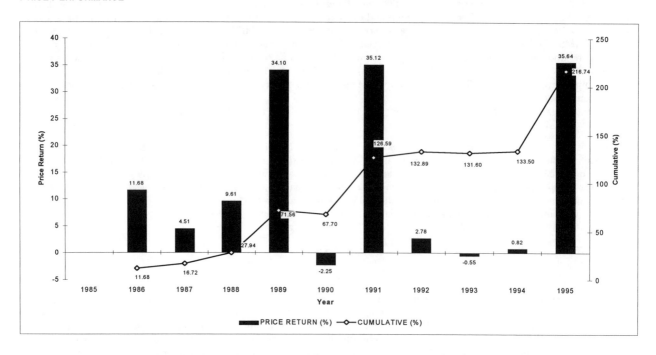

PRICE AND TOTAL RETURN PERFORMANCE

YEAR	VALUE	PRICE RETURN (%)	CUMULATIVE (%)	TOTAL RETURN (%)	MAXIMUM VALUE[1]	DATE	MINIMUM VALUE[1]	DATE
1995	302.04	35.64	216.74	38.13	308.15	NA	221.41	NA
1994	222.67	0.82	133.50	3.13	228.17	NA	204.68	NA
1993	220.85	-0.55	131.60	1.67	224.25	NA	205.84	NA
1992	222.08	2.78	132.89	5.06	222.51	31-Dec	201.62	30-Jun
1991	216.08	35.12	126.59	38.37	216.08	31-Dec	166.17	31-Jan
1990	159.92	-2.25	67.70	0.20	172.47	30-Jun	146.17	30-Sep
1989	163.60	34.10	71.56	36.40	163.60	31-Dec	126.30	28-Feb
1988	122.00	9.61	27.94	11.95	122.20	31-Oct	113.90	31-Mar
1987	111.30	4.51	16.72	6.50	151.40	31-Aug	102.50	30-Nov
1986	106.50	11.68	11.68	14.49	108.90	30-Nov	94.53	31-Jan
1985	95.36							
Average Annual (%)		13.15		15.59				
Compound Annual (%)		12.22		14.66				
Standard Deviation (%)		15.64		15.82				

[1]Maximum/minimum index values for the period 1986-1992 are as of month-end.

SYNOPSIS

The Standard & Poor's (S&P)/BARRA Growth Index is a market value-weighted index that tracks the daily price and monthly total return performance of growth oriented common stocks in the Standard & Poor's 500 (S&P 500) Composite Stock Price Index.

NUMBER OF STOCKS—DECEMBER 31, 1995

184

MARKET VALUE—DECEMBER 31, 1995

US$2,343.3 million

SELECTION CRITERIA

Stocks in the S&P 500 Index are divided according to their price-to-book ratios and are assigned either to the Growth Index or the Value Index, using an asset class factor model, so that the combined indices add up to the S&P 500. By design, approximately 50% of the S&P 500 capitalization is in the Value Index and 50% is in the Growth Index

BACKGROUND

The design of the indices is an outgrowth of research into investment styles in the United States (U.S.) equity market that was performed by William F. Sharpe, Eugene Fama and Kenneth French. They found that the value/growth dimension along with the large/small dimension appears to explain many of the differences in returns for U.S. mutual funds and cross-sectional variability in average stock returns.

In constructing this index and its companion Value Index, the price-to-book ratio value was the attribute selected to characterize value and growth companies due to the fact that it is simple and easy to understand. The ratio tends to be more stable over time and as a consequence, indices based on this measure tend to experience lower turnover.

The index was introduced in May 1992 and recalculated on a monthly total return basis to that date using historically accurate data. Price only closing index values have been calculated daily since January 1993.

BASE DATE

December 31, 1974=10.00

COMPUTATION METHODOLOGY

(1) An aggregate of prices times quantities index formula. Maintenance adjustments to the divisor are made for capitalization changes, namely share issuance, share repurchases, special cash dividends, rights offerings and spin-offs, new listings and delistings. All stock splits and stock dividend adjustments are made on the day before the ex-dividend date. These and all adjustments are made after the close of trading and after the calculation of the closing value of the index. (2) The index is rebalanced semi-annually on January 1, and July 1, based on price-to-book ratios and market capitalizations at the close of trading on November 30 and May 31, respectively. At each semi-annual rebalance, a cutoff value is determined based on the lowest price-to-book ratio of companies that make up the Growth Index. This cutoff value is used to determine whether to place a new member of the S&P 500 Index into the Value or Growth Index. Companies are assigned to the Growth Index if their price-to-book ratio is greater than the most recent semi-annual cutoff value. Otherwise, these new companies are added to the Value Index. (3) The index is adjusted once a month to reflect changes in the S&P 500 Index. (4) When companies are replaced in the S&P 500 Index, they are dropped from the Growth Index.

DERIVATIVE INSTRUMENTS

S&P 500/BARRA Growth Index options trade on The Chicago Board Options Exchange (CBOE).
S&P 500/BARRA Growth Index futures and options trade on the Chicago Mercantile Exchange (CME).

SUBINDICES

None

RELATED INDICES

S&P 500 Composite Stock Price Index
S&P 1500 Supercomposite Index
S&P SmallCap 600 Index
S&P MidCap 400 Index
S&P 100 Index
S&P/BARRA Growth Index
FT/S&P Actuaries World Index
BARRA All-US Price Index
Refer to Appendix 5 for additional indices.

REMARKS

Average price/earnings ratio at December 31, 1995=21.78

PUBLISHER

Standard & Poor's Corporation (S&P Corp.)/BARRA, Inc.

STANDARD & POOR'S (S&P)/BARRA VALUE INDEX

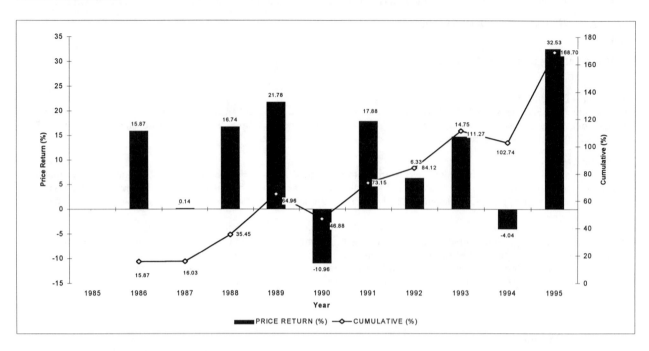

PRICE AND TOTAL RETURN PERFORMANCE

YEAR	VALUE	PRICE RETURN (%)	CUMULATIVE (%)	TOTAL RETURN (%)	MAXIMUM VALUE[1]	DATE	MINIMUM VALUE[1]	DATE
1995	325.13	32.53	168.70	37.00	325.13	NA	245.98	NA
1994	245.32	-4.04	102.74	-0.64	267.16	NA	239.09	NA
1993	255.64	14.75	111.27	18.60	259.11	NA	220.78	NA
1992	222.78	6.33	84.12	10.52	222.44	31-Jul	208.67	31-Mar
1991	209.51	17.88	73.15	22.56	209.51	31-Dec	185.31	31-Jan
1990	177.73	-10.96	46.88	-6.85	198.57	31-May	163.88	31-Oct
1989	199.60	21.78	64.96	26.13	203.60	31-Aug	170.40	28-Feb
1988	163.90	16.74	35.45	21.67	165.70	31-Oct	150.20	31-Jan
1987	140.40	0.14	16.03	3.68	185.30	31-Aug	132.20	30-Nov
1986	140.20	15.87	15.87	21.67	146.20	31-Aug	121.90	31-Jan
1985	121.00							
Average Annual (%)		11.10		15.43				
Compound Annual (%)		10.39		14.71				
Standard Deviation (%)		13.11		13.48				

[1]Maximum/minimum index values for the period 1986-1992 are as of month-end.

SYNOPSIS

The Standard & Poor's (S&P)/BARRA Value Index is a market value-weighted index that tracks the daily price and monthly total return performance of value oriented common stocks in the Standard & Poor's 500 (S&P 500) Composite Stock Price Index.

NUMBER OF STOCKS—DECEMBER 31, 1995

316

MARKET VALUE—DECEMBER 31, 1995

US$2,245.0 million

SELECTION CRITERIA

Stocks in the S&P 500 Index are divided according to their price-to-book ratios and are assigned either to the Value Index or the Growth Index, using an asset class factor model, so that the combined indices add up to the S&P 500. By design, approximately 50% of the S&P 500 capitalization is in the Value Index and 50% is in the Growth Index

BACKGROUND

The design of the indices is an outgrowth of research into investment styles in the United States (U.S.) equity market that was performed by William F. Sharpe, Eugene Fama and Kenneth French. They found that the value/growth dimension along with the large/small dimension appears to explain many of the differences in returns for U.S. mutual funds and cross-sectional variability in average stock returns.

In constructing this index and its companion Growth Index, the price-to-book ratio value was the attribute selected to characterize value and growth companies due to the fact that it is simple and easy to understand. The ratio tends to be more stable over time and as a consequence, indices based on this measure tend to experience lower turnover.

The index was introduced in May 1992 and recalculated on a monthly total return basis to that date using historically accurate data. Price only closing index values have been calculated daily since January 1993.

BASE DATE

December 31, 1974=10.00

COMPUTATION METHODOLOGY

(1) An aggregate of prices times quantities index formula. Maintenance adjustments to the divisor are made for capitalization changes, namely share issuance, share repurchases, special cash dividends, rights offerings and spin-offs, new listings and delistings. All stock splits and stock dividend adjustments are made on the day before the ex-dividend date. These and all adjustments are made after the close of trading and after the calculation of the closing value of the index. (2) The index is rebalanced semi-annually on January 1, and July 1, based on price-to-book ratios and market capitalizations at the close of trading on November 30 and May 31, respectively. At each semi-annual rebalance, a cutoff value is determined based on the lowest price-to-book ratio of companies that make up the Growth Index. This cutoff value is used to determine whether to place a new member of the S&P 500 Index into the Value or Growth Index. Companies are assigned to the Growth Index if their price-to-book ratio is greater than the most recent semi-annual cutoff value. Otherwise, these new companies are added to the Value Index. (3) The index is adjusted once a month to reflect changes in the S&P 500 Index. (4) When companies are replaced in the S&P 500 Index, they are dropped from the Value Index.

DERIVATIVE INSTRUMENTS

S&P 500/BARRA Value Index options trade on The Chicago Board Options Exchange (CBOE).
S&P 500/BARRA Value Index futures and options trade on the Chicago Mercantile Exchange (CME).

SUBINDICES

None

RELATED INDICES

S&P 500 Composite Stock Price Index
S&P 1500 Supercomposite Index
S&P SmallCap 600 Index
S&P MidCap 400 Index
S&P 100 Index
S&P/BARRA Value Index
FT/S&P Actuaries World Index
BARRA All-US Price Index
Refer to Appendix 5 for additional indices.

REMARKS

Average price/earnings ratio at December 31, 1995=14.61

PUBLISHER

Standard & Poor's Corporation (S&P Corp.)/BARRA, Inc.

VALUE LINE ARITHMETIC (VLA) INDEX

PRICE PERFORMANCE

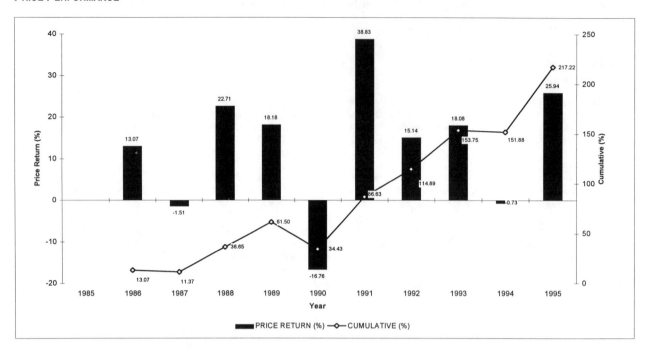

PRICE PERFORMANCE

YEAR	VALUE	PRICE RETURN (%)	CUMULATIVE (%)	MAXIMUM VALUE	DATE	MINIMUM VALUE	DATE
1995	569.91	25.94	217.22	569.91	29-Dec	451.27	3-Jan
1994	452.53	-0.73	151.88	474.33	23-Mar	433.82	12-Dec
1993	455.88	18.08	153.75	455.88	31-Dec	383.53	8-Jan
1992	386.08	15.14	114.89	386.08	31-Dec	335.28	2-Jan
1991	335.30	38.83	86.63	335.30	31-Dec	231.13	14-Jan
1990	241.52	-16.76	34.43	294.73	3-Jan	215.99	17-Oct
1989	290.15	18.18	61.50	306.51	6-Oct	244.60	3-Jan
1988	245.51	22.71	36.65	248.56	21-Oct	201.85	12-Jan
1987	200.08	-1.51	11.37	271.17	25-Aug	176.93	28-Oct
1986	203.14	13.07	13.07	213.82	2-Jul	176.68	10-Jan
1985	179.66						
Average Annual (%)		13.29					
Compound Annual (%)		12.24					
Standard Deviation (%)		15.88					

SYNOPSIS

The Value Line Arithmetic (VLA) Index is an equally-weighted index that tracks the daily price only performance of the common stocks regularly supervised in the *Value Line Investment Survey*.

NUMBER OF STOCKS—DECEMBER 31, 1995

Approximately 1,632

MARKET VALUE—DECEMBER 31, 1995

Not Available

SELECTION CRITERIA

The index is comprised of the common stocks regularly supervised in the *Value Line Investment Survey*. Closed-end funds are excluded as index constituents, including domestic closed-end funds, foreign closed-end funds and closed-end income funds, which number about 35. Over 90% of the stocks comprising the index are listed on the New York Stock Exchange (NYSE).

BACKGROUND

Value Line began to publish the VLA Index in March 1988. It was established at a value equal to the Value Line Composite Index prior to the opening of business on February 1, 1988. At that time, the value of both indices stood at 210.75. Daily index values have been recalculated on a simulation basis to January 1, 1983.

BASE DATE

February 1, 1988=210.75

COMPUTATION METHODOLOGY

An arithmetic average mathematical technique is used by which the closing prices of each stock is divided by the preceding day's close. The changes for all stocks in the group are averaged and the final average change for the day is then multiplied by the prior day's closing index value. The index reflects stock dividends as well as stock splits by adjusting the prior day's stock price.

DERIVATIVE INSTRUMENTS

None

SUBINDICES

None

RELATED INDICES

Value Line Composite Index
Value Line Convertible Index

REMARKS

This benchmark provides a good estimate of the price performance of an equal-dollar portfolio of the stocks covered by Value Line's *Ratings & Reports*.

PUBLISHER

Value Line, Inc.

VALUE LINE COMPOSITE INDEX (XVL)

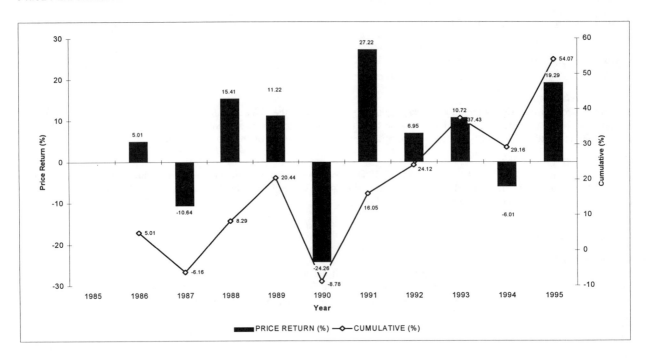

PRICE PERFORMANCE

YEAR	VALUE	PRICE RETURN (%)	CUMULATIVE (%)	MAXIMUM VALUE	DATE	MINIMUM VALUE	DATE
1995	331.04	19.29	54.07	334.83	14-Sep	276.67	3-Jan
1994	277.52	-6.01	29.16	305.87	2-Feb	266.56	9-Dec
1993	295.28	10.72	37.43	295.28	31-Dec	264.52	8-Jan
1992	266.68	6.95	24.12	266.85	12-Feb	238.81	9-Oct
1991	249.34	27.22	16.05	249.34	31-Dec	186.78	15-Jan
1990	195.99	-24.26	-8.78	262.60	3-Jan	179.55	30-Oct
1989	258.78	11.22	20.44	278.69	1-Sep	235.89	10-Jan
1988	232.68	15.41	8.29	239.75	6-Jul	202.69	12-Jan
1987	201.62	-10.64	-6.16	289.02	25-Aug	181.09	4-Dec
1986	225.62	5.01	5.01	246.80	29-May	210.84	10-Jan
1985	214.86						
Average Annual (%)		5.49					
Compound Annual (%)		4.42					
Standard Deviation (%)		15.28					

SYNOPSIS

The Value Line Composite Index (XVL) is an equally-weighted geometrically averaged index that tracks the daily price only performance of the common stocks regularly supervised in the *Value Line Investment Survey*.

NUMBER OF STOCKS—DECEMBER 31, 1995

Approximately 1,632

MARKET VALUE—DECEMBER 31, 1995

Not Available

SELECTION CRITERIA

The index is comprised of the common stocks regularly supervised in the *Value Line Investment Survey*. These include 1,458 industrials, 10 rails and 164 utilities. Closed-end funds are excluded as index constituents, including domestic closed-end funds, foreign closed-end funds and closed-end income funds, which number about 35. Over 90% of the stocks comprising the index are listed on the New York Stock Exchange (NYSE).

BACKGROUND

Weekly values as of Friday were calculated during the period between June 1, 1961 and December 31, 1975. Subsequent to that date, daily values are available.

BASE DATE

June 30, 1961=100.00

COMPUTATION METHODOLOGY

(1) A geometric mean index formula. (2) The index reflects stock dividends as well as stock splits by adjusting the prior day's stock price. (3) The index accommodates additions to and deletions from the *Value Line Investment Survey* through the expansion and contraction of the index.

DERIVATIVE INSTRUMENTS

Value Line Composite Index options and Long-term Equity Participation Securities (LEAPS) trade on the Philadelphia Stock Exchange (PHLX).

SUBINDICES

Value Line Industrial Average
Value Line Railroad Average
Value Line Utility Average

RELATED INDICES

Value Line Arithmetic Index
Value Line Convertible Index

REMARKS

(1) This broadly based benchmark gives equal weight to each stock regardless of number of shares outstanding or share price. Accordingly, the Value Line Arithmetic Averages provide a good estimate of the median price performance of the stocks covered by Value Line's *Ratings & Reports*. (2) Effective May 21, 1988, the computation of the index used as a basis for index options and LEAPS was changed to an unweighted arithmetic index. Previously, it was equally-weighted and geometrically averaged.

PUBLISHER

Value Line, Inc.

WILSHIRE 5000 EQUITY INDEX

PRICE PERFORMANCE

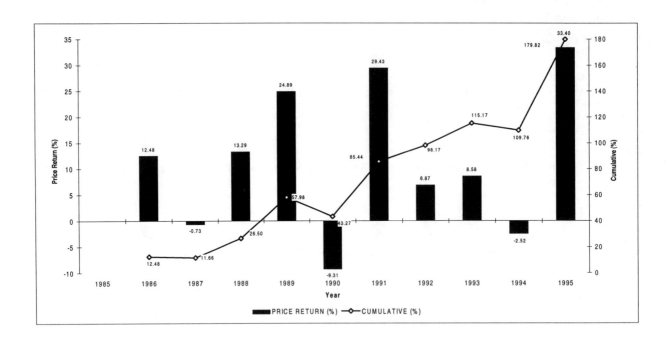

PRICE AND TOTAL RETURN PERFORMANCE

YEAR	VALUE	PRICE RETURN (%)	CUMULATIVE (%)	TOTAL RETURN (%)	MAXIMUM VALUE[1]	DATE	MINIMUM VALUE[1]	DATE
1995	6,057.21	33.40	179.82	36.45	6,084.51	13-Dec	4,529.05	3-Jan
1994	4,540.62	-2.52	109.76	0.00	4,804.31	2-Feb	4,373.58	24-Jun
1993	4,657.83	8.58	115.17	11.28	4,701.68	15-Oct	4,226.70	8-Jan
1992	4,289.74	6.87	98.17	8.97	4,301.52	18-Dec	3,849.10	8-Apr
1991	4,014.10	29.43	85.44	34.20	4,014.87	30-Dec	2,938.58	9-Jan
1990	3,101.36	-9.31	43.27	-6.18	3,518.32	16-Jul	2,772.31	11-Oct
1989	3,419.88	24.89	57.98	29.17	3,440.84	31-Aug	2,857.86	28-Feb
1988	2,738.42	13.29	26.50	17.94	2,750.80	31-Oct	2,517.81	29-Jan
1987	2,417.12	-0.73	11.66	2.27	3,245.83	31-Aug	2,259.44	30-Nov
1986	2,434.95	12.48	12.48	16.09	2,577.65	30-Jun	2,184.11	31-Jan
1985	2,164.69							
Average Annual (%)		11.64		15.02				
Compound Annual (%)		10.84		14.19				
Standard Deviation (%)		14.12		14.63				

[1]Maximum/minimum values for the period 1986-1989 are based on month-end index values.

SYNOPSIS

The Wilshire 5000 Equity Index is a broad based market value-weighted benchmark that measures the daily price only and total return performance of all United States (U.S.)-headquartered, actively traded common stocks with readily available price data traded on the New York Stock Exchange (NYSE), American Stock Exchange (AMEX) and Nasdaq. These shares account for 92% of the U.S. market capitalization.

NUMBER OF STOCKS—DECEMBER 31, 1995

6,927

MARKET VALUE—DECEMBER 31, 1995

US$6,383,599.0 million

SELECTION CRITERIA

The index includes all U.S.-headquartered, actively traded common stocks with readily available price data. Stocks traded in the U.S. but domiciled in other countries are excluded from consideration. Also excluded from consideration are: Preferred stock, convertible preferred stock, participating preferred stock, warrants and rights, Trust Receipts, Royalty Trusts, limited liability companies, OTC Bulletin Board companies, pink sheet-listed companies, closed-end investment companies, limited partnerships and Real Estate Investment Trusts (REITs).

BACKGROUND

The index was created in 1974 and backdated on a monthly basis to December 31, 1970. Daily index value calculations were initiated on December 1, 1979.

BASE DATE

December 31, 1970=1.00

COMPUTATION METHODOLOGY

(1) An aggregate of prices times quantities index formula. Maintenance adjustments to the divisor are made for capitalization changes, new listings and delistings. (2) In the event that an ending price is not available for a given security, the security is dropped from the computation on that date and coverage resumes upon price availability. (3) Cash dividends are reinvested on the ex-dividend date.

DERIVATIVE INSTRUMENTS

None

SUBINDICES

The Wilshire Large Company (Top 750) Equity Index, Wilshire Middle Capitalization Company (Mid Cap 750) Equity Index and the Wilshire Small Company (Next 1750) Equity Index.
The Wilshire Large Company Value and Growth style indices, Wilshire Middle Capitalization Value and Growth style indices and the Wilshire Small Company Value and Growth style indices.
Pacific Stock Exchange Wilshire Small Cap Index.
Capitalization-weighted portfolio indices: Largest 2,500 stocks that make up the Wilshire 5000 Equity Index, next largest 500 stocks, third largest 500 stocks, fourth and fifth largest 500 stocks and the S&P 500.
Nine sector indices according to principal line of business: Capital goods, consumer durables, consumer non-durables and entertainment, energy, financial, materials and services, technology, transportation and utilities. These returns are calculated on an annual buy-and-hold basis and include partial period returns for the year (included after 1984). All portfolios are recreated and rebalanced at the beginning of each year.

RELATED INDICES

Wilshire 5000 Equally Weighted Equity Index (calculated on a price only and total return basis)
Wilshire REIT Index

REMARKS

None

PUBLISHER

Wilshire Associates Inc.

WILSHIRE ASSOCIATES SMALL CAP (WSX) INDEX

PRICE PERFORMANCE

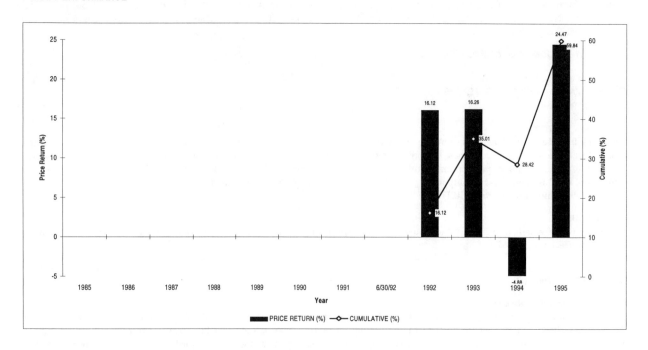

PRICE PERFORMANCE

YEAR	VALUE	PRICE RETURN (%)	CUMULATIVE (%)	MAXIMUM VALUE[1]	DATE	MINIMUM VALUE[1]	DATE
1995	399.61	24.47	59.84	406.17	14-Sep	316.68	30-Jan
1994	321.06	-4.88	28.42	353.82	18-Mar	305.43	9-Dec
1993	337.52	16.26	35.01	337.52	31-Dec	285.35	26-Apr
1992	290.31	16.12	16.12				
6/30/92	250.00						
1991							
1990							
1989							
1988							
1987							
1986							
1985							
Average Annual (%)		7.86					
Compound Annual (%)		7.41					
Standard Deviation (%)[2]		12.54					

[1]Maximum/minimum values for the period 1986-1989 are based on month-end index values.
[2]Standard deviation applicable to the 3 year period 1993-1995.

SYNOPSIS

The Wilshire Associates Small Cap (WSX) Index is a market value-weighted benchmark that measures the continuous price only performance of 250 of the most actively traded United States (U.S.)-headquartered stocks in the small-cap universe. These shares fall within the universe of the Wilshire Small Company (Next 1,750) Equity Index which is derived from the largest 2,500 securities of the Wilshire 5000 Equity Index.

NUMBER OF STOCKS—DECEMBER 31, 1995

250

MARKET VALUE—DECEMBER 31, 1995

US$155,400.0 million

SELECTION CRITERIA

Constituent stocks are drawn from a universe consisting of the smallest 1,750 securities within the largest 2,500 securities of the Wilshire 5000 Equity Index, as measured by market capitalization. Except as noted below, stocks that fall within the smallest 1,750 securities segment are eligible for inclusion in the index. They are selected on the basis of a mathematical model designed to maximize the daily index price movement correlation of the index to the universe of 1,750 securities while at the same time ensuring sufficient liquidity. Shares are replaced in the event trading volume falls below 3,000 per day for six months and replacements must have average daily trading volume in excess of 10,000 shares per day.

Ineligible securities include stocks of the Wilshire Small Company (Next 1,750) Equity Index that fall within the top 10% by market capitalization, stocks in the bottom 20% by market capitalization and stocks in the bottom 25% ranked by trading volume.

BACKGROUND

The index was created specifically as an underlying vehicle for derivative instruments. Daily historical data has been calculated to June 30, 1987.

BASE DATE

June 30, 1992=250.00

COMPUTATION METHODOLOGY

(1) An aggregate of prices times quantities index formula. Maintenance adjustments to the divisor are made for capitalization changes, new listings and delistings. (2) In the event that an ending price is not available for a given security, the security is dropped from the computation on that date and coverage resumes upon price availability. (3) Shares are updated on a monthly basis and replacements are made quarterly, on the day following expiration of the February cycle. The annual restructuring as a result of the annual reranking of the Wilshire 1,750 securities occurs after the May expiration.

DERIVATIVE INSTRUMENTS

Wilshire Small Cap Index options trade on the Pacific Stock Exchange (PSE).

SUBINDICES

None

RELATED INDICES

Wilshire 5000 Equity Index
Wilshire REIT Index

REMARKS

None

PUBLISHER

Wilshire Associates Inc.

WILSHIRE LARGE COMPANY (TOP 750) EQUITY INDEX

TOTAL RETURN PERFORMANCE

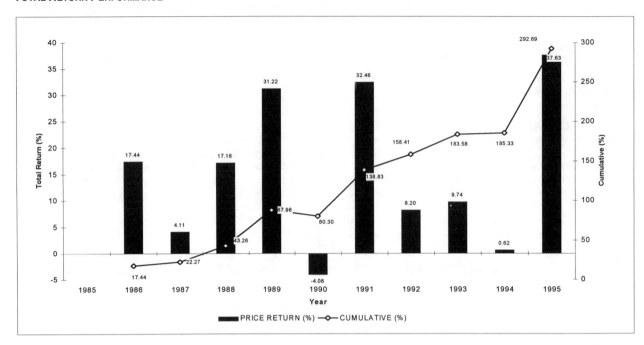

TOTAL RETURN PERFORMANCE

YEAR	VALUE¹	TOTAL RETURN (%)	CUMULATIVE (%)	MAXIMUM VALUE²	DATE	MINIMUM VALUE²	DATE
1995	1,291.37	37.63	292.69	1,291.37	31-Dec	1,029.34	31-Mar
1994	938.33	0.62	185.33	941.24	30-Sep	895.99	31-Mar
1993	932.55	9.74	183.58	932.55	31-Dec	884.20	31-Mar
1992	849.79	8.20	158.41	849.79	31-Dec	765.04	31-Mar
1991	785.38	32.46	138.83	785.38	31-Dec	680.06	30-Jun
1990	592.94	-4.08	80.30	631.12	30-Jun	543.33	30-Sep
1989	618.18	31.22	87.98	618.18	31-Dec	504.60	31-Mar
1988	471.10	17.16	43.26	471.10	31-Dec	428.55	31-Mar
1987	402.09	4.11	22.27	517.76	30-Sep	402.09	31-Dec
1986	386.20	17.44	17.44	397.10	30-Jun	368.87	30-Sep
1985	328.85						
Average Annual (%)		15.45					
Compound Annual (%)		14.66					
Standard Deviation (%)		14.34					

¹Index values computed based on quarterly total rates of return using a 12/31/1977 base value of 100.00.
²Maximum/minimum index values are as of quarter-end, computed based on quarterly total rates of return.

SYNOPSIS

The Wilshire Large Company (Top 750) Equity Index is a market value-weighted index that measures the total return performance of the largest 750 companies derived from the largest 2,500 securities in the Wilshire 5000 Equity Index. These shares, with a median market value of US$3,203.0 million, account for 85% of the Wilshire 5000 Index market capitalization.

NUMBER OF STOCKS—DECEMBER 31, 1995

750

MARKET VALUE—DECEMBER 31, 1995

US$5,160,506.0 million

SELECTION CRITERIA

Constituents represent the top 750 companies that make up the Wilshire 5000 Equity Index and include actively traded United States (U.S.)-headquartered common stocks with readily available price data.

BACKGROUND

The index is derived from the largest 2,500 securities of the Wilshire 5000 Equity Index and a market capitalization that extends down to approximately the US$1.2 billion level. Performance data is available on a quarterly basis.

BASE DATE

April 1988=100.00

COMPUTATION METHODOLOGY

(1) An aggregate of prices times quantities index formula. Maintenance adjustments to the divisor are made daily to eliminate the effect of all types of capitalization changes, new listings and delistings. (2) In the event that an ending price is not available for a given security, the security is dropped from the computation on that date and coverage resumes upon price availability. (3) Cash dividends are reinvested on the ex-dividend date.

DERIVATIVE INSTRUMENTS

None

SUBINDICES

Wilshire Large Company Growth Equity Style Index
Wilshire Large Company Value Equity Style Index

RELATED INDICES

Wilshire 5000 Equity Index
Wilshire 2500 Equity Index
Wilshire MidCap (Mid Cap 750) Equity Index
Wilshire MidCap Growth Equity Style Index
Wilshire MidCap Value Equity Style Index
Wilshire Small Company (Next 1750) Equity Index
Wilshire Small Company Growth Equity Style Index
Wilshire Small Company Value Equity Style Index
Wilshire Small Cap Equity Index
Wilshire REIT Index

REMARKS

The base year coincides with the introduction of Wilshire Asset Management's Equity Style Portfolios, a series of equity portfolios that are designed to track the total return performance of passively managed growth and value styles of equity investing within a universe of large-, middle-capitalization and small-company stocks.

PUBLISHER

Wilshire Associates Inc.

WILSHIRE LARGE COMPANY GROWTH EQUITY STYLE INDEX

TOTAL RETURN PERFORMANCE

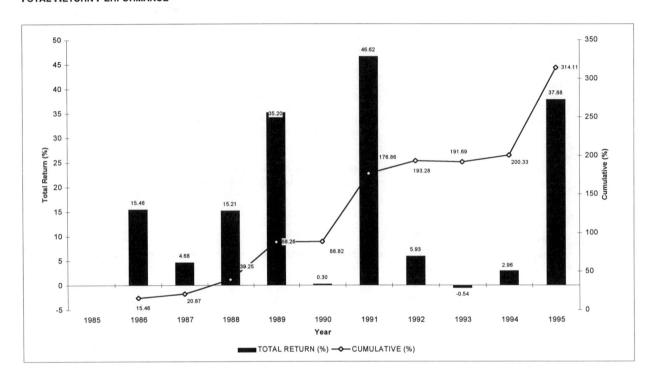

TOTAL RETURN PERFORMANCE

YEAR	VALUE[1]	TOTAL RETURN (%)	CUMULATIVE (%)	MAXIMUM VALUE[2]	DATE	MINIMUM VALUE[2]	DATE
1995	1,364.45	37.88	314.11	1,364.45	31-Dec	1,085.46	31-Mar
1994	989.57	2.96	200.33	989.57	31-Dec	912.83	30-Jun
1993	961.10	-0.54	191.69	961.10	31-Dec	921.42	30-Jun
1992	966.32	5.93	193.28	966.32	31-Dec	863.58	31-Mar
1991	912.22	46.62	176.86	912.22	31-Dec	749.84	30-Jun
1990	622.16	0.30	88.82	662.27	30-Jun	551.60	30-Sep
1989	620.30	35.20	88.26	620.30	31-Dec	493.13	31-Mar
1988	458.81	15.21	39.25	458.81	31-Dec	422.94	31-Mar
1987	398.24	4.68	20.87	522.63	30-Sep	398.24	31-Dec
1986	380.44	15.46	15.46	404.39	30-Jun	357.32	30-Sep
1985	329.49						
Average Annual (%)		16.37					
Compound Annual (%)		15.27					
Standard Deviation (%)		17.33					

[1]Index values computed based on quarterly total rates of return using a 12/31/1977 base value of 100.00.
[2]Maximum/minimum index values are as of quarter-end, computed based on quarterly rates of return.

SYNOPSIS

The Wilshire Large Company Growth Equity Style Index is a market value-weighted portfolio index that measures the total return performance of the largest, growth oriented companies, derived from the top 750 companies within the largest 2,500 companies in the Wilshire 5000 Equity Index.

NUMBER OF STOCKS—DECEMBER 31, 1995

193

MARKET VALUE—DECEMBER 31, 1995

US$1,830,062.0 million

SELECTION CRITERIA

Eligible stocks represent the universe of the top 750 companies of the actively traded United States (U.S.)-headquartered common stocks with readily available price data, which extends down to approximately the US$1.2 billion market capitalization, that make up the Wilshire 5000 Equity Index. Constituent stocks are selected using key variables to assess growth oriented stocks, including sales growth, return on equity and dividend payout. Companies with less than five years of history are excluded from consideration.

BACKGROUND

Wilshire's style indices are created by screening Wilshire's large, mid-cap and small company indices for all companies that embody the characteristics of each style. The selected securities form a portfolio that is maintained for an entire calendar quarter, whereupon securities are purchased and sold in an effort to maintain the portfolio's style focus.

The orientation of each style portfolio is established by eliminating those companies that do not fit the style criteria through a process of elimination as opposed to establishing explicit cutoffs for each measure. All criteria are relative so that the portfolios are not affected by the changing levels of these measures during different market periods.

BASE DATE

April 1988=100.00

COMPUTATION METHODOLOGY

(1) Portfolio results are calculated using a time-weighted total rate of return formula in which the change in portfolio market value during the quarter plus income earned during the period is divided by the market value of the portfolio at the beginning of the period. (2) Style determinations are reviewed each quarter through a screening process, and portfolio purchases and sales are affected at that time. (3) Cash dividends are reinvested as of the end of each quarter.

DERIVATIVE INSTRUMENTS

None

SUBINDICES

None

RELATED INDICES

Wilshire 2500 Equity Index
Wilshire 5000 Equity Index
Wilshire Associates Small Company Growth Equity Style Index
Wilshire Small Company Value Equity Style Index
Wilshire Large Company Value Equity Style Index
Wilshire MidCap Growth Equity Style Index
Wilshire MidCap Value Equity Style Index
Wilshire REIT Index
Wilshire Small Cap Equity Index
Wilshire Small Company (Next 1750) Equity Index
Wilshire MidCap (MidCap 750) Equity Index

REMARKS

Median market capitalization=US$3,475.0 million.

PUBLISHER

Wilshire Associates Inc.

WILSHIRE LARGE COMPANY VALUE EQUITY STYLE INDEX

TOTAL RETURN PERFORMANCE

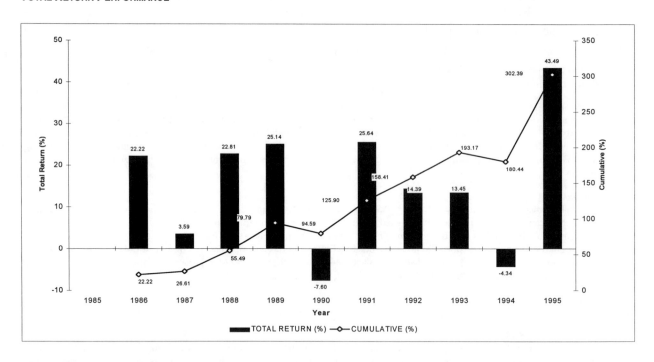

TOTAL RETURN PERFORMANCE

YEAR	VALUE[1]	TOTAL RETURN (%)	CUMULATIVE (%)	MAXIMUM VALUE[2]	DATE	MINIMUM VALUE[2]	DATE
1995	1,571.27	43.49	302.39	1,571.27	31-Dec	1,208.39	31-Mar
1994	1,095.05	-4.34	180.44	1,100.00	30-Sep	1,086.85	30-Jun
1993	1,144.78	13.45	193.17	1,183.61	30-Sep	1,101.57	31-Mar
1992	1,009.04	14.39	158.41	1,009.04	31-Dec	870.26	31-Mar
1991	882.08	25.64	125.90	882.08	31-Dec	782.30	31-Mar
1990	702.06	-7.60	79.79	749.33	30-Jun	643.97	30-Sep
1989	759.84	25.14	94.59	759.84	31-Dec	652.84	31-Mar
1988	607.18	22.81	55.49	607.18	31-Dec	537.07	31-Mar
1987	494.40	3.59	26.61	596.82	30-Sep	494.40	31-Dec
1986	477.26	22.22	22.22	477.26	31-Dec	445.54	31-Mar
1985	390.48						
Average Annual (%)		15.88					
Compound Annual (%)		14.94					
Standard Deviation (%)		15.46					

[1]Index values computed based on quarterly total rates of return using a 12/31/1977 base value of 100.00.
[2]Minimum/maximum index values are as of quarter-end, computed based on quarterly total rates of return.

SYNOPSIS

The Wilshire Large Company Value Equity Style Index is a market value-weighted index that measures the total return performance of the largest, value oriented companies, derived from the top 750 companies within the largest 2,500 companies in the Wilshire 5000 Equity Index.

NUMBER OF STOCKS—DECEMBER 31, 1995

146

MARKET VALUE—DECEMBER 31, 1995

US$988,883.0 million

SELECTION CRITERIA

Eligible stocks represent the universe of the top 750 companies of the actively traded United States (U.S.)-headquartered common stocks with readily available price data, which extends down to approximately the US$1.2 billion market capitalization, that make up the Wilshire 5000 Index. Constituent stocks are selected using key variables to assess value oriented stocks, including price/earnings ratio, price-to-book and yield.

BACKGROUND

Wilshire's style indices are created by screening Wilshire's large, mid-cap and small company indices for all companies that embody the characteristics of each style. The selected securities form a portfolio that is maintained for an entire calendar quarter, whereupon securities are purchased and sold in an effort to maintain the portfolio's style focus.

The orientation of each style portfolio is one which eliminated those companies which do not fit the style criteria through a process elimination as opposed to establishing explicit cutoffs for each measure. All criteria are relative so that the portfolios are not affected by the changing levels of these measures during different market periods.

BASE DATE

April 1988=100.00

COMPUTATION METHODOLOGY

(1) Portfolio results are calculated using a time-weighted total rate of return formula in which the change in portfolio market value during the quarter plus income earned during the period is divided by the market value of the portfolio at the beginning of the period. (2) Style determinations are reviewed each quarter through a screening process, and portfolio purchases and sales are affected at that time. (3) Cash dividends are reinvested as of the end of each quarter.

DERIVATIVE INSTRUMENTS

None

SUBINDICES

None

RELATED INDICES

Wilshire 5000 Equity Index
Wilshire 2500 Equity Index
Wilshire Large Company Growth Equity Style Index
Wilshire MidCap (MidCap 750) Equity Index
Wilshire MidCap Growth Equity Style Index
Wilshire MidCap Value Equity Style Index
Wilshire Small Company (Next 1750) Equity Index
Wilshire Associates Small Company Growth Equity Style Index
Wilshire Small Company Value Equity Style Index
Wilshire Small Cap Equity Index
Wilshire REIT Index

REMARKS

Median market capitalization=US$3,539.0 million.

PUBLISHER

Wilshire Associates Inc.

Wilshire Middle Capitalization Company (MidCap 750) Equity Index

Total Return Performance

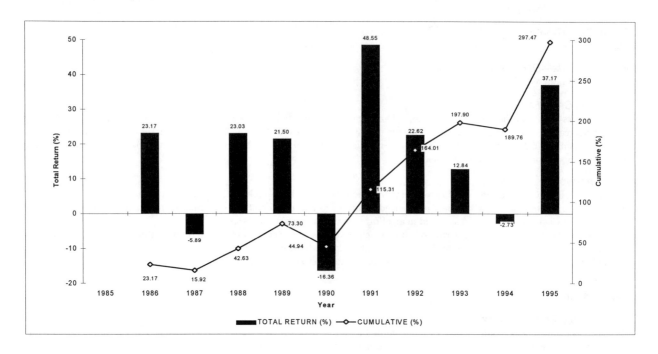

Total Return Performance

YEAR	VALUE[1]	TOTAL RETURN (%)	CUMULATIVE (%)	MAXIMUM VALUE[2]	DATE	MINIMUM VALUE[2]	DATE
1995	1,647.93	32.96	271.82	1,647.93	31-Dec	1,344.54	31-Mar
1994	1,239.44	-0.83	179.65	1,271.61	30-Sep	1,178.18	30-Jun
1993	1,249.76	14.78	181.98	1,249.76	31-Dec	1,138.13	31-Mar
1992	1,088.80	15.28	145.66	1,088.80	31-Dec	933.24	30-Jun
1991	944.50	42.85	113.11	944.50	31-Dec	809.58	31-Mar
1990	661.20	-13.89	49.19	766.51	30-Jun	611.60	30-Sep
1989	767.87	23.48	73.25	792.60	30-Sep	672.16	31-Mar
1988	621.85	21.87	40.31	621.85	31-Dec	581.41	31-Mar
1987	510.27	-0.26	15.13	669.74	30-Sep	510.27	31-Dec
1986	511.61	15.43	15.43	549.73	30-Jun	503.06	30-Sep
1985	443.21						
Average Annual (%)		15.17					
Compound Annual (%)		14.03					
Standard Deviation (%)		16.78					

[1] Index values computed based on quarterly total rates of return using a 12/31/1977 base value of 100.00.
[2] Maximum/minimum index values are as of quarter-end, computed based on quarterly total rates of return.

SYNOPSIS

The Wilshire Middle Capitalization Company (MidCap 750) Equity Index is a market value-weighted index that measures the total return performance of the 750 middle capitalization companies derived from the largest 2,500 securities in the Wilshire 5000 Equity Index. These shares, with a medium market value of US$1,112.0 million, represent 14% of the Wilshire 5000 Equity Index market capitalization.

NUMBER OF STOCKS—DECEMBER 31, 1995
750

MARKET VALUE—DECEMBER 31, 1995
US$903,962.0 million

SELECTION CRITERIA
Constituents are the 501st through 1,250th companies that make up the Wilshire 5000 Equity Index and include the actively traded United States (U.S.)-headquartered common stocks with readily available price data.

BACKGROUND
The index is derived from the largest 2,500 securities of the Wilshire 5000 Equity Index with a market capitalization that falls within a range between US$2.0 billion and US$540.0 million. Performance data is available on a quarterly basis.

BASE DATE
April 1988=100.00

COMPUTATION METHODOLOGY
(1) An aggregate of prices times quantities index formula. Maintenance adjustments to the divisor are made daily to eliminate the effect of all types of capitalization changes, new listings and delistings. (2) In the event that an ending price is not available for a given security, the security is dropped from the computation on that date and coverage resumes upon price availability. (3) Cash dividends are reinvested on the ex-dividend date.

DERIVATIVE INSTRUMENTS
None

SUBINDICES
Wilshire MidCap Growth Equity Style Index
Wilshire MidCap Value Equity Style Index

RELATED INDICES
Wilshire 2500 Equity Index
Wilshire 5000 Equity Index
Wilshire Associates Small Company Growth Equity Style Index
Wilshire Small Company Value Equity Style Index
Wilshire Large Company (Top 750) Equity Index
Wilshire Large Company Growth Equity Style Index
Wilshire Large Company Value Equity Style Index
Wilshire REIT Index
Wilshire Small Cap Equity Index
Wilshire Small Company (Next 1750) Equity Index

REMARKS
The base year coincides with the introduction of Wilshire Asset Management's Equity Style Portfolios, a series of equity portfolios that are designed to track the total return performance of passively managed growth and value styles of equity investing within a universe of large-, middle-capitalization and small company stocks.

PUBLISHER
Wilshire Associates Inc.

WILSHIRE MIDDLE CAPITALIZATION COMPANY GROWTH EQUITY STYLE INDEX

TOTAL RETURN PERFORMANCE

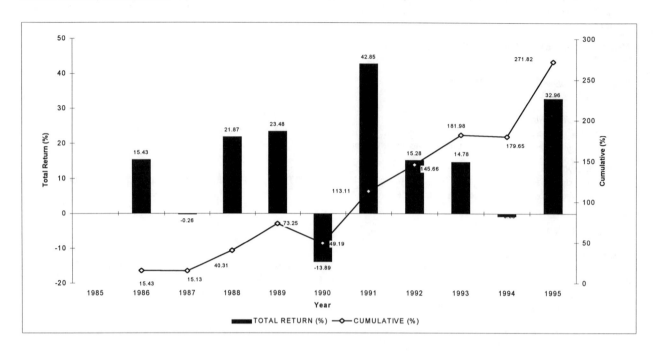

TOTAL RETURN PERFORMANCE

YEAR	VALUE[1]	TOTAL RETURN (%)	CUMULATIVE (%)	MAXIMUM VALUE[2]	DATE	MINIMUM VALUE[2]	DATE
1995	1,751.48	38.96	273.14	1,751.48	31-Dec	1,385.61	31-Mar
1994	1,260.45	0.92	168.53	1,266.40	30-Sep	1,147.83	30-Jun
1993	1,249.01	15.76	166.09	1,249.01	31-Dec	1,098.97	31-Mar
1992	1,079.01	12.28	129.87	1,079.01	31-Dec	889.20	30-Jun
1991	961.02	55.37	104.74	961.02	31-Dec	786.80	31-Mar
1990	618.55	-13.02	31.78	728.08	30-Jun	552.03	30-Sep
1989	711.15	22.01	51.51	739.78	30-Sep	625.61	31-Mar
1988	582.88	14.79	24.18	596.09	30-Jun	569.55	31-Mar
1987	507.80	-5.74	8.18	653.04	30-Jun	507.80	31-Dec
1986	538.70	14.77	14.77	588.33	30-Jun	524.79	30-Sep
1985	469.39						
Average Annual (%)		15.61					
Compound Annual (%)		14.07					
Standard Deviation (%)		20.19					

[1]Index values computed based on quarterly total rates of return using a 12/31/1977 base value of 100.00.
[2]Minimum/maximum index values are as of quarter-end, computed based on quarterly total rates of return.

SYNOPSIS
The Wilshire Middle Capitalization Company Growth Equity Style Index is a market value-weighted index that measures the total return performance of the 750 growth oriented middle-capitalization companies derived from the largest 2,500 securities in the Wilshire 5000 Equity Index.

NUMBER OF STOCKS—DECEMBER 31, 1995
140

MARKET VALUE—DECEMBER 31, 1995
US$190,958.0 million

SELECTION CRITERIA
Eligible stocks represent the universe of the 501st and 1,250th companies that make up the Wilshire 5000 Equity Index of the actively traded United States (U.S.)-headquartered common stocks with readily available price data. Constituent stocks are selected using key variables to assess growth oriented stocks, including sales growth, return on equity and dividend payout. Companies with less than five years of history are excluded from consideration.

BACKGROUND
Wilshire's style indices are created by screening Wilshire's large, mid-cap and small company indices for all companies that embody the characteristics of each style. The selected securities form a portfolio that is maintained for an entire calendar quarter, whereupon securities are purchased and sold in an effort to maintain the portfolio's style focus.

   The orientation of each style portfolio is established by eliminating those companies which do not fit the style criteria through a process of elimination as opposed to establishing explicit cutoffs for each measure. All criteria are relative so that the portfolios are not affected by the changing levels of these measures during different market periods.

BASE DATE
April 1988=100.00

COMPUTATION METHODOLOGY
(1) Portfolio results are calculated using a time-weighted total rate of return formula in which the change in portfolio market value during the quarter plus income earned during the period is divided by the market value of the portfolio at the beginning of the period. (2) Style determinations are reviewed each quarter through a screening process, and portfolio purchases and sales are affected at that time. (3) Cash dividends are reinvested as of the end of each quarter.

DERIVATIVE INSTRUMENTS
None

SUBINDICES
None

RELATED INDICES
Wilshire 2500 Equity Index
Wilshire 5000 Equity Index
Wilshire Associates Small Company Growth Equity Style Index
Wilshire Small Company Value Equity Style Index
Wilshire Large Company (Top 750) Equity Index
Wilshire Large Company Growth Equity Style Index
Wilshire Large Company Value Equity Style Index
Wilshire MidCap Value Equity Style Index
Wilshire Middle Capitalization (MidCap 750) Equity Index
Wilshire REIT Index
Wilshire Small Cap Equity Index
Wilshire Small Company (Next 1750) Equity Index

REMARKS
Median market capitalization=US$1,257.0 million.

PUBLISHER
Wilshire Associates Inc.

WILSHIRE MIDDLE CAPITALIZATION COMPANY VALUE EQUITY STYLE INDEX

TOTAL RETURN PERFORMANCE

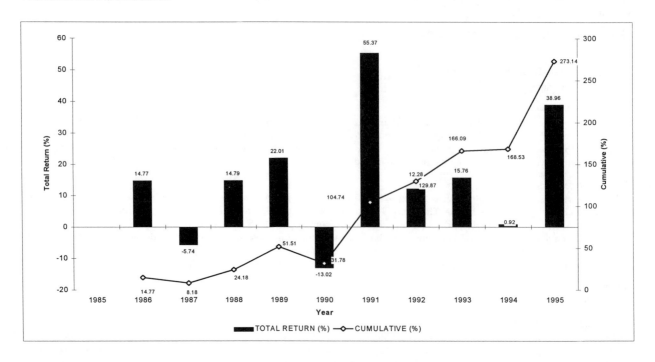

TOTAL RETURN PERFORMANCE

YEAR	VALUE[1]	TOTAL RETURN (%)	CUMULATIVE (%)	MAXIMUM VALUE[2]	DATE	MINIMUM VALUE[2]	DATE
1995	2,204.86	37.17	297.47	2,204.86	31-Dec	1,734.85	31-Mar
1994	1,607.38	-2.73	189.76	1,655.56	30-Sep	1,606.25	30-Jun
1993	1,652.56	12.84	197.90	1,694.59	30-Sep	1,618.61	31-Mar
1992	1,464.54	22.62	164.01	1,464.54	31-Dec	1,230.47	31-Mar
1991	1,194.40	48.55	115.31	1,194.40	31-Dec	961.07	31-Mar
1990	804.04	-16.36	44.94	905.48	31-Mar	742.69	30-Sep
1989	961.34	21.50	73.30	997.75	30-Sep	841.27	31-Mar
1988	791.19	23.03	42.63	791.19	31-Dec	730.78	31-Mar
1987	643.07	-5.89	15.92	783.85	30-Sep	643.07	31-Dec
1986	683.29	23.17	23.17	699.51	30-Jun	653.75	31-Mar
1985	554.73						
Average Annual (%)		16.39					
Compound Annual (%)		14.80					
Standard Deviation (%)		19.91					

[1]Index values computed based on quarterly total rates of return using a 12/31/1977 base value of 100.00.
[1]Minimum/maximum index values are as of quarter-end, computed based on quarterly rates of return.

SYNOPSIS
The Wilshire Middle Capitalization Company Value Equity Style Index is a market value-weighted index that measures the total return performance of the 750 value oriented middle capitalization companies derived from the largest 2,500 securities in the Wilshire 5000 Equity Index.

NUMBER OF STOCKS—DECEMBER 31, 1995
111

MARKET VALUE—DECEMBER 31, 1995
US$136,606.0 million

SELECTION CRITERIA
Eligible stocks represent the universe of the 501st through the 1,250th companies that make up the Wilshire 5000 Equity Index of the actively traded United States (U.S.)-headquartered common stocks with readily available price data. Constituent stocks are selected using key variables to assess value oriented, including price/earnings ratio, price-to-book and yield. Companies with less than five years of history are excluded from consideration.

BACKGROUND
Wilshire's style indices are created by screening Wilshire's large, mid-cap and small company indices for all companies that embody the characteristics of each style. The selected securities form a portfolio that is maintained for an entire calendar quarter, whereupon securities are purchased and sold in an effort to maintain the portfolio's style focus.

The orientation of each style portfolio is established by eliminating those companies which do not fit the style criteria through a process of elimination as opposed to establishing explicit cutoffs for each measure. All criteria are relative so that the portfolios are not affected by the changing levels of these measures during different market periods.

BASE DATE
April 1988=100.00

COMPUTATION METHODOLOGY
(1) Portfolio results are calculated using a time-weighted total rate of return formula in which the change in portfolio market value during the quarter plus income earned during the period is divided by the market value of the portfolio at the beginning of the period. (2) Style determinations are reviewed each quarter through a screening process, and portfolio purchases and sales are affected at that time. (3) Cash dividends are reinvested as of the end of each quarter.

DERIVATIVE INSTRUMENTS
None

SUBINDICES
None

RELATED INDICES
Wilshire 2500 Equity Index
Wilshire 5000 Equity Index
Wilshire Associates Small Company Growth Equity Style Index
Wilshire Small Company Value Equity Style Index
Wilshire Large Company (Top 750) Equity Index
Wilshire Large Company Growth Equity Style Index
Wilshire Large Company Value Equity Style Index
Wilshire MidCap Growth Equity Style Index
Wilshire Middle Capitalization (MidCap 750) Equity Index
Wilshire REIT Index
Wilshire Small Cap Equity Index
Wilshire Small Company (Next 1750) Equity Index

REMARKS
Median market capitalization=US$1,132.0 million.

PUBLISHER
Wilshire Associates Inc.

WILSHIRE SMALL COMPANY (NEXT 1750) EQUITY INDEX

TOTAL RETURN PERFORMANCE

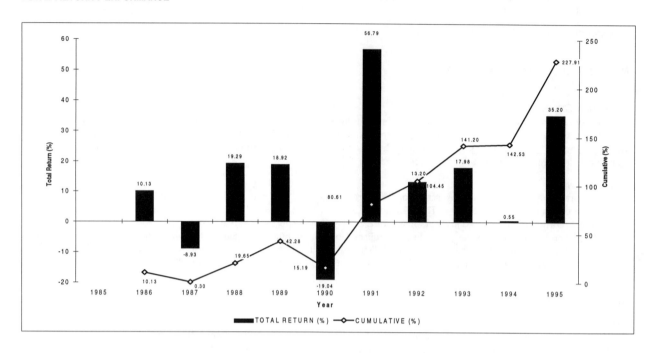

TOTAL RETURN PERFORMANCE

YEAR	VALUE[1]	TOTAL RETURN (%)	CUMULATIVE (%)	MAXIMUM VALUE[2]	DATE	MINIMUM VALUE[2]	DATE
1995	1,609.51	30.26	225.52	1,609.51	31-Dec	1,308.07	31-Mar
1994	1,235.66	-1.37	149.91	1,262.30	30-Sep	1,168.79	30-Jun
1993	1,252.79	17.44	153.37	1,252.79	31-Dec	1,107.50	31-Mar
1992	1,066.75	18.65	115.75	1,066.75	31-Dec	896.44	30-Jun
1991	899.05	45.82	81.83	899.05	31-Dec	777.33	30-Jun
1990	616.56	-18.49	24.70	758.87	30-Jun	579.85	30-Sep
1989	756.40	18.55	52.98	795.45	30-Sep	692.00	31-Mar
1988	638.02	22.55	29.04	642.99	30-Jun	602.61	31-Mar
1987	520.62	-5.14	5.29	704.11	30-Sep	529.65	31-Dec
1986	548.83	11.00	11.00	604.57	30-Jun	542.48	30-Sep
1985	494.45						
Average Annual (%)		13.93					
Compound Annual (%)		12.53					
Standard Deviation (%)		18.47					

[1]Index values computed based on quarterly total rates of return using a 12/31/1977 base value of 100.00.
[2]Maximum/minimum index values are as of quarter-end, computed based on quarterly total rates of return.

SYNOPSIS

The Wilshire Small Company (Next 1750) Equity Index is a market value-weighted index that measures the total return performance of the smallest 1,750 companies derived from the 2,500 largest securities in the Wilshire 5000 Equity Index. These shares, with a median market value of US$393.0 million, represent about 14% of the Wilshire 5000 Equity Index market capitalization.

NUMBER OF STOCKS—DECEMBER 31, 1995

1,750

MARKET VALUE—DECEMBER 31, 1995

US$878,039.0 million

SELECTION CRITERIA

Constituents are the smallest 1,750 companies that make up the top 2,500 securities of the Wilshire 5000 Equity Index and include the actively traded United States (U.S)-headquartered common stocks with readily available price data.

BACKGROUND

The index is derived from the largest 2,500 securities of the Wilshire 5000 Equity Index with a market capitalization that falls within a range that extends between US$540.0 million and US$155.0 million. Performance data is available on a quarterly basis.

BASE DATE

April 1988=100.00

COMPUTATION METHODOLOGY

(1) An aggregate of prices times quantities index formula. Maintenance adjustments to the divisor are made daily to eliminate the effect of all types of capitalization changes, new listings and delistings. (2) In the event that an ending price is not available for a given security, the security is dropped from the computation on that date and coverage resumes upon price availability. (3) Cash dividends are reinvested on the ex-dividend date.

DERIVATIVE INSTRUMENTS

None (a related index, the Wilshire Small Cap Index, serves as an underlying vehicle for index options traded on The Chicago Board Options Exchange (CBOE)).

SUBINDICES

Wilshire Associates Small Company Growth Equity Style Index
Wilshire Associates Small Company Value Equity Style Index

RELATED INDICES

Wilshire 2500 Equity Index
Wilshire 5000 Equity Index
Wilshire Large Company (Top 750) Equity Index
Wilshire Large Company Growth Equity Style Index
Wilshire Large Company Value Equity Style Index
Wilshire MidCap Growth Equity Style Index
Wilshire MidCap Value Equity Style Index
Wilshire Middle Capitalization (Next 750) Equity Index
Wilshire REIT Index
Wilshire Small Cap Equity Index

REMARKS

The base year coincides with the introduction of Wilshire Asset Management's Equity Style Portfolios, a series of equity portfolios that are designed to track the total return performance of passively managed growth and value styles of equity investing within a universe of large-, middle-capitalization and small company stocks.

PUBLISHER

Wilshire Associates Inc.

WILSHIRE SMALL COMPANY GROWTH EQUITY STYLE INDEX

TOTAL RETURN PERFORMANCE

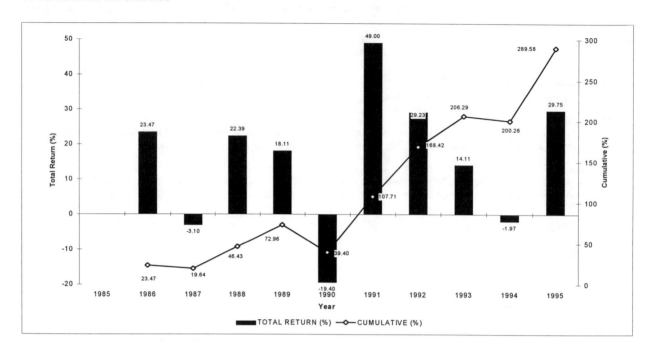

TOTAL RETURN PERFORMANCE

YEAR	VALUE[1]	TOTAL RETURN (%)	CUMULATIVE (%)	MAXIMUM VALUE[2]	DATE	MINIMUM VALUE[2]	DATE
1995	1,593.34	35.20	227.91	1,593.34	31-Dec	1,178.48	31-Mar
1994	1,178.48	0.55	142.53	1,178.48	31-Dec	1,043.17	31-Mar
1993	1,172.03	17.98	141.20	1,172.03	31-Dec	1,002.26	31-Mar
1992	993.42	13.20	104.45	993.42	31-Dec	794.58	30-Jun
1991	877.60	56.79	80.61	877.60	31-Dec	721.04	30-Jun
1990	559.72	-19.04	15.19	715.40	30-Jun	498.06	30-Sep
1989	691.36	18.92	42.28	734.79	30-Sep	628.02	31-Mar
1988	581.39	19.29	19.65	603.72	30-Jun	564.70	31-Mar
1987	487.36	-8.93	0.30	678.96	30-Sep	487.36	31-Dec
1986	535.12	10.13	10.13	595.66	30-Jun	518.23	30-Sep
1985	485.91						
Average Annual (%)		14.41					
Compound Annual (%)		12.61					
Standard Deviation (%)		21.50					

[1]Index values computed based on quarterly total rates of return using a 12/31/1977 base value of 100.00.
[2]Minimum/maximum index values are as of quarter-end, computed based on quarterly rates of return.

SYNOPSIS

The Wilshire Small Company Growth Equity Style Index is a market value-weighted index that measures the total return performance of the smallest 1,750 growth oriented companies derived from the 2,500 largest securities in the Wilshire 5000 Equity Index

NUMBER OF STOCKS—DECEMBER 31, 1995

232

MARKET VALUE—DECEMBER 31, 1995

US$148,127.0 million

SELECTION CRITERIA

Eligible stocks represent the universe of the smallest 1,750 companies that make up the top 2,500 securities of the Wilshire 5000 Equity Index and include the actively traded United States (U.S.)-headquartered common stocks with readily available price data. Constituent stocks are selected using key variables to assess growth oriented stocks, including sales growth, return on equity and dividend payout. Companies with less than two years of history are excluded from consideration.

BACKGROUND

Wilshire's style indices are created by screening Wilshire's large, mid-cap and small company indices for all companies that embody the characteristics of each style. The selected securities form a portfolio that is maintained for an entire calendar quarter, whereupon securities are purchased and sold in an effort to maintain the portfolio's style focus.

The orientation of each style portfolio is established by eliminating those companies which do not fit the style criteria through a process of elimination as opposed to establishing explicit cutoffs for each measure. All criteria are relative so that the portfolios are not affected by the changing levels of these measures during different market periods.

BASE DATE

April 1988=100.00

COMPUTATION METHODOLOGY

(1) Portfolio results are calculated using a time-weighted total rate of return formula in which the change in portfolio market value during the quarter plus income earned during the period is divided by the market value of the portfolio at the beginning of the period. (2) Style determinations are reviewed each quarter through a screening process, and portfolio purchases and sales are affected at that time. (3) Cash dividends are reinvested as of the end of each quarter.

DERIVATIVE INSTRUMENTS

None

SUBINDICES

None

RELATED INDICES

Wilshire 2500 Equity Index
Wilshire 5000 Equity Index
Wilshire Large Company (Top 750) Equity Index
Wilshire Large Company Growth Equity Style Index
Wilshire Large Company Value Equity Style Index
Wilshire MidCap Value Equity Style Index
Wilshire Middle Capitalization (Next 750) Equity Index
Wilshire REIT Index
Wilshire Small Cap Equity Index
Wilshire Small Company (Next 1750) Equity Index
Wilshire Small Company Value Equity Style Index

REMARKS

Median market capitalization=US$511.0 million.

PUBLISHER

Wilshire Associates Inc.

WILSHIRE SMALL COMPANY VALUE EQUITY STYLE INDEX

TOTAL RETURN PERFORMANCE

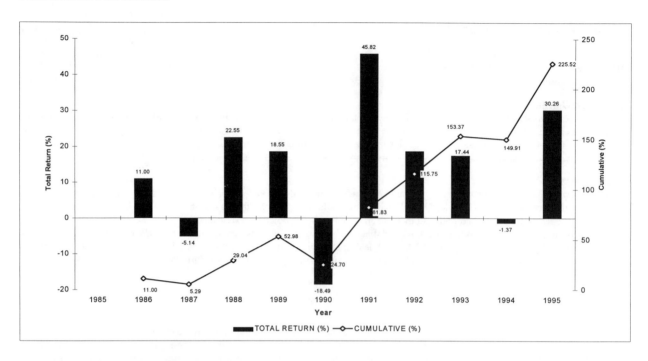

TOTAL RETURN PERFORMANCE

YEAR	VALUE[1]	TOTAL RETURN (%)	CUMULATIVE (%)	MAXIMUM VALUE[2]	DATE	MINIMUM VALUE[2]	DATE
1995	2,675.31	29.75	289.58	2,675.31	31-Dec	2,166.23	31-Mar
1994	2,061.90	-1.97	200.26	2,100.77	30-Sep	2,020.87	31-Mar
1993	2,103.32	14.11	206.29	2,137.52	30-Sep	2,015.23	31-Mar
1992	1,843.25	29.23	168.42	1,843.25	31-Dec	1,530.20	31-Mar
1991	1,426.36	49.00	107.71	1,426.36	31-Dec	1,126.15	31-Mar
1990	957.28	-19.40	39.40	1,132.60	31-Mar	903.44	30-Sep
1989	1,187.71	18.11	72.96	1,245.50	30-Sep	1,059.76	31-Mar
1988	1,005.56	22.39	46.43	1,005.56	31-Dec	922.14	31-Mar
1987	821.58	-3.10	19.64	982.40	30-Sep	821.58	31-Dec
1986	847.90	23.47	23.47	858.00	30-Jun	790.34	31-Mar
1985	686.72						
Average Annual (%)		16.16					
Compound Annual (%)		14.57					
Standard Deviation (%)		19.72					

[1]Index values computed based on quarterly total rates of return using a 12/31/1977 base value of 100.00.
[2]Minimum/maximum index values are as of quarter-end, computed based on quarterly rates of return.

Synopsis

The Wilshire Small Company Value Equity Style Index is a market value-weighted index that measures the total return performance of the smallest 1,750 value oriented companies derived from the 2,500 largest securities in the Wilshire 5000 Equity Index.

Number of Stocks—December 31, 1995

193

Market Value—December 31, 1995

US$110,984.0 million

Selection Criteria

Eligible stocks represent the universe of the smallest 1,750 companies that make up the top 2,500 securities of the Wilshire 5000 Equity Index and include the actively traded United States (U.S.)-headquartered common stocks with readily available price data. Constituents are selected using key variables used to assess value oriented stocks, including price/earnings ratio, price-to-book and yield. Companies with less than two years of history are excluded from consideration.

Background

Wilshire's style indices are created by screening Wilshire's large, mid-cap and small company indices for all companies that embody the characteristics of each style. The selected securities form a portfolio that is maintained for an entire calendar quarter, whereupon securities are purchased and sold in an effort to maintain the portfolio's style focus.

The orientation of each style portfolio is established through a process of eliminating those companies which do not fit the style criteria through a process of elimination as opposed to establishing explicit cutoffs for each measure. All criteria are relative so that the portfolios are not affected by the changing levels of these measures during different market periods.

Base Date

April 1988=100.00

Computation Methodology

(1) Portfolio results are calculated using a time-weighted total rate of return formula in which the change in portfolio market value during the quarter plus income earned during the period is divided by the market value of the portfolio at the beginning of the period. (2) Style determinations are reviewed each quarter through a screening process, and portfolio purchases and sales are affected at that time. (3) Cash dividends are reinvested as of the end of each quarter.

Derivative Instruments

None

Subindices

None

Related Indices

Wilshire 2500 Equity Index
Wilshire 5000 Equity Index
Wilshire Large Company (Top 750) Equity Index
Wilshire Large Company Growth Equity Style Index
Wilshire Large Company Value Equity Style Index
Wilshire MidCap Growth Equity Style Index
Wilshire MidCap Value Equity Style Index
Wilshire Middle Capitalization (Next 750) Equity Index
Wilshire REIT Index
Wilshire Small Cap Equity Index
Wilshire Small Company (Next 1750) Equity Index
Wilshire Small Company Growth Equity Style Index

Remarks

Median market capitalization=US$488.0 million.

Publisher

Wilshire Associates Inc.

ASIA/PACIFIC

AUSTRALIAN ALL ORDINARIES STOCK EXCHANGE INDEX (ASX)

PRICE PERFORMANCE

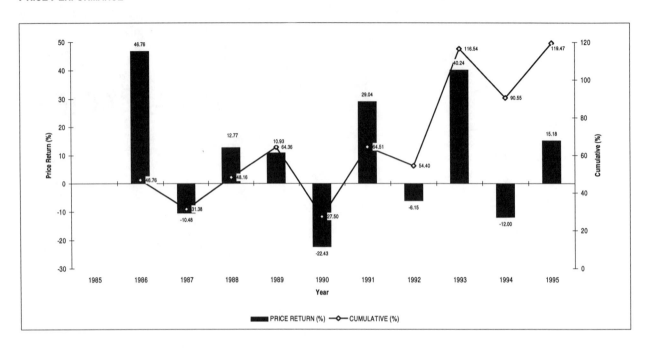

PRICE AND TOTAL RETURN PERFORMANCE

YEAR	VALUE	PRICE RETURN (%)	CUMULATIVE (%)	TOTAL RETURN (%)	MAXIMUM VALUE[1]	DATE	MINIMUM VALUE[1]	DATE
1995	2,203.00	15.18	119.47	20.19	2,225.60	13-Dec	1,823.30	8-Feb
1994	1,912.70	-12.00	90.55	-8.67	2,340.60	3-Feb	1,842.00	12-Dec
1993	2,173.60	40.24	116.54	45.36	2,173.60	31-Dec	1,495.00	13-Jan
1992	1,549.90	-6.15	54.40	-2.31	1,684.50	22-May	1,357.20	16-Nov
1991	1,651.40	29.04	64.51	34.24	1,696.30	8-Nov	1,204.50	16-Jan
1990	1,279.80	-22.43	27.50	-17.52	1,713.70	12-Jan	1,270.70	28-Dec
1989	1,649.80	10.93	64.36	17.40	1,781.80	1-Sep	1,412.90	7-Apr
1988	1,487.20	12.77	48.16	17.88	1,657.60	12-Aug	1,171.60	12-Feb
1987	1,318.80	-10.48	31.38	-7.86	2,306.20	25-Sep	1,467.10	2-Jan
1986	1,473.20	46.76	46.76	52.22	1,464.10	26-Dec	1,001.60	3-Jan
1985	1,003.80							
Average Annual (%)		10.39		15.09				
Compound Annual (%)		8.18		12.85				
Standard Deviation (%)		23.28		23.94				

[1]Maximum/minimum values for the calendar periods 1986-1990 are based on weekly week-ended index values.

SYNOPSIS

The Australian All Ordinaries Stock Exchange Index (ASX) is a broad market capitalization-weighted index that tracks the continuous stock price and total return performance of domestic and overseas-domiciled large capitalization, actively traded, ordinary equity shares that trade on the Australian Stock Exchange (ASX). These shares account for about 94% of the market capitalization of Australian domestic-traded equities.

NUMBER OF STOCKS—DECEMBER 31, 1995
347

MARKET VALUE—DECEMBER 31, 1995
US$230,415.8 million

SELECTION CRITERIA

Eligible securities include listed and ordinary shares, both fully and partly paid shares, rights and delivery shares as well as listed trust units. Constituent shares must achieve a minimum market capitalization of 0.02% of total domestic stocks quoted on the ASX with their index eligible shares only and average normal turnover on the ASX in excess of 0.5% of its quoted shares per month. To maintain the stability of the index, new issues normally require a two- to six-month seasoning period (subject to liquidity, volatility, quality of turnover, distribution of shareholders, etc.), before they are considered eligible for inclusion in the index. Exceptions may apply to some initial offerings and privatizations.

Excluded from the index are shares whose sale is currently prohibited by legislation, company articles or ASX regulations (this does not apply to temporary suspensions but does apply to vendor securities), options, convertible notes and preference shares. A few participating preference and/or convertible securities, however, may be included in the index as secondary issues of ordinary equity provided there is adequate liquidity and they form a substantial part of the company's capital, they are linked to the main equity issue by a fixed ratio, they participate in all pro-rate issues and they must not provide a cash alternative upon their conversion to equity.

BACKGROUND
The ASX Index and related indices were introduced in January 1980. The companion total return index was established with a base value of 1000.00 as of December 31, 1979.

Prior period data covering the period 1936 to 1979 is available for selected ASX price only indices based on recalculations of data produced by the predecessor Sydney and Melbourne indices, with monthly averages available for the period prior to 1958.

This index replaced the Sydney index which had been calculated daily since 1958 as well as the Melbourne index which had been calculated daily since 1960. Previously, the Sydney index tracked monthly share price movements dating back to 1875.

BASE DATE
December 31, 1979=500.00

COMPUTATION METHODOLOGY
(1) An aggregative of prices times quantities index formula. Maintenance adjustments to the divisor are made daily for capitalization changes, new listings and delistings. (2) The value of each security is the last sale price recorded by the Australian Stock Exchange Automated Trading System (SEATS), modified by any subsequent higher bids or lower offers made before trading ends at 16:00 hours (EST). (3) The composition of the index is reviewed on a monthly basis. Mergers, takeovers and other delistings are withdrawn from the index universe between monthly reviews. Suspended companies are retained unless the suspension seems likely to be long-term or terminal in nature. Additions and deletions are kept to a minimum so as to preserve the continuity of the index. Constituent stocks are generally replaced if their market capitalization is reduced to less than 0.01% of the index or their average monthly turnover falls below 0.02% of the index. Normally, 10% to 15% of constituent stocks are replaced each year. (4) Market capitalization is determined on the basis of listed shares. No adjustments are made for cross holdings, controlling, strategic and other long term holdings. Larger index stocks approaching these levels may be assigned a downweighting to reflect their lower availability, but 95% of domestic companies are carried in the index at 100% market capitalization. Some large overseas-domiciled companies with a very low turnover on the Australian market are excluded altogether from the index due to low liquidity. Overseas stocks account for about 2% of the ASX equity turnover and their influence on the ASX indices is limited to a similar level by downweighting these issues to bring their weight in the index in line with their share turnover. (5) Total returns are calculated by reinvesting 100% of dividends at the 16:00 hours (EST) market price on the ex-dividend date.

DERIVATIVE INSTRUMENTS
ASX All Ordinaries index futures and options on futures trade on the Australian Stock Exchange.
ASX All Ordinaries index futures, options on futures and Overnight Options trade on the Sydney Futures Exchange.
ASX Gold subindex futures and options trade on the Australian Stock Exchange.

SUBINDICES
Three broad industry subindices: Industrials, mining, and all resources.
Twenty-four industry subindices: Nineteen industrial groups, three mining groups, oil and gas as well as diversified resources, as follows: All Mining includes gold, other metals and solid fuels; All Resources includes oil and gas and diversified resources; All Industrials includes developers and contractors, building materials, alcohol and tobacco, food and household goods, chemicals, engineering, paper and packaging, retail, transport, media, banks and finance, insurance, entrepreneurial investors, investment and financial services, property trusts, miscellaneous services, miscellaneous industrials and diversified industrial.

RELATED INDICES
ASX 100 Index
ASX 20 Leaders Index
ASX 50 Leaders Index
ASX Midcap Index
ASX Small Cap Index
Trans Tasman 100 Index
The Wardley Index

REMARKS
(1) The index is somewhat concentrated in that the top 10 companies account for about 41% of its market capitalization while the largest 50 companies account for about 75% of its market capitalization. (2) Overseas stocks account for about 2% of ASX equity turnover and their influence on the ASX indices is limited to a similar level by reducing the weighting of the overseas stocks in the index universe.

PUBLISHER
The Australian Stock Exchange Limited.

AUSTRALIAN STOCK EXCHANGE 100 INDEX (ASX 100)

PRICE PERFORMANCE

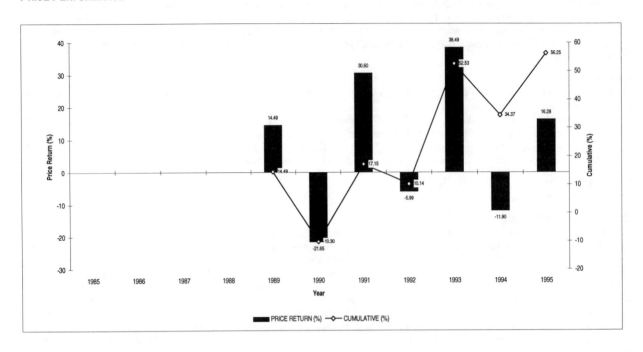

PRICE AND TOTAL RETURN PERFORMANCE

YEAR	VALUE	PRICE RETURN (%)	CUMULATIVE (%)	TOTAL RETURN (%)	MAXIMUM VALUE[1]	DATE	MINIMUM VALUE[1]	DATE
1995	1,741.90	16.28	56.25	21.29	1,767.30	13-Dec	1,438.70	8-Feb
1994	1,498.00	-11.90	34.37	-8.53	1,801.80	31-Jan	1,478.70	30-Nov
1993	1,700.40	38.49	52.53	43.50	1,700.40	31-Dec	1,206.90	31-Jan
1992	1,227.80	-5.99	10.14	-2.15	1,333.80	31-May	1,227.80	31-Dec
1991	1,306.00	30.60	17.15	35.88	1,329.90	31-Oct	1,036.20	31-Jan
1990	1,000.00	-21.65	-10.30	-16.53	1,299.80	31-Jan	1,000.00	31-Dec
1989	1,276.30	14.49	14.49	21.44	1,354.40	31-Aug	1,094.70	31-Mar
1988	1,114.80							
1987								
1986								
1985								
Average Annual (%)		8.62		13.56				
Compound Annual (%)		6.58		11.52				
Standard Deviation (%)		22.43		22.94				

[1]Maximum/minimum values based on month-end index values.

Synopsis

The Australian Stock Exchange 100 Index (ASX 100) is a market capitalization-weighted index that tracks the continuous stock price and total return performance of the 100 largest, actively traded, equity shares on the Australian Stock Exchange (ASX). The shares account for about 74% of the total market capitalization of the ASX All Ordinaries Index. These shares account for about 82% of the market capitalization of domestic Australian-traded equities.

Number of Stocks—December 31, 1995

100

Market Value—December 31, 1995

US$201,618.0 million

Selection Criteria

Constituent stocks include the top 100 companies which are selected on the basis of market capitalization and trading volume.

Eligible securities include listed and ordinary shares, both fully and partly paid shares, rights and delivery shares, and listed trust units which are selected on the basis of market capitalization and trading volume.

For additional information, refer to the Australian All Ordinaries Stock Exchange Index (ASX).

Background

The ASX 100 Index was launched on July 4, 1994 and recalculated to December 31, 1988.

Base Date

December 31, 1990=1000.00

Computation Methodology

(1) An aggregative of prices times quantities index formula. Maintenance adjustments to the divisor are made daily for capitalization changes, new listings and delistings. (2) The value of each security is the last sale price recorded by the Australian Stock Exchange Automated Trading System (SEATS), modified by any subsequent higher bids or lower offers made before trading ends at 16:00 hours (EST). (3) The composition of the index is reviewed on a monthly basis. Mergers, takeovers and other delistings are withdrawn from the index universe between monthly reviews. Suspended companies are retained unless the suspension seems likely to be long-term or terminal in nature. (4) Market capitalization is determined on the basis of listed shares. No adjustments are made for cross holdings, controlling, strategic and other long term holdings. (5) Total returns are calculated by reinvesting 100% of dividends at the 16:00 hours (EST) market price on the ex-dividend date.

Derivative Instruments

None

Subindices

None

Related Indices

ASX All Ordinaries Index
ASX 50 Leaders Index
ASX 20 Leaders Index
ASX Midcap Index
ASX Small Cap Index
Trans Tasman 100 Index
The Wardley Index

Remarks

None

Publisher

The Australian Stock Exchange Limited.

AUSTRALIAN STOCK EXCHANGE MID CAP INDEX

PRICE PERFORMANCE

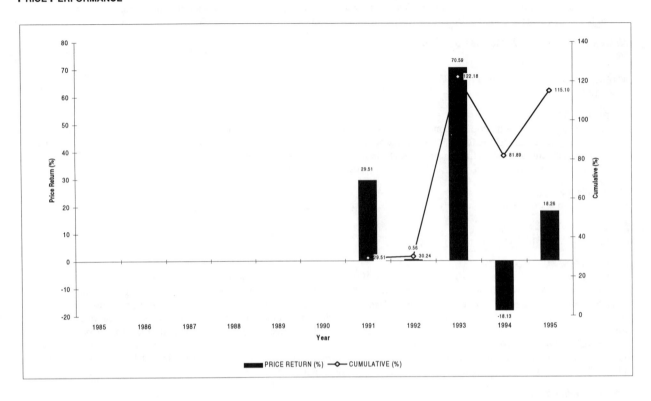

PRICE AND TOTAL RETURN PERFORMANCE

YEAR	VALUE	PRICE RETURN (%)	CUMULATIVE (%)	TOTAL RETURN (%)	MAXIMUM VALUE[1]	DATE	MINIMUM VALUE[1]	DATE
1995	2,151.00	18.26	115.10	23.92	2,151.40	15-Dec	1,691.70	14-Feb
1994	1,818.90	-18.13	81.89	14.74	2,333.70	31-Jan	1,803.60	Nov-96
1993	2,221.80	70.59	122.18	76.99	2,221.80	31-Dec	1,323.60	31-Jan
1992	1,302.40	0.56	30.24	5.26	1,355.80	31-Jul	1,255.70	30-Oct
1991	1,295.10	29.51	29.51	34.75	1,295.10	31-Dec	1,010.30	31-Jan
1990	1,000.00							
1989								
1988								
1987								
1986								
1985								
Average Annual (%)		20.16		15.57				
Compound Annual (%)		16.55		13.57				
Standard Deviation (%)		33.48		27.87				

[1]Maximum/minimum values for the period 12/90-12/94 based on month-end index values.

SYNOPSIS

The Australian Stock Exchange Mid Cap Index is a market capitalization-weighted index that tracks the continuous stock price and total return performance of actively traded middle capitalization equity shares traded on the Australian Stock Exchange (ASX). These shares correspond to the second largest 50 equity shares of the ASX 100 Index.

NUMBER OF STOCKS—DECEMBER 31, 1995
50

MARKET VALUE—DECEMBER 31, 1995
US$30,401.7 million

SELECTION CRITERIA

Constituent stocks include the second largest stocks of the ASX 100 Index selected on the basis of market capitalization and trading volume. Eligible securities include listed and ordinary shares, both fully and partly paid shares, rights and delivery shares as well as listed trust units which are selected on the basis of market capitalization and trading volume.

For additional information, refer to the Australian All Ordinaries Stock Exchange Index.

BACKGROUND
The ASX Mid Cap index was launched in 1995.

BASE DATE
December 31, 1990=1000.00

COMPUTATION METHODOLOGY

(1) An aggregative of prices times quantities index formula. Maintenance adjustments to the divisor are made daily for capitalization changes, new listings and delistings. (2) The value of each security is the last sale price recorded by the Australian Stock Exchange Automated Trading System (SEATS), modified by any subsequent higher bids or lower offers made before trading ends at 16:00 hours (EST). (3) The composition of the index is reviewed on a monthly basis. Mergers, takeovers and other delistings are withdrawn from the index universe between monthly reviews. Suspended companies are retained unless the suspension seems likely to be long-term or terminal in nature. (4) Market capitalization is determined on the basis of listed shares. No adjustments are made for cross holdings, controlling, strategic and other long term holdings. (5) Total returns are calculated by reinvesting 100% of dividends at the 16:00 hours (EST) market price on the ex-dividend date.

DERIVATIVE INSTRUMENTS
None

SUBINDICES
The index is calculated on the basis of price only and total return, including dividends reinvested.
Two broad industry subindices: industrials and resources.

RELATED INDICES
ASX All Ordinaries Index
ASX 100 Index
ASX 50 Leaders Index
ASX 20 Leaders Index
ASX Small Cap Index
Trans Tasman 100 Index
The Wardley Index

REMARKS
None

PUBLISHER
The Australian Stock Exchange Limited.

AUSTRALIAN STOCK EXCHANGE SMALL CAP INDEX

PRICE PERFORMANCE

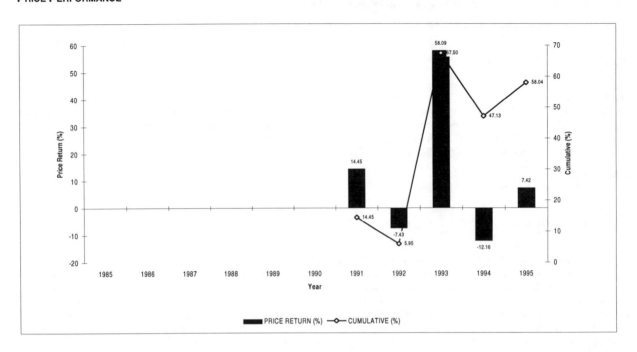

PRICE AND TOTAL RETURN PERFORMANCE

YEAR	VALUE	PRICE RETURN (%)	CUMULATIVE (%)	TOTAL RETURN (%)	MAXIMUM VALUE[1]	DATE	MINIMUM VALUE[1]	DATE
1995	1,580.40	7.42	58.04	12.07	1,580.40	29-Dec	1,358.40	30-Mar
1994	1,471.30	-12.16	47.13	-9.01	1,830.90	31-Jan	1,468.60	Nov-31
1993	1,675.00	58.09	67.50	64.46	1,675.00	31-Dec	1,075.90	31-Jan
1992	1,059.50	-7.43	5.95	-3.68	1,159.80	31-Jan	1,027.90	1-Nov
1991	1,144.50	14.45	14.45	18.90	1,179.30	31-Oct	1,001.80	31-Jan
1990	1,000.00							
1989								
1988								
1987								
1986								
1985								
Average Annual (%)		12.07		16.55				
Compound Annual (%)		9.59		6.74				
Standard Deviation (%)		27.90		29.08				

[1]Maximum/minimum values for the period 12/90-12/94 based on month-end index values.

SYNOPSIS

The Australian Stock Exchange Small Cap Index is a market capitalization-weighted index that tracks the continuous stock price and total return performance of actively traded smaller capitalization equity shares traded on the Australian Stock Exchange (ASX). The shares correspond to the Australian All Ordinaries Stock Exchange Index (ASX) less the shares that make up the ASX 100 Index.

NUMBER OF STOCKS—DECEMBER 31, 1995

220

MARKET VALUE—DECEMBER 31, 1995

US$28,798.01 million

SELECTION CRITERIA

Constituent stocks include all the equity shares of the Australian All Ordinaries Stock Exchange Index less equity shares that make up the ASX 100 Index (i.e. the one hundred largest and most actively traded shares on the ASX). Eligible securities include listed and ordinary shares, both fully and partly paid shares, rights and delivery shares as well as listed trust units. Selection is on the basis of market capitalization and trading volume.

For additional information on selection criteria, refer to the Australian All Ordinaries Stock Exchange Index.

BACKGROUND

The ASX Small Cap Index was launched in 1995.

BASE DATE

December 31, 1990=1000.00

COMPUTATION METHODOLOGY

(1) An aggregative of prices times quantities index formula. Maintenance adjustments to the divisor are made daily for capitalization changes, new listings and delistings. (2) The value of each security is the last sale price recorded by the Australian Stock Exchange Automated Trading System (SEATS), modified by any subsequent higher bids or lower offers made before trading ends at 16:00 hours (EST). (3) The composition of the index is reviewed on a monthly basis. Mergers, takeovers and other delistings are withdrawn from the index universe between monthly reviews. Suspended companies are retained unless the suspension seems likely to be long-term or terminal in nature. (4) Market capitalization is determined on the basis of listed shares. No adjustments are made for cross holdings, controlling, strategic and other long term holdings. (5) Total returns are calculated by reinvesting 100% of dividends at the 16:00 hours (EST) market price on the ex-dividend date.

DERIVATIVE INSTRUMENTS

None

SUBINDICES

Two broad industry subindices: Industrials and resources.

RELATED INDICES

ASX All Ordinaries Index
ASX 100 Index
ASX 50 Leaders Index
ASX 20 Leaders Index
ASX Mid Cap Index
Trans Tasman 100 Index
The Wardley Index

REMARKS

None

PUBLISHER

The Australian Stock Exchange Limited.

AUSTRALIAN STOCK EXCHANGE TWENTY LEADERS INDEX

PRICE PERFORMANCE

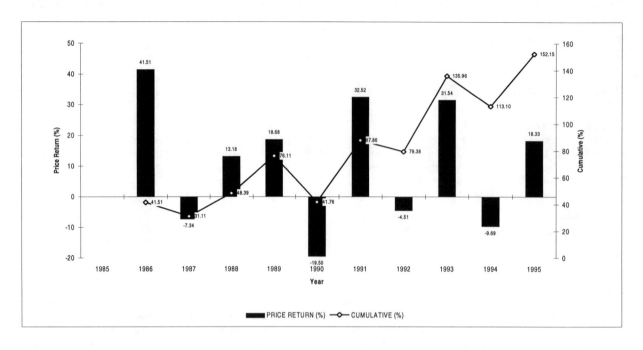

PRICE AND TOTAL RETURN PERFORMANCE

YEAR	VALUE	PRICE RETURN (%)	CUMULATIVE (%)	TOTAL RETURN (%)	MAXIMUM VALUE[1]	DATE	MINIMUM VALUE[1]	DATE
1995	1,201.00	18.33	152.15	23.26	1,227.50	13-Dec	981.20	31-Jan
1994	1,015.00	-9.69	113.10	-6.38	1,195.50	31-Jan	997.50	30-Nov
1993	1,123.90	31.54	135.96	36.07	1,123.90	31-Dec	832.40	31-Jan
1992	854.40	-4.51	79.38	-0.93	925.80	31-May	765.00	31-Oct
1991	894.80	32.52	87.86	37.57	918.10	30-Sep	701.90	31-Jan
1990	675.20	-19.50	41.76	-14.46	860.00	31-Jan	675.20	31-Dec
1989	838.80	18.68	76.11	26.19	889.50	31-Aug	698.60	31-Mar
1988	706.80	13.18	48.39	18.83	748.10	31-Aug	575.30	28-Feb
1987	624.50	-7.34	31.11	-4.16	1,031.90	30-Sep	585.00	31-Oct
1986	674.00	41.51	41.51	47.15	674.00	31-Dec	484.00	28-Feb
1985	476.30							
Average Annual (%)		11.47		16.31				
Compound Annual (%)		9.69		14.49				
Standard Deviation (%)		20.73		21.41				

[1]Maximum/minimum values based on month-end index values.

SYNOPSIS

The Australian Stock Exchange Twenty Leaders Index is a market capitalization-weighted index that tracks the continuous stock price and total return performance of the largest and most actively traded domestic listed ordinary shares with exchange traded options that trade on the Melbourne and Sydney Stock Exchanges. The shares account for about 52% of the market capitalization of the ASX All Ordinaries Index.

NUMBER OF STOCKS—DECEMBER 31, 1995

20

MARKET VALUE—DECEMBER 31, 1995

US$128,534.0 million

SELECTION CRITERIA

The index consists of the 20 largest and most actively traded Australian-listed ordinary shares, with exchange traded options, that trade on the Melbourne and Sydney Stock Exchanges.

BASE DATE

December 31, 1979=250.00

COMPUTATION METHODOLOGY

(1) An aggregative of prices times quantities index formula. Maintenance adjustments to the divisor are made daily for capitalization changes, new listings and delistings. (2) For additional information, refer to the ASX All Ordinaries Index.

DERIVATIVE INSTRUMENTS

Twenty Leaders index futures and options trade on the Australian Stock Exchange.

SUBINDICES

None

RELATED INDICES

ASX All Ordinaries Index
ASX 100 Index
ASX 50 Leaders Index
ASX Mid Cap Index
ASX Small Cap Index
Trans Tasman 100 Index
The Wardley Index

REMARKS

None

PUBLISHER

The Australian Stock Exchange Limited.

DHAKA STOCK EXCHANGE (DSE) ALL SHARE PRICE INDEX

PRICE PERFORMANCE

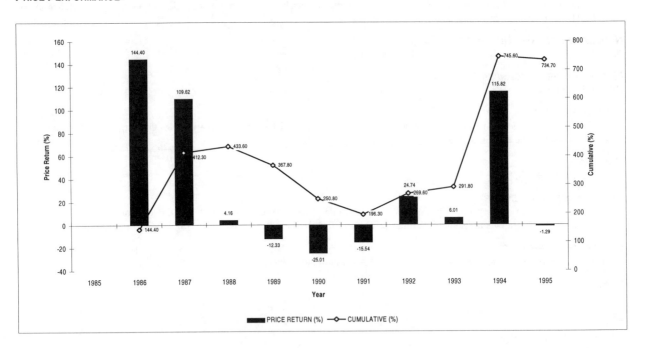

PRICE PERFORMANCE

YEAR	VALUE	PRICE RETURN (%)	CUMULATIVE (%)	MAXIMUM VALUE	DATE	MINIMUM VALUE	DATE
1995	834.70	-1.29	734.70	NA	NA	NA	NA
1994	845.60	115.82	745.60	NA	NA	NA	NA
1993	391.80	6.01	291.80	NA	NA	NA	NA
1992	369.60	24.74	269.60	NA	NA	NA	NA
1991	296.30	-15.54	196.30	NA	NA	NA	NA
1990	350.80	-25.01	250.80	NA	NA	NA	NA
1989	467.80	-12.33	367.80	NA	NA	NA	NA
1988	533.60	4.16	433.60	NA	NA	NA	NA
1987	512.30	109.62	412.30	NA	NA	NA	NA
1986	244.40	144.40	144.40	NA	NA	NA	NA
1985	100.00						
Average Annual (%)		35.06					
Compound Annual (%)		23.64					
Standard Deviation (%)		62.96					

SYNOPSIS

The Dhaka Stock Exchange (DSE) All Share Price Index tracks the daily price only performance of all shares listed on the Dhaka Stock Exchange (DSE) of Pakistan.

NUMBER OF STOCKS—DECEMBER 31, 1995

183

MARKET VALUE—AUGUST 31, 1995

US$1,323.0 million

SELECTION CRITERIA

All shares listed on the Dhaka Stock Exchange are included in the index.

BACKGROUND

None

BASE DATE

1985=100.00

COMPUTATION METHODOLOGY

Not Available

DERIVATIVE INSTRUMENTS

None

SUBINDICES

None

RELATED INDICES

None

REMARKS

None

PUBLISHER

The Dhaka Stock Exchange (DSE).

PEREGRINE GREATER CHINA INDEX

PRICE PERFORMANCE

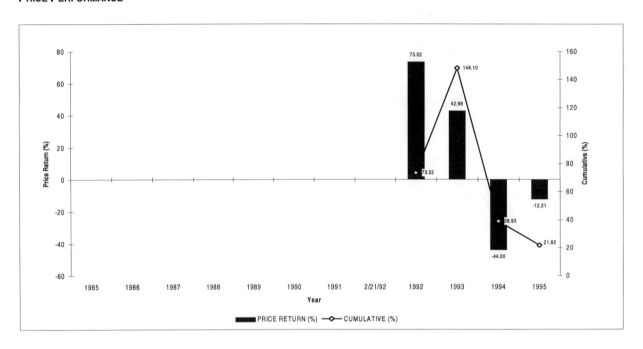

PRICE PERFORMANCE

YEAR	VALUE	PRICE RETURN (%)	CUMULATIVE (%)	MAXIMUM VALUE	DATE	MINIMUM VALUE	DATE
1995	121.83	-12.31	21.83	142.16	4-Aug	115.84	16-Nov
1994	138.93	-44.00	38.93	247.36	3-Jan	134.92	12-Dec
1993	248.10	42.98	148.10	252.43	17-Dec	146.70	23-Jul
1992	173.52	73.52	73.52	208.88	1-Jul	100.00	21-Feb
2/21/92	100.00						
1991							
1990							
1989							
1988							
1987							
1986							
1985							
Average Annual (%)		18.12					
Compound Annual (%)		8.57					
Standard Deviation (%)		60.98					

SYNOPSIS

The Peregrine Greater China Index is a market capitalization-weighted index that tracks the price only performance of Chinese stocks as well as "China play" stocks available for purchase by foreign investors which are listed on the Shanghai, Shenzhen, Hong Kong and New York Stock Exchanges.

NUMBER OF STOCKS—DECEMBER 31, 1995

114

MARKET VALUE—DECEMBER 31, 1995

US$15,300.0 million

SELECTION CRITERIA

Constituent stocks include all "B-Shares" listed on the Shenzhen and Shanghai Stock Exchanges, all "H-Shares" and "N-Shares" listed on the Hong Kong and New York Stock Exchanges as well as Hong Kong-listed "China plays," or companies whose performance is related to economic and financial developments in China.

Stocks that qualify as China plays represent companies that derive a large part of their earnings from China but are listed outside of China. These companies must have a market capitalization in excess of HK$1.0 billion, in addition to the following sector criteria: (1) Manufacturing, construction and services with sales to China that account for at least 30% of total sales, (2) Property development with a net asset value of projects in China that account for at least 30% of total, (3) Banking and finance with a China-related loan portfolio or book assets that account for at least 30% of total; and (4) Transportation, hotels and utilities with earnings from China that represents at least 30% of total earnings.

BACKGROUND

(1) The base date in 1992 coincides with the commencement of "B-Shares" trading on the Shanghai Stock Exchange. (2) The index was expanded to include "B-Shares" listed on the Shanghai and Shenzhen exchanges as these became listed on the respective exchanges.

BASE DATE

February 2, 1992=100.00

COMPUTATION METHODOLOGY

(1) An aggregative of prices times quantities index formula. (2) Shenzhen, Hong Kong and "H-Share" prices are quoted in Hong Kong dollars, and the rest are quoted in U.S. dollars. The New York inter-bank exchange rate is used to convert Hong Kong dollars into U.S. dollars and the U.S. dollar-yen and U.S. dollar-sterling cross-rates from the same source to convert U.S. dollars to yen and sterling, respectively. (3) Market capitalization is computed on the basis of the number of "B-Shares," "H-Shares" and "N-Shares" outstanding. (4) The list of constituent shares is revised quarterly.

DERIVATIVE INSTRUMENTS

None

SUBINDICES

The index is calculated in three currencies: U.S. dollars, Japanese yen and pound sterling.

RELATED INDICES

Peregrine Asia Index
Peregrine Asia Small Cap Index
Peregrine India ADR Index

REMARKS

(1) Hong Kong-listed shares, consisting of 17 "H-Shares" with a market capitalization of US$2.998.0 billion, and 22 Hong Kong Stock Exchange-listed shares with a market capitalization of US$8.7 billion, account for 77.5% of the index. The remaining shares include 26 Shenzhen "B-Shares" with a market capitalization of US$705.0 million, 34 Shanghai listed "B Shares" with a market capitalization of US$1.4 billion and 5 "N-Shares" listed on the New York Stock Exchange with a market capitalization of US$1.3 billion. (Data as of 7/17/95). (2) B-Shares are locally listed shares available for purchase by foreign investors.

PUBLISHER

Peregrine Brokerage Limited.

SHANGHAI (SSE) A-SHARE STOCK PRICE INDEX

PRICE PERFORMANCE

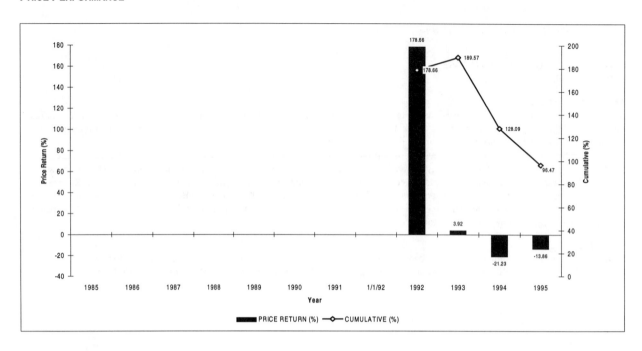

PRICE PERFORMANCE

YEAR	VALUE	PRICE RETURN (%)	CUMULATIVE (%)	MAXIMUM VALUE	DATE	MINIMUM VALUE	DATE
1995	575.19	-13.86	96.47	940.52	22-May	547.54	17-Feb
1994	667.77	-21.23	128.09	1,092.85	13-Sep	321.20	29-Jul
1993	847.75	3.92	189.57	1,615.94	15-Feb	801.26	20-Dec
1992	815.80	178.66	178.66	1,511.27	26-May	292.76	2-Jan
1/1/92	292.76						
1991							
1990							
1989							
1988							
1987							
1986							
1985							
Average Annual (%)		36.87					
Compound Annual (%)		18.39					
Standard Deviation (%)		95.11					

SYNOPSIS
The Shanghai A-Share Stock Price Index is a market capitalization-weighted index that tracks the daily price only performance of all shares listed on the Shanghai Stock Exchange (SSE) and are restricted to local investors.

NUMBER OF STOCKS—DECEMBER 31, 1995
184

MARKET VALUE—DECEMBER 31, 1995
US$28,254.02 million

SELECTION CRITERIA
All A-shares listed on the Shanghai Stock Exchange are included in the index.

BACKGROUND
The index was established at the time of the introduction of "A-Shares" for trading on the SSE.

BASE DATE
January 2, 1992=292.76

COMPUTATION METHODOLOGY
An aggregative of prices times quantities index formula.

DERIVATIVE INSTRUMENTS
None

SUBINDICES
Five industrial sector subindices: Industrial, commercial, utilities, real estate and miscellaneous.

RELATED INDICES
Shanghai B-Share Stock Price Index
Shanghai Composite Stock Price Index

REMARKS
A-Shares are restricted to Chinese investors and are listed locally.

PUBLISHER
The Shanghai Stock Exchange (SSE).

SHANGHAI (SSE) B-SHARE STOCK PRICE INDEX

PRICE PERFORMANCE

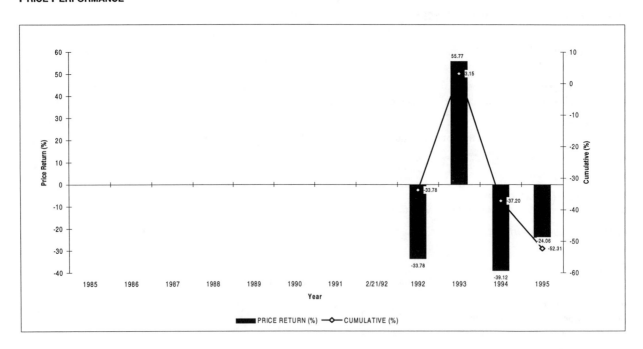

PRICE PERFORMANCE

YEAR	VALUE	PRICE RETURN (%)	CUMULATIVE (%)	MAXIMUM VALUE	DATE	MINIMUM VALUE	DATE
1995	47.69	-24.06	-52.31	63.13	29-Aug	47.69	29-Dec
1994	62.80	-39.12	-37.20	103.90	5-Jan	60.00	15-Dec
1993	103.15	55.77	3.15	103.15	31-Dec	51.39	27-Jul
1992	66.22	-33.78	-33.78	140.85	25-May	56.81	26-Oct
2/21/92	100.00						
1991							
1990							
1989							
1988							
1987							
1986							
1985							
Average Annual (%)		-10.30					
Compound Annual (%)		-16.90					
Standard Deviation (%)		44.48					

SYNOPSIS
The Shanghai B-Share Stock Price Index is a market capitalization-weighted index that tracks the daily price only performance of shares listed on the Shanghai Stock Exchange (SSE) and are available for investment by foreign investors.

NUMBER OF STOCKS—DECEMBER 31, 1995
36

MARKET VALUE—DECEMBER 31, 1995
US$1,082.1 million

SELECTION CRITERIA
All B-shares listed on the Shanghai Stock Exchange.

BACKGROUND
Introduction of the SSE Index coincides with the introduction of the first "B-Share" listing on the SSE.

BASE DATE
February 21, 1992=100.00

COMPUTATION METHODOLOGY
An aggregative of prices times quantities index formula.

DERIVATIVE INSTRUMENTS
None

SUBINDICES
Five industrial sector subindices: Industrial, commercial, utilities, real estate and miscellaneous.

RELATED INDICES
Shanghai A-Share Stock Price Index
Shanghai Composite Stock Price Index

REMARKS
B-Shares are listed locally and are available for purchase by foreign investors.

PUBLISHER
The Shanghai Stock Exchange (SSE).

SHANGHAI (SSE) SHARE STOCK PRICE INDEX

PRICE PERFORMANCE

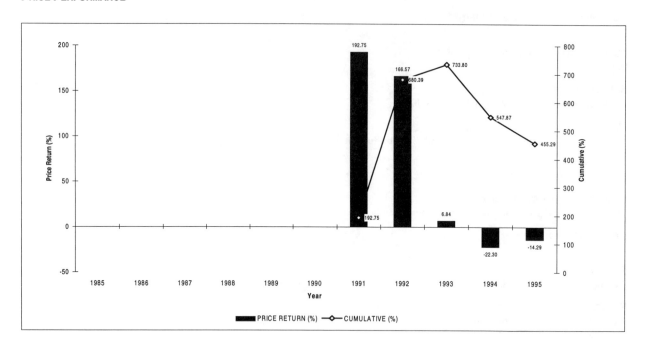

PRICE PERFORMANCE

YEAR	VALUE	PRICE RETURN (%)	CUMULATIVE (%)	MAXIMUM VALUE	DATE	MINIMUM VALUE	DATE
1995	555.29	-14.29	455.29	926.41	22-May	524.43	7-Feb
1994	647.87	-22.30	547.87	1,052.94	13-Sep	325.89	29-Jul
1993	833.80	6.84	733.80	1,558.95	16-Feb	750.46	20-Dec
1992	780.39	166.57	680.39	1,429.01	26-May	292.76	2-Feb
1991	292.75	192.75	192.75	292.75	31-Dec	104.96	17-May
1990	100.00						
1989							
1988							
1987							
1986							
1985							
Average Annual (%)		65.92					
Compound Annual (%)		18.70					
Standard Deviation (%)		104.79					

SYNOPSIS
The Shanghai Share Stock Price Index is a market capitalization-weighted index that tracks the daily price only performance of all A-shares and B-shares listed on the Shanghai Stock Exchange (SSE).

NUMBER OF STOCKS—DECEMBER 31, 1995
220

MARKET VALUE—DECEMBER 31, 1995
US$29,336.1 million

SELECTION CRITERIA
All A-shares and B-shares listed on the SSE are included in the index.

BACKGROUND
The SSE Index was established with a base value of 100 as of December 19, 1990.

BASE DATE
December 19, 1990=100.00

COMPUTATION METHODOLOGY
An aggregative of prices times quantities index formula.

DERIVATIVE INSTRUMENTS
None

SUBINDICES
Five industrial sector subindices: Industrial, commercial, utilities, real estate and miscellaneous.

RELATED INDICES
Shanghai A-Share Stock Price Index
Shanghai B-Share Stock Price Index

REMARKS
A-Shares are listed locally and are restricted to Chinese investors while B-Shares are available for purchase by foreign investors.

PUBLISHER
The Shanghai Stock Exchange (SSE).

HANG SENG CHINA ENTERPRISES INDEX (HSCEI)

PRICE PERFORMANCE

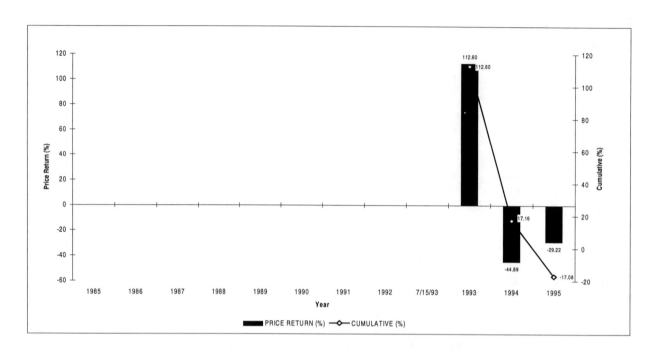

PRICE PERFORMANCE[1]

YEAR	VALUE	PRICE RETURN (%)	CUMULATIVE (%)	MAXIMUM VALUE	DATE	MINIMUM VALUE	DATE
1995	757.12	-29.22	-17.08	1,098.58	12-Jul	684.85	16-Nov
1994	1,069.67	-44.89	17.16	1,947.43	3-Jan	977.62	12-Dec
1993	1,941.12	112.60	112.60	2,176.90	12-Dec	846.77	30-Jul
7/15/93	913.02						
1992							
1991							
1990							
1989							
1988							
1987							
1986							
1985							
Average Annual (%)		-37.06					
Compound Annual (%)		-8.94					
Standard Deviation (%)		11.08					

[1]Statistics applicable to the period 1993-1994.

SYNOPSIS

The Hang Seng China Enterprises Index (HSCEI) is a market capitalization-weighted index that tracks the continuous price only performance of all shares attributable to China enterprises that are listed on the Stock Exchange of Hong Kong Limited (SEHK).

NUMBER OF STOCKS—DECEMBER 31, 1995

17

MARKET VALUE—DECEMBER 31, 1995

US$2,129.2 million

SELECTION CRITERIA

All H-Share companies listed on the SEHK are included in the index. These are shares of Chinese enterprises designed for foreign investors and listed overseas markets, principally in Hong Kong and New York.

BACKGROUND

HSCEI was introduced on August 4, 1994 and backdated to July 15, 1993.

BASE DATE

July 8, 1994=1000.00

COMPUTATION METHODOLOGY

An aggregative of prices times quantities (Laspeyres) index formula. Maintenance adjustments to the divisor are made daily at the end of trading hours for capitalization changes, new listings and delistings.

DERIVATIVE INSTRUMENTS

None

SUBINDICES

None

RELATED INDICES

Hang Seng Index
Hang Seng London Reference Index
Hang Seng Midcap Index

REMARKS

None

PUBLISHER

HSI Services Limited, a subsidiary of Hang Seng Bank.

HANG SENG INDEX (HSI)

PRICE PERFORMANCE

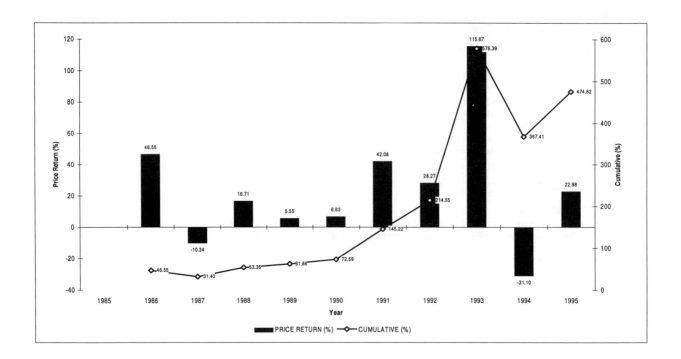

PRICE PERFORMANCE

YEAR	VALUE	PRICE RETURN (%)	CUMULATIVE (%)	MAXIMUM VALUE	DATE	MINIMUM VALUE	DATE
1995	10,073.40	22.98	474.82	10,073.39	31-Dec	6,967.93	23-Jan
1994	8,191.04	-31.10	367.41	12,157.57	4-Feb	7,707.78	12-Dec
1993	11,888.39	115.67	578.39	11,888.39	31-Dec	5,437.80	4-Jan
1992	5,512.39	28.27	214.55	6,447.11	22-Oct	4,301.78	1-Feb
1991	4,297.33	42.08	145.22	4,297.33	31-Dec	2,984.01	16-Jan
1990	3,024.55	6.63	72.59	3,540.43	20-Jul	2,736.55	2-Feb
1989	2,836.57	5.55	61.86	3,309.64	15-May	2,093.61	5-Jun
1988	2,687.44	16.71	53.35	2,719.06	20-Jun	2,286.29	4-Jan
1987	2,302.75	-10.34	31.40	3,944.24	10-May	1,894.94	12-Jul
1986	2,568.30	46.55	46.55	2,568.30	31-Dec	1,559.94	19-Mar
1985	1,752.45						
Average Annual (%)		24.30					
Compound Annual (%)		19.11					
Standard Deviation (%)		39.68					

SYNOPSIS

The Hang Seng Index (HSI) is a market capitalization-weighted index that tracks the continuous price only performance of 33 actively traded large capitalization ordinary shares listed on the Stock Exchange of Hong Kong Limited (SEHK). These shares account for 74% of the domestic market capitalization.

NUMBER OF STOCKS—DECEMBER 31, 1995

33

MARKET VALUE—DECEMBER 31, 1995

US$224,998.0 million

SELECTION CRITERIA

In addition to having a substantial business base in Hong Kong, constituent shares are selected on the basis of their market value and turnover rankings, industry group representation, prevailing and past financial condition of the company, its earnings record and growth prospects as well as the management qualities of the company. More specifically, selected companies must be among those that constitute 90% of the total market value of all ordinary shares listed on the Hong Kong Stock Exchange, based on an average of the previous 12 months, must be among those that account for 90% of the total turnover, based on an aggregate of the previous 24 months, and should have been listed on the SEHK for a minimum of 24 months.

BACKGROUND

The Heng Seng Index was introduced on November 24, 1969. This was followed with the launch of four subindices at the beginning of 1985, using a base date of January 13, 1984.

BASE DATE

July 31, 1964=100.00

COMPUTATION METHODOLOGY

(1) An aggregative of prices times quantities (Laspeyres) index formula. Maintenance adjustments to the divisor are made daily, at the end of trading hours, for capitalization changes, new listings and delistings. (2) Prices are provided by the Stock Exchange of Hong Kong.

DERIVATIVE INSTRUMENTS

(1) HSI index futures trade on the Hong Kong Futures Exchange. (2) HSI Commerce and Industry subindex futures trade on the Hong Kong Futures Exchange. (3) HSI Finance subindex futures trade on the Hong Kong Futures Exchange. (4) HSI Properties subindex futures trade on the Hong Kong Futures Exchange. (5) HSI Utilities subindex futures trade on the Hong Kong Futures Exchange. (6) AMEX Hong Kong 30 index options, Long-Term Equity Anticipation Securities (LEAPS) and Morgan Stanley Call Warrants trade on the American Stock Exchange (AMEX).

SUBINDICES

Four sectoral subindices: Finance, utilities, properties and commerce and industry.

RELATED INDICES

Hang Seng China Enterprises Index
Hang Seng London Reference Index
Hang Seng Midcap Index

REMARKS

The AMEX Hong Kong 30 Index is a market value-weighted index based on the performance of 30 highly capitalized stocks listed on the Stock Exchange of Hong Kong Ltd. which span all major economic sectors and account for about 67% of the exchange's total market capitalization. As of December 31, 1995, 24 member stocks were common to both indices.

PUBLISHER

HSI Services Limited, a subsidiary of Hang Seng Bank.

HANG SENG MIDCAP INDEX

PRICE PERFORMANCE

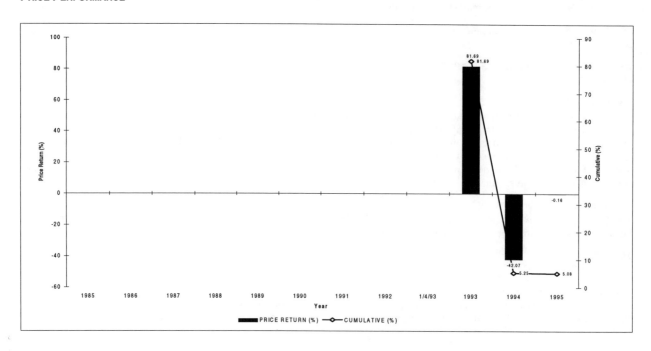

PRICE PERFORMANCE

YEAR	VALUE	PRICE RETURN (%)	CUMULATIVE (%)	MAXIMUM VALUE	DATE	MINIMUM VALUE	DATE
1995	1,209.51	-0.16	5.08	1,302.69	15-Sep	1,038.87	24-Jan
1994	1,211.48	-42.07	5.25	2,173.22	5-Jan	1,155.72	12-Dec
1993	2,091.26	81.69	81.69	2,091.26	31-Dec	1,151.03	4-Jan
1/4/93	1,151.03						
1992							
1991							
1990							
1989							
1988							
1987							
1986							
1985							
Average Annual (%)		13.15					
Compound Annual (%)		1.67					
Standard Deviation (%)		62.94					

SYNOPSIS

The Hang Seng Midcap Index is a market capitalization-weighted index that tracks the continuous price only performance of the 50 most actively traded middle capitalization ordinary shares listed on the Stock Exchange of Hong Kong Limited (SEHK). Constituent shares account for about 90% of the total turnover of mid-cap companies on the SEHK and about 6% the total market capitalization on the exchange.

NUMBER OF STOCKS—DECEMBER 31, 1995

50

MARKET VALUE—DECEMBER 31, 1995

US$18,873.5 million

SELECTION CRITERIA

Constituent shares have an average market capitalization of between HK$2.0 billion and HK$6.0 billion. In addition to having a substantial business base in Hong Kong, constituent shares are selected on the basis of their market value and turnover rankings, industry group representation, prevailing and past financial condition of the company, its earnings record and growth prospects, and management qualities of the company.

Excluded from consideration are constituents in the Hang Seng Index and China Enterprises Index.

BACKGROUND

The index was introduced on July 10, 1995 and daily index values were backdated to January 4, 1993.

BASE DATE

June 1, 1995=1,268.55

COMPUTATION METHODOLOGY

(1) An aggregative of prices times quantities (Laspeyres) index formula. Maintenance adjustments to the divisor are made daily, at the end of trading hours, for capitalization changes, new listings and delistings. (2) The number of issued shares is updated on a monthly basis. (3) Prices are provided by the Stock Exchange of Hong Kong.

DERIVATIVE INSTRUMENTS

None

SUBINDICES

None

RELATED INDICES

Hang Seng Index
Hang Seng China Enterprises Index
Hang Seng London Reference Index

REMARKS

Turnover is expressed as an aggregate of the past 24 months.

PUBLISHER

HSI Services Limited, a subsidiary of Hang Seng Bank.

HONG KONG ALL ORDINARIES INDEX (AOI)

PRICE PERFORMANCE

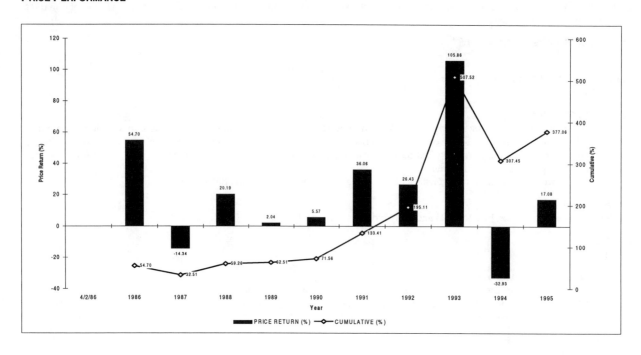

PRICE PERFORMANCE[1]

YEAR	VALUE	PRICE RETURN (%)	CUMULATIVE (%)	MAXIMUM VALUE	DATE	MINIMUM VALUE	DATE
1995	4,770.57	17.08	377.06	4,812.16	17-Oct	3,487.74	23-Jan
1994	4,074.52	-32.93	307.45	6,259.49	4-Jan	3,852.26	12-Dec
1993	6,075.18	105.86	507.52	6,075.18	31-Dec	2,916.05	4-Jan
1992	2,951.06	26.43	195.11	3,409.79	12-Nov	2,333.77	2-Jan
1991	2,334.11	36.06	133.41	2,343.08	15-Nov	1,677.69	16-Jan
1990	1,715.55	5.57	71.56	2,141.20	23-Jul	1,592.01	2-Feb
1989	1,625.05	2.04	62.51	1,967.74	15-May	1,228.56	5-Jun
1988	1,592.61	20.19	59.26	1,657.95	12-Jul	1,262.55	8-Feb
1987	1,325.07	-14.34	32.51	2,495.89	7-Oct	1,090.46	7-Dec
1986	1,546.98	54.70	54.70	1,546.98	31-Dec	1,000.00	2-Apr
4/2/86	1,000.00						
Average Annual (%)		22.07					
Compound Annual (%)		16.91					
Standard Deviation (%)		38.52					

[1]Price performance since 4/2/1986 inception date.

SYNOPSIS
The Hong Kong All Ordinaries Index (AOI) is a comprehensive market capitalization-weighted index that tracks the daily price only performance of domestic ordinary shares listed on the Stock Exchange of Hong Kong Limited (SEHK).

NUMBER OF STOCKS—DECEMBER 31, 1995
521

MARKET VALUE—DECEMBER 31, 1995
US$303,666.7 million

SELECTION CRITERIA
All ordinary shares listed on the Stock Exchange of Hong Kong, except:
(1) Stocks of overseas incorporated companies whose principal activities are carried out abroad; (2) Stocks that have been suspended for over one year; and (3) Stocks that are not traded in Hong Kong dollars.

BACKGROUND
The All Ordinaries Index was launched on February 1, 1989 and index values were backdated to 1986. Effective April 6, 1992, the index was expanded to include seven sectoral subindices, while at the same time, the compilation of the more narrowly based Hong Kong Index was discontinued.

BASE DATE
April 2, 1986=1000.00

COMPUTATION METHODOLOGY
An aggregative of prices times quantities index formula. Maintenance adjustments to the divisor are made daily on the night before the day concerned for capitalization changes, new listings/reactivations and delistings/suspensions. For example, a rights issue is reflected in the index as of the ex-date.

DERIVATIVE INSTRUMENTS
None

SUBINDICES
Seven sectoral subindices: Finance, utilities, properties, consolidated enterprises, industrials, hotels, and miscellaneous companies.

RELATED INDICES
None

REMARKS
None

PUBLISHER
The Stock Exchange of Hong Kong Limited (SEHK).

BOMBAY STOCK EXCHANGE (BSE) 200 INDEX

PRICE PERFORMANCE

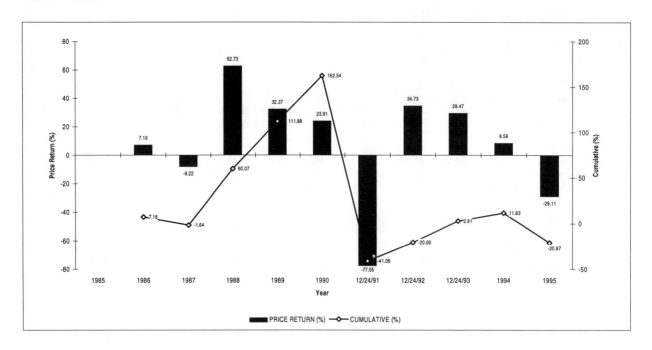

PRICE PERFORMANCE[1]

YEAR	VALUE	PRICE RETURN (%)	CUMULATIVE (%)	MAXIMUM VALUE	DATE	MINIMUM VALUE	DATE
1995	313.68	-29.11	-20.87	441.57	2-Jan	21-Oct	29-Nov
1994	442.50	8.58	11.63	527.63	31-Aug	432.13	13-Dec
12/24/93	407.52	29.47	2.81	407.52	24-Dec	223.50	26-Apr
12/24/92	314.76	34.73	-20.60	591.52	2-Apr	234.79	8-Jan
12/24/91	233.62	-77.55	-41.06	236.80	16-Sep	131.00	3-Jan
1990	1,040.70	23.91	162.54	NA	NA	NA	NA
1989	839.90	32.37	111.88	NA	NA	NA	NA
1988	634.50	62.73	60.07	NA	NA	NA	NA
1987	389.90	-8.22	-1.64	NA	NA	NA	NA
1986	424.80	7.16	7.16	NA	NA	NA	NA
1985	396.40						
Average Annual (%)		8.41					
Compound Annual (%)		-2.31					
Standard Deviation (%)		39.41					

[1]BSE calculations commence in 1991. For prior periods, values are from the Financial Express Bombay Index.

SYNOPSIS
The Bombay Stock Exchange (BSE) 200 Index is a market capitalization-weighted index that tracks the continuous stock price performance of specified and non-specified shares listed on the Bombay Stock Exchange. These shares account for 54% of the total BSE market capitalization (BSE).

NUMBER OF STOCKS—DECEMBER 31, 1995
200

MARKET VALUE—DECEMBER 31, 1995
US$68,205.8 million

SELECTION CRITERIA
Constituent stocks, which are intended to reflect current market trends, are selected on the basis of market capitalization as well as turnover. Eligible securities fall into two categories of listed shares on the Bombay Stock Exchange. These include specified shares, or shares that are settled on a fortnightly basis, as well as of non-specified shares, or cash shares.

BACKGROUND
Launched on May 27, 1994, the index was intended to more accurately portray BSE market trends in light of the phenomenal growth experienced between 1980 and 1994. During this period, the number of listed shares expanded from 992 to 3,585. At the same time, there were newly emerged industry groups as well as a significant expansion in market capitalization. It is intended that the index will serve as an underlying vehicle for stock index futures contracts.

BASE DATE
1989-1990=100.00

COMPUTATION METHODOLOGY
An aggregative of prices times quantities index formula. Maintenance adjustments to the divisor are made as of the ex-date or the effective date for capitalization changes such as bonus issues, rights issues, conversion of debentures, new listings and delistings.

DERIVATIVE INSTRUMENTS
None

SUBINDICES
None

RELATED INDICES
BSE DOLLEX Index
BSE National Index of Equity Prices
BSE Sensitive Index Number of Equity Prices

REMARKS
The Bombay Stock Exchange is closed during the last week of every year.

PUBLISHER
The Bombay Stock Exchange (BSE).

BOMBAY STOCK EXCHANGE (BSE) NATIONAL INDEX OF EQUITY PRICES

PRICE PERFORMANCE

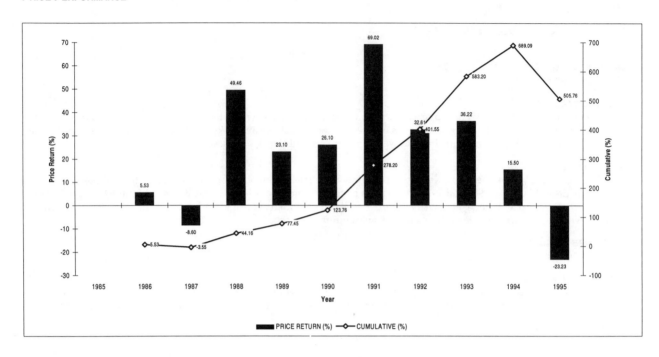

PRICE PERFORMANCE

YEAR	VALUE	PRICE RETURN (%)	CUMULATIVE (%)	MAXIMUM VALUE	DATE	MINIMUM VALUE	DATE
1995	1,430.75	-23.23	505.76	1,860.77	2-Jan	1,342.10	29-Nov
1994	1,863.76	15.50	689.09	2,085.19	7-Oct	1,677.77	5-Jan
1993	613.64	36.22	583.20	1,658.90	13-Dec	948.68	3-May
1992	1,184.60	32.61	401.55	1,991.11	2-Apr	905.17	1-Jan
1991	893.27	69.02	278.20	917.10	20-Nov	491.77	25-Jan
1990	528.51	26.10	123.76	762.72	9-Oct	380.34	31-Jan
1989	419.13	23.10	77.45	421.89	12-Dec	324.20	6-Jan
1988	340.49	49.46	44.16	361.04	2-Dec	206.67	28-Mar
1987	227.81	-8.60	-3.55	267.24	27-Feb	211.02	11-Dec
1986	249.25	5.53	5.53	282.64	28-Feb	229.95	21-Mar
1985	236.19						
Average Annual (%)		22.57					
Compound Annual (%)		19.74					
Standard Deviation (%)		27.06					

SYNOPSIS

The Bombay Stock Exchange (BSE) National Index of Equity Prices is a market capitalization-weighted index that tracks the continuous stock price performance of large specified and non-specified shares listed on India's five major stock exchanges, including the Bombay Stock Exchange, Calcutta Stock Exchange, Delhi Stock Exchange, Ahmedabad Stock Exchange and the Madras Stock Exchange.

NUMBER OF STOCKS—DECEMBER 31, 1995

100

MARKET VALUE—DECEMBER 31, 1995

US$37,688.5 million

SELECTION CRITERIA

Constituent stocks, which are intended to properly represent various industry groups are selected on the basis of market capitalization and turnover. Eligible securities fall into two categories of listed shares on each of the five exchanges. These include specified shares, or shares that are settled on a fortnightly basis, as well as non-specified shares, or cash shares.

Companies that become less prominent and experience thin trading, as well as companies that register continuous losses, are removed from the index.

BACKGROUND

The BSE National Index was launched on January 3, 1989.

BASE DATE

1983-1984=100.00

COMPUTATION METHODOLOGY

(1) An aggregative of prices times quantities index formula. Maintenance adjustments to the divisor are made as of the ex-date or the effective date for capitalization changes such as bonus issues, rights issues, conversion of debentures, new listings and delistings. (2) Closing prices applicable to issues traded on a single exchange are taken from the listed exchange. Closing prices for stocks that are listed on two or more exchanges represent the average price.

DERIVATIVE INSTRUMENTS

None

SUBINDICES

None

RELATED INDICES

BSE Sensitive Index Number of Equity Prices
BSE 200 Index
BSE DOLLEX Index

REMARKS

The Bombay Stock Exchange is closed during the last week of every year.

PUBLISHER

The Bombay Stock Exchange (BSE).

BOMBAY STOCK EXCHANGE (BSE) SENSITIVE INDEX OF EQUITY PRICES

PRICE PERFORMANCE

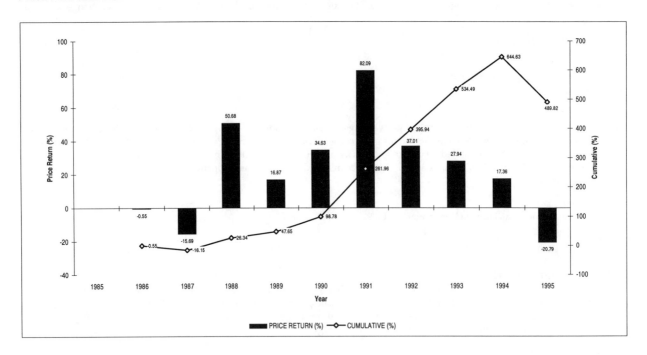

PRICE PERFORMANCE

YEAR	VALUE	PRICE RETURN (%)	CUMULATIVE (%)	MAXIMUM VALUE	DATE	MINIMUM VALUE	DATE
1995	3,110.49	-20.79	489.82	3,932.09	2-Jan	2,922.16	29-Nov
1994	3,926.90	17.36	644.63	4,630.54	12-Sep	3,454.08	5-Jan
1993	3,346.06	27.94	534.49	3,454.81	13-Dec	2,036.81	26-Apr
1992	2,615.37	37.01	395.94	4,467.32	22-Apr	1,949.31	8-Jan
1991	1,908.85	82.09	261.96	1,924.15	19-Nov	956.11	25-Jan
1990	1,048.29	34.63	98.78	1,559.43	9-Oct	659.30	8-Feb
1989	778.64	16.87	47.65	798.01	5-Jul	625.32	6-Jan
1988	666.26	50.68	26.34	719.07	18-Nov	390.00	28-Mar
1987	442.17	-15.69	-16.15	578.75	13-Feb	405.57	10-Dec
1986	524.45	-0.55	-0.55	664.54	27-Feb	482.41	1-Dec
1985	527.36						
Average Annual (%)		22.95					
Compound Annual (%)		19.42					
Standard Deviation (%)		31.01					

SYNOPSIS

The Bombay Stock Exchange (BSE) Sensitive Index of Equity Prices is a capitalization-weighted index that tracks the continuous stock price only performance of 30 larger, actively traded, specified and non-specified shares listed on the Bombay Stock Exchange (BSE). These shares account for 17.8% of the total BSE market capitalization.

NUMBER OF STOCKS—DECEMBER 31, 1995

30

MARKET VALUE—DECEMBER 31, 1995

US$22,640.6 million

SELECTION CRITERIA

Constituent stocks, in addition to properly representing various industry groups, are selected on the basis of market capitalization and turnover. Eligible securities fall into two categories of shares listed on the Bombay Stock Exchange. These include specified shares, or shares that are settled on a fortnightly basis, as well as of non-specified shares, or cash shares.

BACKGROUND

The index was introduced on January 2, 1986.

BASE DATE

1978-1979=100.00

COMPUTATION METHODOLOGY

An aggregative of prices times quantities index formula. Maintenance adjustments to the divisor are made as of the ex-date or the effective date for capitalization changes such as bonus issues, rights issues, conversion of debentures, new listings and delistings.

DERIVATIVE INSTRUMENTS

None

SUBINDICES

None

RELATED INDICES

BSE National Index of Equity Prices
BSE 200
BSE DOLLEX Index

REMARKS

The Bombay Stock Exchange is closed during the last week of every year.

PUBLISHER

The Bombay Stock Exchange (BSE).

The Delhi Stock Exchange (DSE) Sensitive Index of Equity Prices

PRICE PERFORMANCE

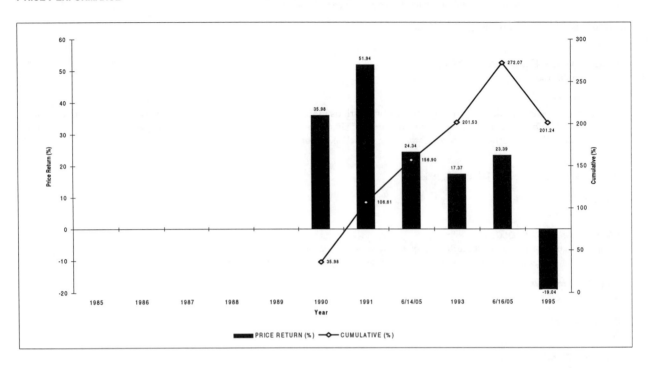

PRICE PERFORMANCE[1]

YEAR	VALUE	PRICE RETURN (%)	CUMULATIVE (%)	MAXIMUM VALUE	DATE	MINIMUM VALUE	DATE
1995	703.55	-19.04	201.24	865.35	3-Jan	679.87	29-Nov
6/16/05	868.98	23.39	272.07	1,011.86	13-Sep	795.65	NA
1993	704.23	17.37	201.53	719.51	13-Dec	430.62	27-Apr
6/14/05	599.99	24.34	156.90	1,255.92	2-Apr	484.92	8-Jan
1991	482.53	51.94	106.61	506.91	18-Sep	274.28	28-Jan
1990	317.57	35.98	35.98	904.96	18-Oct	195.78	9-Feb
1989	233.55	NA	NA	261.43	21-Apr	202.24	29-Nov
1988	NA	NA	NA	NA	NA	NA	NA
1987	180.78	NA	NA	305.19	31-Jan	168.37	30-Nov
1986							
1985							
Average Annual (%)		22.33					
Compound Annual (%)		20.18					
Standard Deviation (%)		23.68					

[1]Statistical measures applicable to the period 1990-1995.

SYNOPSIS

The Delhi Stock Exchange (DSE) Sensitive Index of Equity Prices is a market capitalization-weighted index that tracks the daily stock price performance of 33 shares listed on the Delhi Stock Exchange (DSE). These stocks account for about 22% of the DSE market capitalization.

NUMBER OF STOCKS—DECEMBER 31, 1995
33

MARKET VALUE—DECEMBER 31, 1995
US$1,322.59 million

SELECTION CRITERIA

Constituent stocks are selected from two categories of listed shares on the basis of volume of transactions. The first category, consisting of specified shares, or shares that are settled on a fortnightly basis, consist of 26 companies. The second category, consisting of non-specified shares, or cash shares, consist of seven companies.

BACKGROUND

Since the date of its launch in 1983, the universe of constituent stocks was revised once. The revision, due to the splitting up of one of its component stocks–the DCM group–resulted in the increase in the number of constituent stocks from 26 to 33.

BASE DATE
December 1983=100.00

COMPUTATION METHODOLOGY

An aggregative of prices times quantities index formula. Maintenance adjustments to the divisor are made periodically for capitalization changes, such as bonus issues, rights issues, sub-division, consolidation and conversion of debentures into equity shares.

DERIVATIVE INSTRUMENTS
None

SUBINDICES
None

RELATED INDICES
None

REMARKS

(1) The universe of constituent stocks is currently under review, following the elimination of the Badla system wherein transactions were carried forward from one settlement period to the next without effecting delivery of payment. (2) Specified shares are subject to fortnightly settlements versus payment, while non-specified shares are transacted between Tuesday and Monday of each week for settlement on Saturday of the following week.

PUBLISHER
The Delhi Stock Exchange (DSE).

JAKARTA STOCK EXCHANGE (JSX) COMPOSITE STOCK PRICE INDEX

PRICE PERFORMANCE

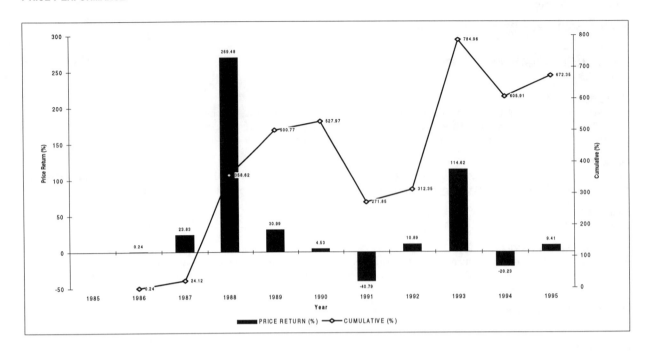

PRICE PERFORMANCE

YEAR	VALUE	PRICE RETURN (%)	CUMULATIVE (%)	MAXIMUM VALUE	DATE	MINIMUM VALUE	DATE
1995	513.85	9.41	672.35	519.18	11-Aug	414.21	19-Apr
1994	469.64	-20.23	605.91	601.83	4-Feb	447.04	13-Dec
1993	588.77	114.62	784.96	588.77	29-Dec	273.31	5-Jan
1992	274.34	10.89	312.35	331.06	19-Jun	246.95	2-Jan
1991	247.39	-40.79	271.85	427.02	25-Feb	224.71	30-Oct
1990	417.79	4.53	527.97	681.94	4-Apr	376.29	5-Dec
1989	399.69	30.99	500.77	507.40	8-Sep	274.08	4-Aug
1988	305.12	269.48	358.62	442.20	21-Dec	82.58	4-Jan
1987	82.58	23.83	24.12	82.58	23-Dec	69.38	14-Jan
1986	66.69	0.24	0.24	69.69	26-Dec	61.56	18-Nov
1985	66.53						
Average Annual (%)		40.30					
Compound Annual (%)		22.68					
Standard Deviation (%)		90.28					

SYNOPSIS

The Jakarta Stock Exchange (JSX) Composite Stock Price Index is a broad based market capitalization-weighted index that tracks the daily stock price only performance of all listed shares on the Jakarta Stock Exchange (JSX), or as it is legally known, PT Bursa Efek Jakarta, of Indonesia.

NUMBER OF STOCKS—DECEMBER 31, 1995

238

MARKET VALUE—DECEMBER 31, 1995

US$66,570.4 million

SELECTION CRITERIA

All listed shares traded on the JSX.

BACKGROUND

The index was introduced in 1982 and backdated to December 31, 1977. At that time, only one share was listed on the exchange.

August 10, 1982 was the fifth anniversary of the reactivation of the JSX. At that time, 13 company shares were listed on the exchange.

BASE DATE

August 10, 1982=100.00

COMPUTATION METHODOLOGY

An aggregative of prices times quantities index formula. Maintenance adjustments to the divisor are made daily for capitalization changes, new listings and delistings.

DERIVATIVE INSTRUMENTS

None

SUBINDICES

None

RELATED INDICES

None

REMARKS

None

PUBLISHER

The Jakarta Stock Exchange (JSX).

HSBC JAMES CAPEL SMALL JAPANESE COMPANIES INDEX

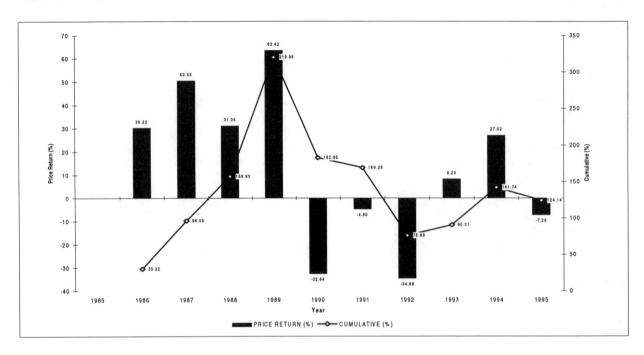

PRICE PERFORMANCE

YEAR	VALUE	PRICE RETURN (%)	CUMULATIVE (%)	MAXIMUM VALUE	DATE	MINIMUM VALUE	DATE
1995	224.14	-7.28	124.14	241.76	3-Jan	167.72	15-Jun
1994	241.74	27.02	141.74	266.53	30-Jun	221.27	31-Jan
1993	190.31	8.20	90.31	257.98	31-May	172.47	31-Jan
1992	175.89	-34.68	75.89	252.09	31-Jan	169.95	30-Nov
1991	269.26	-4.80	169.26	342.02	30-Apr	257.02	31-Jan
1990	282.85	-32.64	182.85	442.60	31-Jul	282.85	31-Dec
1989	419.88	63.42	319.88	419.88	31-Dec	278.67	28-Feb
1988	256.93	31.05	156.93	279.28	30-Jun	218.77	31-Jan
1987	196.05	50.55	96.05	209.88	30-Sep	135.04	31-Jan
1986	130.22	30.22	30.22	146.43	30-Jun	105.06	31-Jan
1985	100.00						
Average Annual (%)		10.09					
Compound Annual (%)		8.41					
Standard Deviation (%)		33.13					

SYNOPSIS

The HSBC James Capel Small Japanese Companies Index is a market capitalization-weighted index that tracks the daily price only performance small companies in Japan.

NUMBER OF STOCKS—DECEMBER 31, 1995

1,695

MARKET VALUE—DECEMBER 31, 1995

US$510,767.1 million

SELECTION CRITERIA

Constituent stocks are limited to a universe of shares with market capitalizations below 40.0 billion Yen (US$386.4 million based on 12/31/95 exchange rates) that constitute the Tokyo Stock Exchange Second Section Index, the Tokyo Stock First Section (TSE-1) Small Index, the JASDAQ Index, the Nikkei Over-the-Counter Stock Average along with mutually exclusive stocks traded on Japan's seven regional exchanges, including Fukuoka, Kyoto, Hiroshima, Nagoya, Niigata, Osaka, and Sapporo.

BACKGROUND

At the end of April 1995, two structural changes to the index were implemented. First, the universe of eligible stocks was expanded to include small companies traded on Japan's regional exchanges. In the process, 365 companies were added. Second, the cut-off point for small companies was revised from a pound-based standard to a Japanese Yen-based standard in order to eliminate the impact of exchange rate fluctuations. The standard was revised from a maximum market capitalization of 250.0 million pounds to 40.0 billion Yen.

BASE DATE

December 31, 1985=100.00

COMPUTATION METHODOLOGY

(1) An aggregative of prices times quantities index formula. Maintenance adjustments to the divisor are made daily for capitalization changes, new listings and delistings. (2) Constituent shares are reviewed on a quarterly basis.

DERIVATIVE INSTRUMENTS

None

SUBINDICES

None

RELATED INDICES

HSBC JC Dragon 300 Index
HSBC JC Latin America 100 Index.
HSBC JC Smaller European Companies Index
HSBC JC Smaller Pan-European Index
Refer to Appendix 5 for additional indices.

REMARKS

None

PUBLISHER

HSBC James Capel.

NAGOYA 25 INDEX

PRICE PERFORMANCE

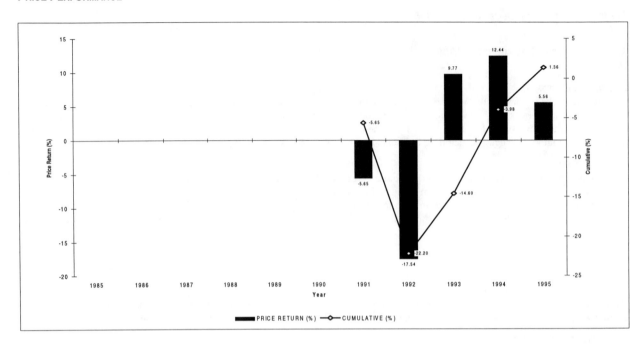

PRICE PERFORMANCE

YEAR	VALUE	PRICE RETURN (%)	CUMULATIVE (%)	MAXIMUM VALUE	DATE	MINIMUM VALUE	DATE
1995	866.64	5.56	1.36	867.74	27-Dec	643.05	13-Jun
1994	820.96	12.44	-3.98	897.37	13-Jun	736.08	4-Jan
1993	730.16	9.77	-14.60	839.25	10-May	634.74	25-Jan
1992	665.19	-17.54	-22.20	829.04	7-Jan	576.27	18-Aug
1991	806.67	-5.65	-5.65	988.92	18-Mar	754.35	3-Jul
1990	854.99	NA	NA	NA	NA	NA	NA
1989	NA	NA	NA	NA	NA	NA	NA
1988	NA	NA	NA	NA	NA	NA	NA
1987	1,000.00						
1986							
1985							
Average Annual (%)		0.46					
Compound Annual (%)		0.14					
Standard Deviation (%)		12.41					

SYNOPSIS
The Nagoya 25 Index is a price-weighted index that tracks the price only performance of leading stocks traded on the First Section of the Tokyo Stock Exchange, Osaka Stock Exchange and Nagoya Stock Exchange.

NUMBER OF STOCKS—DECEMBER 31, 1995
25

MARKET VALUE—DECEMBER 31, 1995
Not Available

SELECTION CRITERIA
Constituents represent widely held common stocks listed on the first sections of the Tokyo Stock Exchange, Osaka Stock Exchange and Nagoya Stock Exchange that are selected to represent the Japanese market as whole. Eligibility is determined on the basis of size, liquidity and trading volume. Stocks must have a market capitalization in excess of 200.0 billion Yen, the number of listed stocks must be equal to or in excess of 300,000 units and trading volume must be equal to or in excess of 300,000 units. In order to properly reflect a variety of industries, at least three issue per industry are selected.

BACKGROUND
Launched in 1988, the index was developed to serve as an underlying vehicle for options trading.

BASE DATE
January 4, 1988=1000.00

COMPUTATION METHODOLOGY
(1) A simple aggregative of actual prices index formula. The divisor is adjusted periodically to reflect non-market changes in the price of the constituent stocks, such as rights offerings, splits, reverse splits, and decreases in capital, or changes in the universe of constituent stocks, so as to maintain its continuity. (2) Stock prices are based on closing quotations on the Tokyo Stock Exchange. (3) The index is monitored on a periodic basis and its constituents may be replaced in the event it is determined that any one of its issues is no longer representative of the market. At that time, a suitable replacement is selected.

DERIVATIVE INSTRUMENTS
Nagoya 25 Index options trade on the Nagoya Stock Exchange.

SUBINDICES
None

RELATED INDICES
None

REMARKS
None

PUBLISHER
Nagoya Stock Exchange.

NIKKEI 225 STOCK AVERAGE

PRICE PERFORMANCE

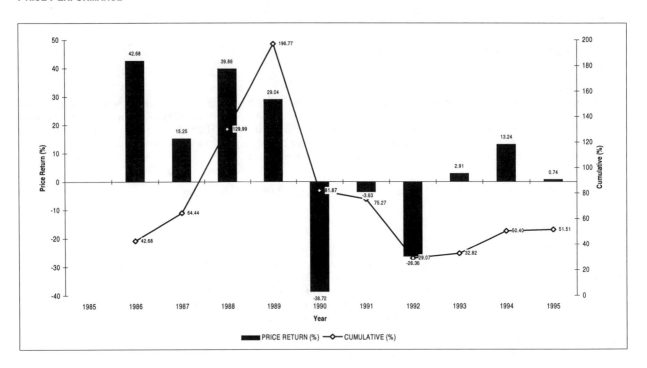

PRICE PERFORMANCE

YEAR	VALUE	PRICE RETURN (%)	CUMULATIVE (%)	MAXIMUM VALUE	DATE	MINIMUM VALUE	DATE
1995	19,868.15	0.74	51.51	20,011.76	27-Dec	14,485.41	3-Jul
1994	19,723.06	13.24	50.40	21,552.81	13-Jun	17,369.74	4-Jan
1993	17,417.24	2.91	32.82	21,148.11	13-Sep	16,078.71	29-Nov
1992	16,924.95	-26.36	29.07	23,801.18	6-Jan	14,309.41	18-Aug
1991	22,983.77	-3.63	75.27	27,146.91	18-Mar	21,456.76	19-Aug
1990	23,848.71	-38.72	81.87	38,712.88	4-Jan	20,221.86	1-Oct
1989	38,915.87	29.04	196.77	37,268.79	30-Nov	30,183.79	5-Jan
1988	30,159.00	39.86	129.99	30,159.00	28-Dec	21,217.04	4-Jan
1987	21,564.00	15.25	64.44	26,646.43	14-Oct	18,544.05	13-Jan
1986	18,710.30	42.68	42.68	18,936.24	20-Aug	12,881.50	21-Jan
1985	13,113.32						
Average Annual (%)		7.50					
Compound Annual (%)		4.24					
Standard Deviation (%)		26.49					

SYNOPSIS

The Nikkei 225 Stock Average is a price-weighted benchmark that tracks the continuous price only performance of 225 actively traded companies listed on the Tokyo Stock Exchange's First Section.

NUMBER OF STOCKS—DECEMBER 31, 1995

225

MARKET VALUE—DECEMBER 31, 1995

Not Available

SELECTION CRITERIA

Constituent shares are selected from the Tokyo Stock Exchange First Section to represent the overall performance of the Japanese stock, with a view toward maintaining the historical continuity of the benchmark. Emphasis is placed on market liquidity, as measured by each issue's trading volume and price fluctuation per trading volume over the preceding 10-year period. The stocks that fall within the top half of the First Section form the "high liquidity group" from which constituent stocks are selected after the stocks have been ranked on the basis of the combination of these two factors. In addition, constituents from the high liquidity group are selected to achieve conformity to the First Section's industrial classifications, based on 36 industry sectors, as described below.

Constituent stocks are deleted from the index due to bankruptcy, merger or acquisition, delisting and removal to the "Seiri-Post" or the TSE Second Section. In addition, constituent stocks are deleted due to relatively low market liquidity. Deletions due to market liquidity considerations are limited to 3% of the number of constituent companies, or an average of six companies per year.

Emphasis for the selection process for replacement stocks is on the maintenance of industrial classifications. This is accomplished by first establishing each industry's distribution within the so called high liquidity group, based on the average number of companies within each group. The result is compared to the ideal number of companies in each distribution group based on the total number of stocks listed on the First Section of the Tokyo Stock Exchange. Additional companies are selected from industries having the largest shortfall, based on market liquidity, as defined above.

Except for newly listed stocks of sufficient import in their impact on the overall market, stocks listed on the TSE First Section for less than three years or have less than 60 million shares outstanding may, in principal, not be considered for inclusion in the index.

BACKGROUND

The index was introduced on September 7, 1950 and recalculated back to May 16, 1949 when the Tokyo Stock Exchange was reopened for trading.

The index was maintained and published by the Tokyo Stock Exchange until the introduction the Tokyo Stock Exchange Index (TOPIX) in 1971. Nihon Keizai Shimbun, Inc. (Nikkei) assumed responsibility for its publication at that time. Joint calculation of the index commenced in May 1975 under an agreement with Dow Jones & Co., during which time the index became known as the Nikkei Dow Average. It was renamed the Nikkei Stock Average in 1985.

The current standards for adding and deleting constituent stocks were announced on December 14, 1990 for implementation October 1, 1991.

BASE DATE

May 16, 1949=176.21

COMPUTATION METHODOLOGY

(1) A simple aggregative of actual prices index formula. The divisor is adjusted periodically to reflect non-market changes in the price of the constituent stocks, such as rights offerings, splits, reverse splits, and decreases in capital or changes in the universe of constituent stocks. (2) Stocks with a par value less than 50.0 Yen are deemed to have a 50.0 Yen par value for index calculation purposes. (3) The composition of the index is reviewed on an annual basis.

DERIVATIVE INSTRUMENTS

(1) Nikkei 225 index futures and options trade on the Osaka Securities Exchange. (2) Nikkei 225 index futures and options trade on the Singapore International Monetary Exchange Ltd. (3) AMEX Japan index options, Long-Term Equity Anticipation Securities (LEAPS), Morgan Stanley Call Warrants, Bear Stearns Strike Reset Call Warrants and Goldman Sachs Indexed Notes trade on the American Stock Exchange in the United States. (4) Nikkei Index options trade on the Chicago Board Options Exchange in the United States. (5) Nikkei 225 futures and options on futures trade on the Chicago Mercantile Exchange in the United States.

SUBINDICES

Thirty-six industry group subindices: Foods, textile products, paper and pulp, chemicals, drugs, petroleum, rubber, glass and ceramics, iron and steel, nonferrous metals, machinery, electric equipment, shipbuilding, motor vehicles, transportation and equipment, precision equipment, other manufacturing, marine and agricultural products, mining, construction, trade, retail stores, banks, securities firms, insurance, other finance, real estate, railroad and bus, trucking, sea transportation, air transportation, warehousing, communication, electric power, gas and services.

RELATED INDICES

Nikkei 300 Index
Nikkei 500 Index
Nikkei All Stock Index
Nikkei Over-the-Counter Stock Average
ISE/Nikkei 50 Stock Index
Refer to Appendix 5 for additional indices.

REMARKS

The stock index options traded on the U.S. American Stock Exchange under the trading symbol (JPN) track the Japan Index, a modified price-weighted index that measures the daily price only performance of most actively traded large capitalization stocks traded on the Tokyo Stock Exchange. The index consists of 210 component stocks that represent a broad cross section of Japanese industries.

PUBLISHER

Nihon Keizai Shimbun, Inc.

NIKKEI STOCK INDEX 300 (NIK 300)

PRICE PERFORMANCE

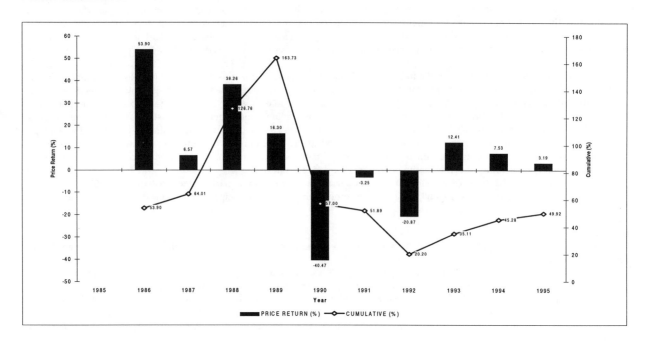

PRICE PERFORMANCE

YEAR	VALUE	PRICE RETURN (%)	CUMULATIVE (%)	MAXIMUM VALUE[1]	DATE	MINIMUM VALUE[1]	DATE
1995	296.33	3.19	49.92	297.64	27-Dec	222.26	13-Jun
1994	287.17	7.53	45.28	311.71	13-Jun	268.22	4-Jan
1993	267.06	12.41	35.11	305.49	25-Oct	234.07	26-Feb
1992	237.58	-20.87	20.20	288.85	31-Jan	222.39	31-Jul
1991	300.23	-3.25	51.89	352.18	28-Feb	300.23	31-Dec
1990	310.32	-40.47	57.00	493.66	31-Jan	283.76	28-Sep
1989	521.28	16.30	163.73	521.28	29-Dec	458.54	30-Jun
1988	448.22	38.26	126.76	448.22	30-Dec	363.64	29-Jan
1987	324.18	6.57	64.01	417.09	29-May	324.18	31-Dec
1986	304.20	53.90	53.90	304.20	31-Dec	194.96	31-Jan
1985	197.66						
Average Annual (%)		7.36					
Compound Annual (%)		4.13					
Standard Deviation (%)		26.75					

[1]Maximum/minimum index values for calendar years 1986-1993 based on month-end values.

SYNOPSIS

The Nikkei Stock Index 300 (NIK 300) Index is a capitalization-weighted index that tracks the continuous price only performance of 300 large capitalization, actively traded, liquid stocks listed on the First Section of the Tokyo Stock Exchange (TSE).

NUMBER OF STOCKS—DECEMBER 31, 1995

300

MARKET VALUE—DECEMBER 31, 1995

Not Available

SELECTION CRITERIA

Constituent stocks are selected on the basis of market capitalization, liquidity, stability and on 36 industrial allocations so as to maintain sectoral relationship to the population of stocks in the First Section.

The universe of eligible stocks is established after eliminating TSE First Section issues that no longer qualify on the basis of any of the following reasons: Conspicuously low traded day ratio, low trading volume and low volume-to-outstanding shares ratio, abrupt shift in ranking based on volume-to-outstanding shares ratio relative to the previous year, absence of dividend payments or posting of losses for a considerable period of time, debt exceeding assets for consecutive accounting periods, and a market capitalization that has become relatively low within its industry group. In addition, stocks that have been listed on the TSE for less than two years are excluded from consideration.

Eligible securities are ranked in average market value order, which is computed over a three-year period.

Index constituents are selected on the basis of an interactive process designed to represent the approximate market value composition ratio that has been established for each of the 36 industry groups.

Stocks are chosen one by one in the order of the largest total market value in each industry. The ratio of the aggregate market value of chosen stocks to the total market value of its industry in the population, or coverage rate, is kept as uniform as possible among each industry type.

Stocks are automatically removed from the index due to bankruptcy, merger, delisting or removal due to excess debt and transfer to the TSE Second Section.

BACKGROUND

The index was calculated on a daily basis to December 31, 1993, and every minute since that date. The basis for selecting constituent stocks was modified in 1993 and implemented in 1994.

Before 1994, the population of stocks that made up the index was reconstituted in its entirety each year. Stocks were selected each year on the basis of market capitalization within each industrial category, based strictly on a ratio of the market value of selected stocks to the population of stocks in the First Section.

BASE DATE

October 1, 1982=100.00

COMPUTATION METHODOLOGY

(1) An aggregative of prices times quantities index formula. Maintenance adjustments to the divisor are made for capitalization changes, new listings and delistings. These are implemented on the day a stock is replaced, on the ex-right date in the event of non-gratis allotments to shareholders, on the day of merger or on the date specified in the market report of the Tokyo Stock Exchange in connection with conversion of warrants, convertible bonds or preferred stock. (2) The number of shares outstanding excludes government owned shares. (3) Component stocks are reviewed in September of each year and changes become effective in early October.

DERIVATIVE INSTRUMENTS

(1) Nikkei 300 Stock index futures and options trade on the Singapore International Monetary Exchange Ltd. (2) Nikkei 300 Stock index options trade on the Osaka Securities Exchange. (3) Nikkei 300 Merrill Lynch Call Warrants trade on the American Stock Exchange in the United States. (4) Nikkei 300 Stock index options and Long-Term Equity Anticipation Securities (LEAPS) trade on the Chicago Board Options Exchange in the United States.

SUBINDICES

Thirty six industrial subsector indices: Foods, textile, paper and pulp, chemicals, drugs, petroleum, rubber, glass and ceramics, iron and steel, nonferrous metals, machinery, electrical equipment, shipbuilding, motor vehicles, transport equipment, other manufacturing, marine products, mining, construction, trade, retail stores, banks, securities firms, insurance, other finance, real estate, railroad and buses, trucking, sea transport, warehousing, communication, electric power, gas and services.

RELATED INDICES

Nikkei 225 Index
Nikkei 500 Index
Nikkei All Stock Index
Nikkei Over-the-Counter Stock Average
ISE/Nikkei 50 Stock Index
Refer to Appendix 5 for additional indices.

REMARKS

(1) Coverage ratio is the market value of selected stocks to the population of stocks that make up the TSE First Section. (2) 32.6% weighting in bank stocks (20.78%) and electrical equipment (11.85%) as of 11/94.

PUBLISHER

Nihon Keizai Shimbun, Inc.

NIKKEI 500 STOCK AVERAGE

PRICE PERFORMANCE

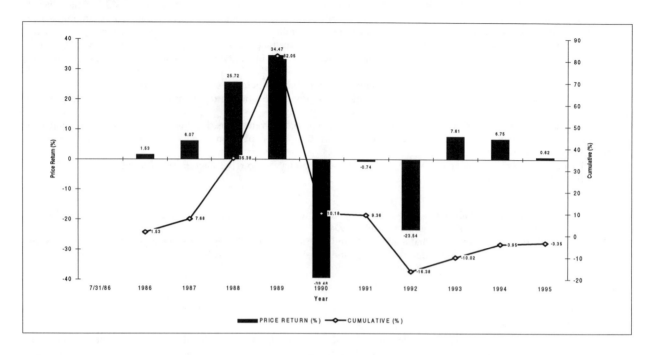

PRICE PERFORMANCE

YEAR	VALUE	PRICE RETURN (%)	CUMULATIVE (%)	MAXIMUM VALUE	DATE	MINIMUM VALUE	DATE
1995	1,277.57	0.62	-3.35	1,280.88	27-Dec	944.96	13-Jun
1994	1,269.71	6.75	-3.95	1,404.03	13-Jun	1,195.53	4-Jan
1993	1,189.44	7.61	-10.02	1,400.93	13-Sep	1,058.03	25-Jan
1992	1,105.29	-23.54	-16.38	1,486.71	6-Jan	923.46	18-Aug
1991	1,445.66	-0.74	9.36	1,759.83	17-Apr	1,380.41	16-Jan
1990	1,456.42	-39.48	10.18	2,394.74	4-Jan	1,310.92	1-Oct
1989	2,406.47	34.47	82.05	2,406.47	29-Dec	1,795.40	4-Jan
1988	1,789.54	25.72	35.38	1,789.75	15-Jun	1,399.80	4-Jan
1987	1,423.44	6.07	7.68	1,748.17	9-Oct	1,316.27	13-Jan
1986	1,342.04	1.53	1.53	1,366.24	20-Aug	1,172.75	22-Oct
7/31/86	1,321.87						
Average Annual (%)		1.94					
Compound Annual (%)		-0.55					
Standard Deviation (%)		22.56					

[1]Statistical measures applicable to the nine year period 12/31/86-12/31/95

SYNOPSIS

The Nikkei 500 Stock Average is a price-weighted index that tracks the continuous price performance of the Tokyo Stock Exchange's First Section.

NUMBER OF STOCKS—DECEMBER 31, 1995

500

MARKET VALUE—DECEMBER 31, 1995

Not Available

SELECTION CRITERIA

Constituent stocks are selected on the basis of trading volume, trading value and market value. Securities are ranked on the basis of each of these factors for the previous three years. The top 500 stocks on the basis of their composite ranking are selected for inclusion in the index.

BACKGROUND

The index was introduced on January 4, 1982.

BASE DATE

January 4, 1972=223.70

COMPUTATION METHODOLOGY

(1) A simple aggregative of actual prices index formula. The divisor that is adjusted periodically to reflect non-market changes in the price of the constituent stocks, such as rights offerings, splits, reverse splits, and decreases in capital, or changes in the universe of constituent stocks, so as to maintain its continuity. Moreover, stocks with a par value less than 50.0 Yen are deemed to have a 50.0 Yen par value for index calculation purposes. (2) Constituent stocks are reselected each year on the basis of a composite ranking that takes into account trading volume, trading value and market value for each of the previous three years.

DERIVATIVE INSTRUMENTS

None

SUBINDICES

Thirty-six industry group subindices: Foods, textile products, paper and pulp, chemicals, drugs, petroleum, rubber, glass and ceramics, iron and steel, nonferrous metals, machinery, electric equipment, shipbuilding, motor vehicles, transportation and equipment, precision equipment, other manufacturing, marine and agricultural products, mining, construction, trade, retail stores, banks, securities firms, insurance, other finance, real estate, railroad and bus, trucking, sea transportation, air transportation, warehousing, communication, electric power, gas and services.

RELATED INDICES

Nikkei 225 Index
Nikkei 300 Index
Nikkei All Stock Index
Nikkei Over-the-Counter Stock Average
ISE/Nikkei 50 Stock Index
Refer to Appendix 5 for additional indices.

REMARKS

None

PUBLISHER

Nihon Keizai Shimbun, Inc.

OSAKA 300 STOCK PRICE INDEX

PRICE PERFORMANCE

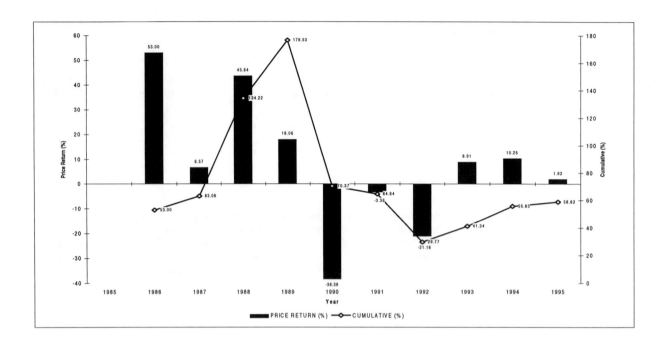

PRICE PERFORMANCE

YEAR	VALUE	PRICE RETURN (%)	CUMULATIVE (%)	MAXIMUM VALUE	DATE	MINIMUM VALUE	DATE
1995	1,365.51	1.92	58.82	1,369.32	27-Dec	1,018.29	13-Jun
1994	1,339.80	10.25	55.83	1,457.73	13-Jun	1,218.50	4-Jan
1993	1,215.20	8.91	41.34	1,400.86	6-Sep	1,063.60	25-Jan
1992	1,115.78	-21.18	29.77	1,466.25	6-Jan	955.27	18-Aug
1991	1,415.57	-3.36	64.64	1,716.58	18-Mar	1,375.16	19-Aug
1990	1,464.82	-38.39	70.37	2,379.77	4-Jan	1,287.83	1-Oct
1989	2,377.54	18.06	176.53	2,394.85	6-Dec	2,026.07	4-Jan
1988	2,013.76	43.64	134.22	2,013.76	28-Dec	1,377.61	4-Jan
1987	1,401.95	6.57	63.06	1,792.68	14-Oct	1,299.97	13-Jan
1986	1,315.46	53.00	53.00	1,339.95	24-Dec	842.15	21-Jan
1985	859.79						
Average Annual (%)		7.94					
Compound Annual (%)		4.73					
Standard Deviation (%)		27.03					

SYNOPSIS
The Osaka 300 Stock Price Index is a market capitalization-weighted index that tracks the price only performance of the large, most actively traded shares listed on the First Section of the Osaka Securities Exchange (OSE).

NUMBER OF STOCKS—DECEMBER 31, 1995
300

MARKET VALUE—DECEMBER 31, 1995
US$1,499,138.2 million

SELECTION CRITERIA
Component stocks include frequently priced issues of large companies with high trading volume that reflect the overall industrial sector scheme of the Osaka market. Deleted issues, due to bankruptcy, merger, delisting from the First Section due to insolvency or other reasons and reassignments to the Second Section, are replaced with high trading volume and frequently priced constituents that maintain the industrial weighting scheme of the Osaka market.

BACKGROUND
The index was introduced on August 1, 1969 after extensive deliberations concerning various deficiencies associated with the price-weighted Osaka 250 Adjusted Stock Average.

BASE DATE
January 4, 1968=100.00

COMPUTATION METHODOLOGY
An aggregative of prices times quantities index formula. Maintenance adjustments to the divisor are made as they impact the market value of constituent shares due to rights offerings, public offerings, private placements, mergers, exercise of stock subscription warrants, conversion of convertible bonds or preferred stock or new listings and delistings.

DERIVATIVE INSTRUMENTS
None

SUBINDICES
Thirty-two industrial subsector indices: Fishery, agriculture and forestry, mining, construction, foods, textiles and apparels, pulp and paper, chemicals, pharmaceutical, oil and coal products, glass and ceramics, iron and steel, non-ferrous metals, metal products, machinery, electric appliances, transportation equipment, precision instruments, other products, electric power and gas, land transportation, marine transportation, air transportation, warehousing and harbor transportation services, communications, wholesale trade, retail trade, banks, insurance, other financing business, real estate and services.

RELATED INDICES
Osaka 250 Adjusted Stock Price Average
Osaka 40 Adjusted Stock Price Average

REMARKS
None

PUBLISHER
Osaka Securities Exchange (OSE).

TOKYO STOCK EXCHANGE PRICE INDEX (TOPIX)

PRICE PERFORMANCE

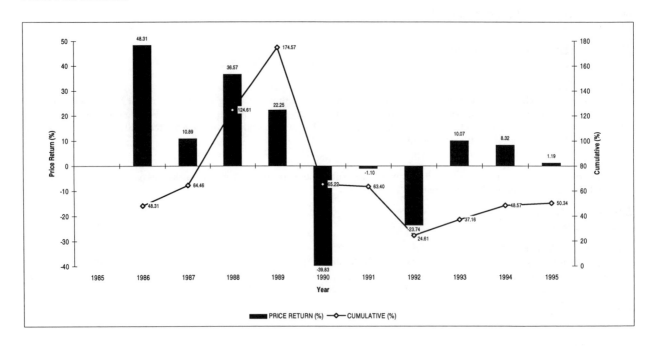

PRICE PERFORMANCE

YEAR	VALUE	PRICE RETURN (%)	CUMULATIVE (%)	MAXIMUM VALUE	DATE	MINIMUM VALUE	DATE
1995	1,577.70	1.19	50.34	1,585.87	27-Dec	1,193.16	13-Jun
1994	1,559.09	8.32	48.57	1,712.73	13-Jun	1,445.97	4-Jan
1993	1,439.31	10.07	37.16	1,698.67	3-Sep	1,250.06	25-Jan
1992	1,307.66	-23.74	24.61	1,763.43	6-Jan	1,102.50	18-Aug
1991	1,714.68	-1.10	63.40	2,028.85	18-Mar	1,638.06	24-Dec
1990	1,733.83	-39.83	65.22	2,867.70	4-Jan	1,523.43	1-Oct
1989	2,881.37	22.25	174.57	2,884.80	18-Dec	2,634.33	27-Mar
1988	2,357.03	36.57	124.61	2,357.03	28-Dec	1,690.44	4-Jan
1987	1,725.83	10.89	64.46	2,258.56	11-Jun	1,557.46	13-Jan
1986	1,556.37	48.31	48.31	1,583.35	20-Aug	1,025.85	21-Jan
1985	1,049.40						
Average Annual (%)		7.29					
Compound Annual (%)		4.16					
Standard Deviation (%)		25.98					

SYNOPSIS
The Tokyo Stock Exchange Price Index (TOPIX) is a broad based capitalization-weighted index that tracks the continuous price only performance of all domestic common stocks listed on the First Section of the Tokyo Stock Exchange (TSE). The First Section is comprised of larger, established companies, that have generally been in existence for five years or more and meet more stringent eligibility criteria relating to the size and business conditions of the issuing company as well as the liquidity of its securities.

NUMBER OF STOCKS—DECEMBER 31, 1995
1,255

MARKET VALUE—DECEMBER 31, 1995
US$3,338,446.9 million

SELECTION CRITERIA
Constituent shares include all stocks that are listed in the First Section of the TSE, excluding foreign shares. In general, the First Section is the marketplace for stocks of larger, seasoned companies. Stocks assigned to the First Section are reviewed at the end of each business year to ensure compliance with listing guidelines. Companies that fail to satisfy First Section listing guidelines are reassigned to the Second Section which is reserved for smaller as well as newly listed companies.

BACKGROUND
The index was introduced on July 1, 1969. Daily index values have been recalculated to May 16, 1949 for the aggregate price index while daily values for each of the subindices are available only from January 4, 1968.

BASE DATE
January 4, 1968=100.00

COMPUTATION METHODOLOGY
(1) An aggregative of prices times quantities index formula. (2) Maintenance adjustments to the divisor due to delistings, mergers, rights offerings, public offerings and private placements which result in the listing of additional shares, are reflected on the day of the event. New listings are reflected in the index one day following the day of listing. The exercise of stock subscription warrants and conversions of a convertible bond or a convertible preferred stock into common stock are made on the last business day of the month.

DERIVATIVE INSTRUMENTS
TOPIX index options and futures trade on the Tokyo Stock Exchange.

SUBINDICES
Twenty-eight industry group subindices: Fishery and forestry, mining, construction, foods, textiles, pulp and paper, chemicals, oil and coal products, rubber products, machinery, electric appliances, transportation equipment, precision instruments, other products, commerce, finance and insurance, real estate, land transportation, marine transportation, air transportation, warehousing and harbor transportation, communication, electric power and gas and services.
TOPIX Large-Sized Companies Subindex
TOPIX Medium-Sized Companies Subindex
TOPIX Small-Sized Companies Subindex

RELATED INDICES
TSE Second Section Stock Price Index
TSE Arithmetic Stock Price Index
Refer to Appendix 5 for additional indices.

REMARKS
None

PUBLISHER
The Tokyo Stock Exchange (TSE).

TOKYO STOCK EXCHANGE PRICE INDEX (TOPIX)—LARGE-SIZED COMPANIES SUBINDEX

PRICE PERFORMANCE

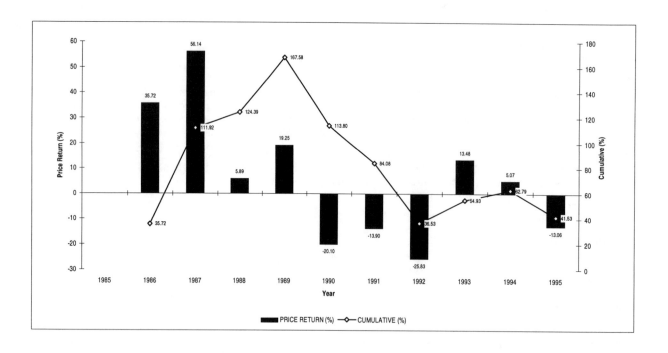

PRICE PERFORMANCE

YEAR	VALUE	PRICE RETURN (%)	CUMULATIVE (%)	MAXIMUM VALUE[1]	DATE	MINIMUM VALUE[1]	DATE
1995	1,396.67	-13.06	41.53	1,611.19	NA	1,215.68	NA
1994	1,606.49	5.07	62.79	1,718.11	13-Jun	1,461.05	4-Jan
1993	1,528.91	13.48	54.93	1,699.40	3-Sep	1,251.44	25-Jan
1992	1,347.31	-25.83	36.53	1,763.75	6-Jan	1,108.78	18-Aug
1991	1,816.57	-13.90	84.08	1,991.94	18-Mar	1,624.42	24-Dec
1990	2,109.84	-20.10	113.80	2,878.18	4-Jan	1,470.88	1-Oct
1989	2,640.58	19.25	167.58	2,910.35	7-Dec	2,469.29	27-Mar
1988	2,214.38	5.89	124.39	2,483.18	28-Dec	1,735.24	4-Jan
1987	2,091.30	56.14	111.92	2,448.70	11-Jun	1,632.90	13-Jan
1986	1,339.35	35.72	35.72	1,644.92	20-Aug	1,006.47	23-Jan
1985	986.83						
Average Annual (%)		6.27					
Compound Annual (%)		3.53					
Standard Deviation (%)		44.68					

[1]Idex values are monthly averages.

SYNOPSIS
The Tokyo Stock Exchange Price Index (TOPIX)—Large-Sized Companies Subindex is a market capitalization weighted index that tracks the continuos price only performance of the largest domestic common stocks listed on the First Section of the Tokyo Stock Exchange (TSE).

NUMBER OF STOCKS—DECEMBER 31, 1995
743

MARKET VALUE—DECEMBER 31, 1995
Not Available

SELECTION CRITERIA
Constituent shares include all stocks of companies that are listed in the First Section of the TSE, excluding foreign shares, with capital in excess of 200.0 million Yen.

BACKGROUND
Until September 1982, large-sized stocks were limited to companies with capital in excess of 10.0 billion Yen.

BASE DATE
January 4, 1968=100.00

COMPUTATION METHODOLOGY
(1) An aggregative of prices times quantities index formula. (2) Maintenance adjustments to the index due to delistings, mergers, rights offerings, public offerings and private placements which result in the listing of additional shares are reflected on the day of the event. New listings are reflected in the index one day following the day of listing. The exercise of stock subscription warrants and conversions of a convertible bond or a convertible preferred stock into common stock are made on the last business day of the month.

DERIVATIVE INSTRUMENTS
None

SUBINDICES
None

RELATED INDICES
TSE Stock Price Index (TOPIX)
TSE Arithmetic Stock Price Index
Refer to Appendix 5 for additional indices.

REMARKS
The First Section is comprised of larger, established companies that have generally been in existence for five years or more and meet more stringent eligibility criteria relating to the size and business conditions of the issuing company as well as the liquidity of its securities.

PUBLISHER
The Tokyo Stock Exchange (TSE).

Tokyo Stock Exchange Price Index (TOPIX)—Medium-Sized Companies Subindex

Price Performance

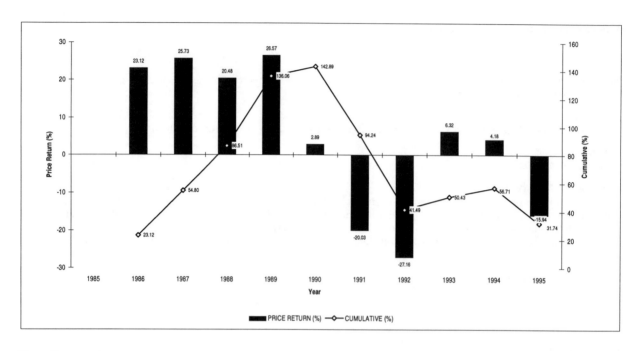

Price Performance

YEAR	VALUE	PRICE RETURN (%)	CUMULATIVE (%)	MAXIMUM VALUE[1]	DATE	MINIMUM VALUE[1]	DATE
1995	1,145.83	-15.94	31.74	1,311.92	NA	959.69	NA
1994	1,363.09	4.18	56.71	1,468.72	17-Jun	1,198.80	4-Jan
1993	1,308.41	6.32	50.43	1,476.45	7-Jun	1,085.92	25-Jan
1992	1,230.67	-27.16	41.49	1,546.20	6-Jan	942.56	18-Aug
1991	1,689.49	-20.03	94.24	1,944.48	17-Apr	1,476.23	24-Dec
1990	2,112.64	2.89	142.89	2,498.68	6-Feb	1,491.10	1-Oct
1989	2,053.22	26.57	136.06	2,502.55	29-Dec	1,706.36	4-Jan
1988	1,622.26	20.48	86.51	1,740.32	23-Jun	1,330.03	4-Jan
1987	1,346.46	25.73	54.80	1,591.74	14-Oct	1,117.11	19-Jan
1986	1,070.92	23.12	23.12	1,176.95	18-Jul	892.94	7-Jan
1985	869.79						
Average Annual (%)		4.62					
Compound Annual (%)		2.79					
Standard Deviation (%)		41.86					

[1]Index values are monthly averages.

SYNOPSIS

The Tokyo Stock Exchange Price Index (TOPIX)—Medium-Sized Companies Subindex is a market capitalization-weighted index that tracks the continuous price only performance of the largest domestic common stocks listed on the First Section of the Tokyo Stock Exchange (TSE).

NUMBER OF STOCKS—DECEMBER 31, 1995
489

MARKET VALUE—DECEMBER 31, 1995
Not Available

SELECTION CRITERIA
Constituent shares include all stocks of companies listed in the First Section of the TSE, excluding foreign shares, with capital in excess of 60.0 million Yen or more but less than 200.0 million Yen.

BACKGROUND
Until September 1982, medium-sized stocks were limited to companies with capital in excess of 3.0 billion Yen but less than 10.0 billion Yen.

BASE DATE
January 4, 1968=100.00

COMPUTATION METHODOLOGY
(1) An aggregative of prices times quantities index formula. (2) Maintenance adjustments to the index due to delistings, mergers, rights offerings, public offerings and private placements which result in the listing of additional shares are reflected on the day of the event. New listings are reflected in the index one day following the day of listing. The exercise of stock subscription warrants and conversions of a convertible bond or a convertible preferred stock into common stock are made on the last business day of the month.

DERIVATIVE INSTRUMENTS
None

SUBINDICES
None

RELATED INDICES
TSE Stock Price Index (TOPIX)
TSE Arithmetic Stock Price Index
Refer to Appendix 5 for additional indices.

REMARKS
The First Section is comprised of larger, established companies that have generally been in existence for five years or more and meet more stringent eligibility criteria relating to the size and business conditions of the issuing company as well as the liquidity of its securities.

PUBLISHER
The Tokyo Stock Exchange (TSE).

TOKYO STOCK EXCHANGE PRICE INDEX (TOPIX)—SMALL-SIZED COMPANIES SUBINDEX

PRICE PERFORMANCE

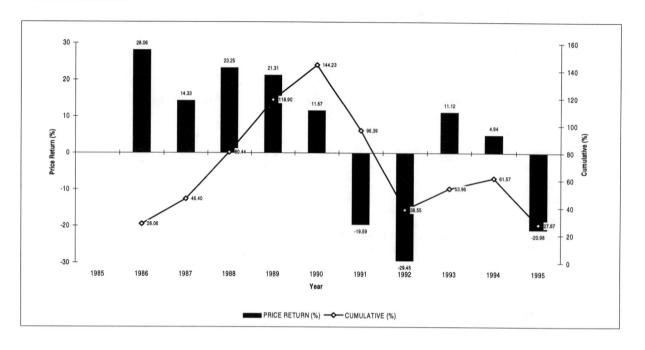

PRICE PERFORMANCE

YEAR	VALUE	PRICE RETURN (%)	CUMULATIVE (%)	MAXIMUM VALUE[1]	DATE	MINIMUM VALUE[1]	DATE
1995	1,788.90	-20.98	27.67	2,116.52	NA	1,788.90	NA
1994	2,263.83	4.94	61.57	2,462.76	17-Jun	2,004.43	4-Jan
1993	2,157.18	11.12	53.96	2,502.30	7-Jun	1,732.40	27-Jan
1992	1,941.25	-29.45	38.55	2,427.22	6-Jan	1,493.10	19-Aug
1991	2,751.66	-19.59	96.39	3,189.04	17-Apr	2,335.51	24-Jan
1990	3,421.97	11.57	144.23	4,038.47	15-Feb	2,438.64	1-Oct
1989	3,067.08	21.31	118.90	3,859.06	29-Dec	2,503.10	6-Jan
1988	2,528.27	23.25	80.44	2,784.16	25-Jun	2,134.47	4-Jan
1987	2,051.33	14.33	46.40	2,528.04	14-Oct	1,717.86	28-Apr
1986	1,794.27	28.06	28.06	2,060.54	14-Jul	1,508.58	13-Jan
1985	1,401.15						
Average Annual (%)		4.46					
Compound Annual (%)		2.47					
Standard Deviation (%)		39.62					

[1]Index values are monthly averages.

SYNOPSIS
The Tokyo Stock Exchange Price Index (TOPIX)—Small-Sized Companies Subindex is a market capitalization-weighted index that tracks the continuous price only performance of the largest domestic common stocks listed on the First Section of the Tokyo Stock Exchange (TSE).

NUMBER OF STOCKS—DECEMBER 31, 1995
326

MARKET VALUE—DECEMBER 31, 1995
Not Available

SELECTION CRITERIA
Constituent shares include all stocks of companies listed in the First Section of the TSE, excluding foreign shares, with capital below 60.0 million Yen.

BACKGROUND
Until September 1982, small-sized companies were limited to companies with capital below 3.0 billion Yen.

BASE DATE
January 4, 1968=100.00

COMPUTATION METHODOLOGY
(1) An aggregative of prices times quantities index formula. (2) Maintenance adjustments to the index due to delistings, mergers, rights offerings, public offerings and private placements which result in the listing of additional shares are reflected on the day of the event. New listings are reflected in the index one day following the day of listing. The exercise of stock subscription warrants and conversions of a convertible bond or a convertible preferred stock into common stock are made on the last business day of the month.

DERIVATIVE INSTRUMENTS
None

SUBINDICES
None

RELATED INDICES
TSE Stock Price Index (TOPIX)
TSE Arithmetic Stock Price Index
Refer to Appendix 5 for additional indices.

REMARKS
The First Section is comprised of larger, established companies that have generally been in existence for five years or more and meet more stringent eligibility criteria relating to the size and business conditions of the issuing company as well as the liquidity of its securities.

PUBLISHER
The Tokyo Stock Exchange (TSE).

TOKYO STOCK EXCHANGE (TSE) SECOND SECTION STOCK PRICE INDEX

PRICE PERFORMANCE

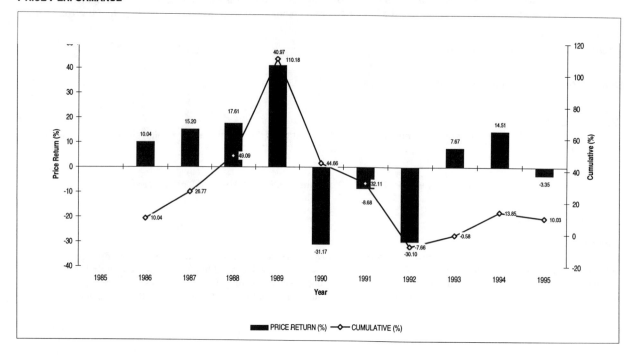

PRICE PERFORMANCE

YEAR	VALUE	PRICE RETURN (%)	CUMULATIVE (%)	MAXIMUM VALUE	DATE	MINIMUM VALUE	DATE
1995	2,062.11	-3.35	10.03	2,130.68	4-Jan	1,441.90	13-Jun
1994	2,133.66	14.51	13.85	2,542.65	6-Jul	1,873.33	4-Jan
1993	1,863.36	7.67	-0.58	2,384.97	7-Jun	1,651.72	26-Jan
1992	1,730.65	-30.10	-7.66	2,459.85	6-Jan	1,502.77	19-Aug
1991	2,475.94	-8.68	32.11	3,423.46	10-May	2,424.50	27-Dec
1990	2,711.15	-31.17	44.66	4,477.16	16-Jul	2,711.15	28-Dec
1989	3,939.15	40.97	110.18	3,939.15	29-Dec	2,774.38	27-Mar
1988	2,794.26	17.61	49.09	3,106.34	23-Jun	2,361.25	4-Jan
1987	2,375.87	15.20	26.77	2,791.54	14-Oct	2,014.69	28-Apr
1986	2,062.35	10.04	10.04	2,337.38	16-Jul	1,857.12	7-Jan
1985	1,874.16						
Average Annual (%)		3.27					
Compound Annual (%)		0.96					
Standard Deviation (%)		22.23					

SYNOPSIS

The Tokyo Stock Exchange (TSE) Second Section Stock Price Index is a broad capitalization-weighted index that tracks the continuous price performance of all domestic common stocks listed on the Second Section of the Tokyo Stock Exchange (TSE).

NUMBER OF STOCKS—DECEMBER 31, 1995

461

MARKET VALUE—DECEMBER 31, 1995

US$149,529.9 million

SELECTION CRITERIA

Constituent shares, which include all stocks listed on the Second Section of the TSE, are smaller, less established companies, and newly listed issuers that do not meet the more stringent eligibility criteria relating to the size and business conditions of the issuing company as well as the liquidity of its securities that are required for First Section listing. Foreign shares are excluded from consideration. Stocks assigned to the Second Section are reviewed at the end of each business year to ensure compliance with listing guidelines. Companies that satisfy First Section listing guidelines are reassigned to the First Section, which is reserved for larger, more established companies.

BACKGROUND

The index tracked a selection of 300 stocks up until March 31, 1985.

BASE DATE

August 18, 1969=100.00

COMPUTATION METHODOLOGY

(1) An aggregative of prices times quantities index formula. (2) Maintenance adjustments to the index due to delistings, mergers, rights offerings, public offerings and private placements which result in the listing of additional shares, are reflected on the day of the event. New listings are reflected in the index one day following the day of listing. The exercise of stock subscription warrants and conversions of a convertible bond or a convertible preferred stock into common stock are made on the last business day of the month.

DERIVATIVE INSTRUMENTS

None

SUBINDICES

None

RELATED INDICES

TSE Price Index (TOPIX)
TSE Arithmetic Stock Price Index
Refer to Appendix 5 for additional indices.

REMARKS

None

PUBLISHER

The Tokyo Stock Exchange (TSE).

KOREA COMPOSITE STOCK PRICE INDEX (KOSPI)

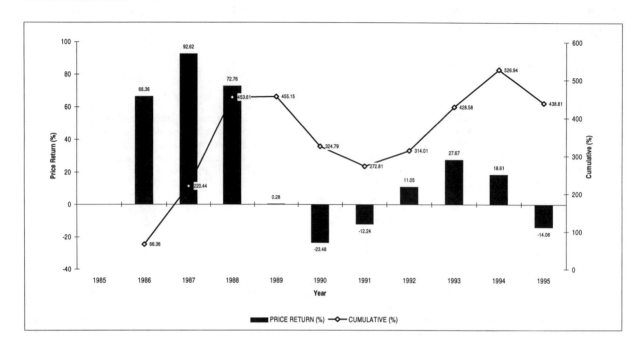

PRICE PERFORMANCE

YEAR	VALUE	PRICE RETURN (%)	CUMULATIVE (%)	MAXIMUM VALUE	DATE	MINIMUM VALUE	DATE
1995	882.94	-14.06	438.81	1,016.66	12-Oct	848.63	24-May
1994	1,027.37	18.61	526.94	1,138.75	8-Nov	855.37	2-Apr
1993	866.18	27.67	428.58	874.10	17-Dec	605.93	6-Mar
1992	678.44	11.05	314.01	691.37	4-Feb	459.07	21-Aug
1991	610.92	-12.24	272.81	763.10	6-Aug	586.51	23-Dec
1990	696.11	-23.48	324.79	928.82	4-Jan	566.27	3-Sep
1989	909.72	0.28	455.15	1,077.77	1-Apr	844.75	11-Dec
1988	907.20	72.76	453.61	922.58	14-Dec	527.89	5-Jan
1987	525.11	92.62	220.44	525.11	26-Dec	264.82	5-Jan
1986	272.61	66.36	66.36	279.67	2-Dec	153.85	24-Jan
1985	163.87						
Average Annual (%)		23.96					
Compound Annual (%)		18.34					
Standard Deviation (%)		40.37					

SYNOPSIS

The Korea Composite Stock Price Index (KOSPI) is a comprehensive capitalization-weighted index that tracks the continuous price performance of all common stocks listed on the Korea Stock Exchange (KSE), including First and Second Sections.

NUMBER OF STOCKS—DECEMBER 31, 1995

714

MARKET VALUE—DECEMBER 31, 1995

US$183,265.9 million

SELECTION CRITERIA

All shares listed on the KSE, including shares traded on the First and Second Sections are included in the index, except newly listed companies.

Listing eligibility is determined on the basis of time period since incorporation, capital size, number of outstanding shares, sales figures, financial health and profitability. Larger, more established companies are generally assigned to the First Section. Newly listed issues are assigned to the Second Section for at least one year after its initial listing.

BACKGROUND

Introduced in 1983, the KOSPI superseded an earlier version that was launched in 1972 which was a price-weighted index consisting of 35 issues selected to represent the market as a whole. The number of issues covered by the index was expanded to include 153 stocks by January 4, 1979. The index was rebased at that time to January 4, 1975 and its calculation continued until the adoption of the present KOSPI in 1983 with its revised 1980 base date.

BASE DATE

January 4, 1980=100.00

COMPUTATION METHODOLOGY

An aggregative of prices times quantities index formula. Maintenance adjustments to the divisor are made whenever the current market value undergoes certain variations such as capitalization changes, new listings, delistings or other factors not strictly related to price changes.

DERIVATIVE INSTRUMENTS

None

SUBINDICES

KSE First and Second Section subindices.

Three subindices are calculated on the basis of company capitalization across both the First and Section Sections, including large-sized, medium-sized and small-sized companies.

Thirty-four subindices by industry groups: Fishing, mining, construction, foods and beverages, textiles, wearing apparel and leather industries, wood and wood products, paper and paper products, chemical petroleum, coal, rubber and plastic products, non-metallic minerals, basic-metal industries, fabricated metals, machinery and equipment, other manufacturers, wholesale trade, transportation and storage, finance and insurance.

RELATED INDICES

Korea Stock Price Index 200
Korea Stock Exchange Bond Index

REMARKS

Foreign investor limitations apply to a single company's outstanding shares.

PUBLISHER

Korea Stock Exchange (KSE).

KOREA COMPOSITE STOCK PRICE INDEX (KOSPI)—LARGE-SIZED COMPANIES SUBINDEX

PRICE PERFORMANCE

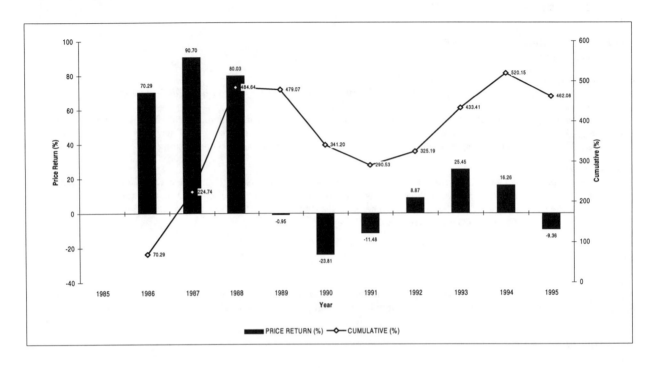

PRICE PERFORMANCE

YEAR	VALUE	PRICE RETURN (%)	CUMULATIVE (%)	MAXIMUM VALUE	DATE	MINIMUM VALUE	DATE
1995	705.41	-9.36	462.08	817.04	12-Oct	670.03	17-Feb
1994	778.29	16.26	520.15	880.52	9-Nov	664.88	2-Apr
1993	669.43	25.45	433.41	674.80	27-Dec	470.18	6-Mar
1992	533.61	8.87	325.19	548.66	8-Feb	356.02	21-Aug
1991	490.12	-11.48	290.53	617.14	6-Aug	446.91	22-Jun
1990	553.71	-23.81	341.20	742.10	4-Jan	446.19	17-Sep
1989	726.73	-0.95	479.07	803.72	1-Apr	668.95	1-Jul
1988	733.72	80.03	484.64	745.09	14-Dec	410.48	5-Jan
1987	407.55	90.70	224.74	407.55	26-Dec	206.86	5-Jan
1986	213.71	70.29	70.29	221.48	2-Dec	115.91	24-Jan
1985	125.50						
Average Annual (%)		24.60					
Compound Annual (%)		18.84					
Standard Deviation (%)		41.23					

SYNOPSIS
The Korea Composite Stock Price Index (KOSPI)—Large-Sized Companies Subindex is a capitalization-weighted index that tracks the price performance of large-sized common stocks listed on the Korea Stock Exchange (KSE), including First and Second Sections, with capital stock in excess of 75.0 billion Won. These shares account for 65% of the domestic market capitalization.

NUMBER OF STOCKS—DECEMBER 31, 1995
99

MARKET VALUE—DECEMBER 31, 1995
US$119,777.4 million

SELECTION CRITERIA
All shares listed on the KSE, including shares traded on the First and Second Sections, with capital stock in excess of 75.0 billion Won, are included in the index, excepting newly listed companies.

BACKGROUND
The Large-Sized Companies Subindex is a component of Korea Stock Price Index.

BASE DATE
January 4, 1980=100.00

COMPUTATION METHODOLOGY
An aggregative of prices times quantities index formula. Maintenance adjustments to the divisor are made whenever the current market value undergoes certain variations such as capitalization changes, new listings, delistings or other factors not strictly related to price changes.

DERIVATIVE INSTRUMENTS
None

SUBINDICES
None

RELATED INDICES
Korea Stock Exchange Composite Index
Korea Stock Price Index 200
Korea Stock Exchange Bond Index

REMARKS
Foreign investor limitations apply to a single company's outstanding shares.

PUBLISHER
Korea Stock Exchange (KSE).

KOREA COMPOSITE STOCK PRICE INDEX (KOSPI)—MEDIUM-SIZED COMPANIES SUBINDEX

PRICE PERFORMANCE

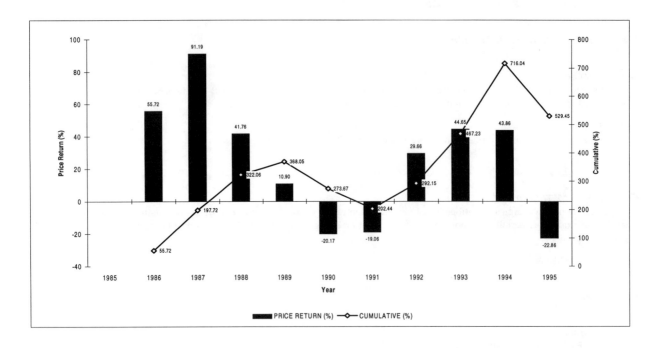

PRICE PERFORMANCE

YEAR	VALUE	PRICE RETURN (%)	CUMULATIVE (%)	MAXIMUM VALUE	DATE	MINIMUM VALUE	DATE
1995	1,355.97	-22.86	529.45	1,787.20	4-Jan	1,314.68	24-May
1994	1,757.91	43.86	716.04	1,795.59	24-Dec	1,117.89	8-Mar
1993	1,221.92	44.65	467.23	1,302.03	20-Nov	837.87	6-Mar
1992	844.76	29.66	292.15	965.07	19-May	633.32	21-Aug
1991	651.51	-19.06	202.44	814.49	15-Mar	635.18	16-Oct
1990	804.95	-20.17	273.67	1,059.67	2-Mar	692.98	24-Sep
1989	1,008.28	10.90	368.05	1,129.58	8-Apr	864.93	19-Jan
1988	909.20	41.76	322.06	940.84	13-Dec	639.63	5-Jan
1987	641.35	91.19	197.72	641.35	26-Dec	328.12	5-Jan
1986	335.45	55.72	55.72	344.36	17-Dec	208.94	6-Jan
1985	215.42						
Average Annual (%)		25.57					
Compound Annual (%)		20.20					
Standard Deviation (%)		37.77					

Synopsis

The Korea Composite Stock Price Index (KOSPI)—Medium-Sized Companies Subindex is a capitalization-weighted index that tracks the price performance of medium-sized common stocks listed on the Korea Stock Exchange (KSE), including First and Second Sections. These shares account for 13% of the domestic market capitalization.

Number of Stocks—December 31, 1995

108

Market Value—December 31, 1995

US$24,323.9 million

Selection Criteria

All shares listed on the KSE, including shares traded on the First and Second Sections, with capital stock between 35.0 and 75.0 billion Won, are included in the index, except newly listed companies.

Background

The Medium-Sized Companies Subindex is a component of Korea Stock Exchange Price Index.

Base Date

January 4, 1980=100.00

Computation Methodology

An aggregative of prices times quantities index formula. Maintenance adjustments to the divisor are made whenever the current market value undergoes certain variations such as capitalization changes, new listings, delistings or other factors not strictly related to price changes.

Derivative Instruments

None

Subindices

None

Related Indices

Korea Stock Exchange Composite Index
Korea Stock Price Index 200
Korea Stock Exchange Bond Index

Remarks

Foreign investor limitations apply to a single company's outstanding shares.

Publisher

Korea Stock Exchange (KSE).

KOREA COMPOSITE STOCK PRICE INDEX (KOSPI)—SMALL-SIZED COMPANIES SUBINDEX

PRICE PERFORMANCE

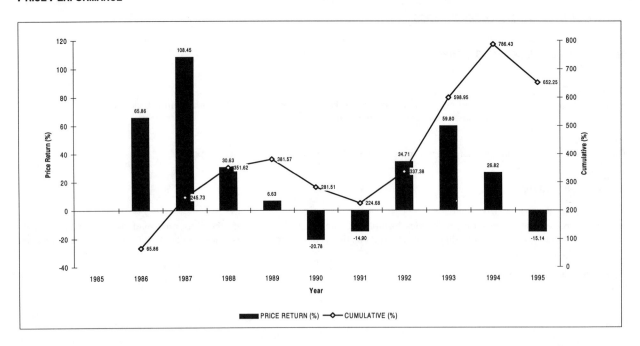

PRICE PERFORMANCE

YEAR	VALUE	PRICE RETURN (%)	CUMULATIVE (%)	MAXIMUM VALUE	DATE	MINIMUM VALUE	DATE
1995	1,748.54	-15.14	652.25	2,227.36	13-Feb	1,628.80	24-May
1994	2,060.42	26.82	786.43	2,074.52	24-Dec	1,394.69	4-Mar
1993	1,624.64	59.80	598.95	1,750.18	22-Dec	1,207.44	6-Jan
1992	1,016.65	34.71	337.38	1,252.07	19-May	749.15	13-Jan
1991	754.68	-14.90	224.68	903.08	16-Mar	692.64	16-Oct
1990	886.79	-20.78	281.51	1,231.57	13-Apr	784.24	27-Sep
1989	1,119.35	6.63	381.57	1,314.37	8-Apr	1,001.20	24-Jan
1988	1,049.75	30.63	351.62	1,079.43	13-Dec	798.54	31-Aug
1987	803.62	108.45	245.73	803.62	26-Dec	381.81	5-Jan
1986	385.52	65.86	65.86	385.52	26-Dec	229.32	4-Jan
1985	232.44						
Average Annual (%)		28.21					
Compound Annual (%)		22.36					
Standard Deviation (%)		41.51					

SYNOPSIS
The Korea Composite Stock Price Index (KOSPI)—Small-Sized Companies Subindex is a capitalization-weighted index that tracks the price performance of small-sized common stocks listed on the Korea Stock Exchange (KSE), including First and Second Sections. These shares account for 21% of the domestic market capitalization.

NUMBER OF STOCKS—DECEMBER 31, 1995
507

MARKET VALUE—DECEMBER 31, 1995
US$38,973.0 million

SELECTION CRITERIA
All shares listed on the KSE, including shares traded on the First and Second Sections, with capital stock below 35.0 billion Won, are included in the index, except newly listed companies.

BACKGROUND
The Small-Sized Companies Subindex is a component of Korea Stock Exchange Price Index.

BASE DATE
January 4, 1980=100.00

COMPUTATION METHODOLOGY
An aggregative of prices times quantities index formula. Maintenance adjustments to the divisor are made whenever the current market value undergoes certain variations such as capitalization changes, new listings, delistings or other factors not strictly related to price changes.

DERIVATIVE INSTRUMENTS
None

SUBINDICES
None

RELATED INDICES
Korea Stock Exchange Composite Index
Korea Stock Exchange Price Index 200
Korea Stock Exchange Bond Index

REMARKS
Foreign investor limitations apply to a single company's outstanding shares.

PUBLISHER
Korea Stock Exchange (KSE).

KOREA STOCK PRICE INDEX 200 (KOSPI 200)

PRICE PERFORMANCE

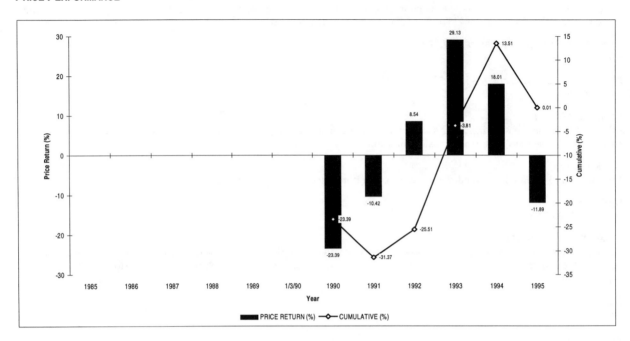

PRICE PERFORMANCE

YEAR	VALUE	PRICE RETURN (%)	CUMULATIVE (%)	MAXIMUM VALUE	DATE	MINIMUM VALUE	DATE
1995	100.01	-11.89	0.01	116.60	12-Oct	95.75	27-May
1994	113.51	18.01	13.51	130.83	9-Nov	95.64	2-Apr
1993	96.19	29.13	-3.81	96.78	27-Dec	65.97	6-Mar
1992	74.49	8.54	-25.51	77.39	1-Feb	50.92	21-Aug
1991	68.63	-10.42	-31.37	85.92	6-Aug	65.48	22-Jun
1990	76.61	-23.39	-23.39	102.00	4-Jan	62.26	17-Sep
1/3/90	100.00						
1989							
1988							
1987							
1986							
1985							
Average Annual (%)		1.66					
Compound Annual (%)		0.00					
Standard Deviation (%)		20.13					

SYNOPSIS

The Korea Stock Price Index 200 (KOSPI 200) is a capitalization-weighted index that tracks the continuous price performance of 200 actively traded large capitalization common stocks listed on the Korea Stock Exchange (KSE). These shares account for 69% of the domestic market capitalization.

NUMBER OF STOCKS—DECEMBER 31, 1995

200

MARKET VALUE—DECEMBER 31, 1995

US$126,736.0 million

SELECTION CRITERIA

Member shares are selected from listings on the First and Second Sections of the Korea Stock Exchange and represent six industrial groups, including manufacturing, electricity and gas, construction, distribution and services, communications and financing.

BACKGROUND

Introduced in 1996, the index has been created to serve as an underlying vehicle for derivative instruments, in particular futures trading.

BASE DATE

January 3, 1990=100.00

COMPUTATION METHODOLOGY

An aggregative of prices times quantities index formula. Maintenance adjustments to the divisor are made whenever the current market value undergoes certain variations such as capitalization changes, new listings, delistings or other factors not strictly related to price changes.

DERIVATIVE INSTRUMENTS

None

SUBINDICES

Five subindices: Production, electronics and communications, circulative service and financial services.

RELATED INDICES

Korea Composite Stock Price Index
Korea Stock Exchange Bond Index

REMARKS

Foreign investor limitations apply to a single company's outstanding shares.

PUBLISHER

Korea Stock Exchange (KSE).

KUALA LUMPUR COMPOSITE INDEX

PRICE PERFORMANCE

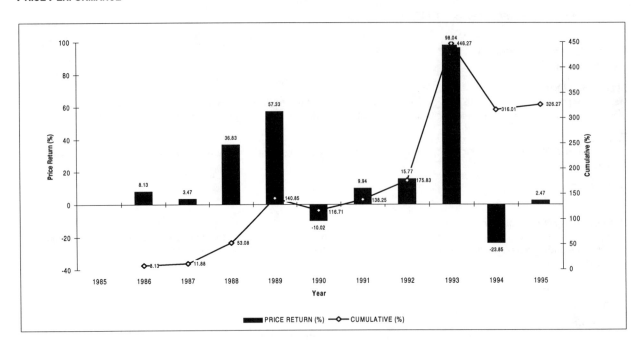

PRICE RETURN (%) —◇— CUMULATIVE (%)

PRICE PERFORMANCE

YEAR	VALUE	PRICE RETURN (%)	CUMULATIVE (%)	MAXIMUM VALUE	DATE	MINIMUM VALUE	DATE
1995	100.01	-11.89	0.01	116.60	12-Oct	95.75	27-May
1994	113.51	18.01	13.51	130.83	9-Nov	95.64	2-Apr
1993	96.19	29.13	-3.81	96.78	27-Dec	65.97	6-Mar
1992	74.49	8.54	-25.51	77.39	1-Feb	50.92	21-Aug
1991	68.63	-10.42	-31.37	85.92	6-Aug	65.48	22-Jun
1990	76.61	-23.39	-23.39	102.00	4-Jan	62.26	17-Sep
1/3/90	100.00						
1989							
1988							
1987							
1986							
1985							
Average Annual (%)		1.66					
Compound Annual (%)		0.00					
Standard Deviation (%)		20.13					

SYNOPSIS

The Kuala Lumpur Composite Index is a market capitalization-weighted index that tracks the continuous stock price only performance of a selected number of larger, actively traded, stocks traded on the Main Board of the Kuala Lumpur Stock Exchange (KLSE). These shares account for about 57% of the total domestic market capitalization.

NUMBER OF STOCKS—DECEMBER 31, 1995

100

MARKET VALUE—DECEMBER 31, 1995

US$125,751.2 million

SELECTION CRITERIA

Constituent stocks listed on the KLSE, regardless of domicile, are eligible for inclusion in the index so long as their major business activities, whether domestic or global, contribute significantly to the Malaysian economy. Moreover, companies are considered for inclusion in the index provided their annual volume and/or market capitalization fall within the first three quartiles established by a universe of Main Board-listed stocks.

Companies that are more than 50% owned by any KLSE Composite index component company and which is defined as a subsidiary company under the Malaysian Companies Act are excluded from consideration.

BACKGROUND

The index was launched on April 4, 1986 and index values have been backdated to 1977.

Prior to the introduction of the Composite Index, the industrial sector index was the only benchmark available for tracking the performance of the Malaysian stock market. The number of constituent stocks was increased to 100 on April 18, 1995. This is intended to be the maximum number of constituent stocks. Also on that date, the index began to be calculated on a continuous basis.

On January 1, 1990 all Singapore companies were delisted from the KLSE.

BASE DATE

January 3, 1977=95.83

COMPUTATION METHODOLOGY

(1) An aggregative of prices times quantities index formula. (2) Companies are considered for withdrawal from the index in the event their annual volume and/or market capitalization fall within the fourth quartile established by a universe of Main Board-listed stocks. (3) Newly listed companies are considered for inclusion in the index after a minimum listing period of three months. (4) Newly listed companies are considered for inclusion in industry subsectors after a minimum listing period of three months in the event the industrial sector is underrepresented in the Composite Index, and otherwise, a minimum period of six months.

DERIVATIVE INSTRUMENTS

None

SUBINDICES

None

RELATED INDICES

KLSE EMAS Index
KLSE Second Board Index

REMARKS

None

PUBLISHER

Kuala Lumpur Stock Exchange (KLSE).

KUALA LUMPUR EMAS INDEX

PRICE PERFORMANCE

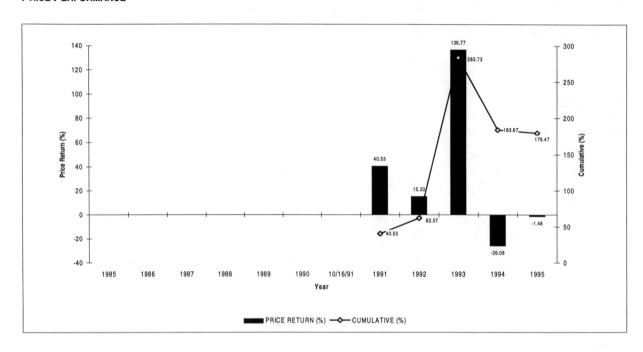

PRICE PERFORMANCE[1]

YEAR	VALUE	PRICE RETURN (%)	CUMULATIVE (%)	MAXIMUM VALUE	DATE	MINIMUM VALUE	DATE
1995	279.47	-1.48	179.47	306.28	4-Aug	237.47	24-Jan
1994	283.67	-26.08	183.67	394.42	4-Jan	259.76	12-Dec
1993	383.73	136.77	283.73	374.77	29-Dec	154.41	13-Jan
1992	162.07	15.33	62.07	165.42	13-Nov	135.16	18-Aug
1991	140.53	40.53	40.53	142.18	12-Nov	131.56	12-Oct
10/16/91	100.00						
1990							
1989							
1988							
1987							
1986							
1985							
Average Annual (%)		31.13					
Compound Annual (%)[1]		7.12					
Standard Deviation (%)		72.45					

[1]Statistical measures applicable to the period 12/31/91-12/31/95.

Synopsis

The Kuala Lumpur EMAS Index is a broad market capitalization-weighted index that tracks the continuous stock price performance of all stocks listed on the Main Board of the Kuala Lumpur Stock Exchange (KLSE). These shares account for 94% of the domestic market capitalization.

Number of Stocks—December 31, 1995

364

Market Value—December 31, 1995

US$206,949.5 million

Selection Criteria

Constituents include all stocks listed on the Main Board of the Kuala Lumpur Stock Exchange, regardless of domicile.

Background

Not Applicable

Base Date

October 16, 1991=100.00

Computation Methodology

An aggregative of prices times quantities index formula.

Derivative Instruments

None

Subindices

Nine sector subindices: Consumer products, industrial products, trading/services, construction, property, finance, plantation, mining and industrial.

Related Indices

KLSE Composite Index
KLSE Second Board Index

Remarks

None

Publisher

Kuala Lumpur Stock Exchange (KLSE).

KUALA LUMPUR SECOND BOARD INDEX

PRICE PERFORMANCE

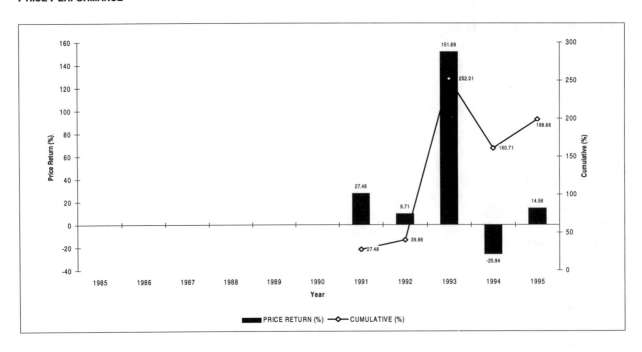

PRICE PERFORMANCE

YEAR	VALUE	PRICE RETURN (%)	CUMULATIVE (%)	MAXIMUM VALUE	DATE	MINIMUM VALUE	DATE
1995	298.66	14.56	198.66	302.07	14-Aug	223.83	24-Jan
1994	260.71	-25.94	160.71	361.00	10-Jan	217.74	7-Jul
1993	352.01	151.69	252.01	346.17	29-Dec	126.84	28-Jan
1992	139.86	9.71	39.86	154.11	18-Dec	109.06	7-Sep
1991	127.48	27.48	27.48	166.54	12-Jun	93.97	16-Jan
1990	100.00						
1989							
1988							
1987							
1986							
1985							
Average Annual (%)		35.50					
Compound Annual (%)		11.56					
Standard Deviation (%)		67.90					

SYNOPSIS

The Kuala Lumpur Second Board Index is a market capitalization-weighted index that tracks the continuous stock price only performance of all stocks listed on the Second Board of the Kuala Lumpur Stock Exchange (KLSE). These shares account for 4% of the domestic market capitalization.

NUMBER OF STOCKS—DECEMBER 31, 1995

150

MARKET VALUE—DECEMBER 31, 1995

US$8,617.8 million

SELECTION CRITERIA

Constituents include all stocks listed on the Second Board of the Kuala Lumpur Stock Exchange, regardless of domicile.

BASE DATE

January 2, 1991=100.00

COMPUTATION METHODOLOGY

An aggregative of prices times quantities index formula.

DERIVATIVE INSTRUMENTS

None

SUBINDICES

None

RELATED INDICES

KLSE Composite Index
KLSE EMAS Index

REMARKS

None

PUBLISHER

Kuala Lumpur Stock Exchange (KLSE).

NEPAL INDEX

PRICE PERFORMANCE

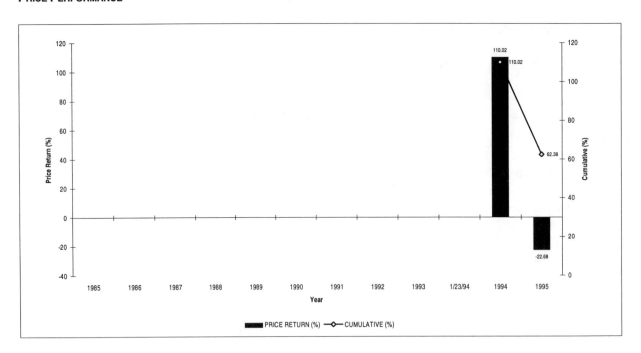

PRICE PERFORMANCE

YEAR	VALUE	PRICE RETURN (%)	CUMULATIVE (%)	MAXIMUM VALUE	DATE	MINIMUM VALUE	DATE
1995	162.38	-22.68	62.38	210.80	2-Jan	149.73	2-Jul
1994	210.02	110.02	110.02	311.45	18-May	100.00	23-Jan
1/23/94	100.00						
1993							
1992							
1991							
1990							
1989							
1988							
1987							
1986							
1985							
Average Annual (%)		55.01					
Compound Annual (%)		44.92					
Standard Deviation (%)		93.84					

SYNOPSIS

The Nepal Index is a capitalization-weighted index that tracks the daily price only performance of equity shares and preference shares listed on the Nepal Stock Exchange (NEPSE) and traded at least once a week. These shares account for about 70% of the combined market capitalization on the NEPSE.

NUMBER OF STOCKS—DECEMBER 31, 1995

30

MARKET VALUE—DECEMBER 31, 1995

US$171.01 million

SELECTION CRITERIA

Constituents are all equity and preference shares that are traded at least once a week on the Nepal Stock Exchange. Companies that cease to trade for a period of one week or more are removed from the index.

BACKGROUND

The index was introduced in April 1994, at which time it tracked nine listed companies.

BASE DATE

January 23, 1994=100.00

COMPUTATION METHODOLOGY

An aggregative of prices times quantities index formula.

DERIVATIVE INSTRUMENTS

None

SUBINDICES

None

RELATED INDICES

None

REMARKS

The banking sector accounts for 41.4% of the Nepalese market capitalization.

PUBLISHER

Capital Nepal.

THE NEW ZEALAND STOCK EXCHANGE (NZSE) MARKET INDEX

PRICE PERFORMANCE

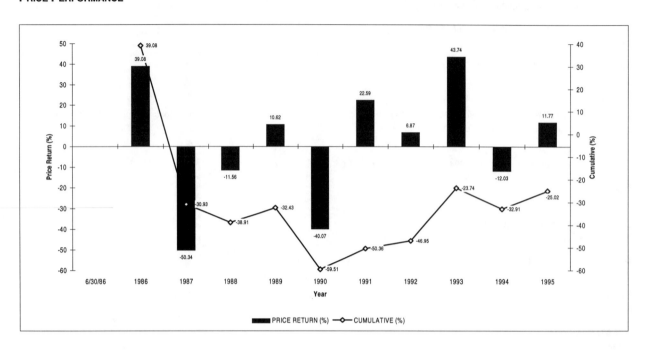

PRICE AND TOTAL RETURN PERFORMANCE[1]

YEAR	VALUE	PRICE RETURN (%)	CUMULATIVE (%)	TOTAL RETURN (%)	MAXIMUM VALUE	DATE	MINIMUM VALUE	DATE
1995	749.79	11.77	-25.02	19.61	767.62	20-Oct	666.93	5-Jan
1994	670.86	-12.03	-32.91	-6.89	854.43	3-Feb	660.34	12-Dec
1993	762.56	43.74	-23.74	51.71	767.05	2-Nov	507.81	21-Jan
1992	530.51	6.87	-46.95	13.41	537.85	17-Jul	456.94	9-Apr
1991	496.42	22.59	-50.36	30.67	510.5	7-Nov	389.33	16-Jan
1990	404.95	-40.07	-59.51	-35.93	700.39	3-Jan	398.90	18-Dec
1989	675.71	10.62	-32.43	18.13	811.79	11-Sep	610.46	4-Jan
1988	610.86	-11.56	-38.91	-6.75	706.51	12-Jan	573.26	29-Feb
1987	690.68	-50.34	-30.93	-48.55	1,390.98	5-Jan	684.42	23-Dec
1986	1,390.78	39.08	39.08	41.55	1,464.63	10-Nov	983.91	10-Jul
6/30/86	1,000.00							
Average Annual (%)		2.18		8.10				
Compound Annual (%)		-2.99		2.69				
Standard Deviation (%)		30.96		32.29				

SYNOPSIS

The New Zealand Stock Exchange (NZSE) Market Index is a market capitalization-weighted index that tracks the continuous stock price (Capital Index) and total return (Gross Index) performance of all domestic New Zealand Stock Exchange (NZSE)-listed and quoted ordinary shares and those securities which can be converted into ordinary shares, including companies that are substantially owned by New Zealand investors.

NUMBER OF STOCKS—DECEMBER 31, 1995

132

MARKET VALUE—DECEMBER 31, 1995

US$32,050.75 million

SELECTION CRITERIA

All classes of equity security of a company are eligible for inclusion in the index. These include convertible notes, specified preferred shares, partly paid shares and warrants. In cases where an equity security other than an ordinary share contributes significantly to the market capitalization of the company and it is sufficiently liquid, it may be included in the index in its own right, with the relevant weight and price being accorded to it.

BACKGROUND

Not Applicable

BASE DATE

June 30, 1986=1000.00

COMPUTATION METHODOLOGY

(1) An aggregative of prices times quantities index formula. Maintenance adjustments to the divisor are made daily for capitalization changes, new listings and delistings. Adjustments are made after the close of trading and after the calculation of the closing index value. (2) Market capitalization is determined on the basis of shares outstanding. Equity securities other than ordinary shares that are included in the index in their own right, are included on the basis of their ordinary share equivalent and thereby increasing the weighting of the ordinary shares in the index. In the case of a convertible or exchangeable security, this equivalent number will be the maximum number of ordinary shares that would be issued on its conversion exchange. In the cases of warrants and partly-paid shares, ordinary share equivalents will be determined by the NZSE at each index revision. Revisions, if any, are communicated to the market at least two weeks before they take effect. (3) New listings are generally eligible for inclusion in the index immediately upon listing. (4) Total rate of return is calculated using gross dividends that are reinvested as of the ex-dividend date.

DERIVATIVE INSTRUMENTS

None

SUBINDICES

Twenty-five industry subindices, each calculated on a price only and total return basis: Agriculture and associated services, automotive, building, chemical and fertilizer, construction, electrical, energy and fuel, engineering, finance and banks, food, forestry and forest products, insurance, investments, liquor and tobacco, meat and by-products, media and communications, medical supplies, miscellaneous services, printing and packaging, property, retail merchants, rubber and plastics, textile and apparel, transport and tourism, and mining.

RELATED INDICES

New Zealand Stock Exchange 30 Index
New Zealand Stock Exchange 40 Index
New Zealand Stock Exchange Smaller Companies Index
New Zealand Stock Exchange Top 10 Index
Trans Tasman 100 Index

REMARKS

Until recently, companies listed under the NZSE's Energy List had been excluded from the Market Index, but tracked in the All Ordinaries Index. The Energy List, consisting of three companies, was created in 1993 or so to enable market trading in the shares of privatized companies that were incorporated with restrictions applicable to the transferability of their shares but which will no longer be available after December 31, 1995. These companies included Power New Zealand Limited and Wairarapa Electricity Limited which have amended their articles of incorporation and are now included in the Market Index. The third company, TrustPower Limited, has voted to amend its articles of incorporation and will be tracked in the Market Index on the first trading day of 1996.

PUBLISHER

The New Zealand Stock Exchange (NZSE).

The New Zealand Stock Exchange—Smaller Companies Index (NZSE–SCI)

Price Performance

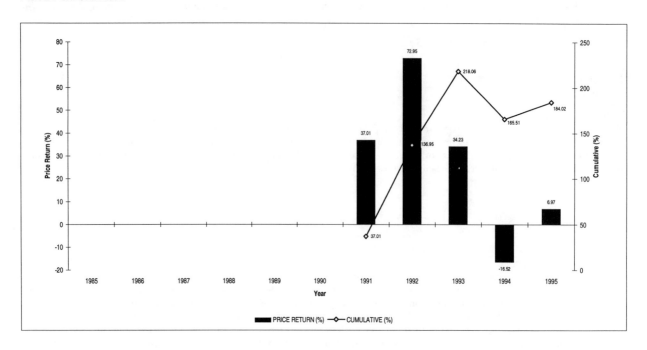

Price and Total Return Performance

YEAR	VALUE	PRICE RETURN (%)	CUMULATIVE (%)	TOTAL RETURN (%)	MAXIMUM VALUE	DATE	MINIMUM VALUE	DATE
1995	4,107.74	6.97	184.02	13.23	4,107.74	29-Dec	3,557.82	22-Mar
1994	3,840.06	-16.52	165.51	-13.54	5,310.35	3-Feb	3,810.13	28-Dec
1993	4,599.99	34.23	218.06	37.67	4,599.99	31-Dec	3,343.20	30-Mar
1992	3,426.97	72.95	136.95	78.64	3,429.64	30-Dec	2,002.35	7-Jan
1991	1,981.49	37.01	37.01	41.76	1,981.49	31-Dec	1,249.13	30-Jan
1990	1,446.28							
1989								
1988								
1987								
1986								
1985								
Average Annual (%)		26.93		31.55				
Compound Annual (%)		11.00		13.06				
Standard Deviation (%)		33.76		34.38				

SYNOPSIS
The New Zealand Stock Exchange—Smaller Companies Index (NZSE–SCI) is a market capitalization-weighted index that tracks the continuous stock price and total return performance of smaller domestic New Zealand Stock Exchange (NZSE)-listed and quoted ordinary shares and those securities which can be converted into ordinary shares. The index is composed of all companies registered in New Zealand or substantially owned by New Zealand investors except those companies that are tracked in the NZSE–40 Index. These shares account for 9% of domestic market capitalization.

NUMBER OF STOCKS—DECEMBER 31, 1995
90

MARKET VALUE—DECEMBER 31, 1995
US$2,878.9 million

SELECTION CRITERIA
All classes of equity security of a company are eligible for inclusion in the index. These include convertible notes, specified preferred shares, partly paid shares and warrants. In cases where an equity security other than an ordinary share contributes significantly to the market capitalization of the company and it is sufficiently liquid, it may be included in the index in its own right, with the relevant weight and price being accorded to it. Constituent stocks are reviewed on a quarterly basis relative to the NZSE–40.

Refer to the NZSE–40 Index for additional information.

BACKGROUND
The index was introduced on May 26, 1993.

BASE DATE
December 28, 1990=1,446.28

COMPUTATION METHODOLOGY
(1) An aggregative of prices times quantities index formula. Maintenance adjustments to the divisor are made daily for capitalization changes, new listings and delistings. Adjustments are made after the close of trading and after the calculation of the closing index value. (2) Market capitalization is determined on the basis of shares outstanding. Equity securities other than ordinary shares that are included in the index in their own right are included on the basis of their ordinary share equivalent and thereby increase the weighting of the ordinary shares in the index. In the case of a convertible or exchangeable security, this equivalent number will be the maximum number of ordinary shares that would be issued on its conversion exchange. In the cases of warrants and partly-paid shares, ordinary share equivalents will be determined by the NZSE at each index revision. Revisions, if any, are communicated to the market at least two weeks before they take effect. (3) New listings are generally eligible for inclusion in the index immediately upon listing. (4) Total rate of return is calculated using gross dividends that are reinvested as of the ex-dividend date.

DERIVATIVE INSTRUMENTS
None

SUBINDICES
None

RELATED INDICES
New Zealand Stock Exchange 30 Index
New Zealand Stock Exchange 40 Index
New Zealand Stock Exchange Market Index
New Zealand Stock Exchange Top 10 Index
Trans Tasman 100 Index

REMARKS
None

PUBLISHER
The New Zealand Stock Exchange (NZSE).

THE NEW ZEALAND STOCK EXCHANGE—30 SELECTION (NZSE–30) INDEX

PRICE PERFORMANCE

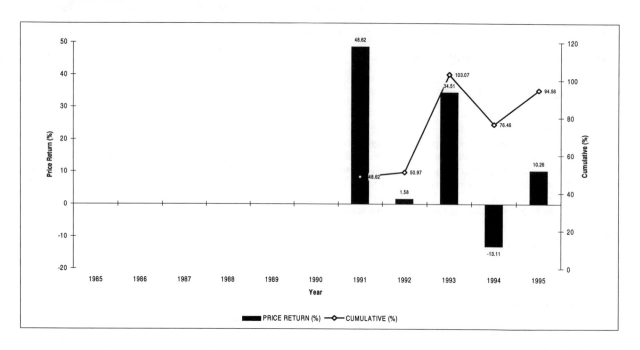

PRICE AND TOTAL RETURN PERFORMANCE

YEAR	VALUE	PRICE RETURN (%)	CUMULATIVE (%)	TOTAL RETURN (%)	MAXIMUM VALUE	DATE	MINIMUM VALUE	DATE
1995	1,945.64	10.26	94.56	18.07	2,002.58	20-Oct	1,747.64	23-Mar
1994	1,764.56	-13.11	76.46	-8.04	2,258.22	3-Feb	1,763.37	29-Dec
1993	2,030.71	34.51	103.07	41.93	2,030.71	31-Dec	1,434.68	21-Jan
1992	1,509.68	1.58	50.97	7.81	1,596.24	2-Jun	1,284.77	30-Oct
1991	1,486.23	48.62	48.62	54.49	1,580.30	7-May	1,136.77	15-Jan
1990	1,000.00							
1989								
1988								
1987								
1986								
1985								
Average Annual (%)		16.37		22.85				
Compound Annual (%)		6.88		9.88				
Standard Deviation (%)		24.97		25.34				

SYNOPSIS
The New Zealand Stock Exchange—30 Selection (NZSE–30) Index is a market capitalization-weighted index that tracks the continuous stock price and total return performance of 30 stocks in the New Zealand Stock Exchange-40 (NZSE-40) Gross Index with the largest float capital. The constituent stocks must be registered in New Zealand or substantially owned by New Zealand investors. These shares account for 61% of the domestic market capitalization.

NUMBER OF STOCKS—DECEMBER 31, 1995
30

MARKET VALUE—DECEMBER 31, 1995
US$19,688.1 million

SELECTION CRITERIA
All classes of equity security of a company are eligible for inclusion in the index. These include convertible notes, specified preferred shares, partly paid shares and warrants. In cases where an equity security other than an ordinary share contributes significantly to the market capitalization of the company and it is sufficiently liquid, it may be included in the index in its own right, with the relevant weight and price being accorded to it. The 30 companies that make up the index are selected from the list of constituent stocks that make up the NZSE–40 Index on the basis of the largest float capital.

Selections, which are reviewed quarterly, are made on the basis of the following additional criteria:
(1) Any stock that has dropped out of the NZSE–40 or to a float capital rank of 36 or below is removed from the index. (2) Any NZSE-40 constituent stock that is not in the NZSE–30 but is ranked 25 or higher by float capital will automatically be introduced into the index. (3) Any additions to or deletions from the index are made on the basis of the liquidity of stocks ranked 25 to 36 in the universe of stocks that make up the NZSE–40.

For additional information, refer to the NZSE–40 Index.

BACKGROUND
Not Applicable

BASE DATE
January 1, 1991=1000.00

COMPUTATION METHODOLOGY
(1) An aggregative of prices times quantities index formula. Maintenance adjustments to the divisor are made daily for capitalization changes, new listings and delistings. Adjustments are made after the close of trading and after the calculation of the closing index value. (2) Market capitalization is determined on the basis of free float, by excluding, as a general rule, all known blocks of shares held, or more or less controlled, by one person or a group of related persons and amounting to 30% or more of the share capital. Equity securities other than ordinary shares that are included in the index in their own right, are included on the basis of their ordinary share equivalent and thereby increasing the weighting of the ordinary shares in the index. In the case of a convertible or exchangeable security, this equivalent number will be the maximum number of ordinary shares that would be issued on its conversion exchange. In the cases of warrants and partly-paid shares, ordinary share equivalents will be determined by the NZSE at each index revision. Revisions, if any, are communicated to the market at least two weeks before they take effect. (3) Total rate of return is calculated using gross dividends that are reinvested as of the ex-dividend date.

DERIVATIVE INSTRUMENTS
None

SUBINDICES
None

RELATED INDICES
New Zealand Stock Exchange 40 Index
New Zealand Stock Exchange Market Index
New Zealand Stock Exchange Smaller Companies Index
New Zealand Stock Exchange Top 10 Index
Trans Trasman 100 Index

REMARKS
The performance of the NZSE–40 is dominated by a handful of stocks, some of which are not readily traded. The capitalization of the top three stocks account for about 50% of the index's market capitalization and the top 10 stocks account for about 73% of market capitalization.

PUBLISHER
The New Zealand Stock Exchange (NZSE).

THE NEW ZEALAND STOCK EXCHANGE—40 (NZSE–40) INDEX

PRICE PERFORMANCE

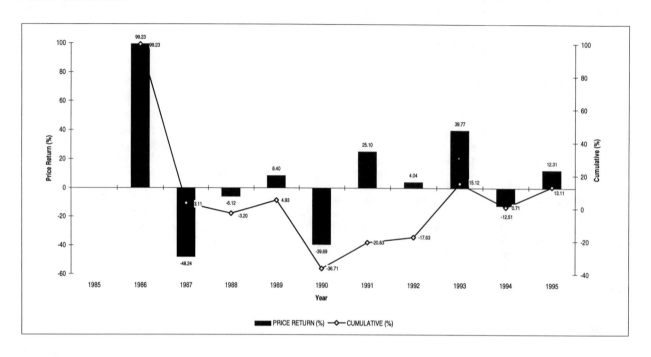

PRICE AND TOTAL RETURN PERFORMANCE[1]

YEAR	VALUE	PRICE RETURN (%)	CUMULATIVE (%)	TOTAL RETURN (%)[2]	MAXIMUM VALUE[3]	DATE	MINIMUM VALUE[3]	DATE
1995	2,149.82	12.31	13.11	20.12	2,206.02	20-Oct	1,901.43	5-Jan
1994	1,914.24	-12.51	0.71	-7.16	2,439.64	3-Feb	1,878.09	12-Dec
1993	2,188.07	39.77	15.12	47.84	2,203.09	2-Nov	1,495.37	21-Jan
1992	1,565.50	4.04	-17.63	10.84	1,589.23	16-Jul	1,365.36	19-Oct
1991	1,504.78	25.10	-20.83	8.92	1,579.75	7-May	1,142.21	15-Jan
1990	1,202.86	-39.69	-36.71		2,072.13	3-Jan	1,173.47	18-Dec
1989	1,994.46	8.40	4.93		2,454.96	5-Sep	1,837.67	5-Jan
1988	1,839.94	-6.12	-3.20		2,624.50	29-Jul	1,625.77	29-Feb
1987	1,959.81	-48.24	3.11		3,794.81	30-Sep	1,959.81	31-Dec
1986	3,786.70	99.23	99.23		3,790.62	28-Nov	1,891.67	31-Jan
1985	1,900.67							
Average Annual (%)		8.23		16.11				
Compound Annual (%)		1.24		7.13				
Standard Deviation (%)		41.79		20.27				

[1]Data prior to September 30, 1991 attribuatable to the Barclays Industrial Share Price Index.
[2]Calculation of total rates of return commenced as of September 30, 1991.
[3]Maximum/minimum index values for the period 1986-1988 are based on month-end values.

SYNOPSIS

The New Zealand Stock Exchange—40 (NZSE–40) Index is a market capitalization-weighted index that tracks the continuous stock price and total return performance of 40 of the largest and most liquid stocks traded on the New Zealand Stock Exchange that are registered in New Zealand or substantially owned by New Zealand investors. These shares account for 96% of the domestic market capitalization.

NUMBER OF STOCKS—DECEMBER 31, 1995

40

MARKET VALUE—DECEMBER 31, 1995

US$30,619.2 million

SELECTION CRITERIA

All classes of equity security of a company are eligible for inclusion in the index. These include convertible notes, specified preferred shares, partly paid shares and warrants. In cases where an equity security other than an ordinary share contributes significantly to the market capitalization of the company and it is sufficiently liquid, it may be included in the index in its own right, with the relevant weight and price being accorded to it.

The 40 companies that make up the index are selected on the basis of the following criteria:
(1) On a quarterly basis, stocks traded on the NZSE are ranked according to their average total market capitalization at the end of each of the preceding six months. The top 50 stocks form an eligible pool from which constituent stocks are selected. (2) Any stock that is not in the NZSE–40 Index and is ranked 30 or higher in the index pool will automatically be adopted as an index constituent. (3) Any additions to or deletions from the index are made on the basis of the liquidity of stocks ranked 31 to 50 in the index pool. That is, additions are selected from the most liquid securities and deletions are selected from the least liquid members of the index.

BACKGROUND

Previously known as the Barclays Industrial Share Price Index, the index had been calculated by Barclays Bank plc on a price only basis until September 30, 1991. Responsibility for the calculation of the index was assumed by the NZSE starting as of that date and calculation of the index on a total return basis commenced.

BASE DATE (ORIGINAL INDEX)

January 31, 1957=100.00

COMPUTATION METHODOLOGY

(1) An aggregative of prices times quantities index formula. Maintenance adjustments to the divisor are made daily for capitalization changes, new listings and delistings. Adjustments are made after the close of trading and after the calculation of the closing index value. (2) Market capitalization is determined on the basis of free float, by excluding, as a general rule, all known blocks of shares held, or more or less controlled, by one person or a group of related persons and amounting to 30% or more of the share capital. Equity securities other than ordinary shares that are included in the index in their own right, are included on the basis of their ordinary share equivalent and thereby increasing the weighting of the ordinary shares in the index. In the case of a convertible or exchangeable security, this equivalent number will be the maximum number of ordinary shares that would be issued on its conversion exchange. In the cases of warrants and partly-paid shares, ordinary share equivalents will be determined by the NZSE at each index revision. Revisions, if any, are communicated to the market at least two weeks before they take effect. (3) Total rate of return is calculated using gross dividends that are reinvested as of the ex-dividend date.

DERIVATIVE INSTRUMENTS

NZSE–40 futures and options contracts trade on the New Zealand Futures and Options Exchange (NZFOE), a subsidiary of the Sydney Futures Exchange.

SUBINDICES

None

RELATED INDICES

New Zealand Stock Exchange 30 Index
New Zealand Stock Exchange Market Index
New Zealand Stock Exchange Smaller Companies Index
New Zealand Stock Exchange Top 10 Index
Trans Tasman 100 Index

REMARKS

(1) The performance of the NZSE–40 is dominated by a handful of stocks, some of which are not readily traded. The capitalization of the top three stocks account for about 50% of the index's market capitalization and the top 10 stocks account for about 73% of market capitalization. (2) Market capitalization was not limited to free float during the period in which the index was computed by Barclays Bank plc.

PUBLISHER

The New Zealand Stock Exchange (NZSE).

KARACHI STOCK EXCHANGE (KSE)-100 INDEX

PRICE PERFORMANCE

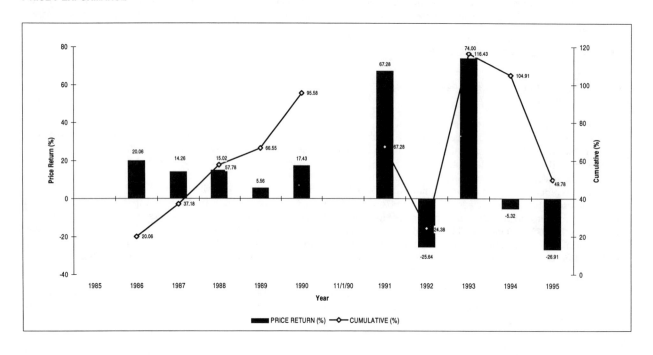

PRICE PERFORMANCE[1]

YEAR	VALUE	PRICE RETURN (%)	CUMULATIVE (%)	MAXIMUM VALUE	DATE	MINIMUM VALUE	DATE
1995	1,497.76	-26.91	49.78	2,090.66	3-Jan	1,402.88	7-Dec
1994	2,049.11	-5.32	104.91	2,661.31	22-Mar	1,936.14	20-Dec
1993	2,164.26	74.00	116.43	2,164.26	31-Dec	1,075.92	20-Apr
1992	1,243.84	-25.64	24.38	1,714.55	7-Jan	1,128.00	20-Sep
1991	1,672.78	67.28	67.28	1,672.78	31-Dec	1,000.00	1-Nov
11/1/90	1,000.00	NM	NM	NA	NA	NA	NA
1990	308.50	17.43	85.29	NA	NA	NA	NA
1989	277.30	5.56	66.55	NA	NA	NA	NA
1988	262.70	15.02	57.78	NA	NA	NA	NA
1987	228.40	14.26	37.18	NA	NA	NA	NA
1986	199.90	20.06	20.06	NA	NA	NA	NA
1985	166.50						
Average Annual (%)		3.23					
Compound Annual (%)		8.41					
Standard Deviation (%)		50.05					

[1]Statistics based on data for the period since 12/31/91. SBP Index values used for the period 1986-1990.

SYNOPSIS

The Karachi Stock Exchange (KSE)-100 Index is a market capitalization-weighted index that tracks the stock price of 100 stocks traded on the Karachi Stock Exchange (KSE) of Pakistan. The stocks account for about 77% of the combined market capitalization on the exchange.

NUMBER OF STOCKS—DECEMBER 31, 1995

100

MARKET VALUE—DECEMBER 31, 1995

US$7,352.5 million

SELECTION CRITERIA

Constituent shares are selected on the basis of market capitalization, as follows:

(1) The largest company in each of the KSE's 27 industry sectors. (2) The largest remaining companies in descending order.

A non-index company that becomes the largest in its industry sector is eligible for inclusion in the index after maintaining its market capitalization leadership position for a full year. Also, a non-index company whose market capitalization exceeds that of the largest in its sector by 10% is eligible for inclusion in the index after a 6-month period. Non-index companies qualify for inclusion strictly on the basis of market capitalization after maintaining its market value position for a period of one year. In addition, newly listed companies or privatized companies with market values equal to 2% of the total market capitalization of the KSE-listed securities qualify for immediate inclusion in the index.

BACKGROUND

The KSE-100 Index superseded the SBP Index which was introduced in 1983 and was comprised of 50 listed companies selected on the basis of market capitalization, turnover and the number of companies in a particular sector. The index was reconstituted as of October 31, 1994, at which time the number of constituent shares was increased to 100 and the foregoing selection criteria was adopted.

BASE DATE

November 1, 1991=1000.00

COMPUTATION METHODOLOGY

(1) An aggregative of prices times quantities index formula. Maintenance adjustments to the divisor are made daily for capitalization changes, new listings and delistings after the close of trading and after the calculation of the closing index value. (2) Index constituents are reviewed semi-annually.

DERIVATIVE INSTRUMENTS

None

SUBINDICES

Twenty-seven industry sector subindices: Mutual funds, modarabas, leasing companies, investment companies/banks, insurance, textile spinning, textile weaving, textile composite, woolen, synthetic and rayon, juste, sugar and allied, cement, tobacco, fuel and energy, engineering, auto and allied engineering, cables and electrical goods, transport and communications, chemicals and pharmaceuticals, paper and board, constructions, leather and tanneries, food and allied, glass and ceramics, and miscellaneous companies.

RELATED INDICES

KSE-All Share Index

REMARKS

None

PUBLISHER

The Karachi Stock Exchange (KSE).

PHILIPPINE STOCK EXCHANGE (PSE) COMPOSITE INDEX

PRICE PERFORMANCE

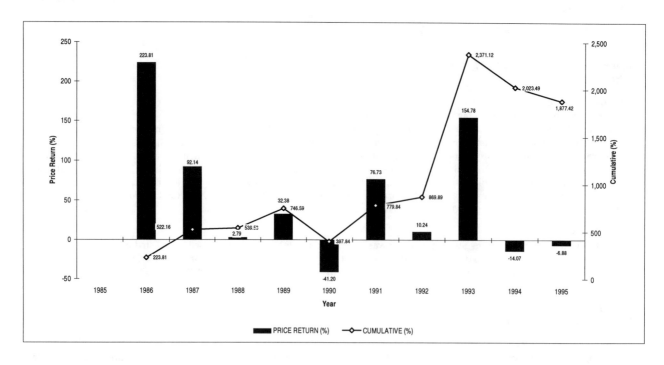

PRICE PERFORMANCE[1]

YEAR	VALUE	PRICE RETURN (%)	CUMULATIVE (%)	MAXIMUM VALUE[2]	DATE	MINIMUM VALUE[2]	DATE
1995	2,594.18	-6.88	1,877.42	2,958.12	10-Jul	2,196.48	20-Nov
1994	2,785.81	-14.07	2,023.49	3,346.79	31-Jan	2,504.88	31-Mar
1993	3,241.86	154.78	2,371.12	3,241.86	31-Dec	1,282.97	31-Jan
1992	1,272.40	10.24	869.89	1,597.74	30-Jun	1,097.17	31-Mar
1991	1,154.26	76.73	779.84	1,161.15	30-Apr	587.46	31-Jan
1990	653.11	-41.20	397.84	1,163.65	31-Mar	516.21	10-Oct
1989	1,110.64	32.38	746.59	1,395.36	30-Nov	804.39	28-Feb
1988	839.00	2.79	539.53	878.78	31-Jan	684.39	31-Oct
1987	816.21	92.14	522.16	1,335.54	31-Jul	439.53	31-Jan
1986	424.81	223.81	223.81	NA	NA	NA	NA
1985	131.19						
Average Annual (%)		53.07					
Compound Annual (%)		99.90					
Standard Deviation (%)		83.91					

[1]Data prior to September 1994 based on Manila Stock Exchange Composite Stock Price Index.
[2]Dates corresponding to actual maximum/minimum values are as of month-end.

SYNOPSIS

The Philippine Stock Exchange (PSE) Composite Index is a market capitalization-weighted index that tracks the daily stock price performance of a selected number of class "A" and class "B" shares listed on the Manila Stock Exchange in the Philippines. The index, which is composed of stocks representative of the commercial/industrial, property, mining and oil sectors of the Philippine economy, accounts for 12% of the domestic market capitalization.

NUMBER OF STOCKS—DECEMBER 31, 1995

41

MARKET VALUE—DECEMBER 31, 1995

US$7,316.3 million

SELECTION CRITERIA

Constituent shares are selected from the four main sectors of the Philippine market, namely the commercial-industrial, property, mining and oil sectors, based on liquidity, market capitalization, and profitability. Other factors include past financial performance, the ability of a company to represent a particular industry so as to provide a cross section of different industries, and companies must be operational or have definite plans for development of their respective projects.

BACKGROUND

The index has roots that date back to the introduction of the Mining Index in 1952. As the early dominance of the Philippine securities markets by mining stocks receded, the index was expanded to include companies in other sectors of the economy.

Up to February 1990, the index represented a numerical average of the weighted prices of the 25 representative companies from each of the main sectors of the market, namely commercial-industrial, mining and oil. Effective February 28, 1990, the Manila Stock Exchange adopted the present computation methodology while maintaining the historical continuity of the index and subindices by adopting their respective closing index values on the new base date.

With the unification of the Manila and Makati Stock Exchanges, the index was recomposed again as of October 4, 1994. Class "B" shares, which had been excluded from previous versions of the index. were added and a new property subindex was created. As of September 30, 1994, the closing values of the previous index were adopted as the base values for the reconstituted index as follows: Composite Index–2,922.21; Commercial/industrial Subindex–4,403.74, Mining Subindex–6,594.75; and Oil Subindex–7.832. The base value for the property subindex was established at 100.00 as of September 30, 1994.

BASE DATE

September 30, 1994=2,922.21

COMPUTATION METHODOLOGY

An aggregative of prices times quantities index formula. Maintenance adjustments to the divisor are made daily for capitalization changes, new listings and delistings.

DERIVATIVE INSTRUMENTS

None

SUBINDICES

Four sector subindices: Commercial/industrial, mining, property and oils.

RELATED INDICES

None

REMARKS

Common "A" Shares may only be sold to Philippine nationals while common "B" shares may be sold to both Philippine and foreign nationals. Non-residents are free to purchase shares in Philippine companies but foreign ownership is restricted to 40% of a company's shares. For this reason, companies divide their share capital into 60% "A" shares and 40% "B" shares.

PUBLISHER

The Philippine Stock Exchange (PSE).

OVERSEA-CHINESE BANKING CORP., LTD. (OCBC) 30-SHARE INDEX

PRICE PERFORMANCE

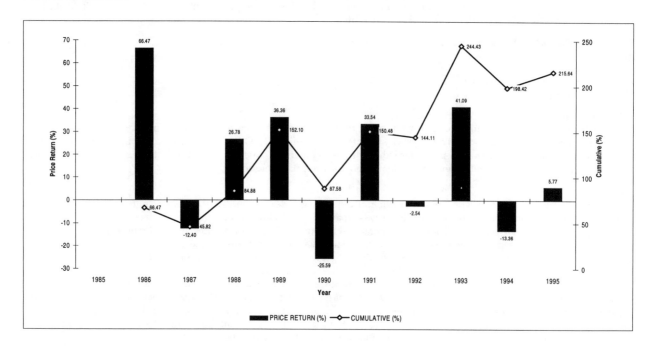

PRICE PERFORMANCE

YEAR	VALUE	PRICE RETURN (%)	CUMULATIVE (%)	MAXIMUM VALUE	DATE	MINIMUM VALUE	DATE
1995	585.17	5.77	215.64	589.78	25-Dec	495.34	23-Jan
1994	553.25	-13.36	198.42	650.60	4-Jan	523.79	13-Dec
1993	638.53	41.09	244.43	640.75	28-Dec	454.21	4-Jan
1992	452.56	-2.54	144.11	477.89	16-Jan	404.27	22-Oct
1991	464.37	33.54	150.48	476.33	31-May	354.74	16-Jan
1990	347.75	-25.59	87.58	503.45	16-Jul	334.55	11-Oct
1989	467.36	36.36	152.10	472.52	26-Jul	341.87	4-Jan
1988	342.74	26.78	84.88	380.23	9-Aug	273.89	4-Jan
1987	270.34	-12.40	45.82	499.09	11-Aug	235.72	7-Dec
1986	308.62	66.47	66.47	331.17	3-Jan	179.92	17-Apr
1985	185.39						
Average Annual (%)		15.61					
Compound Annual (%)		12.18					
Standard Deviation (%)		29.55					

SYNOPSIS
The Oversea-Chinese Banking Corp., Ltd. (OCBC) 30-Share Index is a capitalization-weighted index that tracks the daily price performance of 30 domestic stocks listed on the Stock Exchange of Singapore (SES).

NUMBER OF STOCKS—DECEMBER 31, 1995
30

MARKET VALUE—DECEMBER 31, 1995
Not Available

SELECTION CRITERIA
The 30 stocks are selected from all major sectors of the market, including industrial and commercial, finance, hotels and properties, with the sectoral distribution corresponding to the market as a whole on the basis of market capitalization. In addition, constituent companies are selected on the basis of liquidity and with the intention of avoiding double-counting or over-representation due to parent company and subsidiary relationships.

BACKGROUND
The OCBC 30-Share Index was launched in 1990 following the separation of the Stock Exchange of Singapore (SES) and the Kuala Lumpur Stock Exchange (KLSE). Pursuant to, Malaysian companies were delisted from SES and Singapore companies were delisted from KLSE as of January 1, 1990.

BASE DATE
January 2, 1975=60.00

COMPUTATION METHODOLOGY
An aggregative of prices times quantities index formula.

DERIVATIVE INSTRUMENTS
None

SUBINDICES
None

RELATED INDICES
OCBC Composite Index
OCBC OTC Index

REMARKS
None

PUBLISHER
Oversea-Chinese Banking Corp. Limited/OCBC Investment Research Limited.

Stock Exchange of Singapore (SES) All-Singapore Index

Price Performance

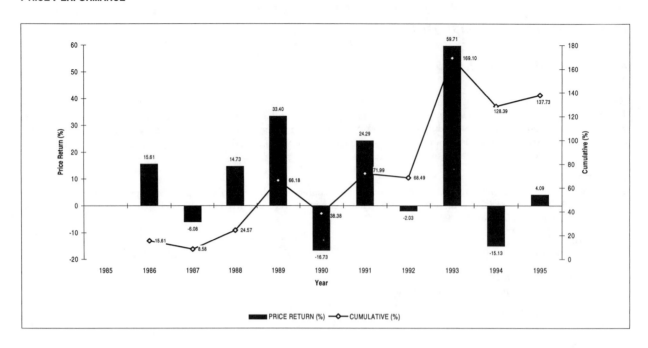

Price Performance

YEAR	VALUE	PRICE RETURN (%)	CUMULATIVE (%)	MAXIMUM VALUE	DATE	MINIMUM VALUE	DATE
1995	555.39	4.09	137.73	558.94	22-Dec	472.90	23-Jan
1994	533.57	-15.13	128.39	641.61	4-Jan	506.84	13-Dec
1993	628.66	59.71	169.10	628.66	31-Dec	394.10	13-Jan
1992	393.63	-2.03	68.49	351.46	22-Oct	416.99	21-Jan
1991	401.80	24.29	71.99	422.43	26-Apr	319.89	8-Jan
1990	323.28	-16.73	38.38	446.87	16-Jul	301.45	11-Oct
1989	388.24	33.40	66.18	389.70	26-Dec	290.53	4-Jan
1988	291.03	14.73	24.57	320.42	8-Aug	253.27	9-Feb
1987	253.66	-6.08	8.58	410.79	11-Aug	231.08	7-Dec
1986	270.09	15.61	15.61	289.59	11-Mar	205.93	28-Apr
1985	233.62						
Average Annual (%)		11.19					
Compound Annual (%)		9.05					
Standard Deviation (%)		23.68					

SYNOPSIS
The Stock Exchange of Singapore (SES) All-Singapore Index is a broad market capitalization-weighted index that tracks the daily price only performance of all the ordinary shares of Singapore companies traded on the Main Board of the Singapore Stock Exchange (SES).

NUMBER OF STOCKS—DECEMBER 31, 1995
212

MARKET VALUE—DECEMBER 31, 1995
US$148,025.2 million

SELECTION CRITERIA
Constituent shares include all the ordinary shares of Singapore companies traded on the Main Board of the Singapore Stock Exchange (SES).

BACKGROUND
The index, which replaced a previous benchmark, was launched on January 1, 1990.

BASE DATE
January 1, 1975=100.00

COMPUTATION METHODOLOGY
An aggregative of prices times quantities index formula. Maintenance adjustments to the divisor are made daily for capitalization changes, new listings and delistings. The base value was established using the average of the daily aggregate market value recorded during the 250 trading days in 1975 applicable to listed companies as of January 2, 1975.

DERIVATIVE INSTRUMENTS
None

SUBINDICES
Four sectoral subindices: Industrial/commercial, financial, hotel and property.

RELATED INDICES
None

REMARKS
The index was launched in 1990 following the separation of the Stock Exchange of Singapore and the Kuala Lumpur Stock Exchange. Pursuant to, Malaysian companies were delisted from SES and Singapore companies were delisted from KLSE as of January 1, 1990.

PUBLISHER
Stock Exchange of Singapore Ltd.

THE STRAITS TIMES INDUSTRIAL (STI) INDEX

PRICE PERFORMANCE

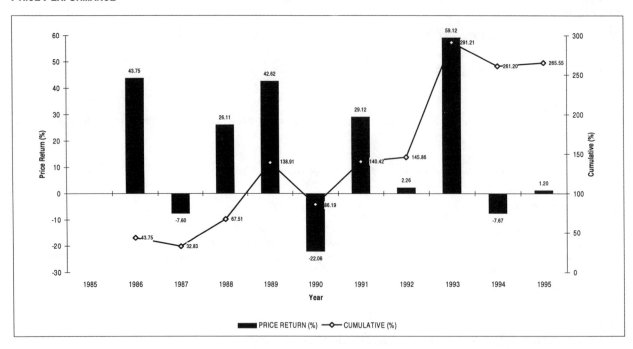

PRICE PERFORMANCE

YEAR	VALUE	PRICE RETURN (%)	CUMULATIVE (%)	MAXIMUM VALUE	DATE	MINIMUM VALUE	DATE
1995	2,266.54	1.20	265.55	2,287.42	22-Dec	1,916.94	23-Jan
1994	2,239.56	-7.67	261.20	2,471.90	4-Jan	2,036.30	21-Mar
1993	2,425.68	59.12	291.21	2,426.85	29-Dec	1,531.11	4-Jan
1992	1,524.40	2.26	145.86	1,545.92	27-Jan	1,310.95	18-Aug
1991	1,490.70	29.12	140.42	1,565.58	3-Jun	1,149.08	16-Jan
1990	1,154.48	-22.06	86.19	1,607.12	27-Mar	1,079.50	11-Oct
1989	1,481.33	42.62	138.91	1,487.76	26-Dec	1,030.69	4-Jan
1988	1,038.62	26.11	67.51	1,177.87	8-Aug	833.61	4-Jan
1987	823.58	-7.60	32.83	1,505.40	26-Aug	700.45	7-Dec
1986	891.30	43.75	43.75	940.64	3-Nov	563.34	28-Apr
1985	620.04						
Average Annual (%)		16.69					
Compound Annual (%)		13.84					
Standard Deviation (%)		27.04					

SYNOPSIS
The Straits Times Industrial (STI) Index is a price-weighted index that tracks the daily price only performance of large, actively traded shares of Singapore companies traded on the Singapore Stock Exchange (SES). These shares account for 48% of the domestic market capitalization.

NUMBER OF STOCKS—DECEMBER 31, 1995
30

MARKET VALUE—DECEMBER 31, 1995
US$71,611.3 million

SELECTION CRITERIA
Constituent shares are selected on the basis of various qualitative and quantitative factors. Qualitative factors include leadership position, liquidity, economic representation and good management and strong earnings growth. Quantitative factors include a market capitalization of at least S$150.0 million or US$100.0 million, trading volume averaging 50,000 shares per day, a record of profitability for the three years prior to inclusion in the index, have a shareholders' fund of at least $30.0 million and not be a chain listing.

Companies experiencing losses for three consecutive years are removed from the index.

BACKGROUND
Constituent shares have not changed since November 3, 1993.

BASE DATE
December 30, 1964=100.00

COMPUTATION METHODOLOGY
A simple aggregative of actual prices index formula. The divisor adjusted to eliminate the effect of bonus and rights issues to keep the current index numbers comparable to the base period.

DERIVATIVE INSTRUMENTS
None

SUBINDICES
None

RELATED INDICES
None

REMARKS
None

PUBLISHER
The Business Times/Times Business Publications Limited.

United Overseas Bank (UOB) Dealing and Automated Quotation System (SESDAQ) Index

Price Performance

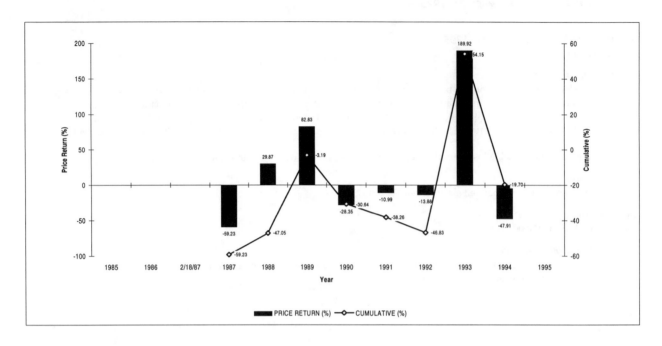

Price Performance

YEAR	VALUE	PRICE RETURN (%)	CUMULATIVE (%)	MAXIMUM VALUE	DATE	MINIMUM VALUE	DATE
1995	100.26	24.86	0.26	108.41	31-Aug	63.09	5-May
1994	80.30	-47.91	-19.70	156.95	4-Jan	76.46	12-Dec
1993	154.15	189.92	54.15	154.15	31-Dec	54.77	4-Jan
1992	53.17	-13.88	-46.83	61.79	2-Jan	48.55	20-Oct
1991	61.74	-10.99	-38.26	84.19	26-Apr	58.22	8-Oct
1990	69.36	-28.35	-30.64	98.96	17-Jul	69.15	21-Dec
1989	96.81	82.83	-3.19	106.92	14-Nov	51.43	2-Mar
1988	52.95	29.87	-47.05	71.29	12-Jul	39.74	9-Feb
1987	40.77	-59.23	-59.23	100.00	18-Feb	34.11	8-Dec
2/18/87	100.00						
1986							
1985							
Average Annual (%)		15.81					
Compound Annual (%)		99.53					
Standard Deviation (%)		65.44					

SYNOPSIS

The United Overseas Bank (UOB) Dealing and Automated Quotation System (SESDAQ) Index is a capitalization-weighted index that tracks the daily price only performance of shares traded on the Stock Exchange of Singapore Dealing and Automated Quotation System (SESDAQ), Singapore's secondary market.

NUMBER OF STOCKS—DECEMBER 31, 1995

46

MARKET VALUE—DECEMBER 31, 1995

US$2,954.8 million

SELECTION CRITERIA

Constituent shares include all companies listed on the Stock Exchange of Singapore Dealing and Automated Quotation System (SESDAQ). These are small- and medium-sized companies that are not eligible for listing on the Main Board.

BACKGROUND

The index was introduced in 1987 concurrent with the launch of the SESDAQ market.

BASE DATE

February 18, 1987=100.00

COMPUTATION METHODOLOGY

An aggregative of prices times quantities index formula. Maintenance adjustments to the divisor are made daily for capitalization changes, new listings and delistings.

DERIVATIVE INSTRUMENTS

None

SUBINDICES

None

RELATED INDICES

UOB Blue Chip Index
UOB OTC Index
UOB Government Bond Index

REMARKS

None

PUBLISHER

United Overseas Bank (UOB).

COLOMBO STOCK EXCHANGE (CSE) ALL SHARE PRICE INDEX

PRICE PERFORMANCE

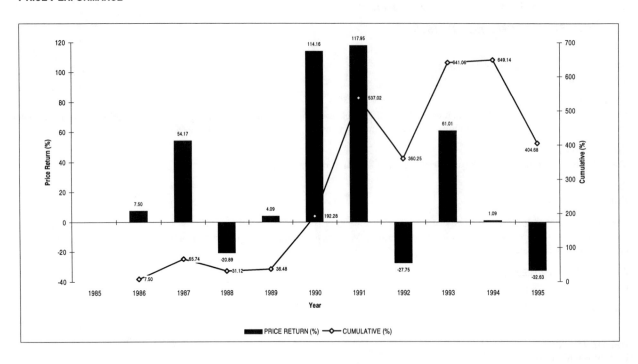

PRICE PERFORMANCE

YEAR	VALUE	PRICE RETURN (%)	CUMULATIVE (%)	MAXIMUM VALUE	DATE	MINIMUM VALUE	DATE
1995	663.73	-32.63	404.68	1,038.86	9-Jan	630.93	24-Oct
1994	985.24	1.09	649.14	1,378.82	2-Mar	911.56	17-Jun
1993	974.62	61.01	641.06	974.62	31-Dec	529.54	16-Feb
1992	605.31	-27.75	360.25	NA	NA	NA	NA
1991	837.79	117.95	537.02	NA	NA	NA	NA
1990	384.39	114.16	192.28	NA	NA	NA	NA
1989	179.49	4.09	36.48	NA	NA	NA	NA
1988	172.44	-20.89	31.12	NA	NA	NA	NA
1987	217.97	54.17	65.74	NA	NA	NA	NA
1986[1]	141.38	7.50	7.50	NA	NA	NA	NA
1985	NA	NA					
Average Annual (%)		27.87					
Compound Annual (%)		17.57					
Standard Deviation (%)		55.96					

[1]1986 price return produced by the CSE Sensitive Index.

SYNOPSIS

The Colombo Stock Exchange (CSE) All Share Price Index is a capitalization-weighted index that tracks the daily price performance of all equity shares traded on the Colombo Stock Exchange (CSE) in Sri Lanka.

NUMBER OF STOCKS—DECEMBER 31, 1995

226

MARKET VALUE—DECEMBER 31, 1995

US$1,998.0 million

SELECTION CRITERIA

Constituents are all equity shares traded on the Colombo Stock Exchange in Sri Lanka.

BACKGROUND

None

BASE DATE

December 31, 1984=100.00

COMPUTATION METHODOLOGY

(1) An aggregative of prices times quantities index formula. Maintenance adjustments to the divisor are made daily for capitalization changes, new listings and delistings. Based on listed companies as of January 2, 1985, the market capitalization for the divisor was computed on the basis of the average market capitalization for the entire calendar year 1985. (2) Last transaction prices on the CSE are used, regardless of when the share price was traded.

DERIVATIVE INSTRUMENTS

None

SUBINDICES

Fourteen sector subindices: Banks, finance and insurance, beverages, food and tobacco, chemicals and pharmaceuticals, construction and engineering, footwear and textiles, hotels and travel, investment trusts, land and property, manufacturing, motors, oil palms, services, stores and supplies and trading.

RELATED INDICES

The CSE Sensitive Index

REMARKS

None

PUBLISHER

Sri Lanka Stock Exchange.

ECONOMIC DAILY NEWS INDEX

PRICE PERFORMANCE

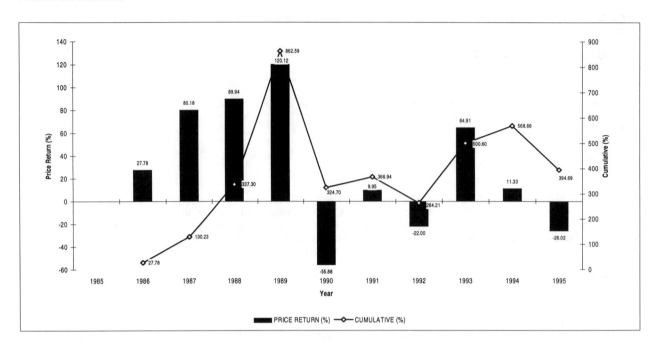

PRICE PERFORMANCE

YEAR	VALUE	PRICE RETURN (%)	CUMULATIVE (%)	MAXIMUM VALUE[1]	DATE	MINIMUM VALUE[1]	DATE
1995	1,835.25	-26.02	394.69	2,280.45	31-Mar	1,678.01	31-Oct
1994	2,480.66	11.33	568.66	2,480.66	31-Dec	1,875.11	31-Mar
1993	2,228.18	64.91	500.60	2,228.18	31-Dec	1,062.34	31-Oct
1992	1,351.18	-22.00	264.21	2,030.24	31-Jan	1,351.18	31-Dec
1991	1,732.30	9.95	366.94	2,206.97	30-Apr	1,427.17	31-Jan
1990	1,575.60	-55.88	324.70	4,248.02	31-Jan	1,027.25	30-Sep
1989	3,571.13	120.12	862.59	4,298.67	31-Oct	1,958.14	31-Jan
1988	1,622.34	89.94	337.30	2,550.86	30-Sep	1,017.22	31-Jan
1987	854.12	80.18	130.23	521.12	31-Jan	1,569.09	30-Sep
1986	474.05	27.78	27.78	392.81	31-Jan	474.05	31-Dec
1985	370.99						
Average Annual (%)		30.03					
Compound Annual (%)		17.34					
Standard Deviation (%)		57.18					

[1]Maximum/minimum index values are as of month-end.

SYNOPSIS
The Economic Daily News Index is a price-weighted index that tracks the daily price only performance of 35 blue chip common stocks listed on the Taiwan Stock Exchange (TSE). These shares account for 24% of the total domestic market capitalization.

NUMBER OF STOCKS—DECEMBER 31, 1995
35

MARKET VALUE—DECEMBER 31, 1995
US$43,599.8 million

SELECTION CRITERIA
Constituent shares represent actively traded stocks of blue chip companies, including manufacturing companies with two or more product lines, with paid capital in excess of NT$1.0 billion, a record of paying normal and steady dividends over the previous three years, and have been listed on the Taiwan Stock Exchange for at least three years. In addition, the trading value of eligible stocks must fall within the top 180 or top two-thirds of all listed companies on the Taiwan Stock Exchange

The maximum number of stocks eligible for inclusion in the index is 40.

BACKGROUND
The index was first published on April 20, 1977 with a sample of 34 stocks. It was recalculated to January 4, 1973. The sample was revised for the first time on April 20, 1977, and six stocks were replaced. The index has since been revised seven times–1978, 1979, 1980, 1986, 1990, 1991 and 1993. The frequency of revisions in recent years is attributable to the expansion in the size of the market and the acceleration of industrial change in Taiwan.

BASE DATE
January 4, 1973=100.00

COMPUTATION METHODOLOGY
A simple aggregative of actual prices index formula.

DERIVATIVE INSTRUMENTS
None

SUBINDICES
None

RELATED INDICES
None

REMARKS
None

PUBLISHER
Economic Daily News.

TAIWAN STOCK EXCHANGE CAPITALIZATION-WEIGHTED STOCK INDEX (TAIEX)

PRICE PERFORMANCE

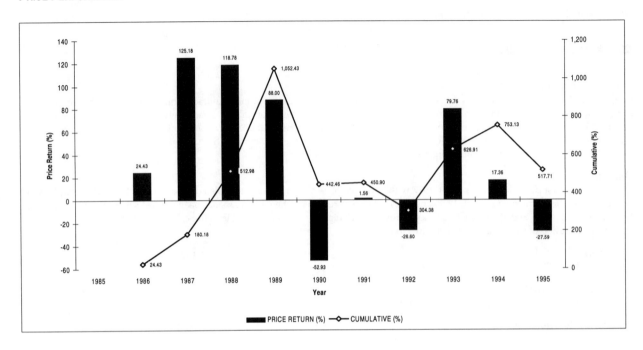

PRICE PERFORMANCE

YEAR	VALUE	PRICE RETURN (%)	CUMULATIVE (%)	MAXIMUM VALUE	DATE	MINIMUM VALUE	DATE
1995	5,158.65	-27.59	517.71	7,124.66	2-Jan	4,503.37	14-Aug
1994	7,124.66	17.36	753.13	7,183.55	3-Oct	5,194.63	19-Mar
1993	6,070.56	79.76	626.91	6,070.56	31-Dec	3,135.56	7-Jan
1992	3,377.06	-26.60	304.38	5,391.63	30-Jan	3,327.67	28-Dec
1991	4,600.67	1.56	450.90	6,305.22	9-May	3,316.26	16-Jan
1990	4,530.16	-52.93	442.46	12,495.34	10-Feb	2,560.47	1-Oct
1989	9,624.18	88.00	1,052.43	10,773.11	25-Sep	4,873.18	5-Jan
1988	5,119.11	118.78	512.98	8,789.73	24-Sep	2,341.06	5-Jan
1987	2,339.86	125.18	180.18	4,673.14	1-Oct	1,063.13	6-Jan
1986	1,039.11	24.43	24.43	1,039.11	19-Dec	839.73	4-Jan
1985	835.12						
Average Annual (%)		34.79					
Compound Annual (%)		19.97					
Standard Deviation (%)		64.07					

SYNOPSIS

The Taiwan Stock Exchange Capitalization Weighted Stock Index (TAIEX) is a broad market capitalization-weighted index that tracks the continuous price only performance of all common stocks listed on the Taiwan Stock Exchange (TSE).

NUMBER OF STOCKS—DECEMBER 31, 1995

328

MARKET VALUE—DECEMBER 31, 1995

US$184,561.4 million

SELECTION CRITERIA

All listed Category A, Category B and Category C shares are included in the index.
    Excluded from the index are preferred stocks and full-delivery stocks.

BACKGROUND

Subindices applicable to Category A and B stocks, as well as eight industry sectors, were established as of January 1981. A non-financials subindex was introduced in December 31, 1986.

BASE DATE

December 29, 1966=100.00

COMPUTATION METHODOLOGY

(1) An aggregative of prices times quantities index formula. Maintenance adjustments to the divisor are made for capitalization changes, new listings and delistings. (2) The base value of the index was established using the 1966 average price of 28 listed issues on the TSE.

DERIVATIVE INSTRUMENTS

None

SUBINDICES

Eleven subindices: Non-financials subindex, excluding banking and insurance companies; Category A shares subindex, Category B shares subindex; and industry subindices covering cement, food, plastics and chemicals, textiles, electric and machinery, pulp and paper, construction, banking and insurance.

RELATED INDICES

Taiwan Stock Exchange Stock Price Average
Taiwan Stock Exchange Industrial Price Average

REMARKS

Stocks listed on the Taiwan Stock Exchange are classified into three categories, Category A, B and C, according to their levels of capital, profitability, capital structure and distribution of shares based on the number of public and non-public registered shareholders. Category C stocks are considered "hi-tech" enterprises.

PUBLISHER

Taiwan Stock Exchange Corporation.

TAIWAN STOCK EXCHANGE COMPOSITE STOCK PRICE AVERAGE

PRICE PERFORMANCE

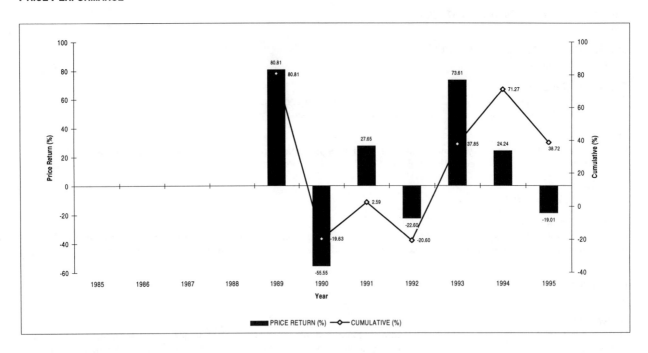

PRICE PERFORMANCE

YEAR	VALUE	PRICE RETURN (%)	CUMULATIVE (%)	MAXIMUM VALUE	DATE	MINIMUM VALUE	DATE
1995	138.72	-19.01	38.72	181.14	5-Jan	119.55	14-Aug
1994	171.27	24.24	71.27	173.03	29-Aug	117.87	12-Mar
1993	137.85	73.61	37.85	137.85	31-Dec	73.98	7-Jan
1992	79.40	-22.60	-20.60	116.39	27-Jan	75.22	16-Sep
1991	102.59	27.65	2.59	124.56	22-Jun	63.65	16-Jan
1990	80.37	-55.55	-19.63	227.22	12-Feb	57.20	1-Oct
1989	180.81	80.81	80.81	233.12	1-Nov	94.52	5-Jan
1988	100.00						
1987							
1986							
1985							
Average Annual (%)		15.59					
Compound Annual (%)		4.79					
Standard Deviation (%)		50.92					

SYNOPSIS
The Taiwan Stock Exchange Composite Stock Price Average is a price-weighted index that tracks the continuous price only performance of 30 common stocks listed on the Taiwan Stock Exchange (TSE). These shares account for about 25% of the total domestic market capitalization on the exchange.

NUMBER OF STOCKS—DECEMBER 31, 1995
30

MARKET VALUE—DECEMBER 31, 1995
US$45,716.63 million

SELECTION CRITERIA
Constituent shares are selected from the universe of Category A, Category B and Category C common stocks that are tracked in the Taiwan Stock Exchange Weighted Stock Index, excluding preferred stocks and full-delivery stocks. The 30 stocks are selected to represent their respective industry by taking into account each company's operating income, trading volume, trading value and turnover ratio.

BACKGROUND
The index is intended to correspond to the Dow Jones Industrial Average (DJIA) in the United States in terms of its computation methodology.

BASE DATE
December 31, 1988=100.00

COMPUTATION METHODOLOGY
A simple aggregative of actual prices index formula. Adjustments are made over the year to reflect stock splits and other capital changes.

DERIVATIVE INSTRUMENTS
None

SUBINDICES
None

RELATED INDICES
Taiwan Stock Exchange Capitalization Weighted Stock Index (TAIEX)
Taiwan Stock Exchange Industrial Price Average

REMARKS
Stocks listed on the Taiwan Stock Exchange are classified into three categories, Category A, B and C, according to their levels of capital, profitability, capital structure and distribution of shares, based on the number of public and non-public registered shareholders. Category C stocks are considered "hi-tech" enterprises.

PUBLISHER
Taiwan Stock Exchange Corporation.

THE SECURITIES EXCHANGE OF THAILAND (SET) INDEX

PRICE PERFORMANCE

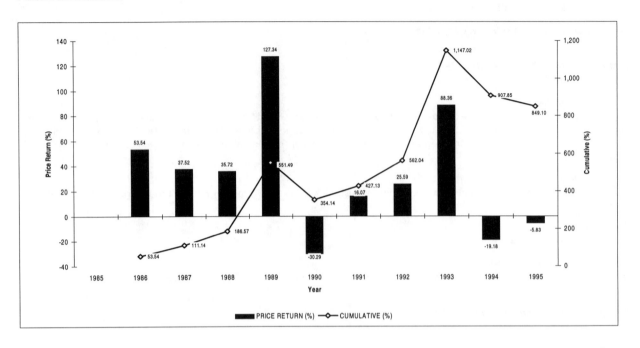

PRICE PERFORMANCE

YEAR	VALUE	PRICE RETURN (%)	CUMULATIVE (%)	MAXIMUM VALUE	DATE	MINIMUM VALUE	DATE
1995	1,280.81	-5.83	849.10	1,472.04	10-Jul	11,335.69	16-Mar
1994	1,360.09	-19.18	907.85	1,753.73	4-Jan	1,196.59	4-Apr
1993	1,682.85	88.36	1,147.02	1,682.85	30-Dec	818.84	1-Jun
1992	893.42	25.59	562.04	963.03	5-Nov	667.84	19-May
1991	711.36	16.07	427.13	908.90	22-Apr	582.48	16-Jan
1990	612.86	-30.29	354.14	1,143.78	25-Jul	544.30	30-Nov
1989	879.19	127.34	551.49	879.19	29-Dec	391.23	3-Jan
1988	386.73	35.72	186.57	471.45	8-Aug	287.71	4-Jan
1987	284.94	37.52	111.14	472.86	16-Oct	203.14	16-Feb
1986	207.20	53.54	53.54	207.98	26-Dec	127.26	19-Jun
1985	134.95						
Average Annual (%)		32.88					
Compound Annual (%)		25.24					
Standard Deviation (%)		48.30					

SYNOPSIS

The Securities Exchange of Thailand (SET) Index is a broad market capitalization-weighted index that tracks the stock price performance of all listed and ordinary shares traded on the Securities Exchange of Thailand (SET).

NUMBER OF STOCKS—DECEMBER 31, 1995

416

MARKET VALUE—DECEMBER 31, 1995

US$135,774.2 million

SELECTION CRITERIA

Eligible securities include all listed and ordinary shares traded on the Securities Exchange of Thailand (SET).

BACKGROUND

The index was introduced in 1975 which coincided with the commencement of operations at the SET.

BASE DATE

April 30, 1975=100.00

COMPUTATION METHODOLOGY

(1) An aggregative of prices times quantities index formula. Maintenance adjustments to the divisor are made daily for capitalization changes, new listings and delistings. (2) Closing prices are used. In the event a closing price is not available, the last available closing price is used.

DERIVATIVE INSTRUMENTS

None

SUBINDICES

Five industry subindices: Banking, finance and securities, commerce, construction materials, and textiles and clothing.

RELATED INDICES

None

REMARKS

Foreign shareholder restrictions apply.

PUBLISHER

The Stock Exchange of Thailand (SET).

ASIA/PACIFIC — REGIONAL

PEREGRINE ASIA INDEX (PAI)—FOREIGN

PRICE PERFORMANCE

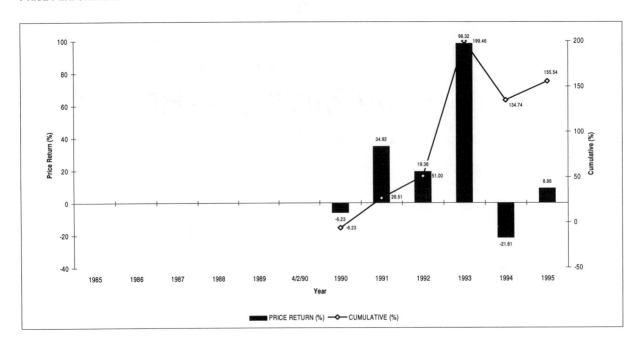

PRICE PERFORMANCE (US$)

YEAR	VALUE	PRICE RETURN (%)	CUMULATIVE (%)	MAXIMUM VALUE	DATE	MINIMUM VALUE	DATE
1995	252.50	8.86	155.54	264.63	10-Jul	200.23	23-Jan
1994	231.95	-21.61	134.74	305.70	5-Jan	217.70	12-Dec
1993	295.90	98.32	199.46	295.90	31-Dec	147.70	4-Jan
1992	149.20	19.36	51.00	165.88	12-Nov	123.40	2-Jan
1991	125.00	34.92	26.51	125.00	31-Dec	89.89	16-Jan
1990	92.65	-6.23	-6.23	115.46	23-Jul	85.74	28-Sep
4/2/90	98.81						
1989							
1988							
1987							
1986							
1985							
Average Annual (%)		22.27					
Compound Annual (%)		16.93					
Standard Deviation (%)		42.12					

SYNOPSIS

The Peregrine Asia Index (PAI)—Foreign is a market capitalization-weighted index that tracks the stock price performance of a universe of Asia-Pacific companies available to foreign investors which are listed in nine markets. The index is intended to be representative of foreign institutional interest in the following nine markets: Hong Kong, India, Indonesia, Korea, Singapore, Malaysia, Thailand, Philippines, and Taiwan.

NUMBER OF STOCKS—DECEMBER 31, 1995

292

MARKET VALUE—DECEMBER 31, 1995

US$428,300.0 million

SELECTION CRITERIA

Constituent stocks are selected on the basis of the following criteria:

(1) Market capitalization and turnover are utilized to make the initial selections which are ultimately designed to be representative of each market. (2) Subsidiaries of other index constituents are eligible for inclusion in the index. (3) New issues with a market capitalization in excess of 1% of the local market's capitalization may be included, if approved, from the second day of trading.

BACKGROUND

Previously known as the Peregrine 100 Index, the PAI was substantially revised in 1994 to include new markets and a substantial number of new companies so as to reflect the rapid changes resulting from privatizations and other initial public offerings.

BASE DATE

May 18, 1990=100.00

COMPUTATION METHODOLOGY

(1) An aggregative of prices times quantities (Laspeyres) index formula. Maintenance adjustments to the divisor are made daily for capitalization changes, new listings and delistings. (2) Market capitalization is determined on the basis of foreign ownership limits or by the number of designated foreign shares. (3) Changes in foreign ownership restrictions are reflected immediately following implementation or as soon as sufficient data is made available to adjust for the changes in ownership restrictions. (4) Constituent stocks are reviewed and revised on a quarterly basis.

DERIVATIVE INSTRUMENTS

None

SUBINDICES

PAI (Combined domestic and Foreign)
PAI-Domestic
Three currencies: U.S dollars, Sterling and Yen denominations.

RELATED INDICES

Peregrine Asia Small Cap Index
Peregrine Greater China Index
Peregrine India ADR Index

REMARKS

The weighting of each market and the corresponding number of issues is as follows: Hong Kong, 22 issues with a market capitalization of US$180.2 billion or 42.9%; India, 46 issues and a market capitalization of US$16.1 billion or 3.8%; Indonesia, 27 issues with a market capitalization of US$17.2 billion or 4.1%; Korea, 38 issues and a market capitalization of US$10.3 billion or 2.5%; Malaysia, 38 issues with a market capitalization of US$71.7 billion or 17.1%; Philippines, 29 issues and a market capitalization of US$18.8 billion or 4.5%; Singapore, 22 issues and a market capitalization of US$6.3 billion or 1.5%; and Thailand, 44 issues and a market capitalization of US$ 42.6 billion or 10.2%. (Data as of 6/12/95).

PUBLISHER

Peregrine Brokerage Limited.

ING BARINGS PAN—ASIA INDEX

PRICE PERFORMANCE

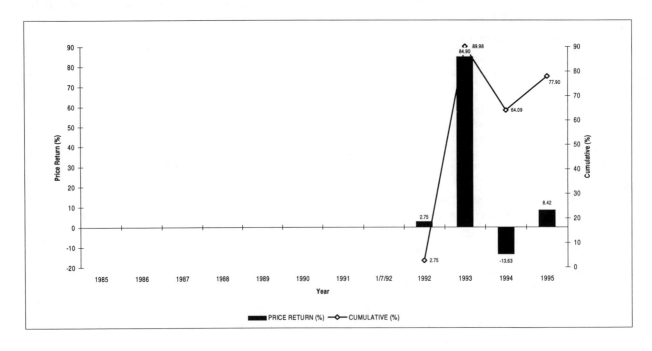

PRICE PERFORMANCE (US$)

YEAR	VALUE	PRICE RETURN (%)	CUMULATIVE (%)	MAXIMUM VALUE[1]	DATE	MINIMUM VALUE[1]	DATE
1995	177.90	8.42	77.90	177.90	31-Dec	150.32	31-Jan
1994	164.09	-13.63	64.09	188.08	31-Jan	157.77	31-Mar
1993	189.98	84.90	89.98	189.98	31-Dec	103.89	31-Jan
1992	102.75	2.75	2.75	114.08	31-May	101.28	31-Jan
1/7/92	100.00						
1991							
1990							
1989							
1988							
1987							
1986							
1985							
Average Annual (%)		20.61					
Compound Annual (%)		15.49					
Standard Deviation (%)		43.87					

[1]Maximum/minimum index values are as of month end.

SYNOPSIS

The ING Barings Pan-Asia Index is a market capitalization-weighted index that tracks the daily price only and total return performance of an investable universe of stocks in the Pan-Asia region, consisting of 13 regional economies.

NUMBER OF STOCKS—DECEMBER 31, 1995

419

MARKET VALUE—DECEMBER 31, 1995

US$364,687.0 million

SELECTION CRITERIA

The index covers 13 regional economies, including Australia, China, Hong Kong, India, Indonesia, Korea, Malaysia, New Zealand, Pakistan, Philippines, Singapore, Taiwan, and Thailand.

Index constituents are selected on the basis of their availability to foreign investors, market capitalization, daily turnover and free-float. They must have a minimum market capitalization greater than 0.5% of the total capitalization of the market, a minimum free float of 10% and a minimum average daily trading value of US$100,000.0 which is confirmed on the basis of trading patterns reviewed over the course of the year.

BACKGROUND

The index and companion indices were launched in 1996. Index values have been backdated to 1992.

BASE DATE

January 7, 1992=100.00

COMPUTATION METHODOLOGY

(1) An aggregative of prices times quantities index formula. Maintenance adjustments to the divisor for capitalization changes, new listings and delistings are made daily on the day they are announced provided this information is known to the index calculators. Otherwise, the capital action is implemented at month-end. Additions and deletions of constituent stocks, other than as a result of a Recomposition Committee meeting, are implemented on the last day of the month. (2) Market capitalization is calculated on the basis of each company's available free float to foreign investors, which is normally updated annually. (3) The composition of the index is reviewed and rebalanced on a quarterly basis. A Recomposition Committee posts the results of the recomposition meetings two weeks in advance of implementing any changes which become effective on the last day of the month. (4) The index is computed using closing prices that coincide with the London time zone. (5) All daily share prices are converted to US dollars using WM/Reuters closing spot rates at 4 PM London Time. (6) Daily total rates of return are computed at the end of each month, with dividends reinvested on the ex-date.

DERIVATIVE INSTRUMENTS

None

SUBINDICES

Asia Index
Emerging Asia Index

RELATED INDICES

ING Barings Asia Convertible Bond Index
ING Barings Eastern Europe Index
ING Barings Emerging Markets World Index

REMARKS

None

PUBLISHER

ING Barings Securities Limited.

HSBC James Capel Dragon 300 Index

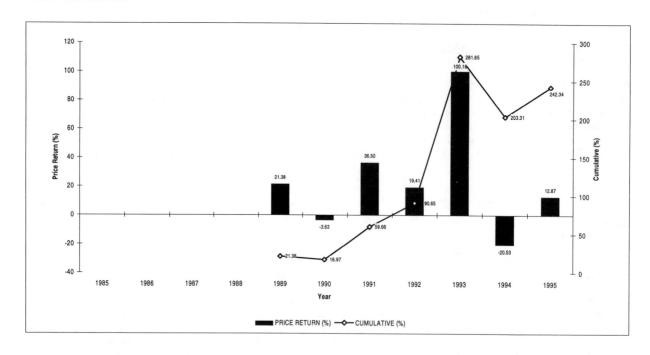

Price Performance (US$)

YEAR	VALUE	PRICE RETURN (%)	CUMULATIVE (%)	MAXIMUM VALUE	DATE	MINIMUM VALUE	DATE
1995	342.34	12.87	242.34	349.47	13-Jul	261.46	23-Jan
1994	303.31	-20.53	203.31	395.19	5-Jan	285.49	12-Dec
1993	381.65	100.18	281.65	381.65	31-Dec	188.92	4-Jan
1992	190.65	19.41	90.65	209.49	11-Nov	159.60	2-Jan
1991	159.66	36.50	59.66	159.66	31-Dec	112.74	16-Jan
1990	116.97	-3.63	16.97	146.83	23-Jul	108.26	28-Sep
1989	121.38	21.38	21.38	124.33	18-May	94.50	5-Jun
1988	100.00						
1987							
1986							
1985							
Average Annual (%)		23.74					
Compound Annual (%)		19.22					
Standard Deviation (%)		38.42					

Synopsis

The HSBC James Capel Dragon 300 Index is a market capitalization-eighted index that tracks the daily price only performance of an investable universe of stocks traded in eight markets in South East Asia. These markets are Hong Kong, Indonesia, Korea, Malaysia, Philippines, Singapore, Taiwan and Thailand.

Number of Stocks—December 31, 1995

300

Market Value—December 31, 1995

US$419,648.0 million

Selection Criteria

In addition to maintaining an accurate representation of the industrial structure, barring legal constraints which may require the deletion of an entire sector, of each component market, constituent stocks are selected on the basis of four overriding considerations, as follows:

(1) Legal constraints–The market capitalization of each constituent security is based on that proportion of its issued capital that is available to foreign investors. (2) Liquidity–Eligible securities must evidence sufficient liquidity such that transactions can be effected with relative ease and sufficient size. (3) Settlement procedures–Eligible securities should be free of potential settlement problems, (4) Accuracy of data.

Base Date

December 31, 1988=100.00

Computation Methodology

(1) An aggregative of prices times quantities index formula. Maintenance adjustments to the divisor are made daily for capitalization changes, new listings and delistings. (2) Capitalization restrictions have been applied as follows: Hong-Kong–None; Indonesia–Capitalization of each security is based on 49% of its issued capital; Korea–Capitalization of each security is based on 10% of its issued capital, except for KEPCO and POSCO in which case a 8% limit applies; Malaysia–Capitalization of each security is based on 30% of its issued capital, except for Telekom Malaysia, Malayan Bank and Tenaga National with 25%, 31% and 2% restrictions respectively; Philippines–Capitalization of each security is based on 100% of its issued capital in the form of "B" shares; Singapore–Capitalization restrictions apply to banks, airlines, newspaper and shipping transport sectors, with limits of 40%, 25%, 49% and 49%, respectively applicable to domestic companies within these sectors; Taiwan–Capitalization of each security is based on 10% of its issued capital; Thailand–Capitalization restrictions are generally held to a maximum of 49%, however further restrictions apply to specific areas of business. (3) Constituent shares are reviewed on a daily and quarterly basis and, if warranted by a significant change in local market practices, modifications are made prior to the quarterly review date.

Derivative Instruments

None

Subindices

Eight South East Asia market subindices: Hong Kong, Indonesia, Korea, Malaysia, Philippines, Singapore, Taiwan and Thailand. Dragon 300 Index, ex-Hong Kong

Related Indices

HSBC JC Japanese Smaller Companies Index
HSBC JC Latin America 100 Index
HSBC JC Smaller European Companies Index
HSBC JC Smaller Pan-European Index
Refer to Appendix 5 for additional indices.

Remarks

None

Publisher

HSBC James Capel.

EUROPE

AUSTRIAN TRADED INDEX (ATX)

PRICE PERFORMANCE

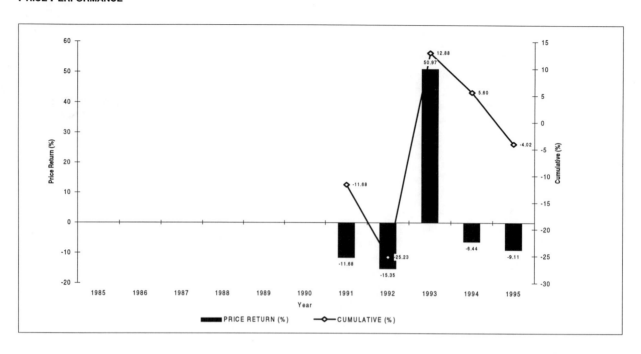

PRICE PERFORMANCE

YEAR	VALUE	PRICE RETURN (%)	CUMULATIVE (%)	MAXIMUM VALUE	DATE	MINIMUM VALUE	DATE
1995	959.79	-9.11	-4.02	1,056.31	2-Jan	882.15	23-Oct
1994	1,056.04	-6.44	5.60	1,222.25	1-Feb	1,011.38	6-Jun
1993	1,128.78	50.97	12.88	1,128.78	31-Dec	712.24	14-Jan
1992	747.70	-15.35	-25.23	1,003.48	5-Jun	682.96	13-Aug
1991	883.25	-11.68	-11.68	1,257.96	16-Apr	883.25	31-Dec
1990	1,000.00						
1989							
1988							
1987							
1986							
1985							
Average Annual (%)		1.68					
Compound Annual (%)		-0.82					
Standard Deviation (%)		27.75					

SYNOPSIS

The Austrian Traded Index (ATX) index is a market value-weighted index that tracks the price only performance of the largest, most liquid, actively traded, domestic stocks on the Vienna Stock Exchange (Weiner Börse). Constituent shares include continuously traded stocks on the so called "Fließhandel," or main market, that accounts for about 70% of total equity turnover in Austria.

NUMBER OF STOCKS—DECEMBER 31, 1995

20

MARKET VALUE—DECEMBER 31, 1995

US$16,973.6 million

SELECTION CRITERIA

ATX constituent stocks are selected on the basis of their trading activity, high level of market capitalization and level of free float.

BACKGROUND

Launched in 1991, the index has become an important stock market barometer of the Austrian equity market. Its design attributes, including real time calculation and dissemination, liquidity, and transparency, permitted the creation of ATX derivative products.

BASE DATE

January 2, 1991=1000.00

COMPUTATION METHODOLOGY

(1) An aggregate of prices times quantities index formula. Maintenance adjustments to the divisor are made for capitalization changes, new listings and delistings. Technical adjustments to the index are made on a quarterly basis to add, delete or otherwise redefine the number of shares outstanding or market weightings for constituent stocks. (2) Stock splits are reflected in the index on the first market day on which the stock is traded in the new minimum denomination. Otherwise, adjustments to capital serve to adjust the ATX before the opening of the market on the day the stock is first listed "ex-right." (3) For computation purposes, however, individual stocks with a minimum free float of less than 25% receive a weighting of less than 25% of their normal market capitalization.

DERIVATIVE INSTRUMENTS

ATX stock index options and futures trade on the Österreichische Termin-Und Optionenborse (ÖTOB).
Long-Term Equity Options (ATX LEOs), with maturities of up to two and a half years, trade on the Osterreichische Termin-Und Optionenborse (ÖTOB).

SUBINDICES

None

RELATED INDICES

ATX 50 Index
ATX-Midcap Index
WBI 30 Index

REMARKS

(1) Market value based on free float market capitalization. (2) In June 1996, the ÖTOB announced plans to launch equity derivatives on a new CECE Index family covering the Hungarian, Czech, Polish and Slovak markets. The CECE Index components account for about 80% of total exchange turnover on each of the respective regional markets.

PUBLISHER

Österreichische Termin-Und Optionenborse (ÖTOB).

THE VIENNA STOCK EXCHANGE SHARE (WEINER BÖRSE) INDEX (WBI)

PRICE PERFORMANCE

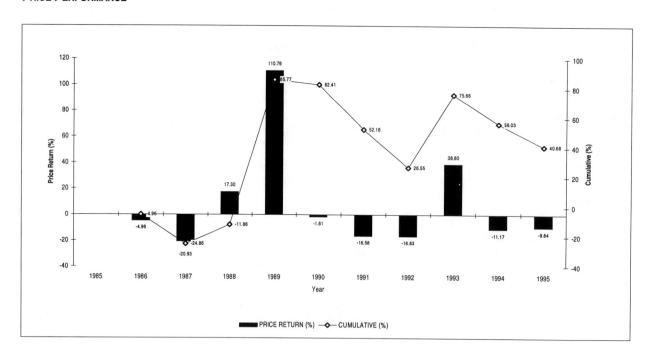

PRICE PERFORMANCE

YEAR	VALUE	PRICE RETURN (%)	CUMULATIVE (%)	MAXIMUM VALUE	DATE	MINIMUM VALUE	DATE
1995	387.36	-9.84	40.68	429.96	2-Jan	369.88	23-Oct
1994	429.64	-11.17	56.03	510.41	1-Feb	413.85	25-Oct
1993	483.67	38.80	75.66	483.67	24-Feb	333.20	15-Jan
1992	348.46	-16.83	26.55	497.93	16-Apr	333.34	18-Dec
1991	418.98	-16.58	52.16	596.05	19-Mar	417.66	23-Dec
1990	502.26	-1.81	82.41	739.21	10-Oct	464.68	25-Sep
1989	511.51	110.76	85.77	543.97	7-Nov	242.67	2-Jan
1988	242.70	17.30	-11.86	248.51	2-Jan	193.96	11-Feb
1987	206.91	-20.93	-24.86	260.37	23-Apr	199.59	11-Nov
1986	261.68	-4.96	-4.96	296.19	26-Nov	256.92	5-Mar
1985	275.35						
Average Annual (%)		8.47					
Compound Annual (%)		3.47					
Standard Deviation (%)		40.28					

SYNOPSIS
The Vienna Stock Exchange Share (Weiner Börse) Index (WBI) is a market value-weighted index that tracks the price only performance of all stocks traded on the main market of the Vienna Stock Exchange (Weiner Börse).

NUMBER OF STOCKS—DECEMBER 31, 1995
113

MARKET VALUE—DECEMBER 31, 1995
US$29,434.2 million

SELECTION CRITERIA
Components include all domestic shares listed for trading on the main market.

BACKGROUND
None

BASE DATE
December 31, 1967=100.00

COMPUTATION METHODOLOGY
An aggregate of prices times quantities index formula. Maintenance adjustments to the divisor are made for capitalization changes, new listings and delistings.

DERIVATIVE INSTRUMENTS
None

SUBINDICES
Sixteen sector indices: Banks, insurance, construction, building materials, breweries, chemicals, utilities, mining and magnesite, machines, transportation and technical manufactured goods, food, paper, commerce and services, conglomerates, real estate and others.

RELATED INDICES
WBI 30 Index
Participation Certificate Index

REMARKS
None

PUBLISHER
The Vienna Stock Exchange (Weiner Börse).

WIENER BÖRSE INDEX 30 (WBI 30) INDEX

PRICE PERFORMANCE

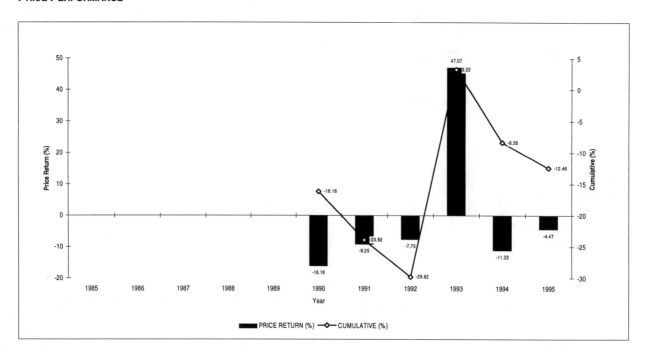

PRICE PERFORMANCE

YEAR	VALUE	PRICE RETURN (%)	CUMULATIVE (%)	MAXIMUM VALUE	DATE	MINIMUM VALUE	DATE
1995	385.59	-4.47	-12.46	416.96	3-Aug	359.89	30-Mar
1994	403.62	-11.22	-8.36	479.75	1-Feb	381.14	25-Oct
1993	454.65	47.07	3.22	454.66	30-Dec	292.24	15-Jan
1992	309.13	-7.75	-29.82	412.87	24-Feb	274.63	13-Aug
1991	335.10	-9.25	-23.92	454.78	16-Apr	326.96	15-Jan
1990	369.26	-16.16	-16.16	608.15	19-Mar	347.86	25-Sep
1989	440.46						
1988							
1987							
1986							
1985							
Average Annual (%)		-0.30					
Compound Annual (%)		-2.19					
Standard Deviation (%)		23.53					

SYNOPSIS
The Wiener Börse Index (WBI 30) Index is a market value-weighted index that tracks the daily total return performance of the largest and most liquid domestic stocks traded on the Vienna Stock Exchange (Weiner Börse). These shares account for 70% of the domestic equity market.

NUMBER OF STOCKS—DECEMBER 31, 1995
30

MARKET VALUE—DECEMBER 31, 1995
US$21,693.8 million

SELECTION CRITERIA
WBI 30 Index constituents are selected on the basis of turnover volume on the stock exchange, market capitalization and representative of the Austrian capital markets.

BACKGROUND
The index was launched on November 3, 1995 to supplement existing benchmarks to more specifically serve as a performance benchmark and for indexation purposes. It was established with a base value corresponding to the value of the WBI Index on October 9, 1995.

BASE DATE
October 9, 1995=393.17

COMPUTATION METHODOLOGY
(1) An aggregate of prices times quantities (Laspeyres) index formula. Maintenance adjustments to the divisor are made daily after the close of trading for capitalization changes, new listings and delistings. (2) The composition of the index, barring extraordinary events, is examined at the beginning of every year by an Expert Committee. (3) Changes in market capitalization are implemented once a year, at the beginning of the calendar year. (4) Total returns are calculated with dividends reinvested directly in the shares of the companies concerned rather than the total index portfolio.

DERIVATIVE INSTRUMENTS
None

SUBINDICES
None

RELATED INDICES
ATX Index
ATX-50 Index
ATX-Midcap Index

REMARKS
In June 1996, the ÖTOB announced plans to launch equity derivatives on a new CECE Index family covering the Hungarian, Czech, Polish and Slovak markets. The CECE Index components account for about 80% of total exchange turnover on each of the respective regional markets.

PUBLISHER
Österreichische Termin-Und Optionenborse (ÖTOB).

BELGIAN (BEL) 20 INDEX

PRICE PERFORMANCE

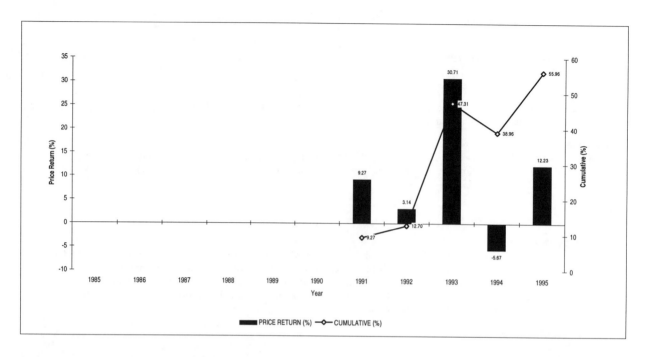

PRICE AND TOTAL RETURN PERFORMANCE

YEAR	VALUE	PRICE RETURN (%)	CUMULATIVE (%)	TOTAL RETURN (%)[1]	MAXIMUM VALUE	DATE	MINIMUM VALUE	DATE
1995	1,559.63	12.23	55.96	16.69	1,559.63	29-Dec	1,271.53	9-Mar
1994	1,389.64	-5.67	38.96	2.08	1,542.65	9-Feb	1,336.39	7-Oct
1993	1,473.10	30.71	47.31	36.22	1,473.53	28-Dec	1,125.46	4-Jan
1992	1,127.02	3.14	12.70	7.51	1,235.40	2-Jun	1,046.07	2-Sep
1991	1,092.72	9.27	9.27	13.90	1,215.78	18-Apr	1,055.23	2-Dec
1990	1,000.00							
1989								
1988								
1987								
1986								
1985								
Average Annual (%)		9.94		15.28				
Compound Annual (%)		9.30		14.72				
Standard Deviation (%)		13.48		13.01				

[1]Total return calculated with gross dividends reinvested.

SYNOPSIS

The Belgian (BEL) 20 Index is a market value-weighted index that tracks the continuous price only performance of 20 large, actively traded Belgian companies listed on the liquid, institutionally oriented, Forward Market segment of the Brussels Stock Exchange.

NUMBER OF STOCKS—DECEMBER 31, 1995

20

MARKET VALUE—DECEMBER 31, 1995

US$63,905.9 million

SELECTION CRITERIA

Constituent shares, which must be Belgian companies listed on the Forward Market for a period of at least six months, are selected on the basis of trading activity and market capitalization. In the selection process, turnover is assigned a weighting of 60% while market capitalization is assigned a weighting of 40%. To avoid duplication, holding companies with a portfolio consisting of over 75% of a BEL 20-listed stock and not ranked within the first 12 stocks, are excluded from the index.

Turnover rankings are calculated using average monthly trading volume on the Forward Market during a 12-month period from December to November of the following year. Market capitalization is calculated once a year based on the Forward Market closing prices on November 30th each year, using the number of issued shares of the listed class rather than the number of listed shares.

BACKGROUND

Launched on March 18, 1991, the index was designed to serve as an underlying product for options and futures contracts traded on the Belgian Futures and Options Exchange (BELFOX). Its design attributes, in addition to real time calculation and dissemination, include stability of constituent stocks, replication, liquidity, and transparency.

BASE DATE

January 1, 1991=1000.00

COMPUTATION METHODOLOGY

(1) An aggregate of prices times quantities index formula. Maintenance adjustments to the divisor are made for capitalization changes, new listings and delistings. Capital events that affect the value of the index by more than 1% are reflected after the close of trading on the Forward Market. (2) Unless circumstances dictate otherwise, the composition of the index is updated once a year, as may be required, on the 3rd Friday of the month of December. (3) Component stocks may not exceed 10% of the global value of the index during a continuous six-month period, otherwise, their weighting factor is limited to 10%.

DERIVATIVE INSTRUMENTS

BEL 20 stock index futures and options trade on the Belgian Futures and Options Exchange (BELFOX).

SUBINDICES

BEL 20 Return Index-Private
BEL 20 Return Index-Institutional

RELATED INDICES

Belgian CATS Market Return Index
Belgian Foreign Forward Markets (CATS) Return Index
Belgian Spot Market Index
Brussels Small Capitalization Return Index
Brussels Medium Capitalization Return Index
B-Gold Index

REMARKS

The official securities market consists of a cash and forward market. While domestic and foreign shares may be traded on both markets, the forward market, which is institutionally oriented, is restricted to large, actively traded securities that are transacted on the Computer Assisted Trading System (CATS). This segment accounts for over 80% of the turnover in domestic stock trading on the Brussels Stock Exchange. The relatively narrow cash market, which is largely reserved for individual investors, accounts for the remaining 20% of turnover.

PUBLISHER

Brussels Stock Exchange.

BELGIAN COMPUTER ASSISTED TRADING SYSTEM (CATS) MARKET RETURN INDEX

TOTAL RETURN PERFORMANCE

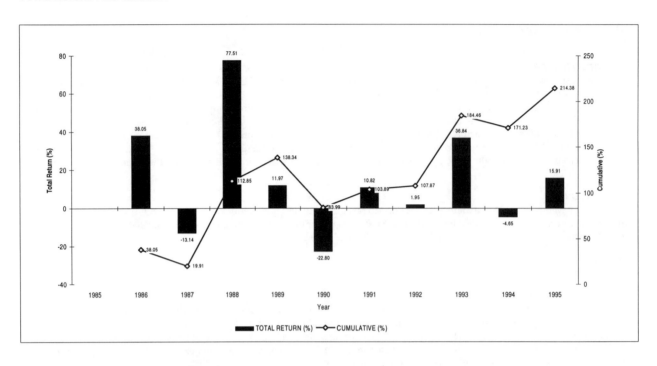

TOTAL RETURN PERFORMANCE

YEAR	VALUE	TOTAL RETURN (%)	CUMULATIVE (%)	MAXIMUM VALUE[1]	DATE	MINIMUM VALUE[1]	DATE
1995	8,401.68	15.91	214.38	8,401.68	29-Dec	6,691.71	8-Mar
1994	7,248.64	-4.65	171.23	7,923.53	20-May	6,953.65	7-Oct
1993	7,602.15	36.84	184.46	7,617.40	30-Dec	5,544.55	4-Jan
1992	5,555.31	1.95	107.87	5,975.34	2-Jun	5,168.79	2-Sep
1991	5,448.98	10.82	103.89	5,824.23	8-Mar	4,573.35	16-Jan
1990	4,917.02	-22.80	83.99	6,532.30	4-Jan	4,862.23	24-Dec
1989	6,369.56	11.97	138.34	6,776.71	26-Sep	5,609.08	4-Jan
1988	5,688.39	77.51	112.85	5,688.39	29-Dec	3,164.03	4-Jan
1987	3,204.52	-13.14	19.91	4,915.06	29-Jul	3,070.85	14-Dec
1986	3,689.29	38.05	38.05	3,715.19	9-Dec	2,525.85	13-Jan
1985	2,672.48						
Average Annual (%)		15.25					
Compound Annual (%)		12.14					
Standard Deviation (%)		29.29					

[1]Maximum/minimum index values for the period 1986-1993 are based on intraday values.

SYNOPSIS
The Belgian Computer Assisted Trading System (CATS) Market Return Index is a market value-weighted index that tracks the total return performance of all the large, actively traded Belgian companies listed on the institutionally oriented Forward Market segment of the Brussels Stock Exchange.

NUMBER OF STOCKS—DECEMBER 31, 1995
56

MARKET VALUE—DECEMBER 31, 1995
US$86,883.8 million

SELECTION CRITERIA
All shares of Belgian companies listed on the Forward Market.

BACKGROUND
The index is calculated every five minutes during the Forward Market session.

BASE DATE
January 1, 1980=1000.00

COMPUTATION METHODOLOGY
An aggregate of prices times quantities index formula. Maintenance adjustments to the divisor are made for capitalization changes, new listings and delistings. Changes to reflect events that affect the market capitalization of constituent stocks or composition of the index, are reflected after the close of trading on the Brussels Stock Exchange on the day preceding the day of the financial operation and prior to the opening of the next trading day.

DERIVATIVE INSTRUMENTS
None

SUBINDICES
None

RELATED INDICES
BEL 20 Index
Belgian Spot Market Index
Belgian Foreign Forward Markets (CATS) Return Index
Brussels Small Capitalization Market Index
Brussels Medium Capitalization Market Index
B-Gold Index

REMARKS
The official securities market consists of a cash and forward market. While domestic and foreign shares may be traded on both markets, the forward market, which is institutionally oriented, is restricted to large, actively traded securities, that are transacted on the Computer Assisted Trading System (CATS). This segment accounts for over 80% of the turnover in domestic stock trading on the Brussels Stock Exchange. The relatively narrow cash market, which is largely reserved for individual investors, accounts for the remaining 20% of turnover.

PUBLISHER
Brussels Stock Exchange.

BELGIAN MEDIUM CAPITALIZATION RETURN INDEX

TOTAL RETURN PERFORMANCE

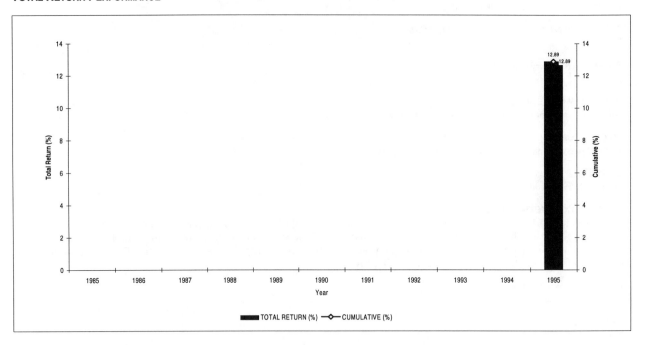

TOTAL RETURN PERFORMANCE

YEAR	VALUE	TOTAL RETURN (%)	CUMULATIVE (%)	MAXIMUM VALUE	DATE	MINIMUM VALUE	DATE
1995	1,128.93	12.89	12.89	1,128.93	29-Dec	1,011.95	2-May
1994	1,000.00						
1993							
1992							
1991							
1990							
1989							
1988							
1987							
1986							
1985							
Average Annual (%)		NM					
Compound Annual (%)		NM					
Standard Deviation (%)		NM					

SYNOPSIS

The Belgian Medium Capitalization Return Index is a market value-weighted index that tracks the daily total return performance of all Belgian stocks traded on the rings market of the Brussels Stock Exchange.

NUMBER OF STOCKS—DECEMBER 31, 1995

73

MARKET VALUE—DECEMBER 31, 1995

US$24,843.7 million

SELECTION CRITERIA

All shares of Belgian companies traded on the rings segment of the cash market, except for any companies that are members of the BEL 20 Index.

BACKGROUND

This segment of the market is open to securities which are the more actively traded than those on the floor market. Moreover, the minimum quotation units are set at a higher level, i.e., 50 shares or BEF 50.000.

BASE DATE

January 1, 1994=1000.00

COMPUTATION METHODOLOGY

(1) An aggregate of prices times quantities index formula. Maintenance adjustments to the divisor are made for capitalization changes, new listings and delistings. Changes to reflect events that affect the market capitalization of constituent stocks or composition of the index, are reflected after the close of trading on the Brussels Stock Exchange on the day preceding the day of the financial operation and prior to the opening of the next trading day. (2) Net dividends are used to compute the total rate of return.

DERIVATIVE INSTRUMENTS

None

SUBINDICES

None

RELATED INDICES

BEL 20 Index
Belgian CATS Market Return Index
Belgian Foreign Forward Markets (CATS) Return Index
Belgian Spot Market Index
Brussels Small Capitalization Return Index
B-Gold Index

REMARKS

The official securities market consists of a cash and forward market. While domestic and foreign shares may be traded on both markets, the cash market is open to issues with lower trading volumes and quotation units while the forward market is intended for institutional investors trading in large, actively traded securities that are transacted on the Computer Assisted Trading System (CATS). The cash market segment, which includes the bond market, the rings market (consisting of securities whose market is broad enough to justify several successive quotations during the day) and the floor market, accounts for about 20% of the turnover in domestic stock trading on the Brussels Stock Exchange.

PUBLISHER

Brussels Stock Exchange.

BELGIAN SMALL CAPITALIZATION RETURN INDEX

PRICE PERFORMANCE

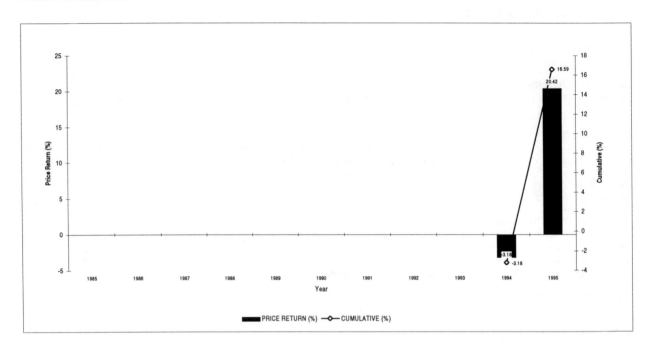

PRICE PERFORMANCE

YEAR	VALUE	PRICE RETURN (%)	CUMULATIVE (%)	MAXIMUM VALUE	DATE	MINIMUM VALUE	DATE
1995	1,165.88	20.42	16.59	1,145.88	29-Dec	910.05	31-Mar
1994	968.16	-3.18	-3.18	1,069.44	24-May	964.94	20-Dec
1993	1,000.00						
1992							
1991							
1990							
1989							
1988							
1987							
1986							
1985							
Average Annual (%)		8.62					
Compound Annual (%)		7.98					
Standard Deviation (%)		16.69					

SYNOPSIS
The Belgian Small Capitalization Return Index is a market value-weighted index that tracks the daily total return performance of small capitalization Belgian stocks traded on the cash market of the Brussels Stock Exchange.

NUMBER OF STOCKS—DECEMBER 31, 1995
127

MARKET VALUE—DECEMBER 31, 1995
US$ 10,977.5 million

SELECTION CRITERIA
All shares of Belgian companies listed on the cash market, except shares of companies listed on both the cash market and forward market.

BACKGROUND
This segment of the market is open to securities which are the least traded in Belgium. Moreover, the minimum quotation units are set at a very low level, i.e., 25 shares or BEF 10.000.

BASE DATE
January 1, 1994=1000.00

COMPUTATION METHODOLOGY
(1) An aggregate of prices times quantities index formula. Maintenance adjustments to the divisor are made for capitalization changes, new listings and delistings. Changes to reflect events that affect the market capitalization of constituent stocks or composition of the index, are reflected after the close of trading on the Brussels Stock Exchange on the day preceding the day of the financial operation and prior to the opening of the next trading day. (2) Net dividends are used to compute the total rate of return.

DERIVATIVE INSTRUMENTS
None

SUBINDICES
None

RELATED INDICES
BEL 20 Index
Belgian CATS Market Return Index
Belgian Foreign Forward Markets (CATS) Return Index
Belgian Spot Market Index
Brussels Medium Capitalization Return Index
B-Gold Index

REMARKS
The official securities market consists of a cash and forward market. While domestic and foreign shares may be traded on both markets, the cash market is open to issues with lower trading volumes and quotation units while the forward market is intended for institutional investors trading in large, actively traded securities that are transacted on the Computer Assisted Trading System (CATS). The cash market segment, which includes the bond market, the rings market (consisting of securities whose market is broad enough to justify several successive quotations during the day) and the floor market, accounts for about 20% of the turnover in domestic stock trading on the Brussels Stock Exchange.

PUBLISHER
Brussels Stock Exchange.

BELGIAN SPOT MARKET INDEX

PRICE PERFORMANCE

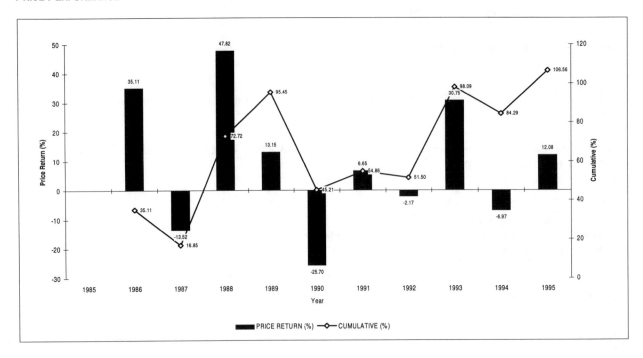

PRICE AND TOTAL RETURN PERFORMANCE

YEAR	VALUE	PRICE RETURN (%)	CUMULATIVE (%)	TOTAL RETURN (%)	MAXIMUM VALUE	DATE	MINIMUM VALUE	DATE
1995	4,230.77	12.08	106.56	12.62	4,230.77	29-Dec	3,679.98	8-Mar
1994	3,774.62	-6.97	84.29	-1.52	4,399.78	19-May	3,620.17	7-Oct
1993	4,057.32	30.75	98.09	35.47	4,057.32	30-Dec	3,097.80	6-Jan
1992	3,103.01	-2.17	51.50	1.58	3,639.07	3-Apr	2,906.66	2-Sep
1991	3,171.73	6.65	54.86	10.43	3,522.78	25-Apr	2,796.93	16-Jan
1990	2,974.09	-25.70	45.21	-23.36	6,077.86	12-Jan	2,954.17	26-Dec
1989	4,003.08	13.15	95.45	16.37	6,215.30	26-Sep	3,509.13	4-Jan
1988	3,537.71	47.82	72.72	52.34	3,537.71	29-Dec	2,366.86	4-Jan
1987	2,393.23	-13.52	16.85	-10.79	3,558.97	13-Aug	2,295.86	18-Dec
1986	2,767.37	35.11	35.11	39.14	2,783.30	9-Nov	1,325.27	15-Jan
1985	2,048.18							
Average Annual (%)		9.72		13.23				
Compound Annual (%)		7.52		11.01				
Standard Deviation (%)		23.05		23.53				

SYNOPSIS

The Belgian Spot Market Index is a market value-weighted index that tracks the daily price only and total return performance of all Belgian stocks traded on the cash market of the Brussels Stock Exchange.

NUMBER OF STOCKS—DECEMBER 31, 1995

205

MARKET VALUE—DECEMBER 31, 1995

US$101,162.4 million

SELECTION CRITERIA

All shares of Belgian companies listed on the cash market of the Brussels Stock Exchange.

BACKGROUND

Calculated daily on the basis of the first price on the cash market and available for dissemination by 3 PM, the index is a comprehensive, total return yardstick for tracking the domestic market as well as market segments.

BASE DATE

January 1, 1980=1000.00

COMPUTATION METHODOLOGY

(1) An aggregate of prices times quantities index formula. Maintenance adjustments to the divisor are made for capitalization changes, new listings and delistings. Changes to reflect events that affect the market capitalization of constituent stocks or composition of the index, are reflected after the close of trading on the Brussels Stock Exchange on the day preceding the day of the financial operation and prior to the opening of the next trading day. (2) Transfers from one industry sector to another are made at the beginning of a new calendar year.

DERIVATIVE INSTRUMENTS

None

SUBINDICES

Seventeen sectoral return (including reinvestment of income dividends) subindices: Food, insurance, banks and financial services, retailing, chemicals, steel, non-ferrous industry, holdings, building, oil, property, metal-electro magnetic, tropicals, electricals, miscellaneous industrial companies, and miscellaneous service companies.

RELATED INDICES

BEL 20 Index
Belgian CATS Market Return Index
Belgian Forward Markets (CATS) Return Index
Brussels Small Capitalization Return Index
Brussels Medium Capitalization Return Index
B-Gold Index

REMARKS

The official securities market consists of a cash and forward market. While domestic and foreign shares may be traded on both markets, the cash market is open to issues with lower trading volumes and quotation units while the forward market is intended for institutional investors trading in large, actively traded securities that are transacted on the Computer Assisted Trading System (CATS). The cash market segment, which includes the bond market, the rings market (consisting of securities whose market is broad enough to justify several successive quotations during the day) and the floor market, accounts for about 20% of the turnover in domestic stock trading on the Brussels Stock Exchange.

PUBLISHER

Brussels Stock Exchange.

CYPRUS STOCK EXCHANGE (CYSE) ALL-SHARE INDEX

PRICE PERFORMANCE

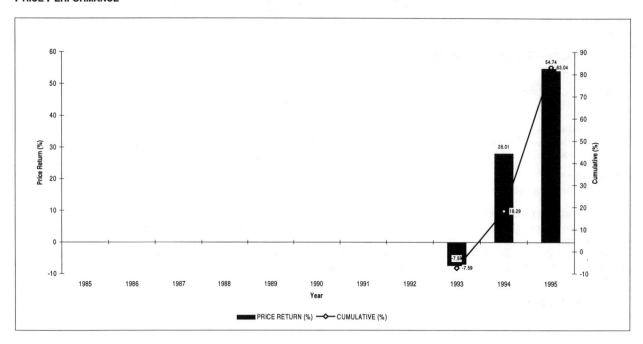

PRICE PERFORMANCE

YEAR	VALUE	PRICE RETURN (%)	CUMULATIVE (%)	MAXIMUM VALUE	DATE	MINIMUM VALUE	DATE
1995	183.04	54.74	83.04	183.04	31-Dec	128.89	31-Jan
1994	118.29	28.01	18.29	118.29	31-Dec	91.99	31-Jan
1993	92.41	-7.59	-7.59	97.22	31-Jan	87.03	31-Jul
1992	100.00						
1991							
1990							
1989							
1988							
1987							
1986							
1985							
Average Annual (%)		25.05					
Compound Annual (%)		22.33					
Standard Deviation (%)		31.27					

[1]Maximum/minimum index values are as of month-end.

SYNOPSIS
The Cyprus Stock Exchange (CYSE) All-Share Index is a market value-weighted index that tracks the daily price only performance of all stocks listed on the Cyprus Stock Exchange (CYSE).

NUMBER OF STOCKS—DECEMBER 31, 1995
70

MARKET VALUE—DECEMBER 31, 1995
US$2,857.8 million

SELECTION CRITERIA
The index includes all full and partly paid shares listed on the Cyprus Stock Exchange, except warrants and debentures.

BACKGROUND
The official Cyprus Stock Exchange was launched on March 29, 1996. Up to that time, an Over-the-Counter (OTC) market operated under the auspices of the Cyprus Chamber of Commerce and Industry.

BASE DATE
December 31, 1992=100.00

COMPUTATION METHODOLOGY
An aggregate of prices times quantities index formula. Maintenance adjustments to the divisor are made for capitalization changes, new listings and delistings.

DERIVATIVE INSTRUMENTS
None

SUBINDICES
Six sectoral subindices: Banking, insurance, investment/finance companies, industrial companies, transportation/hotels and commercial/real estate companies.

RELATED INDICES
Cyprus Stock Exchange Institutional Index

REMARKS
None

PUBLISHER
Cyprus Stock Exchange (CYSE).

PRAGUE STOCK EXCHANGE 50 (PX 50) INDEX

PRICE PERFORMANCE

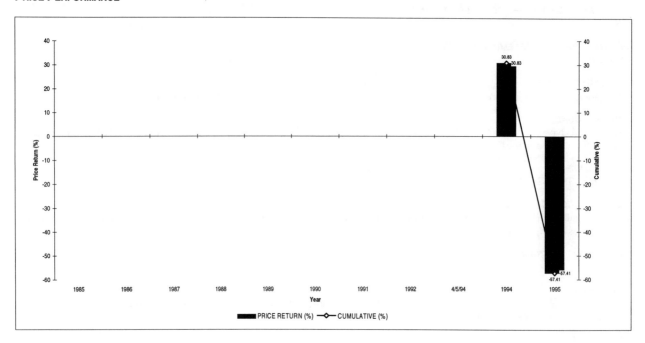

PRICE PERFORMANCE

YEAR	VALUE	PRICE RETURN (%)	CUMULATIVE (%)	MAXIMUM VALUE	DATE	MINIMUM VALUE	DATE
1995	425.90	-23.56	-57.41	586.60	9-Jan	387.2	29-Jun
1994	557.20	-44.28	-44.28	1,244.70	1-Mar	541.1	31-Dec
4/5/94	1,000.00						
1993							
1992							
1991							
1990							
1989							
1988							
1987							
1986							
1985							
Average Annual (%)		NM					
Compound Annual (%)		NM					
Standard Deviation (%)		NM					

SYNOPSIS

The Prague Stock Exchange 50 (PX 50) Index is a market value-weighted index that tracks the daily stock price performance of 50 stocks traded on the Listed Market and Unlisted Market of the Prague Stock Exchange.

NUMBER OF STOCKS—DECEMBER 31, 1995

50

MARKET VALUE—DECEMBER 31, 1995

US$11,076.6 million

SELECTION CRITERIA

Constituent stocks are selected on the basis of market capitalization, liquidity as determined by volume of trades executed, and sectoral representation.

BACKGROUND

Daily trading on the Prague Stock Exchange commenced on April 6, 1994. The PX 50 Index was introduced on the occasion of the first anniversary of the Prague Stock Exchange.

BASE DATE

April 5, 1994=1000.00

COMPUTATION METHODOLOGY

An aggregate of prices times quantities (Paasche) index formula. Maintenance adjustments to the divisor are made for capitalization changes, new listings and delistings.

DERIVATIVE INSTRUMENTS

None

SUBINDICES

None

RELATED INDICES

None

REMARKS

(1) The index combines shares traded on the Listed Market and Unlisted Market due to the fact that only 10 issues were listed for trading on the Listed Market at the time the index was launched. (2) International Finance Corporation (IFC) index calculation standards have been adopted for the construction and calculation of the PX 50 Index.

PUBLISHER

The Prague Stock Exchange.

COPENHAGEN STOCK EXCHANGE (KFX) INDEX

PRICE PERFORMANCE

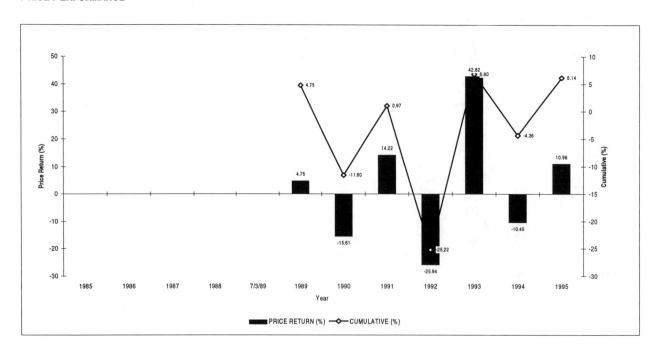

PRICE PERFORMANCE[1]

YEAR	VALUE	PRICE RETURN (%)	CUMULATIVE (%)	MAXIMUM VALUE	DATE	MINIMUM VALUE	DATE
1995	106.14	10.98	6.14	106.43	14-Dec	88.20	29-Mar
1994	95.64	-10.45	-4.36	118.12	2-Feb	91.34	13-Dec
1993	106.80	42.82	6.80	108.19	29-Dec	75.17	14-Jan
1992	74.78	-25.94	-25.22	105.93	15-Jan	70.59	28-Oct
1991	100.97	14.22	0.97	110.92	17-Jul	85.26	7-Jan
1990	88.40	-15.61	-11.60	112.44	20-Jul	88.40	28-Dec
1989	104.75	4.75	4.75	107.33	12-May	103.69	21-Dec
7/3/89	100.00						
1988							
1987							
1986							
1985							
Average Annual (%)		2.67					
Compound Annual (%)		0.22					
Standard Deviation (%)		25.06					

[1]Statistical measures applicable to the six year period 1989-1995.

SYNOPSIS

The Copenhagen Stock Exchange (KFX) Index is a market value-weighted index that tracks the continuous price only performance of domestic stock performance of 20 actively traded Danish-based companies listed on the Copenhagen Stock Exchange. These shares account for 51% of the domestic equity market.

NUMBER OF STOCKS—DECEMBER 31, 1995
20

MARKET VALUE—DECEMBER 31, 1995
US$30,552.8 million

SELECTION CRITERIA

Constituent stocks are selected from a portfolio of 25 companies that are selected on the basis of daily turnover over a 12-month period. Once a year, companies with the greatest frequency of highest daily volumes, combined with the largest market capitalization, are selected for representation in the index. New companies that have not been listed during an entire 12-month period may be eligible for inclusion in the index, provided they have been listed for a minimum of 40 trading days prior to the selection date. (3) Unit trusts, foreign companies and certain holding companies are excluded from the KFX Index.

BACKGROUND

Launched in December 1989, the index was designed to serve as an underlying product for options and futures contracts traded on the Danske Optioner og Futures (FUTOP Clearing Centre). The index was calculated on a daily basis between July 3, 1989 and December 4, 1989 and on a continuous basis thereafter.

BASE DATE
July 3, 1989=100.00

COMPUTATION METHODOLOGY

An aggregate of prices times quantities index formula. Maintenance adjustments to the divisor are made for capitalization changes, new listings and delistings.

DERIVATIVE INSTRUMENTS

KFX index futures and options registered on the FUTOP Clearing Centre trade on the Copenhagen Stock Exchange.

SUBINDICES
None

RELATED INDICES
Total Share Index of the Copenhagen Stock Exchange

REMARKS
None

PUBLISHER
Copenhagen Stock Exchange (CSE).

TOTAL SHARE INDEX OF THE COPENHAGEN STOCK EXCHANGE (CSE)

PRICE PERFORMANCE

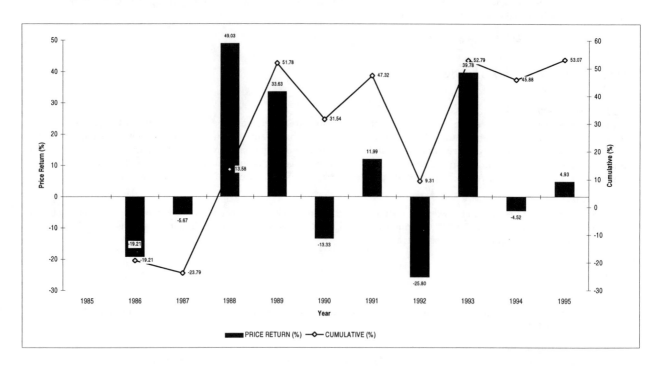

PRICE PERFORMANCE

YEAR	VALUE	PRICE RETURN (%)	CUMULATIVE (%)	MAXIMUM VALUE	DATE	MINIMUM VALUE	DATE
1995	366.30	4.93	53.07	375.44	25-Aug	330.01	29-Mar
1994	349.10	-4.52	45.88	415.79	2-Feb	335.68	20-Dec
1993	365.64	39.78	52.79	367.40	29-Dec	261.90	4-Jan
1992	261.59	-25.80	9.31	365.29	15-Jan	250.42	28-Oct
1991	352.56	11.99	47.32	380.04	2-Aug	302.26	8-Jan
1990	314.80	-13.33	31.54	388.29	20-Jul	310.58	21-Dec
1989	363.22	33.63	51.78	363.22	29-Dec	275.49	27-Feb
1988	271.81	49.03	13.58	271.81	30-Dec	180.69	4-Jan
1987	182.39	-5.67	-23.79	219.76	26-Aug	181.37	8-Dec
1986	193.35	-19.21	-19.21	250.70	18-Apr	186.28	11-Nov
1985	239.31						
Average Annual (%)		7.08					
Compound Annual (%)		4.35					
Standard Deviation (%)		25.92					

SYNOPSIS

The Total Share Index of the Copenhagen Stock Exchange (CSE) is a market value-weighted index that tracks the price only performance of all Danish-based stocks listed on the Copenhagen Stock Exchange (CSE).

NUMBER OF STOCKS—DECEMBER 31, 1995

300

MARKET VALUE—DECEMBER 31, 1995

US$57,193.3 million

SELECTION CRITERIA

The index consists of all domestic companies listed on the CSE, except unit trusts and holding companies, including East Asiatic Holdings and GN Holdings.

Companies with different share classes, i.e., A and B shares, are tracked in the index only once.

BACKGROUND

At the time of its launch on May 1, 1968, the index was limited to a small number of listed stocks. The index was reconstituted twice in the next 15 years. First on January 1, 1973, the index was reconstituted, both as to constituent stocks and subindices, and reset at a value of 100.00. Then, on January 1, 1983, the index was expanded to include all listed companies and the number of subindices was also expanded to five from the previous four. At that time, the value of the index was again reset to 100.00

BASE DATE

January 1, 1983=100.00

COMPUTATION METHODOLOGY

(1) An aggregate of prices times quantities index formula. Maintenance adjustments to the divisor are made daily for capitalization changes, new listings and delistings. Such adjustments take place after trading hours. (2) Bid prices are used to calculate the index, however, these are adjusted for dividends by subtracting 1/360 of the latest paid dividend from the share rate on the first day following the dividend announcement, 2/360 is subtracted on the second day, etc. In the event it is determined that the prospective dividend will differ from the prior period dividend, the calculation is adjusted immediately to reflect the expected or actual dividend.

DERIVATIVE INSTRUMENTS

None

SUBINDICES

Five subindices: Banks, insurance, commerce and service, shipping and industry, and investment trusts.

RELATED INDICES

KFX Index

REMARKS

Danish companies normally pay dividends annually.

PUBLISHER

Copenhagen Stock Exchange (CSE).

FINNISH TRADED STOCK (FOX) INDEX

PRICE PERFORMANCE

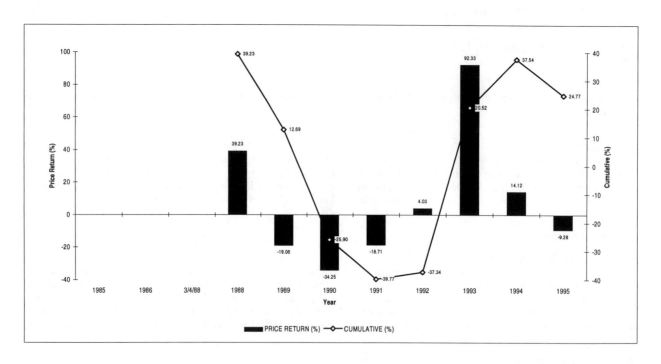

PRICE PERFORMANCE

YEAR	VALUE	PRICE RETURN (%)	CUMULATIVE (%)	MAXIMUM VALUE	DATE	MINIMUM VALUE	DATE
1995	623.87	-9.28	24.77	817.76	14-Sep	563.12	29-Mar
1994	687.68	14.12	37.54	753.24	9-Sep	612.90	3-Jan
1993	602.59	92.33	20.52	622.21	3-Nov	314.92	22-Jan
1992	313.31	4.03	-37.34	361.59	24-Feb	198.31	7-Sep
1991	301.17	-18.71	-39.77	467.40	8-Apr	295.17	23-Dec
1990	370.48	-34.25	-25.90	641.57	6-Feb	357.62	24-Oct
1989	563.46	-19.06	12.69	794.03	17-Apr	541.06	23-Nov
1988	696.16	39.23	39.23	742.38	8-Aug	NA	NA
3/4/88	500.00						
1986							
1985							
Average Annual (%)		8.74					
Compound Annual (%)		2.87					
Standard Deviation (%)		44.20					

SYNOPSIS
The Finnish Traded Stock (FOX) Index is a market value-weighted index that tracks the continuous price only performance of the 25 most actively traded stocks on the Helsinki Stock Exchange.

NUMBER OF STOCKS—DECEMBER 31, 1995
25

MARKET VALUE—DECEMBER 31, 1995
US$23,488.3 million

SELECTION CRITERIA
Index constituents are selected on the basis of median daily trading turnover during the six-month period ending in June and December of each calendar year. The 25 stocks with the highest daily turnover are selected for implementation at the beginning of February and August of each year.

Stocks whose listings can be expected to end during the course of the next six-month period are excluded from consideration.

BACKGROUND
The index was created specifically for the purpose of serving as an underlying vehicle for index futures and options, which commenced trading on May 2, 1988. The index was modified effective with its reconstitution on February 1, 1995 so as to limit the market capitalization of any one company to 20% of the index.

BASE DATE
March 4, 1988=500.00

COMPUTATION METHODOLOGY
(1) An aggregate of prices times quantities index formula. Maintenance adjustments to the divisor are made for capitalization changes, new listings and delistings. (2) For market capitalization calculation purposes, the number of shares outstanding are normally fixed for three months, and updated at the beginning of February, May, August, and November. Market value of constituent shares is limited to 20% of the index. (3) Most recent share prices on the Helsinki Stock Exchange at the time of calculation are used. On expiration date of FOX futures and options, pricing is based on the mean market prices of at least lot-sized deals during continuous trading on the expiration day. When taking the average, the deals are weighted by their volumes.

DERIVATIVE INSTRUMENTS
FOX index futures and options trade on the Finnish Securities and Derivatives Exchange (SOM).

SUBINDICES
None

RELATED INDICES
None

REMARKS
None

PUBLISHER
Finnish Securities and Derivatives Exchange (SOM).

HEX ALL-SHARE PRICE INDEX

PRICE PERFORMANCE

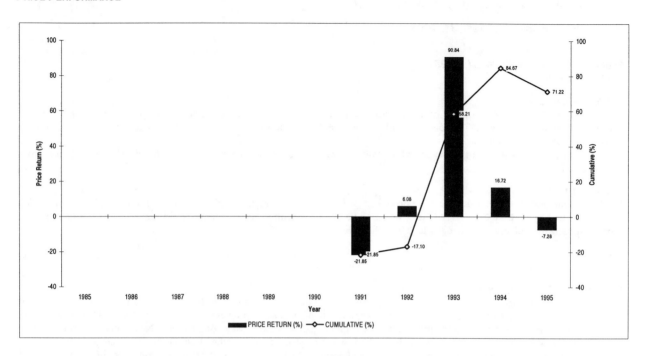

PRICE AND TOTAL RETURN PERFORMANCE

YEAR	VALUE	PRICE RETURN (%)	CUMULATIVE (%)	TOTAL RETURN (%)	MAXIMUM VALUE	DATE	MINIMUM VALUE	DATE
1995	1,712.17	-7.28	71.22	-6.35	2,332.22	14-Sep	1,555.32	29-Mar
1994	1,846.70	16.72	84.67	17.70	1,962.10	3-Feb	1,601.10	3-Jan
1993	1,582.10	90.84	58.21	92.86	1,607.70	3-Nov	843.10	22-Jan
1992	829.00	6.08	-17.10	8.01	935.90	24-Feb	541.00	7-Sep
1991	781.50	-21.85	-21.85	-19.76	1,186.90	8-Apr	765.20	23-Dec
1990	1,000.00							
1989								
1988								
1987								
1986								
1985								
Average Annual (%)		16.90		18.49				
Compound Annual (%)		11.35		13.00				
Standard Deviation (%)		43.79		43.94				

SYNOPSIS
The HEX All-Share Price Index is a market value-weighted index that tracks the continuous price only and total return performance of all stocks, including restricted and unrestricted shares, traded on Finland's Helsinki Stock Exchange.

NUMBER OF STOCKS—DECEMBER 31, 1995
92

MARKET VALUE—DECEMBER 31, 1995
US$43,927.1 million

SELECTION CRITERIA
Constituents include all stocks, including restricted and unrestricted shares, traded on Finland's Helsinki Stock Exchange.

BACKGROUND
The HEX Index and its related indices were introduced on June 1, 1990, with price only index values that have been recalculated on a daily basis to January 1, 1987.

BASE DATE
December 28, 1990=1000.00

COMPUTATION METHODOLOGY
(1) An aggregate of prices times quantities (Paasche) index formula. Maintenance adjustments to the divisor are made for capitalization changes, new listings and delistings. New issues are generally added to the index on the second day of trading while adjustments for bonus issues, subscription issues, etc., are affected either at the time of the first transaction or on the day following payment date. (2) Share prices on the Helsinki Stock Exchange at the time of calculation are used. In the absence of a stock price, the most recently available quotation is used for index computation purposes. (3) Dividends are reinvested as of the ex-dividend date.

DERIVATIVE INSTRUMENTS
None

SUBINDICES
Two main sector subindices: Services and industry.
Seven subsector indices: Banks and finance, insurance and investment, other services, metal and engineering, forest industries, multi-business industry and other industries.

RELATED INDICES
HEX-20 Index
Portfolio HEX Index

REMARKS
None

PUBLISHER
Helsinki Stock Exchange.

CAC-40 (Cotation Automatique Continue) Index

PRICE PERFORMANCE

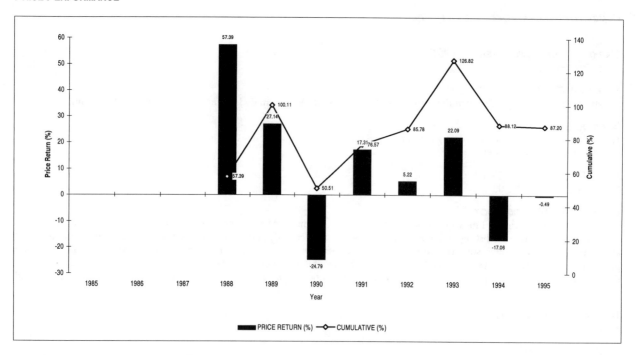

PRICE PERFORMANCE

YEAR	VALUE	PRICE RETURN (%)	CUMULATIVE (%)	MAXIMUM VALUE	DATE	MINIMUM VALUE	DATE
1995	1,871.97	-0.49	87.20	2,017.27	12-May	1,721.14	23-Oct
1994	1,881.15	-17.06	88.12	2,355.93	2-Feb	1,824.42	25-Oct
1993	2,268.22	22.09	126.82	2,281.89	29-Dec	1,772.21	29-Jan
1992	1,857.78	5.22	85.78	2,077.49	11-May	1,611.04	5-Oct
1991	1,765.66	17.31	76.57	1,888.35	23-Sep	1,441.17	14-Jan
1990	1,505.10	-24.79	50.51	2,129.32	20-Apr	1,485.39	25-Sep
1989	2,001.08	27.14	100.11	2,001.08	29-Dec	1,541.01	27-Feb
1988	1,573.94	57.39	57.39	1,573.94	30-Dec	893.82	29-Jan
1987	1,000.00						
1986							
1985							
Average Annual (%)		10.85					
Compound Annual (%)		8.15					
Standard Deviation (%)		26.21					

SYNOPSIS

The CAC-40 (Cotation Automatique Continue) Index is a market value-weighted index that tracks the continuous price only performance of 40 French stocks traded on the Monthly Settlement market (RM) of the Paris Stock Exchange. These shares account for 58% of the domestic equity market.

NUMBER OF STOCKS—DECEMBER 31, 1995

40

MARKET VALUE—DECEMBER 31, 1995

US$291,098.0 million

SELECTION CRITERIA

Constituent companies are selected on the basis of market capitalization and liquidity. Eligible stocks must be among the 100 largest market capitalizations on the Monthly Settlement market and evidence a high level of liquidity as measured by the breadth and depth of the market for each stock based on float, daily trading volume and turnover rates. Equally important, stocks are selected so that the index reflects the full range of companies and industry sectors listed on the Paris Stock Exchange.

BACKGROUND

Launched in June 1988, the CAC-40 is designed to serve as a vehicle for stock index futures and options traded on the Marche a Terme International de France (MATIF) and Marche des Options Negociable de Paris (MONEP).

The index has been recalculated on a daily basis to September 7, 1987.

BASE DATE

December 31, 1987=1000.00

COMPUTATION METHODOLOGY

(1) An aggregate of prices times quantities index formula. Maintenance adjustments to the divisor are made for capitalization changes, new listings and delistings. Adjustments to the base market capitalization are made as warranted as to corporate actions affecting the share capital of component stocks. These include reductions in capital, issuance of bonus shares, cash issues with pre-emptive subscription rights, distributions of assets as well as mergers. (2) Component stocks are reviewed four times each year, but a stock may be eliminated from the index on an earlier date. (3) In the event several types of securities are listed on the Official List or Second Market, only the most actively traded form is considered for inclusion in the index. These are generally ordinary shares. (4) While the index is calculated continuously throughout the trading day, the reference, or official index, is calculated twice daily, at 4 PM when trading on the Paris Stock Exchange floor ends, using floor trading prices, and again at 5 PM when trading ends on the computerized system, using closing prices on the computerized system. The reference index value computed at 5 PM is the base that is used to calculate adjustments following changes in the sample or equity operations affecting component stocks.

DERIVATIVE INSTRUMENTS

CAC-40 index futures and options trade on the Marche a Terme International de France (MATIF) and Marche des Options Negociable de Paris (MONEP).
CAC-40 index short- and long-term options are traded on the MONEP.
CAC-40 index warrants are traded on the European Options Exchange.

SUBINDICES

None

RELATED INDICES

SBF-120 Index
SBF-250 Index
MidCAC Index

REMARKS

The French official list market is made up of two segments, one for cash trading and the other for forward trading on the month-end settlement. Trades on the cash market can be for any quantity while trades on the monthly settlement are for blocks of 5-, 10-, 25-, 50- and 100-shares.

PUBLISHER

The SBF-Bourse de Paris.

MIDCAC INDEX

PRICE PERFORMANCE

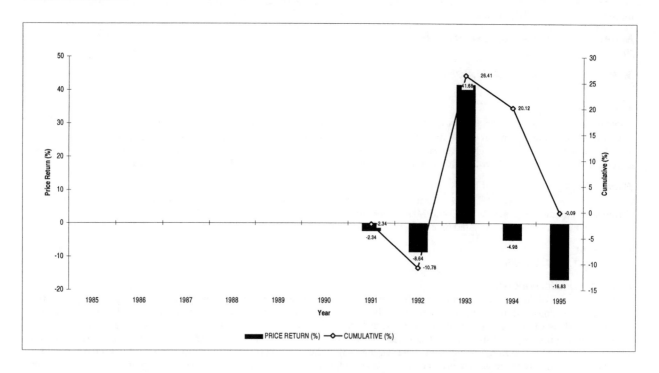

PRICE PERFORMANCE

YEAR	VALUE	PRICE RETURN (%)	CUMULATIVE (%)	MAXIMUM VALUE	DATE	MINIMUM VALUE	DATE
1995	999.06	-16.83	-0.09	1,247.41	6-Jun	957.22	21-Dec
1994	1,201.16	-4.98	20.12	1,450.93	17-Mar	1,195.42	29-Dec
1993	1,264.11	41.68	26.41	1,264.94	31-Dec	886.28	4-Jan
1992	892.25	-8.64	-10.78	1,190.50	25-May	852.59	18-Dec
1991	976.64	-2.34	-2.34	1,188.71	9-Apr	943.76	11-Dec
1990	1,000.00						
1989							
1988							
1987							
1986							
1985							
Average Annual (%)		1.78					
Compound Annual (%)		-0.02					
Standard Deviation (%)		22.96					

SYNOPSIS
The MidCac Index is a market value-weighted index that tracks the price only performance of middle capitalization French stocks traded on the Official List and Second Market of the Paris Stock Exchange. These shares account for 2.8% of the domestic equity market.

NUMBER OF STOCKS—DECEMBER 31, 1995
100

MARKET VALUE—DECEMBER 31, 1995
US$14,055.8 million

SELECTION CRITERIA
Constituent shares, which exclude the 20 highest and 20 lowest capitalization stocks, less frequently traded issues (issues with a trading ratio below 70%) and financial and property companies, are selected on the basis of daily trading value, number of trades and turnover. The universe of eligible Official List and Second Market securities is ranked by capitalization and arrayed into six classes, each of which contains 16.7% of the total number of companies. From this universe, 100 issues are selected in such a way so as to reproduce the equal-weighting of the market capitalization of the six classes, with the most liquid securities in each class given the highest priority.

BACKGROUND
The MIDCAC was introduced in 1995.

BASE DATE
December 31, 1990=1000.00

COMPUTATION METHODOLOGY
(1) An aggregate of prices times quantities index formula. Maintenance adjustments to the divisor are made for capitalization changes, new listings and delistings. Adjustments to the base market capitalization are made as warranted as to corporate actions affecting the share capital of component stocks. These include reductions in capital, issuance of bonus shares, cash issues with pre-emptive subscription rights, distributions of assets as well as mergers. (2) Component stocks are reviewed once each year, however, at the end of each quarter stocks that have been delisted or merged are replaced by the company ranked immediately below in the same economic sector. (3) In the event several types of securities are listed on the Official List or Second Market, only the most actively traded form is considered for inclusion in the index. These are generally ordinary shares. (4) The index is calculated on the basis of opening and closing prices.

DERIVATIVE INSTRUMENTS
None

SUBINDICES
None

RELATED INDICES
CAC-40 Index
SBF-120 Index
SBF-250 Index

REMARKS
Liquidity is measured using median daily trading value, daily number of trades and daily turnover over a prior 12-month period. The three measures are averaged together and each stock's composite rating is used to rank stocks in descending order.

PUBLISHER
The SBF-Bourse de Paris.

SBF-120 INDEX

PRICE PERFORMANCE

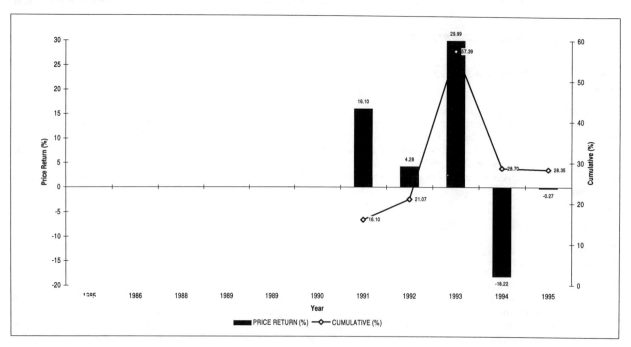

PRICE PERFORMANCE

YEAR	VALUE	PRICE RETURN (%)	CUMULATIVE (%)	MAXIMUM VALUE	DATE	MINIMUM VALUE	DATE
1995	1,283.50	-0.27	28.35	1,374.52	12-May	1,187.74	13-Mar
1994	1,287.03	-18.22	28.70	1,649.57	2-Feb	1,263.75	25-Oct
1993	1,573.85	29.99	57.39	1,580.51	30-Dec	1,180.38	13-Jan
1992	1,210.71	4.28	21.07	1,376.89	11-May	1,068.57	6-Oct
1991	1,160.97	16.10	16.10	1,239.31	23-Sep	952.35	14-Jan
1990	1,000.00						
1989							
1988							
1989							
1986							
1985							
Average Annual (%)		6.38					
Compound Annual (%)		5.12					
Standard Deviation (%)		18.07					

SYNOPSIS

The SBF-120 Index is a market value-weighted index that tracks the continuous price only performance of 120 of actively trade large capitalization French stocks traded on the cash or forward trading segments of the Paris Stock Exchange. These shares account for 80% of the domestic equity market.

NUMBER OF STOCKS—DECEMBER 31, 1995

120

MARKET VALUE—DECEMBER 31, 1995

US$400,692.6 million

SELECTION CRITERIA

Constituent companies are selected on the basis of value of daily trading, volume of daily trading activity, turnover and liquidity or spread expressed as a percentage of bid/asked prices. Eligible stocks are selected from among the 200 largest market capitalizations and rank in the top 150 companies on the basis of trading value, number of trades, daily turnover and spread using the 12 months prior to each quarterly review.

All stocks are ranked in descending order based on the first three criteria and in ascending order based on the fourth. Average rankings are established, and the top 150 ranked stocks are retained. The remaining stocks are ranked on the basis of market capitalization and this universe is used for selecting the 120 index constituents.

Holding companies, whose main asset is a controlling stake in a company already in the sample, are excluded from consideration.

BACKGROUND

The SBF-120 Index was launched in 1993.

BASE DATE

December 31, 1990=1000.00

COMPUTATION METHODOLOGY

(1) An aggregate of prices times quantities index formula. Maintenance adjustments to the divisor are made for capitalization changes, new listings and delistings. Adjustments to the base market capitalization are made as warranted as to corporate actions affecting the share capital of component stocks. These include reductions in capital, issuance of bonus shares, cash issues with pre-emptive subscription rights, distributions of assets as well as mergers. (2) Component stocks are reviewed four times each year, but a stock may be eliminated from the index on an earlier date. (3) In the event several types of securities are listed on the Official List or Second Market, only the most actively traded form is considered for inclusion in the index. These are generally ordinary shares. (4) While the index is calculated continuously throughout the trading day, the reference, or official index, is calculated twice daily, at 4 PM when trading on the Paris Stock Exchange floor ends, using floor trading prices, and again at 5 PM when trading ends on the computerized system, using closing prices on the computerized system. The reference index value computed at 5 PM is the base that is used to calculate adjustments following changes in the sample or equity operations affecting component stocks.

DERIVATIVE INSTRUMENTS

None

SUBINDICES

None

RELATED INDICES

CAC-40 Index
SBF-250 Index
MidCAC Index

REMARKS

The CAC-40 Index is interconnected with the SBF-120 Index such that the SBF-120 Index automatically includes all CAC-40 component stocks.

PUBLISHER

The SBF-Bourse de Paris.

SBF-250 INDEX

PRICE PERFORMANCE

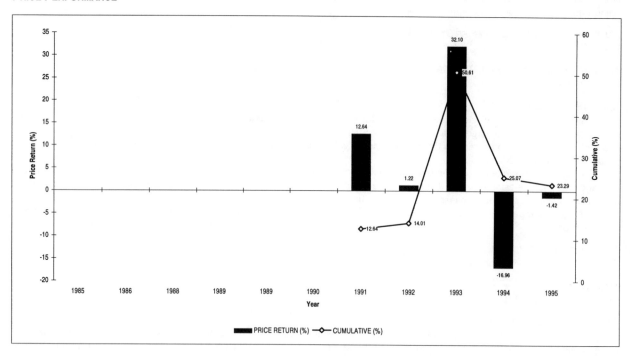

PRICE PERFORMANCE

YEAR	VALUE	PRICE RETURN (%)	CUMULATIVE (%)	MAXIMUM VALUE	DATE	MINIMUM VALUE	DATE
1995	1,232.86	-1.42	23.29	1,322.30	12-May	1,154.41	13-Mar
1994	1,250.66	-16.96	25.07	1,585.20	2-Feb	1,227.86	25-Oct
1993	1,506.09	32.10	50.61	1,510.72	30-Dec	1,116.66	13-Jan
1992	1,140.14	1.22	14.01	1,305.29	11-May	1,027.11	6-Oct
1991	1,126.41	12.64	12.64	1,192.47	1-Oct	950.59	14-Jan
1990	1,000.00						
1989							
1988							
1989							
1986							
1985							
Average Annual (%)		5.51					
Compound Annual (%)		4.28					
Standard Deviation (%)		18.23					

SYNOPSIS

The SBF-250 Index is a market value-weighted index that tracks the price only performance of 250 French stocks listed on the Official List or Second Market segments of the Paris Stock Exchange. These shares account for 94% of the domestic equity market.

NUMBER OF STOCKS—DECEMBER 31, 1995

250

MARKET VALUE—DECEMBER 31, 1995

US$465,675.3 million

SELECTION CRITERIA

Prime consideration in the selection of constituent companies is to replicate the market capitalization of the 12 economic sectors that characterize the structure of economic activity in France, as represented by the sum total of the companies listed on the Paris Stock Exchange. To this end, stocks are ranked by market capitalization is descending order within each sector at the end of each year. Stocks selected within each sector are intended to mirror the identical percentage of its respective sector's market capitalization currently over 90%.

BACKGROUND

Launched in 1993, the SBF-250 Index replaced the CAC General and the INSEE weekly indices, but continues the statistical series generated by these predecessor indices.

BASE DATE

December 31, 1990=1000.00

COMPUTATION METHODOLOGY

(1) An aggregate of prices times quantities index formula. Maintenance adjustments to the divisor are made for capitalization changes, new listings and delistings. Adjustments to the base market capitalization are made as warranted as to corporate actions affecting the share capital of component stocks. These include reductions in capital, issuance of bonus shares, cash issues with pre-emptive subscription rights, distributions of assets as well as mergers. (2) Component stocks are reviewed once each year, however, at the end of each quarter stocks that have been delisted or merged are replaced by the company ranked immediately below in the same economic sector. (3) In the event several types of securities are listed on the Official List or Second Market, only the most actively traded form is considered for inclusion in the index. These are generally ordinary shares. (4) The index is calculated twice a day, on the basis of opening and closing prices.

DERIVATIVE INSTRUMENTS

None

SUBINDICES

Three broad sector subindices: Industrials, services and financials.
Twelve sectoral subindices: Energy, intermediate goods, construction, capital goods, automotive, other consumer goods, food, distribution, other services, property, financial services and investment companies.

RELATED INDICES

CAC-40 Index
CAC-120 Index
MidCAC Index

REMARKS

The CAC-40 and SBF-120 Index are interconnected with the SBF-250 Index such that the SBF-120 Index automatically includes all CAC-40 component stocks and the SBF-250 Index automatically includes all CAC-40 and SBF-120 component stocks .

PUBLISHER

The SBF-Bourse de Paris.

COMMERZBANK SHARE INDEX

PRICE PERFORMANCE

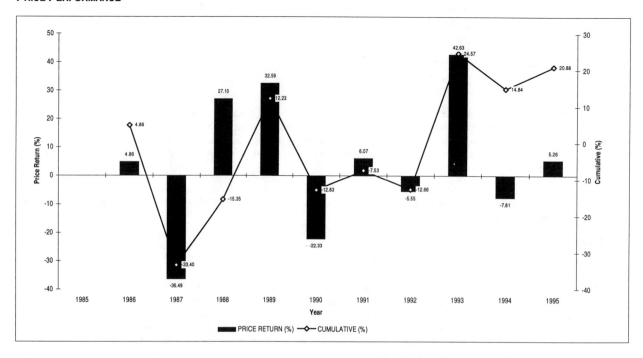

PRICE PERFORMANCE

YEAR	VALUE	PRICE RETURN (%)	CUMULATIVE (%)	MAXIMUM VALUE	DATE	MINIMUM VALUE	DATE
1995	2,358.90	5.26	20.88	2,427.60	19-Sep	2,018.70	30-Mar
1994	2,241.10	-7.81	14.84	2,465.50	2-May	2,116.30	5-Oct
1993	2,431.00	42.63	24.57	2,442.40	27-Dec	1,694.30	14-Jan
1992	1,704.40	-5.55	-12.66	2,043.80	25-May	1,594.60	11-Oct
1991	1,804.50	6.07	-7.53	2,035.20	15-Jan	1,612.50	28-Jan
1990	1,701.20	-22.33	-12.83	2,414.00	3-Apr	1,628.70	28-Sep
1989	2,190.20	32.59	12.23	2,190.20	28-Dec	1,595.70	27-Feb
1988	1,651.90	27.10	-15.35	1,664.30	27-Dec	1,207.90	29-Jan
1987	1,299.70	-36.49	-33.40	2,061.10	17-Aug	1,220.90	10-Nov
1986	2,046.40	4.86	4.86	2,278.80	17-Apr	1,762.40	22-Jul
1985	1,951.50						
Average Annual (%)		4.63					
Compound Annual (%)		1.91					
Standard Deviation (%)		18.75					

SYNOPSIS

The Commerzbank Share Index is a market value-weighted index that tracks the daily price only performance of a selected number of actively traded blue chip German stocks from all areas of trade and industry that are traded on the German stock exchanges. These shares account for about 70% of the aggregate market value of all domestic German shares trading on main and parallel markets.

NUMBER OF STOCKS—DECEMBER 31, 1995

78

MARKET VALUE—DECEMBER 31, 1995

US$403,686.9 million

SELECTION CRITERIA

Constituent securities consist of large capitalization stocks with broad marketability that are selected from all sectors of industry, trade and finance.

Closely held companies are excluded from consideration.

BACKGROUND

The Commerzbank Share Index is the oldest German share index computed on each trading day. Until 1988, the index was calculated on the basis of the mid-session stock prices quoted on the Dusseldorf stock exchange. Since September 1988, however, Frankfurt mid-session prices have been used.

BASE DATE

December 31, 1953=100.00

COMPUTATION METHODOLOGY

An aggregate of prices times quantities index formula. Maintenance adjustments to the divisor are made for capitalization changes, new listings and delistings.

DERIVATIVE INSTRUMENTS

None

SUBINDICES

Twelve sector indices: Major chemicals, other chemicals, electricals/electronics, energy, steel/non-ferrous metals, mechanical engineering, vehicle construction, construction/cement, retail trade, banks, insurance companies and consumer goods/services.

RELATED INDICES

None

REMARKS

None

PUBLISHER

Commerzbank AG.

COMPOSITE DAX PERFORMANCE INDEX

TOTAL RETURN PERFORMANCE

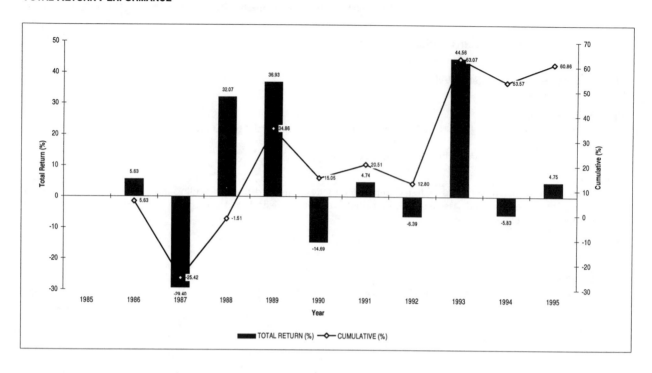

TOTAL RETURN PERFORMANCE[1]

YEAR	VALUE	TOTAL RETURN (%)	CUMULATIVE (%)	MAXIMUM VALUE	DATE	MINIMUM VALUE	DATE
1995	215.70	4.75	60.86	223.78	15-Sep	187.85	28-Mar
1994	205.92	-5.83	53.57	221.73	16-May	195.04	6-Oct
1993	218.66	44.56	63.07	218.66	30-Dec	150.47	14-Jan
1992	151.26	-6.39	12.80	182.02	26-May	142.60	12-Oct
1991	161.59	4.74	20.51	180.30	24-Jun	144.96	16-Jan
1990	154.27	-14.69	15.05	207.31	19-Jul	146.83	28-Sep
1989	180.84	36.93	34.86	180.84	28-Dec	131.36	27-Feb
1988	132.07	32.07	-1.51	132.45	27-Dec	94.02	29-Jan
1987	100.00	-29.40	-25.42	142.40	17-Aug	97.27	10-Nov
1986	141.64	5.63	5.63	152.57	17-Apr	126.04	22-Jul
1985	134.09						
Average Annual (%)		7.24					
Compound Annual (%)		4.87					
Standard Deviation (%)		23.77					

[1]Index was unweighted through 12/31/87.

SYNOPSIS
The Composite DAX Performance Index is a market value-weighted index that tracks the continuous total return performance of all German stocks listed in the official market of the Frankfurt Stock Exchange. These shares account for 92% of the aggregate market value of all domestic German shares trading on the main and parallel markets.

NUMBER OF STOCKS—DECEMBER 31, 1995
347

MARKET VALUE—DECEMBER 31, 1995
US$527,475.6 million

SELECTION CRITERIA
All German stocks listed in the official market of the Frankfurt Stock Exchange

BACKGROUND
The index was retroactively linked to the daily time series of the FWB Index back to January 1, 1970. Values for the sectoral subindices are available since 1974.

BASE DATE
December 31, 1987=100.00

COMPUTATION METHODOLOGY
(1) An aggregate of prices times quantities index formula. Maintenance adjustments to the divisor are made daily for capitalization changes, new listings and delistings. The actual number of shares used to calculate current market capitalization is based on the number of shares listed and declared to be deliverable as of the latest adjustment date. That is, for the 1994-1995 period, the adjustment date was September 16, 1994. (2) Market capitalization is determined on the basis of the listed capital of all share categories, but only the price of ordinary shares is used in the calculation. In the event only preference shares are listed, the preference share price is used. (3) Gross paid dividends are reinvested on the ex-date. Initially, the cash dividend is reinvested arithmetically in the stock. This approach, however, results in an adjustment to the stocks' capital, which is in turn adjusted once a year, on the annual adjustment date, back to actual capital. (4) Frankfurt Stock Exchange prices apply. In the absence of a stock price, the most recently available quotation is used for computation purposes.

DERIVATIVE INSTRUMENTS
None

SUBINDICES
Sixteen industry sectors: Automobiles, construction, chemicals, investment companies, electrical, breweries, mortgage banks, banks, transportation, machinery, paper, utilities, steel, textiles, insurance and retail.

RELATED INDICES
DAX 100 Index
DAX Performance Index
German Bond Index (REX)
Mid Cap DAX (MDAX)

REMARKS
None

PUBLISHER
Deutsche Borse AG.

DAX 100 PERFORMANCE INDEX

TOTAL RETURN PERFORMANCE

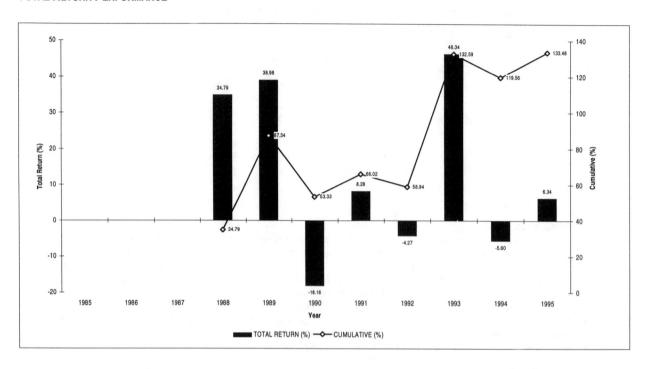

TOTAL RETURN PERFORMANCE

YEAR	VALUE	TOTAL RETURN (%)	CUMULATIVE (%)	MAXIMUM VALUE[1]	DATE	MINIMUM VALUE[1]	DATE
1995	1,167.41	6.34	133.48	1,212.36	15-Sep	994.36	28-Mar
1994	1,097.80	-5.60	119.56	1,166.68	30-Apr	1,062.87	30-Jun
1993	1,162.94	46.34	132.59	1,162.94	31-Dec	809.55	31-Jan
1992	794.70	-4.27	58.94	943.00	31-May	761.67	30-Sep
1991	830.11	8.28	66.02	911.87	31-May	766.89	31-Jan
1990	766.64	-18.16	53.33	1,045.14	31-Mar	727.67	30-Sep
1989	936.71	38.98	87.34	936.71	31-Dec	664.61	28-Feb
1988	673.97	34.79	34.79	673.97	31-Dec	466.64	31-Jan
1987	500.00						
1986							
1985							
Average Annual (%)		13.34					
Compound Annual (%)		11.18					
Standard Deviation (%)		23.73					

[1]Maximum/minimum index values for the period 1988-1994 are as of month-end.

SYNOPSIS
The DAX 100 Performance Index is a market value-weighted index that tracks the continuous total return performance of the 100 most actively traded, large market capitalization German companies traded on the Frankfurt Stock Exchange. These shares account for 78% of the aggregate market value of all domestic German shares trading on the main and parallel markets.

NUMBER OF STOCKS—DECEMBER 31, 1995
100

MARKET VALUE—DECEMBER 31, 1995
US$448,337.4 million

SELECTION CRITERIA
Constituent companies are selected on the basis of stock exchange turnover and market capitalization.

Constituent companies are selected with an emphasis on high free float to ensure the capital of index constituents is actually tradable in the market. In this connection, cross-holdings are taken into consideration.

The composition of the index is monitored once a year to ensure that it continues to mirror the German equity market. Adjustments, if any, are made as of the first Friday after the 14th of September. Strictly defined rules for additions or deletions except in the case of mergers, bankruptcies, takeovers, etc., however, have not been established in an effort to retain flexibility.

BACKGROUND
None

BASE DATE
Dcember 31, 1987=500.00

COMPUTATION METHODOLOGY
(1) An aggregate of prices times quantities index formula. Maintenance adjustments to the divisor are made daily for capitalization changes, new listings and delistings. The actual number of shares used to calculate current market capitalization is based on the number of shares listed and declared to be deliverable as of the latest adjustment date. That is, for the 1994-1995 period, the adjustment date was September 16, 1994. (2) Market capitalization is determined on the basis of the listed capital of all share categories, but only the price of ordinary shares is used in the calculation. In the event only preference shares are listed, the preference share price is used. (3) Gross paid dividends are reinvested on the ex-date. Initially, the cash dividend is reinvested arithmetically in the stock. This approach, however, results in an adjustment to the stocks capital, which is in turn adjusted once a year, on the annual adjustment date, back to actual capital. (4) Frankfurt Stock Exchange prices apply. In the absence of a stock price, the most recently available quotation is used for computation purposes.

DERIVATIVE INSTRUMENTS
None

SUBINDICES
None

RELATED INDICES
Composite DAX (CDAX)
DAX Performance Index
German Bond Index (REX) Index
Mid Cap DAX (MDAX)

REMARKS
None

PUBLISHER
Deutsche Borse AG.

DAX PERFORMANCE INDEX (DEUTCHER AKTIENINDEX)

TOTAL RETURN PERFORMANCE

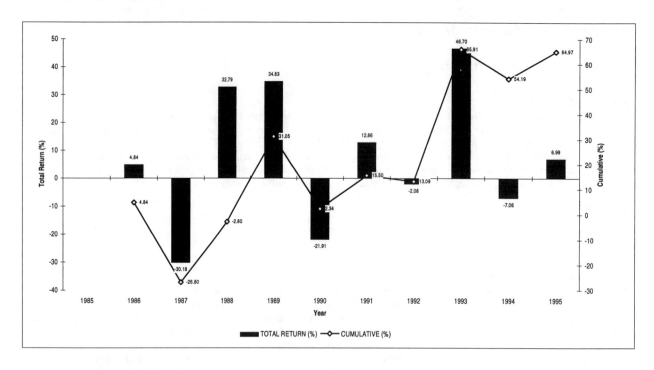

TOTAL RETURN PERFORMANCE[1]

YEAR	VALUE	TOTAL RETURN (%)	CUMULATIVE (%)	MAXIMUM VALUE	DATE	MINIMUM VALUE	DATE
1995	2,253.88	6.99	64.97	2,317.01	15-Sep	1,910.96	Mar-38
1994	2,106.60	-7.06	54.19	2,271.11	16-May	1,960.59	7-Oct
1993	2,266.70	46.70	65.91	2,266.70	30-Dec	1,516.50	13-Jan
1992	1,545.10	-2.08	13.09	1,811.57	25-May	1,420.30	6-Oct
1991	1,578.00	12.86	15.50	1,715.80	11-Jun	1,322.68	16-Jan
1990	1,398.20	-21.91	2.34	1,976.40	30-Mar	1,320.40	28-Sep
1989	1,790.40	34.83	31.05	1,805.00	28-Dec	1,268.70	27-Feb
1988	1,327.90	32.79	-2.80	1,343.80	27-Dec	931.20	28-Jan
1987	1,000.00	-30.18	-26.80	1,571.19	17-Aug	942.50	10-Nov
1986	1,432.30	4.84	4.84	1,594.60	17-Apr	1,244.30	22-Jul
1985	1,366.20						
Average Annual (%)		7.78					
Compound Annual (%)		5.13					
Standard Deviation (%)		24.83					

[1]Index was unweighted through 12/31/87.

SYNOPSIS
The DAX Performance Index (Deutchen Aktienindex) is a market value-weighted index that tracks the continuous total return performance of 30 actively traded, large market capitalization of ordinary and preference shares of German companies traded on the Frankfurt Stock Exchange. These shares account for 61% of the aggregate market value of all domestic German shares trading on the main and parallel markets.

NUMBER OF STOCKS—DECEMBER 31, 1995
30

MARKET VALUE—DECEMBER 31, 1995
US$349,510.85 million

SELECTION CRITERIA
Selection criteria for constituent companies, both ordinary and preference shares, include stock exchange turnover, market capitalization and early availability of opening prices.

Component stocks are selected to reflect the sectoral composition of the German equity market. Emphasis is also on high free float to ensure the capital of index constituents is actually tradable in the market. In this connection, cross-holdings are taken into consideration.

The composition of the index is monitored once a year to ensure that it continues to mirror the German equity market. Adjustments, if any, are made as of the first Friday after the 14th of September. Strictly defined rules for additions or deletions except in the case of mergers, bankruptcies, takeovers, etc., however, have not been established in an effort to retain flexibility.

BACKGROUND
Launched on July 1, 1988, the DAX was designed to mirror the German equity market to serve as an underlying vehicle for stock index futures and options, and to facilitate, through its calculation methodology, replication at lower transaction costs.

Daily index values have been recalculated to January 1, 1980. The DAX Index was linked to the Borsen-Zeitung Index (previously known as the Hardy Index) so that its time series extends back to September 1959. The Borsen-Zeitung Index, which was also comprised of 30 stocks and unweighted and calculated on a total return basis, was discontinued on that date.

BASE DATE
December 31, 1987=1000.00

COMPUTATION METHODOLOGY
(1) An aggregate of prices times quantities index formula. Maintenance adjustments to the divisor are made daily for capitalization changes, new listings and delistings. The actual number of shares used to calculate current market capitalization is based on the number of shares listed and declared to be deliverable as of the latest adjustment date. That is, for the 1994-1995 period, the adjustment date was September 16, 1994. (2) Market capitalization is determined on the basis of the listed capital of all share categories, but only the price of ordinary shares is used in the calculation. In the event only preference shares are listed, the preference share price is used. (3) Gross paid dividends are reinvested on the ex-date. Initially, the cash dividend is reinvested arithmetically in the stock. This approach, however, results in an adjustment to the stocks capital, which is in turn adjusted once a year, on the annual adjustment date, back to actual capital. (4) Frankfurt Stock Exchange prices apply. In the absence of a stock price, the most recently available quotation is used for computation purposes.

DERIVATIVE INSTRUMENTS
DAX index futures and options trade on the Deutsche Terminborse (DTB).
DAX index warrants trade on the European Options Exchange.

SUBINDICES
None

RELATED INDICES
Composite DAX (CDAX)
DAX 100 Index
German Bond Index (REX)
Mid Cap DAX (MDAX)

REMARKS
None

PUBLISHER
Deutshe Borse AG.

MID CAP DAX (MDAX) PERFORMANCE INDEX

TOTAL RETURN PERFORMANCE

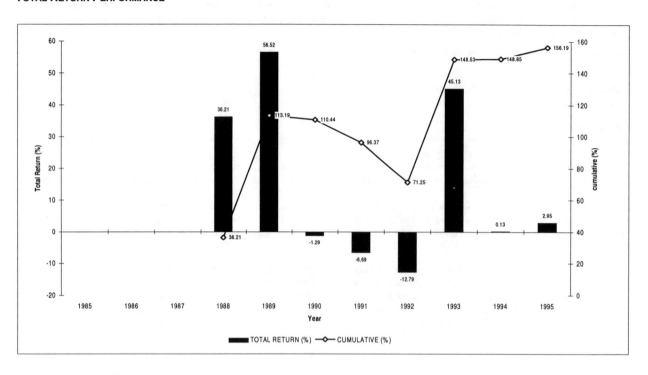

TOTAL RETURN PERFORMANCE

YEAR	VALUE	TOTAL RETURN (%)	CUMULATIVE (%)	MAXIMUM VALUE[1]	DATE	MINIMUM VALUE[1]	DATE
1995	2,561.90	2.95	156.19	2,727.10	31-Jul	2,236.30	31-Mar
1994	2,488.50	0.13	148.85	2,621.20	31-Aug	2,442.50	30-Nov
1993	2,485.30	45.13	148.53	2,485.30	31-Dec	1,753.60	31-Jan
1992	1,712.50	-12.79	71.25	2,189.20	28-Feb	1,705.50	30-Sep
1991	1,963.70	-6.69	96.37	2,294.80	31-May	1,963.70	31-Dec
1990	2,104.40	-1.29	110.44	2,724.10	31-Jul	1,958.00	30-Sep
1989	2,131.90	56.52	113.19	2,131.90	31-Dec	1,448.80	28-Feb
1988	1,362.10	36.21	36.21	1,362.10	31-Dec	914.50	31-Jan
1987	1,000.00						
1986							
1985							
Average Annual (%)		15.02					
Compound Annual (%)		12.48					
Standard Deviation (%)		26.61					

[1]Maximum/minimum index values are as of month-end.

SYNOPSIS

The Mid Cap (MDAX) Performance Index is a market value-weighted index that tracks the continuous total return performance of 70 actively traded, middle sized German companies whose ordinary and preference shares are traded on the Frankfurt Stock Exchange. These shares account for 17.2% of the aggregate market value of all domestic German shares trading on the main and parallel markets..

NUMBER OF STOCKS—DECEMBER 31, 1995
70

MARKET VALUE—DECEMBER 31, 1995
US$98,826.6 million

SELECTION CRITERIA

Selection criteria for constituent companies, both ordinary and preference shares, include stock exchange turnover and market capitalization.

BACKGROUND

The index, which was launched January 19, 1996, has been recalculated to December 30, 1987.

BASE DATE

December 31, 1987=1000.00

COMPUTATION METHODOLOGY

(1) An aggregate of prices times quantities index formula. Maintenance adjustments to the divisor are made daily for capitalization changes, new listings and delistings. The actual number of shares used to calculate current market capitalization is based on the number of shares listed and declared to be deliverable as of the latest adjustment date, which takes place annually. (2) Market capitalization is determined on the basis of the listed capital of all share categories, but only the price of ordinary shares is used in the calculation. In the event only preference shares are listed, the preference share price is used. (3) The weighting of each individual stock is limited to 10% of the index. (4) Gross paid dividends are reinvested on the ex-date. Initially, the cash dividend is reinvested arithmetically in the stock. This approach, however, results in an adjustment to the stocks capital, which is in turn adjusted once a year, on the annual adjustment date, back to actual capital. (5) The index is calculated based on IBIS prices and Frankfurt Stock Exchange prices. In addition, the index is calculated once a day using Kassa prices.

DERIVATIVE INSTRUMENTS
None

SUBINDICES
None

RELATED INDICES
Composite DAX (CDAX)
DAX 100 Index
DAX Performance Index
German Bond Index (REX) Index

REMARKS
None

PUBLISHER
Deutshe Borse AG.

ATHENS STOCK EXCHANGE (ASE) COMPOSITE SHARE INDEX

PRICE PERFORMANCE

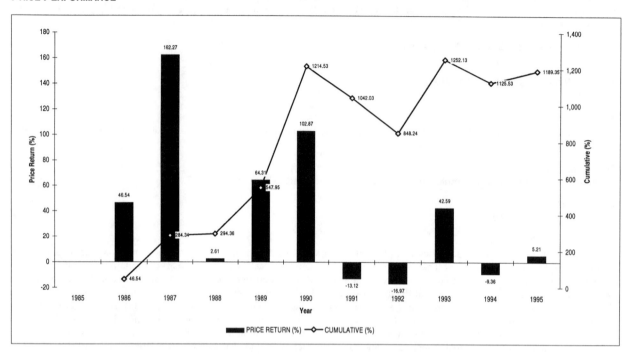

PRICE PERFORMANCE

YEAR	VALUE	PRICE RETURN (%)	CUMULATIVE (%)	MAXIMUM VALUE	DATE	MINIMUM VALUE	DATE
1995	914.15	5.21	1,189.35	992.59	4-Aug	787.15	16-Mar
1994	868.90	-9.36	1,125.53	1,194.58	18-Jan	804.37	22-Nov
1993	958.66	42.59	1,252.13	958.66	31-Dec	667.72	5-Jan
1992	672.30	-16.97	848.24	NA	NA	NA	NA
1991	809.70	-13.12	1,042.03	NA	NA	NA	NA
1990	932.00	102.87	1,214.53	NA	NA	NA	NA
1989	459.40	64.31	547.95	NA	NA	NA	NA
1988	279.60	2.61	294.36	NA	NA	NA	NA
1987	272.50	162.27	284.34	NA	NA	NA	NA
1986	103.90	46.54	46.54	NA	NA	NA	NA
1985	70.90						
Average Annual (%)		38.69					
Compound Annual (%)		29.13					
Standard Deviation (%)		58.35					

SYNOPSIS
The Athens Stock Exchange (ASE) Composite Share Index is a market value-weighted index that tracks the stock price performance of 65 actively traded, large capitalization stocks, listed on the Athens Stock Exchange.

NUMBER OF STOCKS—DECEMBER 31, 1995
65

MARKET VALUE—JULY 4, 1995
US$10,730.85 million

SELECTION CRITERIA
Component stocks are selected on the basis of market capitalization and value of transactions. Selections are reviewed from time to time to ensure that the index continues to represent the market as a whole, although revisions are not made at regular intervals.

Market capitalization and value of transactions data for the six-month period between March 1, 1994 and August 31, 1994 were used as the basis for the initial selection of 65 index constituents.

BACKGROUND
The ASE has been tracking the performance of listed shares since 1955. The present form of the index was introduced on October 3, 1994 in an effort to more properly reflect share price movements with the least number of constituent shares. Previous indices were established with base values of December 31, 1964 and December 31, 1954, respectively.

BASE DATE
December 31, 1980=100.00

COMPUTATION METHODOLOGY
An aggregate of prices times quantities index formula. Maintenance adjustments to the divisor are made for capitalization changes, new listings and delistings.

DERIVATIVE INSTRUMENTS
None

SUBINDICES
Eight sectoral subindices: Banks, insurance companies, leasing corporations, investment corporations, industrial corporations, construction companies, holding companies and commercial and miscellaneous companies.

RELATED INDICES
None

REMARKS
Market value was calculated using the December 31, 1995 exchange rate applied against the market value of constituent securities as of July 4, 1995.

PUBLISHER
The Athens Stock Exchange (ASE).

BUDAPEST STOCK INDEX (BUX)

PRICE PERFORMANCE

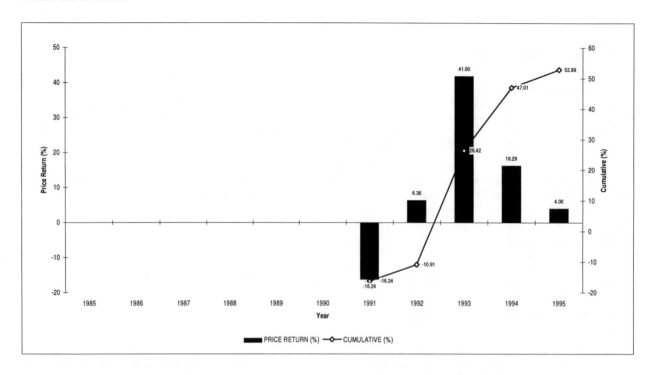

PRICE PERFORMANCE

YEAR	VALUE	PRICE RETURN (%)	CUMULATIVE (%)	MAXIMUM VALUE	DATE	MINIMUM VALUE	DATE
1995	1,528.92	4.00	52.89	1,629.40	25-Sep	1,159.45	31-Jan
1994	1,470.10	16.29	47.01	2,004.73	31-Jan	1,265.21	6-Jan
1993	1,264.15	41.90	26.42	1,307.12	29-Dec	717.75	14-May
1992	890.90	6.36	-10.91	988.42	16-May	830.62	20-Feb
1991	837.60	-16.24	-16.24	1,191.64	2-May	797.69	11-Dec
1990	1,000.00						
1989							
1988							
1987							
1986							
1985							
Average Annual (%)		10.46					
Compound Annual (%)		8.86					
Standard Deviation (%)		21.18					

SYNOPSIS

The BUX Index is a market value-weighted index that tracks the daily price only performance of large, actively traded, shares on the Budapest Stock Exchange of Hungary. These shares account for 58% of the domestic equity market capitalization.

NUMBER OF STOCKS—DECEMBER 31, 1995

21

MARKET VALUE—DECEMBER 31, 1995

US$1,352.7 million

SELECTION CRITERIA

Constituent shares are limited to 25 issues, selected on the basis of the following factors: (1) Face value of issue; (2) Price; (3) Value of transactions; (4) turnover.

Eligibility for inclusion requires that a stock satisfy at least three of these requirements. In the event that more than 25 issues satisfy at least three of these requirements, each factor is weighted and ranked. The 25 stocks with the maximum composite weights are selected for inclusion in the index.

BACKGROUND

The index was adopted as the official index of the Budapest Stock Exchange as of January 1, 1995. Previously, it served as an unofficial benchmark.

The BUX Index tracked six companies at its inception and has since been expanded five times to the present number of issues.

BASE DATE

January 2, 1991=1000.00

COMPUTATION METHODOLOGY

(1) An aggregate of prices times quantities index formula. Maintenance adjustments to the divisor are made for capitalization changes, new listings and delistings. (2) The index is reviewed and updated twice a year, on March 31st and September 30th.

DERIVATIVE INSTRUMENTS

None

SUBINDICES

None

RELATED INDICES

Central European Stock Index

REMARKS

None

PUBLISHER

The Budapest Stock Exchange.

ICELAND STOCK EXCHANGE INDEX (ICEX)

PRICE PERFORMANCE

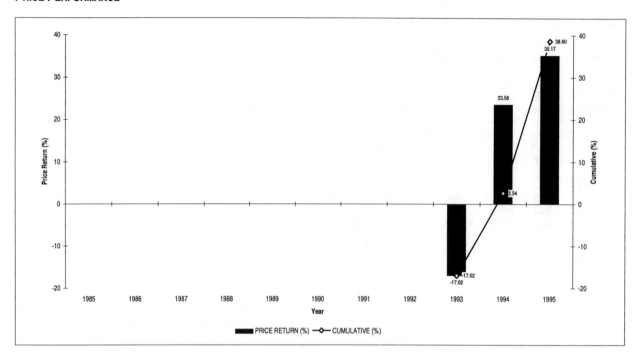

PRICE AND TOTAL RETURN PERFORMANCE

YEAR	VALUE	PRICE RETURN (%)	CUMULATIVE (%)	TOTAL RETURN (%)	MAXIMUM VALUE	DATE	MINIMUM VALUE	DATE
1995	1,386.00	35.17	38.60	39.06	1,386.00	29-Dec	997.70	12-Jan
1994	1,025.40	23.56	2.54	27.10	1,038.20	8-Dec	797.20	6-Apr
1993	829.85	-17.02	-17.02	-14.50	1,004.13	4-Jan	773.57	1-Jun
1992	1,000.00							
1991								
1990								
1989								
1988								
1987								
1986								
1985								
Average Annual (%)		13.91		17.22				
Compound Annual (%)		11.49		14.75				
Standard Deviation (%)		27.40		28.11				

SYNOPSIS
The Iceland Stock Exchange Index (ICEX) is a market value-weighted index that tracks the daily price only and total return performance of all domestic shares listed on the Securities Exchange of Iceland.

NUMBER OF STOCKS—DECEMBER 31, 1995
27

MARKET VALUE—DECEMBER 31, 1995
US$720.99 million

SELECTION CRITERIA
The index includes all shares listed on Securities Exchange of Iceland.

BACKGROUND
The index was launched in February 1994 and recalculated to 1993.

BASE DATE
January 1, 1993=1000.00

COMPUTATION METHODOLOGY
(1) An aggregate of prices times quantities index formula. Maintenance adjustments to the divisor are made for capitalization changes, new listings and delistings. (2) Share prices are the daily closing prices, unless bid/asked prices are higher or lower than the closing prices, in which case the higher or lower prices are used in the calculation of the index.

DERIVATIVE INSTRUMENTS
None

SUBINDICES
None

RELATED INDICES
None

REMARKS
None

PUBLISHER
Iceland Stock Exchange.

Irish Stock Exchange Equity Price (ISEQ) Index

Price Performance

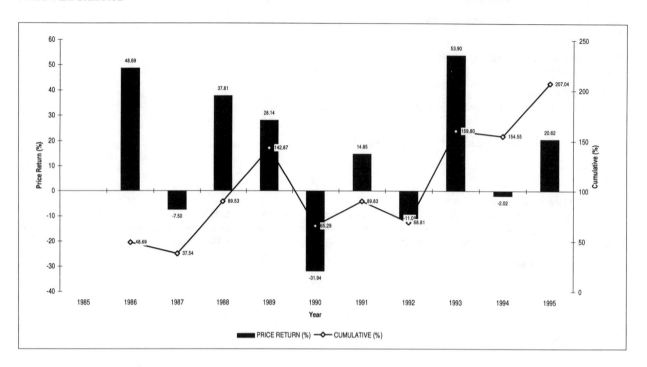

Price and Total Return Performance

YEAR	VALUE	PRICE RETURN (%)	CUMULATIVE (%)	TOTAL RETURN (%)	MAXIMUM VALUE[1]	DATE	MINIMUM VALUE[1]	DATE
1995	2,232.45	20.62	207.04	25.04	2,260.71	7-Dec	1,813.54	14-Mar
1994	1,850.76	-2.02	154.55	1.13	2,082.16	20-Jan	1,694.14	1-Jul
1993	1,888.94	53.90	159.80	59.01	1,888.94	31-Dec	1,222.12	26-Jan
1992	1,227.35	-11.08	68.81	-7.81	1,469.57	17-Jan	1,094.88	19-Oct
1991	1,380.23	14.85	89.83	18.91	1,520.65	15-Mar	1,114.86	25-Jan
1990	1,201.77	-31.94	65.29	-29.24	1,893.10	22-Jan	1,193.66	5-Dec
1989	1,765.87	28.14	142.87	NA	1,781.13	31-Aug	1,506.79	31-Jan
1988	1,378.05	37.81	89.53	NA	1,490.16	31-Jul	1,135.01	31-Jan
1987	1,000.00	-7.50	37.54		1,670.85	30-Sep	982.32	30-Nov
1986	1,081.12	48.69	48.69		1,081.12	30-Dec	742.80	31-Jan
1985	727.08							
Average Annual (%)		15.15		11.17				
Compound Annual (%)		11.87		7.69				
Standard Deviation (%)		27.99		30.45				

[1]Maximum/minimum index values for calendar years 1985-1989 are as of month-end.

SYNOPSIS

The Irish Stock Exchange Equity Price (ISEQ) Index is a market value-weighted index that tracks the periodic price only and daily total return performance of all Official List and Unlisted Securities Market (USM) stocks traded on the Irish Stock Exchange (ISE).

NUMBER OF STOCKS—DECEMBER 31, 1995

65

MARKET VALUE—DECEMBER 31, 1995

US$25,494.4 million

SELECTION CRITERIA

The index includes all Official List and Unlisted Securities Market (USM) stocks traded on the Irish Stock Exchange (ISE). Excluded from the index are UK-registered companies and shares of investment funds.

BACKGROUND

The ISEQ Price Index was initiated on January 4, 1988. Index values have been recalculated on a daily basis to January 1, 1988. A total return index was launched on June 1, 1993 and initiated with a base value of 1000.00 as of January 4, 1988. Price index values have been recalculated to December 31, 1982. Total return values have been calculated since 1988.

BASE DATE

January 4, 1988=1000.00

COMPUTATION METHODOLOGY

(1) An aggregate of prices times quantities index formula. Maintenance adjustments to the divisor are made daily for capitalization changes, new listings and delistings. (2) Total returns are calculated using gross dividends reinvested on the ex-dividend date. (3) The price only index is calculated four times a day while the total return index is calculated daily.

DERIVATIVE INSTRUMENTS

None

SUBINDICES

Two subindices: Financial and all other companies.

RELATED INDICES

None

REMARKS

None

PUBLISHER

Irish Stock Exchange (ISE).

BANCA COMMERCIALE ITALIANA ALL-SHARE (BCI) INDEX

PRICE PERFORMANCE

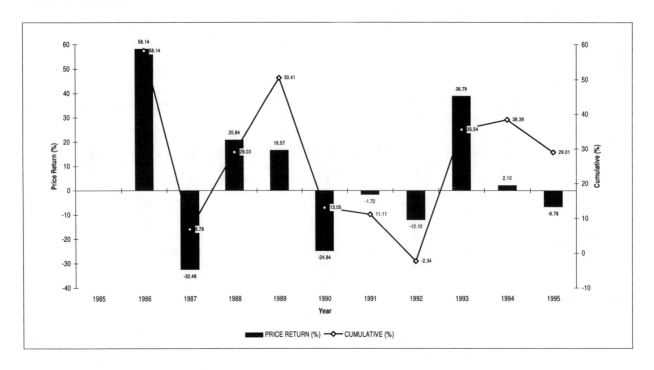

PRICE PERFORMANCE

YEAR	VALUE	PRICE RETURN (%)	CUMULATIVE (%)	MAXIMUM VALUE	DATE	MINIMUM VALUE	DATE
1995	589.60	-6.78	29.01	680.54	10-Feb	547.79	5-Dec
1994	632.48	2.10	38.39	817.17	10-May	581.64	13-Dec
1993	619.48	38.79	35.54	632.86	30-Aug	449.21	11-Jan
1992	446.33	-12.10	-2.34	551.59	6-Feb	354.93	16-Sep
1991	507.79	-1.72	11.11	617.38	3-Jun	482.89	10-Dec
1990	516.69	-24.84	13.05	763.54	14-Jun	500.40	27-Nov
1989	687.44	16.57	50.41	734.83	31-Aug	577.49	28-Feb
1988	589.72	20.84	29.03	593.43	9-Nov	423.91	9-Feb
1987	488.00	-32.48	6.78	767.33	30-Apr	476.26	10-Nov
1986	722.77	58.14	58.14	908.19	20-May	455.69	24-Jan
1985	457.03						
Average Annual (%)		5.85					
Compound Annual (%)		2.58					
Standard Deviation (%)		28.14					

The Banca Commerciale Italiana All-Share (BCI) Index is a market value-weighted index that tracks the daily price only performance of all shares traded on Milan Stock Exchange of Italy.

NUMBER OF STOCKS—DECEMBER 31, 1995
340

MARKET VALUE—DECEMBER 31, 1995
US$209,340.5 million

SELECTION CRITERIA
All shares, both domestic and foreign, traded on the electronic trading system. Unlisted shares are excluded from the index.

BASE DATE
December 31, 1972=100.00

COMPUTATION METHODOLOGY
(1) An aggregate of prices times quantities index formula. Maintenance adjustments to the divisor are made for capitalization changes, new listings and delistings. (2) Official prices from the electronic trading system are used in the index calculation.

DERIVATIVE INSTRUMENTS
None

SUBINDICES
Seven sectoral indices: Banking, financial, insurance, communications, property, industrial and miscellaneous.
Ten subsector indices are calculated for the industrial sector: Food, paper and printing, chemicals, mechanical and electrotechnical engineering, pharmaceutical, building materials, metallurgical, iron and steel, textiles and car/rubber.

RELATED INDICES
BCI 30 Index

REMARKS
None

PUBLISHER
Banca Commerciale Italiana (BCI).

MILAN INDICE DI BORSA (MIB30) INDEX

PRICE PERFORMANCE

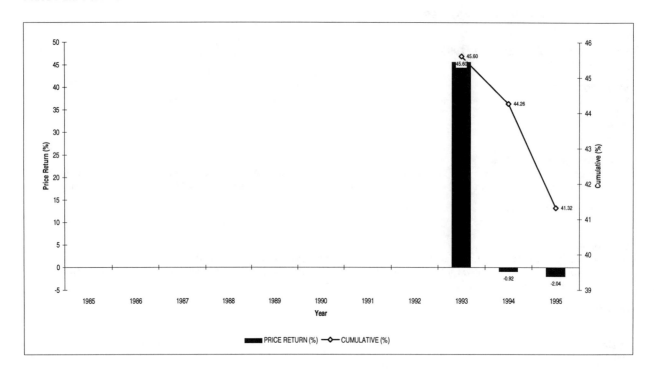

PRICE PERFORMANCE

YEAR	VALUE	PRICE RETURN (%)	CUMULATIVE (%)	MAXIMUM VALUE	DATE	MINIMUM VALUE	DATE
1995	14,132.00	-2.04	41.32	15,895.00	21-Aug	13,094.00	23-Oct
1994	14,426.00	-0.92	44.26	18,836.00	10-May	13,164.00	12-Dec
1993	14,560.00	45.60	45.60	15,089.00	30-Aug	10,041.00	11-Jan
1992	10,000.00						
1991							
1990							
1989							
1988							
1987							
1986							
1985							
Average Annual (%)		14.21					
Compound Annual (%)		12.22					
Standard Deviation (%)		27.19					

SYNOPSIS
The Milan Indice di Borsa (MIB30) Index is a market value-weighted index that tracks the continuous stock price only performance of 30 actively traded large capitalization ordinary, preference or savings shares traded on the Milan Stock Exchange of Italy. These shares account for 73% of the domestic equity market.

NUMBER OF STOCKS—DECEMBER 31, 1995
30

MARKET VALUE—DECEMBER 31, 1995
US$149,212.9 million

SELECTION CRITERIA
Constituent shares are selected on the basis of market capitalization and volume of trading, which are combined into a single factor. The single factor, referred to as the Liquidity and Market Value (LMV), is calculated as follows:
(1) Average market capitalization and average volume of trading for the previous 12-month period are calculated for each listed share and for the stock market as a whole. (2) This is followed by the computation of a ratio (α) of the average market value divided by average volume, for each security and the market as a whole. (3) Finally, the Liquidity Market Value factor is calculated for each stock by adding its average market value to the product of α multiplied by its average trading volume. Shares with the highest Liquidity Market Value factors are selected as index constituents. Multiple share types issued by the same company are excluded and the share class with the highest LMV is selected, shares which have not traded for a significant period are excluded, shares which are likely to fail to satisfy liquidity, market value and official trading requirements during the ensuing period, and shares with a α greater than 10,000.

BACKGROUND
The index was created to serve as an underlying vehicle for derivative instruments. It succeeded the BCI 30 Index, which had been published by Banca Commerciale Italiana.

BASE DATE
December 31, 1992=10,000.00

COMPUTATION METHODOLOGY
(1) An aggregate of prices times quantities index formula. Maintenance adjustments to the divisor are made daily for capitalization changes, new listings and delistings. Maintenance operations are implemented on the day prior to the effective date of the capitalization change. (2) The index is normally revised once a year. More frequent revisions may be made in cases of a suspension or other events that have a series affect on the liquidity of a constituent share.

DERIVATIVE INSTRUMENTS
MIB 30 index futures and options trade on the IDEM, the Italian Derivatives Market.

SUBINDICES
None

RELATED INDICES
IMR (Current)
MIB (historical)
MIB (current)
MIB RNC
MIB Telematico

REMARKS
None

PUBLISHER
Italian Stock Exchange Council.

MILAN INDICE DI BORSA (MIB) INDEX-HISTORICAL

PRICE PERFORMANCE

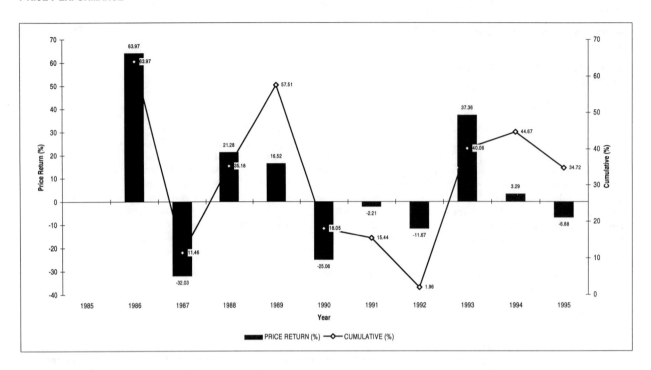

PRICE PERFORMANCE

YEAR	VALUE	PRICE RETURN (%)	CUMULATIVE (%)	MAXIMUM VALUE	DATE	MINIMUM VALUE	DATE
1995	9,138.00	-6.88	34.72	10,556.00	10-Feb	8,491.00	5-Dec
1994	9,813.00	3.29	44.67	12,616.00	10-May	9,015.00	13-Dec
1993	9,500.00	37.36	40.06	9,738.00	30-Aug	6,953.00	11-Jan
1992	6,916.00	-11.67	1.96	8,502.00	6-Feb	5,447.00	16-Sep
1991	7,830.00	-2.21	15.44	9,612.00	3-Jun	7,428.00	10-Dec
1990	8,007.00	-25.06	18.05	11,882.00	14-Jun	7,742.00	27-Nov
1989	10,684.00	16.52	57.51	11,413.00	31-Aug	8,977.00	28-Feb
1988	9,169.00	21.28	35.18	9,251.00	9-Nov	6,578.00	9-Feb
1987	7,560.00	-32.03	11.46	11,802.00	30-Apr	7,375.00	9-Nov
1986	11,122.00	63.97	63.97	13,804.00	20-May	6,763.00	24-Jan
1985	6,783.00						
Average Annual (%)		6.46					
Compound Annual (%)		3.03					
Standard Deviation (%)		29.15					

SYNOPSIS
The Milan Indice di Borsa (MIB) Index-Historical is a market value-weighted historical index that tracks the daily stock price only performance of all ordinary, preference or savings shares listed on the Milan Stock Exchange of Italy.

NUMBER OF STOCKS—DECEMBER 31, 1995
312

MARKET VALUE—DECEMBER 31, 1995
US$205,082.2 million

SELECTION CRITERIA
The index comprises all ordinary, preference or savings shares listed on the Milan Stock Exchange of Italy.

BACKGROUND
This historical MIB Index is unlike the MIB Index-current, the base value of which is reset to 1000.00 the beginning of each year.

BASE DATE
January 2, 1975=1000.00

COMPUTATION METHODOLOGY
(1) An aggregate of prices times quantities index formula. Maintenance adjustments to the divisor are made for capitalization changes, new listings and delistings. (2) Official prices are used for the calculation of the index.

DERIVATIVE INSTRUMENTS
None

SUBINDICES
None

RELATED INDICES
IMR (Current)
MIB (current)
MIB 30 Index
MIB RNC
MIB Telematico

REMARKS
None

PUBLISHER
Italian Stock Exchange Council.

LUXEMBOURG STOCK EXCHANGE INDEX

PRICE PERFORMANCE

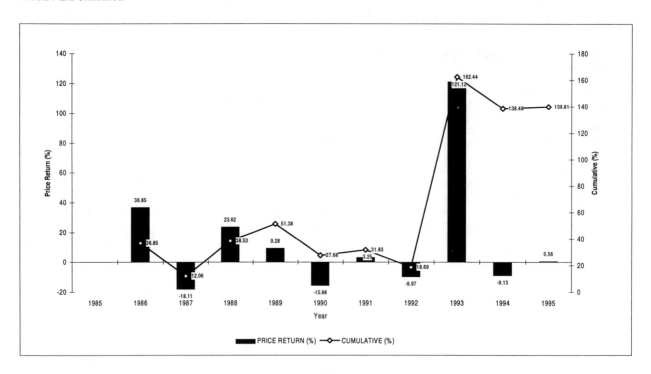

PRICE AND TOTAL RETURN PERFORMANCE

YEAR	VALUE	PRICE RETURN (%)	CUMULATIVE (%)	TOTAL RETURN (%)	MAXIMUM VALUE[1]	DATE	MINIMUM VALUE[1]	DATE
1995	4,325.44	0.56	139.81	-0.13	4,469.23	4-Aug	3,895.06	3-Apr
1994	4,301.38	-9.13	138.48	-7.61	5,132.63	15-Mar	4,290.99	7-Oct
1993	4,733.47	121.12	162.44	104.12	4,770.11	29-Dec	2,138.72	4-Jan
1992	2,140.68	-9.97	18.69	-5.97	2,473.15	23-Jan	2,105.22	18-Dec
1991	2,377.71	3.25	31.83	5.72	2,544.99	30-Sep	2,207.48	31-Jan
1990	2,302.86	-15.66	27.68	-12.14	2,828.49	30-Jun	2,216.24	31-Oct
1989	2,730.41	9.28	51.38	9.33	2,968.23	30-Sep	2,515.29	31-Jan
1988	2,498.63	23.62	38.53	24.13	2,498.63	31-Dec	1,979.99	31-Jan
1987	2,021.16	-18.11	12.06	-16.03	2,521.42	31-Jan	1,996.06	31-Dec
1986	2,468.25	36.85	36.85	40.29	2,796.71	31-May	1,792.74	31-Jan
1985	1,803.66							
Average Annual (%)		14.18		14.17				
Compound Annual (%)		9.14		10.15				
Standard Deviation (%)		41.40		35.99				

[1]Maximum/minimum index values for the period 1986-1991 occured during the month indicated, but not necessarily on the last day of the month.

Synopsis

The Luxembourg Stock Exchange Index is a market value-weighted index that tracks the daily price only and total return performance of a selected number of Luxembourg-based companies traded on the Luxembourg Stock Exchange. These shares account for 25% of the domestic equity market capitalization.

Number of Stocks—December 31, 1995

13

Market Value—December 31, 1995

US$7,691.05 million

Selection Criteria

Constituents are selected to represent the economy of Luxembourg. While there are no fixed capitalization or trading volume criteria, eligible securities are required to evidence reasonable liquidity.

Base Date

January 1, 1985=1000.00

Computation Methodology

(1) An aggregate of prices times quantities index formula. Maintenance adjustments to the divisor are made for capitalization changes, new listings and delistings. (2) Market capitalization is calculated on the basis of the number of shares issued. (3) Securities are priced on the basis of closing prices on the Luxembourg Stock Exchange. (4) Total returns are calculated using gross dividends reinvested as of the ex-dividend date.

Derivative Instruments

None

Subindices

None

Related Indices

None

Remarks

None

Publisher

Luxembourg Stock Exchange.

AMSTERDAM EOE (EOE) INDEX

PRICE PERFORMANCE

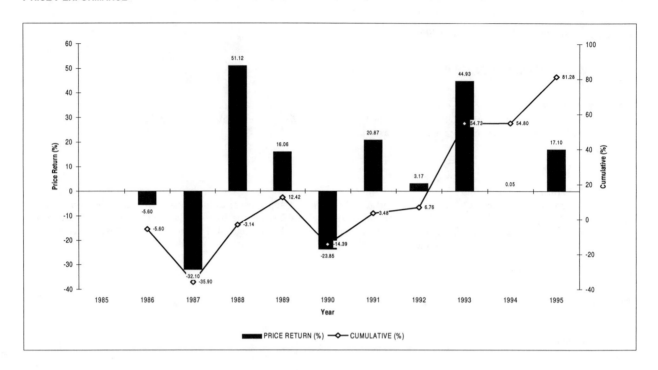

PRICE PERFORMANCE

YEAR	VALUE	PRICE RETURN (%)	CUMULATIVE (%)	MAXIMUM VALUE	DATE	MINIMUM VALUE	DATE
1995	485.35	17.10	81.28	485.35	28-Dec	388.33	23-Mar
1994	414.47	0.05	54.80	438.71	31-Jan	376.69	21-Jun
1993	414.27	44.93	54.73	416.46	27-Dec	286.51	4-Jan
1992	285.84	3.17	6.76	318.56	2-Jun	273.36	30-Oct
1991	277.05	20.87	3.48	286.55	17-Apr	217.62	16-Jan
1990	229.21	-23.85	-14.39	304.64	3-Jan	224.20	8-Nov
1989	301.00	16.06	12.42	328.43	17-Aug	260.18	11-Jan
1988	259.34	51.12	-3.14	259.34	29-Dec	169.29	4-Jan
1987	171.61	-32.10	-35.90	286.05	11-Aug	152.36	10-Nov
1986	252.75	-5.60	-5.60	281.42	22-May	245.27	3-Mar
1985	267.74						
Average Annual (%)		9.18					
Compound Annual (%)		6.13					
Standard Deviation (%)		26.70					

Synopsis

The Amsterdam EOE (EOE) Index is a market value-weighted index that tracks the continuous price only performance of 25 major and most actively traded Dutch stocks listed on the Amsterdam Stock Exchange (ASE). These shares account for 85.5% of the domestic Dutch market.

Number of Stocks—December 31, 1995

25

Market Value—December 31, 1995

US$244,238.8 million

Selection Criteria

The index is limited to shares listed on the Amsterdam Stock Exchange. Constituent shares are mainly nationally oriented companies which have the highest effective turnover on the Dutch market, as measured over the previous three calendar years, that reflect all the important sectors of the Dutch economy. These include transport, food, electronics, energy, banking insurance and chemicals.

Investment funds, holding companies for stocks already included and stocks which, according to the criteria of the Netherlands Central Bureau of Statistics (CBS) are not considered to be Dutch stocks, are excluded from consideration as index constituents.

Background

The index was launched on January 1, 1994 as a continuation of the EOE Nederlandse Aandeleidex (EOE Dutch Stock Index). Its aim is to reflect the general price movement trends on the Amsterdam Stock Exchange as well as to serve as an underlying vehicle for stock index options and futures traded on the EOE-Optiebeurs (Amsterdam Options & Futures Exchange).

Base Date

January 3, 1983=100.00

Computation Methodology

(1) An aggregate of prices times quantities index formula. Maintenance adjustments to the divisor are made for capitalization changes, new listings and delistings. (2) The selection and weighting of the constituent stocks takes place once a year, in February, and changes, if any, are announced at least one month prior to the periodic adjustment. (3) Effective share volume for each of the previous three calendar years is calculated on a weighted basis, with the more recent effective volume assigned a heavier weight. The weight assigned to the most recent year's effective volume is three times the weight assigned to the first year's effective volume and twice the weight assigned to the second year's effective volume. (4) Market capitalization is determined on the basis of the number of outstanding shares according to the most recent official publication of the Amsterdam Stock Exchange. A stock's weighting in the index, however, will not exceed 10%. The weighting of each stock is reflected in the number of shares included in the index, which may be periodically adjusted. (5) Share prices are the prices of transactions concluded in official listing in regular daytime trading, based on values on the Amsterdam Stock Exchange.

Derivative Instruments

Amsterdam EOE index futures and options trade on the EOE-Optiebeurs.

Subindices

None

Related Indices

Amsterdam Midkap-Index
Dutch Top 5 Index
Eurotop 100 Index

Remarks

None

Publisher

Amsterdam EOE-Optiebeurs.

AMSTERDAM MIDKAP-INDEX

PRICE PERFORMANCE

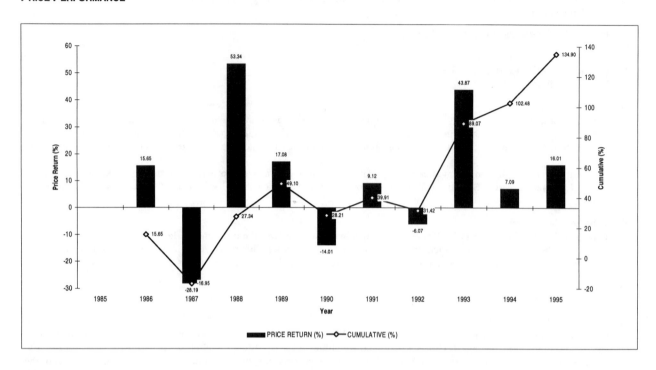

PRICE PERFORMANCE

YEAR	VALUE	PRICE RETURN (%)	CUMULATIVE (%)	MAXIMUM VALUE	DATE	MINIMUM VALUE	DATE
1995	574.62	16.01	134.90	574.87	28-Dec	473.45	23-Mar
1994	495.31	7.09	102.48	507.27	17-Mar	467.06	3-Jan
1993	462.50	43.87	89.07	464.10	27-Dec	320.56	4-Jan
1992	321.47	-6.07	31.42	404.59	2-Jun	309.50	17-Dec
1991	342.24	9.12	39.91	367.16	5-Apr	292.02	16-Jan
1990	313.63	-14.01	28.21	376.56	20-Jul	305.60	28-Sep
1989	364.73	17.08	49.10	391.88	6-Oct	315.72	2-Jan
1988	311.51	53.34	27.34	311.51	29-Dec	199.30	4-Jan
1987	203.15	-28.19	-16.95	323.32	10-Aug	192.44	10-Dec
1986	282.90	15.65	15.65	299.74	21-Aug	247.54	25-Feb
1985	244.62						
Average Annual (%)		11.39					
Compound Annual (%)		8.92					
Standard Deviation (%)		24.56					

SYNOPSIS
The Amsterdam Midkap-Index is a market value-weighted index that tracks the continuous price only performance of 25 stocks that represent the middle section of the Dutch market. These shares account for 5% of the domestic Dutch market.

NUMBER OF STOCKS—DECEMBER 31, 1995
25

MARKET VALUE—DECEMBER 31, 1995
US$14,180.26 million

SELECTION CRITERIA
The index is limited to shares listed on the Amsterdam Stock Exchange. Constituent shares are mainly nationally oriented companies which have the highest effective turnover measured over the previous three calendar years, and fall within the middle section of the Dutch market. That is, the 25 stocks included in the Midkap-Index immediately follow the 25 stocks comprising the Amsterdam EOE-Index.

Stocks that are already included in the Amsterdam EOE Index, investment funds, holding companies for stocks already included and stocks which, according to the criteria of the Netherlands Central Bureau of Statistics (CBS) are not considered to be Dutch stocks, are excluded from consideration as index constituents.

BACKGROUND
The index was launched on October 4, 1995. Its aim is to reflect the price movement of middle-capitalization stocks. Also, it may serve as an underlying vehicle for derivative products.

BASE DATE
January 1983=100.00

COMPUTATION METHODOLOGY
(1) An aggregate of prices times quantities index formula. Maintenance adjustments to the divisor are made for capitalization changes, new listings and delistings. (2) The selection and weighting of the constituent stocks takes place once a year, in February, and changes, if any, are announced at least one month prior to the periodic adjustment. (3) Effective share volume for each of the previous three calendar years is calculated on a weighted basis, with the more recent effective volume assigned a heavier weight. The weight assigned to the most recent year's effective volume is three times the weight assigned to the first year's effective volume and twice the weight assigned to the second year's effective volume. (4) Market capitalization is determined on the basis of the number of outstanding shares according to the most recent official publication of the Amsterdam Stock Exchange. A stock's weighting in the index, however, will not exceed 10%. The weighting of each stock is reflected in the number of shares included in the index, which may be periodically adjusted. (5) Share prices are the prices of transactions concluded in official listing in regular daytime trading, based on values on the Amsterdam Stock Exchange.

DERIVATIVE INSTRUMENTS
Amsterdam Midkap index call and put warrants issued by Rabobank trade on the EOE-Optiebeurs.

SUBINDICES
None

RELATED INDICES
Amsterdam EOE Index
Dutch Top 5 Index
Eurotop 100 Index

REMARKS
None

PUBLISHER
Amsterdam EOE-Optiebeurs.

CENTRAL BUREAU OF STATISTICS (CBS) ALL SHARE INDEX

PRICE PERFORMANCE

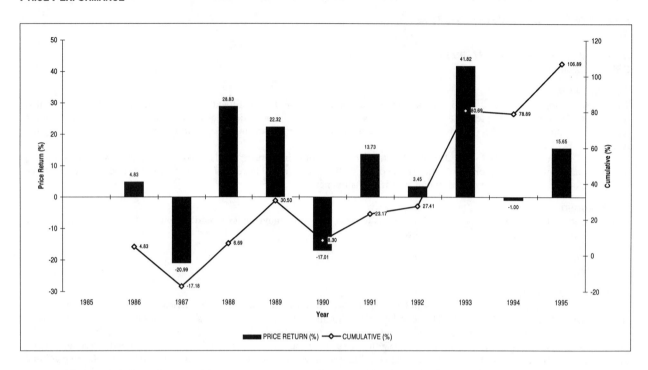

PRICE PERFORMANCE

YEAR	VALUE	PRICE RETURN (%)	CUMULATIVE (%)	MAXIMUM VALUE[1]	DATE	MINIMUM VALUE[1]	DATE
1995	321.50	15.65	106.89	858.54	26-Jul	694.82	23-Mar
1994	278.00	-1.00	78.89	294.80	31-Jan	257.90	27-Jun
1993	280.80	41.82	80.69	280.80	30-Dec	198.60	13-Jan
1992	198.00	3.45	27.41	215.50	9-Jun	189.70	25-Aug
1991	191.40	13.73	23.17	203.10	5-Jun	162.30	16-Jan
1990	168.30	-17.01	8.30	206.30	1-Mar	165.60	11-Aug
1989	202.80	22.32	30.50	210.50	9-Aug	166.60	1-Mar
1988	165.80	28.83	6.69	165.80	31-Dec	133.30	31-Jan
1987	128.70	-20.99	-17.18	194.50	31-Jul	124.00	30-Nov
1986	162.90	4.83	4.83	166.10	31-May	145.80	28-Feb
1985	155.40						
Average Annual (%)		9.16					
Compound Annual (%)		7.54					
Standard Deviation (%)		19.55					

[1]Maximum/minimum index values for the period 1986-1988 are as of month-end.

SYNOPSIS

The Central Bureau of Statistics (CBS) All Share Index is a market value-weighted index that tracks the daily price and total return performance of all Dutch stocks traded on the Amsterdam Stock Exchange (ASE).

NUMBER OF STOCKS—DECEMBER 31, 1995

163

MARKET VALUE—DECEMBER 31, 1995

US$273.29 million

SELECTION CRITERIA

All common shares of Dutch companies listed on the Amsterdam Stock Exchange, excluding shares of investment funds, property funds, holding companies and companies whose principal assets are the share of another company.

BACKGROUND

The CBS All Share Index was introduced on January 1, 1989 to supplement the CBS Tendency Index. The CBS Tendency Index, in turn, was launched on October 1, 1986, as a replacement for the ANP-CBS Index which had been calculated since 1955 by the Netherlands Central Bureau of Statistics (CBS). The calculation of the CBS Tendency Index has also been discontinued.

The new index was designed to better serve the needs of long-term investors while at the same time facilitate portfolio analysis with its total return companion. The index has been recalculated on a daily basis to January 1, 1980. In addition, the All Share Index, both with and without Royal Dutch, has been recalculated on a monthly basis back to December 31, 1952.

BASE DATE

December 31, 1983=100.00

COMPUTATION METHODOLOGY

(1) An aggregate of prices times quantities index formula. Maintenance adjustments to the divisor are made for capitalization changes, new listings and delistings. (2) Closing prices on the ASE are used. In the absence of a stock price, the most recently available quotation is used for computation purposes.

DERIVATIVE INSTRUMENTS

None

SUBINDICES

Two versions of the index are available: One with Royal Dutch Petroleum and one without Royal Dutch in an effort to isolate the impact of this company's significant market capitalization and consequent affect on the performance of the index.

Two subindices: International companies and local companies.

Nine broad economic sector indices: Consumer goods industries, capital goods, basic industries, construction and building, transportation, storage and communication, non-financial services, trade, banking and other financial services and insurance.

RELATED INDICES

None

REMARKS

Royal Dutch Petroleum accounts for 27% of the total market value of domestic equities.

PUBLISHER

Amsterdam Stock Exchange (ASE).

Dutch Top 5 Index (TOPS)

Price Performance

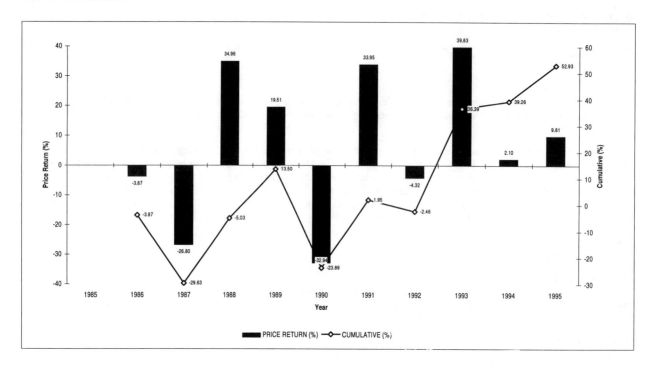

PRICE RETURN (%) — CUMULATIVE (%)

Price Performance

YEAR	VALUE	PRICE RETURN (%)	CUMULATIVE (%)	MAXIMUM VALUE	DATE	MINIMUM VALUE	DATE
1995	810.77	9.81	52.93	858.54	26-Jul	694.82	23-Mar
1994	738.32	2.10	39.26	812.14	18-Apr	704.49	27-Jun
1993	723.11	39.83	36.39	724.48	27-Dec	512.04	13-Jan
1992	517.14	-4.32	-2.46	616.11	11-May	493.85	30-Oct
1991	540.50	33.95	1.95	564.72	14-Nov	393.88	23-Jan
1990	403.51	-32.94	-23.89	610.87	3-Jan	380.08	9-Jan
1989	601.71	19.51	13.50	620.19	8-Sep	504.99	3-Jan
1988	503.47	34.96	-5.03	505.29	27-Dec	371.21	4-Jan
1987	373.05	-26.80	-29.63	654.10	11-Aug	358.87	4-Dec
1986	509.62	-3.87	-3.87	587.06	14-Apr	483.21	29-Oct
1985	530.16						
Average Annual (%)		7.22					
Compound Annual (%)		4.34					
Standard Deviation (%)		25.29					

SYNOPSIS
The Dutch Top 5 Index (TOPS) is a modified equal dollar-weighted index that tracks the continuous price only performance of five Dutch international stocks listed on the Amsterdam Stock Exchange and also on leading international stock exchanges in other European countries as well as the United States. These shares account for 33% of the domestic equity market.

NUMBER OF STOCKS—DECEMBER 31, 1995
5

MARKET VALUE—DECEMBER 31, 1995
US$93,078.02 million

SELECTION CRITERIA
The index, which represents different sectors of industry, including chemicals, transport, electronics, energy and foods, consists of Dutch international stocks listed on the Amsterdam Stock Exchange and also on leading international stock exchanges in other European countries and the United States. These include Akzo Nobel, KLM, Phillips Electronics, Royal Dutch and Unilever.

BACKGROUND
The index was introduced on March 21, 1990 and is designed to serve as an underlying vehicle for stock index options and futures traded on the EOE-Optiebeurs (Amsterdam Options & Futures Exchange).

BASE DATE
December 31, 1989=601.71

COMPUTATION METHODOLOGY
(1) A modified equal dollar-weighted index formula, in which the number of shares representing an investment with 22.5% in each of Akzo Nobel, Phillips Electronics, Royal Dutch and Unilver and 10% in KLM. The index, which was established using share prices as of December 31, 1989, is adjusted periodically to reflect non-market changes in the price of the constituent stocks, such as rights offerings, splits, reverse splits, and decreases in capital, or changes in the universe of constituent stocks, so as to maintain its continuity. (2) The weight distinctions were established on the basis of the effective value of volume recorded over a three-year period to December 31, 1989. Stocks with effective value of volume in excess of Dfl. 7.5 billion were assigned a base weight of 22.5%, while stocks with a n effective value of volume below that level were assigned a base weight of 10%. (3) In the event of stock replacements, the number of shares of the new stock will be such that the total value of the index remains as close as possible to the previous value.

DERIVATIVE INSTRUMENTS
Dutch Top 5 index futures and options trade on the EOE-Optiebeurs.
Dutch Top 5 call and put warrants issued by Citibank are listed on the EOE-Optiebeurs.

SUBINDICES
None

RELATED INDICES
Amsterdam Midkap-Index
Dutch Top 5 Index
Eurotop 100 Index

REMARKS
None

PUBLISHER
Amsterdam EOE-Optiebeurs.

OBX INDEX

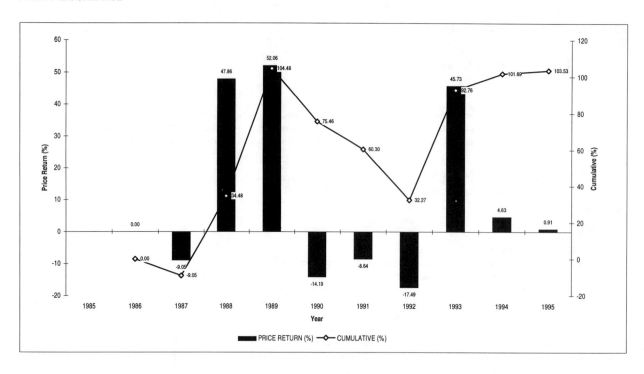

PRICE PERFORMANCE

YEAR	VALUE	PRICE RETURN (%)	CUMULATIVE (%)	MAXIMUM VALUE	DATE	MINIMUM VALUE	DATE
1995	407.06	0.91	103.53	422.39	13-Sep	353.07	9-Mar
1994	403.37	4.63	101.69	433.05	28-Feb	343.94	21-Jun
1993	385.51	45.73	92.76	389.19	29-Dec	262.86	27-Jan
1992	264.53	-17.49	32.27	361.73	17-Jan	212.99	25-Aug
1991	320.60	-8.64	60.30	419.27	26-Aug	292.74	2-Dec
1990	350.91	-14.19	75.46	519.35	2-Aug	336.70	21-Dec
1989	408.96	52.06	104.48	429.04	18-Sep	270.51	2-Jan
1988	268.95	47.86	34.48	273.29	28-Dec	183.18	4-Jan
1987	181.90	-9.05	-9.05	340.43	21-Sep	176.80	10-Nov
1986	200.00						
1985							
Average Annual (%)		11.31					
Compound Annual (%)		8.22					
Standard Deviation (%)		28.78					

Synopsis

The OBX Index is a market value-weighted index that tracks the continuous price only performance of 25 of the most actively traded share classes listed on the Main List of the Oslo Stock Exchange. These shares account for 64% of the Oslo Stock Exchange market capitalization.

Number of Stocks—December 31, 1995

25

Market Value—December 31, 1995

US$29,160.0 million

Selection Criteria

Constituent stocks are selected on the basis of their trading volume involving freely traded shares, over a six-month period and the composition of the index is adjusted twice a year, as of June 1 and December 1. Selected stock classes must also have been traded on at least 60% of the trading days during the period.

Background

The index was designed to serve as an underlying vehicle for trading in derivative financial products. The index, which is now calculated on a continuous basis, was computed daily based on closing prices until the introduction of electronic trading on the Oslo Stock Exchange in the spring of 1988.

Base Date

January 1, 1987=200.00

Computation Methodology

(1) An aggregate of prices times quantities index formula. Maintenance adjustments to the divisor are made for capitalization changes, new listings and delistings. Capitalization changes are reflected in the index as of the "ex-date." (2) For market capitalization calculation purposes, shares with restricted ownership classes will only be valued according to the number of shares that can be freely traded. (3) In the absence of quoted trading prices, the latest available quoted trading price is used. (4) Companies are removed from the index due to trading suspensions or delistings.

Derivative Instruments

OBX index futures and options trade on the Oslo Stock Exchange.

Subindices

None

Related Indices

Oslo Stock Exchange All-Share Index

Remarks

Refer to the Oslo Stock Exchange All-Share Index for information regarding foreign share ownership restrictions.

Publisher

The Oslo Stock Exchange (Oslo Bors).

Oslo Stock Exchange All-Share Index

Total Return Performance

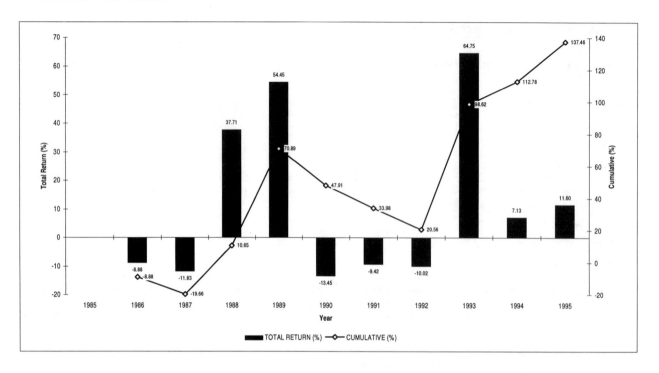

Total Return Performance

YEAR	VALUE	TOTAL RETURN (%)	CUMULATIVE (%)	MAXIMUM VALUE	DATE	MINIMUM VALUE	DATE
1995	732.96	11.60	137.46	749.44	19-Sep	597.53	9-Mar
1994	656.78	7.13	112.78	688.23	4-Feb	567.39	21-Jun
1993	613.08	64.75	98.62	616.59	3-Nov	375.34	27-Jan
1992	372.12	-10.02	20.56	464.24	17-Jan	300.04	25-Aug
1991	413.55	-9.42	33.98	525.34	26-Aug	375.39	2-Dec
1990	456.54	-13.45	47.91	666.35	2-Aug	435.93	21-Dec
1989	527.49	54.45	70.89	544.92	28-Sep	342.79	2-Jan
1988	341.53	37.71	10.65	342.96	28-Dec	248.68	28-Jan
1987	248.00	-11.83	-19.66	442.44	21-Sep	241.76	16-Dec
1986	281.27	-8.88	-8.88				
1985	308.67						
Average Annual (%)		12.21					
Compound Annual (%)		9.03					
Standard Deviation (%)		29.56					

SYNOPSIS

The Oslo Stock Exchange All-Share Index is a market value-weighted index that tracks the continuous total return performance of all Norwegian stocks traded on the Main List of the Oslo Stock Exchange. The index tracks all listed Norwegian share classes, including Class A, Free Class and B-Class shares.

NUMBER OF STOCKS—DECEMBER 31, 1995

182

MARKET VALUE—DECEMBER 31, 1995

US$45,669.3 million

SELECTION CRITERIA

The index includes all stocks traded on the Main List of the Oslo Stock Exchange, including Class A, Free Class and B-Class shares.

BACKGROUND

The index, which is now calculated on a continuous basis, was computed daily based on closing prices until the introduction of electronic trading on the Oslo Stock Exchange in the spring of 1988.

BASE DATE

January 1, 1983=100.00

COMPUTATION METHODOLOGY

(1) An aggregate of prices times quantities index formula. Maintenance adjustments to the divisor are made for capitalization changes, new listings and delistings. (2) Companies are removed from the index due to trading suspensions and lack of trading, following 10 trading days. Companies whose stock has been delisted are immediately removed from the index. (3) Stock splits, ordinary issues, bonus issues and dividend issues which affect share capital are reflected in the index as of the "ex-date." New listings are reflected in the index on the second day of listing. (4) For market capitalization computation of purposes, however, certain companies in which the Norwegian Government has a long-term holding are weighted on the basis of freely transferable shares. In addition, Norse Hydro, the largest listed company on the Oslo Stock Exchange, receives a weighting equal to 50% of its normal market capitalization.

DERIVATIVE INSTRUMENTS

None

SUBINDICES

Four subindices: Banking Index, Insurance Index, Shipping Index and Industry Index.

RELATED INDICES

OBX Index

REMARKS

Foreign ownership of shares carrying voting rights is restricted to 33.3% of the share capital of banks, industrial corporations and insurance companies and 40% of the share capital of shipping companies. Shares carrying voting rights are often designated as A-shares while non-voting shares, which may be owned freely by foreign investors, are designated as B-shares. Some companies have split their shares into two classes, restricted A-shares and free A-shares. The free shares fall within the foreign ownership quota and may be owned freely by foreign investors while the restricted shares may be held by Norwegian Nationals.

PUBLISHER

The Oslo Stock Exchange (Oslo Bors).

WARSAW STOCK EXCHANGE (WIG) INDEX

TOTAL RETURN PERFORMANCE

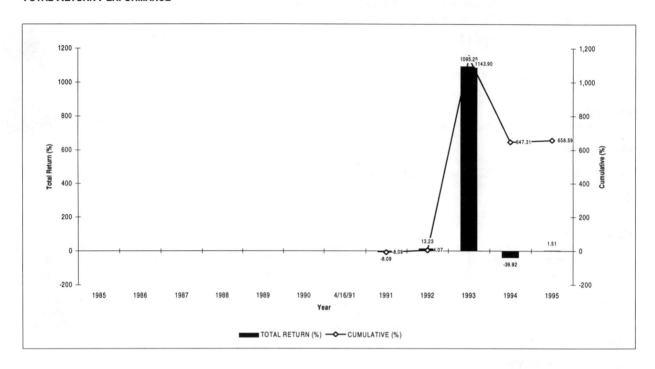

TOTAL RETURN PERFORMANCE

YEAR	VALUE	TOTAL RETURN (%)	CUMULATIVE (%)	MAXIMUM VALUE	DATE	MINIMUM VALUE	DATE
1995	7,585.90	1.51	658.59	9,396.90	12-May	5,904.70	28-Mar
1994	7,473.10	-39.92	647.31	20,760.30	8-Mar	6,716.20	16-Nov
1993	12,439.00	1,095.25	1143.90	12,439.00	30-Dec	1,037.10	4-Jan
1992	1,040.70	13.23	4.07	1,071.00	19-Dec	635.30	23-Jun
1991	919.10	-8.09	-8.09	1,001.90	10-Dec	678.50	1-Oct
4/16/91	1,000.00						
1990							
1989							
1988							
1987							
1986							
1985							
Average Annual (%)		267.52					
Compound Annual (%)		69.50					
Standard Deviation (%)		640.60					

[1] Performance Statistics applicable to the 4-year period 1992-1995.

SYNOPSIS

The Warsaw Stock Exchange (WIG) Index is a market value-weighted index that tracks the daily total return performance of all companies listed on the main market of the Warsaw Stock Exchange (WSE).

NUMBER OF STOCKS—DECEMBER 31, 1995

44

MARKET VALUE—DECEMBER 31, 1995

US$4,416.86 million

SELECTION CRITERIA

All companies listed on the main market, which is limited to larger companies with an established track record, at least 500 shareholders and audited financial statements for the last three financial years.

BACKGROUND

The index was introduced as of April 16, 1991 with the reopening of the WSE.

BASE DATE

April 16, 1991=1000.00

COMPUTATION METHODOLOGY

(1) An aggregate of prices times quantities index formula. Maintenance adjustments to the divisor are made for capitalization changes, new listings and delistings. (2) The market capitalization of constituent companies is limited to 10% of the total market capitalization of the WIG Index and individual sector participation is limited to 30% of WIG. (3) New companies and new issues attributable to listed companies are added to the index at the beginning of each quarter. At the same time, company participations are trimmed down to 10% and individual sectors to 30%, as may be required. (4) Dividends are reinvested as of the "ex-dividend" date.

DERIVATIVE INSTRUMENTS

None

SUBINDICES

None

RELATED INDICES

The Warsaw Stock Exchange WIRR Index
WIG 20 Index

REMARKS

None

PUBLISHER

Warsaw Stock Exchange (WSE).

WARSAW STOCK EXCHANGE WIRR INDEX

TOTAL RETURN PERFORMANCE

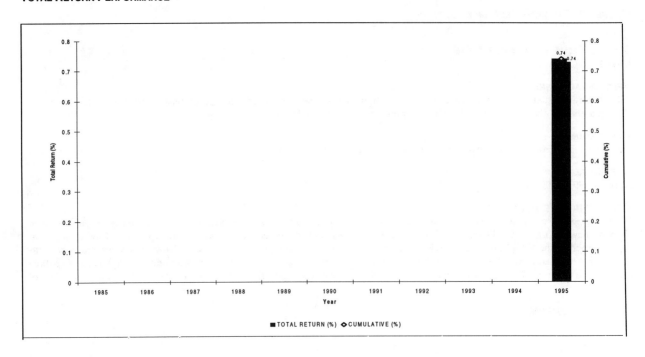

TOTAL RETURN PERFORMANCE

YEAR	VALUE	TOTAL RETURN (%)	CUMULATIVE (%)	MAXIMUM VALUE	DATE	MINIMUM VALUE	DATE
1995	1,007.40	0.74	0.74				
1994	1,000.00						
1993							
1992							
1991							
1990							
1989							
1988							
1987							
1986							
1985							
Average Annual (%)							
Compound Annual (%)							
Standard Deviation (%)							

SYNOPSIS

The Warsaw Stock Exchange WIRR Index is a market value-weighted index that tracks the daily total return performance of all companies listed on the parallel market of the Warsaw Stock Exchange (WSE). These shares account for 1.8% of the combined Main and Parallel markets.

NUMBER OF STOCKS—DECEMBER 31, 1995

9

MARKET VALUE—DECEMBER 31, 1995

US$80.34 million

SELECTION CRITERIA

All companies listed on parallel market, which is open to smaller companies and companies with a shorter track record.

BACKGROUND

None

BASE DATE

December 31, 1994=1000.00

COMPUTATION METHODOLOGY

(1) An aggregate of prices times quantities index formula. Maintenance adjustments to the divisor are made daily for capitalization changes, new listings and delistings. (2) New companies and new issues attributable to listed companies are added to the index at the beginning of each quarter. (3) Dividends are reinvested as of the "ex-dividend" date.

DERIVATIVE INSTRUMENTS

None

SUBINDICES

None

RELATED INDICES

WIG Index
WIG 20 Index

REMARKS

None

PUBLISHER

Warsaw Stock Exchange (WSE).

BANCO TOTTA & ACORES (BT&A) SHARES INDEX

PRICE PERFORMANCE

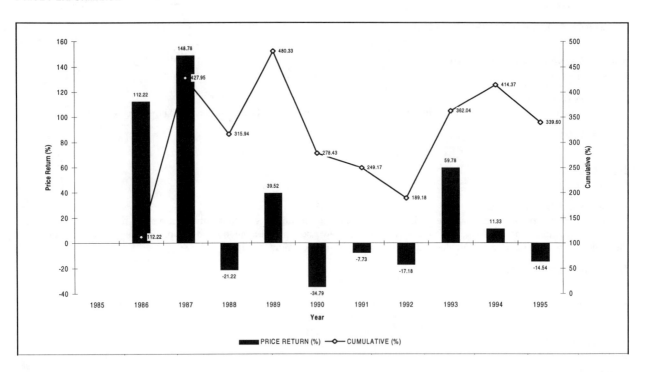

PRICE PERFORMANCE

YEAR	VALUE	PRICE RETURN (%)	CUMULATIVE (%)	MAXIMUM VALUE	DATE	MINIMUM VALUE	DATE
1995	2,489.90	-14.54	339.60	2,911.60	9-Jan	2,412.90	22-Nov
1994	2,913.40	11.33	414.37	3,226.60	18-Feb	2,612.80	20-Jun
1993	2,617.00	59.78	362.04	2,689.00	9-Sep	1,608.20	14-Jan
1992	1,637.90	-17.18	189.18	2,156.40	11-May	1,637.90	31-Dec
1991	1,977.70	-7.73	249.17	2,515.20	18-Mar	1,924.00	5-Dec
1990	2,143.40	-34.79	278.43	3,281.00	4-Jan	2,117.70	20-Dec
1989	3,287.00	39.52	480.33	3,705.10	12-Oct	2,249.80	11-Jan
1988	2,355.90	-21.22	315.94	3,528.60	12-Jan	2,148.00	21-Oct
1987	2,990.30	148.78	427.95	6,812.70	6-Oct	1,220.70	6-Jan
1986	1,202.00	112.22	112.22	1,202.00	31-Dec	572.90	3-Jan
1985	566.40						
Average Annual (%)		27.62					
Compound Annual (%)		15.96					
Standard Deviation (%)		62.00					

SYNOPSIS

The Banco Totta & Acores (BT&A) Shares Index is a price-weighted index that tracks the daily price only performance of large capitalization, actively traded stocks listed on the official market of the Lisbon Stock Exchange (BVL).

NUMBER OF STOCKS—DECEMBER 31, 1995

39

MARKET VALUE—DECEMBER 31, 1995

US$11,183.96 million

SELECTION CRITERIA

Constituent stocks are selected based on transaction amounts, market capitalization, turnover and frequency of transactions. Also, members are selected to reflect all sectors of economic activity in Portugal.

BACKGROUND

The BT&A Index was introduced in 1977.

BASE DATE

March 31, 1977=100.00

COMPUTATION METHODOLOGY

(1) A simple aggregative of actual prices index formula. Adjustments are made over the years to reflect stock splits and other capital changes by reducing the value of the divisor accordingly. (2) In the absence of traded prices, bids and offers may be taken into account in the event they are either higher or lower than the last traded price.

DERIVATIVE INSTRUMENTS

None

SUBINDICES

None

RELATED INDICES

None

REMARKS

None

PUBLISHER

Banco Totta & Acores (BT&A).

BOLSA DE VALORES DE LISBOA (BVL) GENERAL INDEX

TOTAL RETURN PERFORMANCE

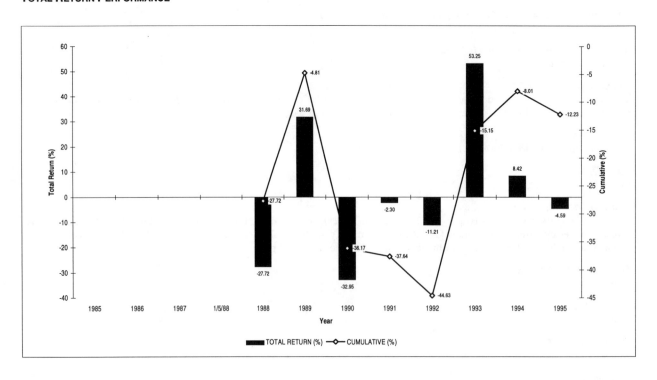

TOTAL RETURN PERFORMANCE

YEAR	VALUE	TOTAL RETURN (%)	CUMULATIVE (%)	MAXIMUM VALUE	DATE	MINIMUM VALUE	DATE
1995	877.69	-4.59	-12.23	933.32	12-May	842.31	22-Nov
1994	919.95	8.42	-8.01	994.46	18-Feb	801.57	20-Jun
1993	848.54	53.25	-15.15	848.54	31-Dec	537.20	13-Jan
1992	553.71	-11.21	-44.63	651.63	11-May	541.60	20-Oct
1991	623.63	-2.30	-37.64	747.69	18-Mar	605.66	16-Jan
1990	638.30	-32.95	-36.17	953.76	4-Jan	627.57	5-Dec
1989	951.91	31.69	-4.81	1,041.59	24-Oct	691.11	22-Jun
1988	722.85	-27.72	-27.72	1,145.10	8-Jan	670.70	21-Oct
1/5/88	1,000.00						
1987							
1986							
1985							
Average Annual (%)		1.82					
Compound Annual (%)		-1.62					
Standard Deviation (%)		29.01					

SYNOPSIS

The Bolsa de Valores de Lisboa (BVL) General Index is a market value-weighted index that tracks the daily total return performance of all stocks traded on the official market of the Lisbon Stock Exchange (BVL). These shares account for 87% of the domestic market capitalization, including the Official Market as well as secondary markets.

NUMBER OF STOCKS—DECEMBER 31, 1995

75

MARKET VALUE—DECEMBER 31, 1995

US$16,004.3 million

SELECTION CRITERIA

Components include all stocks traded on the Market with Official Quotations of the Lisbon Stock Exchange (BVL).

BACKGROUND

The BVL Index was introduced on February 18, 1991. Sectoral indices were introduced on July 15, 1991.

BASE DATE

January 5, 1988=1000.00

COMPUTATION METHODOLOGY

(1) An aggregate of prices times quantities index formula. Maintenance adjustments to the divisor are made daily for capitalization changes, new listings and delistings. (2) Newly admitted stocks, deletions, suspensions, and capital changes are immediately reflected in the index. (3) Latest official price is used in the calculation of the index. For stocks traded on the national trading system, the price considered is the latest official price, regardless of the stock exchange to which the transaction is statistically assigned. (4) The absence of a price quotation for five consecutive stock market sessions results in the withdrawal of a security from the index. (5) Total return is calculated using gross dividends.

DERIVATIVE INSTRUMENTS

None

SUBINDICES

Eight sector indices: Food, beverage and tobacco; paper graphic arts and publishing; chemical industries of oil and coal by-products; manufacturers of metal products, machinery, equipment and transport material; construction and public works; banks and other monetary and financial institutions; real estate and services rendered to companies; all other.

RELATED INDICES

BVL 30 Index
BVL ORF Index

REMARKS

None

PUBLISHER

Bolsa de Valores de Lisboa (BVL).

BOLSA DE VALORES DE LISBOA (BVL) 30 INDEX

TOTAL RETURN PERFORMANCE

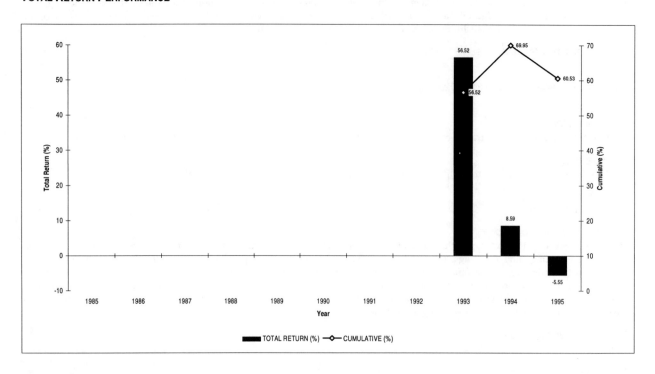

TOTAL RETURN PERFORMANCE

YEAR	VALUE	TOTAL RETURN (%)	CUMULATIVE (%)	MAXIMUM VALUE	DATE	MINIMUM VALUE	DATE
1995	1,605.30	-5.55	60.53	1,740.05	12-May	1,529.44	22-Nov
1994	1,699.54	8.59	69.95	1,863.53	18-Feb	1,447.56	20-Jun
1993	1,565.16	56.52	56.52	1,565.16	31-Dec	980.14	13-Jan
1992	1,000.00						
1991							
1990							
1989							
1988							
1987							
1986							
1985							
Average Annual (%)		19.85					
Compound Annual (%)		17.09					
Standard Deviation (%)		32.53					

SYNOPSIS

The Bolsa de Valores de Lisboa (BVL) 30 Index is a market value-weighted index that tracks the daily total return performance of 30 of the largest and most actively traded stocks on the official market of the Lisbon Stock Exchange (BVL). These shares account for 58% of the domestic equity market.

NUMBER OF STOCKS—DECEMBER 31, 1995

28

MARKET VALUE—DECEMBER 31, 1995

US$10,676.9

SELECTION CRITERIA

Component stocks include companies traded on the Market with Official Quotations of the Lisbon Stock Exchange (BVL) that are selected on the basis of market capitalization and liquidity. A selective indicator based on the number of shares traded and market capitalization, using calendar quarter data as of March, June, September and December, is the basis for ranking stocks for inclusion in the index.

BACKGROUND

The index, introduced on January 11, 1993, was established as a vehicle for trading derivative products.

BASE DATE

January 4, 1993=1000.00

COMPUTATION METHODOLOGY

(1) An aggregate of prices times quantities index formula. Maintenance adjustments to the divisor are made daily for capitalization changes, new listings and delistings. (2) Latest official price is used in the calculation of the index. For stocks traded on the national trading system, the price considered is the latest official price, regardless of the stock exchange to which the transaction is statistically assigned. (3) The absence of a price quotation for five consecutive stock market sessions results in the withdrawal of a security from the index. (4) Index members are reevaluated at the end of each calendar quarter, based on the selection indicator.

DERIVATIVE INSTRUMENTS

None

SUBINDICES

None

RELATED INDICES

BVL General Index
BVL ORF Index

REMARKS

None

PUBLISHER

Bolsa de Valores de Lisboa (BVL).

PORTUGAL STOCK MARKET PSI-20 INDEX

PRICE PERFORMANCE

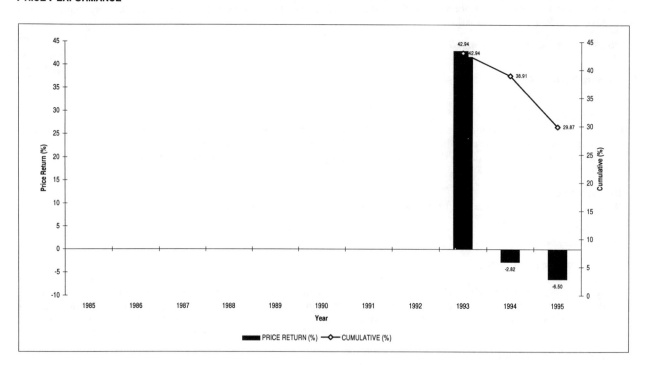

PRICE PERFORMANCE

YEAR	VALUE	PRICE RETURN (%)	CUMULATIVE (%)	MAXIMUM VALUE	DATE	MINIMUM VALUE	DATE
1995	3,896.24	-6.50	29.87	4,227.14	11-Jan	3,722.26	22-Nov
1994	4,167.28	-2.82	38.91	5,141.24	18-Feb	3,662.04	20-Jun
1993	4,288.09	42.94	42.94	4,288.09	31-Dec	2,917.66	14-Jan
1992	3,000.00						
1991							
1990							
1989							
1988							
1987							
1986							
1985							
Average Annual (%)		11.20					
Compound Annual (%)		9.10					
Standard Deviation (%)		27.54					

SYNOPSIS

The Portugal Stock Market PSI-20 Index is a market value-weighted index that tracks the daily price only performance of most liquid stocks listed on the Lisbon Stock Exchange of Portugal.

NUMBER OF STOCKS—DECEMBER 31, 1995

20

MARKET VALUE—DECEMBER 31, 1995

Not Available

SELECTION CRITERIA

Component stocks include companies traded on the Market with Official Quotations of the Lisbon Stock Exchange (BVL) that are selected on the basis of market capitalization and liquidity.

BACKGROUND

The index, introduced in 1995, was established as a vehicle for trading derivative products.

BASE DATE

December 31, 1992=3000.00

COMPUTATION METHODOLOGY

An aggregate of prices times quantities index formula. Maintenance adjustments to the divisor are made for capitalization changes, new listings and delistings.

DERIVATIVE INSTRUMENTS

PSI-20 Index futures trade on the Oporto Stock Exchange (effective June 20, 1996).

SUBINDICES

None

RELATED INDICES

None

REMARKS

With all cash transaction activities transferred to the Lisbon Stock Exchange in 1994, the Oporto Stock Exchange is reorienting itself as Portugal's financial futures market.

PUBLISHER

Oporto Stock Exchange.

CS First Boston ROS 30 Index

PRICE PERFORMANCE

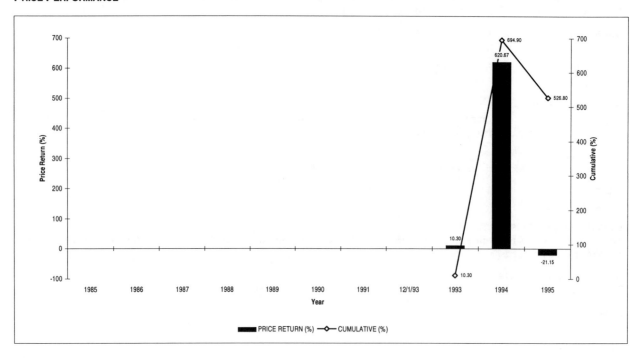

PRICE PERFORMANCE

YEAR	VALUE	PRICE RETURN (%)	CUMULATIVE (%)	MAXIMUM VALUE	DATE	MINIMUM VALUE	DATE
1995	626.80	-21.15	526.80	908.00	6-Jul	426.10	27-Apr
1994	794.90	620.67	694.90	1,706.40	15-Sep	116.60	5-Jan
1993	110.30	10.30	10.30	111.20	15-Dec	100.00	1-Dec
12/1/93	100.00						
1991							
1990							
1989							
1988							
1987							
1986							
1985							
Average Annual (%)		299.76					
Compound Annual (%)		18.97					
Standard Deviation (%)		453.83					

SYNOPSIS
The CS First Boston ROS 30 Index is a market value-weighted index that tracks the daily price only performance, in U.S. dollar terms, of the 30 largest Russian Federation stocks. Based on their full market capitalization, these shares account for an estimated 51% of the domestic market.

NUMBER OF STOCKS—DECEMBER 31, 1995
30

MARKET VALUE—DECEMBER 31, 1995
US$4,121.0 million

SELECTION CRITERIA
Index constituents include the 30 largest traded Russian Federation stocks, on the basis of free float market capitalization, that are available for purchase by all market participants, including foreigners. The index is structured so that no single industry sector dominates its performance. Therefore, exposure to any one sector is limited to 50% of the total market capitalization of the index. In the event the market capitalization of any one sector exceeds the 50% level for 22 days in the course of a quarter, the smallest company selected from the overweighted sector will be removed and replaced by the next largest company outside the index.

Preference shares, shares of companies which are more than 50% owned by an index constituent and companies whose shares have not been traded on three or more days during the quarter are excluded from the index.

BACKGROUND
After a review by the London Stock Exchange, CS First Boston implemented a number of changes to the computation of the index in November 1995. A slight rule change with regard to selection criteria was introduced in January 1996 pursuant to which shares must trade 12 times over the previous 12-months rather than three times in the last quarter.

BASE DATE
September 1, 1994=100.00

COMPUTATION METHODOLOGY
(1) An aggregate of prices times quantities index formula. Maintenance adjustments to the divisor are made for capitalization changes, new listings and delistings. (2) Market capitalization of constituent companies is calculated on the basis of free float of voting shares. For example, in the case of a company that restricts the sale of its shares to foreigners, only the segment that is available for purchase by foreigners is used to calculate free float market capitalization both for constituent selection and index calculation purposes. In cases where a company's share capital has been specifically removed from circulation, such as cases involving stakes held by the government, such segments are not included in the calculation of free float. (3) Index constituents as well as free float are reviewed on a quarterly basis, using publicly available and company supplied information. (4) The use of the last traded price provided by a price quotation service for index calculation purposes is preferable. In the absence of such prices, however, the last traded price from trades transacted by CS First Boston during the day are used. Otherwise, prices that CS First Boston would have considered for use had trades actually taken place during the day, are utilized. In the event CS First Boston must resort to the last pricing option, which is frequently the case, and a price change in one day of more than 25% is experienced, such movement must be confirmed by reference to two other pricing sources, such as quotes by competing brokers, either on Reuters or Bloomberg, or prices published in Moscow newspapers.

DERIVATIVE INSTRUMENTS
None

SUBINDICES
None

RELATED INDICES
CS First Boson ROS 30 Ruble Index
CS First Boston Convertible Securities Index
CS First Boston High Yield Index

REMARKS
(1) There is, at present, no formal Russian Federation stock exchange and the over-the-counter trading system is still in its infancy. Combined with the absence of firm bid and/or offer quotations, the availability of reliable pricing information is restricted. (2) Market value refers to free float. The equivalent market capitalization of the thirty stocks is US$11,143.0 million.

PUBLISHER
CS First Boston.

MOSCOW TIMES STOCK INDEX

PRICE PERFORMANCE

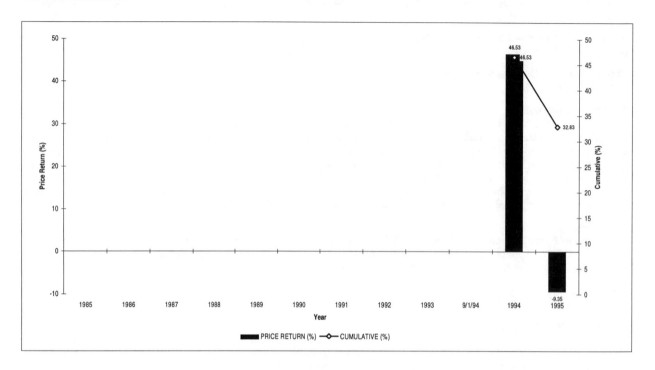

PRICE PERFORMANCE

YEAR	VALUE	PRICE RETURN (%)	CUMULATIVE (%)	MAXIMUM VALUE	DATE	MINIMUM VALUE	DATE
1995	132.83	-9.35	32.83	196.13	7-Jul	104.03	10-Feb
1994	146.53	46.53	46.53	166.17	12-Oct	100.00	1-Sep
9/1/94	100.00						
1993							
1992							
1991							
1990							
1989							
1988							
1987							
1986							
1985							
Average Annual (%)		27.96					
Compound Annual (%)		NM					
Standard Deviation (%)		NM					

SYNOPSIS

The Moscow Times Stock Index is a market value-weighted index that tracks the daily price only performance of large, actively traded Russian Federation stocks. These shares account for an estimated 56% of the domestic equity market capitalization.

NUMBER OF STOCKS—DECEMBER 31, 1995

50

MARKET VALUE—DECEMBER 31, 1995

US$12,272.0 million

SELECTION CRITERIA

Index constituents include at least 30 of the top Russian companies that are selected on the basis of the following criteria:

(1) Investability–At least 25% of the shares must be publicly available for investment and not restricted to a single party or parties acting in concert. Unless there is evidence to the contrary, two or more holders with control of over 75% of a single security may be deemed as to acting in concert. (2) Price–An accurate and reliable price for the determination of a security's market value must be in evidence. Three separate licensed financial market participants acting as market makers must be able to provide an independent buy or sell price for the stock on a daily basis; (3) Liquidity–Securities that do not trade for at least one day during a 60-day period preceding the quarterly review meetings may be excluded from eligibility as an index constituent. Also, the initial share offer, which may be defined as the company's privatization auction, must be completed and shares subsequently traded for at least three months prior to being eligible for inclusion in the index.

Companies whose stock prices are solely a direct derivation of an underlying stock or other security holdings and companies whose primary business activity is not transparent or which do not appear to be involved in a substantial business activity are not eligible for inclusion in the index.

BACKGROUND

The Moscow Times Index Advisory Board oversees the index and criteria for inclusion.

BASE DATE

September 1, 1994=100.00

COMPUTATION METHODOLOGY

(1) An aggregate of prices times quantities index formula. Maintenance adjustments to the divisor are made for capitalization changes, new listings and delistings. (2) The index is calculated in Rubles, using the average of bid and/or offer quotations received from at least three market makers, and, whenever possible, five market makers. In the event quotations are available from five market makers, the highest and lowest prices will be excluded. In computing average bid and/or offer quotations, the quotations of each market maker are averaged first, followed by the computation of an average of the bid and/or offer quotations for all market makers. (3) The market capitalization of constituent companies is updated one week after information regarding a change in market capitalization becomes available. (4) Index constituents are reviewed on a quarterly basis.

DERIVATIVE INSTRUMENTS

None

SUBINDICES

None

RELATED INDICES

Moscow Times Dollar Adjusted Stock Index

REMARKS

There is, at present, no formal Russian Federation stock exchange and the over-the-counter trading system is still in its infancy. Combined with the absence of firm bid and/or offer quotations, the availability of reliable pricing information is restricted.

PUBLISHER

The Moscow Times/Skate-Press.

Slovak Share Index (SAX)

TOTAL RETURN PERFORMANCE

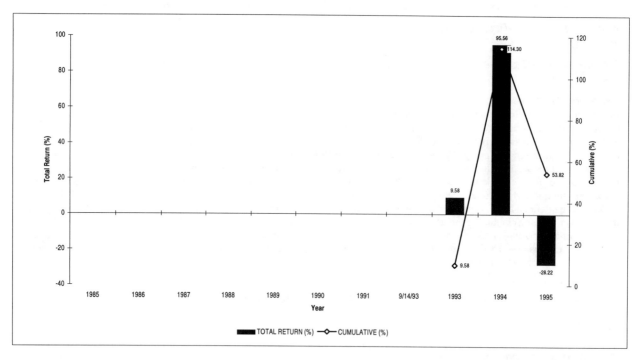

TOTAL RETURN PERFORMANCE

YEAR	VALUE	TOTAL RETURN (%)	CUMULATIVE (%)	MAXIMUM VALUE	DATE	MINIMUM VALUE	DATE
1995	153.82	-28.22	53.82	216.25	2-Jan	147.08	12-Dec
1994	214.30	95.56	114.30	405.50	23-Feb	109.60	3-Jan
1993	109.58	9.58	9.58	114.39	21-Dec	100.00	14-Sep
9/14/93	100.00						
1991							
1990							
1989							
1988							
1987							
1986							
1985							
Average Annual (%)		25.64					
Compound Annual (%)		15.44					
Standard Deviation (%)		63.44					

SYNOPSIS

The Slovak Share Index (SAX) Index is a market value-weighted index that tracks the daily total return performance of the largest and most actively traded shares listed on the Main and Junior Markets of the Bratislava Stock Exchange (BSE). These companies account for about 93% of the BSE's listed market capitalization.

NUMBER OF STOCKS—DECEMBER 31, 1995

12

MARKET VALUE—DECEMBER 22, 1995

US$1,159.0 million

SELECTION CRITERIA

Companies are selected on the basis of market capitalization and trading volume so as to reflect the price movement of the market as a whole. The 12 constituent companies, are as follows: Nafta, Slovnaft, Ozeta, Biotika, VUB, VSZ, IRB, Slovenska poist'ovna, Chirana, Slovenske lodenice, Provazske stronjarne, and Plastika.

BACKGROUND

At its inception, the SAX Index was comprised of eight firms. Expanded trading activity on the BSE promoted the addition of four constituent companies as of May 12, 1995. This development strengthened the sectoral structure of the index so as to more properly reflect the Slovak economy.

BASE DATE

September 14, 1993=100.00

COMPUTATION METHODOLOGY

(1) An aggregate of prices times quantities index formula. (2) Average daily prices are currently used, however, with improving liquidity, index calculation will revert to closing prices.

DERIVATIVE INSTRUMENTS

None

SUBINDICES

None

RELATED INDICES

None

REMARKS

(1) Four constituent companies were added to index as of May 12, 1995. These are: Chirana, Slovenske lodenice, Provazske stronjarne, and Plastika. (2) The trading volume of Nafta accounts for about 63% of the trading volume of the BSE Automated Bourse Trading System (ABTS). (3) The four largest index components, including Nafta, Slovnaft, VSZ and VUB account for 79% of the SAX's market capitalization. (4) The BSE listed 829 Unlisted Shares as of December 22, 1995 with a market capitalization of US$4,116.7 million. (5) Market value is as of the last trading day of the year on December 22, 1995. Exchange rate is as of December 31, 1995.

PUBLISHER

The Bratislava Stock Exchange (BSE).

IBEX-35 INDEX

PRICE PERFORMANCE

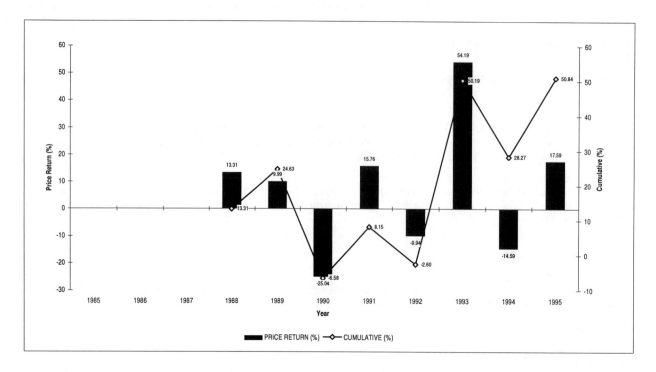

PRICE PERFORMANCE

YEAR	VALUE	PRICE RETURN (%)	CUMULATIVE (%)	MAXIMUM VALUE	DATE	MINIMUM VALUE	DATE
1995	3,630.76	17.59	50.84	3,633.80	22-Dec	2,865.10	23-Mar
1994	3,087.68	-14.59	28.27	3,980.53	31-Jan	3,036.08	29-Dec
1993	3,615.20	54.19	50.19	3,631.45	27-Dec	2,354.00	4-Jan
1992	2,344.60	-9.94	-2.60	2,857.18	28-Feb	1,873.58	5-Oct
1991	2,603.30	15.76	8.15	2,897.60	5-Jun	2,151.20	14-Jan
1990	2,248.80	-25.04	-6.58	3,042.30	3-Jan	2,060.70	28-Sep
1989	3,000.00	9.99	24.63	3,374.30	27-Sep	2,682.00	1-Mar
1988	2,727.50	13.31	13.31	3,060.70	15-Jun	2,385.90	4-Jan
1987	2,407.10						
1986							
1985							
Average Annual (%)		7.66					
Compound Annual (%)		5.27					
Standard Deviation (%)		24.61					

The IBEX-35 Index is a market value-weighted index that tracks the continuous stock price only performance of the most actively traded stocks traded on the continuous market of the four Spanish stock markets, including Bolsa de Madrid, Bolsa de Barcelona, Bolsa de Bilbao, and Bolsa de Valencia.

NUMBER OF STOCKS—DECEMBER 31, 1995
35

MARKET VALUE—DECEMBER 31, 1995
US$115,258.05 million

SELECTION CRITERIA
Component stocks represent the most liquid companies traded on the continuous market in Spain.

BACKGROUND
Introduced in January 1991, the IBEX-35 was developed for the purpose of trading derivative products. The index actually dates back to 1987 when it was called Fiex.

BASE DATE
December 31, 1989=3000.00

COMPUTATION METHODOLOGY
(1) An aggregate of prices times quantities index formula. Maintenance adjustments to the divisor are made for capitalization changes, new listings and delistings. (2) The composition of the index is revised on a semi-annual basis. (3) The price per share for each constituent company is based on the last transaction on the continuous market.

DERIVATIVE INSTRUMENTS
IBEX-35 Index futures and options trade on the Mercado Espanol de Futuros Financieros (MEFF) Renta Variable.

SUBINDICES
None

RELATED INDICES
None

REMARKS
None

PUBLISHER
Sociedad de Bolsas S.A.

MADRID GENERAL INDEX

PRICE PERFORMANCE

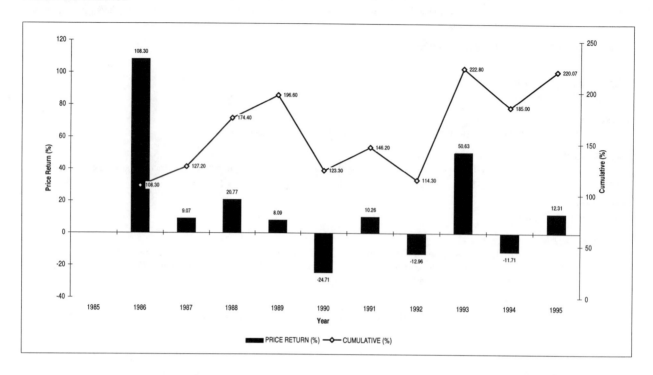

PRICE AND TOTAL RETURN PERFORMANCE

YEAR	VALUE	PRICE RETURN (%)	CUMULATIVE (%)	TOTAL RETURN (%)	MAXIMUM VALUE	DATE	MINIMUM VALUE	DATE
1995	320.07	12.31	220.07	16.19	320.21	22-Dec	261.84	23-Mar
1994	285.00	-11.71	185.00	-9.24	358.57	3-Feb	279.00	29-Dec
1993	322.80	50.63	222.80	55.87	323.71	27-Dec	213.76	4-Jan
1992	214.30	-12.96	114.30	-7.37	266.51	28-Feb	179.48	5-Oct
1991	246.20	10.26	146.20	14.95	289.22	18-Mar	213.78	14-Jan
1990	223.30	-24.71	123.30	-22.54	309.74	16-Jul	209.37	28-Sep
1989	296.60	8.09	196.60	11.23	328.55	13-Sep	268.61	1-Mar
1988	274.40	20.77	174.40	24.71	301.63	15-Jun	225.50	4-Jan
1987	227.20	9.07	127.20	12.46	328.36	10-Jun	201.08	4-Dec
1986	208.30	108.30	108.30	115.90	208.83	19-Dec	100.83	3-Jan
1985	100.00							
Average Annual (%)		17.00		21.22				
Compound Annual (%)		12.34		16.40				
Standard Deviation (%)		38.23		39.55				

SYNOPSIS
The Madrid General Index is a market value-weighted index that tracks the daily stock price only and total return performance of liquid, actively traded, large capitalization common stocks traded on the Madrid Stock Exchange. These shares account for 72% of the Madrid stock market capitalization.

NUMBER OF STOCKS—DECEMBER 31, 1995
106

MARKET VALUE—DECEMBER 31, 1995
US$136,310.0 million

SELECTION CRITERIA
Constituent shares are selected for inclusion in the index at the end of each year on the basis of market capitalization, liquidity and frequency of trading within each of nine industry sectors.

BACKGROUND
The index dates back to December 1940, and until 1985 it was rebased to a value of 100.00 on a yearly basis.

BASE DATE
December 31, 1985=100.00

COMPUTATION METHODOLOGY
(1) An aggregate of prices times quantities index formula. Maintenance adjustments to the divisor are made for capitalization changes, new listings and delistings. (2) The weighting of each sector in the index is determined by the sector's market capitalization. The weighting of each share in its respective sector is determined by its percentage of the sector's capitalization. (3) Total returns are calculated using net dividends. Adjustments for dividends are made on a daily basis, by estimating the net dividend amount paid during the previous year. The amount obtained by dividing that sum by 365 days and multiplying it by the number of days that have passed is deducted from the daily share price. On the day the dividend is actually paid, the net amount paid is worked out and the fall in the share price from discounting the dividend is corrected.

DERIVATIVE INSTRUMENTS
None

SUBINDICES
Nine sector indices: Banks and insurance companies, utilities, food, construction, portfolio investment, metal-working, oil-chemicals, communications, other industries and services.

RELATED INDICES
Madrid General Long Price Index (Same as Madrid General Price Index, but base date is December 31, 1940=100.00)
Madrid General Long Total Index (Same as Madrid General Price Index, but base date is December 31, 1940=100.00)
Madrid General CPI Adusted Indices

REMARKS
None

PUBLISHER
The Madrid Stock Exchange.

OMX Index

PRICE PERFORMANCE

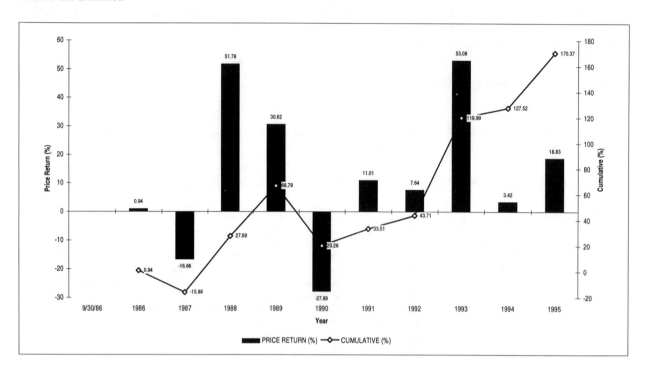

PRICE PERFORMANCE[1]

YEAR	VALUE	PRICE RETURN (%)	CUMULATIVE (%)	MAXIMUM VALUE	DATE	MINIMUM VALUE	DATE
1995	1,351.85	18.83	170.37	1,477.85	19-Sep	1,092.64	9-Mar
1994	1,137.59	3.42	127.52	1,238.43	31-Jan	1,021.08	6-Jul
1993	1,099.94	53.08	119.99	1,123.14	4-Nov	693.42	25-Jan
1992	718.54	7.64	43.71	753.09	3-Jun	482.06	6-Oct
1991	667.54	11.01	33.51	837.29	11-Jul	549.93	8-Jan
1990	601.32	-27.89	20.26	927.85	4-Jul	554.13	28-Nov
1989[2]	833.93	30.62	66.79	880.78	29-Aug	610.03	2-Jan
1988	638.43	51.78	27.69	642.56	29-Dec	414.78	4-Jan
1987	420.62	-16.66	-15.88	654.98	8-Oct	400.94	3-Dec
1986[3]	504.71	0.94	0.94	504.71	30-Dec	499.29	29-Dec
9/30/86	500.00						
Average Annual (%)		14.65					
Compound Annual (%)		10.35					
Standard Deviation (%)		27.63					

[1]Statistical measures applicable to the period 1987-1995.
[2]Low index value occured on 1/2/1989 and 1/4/1989.
[3]1986 index values for the period 12/18/1986-12/31/1986.

The OMX Index is a market value-weighted index that tracks the stock price performance of the most liquid issues traded on the Stockholm Stock Exchange (SSE). These shares account for 61% of the aggregate market value of all shares trading on the main, O-T-C as well as unofficial markets.

Number of Stocks—December 31, 1995
30

Market Value—December 31, 1995
US$108,638.35 million

Selection Criteria
Constituent stocks are selected on the basis of traded volume during a six-month period beginning seven months prior to the beginning of the calendar half-year, as follows:

(1) A stock's trading volume, as calculated in Swedish Krona, must place it within the 45 most traded stocks on the SSE. Otherwise, the constituent is replaced by a non-index stock with the highest traded volume; (2) If a non-index SSE-listed constituent stock is among the 15 most-traded stocks, it shall replace an index constituent with the lowest traded volume; (3) A stock may be excluded from consideration in the event that a significant portion of its trading volume is attributable to a few transactions or to transactions that have occurred within a limited time period; (4) A stock may be removed from the index in the event that its trading volume is so low that price information is no longer satisfactory, i.e., price paid deviates from the bid-asked spread by a significant amount. Also, constituent stocks may be replaced in the event of delistings and takeover situations.

Background
The OMX was launched in September 1986 to serve as a trading vehicle for stock index futures and options.

Base Date
September 30, 1986=500.00

Computation Methodology
(1) An aggregate of prices times quantities index formula. Maintenance adjustments to the divisor are made for capitalization changes, new listings and delistings. (2) Index constituents are reviewed twice a year, however more frequent modifications are preceded by announcements made two trading days prior to implementation.

Derivative Instruments
OMX index futures and options trade on OM Stockholm AB, a wholly-owned subsidiary of OM Gruppen AB.
OMX Flex derivative products trade on OM Stockholm AB, a wholly-owned subsidiary of OM Gruppen AB.
OMX index futures and options trade on the London Securities and Derivatives Exchange (OMLX).

Subindices
None

Related Indices
None

Remarks
None

Publisher
OM Stockholm AB.

THE STOCKHOLM STOCK EXCHANGE GENERAL (SX-GENERAL) INDEX

PRICE PERFORMANCE

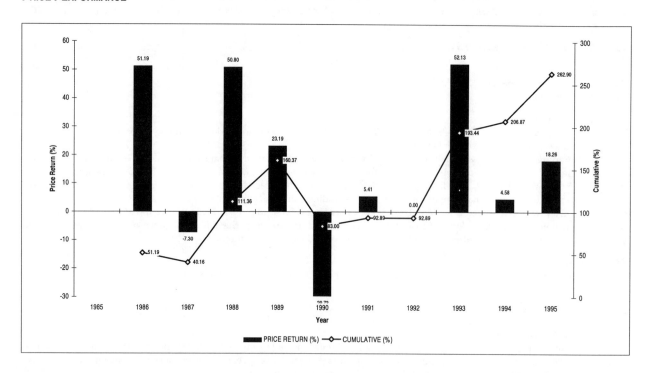

PRICE PERFORMANCE

YEAR	VALUE	PRICE RETURN (%)	CUMULATIVE (%)	MAXIMUM VALUE	DATE	MINIMUM VALUE	DATE
1995	1,716.16	18.26	262.90	1,850.84	19-Sep	1,419.02	29-Mar
1994	1,451.20	4.58	206.87	1,582.00	31-Jan	1,318.50	6-Jul
1993	1,387.70	52.13	193.44	1,415.20	3-Nov	874.10	28-Jan
1992	912.20	0.00	92.89	909.90	11-May	640.80	5-Oct
1991	912.20	5.41	92.89	1,138.70	11-Jul	803.70	8-Jan
1990	865.40	-29.72	83.00	1,308.40	5-Jul	807.10	27-Nov
1989	1,231.30	23.19	160.37	1,349.10	16-Aug	953.10	2-Jan
1988	999.50	50.80	111.36	999.50	30-Dec	652.40	4-Jan
1987	662.80	-7.30	40.16	987.40	8-Oct	607.90	11-Nov
1986	715.00	51.19	51.19	760.10	7-Nov	478.20	20-Jan
1985	472.90						
Average Annual (%)		16.85					
Compound Annual (%)		13.76					
Standard Deviation (%)		27.76					

SYNOPSIS

The Stockholm Stock Exchange General (SX-General) Index is a broad market value-weighted index that tracks the continuous stock price performance of all classes of stock traded on the A-list of the Stockholm Stock Exchange (SSE), including convertible participation notes. These shares account for 97% of the aggregate market value of all shares trading on the main, O-T-C as well as unofficial markets.

NUMBER OF STOCKS—DECEMBER 31, 1995

126

MARKET VALUE—DECEMBER 31, 1995

US$171,380.0 million

SELECTION CRITERIA

All securities, including convertible participation notes, listed and traded on the A-List of the Stockholm Stock Exchange, Sweden's dominant market for the largest and most heavily traded securities.

BACKGROUND

None

BASE DATE

December 31, 1979=100.00

COMPUTATION METHODOLOGY

(1) An aggregate of prices times quantities index formula. Maintenance adjustments to the divisor are made daily upon first quotation following capitalization changes, new listings and delistings. New companies are added to the index on the second day of trading after registration. (2) Most recent price paid is used in the calculation of the index. In the event there is no paid price for the day, the most recent bid price is used. In the absence of a most recent bid price, the paid price or bid of the previous day is used.

DERIVATIVE INSTRUMENTS

None

SUBINDICES

Nine industrial sector subindices: Engineering, forest products, chemicals and pharmaceuticals, wholesale and retail trade, services, real estate and construction, investment companies, banks and insurance as well as miscellaneous industries.
SX-16 Index
SX-70 Index

RELATED INDICES

SX-O Index
SX-OTC Index

REMARKS

None

PUBLISHER

The Stockholm Fondbors AB.

THE STOCKHOLM STOCK EXCHANGE O-LIST INDEX

PRICE PERFORMANCE

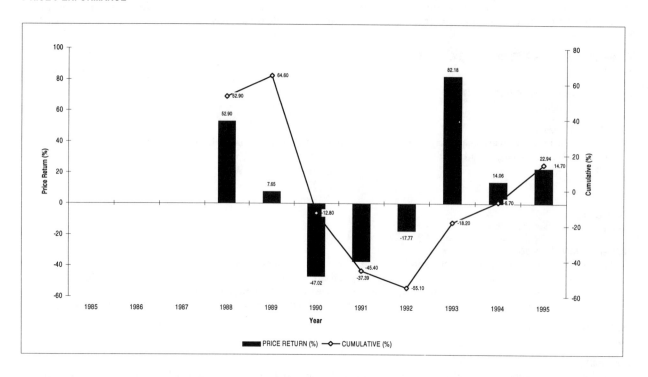

PRICE PERFORMANCE

YEAR	VALUE	PRICE RETURN (%)	CUMULATIVE (%)	MAXIMUM VALUE	DATE	MINIMUM VALUE	DATE
1995	114.70	22.94	14.70	114.70	29-Dec	86.70	29-Mar
1994	93.30	14.06	-6.70	103.00	19-May	81.30	18-Jul
1993	81.80	82.18	-18.20	84.40	3-Nov	44.10	25-Jan
1992	44.90	-17.77	-55.10	65.60	27-Jan	34.40	29-Sep
1991	54.60	-37.39	-45.40	91.90	19-Feb	60.70	19-Dec
1990	87.20	-47.02	-12.80	163.30	9-Jan	83.50	21-Jan
1989	164.60	7.65	64.60	174.80	15-Aug	143.10	2-Jan
1988	152.90	52.90	52.90	152.90	30-Dec	99.20	4-Jan
1987	100.00						
1986							
1985							
Average Annual (%)		9.69					
Compound Annual (%)		1.73					
Standard Deviation (%)		43.93					

SYNOPSIS
The Stockholm Stock Exchange O-list Index is a market value-weighted index that tracks the continuous stock price performance of all outstanding stock of all classes or series listed on the O-list of the Stockholm Stock Exchange (SSE). These shares account for 2% of the aggregate market value of all shares trading on the main, O-T-C as well as unofficial markets.

NUMBER OF STOCKS—DECEMBER 31, 1995
47

MARKET VALUE—DECEMBER 31, 1995
US$3,740.0 million

SELECTION CRITERIA
All securities listed and traded on Stockholm's Stock Exchange O-List, Sweden's unofficial parallel market which deals in unlisted shares, both on and off the exchange floor.

BACKGROUND
None

BASE DATE
December 31, 1987=100.00

COMPUTATION METHODOLOGY
(1) An aggregate of prices times quantities index formula. Maintenance adjustments to the divisor are made daily upon first quotation following capitalization changes, new listings and delistings. New companies are added to the index on the second day of trading after registration. (2) Most recent price paid is used in the calculation of the index. In the event there is no paid price for the day, the most recent bid price is used. In the absence of a most recent bid price, the paid price or bid of the previous day is used.

DERIVATIVE INSTRUMENTS
None

SUBINDICES
None

RELATED INDICES
SX-OTC Index
The Stockholm Stock Exchange General (SX-General) Index

REMARKS
None

PUBLISHER
The Stockholm Fondbors AB.

THE STOCKHOLM STOCK EXCHANGE OTC INDEX

PRICE PERFORMANCE

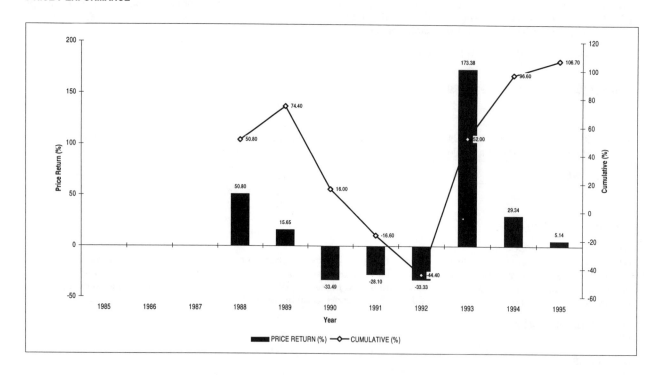

PRICE PERFORMANCE

YEAR	VALUE	PRICE RETURN (%)	CUMULATIVE (%)	MAXIMUM VALUE	DATE	MINIMUM VALUE	DATE
1995	206.70	5.14	106.70	229.50	21-Sep	188.40	6-Jun
1994	196.60	29.34	96.60	202.40	21-Feb	151.50	3-Jan
1993	152.00	173.38	52.00	152.30	28-Dec	54.10	4-Jan
1992	55.60	-33.33	-44.40	88.00	7-Feb	48.10	21-Dec
1991	83.40	-28.10	-16.60	122.40	18-Mar	78.00	19-Dec
1990	116.00	-33.49	16.00	170.80	2-Jan	112.80	27-Dec
1989	174.40	15.65	74.40	188.60	10-Oct	142.00	3-Jan
1988	150.80	50.80	50.80	152.50	16-Dec	96.10	13-Jan
1987	100.00						
1986							
1985							
Average Annual (%)		22.42					
Compound Annual (%)		9.50					
Standard Deviation (%)		68.42					

SYNOPSIS
The Stockholm Stock Exchange OTC Index is a market value-weighted index that tracks the continuous stock price performance of all outstanding stock of all classes or series listed on the over-the-counter (O-T-C) market of the Stockholm Stock Exchange (SSE). These shares account for 1% of the aggregate market value of all shares trading on the main, O-T-C as well as unofficial markets.

NUMBER OF STOCKS—DECEMBER 31, 1995
50

MARKET VALUE—DECEMBER 31, 1995
US$2,040.0 million

SELECTION CRITERIA
All securities listed and traded on the O-T-C market of the Stockholm Stock Exchange, Sweden's market for small and medium sized companies.

BASE DATE
December 31, 1987=100.00

COMPUTATION METHODOLOGY
(1) An aggregate of prices times quantities index formula. Maintenance adjustments to the divisor are made daily upon first quotation following capitalization changes, new listings and delistings. New companies are added to the index on the second day of trading after registration. (2) Most recent price paid is used in the calculation of the index. In the event there is no paid price for the day, the most recent bid price is used. In the absence of a most recent bid price, the paid price or bid of the previous day is used.

DERIVATIVE INSTRUMENTS
None

SUBINDICES
None

RELATED INDICES
SX-O Index
The Stockholm Stock Exchange General (SX-General) Index

REMARKS
None

PUBLISHER
The Stockholm Fondbors AB.

Swiss Market Index (SMI)

Price Performance

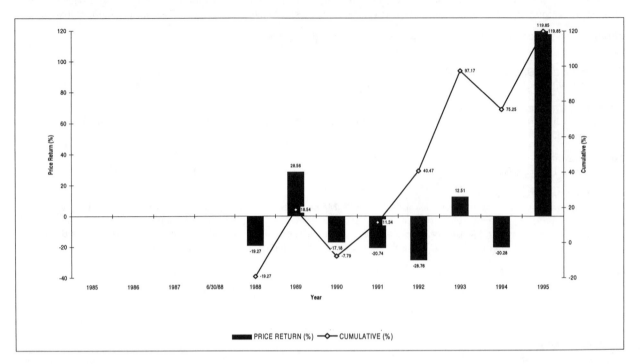

Price Performance

YEAR	VALUE	PRICE RETURN (%)	CUMULATIVE (%)	MAXIMUM VALUE	DATE	MINIMUM VALUE	DATE
1995	3,297.70	25.45	119.85	3,317.10	27-Dec	2,450.30	13-Mar
1994	2,628.80	-11.12	75.25	3,178.40	31-Jan	2,458.60	27-Oct
1993	2,957.60	40.37	97.17	2,972.60	27-Dec	2,049.50	11-Jan
1992	2,107.00	26.16	40.47	2,107.00	30-Dec	1,690.30	8-Jan
1991	1,670.10	20.75	11.34	1,742.80	31-May	1,287.60	14-Jan
1990	1,383.10	-22.21	-7.79	1,860.40	13-Jul	1,351.00	28-Sep
1989	1,778.10	23.87	18.54	1,910.02	28-Aug	1,433.60	27-Feb
1988	1,435.40	-4.31	-4.31	NA	NA	NA	NA
6/30/88	1,500.00						
1987							
1986							
1985							
Average Annual (%)		13.1⌣					
Compound Annual (%)		11.07					
Standard Deviation (%)[1]		22.57					

[1]Standard deviation applies to calendar years 1989-1995

SYNOPSIS

The Swiss Market Index (SMI) is a market value-weighted index that tracks the continuous stock price only and daily total return performance of the largest permanent and most actively traded Swiss securities on the Zurich, Geneva and Basle Stock Exchanges of Switzerland. These shares account for 70% of the domestic equity market capitalization.

NUMBER OF STOCKS—DECEMBER 31, 1995

21

MARKET VALUE—DECEMBER 31, 1995

US$278,960.8 million

SELECTION CRITERIA

Components, which many number between 20 and 24 securities, include the most liquid securities of highly capitalized Swiss companies which are permanently traded on the Zurich, Geneva and Basle Stock Exchanges and may be held by foreigners. Turnover is the most important determinant in the selection of constituent shares, but sector mix of the index as a whole and market capitalization may also be taken into consideration.

BACKGROUND

The SMI, which was designed to serve as an underlying vehicle for stock index futures and options, was introduced in August 1988 and recalculated to December 30, 1987. A total return version of the index was introduced on January 4, 1993 with a base date of June 30, 1988.

BASE DATE

June 30, 1988 = 1500.00

COMPUTATION METHODOLOGY

(1) An aggregate of prices times quantities (Laspeyres) index formula. Maintenance adjustments to the divisor are made daily after the close of trading for capitalization changes, new listings and delistings. (2) Newly listed securities are generally added to the index on the second day of trading, using the closing price on the first day of trading for the index adjustment. (3) Market capitalization is determined on the basis of the actual number of shares outstanding. Such a determination is made twice a year, on June 15 and December 15. Modifications to market capitalizations are reflected at the beginning of the following month. (4) Prices based on quotations on the Zurich, Geneva and Basle Stock Exchanges and pre-bourse markets. On local market holidays the prices on the active exchanges are used. In the absence of a transaction, the last buyer's price or previous days value is utilized. (5) Total returns are calculated with dividends reinvested on the ex-dividend date.

DERIVATIVE INSTRUMENTS

SMI Index futures and options trade on the Swiss Options and Financial Futures Exchange AG (SOFFEX).
SMI Long-Term options trade on SOFFEX.

SUBINDICES

None

RELATED INDICES

Swiss Bid/Ask Index (SBAI)
Swiss Bond Index
Swiss Price Index

REMARKS

None

PUBLISHER

Association Tripartite Bourses (ATB).

Swiss Performance Index (SPI)

Price Performance

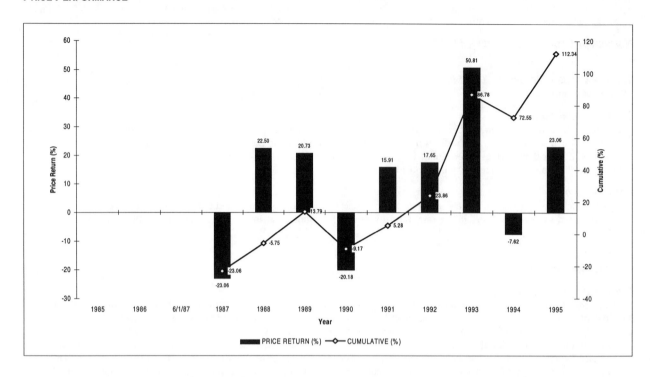

Price Performance

YEAR	VALUE	PRICE RETURN (%)	CUMULATIVE (%)	MAXIMUM VALUE	DATE	MINIMUM VALUE	DATE
1995	2,123.43	23.06	112.34	2,131.68	27-Dec	1,614.34	13-Mar
1994	1,725.53	-7.62	72.55	2,007.47	31-Jan	1,630.54	27-Oct
1993	1,867.84	50.81	86.78	1,873.54	27-Dec	1,221.25	11-Jan
1992	1,238.57	17.65	23.86	1,238.60	30-Dec	1,003.40	8-Jan
1991	1,052.80	15.91	5.28	1,129.10	19-Jul	843.50	14-Jan
1990	908.30	-20.18	-9.17	1,231.00	13-Jul	884.70	27-Nov
1989	1,137.90	20.73	13.79	1,226.60	28-Aug	194.90	27-Feb
1988	942.50	22.50	-5.75	943.70	2-Nov	753.40	13-Jan
1987	769.40	-23.06	-23.06	1,206.20	NA	736.50	NA
6/1/87	1,000.00						
1986							
1985							
Average Annual (%)		11.74					
Compound Annual (%)		9.26					
Standard Deviation (%)[1]		21.35					

[1] Standard deviation applies to calendar years 1988-1995

SYNOPSIS

The Swiss Performance Index (SPI) is a broad based market value-weighted index that tracks the continuous stock price and daily total return performance of all securities quoted on the main and official parallel markets of the Zurich, Geneva and Basle Stock Exchanges of Switzerland.

NUMBER OF STOCKS—DECEMBER 31, 1995

338

MARKET VALUE—DECEMBER 31, 1995

US$396,860.7 million

SELECTION CRITERIA

All bearer stocks, registered stocks and certificates of participation listed in Zurich, Geneva and Basle and on the official parallel markets in Zurich and Geneva (marche annexe).

BACKGROUND

The SPI, which was previously known as the "SwissIndex," was introduced on September 1, 1987 as a total return index and recalculated to December 29, 1983. A price only version of the index was introduced later with a base value of 1000.00 as of December 31, 1993.

BASE DATE

June 1, 1987=1000.00

COMPUTATION METHODOLOGY

(1) An aggregate of prices times quantities (Laspeyres) index formula. Maintenance adjustments to the divisor are made daily after the close of trading for capitalization changes, new listings and delistings. (2) Newly listed securities are generally added to the index on the second day of trading, using the closing price on the first day of trading for the index adjustment. (3) Market capitalization is determined on the basis of the number of shares authorized, including shares held in reserve, regardless of the number of shares that are actually in circulation. (4) The classification of securities according to economic sector is based on the main field of operations. (5) Prices based on quotations on the Zurich, Geneva and Basle Stock Exchanges and pre-bourse markets. On local market holidays the prices on the active exchanges are used. In the absence of a transaction, the last buyer's price or previous day's value is utilized. (6) Total returns are calculated with dividends reinvested on the ex-dividend date.

DERIVATIVE INSTRUMENTS

None

SUBINDICES

Two broad based subindices: Services and industrial companies.

Thirteen sectoral subindices within the services and industrial sectors: Services Sector–Banks, insurance companies, transportation, retailers and miscellaneous services; Industrial Sector–Machinery, utilities, chemicals, food, electronics, building contractors and materials, and miscellaneous industrial companies.

Swiss Middle Companies Index
Swiss Middle and Large Companies Index
Swiss Large Companies Index
Swiss Small Companies Index
Swiss Small and Middle Companies Index

RELATED INDICES

Swiss Bid/Ask Index (SBAI)
Swiss Bond Index
Swiss Market Index

REMARKS

None

PUBLISHER

Association Tripartite Bourses (ATB).

ISTANBUL STOCK EXCHANGE (ISE) COMPOSITE INDEX

PRICE PERFORMANCE

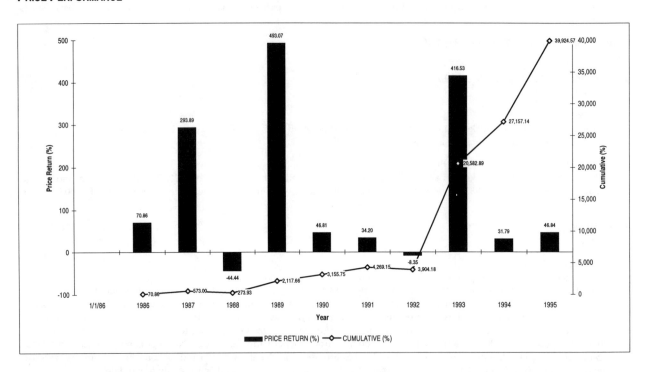

PRICE PERFORMANCE

YEAR	VALUE	PRICE RETURN (%)	CUMULATIVE (%)	MAXIMUM VALUE[1]	DATE	MINIMUM VALUE[1]	DATE
1995	40,024.57	46.84	39,924.57	54,565.03	21-Apr	24,644.31	23-Jan
1994	27,257.14	31.79	27,157.14	27,257.14	31-Dec	14,087.16	31-Mar
1993	20,682.89	416.53	20,582.89	20,682.89	31-Dec	4,383.01	31-Jan
1992	4,004.18	-8.35	3,904.18	4,926.19	31-Jan	3,297.36	30-May
1991	4,369.15	34.20	4,269.15	5,102.57	28-Feb	2,746.84	31-Oct
1990	3,255.75	46.81	3,155.75	5,384.48	31-Jul	3,255.75	31-Dec
1989	2,217.66	493.07	2,117.66	2,217.66	31-Dec	379.74	31-Jan
1988	373.93	-44.44	273.93	857.74	31-Jan	402.12	31-Oct
1987	673.00	293.89	573.00	1,149.03	31-Aug	216.90	31-Jan
1986[2]	170.86	70.86	70.86	170.86	31-Dec	100.00	31-Jan
1/1/86	100.00						
Average Annual (%)		138.12					
Compound Annual (%)		82.07					
Standard Deviation (%)		190.28					

[1]Maximum/minimum values are based on month end index values.
[2]1986 price only performance since 1/31/1986 inception date.

SYNOPSIS

The Istanbul Stock Exchange (ISE) Composite Index is a market value-weighted index that tracks the daily price only performance of actively traded large capitalization stocks listed on the Istanbul Stock Exchange (ISE). These shares account for about 85% of listed shares as measured on the basis of trading volume and market capitalization.

NUMBER OF STOCKS—DECEMBER 31, 1995
100

MARKET VALUE—DECEMBER 31, 1995
US$3,141.0 million

SELECTION CRITERIA
Constituent stocks are selected on the basis of market value open to the public, average daily trading value and average daily number of trading contracts.

BACKGROUND
From its inception and continuing to October 26, 1987, the ISE Composite Index was calculated on a weekly basis and daily thereafter. Until the end of 1990, the index was market value-weighted. It was modified in 1991 and the market value-weighting methodology was replaced by a combination of flotation and number of shares outstanding of each constituent company as a weighting factor. At the same time, two subindices were introduced.

BASE DATE
January 1986=100.00

COMPUTATION METHODOLOGY
(1) An aggregate of prices times quantities index formula, using flotation weights. Maintenance adjustments to the divisor are made for capitalization changes, new listings and delistings. (2) Flotation weight is determined on the basis of the publicly held portion, and is reviewed on a quarterly basis. (3) The index is adjusted as required to take into account increases in capital. (4) The index composition is reviewed quarterly, at which time constituent stocks may be added or deleted. (5) Last available price is used in the event a constituent stock ceases to trade or is suspended.

DERIVATIVE INSTRUMENTS
None

SUBINDICES
Two industrial subindices: Industrials Index, consisting of industrial and commercial companies and the Financials Index, consisting of banks, holding companies, insurance companies, leasing and factoring companies. Each of the indices are calculated in Turkish Lira terms and U.S. dollar terms. In calculating the indices in U.S. dollar terms, the Central Bank's effective US$ buying rates are used.

RELATED INDICES
The index is calculated daily on the basis of closing prices as well as the weighted average prices.

REMARKS
Market value of index constituents is based on flotation weights.

PUBLISHER
Istanbul Stock Exchange (ISE).

FINANCIAL TIMES ORDINARY SHARE INDEX (30 SHARE INDEX)

PRICE PERFORMANCE

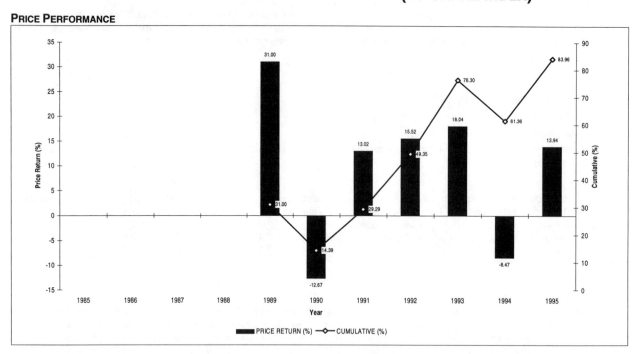

PRICE PERFORMANCE

YEAR	VALUE	PRICE RETURN (%)	CUMULATIVE (%)	MAXIMUM VALUE	DATE	MINIMUM VALUE	DATE
1995	2,690.10	13.94	83.86	2,690.10	29-Dec	2,238.30	23-Jan
1994	2,360.90	-8.47	61.36	2,713.60	2-Feb	2,240.60	24-Jun
1993	2,579.40	18.04	76.30	2,598.70	29-Dec	2,124.70	19-Jan
1992	2,185.20	15.52	49.35	2,185.20	31-Dec	1,670.00	1-Sep
1991	1,891.60	13.02	29.29	NA	NA	NA	NA
1990	1,673.70	-12.67	14.39	NA	NA	NA	NA
1989	1,916.60	31.00	31.00	NA	NA	NA	NA
1988	1,463.10	NA	NA	NA	NA	NA	NA
1987		NA	NA	NA	NA	NA	NA
1986		NA	NA	NA	NA	NA	NA
1985							
Average Annual (%)		10.05					
Compound Annual (%)		9.09					
Standard Deviation (%)		15.36					

SYNOPSIS

The Financial Times Ordinary Share Index (30 Share Index) is an equally-weighted, geometrically averaged index that tracks the continuous price only performance of 30 stocks that represent the most heavily traded domestic "blue chip" stocks listed on the London Stock Exchange.

NUMBER OF STOCKS—DECEMBER 31, 1995

30

MARKET VALUE—DECEMBER 31, 1995

Not Available

SELECTION CRITERIA

The 30 constituent companies are selected to properly represent a cross section of British industry and commerce.

BACKGROUND

Calculated since 1935, the Financial Times Index has been one of the most widely quoted measures of the behavior of the London Stock Exchange. It was known as the 30-Share Index until its name was changed to the Industrial Ordinary Share Index and, in 1984, to the Financial Times Ordinary Share Index with the addition of its first financial share. The index was established by the *Financial News*, which was subsequently absorbed into the *Financial Times*.

At its inception, the index was designed to be representative of British industry and the constituent shares included six companies that were allocated to heavy industry, four to textiles, three to motors and aviation, three to electrical manufacturing and radio, three to building materials, six to food, drink and tobacco, two to retail stores and three to miscellaneous industries. Over the years, the composition of the index has shifted toward companies in the service trades, with the addition of the first oil company in March 1977, the first telecommunications company on December 4, 1984 and the first financial company–National Westminster Bank–also on December 4, 1984.

The index, which was calculated once a day, is now computed on a continuous basis. The number of constituent shares, however, has remained at 30, having been chosen originally as the best compromise between ease and speed of calculation and the need to minimize the undue influence of a single company.

BASE DATE

July 1, 1935=100.00

COMPUTATION METHODOLOGY

(1) A geometric mean index formula. (2) Prices are based on quotations on the London Stock Exchange Automated Quotation System (SEAQ).

DERIVATIVE INSTRUMENTS

None

SUBINDICES

None

RELATED INDICES

FT-Actuaries Fixed Interest Index
FT-Fixed Interest Index
FT-SE Actuaries All-Share Index
FT-SE Actuaries Fledgling Index
FT-SE Eurotrack 100 Index
FT-SE Eurotrack 200 Index
FT/S&P Actuaries World Index
Refer to Appendix 5 for additional indices.

REMARKS

FT-SE International was established by the *Financial Times* and the London Stock Exchange in 1995 to manage and develop the FT-SE and FT-Actuaries indices. Responsibility for the FT/S&P Actuaries World Index, which is co-published by the Financial Times Ltd., Goldman Sachs & Co. and Standard and Poor's, is scheduled for 1996. Responsibility for the Financial Times Ordinary Index, however, continues to reside with the *Financial Times*. Related indices include a partial list of the more commonly publicized benchmarks under the auspices of FT-SE International.

PUBLISHER

The Financial Times Ltd.

FINANCIAL TIMES-STOCK EXCHANGE 100 (FT-SE 100) INDEX

PRICE PERFORMANCE

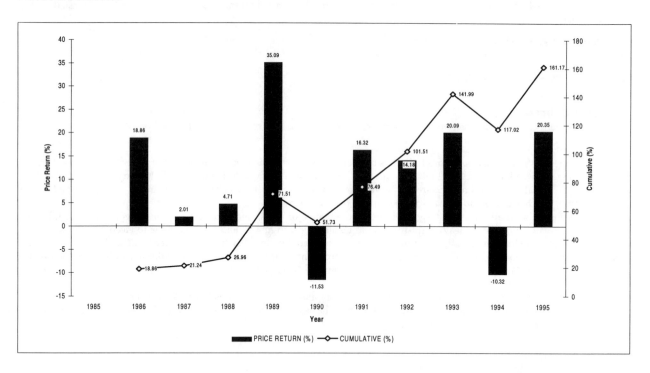

PRICE PERFORMANCE

YEAR	VALUE	PRICE RETURN (%)	CUMULATIVE (%)	MAXIMUM VALUE	DATE	MINIMUM VALUE	DATE
1995	3,689.30	20.35	161.17	3,689.30	29-Dec	2,954.20	23-Jan
1994	3,065.60	-10.32	117.02	3,520.30	2-Feb	2,876.60	24-Jun
1993	3,418.40	20.09	141.99	3,462.00	29-Dec	2,737.60	19-Jan
1992	2,846.50	14.18	101.51	2,847.80	29-Dec	2,281.00	25-Aug
1991	2,493.10	16.32	76.49	2,679.60	2-Sep	2,054.80	16-Jan
1990	2,143.40	-11.53	51.73	2,463.70	3-Jan	1,990.30	24-Sep
1989	2,422.70	35.09	71.51	2,423.90	8-Sep	1,782.80	3-Jan
1988	1,793.40	4.71	26.96	1,879.30	22-Jun	1,694.50	8-Feb
1987	1,712.70	2.01	21.24	2,443.40	16-Jul	1,565.20	9-Nov
1986	1,679.00	18.86	18.86	1,717.60	3-Apr	1,370.10	14-Jan
1985	1,412.60						
Average Annual (%)		10.97					
Compound Annual (%)		10.08					
Standard Deviation (%)		14.65					

SYNOPSIS

The Financial Times-Stock Exchange 100 (FT-SE 100) Index is a market value-weighted index that tracks the continuous price only and daily total return performance of the 100 most highly capitalized British stocks traded on the London Stock Exchange. The index consists of shares that must qualify for inclusion in the FT-SE Actuaries All-Share Index and represents 73% of this benchmark. Its shares also account for about 75% of the capitalization of the UK equity market.

NUMBER OF STOCKS—DECEMBER 31, 1995
100

MARKET VALUE—DECEMBER 31, 1995
US$963,501.6 million

SELECTION CRITERIA

Constituent companies, which must qualify for inclusion in the FT-SE Actuaries All-Share Index, represent the largest 100 UK-registered companies, including Investment Trusts (companies whose business is that of holding equity and other investments) whose classes of ordinary share prices are quoted on the London Stock Exchange on the basis of market capitalization. In the process of identifying and tracking the 100 most highly capitalized stocks, the entire quoted equity capital of a constituent company is included in the calculation of market capitalization. In the event that there are two or more classes of equity, the equivalent capitalization of the most marketable class will be used. The FT-SE Actuaries UK Indices Committee is responsible for making determinations regarding the eligibility of UK companies to be included in the index. These are made on the basis of a quarterly review conducted in March, June, September and December. Any constituent which has risen to the 90th or above position in market capitalization during the quarter will be adopted while any security that has fallen to the 111th place or below in terms of market capitalization during the quarter will be deleted. Changes are implemented on the first business day following the end of the calendar quarter. Major new issues, accounting for 1% or more of the total market capitalization of the FT-SE Actuaries All-Share Index and replacements due to suspensions, takeovers, merges, etc., may be added prior to the calendar quarter reviews.

Eligible securities must be sufficiently liquid to be traded. These are evaluated on the basis of the following guidelines: (1) At least 25% of the shares in issue must be publicly available for investment and not held in the hands of a single party or parties acting in concert. Two or more identifiable holders of more than 75% of a single security may be deemed to be acting in concert. (2) Accurate and reliable prices. A sterling-denominated firm quotation must exist on the SEAQ or the Stock Exchange Alternative Trading Service (SEATS), for infrequently traded shares, for a company to be included. (3) Eligible listed companies are ranked by market capitalization and the largest companies, consisting of 98%-99% of all eligible companies, are selected for inclusion. (4) Except for large new issues, securities must trade on at least 100 business days during the 12-month period prior to the annual review of constituents. To be eligible, new issues must trade with the same minimum frequency in proportion to the period since first traded (i.e., securities traded for 6 months must trade for a minimum of 50 days).

Subsidiaries of companies already included, convertible preference shares, loan stocks, funds whose prices are a direct derivation of underlying holdings and non-dividend paying and/or companies with a large static shareholder base are not eligible.

BACKGROUND

The index, also known as the "Footsie," was introduced on January 4, 1984 to provide a real time indicator of trends in the UK equity market and to serve as a vehicle for options and futures trading. For this reason a base value of 1000.00 was chosen, thereby making the index more tradable on the futures or options markets as a high base contract figure usually produces whole number changes every day. Daily total return calculations were initiated as of December 31, 1992, with a base value of 1000.00.

BASE DATE

December 31, 1983=1000.00

COMPUTATION METHODOLOGY

(1) An aggregate of prices times quantities index formula. Maintenance adjustments to the divisor are made daily for capitalization changes, new listings and delistings. (2) The removal and replacement of constituents due to delistings, mergers, takeovers, restructurings or other similar events, are normally affected simultaneously on the day following the day on which the event justifying the removal is announced. Announcements after the close of business are normally made on the following business day. Suspended member stocks of the 100 Index may be removed after the close of trading on the second day. Otherwise, delistings are normally removed at a price of zero on the 11th trading day. A reserve list of the highest ranking non-constituent companies is maintained and published regularly. (3) The entire quoted equity capital of a constituent is included in the calculation of market capitalization. In the event that there are two or more classes of equity, the equivalent capitalization of the most marketable class will be used. Adjustments to reflect major changes in market capitalization are made before the start of business on the day on which the change takes effect. Less significant changes are implemented before the start of business on the day following the announcement. The value of a stapled unit, in which the shares of two separate companies or different types of shares are stapled together so as to be tradable as a single instrument or unit, is included to the extent it is deemed eligible. (4) Industry sector classifications may change from time to time and will be implemented after the close of business on the last day of each quarter. (5) Actual mid-prices as quoted on the SEAQ or SEATS are used. Prices are taken between 2:30 and 3 PM each day and monitored and adjusted for late changes. (6) Total returns are calculated using gross dividends reinvested as of the ex-dividend date.

DERIVATIVE INSTRUMENTS

FT-SE 100 index futures and options contracts trade on the London International Financial Futures Exchange Ltd. (LIFFE).
FT-SE 100 flex futures and options trade on the OMLX, the London Securities and Derivatives Exchange.
FT-SE 100 flex options contracts trade on the London International Financial Futures Exchange Ltd. (LIFFE)
FT-SE 100 index options contracts trade on the Chicago Board Options Exchange (CBOE).
FT-SE 100 index futures contracts and options on futures trade on the Chicago Mercantile Exchange (CME).

SUBINDICES

None

RELATED INDICES

FT-Actuaries Fixed Interest Index   FT-SE Actuaries All-Share Index   FT-SE Eurotrack 100 Index   FT/S&P Actuaries World Index
FT Fixed Interest Index   FT-SE Actuaries Fledgling   FT-SE Eurotrack 200 Index   Refer to Appendix 5 for additional indices.

REMARKS

(1) In addition to the UK Indices Committee, a Steering Committee is responsible for maintaining the ground rules for the management of the UK series of indices along with the FT-SE Eurotrack 100 and 200 Indices and the FT-SE Actuaries classification system, an Industry Classification Committee is responsible for the actual industrial classification of constituents and an independent auditor is retained to ensure all recommended changes are made in accordance with the applicable guidelines. (2) FT-SE International was established by the *Financial Times* and the London Stock Exchange in 1995 to manage and develop the FT-SE and FT-Actuaries indices. Responsibility for the FT/S&P Actuaries World Index, which is co-published by the Financial Times Ltd., Goldman Sachs & Co. and S&P, is scheduled for 1996. (3) Related indices include a partial list of commonly publicized benchmarks.

PUBLISHER

FT-SE International Ltd.

FINANCIAL TIMES-STOCK EXCHANGE ACTUARIES 350 (FT-SE ACTUARIES 350) INDEX

PRICE PERFORMANCE

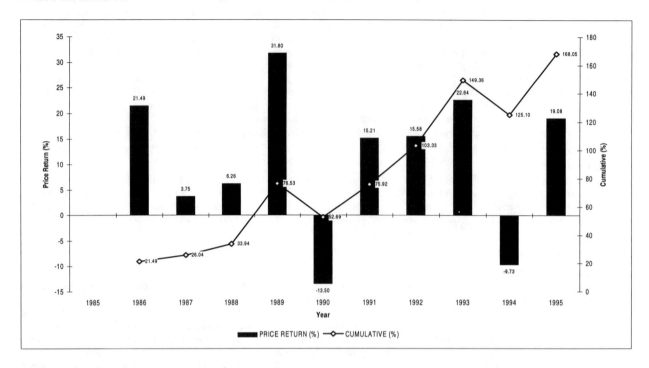

PRICE PERFORMANCE

YEAR	VALUE	PRICE RETURN (%)	CUMULATIVE (%)	MAXIMUM VALUE[1]	DATE	MINIMUM VALUE[1]	DATE
1995	1,830.60	19.08	168.05	1,830.60	29-Dec	1,482.40	23-Jan
1994	1,537.30	-9.73	125.10	1,778.30	2-Feb	1,451.30	24-Jun
1993	1,703.00	22.64	149.36	1,721.50	29-Dec	1,348.70	19-Jan
1992	1,388.60	15.58	103.33	1,388.90	29-Dec	1,103.10	25-Aug
1991	1,201.40	15.21	75.92	1,298.30	6-Sep	1,018.10	18-Jan
1990	1,042.80	-13.50	52.69	1,220.50	5-Jan	968.00	28-Sep
1989	1,205.60	31.80	76.53	1,219.00	8-Sep	924.00	6-Jan
1988	914.70	6.26	33.94	957.80	1-Jul	876.80	12-Feb
1987	860.80	3.75	26.04	1,217.60	17-Jul	786.50	30-Nov
1986	829.70	21.49	21.49	829.70	31-Dec	672.10	24-Jan
1985	682.94						
Average Annual (%)		11.26					
Compound Annual (%)		10.36					
Standard Deviation (%)		14.48					

[1]Maximum/minimum index values for the period 1986-1991 based on weekly values.

SYNOPSIS
The Financial Times-Stock Exchange Actuaries 350 (FT-SE Actuaries 350) Index is a market value-weighted index that tracks the continuous price only and daily total return performance of the 350 most highly capitalized British stocks traded on the London Stock Exchange that are included in both the FT-SE 100 Index and FT-SE Mid 250 Index. The index consists of shares that must qualify for inclusion in the FT-SE Actuaries All-Share Index and represents 93% of this benchmark. Its shares account for 92% of the UK equity market.

NUMBER OF STOCKS—DECEMBER 31, 1995
350

MARKET VALUE—DECEMBER 31, 1995
US$1,222,668.5 million

SELECTION CRITERIA
Constituents, which must qualify for inclusion in the FT-SE Actuaries All-Share Index, are members of the FT-SE 100 and FT-SE Mid 250 indices. They represent the largest 350 UK-registered companies based on of market capitalization, including Investment Trusts whose classes of ordinary share prices are quoted on the London Stock Exchange. The FT-SE Actuaries UK Indices

Committee is responsible for making determinations regarding the eligibility of UK companies to be included. Such determinations are made on the basis of a quaterly review conducted in March, June, September and December, to ensure continued eligibility.

Eligible securities must be sufficiently liquid to be traded. These are evaluated on the basis of the following guidelines: (1) At least 25% of the shares in issue must be publicly available for investment and not held in the hands of a single party or parties acting in concert. Two or more identifiable holders of more than 75% of a single security may be deemed to be acting in concert. (2) Accurate and reliable prices. A sterling-denominated firm quotation must exist on the Stock Exchange Automated Quotations System (SEAQ) or the Stock Exchange Alternative Trading Service (SEATS), for infrequently traded shares, for a company to be included. (3) Eligible companies are ranked by market capitalization and the largest companies, consisting of 98%-99% of all eligible companies, are selected. (4) Except for large new issues, securities must trade on at least 100 business days during the 12-month period prior to the annual review. To be eligible, new issues must trade with the same minimum frequency in proportion to the period since first traded (i.e., securities traded for 6 months must trade for a minimum of 50 days).

Subsidiaries of companies already included, convertible preference shares, loan stocks, funds whose prices are a direct derivation of underlying holdings and non-dividend paying and/or companies with a large static shareholder base, are not eligible. Refer to the FT-SE 100 Index and FT-SE Mid 250 Index for additional information.

BACKGROUND

The index was launched in October 1992 following a detailed review of UK indices, with a base value set to coincide with the closing level of the FT All-Share Index as of December 31, 1985. The total return index was introduced in July 1993, with a base value of 1000.00 as of December 31, 1992.

BASE DATE

December 31, 1985=682.94

COMPUTATION METHODOLOGY

(1) An aggregate of prices times quantities index formula. Maintenance adjustments to the divisor are made daily for capitalization changes, new listings and delistings. (2) The removal and replacement of constituents due to delistings, mergers, takeovers, restructurings or other similar events, are normally affected simultaneously on the day following the day on which the event justifying the removal is announced. Announcements after the close of business are normally deemed to be made on the following business day. Suspended stocks that are members of the FT-SE 100 Index may be removed after the close of trading on the second day. Otherwise, delistings are normally removed at a price of zero on the 11th trading day. (3) The entire quoted equity capital of a constituent company is included in the calculation of market capitalization. In the event that there are two or more classes of equity, the equivalent capitalization of the most marketable class will be used. Adjustments to reflect major changes in market capitalization are made before the start of business on the day on which the change takes effect. Less significant changes are implemented before the start of business on the day following the announcement of the change. The value of a stapled unit, where shares of two separate companies or different types of shares are stapled together so as to be tradable as a single instrument or unit, is included in the index to the extent it is deemed eligible for participation. (4) Industry sector classifications of a constituent may change from time to time. Such changes will be implemented after the close of business on the last day of each quarter. (5) Exact mid-prices as quoted on the SEAQ or SEATS are used. Prices are taken between 2:30 and 3 PM each day and monitored and adjusted for late changes. (6) Total returns are calculated using gross dividends reinvested as of the ex-dividend date.

DERIVATIVE INSTRUMENTS

FT-SE Actuaries 350 flex futures and options contracts trade on the OMLX, the London Securities and Derivatives Exchange.
FT-SE 350 Actuaries Industry Baskets flex futures and options contracts trade on the OMLX, the London Securities and Derivatives Exchange.

SUBINDICES

FT-SE 100 Index   FT-SE 350 Higher Yield Index   FT-SE 350 Lower Yield Index   FT-SE Mid 250 Index
Thirty-seven industrial group subindices: Extractive industries, integrated oil, oil exploration and production, building and construction, building materials and merchandise, chemicals, diversified industrials, electronic and electronic equipment, engineering, engineering vehicles, paper, packaging and printing, textiles and apparel, breweries, spirits, wines and ciders, food producers, household goods, health care, pharmaceuticals, tobacco, distributors, leisure and hotels, media, food retailers, general retailers, support services, transportation, other services and business, electricity, gas distribution, telecommunications, water, retail banks, merchant banks, insurance, life insurance, other financial, and property.

RELATED INDICES

FT-Actuaries Fixed Interest Index FT-SE Actuaries All-Share Index   FT-SE Eurotrack 100 Index   FT/S&P Actuaries World Index
FT Fixed Interest Index FT-SE Actuaries Fledgling Index FT-SE Eurotrack 200 Index   Refer to Appendix 5 for additional indices.

REMARKS

(1) In addition to the UK Indices Committee, a Steering Committee is responsible for maintaining the ground rules for the management of the UK series of indices along with the FT-SE Eurotrack 100 and 200 indices and the FT-SE Actuaries classification system, an Industry Classification Committee is responsible for the actual industrial classification of constituents and an independent auditor is retained to ensure that all recommended changes are made in accordance with the applicable guidelines. (2) FT-SE International was established by the *Financial Times* and the London Stock Exchange in 1995 to manage and develop the FT-SE and FT-Actuaries indices. Responsibility for the FT/S&P Actuaries World Index, co-published by the Financial Times Ltd., Goldman Sachs & Co. and S&P, is scheduled for 1996. (3) Related indices include a partial list of commonly publicized benchmarks.

PUBLISHER

FT-SE International Ltd.

FT-SE ACTUARIES ALL-SHARE INDEX

PRICE PERFORMANCE

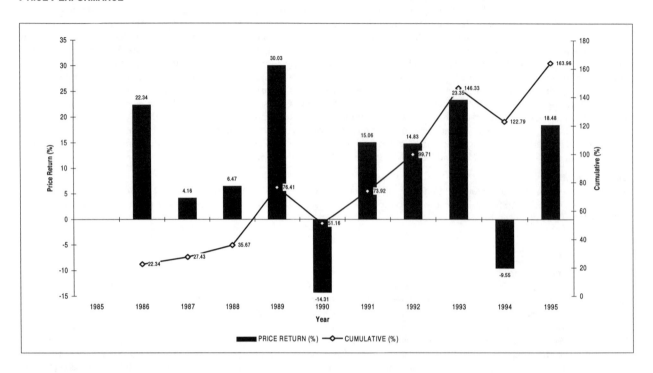

PRICE PERFORMANCE

YEAR	VALUE	PRICE RETURN (%)	CUMULATIVE (%)	MAXIMUM VALUE	DATE	MINIMUM VALUE	DATE
1995	1,802.56	18.48	163.96	1,802.56	29-Dec	1,469.23	23-Jan
1994	1,521.44	-9.55	122.79	1,764.11	2-Feb	1,445.85	24-Jun
1993	1,682.17	23.35	146.33	NA	NA	NA	NA
1992	1,363.79	14.83	99.71	NA	NA	NA	NA
1991	1,187.70	15.06	73.92	NA	NA	NA	NA
1990	1,032.25	-14.31	51.16	NA	NA	NA	NA
1989	1,204.70	30.03	76.41	NA	NA	NA	NA
1988	926.50	6.47	35.67	NA	NA	NA	NA
1987	870.22	4.16	27.43	NA	NA	NA	NA
1986	835.48	22.34	22.34	NA	NA	NA	NA
1985	682.90						
Average Annual (%)		11.08					
Compound Annual (%)		10.19					
Standard Deviation (%)		14.38					

SYNOPSIS

The FT-SE Actuaries All-Share Index is a market value-weighted index that tracks the daily price only and total return performance of the major capital and industry segments of the UK equity market. These shares incorporate 99% of the UK equity market.

NUMBER OF STOCKS—DECEMBER 31, 1995
899

MARKET VALUE—DECEMBER 31, 1995
US$1,315,760.0 million

SELECTION CRITERIA

The index incorporates, on the basis of market capitalization, 98%-99% of all classes of eligible ordinary shares of UK-registered companies traded on the London Stock Exchange, including Investment Trusts and companies comprised within and traded as part of a stapled unit. The number of constituents can vary throughout the year. The index is composed of the FT-SE 100 and FT-SE Mid 250, FT-SE Actuaries 350 and the FT-SE SmallCap indices. The FT-SE Actuaries UK Indices Committee maks determinations regarding the eligibility of UK companies. These are made once a year and implemented after the close of business on December 31st. However, quarterly changes made to the FT-SE 100 and FT-SE Mid 250, FT-SE-Actuaries 350 and the FT-SE SmallCap indices are made automatically to the FT-SE Actuaries All-Share Index. The index aims to maintain stability of constituents while representing the UK equity market by including and excluding securities that have significant increases or decreases in value. Also, more frequent changes are made due to delistings, suspensions, mergers, restructurings, takeovers, sizable new issues, etc.

Eligible securities must be sufficiently liquid to be traded. These are evaluated on the basis of the following guidelines: (1) At least 25% shares in issue must be publicly available for investment and not held in the hands of a single party or parties acting in concert. Two or more identifiable holders of more than 75% of a single security may be deemed to be acting in concert; (2) Accurate and reliable prices. A sterling-denominated firm quotation must exist on the Stock Exchange Automated Quotations System (SEAQ) or the Stock Exchange Alternative Trading Service (SEATS), for infrequently traded shares, for a company to be included. (3) Eligible listed companies are ranked by market capitalization and the largest companies, consisting of 98%-99% of all eligible companies, are selected for inclusion. Shares listed in the Alternative Investment Market (AIM) are ineligible. (4) Except for large new issues, securities must trade on at least 100 business days during the 12 month period prior to the annual review. To be eligible, new issues must trade with the same minimum frequency in proportion to the period since first traded (i.e., securities traded for 6 months must trade for a minimum of 50 days).

Subsidiaries of companies in the index, convertible preference shares, loan stocks, funds whose prices are a direct derivation of underlying holdings and non-dividend paying and/or companies with a large static shareholder base, are not eligible. Refer to the FT-SE 100, FT-SE Mid 250, FT-SE-Actuaries 350 and the FT-SE SmallCap indices for additional information.

BACKGROUND
The index dates back to 1929 when the Institute of Actuaries in London and the Faculty of Actuaries in Edinburgh began to compile a broadly based Actuaries Investment Index covering about 200 shares and was produced monthly. Itwas expanded in 1962 to 636 companies and the calculation frequency to once daily. The number of constituents has since been expanded to almost 900 companies. Daily total return performance calculations were initiated as of December 31, 1992, with a base value of 1000.00.

BASE DATE
April 10, 1962=100.00

COMPUTATION METHODOLOGY
(1) An aggregate of prices times quantities index formula. Maintenance adjustments to the divisor are made daily for capitalization changes, new listings and delistings. (2) Removal and replacements due to delistings, mergers, takeovers, restructurings or similar events, are normally affected simultaneously on the day following the day on which the event is announced. Announcements after the close of business are made on the following business day. Suspended stocks that are members of the FT-SE 100 Index may be removed after the close of trading on the second day at their suspended price. Otherwise, delistings are normally removed at a price of zero on the 11th trading day. (3) Except for constituent changes affecting the FT-SE 100, FT-SE Mid 250, FT-SE Actuaries 350 and FT-SE SmallCap indices, stocks which fall out due to suspensions, takeovers, mergers, etc., are not replaced prior to the annual review. (4) Large new issues may qualify for accelerated entry if they account for 1% more of the total market capitalization of the FT-SE Actuaries All-Share Index. New issues of smaller companies may qualify for accelerated entry if they represent 0.25% or more of the total capitalization of the FT-SE SmallCap Index. (5) The entire quoted equity capital of a constituent company is included in the calculation of market capitalization. In the event that there are two or more classes of equity, the equivalent capitalization of the most marketable class will be used. Adjustments to reflect major changes in market capitalization are made before the start of business on the day the change takes effect. Less significant changes are implemented before the start of business on the day following the announcement. The value of a stapled unit is included to the extent it is eligible. (6) Industry sector classifications change from time to time and are implemented after the close of business on the last day of each quarter. (7) Actual mid-prices as quoted on the SEAQ or SEATS are used. Prices are taken between 2:30 and 3 PM each day and monitored and adjusted for late changes. (8) Total returns are calculated using gross dividends reinvested as of the ex-dividend date.

DERIVATIVE INSTRUMENTS
None

SUBINDICES
FT-SE 100 Index   FT-SE Actuaries 350 Index   FT-SE Mid 250 Index   FT-SE SmallCap Index
Eight economic sector subindices: Mineral extracting, general industrials, consumer goods, services, utilities, non-financial companies, financials and investment trusts.
Thirty-seven industrial subindices: Extractive industries, integrated oil, oil exploration/production, building/construction, building materials/merchants, chemicals, diversified industrials, electronic/electronic equipment, engineering, engineering vehicles, paper, packaging/printing, textiles/apparel, breweries, spirits, wines/ciders, food producers, household goods, health care, pharmaceuticals, tobacco, distributors, leisure/hotels, media, food retailers, general retailers, support services, transportation, other services and business, electricity, gas distribution, telecommunications, water, retail banks, merchant banks, insurance, life insurance, other financial, and property.

RELATED INDICES
FT-Actuaries Fixed Interest Index FT Fixed Interest Index FT-SE Actuaries Fledgling Index FT-SE Eurotrack 100 Index
FT-SE Eurotrack 200 Index   FT/S&P Actuaries World Index Refer to Appendix 5 for additional indices.

REMARKS
(1) In addition to the UK Indices Committee, a Steering Committee is responsible for maintaining the ground rules for the management of the UK series of indices along with the FT-SE Eurotrack 100 and 200 indices and the FT-SE Actuaries classification system, an Industry Classification Committee is responsible for the actual industrial classification of constituents and an independent auditor is retained to ensure changes are made in accordance with the applicable guidelines. (2) FT-SE International was established by the *Financial Times* and the London Stock Exchange in 1995 to manage and develop the FT-SE and FT-Actuaries indices. Responsibility for the FT/S&P Actuaries World Index, co-published by the Financial Times Ltd., Goldman Sachs & Co. and S&P, is scheduled for 1996. (3) Related indices include a partial list of commonly publicized benchmarks.

PUBLISHER
FT-SE International Ltd.

FT-SE ACTUARIES FLEDGLING INDEX

PRICE PERFORMANCE

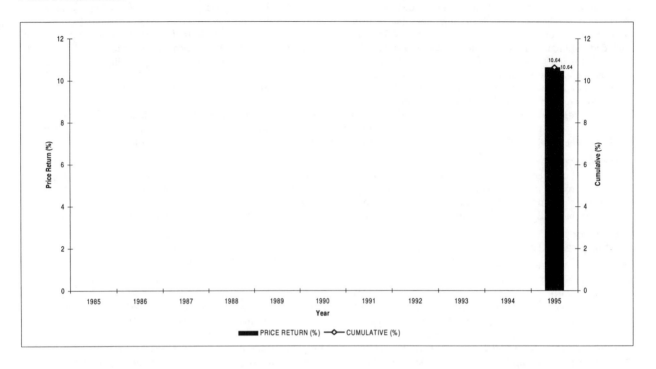

PRICE PERFORMANCE

YEAR	VALUE	PRICE RETURN (%)	CUMULATIVE (%)	MAXIMUM VALUE	DATE	MINIMUM VALUE	DATE
1995	1,106.40	10.64	10.64	1,106.40	29-Dec	949.00	13-Mar
1994	1,000.00						
1993							
1992							
1991							
1990							
1989							
1988							
1987							
1986							
1985							
Average Annual (%)		10.64					
Compound Annual (%)		NM					
Standard Deviation (%)		NM					

SYNOPSIS
The FT-SE Actuaries Fledgling Index is a market value-weighted index that tracks the daily price only and total return performance of UK-listed ordinary equity shares traded on the London Stock Exchange that are too small to be included in the FT-SE Actuaries All-Share Index. These shares account for less than 1% of the UK equity market.

NUMBER OF STOCKS—DECEMBER 31, 1995
549 companies

MARKET VALUE—DECEMBER 31, 1995
US$245.5 million

SELECTION CRITERIA
Index components include UK-registered companies with ordinary issued shares that satisfy the following guidelines, but are too small to be included in the FT-SE Actuaries All-Share Index (i.e., on the basis of market capitalization, these companies fall outside of the 98%-99% of companies captured in the All-Share Index).

The FT-SE Actuaries UK Indices Committee is responsible for making determinations regarding the eligibility of UK companies to be included in the index. Such determinations are made once a year, on the basis of investability, price, size as well as liquidity considerations, and are implemented after the close of business on December 31st.

The index is limited to UK-registered eligible listed shares, including Investment Trusts (companies whose business is that of holding equity and other investments), whose classes of ordinary share prices are quoted on the London Stock Exchange. Eligible securities must be sufficiently liquid to be traded. These are evaluated on the basis of the following guidelines: (1) Investability-At least 25% of the shares in issue must be publicly available for investment and not held in the hands of a single party or parties acting in concert. Two or more identifiable holders of more than 75% of a single security may be deemed to be acting in concert; (2) Price-Accurate and reliable prices must be in evidence. A sterling-denominated firm quotation must exist on the Stock Exchange Automated Quotations System (SEAQ) or the Stock Exchange Alternative Trading Service (SEATS), for infrequently traded shares, for a company to be included in the index; (3) Liquidity-Except for large new issues, securities must trade on at least 50 business days during the 12-month period prior to the annual review of constituents. To be eligible, new issues must trade with the same minimum frequency in proportion to the period since first traded (i.e., securities traded for 6 months must trade for a minimum of 50 days).

Subsidiaries of companies that are already included in the index, convertible preference shares, loan stocks, funds whose prices are a direct derivation of underlying holdings (i.e., Unit Trusts), and non-dividend paying companies and/or companies with a large static shareholder base, are not eligible for inclusion in the index. Shares listed in the recently introduced Alternative Investment Market (AIM) are also ineligible for inclusion in the index.

BACKGROUND
The index was introduced in January 1995.

BASE DATE
December 31, 1994=1000.00

COMPUTATION METHODOLOGY
(1) An aggregate of prices times quantities index formula. Maintenance adjustments to the divisor are made daily for capitalization changes, new listings and delistings. (2) The removal of constituents due to delistings, mergers, takeovers, restructurings or other similar events, are normally affected simultaneously on the day following the day on which the event justifying the removal is announced. Announcements after the close of business are normally deemed to be made on the following business day. Suspended stocks are normally removed at a price of zero on the 11th trading day. (3) The entire quoted equity capital of a constituent company is included in the calculation of market capitalization. In the event that there are two or more classes of equity, the equivalent capitalization of the most marketable class will be used. Adjustments to reflect major changes in market capitalization are made before the start of business on the day on which the change takes effect. Less significant changes are implemented before the start of business on the day following the announcement of the change. The value of a stapled unit, in which the shares of two separate companies or different types of shares are stapled together so as to be tradable as a single instrument or unit, is included in the index to the extent it is deemed eligible for participation. (4) Actual mid-prices as quoted on the SEAQ or SEATS are used. Prices are taken between 2:30 and 3 PM each day and monitored and adjusted for late changes. (5) Total returns are calculated using gross dividends reinvested as of the ex-dividend date.

DERIVATIVE INSTRUMENTS
None

SUBINDICES
None

RELATED INDICES
FT-Actuaries Fixed Interest Index
FT Fixed Interest Index
FT-SE Actuaries All-Share Index
FT-SE Eurotrack 100 Index
FT-SE Eurotrack 200 Index
FT/S&P Actuaries World Index
Refer to Appendix 5 for additional indices.

REMARKS
(1) In addition to the UK Indices Committee, a Steering Committee is responsible for maintaining the ground rules for the management of the UK series of indices along with the FT-SE Eurotrack 100 and 200 indices and the FT-SE Actuaries classification system, an Industry Classification Committee is responsible for the actual industrial classification of constituents and an independent auditor is retained to ensure that all recommended changes are made in accordance with the applicable guidelines. (2) FT-SE International was established by the *Financial Times* and the London Stock Exchange in 1995 to manage and develop the FT-SE and FT-Actuaries indices. Responsibility for the FT/S&P Actuaries World Index is scheduled for 1996. (3) Related indices include a partial list of the more commonly publicized benchmarks.

PUBLISHER
FT-SE International Ltd.

FINANCIAL TIMES-STOCK EXCHANGE ALTERNATIVE INVESTMENT MARKET (FT-SE AIM) INDEX

PRICE PERFORMANCE

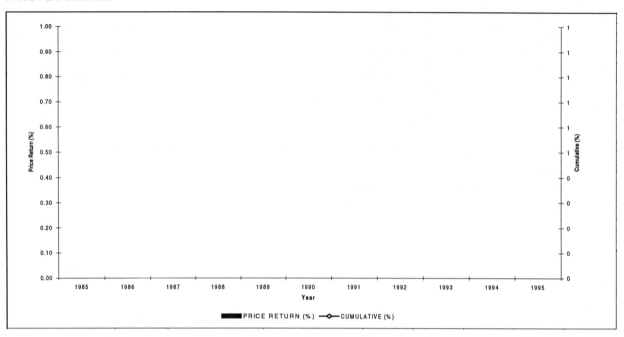

PRICE PERFORMANCE

YEAR	VALUE	PRICE RETURN (%)	CUMULATIVE (%)	MAXIMUM VALUE	DATE	MINIMUM VALUE	DATE
1995	1,000.00						
1994							
1993							
1992							
1991							
1990							
1989							
1988							
1987							
1986							
1985							
Average Annual (%)							
Compound Annual (%)							
Standard Deviation (%)							

Synopsis

The Financial Times-Stock Exchange Alternative Investment Market (FT-SE AIM) Index is a market value-weighted index that tracks the continuous price only and daily total return performance of the eligible companies in the Alternative Investment Market (AIM) of the London Stock Exchange.

Number of Stocks—December 31, 1995
107

Market Value—December 31, 1995
US$3,072.14 million

Selection Criteria

All classes of ordinary issued shares, with a sterling-denominated firm quotation on the Stock Exchange Automated Quotations System (SEAQ) or the Stock Exchange Alternative Trading Service (SEATS) Plus are eligible for inclusion in the index. Companies whose business consists of holding equity and other investments, such as unit investment trusts, are eligible for inclusion in the index. Investment trusts with split-capital structures and funds whose prices are a direct derivation of underlying holdings, such as unit trusts, are excluded from consideration as index constituents.

Background

The index was introduced in 1996 in response to the launch in June 1995 of the Alternative Investment Market (AIM) for small and fast growing companies.

Base Date

December 31, 1995=1,000.00

Computation Methodology

(1) An aggregate of prices times quantities index formula. Maintenance adjustments to the divisor are made for capitalization changes, new listings and delistings. Simultaneous changes due to delistings, mergers, restructurings and takeovers are effected before the start of the business day on which the event justifying the change was announced. (2) Adjustments to reflect major changes in market capitalization are made before the start of business on the day on which the change takes effect. Less significant changes are implemented before the start of business on the day following the announcement of the change. (3) Unless they represent 5% or more of its market capitalization, new issues and newly listed AIM securities are eligible for inclusion in the index until the next annual review date. Otherwise, the security will be added to the index within 10 days of being listed on AIM. (4) Suspended companies may remain in the index and valued at the price at which they were suspended, for up to 20 business days. Thereafter, the index member is deleted from the index either at its suspended price or at zero value. (5) The market capitalization of constituent companies is calculated on the basis of each company's entire quoted equity capital. In the event a company has two or more classes of equity, significant and liquid secondary lines are included in the market value calculation using the market price applicable to the second line. A secondary line is priced separately if its nominal value is greater than 20% of the aggregate capital of the company. (6) Index constituents are reviewed once a year, in December, and any changes are implemented at the end of the calendar year. Quarterly reviews are anticipated during 1996 and 1997 in response to anticipated rapid growth in the AIM market. (7) Latest published price is used for index calculation purposes. (8) Total returns are calculated using gross dividends reinvested as of the ex-dividend date.

Derivative Instruments
None

Subindices
None

Related Indices
FT-Actuaries Fixed Interest Index
FT Fixed Interest Index
FT-SE Actuaries All-Share Index
FT-SE Eurotrack 100 Index
FT-SE Eurotrack 200 Index
FT-SE Fledgling Index
FT/S&P Actuaries World Index
Refer to Appendix 5 for additional indices.

Remarks

(1) In addition to the UK Indices Committee, a Steering Committee is responsible for maintaining the ground rules for the management of the UK series of indices along with the FT-SE Eurotrack 100 and 200 indices and the FT-SE Actuaries classification system, an Industry Classification Committee is responsible for the actual industrial classification of constituents and an independent auditor is retained to ensure that all recommended changes are made in accordance with the applicable guidelines. (2) FT-SE International was established by the *Financial Times* and the London Stock Exchange in 1995 to manage and develop the FT-SE and FT-Actuaries indices. Responsibility for the FT/S&P Actuaries World Index, to be co-published by the Financial Times Ltd., Goldman Sachs & Co. and Standard and Poor's, is scheduled for 1996. (3) Related indices include a partial list of the more commonly publicized benchmarks.

Publisher
FT-SE International Ltd.

FINANCIAL TIMES-STOCK EXCHANGE MID 250 (FT-SE MID 250) INDEX

PRICE PERFORMANCE

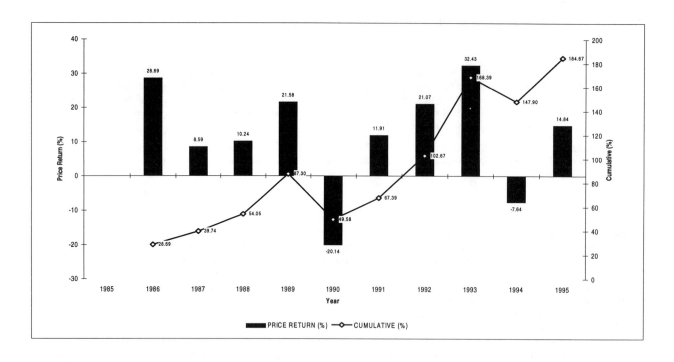

PRICE PERFORMANCE

YEAR	VALUE	PRICE RETURN (%)	CUMULATIVE (%)	MAXIMUM VALUE[1]	DATE	MINIMUM VALUE[1]	DATE
1995	4,021.30	14.84	184.67	4,021.30	29-Dec	3,300.90	8-Mar
1994	3,501.80	-7.64	147.90	4,152.80	3-Feb	3,363.40	27-Jun
1993	3,791.30	32.43	168.39	3,807.00	29-Dec	2,876.30	13-Jan
1992	2,862.90	21.07	102.67	2,862.90	31-Dec	2,157.80	16-Sep
1991	2,364.60	11.91	67.39	2,641.80	6-Sep	2,028.70	18-Jan
1990	2,112.90	-20.14	49.58	2,709.40	5-Jan	1,960.40	28-Sep
1989	2,645.80	21.58	87.30	2,768.70	8-Sep	2,198.70	6-Jan
1988	2,176.10	10.24	54.05	2,304.70	14-Oct	2,053.60	5-Feb
1987	1,974.00	8.59	39.74	2,804.00	9-Oct	1,750.60	4-Dec
1986	1,817.90	28.69	28.69	1,817.90	31-Dec	1,389.20	24-Jan
1985	1,412.60						
Average Annual (%)		12.16					
Compound Annual (%)		11.03					
Standard Deviation (%)		16.03					

[1]Maximum/minimum index values for the period 1986-1991 based on weekly values.

SYNOPSIS
The Financial Times-Stock Exchange Mid 250 (FT-SE Mid 250) Index is a market value-weighted index that tracks the continuous price only and daily total return performance of the second tier, middle capitalization British stocks traded on the London Stock Exchange. The index consists of shares that must qualify for inclusion in the FT-SE Actuaries All-Share Index and represents 20% of this benchmark. Its shares also account for about 19% of the UK equity market.

NUMBER OF STOCKS—DECEMBER 31, 1995
250

MARKET VALUE—DECEMBER 31, 1995
US$259,166.9 million

SELECTION CRITERIA
Constituents, which must qualify for inclusion in the FT-SE Actuaries All-Share Index, represent the largest 250 UK-registered companies based on market capitalization, outside the FT-SE 100 Index, including Investment Trusts whose classes of ordinary share prices are quoted on the London Stock Exchange. In the process of identifying and tracking the next 250 most highly capitalized stocks, the entire quoted equity capital of a constituent company is included in the calculation of market capitalization. In the event that there are two or more classes of equity, the equivalent capitalization of the most marketable class will be used. The FT-SE Actuaries UK Indices Committee is responsible for making determinations regarding the eligibility of UK companies to be

included. These are made based on quarterly reviews in March, June, September and December, to ensure continued eligibility. Any constituent which has risen to the 325th or above position in market capitalization during the quarter will be adopted. Any security that has fallen to the 376th place or below in market capitalization during the quarter will be deleted. Likewise, companies deleted from the FT-SE 100 at the periodic review are normally included in the FT-SE Mid 250 while companies added to the FT-SE 100 are deleted from the FT-SE Mid 250. Changes are implemented on the first business day following the end of the calendar quarter.

Eligible securities for inclusion must be sufficiently liquid. These are evaluated on the basis of the following guidelines: (1) At least 25% of the of the shares in issue must be publicly available for investment and not held in the hands of a single party or parties acting in concert. Two or more identifiable holders of more than 75% of a single security may be deemed to be acting in concert. (2) Accurate and reliable prices. A sterling-denominated firm quotation must exist on Stock Exchange Automated Quotations System (SEAQ) or the Stock Exchange Alternative Trading Service (SEATS), for infrequently traded shares. (3) Eligible listed companies are ranked by market capitalization and the largest companies, consisting of 98%-99% of eligible companies, are selected. (4) Except for large new issues, securities must trade on at least 100 business days during the 12-month period prior to the annual review of constituents. To be eligible, new issues must trade with the same minimum frequency in proportion to the period since first traded (i.e., securities traded for 6 months must trade for a minimum of 50 days).

Subsidiaries of companies included in the index, members of the FT-SE 100 Index, convertible preference shares, loan stocks, funds whose prices are a direct derivation of underlying holdings and non-dividend paying and/or companies with a large static shareholder base, are not eligible.

BACKGROUND

The index was launched in October 1992 following a detailed review of UK indices, with a base value set to coincide with the closing level of the FT-SE 100 as of January 31, 1985. The total return index was introduced in July 1993, with a base value of 1000.00 as of December 31, 1992.

BASE DATE

January 31, 1985=1412.60

COMPUTATION METHODOLOGY

(1) An aggregate of prices times quantities index formula. Maintenance adjustments to the divisor are made daily for capitalization changes, new listings and delistings. (2) The removal and replacement of constituents due to delistings, mergers, takeovers, restructurings or other similar events, are normally affected simultaneously on the day following the day the event is announced. Announcements after the close of business are normally deemed to be made on the following business day. Suspended stocks that are members of the FT-SE 100 Index may be removed after the close of trading on the second day at their suspended price. Otherwise, delistings are normally removed at a price of zero on the 11th trading day. A reserve list consisting of the highest ranking, non-constituent companies is maintained and published regularly. (3) The entire quoted equity capital of a constituent company is included in the calculation of market capitalization. In the event that there are two or more classes of equity, the equivalent capitalization of the most marketable class will be used. Adjustments to reflect major changes in market capitalization are made before the start of business on the day on which the change takes effect. Less significant changes are implemented before the start of business on the day following the announcement of the change. The value of a stapled unit, in which the shares of two separate companies or different types of shares are stapled together so as to be tradable as a single instrument or unit, is included in the index to the extent it is deemed eligible for participation. (4) Industry sector classifications of a constituent may change from time to time. Such changes will be implemented after the close of business on the last day of each quarter. (5) Actual mid-prices as quoted on the SEAQ or SEATS are used. Prices are taken between 2:30 and 3 PM each day and monitored and adjusted for late changes. (6) Total returns are calculated using gross dividends reinvested as of the ex-dividend date.

DERIVATIVE INSTRUMENTS

FT-SE Mid 250 index futures contracts trade on the London International Financial Futures Exchange Ltd. (LIFFE).
FT-SE Mid 250 index futures and options trade on the OMLX, The London Securities and Derivatives Exchange.
FT-SE Mid 250 index flex futures and options trade on the OMLX, The London Securities and Derivatives Exchange.

SUBINDICES

FT-SE Mid 250 ex-Investment Trusts

RELATED INDICES

FT-Actuaries Fixed Interest Index   FT-SE Actuaries Fledgling Index   FT-SE Eurotrack 100 Index   FT/S&P Actuaries World Index
FT Fixed Interest Index   FT-SE Actuaries All-Share Index   FT-SE Eurotrack 200 Index   Refer to Appendix 5 for additional indices.

REMARKS

(1) In addition to the UK Indices Committee, a Steering Committee is responsible for maintaining the ground rules for the management of the UK series of indices along with the FT-SE Eurotrack 100 and 200 indices and the FT-SE Actuaries classification system, an Industry Classification Committee is responsible for the actual industrial classification of constituents and an independent auditor is retained to ensure that all recommended changes are made in accordance with the applicable guidelines. (2) FT-SE International was established by the *Financial Times* and the London Stock Exchange in 1995 to manage and develop the FT-SE and FT-Actuaries indices. Responsibility for the FT/S&P Actuaries World Index, which is co-published by the Financial Times Ltd., Goldman Sachs & Co. and S&P, is scheduled for 1996. (3) Related indices include a list of commonly publicized benchmarks.

PUBLISHER

FT-SE International Ltd.

FT-SE SMALLCAP INDEX

PRICE PERFORMANCE

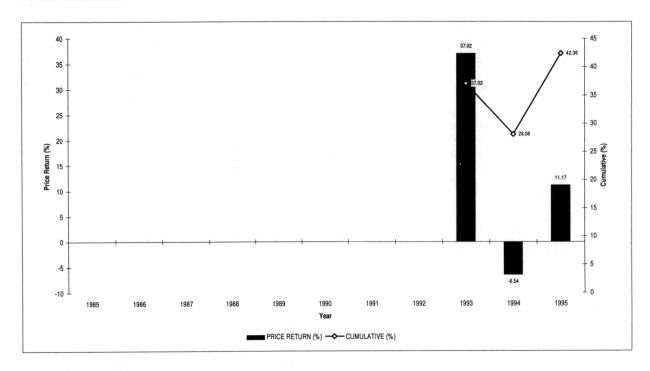

PRICE PERFORMANCE

YEAR	VALUE	PRICE RETURN (%)	CUMULATIVE (%)	MAXIMUM VALUE	DATE	MINIMUM VALUE	DATE
1995	1,941.55	11.17	42.36	1,993.11	11-Sep	1,678.61	13-Mar
1994	1,746.41	-6.54	28.06	2,094.98	4-Feb	1,727.68	14-Dec
1993	1,868.68	37.02	37.02				
1992	1,363.79						
1991							
1990							
1989							
1988							
1987							
1986							
1985							
Average Annual (%)		13.88					
Compound Annual (%)		12.50					
Standard Deviation (%)		21.91					

SYNOPSIS

The FT-SE SmallCap Index is a market value-weighted index that tracks the daily price only and total return performance of smaller capitalization UK equities within the FT-SE Actuaries All-Share Index that are traded on the London Stock Exchange and which do not qualify for inclusion in the FT-SE Actuaries 350 Index due to their size. These shares account for less than 1% of the All-Share Index and 0.01% of the UK equity market.

NUMBER OF STOCKS—DECEMBER 31, 1995
549

MARKET VALUE—DECEMBER 31, 1995
US$101.1 million

SELECTION CRITERIA

The constituents consists of UK-registered companies within the FT-SE Actuaries All-Share Index not large enough to qualify for inclusion in the FT-SE Actuaries 350 Index, an index that tracks the 350 most highly capitalized British stocks. The FT-SE Actuaries UK Indices Committee is responsible for making determinations regarding the eligibility of UK companies. These are made once a year, based on investability, price, size and liquidity, and are implemented after the close of business on December 31st. Quarterly changes to the FT-SE 100 and FT-SE Mid 250, however, may affect the FT-SE SmallCap Index. Also, new issues, amounting to 0.25% or more of the total market capitalization of the FT-SE SmallCap Index are eligible as of the next quarterly review date.

Eligible securities must be sufficiently liquid to be traded. These are evaluated on the basis of the following guidelines:

(1) At least 25% of the shares in issue must be publicly available for investment and not held in the hands of a single party or parties acting in concert. Two or more identifiable holders of more than 75% of a single security may be deemed to be acting in concert. (2) Accurate and reliable prices. A sterling-denominated firm quotation must exist on Stock Exchange Automated Quotations System (SEAQ) or the Stock Exchange Alternative Trading Service (SEATS), for infrequently traded shares. (3) Eligible listed companies are ranked by market capitalization and the largest companies, consisting of 98%-99% of all eligible companies, are selected. Shares listed in Alternative Investment Market (AIM) are ineligible. (4) Except for large new issues, securities must trade on at least 100 business days during the 12-month period prior to the annual review of constituents. To be eligible, new issues must trade with the same minimum frequency in proportion to the period since first traded (i.e., securities traded for 6 months must trade for a minimum of 50 days).

Subsidiaries of companies in the index, convertible preference shares, loan stocks, funds whose prices are a direct derivation of underlying holdings and non-dividend paying and/or companies with a large static shareholder base, are not eligible. Refer to the FT-SE Actuaries All-Share, FT-SE 100 and FT-SE Mid 250 indices for additional information.

BACKGROUND
The index was launched in 1993.

BASE DATE
December 31, 1992=1363.79

COMPUTATION METHODOLOGY
(1) An aggregate of prices times quantities index formula. Maintenance adjustments to the divisor are made daily for capitalization changes, new listings and delistings. (2) Except for eligible new issues and constituent changes affecting the FT-SE 100 Index and FT-SE Mid 250 Index, stocks which fall out of the index due to suspensions, takeovers, mergers, etc., are not be replaced. (3) The removal and replacement of constituents due to delistings, mergers, takeovers, restructurings or other similar events, are normally affected simultaneously on the day following the day on which the event justifying the removal is announced. Announcements after the close of business are normally deemed to be made on the following business day. Suspended stocks that are members of the FT-SE 100 Index may be removed after the close of trading on the second day. Otherwise, delistings are normally removed at a price of zero on the 11th trading day. A reserve list consisting of the highest ranking, non-constituent companies is maintained and published regularly. (4) The entire quoted equity capital of a constituent company is included in the calculation of market capitalization. In the event that there are two or more classes of equity, the equivalent capitalization of the most marketable class will be used. Adjustments to reflect major changes in market capitalization are made before the start of business on the day on which the change takes effect. Less significant changes are implemented before the start of business on the day following the announcement of the change. The value of a stapled unit, in which the shares of two separate companies or different types of shares are stapled together so as to be tradable as a single instrument or unit, is included in the index to the extent it is deemed eligible for participation. (5) Industry sector classifications of a constituent may change from time to time. Such changes will be implemented after the close of business on the last day of each quarter. (6) Actual mid-prices as quoted on the SEAQ or SEATS are used. Prices are taken between 2:30 and 3 PM each day and monitored and adjusted for late changes. (7) Total returns are calculated using gross dividends reinvested as of the ex-dividend date.

DERIVATIVE INSTRUMENTS
None

SUBINDICES
FT-SE SmallCap Index, ex-investment trusts

RELATED INDICES
FT-Actuaries Fixed Interest Index
FT Fixed Interest Index
FT-SE Actuaries All-Share Index
FT-SE Actuaries Fledgling Index
FT-SE Eurotrack 100 Index
FT-SE Eurotrack 200 Index
FT/S&P Actuaries World Index
Refer to Appendix 5 for additional indices.

REMARKS
(1) In addition to the UK Indices Committee, a Steering Committee is responsible for maintaining the ground rules for the management of the UK series of indices along with the FT-SE Eurotrack 100 and 200 indices and the FT-SE Actuaries classification system, an Industry Classification Committee is responsible for the actual industrial classification of constituents and an independent auditor is retained to ensure that all recommended changes are made in accordance with the applicable guidelines. (2) FT-SE International was established by the *Financial Times* and the London Stock Exchange in 1995 to manage and develop the FT-SE and FT-Actuaries indices. Responsibility for the FT/S&P Actuaries World Index, which is co-published by the Financial Times Ltd., Goldman Sachs & Co. and Standard and Poor's, is scheduled for 1996. (3) Related indices include a partial list of the more commonly publicized benchmarks.

PUBLISHER
FT-SE International Ltd.

HOARE GOVETT SMALLER COMPANIES (HGSC) INDEX

TOTAL RETURN PERFORMANCE

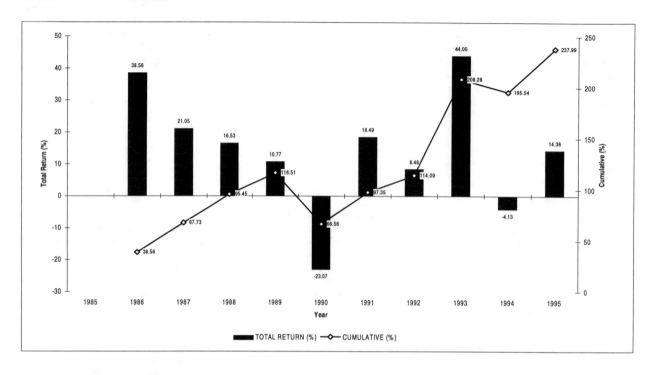

TOTAL RETURN PERFORMANCE

YEAR	VALUE	TOTAL RETURN (%)	CUMULATIVE (%)	MAXIMUM VALUE[1]	DATE	MINIMUM VALUE[1]	DATE
1995	2,439.32	14.36	237.99	2,439.32	31-Dec	2,069.71	28-Feb
1994	2,132.96	-4.13	195.54	2,451.73	31-Jan	2,132.96	31-Dec
1993	2,224.89	44.00	208.28	2,224.89	31-Dec	1,658.64	31-Jan
1992	1,545.08	8.48	114.09	1,621.90	31-May	1,260.87	31-Aug
1991	1,424.31	18.49	97.35	1,537.79	30-Sep	1,145.93	31-Jan
1990	1,202.06	-23.07	66.56	1,554.72	31-Jan	1,188.89	30-Sep
1989	1,562.59	10.77	116.51	1,728.80	31-Aug	1,518.98	31-Oct
1988	1,410.60	16.53	95.45	1,489.92	31-Oct	1,301.33	31-Jan
1987	1,210.51	21.05	67.73	1,740.44	30-Sep	1,085.79	31-Jan
1986	1,000.00	38.56	38.56	1,000.00	31-Dec	746.36	31-Jan
1985	721.71						
Average Annual (%)		14.50					
Compound Annual (%)		12.95					
Standard Deviation (%)		19.21					

[1]Maximum/minimum index values are as of month-end.

Synopsis

The Hoare Govett Smaller Companies (HGSC) Index is a market value-weighted index that tracks the daily stock price and total return performance of the lowest 10th by market capitalization of UK-listed stocks on the London Stock Exchange.

Number of Stocks—December 31, 1995

1,557

Market Value—December 31, 1995

US$136,360.4 million

Selection Criteria

Constituent stocks represent the entire universe of stocks that make up the lowest 10th, by market capitalization, of stocks listed on the London Stock Exchange. There are no restrictions imposed on any stocks on the basis of market capitalization, equity float capital, partial ownership by another quoted company, liquidity or trading volume.

Background

The index was introduced at the beginning of 1987 and backdated to 1955, using monthly data from the London Share Price Database (LSPD), which includes a comprehensive record of prices, capital changes and dividends for all UK-registered sterling-denominated shares traded on the London Stock Exchange since 1975.

Base Date

December 31, 1986=1000.00

Computation Methodology

(1) An aggregate of prices times quantities index formula. Maintenance adjustments to the divisor are made for capitalization changes, new listings and delistings. (2) The index is rebalanced only once a year. This process takes place at the beginning of the year with additions and deletions, as may be required, to maintain the index's lowest one 10th composition.

Derivative Instruments

None

Subindices

HGSC, excluding investment trusts.
Eight economic sector subindices (corresponding to the FT-SE All-Share Index): Mineral extracting, general industrials, consumer goods, services, utilities, non-financial companies, financials and investment trusts.
Thirty-seven industrial group subindices (also corresponding to the FT-SE All-Share Index): Extractive industries, integrated oil, oil exploration and production, building and construction, building materials and merchants, chemicals, diversified industrials, electronic and electronic equipment, engineering, engineering vehicles, paper, packaging and printing, textiles and apparel, breweries, spirits, wines and ciders, food producers, household goods, health care, pharmaceuticals, tobacco, distributors, leisure and hotels, media, food retailers, general retailers, support services, transportation, others services and business, electricity, gas distribution, telecommunications, water, retail banks, merchant banks, insurance, life insurance, other financial, and property.

Related Indices

HG 1000 Index

Remarks

(1) Number of stocks as well as market values are as of January 1, 1996 and represent the composition of the index subsequent to its annual reconstitution. The index started in 1995 with 1,452 constituent shares attributable to 1,387 companies with a combined market capitalization of US$89.4 billion. (2) The average market capitalization of index constituents is US$63.49 billion; the largest company has a market capitalization of US$289.24 billion and the smallest has a market capitalization of US$353.0 million. (3) An Extended HSSC Index, covering Unlisted Securities Market (USM) securities that fall within the HGSC market capitalization limit, has been discontinued due to the abolition of the USM in 1995.

Publisher

Hoare Govett Securities Ltd./ABN-AMRO.

EUROPE — REGIONAL

Eurotop 100 (E100) Index

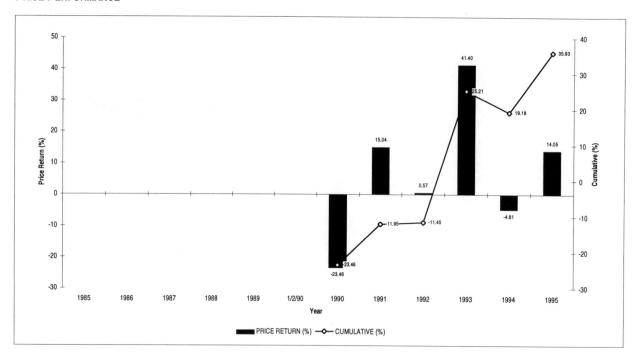

Price Performance (ECU)

YEAR	VALUE	PRICE RETURN (%)	CUMULATIVE (%)	MAXIMUM VALUE	DATE	MINIMUM VALUE	DATE
1995	1,344.01	14.05	35.93	1,344.19	27-Dec	1,117.34	9-Mar
1994	1,178.46	-4.81	19.18	1,311.01	2-Feb	1,136.46	5-Oct
1993	1,238.02	41.40	25.21	1,239.00	30-Dec	862.73	13-Jan
1992	875.56	0.57	-11.45	976.55	25-May	772.52	5-Oct
1991	870.57	15.04	-11.95	955.56	5-Jun	729.57	14-Jan
1990	756.76	-23.46	-23.46	1,025.93	4-Jan	743.10	8-Nov
1/2/90	988.77						
1989							
1988							
1987							
1986							
1985							
Average Annual (%)		4.79					
Compound Annual (%)		2.97					
Standard Deviation (%)		24.23					

Synopsis

The Eurotop 100 (E100) Index is an effective share turnover-weighted index, calculated in the European Currency Unit (ECU), that tracks the continuous price only performance of the 100 most actively traded stocks in nine European countries.

Number of Stocks—December 31, 1995

100

Market Value—December 31, 1995

US$1,550,980.9 million

Selection Criteria

The index includes the nine European member states of the Organization for Economic Cooperation and Development (OECD) with a total market capitalization in excess of 2.5% of the total market capitalization of all countries included in the index. These are: United Kingdom (UK), Germany, France, Switzerland, The Netherlands, Italy, Spain, Sweden and Belgium.

The exchange capitalization in ECU of local stocks in the country at the end of the previous calendar year is determined. The relevant country's stock exchange is selected on the basis of the highest effective volume in local shares over a period of three calendar years.

Constituent stocks are limited to local issues, and shares that may only be owned by local residents are excluded from consideration. Constituent stocks are selected and assigned base weightings using as criteria the effective share volumes on the selected local stock exchange over a period of three years. The weighting of each stock reflects the number of shares included in the index. The selection of stocks and their base weightings are adjusted annually on the basis of effective share volumes over the past three full calendar years.

Stock regarded as investment funds are excluded from consideration. Moreover, companies with multiple share listings are screened on the basis of the highest effective volume over the last three calendar years.

Background

The index was launched in June 1990. Created as a vehicle for stock index option and futures trading, the index seeks to closely track developments in the European markets.

Base Date

January 1, 1990=1000.00

Computation Methodology

(1) The index is calculated as the sum of the prices multiplied by the corresponding weights, divided by 100. (2) The weights of constituent stocks may be revised to take stock dividends, bonus payments and rights issues, provided such actions have an impact of more than 0.01 index points (ECU). (3) Additions or removals from the index, as well as base weightings of the countries in the index, are implemented no more frequently than once every two years (in even calendar years). Such adjustments are made only when countries must be added to or deleted from the index, in accordance with the index rules, or the number of stocks to be included from one or more countries must be changed by at least two stocks. (4) Countries in the index are assigned a base weighting derived from a combination of their total exchange capitalization (90%) and gross national product (10%). (5) The selection of stocks and their base weightings are adjusted annually on the basis of effective share volumes over the past three full calendar years. (6) The most recently published transaction prices as provided by the relevant stock exchange and the most recent ask price of each relevant currency as provided by Reuters is used in the calculation of the index. (7) Index values are calculated in the European Currency Unit (ECU) and converted to multiple currencies, including U.S. dollars and Swiss Francs. The official closing value of the index is calculated after the last relevant stock exchange has customarily ceased normal regulated trading.

Derivative Instruments

Eurotop 100 index futures and options trade on the Amsterdam OEO-Optiebeurs.
Eurotop 100 index options trade on the American Stock Exchange (AMEX).
Eurotop 100 futures trade on the New York Mercantile Exchange (NYME).

Subindices

Ten currency subindices: U.S. dollars as well as each of the currencies applicable to the participating countries.

Related Indices

Amsterdam EOE-Index
Amsterdam Midkap-Index
Dutch Top 5 Index

Remarks

The following local stock exchanges have been designated for use in the calculation of market capitalizations and stock selection: United Kingdom, London Stock Exchange; Germany, Frankfurt Stock Exchange; France, Paris Stock Exchange; Switzerland, Zurich Stock Exchange; Italy, Milan Stock Exchange; The Netherlands, Amsterdam Stock Exchange; Sweden, Stockholm Stock Exchange; Spain, Madrid Stock Exchange; and Belgium, Brussels Stock Exchange.

Publisher

Amsterdam EOE-Optiebeurs.

FT-SE EUROTRACK 100 INDEX

PRICE PERFORMANCE

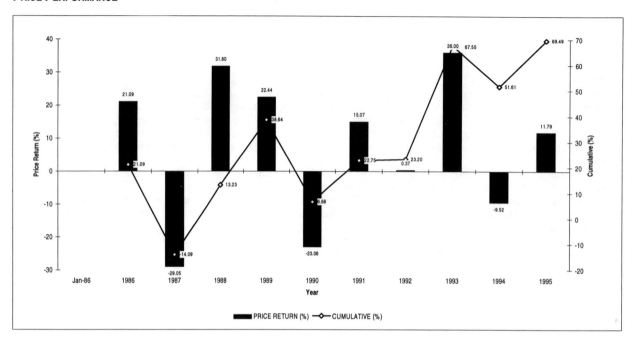

PRICE PERFORMANCE (DM)

YEAR	VALUE	PRICE RETURN (%)	CUMULATIVE (%)	MAXIMUM VALUE	DATE	MINIMUM VALUE	DATE
1995	1,490.40	11.79	69.49	1,492.17	28-Dec	1,229.04	13-Mar
1994	1,333.16	-9.52	51.61	1,539.91	31-Jan	1,282.50	6-Oct
1993	1,473.36	36.00	67.55	1,473.36	31-Dec	1,063.27	13-Jan
1992	1,083.35	0.37	23.20	1,198.94	29-May	937.42	5-Oct
1991	1,079.41	15.07	22.75	1,164.11	5-Jun	901.01	16-Jan
1990	938.05	-23.06	6.68	1,269.70	5-Jun	937.25	28-Dec
1989	1,219.13	22.44	38.64	1,232.15	8-Sep	979.51	27-Feb
1988	995.69	31.80	13.23	995.69	30-Dec	735.49	3-Feb
1987	755.45	-29.05	-14.09	1,136.65	14-Aug	725.73	10-Nov
1986	1,064.81	21.09	21.09	1,099.72	5-Sep	872.05	30-Jan
Jan-86	879.35						
Average Annual (%)		7.69					
Compound Annual (%)		5.42					
Standard Deviation (%)		22.35					

SYNOPSIS

The FT-SE Eurotrack 100 Index is a market value-weighted, Deutsch Mark-denominated index that tracks the continuous price only performance of the 100 most highly capitalized Continental European stocks (excluding the United Kingdom) of 11 countries traded on the London Stock Exchange Automated Quotation (SEAQ) and SEAQ International Systems.

NUMBER OF STOCKS—DECEMBER 31, 1995
100

MARKET VALUE—DECEMBER 31, 1995
US$1,149,384.2 million

SELECTION CRITERIA

Eligible securities are selected on the basis of country weights so as to maintain a close correlation to the FT/S&P Actuaries World Index-Europe (excluding the UK) and market capitalizations in 11 European countries. These include Germany, France, The Netherlands, Switzerland, Italy, Spain, Belgium, Sweden, Ireland, Norway, and Denmark.

In the process of identifying and tracking the 100 most highly capitalized stocks, the entire quoted equity capital of a constituent company is included in the calculation of market capitalization. In the event that there are two or more classes of equity, the equivalent capitalization of the most marketable class is used. Where both an ADR line and the ordinary line of a company have firm quotes available, the ordinary line is considered. The market capitalization of constituent companies is reviewed on a quarterly basis to ensure continued eligibility. Any constituent that falls to the 111th place or below is deleted. Constituents that fall to a level below 101st place and 110th place inclusive, are deleted only if it is necessary to create a vacancy for a security which has risen to 90th place or better, in terms of market capitalization, during the course of the quarter. Changes are implemented on the first business day following the end of the calendar quarter.

A stock ceases to be eligible for inclusion in the index if less than 25% is in public hands, unless a country is deemed to be underweight, in which case a 10% eligibility standard is applied.

BACKGROUND

The FT-SE Eurotrack 100 Index was introduced on October 29, 1990. It was designed to provide a real time indicator of price trends in the major underlying European markets based on stocks trading on the London Stock Exchange pursuant to a common set of dealing rules and, at the same time, to serve as a vehicle for options and futures trading. Index futures and options were listed on the London International Financial Futures Exchange Ltd. (LIFFE), but these have ceased to trade.

Liquidity and ease of settlement were important considerations in the construction of the index and these were satisfied by ensuring that constituent stocks have firm quotes on the SEAQ (UK and Irish securities) and SEAQ International (European securities, excluding UK and Ireland), that they meet minimum market capitalization guidelines and that they are relatively easy to settle.

The index was reconstructed by James Capel Quantitative Research, with data and methodology audited by the WM Company, back to December 31, 1985, using rules in effect as of 1990 to establish appropriate country weights and market capitalization data as of that date.

BASE DATE

December 31, 1985=1000.00

COMPUTATION METHODOLOGY

(1) An aggregate of prices times quantities index formula. Maintenance adjustments to the divisor are made for capitalization changes, new listings and delistings. (2) The index is denominated in Deutsch Marks (DM). It is also calculated in U.S. dollars and British pounds. (3) Country weightings are reviewed and adjusted on a quarterly basis, as may be required, on the first business day following the end of the calendar quarter. (4) Market capitalization computations reflect any legal restrictions applicable to shares which can be held by non-domestic investors. Additions and removals are made during the course of the quarter, as appropriate, due to major new issues, amounting to 1.5% or more of the market capitalization of the index, or suspensions of existing constituent companies, splits, as well as takeovers. Replacements are selected from a list consisting of the highest capitalized stocks from the most underweighted country. (5) The official index closing price is normally set at 15.30 PM London Time.

DERIVATIVE INSTRUMENTS

None

SUBINDICES

Eleven country subindices, calculated in the home currency of the respective country: Germany; France; The Netherlands; Switzerland; Italy; Spain; Belgium; Sweden; Ireland; Norway; and Denmark.

RELATED INDICES

FT-Actuaries Fixed Interest Index
FT Fixed Interest Index
FT-SE-Actuaries All-Share Index
FT-SE Actuaries Fledgling Index
FT-SE Eurotrack 200 Index
FT/S&P Actuaries World Index
Refer to Appendix 5 for additional indices.

REMARKS

FT-SE International was established by the *Financial Times* and the London Stock Exchange in 1995 to manage and develop the FT-SE and FT-Actuaries indices. Responsibility for the FT/S&P Actuaries World Index, which is co-published by the Financial Times Ltd., Goldman Sachs & Co. and Standard and Poor's, is scheduled for 1996.

PUBLISHER

FT-SE International Ltd.

FT-SE EUROTRACK 200 INDEX

PRICE PERFORMANCE

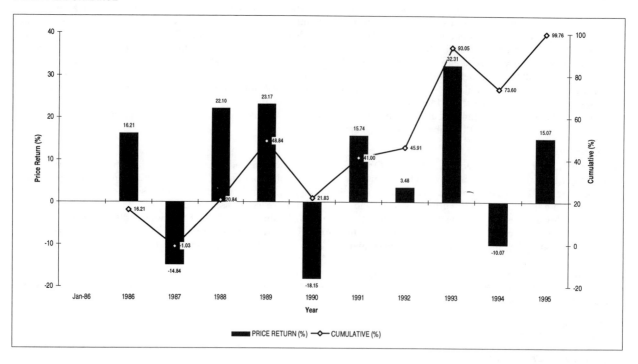

PRICE PERFORMANCE

YEAR	VALUE	PRICE RETURN (%)	CUMULATIVE (%)	MAXIMUM VALUE	DATE	MINIMUM VALUE	DATE
1995	1,600.60	15.07	99.76	1,602.58	27-Dec	1,323.28	9-Mar
1994	1,391.00	-10.07	73.60	1,607.16	2-Feb	1,339.81	6-Oct
1993	1,546.84	32.31	93.05	1,552.43	29-Dec	1,143.97	13-Jan
1992	1,169.11	3.48	45.91	1,248.99	11-May	1,010.09	5-Oct
1991	1,129.81	15.74	41.00	1,198.60	3-Sep	938.62	16-Jan
1990	976.20	-18.15	21.83	1,231.33	17-Jul	947.60	29-Sep
1989	1,192.63	23.17	48.84	1,221.96	3-Sep	968.83	2-Jan
1988	968.27	22.10	20.84	970.75	29-Dec	790.87	10-Nov
1987	793.03	-14.84	-1.03	1,143.99	17-Jul	747.92	10-Nov
1986	931.17	16.21	16.21	968.59	22-Apr	790.71	3-Feb
Jan-86	801.28						
Average Annual (%)		8.50					
Compound Annual (%)		7.16					
Standard Deviation (%)		17.47					

SYNOPSIS
The FT-SE Eurotrack 200 Index is a market-value weighted, European Currency Unit (ECU)-denominated, index that tracks the continuous price only performance of the 200 most highly capitalized European stocks traded on London's Stock Exchange Automated Quotation (SEAQ) and SEAQ International Systems. The FT-SE 100 Index and the FT-SE Eurotrack 100 Index are combined to form the index.

NUMBER OF STOCKS—DECEMBER 31, 1995
200

MARKET VALUE—DECEMBER 31, 1995
US$1,729,948.4 million

SELECTION CRITERIA
All constituent shares in the FT-SE 100 Index and the FT-SE Eurotrack 100 Index which consist of the most highly capitalized stocks traded on London's Stock Exchange Automated Quotation (SEAQ) and SEAQ International Systems from the following twelve European countries: The United Kingdom (UK), Germany, France, The Netherlands, Switzerland, Italy, Spain, Belgium, Sweden, Ireland, Norway and Denmark.

Any changes made to the FT-SE 100 Index and FT-SE Eurotrack 100 Index, in accordance to selection and maintenance rules, are also made to the FT-SE Eurotrack 200 Index.

Refer to the FT-SE 100 and FT-SE Eurotrack 100 indices for additional information.

BACKGROUND
The FT-SE Eurotrack 200 Index was introduced on February 25, 1991. It was designed to provide a real time indicator of price trends in the major underlying European markets based on stocks trading on the London Stock Exchange pursuant to a common set of dealing rules and, at the same time, to serve as a vehicle for options and futures trading. Index futures and options were listed on the London International Financial Futures Exchange Ltd. (LIFFE), but these have ceased to trade.

Liquidity and ease of settlement were important considerations in the construction of the index and these were satisfied by ensuring that constituent stocks have firm quotes on the SEAQ (UK and Irish securities) and SEAQ International (European securities, excluding UK and Ireland), that they meet minimum market capitalization guidelines and that they are relatively easy to settle.

BASE DATE
October 26, 1990=1000.00

COMPUTATION METHODOLOGY
(1) An aggregate of prices times quantities index formula. Maintenance adjustments to the divisor are made for capitalization changes, new listings and delistings. (2) The index is denominated in European Currency Units (ECU). (3) The FT-SE Eurotrack constituents, using their natural weights which are established so as to maintain close correlation to the FT/S&P Actuaries World Index-Europe, are combined with the FT-SE 100 constituents which are weighted by applying a "Weighting Restraint Factor" (WRF) to the capitalization of each FT-SE 100 constituent. The WRF factor represents the ratio of the UK and Continental Europe within Europe, multiplied by the market capitalization of the FT-SE 100 Index, which is in turn divided by the market capitalization of the FT-SE 100. The result is the percentage of FT-SE 100 shares to be included in the FT-SE Eurotrack 200 Index on a quarterly basis. (4) Index weightings are reviewed and adjusted on a quarterly basis, as may be required, on the first business day following the end of the calendar quarter.

DERIVATIVE INSTRUMENTS
None

SUBINDICES
None

RELATED INDICES
FT-Actuaries Fixed Interest Index
FT Fixed Interest Index
FT-SE Actuaries Fledgling Index
FT-SE Eurotrack 100 Index
FT-SE Actuaries All-Share Index
FT/S&P Actuaries World Index
Refer to Appendix 5 for additional indices.

REMARKS
FT-SE International was established by the *Financial Times* and the London Stock Exchange in 1995 to manage and develop the FT-SE and FT-Actuaries indices. Responsibility for the FT/S&P Actuaries World Index, which is co-published by the Financial Times Ltd., Goldman Sachs & Co. and Standard and Poor's, is scheduled for 1996.

PUBLISHER
FT-SE International Ltd.

HSBC JAMES CAPEL SMALLER EUROPEAN COMPANIES INDEX

PRICE PERFORMANCE

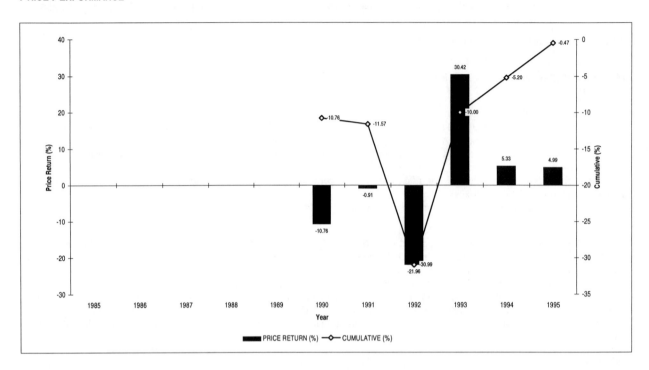

PRICE PERFORMANCE

YEAR	VALUE	PRICE RETURN (%)	CUMULATIVE (%)	MAXIMUM VALUE	DATE	MINIMUM VALUE	DATE
1995	99.53	4.99	-0.47	106.22	4-Aug	92.50	7-Feb
1994	94.80	5.33	-5.20	100.69	22-Aug	90.68	3-Jan
1993	90.00	30.42	-10.00	90.91	28-Dec	68.40	4-Jan
1992	69.01	-21.96	-30.99	92.33	19-May	68.55	24-Nov
1991	88.43	-0.91	-11.57	99.85	6-Mar	79.30	19-Aug
1990	89.24	-10.76	-10.76	113.94	31-Jul	86.88	25-Dec
1989	100.00						
1988							
1987							
1986							
1985							
Average Annual (%)		1.19					
Compound Annual (%)		-0.08					
Standard Deviation (%)		17.71					

SYNOPSIS

The HSBC James Capel Smaller European Companies Index is a market value-weighted index that tracks the daily price only performance of a universe of small company stocks listed on 17 European markets (excluding the United Kingdom) with an internationally recognized exchange.

NUMBER OF STOCKS—DECEMBER 31, 1995

1,168

MARKET VALUE—DECEMBER 31, 1995

US$364,230.4 million

SELECTION CRITERIA

The index consists of small companies listed in the following markets: Austria, Belgium, Denmark, Finland, France, Germany, Greece, Ireland, Italy, Luxembourg, The Netherlands, Norway, Portugal, Spain, Sweden, Switzerland, and Turkey.

Constituents are selected on the basis of their combined full market capitalization, which must lie within a range of 50.0 million pounds and 500.0 million pounds. An official quotation is required for eligibility, however, liquidity factors are not taken into consideration.

BACKGROUND

The index has been backdated to December 31, 1985.

BASE DATE

December 31, 1989=100.00

COMPUTATION METHODOLOGY

(1) An aggregate of prices times quantities index formula. Maintenance adjustments to the divisor are made for capitalization changes, new listings and delistings. (2) Market capitalization is calculated on the basis of each company's fully issued capital, regardless of the level of free float. Small changes in a company's market capitalization relative to the minimum and maximum guidelines for small companies are not likely to lead to a rebalancing of the index. (3) The index is monitored daily and rebalanced quarterly.

DERIVATIVE INSTRUMENTS

None

SUBINDICES

Seventeen market indices: Austria, Belgium, Denmark, Finland, France, Germany, Greece, Ireland, Italy, Luxembourg, The Netherlands, Norway, Portugal, Spain, Sweden, Switzerland, and Turkey.

Smaller Pan-European Companies Index, including the UK, which is achieved by combining the JC Trixie Index and the Smaller European Index.

RELATED INDICES

HSBC JC Dragon 300 Index
HSBC JC Japanese Smaller Companies Index
HSBC JC Latin America 100 Index
HSBC JC Tiger Index
Refer to Appendix 5 for additional indices.

REMARKS

None

PUBLISHER

HSBC James Capel & Co. Limited.

ING BARINGS SPECIAL EASTERN EUROPE INDEX

PRICE PERFORMANCE

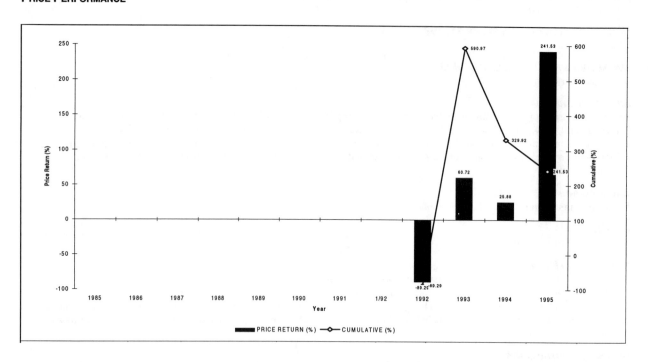

PRICE PERFORMANCE (US$)

YEAR	VALUE	PRICE RETURN (%)	CUMULATIVE (%)	MAXIMUM VALUE[1]	DATE	MINIMUM VALUE[1]	DATE
1995	79.44	-20.56	241.53	90.96	31-Jul	74.36	Mar-95
1994	100.00	-37.78	329.92	257.39	28-Feb	100.00	31-Dec
1993	160.72	833.33	590.97	160.72	31-Dec	16.17	28-Feb
1992	17.22	-25.97	-25.97	23.90	28-Feb	15.02	30-Jun
Jan-92	23.26						
1991							
1990							
1989							
1988							
1987							
1986							
1985							
Average Annual (%)		191.24					
Compound Annual (%)		35.94					
Standard Deviation (%)		430.78					

[1]Maximum/minimum index values are as of month-end.

SYNOPSIS
The ING Barings Special Eastern Europe Index is a market value-weighted index that tracks the daily price only performance of an investable universe of equity shares in four Eastern European countries, including the Czech Republic, Hungary, Poland, and Russia.

NUMBER OF STOCKS—DECEMBER 31, 1995
72

MARKET VALUE—DECEMBER 31, 1995
US$7,253.1 million

SELECTION CRITERIA
Constituents are selected on the basis of the following guidelines:
(1) Market capitalization of at least 0.5% of the total capitalization of the market. (2) Average daily traded value of at least US$250,000.0. In the case of Russia, in lieu of the daily traded value requirement, an alternative liquidity indicator of a minimum of 10 brokers quoting indicative prices on Reuters is applicable. (3) Free float of at least 10%.

BACKGROUND
The index, an extension of the ING Barrings Emerging Markets Index (BEMI), was launched on September 29, 1995 in response to increasing foreign investment in the Central and Eastern European Region, with index values recalculated to January 1992. Due to low or uncertain levels of liquidity associated with the region, the selection guidelines employed in the BEMI could not be applied to this index and were modified accordingly.

BASE DATE
December 31, 1994=100.00

COMPUTATION METHODOLOGY
(1) An aggregate of prices times quantities (Paasche) index formula. Maintenance adjustments to the divisor are made for capitalization changes, new listings and delistings. Additions and deletions of constituent stocks, other than as a result of a Recomposition Committee meeting, are implemented on the last day of the month. (2) Market capitalization is calculated on the basis of each company's available free float to foreign investors, which is normally updated annually. (3) The composition of the index is reviewed and rebalanced on a quarterly basis. A Recomposition Committee posts the results of the recomposition meetings two weeks in advance of implementing any changes, which become effective on the last day of the month. (4) The long-term stability and continuity of the index is maintained in the event that a country exceeds the index criteria by expanding the index so that it may be calculated both with and without the ineligible constituent country. (5) The index is computed using closing prices that coincide with the London time zone. (6) All daily share prices are converted to U.S. dollars using WM/Reuters closing spot rates at 4 PM, London Time.

DERIVATIVE INSTRUMENTS
None

SUBINDICES
Four standalone country indices: Czech Republic, Hungary, Poland and Russia.
Extended BEMI, including the three additional ineligible countries.
Two equal-weighted BEMI indices are calculated, one that is rebalanced quarterly and a second that is rebalanced annually.

RELATED INDICES
Baring Emerging Markets World Index (BEMI)
Extended BEMI, including Czech Republic, Hungary, Poland and Russia
Baring Asian Convertible Bond Index
Baring Pan Asia Index

REMARKS
(1) ING Baring offers the flexibility to create customized or modified indices, including use of standalone indices to create customized benchmarks. (2) Exchange rates per ING Baring Securities Limited. (3) Market value of constituent securities represents available capitalization, which is equivalent to US$22,061.3 million of total market value.

PUBLISHER
ING Baring Securities Limited.

NOMURA RESEARCH INSTITUTE (NRI) EAST EUROPEAN INDEX

PRICE PERFORMANCE

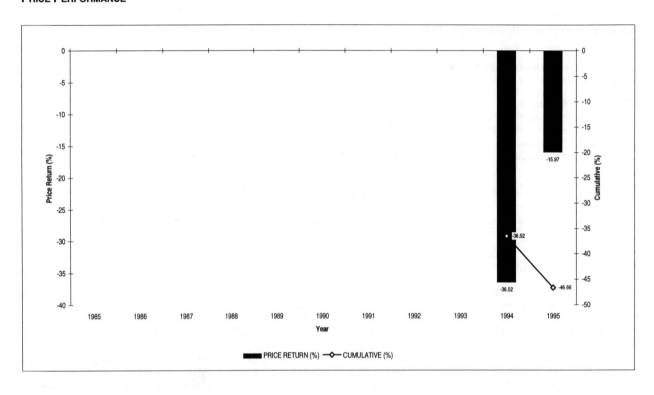

PRICE PERFORMANCE

YEAR	VALUE	PRICE RETURN (%)	CUMULATIVE (%)	MAXIMUM VALUE	DATE	MINIMUM VALUE	DATE
1995	53.34	-15.97	-46.66	63.31	5-Jan	51.71	29-Nov
1994	63.48	-36.52	-36.52	152.70	2-Mar	61.04	16-Dec
1993	100.00						
1992							
1991							
1990							
1989							
1988							
1987							
1986							
1985							
Average Annual (%)		-26.25					
Compound Annual (%)		-26.97					
Standard Deviation (%)		14.53					

SYNOPSIS

The Nomura Research Institute (NRI) East European Index is a market value-weighted index that tracks the daily stock price only performance of companies whose shares are traded on the main or "listed" markets of the Czech Republic, Hungary, Poland and Slovakia.

NUMBER OF STOCKS—DECEMBER 31, 1995

149

MARKET VALUE—DECEMBER 31, 1995

US$19,575.0 million

SELECTION CRITERIA

All stocks listed on the main or "listed" market of the Czech Republic, Hungary, Poland and Slovakia are eligible for inclusion in the index.

BACKGROUND

None

BASE DATE

December 31, 1993=100.00

COMPUTATION METHODOLOGY

(1) An aggregate of prices times quantities index formula. Maintenance adjustments to the divisor are made for capitalization changes, new listings and delistings. (2) Official close of day prices are used.

DERIVATIVE INSTRUMENTS

None

SUBINDICES

Four market subindices: Czech Republic, Hungary, Poland and Slovakia.
Economic sector indices for the composite index and individual country indices.

RELATED INDICES

NRI-AP200 Equity Index
NRI European Multimedia Index
Russell/NRI Japanese Equity Style Index Series
Russell/NRI Japanese Total Market Index

REMARKS

The number of listed stocks, market capitalization and NRI weighting applicable to each of the markets are, as follows: Czech Republic, 63 issues with a market capitalization of US$11,991.0 million and a weight of 47.59%; Hungary, 15 issues with a market capitalization of US$2,009.0 million and a weight of 10.26%; Poland, 53 issues with a market capitalization of US$4,415.0 million and a weight of 22.56%; and Slovakia, 18 issues with a market capitalization of US$1,160.0 million and a weight of 5.92%.

PUBLISHER

Nomura International plc/Nomura Research Institute, Ltd.

NORDIC SECURITIES MARKET INDEX

PRICE PERFORMANCE

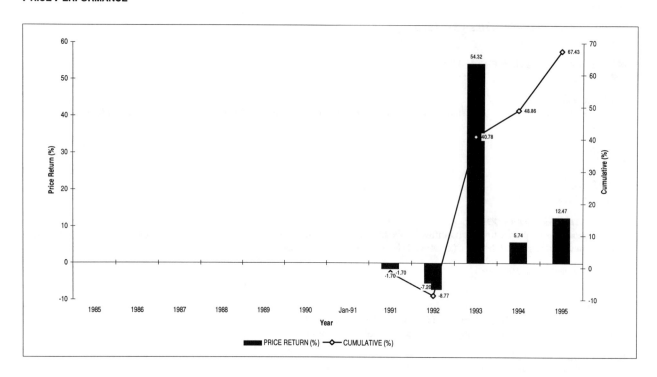

PRICE PERFORMANCE

YEAR	VALUE	PRICE RETURN (%)	CUMULATIVE (%)	MAXIMUM VALUE[1]	DATE	MINIMUM VALUE[1]	DATE
1995	596.13	12.47	67.43	638.47	19-May	505.79	31-Mar
1994	530.03	5.74	48.86	572.49	31-Jan	497.20	30-Jun
1993	501.24	54.32	40.78	503.99	31-Oct	325.85	31-Jan
1992	324.81	-7.20	-8.77	369.26	31-Jan	269.88	30-Sep
1991	350.01	-1.70	-1.70	415.69	31-Jul	350.01	31-Dec
Jan-91	356.05						
1990							
1989							
1988							
1987							
1986							
1985							
Average Annual (%)		12.73					
Compound Annual (%)		10.86					
Standard Deviation (%)		24.41					

[1]Maximum/minimum index values are as of month-end.

SYNOPSIS

The Nordic Securities Market Index is a weighted composite index that tracks the stock performance of the domestic shares listed on the stock exchanges of Denmark, Finland, Norway and Sweden, by combining the leading stock market indices in each of these markets.

NUMBER OF STOCKS—DECEMBER 31, 1995

700

MARKET VALUE—DECEMBER 31, 1995

US$318,169.7 million

SELECTION CRITERIA

The index consists of all shares that make up each market's broad based securities market index. These include Denmark's Copenhagen CSE Index (CSI) of all Danish based stocks traded on the Copenhagen Stock Exchange, Finland's Helsinki HEX All-Share Index (HEX) of all stocks, including restricted and unrestricted shares, traded on the Helsinki Stock Exchange, Norway's Oslo OSI Index (OSI) of stocks traded on the Main List of the Oslo Stock Exchange, including Class A, Free Class and B-Class shares and Sweden's Stockholm SX Index (SSI) of all classes of stock traded on the A-list of the Stockholm Stock Exchange.

BACKGROUND

None

BASE DATE

January 1, 1983=100.00

COMPUTATION METHODOLOGY

A weighted average of the national indices. The index value of each component index is weighted by the combined market capitalization of the component stocks that make up each index, which are converted into a common currency by using the European Currency Unit (ECU), and dividing the result by the product of the respective index values.

DERIVATIVE INSTRUMENTS

None

SUBINDICES

None

RELATED INDICES

None

REMARKS

The index provides a guide, but not precise measure of the aggregate performance of shares traded on the four Nordic stock markets. The individual indices that make up the Nordic Index are each calculated using a market value-weighted index formula. The Copenhagen CSE Index, Helsinki HEX All-Share Index and Stockholm SX-General Index are each included on the basis of price only performance results while the Olso Stock Exchange Index is included on the basis of total return performance.

PUBLISHER

The Nordic Stock Exchanges.

CENTRAL/LATIN AMERICA

BUENOS AIRES STOCK EXCHANGE VALUE INDEX—COMPOSITE

PRICE PERFORMANCE

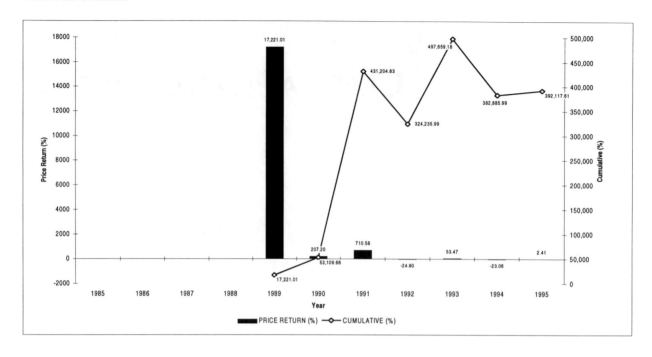

PRICE PERFORMANCE

YEAR	VALUE	PRICE RETURN (%)	CUMULATIVE (%)	MAXIMUM VALUE	DATE	MINIMUM VALUE	DATE
1995	16,237.81	2.41	392,117.61	16,531.10	2-Jan	9,831.09	9-Mar
1994	15,855.62	-23.06	382,885.99	25,470.33	16-Feb	1,513.31	27-Dec
1993	20,607.23	53.47	497,659.18	20,607.23	30-Dec	12,167.66	8-Mar
1992	13,427.51	-24.80	324,235.99	25,740.10	1-Jun	10,575.75	23-Nov
1991	17,856.02	710.58	431,204.83	17,900.14	16-Oct	2,030.57	21-Jan
1990	2,202.88	207.20	53,109.66	2,814.06	7-Aug	401.91	8-Jan
1989	717.09	17,221.01	17,221.01	717.09	28-Dec	4.02	3-Feb
1988	4.14						
1987							
1986							
1985							
Average Annual (%)		2,592.40					
Compound Annual (%)		226.11					
Standard Deviation (%)		6,455.89					

SYNOPSIS
The Buenos Aires Stock Exchange Value Index–Composite is a market value-weighted index that tracks the daily stock price performance of all common shares listed on the Buenos Aires Stock Exchange (BASE).

NUMBER OF STOCKS—DECEMBER 31, 1995
149

MARKET VALUE—DECEMBER 31, 1994
US$37,783.0 million

SELECTION CRITERIA
All common shares listed on the Buenos Aires Stock Exchange (BASE).

BACKGROUND
None

BASE DATE
December 31, 1977=0.00001

COMPUTATION METHODOLOGY
An aggregative of prices times quantities index formula. Maintenance adjustments to the divisor are made for capitalization changes, new listings and delistings.

DERIVATIVE INSTRUMENTS
None

SUBINDICES
Sixteen sector subindices: Food, banks, insurance, beverages, trade and imports, construction, finance, raw materials, chemicals, manufacturing, metals, paper and printing, utilities, textiles and miscellaneous companies.

RELATED INDICES
An inflation adjusted index is calculated, using a base value of 100.00, as of December 31, 1977.
Burcap Index
Merval Index

REMARKS
None

PUBLISHER
The Buenos Aires Stock Exchange (BASE).

MERVAL INDEX

PRICE PERFORMANCE

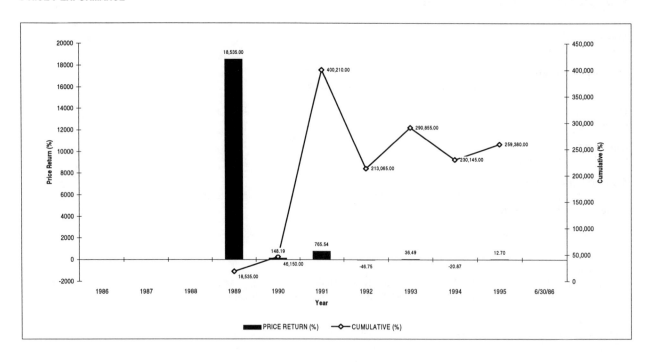

PRICE PERFORMANCE

YEAR	VALUE	PRICE RETURN (%)	CUMULATIVE (%)	MAXIMUM VALUE	DATE	MINIMUM VALUE	DATE
1995	518.96	12.70	259,380.00	518.96	28-Dec	262.11	8-Mar
1994	460.49	-20.87	230,145.00	727.85	16-Feb	436.97	28-Dec
1993	581.91	36.49	290,855.00	581.91	30-Dec	356.56	10-May
1992	426.33	-46.75	213,065.00	890.41	1-Jun	315.38	16-Oct
1991	800.62	765.54	400,210.00	854.70	1-Nov	83.85	21-Jan
1990	92.50	148.19	46,150.00	142.79	7-Aug	17.48	8-Jan
1989	37.27	18,535.00	18,535.00	37.27	28-Dec	0.17	3-Feb
1988	0.20	NA	NA	NA	NA	NA	NA
1987	NA	NA	NA	NA	NA	NA	NA
1986	NA	NA	NA	NA	NA	NA	NA
6/30/86	0.01						
Average Annual (%)		2,775.76					
Compound Annual (%)		207.42					
Standard Deviation (%)		6,954.91					

SYNOPSIS
The Merval Index is a theoretical quantity-weighted index that tracks the continuous stock price performance of selected common shares listed on the Buenos Aires Stock Exchange (BASE).

NUMBER OF STOCKS—DECEMBER 31, 1995
Not Available

MARKET VALUE—DECEMBER 31, 1995
Not Available

SELECTION CRITERIA
Constituents are selected from the universe of stocks traded on the BASE, on the basis their market participation computed over a six-month period. All traded securities are arrayed by their participation coefficient and from this universe, index constituents are selected until a cumulative level of participation of 80% has been achieved.

BACKGROUND
None

BASE DATE
June 30, 1986=0.01

COMPUTATION METHODOLOGY
(1) The index value is the summation of each security's price quotation multiplied by each security's theoretical quantity. The theoretical quantity is computed in a number of steps. First, a participation coefficient based on relative trading value and number of transactions is calculated. All securities are arrayed by their participation coefficient and from this universe, index constituents are selected until a cumulative level of participation of 80% has been achieved. Second, each security's adjusted participation coefficient is computed by dividing each security's relative participation coefficient by the sum of the participation coefficients of all selected securities. Finally, the theoretical quantity for each security is computed by dividing the closing index value as of the prior quarter-end by each security's price quotation and multiplying the result by the adjusted participation coefficient. (2) Constituent companies and their weights are revised quarterly, on the basis of trading value and number of transactions measured during the previous six months.

DERIVATIVE INSTRUMENTS
None

SUBINDICES
None

RELATED INDICES
The Buenos Aires Stock Exchange Value Index–Composite Index
Burcap Index

REMARKS
None

PUBLISHER
The Buenos Aires Stock Exchange (BASE).

SECURITIES EXCHANGE OF BARBADOS SHARE INDEX

PRICE PERFORMANCE

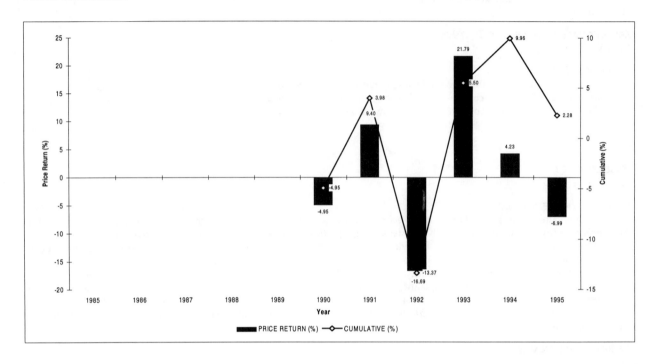

PRICE PERFORMANCE

YEAR	VALUE	PRICE RETURN (%)	CUMULATIVE (%)	MAXIMUM VALUE[1]	DATE	MINIMUM VALUE[1]	DATE
1995[2]	1,297.63	-6.99	2.28	1,510.02	28-Feb	1,295.64	30-Nov
1994	1,395.18	4.23	9.96	1,395.18	31-Dec	1,347.91	31-Jan
1993	1,338.58	21.79	5.50	1,338.58	31-Dec	1,098.81	31-Jan
1992	1,099.13	-16.69	-13.37	1,260.73	31-Mar	1,089.40	31-Oct
1991	1,319.25	9.40	3.98	1,382.07	31-Aug	1,221.18	31-Jan
1990	1,205.95	-4.95	-4.95	1,293.52	28-Feb	1,205.95	31-Dec
1989	1,268.75	NA	NA	1,273.13	30-Nov	1,252.81	31-Aug
1988	NA	NA	NA	NA	NA	NA	NA
1987	1,000.00						
1986							
1985							
Average Annual (%)		1.13					
Compound Annual (%)		0.38					
Standard Deviation (%)		13.60					

[1]Maximum/minimum values are month-end index values. 1989 maximum/minimum values based on period 8/31/1989-12/31/1989.
[2]In July 1995 the index calculation methodology was modified and the continuity of the index was interrupted.

SYNOPSIS

The Securities Exchange of Barbados Share Index is a market value-weighted index that tracks the price performance of ordinary shares listed on the Securities Exchange of Barbados.

NUMBER OF STOCKS—DECEMBER 31, 1995

18

MARKET VALUE—DECEMBER 31, 1995

US$490.53 million

SELECTION CRITERIA

Constituent shares include all ordinary shares listed on the Securities Exchange of Barbados.

BACKGROUND

The stock exchange was founded on June 1, 1987 and the index was introduced shortly thereafter. Index values are available to August 1989. In June 1995, the index calculation methodology was modified to bring the calculation in line with other regional exchanges.

BASE DATE

January 1, 1988=1000.00

COMPUTATION METHODOLOGY

An aggregative of prices times quantities index formula. Maintenance adjustments to the divisor are made for capitalization changes, new listings and delistings.

DERIVATIVE INSTRUMENTS

None

SUBINDICES

None

RELATED INDICES

None

REMARKS

Two companies, Barbados External Telecommunications and CIBC W.I. Holdings account for 52% of the market capitalization of the index.

PUBLISHER

Securities Exchange of Barbados.

IBV Profitability Index of Rio de Janeiro Stock Exchange (IBV)

Price Performance

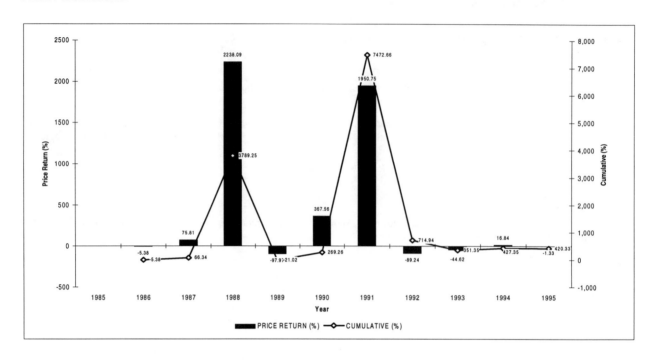

Price Performance

YEAR	VALUE[1]	PRICE RETURN (%)	CUMULATIVE (%)	MAXIMUM VALUE[2]	DATE	MINIMUM VALUE[2]	DATE
1995	16,247.00	-1.33	420.33	18,517.00	19-Sep	9,119.00	9-Mar
1994	16,466.00	16.84	427.35	20,266.00	30-Sep	1,419.50	3-Jan
1993	14,093.00	-44.62	351.35	NA	NA	NA	NA
1992	25,446.00	-89.24	714.94	NA	NA	NA	NA
1991	236,451.00	1,950.75	7,472.66	NA	NA	NA	NA
1990	11,530.00	367.56	269.26	NA	NA	NA	NA
1989	2,466.00	-97.97	-21.02	NA	NA	NA	NA
1988	121,439.00	2,238.09	3,789.25	121,439.00	29-Dec	5,319.00	4-Jan
1987	5,193.95	75.81	66.34	5,815.99	16-Oct	1,852.88	16-Mar
1986	2,954.33	-5.38	-5.38	5,979.74	2-May	2,658.34	9-Dec
1985	3,122.43						
Average Annual (%)		441.05					
Compound Annual (%)		17.93					
Standard Deviation (%)		883.80					

[1]Due to the high levels of Brazilian inflation, the IBV's index value was divided by 1,000 as of October 23, 1989. Index values for calendar year-ends 1986-1988 were adjusted similarly by dividing these by 1,000.

[2]Maximum/minimum values for the calendar periods following 1989 are based on month-end values.

SYNOPSIS
The IBV Profitability Index of Rio de Janeiro Stock Exchange (IBV) Index is a market value-weighted price only index that tracks the daily performance of the most actively traded stocks listed on the Rio de Janeiro Stock Exchange. Consisting of an average of 60 stocks, the index has historically represented in excess of 90% of the traded turnover on the Rio de Janeiro Stock Exchange.

NUMBER OF STOCKS—DECEMBER 31, 1995
About 60

MARKET VALUE—DECEMBER 31, 1995
Not Available

SELECTION CRITERIA
Constituent stocks are selected on the basis of their liquidity in the preceding 12-month period. Qualification for inclusion in the index is assessed using the following factors:
(1) A stock must have been traded in at least 80% of the trading sessions within the previous 12 months. (2) A stock must display a record of at least 1,000 transactions. (3) A stock must be continuously traded. Its absence five times from five or more consecutive trading sessions disqualifies it from consideration as an index constituent.

BACKGROUND
Introduced on August 18, 1955, the IBV was constructed on the basis of a traded value-weighted portfolio. It was redesigned in 1986 and transformed into a capitalization-weighted index in an effort to adopt a methodology more common among international exchanges, achieve greater academic support, and support the needs of the derivatives market. Due to the high levels of Brazilian inflation, the IBV's Index value was divided by 1,000 as of October 23, 1989.

BASE DATE
December 12, 1983=100.00

COMPUTATION METHODOLOGY
(1) An aggregative of prices times quantities index formula. Maintenance adjustments to the divisor are made for capitalization changes, new listings and delistings. (2) Constituent stocks are reviewed annually in June and a new portfolio of qualified stocks is established on the first trading day in July. (3) Constituent stocks are also reviewed on a quarterly basis. Stocks failing to qualify are removed from the index. (4) Market capitalization is defined using the number of outstanding shares held by the public or non-controlling shareholders.

DERIVATIVE INSTRUMENTS
None

SUBINDICES
Seven sectoral subindices: Consumer goods, finance, mining, chemicals and petrochemicals, services, iron and steel and commerce. Subindices that track the performance of securities issued by government controlled companies and "private sector" companies.

RELATED INDICES
Inflation adjusted IBV Index
I-SENN Index
Rio de Janeiro Stock Exchange Price Index (IPBV)

REMARKS
None

PUBLISHER
The Rio de Janeiro Stock Exchange.

I-SENN INDEX

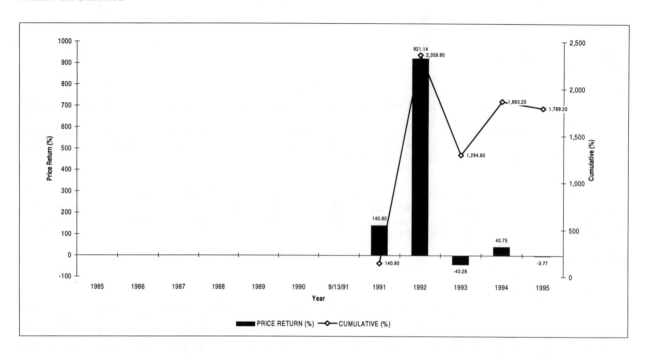

PRICE PERFORMANCE[1]

YEAR	VALUE	PRICE RETURN (%)	CUMULATIVE (%)	MAXIMUM VALUE	DATE	MINIMUM VALUE	DATE
1995	18,892.00	-3.77	1,789.20	21,494.00	18-Sep	10,647.00	9-Mar
1994	19,632.00	40.75	1,863.20	146,457.00	29-Jun	1,337.00	5-Jul
1993	13,948.00	-43.28	1,294.80	102,414.00	26-Nov	7,615.00	29-Apr
1992	24,589.00	921.14	2,358.90	24,589.00	30-Dec	2,704.00	2-Jan
1991	2,408.00	140.80	140.80	2,408.00	30-Dec	894.00	26-Sep
9/13/91	1,000.00						
1990							
1989							
1988							
1987							
1986							
1985							
Average Annual (%)		263.91					
Compound Annual (%)		108.48					
Standard Deviation (%)		462.89					

[1]Performance measures appliable to the 4-year period 1992-1995.

The I-SENN Index is a traded value-weighted price only index that tracks the continuous performance of the 50 most actively traded stocks listed on Brazil's eight stock exchanges, including Belo Horizonte, Curitiba, Fortaleza, Porto Alegre, Recife, Rio de Janeiro, Salvador and Santos that are integrated by the national electronic system–the Sistema Electronico de Negociacao Nacional (SENN).

NUMBER OF STOCKS—DECEMBER 31, 1995
50

MARKET VALUE—DECEMBER 31, 1995
Not Available

SELECTION CRITERIA
Constituent stocks represent the most traded stocks over the previous 12 months, on the basis of traded value in Curzerios Reais.

Each quarter, the portfolio of securities that comprise the index is reviewed and adjusted based on trading value achieved over the previous 12 months. Adjustments are implemented on the last trading day of March, June, September and December of each year.

BACKGROUND
None

BASE DATE
September 16, 1991=1000.00

COMPUTATION METHODOLOGY
(1) A base-weighted aggregate index formula in which stock prices are weighted by a theoretical quantity value representing relative trading volume rather than market capitalization, which is adjusted to eliminate the effect of dividends and rights offerings. (2) The portfolio of constituent stocks is reviewed four times a year, based on traded value over the previous 12 months.

DERIVATIVE INSTRUMENTS
I-SENN index futures and options trade on the Rio de Janeiro Stock Exchange and the Bolsa de Mercadorias & Futuros (BM&F).

SUBINDICES
None

RELATED INDICES
IBV Index
Rio de Janeiro Stock Exchange Price Index (IPBV)

REMARKS
None

PUBLISHER
The Rio de Janeiro Stock Exchange.

THE SAO PAULO STOCK EXCHANGE INDEX (BOVESPA)

PRICE PERFORMANCE

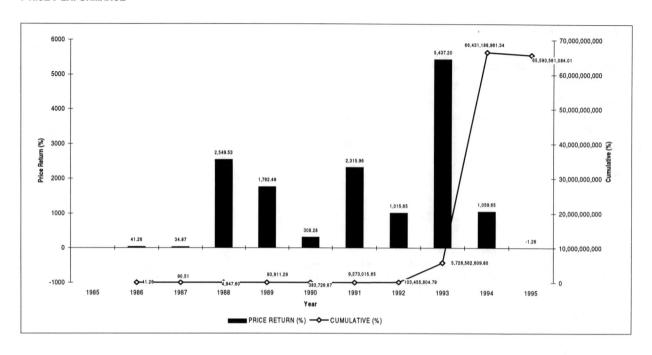

PRICE PERFORMANCE

YEAR	VALUE	PRICE RETURN (%)	CUMULATIVE (%)	DOLLAR ADJUSTED[1]	MAXIMUM VALUE[2]	DATE	MINIMUM VALUE[2]	DATE
1995	42,990.02	-1.26	65,593,561,084.01	-13.91	48,612.27	19-Sep	21,382.76	9-Mar
1994	43,539.00	1,059.65	66,431,186,961.34	59.59	54,840.00	30-Sep	7,405.50	31-Jan
1993	3,754.50	5,437.20	5,728,562,609.80	111.24	3,754.50	31-Dec	92.85	31-Jan
1992	67.81	1,015.65	103,455,804.79	-3.66	67.81	31-Dec	11.21	31-Jan
1991	6.08	2,315.96	9,273,015.65	288.63	6.08	31-Dec	0.47	31-Jan
1990	0.25	308.28	383,726.67	-72.73	0.30	31-Jul	0.07	31-Mar
1989	0.06	1,762.49	93,911.29	24.06	0.06	31-Dec	0.00	31-Jan
1988	0.00	2,549.53	4,947.60	151.14	0.00	31-Dec	0.00	31-Jan
1987	0.00	34.87	90.51	-71.99	0.00	30-Sep	0.00	31-Jan
1986	0.00	41.26	41.26	-0.52	0.00	30-Apr	0.00	31-Jan
1985	0.00							
Average Annual (%)		1,452.36		47.19				
Compound Annual (%)		661.53		9.91				
Standard Deviation (%)		1,689.58		9.47				

[1]Dollar adjusted price returns adjusted by the variation of the Real$/US$ based on monthly closing commercial dollar selling rates.
[2]Refer to Background Information for index value adjustments. Based on month-end values.

SYNOPSIS
The Sao Paulo Stock Exchange Index (BOVESPA) is a market value-weighted index that tracks the daily price only performance of the most actively traded stocks in the cash market of the Sao Paulo Stock Exchange. These shares account for about 80% of the BOVESPA trading volume and 66% of the stock exchange's market capitalization.

NUMBER OF STOCKS—DECEMBER 31, 1995
49

MARKET VALUE—DECEMBER 31, 1995
US$97,365.4 million

SELECTION CRITERIA
The portfolio of constituent stocks are selected on the basis of trading volume and must satisfy the following criteria which is evaluated over the preceding 12-month period:
(1) A stock must experience trading volume in excess of 0.1% of the combined trading volume on the BOVESPA Stock Exchange. (2) A stock must participate in at least 80% of the floor trading sessions. (3) Trading volume statistics are calculated on a quarterly basis for each stock and are arrayed from highest to lowest. Stocks are added to the portfolio of constituent stocks until a cumulative trading volume of 80% has been reached.

BACKGROUND
BOVESPA was initiated in 1968 after discussions to create a "national index" did not materialize for technical reasons. Until May 11, 1992, the index was calculated on a weekly basis.

It was adjusted several times to accommodate the number of digits available for computation in the central computers. It was divided by 100 on October 3, 1983, and by 10 on December 2, 1985, August 29, 1988, April 14, 1989, January 12, 1990, May 28, 1991, January 21, 1992, January 26, 1993 and August 27, 1993 and again on February 10, 1994.

BASE DATE
January 2, 1968=100.00

COMPUTATION METHODOLOGY
(1) An aggregative of prices times quantities index formula. Maintenance adjustments to the divisor are made for capitalization changes, new listings and delistings. (2) The portfolio of constituent stocks is reviewed every four months, based on trading volume and value over the previous 12 months. The number of stocks in the index is not fixed. (3) On a quarterly basis, the portfolio of securities is deemed to be sold and the proceeds reinvested in the new portfolio for the ensuing four-month period. (4) A stock's trading index is the square root of the number of shares traded in the cash market in the last 12 months divided by the total number of shares traded in the cash market multiplied by the dollar volume, in Brazilian currency, of trading in the stock divided by the total dollar volume, in Brazilian currency.

DERIVATIVE INSTRUMENTS
BOVESPA index futures trade on the Bolsa Brasileira de Futuros.
BOVESPA index futures trade on the Bolsa de Mercadorias & Futuros (BM&F).

SUBINDICES
A subindex comprising the most actively traded stocks within the portfolio of constituent shares which, at December 31, 1993, included the following three companies: Electrobras PNB, Telebras and Vale do Rio Doce PN.
A subindex comprising the remaining shares that make up the index.

RELATED INDICES
None

REMARKS
None

PUBLISHER
The Sao Paulo Stock Exchange.

INDICE DE PRECIOS SELECTIVO DE ACCIONES (IPSA)

PRICE PERFORMANCE

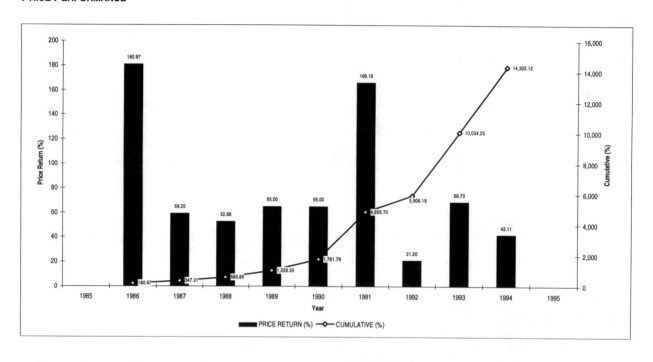

PRICE PERFORMANCE

YEAR	VALUE	PRICE RETURN (%)	CUMULATIVE (%)	MAXIMUM VALUE[1]	DATE	MINIMUM VALUE[1]	DATE
1995	100.00	NM	NM	114.11	11-Jul	78.25	3-Sep
1994	19,764.03	42.11	14,302.12	21,459.69	31-Oct	14,276.83	31-Mar
1993	13,907.23	68.73	10,034.25	13,907.23	31-Dec	8,335.41	30-Apr
1992	8,242.30	21.20	5,906.19	9,165.14	31-Jul	6,613.01	31-Jan
1991	6,800.71	166.18	4,855.70	7,524.76	30-Sep	3,039.60	31-Jan
1990	2,554.93	65.00	1,761.79	2,554.93	31-Dec	1,270.17	30-Nov
1989	1,548.44	65.00	1,028.35	1,548.44	31-Dec	1,064.58	31-Jan
1988	938.45	52.88	583.85	938.45	31-Dec	598.75	31-May
1987	613.85	59.20	347.31	748.04	30-Sep	432.28	31-Jan
1986	385.58	180.97	180.97	385.58	31-Dec	150.53	31-Jan
1985	137.23						
Average Annual (%)		72.13					
Compound Annual (%)		73.71					
Standard Deviation (%)		55.07					

[1]Maximum/minimum index values based on month end.

SYNOPSIS
The Indice de Precios Selectivo de Acciones (IPSA) Index is a market value-weighted price only index that tracks the performance of the largest, most actively traded, stocks listed on Santiago Stock Exchange.

NUMBER OF STOCKS—DECEMBER 31, 1995
40

MARKET VALUE—DECEMBER 31, 1995
Not Available

SELECTION CRITERIA
Constituents are selected on the basis of market capitalization which is computed on the basis of each stock's average market capitalization during the previous four quarters. Market capitalizations attributable to the most recent quarters are weighted more heavily in the computation.

BACKGROUND
The index was created in July 1977.

BASE DATE
December 31, 1995=100.00

COMPUTATION METHODOLOGY
Constituent shares are reviewed on a quarterly basis and the index is reconstituted accordingly. It is rebased to 100.00 at the beginning of each year.

DERIVATIVE INSTRUMENTS
IPSA index futures trade on the Santiago Stock Exchange.

SUBINDICES
None

RELATED INDICES
Indice General de Precios de Acciones (IGPA)
INTER-10

REMARKS
None

PUBLISHER
Bolsa de Comercio de Santiago (Santiago Stock Exchange).

INDICE GENERAL DE PRECIOS DE ACCIONES (IGPA)

PRICE PERFORMANCE

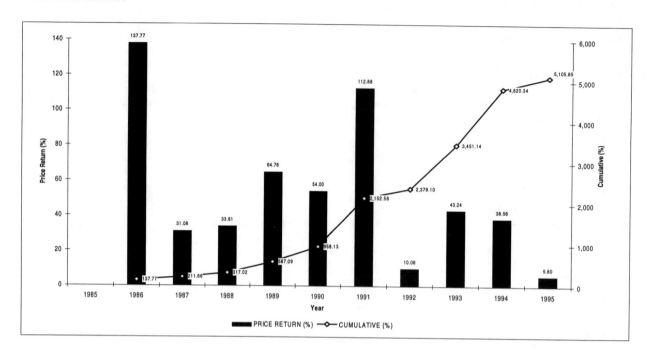

PRICE PERFORMANCE

YEAR	VALUE	PRICE RETURN (%)	CUMULATIVE (%)	MAXIMUM VALUE[1]	DATE	MINIMUM VALUE[1]	DATE
1995	5,739.97	5.80	5,105.85	6,363.15	11-Jul	4,569.33	9-Mar
1994	5,425.17	38.56	4,820.34	5,755.07	21-Nov	3,896.85	4-Apr
1993	3,915.49	43.24	3,451.14	3,969.89	28-Dec	2,612.59	10-May
1992	2,733.46	10.06	2,379.10	3,063.12	3-Apr	2,365.44	21-Jan
1991	2,483.69	112.88	2,152.58	3,023.27	8-Oct	1,135.17	15-Jan
1990	1,166.69	54.00	958.13	1,177.53	20-Dec	763.80	2-Jan
1989	757.59	64.76	587.09	757.59	31-Dec	498.10	31-Jan
1988	459.81	33.81	317.02	459.81	31-Dec	341.99	31-May
1987	343.64	31.08	211.66	409.66	30-Sep	265.20	31-May
1986	262.16	137.77	137.77	262.16	31-Dec	118.13	31-Jan
1985	110.26						
Average Annual (%)		53.20					
Compound Annual (%)		48.47					
Standard Deviation (%)		42.34					

[1]Maximum/minimum values for the period 1986-1990 are based on month-end values.

SYNOPSIS
The Indice General de Precios de Acciones (IGPA) Index is a market value-weighted price only index that tracks the performance of most of the traded stocks listed on Santiago Stock Exchange for which information is available.

NUMBER OF STOCKS—DECEMBER 31, 1995
170

MARKET VALUE—DECEMBER 31, 1995
Not Available

SELECTION CRITERIA
Constituents represent most of the stocks traded on the Santiago Stock Exchange for which information is available. Stocks are selected from five basic industrial sectors, including finance, agriculture, mining, industrial and services in an effort to achieve broad representation.

BACKGROUND
The index was created in 1958. It was later modified by expanding coverage from a fixed number of stocks.

BASE DATE
December 31, 1980=100.00

COMPUTATION METHODOLOGY
An aggregative of prices times quantities index formula. Maintenance adjustments to the divisor are made for capitalization changes, new listings and delistings.

DERIVATIVE INSTRUMENTS
None

SUBINDICES
Five sector subindices: Finance, agriculture, mining, industrial and services.
Industrial and services subindices are further divided into 12 sector subindices.

RELATED INDICES
Indice de Precios Selectivo de Acciones (IPSA)
INTER-10

REMARKS
None

PUBLISHER
Bolsa de Comercio de Santiago (Santiago Stock Exchange).

INDEX OF THE BOLSA DE BOGOTA (IBB)

PRICE PERFORMANCE

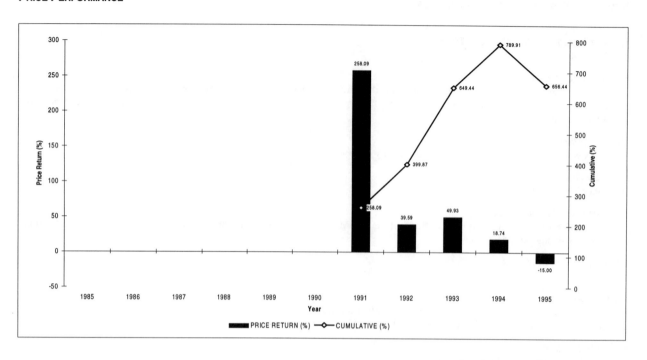

PRICE PERFORMANCE

YEAR	VALUE	PRICE RETURN (%)	CUMULATIVE (%)	MAXIMUM VALUE	DATE	MINIMUM VALUE	DATE
1995	756.44	-15.00	656.44	1,022.47	18-Jan	665.68	17-Nov
1994	889.91	18.74	789.91	1,059.45	22-Mar	745.84	1-Mar
1993	749.44	49.93	649.44	749.44	30-Dec	400.82	17-Mar
1992	499.87	39.59	399.87	549.16	16-Oct	359.68	1-Feb
1991	358.09	258.09	258.09	358.09	30-Dec	99.98	1-Feb
1990	100.00						
1989							
1988							
1987							
1986							
1985							
Average Annual (%)		70.27					
Compound Annual (%)		49.88					
Standard Deviation (%)		107.89					

SYNOPSIS
The Index of the Bolsa de Bogota (IBB) is a market value-weighted index that tracks the stock price performance of the 20 most actively traded shares on the Bogota Stock Exchange of Colombia. These shares account for 69% of the Bogota Stock Exchange capitalization.

NUMBER OF STOCKS—DECEMBER 31, 1995
20

MARKET VALUE—DECEMBER 31, 1995
US$7,125.55 million

SELECTION CRITERIA
Constituent stocks are selected on the basis of trading volume measured over the previous 48 bi-weekly periods. Selected stocks are reviewed twice per month.

BACKGROUND
The IBB replaced a previous index that was established as of March 15, 1976 and calculated to the end of 1990.

BASE DATE
January 2, 1991=100.00

COMPUTATION METHODOLOGY
A weighted average index formula is used.

DERIVATIVE INSTRUMENTS
None

SUBINDICES
None

RELATED INDICES
Indicador de Rentabilidad de la Bolsa Bogota (IRBB Bond Price Index)

REMARKS
None

PUBLISHER
Bolsa de Bogota, S.A.

BOLSA NACIONAL DE VALORES INDICE ACCIONARIO (BNV)

PRICE PERFORMANCE

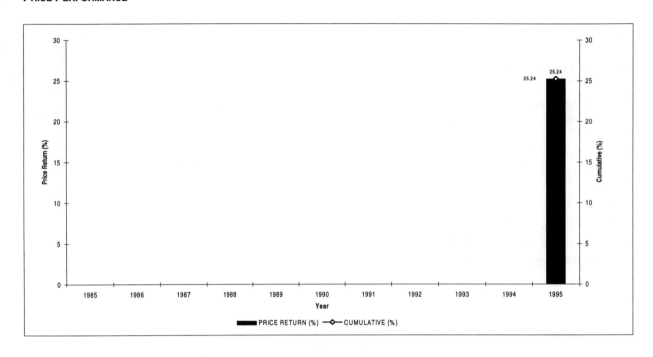

PRICE PERFORMANCE

YEAR	VALUE	PRICE RETURN (%)	CUMULATIVE (%)	MAXIMUM VALUE	DATE	MINIMUM VALUE	DATE
1995	1,252.36	25.24	25.24	1,257.70	14-Dec	1,000.00	1-Jan
1994	1,000.00						
1993							
1992							
1991							
1990							
1989							
1988							
1987							
1986							
1985							
Average Annual (%)		25.24					
Compound Annual (%)		25.24					
Standard Deviation (%)		NM					

SYNOPSIS

The Bolsa Nacional de Valores Indice Accionario (BNV) Index is a market value-weighted index that tracks the price only performance of all the stocks listed on the Costa Rica Stock Exchange.

NUMBER OF STOCKS—DECEMBER 31, 1995

28

MARKET VALUE—DECEMBER 31, 1995

US$1,872.2 million

SELECTION CRITERIA

All domestic and foreign stocks listed on the stock exchange.

BACKGROUND

The index was introduced in 1995.

COMPUTATION METHODOLOGY

An aggregative of prices times quantities index formula (Paasche). Maintenance adjustments to the divisor are made for capitalization changes, new listings and delistings.

DERIVATIVE INSTRUMENTS

None

SUBINDICES

None

RELATED INDICES

None

REMARKS

None

PUBLISHER

Bolsa National de Valores.

INDICE ACCIONARIO DE LA BOLSA DE VALORES DE QUITO 8 (I.A.Q. 8)

PRICE PERFORMANCE

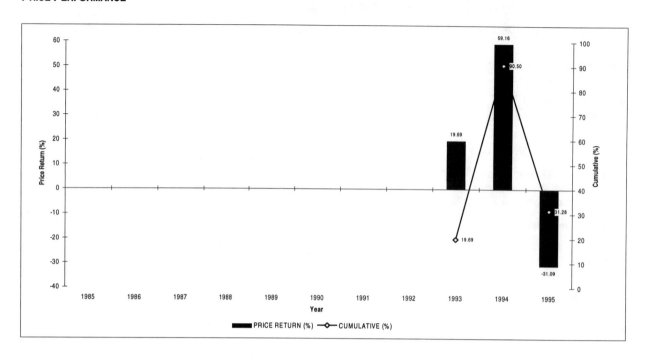

PRICE PERFORMANCE

YEAR	VALUE	PRICE RETURN (%)	CUMULATIVE (%)	MAXIMUM VALUE	DATE	MINIMUM VALUE	DATE
1995	161.61	-31.09	31.28	242.46	NA	137.51	NA
1994	234.51	59.16	90.50	244.65	NA	108.11	NA
1993	147.34	19.69	19.69				
1992	123.10						
1991							
1990							
1989							
1988							
1987							
1986							
1985							
Average Annual (%)		15.92					
Compound Annual (%)		9.50					
Standard Deviation (%)		45.24					

SYNOPSIS

The Indice Accionario de la Bolsa de Valores de Quito 8 (I.A.Q. 8) Index is a market value-weighted index that tracks the stock price performance of the eight largest stocks traded on the Quito Stock Exchange.

NUMBER OF STOCKS—DECEMBER 31, 1995

8

MARKET VALUE—DECEMBER 31, 1995

Not Available

SELECTION CRITERIA

Constituent stocks are selected on the basis of market capitalization.

BACKGROUND

Not Available

BASE DATE

Not Available

COMPUTATION METHODOLOGY

An aggregative of prices times quantities index formula.

DERIVATIVE INSTRUMENTS

None

SUBINDICES

None

RELATED INDICES

Indice Diario de Volumen (IVQ)
Indice de Rendimeinto (RBQ)

REMARKS

None

PUBLISHER

Bolsa de Valores de Quito.

JAMAICA STOCK EXCHANGE (JSE) MARKET INDEX

PRICE PERFORMANCE

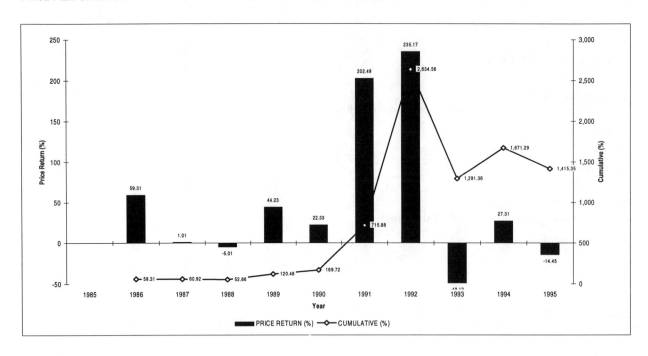

PRICE PERFORMANCE

YEAR	VALUE	PRICE RETURN (%)	CUMULATIVE (%)	MAXIMUM VALUE	DATE	MINIMUM VALUE	DATE
1995	14,266.99	-14.45	1,415.35	24,907.11	23-Jan	14,087.68	20-Dec
1994	16,676.70	27.31	1,671.29	17,024.96	6-Jun	10,648.64	26-Jan
1993	13,099.70	-49.12	1,291.36	32,421.70	28-Jan	12,822.30	28-Dec
1992	25,745.90	235.17	2,634.56	25,745.90	31-Dec	6,582.30	27-Apr
1991	7,681.50	202.49	715.88	8,506.90	11-Nov	2,378.60	16-Jan
1990	2,539.40	22.33	169.72	2,539.40	27-Dec	1,897.95	27-Feb
1989	2,075.80	44.23	120.48	2,592.30	7-Sep	1,396.90	26-Jan
1988	1,439.20	-5.01	52.86	1,572.09	21-Jan	1,295.70	29-Sep
1987	1,515.10	1.01	60.92	1,938.85	26-Feb	1,515.10	31-Dec
1986	1,499.90	59.31	59.31	1,499.90	23-Dec	874.70	29-Apr
1985	941.50						
Average Annual (%)		52.33					
Compound Annual (%)		31.24					
Standard Deviation (%)		93.27					

SYNOPSIS

The Jamaica Stock Exchange (JSE) Market Index is a market value-weighted index that tracks the price only performance of ordinary shares listed on the Jamaica Stock Exchange.

NUMBER OF STOCKS—DECEMBER 31, 1995

48

MARKET VALUE—DECEMBER 31, 1995

US$1,390.59 million

SELECTION CRITERIA

All ordinary shares listed on the Jamaica Stock Exchange.

BACKGROUND

None

BASE DATE

June 30, 1969=100.00

COMPUTATION METHODOLOGY

(1) An aggregative of prices times quantities index formula. Maintenance adjustments to the divisor are made for capitalization changes, new listings and delistings. (2) Last sale price is used.

DERIVATIVE INSTRUMENTS

None

SUBINDICES

None

RELATED INDICES

None

REMARKS

None

PUBLISHER

The Jamaica Stock Exchange.

PANAMA STOCK EXCHANGE GENERAL INDEX (PSE)

PRICE PERFORMANCE

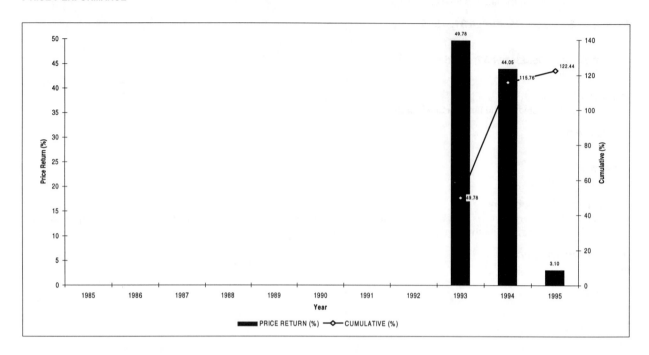

PRICE PERFORMANCE[1]

YEAR	VALUE	PRICE RETURN (%)	CUMULATIVE (%)	MAXIMUM VALUE	DATE	MINIMUM VALUE	DATE
1995	222.44	3.10	122.44	223.61	4-Dec	214.80	28-Mar
1994	215.76	44.05	115.76	217.46	10-Oct	149.41	15-Jan
1993	149.78	49.78	49.78	149.78	31-Dec	100.00	1-Jan
1992	100.00						
1991							
1990							
1989							
1988							
1987							
1986							
1985							
Average Annual (%)		32.31					
Compound Annual (%)		30.54					
Standard Deviation (%)		25.46					

[1]Due to the absence of trading activity, index values remained unchanged at 100.00 through the end of March 1993.

SYNOPSIS
The Panama Stock Exchange General Index (PSE) is a market value-weighted index that tracks the daily stock price performance of stocks traded on the The Bolsa de Valores de Panama, S.A. (Panama Stock Exchange).

NUMBER OF STOCKS—DECEMBER 31, 1995
18

MARKET VALUE—DECEMBER 31, 1995
US$831.0 million

SELECTION CRITERIA
Constituent stocks represent Panama's "Blue Chip" companies. They are selected on the basis of market capitalization, trading volume, profit history, growth and quality of management.

BACKGROUND
The Bolsa de Valores de Panama, S.A. started operations June 26, 1990. The establishment of the index followed shortly thereafter. The index was initiated with 10 companies. An 11th company was added in 1995.

BASE DATE
December 31, 1992=100.00

COMPUTATION METHODOLOGY
An aggregative of prices times quantities index formula. Maintenance adjustments to the divisor are made for capitalization changes, new listings and delistings.

DERIVATIVE INSTRUMENTS
None

SUBINDICES
None

RELATED INDICES
None

REMARKS
None

PUBLISHER
The Bolsa de Valores de Panama, S.A.

INDICE GENERAL (IGBVL)

PRICE PERFORMANCE

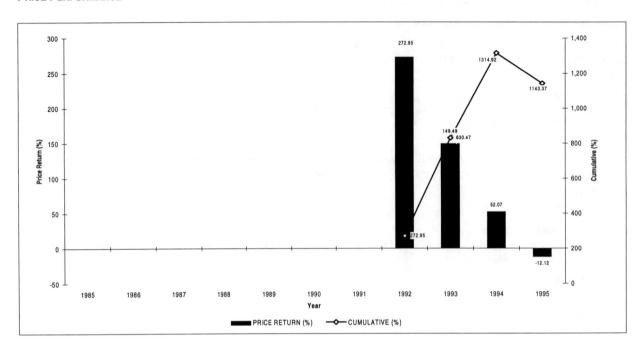

PRICE PERFORMANCE

YEAR	VALUE	PRICE RETURN (%)	CUMULATIVE (%)	MAXIMUM VALUE	DATE	MINIMUM VALUE	DATE
1995	1,243.37	-12.12	1,143.37	1,517.06	17-Jul	907.83	9-Mar
1994	1,414.92	52.07	1,314.92	1,528.86	2-Nov	947.46	5-Jan
1993	930.47	149.49	830.47	1,061.41	28-Oct	328.13	26-Jan
1992	372.95	272.95	272.95				
1991	100.00						
1990							
1989							
1988							
1987							
1986							
1985							
Average Annual (%)		115.59					
Compound Annual (%)		87.78					
Standard Deviation (%)		124.17					

SYNOPSIS

The Indice General (IGBVL) Index is a traded value-weighted index that tracks the performance of the largest and most actively traded stocks listed on Lima Stock Exchange with American Depositary Receipts.

NUMBER OF STOCKS—DECEMBER 31, 1995

63

MARKET VALUE—DECEMBER 31, 1995

US$7,223.1 million

SELECTION CRITERIA

Not Available

BACKGROUND

The index has been calculated since December 31, 1981.

BASE DATE

December 31, 1981=100.00

COMPUTATION METHODOLOGY

Not Available

DERIVATIVE INSTRUMENTS

None

SUBINDICES

Eight sectoral subindices and four industrial subindices are calculated.

RELATED INDICES

Indice Selectivo (ISBVL)

REMARKS

None

PUBLISHER

Bolsa de Valores de Lima.

INDICE SELECTIVO (ISBVL)

PRICE PERFORMANCE

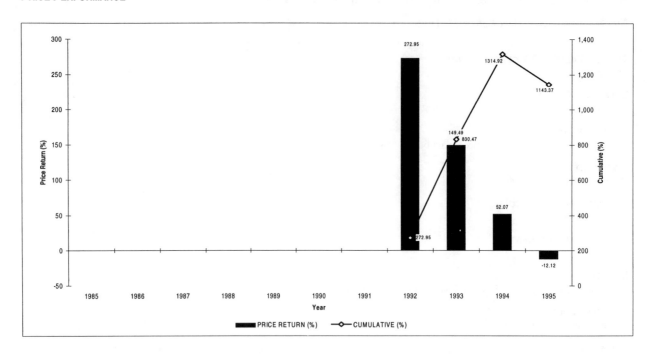

PRICE PERFORMANCE

YEAR	VALUE	PRICE RETURN (%)	CUMULATIVE (%)	MAXIMUM VALUE	DATE	MINIMUM VALUE	DATE
1995	1,686.32	0.44	1,586.32	1,922.64	8-Sep	1,073.77	9-Mar
1994	1,678.91	70.30	1,578.91	1,841.13	18-Oct	1,010.93	6-Jan
1993	985.86	102.64	885.86	1,021.88	29-Oct	389.64	12-Jan
1992	486.52	386.52	386.52	486.52	30-Dec	94.22	7-Jan
1991	100.00						
1990							
1989							
1988							
1987							
1986							
1985							
Average Annual (%)		139.97					
Compound Annual (%)		102.64					
Standard Deviation (%)		169.81					

SYNOPSIS

The Indice Selectivo (ISBVL) Index tracks the performance of 15 leading companies whose shares are traded on the Lima Stock Exchange.

NUMBER OF STOCKS—DECEMBER 31, 1995

15

MARKET VALUE—DECEMBER 31, 1995

US$4,732.1 million

SELECTION CRITERIA

Not Available

BACKGROUND

The index was introduced in July 1993.

BASE DATE

December 31, 1991=100.00

COMPUTATION METHODOLOGY

Not Available

DERIVATIVE INSTRUMENTS

None

SUBINDICES

None

RELATED INDICES

Indice General (IGBVL)

REMARKS

None

PUBLISHER

Bolsa de Valores de Lima.

TRINIDAD & TOBAGO STOCK EXCHANGE DAILY INDEX OF STOCK MARKET VALUES

PRICE PERFORMANCE

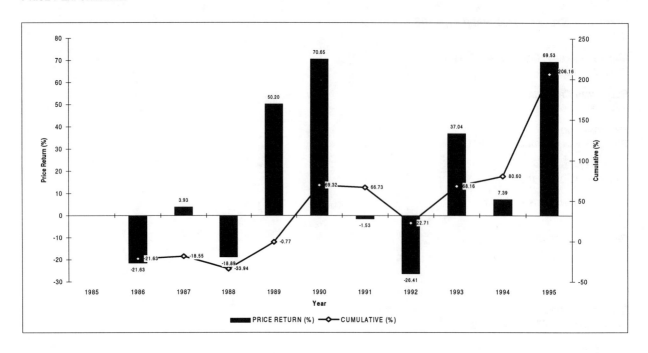

PRICE PERFORMANCE

YEAR	VALUE	PRICE RETURN (%)	CUMULATIVE (%)	MAXIMUM VALUE	DATE	MINIMUM VALUE	DATE
1995	150.20	69.53	206.16	159.70	3-Nov	89.00	3-Jan
1994	88.60	7.39	80.60	90.10	15-Apr	82.10	14-Jan
1993	82.50	37.04	68.16	82.50	29-Dec	59.00	2-Apr
1992	60.20	-26.41	22.71	81.20	3-Jan	60.20	30-Dec
1991	81.80	-1.53	66.73	90.20	28-Aug	74.50	15-Mar
1990	83.07	70.65	69.32	83.07	28-Dec	48.78	2-Jan
1989	48.68	50.20	-0.77	51.07	23-Aug	31.84	NA
1988	32.41	-18.89	-33.94	39.96	NA	32.41	NA
1987	39.96	3.93	-18.55	41.68	NA	38.69	NA
1986	38.45	-21.63	-21.63	49.44	NA	38.08	NA
1985	49.06						
Average Annual (%)		17.03					
Compound Annual (%)		11.84					
Standard Deviation (%)		37.14					

SYNOPSIS
The Trinidad & Tobago Stock Exchange Daily Index of Stock Market Values is a market value-weighted index that tracks the price performance of ordinary shares listed on the Trinidad and Tobago Stock Exchange.

NUMBER OF STOCKS—DECEMBER 31, 1995
24

MARKET VALUE—DECEMBER 31, 1995
US$1,111.21 million

BACKGROUND
None

BASE DATE
January 1, 1983=100.00

COMPUTATION METHODOLOGY
An aggregative of prices times quantities index formula. Maintenance adjustments to the divisor are made for capitalization changes, new listings and delistings.

DERIVATIVE INSTRUMENTS
None

SUBINDICES
Five sectoral subindices: Commercial banks, conglomerates, manufacturing I, manufacturing II, and property and trading.

RELATED INDICES
None

REMARKS
The Stock Exchange is open for trading on Tuesday, Wednesday and Friday of each week.

PUBLISHER
Trinidad and Tobago Stock Exchange.

BOLSA DE VALORES DE CARACAS INDICE DE CAPITALIZATION

PRICE PERFORMANCE

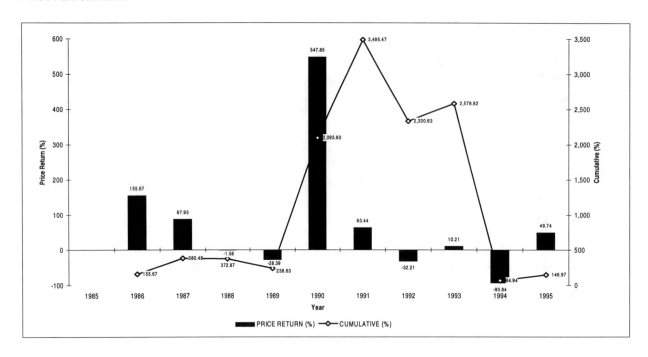

PRICE PERFORMANCE

YEAR	VALUE[1]	PRICE RETURN (%)	CUMULATIVE (%)	MAXIMUM VALUE[2]	DATE	MINIMUM VALUE[2]	DATE
1995	2,019.39	49.74	146.97	2,019.39	29-Dec	1,168.34	11-Jul
1994	1,348.63	-93.84	64.94	1,600.49	21-Sep	959.69	26-Jan
1993	21,903.36	10.21	2,578.82	NA	NA	9,060.09	16-Mar
1992	19,874.07	-32.21	2,330.63	34,142.60	3-Feb	19,125.61	30-Nov
1991	29,316.56	63.44	3,485.47	30,557.60	13-Nov	18,144.76	2-Jan
1990	17,937.60	547.85	2,093.80	17,937.60	31-Dec	2,486.69	31-Jan
1989	2,768.80	-28.39	238.63	4,606.37	31-Jan	2,111.92	30-Jul
1988	3,866.44	-1.58	372.87	4,764.14	28-Feb	3,762.63	30-Nov
1987	3,928.64	87.93	380.48	3,928.64	31-Dec	2,628.05	31-Jan
1986	2,090.47	155.67	155.67	2,090.47	31-Dec	890.37	31-Jan
1985	817.65						
Average Annual (%)		84.31					
Compound Annual (%)		9.46					
Standard Deviation (%)		180.05					

[1]Revised index base value of 1000.00 as of December 31, 1993 not shown, but price performance data for 1993 and beyond are calculated using the new base value.
[2]Maximum/minimum index values for the period 1986-1990 are based on month-end values.

SYNOPSIS
The Bolsa de Valores de Caracas Indice de Capitalization is a price only index that tracks the performance of 19 stocks listed on the Caracas Stock Exchange.

NUMBER OF STOCKS—DECEMBER 31, 1995
19

MARKET VALUE—DECEMBER 31, 1995
Not Available

SELECTION CRITERIA
Not Available

BACKGROUND
Various indices have been modified and replaced over the years. The latest index, which superseded the Indice Bolsa de Valores de Caracas with its base value of 100.00 as of January 1971, was introduced in January 1994.

BASE DATE
December 31, 1993=1000.00

COMPUTATION METHODOLOGY
Not Available

DERIVATIVE INSTRUMENTS
Not Available

SUBINDICES
Not Available

RELATED INDICES
Not Available

REMARKS
None

PUBLISHER
Bolsa de Valores de Caracas.

LATIN AMERICA — REGIONAL

HSBC James Capel Latin America 100 Index

PRICE PERFORMANCE

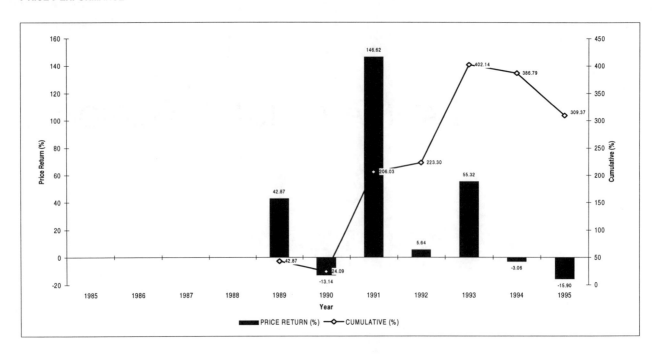

PRICE PERFORMANCE (US$)

YEAR	VALUE	PRICE RETURN (%)	CUMULATIVE (%)	MAXIMUM VALUE[1]	DATE	MINIMUM VALUE[1]	DATE
1995	409.37	-15.90	309.37	486.79	2-Jan	271.08	9-Mar
1994	486.79	-3.06	386.79	625.78	23-Sep	423.14	20-Apr
1993	502.14	55.32	402.14	502.15	31-Dec	311.86	28-Feb
1992	323.30	5.64	223.30	396.77	31-May	291.02	30-Sep
1991	306.03	146.62	206.03	306.03	31-Dec	141.27	31-Jan
1990	124.09	-13.14	24.09	149.84	28-Feb	109.45	31-Mar
1989	142.87	42.87	42.87	157.33	30-Apr	89.93	31-Jan
1988	100.00						
1987							
1986							
1985							
Average Annual (%)		31.19					
Compound Annual (%)		22.31					
Standard Deviation (%)		57.81					

[1]Maximum/minimum values based on month-end values.

SYNOPSIS

The HSBC James Capel Latin America 100 Index is a market value-weighted index that tracks the daily price performance of an investable universe of stocks traded in seven markets in Latin America and Mexico. These markets are Argentina, Brazil, Chile, Columbia, Mexico, Peru and Venezuela.

NUMBER OF STOCKS—DECEMBER 31, 1995

100

MARKET VALUE—DECEMBER 31, 1995

US$172,379.1 million

SELECTION CRITERIA

In addition to maintaining an accurate representation of the industrial structure of each component market, constituent stocks are selected on the basis of the following overriding considerations:

(1) Legal constraints–Market capitalization of each constituent security is based on that proportion of its issued capital that is available to foreign investors; (2) Liquidity–Eligibility is limited to securities that are traded on the official exchanges in Latin America. Two or more lines of stock may be included in the index in the event a company has two or more actively traded lines of stock; (3) Trading volume; (4) Cross ownership–Companies with significant ownership positions by other companies may be excluded from the index; and (5) Accuracy of data.

BACKGROUND

None

BASE DATE

December 31, 1988=100.00

COMPUTATION METHODOLOGY

(1) An aggregative of prices times quantities index formula. Maintenance adjustments to the divisor are made daily for capitalization changes, new listings and delistings. (2) Market capitalization is calculated on the basis of each company's full issued capital. (3) Constituent shares are reviewed on a daily and quarterly basis and, if warranted by a significant change in local market practices, modifications are made prior to the quarterly review date.

DERIVATIVE INSTRUMENTS

None

SUBINDICES

Seven market subindices: Argentina, Brazil, Chile, Columbia, Mexico, Peru and Venezuela. In addition, the index is calculated without the Mexico market.

RELATED INDICES

HSBC JC Dragon 300 Index
HSBC JC Japanese Smaller Companies Index
HSBC JC Smaller European Companies Index
HSBC JC Smaller Pan-European Index
Refer to Appendix 5 for additional indices.

REMARKS

None

PUBLISHER

HSBC James Capel.

AFRICA/MIDDLE EAST

BOTSWANA SHARE MARKET INDEX

PRICE PERFORMANCE

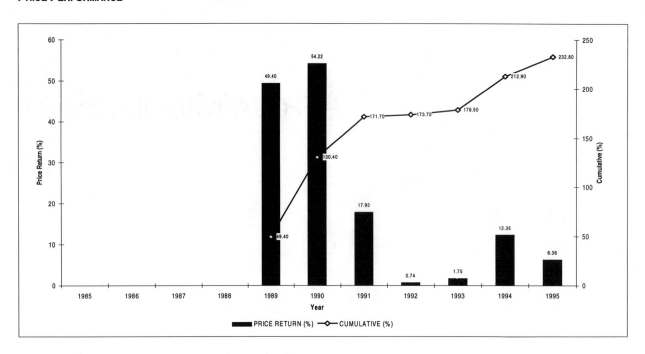

PRICE PERFORMANCE

YEAR	VALUE	PRICE RETURN (%)	CUMULATIVE (%)	MAXIMUM VALUE	DATE	MINIMUM VALUE	DATE
1995	332.80	6.36	232.80	NA	NA	NA	NA
1994	312.90	12.35	212.90	NA	NA	NA	NA
1993	278.50	1.75	178.50	NA	NA	NA	NA
1992	273.70	0.74	173.70	NA	NA	NA	NA
1991	271.70	17.93	171.70	NA	NA	NA	NA
1990	230.40	54.22	130.40	NA	NA	NA	NA
1989	149.40	49.40	49.40	NA	NA	NA	NA
1988	100.00						
1987							
1986							
1985							
Average Annual (%)		20.39					
Compound Annual (%)		18.74					
Standard Deviation (%)		22.31					

SYNOPSIS

The Botswana Share Market Index is a comprehensive market value-weighted index that tracks the daily price only performance of all stocks listed on the Botswana Share Market.

NUMBER OF STOCKS—DECEMBER 31, 1995

12

MARKET VALUE—DECEMBER 31, 1995

US$397.70 million

SELECTION CRITERIA

Constituent shares include all stocks listed on the Botswana Share Market, including Barclays Bank, BIHL, ENGEN, First National Bank of Botswana, Inco, Kgolo Ya Sechaba, PEP, Real Estate Development Company, Sechaba, Sefalana and Standard Chartered Bank.

BACKGROUND

None

BASE DATE

June 19, 1989=100.00

COMPUTATION METHODOLOGY

(1) An aggregative of prices times quantities index formula. Maintenance adjustments are made for capitalization changes, new listings and delistings. (2) Bid prices were used to compute the index to May 1994 and the greater of the bid and last price thereafter.

DERIVATIVE INSTRUMENTS

None

SUBINDICES

None

RELATED INDICES

None

REMARKS

None

PUBLISHER

Stockbrokers Botswana Ltd.

BVA GENERAL INDEX

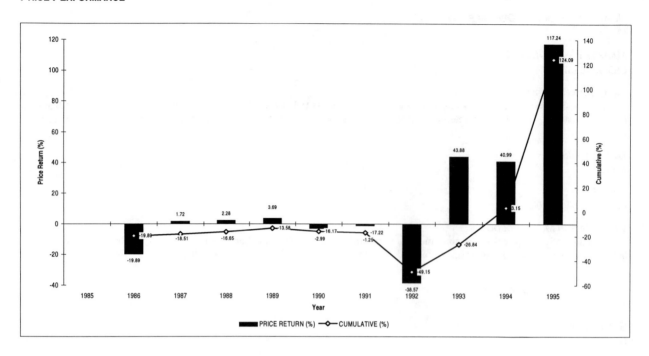

PRICE PERFORMANCE

YEAR	VALUE	PRICE RETURN (%)	CUMULATIVE (%)	MAXIMUM VALUE	DATE	MINIMUM VALUE	DATE
1995	277.20	117.24	124.09	NA	NA	NA	NA
1994	127.60	40.99	3.15	NA	NA	NA	NA
1993	90.50	43.88	-26.84	NA	NA	NA	NA
1992	62.90	-38.57	-49.15	NA	NA	NA	NA
1991	102.40	-1.25	-17.22	NA	NA	NA	NA
1990	103.70	-2.99	-16.17	NA	NA	NA	NA
1989	106.90	3.69	-13.58	NA	NA	NA	NA
1988	103.10	2.28	-16.65	NA	NA	NA	NA
1987	100.80	1.72	-18.51	NA	NA	NA	NA
1986	99.10	-19.89	-19.89	NA	NA	NA	NA
1985	123.70						
Average Annual (%)		14.71					
Compound Annual (%)		8.40					
Standard Deviation (%)		43.59					

SYNOPSIS
The BVA General Index tracks the stock price performance of shares listed on the Abidjan Stock Exchange.

NUMBER OF STOCKS—DECEMBER 31, 1995
31

MARKET VALUE—DECEMBER 31, 1995
US$867.0 million

SELECTION CRITERIA
All shares listed on the Abidjan Stock Exchange.

BACKGROUND
None

BASE DATE
December 31, 1985=100.00

COMPUTATION METHODOLOGY
Not Available

DERIVATIVE INSTRUMENTS
None

SUBINDICES
None

RELATED INDICES
None

REMARKS
None

PUBLISHER
Abidjan Stock Exchange.

Ghana Stock Exchange (GSE) All-Share Index

PRICE PERFORMANCE

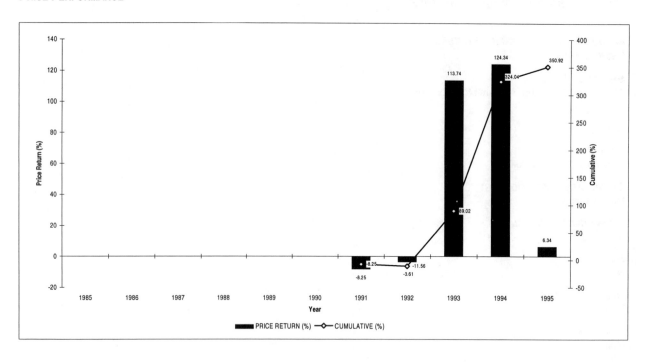

PRICE PERFORMANCE

YEAR	VALUE	PRICE RETURN (%)	CUMULATIVE (%)	MAXIMUM VALUE	DATE	MINIMUM VALUE	DATE
1995	317.00	6.34	350.92	NA	NA	NA	NA
1994	298.10	124.34	324.04	NA	NA	NA	NA
1993	132.88	113.74	89.02	NA	NA	NA	NA
1992	62.17	-3.61	-11.56	NA	NA	NA	NA
1991	64.50	-8.25	-8.25	NA	NA	NA	NA
1990	70.30						
1989							
1988							
1987							
1986							
1985							
Average Annual (%)		46.51					
Compound Annual (%)		35.15					
Standard Deviation (%)		66.52					

SYNOPSIS

The Ghana Stock Exchange (GSE) All-Share Index is a market value-weighted index that tracks the price only performance of all shares listed on the Ghana Stock Exchange (GSE).

NUMBER OF STOCKS—DECEMBER 31, 1995

19

MARKET VALUE—DECEMBER 31, 1995

US$1,680.0 million

SELECTION CRITERIA

The index consists of all shares listed on the Ghana Stock Exchange.

BACKGROUND

None

BASE DATE

September 1, 1994=100.00

COMPUTATION METHODOLOGY

An aggregative of prices times quantities index formula. Maintenance adjustments are made for capitalization changes, new listings and delistings.

SUBINDICES

None

RELATED INDICES

None

REMARKS

None

PUBLISHER

Ghana Stock Exchange (GSE).

TEL AVIV STOCK EXCHANGE GENERAL SHARE INDEX

PRICE PERFORMANCE

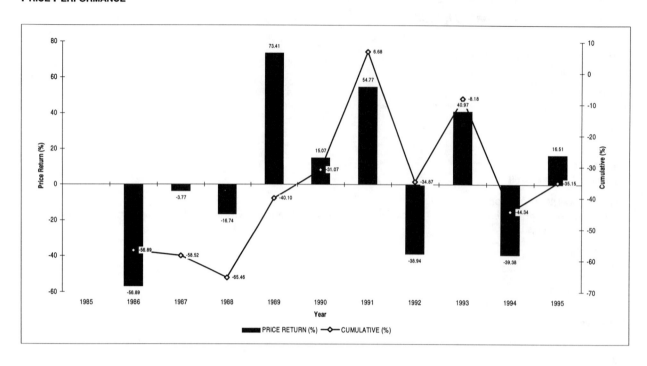

PRICE PERFORMANCE[1]

YEAR	VALUE	PRICE RETURN (%)	CUMULATIVE (%)	MAXIMUM VALUE	DATE	MINIMUM VALUE	DATE
1995	190.82	16.51	-35.15	196.27	23-Aug	137.50	28-Feb
1994	163.77	-39.38	-44.34	289.03	16-Jan	145.03	4-Jul
1993	270.15	40.97	-8.18	273.11	26-Dec	184.17	23-Feb
1992	191.64	-38.94	-34.87	191.64	31-Dec	99.87	6-Jan
1991	313.88	54.77	6.68	363.18	3-Oct	196.46	7-Jan
1990	202.80	15.07	-31.07	240.00	23-Jul	164.51	21-Mar
1989	176.24	73.41	-40.10	179.19	11-Dec	105.92	3-Jan
1988	101.63	-16.74	-65.46	104.87	16-Nov	90.25	8-Feb
1987	122.06	-3.77	-58.52	135.34	28-Apr	99.37	4-Jan
1986	126.84	-56.89	-56.89	126.84	31-Dec	96.75	3-Feb
1985	294.23						
Average Annual (%)		4.50					
Compound Annual (%)		-4.24					
Standard Deviation (%)		43.41					

[1]Index reset to 100.00 at the beginning of 1986,1987,1988, 1989 and 1992.

SYNOPSIS

The Tel Aviv Stock Exchange General Share Index is a market value-weighted index that tracks the continuous stock price performance of all domestic and foreign common stocks and convertible securities traded on the Tel Aviv Stock Exchange (TSE).

NUMBER OF STOCKS—DECEMBER 31, 1995

1,019

MARKET VALUE—DECEMBER 31, 1995

US$36,523.13 million

SELECTION CRITERIA

Constituents consist of all domestic common stock and convertible securities traded on the Tel Aviv Stock Exchange.
Non-marketable securities due to prolonged trade suspension are not eligible for inclusion in the index.

BACKGROUND

None

BASE DATE

January 1, 1992=100.00

COMPUTATION METHODOLOGY

(1) An aggregative of prices times quantities index formula. Maintenance adjustments are made daily for capitalization changes, new listings and delistings. (2) Market capitalization is determined on the basis of the same class of shares listed for trade on the TSE.

DERIVATIVE INSTRUMENTS

None

SUBINDICES

Various sector indices.

RELATED INDICES

CCM Index
MAOF-25 Index
TA-100

REMARKS

The index includes seven foreign stocks with a market value of US$63.8 million as of December 31, 1995.

PUBLISHER

The Tel Aviv Stock Exchange (TSE).

TEL AVIV STOCK EXCHANGE MAOF-25 INDEX

PRICE PERFORMANCE

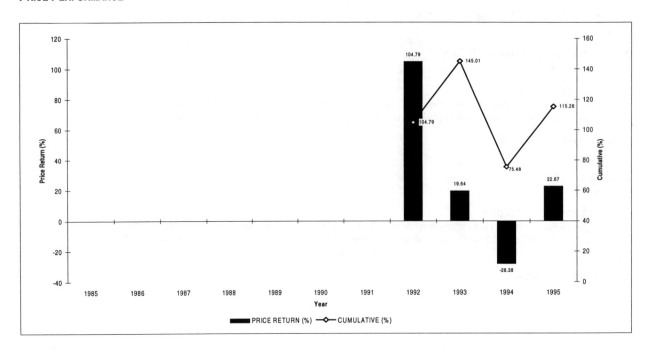

PRICE PERFORMANCE

YEAR	VALUE	PRICE RETURN (%)	CUMULATIVE (%)	MAXIMUM VALUE	DATE	MINIMUM VALUE	DATE
1995	215.26	22.67	115.26	217.28	27-Dec	145.73	28-Feb
1994	175.48	-28.38	75.48	249.71	3-Jan	153.30	4-Jul
1993	245.01	19.64	145.01	257.72	10-Nov	178.08	22-Jul
1992	204.79	104.79	104.79	204.79	31-Dec	102.42	2-Jan
1991	100.00						
1990							
1989							
1988							
1987							
1986							
1985							
Average Annual (%)		29.68					
Compound Annual (%)		21.13					
Standard Deviation (%)		55.26					

SYNOPSIS

The Tel Aviv Stock Exchange MAOF-25 Index is a market value-weighted index that tracks the continuous stock price performance of the 25 largest capitalization stocks traded in the Semi-Continuous Auction System in Israel. These shares account for 54% of the common stocks and convertible securities listed on the Tel Aviv Stock Exchange (TSE).

NUMBER OF STOCKS—DECEMBER 31, 1995

25

MARKET VALUE—DECEMBER 31, 1995

US$25,933.01 million

SELECTION CRITERIA

Constituent shares, which are comprised of shares designated for trade in the Semi-Continuous Auction System ("Mishtanim") in the next half year, are selected on the basis of market capitalization as of June 30th and December 31st of each year, provided eligible shares are continuously traded and/or these eligible shares have not been suspended for a period greater than five days.

Shares designated for inclusion in the index must have a market value that is at least 20% greater than the market value of any shares that they may replace.

BACKGROUND

None

BASE DATE

January 1, 1992=100.00

COMPUTATION METHODOLOGY

(1) An aggregative of prices times quantities index formula. Maintenance adjustments are made for capitalization changes, new listings and delistings. (2) Market capitalization is determined on the basis of the same class of shares listed for trade on the TSE. (3) The weight of each share in the index is determined on the basis of the ratio of the stock's market capitalization relative to the market capitalization of all constituent shares. To the extent that a share's weight in the index exceeds 9.5%, its weight is capped at that level and the residual is apportioned among shares whose weight in the index falls below 9.5%. (4) The last transaction price in the Semi-Continuous Auction Market is used to compute the index. In the absence of transactions, the index is computed using closing prices or interim prices in the computerized call market (Meretz).

DERIVATIVE INSTRUMENTS

MAOF-25 Index options trade on the Tel Aviv Stock Exchange (TSE).

SUBINDICES

None

RELATED INDICES

General Shares Index
TA-100
CCM Index

REMARKS

Under the Semi-Continuous Auction System, transactions are carried out in predetermined order during two to six trading rounds and are concluded between two Tel Aviv Stock Exchange members at mutually agreed upon prices. During each round, a number of transactions can be executed, each at different prices.

PUBLISHER

The Tel Aviv Stock Exchange (TSE).

THE AMMAN FINANCIAL MARKET (AFM) PRICE INDEX

PRICE PERFORMANCE

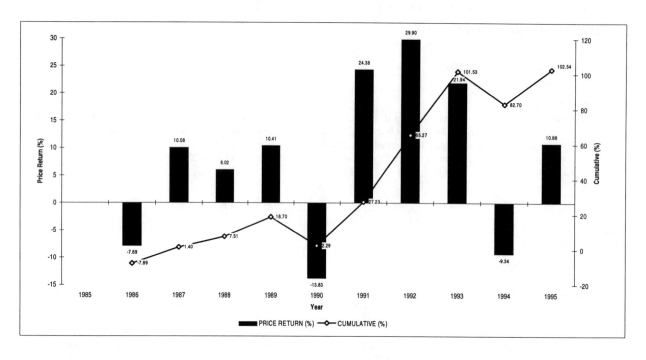

PRICE PERFORMANCE

YEAR	VALUE	PRICE RETURN (%)	CUMULATIVE (%)	MAXIMUM VALUE	DATE	MINIMUM VALUE	DATE
1995	159.20	10.86	102.54	166.80	4-Jun	139.05	22-Mar
1994	143.60	-9.34	82.70	165.50	28-Feb	143.60	31-Dec
1993	158.40	21.94	101.53	181.60	7-Jul	131.00	20-Feb
1992	129.90	29.90	65.27	129.90	31-Dec	100.60	1-Jan
1991	100.00	24.38	27.23	100.00	31-Dec	89.10	1-Aug
1990	80.40	-13.83	2.29	95.00	31-May	80.20	30-Nov
1989	93.30	10.41	18.70	93.30	31-Dec	84.50	30-Apr
1988	84.50	6.02	7.51	85.30	30-Nov	76.20	30-Apr
1987	79.70	10.08	1.40	79.90	31-Dec	71.30	31-Jan
1986	72.40	-7.89	-7.89	76.90	28-Feb	69.70	31-Jul
1985	78.60						
Average Annual (%)		8.25					
Compound Annual (%)		7.31					
Standard Deviation (%)		14.88					

SYNOPSIS
The Amman Financial Market (AFM) Price Index is a market value-weighted index that tracks the daily stock price performance of the 60 most liquid stocks traded on the Amman Stock Exchange of Jordan. These shares account for 86% of the stock market capitalization.

NUMBER OF STOCKS—DECEMBER 31, 1995
60

MARKET VALUE—DECEMBER 31, 1995
US$4,038.4 million

SELECTION CRITERIA
Stocks are selected on the basis of liquidity in the regular market.

BACKGROUND
None

BASE DATE
December 31, 1991=100.00

COMPUTATION METHODOLOGY
An aggregative of prices times quantities index formula. Maintenance adjustments are made for capitalization changes, new listings and delistings.

DERIVATIVE INSTRUMENTS
None

SUBINDICES
Four industry subindices: Banking and finance companies, insurance, services and industrial companies.

RELATED INDICES
AFM Unweighted Index

REMARKS
The Amman Financial Market began to publish the unweighted index at the beginning of 1996.

PUBLISHER
Amman Financial Market (AFM).

NAIROBI STOCK EXCHANGE 20 INDEX

PRICE PERFORMANCE

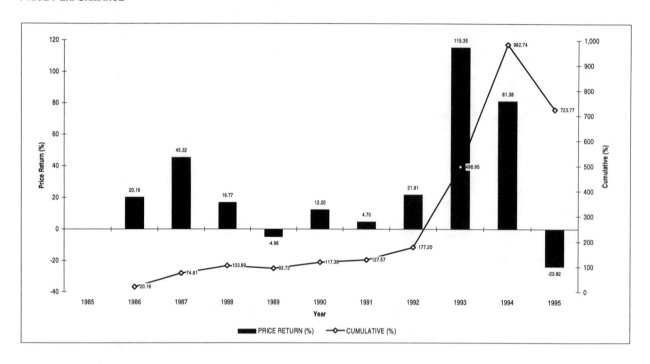

PRICE PERFORMANCE

YEAR	VALUE	PRICE RETURN (%)	CUMULATIVE (%)	MAXIMUM VALUE	DATE	MINIMUM VALUE	DATE
1995	3,468.90	-23.92	723.77	NA	NA	NA	NA
1994	4,559.40	81.38	982.74	NA	NA	NA	NA
1993	2,513.74	115.35	496.95	NA	NA	NA	NA
1992	1,167.29	21.81	177.20	NA	NA	NA	NA
1991	958.30	4.70	127.57	NA	NA	NA	NA
1990	915.30	12.20	117.36	NA	NA	NA	NA
1989	815.80	-4.98	93.73	NA	NA	NA	NA
1988	858.60	16.77	103.89	NA	NA	NA	NA
1987	735.30	45.32	74.61	NA	NA	NA	NA
1986	506.00	20.16	20.16	NA	NA	NA	NA
1985	421.10						
Average Annual (%)		28.88					
Compound Annual (%)		23.48					
Standard Deviation (%)		41.60					

SYNOPSIS
The Nairobi Stock Exchange 20 Index is a price-weighted index that tracks the price only performance of all shares listed on the Nairobi Stock Exchange.

NUMBER OF STOCKS—DECEMBER 31, 1995
56

MARKET VALUE—DECEMBER 31, 1995
US$1,889.0 million

SELECTION CRITERIA
All Shares listed on the Nairobi Stock Exchange.

BACKGROUND
None

BASE DATE
Not Available

COMPUTATION METHODOLOGY
Not Available

DERIVATIVE INSTRUMENTS
None

SUBINDICES
None

RELATED INDICES
None

REMARKS
None

PUBLISHER
Nairobi Stock Exchange.

KUWAIT STOCK EXCHANGE (KSE) INDEX

PRICE PERFORMANCE

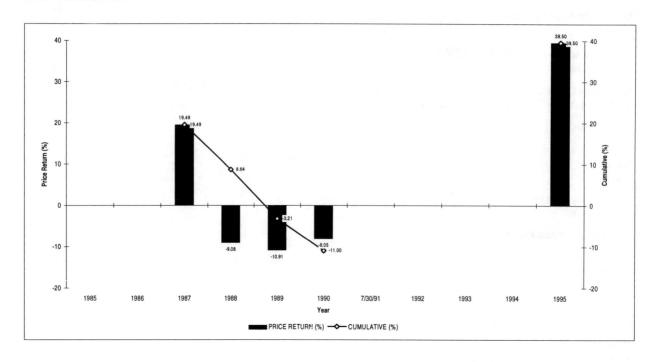

PRICE PERFORMANCE

YEAR	VALUE	PRICE RETURN (%)	CUMULATIVE (%)	MAXIMUM VALUE	DATE	MINIMUM VALUE	DATE
1995	1,365.70	39.50	39.50	NA	NA	NA	NA
1994	979.00	NA	NA	1,002.00	12-Feb	932.00	30-Jun
1993	NA	NA	NA	NA	NA	NA	NA
1992	NA	NA	NA	NA	NA	NA	NA
7/30/91	NA	NA	NA	NA	NA	NA	NA
1990	890.00	-8.05	-11.00	944.00	2-Jan	873.00	14-May
1989	967.94	-10.91	-3.21	1,066.20	2-Jan	932.48	22-Jul
1988	1,086.42	-9.08	8.64	1,182.97	3-Jan	1,021.05	24-May
1987	1,194.90	19.49	19.49	1,340.64	14-Apr	969.19	18-Jan
1986	1,000.00						
1985							
Average Annual (%)		6.19					
Compound Annual (%)		NM					
Standard Deviation (%)		NM					

SYNOPSIS
The Kuwait Stock Exchange (KSE) Index is a broad market value-weighted index that tracks the stock price performance of all shares traded on the Kuwait Stock Exchange (KSE).

NUMBER OF STOCKS—DECEMBER 31, 1995
51

MARKET VALUE—DECEMBER 31, 1994
US$6,381.5 million

SELECTION CRITERIA
Constituent shares include all listed companies on the Kuwait Stock Exchange.

BACKGROUND
The KSE Index was introduced on January 1, 1987. The Kuwait Stock Exchange ceased to operate due to the Iraqi invasion on August 2, 1990. It was officially reopened on September 28, 1992 and the index was restarted on February 12, 1994 based on the closing prices of listed shares as of December 31, 1993.

BASE DATE
December 31, 1986=100.00

COMPUTATION METHODOLOGY
A price-weighted calculation methodology is employed using a ratio of the average of daily closing share prices to the average of closing share prices as of December 31, 1986.

DERIVATIVE INSTRUMENTS
None

SUBINDICES
None

RELATED INDICES
None

REMARKS
The KSE was closed between August 2, 1990 and September 28, 1992 due to the Iraqi invasion of Kuwait.

PUBLISHER
Kuwait Stock Exchange (KSE).

STOCK EXCHANGE OF MAURITIUS INDEX (SEMDEX)

PRICE PERFORMANCE

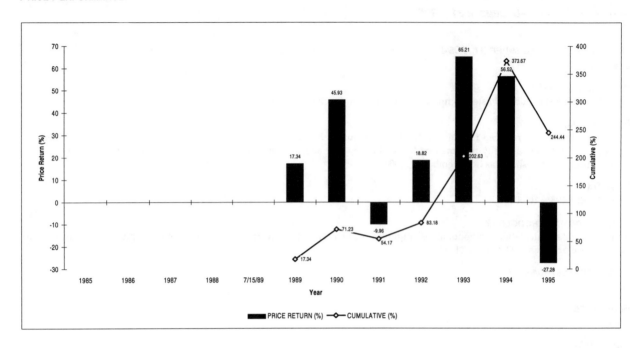

PRICE PERFORMANCE

YEAR	VALUE	PRICE RETURN (%)	CUMULATIVE (%)	MAXIMUM VALUE	DATE	MINIMUM VALUE	DATE
1995	344.44	-27.28	244.44	484.37	1-Feb	314.11	15-Nov
1994	473.67	56.52	373.67	473.72	14-Oct	307.33	10-Jan
1993	302.63	65.21	202.63	302.63	21-Dec	186.06	12-Jan
1992	183.18	18.82	83.18	191.49	12-Nov	148.24	14-Apr
1991	154.17	-9.96	54.17	179.03	22-Aug	119.81	10-Jan
1990	171.23	45.93	71.23	473.72	9-Jan	148.12	24-Aug
1989	117.34	17.34	17.34	119.51	11-Oct	100.00	5-Jul
7/15/89	100.00						
1988							
1987							
1986							
1985							
Average Annual (%)		27.69					
Compound Annual (%)		19.32					
Standard Deviation (%)		28.45					

SYNOPSIS

The Stock Exchange of Mauritius Index (SEMDEX) is a broad market value-weighted index that tracks the daily stock price performance of all domestic shares listed on the Stock Exchange of Mauritius Ltd.

NUMBER OF STOCKS—DECEMBER 31, 1995

28

MARKET VALUE—DECEMBER 31, 1995

US$1,381.0 million

SELECTION CRITERIA

All domestic companies listed on the Stock Exchange of Mauritius.

BACKGROUND

The establishment of the index coincided with the date of the Mauritius Stock Exchange's first trading session.

BASE DATE

July 5, 1989=100.00

COMPUTATION METHODOLOGY

An aggregative of prices times quantities index formula. Maintenance adjustments are made for capitalization changes, new listings and delistings.

DERIVATIVE INSTRUMENTS

None

SUBINDICES

None

RELATED INDICES

None

REMARKS

None

PUBLISHER

The Stock Exchange of Mauritius Ltd.

INDICE MOYEN GENERAL ANNUAL

PRICE PERFORMANCE

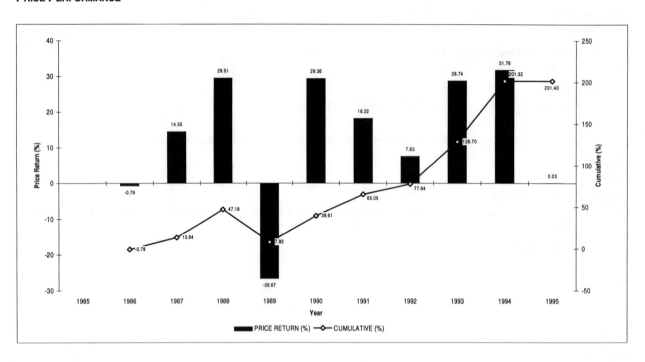

PRICE PERFORMANCE

YEAR	VALUE	PRICE RETURN (%)	CUMULATIVE (%)	MAXIMUM VALUE	DATE	MINIMUM VALUE	DATE
1995	342.39	0.03	201.40	NA	NA	NA	NA
1994	342.30	31.76	201.32	NA	NA	NA	NA
1993	259.80	28.74	128.70	NA	NA	NA	NA
1992	201.80	7.63	77.64	NA	NA	NA	NA
1991	187.50	18.22	65.05	NA	NA	NA	NA
1990	158.60	29.36	39.61	NA	NA	NA	NA
1989	122.60	-26.67	7.92	NA	NA	NA	NA
1988	167.20	29.51	47.18	NA	NA	NA	NA
1987	129.10	14.55	13.64	NA	NA	NA	NA
1986	112.70	-0.79	-0.79	NA	NA	NA	NA
1985	113.60						
Average Annual (%)		13.23					
Compound Annual (%)		11.66					
Standard Deviation (%)		18.65					

SYNOPSIS

The Indice Moyen General Annual Index is an index that tracks the price only performance of shares listed on the Casablanca Stock Exchange.

NUMBER OF STOCKS—DECEMBER 31, 1994

61

MARKET VALUE—DECEMBER 31, 1995

US$4,376.0 million

SELECTION CRITERIA

Not Available

BACKGROUND

None

BASE DATE

Not Available

COMPUTATION METHODOLOGY

Not Available

DERIVATIVE INSTRUMENTS

None

SUBINDICES

None

RELATED INDICES

None

REMARKS

None

PUBLISHER

Casablanca Stock Exchange.

NAMIBIA STOCK EXCHANGE (NSE) INDEX

PRICE PERFORMANCE

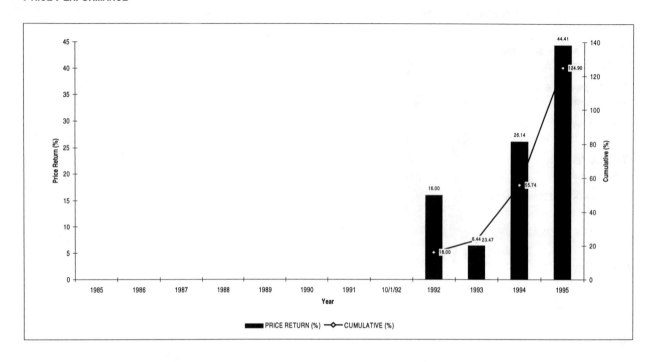

PRICE PERFORMANCE[1]

YEAR	VALUE	PRICE RETURN (%)	CUMULATIVE (%)	MAXIMUM VALUE[2]	DATE	MINIMUM VALUE[2]	DATE
1995	224.90	44.41	124.90	NA	NA	NA	NA
1994	155.74	26.14	55.74	193.82	30-Sep	133.49	31-Jan
1993	123.47	15.63	23.47	123.47	31-Dec	97.04	31-May
1992	116.00	16.00	16.00	NA	NA	NA	NA
10/1/92	100.00						
1991							
1990							
1989							
1988							
1987							
1986							
1985							
Average Annual (%)		28.61					
Compound Annual (%)		24.69					
Standard Deviation (%)		18.99					

[1]Performance statistics applicable to the 3-year period 1993-1995.
[2]Based on month-end index values. Index values for 3/1993 and 7/1993 not applicable.

SYNOPSIS

The Namibia Stock Exchange (NSE) Index is a market value-weighted index that tracks the daily stock price performance of all domestic and foreign shares of companies listed on the Namibian Stock Exchange.

NUMBER OF STOCKS—DECEMBER 31, 1995

26

MARKET VALUE—DECEMBER 31, 1995

US$19,100.9 million

SELECTION CRITERIA

All companies listed on the Namibian Stock Exchange.

BACKGROUND

The index commenced on October 1, 1992, at the time the NSE was established. Initially, the index was computed by:
(1) Dividing each listed stock's current price by its initial listing price; (2) Averaging the results for all listed stocks. New listings were automatically added to the index at a value of 1.00 and this approach served to depress the overall performance of the index. The modified base-weighted aggregative index formula went into effect as of July 1, 1995.

BASE DATE

October 1, 1992=100.00

COMPUTATION METHODOLOGY

An aggregative of prices times quantities index formula. Maintenance adjustments are made for capitalization changes, new listings and delistings.

DERIVATIVE INSTRUMENTS

None

SUBINDICES

A subindex that tracks the performance of 10 local companies with operations in Namibia.

RELATED INDICES

None

REMARKS

Industry sector indices are planned for introduction in the future.

PUBLISHER

Namibian Stock Exchange.

NIGERIA STOCK EXCHANGE (NSE) ALL-SHARE INDEX

PRICE PERFORMANCE

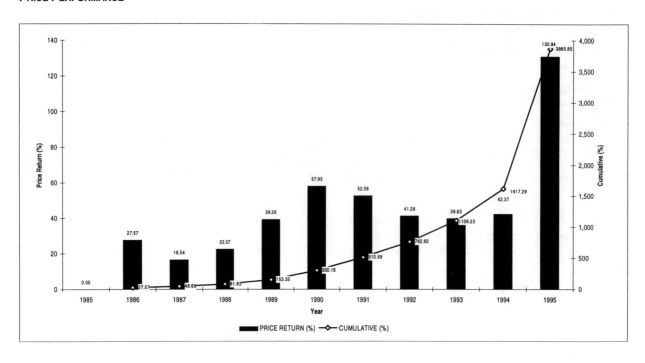

PRICE PERFORMANCE

YEAR	VALUE	PRICE RETURN (%)	CUMULATIVE (%)	MAXIMUM VALUE[1]	DATE	MINIMUM VALUE[1]	DATE
1995	5,092.15	130.94	3,865.85	5,108.07	15-Nov	2,216.60	1-Feb
1994	2,205.00	42.37	1,617.29	2,205.00	31-Dec	1,666.30	31-Jan
1993	1,548.80	39.83	1,106.23	1,548.80	31-Dec	1,113.40	31-Jan
1992	1,107.60	41.28	762.62	1,107.60	31-Dec	794.00	31-Jan
1991	784.00	52.59	510.59	784.00	31-Dec	528.70	31-Jan
1990	513.80	57.95	300.16	513.80	31-Dec	249.30	28-Feb
1989	325.30	39.26	153.35	325.30	31-Dec	240.00	31-Jan
1988	233.60	22.37	81.93	233.60	31-Dec	190.80	31-Jan
1987	190.90	16.54	48.68	194.90	30-Sep	57.50	30-Apr
1986	163.80	27.57	27.57	163.80	31-Dec	143.60	31-Jan
1985	128.40						
Average Annual (%)		47.07					
Compound Annual (%)		44.49					
Standard Deviation (%)		32.10					

[1]Maximum/minimum index values for the period 1985-1994 are as of month-end.

SYNOPSIS

The Nigeria Stock Exchange (NSE) All-Share Index is a market value-weighted index that tracks the daily stock price performance of all First Tier common shares listed on the Nigerian Stock Exchange (NSE).

NUMBER OF STOCKS—DECEMBER 31, 1995

161

MARKET VALUE—DECEMBER 31, 1995

US$1,952.47 million

SELECTION CRITERIA

The index consists of all stocks listed on First Tier of Nigerian Stock Exchange. Preference stocks are not eligible for consideration as index constituents.

BACKGROUND

The NSE commenced operations on June 5, 1961.

BASE DATE

January 3, 1984=100.00

COMPUTATION METHODOLOGY

An aggregative of prices times quantities index formula. Maintenance adjustments are made for capitalization changes, new listings and delistings.

DERIVATIVE INSTRUMENTS

None

SUBINDICES

None

RELATED INDICES

None

REMARKS

The NSE plans to introduce sectoral indices in 1996.

PUBLISHER

The Nigerian Stock Exchange (NSE).

MUSCAT SECURITIES MARKET (MSM) PRICE INDEX

PRICE PERFORMANCE

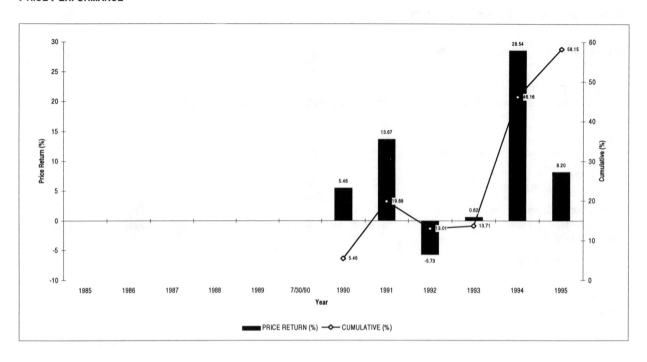

PRICE RETURN (%) —O— CUMULATIVE (%)

PRICE PERFORMANCE[1]

YEAR	VALUE	PRICE RETURN (%)	CUMULATIVE (%)	MAXIMUM VALUE[2]	DATE	MINIMUM VALUE[2]	DATE
1995	158.15	8.20	58.15	NA	NA	NA	NA
1994	146.16	28.54	46.16	149.86	31-Oct	115.35	31-Jan
1993	113.71	0.62	13.71	113.71	31-Dec	104.83	31-Jul
1992	113.01	-5.73	13.01	117.89	31-Mar	104.11	31-Oct
1991	119.88	13.67	19.88	126.46	30-Jun	106.76	31-Jan
1990	105.46	5.46	5.46	105.46	31-Dec	NA	NA
7/30/90	100.00						
1989							
1988							
1987							
1986							
1985							
Average Annual (%)		9.40					
Compound Annual (%)		8.44					
Standard Deviation (%)		13.15					

[1]Statistical measures applicable to the 5-year period 1991-1995.
[2]Maximum/minimum index values are as of month-end.

Synopsis
The Muscat Securities Market (MSM) Price Index is a market value-weighted index that tracks the daily stock price performance of all Regular Market and some Parallel Market companies traded on the Muscat Securities Market (MSM).

Number of Stocks—December 31, 1995
80

Market Value—December 31, 1995
US$1,980.0 million

Selection Criteria
All companies listed on the Regular Market as well as some Parallel Market companies. These are well established companies that have published audited financial statements for at least two years.

Background
None

Base Date
July 1990=100.00

Computation Methodology
An aggregative of prices times quantities index formula.

Derivative Instruments
None

Subindices
Four industry sector indices: Industrial, banking and investment, insurance and services.

Related Indices
None

Remarks
None

Publisher
The Muscat Securities Market (MSM).

ALSI 40 INDEX

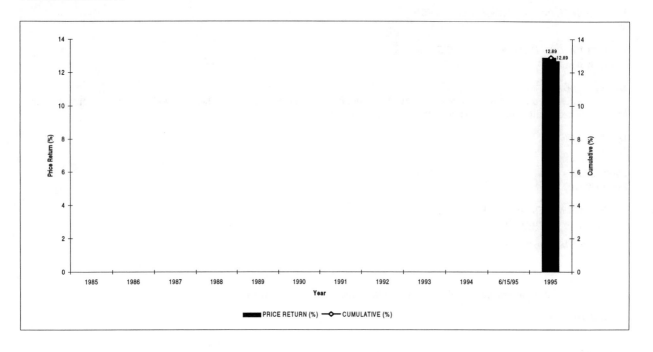

PRICE PERFORMANCE

YEAR	VALUE	PRICE RETURN (%)	CUMULATIVE (%)	MAXIMUM VALUE	DATE	MINIMUM VALUE	DATE
1995	5,644.69	12.89	12.89	5,788.89	12-Dec	4,946.71	3-Jul
6/15/95	5,000.00						
1994							
1993							
1992							
1991							
1990							
1989							
1988							
1987							
1986							
1985							
Average Annual (%)		NM					
Compound Annual (%)		NM					
Standard Deviation (%)		NM					

SYNOPSIS

The ALSI 40 Index is a market value-weighted index that tracks the stock price only performance of the largest and most liquid 40 South African traded shares on the Johannesburg Stock Exchange (JSE). These shares account for 59% of the domestic market capitalization.

NUMBER OF STOCKS—DECEMBER 31, 1995

40

MARKET VALUE—DECEMBER 31, 1995

US$144,707.9 million

SELECTION CRITERIA

Constituent companies must be eligible for inclusion in the JSE-Actuaries All Share Index, i.e., they must be ordinary shares of operating companies that are listed on the Johannesburg Stock Exchange.

Companies are selected on the basis of market capitalization and liquidity, each of which is assigned equal weighting in the selection process. Market capitalization and liquidity are determined using average weekly market capitalization and trading activity for the previous 12-month period, calculated on the last business day of each week. Market capitalization and liquidity for newly listed shares are calculated over the time for which the new shares have been listed.

Companies are arranged in rank order, by market capitalization and liquidity, and those that rank in the top 40 are selected for inclusion in the index.

BACKGROUND

The index was developed in conjunction with the Actuarial Society, the Johannesburg Stock Exchange and the South African Futures Exchange and was introduced on June 16, 1995 to supplement the JSE Actuaries equity indices and more properly serve as an underlying vehicle for derivative products.

BASE DATE

June 15, 1995=5000.00

COMPUTATION METHODOLOGY

(1) An aggregative of prices times quantities index formula. Maintenance adjustments are made for capitalization changes, new listings and delistings. (2) The index constituents are reviewed every six months, on June 1 and December 1 of each year and revisions take effect on the first business day following the mid-month expiration of Safex stock index futures contracts. (3) Index constituents are removed due to takeovers, mergers and suspensions and replaced by the next most eligible shares. (4) Latest available ordinary share prices are used or, in the absence of a share price, bid or asked prices. (5) Market capitalization is determined on the basis of the total number of ordinary shares of all classes that the company has issued and listed on the JSE. Only fully paid shares are taken into account. Partly paid shares held by employees and directors are excluded. In the event share capital consists of both "S" and ordinary shares, the combined number of shares is used to compute market capitalization. The effective date of changes in the number of eligible shares for index computation purposes is determined by the JSE Committee.

DERIVATIVE INSTRUMENTS

JSE-Actuaries All Share Index futures and options on futures trade on the South African Futures Exchange.

SUBINDICES

None

RELATED INDICES

JSE Top Forty Company All Share Index (ALSI 40)
JSE Top Ten Company Gold Index (GLDI 10)
JSE Top Thirty Financial/Industrial Index (FNDI 30)
JSE Top Twenty Five Company Industrial Index (INDI 25)
JSE-Actuaries All Share Index
JSE-Actuaries Bond Index

REMARKS

Derivative products are based on the JSE-Actuaries All Share Equity Index prior to its substantial modification in March 1995, at which time the number of index participants was expanded from 80% of the shares in each sector of the market (Old Index). Equity index products will continue to be based on the old benchmark until their expiration in March 1996 and the Old Index will continue to be calculated until then. Thereafter, all equity index products will be based on the new index and the JSE will cease publication of the Old Index.

PUBLISHER

The Johannesburg Stock Exchange (JSE).

GLDI 10 INDEX

PRICE PERFORMANCE

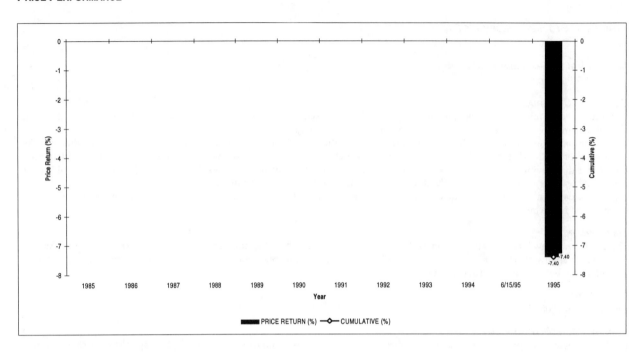

PRICE PERFORMANCE

YEAR	VALUE	PRICE RETURN (%)	CUMULATIVE (%)	MAXIMUM VALUE	DATE	MINIMUM VALUE	DATE
1995	926.01	-7.40	-7.40	1,097.88	21-Aug	838.75	30-Oct
6/15/95	1,000.00						
1994							
1993							
1992							
1991							
1990							
1989							
1988							
1987							
1986							
1985							
Average Annual (%)		NM					
Compound Annual (%)		NM					
Standard Deviation (%)		NM					

SYNOPSIS

The GLDI 10 Index is a market value-weighted index that tracks the stock price only performance of the 10 largest and most liquid South African-traded gold mining shares listed on the Johannesburg Stock Exchange (JSE).

NUMBER OF STOCKS—DECEMBER 31, 1995

40

MARKET VALUE—DECEMBER 31, 1995

US$10,934.8 million

SELECTION CRITERIA

Gold mining companies must be eligible for inclusion in the JSE-Actuaries All Share Index, i.e., they must be ordinary shares of operating companies that are listed on the Johannesburg Stock Exchange.

Companies are selected on the basis of market capitalization and liquidity, each of which is assigned equal weighting in the selection process. Market capitalization and liquidity are determined using average weekly market capitalization and trading activity for the previous 12-month period, calculated on the last business day of each week. Market capitalization and liquidity for newly listed shares are calculated over the time for which the new shares have been listed.

Companies are arranged in rank order, by market capitalization and liquidity, and those that rank in the top 10 are selected for inclusion in the index.

BACKGROUND

The index, along with several companion indices, was developed in conjunction with the Actuarial Society, the Johannesburg Stock Exchange and the South African Futures Exchange and was introduced on June 16, 1995 to supplement the JSE Actuaries equity indices and more properly serve as an underlying vehicle for derivative products.

BASE DATE

June 15, 1995=1000.00

COMPUTATION METHODOLOGY

(1) An aggregative of prices times quantities index formula. Maintenance adjustments are made for capitalization changes, new listings and delistings. (2) The index constituents are reviewed every six months, on June 1 and December 1 of each year and revisions take effect on the first business day following the mid-month expiration of Safex stock index futures contracts. (3) Index constituents are removed due to takeovers, mergers and suspensions and replaced by the next most eligible shares. (4) Latest available ordinary share prices are used or, in the absence of a share price, bid or asked prices. (5) Market capitalization is determined on the basis of the total number of ordinary shares of all classes that the company has issued and listed on the JSE. Only fully paid shares are taken into account. Partly paid shares held by employees and directors are excluded. In the event share capital consists of both "S" and ordinary shares, the combined number of shares is used to compute market capitalization. The effective date of changes in the number of eligible shares for index computation purposes is determined by the JSE Committee.

DERIVATIVE INSTRUMENTS

JSE-Actuaries All Gold Index futures and options on futures trade on the South African Futures Exchange.

SUBINDICES

None

RELATED INDICES

JSE-Actuaries All Share Index
JSE-Actuaries Bond Index
JSE Top Forty Company All Share Index (ALSI 40)
JSE Top Thirty Financial/Industrial Index (FNDI 30)
JSE Top Twenty Five Company Industrial Index (INDI 25)

REMARKS

Derivative products are based on the JSE-Actuaries All Share Equity All Gold subindex prior to its substantial modification in March 1995, at which time the number of index participants was expanded from 80% of the shares in each sector of the market (Old Index). Equity index products will continue to be based on the old benchmark until their expiration in March 1996 and the Old Index will continue to be calculated until then. Thereafter, all equity index products will be based on the new index and the JSE will cease publication of the Old Index.

PUBLISHER

The Johannesburg Stock Exchange (JSE).

INDI 25 INDEX

PRICE PERFORMANCE

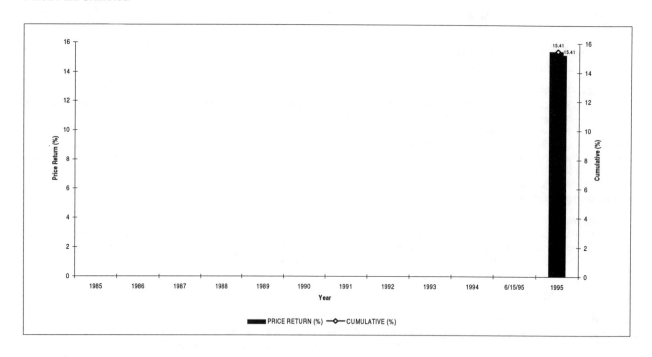

PRICE PERFORMANCE

YEAR	VALUE	PRICE RETURN (%)	CUMULATIVE (%)	MAXIMUM VALUE	DATE	MINIMUM VALUE	DATE
1995	7,501.92	15.41	15.41	7,556.86	7-Dec	6,501.64	3-Jul
6/15/95	6,500.00						
1994							
1993							
1992							
1991							
1990							
1989							
1988							
1987							
1986							
1985							
Average Annual (%)		NM					
Compound Annual (%)		NM					
Standard Deviation (%)		NM					

SYNOPSIS

The INDI 25 Index is a market value-weighted index that tracks the stock price only performance of the 25 largest and most liquid South African-traded industrial company shares listed on the Johannesburg Stock Exchange (JSE).

NUMBER OF STOCKS—DECEMBER 31, 1995

25

MARKET VALUE—DECEMBER 31, 1995

US$72,696.6 million

SELECTION CRITERIA

Industrial companies must be eligible for inclusion in the JSE-Actuaries All Share Index, i.e., they must be ordinary shares of operating companies that are listed on the Johannesburg Stock Exchange.

Companies are selected on the basis of market capitalization and liquidity, each of which is assigned equal weighting in the selection process. Market capitalization and liquidity are determined using average weekly market capitalization and trading activity for the previous 12-month period, calculated on the last business day of each week. Market capitalization and liquidity for newly listed shares are calculated over the time for which the new shares have been listed.

Companies are arranged in rank order, by market capitalization and liquidity, and those that rank in the top 10 are selected for inclusion in the index.

BACKGROUND

The index, along with several companion indices, was developed in conjunction with the Actuarial Society, the Johannesburg Stock Exchange and the South African Futures Exchange and was introduced on June 16, 1995 to supplement the JSE Actuaries equity indices and more properly serve as an underlying vehicle for derivative products.

BASE DATE

June 15, 1995=6500.00

COMPUTATION METHODOLOGY

(1) An aggregative of prices times quantities index formula. Maintenance adjustments are made for capitalization changes, new listings and delistings. (2) The index constituents are reviewed every six months, on June 1 and December 1 of each year and revisions take effect on the first business day following the mid-month expiration of Safex stock index futures contracts. (3) Index constituents are removed due to takeovers, mergers and suspensions and replaced by the next most eligible shares. (4) Latest available ordinary share prices are used or, in the absence of a share price, bid or asked prices. (5) Market capitalization is determined on the basis of the total number of ordinary shares of all classes that the company has issued and listed on the JSE. Only fully paid shares are taken into account. Partly paid shares held by employees and directors are excluded. In the event share capital consists of both "S" and ordinary shares, the combined number of shares is used to compute market capitalization. The effective date of changes in the number of eligible shares for index computation purposes is determined by the JSE Committee.

DERIVATIVE INSTRUMENTS

JSE-Actuaries Industrial Index futures and options on futures trade on the South African Futures Exchange.

SUBINDICES

None

RELATED INDICES

JSE-Actuaries All Share Index
JSE Actuaries Bond Index
JSE Top Forty Company All Share Index (ALSI 40)
JSE Top Ten Company Gold Index (INDI 25)
JSE Top Thirty Financial/Industrial Index (FNDI 30)

REMARKS

Derivative products are based on the JSE-Actuaries All Share Equity Industrial subindex prior to its substantial modification in March 1995, at which time the number of index participants was expanded from 80% of the shares in each sector of the market (Old Index). Equity index products will continue to be based on the old benchmark until their expiration in March 1996 and the Old Index will continue to be calculated until then. Thereafter, all equity index products will be based on the new index and the JSE will cease publication of the Old Index.

PUBLISHER

The Johannesburg Stock Exchange (JSE).

JOHANNESBURG STOCK EXCHANGE (JSE)-ACTUARIES ALL GOLD SUBINDEX

PRICE PERFORMANCE

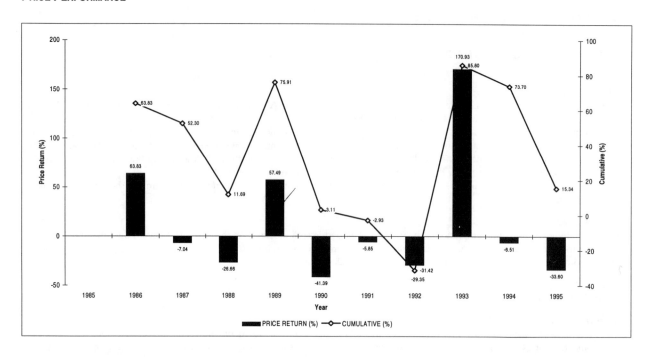

PRICE PERFORMANCE

YEAR	VALUE	PRICE RETURN (%)	CUMULATIVE (%)	MAXIMUM VALUE[1]	DATE	MINIMUM VALUE[1]	DATE
1995	1,343.51	-33.60	15.34	1,984.91	3-Nov	1,250.23	30-Oct
1994	2,023.30	-6.51	73.70	2,535.07	7-Sep	1,748.93	14-Feb
1993	2,164.16	170.93	85.80	2,183.86	27-Dec	770.83	20-Jan
1992	798.79	-29.35	-31.42	1,327.26	21-Jan	745.73	10-Nov
1991	1,130.69	-5.85	-2.93	1,469.50	5-Jul	970.54	25-Feb
1990	1,201.00	-41.39	3.11	2,250.00	2-Feb	1,111.41	18-Dec
1989	2,049.00	57.49	75.91	2,254.00	12-Dec	1,293.00	3-Jan
1988	1,301.00	-26.66	11.69	1,343.00	30-Sep	1,207.00	30-Apr
1987	1,774.00	-7.04	52.30	2,410.00	31-Jul	1,774.00	31-Dec
1986	1,908.30	63.83	63.83	1,954.00	30-Nov	1,142.10	31-May
1985	1,164.80						
Average Annual (%)		14.19					
Compound Annual (%)		1.44					
Standard Deviation (%)		65.93					

[1]Maximum/minimum index values for the period 1986-1988 are as of month-end.

SYNOPSIS
The Johannesburg Stock Exchange (JSE)-Actuaries All Gold Subindex is a market value-weighted index that tracks several times per day the stock price performance of ordinary gold mining shares listed on the Johannesburg Stock Exchange (JSE).

NUMBER OF STOCKS—DECEMBER 31, 1995
48

MARKET VALUE—DECEMBER 31, 1995
US$13,938.9 million

SELECTION CRITERIA
The index includes all the ordinary shares of Sourth African gold mining stocks listed on the Johannesburg Stock Exchange. Generally, index participation is limited to operating companies.

BACKGROUND
The JSE-Actuaries All Gold Subindex, a component of the JSE-Actuaries All Share Index, was substantially modified in March 1995, at which time the number of index participants was expanded from 80% of the shares in each sector of the market (Old Index), by market capitalization, to include all South African-listed operating companies. At the same time, the Actuarial Society, the Johannesburg Stock Exchange and the South African Futures Exchange announced the development of four narrowly based indices that could more properly serve as underlying vehicles for derivative products. These were introduced on June 16, 1995.

The JSE along with several sectoral indices were launched on November 1, 1978. The index was linked to the Rand Daily Mail (RDM) indices, including the RDM 100 and RDM Gold Index, which were the most widely accepted indicators in South Africa at the time. Thus, the values of the JSE at the end of September 1978 were linked to the RDM values as of that date. Historical continuity was maintained and index values are available to 1960.

BASE DATE
January 1, 1960=100.00

COMPUTATION METHODOLOGY
(1) An aggregative of prices times quantities index formula. Maintenance adjustments are made for capitalization changes, new listings and delistings. (2) Latest available ordinary share prices are used or, in the absence of a share price, bid or asked prices. (3) Market capitalization is determined on the basis of the total number of ordinary shares of all classes that the company has issued and listed on the JSE. Only fully paid shares are taken into account. Partly paid shares held by employees and directors are excluded. In the event share capital consists of both "S" and ordinary shares, the combined number of shares is used to compute market capitalization. The effective date of changes in the number of eligible shares for index computation purposes is determined by the JSE Committee.

DERIVATIVE INSTRUMENTS
JSE-Actuaries All Gold index futures and options on futures trade on the South African Futures Exchange.

SUBINDICES
Five sectoral subindices: Gold-Rand and others, Gold-Evander, Gold-Klerksdorp, Gold-O.F.S. and Gold-West Wilts.

RELATED INDICES
JSE-Actuaries All Share Equity Index
JSE Top Forty Company All Share Index (ALSI 40)
JSE Top Ten Company Gold Index (GLDI 10)
JSE Top Twenty-Five Company Industrial Index (INDI 25)
JSE Top Thirty Company Financial/Industrial (FNDI 30)
JSE Actuaries Bond Index

REMARKS
Derivative products are based on the Old Index and will continue until their expiration in March 1996. The Old Index will continue to be calculated until then. Thereafter, all equity index products will be based on the new indices and the JSE will cease publication of the Old Index.

PUBLISHER
The Johannesburg Stock Exchange (JSE).

JOHANNESBURG STOCK EXCHANGE (JSE)-ACTUARIES (JSE ACTUARIES) ALL SHARE INDEX

PRICE PERFORMANCE

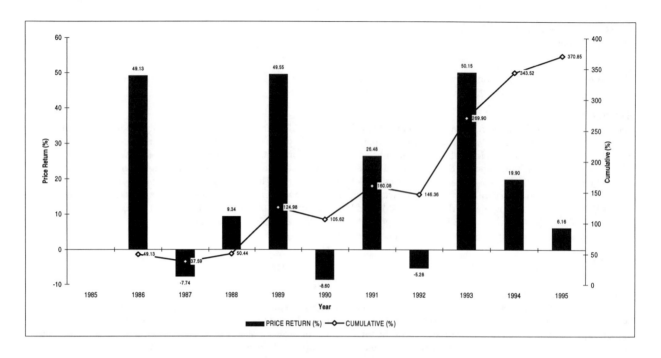

PRICE PERFORMANCE

YEAR	VALUE	PRICE RETURN (%)	CUMULATIVE (%)	MAXIMUM VALUE	DATE	MINIMUM VALUE	DATE
1995	6,228.42	6.16	370.85	6,283.28	12-Dec	5,054.13	31-Jan
1994	5,866.90	19.90	343.52	6,053.80	7-Sep	4,691.63	14-Feb
1993	4,893.00	50.15	269.90	4,892.99	31-Dec	3,249.09	5-Jan
1992	3,258.80	-5.28	146.36	3,743.55	4-Jun	2,925.82	15-Oct
1991	3,440.30	26.48	160.08	3,580.27	13-Nov	2,526.00	30-Jan
1990	2,720.00	-8.60	105.62	3,392.00	20-Mar	2,546.00	15-Nov
1989	2,976.00	49.55	124.98	2,976.00	31-Dec	2,158.00	31-Jan
1988	1,990.00	9.34	50.44	1,990.00	31-Dec	1,518.00	28-Feb
1987	1,820.00	-7.74	37.59	2,704.00	31-Aug	1,820.00	31-Dec
1986	1,972.70	49.13	49.13	1,999.00	30-Nov	1,358.60	30-Apr
1985	1,322.80						
Average Annual (%)		18.91					
Compound Annual (%)		16.76					
Standard Deviation (%)		24.02					

SYNOPSIS

The Johannesburg Stock Exchange (JSE)-Actuaries (JSE Actuaries) All Share Index is a market value-weighted index that tracks several times per day the stock price performance of ordinary shares listed on the Johannesburg Stock Exchange (JSE) in South Africa.

NUMBER OF STOCKS—DECEMBER 31, 1995

536

MARKET VALUE—DECEMBER 31, 1995

US$244,984.7 million

SELECTION CRITERIA

The index includes all South African ordinary shares listed on the Johannesburg Stock Exchange. Generally, index participation is limited to operating companies.

BACKGROUND

The JSE-Actuaries All Share Equity Index was substantially modified in March 1995, at which time the number of index participants was expanded from 80% of the shares in each sector of the market (Old Index), by market capitalization, to include all South African-listed operating companies. At the same time, the Actuarial Society, the Johannesburg Stock Exchange and the South African Futures Exchange announced the development of four narrowly based indices that could more properly serve as underlying vehicles for derivative products. These were introduced on June 16, 1995.

The JSE along with several sectoral indices were launched on November 1, 1978. The index was linked to the Rand Daily Mail (RDM) indices, including the RDM 100 and RDM Gold Index, which were the most widely accepted indicators in South Africa at the time. Thus, the values of the JSE at the end of September 1978 were linked to the RDM values as of that date. Historical continuity was maintained and index values are available to 1960.

BASE DATE

January 1, 1960=100.00

COMPUTATION METHODOLOGY

(1) An aggregative of prices times quantities index formula. Maintenance adjustments are made for capitalization changes, new listings and delistings. (2) Latest available ordinary share prices are used or, in the absence of a share price, bid or asked prices. (3) Market capitalization is determined on the basis of the total number of ordinary shares of all classes that the company has issued and listed on the JSE. Only fully paid shares are taken into account. Partly paid shares held by employees and directors are excluded. In the event share capital consists of both "S" and ordinary shares, the combined number of shares is used to compute market capitalization. The effective date of changes in the number of eligible shares for index computation purposes is determined by the JSE Committee.

DERIVATIVE INSTRUMENTS

JSE-Actuaries All Share index futures and options on futures trade on the South African Futures Exchange.
JSE-Actuaries All Gold index futures and options on futures trade on the South African Futures Exchange.
JSE-Actuaries Industrial index futures and options on futures trade on the South African Futures Exchange.

SUBINDICES

Seven composite indices: All gold, metals and minerals, financial, industrial, mining producers, mining finance, and financial and industrial.

Thirty-six sectoral subindices. Coal, diamonds, Gold-Rand and others, Gold-Evander, Gold-Klerksdorp, Gold-O.F.S., Gold-West Wilts, copper, manganese, pantinum, other metals and minerals, mining houses, mining holdings, banks and other financial services, insurance, investment trusts, property, property trusts, property loan stock, industrial holdings, beverages, hotels and leisure, building and construction, chemicals and oils, clothing, footwear and textiles, electronics and electrical battery, engineering, food, furniture and household goods, motors, pulp, paper and packaging, pharmaceutical and medical, printing and publishing, steel and allied, retailers and wholesalers and transportation.

RELATED INDICES

JSE Top Forty Company All Share Index (ALSI 40)
JSE Top Ten Company Gold Index (GLDI 10)
JSE Top Twenty-Five Company Industrial Index (INDI 25)
JSE Actuaries Top Thirty Company Financial/Industrial (FNDI 30)
JSE Actuaries Bond Index

REMARKS

Derivative products are based on the Old Index and will continue until their expiration in March 1996. The Old Index will continue to be calculated until then. Thereafter, all equity index products will be based on the new indices and the JSE will cease publication of the Old Index.

PUBLISHER

The Johannesburg Stock Exchange (JSE).

SWAZILAND STOCK MARKET (SSM) INDEX

PRICE PERFORMANCE

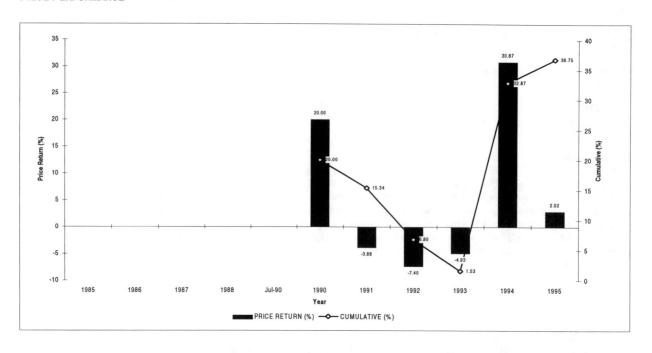

PRICE PERFORMANCE[1]

YEAR	VALUE	PRICE RETURN (%)	CUMULATIVE (%)	MAXIMUM VALUE	DATE	MINIMUM VALUE	DATE
1995	136.75	2.92	36.75	137.55	22-Jan	126.25	6-Jan
1994	132.87	30.87	32.87	132.87	16-Dec	106.26	29-Aug
1993	101.53	-4.93	1.53	116.02	20-Dec	99.31	12-Nov
1992	106.80	-7.40	6.80	115.34	3-Jan	106.80	25-Sep
1991	115.34	-3.88	15.34	125.00	4-Jan	115.34	8-Mar
1990	120.00	20.00	20.00	120.00	9-Nov	115.00	13-Jul
Jul-90	100.00						
1988							
1987							
1986							
1985							
Average Annual (%)		3.51					
Compound Annual (%)		2.65					
Standard Deviation (%)		15.76					

[1]Statistical measures applicable to the 5-year period 1991-1995.

SYNOPSIS
The Swaziland Stock Market (SSM) Index is a market value-weighted index that tracks the daily price only performance all stocks listed on the Swaziland Stock Market Limited.

NUMBER OF STOCKS—DECEMBER 31, 1995
4

MARKET VALUE—DECEMBER 31, 1995
US$338.9 million

SELECTION CRITERIA
Constituent shares include all stocks listed on the Swaziland Stock market Limited, including Lonrho, RSSC, Standard Chatered Bank and Swazi-Spa.

BACKGROUND
The index was initiated in 1990 with a single listing. Additional single listings were added in 1991, 1993 and 1994.

BASE DATE
July 1990=100.00

COMPUTATION METHODOLOGY
An aggregative of prices times quantities index formula. Maintenance adjustments are made for capitalization changes, new listings and delistings.

DERIVATIVE INSTRUMENTS
None

SUBINDICES
None

RELATED INDICES
None

REMARKS
None

PUBLISHER
Swaziland Stockbrokers Ltd.

ZIMBABWE STOCK EXCHANGE (ZSE) INDUSTRIAL AND MINING INDEX

PRICE PERFORMANCE

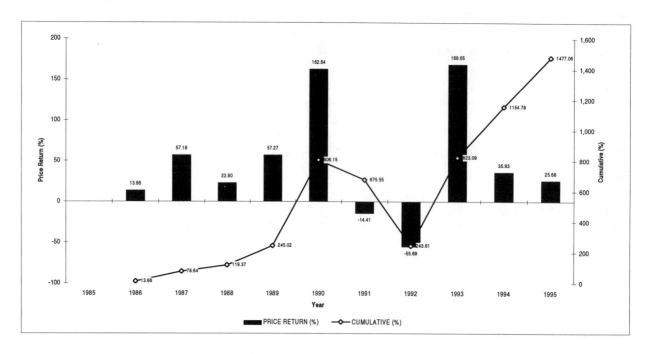

PRICE PERFORMANCE

YEAR	VALUE	PRICE RETURN (%)	CUMULATIVE (%)	MAXIMUM VALUE	DATE	MINIMUM VALUE	DATE
1995	3,972.62	25.68	1,477.06	NA	NA	NA	NA
1994	3,160.80	35.93	1,154.78	NA	NA	NA	NA
1993	2,325.26	168.65	823.09	NA	NA	NA	NA
1992	865.55	-55.69	243.61	NA	NA	NA	NA
1991	1,953.60	-14.41	675.55	NA	NA	NA	NA
1990	2,282.60	162.64	806.15	NA	NA	NA	NA
1989	869.10	57.27	245.02	NA	NA	NA	NA
1988	552.60	22.80	119.37	NA	NA	NA	NA
1987	450.00	57.18	78.64	NA	NA	NA	NA
1986	286.30	13.66	13.66	NA	NA	NA	NA
1985	251.90						
Average Annual (%)		47.37					
Compound Annual (%)		31.76					
Standard Deviation (%)		70.69					

SYNOPSIS

The Zimbabwe Stock Exchange (ZSE) Industrial and Mining Index is a market value-weighted index that tracks the daily stock price performance of common and preferred shares listed on the Zimbabwe Stock Exchange (ZSE).

NUMBER OF STOCKS—DECEMBER 31, 1995

64

MARKET VALUE—DECEMBER 31, 1995

US$2,038.0 million

SELECTION CRITERIA

All common and preferred stocks listed on the Zimbabwe Stock Exchange.

BACKGROUND

None

BASE DATE

December 31, 1966=100.00

COMPUTATION METHODOLOGY

(1) An aggregative of prices times quantities index formula. Maintenance adjustments are made for capitalization changes, new listings and delistings. (2) Mid-market prices are used.

DERIVATIVE INSTRUMENTS

None

SUBINDICES

Industrial and mining subindices.

RELATED INDICES

None

REMARKS

Consideration is being given to the introduction of a composite index.

PUBLISHER

Zimbabwe Stock Exchange (ZSE).

WORLD

Dow Jones Global Stock Index

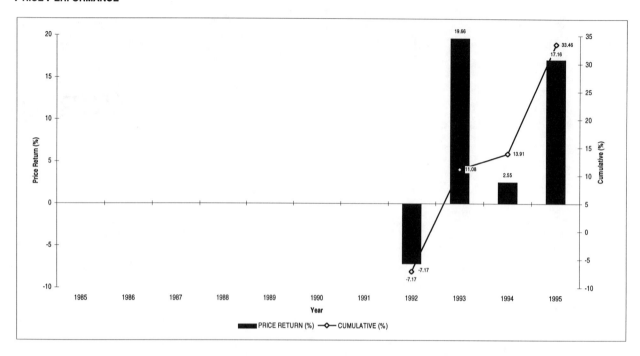

Price Performance (US$)

YEAR	VALUE	PRICE RETURN (%)	CUMULATIVE (%)	MAXIMUM VALUE	DATE	MINIMUM VALUE	DATE
1995	133.46	17.16	33.46	133.69	27-Dec	109.36	23-Jan
1994	113.91	2.55	13.91	119.86	2-Sep	110.55	4-Apr
1993	111.08	19.66	11.08	114.02	6-Sep	91.47	13-Jan
1992	92.83	-7.17	-7.17	101.80	6-Jan	85.68	8-Apr
1991	100.00						
1990							
1989							
1988							
1987							
1986							
1985							
Average Annual (%)		3.22					
Compound Annual (%)		2.93					
Standard Deviation (%)		12.65					

SYNOPSIS

The Dow Jones Global Stock Index is a market capitalization-weighted index that tracks the daily stock price only performance of equity securities on a worldwide basis. Twenty-five countries are represented in the index, inlcuding companies in North America, Latin America, Asia, Europe and Africa.

NUMBER OF STOCKS—DECEMBER 31, 1995

2,654

MARKET VALUE—DECEMBER 31, 1995

US$11,522,603.8 million

SELECTION CRITERIA

Constituents stocks are selected from 25 countries, including Australia, Austria, Belgium, Canada, Denmark, Finland, France, Germany, Hong Kong, Indonesia, Ireland, Italy, Japan, Malaysia, Mexico, The Netherlands, New Zealand, Norway, Singapore, Spain, Sweden, Switzerland, Thailand, United Kingdom and the United States, and represent about 80% of each country's market capitalization and must be readily marketable, common or ordinary shares, with the usual participation rights, including dividends.

Index members are included and accounted for in the country index based on the country in which each company is incorporated. Selections are made using objective as well as subjective criteria, as follows:

(1) A stock must be readily marketable. Shares in which there is very low trading volume or isolated trades are excluded; also, companies controlled by the government, a family, an individual or another corporation are subject to review before being included. (2) At least 25% of an issue must be available for ownership by foreigners collectively, without restrictions. In cases of significant restriction on foreign ownership of a specific stock or class of issues, an issue is tracked in the index in the same proportion that shares are available to foreign investors. (3) All eligible stock issues are ranked in market capitalization order and constituents are selected on the basis of the highest capitalizations within each industry in each market, until approximately 80% of its market capital is represented in the index. Exceptions may be made for certain well known corporations with long track records that may not qualify on the basis of the strict application of these guidelines. Such exceptions account for a minor portion of the market's total capitalization.

With limited exceptions, preferred stock, mutual fund shares and closed-end funds are not eligible for inclusion. An exception may be made in the event a closed-end fund provides the dominant vehicle for an investor to participate in a specific industry.

BACKGROUND

The Dow Jones Global Stock Index expanded on the existing Dow Jones Equity Market Index introduced in 1988 and which represents the World Index's U.S. component.

BASE DATE

December 31, 1991=100.00

COMPUTATION METHODOLOGY

(1) A base-weighted aggregate index formula is used, with the divisor market capitalization adjusted daily to eliminate the effect of all types of capitalization changes, new listings and delistings to keep the current index numbers comparable to the base period. (2) The index is reviewed periodically to assure that each nation has approximately 80% of its market capital represented and ensure proper industrial classification, based on each company's dominant line of business. (3) The official close of the index is at 4 PM. Currency values then prevailing are used in the calculation of the index each day.

DERIVATIVE INSTRUMENTS

None

SUBINDICES

Country indices are calculated in each country's own currency and the U.S. dollar.
Regional indices, in U.S. dollars, are calculated for Asia/Pacific, Europe and the Americas.
The World index is calculated on the basis of the U.S. dollar, British pound, German mark and Japanese yen.
Subindices are calculated for nine economic sectors and 124 industry groups. The economic sectors include basic materials, consumer cyclical, consumer non-cyclical, energy, financial, industrial, technology, utilities and independent companies, or multi-industry companies.

RELATED INDICES

Dow Jones Composite Average
Dow Jones Equity Market Index
Dow Jones Industrial Average
Dow Jones Transportation Average
Dow Jones Utilities Average
For additional indices, refer to Appendix 2.

REMARKS

(1) Three additional countries–Philippines, South Korea and South Africa– were added to the index in the first quarter of 1996, bringing the total to 28 countries and an estimated 2,767 securities. The market capitalization of South Korea, due to allowable foreign ownership restrictions, is limited to 15%. In addition, the calculation frequency of the World Index along with South Korea and Asia/Pacific subindices will be expanded to include Saturdays since the South Korean market is open for trading on Saturdays. (2) Taiwan was added to the index as of April 1, 1996, with about 100 Taiwan stocks.

PUBLISHER

Dow Jones & Company, Inc.

FINANCIAL TIMES/STANDARD & POOR'S (FT/S&P) ACTUARIES WORLD INDEX

PRICE PERFORMANCE

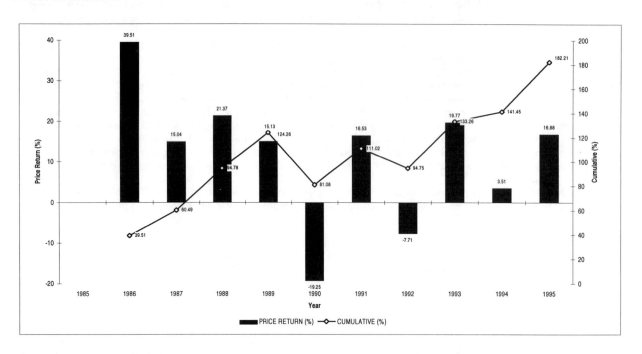

PRICE PERFORMANCE (US$)

YEAR	VALUE	PRICE RETURN (%)	CUMULATIVE (%)	MAXIMUM VALUE	DATE	MINIMUM VALUE[1]	DATE
1995	202.29	16.88	182.21	202.52	27-Dec	165.92	23-Jan
1994	173.07	3.51	141.45	180.80	31-Aug	166.19	4-Apr
1993	167.20	19.77	133.26	170.68	15-Oct	137.32	13-Jan
1992	139.60	-7.71	94.75	152.88	7-Jan	130.66	8-Apr
1991	151.26	16.53	111.02	151.26	31-Dec	123.28	16-Jan
1990	129.80	-19.25	81.08	162.05	4-Jan	118.33	28-Sep
1989	160.75	15.13	124.26	160.75	29-Dec	136.68	15-Jun
1988	139.62	21.37	94.78	139.07	9-Dec	114.13	25-Jan
1987	115.04	15.04	60.49	NA	NA	NA	NA
1986	100.00	39.51	39.51	NA	NA	NA	NA
1985	71.68						
Average Annual (%)		12.08					
Compound Annual (%)		10.93					
Standard Deviation (%)		16.35					

[1]1988 minimum index value based on data commencing as of that date.

SYNOPSIS

The Financial Times/Standard & Poor's (FT/S&P) Actuaries World Index is a market capitalization-weighted index that tracks the daily stock price and total return performance of investable securities worldwide. The index, which consists principally of common or ordinary shares, aims to capture approximately 85% of the total market capitalization available to foreign investors in each of 26 countries in Africa, Asia/Pacific, Europe, Latin America and North America. These include Australia, Austria, Belgium, Brazil, Canada, Denmark, Finland, France, Germany, Hong Kong, Ireland, Italy, Japan, Malaysia, Mexico, The Netherlands, New Zealand, Norway, Singapore, South Africa, Spain, Sweden, Switzerland, Thailand, United Kingdom, and the United States.

NUMBER OF STOCKS—DECEMBER 31, 1995

2,396

MARKET VALUE—DECEMBER 31, 1995

US$11,820,000.0 million

SELECTION CRITERIA

The index is designed to serve as a comprehensive benchmark that is consistent, flexible, accurate, investable, representative and user-driven.

A top down approach is employed. Constituent stocks are, in most cases, selected on the basis of the country they are legally registered or have their main market listing and are recognized for taxation purposes, after a determination of individual country eligibility and the overall economic sectoral make-up of the investable universe has been established. Decisions effecting overall policies and objectives as well as the operation of the index reside with a World Index Policy Committee.

Country selection is based on the following criteria:

(1) Direct equity investments by foreign nationals must be permitted. (2) Accurate and timely data must be available. (3) No significant exchange controls should exist which would prevent the timely repatriation of capital or dividends. (4) Significant international investor interest in the local equity market. (5) The existence of adequate liquidity.

Security selection is based on the following guidelines:

(1) Determination of the investable universe defined as the aggregate capitalization of all equity securities listed on the exchanges monitored within each selected country selected, after adjustments for ineligible securities, market capitalization modifications due to partial restrictions on foreign ownership. The economic sectoral make-up of the investable universe is also established. (2) Index constituents are allocated to one of 97 industry subsectors, which are combined to form 36 industry groups and seven economic sectors. While exceptions apply, constituents are generally classified according to the business area that represents the greatest share of group revenue. (3) Determination of a market's minimum company size which represents the smallest sized company after the aggregate capitalization of all equity securities listed on the exchanges monitored within each selected country has been adjusted by excluding the bottom 5% of any market's capitalization. (4) Determination of large company cut-off. The average size of the companies constituting the remaining 95% of the market's available equity.

Stock selection, which is aimed at achieving an 85% investable universe sample after application of the investability screens, within an acceptable band of 82%-88% so as to limit turnover to 5%-7% for the larger markets, proceeds on the basis of the following steps: First, stocks with a market capitalization greater than the large company cut-off are automatically selected for inclusion. Second, the sectoral composition of this universe of securities is determined. Next, the remaining stocks in the investable universe are selected in descending order of size within economic sectors such that any divergences in economic sector weights between the selected index universe and the investable universe are minimized. The selection process continues until the aggregate capitalization of the sample represents as closely as possible 85% of the capitalization of the investable universe.

Securities are excluded from consideration if they fall within the bottom 5% of any market's capitalization and in the event foreign investors are barred entirely from their ownership, the security is deemed to be illiquid, i.e., fails to trade for more than 15 working days within each of two successive quarters, or in the event that the size of one line of capital, in cases of a company with multiple lines of equity capital, is less than 50% of the market's minimum market size or the size of the line is between 50% and 100% of the market's minimum size but is less than 25% of the company's main line of equity.

Companies whose business is that of holding equity and other investments, such as UK Investment Trusts, are eligible for inclusion in the index. Split capital investment trusts and investment vehicles whose price is a direct derivation of underlying holdings, however, are excluded from consideration.

BACKGROUND

The FT/S&P Actuaries World Index was co-founded by the *Financial Times*, Goldman Sachs & Co. and Natwest Securities Ltd. in conjunction with the Institute of Actuaries and the Faculty of Actuaries. In 1995, Standard & Poor's replaced Natwest Securities. Following a transition period, the *Financial Times* and S&P will jointly calculate the index.

Launched in 1987 with about 2,400 companies from 23 countries, the index has been expanded with the addition of Finland in 1987 and Thailand and Brazil in November 1994. The index has been recalculated back to December 31, 1985. It is published on a daily basis, on any weekday when one or more of its constituent markets is open for trading, at approximately 21:30 London Time

BASE DATE

December 31, 1986=100.00

Continued on next page

COMPUTATION METHODOLOGY

(1) Aggregate market value weighted arithmetic average of the price ratios index formula is used. Maintenance adjustments to the divisor are made daily for capitalization changes, new listings and delistings. Individual country indices are calculated in local currency. Composite indices for regional areas and the world are calculated as the weighted average performance of countries within a region or the world, using common currencies which include U.S. dollars, Pound Sterling, Japanese Yen and German Deutsch Marks. (2) Additions and deletions, which are either implemented immediately or, more likely at the next quarter end, are made to reflect changes in the composition of the investable universe or economic sectors, relative importance of constituent and non-constituent companies, levels of market representation due to market events, availability of a new eligible security whose total market capitalization is 1% or more of the current capitalization of the relevant index and is greater than the large company cut-off, creation of a new company as a result of an existing constituent's spin-off to existing shareholders as well as changes in circumstances regarding a constituent's investability and free float. (3) Companies are deleted immediately due to mergers or acquisitions and may be replaced prior to quarter end by the purchasing company provided the company is eligible under the selection guidelines. (4) Suspended stocks are considered for deletion after an interval of 10 days, and are written down to the lowest unit of currency in that market on the day prior to deletion. (5) New countries are added to the index at the end of a calendar year. (6) The market capitalization of securities subject to partial restrictions on foreign ownership is computed on the basis of that portion which is available to foreign investors. With some exceptions for securities with existing free float of more than 10%, the full market capitalization of a security is eligible for inclusion in the index, however, 25% or more of the security must be publicly available for investment and is not in the hands of a single party or parties "acting in concert." A government's share ownership is included in this total if these holdings have a stock exchange listing and could be offered to the public. Two or more identifiable holders of more than 75% of a single security may be deemed to be acting in concert unless evidence is available to the contrary. Consideration is also given to the impact on investability due to "strategic" foreign holdings, which may serve to reduce the investability weight or lead to a company being excluded from consideration. (7) The index is normally computed using closing mid-market or last trade prices. With regard to Mexico, closing prices are unavailable at the normal transmission time from New York. Consequently, there is a one-day lag in Mexican data and calculations. (8) Exchange rates, using WM/Reuters Sport Rates, are collected at approximately 17 hours London Time. (9) Up-to-date indicated annualized dividend rates, adjusted for any interim changes and updated for any firm and precise forecasts are used, on a daily prorated basis, for total rate of return calculations. All dividends are grossed-up by each country's corporation tax rate. (10) The index is recalculated in the event of errors or distortions that are deemed to be significant, generally on the order of 25 basis points for a country index and 10 basis points for the world index.

DERIVATIVE INSTRUMENTS

Country Baskets Index Fund, Inc. series of shares for Australia, France, Germany, Hong Kong, Italy, Japan, South Africa, the United Kingdom and the United States trade on the New York Stock Exchange (NYSE).

SUBINDICES

FT-Actuaries World Index–Large Companies
FT-Actuaries World Index–Medium Small Companies
Currency subindices: Local currency, U.S. dollar terms and UK pound sterling.
Regional and special areas indices: Americas, Europe, Nordic countries, Pacific Basin, Euro-Pacific, and North America, Europe ex-UK, Pacific ex UK World ex-US, World ex-UK and World ex-Japan, Europe ex-UK, Pacific ex UK, World ex-US, World ex-UK and World ex-Japan.
National indices: Australia, Austria, Belgium, Brazil, Canada, Denmark, Finland, France, Germany, Hong Kong, Ireland, Italy, Japan, Malaysia, Mexico, The Netherlands, New Zealand, Norway, Singapore, South Africa, Spain, Sweden, Switzerland, Thailand, United Kingdom, and the United States.
Seven economic sector subindices: Basic industries, capital goods, consumer goods/services, energy, financing, insurance and real estate, transportation and storage, and utilities
Thirty-six industry subgroup indices and 97 subsector indices. Subgroup indices are: Commercial banks and other banks, financial institutions and services, life/agents and brokers insurance, multiline/property and casualty insurance, real estate, diversified holding companies, oil, other energy, utilities, transportation and storage, automobiles, household durables and appliances, textiles and wearing apparel, beverage industries/tobacco manufacturers, health and personal care, food and grocery products, entertainment/leisure time/toys. media, business services and computer software, retail trade, wholesale trade, diversified consumer goods/services, aerospace/defense, computers, telecommunications, equipment and office equipment, electrical equipment, electronics and instrumentation/control equipment, machinery and engineering services, heavy engineering and shipbuilding, auto components, diversified industrial (manufacturing), construction and building materials, chemicals, mining, metal and minerals, precious metals and minerals, forestry and paper products and fabricated metal products.

RELATED INDICES

Refer to Appendix 5 for indices published by the Financial Times, Goldman Sachs and Standard & Poor's.

REMARKS

(1) FT-Actuaries World Index market weights as of December 31, 1995 are, as follows: North America/Latin America-U.S.41.8%, Canada 1.4%, Mexico 0.3%, Brazil 0.4%; Europe-Austria 0.1%, Belgium 0.7%, Denmark 0.3%, Finland 0.3%, France 3.2%, Germany 3.4%, Ireland 0.2%, Italy 1.2%, The Netherlands 2.0%, Norway 0.2%, Spain 1.0%, Sweden 1.1%, Switzerland 2.8%, United Kingdom 9.3%; Pacific-Australia 1.4%, Hong Kong 1.9%, Japan 24.1%, Malaysia 1.0%, New Zealand 0.2%, Singapore 0.5%, Thailand 0.2%; Africa-South Africa 1.2%. (2) In addition to the subindices noted above, FT/S&P offers the flexibility to create customized indices and portfolios. (3) FT-Actuaries World Index-Large Companies and Medium-Small Companies subindices consist, within each country, of companies that make up the top 75% and the bottom 25%, respectively. Each of these subindices, rebalanced twice a year in March and September, are also calculated for the seven sector and 36 industry groups. (4) FT-SE International was established by the *Financial Times* and the London Stock Exchange in 1995 to manage and develop the FT-SE and FT-Actuaries indices. Responsibility for the FT/S&P Actuaries World Index, which is jointly co-published by the Financial Times Ltd., Goldman Sachs & Co. and Standard and Poor's, is scheduled for 1996

PUBLISHER

Financial Times Ltd., Goldman Sachs & Co. and Standard & Poor's.

ING BARINGS EMERGING MARKETS WORLD INDEX (BEMI)

PRICE PERFORMANCE

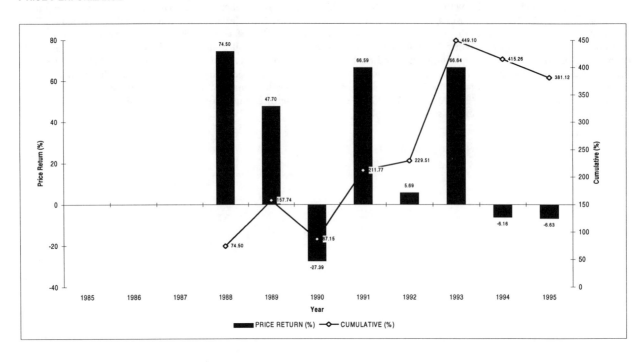

PRICE PERFORMANCE (US$)

YEAR	VALUE	PRICE RETURN (%)	CUMULATIVE (%)	MAXIMUM VALUE[1]	DATE	MINIMUM VALUE[1]	DATE
1995	147.56	-6.63	381.12	158.07	2-Jan	117.15	10-Mar
1994	158.03	-6.16	415.26	191.79	26-Sep	141.65	21-Apr
1993	168.41	66.64	449.10	168.41	31-Dec	99.81	4-Feb
1992	101.06	5.69	229.51	112.80	31-Mar	93.81	30-Sep
1991	95.62	66.59	211.77	NA	NA	NA	NA
1990	57.40	-27.39	87.15	NA	NA	NA	NA
1989	79.05	47.70	157.74	NA	NA	NA	NA
1988	53.52	74.50	74.50	NA	NA	NA	NA
1987	30.67						
1986							
1985							
Average Annual (%)		27.62					
Compound Annual (%)		21.70					
Standard Deviation (%)		40.47					

[1] Maximum/minimum index values for 1992 are as of quarter-end. Based on London closing prices.

SYNOPSIS

The ING Barings Emerging Markets World Index (BEMI) is a market capitalization-weighted index that tracks the twice daily price only and total return performance of an investable universe of global emerging markets in Asia, Europe and Latin America. The 18 countries included: Argentina, Brazil, Chile, China, Colombia, Greece, Indonesia, Korea, Malaysia, Mexico, Pakistan, Peru, Philippines, Portugal, South Africa, Taiwan, Thailand and Turkey.

NUMBER OF STOCKS—DECEMBER 31, 1995
396

MARKET VALUE—DECEMBER 31, 1995
US$192,300.0 million

SELECTION CRITERIA

Country inclusion is based upon Barings' definition of an emerging market. A country must satisfy three conditions: (1) Have a minimum GDP per capita of US$400.0 and a maximum level of about US$10,000.0. (2) Have an open stock market with a minimum of 100 listed companies. (3) A minimum market trading value of US$2,000.0 million, achieved in at least one of the last three years.

Constituents are selected on the basis of their availability to foreign investors, market capitalization, daily turnover and free-float. More specifically, stocks must meet a one year seasoning requirement, except for privatization issues which must still meet the other conditions for eligibility, they must have a market capitalization greater than 1% of the Baring Securities database for that country, except shares that rank first or second in their industry sector may be included if they have a minimum capitalization of 0.5%, a minimum free float of 10% and a minimum average daily trading value of US$100,000.0 confirmed on the basis of trading patterns reviewed over the course of the year.

BACKGROUND

Designed to create a measure of foreign institutional investability, BEMI was launched in October 1992. It was established with a base value of 100.00 as of July 1, 1992 and backdated to December 31, 1987. When first launched, the index consisted of 12 qualifying emerging markets with a population of 206 companies. Pakistan, Peru and Venezuela were each added during the 1994 calendar year. China and Colombia were subsequently added.

BASE DATE

July 1, 1992=100.00

COMPUTATION METHODOLOGY

(1) Aggregate market value weighted-arithmetic average of the price ratios Paasche index formula is used. Maintenance adjustments to the divisor are made for capitalization changes, new listings and delistings. Additions and deletions of constituent stocks, other than as a result of a Recomposition Committee meeting, are implemented on the last day of the month. (2) Market capitalization is calculated on the basis of each company's available free float to foreign investors, which is normally updated annually. (3) The composition of the index is reviewed and rebalanced on a quarterly basis. A Recomposition Committee posts the results of the recomposition meetings two weeks in advance of implementing any changes, which become effective on the last day of the month. (4) The long-term stability and continuity of the index is maintained in the event that a country exceeds the index criteria by expanding the index so that it may be calculated both with and without the ineligible constituent country. (5) The index is computed using closing prices that coincide with the London time zone such that Latin American closing share prices are as of the prior day. A second BEMI closing price, based on 4 PM New York Time, was introduced in 1995. (6) All daily share prices are converted to U.S. dollars using WM/Reuters Closing Spot Rates as of 4 PM London Time. (7) Total rates of return are calculated daily at month-end.

DERIVATIVE INSTRUMENTS

None

SUBINDICES

Various regional indices: Asia, Europe and Latin America.
A number of standalone country indices, that have either exceeded BEMI country criteria or have not yet met the criteria: India, Jordan and Poland.
Extended BEMI, including the three additional ineligible countries.
Two equal-weighted BEMI indices are calculated, one is rebalanced quarterly and a second is rebalanced annually.
Eleven sector indices: Agriculture/food, basic materials, capital equipment, consumer goods, energy, financial, multi-industry, real estate/property, services, transport and utilities.

RELATED INDICES

Barings Asian Convertible Bond Index
Barings Pan Asia Index
Baring Special Eastern Europe Index

REMARKS

(1) ING Barings offers the flexibility to created customized or modified indices, including use of standalone indices to create customized benchmarks. (2) BEMI market weights on the basis of available capitalization as of December 31, 1995 are, as follows: Europe-Greece 1.37%, Portugal 1.78%, Turkey 1.17%; Latin America-Argentina 5.56%, Brazil 13.78%, Chile 5.80%, Colombia 0.86%, Mexico 9.52%, Peru 2.32%; Asia/Pacific-China 1.21%, Indonesia 5.49%, Korea 4.97%, Malaysia 13.20%, Pakistan 0.39%, Philippines 3.04%, Taiwan 6.35%, Thailand 7.61%; Africa-South Africa-15.58%.

PUBLISHER

ING Baring Securities Limited.

INTERNATIONAL FINANCE CORPORATION (IFC) GLOBAL INDEX

PRICE PERFORMANCE

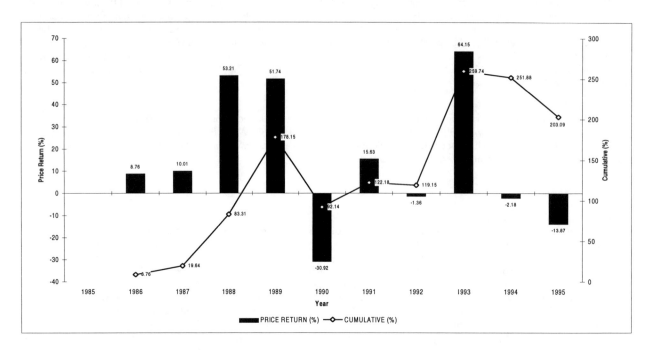

PRICE AND TOTAL RETURN PERFORMANCE (US$)

YEAR	VALUE	PRICE RETURN (%)	CUMULATIVE (%)	TOTAL RETURN (%)	MAXIMUM VALUE[1]	DATE	MINIMUM VALUE[1]	DATE
1995	370.40	-13.87	203.09	-12.32	397.45	31-Jul	351.86	15-Nov
1994	430.00	-2.18	251.88	-0.50	511.90	23-Sep	410.90	6-May
1993	439.60	64.15	259.74	67.50	393.98	31-Dec	267.02	31-Jan
1992	267.80	-1.36	119.15	0.30	305.67	31-Mar	254.51	30-Sep
1991	271.50	15.63	122.18	17.60	271.52	31-Dec	225.47	31-Jan
1990	234.80	-30.92	92.14	-29.90	380.19	31-Jan	205.72	30-Sep
1989	339.90	51.74	178.15	54.70	340.67	30-Sep	238.97	31-Jan
1988	224.00	53.21	83.31	58.20	255.86	30-Sep	160.63	31-Jan
1987	146.20	10.01	19.64	13.50	227.37	30-Sep	133.09	31-Jan
1986	132.90	8.76	8.76	12.80	150.72	31-May	119.62	31-Jan
1985	122.20							
Average Annual (%)		15.52		18.19				
Compound Annual (%)		11.73		14.24				
Standard Deviation (%)		31.26		32.20				

[1]Maximum/minmum index values for the calendar years 1986-1993 are as of month-end.

SYNOPSIS
The International Finance Corporation (IFC) Global Index is a market value-weighted index that tracks the daily price only and total return performance of common stocks and other such securities in emerging markets domiciled in 27 countries. The index targets 60% to 75% of the total market capitalization of all shares listed on the local stock exchange.

NUMBER OF STOCKS—DECEMBER 31, 1995
1,590

MARKET VALUE—DECEMBER 31, 1995
US$1,084,602.0 million

SELECTION CRITERIA
Country inclusion is based upon IFC's definition of an emerging market which represents any stock market located in a developing country. Using the World Bank's GNP per capita criterion, a developing country is one with a per capita GNP level of US$8,956.0 or less based on 1994 data. (See Remarks for market weights.) There is no predetermined criteria for selecting an emerging market. Most have had at least 30-50 listed companies with a market capitalization of US$1,000.0 million or more and annual value traded of US$100.0 million or more.

Selection is based on the following, which is reviewed for implementation by an Advisory Panel of experts:
(1) With some exceptions, companies listing stocks must be legally domiciled in their home markets. (2) Eligible securities include common and preferred stocks, participation certificates and other such securities that represent an equity interest in a qualified

company, regardless of voting status. (3) Constituents represent the most actively traded shares, based on frequency of trading, trading value during the course of the year and prospects for continued trading. Using the trading criteria, stocks are selected until market capitalization coverage reaches the target of 60% to 75% of the local total market capitalization. The IFC index may fall below the targeted range in some markets which include listed mutual funds, investment trusts and unlisted classes of shares in the definition of market capitalization. (4) Industry diversification may influence selection of constituents, particularly if several stocks meet the liquidity and size criteria. Investment trusts, unit trusts, mutual funds and closed-end funds are not eligible for inclusion.

BACKGROUND

Initiated in mid-1981 with historical data to December 1975, the original IFC series of indices were based on the 10-20 most active stocks in each of 10 emerging markets. The index was equal-weighted and calculated once a year, using month-end prices. In late 1985, the IFC decided to implement substantial modifications wich were implemented as of January 1987, using a base date of December 1984. A capitalization-weighted calculation methodology was adopted, frequency of calculation was accelerated to monthly, the timelines of calculation was improved and the number of markets was expanded to 17, stock coverage was increased and regional indices for Latin America and Asia were introduced. Beginning in 1988, frequency of calculation was advanced to weekly. By that time, market coverage had been expanded to 20 markets. Between 1988 and 1992, the IFC expanded stock coverage by adding the number of data variables available for each stock and introducing a detailed series of industry and sector subindices.

In March 1993, the IFC introduced a new, companion set of indices, designed to serve as additional benchmarks for international portfolio managers by limiting coverage to an investable universe of securities. IFC introduced three tradable indices in 1994, including the IFC100, Asia50 and Latin50. IFC commenced daily calculation of its IFCG and IFCI indices in the fall of 1995 and, in January 1996, adjustments for cross-holding of shares was implemented. Monthly indices are available from the end of 1975, weekly indices from the end of 1988 and daily values as of December 1995.

BASE DATE

December 31,1984=100.00

COMPUTATION METHODOLOGY

(1) Aggregate market value weighted arithmetic average of the price ratios Paasche index formula is used. Maintenance adjustments to the divisor are made daily for capitalization changes, new listings and delistings. The index is calculated in local currency and U.S. dollar terms. (2) The index is computed using the last transaction price recorded on the "main board" of the local stock exchange. The last transaction price is carried forward in the event a stock did not trade on the index calculation date. (3) Market capitalization is determined on the basis of number of shares outstanding. Both shares issued and outstanding are used and are differentiated by class or series if a constituent company's share capital is denominated in different classes or series. As such, only the selected share class is included in the index. Constituent stocks are adjusted for cross-holding conditions (effective January 1996) by adjusting downward the market capitalization of "owner stocks" based on the value of the cross-owned stock that is circulating and not held by other companies. (4) Constituents are not adjusted on the basis of float conditions. (5) Cash dividends are recorded on the ex-dividend date, using gross cash dividends. (6) Markets and constituents are reviewed on an annual basis. Stocks may be added in advance due to an initial public offering of significant size (i.e., 10% or more of index capitalization) that is likely to satisfy the liquidity criteria. Additions are recorded at the first closing transaction price at the addition date. Also, deletions due to delistings, suspensions or corporate mergers take effect at the time of delistings at the last recorded transaction price. In the event of bankruptcy, stocks are deemed to have a value of 1/1000 of the national currency unit. (7) Since October 1994, WM/Reuters Closing Spot Rates as of 4 PM London Time are used for currency conversions. (8) Corrected pricing information or other data are entered upon receipt. Changes to index results of 0.5% or more from the last reported level are publicly announced.

DERIVATIVE INSTRUMENTS
None

SUBINDICES

IFC Investable Index   IFC100 Index   Asia50 Index   Latin50 Index

Individual country indices and markets: East Asia, South Asia, Europe/Mideast/Africa, and Latin America.

Regional indices: Latin America, Asia, Europe, Mideast and Africa (EMEA).

Nine sector subindices on a composite index basis: Agriculture, construction, manufacturing, transportation/communications and utility, wholesale/retail trade, finance/insurance/real estate, services and other/diversified holding companies.

Twenty-three industry subindices: Metal mining, general building contractors, food and kindred products, textile mill products, apparel and other textile products, paper and allied products, chemical and allied products, petroleum refining and related products, rubber and miscellaneous, plastics products, cement and glass product, primary metal industries, fabricated metal industries, fabricated metal products, electric and electronic equipment, transportation equipment, miscellaneous manufacturing, water transportation, communications, electric, gas or sanitary services, banking, credit agencies other than banks, security and commodity brokers, insurance and hotels and other lodging places.

RELATED INDICES
None

REMARKS

(1) IFC market weights as of December 31, 1995: Latin America-Argentina 2.0%, Brazil 8.7%, Chile 4.4%, Colombia 0.8%, Mexico 5.6%, Peru 0.7%, Venezuela 0.2%; East Asia-China 2.3%, Korea 11.4%, Philippines 2.9%, Taiwan 10.4%; South Asia-India 5.3%, Indonesia 3.5%, Malaysia 13.1%, Pakistan 0.6%, Sri-Lanka 0.1%, Thailand 8.8%; Europe/Mideast/Africa-Czech Republic 0%, Greece 0.9%, Hungary 0.1%, Jordan 0.3%, Nigeria 0.1%, Poland 0.2%, Portugal 1%, South Africa 15%, Turkey 1.3%, Zimbabwe 0.1%. (2) The composite index includes constituents of all IFC market indices, but there may be delays between the introduction of a new market and its inclusion. (3) One company's shares may be substituted for another with similar trading characteristics.

PUBLISHER

International Finance Corporation (IFC).

INTERNATIONAL FINANCE CORPORATION (IFC) INVESTABLE INDEX

PRICE PERFORMANCE

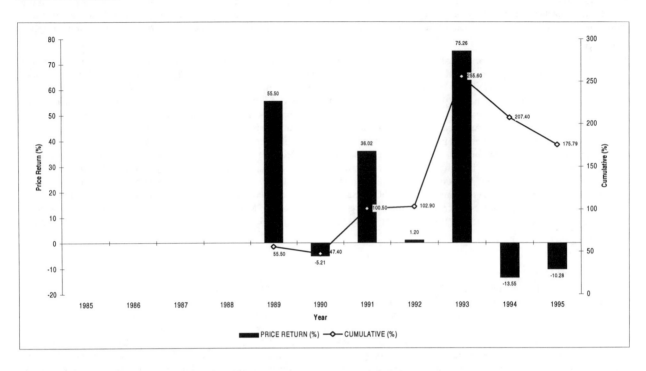

PRICE AND TOTAL RETURN PERFORMANCE (US$)

YEAR	VALUE	PRICE RETURN (%)	CUMULATIVE (%)	TOTAL RETURN (%)	MAXIMUM VALUE[1]	DATE	MINIMUM VALUE[1]	DATE
1995	275.79	-10.28	175.79	-8.40	280.6	31-Jul	261.37	31-Mar
1994	307.40	-13.55	207.40	-12.00	NA	NA	NA	NA
1993	355.60	75.26	255.60	79.60	NA	NA	NA	NA
1992	202.90	1.20	102.90	3.30	NA	NA	NA	NA
1991	200.50	36.02	100.50	39.50	NA	NA	NA	NA
1990	147.40	-5.21	47.40	-2.20	NA	NA	NA	NA
1989	155.50	55.50	55.50	61.50	NA	NA	NA	NA
1988	100.00							
1987								
1986								
1985								
Average Annual (%)		13.89		16.13				
Compound Annual (%)		10.68		12.66				
Standard Deviation (%)		35.60		36.95				

[1]Maximum/minimum index values for 1995 are as of month-end.

SYNOPSIS
The International Finance Corporation (IFC) Investable Index is a market value weighted index that tracks the daily stock price and total return performance of investable emerging market equity securities domiciled in 26 countries in Europe, Middle East, Africa and Latin America that are available for purchase by foreign institutional investors.

NUMBER OF STOCKS—DECEMBER 31, 1995
1,136

MARKET VALUE—DECEMBER 31, 1995
US$605,550.90 million

SELECTION CRITERIA
Country inclusion is based upon IFC's definition of an emerging market, which represents any stock market located in a developing country. Using the World Bank's GNP per capita criterion, a developing country is one with a per capita GNP level of US$ 8,625.0 or less based on 1993 data. (See Remarks for market weights.) There is no predetermined criteria for selecting an emerging market. Most have had at least 30- to 50-listed companies with a market capitalization of US$1,000.0 million or more and annual value traded of US$100.0 million or more.

Constituents are selected on the following guidelines which are reviewed by an Advisory Panel of experts:

(1) With some exceptions, companies listing stocks must be legally domiciled in their home markets. (2) Eligible securities include common stocks, preferred stocks, participation certificates and other such securities that represent an equity interest in a qualified company, regardless of voting status. Investment trusts, unit trusts, mutual funds and closed-end funds are not eligible. (3) Stocks are selected on the basis of the ability of foreign institutions to buy and sell shares at the local stock exchange and repatriate capital gains and dividend income without undue constraint. For each security, IFC creates a "degree open factor" with a value from zero to one which indicates the amount of the security foreigners may legally own due to any corporate by-law, corporate charter, industry limitations on foreign ownership, the amount of company capital a single foreign investor may hold and separate limits on the amount that such an investor may hold collectively. In addition, each stock must have an average minimum investable market capitalization of US$25.0 million for a 12-month period prior to inclusion and must trade at least US$10.0 million over the prior year. A number of exceptions may apply, however, including cases involving smaller, less liquid emerging markets in which few, if any, stocks will qualify. In such cases, IFC calculates an index based on the five most liquid shares open to foreign investors. (4) Industry diversification may influence the selection of constituent stocks.

BACKGROUND
The index was created in late 1992 and introduced in March 1993. For additional information, refer to the IFC Global Index.

BASE DATE
December 31, 1988=100.00

COMPUTATION METHODOLOGY
(1) Aggregate market value-weighted arithmetic average of the price ratios Paasche index formula is used. Maintenance adjustments to the divisor are made daily for capitalization changes, new listings and delistings. The index is calculated in local currency and U.S. dollar terms. (2) The index is computed using the last transaction price recorded on the "main board" of the local stock exchange. The last transaction price is carried forward in the event a stock did not trade on the index calculation date. (3) Market capitalization is determined on the basis of the number of shares outstanding, adjusted by its degree open factor. For example, if national law restricts foreign portfolio investment to an aggregate of 10% of a company's outstanding shares, then the degree of open factor is 0.10 and only 10% of the company's market capitalization is taken into consideration in the computation. Both shares issued and shares outstanding are used and these are differentiated by class or series if a constituent company's share capital is denominated in different classes or series. As such, only the selected share class is included in the index. (4) Cash dividends are recorded on the ex-dividend date, using gross cash dividends. (5) Markets and constituent stocks are reviewed on an annual basis, including changes in investability status. Stocks may be added to the index in advance, however, due to an initial public offering of significant size (i.e., 10% or more of the IFC index capitalization) that at the same time is likely to satisfy the liquidity criteria. Also, deletions due to failure to satisfy minimum size and liquidity conditions, declines in failure to delistings, suspensions or corporate mergers take effect at the time of such delistings. (6) Additions are recorded at the first closing transaction price at the addition date. Also, deletions due to delistings, suspensions or corporate mergers take effect at the time of such delistings at the last recorded transaction price. In the event of bankruptcy, stocks are deemed to have a value of 1/1000 of the national currency unit. (7) Since October 1994, WM/Reuters Closing Spot Rates as of 4 PM London Time are used for currency conversions. (8) Corrected pricing information or other data are entered upon receipt. Changes to index results of 0.5% or more from the last level are publicly announced.

DERIVATIVE INSTRUMENTS
None

SUBINDICES
IFC100 Index	Asia50 Index	Latin50 Index

Individual country indices and markets: East Asia, South Asia, Europe/Mideast/Africa, and Latin America.
Regional indices: Latin America, Asia, Europe, Mideast and Africa (EMEA).
Nine sector subindices on a composite index basis: Agriculture, construction, manufacturing, transportation/communications and utility, wholesale/retail trade, finance/insurance/real estate, services and other/diversified holding companies.
Twenty-three industry subindices: Metal mining, general building contractors, food and kindred products, textile mill products, apparel and other textile products, paper and allied products, chemical and allied products, petroleum refining and related products, rubber and miscellaneous, plastics products, cement and glass product, primary metal industries, fabricated metal industries, fabricated metal products, electric and electronic equipment, transportation equipment, miscellaneous manufacturing, water transportation, communications, electric, gas or sanitary services, banking, credit agencies other than banks, security and commodity brokers, insurance and hotels and other lodging places.

RELATED INDICES
IFC Global Index

REMARKS
(1) Market weights as of December 31, 1995: Latin America-Argentina 3.6%, Brazil 10.5%, Chile 1.9%, Colombia 1.3%, Mexico 9.2%, Peru 1.1%, Venezuela 0.4%; East Asia-China 0.3%, Korea 2.8%, Philippines 2.8%, Taiwan 2.8%; South Asia-India 2.2%, Indonesia 3.2%, Malaysia 19.7%, Pakistan 0.8%, Sri-Lanka 0.1%, Thailand 4.7%; Europe/Mideast/Africa-Czech Republic 0%, Greece 1.6%, Hungary 0.1%, Jordan 0.2%, Nigeria 0%, Poland 0.3%, Portugal 1.4%, South Africa 26.7%, Turkey 2.3%, Zimbabwe 0%. (2) The composite index includes the constituents of all IFC market indices, but there may be some delays between the introduction of a new market and its inclusion. (3) One company's shares may be substituted for another with similar trading characteristics.

PUBLISHER
International Finance Corporation (IFC).

INTERNATIONAL FINANCE CORPORATION (IFC) TRADEABLE ASIA50 INDEX

PRICE PERFORMANCE

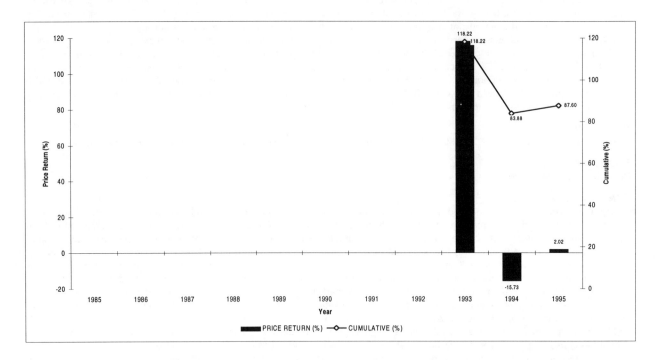

PRICE PERFORMANCE (US$)

YEAR	VALUE	PRICE RETURN (%)	CUMULATIVE (%)	MAXIMUM VALUE	DATE	MINIMUM VALUE	DATE
1995	1,875.98	2.02	87.60	2,123.19	5-Jun	1,554.22	24-Jan
1994	1,838.84	-15.73	83.88	2,276.23	5-Jan	1,605.14	4-Apr
1993	2,182.17	118.22	118.22	2,182.17	31-Dec	987.58	13-Jan
1992	1,000.00						
1991							
1990							
1989							
1988							
1987							
1986							
1985							
Average Annual (%)		34.83					
Compound Annual (%)		23.33					
Standard Deviation (%)		72.75					

SYNOPSIS

The International Finance Corporation (IFC) Tradeable Asia50 Index is a tradeable, market value-weighted index that tracks the daily stock price only performance of the largest and most liquid emerging market equity securities domiciled in eight markets in Asia that are available for purchase by foreign institutional investors. Markets include Korea, Taiwan, India, Indonesia, Korea, Malaysia, Philippines and Thailand.

NUMBER OF STOCKS—DECEMBER 31, 1995

50

MARKET VALUE—DECEMBER 31, 1995

US$94,107.0 million

SELECTION CRITERIA

Index constituents are selected from the universe of stocks that are eligible for inclusion in the IFC Investable Index on the basis of the following guidelines:
(1) Trading on over 95% of the local stock exchange's total trading days in the previous year. (2) A minimum trading value of US$5.0 million per month for at least 11 months in the preceding year, and a minimum total trading value of US$100.0 million for the year. (3) A minimum average investable market capitalization of US$200.0 million in the previous year.

Qualifying Asian stocks are ranked on the basis of total value traded. The top 50 stocks are selected as index constituents.

For additional information, refer to the IFC Global and Investable indices.

BACKGROUND

The index was created in 1994 to serve as an underlying investment vehicle for derivative products that are scheduled for introduction in the future.

BASE DATE

December 31, 1993=1,000.00

COMPUTATION METHODOLOGY

(1) Aggregate market value-weighted arithmetic average of the price ratios Paasche index formula is used. Maintenance adjustments to the divisor are made daily for capitalization changes, new listings and delistings. The index is calculated in local currency and U.S. dollar terms. (2) The index is computed using the last transaction price recorded on the "main board" of the local stock exchange. The last transaction price is carried forward in the event a stock did not trade on the index calculation date. (3) Market capitalization is determined on the basis of the number of shares outstanding, adjusted by its degree open factor. For example, if national law restricts foreign portfolio investment to an aggregate of 10% of a company's outstanding shares, then the degree of open factor is 0.10 and only 10% of the company's market capitalization is taken into consideration in the computation of the index. Both shares issued and shares outstanding are used and these are differentiated by class or series if a constituent company's share capital is denominated in different classes or series. As such, only the selected share class is included in the index. (4) Markets and constituent stocks are reviewed on an annual basis, including changes in investability status, and a new universe of index constituents takes effect on April 1 of each year. The previous year's universe of index constituents is ranked on the basis of market capitalization and the bottom 10% of stocks are eligible for replacement, including any stocks that no longer satisfy minimum size and liquidity conditions. (5) WM/Reuters Closing Spot Rates as of 4 PM London Time are used for currency conversions. (6) Corrected pricing information or other securities data are entered into the database upon receipt. Changes to index results of 0.5% or more form the last reported index level are publicly announced.

DERIVATIVE INSTRUMENTS

None

SUBINDICES

None

RELATED INDICES

IFC Global Index
IFC Investable Index

REMARKS

(1) Total rates of return are not calculated at the present time. (2) Asia50 market weights as of April 16, 1996 (market capitalization=US$116,281.8 million) are, as follows: China 9.18%, India 0.61%, Indonesia 2.79%, Korea 6.01%, Malaysia 59.82%, Philippines 8.0% and Thailand 13.59%.

PUBLISHER

International Finance Corporation (IFC).

INTERNATIONAL FINANCE CORPORATION (IFC) TRADEABLE LATIN50 INDEX

PRICE PERFORMANCE

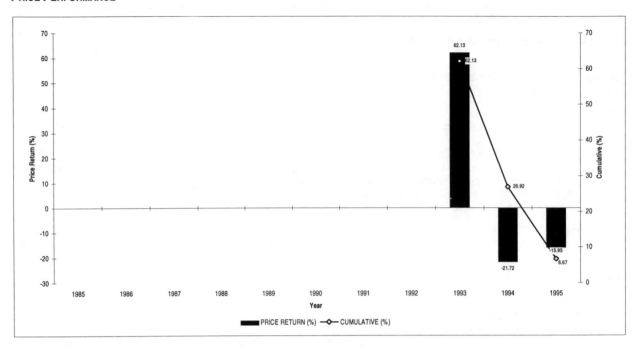

PRICE PERFORMANCE (US$)

YEAR	VALUE	PRICE RETURN (%)	CUMULATIVE (%)	MAXIMUM VALUE	DATE	MINIMUM VALUE	DATE
1995	1,066.68	-15.95	6.67	1,262.74	2-Jan	619.95	9-Mar
1994	1,269.17	-21.72	26.92	1,937.52	14-Feb	1,133.86	27-Dec
1993	1,621.27	62.13	62.13	1,621.27	31-Dec	922.24	24-Feb
1992	1,000.00						
1991							
1990							
1989							
1988							
1987							
1986							
1985							
Average Annual (%)		8.15					
Compound Annual (%)		2.18					
Standard Deviation (%)		46.83					

SYNOPSIS

The International Finance Corporation (IFC) Tradeable Latin50 Index is a tradeable, market value-weighted index that tracks the daily stock price only performance of the largest and most liquid emerging market equity securities domiciled in seven markets in Latin America that are available for purchase by foreign institutional investors. Markets include Argentina, Brazil, Chile, Colombia, Mexico, Peru and Venezuela.

NUMBER OF STOCKS—DECEMBER 31, 1995
50

MARKET VALUE—DECEMBER 31, 1995
US$104,511.0 million

SELECTION CRITERIA

Index constituents are selected from the universe of stocks that are eligible for inclusion in the IFC Investable Index on the basis of the following guidelines:

(1) Trading on over 95% of the local stock exchange's total trading days in the previous year. (2) A minimum trading value of US$5.0 million per month for at least 11months in the preceding year, and a minimum total trading value of US$100.0 million for the year. (3) A minimum average investable market capitalization of US$200.0 million in the previous year.

Qualifying Latin American stocks are ranked on the basis of total value traded. The top 50 stocks are selected as index constituents.

For additional information, refer to the IFC Global and Investable indices.

BACKGROUND

The index was created in 1994 to serve as an underlying investment vehicle for derivative products that are scheduled for introduction in the future.

BASE DATE
December 31, 1993=1,000.00

COMPUTATION METHODOLOGY

(1) Aggregate market value-weighted arithmetic average of the price ratios Paasche index formula is used. Maintenance adjustments to the divisor are made daily for capitalization changes, new listings and delistings. The index is calculated in local currency and U.S. dollar terms. (2) The index is computed using the last transaction price recorded on the "main board" of the local stock exchange. The last transaction price is carried forward in the event a stock did not trade on the index calculation date. (3) Market capitalization is determined on the basis of the number of shares outstanding adjusted by its degree open factor. For example, if national law restricts foreign portfolio investment to an aggregate of 10% of a company's outstanding shares, then the degree of open factor is 0.10 and only 10% of the company's market capitalization is taken into consideration in the computation of the index. Both shares issued and shares outstanding are used and these are differentiated by class or series if a constituent company's share capital is denominated in different classes or series. As such, only the selected share class is included in the index. (4) Markets and constituent stocks are reviewed on an annual basis, including changes in investability status, and a new universe of index constituents takes effect on April 1 of each year. The previous year's universe of index constituents is ranked on the basis of market capitalization and the bottom 10% of stocks are eligible for replacement, including any stocks that no longer satisfy minimum size and liquidity conditions. (5) WM/Reuters Closing Spot Rates as of 4 PM London Time are used for currency conversions. (6) Corrected pricing information or other securities data are entered into the database upon receipt. Changes to index results of 0.5% or more form the last reported index level publicly announced.

DERIVATIVE INSTRUMENTS
None

SUBINDICES
None

RELATED INDICES
IFC Global Index
IFC Investable Index

REMARKS

(1) Total rates of return are not calculated at the present time. (2) Latin50 market weights as of April 16, 1996 (market capitalization=US$130975.3 million) are, as follows: Argentina 12.71%, Brazil 37.82%, Chile 12.60%, Colombia 0.39%, Mexico 34.18% and Peru 2.30%.

PUBLISHER
International Finance Corporation (IFC).

INTERNATIONAL FINANCE CORPORATION (IFC) TRADEABLE100 INDEX

PRICE PERFORMANCE

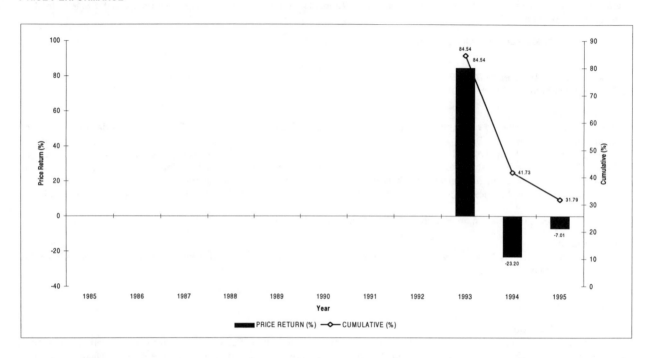

PRICE PERFORMANCE (US$)

YEAR	VALUE	PRICE RETURN (%)	CUMULATIVE (%)	MAXIMUM VALUE	DATE	MINIMUM VALUE	DATE
1995	1,317.89	-7.01	31.79	1,410.68	2-Jan	1,026.61	9-Mar
1994	1,417.29	-23.20	41.73	1,912.11	23-Sep	1,336.77	27-Dec
1993	1,845.37	84.54	84.54	1,845.37	31-Dec	968.83	2-Feb
1992	1,000.00						
1991							
1990							
1989							
1988							
1987							
1986							
1985							
Average Annual (%)		18.11					
Compound Annual (%)		9.64					
Standard Deviation (%)		58.09					

Synopsis

The International Finance Corporation (IFC) Tradeable100 Index is a tradeable, market value-weighted index that tracks the daily stock price only performance of the largest and most liquid emerging market equity securities domiciled in 14 markets in Asia, Europe and Latin America that are available for purchase by foreign institutional investors. Markets include Argentina, Brazil, Chile, India, Indonesia, Korea, Malaysia, Mexico, Peru, Taiwan, Philippines, Thailand, South Africa and Turkey.

Number of Stocks—December 31, 1995
100

Market Value—December 31, 1995
US$276,691.0 million

Selection Criteria
Index constituents are selected from the universe of stocks that are eligible for inclusion in the IFC Investable Index on the basis of the following guidelines:
(1) Trading on over 95% of the local stock exchange's total trading days in the previous year. (2) A minimum trading value of US$5.0 million per month for at least 11 months in the preceding year, and a minimum total trading value of US$100.0 million for the year. (3) A minimum average investable market capitalization of US$200.0 million in the previous year.
    Qualifying stocks are ranked on the basis of total value traded. The top 100 stocks are selected as index constituents.
    For additional information, refer to the IFC Global and Investable indices.

Background
The index was created in 1994 to serve as an underlying investment vehicle for derivative products that are scheduled for introduction in the future.

Base Date
December 31, 1993=1,000.00

Computation Methodology
(1) Aggregate market value-weighted arithmetic average of the price ratios Paasche index formula is used. Maintenance adjustments to the divisor are made daily for capitalization changes, new listings and delistings. The index is calculated in local currency and U.S. dollar terms. (2) The index is computed using the last transaction price recorded on the "main board" of the local stock exchange. The last transaction price is carried forward in the event a stock did not trade on the index calculation date. (3) Market capitalization is determined on the basis of the number of shares outstanding, adjusted by its degree open factor. For example, if national law restricts foreign portfolio investment to an aggregate of 10% of a company's outstanding shares, then the degree of open factor is 0.10 and only 10% of the company's market capitalization is taken into consideration in the computation of the index. Both shares issued and shares outstanding are used and these are differentiated by class or series if a constituent company's share capital is denominated in different classes or series. As such, only the selected share class is included in the index. (4) Markets and constituent stocks are reviewed on an annual basis, including changes in investability status, and a new universe of index constituents takes effect on April 1 of each year. The previous year's universe of index constituents is ranked on the basis of market capitalization and the bottom 10% of stocks are eligible for replacement, including any stocks that no longer satisfy minimum size and liquidity conditions. (5) WM/Reuters Closing Spot Rates as of 4 PM London Time are used for currency conversions. (6) Corrected pricing information or other securities data are entered into the database upon receipt. Changes to index results of 0.5% or more form the last reported index level publicly announced.

Derivative Instruments
None

Subindices
Asia50 Index
Latin50 Index

Related Indices
IFC Global Index
IFC Investable Index

Remarks
(1) The Asia50 Tradeable and Latin50 Tradeable indices are not pure subindices in that each index includes or excludes stocks that are tracked in the IFC Tradeable100 Index. (2) Total rates of return are not calculated at the present time. (3) IFC100 market weights as of April 16, 1996 (market capitalization=US$276,690.72 million) are, as follows: Turkey 1.15%, Argentina 6.25%, Brazil 11.85%, Chile 5.96%, Mexico 15.52%, Peru 1.09, China 3.86%, India 0.26%, Indonesia 0.25%, Korea 2.52%, Malaysia 23.21%, Philippines 2.73%, Thailand 5.63%, South Africa 19.71%.

Publisher
International Finance Corporation (IFC).

MORGAN STANLEY CAPITAL INTERNATIONAL (MSCI)
EMERGING MARKETS FREE GLOBAL INDEX

PRICE PERFORMANCE

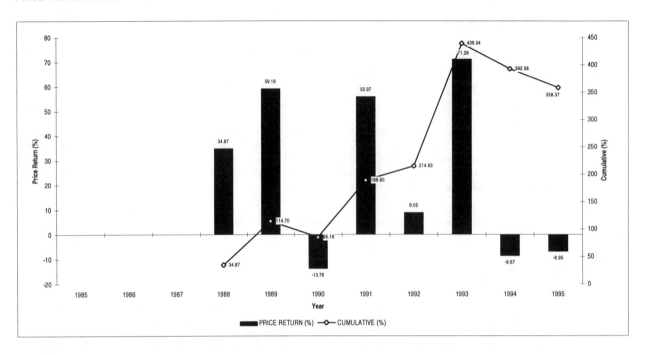

PRICE AND TOTAL RETURN PERFORMANCE (US$)

YEAR	VALUE	PRICE RETURN (%)	CUMULATIVE (%)	TOTAL RETURN (%)[1]	MAXIMUM VALUE	DATE	MINIMUM VALUE	DATE
1995	458.37	-6.95	358.37	-5.21	495.54	13-Jul	395.70	9-Mar
1994	492.58	-8.67	392.58	-7.32	587.11	16-Sep	453.77	9-May
1993	539.34	71.26	439.34	74.84	539.34	31-Dec	313.65	4-Jan
1992	314.93	9.05	214.93	11.40	353.79	17-Apr	285.65	24-Aug
1991	288.80	55.97	188.80	59.91	288.80	31-Dec	175.34	16-Jan
1990	185.16	-13.76	85.16	-10.55	257.37	1-Aug	178.96	30-Nov
1989	214.70	59.19	114.70	64.96	214.70	29-Dec	131.00	19-Jan
1988	134.87	34.87	34.87	40.43	138.26	9-Nov	99.84	4-Jan
1987	100.00							
1986								
1985								
Average Annual (%)		25.12		28.56				
Compound Annual (%)		20.96		24.22				
Standard Deviation %)		34.38		35.54				

[1]Total return based on reinvestment of gross dividends.

SYNOPSIS
The Morgan Stanley Capital International (MSCI) Emerging Markets Free Global Index is a market capitalization-weighted index that tracks the daily stock price and total return performance of unrestricted common stocks or ordinary shares of emerging markets domiciled in 22 countries generally open to foreign investment, in local currency and U.S. dollar terms. It aims to capture 60% of the total market capitalization at both the participating country and industry level. (See Remarks for market weights.).

NUMBER OF STOCKS—DECEMBER 31, 1995
890

MARKET VALUE—DECEMBER 31, 1995
US$690,000.0 million

SELECTION CRITERIA
An emerging market is defined on the basis of Gross Domestic Product (GDP) Per Capita, which is substantially below the average for developed economies. The average emerging market covered by the MSCI EMI has a GDP Per Capita of $3,100.0, versus an average of $20,535.0 for 21 developed markets covered by MSCI. The universe of constituents in each market is generally selected from the most actively traded exchanges. With exceptions, member securities are limited to common or ordinary shares. With regard to Mexico, Venezuela and the Philippines, constituents exclude companies and share classes closed to foreign investors, such as C shares of financial companies as well as other types of companies in Mexico, all companies except banks in Venezuela, B

shares and undifferentiated shares in the Philippines. Korea, which is liberalizing restrictions applicable to foreign investment, is included at 20% of its market capitalization. Taiwan is excluded in its entirety due to the severity of restrictions that apply to foreign investors. The following guidelines apply to selection: (1) Securities are selected on the basis of a dynamic optimization process which involves maximizing float and liquidity, reflecting accurately the market's size and industry profile and minimizing cross ownership. (2) To achieve a high level of tracking and accurately reflect country-wide performance and industry characteristics of each country's overall market, MSCI aims to capture 60% of the capitalization of each industry group, as defined by local practice. From the universe of available stocks in each industry group, stocks are selected up to approximately the 60% level, subject to liquidity, float and cross-ownership considerations. In addition, a stock may be assessed by sales, net income and industry output. Percent of coverage may deviate from this target. (3) Maximum liquidity is balanced using factors such as overall industry representation. Liquidity, measured by trading value as reported by the local exchange, is assessed over time based on an absolute as well as relative basis. While a hard-and-fast liquidity yardstick is not utilized, trading values are monitored to establish a "normal" level across short-term market peaks and troughs. (4) Maximum float, or the percentage of a company's shares freely tradable, is an optimization parameter but not a hard-and-fast rule. With exceptions, constituents are included at 100% of market capitalization. (5) Stocks with cross-ownership positions are avoided or minimized. (6) A representative sample of large, medium and small companies is included. (7) Maintains, country weights in regional and international indices reflective of the true size of the markets. Small and highly illiquid securities, non-domiciled companies and investment trusts are excluded.

BACKGROUND
In 1988, the index was expanded to include emerging markets. Covered initially were: Argentina, Brazil, Chile, Greece, Indonesia, Jordan, Korea, Malaysia, Mexico, Philippines, Portugal, Taiwan, Thailand and Turkey. This was expanded January 1, 1993 to include Columbia, India, Pakistan, Peru, Sri-Lanka and Venezuela. Israel, Poland and South Africa were added as of March 1, 1995.

BASE DATE
January 1, 1988=100.00

COMPUTATION METHODOLOGY
(1) Aggregate market value-weighted arithmetic average of the price ratios Laspeyres index formula is used. Maintenance adjustments to the divisor are made daily as they occur for capitalization changes, new listings and delistings. Individual country indices are calculated in local currency and converted to U.S. dollars. (2) Structural changes due to industry composition or regulations generally take place one year to 18 months. These are implemented yearly on the first business day in March, June, September and December and are announced at least two weeks in advance. (3) Companies may be deleted because they have diversified from their industry classification, the industry has evolved in a different direction from the company's thrust, or a better industry representative exists in the form of a new issue or existing company. (4) New issues generally undergo a "seasoning" period of one year to 18 months prior to eligibility. New issues due to an initial public offering of significant size that change a country's market and industry profiles, and generate strong investor interest likely to assure a high level of liquidity, may be included immediately. (5) The market capitalization of constituents is weighted on the basis of their full market value, i.e., without adjustments for "long term holdings" or partial foreign investment restrictions. To address the issue of restriction on foreign ownership, an additional series of "Free" indices are calculated for countries and markets with restrictions on foreign ownership of shares. (6) While exceptions apply, the index is computed using the last transaction price recorded on the dominant stock exchange in each market. (7) Exchange rates are taken daily at 4 PM London Time. Representative rates are selected for each currency based on a number of "snapshots" of the latest contributed quotations taken from the Reuters service at short intervals around 4 PM. WM/Reuters provide closing bid and offer rates which are used to calculate the mid-point to five decimal places. MSCI uses its own timing and sources for currency exchange rates in some Latin American countries. (8) Dividends are recognized on the ex-dividend date and factored into the return in the form of a dividend receivable. Dividends are deemed to be received on the payment date while the reinvestment of dividends occurs at the end of the month in which the payment date falls.

DERIVATIVE INSTRUMENTS
World Equity Benchmark Shares Foreign Fund, Inc. (WEBS) series of shares for Malaysia and Mexico (Free) trade on the AMEX.

SUBINDICES
Individual country, regional, international and combined indices for the Far East, Latin America and Asia.
Eight economic sectors: Energy, materials, capital equipment, consumer goods, services, finance, multi-industry and gold mines.
Thirty-eight industry group subindices: Energy sources, utilities-electric and gas, building materials and components, chemicals, forest products and paper, non-ferrous metals, steel, miscellaneous materials and commodities, aerospace and military technology, construction and housing, data processing and reproduction, electrical and electronics, electronic components-instruments, energy equipment and services, industrial components, machinery and engineering, appliances and household durables, automobiles, beverages and tobacco, food and household products, health and personal care, recreation and other consumer goods, textiles and apparel, broadcasting and publishing, business and public services, leisure and tourism, merchandising, telecommunications, transportation-airlines, transportation-road and rail, transportation-shipping, wholesale and international trade, banking, financial services, insurance, real estate, multi-industry and gold mines.

RELATED INDICES
MSCI Emerging Markets Global Index   MSCI World Index   Refer to Appendix 5 for additional indices.

REMARKS
(1) Index market weights as of December 31, 1995: Asia-India 5.8%, Indonesia 5.4%, Korea 3.3%, Malaysia 16.7%, Pakistan 0.6%, Philippines 3.0%, Sri-Lanka 0.2%, Taiwan 0.0%, Thailand 9.9%; Latin America-Argentina 3.8%, Brazil 11.2%, Chile 5.4%, Colombia 0.8%, Mexico 8.8%, Peru 1.3%, Venezuela 0.4%; Europe/Middle East-Greece 1.3%, Israel 2.8%, Jordan 0.2%, Poland 0.3%, Portugal 2.9%, Turkey 1.3%; Africa-South Africa 16.4%. (2) GDP based on The World Bank 1992, except Taiwan is on brokers' estimates.

PUBLISHER
Morgan Stanley Capital International (MSCI).

MORGAN STANLEY CAPITAL INTERNATIONAL (MSCI)
EMERGING MARKETS GLOBAL INDEX

PRICE PERFORMANCE

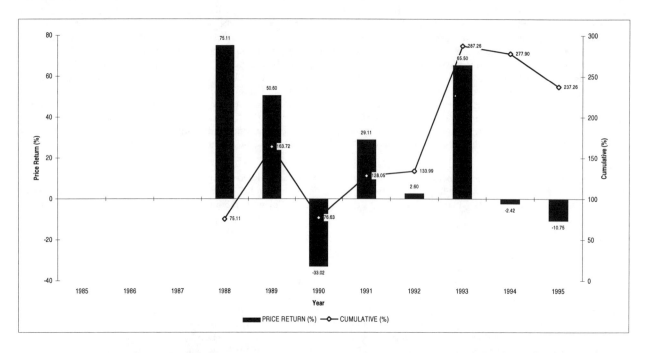

PRICE AND TOTAL RETURN PERFORMANCE (US$)

YEAR	VALUE	PRICE RETURN (%)	CUMULATIVE (%)	TOTAL RETURN (%)[1]	MAXIMUM VALUE	DATE	MINIMUM VALUE	DATE
1995	337.26	-10.75	237.26	-9.20	378.53	2-Jan	312.82	9-Mar
1994	377.90	-2.42	277.90	-1.07	433.25	19-Sep	341.25	20-Apr
1993	387.26	65.50	287.26	68.76	387.26	31-Dec	232.69	29-Jan
1992	233.99	2.60	133.99	4.56	263.02	24-Mar	213.01	23-Sep
1991	228.05	29.11	128.05	31.69	228.05	31-Dec	154.72	16-Jan
1990	176.63	-33.02	76.63	-31.45	301.92	9-Feb	155.55	1-Oct
1989	263.72	50.60	163.72	53.52	271.25	12-Oct	173.27	5-Jan
1988	175.11	75.11	75.11	79.08	202.02	26-Sep	99.95	4-Jan
1987	100.00							
1986								
1985								
Average Annual (%)		22.09		24.49				
Compound Annual (%)		16.41		18.67				
Standard Deviation (%)		39.01		39.91				

[1]Total return based on reinvestment of gross dividends.

SYNOPSIS

The Morgan Stanley Capital International (MSCI) Emerging Markets Global Index is a market capitalization-weighted index that tracks the daily stock price and total return performance of largely common stocks or ordinary shares in emerging markets domiciled in 23 countries regardless of restrictions on investment by foreigners, in local currency and U.S. dollar. The index aims to capture 60% of the total market capitalization at the participating country and industry level. (See Remarks for market weights).

NUMBER OF STOCKS—DECEMBER 31, 1995
977

MARKET VALUE—DECEMBER 31, 1995
US$893,000.0 million

SELECTION CRITERIA

An emerging market is defined on the basis of Gross Domestic Product (GDP) Per Capita, which is substantially below the average for developed economies. The average emerging market covered by the MSCI EMI has a GDP Per Capita of $3,100.0, versus an average of $20,535.0 for 21 developed markets covered by MSCI. The universe of constituents in each market is generally selected from the most actively traded exchanges and, with some exceptions, securities are limited to common or ordinary shares. Index constituents are selected on the basis of a dynamic optimization process which involves maximizing float and liquidity, reflecting accurately the market's character in terms of the size as measured by market capitalization, and industry representation so as to mirror the local market, and minimize cross-ownership. The following guidelines apply:

(1) To achieve a proper balance between a high level of tracking, liquidity and restricted float considerations, MSCI aims to capture 60% of each country's market capitalization. (2) To assure that the index reflects the industry characteristics of each country's overall market, MSCI aims to capture 60% of the capitalization of each industry group, as defined by local practice. From the universe of available stocks in each industry group, stocks are selected up to approximately the 60% level, subject to liquidity, float and cross-ownership considerations. In addition to market capitalization, a stock's importance may be assessed by such measures as sales, net income, and industry output. (3) Maximum liquidity is balanced by the consideration of other factors, such as overall industry representation. Liquidity, measured by trading value as reported by the local exchange, is assessed over time based on an absolute as well as relative basis. While a hard-and-fast liquidity yardstick is not utilized, trading values are monitored to establish a "normal" level across short-term market peaks and troughs. (4) Maximum float, or the percentage of a company's shares that are freely tradable, is an important optimization parameter but not a hard-and-fast rule for stock selection. While some exceptions are made, index constituents are included at 100% of market capitalization. (5) Stocks with cross-ownership positions are avoided or minimized. (6) A representative sample of large, medium and small companies is included in the index. (7) Maintains, to the extent possible, country weights in regional and international indices reflective of the true size of markets.

Small and highly illiquid securities, non-domiciled companies as well as investment trusts are excluded from consideration.

BACKGROUND

In 1988, MSCI expanded the MSCI World Index to include coverage of emerging markets. Initially, the following emerging markets were covered: Argentina, Brazil, Chile, Greece, Indonesia, Jordan, Korea, Malaysia, Mexico, Philippines, Portugal, Taiwan, Thailand and Turkey. The index was expanded as of January 1, 1993 to include Columbia, India, Pakistan, Peru, Sri-Lanka, and Venezuela. Israel, Poland and South Africa were added as of March 1, 1995.

BASE DATE

January 1, 1988=100.00

COMPUTATION METHODOLOGY

(1) Aggregate market value-weighted arithmetic average of the price ratios Laspeyres index formula is used. Maintenance adjustments to the divisor are made daily for capitalization changes, new listings and delistings, as they occur. Individual country indices are calculated in local currency and converted to U.S. dollars. (2) Structural changes due to industry composition or regulations generally take place every one year to 18 months. These are implemented on the first business day in March, June, September and December of each year and are announced at least two weeks in advance. (3) Companies may be deleted because they have diversified away from their industry classification, because the industry has evolved in a different direction from the company's thrust, or because a better industry representative exists in the form of a new issue or existing company. (4) New issues generally undergo a "seasoning" period of one year to 18 months prior to eligibility for inclusion in the index. New issues due to an initial public offering of significant size that change a country's market and industry profiles, and generate strong investor interest that is likely to assure a high level of liquidity, may be included in the index immediately. (5) The market capitalization of constituent companies is weighted on the basis of their full market value, i.e., without adjustments for "long term holdings" or partial foreign investment restrictions. To address the issue of restriction on foreign ownership, an additional series of "Free" indices are calculated for countries and markets with restrictions on foreign ownership of shares. (6) While some exceptions apply, the index is computed using the last transaction price recorded on the dominant stock exchange in each market. (7) WM/Reuters Closing Spot Rates as of 4 PM London Time are used for currency conversions. Due to the high volatility of currencies in some Latin American countries, MSCI uses its own timing and sources for currency exchange rates applicable to these markets. (8) Dividends are recognized on the ex-dividend date and factored into the index return in the form of a dividend receivable. Dividends are deemed to be received on the payment date while the reinvestment of dividends occurs at the end of the month in which the payment date falls.

DERIVATIVE INSTRUMENTS

World Equity Benchmark Shares Foreign Fund, Inc. (WEBS) series of shares for Malaysia and Mexico (Free) trade on the American Stock Exchange (AMEX).

SUBINDICES

MSCI Emerging Markets Free Index.
Individual country, various regional and special areas indices for the Far East, Latin America and Asia.
Eight international economic sector subindices and 38 industry group subindices. Refer to MSCI World Index for information.

RELATED INDICES

MSCI World Index   Refer to Appendix 5 for additional indices.

REMARKS

(1) Index market weights as of December 31, 1995: Asia-India 4.5%, Indonesia 4.2%, Korea 22.8%, Malaysia 12.9%, Pakistan 0.5%, Philippines 2.9%, Sri Lanka 0.1%, Taiwan 11.7%, Thailand 7.6%; Latin America-Argentina 2.9%, Brazil 8.6%, Chile 4.1%, Colombia 0.6%, Mexico 6.6%, Peru 1.0%, Venezuela 0.3%; Europe/Middle East-Greece 1.0%, Israel 2.2%, Jordan 0.2%, Poland 0.2%, Portugal 1.6%, Turkey 1.0%; Africa-South Africa 12.7%. (2) Customized indices and portfolios, including the integration with MSCI's World indices, to permit investors to assess performance and valuation measures on a geographic and industry basis are offered. (3) GDP data based on The World Bank, 1992, except Taiwan which is based on brokers' estimates.

PUBLISHER

Morgan Stanely Capital International (MSCI).

MORGAN STANLEY CAPITAL INTERNATIONAL (MSCI) EUROPE AUSTRALIA AND FAR EAST (EAFE) INDEX

PRICE PERFORMANCE

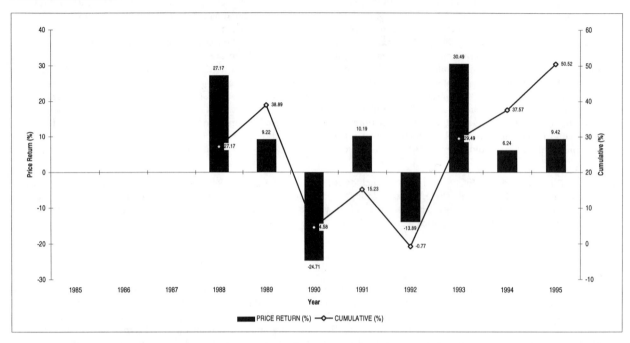

PRICE AND TOTAL RETURN PERFORMANCE (US$)

YEAR	VALUE	PRICE RETURN (%)	CUMULATIVE (%)	TOTAL RETURN (%)[1]	MAXIMUM VALUE	DATE	MINIMUM VALUE	DATE
1995	1,135.63	9.42	50.52	11.55	1,137.08	27-Dec	970.02	23-Jan
1994	1,037.86	6.24	37.57	8.06	1,094.35	2-Sep	974.95	13-Jan
1993	976.90	30.49	29.49	32.94	1,005.25	25-Oct	730.71	13-Jan
1992	748.62	-13.89	-0.77	-11.85	890.30	6-Jan	711.49	9-Apr
1991	869.35	10.19	15.23	12.50	905.66	18-Feb	745.37	16-Jan
1990	788.98	-24.71	4.58	-23.20	1,054.33	4-Jan	717.24	28-Sep
1989	1,047.86	9.22	38.89	10.80	1,053.20	27-Dec	856.97	15-Jun
1988	959.40	27.17	27.17	28.59	963.24	24-Nov	731.91	15-Jan
1987	754.45	NA	NA	24.93	NA	NA	NA	NA
1986	NA	NA	NA	69.94	NA	NA	NA	NA
1985	NA							
Average Annual (%)		6.77		16.43				
Compound Annual (%)		5.24		13.95				
Standard Deviation (%)		18.60		25.53				

[1]Total return based on reinvestment of gross dividends.

SYNOPSIS
The Morgan Stanley Capital International (MSCI) Europe Australia and Far East (EAFE) Index is a market capitalization-weighted index that tracks the daily price and total return performance of common or ordinary shares in developed markets in Europe, Australia and the Far East. The index, which aims to capture 60% of the total market capitalization at both the participating country and industry level, includes securities domiciled in 21 countries. (See Remarks for market weights.)

NUMBER OF STOCKS—DECEMBER 31, 1995
1,112

MARKET VALUE—DECEMBER 31, 1995
US$5,258,900.0 million

SELECTION CRITERIA
The index is designed to accurately represent the buyable opportunities in the markets covered by balancing the inclusiveness of an "all share" index against the replicability of a "blue chip" index.

The universe of constituent securities in each market is generally limited to common or ordinary shares that are selected on the basis of a dynamic optimization process which involves maximizing float and liquidity, reflecting accurately the market's character in terms of the size as measured by market capitalization, and industry representation so as to mirror the local market, and minimizing cross-ownership. The following guidelines apply:

(1) To achieve a proper balance between a high level of tracking, liquidity and restricted float considerations, MSCI aims to capture 60% of each country's market capitalization. (2) To assure that the index reflects the industry characteristics of each country's overall market, MSCI aims to capture 60% of the capitalization of each industry group, as defined by local practice. From the universe of available stocks in each industry group, stocks are selected up to approximately the 60% level, subject to liquidity, float and cross-ownership considerations. In addition to market capitalization, a stock's importance may be assessed by such measures as sales, net income, and industry output. (3) Maximization of liquidity is balanced by the consideration of other factors, such as overall industry representation. Liquidity, measured by trading value as reported by the local exchange, is assessed over time based on an absolute as well as relative basis. While a hard-and-fast liquidity yardstick is not utilized, trading values are monitored to establish a "normal" level across short-term market peaks and troughs. (4) Maximum float, or the percentage of a company's shares that are freely tradable, is an important optimization parameter but not a hard-and-fast rule for stock selection. While some exceptions are made, index constituents are included at 100% of market capitalization. (5) Stocks with cross-ownership positions are avoided or minimized. (6) A representative sample of large, medium and small companies is included in the index.

Non-domiciled companies as well as investment trusts are excluded from consideration as index constituents.

BACKGROUND
The index is a component of the Morgan Stanley Capital International Index, the first international performance benchmark designed to track the world's developed markets. It was created in 1968 by Capital International, S.A., the Swiss subsidiary of the Capital Group, Inc. The rights to the index were acquired in 1986 by Morgan Stanley. In 1988, MSCI expanded the index to include coverage of emerging markets.

Historical data for some indices go back to 1959.

BASE DATE
January 1, 1970=100.00

COMPUTATION METHODOLOGY
(1) Aggregate market value-weighted arithmetic average of the price ratios Laspeyres index formula is used. Maintenance adjustments to the divisor are made daily for capitalization changes, new listings and delistings, as they occur. Individual country indices are calculated in local currency and converted to U.S. dollars. (2) Structural changes due to industry composition or regulations generally take place every one year to 18 months. These are implemented on the first business day in March, June, September and December of each year and are announced at least two weeks in advance. (3) Companies may be deleted because they have diversified away from their industry classification, because the industry has evolved in a different direction from the company's thrust, or because a better industry representative exists in the form of a new issue or existing company. (4) New issues generally undergo a "seasoning" period of one year to 18 months prior to eligibility for inclusion in the index. New issues due to an initial public offering of significant size that change a country's market and industry profiles, and generate strong investor interest likely to assure a high level of liquidity, may be included in the index immediately. (5) The market capitalization of constituent companies is weighted on the basis of their full market value, i.e., without adjustments for "long term holdings" or partial foreign investment restrictions. To address the issue of restriction on foreign ownership, an additional series of "Free" indices are calculated for countries and markets with restrictions on foreign ownership of shares. (6) While some exceptions apply, the index is computed using the last transaction price recorded on the dominant stock exchange in each market. (7) WM/Reuters Closing Spot Rates as of 4 PM London Time are used for currency conversions. (8) Dividends are recognized on the ex-dividend date and factored into the index return in the form of a dividend receivable. Dividends are deemed to be received on the payment date while the reinvestment of dividends occurs at the end of the month in which the payment date falls.

DERIVATIVE INSTRUMENTS
World Equity Benchmark Shares Foreign Fund, Inc. (WEBS) series of shares for Australia, Austria, Belgium, France, Germany, Hong Kong, Italy, Japan, Malaysia, The Netherlands, Singapore (Free), Spain, Sweden, Switzerland, and the United Kingdom trade on the American Stock Exchange (AMEX).

SUBINDICES
Various international, special areas indices, national indices, free regional and country indices, hedged indices, combined indices, Small Cap indicators, eight international economic sector subindices and 38 industry group indices. Refer to MSCI World Index for additional information.

RELATED INDICES
MSCI Emerging Markets Index
Refer to Appendix 5 for additional indices.

REMARKS
MSCI EAFE Index market weights as of December 31, 1995 are, as follows: Europe-Austria 0.4%, Belgium 1.1%, Denmark 0.2%, Finland 0.5%, France 6.3%, Germany 6.9%, Ireland 0.3%, Italy 2.2%, The Netherlands 4.0%, Norway 0.5%, Spain 1.8%, Sweden 2.0%, Switzerland 5.9%, United Kingdom 16.9%; Pacific-Australia 2.6%, Hong Kong 3.1%, Japan 40.9%, Malaysia 2.2%, New Zealand 0.4%, Singapore 1.2%.

PUBLISHER
Morgan Stanley Capital International (MSCI).

MORGAN STANLEY CAPITAL INTERNATIONAL (MSCI) WORLD INDEX

PRICE PERFORMANCE

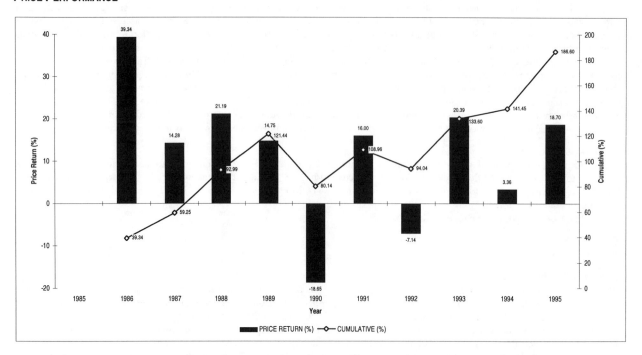

PRICE AND TOTAL RETURN PERFORMANCE (US$)

YEAR	VALUE	PRICE RETURN (%)	CUMULATIVE (%)	TOTAL RETURN (%)[1]	MAXIMUM VALUE	DATE	MINIMUM VALUE	DATE
1995	734.28	18.70	186.60	21.32	734.29	27-Dec	596.21	23-Jan
1994	618.59	3.36	141.45	5.58	644.01	2-Sep	592.36	4-Apr
1993	598.50	20.39	133.60	23.13	607.10	15-Oct	488.58	13-Jan
1992	497.13	-7.14	94.04	-4.66	543.46	6-Jan	467.53	8-Apr
1991	535.36	16.00	108.96	18.97	535.36	31-Dec	439.09	16-Jan
1990	461.53	-18.65	80.14	-16.52	571.02	4-Jan	423.15	28-Sep
1989	567.34	14.75	121.44	17.19	567.34	29-Dec	480.70	15-Jun
1988	494.43	21.19	92.99	23.95	494.43	30-Dec	401.02	21-Jan
1987	407.99	14.28	59.25	16.76	495.90	28-Aug	356.80	2-Jan
1986	357.00	39.34	39.34	42.80	360.80	2-Sep	249.80	24-Jan
1985	256.20							
Average Annual (%)		12.22		14.85				
Compound Annual (%)		11.10		13.72				
Standard Deviation (%)		16.18		16.50				

[1]Total return based on reinvestment of gross dividends.

SYNOPSIS

The Morgan Stanley Capital International (MSCI) World Index is a market capitalization-weighted index that tracks the daily price and total return performance of international common or ordinary shares in developed markets worldwide. The index, which aims to capture 60% of the total market capitalization at both the participating country and industry level, includes securities domiciled in 22 development countries in Asia/Pacific, Europe and North American. (See Remarks for market weights.)

NUMBER OF STOCKS—DECEMBER 31, 1995
1,579

MARKET VALUE—DECEMBER 31, 1995
US$9,219,000.0 million

SELECTION CRITERIA

The index is designed to accurately represent the buyable opportunities in the markets covered by balancing the inclusiveness of an "all share" index against the replicability of a "blue chip" index. The universe of constituents in each market is generally limited to common or ordinary shares selected on the basis of a dynamic optimization process which involves maximizing float and liquidity, reflecting accurately the market's character as measured by market capitalization, and industry representation so as to mirror the local market and minimize cross-ownership.

The following guidelines apply: (1) To achieve a proper balance between a high level of tracking, liquidity and restricted float considerations, MSCI aims to capture 60% of each country's market capitalization. (2) To assure that the index reflects the industry characteristics of each country's overall market, MSCI aims to capture 60% of the capitalization of each industry group, as defined by local practice. From the universe of available stocks in each industry group, stocks are selected up to approximately the 60% level, subject to liquidity, float and cross-ownership considerations. In addition, a stock may be assessed by sales, net income, and industry output. (3) Maximization of liquidity is balanced by factors, such as overall industry representation. Liquidity, measured by trading value reported by the local exchange, is assessed over time on an absolute and a relative basis. While a hard-and-fast liquidity yardstick is not utilized, trading values are monitored to establish a "normal" level across short-term market peaks and troughs. (4) Maximum float, or the percentage of a company's shares freely tradable, is an important optimization parameter but not a hard-and-fast rule. With exceptions, constituents are included at 100% of market capitalization. (5) Stocks with cross-ownership positions are avoided or minimized. (6) A representative sample of large, medium and small companies is included.

Non-domiciled companies and investment trusts are excluded.

BACKGROUND

The index, the first international performance benchmark designed to track the world's developed markets, was created in 1968 by Capital International, S.A., the Swiss subsidiary of the Capital Group, Inc. The rights to the index were acquired in 1986 by Morgan Stanley. In 1988, MSCI expanded the index to include coverage of emerging markets. Historical data for some indices go back to 1959.

BASE DATE
January 1, 1970=100.00

COMPUTATION METHODOLOGY

(1) Aggregate market value-weighted arithmetic average of the price ratios Laspeyres index formula is used. Maintenance adjustments to the divisor are made daily for capitalization changes, new listings and delistings, as they occur. Individual country indices are calculated in local currency and converted to U.S. dollars. (2) Structural changes due to industry composition or regulations generally take place every one year to 18 months. These are implemented on the first business day in March, June, September and December of each year and are announced at least two weeks in advance. (3) Companies may be deleted if they have diversified away from their industry classification, if the industry has evolved in a different direction from the company's thrust, or if a better industry representative exists in the form of a new issue or existing company. (4) New issues generally undergo

Continued on next page

a "seasoning" period of one year to 18 months prior to eligibility. New issues due to an initial public offering of significant size that change a country's market and industry profiles and generate strong investor interest likely to assure a high level of liquidity, may be included immediately. (5) The market capitalization of constituents is weighted on the basis of their full market value, i.e., without adjustments for "long term holdings" or partial foreign investment restrictions. To address the issue of restriction on foreign ownership, an additional series of "Free" indices are calculated for countries and markets with restrictions on foreign ownership of shares. (6) While exceptions apply, the index is computed using the last transaction price recorded on the dominant stock exchange in each market. (7) WM/Reuters Closing Spot Rates as of 4 PM London Time are used for currency conversions. MSCI uses its own timing and sources for currency exchange rates for some Latin American countries. (8) Dividends are recognized on the ex-dividend date and factored into the return in the form of a dividend receivable. Dividends are deemed to be received on the payment date while the reinvestment of dividends occurs at the end of the month in which the payment date falls.

DERIVATIVE INSTRUMENTS
World Equity Benchmark Shares Foreign Fund, Inc. (WEBS) series of shares for Australia, Austria, Belgium, Canada, France, Germany, Hong Kong, Italy, Japan, Malaysia, Mexico (Free), The Netherlands, Singapore (Free), Spain, Sweden, Switzerland and the United Kingdom trade on the American Stock Exchange (AMEX).

SUBINDICES
Various international, special areas and national indices, i.e., North America, Europe, Australia and Far East (EAFE), Europe, ex-UK, Nordic Countries, Pacific countries, Far East and EASEA (EAFE, ex-Japan), World, ex-USA, EAFE+Canada and Kakusai Index (World ex-Japan).
Free regional and country indices: The World Index Free, EAFE Free, Pacific Free and Far East Free and Singapore.
GDP Weighted Indices: The World Index, EAFE and Europe.
Hedged indices.
Combined Indices in which developed and emerging markets are combined: All Country World Index, EAFE+Emerging Markets, EAFE+Emerging Markets Free, Combined Far East Free, Combined Far East ex-Japan, Combined Far East Free ex Japan, Combined Asia Free ex-Japan and Combined Pacific Free ex-Japan.
Small Cap Indicators: Australia, Austria, Belgium, Denmark, Finland, France, Germany, Greece, Hong Kong, Ireland, Italy, Malaysia, The Netherlands, New Zealand, Norway, Singapore, Spain, Sweden, Switzerland, United Kingdom, Europe and Pacific.
Eight international economic sector subindices: Energy, materials, capital equipment, consumer goods, services, finance, multi-industry and gold mines.
Thirty-eight industry group subindices: Energy sources, utilities-electric and gas, building materials and components, chemicals, forest products and paper, non-ferrous metals, steel, miscellaneous materials and commodities, aerospace and military technology, construction and housing, data processing and reproduction, electrical and electronics, electronic components-instruments, energy equipment and services, industrial components, machinery and engineering, appliances and household durables, automobiles, beverages and tobacco, food and household products, health and personal care, recreation and other consumer goods, textiles and apparel, broadcasting and publishing, business and public services, leisure and tourism, merchandising, telecommunications, transportation-airlines, transportation-road and rail, transportation-shipping, wholesale and international trade, banking, financial services, insurance, real estate, multi-industry and gold mines.

RELATED INDICES
MSCI Emerging Markets Index
Refer to Appendix 5 for additional indices.

REMARKS
(1) Index market weights as of December 31, 1995: Europe-Austria 0.2%, Belgium 0.7%, Denmark 0.5%, Finland 0.3%, France 3.6%, Germany 3.9%, Ireland 0.2%, Italy 1.3%, The Netherlands 0.3%, Norway 1.0%, Spain 1.0%, Sweden 1.2%, Switzerland 3.4%, United Kingdom 9.6%; Pacific-Australia 1.5%, Hong Kong 1.8%, Japan 23.4%, Malaysia 1.2%, New Zealand 0.2%, Singapore 0.7%; North America-Canada 2.2%, United States 40.8%. (2) Subindices include a partial list of performance benchmarks. Customized indices and portfolios to permit investors to assess performance and valuation measures on a geographic and industry basis are offered. (3) Free indices, in which ownership restrictions prevent foreign invements in industries and/or companies. The Free indices exclude securities which are not readily purchasable by non-local investors. (4) GDP Weighted Indices are weighted by Gross Domestic Product (GDP) rather than market capitalization. (5) Hedged indices are ones in which the performance of international equity markets is captured while neutralizing the effects of currency fluctuations vis-a-vis the U.S. dollar by using a 30-day forward rate to construct the hedge. A full series of hedged indices is calculated in U.S. dollars, without dividends reinvested. The base date is

January 1, 1988. (6) Small Cap Indicators were introduced in 1994 for 19 of 22 developed markets as a precursor to the introduction of a Small Cap Index. The indicators track the performance of smaller companies with total market value less than US$800.0 million as of June 30, 1994.

PUBLISHER
Morgan Stanley Capital International (MSCI).

SALOMON BROTHERS WORLD EQUITY INDEX-
BROAD MARKET INDEX (SBWEI-BMI)

PRICE PERFORMANCE

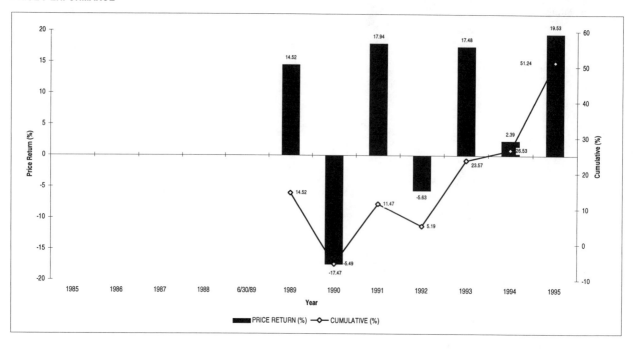

PRICE AND TOTAL RETURN PERFORMANCE (US$)[1]

YEAR	VALUE	PRICE RETURN (%)	CUMULATIVE (%)	TOTAL RETURN (%)	MAXIMUM VALUE	DATE	MINIMUM VALUE	DATE
1995	143.78	19.53	51.24	22.42	143.80	27-Dec	116.74	23-Jan
1994	120.29	2.39	26.53	4.77	125.50	31-Aug	116.08	4-Apr
1993	117.48	17.48	23.57	20.26	119.70	15-Oct	98.44	13-Jan
1992	100.00	-5.63	5.19	-2.98	107.47	6-Jan	93.06	8-Apr
1991	105.97	17.94	11.47	21.19	105.97	31-Dec	85.84	14-Jan
1990	89.85	-17.47	-5.49	-15.07	110.06	4-Jan	82.21	28-Sep
1989	108.87	14.52	14.52	15.83	108.87	29-Dec	95.07	30-Jun
6/30/89	95.07							
1988								
1987								
1986								
1985								
Average Annual (%)		5.71		8.43				
Compound Annual (%)		4.74		4.41				
Standard Deviation (%)		15.21		15.46				

[1]Statistical measures applicable to the six year period 1990-1995.

SYNOPSIS

The Salomon Brothers World Equity Index-Broad Market Index (SBWEI-BMI) is a liquid, market value-weighted index that tracks the daily stock price and monthly total return performance of the world's equity markets. The index covers issues domiciled in 22 countries, including Australia, Austria, Belgium, Canada, Denmark, Finland, France, Germany, Hong Kong, Ireland, Italy, Japan, Malaysia, The Netherlands, New Zealand, Norway, Singapore, Spain, Sweden, Switzerland, United Kingdom and the United States.

NUMBER OF STOCKS—DECEMBER 31, 1995
6,588

MARKET VALUE—DECEMBER 31, 1995
US$9,960,909.1 million

SELECTION CRITERIA

Country selections are based on the size of the country's equity market, the freedom of capital movement and the ability to repatriate dividends. For stock selection, the index employs a top-down approach in which constituents are limited to stock issues that a non-domiciled investor may purchase, with available market capitalization, or float, in excess of US$100.0 million. With few exceptions, issues are included in the index of their country of incorporation.

Available capital is determined after removal of four types of unavailable capital, determined as follows:
(1) Corporate cross holdings–All identifiable holdings of any size held by other companies that are members of the index. (2) Private control blocks–All individual, corporate or personal and family trust or group holdings equal to or greater than 10% of an issuer's total shares outstanding. (3) Government holdings–All shares held by the government of the company's country of domicile. (4) Legally restricted shares–Complete or partial restrictions non-domiciled ownership or voting rights of company shares.

All issues of a company are removed once its combined available market capitalization falls below US$75.0 million. All eligible issues of a company are added once its combined available market capitalization equals to or exceeds US$100.0 million. Investment trusts, unit trusts, mutual fund shares, closed-end funds, equity warrants and convertible bonds are not eligible.

BACKGROUND

Originally jointly compiled by Salomon Brothers and Frank Russell Company, the SBWEI has been recalculated back to June 30, 1989.

BASE DATE

December 31, 1992=100.00

COMPUTATION METHODOLOGY

(1) Aggregate market value-weighted arithmetic average of the price ratios index formula is used. Maintenance adjustments to the divisor are made for capitalization changes, new listings and delistings. The index is calculated in local currency and U.S. dollar terms. (2) Available market capitalization, or float capitalization, is calculated once a year on the basis of price multiplied by total shares outstanding multiplied by the share availability factor, which is determined as of the last business day each May. (3) Shares outstanding due to ordinary changes in share capital are updated monthly. Otherwise, the ex-dividend date applies. (4) Changes to the constituent list are effective July 1 each year and are preannounced. Delisted issues are not replaced prior to the annual reconstitution. Large, newly formed companies, spin-offs from index constituents and privatizations falling within the top quartile of their country's capitalization range enter the index at the next month-end following their official listing. (5) Deletions due to mergers, acquisitions and restructurings are deleted from the index on the last trading day of the month in which the event takes place. Until such time, the issue is carried at its last available price. (6) Pricing sources include Ausstock for Australia, Nikkei for Japan, Toronto Stock Exchange for Canada, Interactive Data Services, Inc. for the United States and Extel for all other securities. If trading in a stock is halted, the last bid price or suspension price is used. (7) Gross dividends are tabulated daily, accumulated and reinvested at month-end. (8) WM/Reuters Closing Spot Rates as of 4 PM London Time are used for currency conversions.

DERIVATIVE INSTRUMENTS

None

SUBINDICES

Extended Market Index (EMI)
GDP-Weighted World Equity Index
Primary Market Index (PMI)
Various individual country, currency and regional indices.
Seven international economic sector indices: Basic industry, capital spending, consumer staple, consumer cyclical, energy, financial and utilities.
Thirty-nine international industry groups. Aerospace and defense, auto components, automobiles, beverages, multinational banks, regional banks, chemicals, construction and buildings, consumer electronics, energy, industrial electronics, engineering, specialty financial, food manufacturing, food retailing, household products, industrial materials, insurance, manufacturing, mining and commodities, media and agencies, merchandising, miscellaneous, multi-industry, office equipment, paper and packaging, pharmaceuticals, property, shipping and containers, steel and metal products, tobacco, air transport, land transport, communications equipment, communications networks, textiles, trade companies, and water, power and light.

RELATED INDICES

Salomon Brothers Broad Investment Grade Bond Index
Salomon Brothers Convertible Securities Index
Salomon Brothers High Yield Index

Salomon Brothers World Government Bond Index
Salomon Brothers World Money Market Index
Refer to Appendix 5 for additional indices.

REMARKS

(1) SBWEI-BMI market weights on the basis of available capitalization as of December 31, 1995 are, as follows: Europe-Australia 1.58%, Austria 0.12%, Belgium 0.47%, Denmark 0.32%, Finland 0.30%, France 2.53%, Germany 3.16%, Ireland 0.18%, Italy 0.96%, The Netherlands 2.21%, Norway 0.21%, Spain 0.73%, Sweden 0.94%, Switzerland 2.95%, United Kingdom 11.18%; Asia/Pacific-Australia 1.58%, Hong Kong 1.55%, Japan 20.08%, Malaysia 0.89%, New Zealand 0.16%, Singapore 0.56%; North America-Canada 2.11%, United States 46.82%. (2) Customized subindices by country and regions are available.

PUBLISHER

Salomon Brothers Inc.

SALOMON BROTHERS WORLD EQUITY INDEX-EXTENDED MARKET INDEX (SBWEI-EMI)

PRICE PERFORMANCE

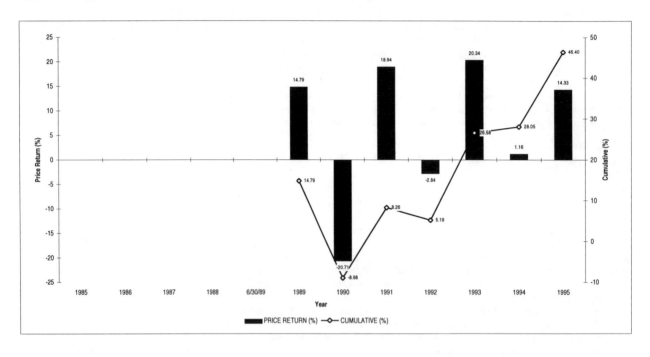

PRICE AND TOTAL RETURN PERFORMANCE (US$)[1]

YEAR	VALUE	PRICE RETURN (%)	CUMULATIVE (%)	TOTAL RETURN (%)	MAXIMUM VALUE	DATE	MINIMUM VALUE	DATE
1995	139.18	14.33	46.40	16.75	139.18	27-Dec	118.44	23-Jan
1994	121.74	1.16	28.05	3.17	129.29	2-Feb	116.45	12-Dec
1993	120.34	20.34	26.58	22.75	123.96	15-Oct	99.36	4-Jan
1992	100.00	-2.84	5.19	-0.38	105.47	7-Feb	93.13	12-Aug
1991	102.92	18.94	8.26	21.96	103.78	17-Apr	81.32	16-Jan
1990	86.53	-20.71	-8.98	-18.68	110.37	4-Jan	81.30	28-Sep
1989	109.13	14.79	14.79	16.05	109.13	29-Dec	95.07	30-Jun
6/30/89	95.07							
1988								
1987								
1986								
1985								
Average Annual (%)		7.67		7.60				
Compound Annual (%)		4.14		6.52				
Standard Deviation (%)		15.83		16.08				

[1]Statistical measures applicable to the 6-year period 1990-1995.

SYNOPSIS

The Salomon Brothers World Equity Index-Extended Market Index (SBWEI-EMI) is a liquid market value-weighted index that tracks the daily stock price and monthly total return performance of small capitalization stocks in 20 markets throughout the world's equity markets. These markets include Australia, Austria, Belgium, Canada, Denmark, Finland, France, Germany, Hong Kong, Ireland, Italy, Japan, Malaysia, The Netherlands, New Zealand, Norway, Singapore, Spain, Sweden, Switzerland, United Kingdom and the United States.

NUMBER OF STOCKS—DECEMBER 31, 1995
4,959

MARKET VALUE—DECEMBER 31, 1995
US$1,978,074.0 million

SELECTION CRITERIA
Index constituents are selected from the universe of stocks that make up the Salomon Brothers World Equity-Broad Market Index (BMI), and represent the bottom 20% of its available capital in each country. Eligible companies, however, are selected on the basis of their rankings by total market capitalization and those stocks falling within the bottom 20% of the cumulative available capital are selected as index constituents.

In an effort to minimize annual movement between the small-capitalization and large-capitalization components of the SMWEI, issues migrate into the SBWEI-Primary Market Index (PMI) if their total capitalization rank places them within the top 75% of the cumulative available capital of the SBWEI-Broad Market Index (BMI). Conversely, issues migrate from the PMI to the EMI if their total capitalization rank falls below the top 85% of the cumulative available capital of the BMI.

For additional information, refer to the Salomon Brothers-World Equity Index-BMI.

BACKGROUND
The SBWEI has been recalculated back to June 30, 1989.

BASE DATE
December 31, 1992=100.00

COMPUTATION METHODOLOGY
(1) Aggregate market value-weighted arithmetic average of the price ratios index formula is used. Maintenance adjustments to the divisor are made for capitalization changes, new listings and delistings. The index is calculated in local currency and U.S. dollar terms. (2) Available market capitalization, or float capitalization, is calculated once a year on the basis of price multiplied by total shares outstanding multiplied by the share availability factor, which is determined as of the last business day each May. (3) Shares outstanding due to ordinary changes in share capital are updated monthly. Otherwise, the ex-dividend date applies. (4) Changes to the constituent list are effective July 1 each year and are preannounced. Delisted issues are not replaced prior to the annual reconstitution. Large, newly formed companies, spin-offs from index constituents and privatizations falling within the top quartile of their country's capitalization range enter the index at the next month-end following their official listing. (5) Deletions due to mergers, acquisitions and restructurings are deleted from the index on the last trading day of the month in which the event takes place. Until such time, the issue is carried at its last available price. (6) Pricing sources include Ausstock for Australia, Nikkei for Japan, Toronto Stock Exchange for Canada, Interactive Data Services, Inc. for the United States and Extel for all other securities. If trading in a stock is halted, the last bid price or suspension price is used. (7) Gross dividends are tabulated daily, accumulated and reinvested at month-end. (8) WM/Reuters Closing Spot Rates as of 4 PM London Time are used for currency conversions.

DERIVATIVE INSTRUMENTS
None

SUBINDICES
GDP-Weighted World Equity Index
Various individual country, currency and regional indices.
Seven international economic sector and 39 international industry group subindices.

RELATED INDICES
Salomon Brothers Broad Investment Grade Bond Index
Salomon Brothers Convertible Securities Index
Salomon Brothers High Yield Index
Salomon Brothers World Equity Index
Salomon Brothers World Government Bond Index
Salomon Brothers World Money Market Index
Refer to Appendix 5 for additional indices.

REMARKS
(1) SBWEI-EMI market weights on the basis of available capitalization as of December 31, 1995 are, as follows: Europe-Austria 0.13%, Belgium 0.47%, Denmark 0.30%, Finland 0.30%, France 2.49%, Germany 2.77%, Ireland 0.15%, Italy 0.84%, The Netherlands 2.06%, Norway 0.22%, Spain 0.64%, Sweden 0.96%, Switzerland 2.58%, United Kingdom 10.78%; Asia/Pacific-Australia 1.69%, Hong Kong 1.50%, Japan 20.26%, Malaysia 0.95%, New Zealand 0.15%, Singapore 0.55%; North America-Canada 2.10%, United States 48.11%. (2) Customized subindices by country and regions are available.

PUBLISHER
Salomon Brothers Inc.

SALOMON BROTHERS WORLD EQUITY INDEX-PRIMARY MARKET INDEX (SBWEI-PMI)

PRICE PERFORMANCE

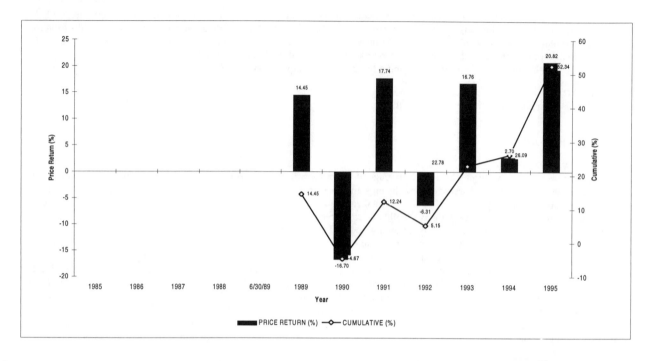

PRICE AND TOTAL RETURN PERFORMANCE (US$)[1]

YEAR	VALUE	PRICE RETURN (%)	CUMULATIVE (%)	TOTAL RETURN (%)	MAXIMUM VALUE	DATE	MINIMUM VALUE	DATE
1995	144.88	20.82	52.34	23.84	145.06	27-Dec	116.29	23-Jan
1994	119.91	2.70	26.09	5.17	124.68	31-Aug	114.69	4-Apr
1993	116.76	16.76	22.78	19.62	118.64	15-Oct	98.16	13-Jan
1992	100.00	-6.31	5.15	-3.62	108.29	6-Jan	93.03	8-Apr
1991	106.74	17.74	12.24	21.04	106.74	31-Dec	86.75	9-Jan
1990	90.66	-16.70	-4.67	-14.20	110.01	4-Jan	82.44	28-Sep
1989	108.84	14.45	14.45	15.78	108.84	29-Dec	95.10	30-Jun
6/30/89	95.10							
1988								
1987								
1986								
1985								
Average Annual (%)		5.83		8.64				
Compound Annual (%)		4.88		4.54				
Standard Deviation (%)		15.17		15.42				

[1]Statistical measures applicable to the 6-year period 1990-1995.

SYNOPSIS

The Salomon Brothers World Equity Index-Primary Market Index (SBWEI-PMI) is a liquid market value-weighted index that tracks the daily stock price and monthly total return performance of large capitalization stocks in 22 of the world's equity markets. These markets include Australia, Austria, Belgium, Canada, Denmark, Finland, France, Germany, Hong Kong, Ireland, Italy, Japan, Malaysia, The Netherlands, New Zealand, Norway, Singapore, Spain, Sweden, Switzerland, United Kingdom and the United States.

NUMBER OF STOCKS—DECEMBER 31, 1995
1,629

MARKET VALUE—DECEMBER 31, 1995
US$7,982,835.0 million

SELECTION CRITERIA

Index constituents are selected from the universe of stocks that make up the Salomon Brothers World Equity-Broad Market Index (BMI), and represent the top 80% of its available capital in each country. Eligible companies, however, are selected on the basis of their rankings by total market capitalization and those stocks falling within the top 80% of the cumulative available capital are selected as index constituents.

In an effort to minimize annual movement between the small-capitalization and large-capitalization components of the SBWEI, issues migrate into the PMI large capitalization index if their total capitalization rank places them within the top 75% of the cumulative available capital of the SBWEI-Broad Market Index (BMI). Conversely, issues migrate from the PMI to the SBWEI-Extended Market Index (EMI) if their total capitalization rank falls below the top 85% of the cumulative available capital of the BMI.

For additional information, refer to the Salomon Brothers World Equity Index-BMI.

BACKGROUND

The SBWEI has been recalculated back to June 30, 1989.

BASE DATE

December 31, 1992=100.00

COMPUTATION METHODOLOGY

(1) Aggregate market value-weighted arithmetic average of the price ratios index formula is used. Maintenance adjustments to the divisor are made for capitalization changes, new listings and delistings. The index is calculated in local currency and U.S. dollar terms. (2) Available market capitalization, or float capitalization, is calculated once a year on the basis of price multiplied by total shares outstanding multiplied by the share availability factor, which is determined as of the last business day each May. (3) Shares outstanding due to ordinary changes in share capital are updated monthly. Otherwise, the ex-dividend date applies. (4) Changes to the constituent list are effective July 1 each year and are preannounced. Delisted issues are not replaced prior to the annual reconstitution. Large, newly formed companies, spin-offs from index constituents and privatizations falling within the top quartile of their country's capitalization range enter the index at the next month-end following their official listing. (5) Deletions due to mergers, acquisitions and restructurings are deleted from the index on the last trading day of the month in which the event takes place. Until such time, the issue is carried at its last available price. (6) Pricing sources include Ausstock for Australia, Nikkei for Japan, Toronto Stock Exchange for Canada, Interactive Data Services, Inc. for the United States and Extel for all other securities. If trading in a stock is halted, the last bid price or suspension price is used. (7) Gross dividends are tabulated daily, accumulated and reinvested at month-end. (8) WM/Reuters Closing Spot Rates as of 4 PM London Time are used for currency conversions.

DERIVATIVE INSTRUMENTS

None

SUBINDICES

GDP-Weighted World Equity Index
Various individual country, currency and regional indices.
Seven international economic sector and 39 international industry group subindices.

RELATED INDICES

Salomon Brothers Broad Investment Grade Bond Index
Salomon Brothers Convertible Securities Index
Salomon Brothers High Yield Index
Salomon Brothers World Government Bond Index
Salomon World Money Market Index
Refer to Appendix 5 for additional indices.

REMARKS

(1) SBWEI-PMI market weights on the basis of available capitalization as of December 31, 1995 are, as follows: Europe-Austria 0.11%, Belgium 0.47%, Denmark 0.32%, Finland 0.30%, France 2.54%, Germany 3.26%, Ireland 0.18%, Italy 0.98%, The Netherlands 2.24%, Norway 0.20%, Spain 0.75%, Sweden 0.93%, Switzerland 3.05%, United Kingdom 11.27%; Asia/Pacific-Australia 1.56%, Hong Kong 1.57%, Japan 20.04%, Malaysia 0.88%, New Zealand 0.16%, Singapore 0.56%; North America-Canada 2.11%, United States 46.50%. (2) Customized indices and regions are also available upon request.

PUBLISHER

Salomon Brothers Inc.

9

INDEX PROFILES — BONDS
NORTH AMERICA

BOND BUYER MUNICIPAL BOND INDEX (BBI)

PRICE PERFORMANCE

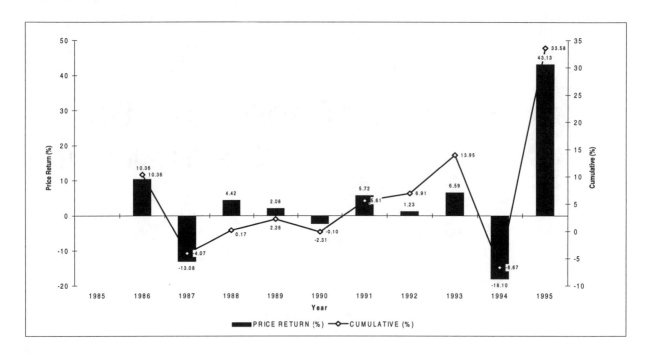

PRICE PERFORMANCE

YEAR	VALUE	PRICE RETURN (%)	CUMULATIVE (%)	MAXIMUM VALUE	DATE	MINIMUM VALUE	DATE
1995	122.06	43.13	33.58	122.06	29-Dec	85.03	3-Jan
1994	85.28	-18.10	-6.67	104.78	31-Jan	80.81	22-Nov
1993	104.13	6.59	13.95	106.56	15-Oct	97.34	12-Jan
1992	97.69	1.23	6.91	101.22	29-Jul	93.41	28-Oct
1991	96.50	5.72	5.61	96.50	31-Dec	90.69	16-Jan
1990	91.28	-2.31	-0.10	93.38	2-Jan	87.66	11-Oct
1989	93.44	2.08	2.26	95.19	1-Aug	89.13	21-Mar
1988	91.53	4.42	0.17	92.44	31-Oct	86.81	23-May
1987	87.66	-13.08	-4.07	103.03	5-Mar	76.31	19-Oct
1986	100.84	10.36	10.36	101.72	4-Dec	91.13	13-Jan
1985	91.38						
Average Annual (%)		4.01					
Compound Annual (%)		2.94					
Standard Deviation (%)		16.37					

SYNOPSIS

The Bond Buyer Municipal Bond Index (BBI) is a modified price-weighted index that tracks the twice-daily price only performance of long-term, high quality, actively traded, general obligation and revenue bonds that pay semi-annual interest at fixed coupon rates.

NUMBER OF BONDS—DECEMBER 31, 1995

40

MARKET VALUE—DECEMBER 31, 1995

Not Available

SELECTION CRITERIA

Constituent bonds must have a principal value of at least $50 million, except term housing bonds which must have a principal value of at least $75.0 million, must be rated either A- or better by Standard & Poor's or A or better by Moody's Investors Service at the time of entry into the index, must have a remaining maturity of at least 19 years at the time of entry into the index, must be callable between seven and 16 years from the date of the bond's initial inclusion in the index and it must be reoffered, at a price between 95 and 105, out of syndicate, and eligible for dealer-to-dealer broker trading at least one business day prior to inclusion in the index. Private placements and bonds with unusual or extraordinary features are excluded from consideration. No more than two bonds from the same issuer are included in the index.

The composition of the index is revised on a regular basis as new bonds meeting the criteria of the index are issued and existing bonds mature or are dropped from the index due to a default, a rating downgrade below A- by either Standard & Poor's or Moody's, more than two bonds from any one issuer are considered for inclusion, a bond's price was equal to or greater than 102 for two consecutive days immediately preceding the date on which the index composition changes, and the bond includes a provision for extraordinary redemption in the official statement, and a bond is inactively traded. Revisions occur twice a month, on the 15th and the last business day of the month.

BACKGROUND

The index which serves as a short-term price-performance indicator of the municipal bond market, was created by the Chicago Board of Trade (CBOT) to be the basis for the Municipal Bond Index futures contract, and is designed to reflect current market conditions. From July 2, 1984 to September 30, 1993, the index was calculated once a day, using prices as of 3 PM (EST). Since October 1, 1993, the index has been calculated twice a day, at 12 PM as well as 3 PM.

From March 1, 1995 to June 30, 1995, a new version of the index had been calculated. The new version uses a coefficient that was reset to 1.000 on March 1, 1995 and adjusted thereafter according to Board of Trade regulations. Calculation of the original version of the index ceased as of July 1, 1995.

BASE DATE

December 12, 1983=82 22/32nds

COMPUTATION METHODOLOGY

(1) A modified form of price index formula, in which the sum of the current converted dollar price of each bond is divided by 40 and multiplied by a coefficient that serves to maintain the continuity of the index in light of changes to its composition. The average converted price is then rounded to the nearest 1/32 point to arrive at the daily BBI Index value. (2) The conversion factor for each bond is the price at which one dollar face value of the bond will yield a standard 8% coupon rate. The coupon is the bond's actual coupon rounded to the nearest 1/8 percent. The time to maturity is calculated in complete three-month increments from the first business day of the quarter following the bond's reoffer date to the first call-at-par date. (3) Price quotations are provided by municipal bond dealer-to-dealer brokers, which include Cantor Fitzgerald Municipal Brokers, Inc., Chapdelaine & Co., J.J. Kenny Drake & Co., J.F. Hartfield & Co., Titus & Donnelly Inc. and Municipal Partners Inc. At least four municipal bond brokers evaluate the index components on a daily basis, between the hours of 1:45 PM and 2 PM Chicago Time. Each broker's price evaluation is defined as the broker's assessment of the price at which $100,000.0 face value of each bond could be sold in the cash market. The price evaluation is expressed as a percentage of face value. A median price evaluation is determined by dropping the highest and lowest average dollar bid prices and calculating the mean of the remaining price evaluations.

DERIVATIVE INSTRUMENTS

Bond Buyer Municipal Bond index futures and options trade on the Chicago Board of Trade (CBOT).

SUBINDICES

None

RELATED INDICES

Bond Buyer 11 Bond Index
Bond Buyer 20 Bond Index
Bond Buyer Revenue Bond Index

REMARKS

Trading volume is determined on the basis of dealer-to-dealer trades matched by the National Securities Clearing Corporation.

PUBLISHER

The Bond Buyer.

CS First Boston High Yield Index

TOTAL RETURN PERFORMANCE

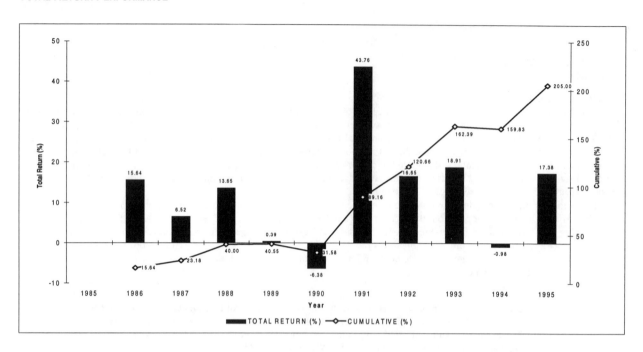

TOTAL RETURN PERFORMANCE

YEAR	VALUE	TOTAL RETURN (%)	CUMULATIVE (%)	MAXIMUM VALUE[1]	DATE	MINIMUM VALUE[1]	DATE
1995	305.00	17.38	205.00	305.00	31-Dec	262.56	31-Jan
1994	259.83	-0.98	159.83	267.46	28-Feb	255.85	30-Jun
1993	262.39	18.91	162.39	262.39	31-Dec	226.68	31-Jan
1992	220.66	16.65	120.66	220.66	31-Dec	196.86	31-Jan
1991	189.16	43.76	89.16	189.16	31-Dec	135.18	31-Jan
1990	131.58	-6.38	31.58	149.45	31-Jul	128.37	31-Oct
1989	140.55	0.39	40.55	147.91	31-Jul	140.55	31-Dec
1988	140.00	13.65	40.00	140.00	31-Dec	127.39	31-Jan
1987	123.18	6.52	23.18	123.38	31-Aug	115.75	31-Oct
1986	115.64	15.64	15.64	115.78	31-Oct	101.00	31-Jan
1985	100.00						
Average Annual (%)		12.56					
Compound Annual (%)		11.80					
Standard Deviation (%)		14.11					

[1]Maximum/minimum index values are as of month-end.

SYNOPSIS

The CS First Boston High Yield Index is a market value-weighted index that tracks the monthly price only and total return performance of the publicly traded high yield debt market in the United States (U.S.).

NUMBER OF BONDS—DECEMBER 31, 1995

687

MARKET VALUE—DECEMBER 31, 1995

US$127,397.0 million

SELECTION CRITERIA

The index consists of publicly traded U.S. dollar-denominated debt issues rated BBB or Ba1 or below with par amounts in excess of US$75.0 million, excepting split rated BBB debt issues which are subject to a US$125.0 million market value, without any maturity restrictions. Moreover, new issues with par amounts greater than US$75.0 million are automatically added to the index at the time of issuance, fallen angels with market values greater than US$75.0 million are added to the index two months after being downgraded and private issues which become publicly registered are considered a new issue one month after the effective date and are added to the index provided the par amount exceeds US$75.0 million.

Excluded from the index are called, retired, exchanged or upgraded issues, defaulted issues when their market value falls below US$20.0 million for six consecutive months and non-defaulted issues with a market value below US$50.0 million for six consecutive months.

BACKGROUND

In addition to the month-end index calculations, a daily flash index has been published since 1995. The flash index consists of the 50 most actively traded bonds that are selected to mirror the composition of the broad index.

BASE DATE

January 1, 1986=100.00

COMPUTATION METHODOLOGY

(1) An aggregate of prices times quantities index formula. For total rate of return calculations, coupon received or accrued is taken into account. (2) Interest received during the month is reinvested at a rate of 4%.

DERIVATIVE INSTRUMENTS

None

SUBINDICES

Various subindices by ratings tiers, security type, issue size, debt type and industry groups.

RELATED INDICES

CS First Boston Convertible Securities Index
CS First Boston ROS 30

REMARKS

Issuers with two or more high yield debt issues outstanding are limited to the two largest issues.

PUBLISHER

CS First Boston.

LEHMAN BROTHERS ADJUSTABLE RATE MORTGAGE (ARM) INDEX

TOTAL RETURN PERFORMANCE

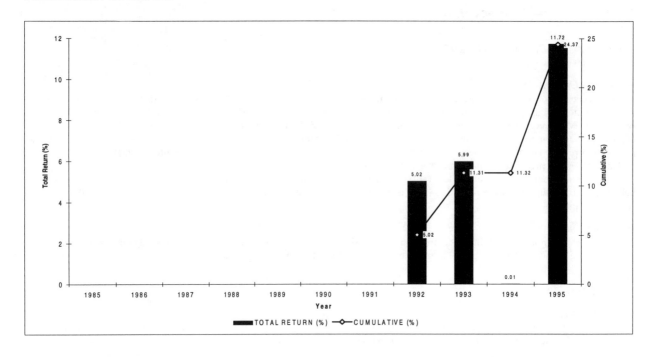

TOTAL RETURN PERFORMANCE

YEAR	VALUE	TOTAL RETURN (%)	CUMULATIVE (%)	MAXIMUM VALUE[1]	DATE	MINIMUM VALUE[1]	DATE
1995	124.37	11.72	24.37	124.37	31-Dec	113.17	31-Jan
1994	111.32	0.01	11.32	111.70	28-Feb	110.14	31-May
1993	111.31	5.99	11.31	111.31	31-Dec	106.09	31-Jan
1992	105.02	5.02	5.02	105.02	31-Dec	99.82	31-Mar
1991	100.00						
1990							
1989							
1988							
1987							
1986							
1985							
Average Annual (%)		5.69					
Compound Annual (%)		5.60					
Standard Deviation (%)		4.80					

[1]Maximum/minimum index values are as of month-end.

SYNOPSIS

The Lehman Brothers ARM Index is a market value-weighted index that tracks the monthly price only, coupon, paydown and total return performance of all U.S. Government agency guaranteed securities with coupons that adjust periodically based on a spread over a published index, regardless of minimum size or maturity.

NUMBER OF BONDS—DECEMBER 31, 1995

Not Available

MARKET VALUE—DECEMBER 31, 1995

US$182,786.0 million

SELECTION CRITERIA

Index eligible issues must satisfy index type and coupon reset frequency requirements. To be eligible, an index type must represent at least 1.5% of the total outstanding agency ARM market and coupon reset frequencies must represent at least 2% of the total qualifying index type. Convertible and non-convertible securities as well as securities backed by single and multifamily mortgages are included.

The index includes graduated payment mortgages (GPMs) but excludes Graduated Equity Mortgages (GEMs). Also excluded are securities with insufficient data or an initial reset period of more than one year longer than the subsequent reset frequency, multifamily securities backed by balloon mortgages or are tied to an index other than the Eleventh District Cost of Funds (COFI-11) Index.

BACKGROUND

The index was introduced in 1993. For additional information, refer to the Lehman Brothers Aggregate Bond Index.

BASE DATE

December 31, 1992=100.00

COMPUTATION METHODOLOGY

(1) An aggregate of prices times quantities index formula, including gain/loss on repayments of principal and currency conversions, where applicable, as well as coupon received or accrued for total rate of return calculations. (2) Returns are based on a universe of securities established at the beginning of each month and held constant until the beginning of the next month. Securities that become ineligible for inclusion in the index during the month due to downgrades, redemptions or calls, securities falling below one year in maturity or newly eligible securities are maintained in a second, statistical universe. The statistical universe drives the production of portfolio statistics during the course of the month, i.e., coupon, duration, maturity, yield and price, and is also used to update the returns universe at the end of each month. (3) Intramonth cash flows are reinvested at month-end. If a security is no longer outstanding at the end of the month, the ending price is the level at which it exited the market. (4) Over 300 representative ARM securities are priced daily by the Lehman trading desk with bid-side prices, option-adjusted spreads or net effective margins. Over 20,000 security pools are priced daily as of 3 PM (EST) based on these levels using a proprietary pricing model and the Treasury yield curve. Prices are for the earliest settlement month and standard Public Security Association (PSA) settlement. (5) The index is rebalanced each month. Sectors are added or deleted from the index each month on the basis of their selection criteria, eligibility or failure to meet eligibility requirements over a consecutive three-month period.

DERIVATIVE INSTRUMENTS

None

SUBINDICES

COFI-11 Conventional ARM Index
6 Month CD Conventional ARM Index
6 Month Libor Conventional ARM Index
1 Year CMT GNMA ARM Index
Year CMT Conventional ARM Index

RELATED INDICES

Lehman Aggregate Bond Index
Lehman Commodity Index
Lehman Emerging Americas Bond Index
Lehman Global Bond Index
Lehman High Yield Composite Bond Index
Lehman Municipal Bond Index
Lehman Mutual Fund Indices
Refer to Appendix 5 for additional indices.

REMARKS

In addition to the subindices noted above, various additional subindices are available by payment frequency and conversion features. To supplement commonly used indices, Lehman offers the flexibility to create customized indices that meet specific investor requirements.

PUBLISHER

Lehman Brothers.

LEHMAN BROTHERS AGGREGATE BOND INDEX

TOTAL RETURN PERFORMANCE

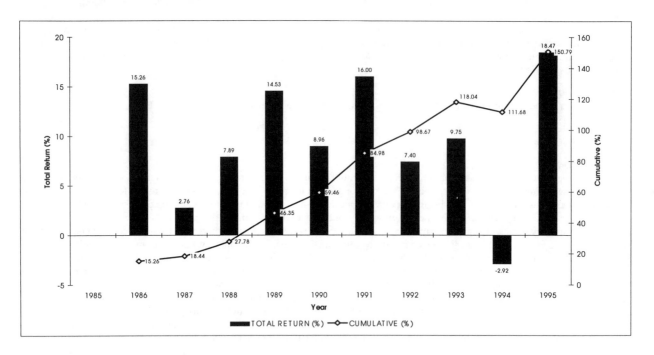

TOTAL RETURN AND PRICE PERFORMANCE

YEAR	VALUE	TOTAL RETURN (%)	CUMULATIVE (%)	PRICE RETURN (%)	MAXIMUM VALUE[1]	DATE	MINIMUM VALUE[1]	DATE
1995	680.66	18.47	150.79	10.43	680.66	31-Dec	585.89	31-Jan
1994	574.52	-2.92	111.68	-9.52	599.77	31-Jan	570.15	31-May
1993	591.78	9.75	118.04	2.93	593.64	31-Oct	549.55	31-Jan
1992	539.21	7.40	98.67	-0.20	539.21	31-Dec	495.22	31-Jan
1991	502.05	16.00	84.98	6.75	502.05	31-Dec	438.14	31-Jan
1990	432.79	8.96	59.46	-0.33	432.79	31-Dec	390.43	30-Apr
1989	397.20	14.53	46.35	4.71	397.20	31-Dec	249.25	28-Feb
1988	346.81	7.89	27.78	-1.42	346.81	31-Dec	329.52	31-May
1987	321.46	2.76	18.44	-6.00	321.46	31-Dec	308.08	31-May
1986	312.84	15.26	15.26	5.18	312.84	31-Dec	272.92	31-Jan
1985	271.41							
Average Annual (%)		9.81		1.25				
Compound Annual (%)		9.63		1.09				
Standard Deviation (%)		6.56		6.01				

[1]Maximum/minimum index values are as of month-end.

SYNOPSIS

The Lehman Brothers Aggregate Bond Index is a market value-weighted index that tracks the daily price only, coupon, paydowns, and total return performance of fixed-rate, publicly placed, dollar-denominated and nonconvertible, investment grade, debt issues with at least $100.0 million par amount outstanding and with at least one year to final maturity.

NUMBER OF BONDS—DECEMBER 31, 1995
5,343

MARKET VALUE—DECEMBER 31, 1995
US$4,536,000.0 million

SELECTION CRITERIA

Constituents include fixed-rate, publicly placed debt that is registered with the Securities and Exchange Commission (SEC), including securities that carry a coupon that steps up or changes according to a predetermined schedule and zero coupon bonds, dollar-denominated and nonconvertible investment grade issues with at least $100.0 million par amount outstanding and with at least one year to maturity without any restrictions as to final maturity, as follows: U.S. Treasury obligations, excluding flower bonds and foreign-targeted issues, U.S. Government agencies and quasi-federal corporations and corporate debt guaranteed by the

U.S. Government, corporate debt, including Yankees and Yankee securities that are issued or guaranteed by foreign sovereign governments, municipalities, or government agencies or international agencies, securities backed by mortgage pools of the Government National Mortgage Association (GNMA), Federal Home Loan Mortgage Corporation (FHLMC), and Federal National Mortgage Association (FNMA), as well as asset-backed securities, including credit card, auto and home equity loans.

Non-fixed rate securities or stripped securities or securities with esoteric or one-of-a-kind features such as structured notes or range notes with coupons that depend on market indices and private placement securities, including 144A securities, are not eligible for inclusion in the index.

BACKGROUND

The index, which combines the Lehman Government/Corporate Bond Index (introduced in 1972), the Mortgage-Backed Securities Index and the Asset-Backed Securities Index, was introduced in 1986 with monthly data going back to December 31, 1975. Par amount outstanding requirements for inclusion in the index have been modified over the years and was last increased from $50.0 million to $100.0 million for all issues, effective as of January 1, 1994. The Lehman family of indices is designed to incorporate the concepts of an investable universe of securities, clearly defined investment styles, low turnover and transparency.

BASE DATE

December 31, 1975=100.00

COMPUTATION METHODOLOGY

(1) An aggregate of prices times quantities index formula, including gain/loss on repayments of principal and currency conversions, where applicable, as well as coupon received or accrued for total rate of return calculations. (2) Returns are based on a universe of securities established at the beginning of each month and held constant until the beginning of the next month. Securities that become ineligible for inclusion in the index during the month due to downgrades, redemptions or calls, securities falling below one year in maturity or newly eligible securities are maintained in a second, statistical universe. The statistical universe drives the production of portfolio statistics during the course of the month, i.e., coupon, duration, maturity, yield and price, and is also used to update the returns universe at the end of each month. (3) Intramonth cash flows are reinvested at month-end. If a security is no longer outstanding at the end of the month, the ending price is the level at which it exited the market. (4) Bonds are priced on the bid side at 3 PM (EST) each day, except that corporate bonds new to the index are initially priced on the offer side. Bonds are predominantly trader priced (about 99% of the market value of the index is priced by traders). Remaining issues, which consist of smaller, less liquid securities, are priced using matrix pricing algorithms that take into account sector, quality, duration, option features as well as issuer specific factors. (5) The final maturity requirement of at least one year is determined regardless of call features and mortgage and asset-backed securities must have a remaining average life of at least one year.

DERIVATIVE INSTRUMENTS

None

SUBINDICES

Asset-Backed Securities Index
Agency Bond Index
1-3 Year Government Index
20+ Year Treasury Index
Corporate Bond Index
Government/Corporate Bond Index
Government Bond Index
Mortgage-Backed Securities Index
Treasury Bond Index

RELATED INDICES

Lehman Adjustable Rate Mortgage Index
Lehman Commodity Index
Lehman Emerging Americas Bond Index
Lehman Global Bond Index
Lehman High Yield Composite Bond Index
Lehman Municipal Bond Index
Lehman Mutual Fund Indices
Refer to Appendix 5 for additional indices.

REMARKS

(1) In addition to the major subindices noted above, each of Lehman's subindices include intermediate and long-term components, comprised of maturities of one- to 10-years and maturities greater than 10 years, respectively, as well as additional maturity, quality and sector breakdowns. To supplement commonly used indices, Lehman offers the flexibility to create customized indices that meet specific investor requirements. (2) Investment grade debt ratings are based on determinations by Moody's Investors Service. A Standard & Poor's rating is used in the event a Moody's rating is not available, followed by a Fitch Investor's Service rating in the absence of both a Moody's and S&P rating. The Moody's rating prevails in the event of split-rated issues.

PUBLISHER

Lehman Brothers.

LEHMAN BROTHERS CORPORATE BOND INDEX

TOTAL RETURN PERFORMANCE

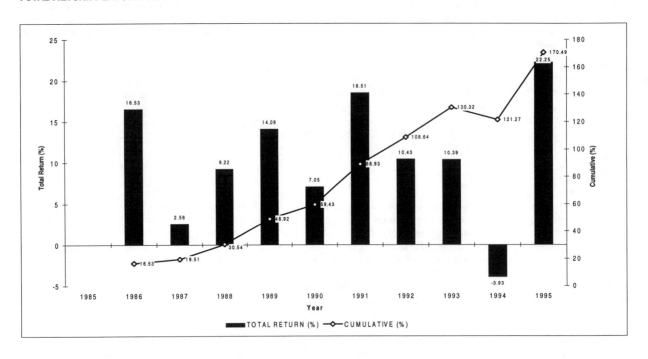

TOTAL RETURN AND PRICE PERFORMANCE

YEAR	VALUE	TOTAL RETURN (%)	CUMULATIVE (%)	PRICE RETURN (%)	MAXIMUM VALUE[1]	DATE	MINIMUM VALUE[1]	DATE
1995	824.23	22.25	170.49	8.12	824.23	31-Dec	688.54	31-Jan
1994	674.24	-3.93	121.27	-11.15	715.46	31-Jan	666.50	31-May
1993	701.84	10.39	130.32	4.14	706.41	31-Oct	640.34	31-Jan
1992	635.76	10.43	108.64	0.12	625.76	31-Dec	568.53	31-Jan
1991	575.72	18.51	88.93	8.54	575.72	31-Dec	491.96	31-Jan
1990	485.81	7.05	59.43	-2.36	485.81	31-Dec	448.15	31-Jan
1989	453.80	14.09	48.92	4.15	453.80	31-Dec	401.37	28-Feb
1988	397.77	9.22	30.54	-0.49	397.77	31-Dec	275.61	31-May
1987	364.18	2.56	19.51	-6.58	364.18	31-Dec	350.03	31-May
1986	355.10	16.53	16.53	5.94	355.10	31-Dec	306.99	31-Jan
1985	304.72							
Average Annual (%)		10.71		1.04				
Compound Annual (%)		10.46		0.85				
Standard Deviation (%)		7.72		6.42				

[1]Maximum/minimum index values are as of month-end.

SYNOPSIS

The Lehman Brothers Corporate Bond Index is a market value-weighted index that tracks the daily price only, coupon and total return performance of fixed-rate, publicly placed Securities and Exchange Commission (SEC)-registered, dollar-denominated and nonconvertible, investment grade corporate debt issues with at least $100.0 million par amount outstanding and one year to final maturity.

NUMBER OF BONDS—DECEMBER 31, 1995
3,387

MARKET VALUE—DECEMBER 31, 1995
US$793,223.0 million

SELECTION CRITERIA

Constituents include fixed-rate corporate debt issues that are publicly placed and registered with the Securities and Exchange Commission, including securities that carry a coupon that steps up or changes according to a predetermined schedule and zero coupon bonds, dollar-denominated and nonconvertible investment grade issues with at least $100.0 million par amount outstanding and at least one year to maturity without any restrictions as to final maturity, as follows: Corporate debt issued by companies in the industrial, financial and utility sectors as well as Yankees and Yankee securities that are issued or guaranteed by foreign sovereign governments, municipalities, or government agencies or international agencies.

Non-fixed rate securities or stripped securities or securities with esoteric or one-of-a-kind features such as structured notes or range notes with coupons that depend on market indices and private placement securities, including 144A securities, are not eligible for inclusion in the index.

BACKGROUND

The index is a component of the Lehman Brothers Aggregate Bond Index. For additional information, refer to the Lehman Brothers Aggregate Bond Index.

BASE DATE

December 31, 1972=100.00

COMPUTATION METHODOLOGY

(1) An aggregate of prices times quantities index formula, including gain/loss on repayments of principal and currency conversions, where applicable, as well as coupon received or accrued for total rate of return calculations. (2) Returns are based on a universe of securities established at the beginning of each month and held constant until the beginning of the next month. Securities that become ineligible for inclusion in the index during the month due to downgrades, redemptions or calls, securities falling below one year in maturity or newly eligible securities are maintained in a second, statistical universe. The statistical universe drives the production of portfolio statistics during the course of the month, i.e., coupon, duration, maturity, yield and price, and is also used to update the returns universe at the end of each month. (3) Intramonth cash flows are reinvested at month-end. If a security is no longer outstanding at the end of the month, the ending price is the level at which it exited the market. (4) Bonds are priced on the bid side at 3 PM (EST) each day, except that corporate bonds new to the index are initially priced on the offer side. Bonds are predominantly trader priced (about 99% of the market value of the index priced by traders). Remaining issues, which consist of smaller, less liquid securities, are priced using matrix pricing algorithms that take into account sector, quality, duration, option features as well as issuer specific factors. (5) The final maturity requirement of at least one year is determined regardless of call features and mortgage and asset-backed securities must have a remaining average life of at least one year.

DERIVATIVE INSTRUMENTS

None

SUBINDICES

Sector subindices: Industrial, utility, finance and Yankee bonds.

RELATED INDICES

Lehman Adjustable Rate Mortgage Index
Lehman Commodity Index
Lehman Emerging Americas Bond Index
Lehman Global Bond Index
Lehman High Yield Composite Bond Index
Lehman Municipal Bond Index
Lehman Mutual Fund Indices
Refer to Appendix 5 for additional indices.

REMARKS

(1) In addition to the major subindices noted above, each of Lehman's subindices include intermediate and long-term components, comprised of maturities of one- to 10-years and maturities greater than 10 years, respectively, as well as additional maturity, quality and sector breakdowns. To supplement commonly used indices, Lehman offers the flexibility to create customized indices that meet specific investor requirements. (2) Investment grade debt ratings are based on determinations by Moody's Investors Service. A Standard & Poor's rating is used in the event a Moody's rating is not available, followed by a Fitch Investor's Service ratings in the absence of both a Moody's and S&P rating. The Moody's rating prevails in the event of split-rated issues.

PUBLISHER

Lehman Brothers.

LEHMAN BROTHERS GOVERNMENT/CORPORATE BOND INDEX

TOTAL RETURN PERFORMANCE

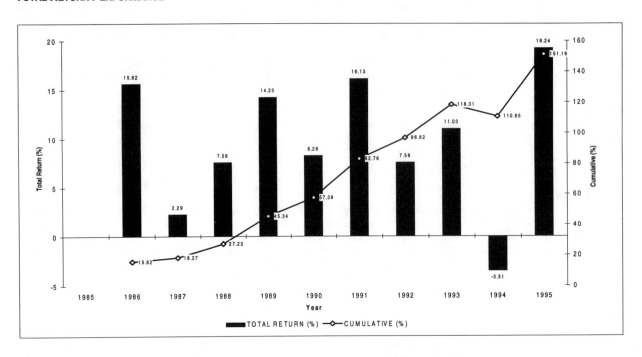

TOTAL RETURN AND PRICE PERFORMANCE

YEAR	VALUE	TOTAL RETURN (%)	CUMULATIVE (%)	PRICE RETURN (%)	MAXIMUM VALUE[1]	DATE	MINIMUM VALUE[1]	DATE
1995	777.52	19.24	151.19	11.28	777.52	31-Dec	664.57	31-Jan
1994	652.05	-3.51	110.65	-10.04	685.93	31-Jan	647.78	30-Nov
1993	675.76	11.03	118.31	3.74	680.51	31-Oct	621.86	31-Jan
1992	608.62	7.58	96.62	-0.25	608.62	31-Dec	547.24	31-Mar
1991	565.73	16.13	82.76	6.96	565.73	31-Dec	492.64	31-Jan
1990	487.17	8.28	57.39	-0.75	487.17	31-Dec	440.65	30-Apr
1989	449.90	14.23	45.34	4.66	449.90	31-Dec	396.07	28-Feb
1988	393.84	7.58	27.23	-1.54	397.00	31-Oct	374.48	31-May
1987	366.09	2.29	18.27	-6.35	366.09	31-Dec	345.90	30-Sep
1986	357.88	15.62	15.62	5.54	357.88	31-Dec	311.37	31-Jan
1985	309.54							
Average Annual (%)		9.85		1.33				
Compound Annual (%)		9.65		1.14				
Standard Deviation (%)		6.91		6.40				

[1]Maximum/minimum index values are as of month-end.

SYNOPSIS

The Lehman Brothers Government/Corporate Bond Index is a market value-weighted index that tracks the daily price only, coupon and total return performance of fixed-rate, publicly placed, investment grade, debt issues of the U.S. Treasury, U.S. Government agencies and quasi-federal corporations and corporate debt guaranteed by the U.S. Government, and non-convertible domestic corporate debt with at least US$100.0 million par amount outstanding and one year to final maturity.

NUMBER OF BONDS—DECEMBER 31, 1995
4,616

MARKET VALUE—DECEMBER 31, 1995
US$ 3,187,884.0 million

SELECTION CRITERIA

Constituent issues include fixed-rate public obligations of the U.S. Treasury, U.S. Government agencies and quasi-federal corporations and corporate debt guaranteed by the U.S. Government as well as corporate debt issues that are publicly placed and registered with the Securities and Exchange Commission, including securities that carry a coupon that steps up or changes according to a predetermined schedule and zero coupon bonds, dollar-denominated and nonconvertible, investment grade issues with at least $100.0 million par amount outstanding and at least one year to maturity without any restrictions as to final maturity. In addition to corporate debt issued by companies in the industrial, financial and utility sectors, the index consists of Yankees and Yankee securities that are issued or guaranteed by foreign sovereign governments, municipalities, or government agencies or international agencies.

Flower bonds, foreign targeted issues, non-fixed rate securities or stripped securities or securities with esoteric or one-of-a-kind features such as structured notes or range notes with coupons that depend on market indices and private placement securities, including 144A securities, are not eligible for inclusion in the index.

BACKGROUND

Introduced in 1972, the index, which is a component of the Lehman Brothers Aggregate Bond Index, combines the Lehman Government and Corporate Bond indices. As of August 31, 1988, the index was expanded to include the Yankee Bond Index, with its SEC-registered, U.S. dollar-denominated debt issued or guaranteed by foreign sovereign governments, municipalities, government agencies or supranational entities. Daily return and related statistical data have been calculated since January 1989. For additional information, refer to the Lehman Brothers Aggregate Bond Index.

BASE DATE

December 31, 1972=100.00

COMPUTATION METHODOLOGY

(1) An aggregate of prices times quantities index formula, including gain/loss on repayments of principal and currency conversions, where applicable, as well as coupon received or accrued for total rate of return calculations. (2) Returns are based on a universe of securities established at the beginning of each month and held constant until the beginning of the next month. Securities that become ineligible for inclusion in the index during the month due to downgrades, redemptions or calls, securities falling below one year in maturity or newly eligible securities are maintained in a second, statistical universe. The statistical universe drives the production of portfolio statistics during the course of the month, i.e., coupon, duration, maturity, yield and price, and is also used to update the returns universe at the end of each month. (3) Intramonth cash flows are reinvested at month-end. If a security is no longer outstanding at the end of the month, the ending price is the level at which it exited the market. (4) Bonds are priced on the bid side at 3 PM (EST) each day, except that corporate bonds new to the index are initially priced on the offer side. Bonds are predominantly trader priced (about 99% of the market value of the index priced by traders). Remaining issues, which consist of smaller, less liquid securities, are priced using matrix pricing algorithms that take into account sector, quality, duration, option features as well as issuer specific factors. (5) The final maturity requirement of at least one year is determined regardless of call features and mortgage and asset-backed securities must have a remaining average life of at least one year.

DERIVATIVE INSTRUMENTS

None

SUBINDICES

Corporate Index
Government Index

RELATED INDICES

Lehman Adjustable Rate Mortgage Index
Lehman Commodity Index
Lehman Emerging Americas Bond Index
Lehman Global Bond Index
Lehman High Yield Composite Bond Index
Lehman Municipal Bond Index
Lehman Mutual Fund Indices
Refer to Appendix 5 for additional indices.

REMARKS

(1) In addition to the major subindices noted above, each of Lehman's subindices include intermediate and long-term components comprised of maturities of one- to 10-years and maturities greater than 10 years, respectively, as well as additional maturity, quality and sector breakdowns. Sector breakdowns include industrial, utility, finance and Yankee bonds. To supplement commonly used indices, Lehman offers the flexibility to create customized indices that meet specific investor requirements. (2) Investment grade debt ratings are based on determinations by Moody's Investors Service. A Standard & Poor's rating is used in the event a Moody's rating is not available, followed by a Fitch Investor's Service ratings in the absence of both a Moody's and S&P rating. The Moody's rating prevails in the event of split-rated issues.

PUBLISHER

Lehman Brothers.

LEHMAN BROTHERS HIGH YIELD COMPOSITE BOND INDEX

TOTAL RETURN PERFORMANCE

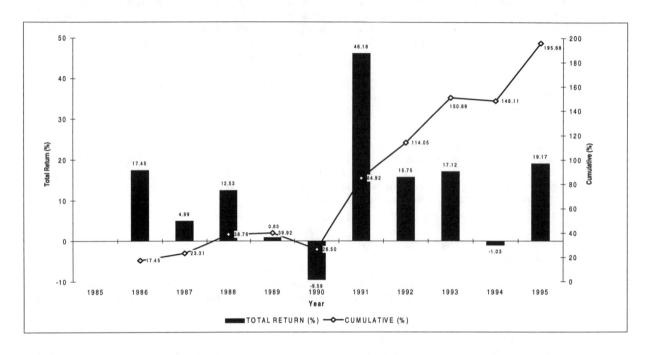

TOTAL RETURN PERFORMANCE

YEAR	VALUE	TOTAL RETURN (%)	CUMULATIVE (%)	MAXIMUM VALUE[1]	DATE	MINIMUM VALUE[1]	DATE
1995	419.42	19.17	195.68	419.42	31-Dec	356.71	31-Jan
1994	351.94	-1.03	148.11	363.32	31-Jan	346.29	30-Apr
1993	355.60	17.12	150.69	355.60	31-Dec	312.46	31-Jan
1992	303.63	15.75	114.05	303.63	31-Dec	271.55	31-Jan
1991	262.31	46.18	84.92	158.59	30-Nov	184.37	31-Jan
1990	179.44	-9.59	26.50	208.90	31-Jul	173.04	31-Oct
1989	198.47	0.83	39.92	106.85	31-Aug	198.16	30-Nov
1988	196.83	12.53	38.76	196.83	31-Dec	180.76	31-Jan
1987	174.91	4.99	23.31	178.39	31-Mar	166.02	31-Oct
1986	166.60	17.45	17.45	167.08	30-Nov	143.72	31-Jan
1985	141.85						
Average Annual (%)		12.34					
Compound Annual (%)		11.45					
Standard Deviation (%)		15.27					

[1]Maximum/minimum index values are as of month-end.

SYNOPSIS

The Lehman Brothers High Yield Composite Bond Index is a market value-weighted index that tracks the daily price only, coupon and total return performance of non-investment grade fixed-rate, publicly placed, dollar-denominated and nonconvertible debt registered with the U.S. Securities and Exchange Commission (SEC).

NUMBER OF BONDS—DECEMBER 31, 1995
835

MARKET VALUE—DECEMBER 31, 1995
US$164,012.0 million

SELECTION CRITERIA

Eligible securities include non-investment grade, publicly placed, dollar-denominated and nonconvertible debt registered with the U.S. Securities and Exchange Commission (SEC) at least $100.0 million par amount outstanding and at least one year to final maturity, including corporate bonds, Yankee and global bonds of issuers in G-7 countries, original issue zero coupon bonds and step-up coupon structures.

Defaulted securities are included in the broad-based index. Pay-in-kind (PIK) bonds, Eurobonds, 144A bonds and emerging market debt are excluded form consideration.

BACKGROUND

The index was introduced in January 1986. The inception date for the industrial sector and subsector indices is December 31, 1992. For additional information, refer to the Lehman Brothers Aggregate Bond Index.

The par amount outstanding requirement for inclusion in the index was modified in January 1993, at which time it increased from $50.0 million to $100.0 million.

BASE DATE

December 31, 1982=100.00

COMPUTATION METHODOLOGY

(1) An aggregate of prices times quantities index formula, including gain/loss on repayments of principal and currency conversions, where applicable, as well as coupon received or accrued for total rate of return calculations. (2) Returns are based on a universe of securities established at the beginning of each month and held constant until the beginning of the next month. Securities that become ineligible for inclusion in the index during the month due to downgrades, redemptions or calls, securities falling below one year in maturity or newly eligible securities are maintained in a second, statistical universe. The statistical universe drives the production of portfolio statistics during the course of the month, i.e., coupon, duration, maturity, yield and price, and is also used to update the returns universe at the end of each month. (3) Intramonth cash flows are reinvested at month-end. If a security is no longer outstanding at the end of the month, the ending price is the level at which it exited the market. (4) Bonds are priced on the bid side at 3 PM (EST) each day, except that corporate bonds new to the index are initially priced on the offer side. Bonds are predominantly trader priced (about 99% of the market value of the index priced by traders). Remaining issues, which consist of smaller, less liquid securities, are priced using matrix pricing algorithms that take into account sector, quality, duration, option features as well as issuer specific factors. (5) The final maturity requirement of at least one year is determined regardless of call features and mortgage and asset-backed securities must have a remaining average life of at least one year.

DERIVATIVE INSTRUMENTS

None

SUBINDICES

High Yield Index, ex defaulted securities

RELATED INDICES

Lehman Adjustable Rate Mortgage Index
Lehman Aggregate Bond Index
Lehman Commodity Index
Lehman Emerging Americas Bond Index
Lehman Global Bond Index
Lehman Municipal Bond Index
Lehman Mutual Fund Indices
Refer to Appendix 5 for additional indices.

REMARKS

(1) In addition to the major subindices noted above, each of Lehman's subindices include intermediate and long-term components, comprised of maturities of one- to 10- years and maturities greater than 10 years, respectively, as well as additional security type, maturity, quality and sector breakdowns. To supplement commonly used indices, Lehman offers the flexibility to create customized indices that meet specific investor requirements. (2) Non-investment grade debt ratings of Ba1 or lower, including defaulted securities, are based on determinations by Moody's Investors Service. A Standard & Poor's rating of BB+ or lower is used in the event a Moody's rating is not available, followed by a Fitch Investor's Service ratings in the absence of both a Moody's and S&P rating. The Moody's rating prevails in the event of split-rated issues. (3) A small number of unrated bonds is included in the index, however, these must have previously held a high yield rating or have been associated with a high yield issuer, and must trade accordingly.

PUBLISHER

Lehman Brothers.

LEHMAN BROTHERS MORTGAGE-BACKED SECURITIES INDEX

TOTAL RETURN PERFORMANCE

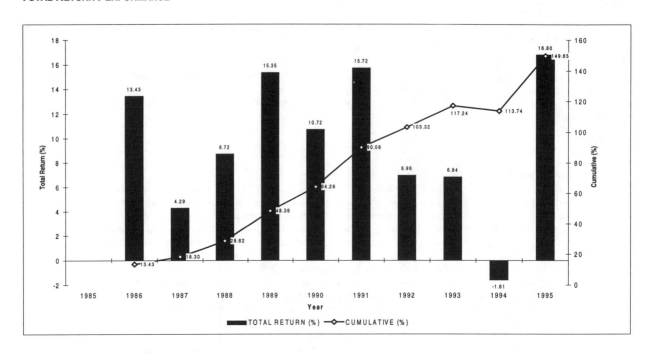

TOTAL RETURN AND PRICE PERFORMANCE

YEAR	VALUE	TOTAL RETURN (%)	CUMULATIVE (%)	PRICE RETURN (%)	MAXIMUM VALUE[1]	DATE	MINIMUM VALUE[1]	DATE
1995	697.95	16.80	149.65	8.55	697.95	31-Dec	610.33	31-Jan
1994	597.54	-1.61	113.74	-8.40	613.35	31-Jan	591.17	31-May
1993	607.33	6.84	117.24	1.12	607.33	31-Dec	575.90	31-Jan
1992	568.43	6.96	103.32	-0.08	568.43	31-Dec	525.28	31-Jan
1991	531.42	15.72	90.08	6.26	531.42	31-Dec	466.21	31-Jan
1990	459.23	10.72	64.26	0.80	459.23	31-Dec	411.86	31-Jan
1989	414.76	15.35	48.36	4.89	414.76	31-Dec	363.47	28-Feb
1988	359.57	8.72	28.62	-1.12	366.80	31-Oct	343.10	31-Jan
1987	330.73	4.29	18.30	-4.71	330.73	31-Dec	314.04	31-May
1986	317.12	13.43	13.43	3.37	317.12	31-Dec	280.67	31-Jan
1985	279.57							
Average Annual (%)		9.72		1.07				
Compound Annual (%)		9.58		0.95				
Standard Deviation (%)		5.84		5.08				

[1]Maximum/minimum index values are as of month-end.

SYNOPSIS

The Lehman Brothers Mortgage-Backed Securities Index is a market value-weighted index that tracks the daily price only, coupon, paydown and total return performance of publicly placed, fixed-rate securities backed by mortgage pools of the Government National Mortgage Association (GNMA), Federal Home Loan Mortgage Corporation (FHLMC) and Federal National Mortgage Association (FNMA).

NUMBER OF BONDS—DECEMBER 31, 1995

603

MARKET VALUE—DECEMBER 31, 1995

US$1,291,196.0 million

SELECTION CRITERIA

Issues include publicly placed, fixed-rate securities backed by mortgage pools of the Government National Mortgage Association (GNMA), Federal Home Loan Mortgage Corporation (FHLMC) and Federal National Mortgage Association (FNMA) with at least one year to maturity and an outstanding par value of at least $100.0 million.

The index includes graduated payment mortgages (GPMs) but excludes Graduated Equity Mortgages (GEMs).

BACKGROUND

The index, which forms part of the Lehman Aggregate Bond Index, was introduced in January 1986 with monthly returns dating back to 1976. Daily return and related statistical data have been calculated since January 1989. For additonal information, refer to the Lehman Aggregate Bond Index.

BASE DATE

December 31, 1975=100.00

COMPUTATION METHODOLOGY

(1) An aggregate of prices times quantities index formula, including gain/loss on repayments of principal and currency conversions, where applicable, as well as coupon received or accrued for total rate of return calculations. (2) Returns are based on a universe of securities established at the beginning of each month and held constant until the beginning of the next month. Securities that become ineligible for inclusion in the index during the month due to downgrades, redemptions or calls, securities falling below one year in maturity or newly eligible securities are maintained in a second, statistical universe. The statistical universe drives the production of portfolio statistics during the course of the month, i.e., coupon, duration, maturity, yield and price, and is also used to update the returns universe at the end of each month. (3) Intramonth cash flows are reinvested at month-end. If a security is no longer outstanding at the end of the month, the ending price is the level at which it exited the market. (4) Bonds are priced on the bid side at 3 PM (EST) each day, except that corporate bonds new to the index are initially priced on the offer side. Bonds are predominantly trader priced (about 99% of the market value of the index priced by traders). Remaining issues, which consist of smaller, less liquid securities, are priced using matrix pricing algorithms that take into account sector, quality, duration, option features as well as issuer specific factors. (5) The final maturity requirement of at least one year is determined regardless of call features and mortgage and asset-backed securities must have a remaining average life of at least one year.

DERIVATIVE INSTRUMENTS

None

SUBINDICES

GNMA Index
FHLMC Index
FNMA Index

RELATED INDICES

Lehman Adjustable Rate Mortgage Index
Lehman Commodity Index
Lehman Emerging Americas Bond Index
Lehman Global Bond Index
Lehman High Yield Composite Bond Index
Lehman Municipal Bond Index
Lehman Mutual Fund Indices
Refer to Appendix 5 for additional indices.

REMARKS

In addition to the major subindices noted above, Lehman's mortgage backed-securities subindices include various price and coupon sectors for GNMA 30-year and 15-year mortgages, conventional 30-year and 15-year mortgages and Balloon mortgages. To supplement commonly used indices, Lehman offers the flexibility to create customized indices that meet specific investor requirements.

PUBLISHER

Lehman Brothers.

LEHMAN BROTHERS MUNICIPAL BOND INDEX

TOTAL RETURN PERFORMANCE

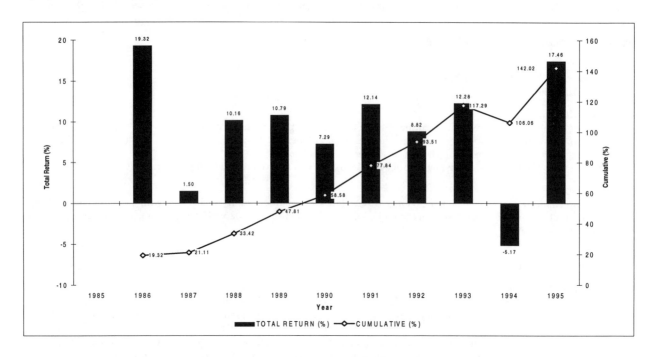

TOTAL RETURN PERFORMANCE

YEAR	VALUE	TOTAL RETURN (%)	CUMULATIVE (%)	MAXIMUM VALUE[1]	DATE	MINIMUM VALUE[1]	DATE
1995	399.70	17.46	142.02	399.70	31-Dec	350.03	31-Jan
1994	340.30	-5.17	106.06	362.95	31-Jan	332.98	30-Nov
1993	358.85	12.28	117.29	358.85	31-Dec	323.31	31-Jan
1992	319.59	8.82	93.51	319.59	31-Dec	294.37	31-Jan
1991	293.70	12.14	77.84	293.70	31-Dec	265.42	31-Jan
1990	261.90	7.29	58.58	261.90	31-Dec	242.96	31-Jan
1989	244.11	10.79	47.81	244.11	31-Dec	221.80	31-Mar
1988	220.34	10.16	33.42	220.34	31-Dec	206.89	31-Mar
1987	200.01	1.50	21.11	203.98	28-Feb	190.74	31-May
1986	197.05	19.32	19.32	197.59	30-Nov	174.87	31-Jan
1985	165.15						
Average Annual (%)		9.46					
Compound Annual (%)		9.24					
Standard Deviation (%)		7.16					

[1]Maximum/minimum index values are as of month-end.

SYNOPSIS

The Lehman Brothers Municipal Bond Index is a market value-weighted index that tracks the mid-month and monthly price only, coupon and total return performance of investment grade, tax-exempt bonds, with a remaining maturity of at least one year, including state and local general obligation, revenue, insured and prerefunded bonds.

NUMBER OF BONDS—DECEMBER 31, 1995
26,608

MARKET VALUE—DECEMBER 31, 1995
US$436,992.0 million

SELECTION CRITERIA

Municipal government obligations, revenue, prefunded and insured bonds must have a minimum Moody's Investors Service credit rating of Baa3 with an outstanding par value of at least $3.0 million and be issued as part of a deal of at least $50.0 million. In addition, the bonds must have been issued within the last five years and have a remaining maturity of at least one year (refer to Background for revisions effective January 1, 1996).

BACKGROUND

The index was introduced in 1980. Quality and outstanding par value guidelines for eligibility were modified as of July 1993 so as to more accurately reflect the bond marketplace, and again as of January 1, 1996. On that date, coverage was expanded by about 2,750 bonds to include zero coupon bonds and bonds subject to the alternative minimum tax (AMT). The selection criteria was further modified to allow the inclusion of all bonds issued after January 1, 1991, thus eliminating the five year rolling issuance requirement.

Bonds with floating coupons are excluded from the index.

For additional information, refer to the Lehman Brothers Aggregate Bond Index.

BASE DATE

December 31, 1979=100.00

COMPUTATION METHODOLOGY

(1) An aggregate of prices times quantities index formula, including gain/loss on repayments of principal and currency conversions, where applicable, as well as coupon received or accrued for total rate of return calculations. (2) Returns are based on a universe of securities established at the beginning of each month and held constant until the beginning of the next month. Securities that become ineligible for inclusion in the index during the month due to downgrades, redemptions or calls, securities falling below one year in maturity or newly eligible securities are maintained in a second, statistical universe. The statistical universe drives the production of portfolio statistics during the course of the month, i.e., coupon, duration, maturity, yield and price, and is also used to update the returns universe at the end of each month. (3) Intramonth cash flows are reinvested at month-end. If a security is no longer outstanding at the end of the month, the ending price is the level at which it exited the market. (4) Muller Data Corporation serves as the pricing source for index securities. Pricing of securities in the index is evaluated twice a month. Month end pricing takes place as of 4 PM (EST) on the last business day of the month. (5) The final maturity requirement of at least one year is determined regardless of call features and mortgage and asset-backed securities must have a remaining average life of at least one year.

DERIVATIVE INSTRUMENTS

None

SUBINDICES

GO Bond Index
Revenue Bond Index
Prerefunded Index
Insured Bond Index
AMT Bond Index
California Tax-exempt Bond Index
New York Tax-exempt Bond Index

RELATED INDICES

Lehman Adjustable Rate Mortgage Index
Lehman Aggregate Bond Index
Lehman Commodity Index
Lehman Emerging Americas Bond Index
Lehman Global Bond Index
Lehman High Yield Composite Bond Index
Lehman Mutual Fund Indices
Refer to Appendix 5 for additional indices.

REMARKS

(1) In addition to the major subindices noted above, subindices based on maturity, quality and revenue source are calculated. To supplement commonly used indices, Lehman offers the flexibility to create customized indices that meet specific investor requirements. (2) Investment grade debt ratings are based on determinations by Moody's Investors Service. A Standard & Poor's rating is used in the event a Moody's rating is not available, followed by a Fitch Investor's Service rating in the absence of both a Moody's and S&P rating. The Moody's rating prevails in the event of split-rated issues.

PUBLISHER

Lehman Brothers.

LEHMAN BROTHERS U.S. GOVERNMENT BOND INDEX

TOTAL RETURN PERFORMANCE

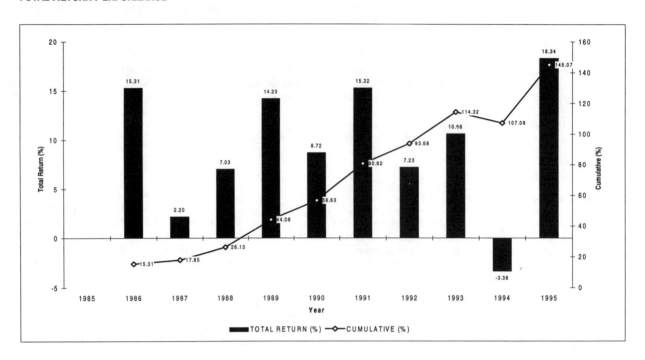

TOTAL RETURN AND PRICE PERFORMANCE

YEAR	VALUE	TOTAL RETURN (%)	CUMULATIVE (%)	PRICE RETURN (%)	MAXIMUM VALUE[1]	DATE	MINIMUM VALUE[1]	DATE
1995	786.99	18.34	145.07	10.64	786.99	31-Dec	677.40	31-Jan
1994	665.02	-3.38	107.09	-9.69	697.67	31-Jan	661.00	30-Nov
1993	688.25	10.66	114.32	3.62	693.20	31-Oct	635.17	31-Jan
1992	621.96	7.23	93.68	-0.37	621.96	31-Dec	569.89	31-Mar
1991	580.04	15.32	80.62	6.42	580.04	31-Dec	508.40	31-Jan
1990	503.00	8.72	56.63	-0.17	503.00	31-Dec	452.90	30-Apr
1989	462.67	14.23	44.08	4.80	462.67	31-Dec	406.86	31-Mar
1988	405.05	7.03	26.13	-1.86	405.05	31-Dec	386.06	31-May
1987	378.44	2.20	17.85	-6.29	378.44	31-Dec	358.21	30-Sep
1986	370.31	15.31	15.31	5.41	370.31	31-Dec	322.86	31-Jan
1985	321.13							
Average Annual (%)		9.57		1.25				
Compound Annual (%)		9.38		1.08				
Standard Deviation (%)		6.67		6.16				

[1]Maximum/minimum index values are as of month-end.

SYNOPSIS

The Lehman Brothers U.S. Government Bond Index is a market value-weighted index that tracks the daily price only, coupon, and total return performance of fixed-rate, publicly placed, dollar-denominated obligations issued by the U.S. Treasury, U.S. Government agencies, quasi-federal corporations, and corporations whose debt is guaranteed by the U.S. Government with at least $100.0 million par amount outstanding and one year to final maturity.

NUMBER OF BONDS—DECEMBER 31, 1995

1,229

MARKET VALUE—DECEMBER 31, 1995

US$2,394,662.0 million

SELECTION CRITERIA

Constituents include all public obligations of the U.S. Treasury, U.S. Government agencies and quasi-federal corporations and corporate debt guaranteed by the U.S. Government with at least $100.0 million par amount outstanding and with at least one year to maturity without any restrictions as to final maturity.

Flower bonds and foreign-targeted issues are not eligible for inclusion in the index.

BACKGROUND

The index is a component of the Lehman Brothers Aggregate Bond Index. For additional information, refer to the Lehman Brothers Aggregate Bond Index.

BASE DATE

December 31, 1995=100.00

COMPUTATION METHODOLOGY

(1) An aggregate of prices times quantities index formula, including gain/loss on repayments of principal and currency conversions, where applicable, as well as coupon received or accrued for total rate of return calculations. (2) Returns are based on a universe of securities established at the beginning of each month and held constant until the beginning of the next month. Securities that become ineligible for inclusion in the index during the month due to downgrades, redemptions or calls, securities falling below one year in maturity or newly eligible securities are maintained in a second, statistical universe. The statistical universe drives the production of portfolio statistics during the course of the month, i.e., coupon, duration, maturity, yield and price, and is also used to update the returns universe at the end of each month. (3) Intramonth cash flows are reinvested at month-end. If a security is no longer outstanding at the end of the month, the ending price is the level at which it exited the market. (4) Bonds are priced on the bid side at 3 PM (EST) each day, except that corporate bonds new to the index are initially priced on the offer side. Bonds are predominantly trader priced (about 99% of the market value of the index priced by traders). Remaining issues, which consist of smaller, less liquid securities, are priced using matrix pricing algorithms that take into account sector, quality, duration, option features as well as issuer specific factors. (5) The final maturity requirement of at least one year is determined regardless of call features and mortgage and asset-backed securities must have a remaining average life of at least one year.

DERIVATIVE INSTRUMENTS

None

SUBINDICES

Agency Bond Index
20 Years Treasury Bond Index
1-3 Year Treasury Bond Index
Treasury Bond Index

RELATED INDICES

Lehman Adjustable Rate Mortgage Index
Lehman Commodity Index
Lehman Emerging Americas Bond Index
Lehman Global Bond Index
Lehman High Yield Composite Bond Index
Lehman Municipal Bond Index
Lehman Mutual Fund Indices
Refer to Appendix 5 for additional indices.

REMARKS

In addition to the major subindices noted above, each of Lehman's subindices include intermediate and long-term components, comprised of maturities of one- to 10- years and maturities greater than 10 years, respectively, as well as additional maturity, quality and sector breakdowns. To supplement commonly used indices, Lehman offers the flexibility to create customized indices that meet specific investor requirements.

PUBLISHER

Lehman Brothers.

MERRILL LYNCH HIGH YIELD MASTER INDEX

TOTAL RETURN PERFORMANCE

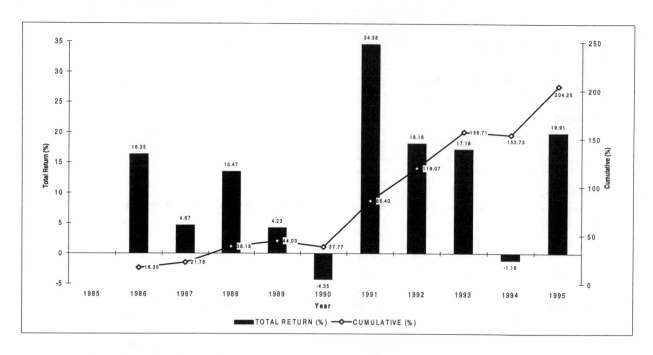

TOTAL RETURN AND PRICE PERFORMANCE

YEAR	VALUE	TOTAL RETURN (%)	CUMULATIVE (%)	PRICE RETURN (%)	MAXIMUM VALUE[1]	DATE	MINIMUM VALUE[1]	DATE
1995	385.10	19.91	204.25	8.59	385.10	31-Dec	325.69	31-Jan
1994	321.16	-1.16	153.73	-10.57	332.06	31-Jan	314.08	30-Jun
1993	324.94	17.18	156.71	5.76	324.94	31-Dec	284.12	31-Jan
1992	277.29	18.16	119.07	5.56	277.29	31-Dec	242.88	31-Mar
1991	234.68	34.58	85.40	18.38	234.68	31-Dec	176.85	31-Jan
1990	174.38	-4.35	37.77	-16.56	190.14	31-Jul	170.46	30-Apr
1989	182.31	4.23	44.03	-8.26	186.77	31-Aug	177.53	28-Feb
1988	174.91	13.47	38.18	0.36	174.91	31-Dec	158.36	31-May
1987	154.14	4.67	21.78	-7.25	156.03	31-Aug	148.37	31-May
1986	147.27	16.35	16.35	3.13	147.27	31-Dec	127.44	31-Jan
1985	126.58							
Average Annual (%)		12.30		-0.09				
Compound Annual (%)		11.77		-0.58				
Standard Deviation (%)		11.60		10.50				

[1]Maximum/minimum index values are as of month-end.

SYNOPSIS

The Merrill Lynch High Yield Master Index is a market value-weighted index that tracks the daily price only, income and total return performance of non-investment grade publicly placed, nonconvertible, fixed-rate, coupon-bearing, United States (U.S.) domestic debt, with outstanding par amounts greater than or equal to $50.0 million, and a term-to-maturity greater than or equal to one year.

NUMBER OF BONDS—DECEMBER 31, 1995

849

MARKET VALUE—DECEMBER 31, 1995

US$155,062.5 million

SELECTION CRITERIA

Eligible securities include publicly placed, nonconvertible, fixed-rate, coupon-bearing debt obligations with outstanding par amounts greater than or equal to $50.0 million and a term-to-maturity greater than or equal to one year, which are rated, on a composite basis, by Standard & Poor's and Moody's, less than BBB-/Baa3 and below, but not in default.

DIBs and PIKS are excluded from consideration.

BACKGROUND

The index is a companion to the Merrill Lynch Global Bond Index. To improve liquidity and pricing quality, the minimum par outstanding requirement for eligible issues was increased from $25.0 million to $50.0 million effective March 1, 1991.

Monthly data is available to October 31, 1986. Thereafter, daily index values are available

For additional information, refer to the Merrill Lynch Global Bond Index.

BASE DATE

October 31, 1984=100.00

COMPUTATION METHODOLOGY

(1) An aggregate of prices times quantities index formula, including gain/loss on repayments of principal and currency conversions, where applicable, as well as coupon received or accrued for total rate of return calculations. (2) Daily price and total return calculations are based on the theory that the portfolio of securities that make up the index is purchased in its entirety at approximately 3 PM (EST) on the initial day and held until the same time on the following day, when it is sold. Price and total returns for a one day period represent the sum of the weighted average price return, weighted average accrued interest return, and weighted average coupon return, weighted by the market value of the outstanding amount of each bond in the index. Total return for extended intervals are calculated by "chain-linking" the periodic rates of return. Transaction costs are not included in the calculations of price and total returns. (3) Except for mortgage and asset backed principal pay downs, which are assumed to occur on the 30th of the month, accrued interest and cash flows are assumed to be reinvested on a daily basis. (4) Bonds are generally priced on the basis of bid-side prices obtained from Merrill Lynch's trading floors. These are either hand priced or matrix priced, using price quotes taken at approximately 3 PM (EST). (5) Market values, for total return calculation purposes, are based on the outstanding amounts of each bond, which are reviewed regularly to account for full and partial retirement of debt, calls, sinking-fund requirements, tenders or re-opening of issues. (6) New issues enter the index on the first business day following settlement while bonds that no longer meet the index or subindex criterion are removed from the index one day, or two days, respectively, following such a determination. Bonds are removed from the index when they no longer satisfy the size, rating or maturity criteria.

DERIVATIVE INSTRUMENTS

None

SUBINDICES

Various subindices by industry group, credit quality and maturity.

RELATED INDICES

Merrill Lynch Capital Markets Index
Merrill Lynch Convertible Securities Index
Merrill Lynch Currency Indices
Merrill Lynch Energy and Metals Index
Merrill Lynch Global Bond Index
Merrill Lynch Institutional Municipal Index
Merrill Lynch Money Market Instrument Indices
Refer to Appendix 5 for additional indices.

REMARKS

(1) A composite rating is calculated by averaging the ratings assigned by Moody's and S&P. In the event the average rating falls between two adjacent split-rated issues, the composite rating is the lower of the two (2) To improve the liquidity and pricing quality of the index, new selection criteria were implemented starting April 30, 1996. The minimum par amount outstanding requirement for bonds was increased to US$100.0 million, with the exception of the U.S. Asset Backed Master which remains at US$25.0 million. Additionally, the US$200.0 million minimum requirement for each generic mortgage coupon was dropped and replaced by a US$100.0 million minimum applied to each seasoning category within a generic coupon. The exclusion of smaller issues is expected to have minimal impact on the market coverage and risk profile of the indices as these are market value-weighted.

PUBLISHER

Merrill Lynch & Co.

MERRILL LYNCH INSTITUTIONAL MUNICIPAL INDEX

TOTAL RETURN PERFORMANCE

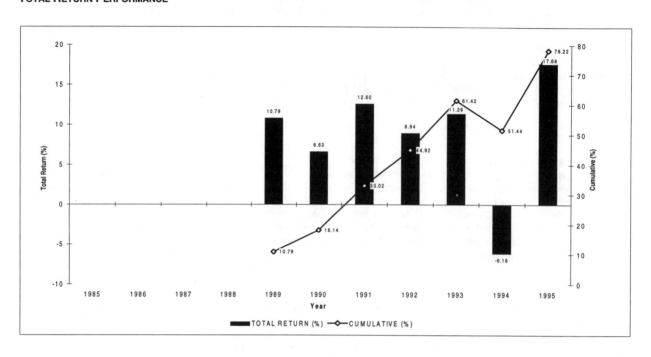

TOTAL RETURN AND PRICE PERFORMANCE

YEAR	VALUE	TOTAL RETURN (%)	CUMULATIVE (%)	PRICE RETURN (%)	MAXIMUM VALUE[1]	DATE	MINIMUM VALUE[1]	DATE
1995	178.22	17.68	78.22	4.77	178.22	31-Dec	155.96	31-Jan
1994	151.44	-6.18	51.44	-11.98	163.02	31-Jan	148.75	30-Nov
1993	161.42	11.39	61.42	4.77	161.42	31-Dec	146.83	31-Jan
1992	144.92	8.94	44.92	2.05	144.92	31-Dec	132.82	29-Feb
1991	133.02	12.60	33.02	5.12	133.02	31-Dec	119.80	31-Jan
1990	118.14	6.63	18.14	-0.73	118.14	31-Dec	108.62	30-Apr
1989	110.79	10.79	10.79	3.23	110.79	31-Dec	100.00	28-Feb
1988	100.00							
1987								
1986								
1985								
Average Annual (%)		8.84		1.03				
Compound Annual (%)		8.60		0.60				
Standard Deviation (%)		7.45		6.10				

[1]Maximum/minimum index values are as of month-end.

SYNOPSIS

The Merrill Lynch Institutional Municipal Index is a modified equal-weighted index that tracks the daily price only, income and total return performance of the domestic United States (U.S.) municipal market which consists of a selected number of investment grade, publicly traded fixed-rate and coupon-bearing municipal securities with a maturity of at least one year.

NUMBER OF BONDS—DECEMBER 31, 1995

375

MARKET VALUE—DECEMBER 31, 1995

US$100,020.0 million

SELECTION CRITERIA

A matrix technique is employed to model the performance and characteristics of the municipal market with a smaller number of municipal securities. Index members are selected from a universe consisting of investment grade, publicly traded fixed-rate and coupon-bearing municipal securities with a maturity of at least one year on the basis of their fit into established matrix blocks that are assigned a specific weight and set of sector, maturity and quality characteristics. Securities are placed in these blocks based on their fit to the block criteria.

BACKGROUND

The index is a component of the Merrill Lynch Global Bond Index, with monthly data to December 31, 1992. Daily index values are available thereafter.

For additional information, refer to the Merrill Lynch Global Bond Index.

BASE DATE

December 31, 1988=100.00

COMPUTATION METHODOLOGY

(1) A modified equal weighting index formula, in which the individual securities are equal weighted within matrix blocks that are, in turn, weighted on the basis of sector, maturity and quality characteristics. (2) Accrued interest and cash flows are assumed to be reinvested on a daily basis in the market. (3) Bid-side prices are obtained for each of the bonds in the index for both the beginning and the end of the measurement period. Securities prices are obtained from Merrill Lynch's trading floors. In addition, municipal bonds are hand priced twice weekly. Spreads calculated from the hand prices are applied to a municipal yield curve to generate alternate daily pricing.

DERIVATIVE INSTRUMENTS

None

SUBINDICES

Bank Trust Index
Insurance Company Index
Five municipal bond mutual fund indices: California Mutual Fund Index, Insured Bond Index, Mutual Fund Index, New York Mutual Fund Index and Intermediate Mutual Fund Index.

RELATED INDICES

Merrill Lynch Capital Markets Index
Merrill Lynch Convertible Securities Index
Merrill Lynch Currency Indices
Merrill Lynch Energy and Metals Index
Merrill Lynch Global Bond Index
Merrill Lynch Money Market Instrument Indices
Refer to Appendix 5 for additional indices.

REMARKS

(1) Investment quality determination rely on quality ratings of BBB- by Standard & Poor's (S&P) and/or Baa3 and above by Moody's Investors Service. A composite rating is calculated by averaging the ratings assigned by Moody's and S&P. In the event the average rating falls between two adjacent split-rated issues, the composite rating is the lower of the two. (2) Subindices refers to a partial list of performance benchmarks. Numerous subindices are available based on municipal sector, maturity and quality considerations.

PUBLISHER

Merrill Lynch & Co.

MERRILL LYNCH MORTGAGE MASTER BOND INDEX

TOTAL RETURN PERFORMANCE

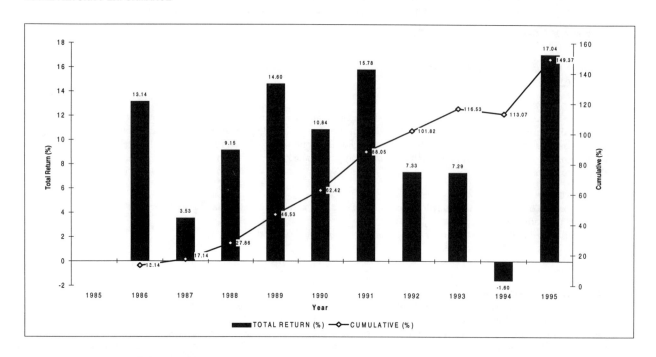

TOTAL RETURN AND PRICE PERFORMANCE

YEAR	VALUE	TOTAL RETURN (%)	CUMULATIVE (%)	PRICE RETURN (%)	MAXIMUM VALUE[1]	DATE	MINIMUM VALUE[1]	DATE
1995	688.32	17.04	149.37	8.79	688.32	31-Dec	601.01	31-Jan
1994	588.10	-1.60	113.07	-8.28	603.60	31-Jan	579.46	30-Apr
1993	597.67	7.29	116.53	1.54	597.67	31-Dec	564.51	31-Jan
1992	557.07	7.33	101.82	0.11	557.07	31-Dec	513.82	31-Jan
1991	519.05	15.78	88.05	6.21	519.05	31-Dec	454.67	31-Jan
1990	448.30	10.84	62.42	0.91	448.30	31-Dec	400.47	31-Jan
1989	404.46	14.60	46.53	4.12	404.46	31-Dec	357.03	28-Feb
1988	352.91	9.15	27.86	-0.98	360.24	31-Oct	334.34	31-May
1987	323.32	3.53	17.14	-5.64	323.32	31-Dec	304.56	30-Sep
1986	312.30	13.14	13.14	1.31	312.30	31-Dec	277.10	31-Jan
1985	276.02							
Average Annual (%)		9.71		0.81				
Compound Annual (%)		9.57		0.69				
Standard Deviation (%)		5.83		5.08				

[1]Maximum/minimum index values are as of month-end.

SYNOPSIS

The Merrill Lynch Mortgage Master Bond Index is a market value-weighted index that tracks the daily price only, income and total return performance of publicly placed fixed-rate, coupon-bearing, mortgage pass-through securities issued by U.S. Government agencies, including Government National Mortgage Association (GNMA), Federal Home Loan Mortgage Corporation (FHLMC) and Federal National Mortgage Association (FNMA) with original terms to maturity of 15 and 30 years.

NUMBER OF BONDS—DECEMBER 31, 1995
228

MARKET VALUE—DECEMBER 31, 1995
US$1,269,555.0 million

SELECTION CRITERIA

Eligible securities include U.S. Government agency mortgage pass-through securities with outstanding par amounts greater than or equal to $200.0 million per coupon for generic mortgage backed securities with various maturities.

FHA project notes, collateralized mortgage obligations (CMOs), 1/4-coupon pass-throughs, GNMA IIs, mobile-home, graduated payment mortgages, stripped interest only (IOs) and stripped principal only (POs) are excluded from consideration as index constituents.

BACKGROUND

The index represents a component of the Merrill Lynch Domestic Master Bond Index which is, in turn, a member of the Merrill Lynch Global Bond Index.

The Mortgage Master Index was established as of December 31, 1975 and monthly data is available to March 31, 1989. Thereafter, the index was computed on a daily basis. Price only returns are available since October 31, 1985.

For additional information, refer to the Merrill Lynch Global Bond Index.

BASE DATE

December 31, 1975=100.00

COMPUTATION METHODOLOGY

(1) An aggregate of prices times quantities index formula, including gain/loss on repayments of principal and currency conversions, where applicable, as well as coupon received or accrued for total rate of return calculations. (2) Daily price and total return calculations are based on the theory that the portfolio of securities that make up the index is purchased in its entirety at approximately 3 PM (EST) on the initial day and held until the same time on the following day, when it is sold. Price and total returns for a one day period represent the sum of the weighted average price return, weighted average accrued interest return, and weighted average coupon return, weighted by the market value of the outstanding amount of each bond in the index. Total return for extended intervals are calculated by "chain-linking" the periodic rates of return. Transaction costs are not included in the calculations of price and total returns. (3) Except for mortgage and asset backed principal pay-downs, which are assumed to occur on the 30th of the month, accrued interest and cash flows are assumed to be reinvested on a daily basis. (4) Bonds are generally priced on the basis of bid-side prices obtained from Merrill Lynch's trading floors. These are either hand priced or matrix priced, using price quotes taken at approximately 3 PM (EST). (5) Market values, for total return calculation purposes, are based on the outstanding amounts of each bond, which are reviewed regularly to account for full and partial retirement of debt, calls, sinking-fund requirements, tenders or re-opening of issues. (6) New issues enter the index on the first business day following settlement while bonds that no longer meet the index or subindex criterion are removed from the index one day, or two days, respectively, following such a determination. Bonds are removed from the index when they no longer satisfy the size, rating or maturity criteria.

DERIVATIVE INSTRUMENTS

None

SUBINDICES

Various subindices based on issuer/agency and final maturity.

RELATED INDICES

Merrill Lynch Capital Markets Index
Merrill Lynch Convertible Securities Index
Merrill Lynch Currency Indices
Merrill Lynch Energy and Metals Index
Merrill Lynch Institutional Municipal Index
Merrill Lynch Money Market Instrument Indices
Refer to Appendix 5 for additional indices.

REMARKS

To improve the liquidity and pricing quality of the index, new selection criteria were implemented starting April 30, 1996. The minimum par amount outstanding requirement for bonds were increased to US$100.0 million, with the exception of the U.S. Asset Backed Master which remains at US$25.0 million. Additionally, the US$200.0 million minimum requirement for each generic mortgage coupon was dropped and replaced by a US$100.0 million minimum applied to each seasoning category within a generic coupon. The exclusion of smaller issues is expected to have minimal impact on the market coverage and risk profile of the indices as these are market value-weighted.

PUBLISHER

Merrill Lynch & Co.

MERRILL LYNCH U.S. CORPORATE & GOVERNMENT MASTER BOND INDEX

TOTAL RETURN PERFORMANCE

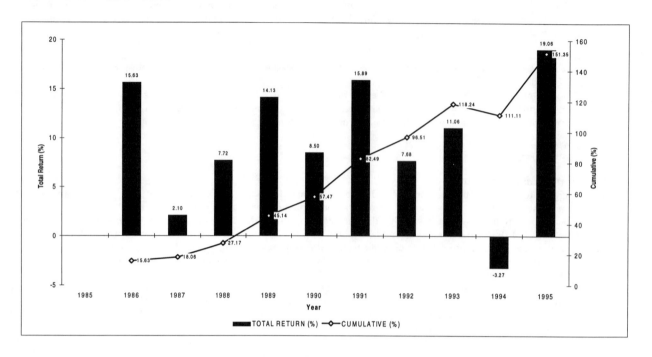

TOTAL RETURN AND PRICE PERFORMANCE

YEAR	VALUE	TOTAL RETURN (%)	CUMULATIVE (%)	PRICE RETURN (%)	MAXIMUM VALUE[1]	DATE	MINIMUM VALUE[1]	DATE
1995	751.55	19.06	151.35	11.02	751.55	31-Dec	642.96	31-Jan
1994	631.24	-3.27	111.11	-9.88	662.03	31-Jan	625.80	30-Jun
1993	652.55	11.06	118.24	3.67	657.04	31-Oct	600.01	31-Jan
1992	587.59	7.68	96.51	-0.22	587.59	31-Dec	537.56	31-Jan
1991	545.66	15.89	82.49	6.68	545.66	31-Dec	475.90	31-Jan
1990	470.84	8.50	57.47	-0.64	470.84	31-Dec	425.38	30-Apr
1989	433.98	14.13	45.14	4.44	433.98	31-Dec	382.17	28-Feb
1988	380.26	7.72	27.17	-1.46	382.77	31-Oct	365.14	31-Jan
1987	353.01	2.10	18.06	-6.57	353.01	31-Dec	333.45	30-Sep
1986	345.76	15.63	15.63	5.47	345.76	31-Dec	300.44	31-Jan
1985	299.01							
Average Annual (%)		9.85		1.25				
Compound Annual (%)		9.65		1.07				
Standard Deviation (%)		6.81		6.30				

[1]Maximum/minimum index values are as of month-end.

SYNOPSIS

The Merrill Lynch U.S. Corporate & Government Master Bond Index is a market value-weighted index that tracks the daily price only, income and total return performance of publicly placed, nonconvertible, fixed-rate, coupon-bearing, investment grade United States (U.S.) domestic debt.

NUMBER OF BONDS—DECEMBER 31, 1995
6,658

MARKET VALUE—DECEMBER 31, 1995
US$3,433,577.2 million

SELECTION CRITERIA

Eligible securities include U.S. Government and investment grade corporate securities with outstanding par amounts greater than or equal to $25.0 million for corporate and Treasury securities, with term-to-maturity greater than or equal to one year, which are rated BBB-/Baa3 and above, on a composite basis, by Standard & Poors' and Moody's Investors Service.

Floating-rate debt, equipment trust certificates and Title 11 securities are excluded from consideration as index constituents.

BACKGROUND

The index is a component of the Merrill Lynch U.S. Domestic Master Bond Index which, in turn, forms part of the Merrill Global Bond Index. It was established as of December 31, 1972 and monthly total return data is available to October 31, 1986. Price return index values are available as of January 31, 1976. The index has been computed on a daily basis since October 31, 1986.

For additional information, refer to the Merrill Lynch Global Bond Index.

BASE DATE

December 31, 1972=100.00

COMPUTATION METHODOLOGY

(1) An aggregate of prices times quantities index formula, including gain/loss on repayments of principal and currency conversions, where applicable, as well as coupon received or accrued for total rate of return calculations. (2) Daily price and total return calculations are based on the theory that the portfolio of securities that make up the index is purchased in its entirety at approximately 3 PM (EST) on the initial day and held until the same time on the following day, when it is sold. Price and total returns for a one day period represent the sum of the weighted average price return, weighted average accrued interest return, and weighted average coupon return, weighted by the market value of the outstanding amount of each bond in the index. Total return for extended intervals is calculated by "chain-linking" the periodic rates of return. Transaction costs are not included in the calculations of price and total returns. (3) Except for mortgage and asset backed principal pay downs, which are assumed to occur on the 30th of the month, accrued interest and cash flows are assumed to be reinvested on a daily basis. (4) Bonds are generally priced on the basis of bid-side prices obtained from Merrill Lynch's trading floors and are hand priced or matrix priced, using price quotes taken at approximate-ly 3 PM (EST). (5) Market values, for total return calculations, are based on the outstanding amounts of each bond, and are reviewed regularly to account for full and partial retirement of debt, calls, sinking-fund requirements, tenders or re-opening of issues. (6) New issues enter on the first business day following settlement while bonds that no longer meet the index or subindex criterion are removed from the index one day, or two days, respectively, following such a determination. Bonds are removed from the index when they no longer satisfy the size, rating or maturity criteria.

DERIVATIVE INSTRUMENTS

None

SUBINDICES

Government Master
Corporate Master
Treasury Master
Agency Master

RELATED INDICES

Merrill Lynch Capital Markets Index
Merrill Lynch Convertible Securities Index
Merrill Lynch Currency Indices
Merrill Lynch Energy and Metals Index
Merrill Lynch High Yield Master Index
Merrill Lynch Institutional Municipal Index
Merrill Lynch Money Market Instrument Indices
Refer to Appendix 5 for additional indices.

REMARKS

(1) A composite rating is calculated by averaging the ratings assigned by Moody's and S&P. In the event the average rating falls between two adjacent split-rated issues, the composite rating is the lower of the two. (2) Subindices refers to a partial list of commonly used performance benchmarks. In addition to numerous subindices which are compiled along sector, industry, maturity, quality and coupon lines, Merrill offers the flexibility to create custom indices. (3) To improve the liquidity and pricing quality of the index, new selection criteria were implemented starting April 30, 1996. The minimum par amount outstanding requirement for bonds was increased to US$100.0 million, with the exception of the U.S. Asset Backed Master which remains at US$25.0 million. Additionally, the US$200.0 million minimum requirement for each generic mortgage coupon was dropped and replaced by a US$100.0 million minimum applied to each seasoning category within a generic coupon. The exclusion of smaller issues is expected to have minimal impact on the market coverage and risk profile of the indices as these are market value-weighted.

PUBLISHER

Merrill Lynch & Co.

MERRILL LYNCH U.S. DOMESTIC CORPORATE BOND INDEX

TOTAL RETURN PERFORMANCE

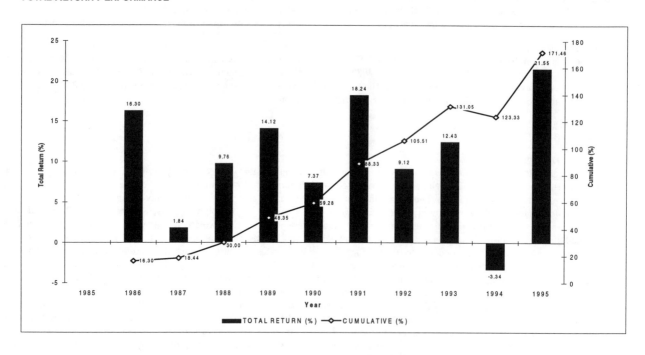

TOTAL RETURN AND PRICE PERFORMANCE

YEAR	VALUE	TOTAL RETURN (%)	CUMULATIVE (%)	PRICE RETURN (%)	MAXIMUM VALUE	DATE	MINIMUM VALUE	DATE
1995	819.75	21.55	171.46	12.67	819.75	31-Dec	687.28	31-Jan
1994	674.41	-3.34	123.33	-10.62	709.45	31-Jan	666.63	30-Jun
1993	697.73	12.43	131.05	4.25	702.32	31-Oct	634.09	31-Jan
1992	620.59	9.12	105.51	0.41	620.59	31-Dec	565.22	31-Mar
1991	568.73	18.24	88.33	8.13	568.73	31-Dec	486.44	31-Jan
1990	481.00	7.37	59.28	-2.28	481.00	31-Dec	439.83	30-Apr
1989	447.98	14.12	48.35	3.90	447.98	31-Dec	395.42	28-Feb
1988	392.57	9.76	30.00	-0.15	393.74	31-Oct	366.81	31-May
1987	357.67	1.84	18.44	-7.34	357.67	31-Dec	336.77	30-Sep
1986	351.20	16.30	16.30	5.53	351.20	31-Dec	303.11	31-Jan
1985	301.98							
Average Annual (%)		10.74		1.45				
Compound Annual (%)		10.50		1.23				
Standard Deviation (%)		7.53		7.00				

[1]Maximum/minimum index values are as of month-end.

SYNOPSIS

The Merrill Lynch U.S. Domestic Corporate Bond Index is a market value-weighted index that tracks the daily price only, income and total return performance of publicly placed, nonconvertible, fixed-rate, coupon-bearing, investment grade United States (U.S.) domestic debt.

NUMBER OF BONDS—DECEMBER 31, 1995
4,216

MARKET VALUE—DECEMBER 31, 1995
US$823,976.2 million

SELECTION CRITERIA

Eligible securities include investment grade corporate securities with outstanding par amounts greater than or equal to $25.0 million with term-to-maturity greater than or equal to one year which are rated BBB-/Baa3 and above, on a composite basis, by Standard & Poors' and Moody's Investors Service.

Floating-rate debt, equipment trust certificates and Title 11 securities are excluded from consideration as index components.

BACKGROUND

The index represents a component of the Merrill Lynch U.S. Domestic Master Bond Index, which, in turn, forms part of the Merrill Lynch Global Bond Index.

Price only index values have been computed since January 31, 1976 and monthly data is available to October 31, 1986. Thereafter, the index was computed on a daily basis. Some subindices, however, have been computed since December 31, 1972.

For additional information, refer to the Merrill Lynch Global Bond Index.

BASE DATE

December 31, 1972=100.00

COMPUTATION METHODOLOGY

(1) An aggregate of prices times quantities index formula, including gain/loss on repayments of principal and currency conversions, where applicable, as well as coupon received or accrued for total rate of return calculations. (2) Daily price and total return calculations are based on the theory that the portfolio of securities that make up the index is purchased in its entirety at approximately 3 PM (EST) on the initial day and held until the same time on the following day, when it is sold. Price and total returns for a one day period represent the sum of the weighted average price return, weighted average accrued interest return, and weighted average coupon return, weighted by the market value of the outstanding amount of each bond in the index. Total return for extended intervals is calculated by "chain-linking" the periodic rates of return. Transaction costs are not included in the calculations of price and total returns. (3) Except for mortgage and asset backed principal pay downs, which are assumed to occur on the 30th of the month, accrued interest and cash flows are assumed to be reinvested on a daily basis in the market. (4) Bonds are generally priced on the basis of bid-side prices obtained from Merrill Lynch's trading floors. These are either hand priced or matrix priced, using price quotes taken at approximately 3 PM (EST). (5) Market values, for total return calculation purposes, are based on the outstanding amounts of each bond, which are reviewed regularly to account for full and partial retirement of debt, calls, sinking-fund requirements, tenders or re-opening of issues. (6) New issues enter the index on the first business day following settlement while bonds that no longer meet the index or subindex criterion are removed from the index one day, or two days, respectively, following such a determination. Bonds are removed from the index when they no longer satisfy the size, rating or maturity criteria.

DERIVATIVE INSTRUMENTS

None

SUBINDICES

Various subindices representing industries, maturities and qualities.

RELATED INDICES

Merrill Lynch Capital Markets Index
Merrill Lynch Convertible Securities Index
Merrill Lynch Currency Indices
Merrill Lynch Energy and Metals Index
Merrill Lynch High Yield Master Index
Merrill Lynch Institutional Municipal Index
Merrill Lynch Money Market Instrument Indices
Refer to Appendix 5 for additional indices.

REMARKS

(1) A composite rating is calculated by averaging the ratings assigned by Moody's and S&P. In the event the average rating falls between two adjacent split-rated issues, the composite rating is the lower of the two. (2) To improve the liquidity and pricing quality of the index, new selection criteria were implemented starting April 30, 1996. The minimum par amount outstanding requirement for bonds were increased to US$100.0 million, with the exception of the U.S. Asset Backed Master which remains at US$25.0 million. Additionally, the US$200.0 million minimum requirement for each generic mortgage coupon was dropped and replaced by a US$100.0 million minimum applied to each seasoning category within a generic coupon. The exclusion of smaller issues is expected to have minimal impact on the market coverage and risk profile of the indices as these are market value-weighted.

PUBLISHER

Merrill Lynch & Co.

MERRILL LYNCH U.S. DOMESTIC MASTER BOND INDEX

TOTAL RETURN PERFORMANCE

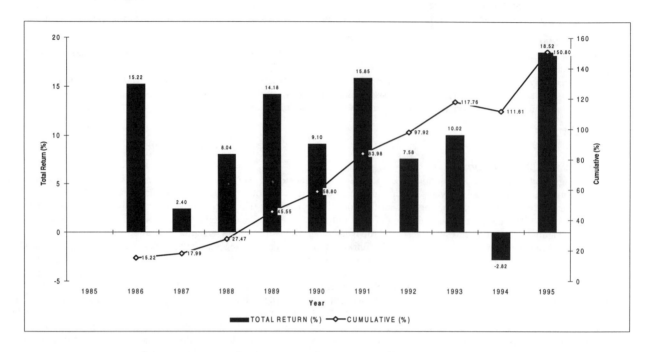

TOTAL RETURN AND PRICE PERFORMANCE

YEAR	VALUE	TOTAL RETURN (%)	CUMULATIVE (%)	PRICE RETURN (%)	MAXIMUM VALUE¹	DATE	MINIMUM VALUE¹	DATE
1995	670.59	18.52	150.80	10.42	670.59	31-Dec	576.81	31-Jan
1994	565.80	-2.82	111.61	-9.46	589.98	31-Jan	561.11	30-Apr
1993	582.25	10.02	117.76	3.08	583.92	31-Oct	539.26	31-Jan
1992	529.20	7.58	97.92	-0.14	529.20	31-Dec	485.27	31-Jan
1991	491.92	15.85	83.98	6.54	491.92	4-Mar	429.57	31-Jan
1990	424.61	9.10	58.80	-0.25	424.61	31-Dec	382.47	30-Apr
1989	389.18	14.18	45.55	4.34	389.18	8-Dec	343.10	28-Feb
1988	340.84	8.04	27.47	-1.37	344.26	31-Oct	323.23	31-May
1987	315.48	2.40	17.99	-6.33	315.48	31-Dec	297.79	30-Sep
1986	308.08	15.22	15.22	NA	308.08	31-Dec	268.62	31-Jan
1985	267.38							
Average Annual (%)		9.81		0.76				
Compound Annual (%)		9.63		0.53				
Standard Deviation (%)		6.53		6.19				

¹Maximum/minimum index values are as of month-end.

SYNOPSIS

The Merrill Lynch U.S. Domestic Master Bond Index is a market value-weighted index that tracks the daily price only, income and total return performance of publicly placed, nonconvertible, fixed-rate, coupon-bearing, investment grade United States (U.S.) domestic debt.

NUMBER OF BONDS—DECEMBER 31, 1995

6,886

MARKET VALUE—DECEMBER 31, 1995

US$4,703132.25 million

SELECTION CRITERIA

Eligible securities include U.S. Government, mortgage pass-through and investment grade corporate securities with outstanding par amounts greater than or equal to $25.0 million for corporate and Treasury securities and $200.0 million per coupon for generic mortgage-backed securities, with term to maturity greater than or equal to one year, which are rated BBB-/Baa3 and above, on a composite basis, by Standard & Poors' and Moody's Investors Service.

World Bank, Yankee and Canadian corporate issues are included in the index. Floating-rate debt, equipment trust certificates, Title 11 securities, GNMA series II, mobile-home, and graduated payment and 1/4-coupon mortgages are excluded from consideration as index constituents.

BACKGROUND

The Merrill Lynch Domestic Master Bond Index, which represents the major U.S. domestic component of the Merrill Lynch Global Bond Index, was established as of December 31, 1975 and monthly data is available to March 31, 1989. Thereafter, the index was computed on a daily basis. Some subindices, however, have been computed since December 31, 1972.

For additional information, refer to the Merrill Lynch Global Bond Index.

BASE DATE

December 31, 1975=100.00

COMPUTATION METHODOLOGY

(1) An aggregate of prices times quantities index formula, including gain/loss on repayments of principal and currency conversions, where applicable, as well as coupon received or accrued for total rate of return calculations. (2) Daily price and total return calculations are based on the theory that the portfolio of securities that make up the index is purchased in its entirety at approximately 3 PM (EST) on the initial day and held until the same time on the following day, when it is sold. Price and total returns for a one day period represent the sum of the weighted average price return, weighted average accrued interest return, and weighted average coupon return, weighted by the market value of the outstanding amount of each bond in the index. Total return for extended intervals are calculated by "chain-linking" the periodic rates of return. Transaction costs are not included in the calculations of price and total returns. (3) Except for mortgage and asset backed principal pay downs, which are assumed to occur on the 30th of the month, accrued interest and cash flows are assumed to be reinvested on a daily basis in the market. (4) Bonds are generally priced on the basis of bid-side prices obtained from Merrill Lynch's trading floors. These are either hand priced or matrix priced, using price quotes taken at approximately 3 PM (EST). (5) Market values, for total return calculation purposes, are based on the outstanding amounts of each bond, which are reviewed regularly to account for full and partial retirement of debt, calls, sinking-fund requirements, tenders or re-opening of issues. (6) New issues enter the index on the first business day following settlement while bonds that no longer meet the index or subindex criterion are removed from the index one day, or two days, respectively, following such a determination. Bonds are removed from the index when they no longer satisfy the size, rating or maturity criteria.

DERIVATIVE INSTRUMENTS

None

SUBINDICES

Agency Master
Corporate Master
Government Master
Mortgage Master
Treasury Master

RELATED INDICES

Merrill Lynch Capital Markets Index
Merrill Lynch Convertible Securities Index
Merrill Lynch Currency Indices
Merrill Lynch Energy and Metals Index
Merrill Lynch High Yield Master Index
Merrill Lynch Institutional Municipal Index
Merrill Lynch Money Market Instrument Indices
Refer to Appendix 5 for additional indices.

REMARKS

(1) A composite rating is calculated by averaging the ratings assigned by Moody's and S&P. In the event the average rating falls between two adjacent split-rated issues, the composite rating is the lower of the two. (2) Subindices refers to a partial list of commonly used performance benchmarks. In addition to numerous subindices which are compiled along sector, industry, maturity, quality and coupon lines, Merrill offers the flexibility to create custom indices. (3) To improve the liquidity and pricing quality of the index, new selection criteria were implemented starting April 30, 1996. The minimum par amount outstanding requirement for bonds were increased to US$100.0 million, with the exception of the U.S. Asset Backed Master which remains at US$25.0 million. Additionally, the US$200.0 million minimum requirement for each generic mortgage coupon was dropped and replaced by a US$100.0 million minimum applied to each seasoning category within a generic coupon. The exclusion of smaller issues is expected to have minimal impact on the market coverage and risk profile of the indices as these are market value-weighted.

PUBLISHER

Merrill Lynch & Co.

MERRILL LYNCH U.S. GOVERNMENT MASTER BOND INDEX

TOTAL RETURN PERFORMANCE

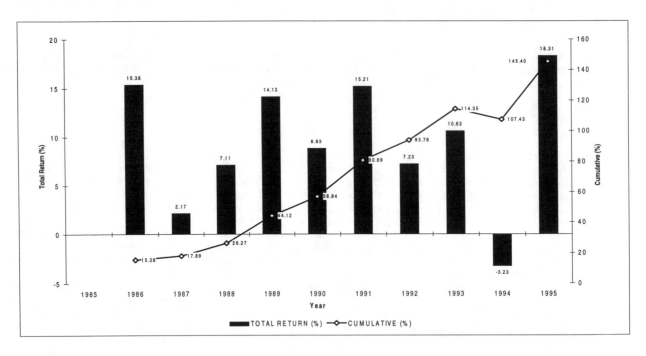

TOTAL RETURN AND PRICE PERFORMANCE

YEAR	VALUE	TOTAL RETURN (%)	CUMULATIVE (%)	PRICE RETURN (%)	MAXIMUM VALUE[1]	DATE	MINIMUM VALUE[1]	DATE
1995	747.32	18.31	145.40	10.52	747.32	31-Dec	643.30	31-Jan
1994	631.67	-3.23	107.43	-9.64	661.77	31-Jan	626.79	30-Jun
1993	652.76	10.63	114.35	3.50	652.76	31-Dec	602.41	31-Jan
1992	590.04	7.23	93.76	-0.42	590.04	31-Dec	540.90	31-Mar
1991	550.25	15.21	80.69	6.26	550.25	31-Dec	482.66	31-Jan
1990	477.62	8.83	56.84	-0.15	477.62	31-Dec	429.96	30-Apr
1989	438.87	14.13	44.12	4.63	438.07	31-Dec	386.19	28-Feb
1988	384.53	7.11	26.27	-1.86	387.47	31-Oct	366.38	31-May
1987	359.01	2.17	17.89	-6.33	359.01	31-Dec	345.39	31-May
1986	351.38	15.38	15.38	5.42	351.38	31-Dec	306.09	31-Jan
1985	304.53							
Average Annual (%)		9.58		1.19				
Compound Annual (%)		9.39		1.02				
Standard Deviation (%)		6.62		6.10				

[1]Maximum/minimum index values are as of month-end.

SYNOPSIS

The Merrill Lynch U.S. Government Master Bond Index is a market value-weighted index that tracks the daily price only, income and total return performance of publicly placed, nonconvertible, fixed-rate, coupon-bearing, U.S. Government debt, including Treasury and U.S. Government agency securities.

NUMBER OF BONDS—DECEMBER 31, 1995

2,442

MARKET VALUE—DECEMBER 31, 1995

US$2,609,601.0 million

SELECTION CRITERIA

Eligible securities include U.S. Government securities with outstanding par amounts greater than or equal to $25.0 million with term to maturity greater than or equal to one year.

U.S. Government agency issues include World Bank Government Bonds and TVA bonds. Floating-rate debt is excluded from consideration as an index constituent.

BACKGROUND

The index is a component of the Merrill Lynch Domestic Master Bond Index which, in turn, forms part of the Merrill Lynch Global Bond Index.

Total return monthly data is available to October 31, 1986. Price return index values are available as of February 29, 1976. Subsequent to October 31, 1986 the index was computed on a daily basis.

For additional information, refer to the Merrill Lynch Global Bond Index.

BASE DATE

December 31, 1972=100.00

COMPUTATION METHODOLOGY

(1) An aggregate of prices times quantities index formula, including gain/loss on repayments of principal and currency conversions, where applicable, as well as coupon received or accrued for total rate of return calculations. (2) Daily price and total return calculations are based on the theory that the portfolio of securities that make up the index is purchased in its entirety at approximately 3 PM (EST) on the initial day and held until the same time on the following day, when it is sold. Price and total returns for a one day period represent the sum of the weighted average price return, weighted average accrued interest return, and weighted average coupon return, weighted by the market value of the outstanding amount of each bond in the index. Total return for extended intervals is calculated by "chain-linking" the periodic rates of return. Transaction costs are not included in the calculations of price and total returns. (3) Except for mortgage and asset backed principal pay downs, which are assumed to occur on the 30th of the month, accrued interest and cash flows are assumed to be reinvested on a daily basis in the market. (4) Bonds are generally priced on the basis of bid-side prices obtained from Merrill Lynch's trading floors. These are either hand priced or matrix priced, using price quotes taken at approximately 3 PM (EST). (5) Market values, for total return calculation purposes, are based on the outstanding amounts of each bond, which are reviewed regularly to account for full and partial retirement of debt, calls, sinking-fund requirements, tenders or re-opening of issues. (6) New issues enter the index on the first business day following settlement while bonds that no longer meet the index or subindex criterion are removed from the index one day, or two days, respectively, following such a determination. Bonds are removed from the index when they no longer satisfy the size, rating or maturity criteria.

DERIVATIVE INSTRUMENTS

None

SUBINDICES

Treasury Master
Agency Master

RELATED INDICES

Merrill Lynch Capital Markets Index
Merrill Lynch Convertible Securities Index
Merrill Lynch Currency Indices
Merrill Lynch Energy and Metals Index
Merrill Lynch High Yield Master Index
Merrill Lynch Institutional Municipal Index
Merrill Lynch Money Market Instrument Indices
Refer to Appendix 5 for additional indices.

REMARKS

(1) A composite rating is calculated by averaging the ratings assigned by Moody's and S&P. In the event the average rating falls between two adjacent split-rated issues, the composite rating is the lower of the two. (2) Subindices refers to a partial list of commonly used performance benchmarks. In addition to numerous subindices which are compiled along sector, industry, maturity, quality and coupon lines, Merrill offers the flexibility to create custom indices. (3) To improve the liquidity and pricing quality of the index, new selection criteria were implemented starting April 30, 1996. The minimum par amount outstanding requirement for bonds was increased to US$100.0 million, with the exception of the U.S. Asset Backed Master which remain at US$25.0 million. Additionally, the US$200.0 million minimum requirement for each generic mortgage coupon was dropped and replaced by a US$100.0 million minimum applied to each seasoning category within a generic coupon. The exclusion of smaller issues is expected to have minimal impact on the market coverage and risk profile of the indices as these are market value-weighted.

PUBLISHER

Merrill Lynch & Co.

SALOMON BROTHERS BROAD INVESTMENT-GRADE (BIG) BOND INDEX

TOTAL RETURN PERFORMANCE

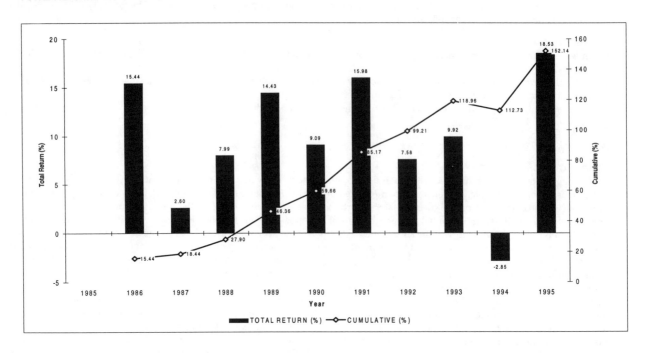

TOTAL RETURN AND PRICE PERFORMANCE

YEAR	VALUE	TOTAL RETURN (%)	CUMULATIVE (%)	PRICE RETURN (%)	MAXIMUM VALUE[1]	DATE	MINIMUM VALUE[1]	DATE
1995	553.37	18.53	152.14	11.24	553.37	31-Dec	476.53	31-Jan
1994	466.87	-2.85	112.73	0.13	487.04	31-Jan	462.52	30-Jun
1993	480.55	9.92	118.96	-0.02	481.89	31-Oct	446.05	31-Jan
1992	437.20	7.58	99.21	0.91	437.20	31-Dec	401.20	31-Jan
1991	406.40	15.98	85.17	2.31	406.40	31-Dec	354.64	31-Jan
1990	350.40	9.09	59.66	0.85	350.40	31-Dec	315.95	30-Apr
1989	321.21	14.43	46.36	-0.49	321.21	31-Dec	297.44	31-May
1988	280.70	7.99	27.90	-0.71	283.90	31-Oct	267.11	31-May
1987	259.93	2.60	18.44	0.46	259.93	31-Dec	245.66	30-Sep
1986	253.35	15.44	15.44	-0.40	253.35	31-Dec	220.72	31-Jan
1985	219.47							
Average Annual (%)		9.87		1.43				
Compound Annual (%)		9.69		1.37				
Standard Deviation (%)		6.57		3.56				

[1]Maximum/minimum index values are as of month-end.

SYNOPSIS

The Salomon Brothers Broad Investment-Grade (BIG) Bond Index is a broad market value-weighted index that tracks the daily and monthly price only and total return performance of institutionally-traded investment grade, fixed rate bonds issued in the United States, including U.S. Treasury, Government-sponsored (agency and supranational), mortgage and investment-grade corporate issues with a maturity of one year or longer.

NUMBER OF BONDS—DECEMBER 31, 1995
4,892

MARKET VALUE—DECEMBER 31, 1995
US$4,496,063.9 million

SELECTION CRITERIA

Qualifying securities consist of U.S. Treasury issues, U.S. agency, including supranationals issued as Yankee or Global bonds, corporates, including Yankees and Globals, mortgage pass-throughs, including 30-year and 15-year GNMA, FNMA and FHLMC securities and FNMA and FHLMC balloon mortgages, with a minimum maturity of one year or longer, a minimum Standard & Poor's or Moody's Investors Service quality of BBB-/Baa3 or better. Constituent bonds must also satisfy varying guidelines for minimum par amount outstanding. The minimum par amount outstanding for U.S. Treasuries and mortgages as well as corporates and Government-sponsored issues is US$1.0 billion and US$100.0 million, respectively. A corporate- or Government-sponsored bond is removed if it falls below US$75.0 million.

144A securities are eligible for inclusion in the index while floating or variable rate bonds, illiquid private placement type securities for which accurate information on outstanding, market coupon and maturity structure may be difficult to obtain, and derivative type securities that result in "double counting" of principal, such as U.S. Treasury zero-coupon bonds, CMOs and mortgage STRIPs, are excluded from consideration.

BACKGROUND

The Salomon Brothers fixed income indices, which were introduced in 1985, are designed to provide a reliable and fair benchmark for the investment-grade bond manager and be fully compatible with the techniques for the management of active, structured and passive portfolios. In addition to maintaining simple and objective selection criteria, the index is intended to offer a comprehensive, yet replicable, universe of securities that are free of markets or market segments that have established barriers to entry or foreign ownership restrictions. Through its Targeted Index Matrix (TIM), Salomon provides a generalized framework for constructing customized indices along a broad spectrum of duration and quality combinations available in the investment grade, fixed income market.

BIG Index requirements for inclusion on the basis of par amount outstanding have been modified over the years. The present entry and exit levels took effect in January 1995. In addition, the index has been enhanced over the years with regard to computation methodology, treatment of transaction costs, determination of quality ratings, expansion of industry sectors and introduction of additional security types.

BASE DATE

December 31, 1979=100.00

COMPUTATION METHODOLOGY

(1) An aggregate of prices times quantities index formula, including gain/loss on repayments of principal and currency conversions, where applicable, as well as coupon received or accrued for total rate of return calculations. (2) Price only and total returns are calculated based on the assumption that each security, which is market capitalization-weighted using the issue's market value at the beginning of the period, is purchased at the beginning of the period and sold at the end of the measurement period. (3) The securities in which Salomon Brothers traders make active markets are individually priced at month-end by those traders using bid-side prices for existing index constituents and offer prices for all newly added securities to reflect transaction costs and facilitate replication as of 5 PM (NY Time). For daily return calculations only, most corporate issues are matrix-priced. (4) New issues are monitored on a daily basis and eligible issues are included at the beginning of the month following their first settlement date. Bonds that no longer satisfy maturity, amount outstanding or credit rating criteria are removed from the index at the end of each month. The index is also adjusted monthly for changes in the amount outstanding due to calls, tenders, sinking funds, or principal paydowns. (5) New issues enter the index at the offer price. (6) Intramonth cash flows payments are reinvested continuously at the daily average of the one month Treasury bill for the calculation period. (7) Calendar month-end settlement dates are assumed for month-end calculations and same day settlements for daily index calculations.

DERIVATIVE INSTRUMENTS

None

SUBINDICES

Corporate Index
Mortgage Index
Treasury/Government Sponsored/Corporate Index
Treasury/Government Sponsored Index

RELATED INDICES

Salomon Brothers Convertible Securities Index
Salomon Brothers High Yield Market Index
Salomon Brothers World Equity Index
Salomon Brothers World Government Bond Index
Salomon Brothers World Money Market Index
Refer to Appendix 5 for additional indices.

REMARKS

Subindices include a partial list of commonly used performance benchmarks.
Various subindices by quality, maturity and market/security segment are also available.

PUBLISHER

Salomon Brothers Inc

SALOMON BROTHERS BROAD INVESTMENT-GRADE (BIG) CORPORATE BOND INDEX

TOTAL RETURN PERFORMANCE

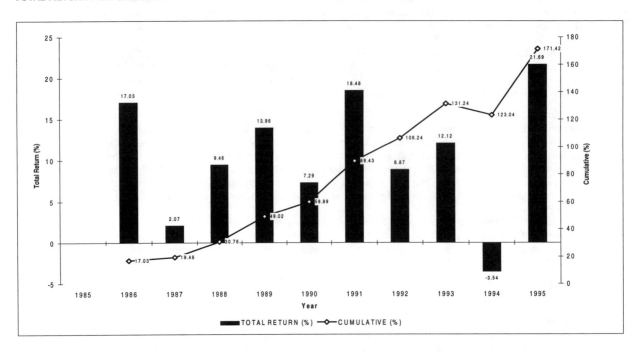

TOTAL RETURN AND PRICE PERFORMANCE

YEAR	VALUE	TOTAL RETURN (%)	CUMULATIVE (%)	PRICE RETURN (%)	MAXIMUM VALUE[1]	DATE	MINIMUM VALUE[1]	DATE
1995	602.67	21.69	171.42	13.00	602.67	31-Dec	505.74	Jan-96
1994	495.24	-3.54	123.04	0.20	522.74	31-Jan	489.81	30-Jun
1993	513.44	12.12	131.24	-0.02	516.22	31-Oct	468.95	31-Jan
1992	457.94	8.87	106.24	1.03	457.94	31-Dec	416.76	31-Jan
1991	420.62	18.48	89.43	2.39	420.62	31-Dec	359.49	31-Jan
1990	355.01	7.29	59.89	0.74	355.01	31-Dec	327.45	31-Jan
1989	330.88	13.96	49.02	-0.67	330.88	31-Dec	292.96	28-Feb
1988	290.35	9.46	30.76	-0.69	290.35	31-Dec	273.64	31-May
1987	265.25	2.07	19.46	0.84	266.86	28-Feb	248.81	30-Sep
1986	259.86	17.03	17.03	0.29	259.86	31-Dec	223.52	31-Jan
1985	222.04							
Average Annual (%)		10.74		1.71				
Compound Annual (%)		10.50		1.64				
Standard Deviation (%)		7.66		4.07				

[1]Maximum/minimum index values are as of month-end.

SYNOPSIS

The Salomon Brothers Broad Investment-Grade (BIG) Corporate Bond Index is a market value-weighted index that tracks the daily and monthly price only and total return performance of institutionally-traded investment grade, corporate fixed-rate bonds issued in the United States with a maturity of one year or longer.

NUMBER OF BONDS—DECEMBER 31, 1995
3,692

MARKET VALUE—DECEMBER 31, 1995
US$854,604.75 million

SELECTION CRITERIA

Qualifying securities consist of corporate bonds, including Yankees and Globals, with a minimum maturity of one year or longer, a minimum Standard & Poor's or Moody's Investors Service quality of BBB-/Baa3 or better, and a minimum par amount of US$1.0 billion. A corporate bond is removed if its amount falls below US$75.0 million.

144A securities are eligible for inclusion in the index while floating or variable rate bonds, illiquid private placement type securities for which accurate information on outstanding, market coupon and maturity structure may be difficult to obtain, are excluded from consideration.

BACKGROUND

The Corporate Index is a subindex of the Salomon Brothers Broad Investment Grade Bond Index, which was introduced in 1985. For additional information, refer to the Salomon Brothers Broad Investment-Grade (BIG) Bond Index.

Requirements for inclusion on the basis of par amount outstanding have been modified over the years. The present entry and exit levels took effect in January 1995. In addition, the index has been enhanced over the years with regard to computation methodology, treatment of transaction costs, determination of quality ratings, expansion of industry sectors and introduction of additional security types.

BASE DATE
December 31, 1979=100.00

COMPUTATION METHODOLOGY

(1) An aggregate of prices times quantities index formula, including gain/loss on repayments of principal and currency conversions, where applicable, as well as coupon received or accrued for total rate of return calculations. (2) Price only and total returns are calculated based on the assumption that each security, which is market capitalization-weighted using the issue's value at the beginning of the period, is purchased at the beginning of the period and sold at the end of the measurement period. (3) The securities in which Salomon Brothers traders make active markets are individually priced at month-end by those traders, using bid-side prices for existing index constituents and offer prices for all newly added securities to reflect transaction costs and facilitate replication as of 5 PM (NY Time). For daily return calculations only, most corporate issues are matrix-priced. (4) New issues are monitored on a daily basis and eligible issues are included at the beginning of the month following their first settlement date. Bonds that no longer satisfy maturity, amount outstanding or credit rating criteria are removed from the index at the end of each month. The index is also adjusted monthly for changes in the amount outstanding due to calls, tenders, sinking funds, or principal paydowns. (5) New issues enter the index at the offer price. (6) Intramonth cash flows payments are reinvested continuously at the daily average of the one month Treasury bill for the calculation period. (7) Calendar month-end settlement dates are assumed for month-end calculations and same day settlements for daily index calculations.

DERIVATIVE INSTRUMENTS
None

SUBINDICES
Corporate High Grade Index

RELATED INDICES
Salomon Brothers Convertible Securities Index
Salomon Brothers High Yield Market Index
Salomon Brothers World Equity Index
Salomon Brothers World Government Bond Index
Salomon Brothers World Money Market Index
Refer to Appendix 5 for additional indices.

REMARKS

Subindices include a partial list of commonly used performance benchmarks. Various subindices by quality, maturity and market/security segment are also available.

PUBLISHER
Salomon Brothers Inc.

SALOMON BROTHERS BROAD INVESTMENT-GRADE (BIG) MORTGAGE INDEX

TOTAL RETURN PERFORMANCE

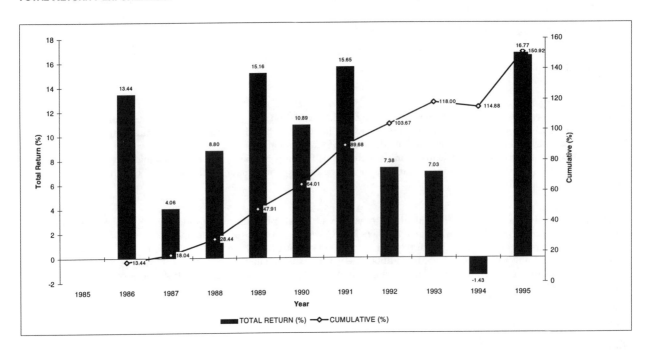

TOTAL RETURN AND PRICE PERFORMANCE

YEAR	VALUE	TOTAL RETURN (%)	CUMULATIVE (%)	PRICE RETURN (%)	MAXIMUM VALUE[1]	DATE	MINIMUM VALUE[1]	DATE
1995	581.65	16.77	150.92	8.42	581.65	31-Dec	509.27	31-Jan
1994	498.12	-1.43	114.88	0.17	507.23	28-Feb	491.60	30-Apr
1993	505.34	7.03	118.00	0.12	505.34	31-Dec	478.63	31-Jan
1992	472.13	7.38	103.67	0.52	472.13	31-Dec	435.23	31-Jan
1991	439.70	15.65	89.68	1.40	439.70	31-Dec	385.75	31-Jan
1990	380.20	10.89	64.01	0.88	380.20	31-Dec	340.38	31-Jan
1989	342.86	15.16	47.91	-0.22	342.86	31-Dec	301.03	28-Feb
1988	297.73	8.80	28.44	-1.31	303.64	31-Oct	283.14	31-May
1987	273.64	4.06	18.04	0.36	273.64	31-Dec	260.14	31-May
1986	262.97	13.44	13.44	-0.51	262.97	31-Dec	232.70	31-Jan
1985	231.81							
Average Annual (%)		9.78		0.98				
Compound Annual (%)		9.64		0.95				
Standard Deviation (%)		5.77		2.72				

[1]Maximum/minimum index values are as of month-end.

SYNOPSIS

The Salomon Brothers Broad Investment-Grade (BIG) Mortgage Index is a market value-weighted index that tracks the daily and monthly principal only and total return performance of institutionally-traded Government National Mortgage Association (GNMA), Federal Home Loan Mortgage Corporation (FHLMC) and Federal National Mortgage Association (FNMA) mortgage pass-through securities along with FNMA and FHLMC balloon mortgages with a maturity of one year or longer.

NUMBER OF BONDS—DECEMBER 31, 1995
145

MARKET VALUE—DECEMBER 31, 1995
US$1,272,972.5 million

SELECTION CRITERIA

Qualifying securities consist of 30-year and 15-year GNMA, FNMA and FHLMC securities and FNMA and FHLMC balloon mortgages, with a minimum maturity of one year or longer, and a minimum amount outstanding of US$1.0 billion, based on the aggregate of mortgage pools by coupon within agency or product type.

Derivative type securities that result in "double counting" of principal, such as collateralized mortgage obligations (CMOs) and stripped interest only (IOs) and stripped principal only (POs), are excluded from consideration.

BASE DATE
December 31, 1979=100.00

BACKGROUND

The Mortgage Index is a subindex of the Salomon Brothers Broad Investment-Grade Bond Index which was introduced in 1985. For additional information, refer to the Salmon Brothers BIG Index.

Requirements for inclusion on the basis of par amount outstanding have been modified over the years. The present entry and exit levels took effect in January 1995. In addition, the index has been enhanced over the years with regard to computation methodology, treatment of transaction costs, and introduction of additional security types.

COMPUTATION METHODOLOGY

(1) An aggregate of prices times quantities index formula, including gain/loss on repayments of principal and currency conversions, where applicable, as well as coupon received or accrued for total rate of return calculations. (2) Scheduled principal amortization and unscheduled principal prepayments are taken into account in the calculation of price-only as well as total rate of return performance. (3) Securities are trader priced at the end of every month, quoted for standard Public Securities Association (PSA) settlement dates which occur on a variety of dates throughout the month. Prices are adjusted for principal paydowns and also are adjusted for carry, using the one month London Interbank Offered Rate (LIBOR). (4) The index is reweighted each month to reflect new issuance and principal paydowns. (5) New issues are monitored on a daily basis and eligible issues are included at the beginning of the month following their first settlement date. Bonds that no longer satisfy maturity and amount outstanding criteria are removed from the index at the end of each month. The index is also adjusted monthly for changes in the amount outstanding due to principal paydowns. (6) New issues enter the index at the offer price. (7) Intramonth cash flows payments are reinvested continuously at the monthly average of the daily one month Treasury bill rate. (8) Calendar month end settlement dates are assumed for month-end calculations and same day settlements for daily index calculations.

DERIVATIVE INSTRUMENTS
None

SUBINDICES
GNMA Index
FHLMC Index
FNMA Index

RELATED INDICES
Salomon Brothers Convertible Securities Index
Salomon Brothers High Yield Master Index
Salomon Brothers World Equity Index
Salomon Brothers World Government Bond Index
Salomon Brothers World Money Market Index
Refer to Appendix 5 for additional indices.

REMARKS

Subindices include a partial list of commonly used performance benchmarks. Various subindices by quality, maturity and market/security segment are also available, including new, moderately seasoned and seasoned mortgage pools.

PUBLISHER
Salomon Brothers Inc.

SALOMON BROTHERS BROAD INVESTMENT-GRADE (BIG) TREASURY/GOVERNMENT SPONSORED BOND INDEX

TOTAL RETURN PERFORMANCE

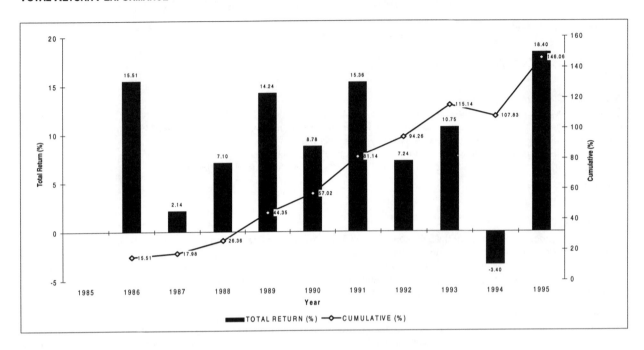

TOTAL RETURN AND PRICE PERFORMANCE

YEAR	VALUE	TOTAL RETURN (%)	CUMULATIVE (%)	PRICE RETURN (%)	MAXIMUM VALUE[1]	DATE	MINIMUM VALUE[1]	DATE
1995	533.71	18.40	146.06	10.63	533.71	31-Dec	459.61	31-Jan
1994	450.78	-3.40	107.83	0.08	473.07	31-Jan	447.39	30-Jun
1993	466.64	10.75	115.14	-0.10	469.74	31-Oct	430.81	31-Jan
1992	421.35	7.24	94.26	1.08	421.35	31-Dec	386.01	31-Mar
1991	392.89	15.36	81.14	2.78	392.89	31-Dec	344.19	31-Jan
1990	340.57	8.78	57.02	0.87	340.57	31-Dec	306.72	30-Apr
1989	313.09	14.24	44.35	-0.56	313.09	31-Dec	275.61	28-Feb
1988	274.07	7.10	26.36	-0.42	276.20	31-Oct	261.77	31-May
1987	255.90	2.14	17.98	0.39	255.90	31-Dec	242.60	30-Sep
1986	250.54	15.51	15.51	-0.59	250.54	31-Dec	218.19	31-Jan
1985	216.90							
Average Annual (%)		9.61		1.42				
Compound Annual (%)		9.42		1.37				
Standard Deviation (%)		6.71		3.39				

[1]Maximum/minimum index values are as of month-end.

SYNOPSIS

The Salomon Brothers Broad Investment-Grade (BIG) Treasury/Government Sponsored Bond Index is a market value-weighted index that tracks the daily and monthly principal only and total return performance of institutionally-traded fixed rate U.S. Treasury notes and bonds as well as Government-sponsored agency and supranational debt issues with a maturity of one year or longer.

NUMBER OF BONDS—DECEMBER 31, 1995

1,055

MARKET VALUE—DECEMBER 31, 1995

US$2,368,486.7 million

SELECTION CRITERIA

Qualifying securities consist of U.S. Treasury issues, U.S. agency, including supranationals issued as Yankee or Global bonds, with a minimum maturity of one year or longer and minimum par amount outstanding of US$1.0 billion. U.S. Treasury issues and Government-sponsored bonds are removed from the index if their part amounts fall below US$1.0 billion and US$75.0 million, respectively.

Floating or variable rate bonds as well as derivative type securities that result in "double counting" of principal, such as U.S. Treasury zero-coupon bonds, are excluded from consideration.

BACKGROUND

The Treasury/Government Sponsored Index is a subindex of the Salomon Brothers Broad Investment Grade Bond index, which was introduced in 1985. For additional information, refer to the Salomon Brothers Big Index.

Requirements for inclusion on the basis of par amount outstanding have been modified over the years. The present entry and exit levels took effect in January 1995. In addition, the index has been enhanced over the years with regard to computation methodology, treatment of transaction costs, determination of quality ratings, expansion of industry sectors and introduction of additional security types.

BASE DATE

December 31, 1979=100.00

COMPUTATION METHODOLOGY

(1) An aggregate of prices times quantities index formula, including gain/loss on repayments of principal and currency conversions, where applicable, as well as coupon received or accrued for total rate of return calculations. (2) Price only and total returns are calculated based on the assumption that each security, which is market capitalization weighted using the issue's market value at the beginning of the period, is purchased at the beginning of the period and sold at the end of the measurement period. (3) The securities in which Salomon Brothers traders make active markets are individually priced at month-end by those traders, using bid-side prices for existing index constituents and offer prices for all newly added securities to reflect transaction costs and facilitate replication as of 5 PM (NY Time). For daily return calculations only, most corporate issues are matrix-priced. (4) New issues are monitored on a daily basis and eligible issues are included at the beginning of the month following their first settlement date. Bond that no longer satisfy maturity, amount outstanding or credit rating criteria are removed from the index at the end of each month. The index is also adjusted monthly for changes in the amount outstanding due to calls, tenders, sinking funds, or principal paydowns. (5) New issues enter the index at the offer price. (6) Intramonth cash flows payments are reinvested continuously at the daily average of the one month Treasury bill for the calculation period. (7) Calendar month end settlement dates are assumed for month-end calculations and same day settlements for daily index calculations.

DERIVATIVE INSTRUMENTS

None

SUBINDICES

Treasury Index
Government Sponsored Debt Index

RELATED INDICES

Salomon Brothers Convertible Securities Index
Salomon Brothers High Yield Market Index
Salomon Brothers World Equity Index
Salomon Brothers World Government Bond Index
Salomon Brothers World Money Market Index
Refer to Appendix 5 for additional indices.

REMARKS

Subindices include a partial list of commonly used performance benchmarks. Various subindices by quality, maturity and market/security segment are also available.

PUBLISHER

Salomon Brothers Inc.

SALOMON BROTHERS HIGH-YIELD MARKET INDEX

TOTAL RETURN PERFORMANCE

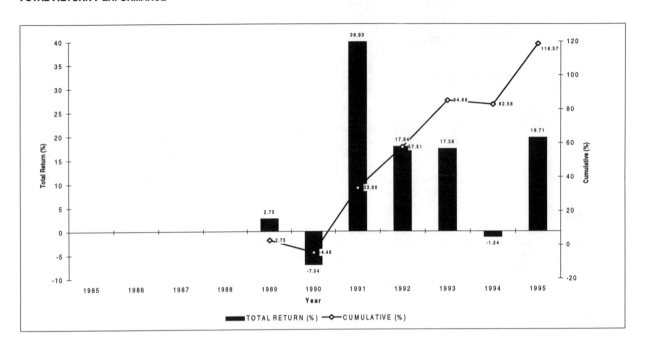

TOTAL RETURN AND PRICE PERFORMANCE

YEAR	VALUE	TOTAL RETURN (%)	CUMULATIVE (%)	PRICE RETURN (%)	MAXIMUM VALUE[1]	DATE	MINIMUM VALUE[1]	DATE
1995	218.57	19.71	118.57	9.39	218.57	31-Dec	185.22	31-Jan
1994	182.58	-1.24	82.58	-9.94	188.89	31-Jan	179.37	30-Apr
1993	184.88	17.38	84.88	7.10	184.88	31-Dec	161.35	31-Jan
1992	157.51	17.84	57.51	6.86	157.51	31-Dec	137.52	31-Jan
1991	133.66	39.93	33.66	25.65	133.36	31-Dec	98.00	31-Jan
1990	95.52	-7.04	-4.48	NA	105.37	31-Jul	92.69	31-Oct
1989	102.75	2.75	2.75	NA	106.65	31-Jul	101.75	31-Jan
1988	100.00							
1987								
1986								
1985								
Average Annual (%)		12.76		7.81				
Compound Annual (%)		11.82		7.21				
Standard Deviation (%)		15.93		12.62				

[1]Maximum/minimum index values are as of month-end.

SYNOPSIS

The Salomon Brothers High-Yield Market Index is a market value-weighted index that tracks the daily price only and total return performance of tradable, publicly placed, fixed coupon, nonconvertible, non-investment grade corporate debt issued in the United States with at least one year to final maturity.

NUMBER OF BONDS—DECEMBER 31, 1995

1,001

MARKET VALUE—DECEMBER 31, 1995

US$184,726.0 million

SELECTION CRITERIA

Constituents include all publicly placed, fixed coupon, nonconvertible, corporate debt issued in the United States with at least US$50.0 billion par amount outstanding and at least one year to final maturity. In addition to cash-pay and deferred-interest securities, the index includes bonds issued under Rule 144A after they have been fully registered with the Securities and Exchange Commission (SEC). To be eligible, issues must either be rated no higher than BB+ by Standard & Poor's Corporation or Ba1 by Moody's Investors Service.

BACKGROUND

Refer to the Salomon Brothers BIG Index.

BASE DATE

December 31, 1988=100.00

COMPUTATION METHODOLOGY

(1) An aggregate of prices times quantities index formula, including gain/loss on repayments of principal and currency conversions, where applicable, as well as coupon received or accrued for total rate of return calculations. (2) Price only and total returns are calculated based on the assumption that each security, which is market capitalization-weighted using the issue's value at the beginning of the period, is purchased at the beginning of the period and sold at the end of the measurement period. (3) The securities in which Salomon Brothers traders make active markets are individually priced at month-end by those traders, using bid-side prices for existing index constituents and offer prices for all newly added securities to reflect transaction costs and facilitate replication as of 5 PM (NY Time). For daily return calculations only, most corporate issues are matrix-priced. (4) New issues are monitored on a daily basis and eligible issues are included at the beginning of the month following their first settlement date. Bonds that no longer satisfy maturity, amount outstanding or credit rating criteria are removed from the index at the end of each month. The index is also adjusted monthly for changes in the amount outstanding due to calls, tenders, sinking funds, or principal paydowns. (5) New issues enter the index at the offer price. (6) Intramonth cash flows payments are reinvested continuously at the daily average of the one month Treasury bill for the calculation period. (7) Calendar month-end settlement dates are assumed for month-end calculations and same day settlements for daily index calculations.

DERIVATIVE INSTRUMENTS

None

SUBINDICES

Extended High-Yield Market Index
High Yield Cash-Pay Index
Composite High Yield Index
Bankrupt/Default Index
Deferred-Interest Index
Distressed Index
Safest of High-Yields Index

RELATED INDICES

Salomon Brothers Broad Investment-Grade (BIG) Bond Index
Salomon Brothers Convertible Securities Index
Salomon Brothers World Equity Index
Salomon Brothers World Government Bond Index
Salomon Brothers World Money Market Index
Refer to Appendix 5 for additional indices.

REMARKS

(1) Subindices include a partial list of commonly used performance benchmarks. Various subindices by varying maturities, including short, intermediate and long, varying industries as well as credit qualities. (2) Quality sector designations for split-rated debt issues are determined on the basis of Standard & Poor's (S&P) ratings. In the event a bond is rated by Moody's Investors Service and an S&P rating is not available, Salomon assigns an equivalent S&P rating and places the bond in the corresponding quality sector.

PUBLISHER

Salomon Brothers Inc.

WORLD

BLOOMBERG/EUROPEAN FEDERATION OF FINANCIAL ANALYST SOCIETIES (EFFAS) ALL GOVERNMENT BOND INDEX—U.S. GOVERNMENT

TOTAL RETURN PERFORMANCE

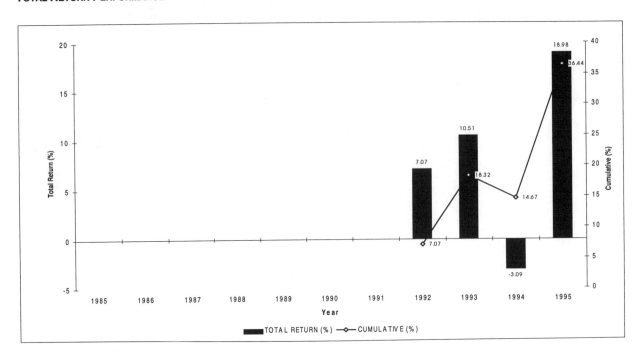

TOTAL RETURN AND PRICE PERFORMANCE

YEAR	VALUE	TOTAL RETURN (%)	CUMULATIVE (%)	PRICE RETURN (%)	MAXIMUM VALUE[1]	DATE	MINIMUM VALUE[1]	DATE
1995	136.44	18.98	36.44	11.21	136.435	29-Dec	114.551	3-Jan
1994	114.67	-3.09	14.67	-9.31	120.243	28-Jan	112.129	9-May
1993	118.32	10.51	18.32	3.39	120.026	15-Oct	106.465	7-Jan
1992	107.07	7.07	7.07	1.19	107.556	5-Oct	96.928	13-Mar
1991	100.00							
1990								
1989								
1988								
1987								
1986								
1985								
Average Annual (%)		8.37		1.62				
Compound Annual (%)		8.08		1.35				
Standard Deviation (%)		9.13		8.46				

[1]Maximum/minimum index values are as of month-end.

SYNOPSIS

The Bloomberg/European Federation of Financial Analyst Societies (EFFAS) All Government Bond Index—U.S. Government is the U.S. Government component of an investable market value-weighted index that tracks the daily principal only, gross price and total return of all publicly placed, fixed rate domestic government bonds denominated in 20 local currencies along with the European Currency Unit (ECU), with a final maturity in excess of one year, issued by 20 countries in Europe, Far East and North America.

NUMBER OF BONDS—DECEMBER 31, 1995
173

MARKET VALUE—DECEMBER 31, 1995
US$2,302,000.0 million

SELECTION CRITERIA

The index consists of liquid, comparable, publicly placed, fixed rate, non-convertible, domestic government bonds denominated in local currencies, with a final maturity in excess of one year. The 20 countries include: Australia, Austria, Belgium, Canada, Denmark, Finland, France, Germany, Ireland, Italy, Japan, The Netherlands, New Zealand, Norway, Portugal, Spain, Sweden, Switzerland, United Kingdom and the United States.

Callable bonds, serial redemption bonds and zero coupon bonds are eligible for inclusion in the index.

Excluded from eligibility are the following bond types:

(1) Bonds with cash flow uncertainty. These include: Floating rate bonds, index-linked bonds, callable bonds, puttable bonds, extendible bonds, bonds with sinking funds, bonds with warrants attached, mortgage or asset backed securities, including strips, dual-currency bonds and bonds with different tax status or special privileges. (2) Certain small or tightly held issues. (3) Illiquid bonds, such that there is an absence of Bloomberg Generic (BGN) prices.

BACKGROUND

The index was conceived and developed in an effort to address the need for a satisfactory portfolio performance yardstick for the day-to-day comparison of individual bond markets prior to the introduction of worldwide Government bond indices by various organizations in the U.S. and overseas. The European Federation of Financial Analysts Society undertook this effort along with Datastream, which was subsequently replaced by Bloomberg.

The index currently tracks each individual market, however, a global bond index is currently being tested and a Euro, international and corporate bond indices are under development.

BASE DATE

December 31, 1991=100.00

COMPUTATION METHODOLOGY

(1) An aggregate of prices times quantities index formula, including gain/loss on repayments of principal and currency conversions, if applicable, as well as coupon received or accrued for total rate of return calculations. (2) Intramonth cash flow payments due to coupon payments and redemptions are reinvested across the maturity sector at the time they are received. (3) Bond are priced using the official market or close of trading in each country. In the event two-way bid and offered prices are quoted for bonds, the average of the bid and offered prices are used. Government securities that are not priced for three consecutive business days are dropped from the index. Similarly, a security that is suspended is removed from the index after the third consecutive business day. (4) The index constituents are reviewed on a monthly basis, with new issues added to the index at the next selection date once the amount of the issue is known and a reliable price is available following the issue date . (5) Defaulted securities, if any, are removed from the index at the last available price as soon as the bond is known to have gone into default. (6) Partly paid securities are treated as fully paid for index performance calculation purposes. (7) A bond that has been called is left in the index until either it is redeemed or the constituents are reviewed at the end of the month at which time it is removed. (8) Calculations are based on the normal settlement date for the local market.

DERIVATIVE INSTRUMENTS

None

SUBINDICES

Bellwether Bond Index
Tracker Bond Index
Six subindices for the following maturity bonds: One- to three-years, three- to five-years, five- to seven-years, seven- to 10-years, over 10-years, perpetual and all maturity sectors combined.
Cross-currency total rates of return.

RELATED INDICES

Bloomberg Real Estate Index
Bloomberg State Common Stock Indices
Refer to Appendix 5 for additional indices.

REMARKS

(1) The number of bonds and market value are applicable to the U.S. Government component of the index. Refer to Appendix 5 for the number of bonds, market value and performance of the various other bond indices. (2) The Tracker Bond Index is a proxy for the All Bond Index. It consists of larger bonds and excludes illiquid issues or issues with special features. Selected on the basis of market capitalization, the index covers 20 or more issues and at least 25% of the group by market value or at least 50% of the group by market value, including any bonds that represent more than 5% of the market. (3) The Bellwether Bond Index consists of the most liquid issues in each market. The index includes up to five securities that are selected on the basis of market value, the greatest number of market makers, and a price spread that is less than the average for the Tracker Index.

PUBLISHER

Bloomberg Financial Services.

EMERGING MARKETS BOND INDEX PLUS (EMBI+)

TOTAL RETURN PERFORMANCE

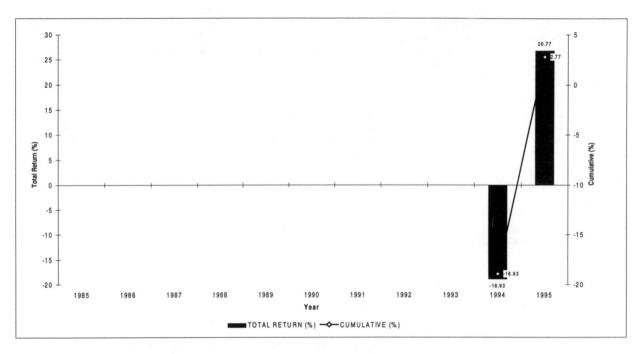

TOTAL RETURN PERFORMANCE (US$)

YEAR	VALUE	TOTAL RETURN (%)	CUMULATIVE (%)	MAXIMUM VALUE	DATE	MINIMUM VALUE	DATE
1995	102.77	26.77	2.77	102.77	29-Dec	62.12	9-Mar
1994	81.07	-18.93	-18.93	101.64	13-Jan	75.26	21-Apr
1993	100.00						
1992							
1991							
1990							
1989							
1988							
1987							
1986							
1985							
Average Annual (%)		3.92					
Compound Annual (%)		1.38					
Standard Deviation (%)		32.31					

SYNOPSIS
The Emerging Markets Bond Index Plus (EMBI+) is a liquid, market value-weighted, index that tracks the daily price only, income and total return performance of traded external debt instruments in 14 emerging markets, including U.S dollar and other external currency denominated Brady bonds, loans, Eurobonds and local market instruments.

NUMBER OF BONDS—DECEMBER 31, 1995
49

MARKET VALUE—DECEMBER 31, 1995
US$110,002.0 million

SELECTION CRITERIA
Emerging market countries are defined on the basis of their ability to repay external currency-denominated debt, using a Standard & Poor's and Moody's Investors Service rating ceiling of BBB+/Baa1.

Within eligible markets, bonds, including corporate external currency denominated bonds which are subject to a country's sovereign credit ceiling, are selected after satisfying the following criteria:
(1) A bond must satisfy a minimum face amount outstanding requirement, which varies by liquidity rating. (2) A bond must be rated BBB+/Baa1 or below. (3) A bond must have three or more years remaining to maturity. (4) A bond must be able to settle internationally, as in Euroclear, for example.

After establishing its eligibility, the liquidity of each instrument is assessed using the following five point scale:
(1) L1-Benchmark–Minimum US$2.0 billion face amount outstanding, an average bid/asked spread of <3/8 point, and quotations by all six designated brokers 75% of the time. (2) L2–Minimum US$1.0 billion face amount outstanding, an average bid/asked spread of <3/4 point and quotations by at least three of the six designated brokers 75% of the time. (3) L3–Minimum US$500.0 million face amount outstanding, an average bid/asked spread of <1.5 points and quotations by at least two of the six designated brokers 75% of the time. (4) L4–Minimum US$500.0 million face amount outstanding, an average bid/asked spread of <3 points and price quotations by at least one of six designated brokers at least 25% of the time. (5) L5-Illiquid–The bond is rarely or never quoted by designated brokers.

Instruments must be rated L1 or L2 or L3 to be eligible for inclusion in the index. Debt obligations that fail to maintain these liquidity ratings or their remaining life falls below one year, are dropped from the index.

BACKGROUND
Introduced in 1995, the EMBI+ expands upon J. P. Morgan's EMBI Index, which was designed to capture the highly liquid segment of the Brady bond market, by loosening liquidity criteria to allow for a broader range of fixed income assets in emerging markets.

In September 1995, revised liquidity definitions were implemented in an effort to further stabilize the composition of the index along with its companion EMBI Index. These involved the introduction of minimum face amounts outstanding, requirements applicable to the addition and deletion of instruments as well as minimum time to maturity.

The index is designed to serve as investable and replicable, transparent, accurate and reliable and timely in terms of its publication.

BASE DATE
December 31, 1991=100.00

COMPUTATION METHODOLOGY
(1) An aggregate of prices times quantities index formula, including gain/loss on repayments of principal and currency conversions, if applicable, as well as coupon received or accrued for total rate of return calculations. Daily returns are calculated for each market and in turn, the composite index is calculated using the market capitalization-weighted average of the daily returns of each market. (2) The index calculation takes into account all existing trading conventions, day-count bases, ex-periods and multiple series. (3) Special considerations and approximations apply to nonperforming and partially performing instruments. (4) Market capitalization is the outstanding portion of a debt instrument that an investor can easily purchase multiplied by its price. (5) Cash in the form of coupon payments and amortizations, if any, are reinvested in the instrument when received. (6) The index is rebalanced at the end of each month. (7) Instruments rated L1 or L2 or L3 must maintain liquidity ratings for one month, three months and six months, respectively, before they are added to the index. Debt obligations that decline to L4 and L5 liquidity ratings are dropped from the index after six months or one month, respectively. Exceptions are made for bonds that represent the last instrument in a given country, in which case it is dropped in the first month in which it falls to a L5 liquidity rating or the sixth consecutive month in which it is rated L4. Once dropped, a debt instrument is not eligible to reenter the index for a period of 12 months.

DERIVATIVE INSTRUMENTS
None

SUBINDICES
EMBI Index
Latin Eurobond Index (LEI)
South Africa Bond Index (SABI)
Various subindices by liquidity ratings, security type, geographic regions, single countries and currencies.

RELATED INDICES
J. P. Morgan Cash Index
J. P. Morgan Commodity Index
J. P. Morgan ECU Index
J. P. Morgan Global Government Bond Index

REMARKS
(1) EMBI+ weights on the basis of market capitalization as of December 31, 1995 are, as follows: Argentina 21.11%, Brazil 28.57%, Bulgaria 1.94%, Ecuador 2.19%, Mexico 18.99%, Morocco 1.49%, Nigeria 0.93%, Panama 0.41%, Peru 1.22%, Philippines 2.91%, Poland 4.27%, Russia 7.0%, South Africa 0.74% and Venezuela 8.23%. (2) A determination regarding the classification of an emerging market with a split rating is still pending.

PUBLISHER
J.P. Morgan Securities Inc.

J.P. Morgan ECU Bond Index

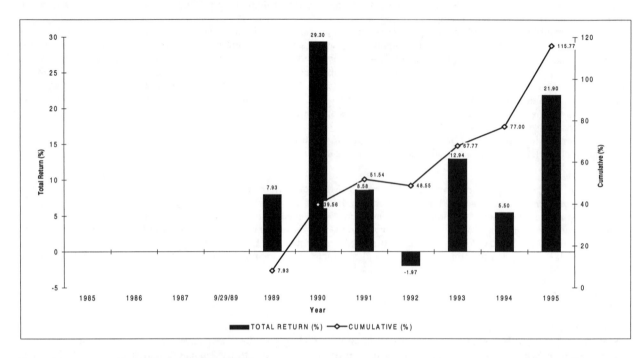

TOTAL RETURN AND PRICE PERFORMANCE (US$)

YEAR	VALUE	TOTAL RETURN (%)	CUMULATIVE (%)	PRICE RETURN (%)	MAXIMUM VALUE[1]	DATE	MINIMUM VALUE[1]	DATE
1995	199.91	21.90	115.77	13.55	199.91	31-Dec	168.62	31-Jan
1994	163.99	5.50	77.00	-2.68	167.11	31-Oct	154.92	28-Feb
1993	155.44	12.94	67.77	4.94	155.44	31-Dec	139.29	31-Jul
1992	137.63	-1.97	48.55	-10.05	150.45	31-Aug	132.04	31-Mar
1991	140.40	8.58	51.54	3.58	140.40	31-Dec	111.53	30-Jun
1990	129.30	29.30	39.56	13.51	129.30	31-Dec	97.02	28-Feb
1989	100.00	7.93	7.93	NA	100.00	31-Dec	92.65	29-Sep
9/29/89	92.65							
1987								
1986								
1985								
Average Annual (%)		13.47		3.81				
Compound Annual (%)		13.09		3.46				
Standard Deviation (%)[2]		11.35		9.21				

[1]Maximum/minimum index values are as of month-end.
[2]Standard deviation applicable to the 6-year period 1990-1995.

SYNOPSIS

The J. P. Morgan ECU Bond Index is a tradeable market value-weighted index that tracks the daily price only and total return performance of a basket of regularly traded, fixed rate bonds issued by corporate, sovereign and supernational organizations and denominated in the European Currency Unit (ECU).

NUMBER OF BONDS—DECEMBER 31, 1995
18

MARKET VALUE—DECEMBER 31, 1995
US$48,394.0 million

SELECTION CRITERIA

Eligible bonds consist of corporate, sovereign and supernational issues that are denominated in the European Currency Unit (ECU). They must have a maturity of not less than three years and not more than 10 years and can be traded in size and at acceptable bid/offer spreads which are on the order of 10 basis points in price terms. A reasonable distribution of bonds throughout the three-year to 10-year maturity spectrum is sought, with benchmark issues for the three-, five-, seven- and ten-year maturities present in the index basket at all times.

Bonds are included in the index for a period of no less than four months. Once excluded, a bond is not permitted to reenter the index for a period of six months.

BACKGROUND

The index, which was introduced 1991, embodies the attributes that also characterize the J.P. Morgan Government Bond Index in terms of its construction methodology, representativeness, investability and replicability. The index has been recalculated back to October 1, 1989 on a daily basis.

BASE DATE
December 29, 1989=100.00

COMPUTATION METHODOLOGY

(1) An aggregate of prices times quantities index formula, including gain/loss on repayments of principal and currency conversions, if applicable, as well as coupon received or accrued for total rate of return calculations. Transaction costs and taxes are not taken into consideration. (2) Market weights are based on liquidity considerations or tradable market value. (3) The computation of the index is based upon a selected basket of eligible securities which, for the purpose of performance measurement simplification and to facilitate replication, is adjusted at the beginning of each month. The composition of the index, or the basket, is reviewed at the beginning of each month to take account of the evolution of the market and adjustments may be made to reflect changes in liquidity, credit ratings or amounts outstanding of individual issues, new issues and the emergence of new benchmarks. (4) The market capitalization of a given bond is reviewed each month to take into account reopenings, conversions, strips, etc. (5) Maturity guidelines are applied to the life of the bond, which is defined as the period between settlement and maturity. (6) Accrued interest calculations reflect domestic settlement procedures and ex-dividend conventions in each market. Coupons are reinvested on a daily basis into the country or sector index in proportion to the latest market value of the constituents. (7) Mid prices are used for all calculations. Price data are provided by J.P. Morgan market makers. ECU prices are based on J.P. Morgan's data from April 1990. Data prior to that date have been obtained from a variety of external sources and validated by J.P. Morgan prior to being used. (8) Foreign exchange rates are based on WM/Reuters Closing Spot Rates as of 4 PM London Time.

DERIVATIVE INSTRUMENTS
None

SUBINDICES
Two quality subindices: Triple-A index and a non-triple A rated index.

RELATED INDICES
J. P. Morgan Cash Index
J. P. Morgan Commodity Index
J. P. Morgan Emerging Markets Bond Index
J. P. Morgan Global Government Bond Index

REMARKS

Bond ratings from Moody's and Standard & Poor's are used for the classification of debt issues within the subindices. In the event of a split rating, the lower of the two ratings are utilized for quality classification purposes. Bonds without assigned ratings from Moody's Investors or Standard & Poor's are excluded from eligibility in the triple-A subindex, excepting certain sovereign credits, such as the French Treasury Obligation Assimilable du Tre[mar1]' sor (OATs), which, according to J.P. Morgan, are assigned a paripassu status of Triple-A.

PUBLISHER
J. P. Morgan Securities Inc.

J.P. MORGAN GLOBAL GOVERNMENT BOND INDEX

TOTAL RETURN PERFORMANCE

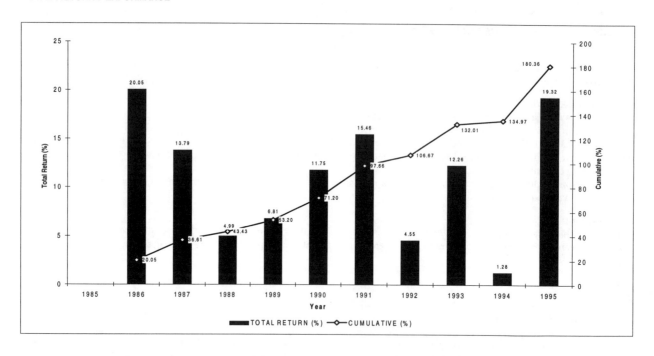

TOTAL RETURN AND PRICE PERFORMANCE (US$)

YEAR	VALUE	TOTAL RETURN (%)	CUMULATIVE (%)	PRICE RETURN (%)	MAXIMUM VALUE	DATE	MINIMUM VALUE	DATE
1995	205.22	19.32	180.36	11.64	205.22	29-Dec	171.05	9-Jan
1994	172.00	1.28	134.97	-5.77	174.41	18-Oct	165.78	18-Apr
1993	169.83	12.26	132.01	4.90	172.16	12-Oct	150.79	4-Jan
1992	151.28	4.55	106.67	-3.28	158.93	8-Sep	138.56	13-Mar
1991	144.69	15.46	97.66	6.53	144.69	31-Dec	123.25	18-Jun
1990	125.32	11.75	71.20	2.65	126.17	12-Dec	107.68	13-Mar
1989	112.14	6.81	53.20	-1.58	112.41	22-Dec	102.46	21-Mar
1988	104.99	4.99	43.43	-3.11	106.00	6-Dec	97.73	8-Jan
1987	100.00	13.79	36.61	4.50	100.00	31-Dec	87.88	1-Jan
1986	87.88	20.05	20.05	10.72	87.88	31-Dec	72.04	13-Jan
1985	73.20							
Average Annual (%)		11.03		2.72				
Compound Annual (%)		10.86		2.56				
Standard Deviation (%)		6.42		6.02				

SYNOPSIS

The J.P. Morgan Global Government Bond Index is a tradeable market value-weighted index that tracks the daily price, interest, total return and currency performance of actively traded, fixed-rate domestic government bonds, with maturities greater than one year, that have been issued by 13 countries. These include Australia, Belgium, Canada, Denmark, France, Germany, Italy, Japan, The Netherlands, Spain, Sweden, United Kingdom and the United States

NUMBER OF BONDS—DECEMBER 31, 1995

510

MARKET VALUE—DECEMBER 31, 1995

US$4,792,995.0 million

SELECTION CRITERIA
Eligible markets are selected on the basis of credit quality, accessibility to foreign investors, liquidity, investment diversification opportunities and level of institutional trading activity. Within each eligible market, bonds, in turn, consist of a universe of issues that are readily available for purchase at actively quoted prices. These instruments, which must be tradable and redeemable for cash and whose appeal is not limited exclusively to domestic investors for local tax or regulatory reasons, include fixed-rate government bonds with final maturities greater than one year, which are regularly traded in size at acceptable bid-offer spreads. Straight, put, call sinking fund, purchase fund, extendible, conversion and double-dated bonds are all eligible for inclusion in the index.

Index linked issues and floaters, perpetual bonds, irredeemable bonds, convertible securities, private placements and special instruments, such as flower bonds in the U.S. and medium term discount bonds in Japan, are excluded from consideration.

BACKGROUND
The index was introduced on December 4, 1989. Daily index values are available to December 31, 1995 and to December 31, 1987 for Ireland, Italy, New Zealand, Spain and Sweden.

BASE DATE
December 31, 1987=100.00

COMPUTATION METHODOLOGY
(1) An aggregate of prices times quantities index formula, including gain/loss on repayments of principal and currency conversions, if applicable, as well as coupon received or accrued for total rate of return calculations. Transaction costs and taxes are excluded. (2) Market weights are based on liquidity considerations or tradable market value. Modifications in the individual weights are made at the beginning of each month to reflect purchase and sinking fund redemptions, reopenings, buy-ins, reverse auctions, and STRIP activity. (3) Each issue remains in the index for a minimum of six months. Issues that are dropped from the index are not permitted to reenter the index for a period of six months. (4) Accrued interest calculations reflect domestic settlement procedures and ex-dividend conventions in each market. Coupons are reinvested on a daily basis into the country or sector index in proportion to the latest market value of the constituents. (5) Prices represent closing transaction prices, usually bid prices, supplied by J.P. Morgan in its capacity as market-maker or dealing official fixing prices from the local exchange. (6) Foreign exchange rates are based on WM/Reuters Closing Spot Rates as of 4 PM London Time.

DERIVATIVE INSTRUMENTS
None

SUBINDICES
Three liquidity sector subindices: "Benchmark," "Active," and "Traded."
Additional government bond indices: Ireland and New Zealand along with ECU-denominated bonds.
G-5 Government Bond Index, comprised of France, Germany, Japan, United Kingdom and the United States.
G-7 Government Bond Indices, comprised of G-5 plus Canada and Italy.

RELATED INDICES
J. P. Morgan Cash Index
J. P. Morgan Commodity Index
J. P. Morgan ECU Index
J. P. Morgan Emerging Markets Bond Index

REMARKS
(1) "Benchmark" issues include bonds that are widely recognized market indicators whose terms set a standard for the market. Benchmark bonds usually have the greatest liquidity, experience the highest turnover and are the most frequently quoted. They are the most recent sizable issue, current coupon issue, often the latest or most recently recognized issue, and usually consist of only one bond in any given maturity sector. "Active" issues include all benchmark issues along with bonds that have significant daily turnover and characterized by the fact that they may have been a benchmark issue earlier, actively quoted side-issues so that the universe spans the yield curve. "Traded" issues include all active issues plus other issues with prices that change regularly for which a two way market exists available for investment. The number of bonds referred above apply to the number of traded issues. (2) In addition to the more widely used customized indices, over 800 subindices and associated statistics are published, including customized indices and indices by return type, including total return, principal, interest and currency return, weighting schemes, maturity sectors, local currency, any of 67 base currencies and currency-hedged indices.

PUBLISHER
J.P. Morgan Securities Inc.

LEHMAN BROTHERS EMERGING AMERICAS BOND INDEX

TOTAL RETURN PERFORMANCE

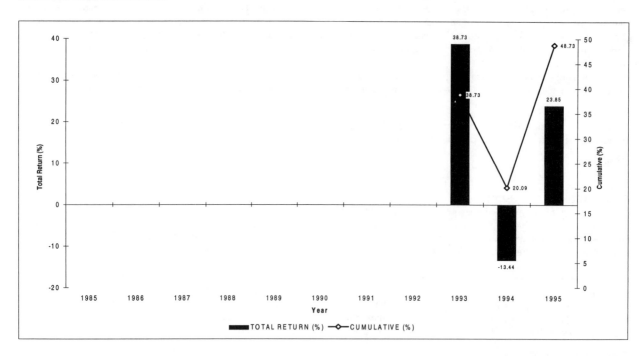

TOTAL RETURN PERFORMANCE (US$)

YEAR	VALUE	TOTAL RETURN (%)	CUMULATIVE (%)	MAXIMUM VALUE[1]	DATE	MINIMUM VALUE[1]	DATE
1995	148.73	23.85	48.73	148.73	31-Dec	106.29	31-Mar
1994	120.09	-13.44	20.09	139.29	31-Jan	117.87	30-Jun
1993	138.73	38.73	38.73	138.73	31-Dec	101.31	31-Jan
1992	100.00						
1991							
1990							
1989							
1988							
1987							
1986							
1985							
Average Annual (%)		16.38					
Compound Annual (%)		14.15					
Standard Deviation (%)		26.87					

[1]Maximum/minimum index values are as of month-end.

SYNOPSIS

The Lehman Brothers Emerging Americas Bond Index is a market value-weighted index that tracks the monthly price only, coupon, paydowns, and total return performance of publicly traded, nonconvertible, U.S. dollar-denominated debt issues of public and private entities in Argentina, Brazil, Mexico and Venezuela.

NUMBER OF BONDS—DECEMBER 31, 1995

155

MARKET VALUE—DECEMBER 31, 1995

US$105,882.0 million

SELECTION CRITERIA

Eligible securities include publicly traded, public and private, nonconvertible, U.S. dollar-denominated issues in Argentina, Brazil, Mexico and Venezuela. These consist of international issues, namely Eurobonds, Yankees and globals, Brady bonds and locally issued debt obligations which must have a remaining maturity of one year or more and have a minimum par amount outstanding of $100.0 million. Brady bonds and locally issued bonds must have at least $1.0 billion (outstanding amounts in similar series are aggregated) and $500.0 million outstanding par amounts, respectively. Issues with fixed, floating and hybrid coupons, as well as pay-in-kind (PIK) bonds, are eligible for inclusion in the index.

Private placements and 144A securities, however, are excluded from the index unless they have qualifying Eurobond tranches.

BACKGROUND

The index was introduced in 1994. For additional information, refer to the Lehman Brothers Aggregate Bond Index.

BASE DATE

December 31, 1993=100.00

COMPUTATION METHODOLOGY

(1) An aggregate of prices times quantities index formula, including gain/loss on repayments of principal and currency conversions, if applicable, as well as coupon received or accrued for total rate of return calculations. (2) Returns are based on a universe of securities established at the beginning of each month and held constant until the beginning of the next month. Securities that become ineligible for inclusion in the index during the month due to downgrades, redemptions or calls, securities falling below one year in maturity or newly eligible securities are maintained in a second, statistical universe. The statistical universe drives the production of portfolio statistics during the course of the month, i.e., coupon, duration, maturity, yield and price, and is also used to update the returns universe at the end of each month. (3) Intramonth cash flows are reinvested at month-end. If a security is no longer outstanding at the end of the month, the ending price is the level at which it exited the market. (4) Securities are priced by Lehman Brothers traders. (5) The final maturity requirement of at least one year is determined regardless of call features and mortgage and asset-backed securities must have a remaining average life of at least one year.

DERIVATIVE INSTRUMENTS

None

SUBINDICES

Various subindices by country, issue and issuer type and fixed as well as floating rates of interest.

RELATED INDICES

Lehman Adjustable Rate Mortgage Index
Lehman Aggregate Bond Index
Lehman Commodity Index
Lehman Emerging Americas Bond Index
Lehman Global Bond Index
Lehman High Yield Composite Bond Index
Lehman Municipal Bond Index
Lehman Mutual Fund Indices
Refer to Appendix 5 for additional indices.

REMARKS

(1) To supplement commonly used indices, Lehman offers the flexibility to create customized indices that meet specific investor requirements. (2) For cash flow yields, floating coupons are assumed to be current LIBOR plus a contractual spread.

PUBLISHER

Lehman Brothers.

LEHMAN BROTHERS EUROBOND INDEX

TOTAL RETURN PERFORMANCE

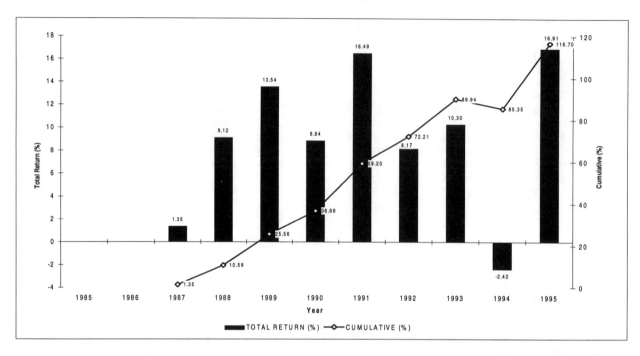

TOTAL RETURN PERFORMANCE

YEAR	VALUE	TOTAL RETURN (%)	CUMULATIVE (%)	MAXIMUM VALUE[1]	DATE	MINIMUM VALUE[1]	DATE
1995	216.70	16.91	116.70	216.70	31-Dec	188.48	31-Jan
1994	185.35	-2.42	85.35	192.57	31-Jan	183.52	30-Apr
1993	189.94	10.30	89.94	190.48	31-Oct	176.17	31-Jan
1992	172.21	8.17	72.21	172.60	30-Sep	158.08	31-Jan
1991	159.20	16.49	59.20	159.20	31-Dec	138.30	31-Jan
1990	136.66	8.84	36.66	136.66	31-Dec	123.87	31-Jan
1989	125.56	13.54	25.56	125.56	31-Dec	111.47	28-Feb
1988	110.59	9.12	10.59	110.93	31-Oct	104.31	31-Oct
1987	101.35	1.35	1.35	101.35	31-Dec	96.89	30-Sep
1986	100.00						
1985							
Average Annual (%)		9.14					
Compound Annual (%)		8.97					
Standard Deviation (%)		7.05					

[1]Maximum/minimum index values are as of month-end.

SYNOPSIS

The Lehman Brothers Eurobond Index is a market value-weighted index that tracks the monthly price only, coupon and total return performance of non-SEC registered corporate, sovereign and supranational issues, including government guaranteed, fixed-rate, U.S. dollar-denominated, nonconvertible, investment grade debt traded on the Eurobond market.

NUMBER OF BONDS—DECEMBER 31, 1995
666

MARKET VALUE—DECEMBER 31, 1995
US$275638.0 million

SELECTION CRITERIA

Eligible securities include investment grade, non-Securities Exchange Commission (SEC)-registered (except for global issues which can be settled either in Europe or the United States) corporate, sovereign and supranational issues, including government guaranteed, fixed-rate, U.S. dollar-denominated, nonconvertible debt traded on the Eurobond market, with at least one year remaining to maturity and an outstanding par value of $100.0 million, or $200.0 million in the case of Japanese ex-warrant bonds. Eurobonds issued as part of Euro-medium term note programs may be included as are Dragon bonds.

Equity linked securities, convertible securities, securities that have floating rates of interest and warrants, however, are excluded from the index.

BACKGROUND

The index was revised in April 1994 to reflect changes in the Eurobond market by adding Dragon and global bonds. For additional information, refer to the Lehman Brothers Aggregate Bond Index.

BASE DATE

December 31, 1986=100.00

COMPUTATION METHODOLOGY

(1) An aggregate of prices times quantities index formula, including gain/loss on repayments of principal and currency conversions, if applicable, as well as coupon received or accrued for total rate of return calculations. (2) Returns are based on a universe of securities established at the beginning of each month and held constant until the beginning of the next month. Securities that become ineligible for inclusion in the index during the month due to downgrades, redemptions or calls, securities falling below one year in maturity or newly eligible securities are maintained in a second, statistical universe. The statistical universe drives the production of portfolio statistics during the course of the month, i.e., coupon, duration, maturity, yield and price, and is also used to update the returns universe at the end of each month. (3) Intramonth cash flows are reinvested at month-end. If a security is no longer outstanding at the end of the month, the ending price is the level at which it exited the market. (4) Bonds are priced on the bid side at 3 PM (EST), except that corporate bonds new to the index are initially priced on the offer side. Bonds are predominantly trader priced, with about 99% of the market value of the index priced by traders. Remaining issues, which consist of smaller, less liquid securities, are priced using matrix pricing algorithms that take into account sector, quality, duration, option features as well as issuer specific factors. (5) The final maturity requirement of at least one year is determined regardless of call features and mortgage and asset-backed securities must have a remaining average life of at least one year.

DERIVATIVE INSTRUMENTS

None

SUBINDICES

Subindices are calculated by each issuer type, including sovereign, corporate and supranational, varying credit ratings, country of issue and global issues.

RELATED INDICES

Lehman Adjustable Rate Mortgage Index
Lehman Aggregate Bond Index
Lehman Commodity Index
Lehman Emerging Americas Bond Index
Lehman Global Bond Index
Lehman High Yield Composite Bond Index
Lehman Municipal Bond Index
Lehman Mutual Fund Indices
Refer to Appendix 5 for additional indices.

REMARKS

(1) In addition to the major subindices noted above, Lehman's subindices include additional maturity, quality and sector breakdowns. To supplement commonly used indices, Lehman offers the flexibility to create customized indices that meet specific investor requirements. (2) Debt instruments must be rated investment grade or above by Moody's Investors Service, or another rating agency in the event a Moody's rating is not available. In a small number of cases, unrated investment quality bonds may be included in the index, provided they are widely perceived as investment grade and are trading accordingly.

PUBLISHER

Lehman Brothers.

LEHMAN BROTHERS GLOBAL BOND INDEX

TOTAL RETURN PERFORMANCE

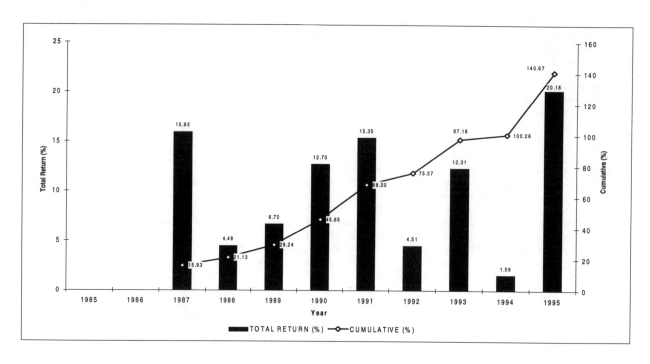

TOTAL RETURN PERFORMANCE (US$)

YEAR	VALUE	TOTAL RETURN (%)	CUMULATIVE (%)	MAXIMUM VALUE[1]	DATE	MINIMUM VALUE[1]	DATE
1995	240.67	20.18	140.67	240.67	31-Dec	104.45	31-Jan
1994	200.26	1.56	100.26	202.31	30-Nov	194.37	31-May
1993	197.18	12.31	97.18	197.18	31-Dec	178.58	31-Jan
1992	175.57	4.51	75.57	182.45	31-Aug	162.62	31-Mar
1991	168.00	15.35	68.00	168.00	31-Dec	143.65	31-Jul
1990	145.65	12.70	45.65	145.65	31-Dec	125.16	30-Apr
1989	129.24	6.70	29.24	129.24	31-Dec	118.40	31-May
1988	121.13	4.49	21.13	121.94	30-Nov	112.79	31-Aug
1987	115.93	15.93	15.93	115.93	31-Dec	102.09	30-Sep
1986	100.00						
1985							
Average Annual (%)		10.41					
Compound Annual (%)		10.25					
Standard Deviation (%)		6.34					

[1]Maximum/minimum index values are as of month-end.

SYNOPSIS

The Lehman Brothers Global Bond Index is a market value-weighted index that tracks the daily price, coupon, currency and total return performance of fixed-rate, nonconvertible, local currency-denominated sovereign fixed income securities of 19 developed countries along with European Currency Unit (ECU)-denominated debt.

NUMBER OF BONDS—DECEMBER 31, 1995

799

MARKET VALUE—DECEMBER 31, 1995

US$ 5,264,341.0 million

SELECTION CRITERIA

Constituents include fixed-rate, nonconvertible, local currency-denominated sovereign fixed income securities of 19 developed countries along with ECU-denominated debt, with par amounts outstanding of $100.0 million and at least one year remaining to maturity. Countries include Canada, France, Germany, Italy, Japan, United Kingdom, United States, Australia, Belgium, Denmark, The Netherlands, Spain, Sweden, Austria, Finland, Ireland, New Zealand, Norway, Portugal, and the ECU.

Excluded from the index are securities from countries classified as emerging markets as well as some illiquid issues.

BACKGROUND

The index was introduced in April 1992 with data going back to December 31, 1986. The inception date for the industrial sector and subsector indices is December 31, 1992. For additional information, refer to the Lehman Brothers Aggregate Bond Index.

The par amount outstanding requirement for inclusion in the index was modified in January 1993, at which time it increased from $50.0 million to $100.0 million.

BASE DATE

December 31, 1986=100.00

COMPUTATION METHODOLOGY

(1) An aggregate of prices times quantities index formula, including gain/loss on repayments of principal and currency conversions, if applicable, as well as coupon received or accrued for total rate of return calculations. (2) Returns are based on a universe of securities established at the beginning of each month and held constant until the beginning of the next month. Securities that become ineligible for inclusion in the index during the month due to downgrades, redemptions or calls, securities falling below one year in maturity or newly eligible securities are maintained in a second, statistical universe. The statistical universe drives the production of portfolio statistics during the course of the month, i.e., coupon, duration, maturity, yield and price, and is also used to update the returns universe at the end of each month. (3) Intramonth cash flows are reinvested at month-end. If a security is no longer outstanding at the end of the month, the ending price is the level at which it exited the market. (4) Prices are provided by Lehman Brothers trading desks in London, New York and Tokyo. Additional prices are provided by outside sources in the local markets while currency rates are based on the WM/Reuters closing spot rates. Some illiquid issues are excluded to ensure pricing accuracy. (5) Country components are weighted according to market capitalization, except Japan which is weighted on the basis of the market value of the 40 largest Japanese government bonds.

DERIVATIVE INSTRUMENTS

None

SUBINDICES

G-7 Index
Majors Index, which includes the G-7 Index along with Australia, Belgium, Denmark, The Netherlands, Spain and Sweden. These are available on a hedged or unhedged basis.
Subindices for any of the countries tracked, in any currency, including ECU.

RELATED INDICES

Lehman Adjustable Rate Mortgage Index
Lehman Aggregate Bond Index
Lehman Commodity Index
Lehman Emerging Americas Bond Index
Lehman High Yield Composite Bond Index
Lehman Municipal Bond Index
Lehman Mutual Fund Indices
Refer to Appendix 5 for additional indices.

REMARKS

(1) To supplement commonly used indices, Lehman offers the flexibility to create customized indices that meet specific investor requirements. (2) Investment grade debt ratings are based on determinations by Moody's Investors Service. A Standard & Poor's rating is used in the event a Moody's rating is not available, followed by a Fitch Investor's Service ratings in the absence of both a Moody's and S&P rating. The Moody's rating prevails in the event of split-rated issues.

PUBLISHER

Lehman Brothers.

LOMBARD ODIER & CIE (LOC) GLOBAL
WORLD GOVERNMENT BOND INDEX

TOTAL RETURN PERFORMANCE

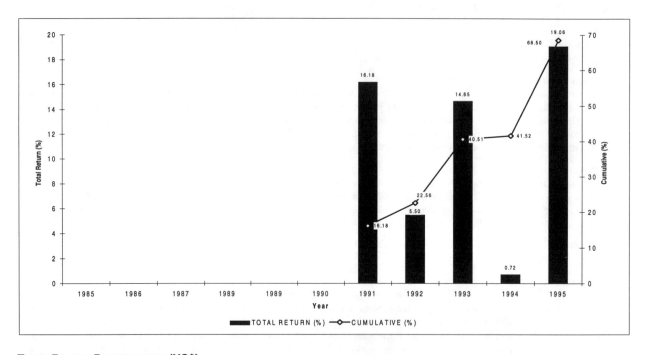

TOTAL RETURN PERFORMANCE (US$)

YEAR	VALUE	TOTAL RETURN (%)	CUMULATIVE (%)	MAXIMUM VALUE	DATE	MINIMUM VALUE	DATE
1995	391.15	19.06	68.50	391.60	28-Dec	326.75	6-Jan
1994	328.52	0.72	41.52	333.49	17-Oct	319.65	5-Apr
1993	326.18	14.65	40.51	332.57	12-Oct	283.42	4-Jan
1992	284.51	5.50	22.56	297.93	7-Sep	259.09	12-Mar
1991	269.69	16.18	16.18	269.69	31-Dec	229.35	13-Jun
1990	232.14						
1989	NA						
1989	NA						
1987	NA						
1986	NA						
1985	NA						
Average Annual (%)		11.22					
Compound Annual (%)		11.00					
Standard Deviation (%)		7.76					

SYNOPSIS
The Lombard Odier & Cie (LOC) Global World Government Bond Index is a market value-weighted index that tracks the daily unhedged price-only and total return performance of 17 central government straight fixed coupon bearing bonds with maturities in excess of one year, expressed in U.S. dollar as well as in Swiss Franc terms.

NUMBER OF BONDS—DECEMBER 31, 1995
217

MARKET VALUE—DECEMBER 31, 1995
Not Available

SELECTION CRITERIA
The index, which comprises government bonds issued by Belgium, Canada, Australia, Denmark, Finland, Holland, Italy, Germany, France, Japan, New Zealand, Norway, Spain, Sweden, Switzerland, United Kingdom and the United States, relies on a sample of representative, liquid bonds that are selected in each market on the basis of the following principals:

(1) Representativeness–Each issue must meet certain liquidity criteria. (2) Consistency–Consistent average maturities and durations. (3) Replicability–Investors must be able to replicate the index to match its performance. (4) Reliability–In terms of accuracy and the consistent application of methodology.

Within these broader principals, eligibility of bonds is determined on the basis of the following criteria:

(1) Minimum bond size of 100.0 million SFR or equivalent. Moreover, a bond must be generally available for investment and regularly traded in size at acceptable bid offer spreads. (2) A consistent average maturity and duration. With some exceptions, most bonds have an average maturity of between six and seven years. Exceptions include the United States and Canada where the average maturity is between eight and nine years.

BACKGROUND
The World Government Bond Index along with its companion indices, which forms part of the LOC Global Government Bond Indices, were created in 1983.

BASE DATE
December 31, 1982=100.00

COMPUTATION METHODOLOGY
(1) Index formula aggregates by market value the arithmetic average of the daily price changes, within each market, along with adjustments for accrued interest and currency value fluctuations. (2) Market capitalization is updated once a year. (3) The index is rebalanced every quarter. (4) Average daily bid prices are obtained from several sources, including major market makers, Telekurs and Bloomberg.

DERIVATIVE INSTRUMENTS
None

SUBINDICES
LOC European Government Bond Index
LOC World Bond Index, ex-Switzerland
LOC Individual Bond Market indices, denominated in local currencies.

RELATED INDICES
LOC European Government Bond Index
LOC Individual Bond Market indices: Government Bonds and Euro-Bonds

REMARKS
None

PUBLISHER
Lombard Odier & Cie (LOC).

MERRILL LYNCH BRADY BOND INDEX

TOTAL RETURN PERFORMANCE

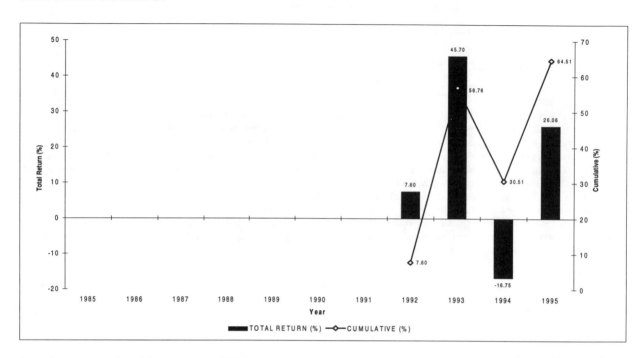

TOTAL RETURN AND PRICE PERFORMANCE (US$)

YEAR	VALUE	TOTAL RETURN (%)	CUMULATIVE (%)	PRICE RETURN (%)	MAXIMUM VALUE	DATE	MINIMUM VALUE	DATE
1995	164.51	26.06	64.51	13.08	164.51	31-Dec	116.05	31-Mar
1994	130.51	-16.75	30.51	-23.40	158.32	31-Jan	126.70	30-Jun
1993	156.76	45.70	56.76	34.53	156.76	31-Dec	108.16	31-Jan
1992	107.60	7.60	7.60	-1.64	107.60	31-Dec	100.15	31-Mar
1991	100.00							
1990								
1989								
1988								
1987								
1986								
1985								
Average Annual (%)		15.65		5.64				
Compound Annual (%)		13.25		3.47				
Standard Deviation (%)		26.62		24.40				

SYNOPSIS

The Merrill Lynch Brady Bond Index is a market value-weighted index that tracks the daily price only, income, currency and total return performance of dollar-denominated rescheduled loans that have been exchanged for Brady bonds in nine countries in Latin America, Eastern Europe and Asia/Pacific.

NUMBER OF BONDS—DECEMBER 31, 1995

39

MARKET VALUE—DECEMBER 31, 1995

US$71,138.4 million

SELECTION CRITERIA
The index includes fixed and floating rate securities, without restrictions as to outstanding par amounts, maturity range or quality guidelines attributable to the nine following countries: Argentina, Bulgaria, Brazil, Ecuador, Mexico, Nigeria, Philippines, Poland and Venezuela.

BACKGROUND
This index is a separate component of the Merrill Lynch Global Bond Index. It replaced the International Emerging Market Index which, in addition to Brady Bonds, tracked the sovereign debt of international emerging markets that had not been restructured as well as new issue bonds. Daily data is available since inception.

For additional information, refer to the Merrill Lynch Global Bond Index.

BASE DATE
December 30, 1994=100.00

COMPUTATION METHODOLOGY
(1) Index formula is an aggregate value-weighted arithmetic average of the price ratios, coupon received or accrued (for total rate of return calculations), gain/loss on repayments of principal and, where applicable, currency value fluctuations. (2) Daily price and total return calculations are based on the theory that the portfolio of securities that make up the index is purchased in its entirety at approximately 3 PM (EST) on the initial day and held until the same time on the following day, when it is sold. Price and total returns for a one day period represent the sum of the weighted average price return, weighted average accrued interest return, and weighted average coupon return, weighted by the market value of the outstanding amount of each bond in the index. Total returns for all non-U.S. dollar bond indices are denominated in local currency, while multicurrency indices are denominated in U.S. dollars. Foreign currency return is computed as the difference in the spot exchange rates expressed from one period to the next divided by the exchange rate at the beginning of the period. Total return for extended intervals are calculated by "chain-linking" the periodic rates of return. Transaction costs are not included in the calculations of price and total returns. (3) Except for mortgage- and asset-backed principal paydowns which are assumed to occur on the 30th of the month, accrued interest and cash flows are assumed to be reinvested on a daily basis in the market. (4) Bonds are generally priced on the basis of bid-side prices obtained from Merrill Lynch's trading floors. These are either hand priced or matrix priced, using price quotes taken at approximately 3 PM (EST). Non-U.S. dollar government bonds are priced using Merrill Lynch's international government bond trading desks, supplemented by prices from external sources. Foreign exchange rates are as of the London close as posted by the WM Company. (5) Market values, for total return calculation purposes, are based on the outstanding amounts of each bond, which are reviewed regularly to account for full and partial retirement of debt, calls, sinking-fund requirements, tenders or re-opening of issues. (6) New issues enter the index on the first business day following settlement while bonds that no longer meet the index or subindex criterion are removed from the index one day, or two days, respectively, following such a determination. Bonds are removed from the index when they no longer satisfy the size, rating or maturity criteria.

DERIVATIVE INSTRUMENTS
None

SUBINDICES
Latin America, non-Latin America regional indices as well as country indices.

RELATED INDICES
Merrill Lynch Capital Markets Index
Merrill Lynch Convertible Securities Index
Merrill Lynch Currency Indices
Merrill Lynch Energy & Metals Index
Merrill Lynch Global Bond Index
Merrill Lynch High Yield Master Index
Merrill Lynch Institutional Municipal Index
Merrill Lynch Money Market Instruments Indices
Refer to Appendix 5 for additional indices.

REMARKS
Subindices refers to a partial list of commonly used performance benchmarks. In addition to numerous subindices which are compiled along sector, industry, maturity, quality and coupon lines, Merrill offers the flexibility to create custom indices.

PUBLISHER
Merrill Lynch & Co.

MERRILL LYNCH CANADIAN BOND MASTER INDEX

TOTAL RETURN PERFORMANCE

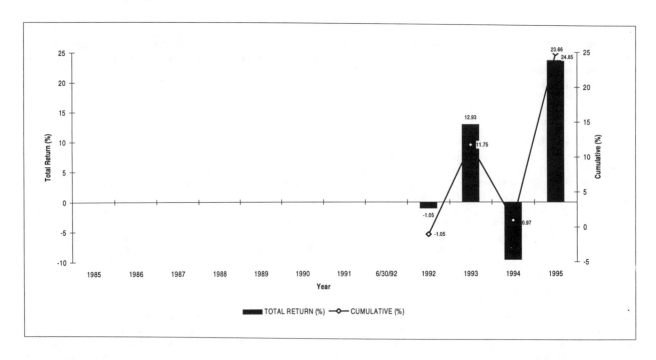

TOTAL RETURN AND PRICE PERFORMANCE (US$)[1]

YEAR	VALUE	TOTAL RETURN (%)	CUMULATIVE (%)	PRICE RETURN (%)	MAXIMUM VALUE[2]	DATE	MINIMUM VALUE[2]	DATE
1995	124.85	23.66	24.85	13.69	124.85	31-Dec	100.59	31-Jan
1994	100.97	-9.65	0.97	-15.65	99.29	31-Jan	82.76	31-Dec
1993	111.75	12.93	11.75	3.71	98.35	28-Feb	94.05	30-Sep
1992	98.95	-1.05	-1.05	-5.40	105.20	31-Jul	92.24	30-Nov
6/30/92	100.00							
1991								
1990								
1989								
1988								
1987								
1986								
1985								
Average Annual (%)		8.98		0.58				
Compound Annual (%)		8.06		-0.18				
Standard Deviation (%)		17.00		14.92				

[1]Statistical measures applicable to the three year period 1993-1995.
[2]Maximum/minimum index values are as of month-end.

SYNOPSIS

The Merrill Lynch Canadian Bond Master Index is a market value-weighted index that tracks the daily price only, income, currency and total return performance of the aggregate Canadian fixed income market, including all publicly placed Canadian government, provincial and corporate fixed-rate, investment grade, coupon bearing bonds, with final maturities greater than or equal to one year.

NUMBER OF BONDS—DECEMBER 31, 1995
448

MARKET VALUE—DECEMBER 31, 1995
US$250,596.9 million

SELECTION CRITERIA

Eligible securities include all publicly placed Canadian government, provincial and corporate fixed-rate, bonds with outstanding par amounts greater than or equal to $25.0 million, a term to maturity greater than or equal to one year, and ratings of BBB and above by Standard & Poor's and Moody's. Some bonds, however, may not be rated.

BACKGROUND

The index, which is a component of the Merrill Lynch Global Bond Index, was created to meet the specific needs of Canadian market investors. At that time, Canadian provincial and corporate debt instruments were added to the already existing Canadian Government Iindex which had been tracked since December 31, 1985. For additional information, refer to the Merrill Lynch Global Bond Index.

BASE DATE

June 30, 1992=100.00

COMPUTATION METHODOLOGY

(1) An aggregate of prices times quantities index formula, including gain/loss on repayments of principal and currency conversions, where applicable, as well as coupon received or accrued for total rate of return calculations. (2) Daily price and total return calculations are based on the theory that the portfolio of securities that make up the index is purchased in its entirety at approximately 3 PM (EST) on the initial day and held until the same time on the following day, when it is sold. Price and total returns for a one day period represent the sum of the weighted average price return, weighted average accrued interest return, and weighted average coupon return, weighted by the market value of the outstanding amount of each bond in the index. Total returns for all non-U.S. dollar bond indices are denominated in local currency, while multicurrency indices are denominated in U.S. dollars. Foreign currency return is computed as the difference in the spot exchange rates expressed from one period to the next divided by the exchange rate at the beginning of the period. Total return for extended intervals are calculated by "chain-linking" the periodic rates of return. Transaction costs are not included in the calculations of price and total returns. (3) Except for mortgage and asset backed principal paydowns which are assumed to occur on the 30th of the month, accrued interest and cash flows are assumed to be reinvested on a daily basis in the market. (4) Bonds are generally priced on the basis of bid-side prices obtained from Merrill Lynch's trading floors. These are either hand priced or matrix priced, using price quotes taken at approximately 3 PM (EST). Non-U.S. dollar government bonds are priced using Merrill Lynch's international government bond trading desks, supplemented by prices from external sources. Foreign exchange rates are as of the London close as posted by the WM Company. (5) Market values, for total return calculation purposes, are based on the outstanding amounts of each bond, which are reviewed regularly to account for full and partial retirement of debt, calls, sinking-fund requirements, tenders or re-opening of issues. (6) New issues enter the index on the first business day following settlement while bonds that no longer meet the index or subindex criterion are removed from the index one day, or two days, respectively, following such a determination. Bonds are removed from the index when they no longer satisfy the size, rating or maturity criteria.

DERIVATIVE INSTRUMENTS

None

SUBINDICES

Three subindices: Canadian Government, Provincial, and corporate sectors

RELATED INDICES

Merrill Lynch Capital Markets Index
Merrill Lynch Convertible Securities Index
Merrill Lynch Currency Indices
Merrill Lynch Energy and Metals Index

Merrill Lynch High Yield Master Index
Merrill Lynch Institutional Municipal Index
Merrill Lynch Money Market Instrument Indices
Refer to Appendix 5 for additional indices.

DERIVATIVE INSTRUMENTS

None

REMARKS

(1) A composite credit rating is calculated by averaging the ratings assigned by Moody's and S&P. In the event the average rating falls between two adjacent split-rated issues, the composite rating is the lower of the two. (2) Subindices refers to a partial list of commonly used performance benchmarks. In addition to numerous subindices which are compiled along sector, industry, maturity, quality and coupon lines, Merrill offers the flexibility to create custom indices. (3) To improve the liquidity and pricing quality of the index, new selection criteria were implemented starting April 30, 1996. The minimum par amount outstanding requirement for bonds were increased to US$100.0 million, with the exception of the U.S. Asset Backed Master which remains at US$25.0 million. Additionally, the US$200.0 million minimum requirement for each generic mortgage coupon was dropped and replaced by a US$100.0 million minimum applied to each seasoning category within a generic coupon. The exclusion of smaller issues is expected to have minimal impact on the market coverage and risk profile of the indices as these are market value-weighted.

PUBLISHER

Merrill Lynch & Co.

MERRILL LYNCH EURODOLLAR BOND INDEX

TOTAL RETURN PERFORMANCE

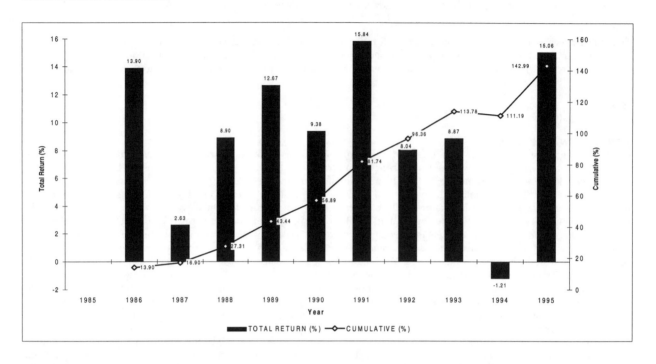

TOTAL RETURN AND PRICE PERFORMANCE

YEAR	VALUE	TOTAL RETURN (%)	CUMULATIVE (%)	PRICE RETURN (%)	MAXIMUM VALUE[1]	DATE	MINIMUM VALUE[1]	DATE
1995	359.25	15.06	142.99	7.03	359.25	31-Dec	317.08	31-Jan
1994	312.23	-1.21	111.19	-8.28	319.31	31-Jan	307.63	30-Apr
1993	316.06	8.87	113.78	1.21	316.37	31-Oct	294.40	31-Jan
1992	290.30	8.04	96.36	-0.42	290.92	30-Sep	266.92	31-Jan
1991	268.69	15.84	81.74	6.06	268.69	31-Dec	234.35	31-Jan
1990	231.95	9.38	56.89	0.00	231.95	31-Dec	210.33	31-Jan
1989	212.07	12.67	43.44	3.02	212.07	31-Dec	189.61	28-Feb
1988	188.22	8.90	27.31	-0.71	188.71	31-Oct	177.18	31-Jan
1987	172.83	2.63	16.90	-6.72	172.83	31-Dec	166.01	31-May
1986	168.39	13.90	13.90	3.42	168.39	31-Dec	148.74	31-Jan
1985	147.84							
Average Annual (%)		9.41		0.46				
Compound Annual (%)		9.28		0.35				
Standard Deviation (%)		5.43		4.95				

[1]Maximum/minimum index values are as of month-end.

SYNOPSIS

The Merrill Lynch Eurodollar Bond Index is a market value-weighted index that tracks the daily price, income and total return performance of publicly placed nonconvertible, fixed-rate, coupon-bearing, investment grade U.S. dollar-denominated debt issued by U.S. and foreign governments, agencies and corporations.

NUMBER OF BONDS—DECEMBER 31, 1995
500

MARKET VALUE—DECEMBER 31, 1995
US$157,604.5 million

SELECTION CRITERIA

Eligible securities include U.S. dollar-denominated debt issued by U.S. and foreign governments, agencies and corporations, with outstanding par amounts greater than or equal to $25.0 million and term-to-maturity greater than or equal to one year which are rated BBB-/Baa3 and above, on a composite basis, by Standard & Poor's and Moody's Investors Service.

U.S. Government agency securities and index linked bonds are excluded from consideration as index constituents.

BACKGROUND

The index represents a component of the Merrill-Lynch U.S. Domestic Master Bond Index, which, in turn, forms part of the Merrill Lynch Global Bond Index. Monthly data is available to April 30, 1990. Thereafter, the index was computed on a daily basis.

For additional information, refer to the Merrill Lynch Global Bond Index.

BASE DATE

December 31, 1982=100.00

COMPUTATION METHODOLOGY

(1) Index formula is an aggregate value-weighted arithmetic average of the price ratios, coupon received or accrued (for total rate of return calculations), gain/loss on repayments of principal and, where applicable, currency value fluctuations. (2) Daily price and total return calculations are based on the theory that the portfolio of securities that make up the index is purchased in its entirety at approximately 3 PM (EST) on the initial day and held until the same time on the following day, when it is sold. Price and total returns for a one day period represent the sum of the weighted average price return, weighted average accrued interest return, and weighted average coupon return, weighted by the market value of the outstanding amount of each bond in the index. Total return for extended intervals are calculated by "chain-linking" the periodic rates of return. Transaction costs are not included in the calculations of price and total returns. (3) Except for mortgage- and asset-backed principal paydowns which are assumed to occur on the 30th of the month, accrued interest and cash flows are assumed to be reinvested on a daily basis in the market. (4) Bonds are generally priced on the basis of bid-side prices obtained from Merrill Lynch's trading floors. These are either hand priced or matrix priced, using price quotes taken at approximately 3 PM (EST). (5) Market values, for total return calculation purposes, are based on the outstanding amounts of each bond, which are reviewed regularly to account for full and partial retirement of debt, calls, sinking-fund requirements, tenders or re-opening of issues. (6) New issues enter the index on the first business day following settlement while bonds that no longer meet the index or subindex criterion are removed from the index one day, or two days, respectively, following such a determination. Bonds are removed from the index when they no longer satisfy the size, rating or maturity criteria.

DERIVATIVE INSTRUMENTS

None

SUBINDICES

Various subindices representing par amounts outstanding, credit ratings and maturities.

RELATED INDICES

Merrill Lynch Capital Markets Index
Merrill Lynch Convertible Securities Index
Merrill Lynch Currency Indices
Merrill Lynch Energy & Metals Index
Merrill Lynch High Yield Master Index
Merrill Lynch Institutional Municipal Index
Merrill Lynch Money Market Instruments Indices
Refer to Appendix 5 for additional indices.

REMARKS

(1) A composite rating is calculated by averaging the ratings assigned by Moody's and S&P. In the event the average rating falls between two adjacent split-rated issues, the composite rating is the lower of the two. Some non-U.S. bonds are not rated by Standard & Poor's or Moody's Investors Service. (2) To improve the liquidity and pricing quality of the index, new selection criteria were implemented starting April 30, 1996. The minimum par amount outstanding requirement for bonds were increased to US$100.0 million, with the exception of the U.S. Asset Backed Master which remain at US$25.0 million. Additionally, the US$200.0 million minimum requirement for each generic mortgage coupon was dropped and replaced by a US$100.0 million minimum applied to each seasoning category within a generic coupon. The exclusion of smaller issues is expected to have minimal impact on the market coverage and risk profile of the indices as these are market value-weighted.

PUBLISHER

Merrill Lynch & Co.

MERRILL LYNCH GLOBAL BOND INDEX

TOTAL RETURN PERFORMANCE

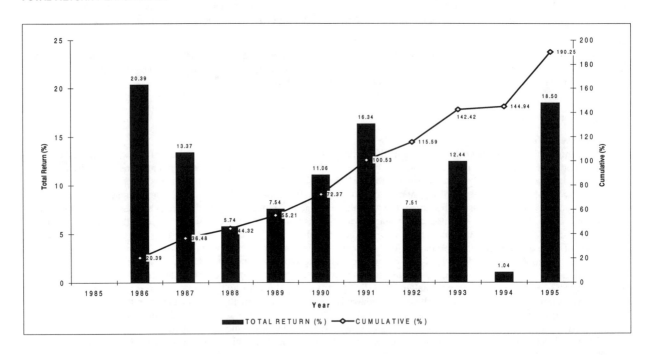

TOTAL RETURN AND PRICE PERFORMANCE (US$)

YEAR	VALUE	TOTAL RETURN (%)	CUMULATIVE (%)	PRICE RETURN (%)	MAXIMUM VALUE	DATE	MINIMUM VALUE	DATE
1995	290.25	18.50	190.25	10.57	290.25	31-Dec	248.92	31-Jan
1994	244.94	1.04	144.94	-5.84	245.48	31-Jan	239.07	31-May
1993	242.42	12.44	142.42	5.28	242.42	31-Dec	219.30	31-Jan
1992	215.59	7.51	115.59	-0.10	218.74	30-Sep	195.95	31-Mar
1991	200.53	16.34	100.53	7.30	200.53	31-Dec	173.28	31-Mar
1990	172.37	11.06	72.37	1.90	172.37	31-Dec	149.87	30-Apr
1989	155.21	7.54	55.21	-1.24	155.21	31-Dec	142.11	31-Mar
1988	144.32	5.74	44.32	-2.87	145.18	30-Nov	135.89	31-Aug
1987	136.48	13.37	36.48	4.19	136.48	31-Dec	121.81	30-Sep
1986	120.39	20.39	20.39	9.96	120.39	31-Dec	101.12	31-Jan
1985	100.00							
Average Annual (%)		11.39		2.91				
Compound Annual (%)		11.24		2.78				
Standard Deviation (%)		6.05		5.50				

¹Maximum/minimu index values are as of month-end.

SYNOPSIS

The Merrill Lynch Global Bond Index, a market value-weighted index, tracks the daily price only, income, currency and total return performance of publicly placed nonconvertible, fixed-rate, coupon-bearing U.S. and non-U.S. dollar-denominated investment grade debt.

NUMBER OF BONDS—DECEMBER 31, 1995
8,472

MARKET VALUE—DECEMBER 31, 1995
US$8,617,516.2 million

SELECTION CRITERIA

Eligible securities consist of U.S. Treasury and U.S. Government agency securities, mortgage pass-through securities, investment grade corporate securities, including Canadian and Yankee issues, Global government and Eurobond issues, including U.S. dollar-denominated bonds issued by U.S. and foreign governments, agencies and corporations, and non-U.S dollar government and Eurobonds, with outstanding par amounts greater than or equal to $25.0 million for corporate and Treasury securities and $200.0 million per coupon for generic mortgage backed securities, and term to maturity greater than or equal to one year.

World Bank, Yankee and Canadian issues are included. Floating-rate debt, index-linked debt, equipment trust certificates, Title 11 securities, GNMA series II, mobile home, and graduated payment and 1/4-coupon mortgages are excluded.

BACKGROUND

The Merrill Lynch Global Bond Index comprises the Global Dollar Bond Index and the Non-U.S. Dollar Bond Index. Together, these cover the domestic and international bond markets, with performance that can be denominated in a variety of currencies. The domestic indices track the U.S. Government, corporate, asset backed and mortgage markets while the international series includes global government bond, Eurobond and a series of currency indices. In addition, Merrill also compiles STRIPS, Treasury yield-curve, selected money market, municipal bond, high yield and convertible securities indices. A number of Master indices aggregate bonds into commonly used benchmarks that represent broad markets along domestic and global lines. (i.e., the U.S. domestic market includes the U.S. Domestic Master Index, which covers corporate, government and mortgage securities, Corporate and Government Master Index, Corporate Master, Government Master, Agency Master, Treasury Master, Mortgage Master, Asset Backed Master, Municipal Master and High Yield Master and the global bond market includes the Global Government and Eurobond, Global Government Bond, Global Government Bond Expanded, Global Eurobond, Global Dollar Bond indices and Non-U.S. Dollar Bond, Non-U.S. Dollar Government Bond, Non-U.S. Dollar Eurobond and Brady Bond Master indices. In addition, subindices are compiled along sector, industry, maturity, quality and coupon lines. Merrill Lynch computes more than 1,000 master and subindices. The Merrill Lynch Global Bond Index offers the flexibility to create custom indices and tailoring a benchmark by combining two or more subindices to create a "custom index" by using the Merrill Lynch Global Index System on Bloomberg Financial Markets System. The index has been modified and expanded over time. Some of its components have been calculated on a daily or monthly basis, back to December 31, 1972. Others were initiated with subsequent base dates. The inception date for the Global Bond Index is 1985. Monthly data is available to May 31, 1990 and thereafter, daily index values are computed.

BASE DATE

December 31, 1985=100.00

COMPUTATION METHODOLOGY

(1) An aggregate of prices times quantities index formula, including gain/loss on repayments of principal and currency conversions, if applicable, as well as coupon received or accrued for total rate of return. (2) Daily price and total return calculations are based on the theory that the portfolio of securities that make up the index is purchased in its entirety at approximately 3 PM (EST) on the initial day and held until the same time on the following day, when it is sold. Price and total returns for a one day period represent the sum of the weighted average price return, weighted average accrued interest return, and weighted average coupon return, weighted by the market value of the outstanding amount of each bond in the index. Total returns for all non-U.S. dollar bond indices are denominated in local currency, while multicurrency indices are denominated in U.S. dollars. Foreign currency return is computed as the difference in the spot exchange rates expressed from one period to the next divided by the exchange rate at the beginning of the period. Total return for extended intervals are calculated by "chain-linking" the periodic rates of return. Transaction costs are not included in the calculations of price and total returns. (3) Except for mortgage and asset backed principal paydowns which are assumed to occur on the 30th of the month, accrued interest and cash flows are assumed to be reinvested on a daily basis in the market. (4) Bonds are generally priced on the basis of bid-side prices obtained from Merrill Lynch's trading floors. These are either hand priced or matrix priced, using price quotes taken at approximately 3 PM (EST). Non-U.S. dollar government bonds are priced using Merrill Lynch's international government bond trading desks, supplemented by prices from external sources. Foreign exchange rates are as of the London close as posted by the WM Company. (5) Market values, for total return are on the outstanding amounts of each bond, which are reviewed regularly to account for full and partial retirement of debt, calls, sinking-fund requirements, tenders or re-opening of issues. (6) New issues enter on the first business day following settlement while bonds no longer meeting the index or subindex criterion are removed one day, or two days, respectively, following such a determination. Bonds are removed when they no longer satisfy the size, rating or maturity criteria.

DERIVATIVE INSTRUMENTS

None

SUBINDICES

Corporate and Government Master	Government Master	U.S. Domestic Master
Corporate Master	Mortgage Master	

RELATED INDICES

Merrill Lynch Capital Markets Index	Merrill Lynch High Yield Master Index
Merrill Lynch Convertible Securities Index	Merrill Lynch Institutional Municipal Index
Merrill Lynch Currency Indices	Merrill Lynch Money Market Instruments Indices
Merrill Lynch Energy & Metals Index	Refer to Appendix 5 for additional indices.

REMARKS

(1) Investment grade issues are rated BBB-/Baa3 and above, on a composite basis, by Standard & Poor's and Moody's Investors Service and is calculated by averaging the ratings assigned by Moody's and S&P. When the average rating falls between two adjacent split-rated issues, the rating is the lower of the two. Some non-U.S. bonds are not rated. (2) Subindices are a partial list of commonly used benchmarks. (3) To improve the liquidity and pricing quality, new selection criteria were implemented April 30, 1996. The minimum par amount outstanding requirement for bonds was increased to US$100.0 million; the U.S. Asset Backed Master remains at US$25.0 million. The US$200.0 million minimum requirement for each generic mortgage coupon was replaced by a US$100.0 million minimum applied to each seasoning category within a generic coupon. The exclusion of smaller issues is expected to have minimal impact on the market coverage and risk profile of the indices as these are market value-weighted.

PUBLISHER

Merrill Lynch & Co.

MERRILL LYNCH GLOBAL GOVERNMENT BOND INDEX

TOTAL RETURN PEFORMANCE

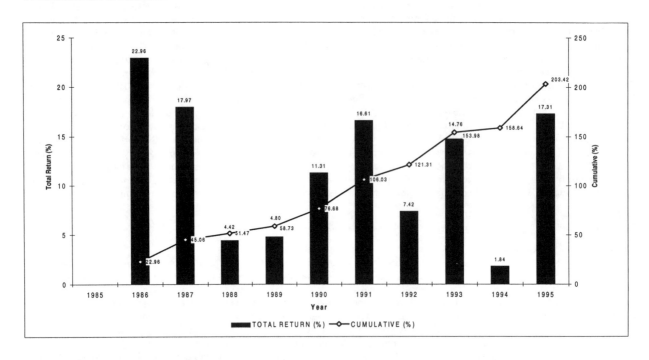

TOTAL RETURN AND PRICE PERFORMANCE (US$)

YEAR	VALUE	TOTAL RETURN (%)	CUMULATIVE (%)	PRICE RETURN (%)	MAXIMUM VALUE[1]	DATE	MINIMUM VALUE[1]	DATE
1995	303.42	17.31	203.42	10.096	303.86	30-Jun	262.36	31-Jan
1994	258.64	1.84	158.64	-4.751	260.19	31-Oct	250.59	31-May
1993	253.98	14.76	153.98	7.51	253.98	31-Dec	225.22	31-Jan
1992	221.31	7.42	121.31	-0.02	226.00	30-Sep	199.75	31-Mar
1991	206.03	16.61	106.03	7.94	206.03	31-Dec	175.80	31-Mar
1990	176.68	11.31	76.68	2.54	176.68	31-Dec	151.11	30-Apr
1989	158.73	4.80	58.73	-3.38	158.73	31-Dec	147.35	31-May
1988	151.47	4.42	51.47	-3.67	152.70	30-Nov	140.86	31-Aug
1987	145.06	17.97	45.06	8.84	145.06	31-Dec	126.32	30-Sep
1986	122.96	22.96	22.96	13.04	122.96	31-Dec	101.37	31-Jan
1985	100.00							
Average Annual (%)		11.94		3.81				
Compound Annual (%)		11.74		3.63				
Standard Deviation (%)		7.05		6.48				

[1]Maximum/minimum index values are as of month-end.

SYNOPSIS

The Merrill Lynch Global Government Bond Index is a market value-weighted index that tracks the daily price only, income, currency and total return performance of publicly placed, nonconvertible, fixed-rate, coupon-bearing U.S. dollar and non-U.S. dollar-denominated debt issued by 15 governments in North America, Europe and Asia/Pacific.

NUMBER OF BONDS—DECEMBER 31, 1995

618

MARKET VALUE—DECEMBER 31, 1995

US$5,048,722.0 million

SELECTION CRITERIA

Eligible securities include U.S. dollar and non-U.S. dollar-denominated debt issued by the governments of Australia, Belgium, Canada, Denmark, France, Germany, Ireland, Italy, Japan, Netherlands, New Zealand, Spain, Sweden, Switzerland, United

Kingdom (UK) and the United States (U.S.) with outstanding par amounts greater than or equal to $25.0 million with term-to-maturity greater than or equal to one year.

U.S. Government agency securities, and index linked bonds are excluded from consideration as index constituents.

BACKGROUND

The index represents a component of the Merrill Lynch Global Bond Index. The index was originally composed of bonds from nine countries: Australia, Canada, The Netherlands, France, German, Japan, Switzerland, UK and the U.S. It was expanded, effective October 1, 1993, to cover eight additional government markets, including Belgian, Danish, Irish, Italian, New Zealand, Portuguese, Spanish and Swedish government bonds. To ensure an ongoing consistent measure of performance, the eight additional government markets are tracked in two supplemental indices, namely the Global Government Bond Index II and the Non-U.S Dollar Government Bond Index II, with daily data to September 30, 1993. Monthly index values are available to January 31, 1990. Thereafter, the index was computed on a daily basis.

For additional information, refer to the Merrill Lynch Global Bond Index.

BASE DATE

December 31, 1985=100.00

COMPUTATION METHODOLOGY

(1) An aggregate of prices times quantities index formula, including gain/loss on repayments of principal and currency conversions, if applicable, as well as coupon received or accrued for total rate of return calculations. (2) Daily price and total return calculations are based on the theory that the portfolio of securities that make up the index is purchased in its entirety at approximately 3 PM (EST) on the initial day and held until the same time on the following day, when it is sold. Price and total returns for a one day period represent the sum of the weighted average price return, weighted average accrued interest return, and weighted average coupon return, weighted by the market value of the outstanding amount of each bond in the index. Total returns for all non-U.S. dollar bond indices are denominated in local currency, while multicurrency indices are denominated in U.S. dollars. Foreign currency return is computed as the difference in the spot exchange rates expressed from one period to the next divided by the exchange rate at the beginning of the period. Total return for extended intervals are calculated by "chain-linking" the periodic rates of return. Transaction costs are not included in the calculations of price and total returns. (3) Except for mortgage and asset backed principal paydowns which are assumed to occur on the 30th of the month, accrued interest and cash flows are assumed to be reinvested on a daily basis in the market. (4) Bonds are generally priced on the basis of bid-side prices obtained from Merrill Lynch's trading floors. These are either hand priced or matrix priced, using price quotes taken at approximately 3 PM (EST). Non-U.S. dollar government bonds are priced using Merrill Lynch's international government bond trading desks, supplemented by prices from external sources. Foreign exchange rates are as of the London close as posted by the WM Company. (5) Market values, for total return calculation purposes, are based on the outstanding amounts of each bond, which are reviewed regularly to account for full and partial retirement of debt, calls, sinking-fund requirements, tenders or re-opening of issues. (6) New issues enter the index on the first business day following settlement while bonds that no longer meet the index or subindex criterion are removed from the index one day, or two days, respectively, following such a determination. Bonds are removed from the index when they no longer satisfy the size, rating or maturity criteria.

DERIVATIVE INSTRUMENTS

None

SUBINDICES

Various subindices by security type and issuer, country, maturity, quality considerations as well as currency.

RELATED INDICES

Merrill Lynch Capital Markets Index
Merrill Lynch Convertible Securities Index
Merrill Lynch Currency Indices
Merrill Lynch Energy & Metals Index
Merrill Lynch High Yield Master Index
Merrill Lynch Institutional Municipal Index
Merrill Lynch Money Market Instruments Indices
Refer to Appendix 5 for additional indices.

REMARKS

(1) A composite rating is calculated by averaging the ratings assigned by Moody's and S&P. In the event the average rating falls between two adjacent split-rated issues, the composite rating is the lower of the two. Some non-U.S. bonds are not rated by Standard & Poor's or Moody's Investors Service. (2) To improve the liquidity and pricing quality of the index, new selection criteria were implemented starting April 30, 1996. The minimum par amount outstanding requirement for bonds was increased to US$100.0 million, with the exception of the U.S. Asset Backed Master which remains at US$25.0 million. Additionally, the US$200.0 million minimum requirement for each generic mortgage coupon was dropped and replaced by a US$100.0 million minimum applied to each seasoning category within a generic coupon. The exclusion of smaller issues is expected to have minimal impact on the market coverage and risk profile of the indices as these are market value-weighted.

PUBLISHER

Merrill Lynch & Co.

SALOMON BROTHERS BRADY BOND INDEX

TOTAL RETURN PERFORMANCE

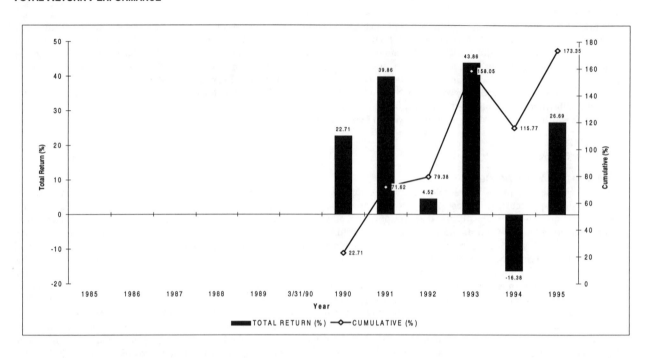

TOTAL RETURN AND PRICE PERFORMANCE (US$)

YEAR	VALUE	TOTAL RETURN (%)	CUMULATIVE (%)	PRICE RETURN (%)	MAXIMUM VALUE[1]	DATE	MINIMUM VALUE[1]	DATE
1995	273.35	26.69	173.35	13.70	273.35	31-Dec	191.83	31-Mar
1994	215.77	-16.38	115.77	-5.48	258.83	31-Jan	205.64	30-Jun
1993	258.05	43.86	158.05	32.89	258.05	31-Dec	180.80	31-Jan
1992	179.38	4.52	79.38	-4.13	187.04	31-Aug	171.59	31-Mar
1991	171.62	39.86	71.62	25.89	171.62	31-Dec	124.58	31-Jan
1990	122.71	22.71	22.71	10.26	122.71	31-Dec	104.90	30-Apr
3/31/90	100.00							
1989								
1988								
1987								
1986								
1985								
Average Annual (%)		23.09		13.93				
Compound Annual (%)		21.11		13.01				
Standard Deviation (%)[2]		25.35		17.29				

[1]Maximum/minimum index values are as of month-end.
[2]Standard deviation appliable to the 5-year period 1991-1995.

SYNOPSIS

The Salomon Brothers Brady Bond Index is a market value-weighted index that tracks the daily and monthly price only and total return performance of tradable emerging market debt that has been restructured under the Brady Plan, including all fixed and floating rate U.S. dollar-denominated Brady bonds issued by countries in Africa, Latin America, Eastern Europe and Asia/Pacific.

NUMBER OF BONDS—DECEMBER 31, 1995

Not Available

MARKET VALUE—DECEMBER 31, 1995

US$80,371.2 million

SELECTION CRITERIA

The index is comprised of all fixed and floating rate U.S. dollar-denominated Brady bonds with minimum par amounts outstanding of $500.0 million that have been issued by the following countries: Argentina, Brazil, Bulgaria, Mexico, Nigeria, Philippines, Poland and Venezuela.

BACKGROUND

At its inception in April 1990, the index tracked the first Brady bond issued by Mexico. It was expanded to include newly issued Brady bonds with a minimum par amount outstanding of $200.0 million until the threshold was increased to $500.0 million as of February 1994. The new guideline disqualified Uruguay and Costa Rica Brady bonds.

For additional information, refer to the Salomon Brothers BIG Index.

BASE DATE

March 31, 1990=100.00

COMPUTATION METHODOLOGY

(1) An aggregate of prices times quantities index formula, including gain/loss on repayments of principal and currency conversions, if applicable, as well as coupon received or accrued for total rate of return calculations. (2) Price only and total returns are calculated based on the assumption that each security, which is market capitalization-weighted using the issue's market value at the beginning of the period, is purchased at the beginning of the period and sold at the end of the measurement period. (3) The securities in which Salomon Brothers' traders make active markets are individually priced at month-end by those traders, using bid-side prices for existing index constituents and offer prices for all newly added securities to reflect transaction costs and facilitate replication as of 5 PM. For daily return calculations only, most corporate issues are matrix-priced. (4) New issues are monitored on a daily basis and eligible issues are included at the beginning of the month following their first settlement date. Bonds that no longer satisfy maturity, amount outstanding or credit rating criteria are removed from the index at the end of each month. The index is also adjusted monthly for changes in the amount outstanding due to calls, tenders, sinking funds or principal paydowns. (5) New issues enter the index at the offer price. (6) Intramonth cash flows payments are reinvested continuously at the daily average of the one month Treasury bill for the calculation period. (7) Calendar month-end settlement dates are assumed for month-end calculations and same day settlements for daily index calculations.

DERIVATIVE INSTRUMENTS

None

SUBINDICES

Eight country subindices: Argentina, Brazil, Bulgaria, Mexico, Nigeria, Philippines, Poland and Venezuela.
Fixed-rate and floating rate subindices.
Latin American and Non-Latin American subindices.

RELATED INDICES

Salomon Brothers Broad Investment-Grade Bond Index
Salomon Brothers Convertible Securities Index
Salomon Brothers High Yield Market Index
Salomon Brothers World Equity Index
Salomon Brothers World Government Bond Index
Salomon Brothers World Money Market Index
Refer to Appendix 5 for additional indices.

REMARKS

None

PUBLISHER

Salomon Brothers Inc.

SALOMON BROTHERS EURODOLLAR BOND INDEX

TOTAL RETURN PERFORMANCE

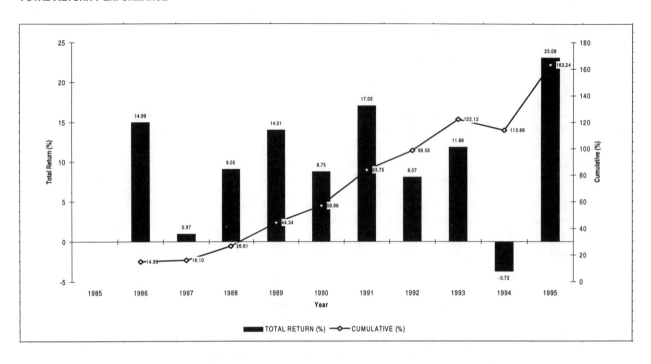

TOTAL RETURN PERFORMANCE

YEAR	VALUE	TOTAL RETURN (%)	CUMULATIVE (%)	MAXIMUM VALUE[1]	DATE	MINIMUM VALUE[1]	DATE
1995	596.19	23.09	163.24	596.19	31-Dec	492.63	31-Jan
1994	484.34	-3.72	113.86	511.16	31-Jan	479.92	30-Nov
1993	503.06	11.86	122.12	506.28	29-Oct	460.86	29-Jan
1992	449.74	8.07	98.58	452.14	30-Sep	411.38	31-Mar
1991	416.15	17.05	83.75	416.15	31-Dec	359.87	31-Jan
1990	355.52	8.75	56.98	355.52	31-Dec	321.57	31-Jan
1989	326.90	14.01	44.34	326.04	30-Nov	288.01	28-Feb
1988	286.74	9.05	26.61	289.49	31-Oct	272.10	29-Jan
1987	262.94	0.97	16.10	264.66	27-Feb	250.05	30-Sep
1986	260.42	14.99	14.99	260.42	31-Dec	220.41	31-Jan
1985	226.48						
Average Annual (%)		10.41					
Compound Annual (%)		10.16					
Standard Deviation (%)		7.75					

[1]Maximum/Minimum index values are as of month-end.

SYNOPSIS

The Salomon Brothers Eurodollar Bond Index is a market value-weighted index that tracks the daily and monthly principal only and total return performance of tradable investment grade, fixed rate Eurodollar bonds with minimum maturities of one year or longer. Securities include sovereign and sovereign guaranteed debt, supranational issues, local government and corporate issues as well as asset-backed transactions.

NUMBER OF BONDS—DECEMBER 31, 1995
652

MARKET VALUE—DECEMBER 31, 1995
US$292,231.0 million

SELECTION CRITERIA

Eligible securities consist of Eurobonds, global bonds, Dragon bonds and certain Euro Medium-Term notes and asset-backed bonds with a minimum maturity of one year or longer and minimum par amounts outstanding of US$150.0 million with minimum denominations of US$100,000.0. In addition, a minimum Standard & Poor's or Moody's Investors Service investment grade quality of BBB-/Baa3 or better is required for eligibility.

Bullet bonds, securities with sinking fund features, puttable, extendible or callable bonds are eligible for inclusion in the index.

Zero-coupon bonds are excluded from all but the Eurodollar subindex.

BACKGROUND

The index is one of several Eurobond indices that, in addition to the Eurodollar market, measures the performance of Eurosterling, Euroyen and Euro-Deutschemark bonds. It was reconstituted in January 1994, in terms of index design and calculation methodology, as part of a redefinition of the Eurobond and Foreign bond sectors of the Salomon World Bond Index that is in the process of being phased out. Historical data based on the design and calculation methodology applicable to the World Bond Index is available to December 31, 1977.

For additional information, refer to the Salomon Brothers BIG Index.

BASE DATE

June 30, 1993=100.00

COMPUTATION METHODOLOGY

(1) An aggregate of prices times quantities index formula, including gain/loss on repayments of principal and currency conversions, if applicable, as well as coupon received or accrued for total rate of return calculations. (2) Price only and total returns are calculated based on the assumption that each security, which is market capitalization-weighted using the issue's market value at the beginning of the period, is purchased at the beginning of the period and sold at the end of the measurement period. (3) Securities are individually priced by Salomon Brothers' traders on a daily basis and at month-end. (4) New issues are monitored on a daily basis and eligible issues are included at the beginning of the month following their first settlement date. Bonds that no longer satisfy maturity, amount outstanding or credit rating criteria are removed from the index at the end of each month. The index is also adjusted monthly for changes in the amount outstanding due to calls, tenders, sinking funds or principal paydowns. (5) New issues enter the index at the offer price. (6) Cash flows due to scheduled payments are reinvested at the daily average of the local one-month interbank rate from payment date to month-end. (7) Calendar month-end settlement dates are assumed for month-end calculations and same day settlements for daily index calculations. (8) Currency exchange rates are based on WM/Reuters Closing Spot Rates, which are the median rates based on observations taken at regular intervals around the London 4 PM fixing time.

DERIVATIVE INSTRUMENTS

None

SUBINDICES

Regularly calculated sectors: Sovereign and Sovereign Guaranteed, Supranational, Official and Agency, Corporate, Financial and Asset-Backed.

RELATED INDICES

Salomon Brothers Broad Investment-Grade Bond Index
Salomon Brothers Convertible Securities Index
Salomon Brothers High Yield Market Index
Salomon Brothers World Equity Index
Salomon Brothers World Government Bond Index
Salomon Brothers World Money Market Index
Refer to Appendix 5 for additional indices.

REMARKS

(1) In addition to the subindices noted above, various subindices are based on credit, issuer nationality and type and maturity sectors. For both the Eurodollar and Eurosterling subindices, additional subindices are calculated for bonds issued by non-U.S. entities. (2) Also calculated are the following related Eurobond Indices: Eurosterling Bond Index, Euroyen Bond Index and Euro-Deutschemark Bond Index

PUBLISHER

Salomon Brothers Inc.

SALOMON BROTHERS WORLD GOVERNMENT BOND INDEX (WGBI)

TOTAL RETURN PERFORMANCE

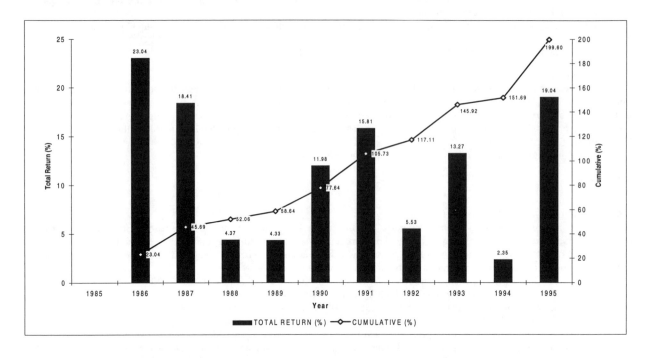

TOTAL RETURN AND PRICE PERFORMANCE (US$)

YEAR	VALUE	TOTAL RETURN (%)	CUMULATIVE (%)	PRICE RETURN (%)	MAXIMUM VALUE[1]	DATE	MINIMUM VALUE[1]	DATE
1995	381.24	19.04	199.60	11.24	381.24	31-Dec	326.99	31-Jan
1994	320.27	2.35	151.69	-4.60	323.84	31-Oct	310.55	31-May
1993	312.93	13.27	145.92	7.96	313.06	30-Sep	281.09	31-Jan
1992	276.27	5.53	117.11	-2.05	286.85	30-Sep	253.00	31-Mar
1991	261.79	15.81	105.73	7.04	261.79	31-Dec	223.35	31-Mar
1990	226.05	11.98	77.64	3.06	226.05	31-Dec	193.60	30-Apr
1989	201.87	4.33	58.64	-3.68	201.87	31-Dec	186.62	31-May
1988	193.50	4.37	52.06	-3.61	195.49	30-Nov	179.41	31-Aug
1987	185.39	18.41	45.69	9.57	185.39	31-Dec	161.27	31-Jan
1986	156.57	23.04	23.04	13.57	156.57	31-Dec	129.01	31-Jan
1985	127.25							
Average Annual (%)		11.81		3.85				
Compound Annual (%)		11.60		3.64				
Standard Deviation (%)		7.31		6.90				

[1]Maximum/minimum index values are as of month-end.

SYNOPSIS
The Salomon Brothers World Government Bond Index (WGBI) is a market value-weighted index that tracks the daily price only, total return and currency performance of fixed-rate sovereign debt issued in the domestic market in local currency by 14 governments, with a minimum maturity of one year or longer. The index is comprised of bonds issued by the following governments: Australia, Austria, Belgium, Canada, Denmark, France, Germany, Italy, Japan, The Netherlands, Spain, Sweden, United Kingdom (UK) and the United States (US).

NUMBER OF BONDS—DECEMBER 31, 1995
829

MARKET VALUE—DECEMBER 31, 1995
US$6,093,165.3 million

SELECTION CRITERIA
Country eligibility is determined on the basis of market capitalization and investability criteria. A market's eligible issues must total at least US$20.0 billion, DM30.0 billion and 2.5 trillion Yen for a period of three consecutive months. Security eligibility is determined on the basis of minimum amount outstanding, which varies by market, as follows: Australia A$250.0 million, Austria Sch3.0 billion, Belgium Bfr15.0 billion, Canada C$250.0 million, Denmark Dkr1500.0 million, France Ffr10.0 billion, Germany DM

500.0 million, Ireland Pun200.0 million, Italy Lir500.0 million, Japan 200.0 billion Yen, The Netherlands Dfl500.0 million, New Zealand NZ$100.0 million, Norway Nok5.0 billion, Portugal Esc50.0 billion, Spain Pta100.0 billion, Sweden Skr1.0 billion, United Kingdom 250.0 million Pounds and the United States $1.0 billion public amount outstanding.

Bullet bonds, securities with sinking fund features, puttable, extendible or callable bonds are eligible for inclusion in the index. Also, markets may be withdrawn from participation in the index. This occurs at the end of the following quarter when the market capitalization of eligible securities falls below one-half of all of the entry criteria levels for six consecutive months.

BACKGROUND

The index, which was intended to replace the World Government Bond Index, has changed considerably since its introduction in 1986. It has been expanded over the years to accommodate eligible countries and securities and its minimum entry requirements have been increased. Moreover, Salomon introduced after-tax indices in 1987 as well as currency hedged indices in 1988.

For additional information, refer to the Salomon Brothers BIG Index.

BASE DATE

December 31, 1994=100.00

COMPUTATION METHODOLOGY

(1) An aggregate of prices times quantities index formula, including gain/loss on repayments of principal and currency conversions, if applicable, as well as coupon received or accrued for total rate of return calculations. (2) Price only and total returns are calculated based on the assumption that each security, which is market capitalization-weighted using the issue's market value at the beginning of the period, is purchased at the beginning of the period and sold at the end of the measurement period. (3) Salomon Brothers' traders furnish prices on a daily basis and at month-end for Canada, France, Germany, Japan, The Netherlands, Spain, United Kingdom and the United States. Significant market makers provide prices for Australia, Austria, Belgium, Denmark, Finland, Ireland, Italy, New Zealand, Norway, Portugal, Sweden and Switzerland. All prices are as of the local market close. Canadian and U.S. securities are priced at 5 PM NYT for the monthly calculation and at 3 PM NYT for the daily calculations. (4) New markets that satisfy the eligibility criteria are added to the index at the beginning of the following quarter. Similarly, markets whose market capitalization of eligible issues falls below one-half of all the entry criteria levels for a period of six consecutive months, are removed from the index at the beginning of the following quarter. (5) Bonds that no longer satisfy the maturity criteria are removed from the index along with called or tendered bonds. (6) New issues enter the index at the offer price. 7) Cash flows due to scheduled payments are reinvested at the local short-term interest rates from payment date to month-end. (8) Calendar month-end settlement dates are assumed for month-end calculations and same day settlements for daily index calculations. (9) Currency exchange rates are based on WM/Reuters Closing Spot Rates, which are the median rates based on observations taken at regular intervals around the London 4 PM fixing time.

DERIVATIVE INSTRUMENTS

None

SUBINDICES

After-Tax Bond Index
Currency-Hedged Bond Index
European Government Bond Composite Index
European World Government Bond Index
Global Government Bond Composite Index
Group-of-Five (G-5) Index
Group-of-Seven (G-7) Index
Nonbase Currency Government Bond Index
World Government Bond Ten-Market Index (WGBI-10)

RELATED INDICES

Salomon Brothers Broad Investment-Grade Bond Index
Salomon Brothers Convertible Securities Index
Salomon Brothers High Yield Market Index
Salomon Brothers World Equity Index
Salomon Brothers World Money Market Index
Refer to Appendix 5 for additional indices.

REMARKS

Subindices include a partial list of performance benchmarks. Additional subindices track the performance of bond markets that do not qualify for inclusion in the WGBI based on current selection criteria, including Finland, Ireland, New Zealand, Norway, Portugal and Switzerland. Various subindices by quality, maturity and market/security segment are also available.

PUBLISHER

Salomon Brothers Inc.

10

INDEX PROFILES —
MONEY MARKET INSTRUMENTS
NORTH AMERICA

J.P. Morgan Cash Index

TOTAL RETURN PERFORMANCE

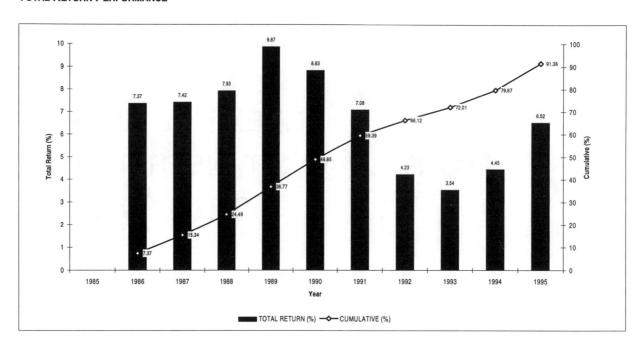

TOTAL RETURN PERFORMANCE

YEAR	VALUE	TOTAL RETURN (%)	CUMULATIVE (%)	MAXIMUM VALUE	DATE	MINIMUM VALUE	DATE
1995	165.93	6.52	91.38	165.93	31-Dec	156.78	31-Jan
1994	155.77	4.45	79.67	155.77	31-Dec	149.62	31-Jan
1993	149.13	3.54	72.01	149.13	31-Dec	144.51	31-Jan
1992	144.03	4.23	66.12	144.03	31-Dec	138.70	31-Jan
1991	138.19	7.08	59.39	138.19	31-Dec	130.03	31-Jan
1990	129.05	8.83	48.85	129.05	31-Dec	119.48	31-Jan
1989	118.58	9.87	36.77	118.58	31-Dec	108.82	31-Jan
1988	107.93	7.93	24.49	107.93	31-Dec	100.73	31-Jan
1987	100.00	7.42	15.34	100.00	31-Dec	93.60	31-Jan
1986	93.09	7.37	7.37	93.09	31-Dec	87.29	31-Jan
1985	86.70						
Average Annual (%)		6.72					
Compound Annual (%)		6.71					
Standard Deviation (%)		2.06					

SYNOPSIS

The J.P. Morgan Cash Index tracks the daily total return performance of constant maturity euro-currency deposits, including one-, two-, three-, six- and 12-month deposits, for 11 markets. These markets include Australia, Belgium, Canada, France, Germany, Italy, Japan, The Netherlands, Spain and the United States.

NUMBER OF ISSUES—DECEMBER 31, 1995

1

MARKET VALUE—DECEMBER 31, 1995

Not Applicable

SELECTION CRITERIA

Euro-currency deposits for the 11 markets deemed to be the most important for the international investor.

BACKGROUND

The J.P. Morgan Cash Index was introduced in December 1990, as a complement to the J.P. Morgan Governfment Bond Index, to serve as a reliable performance benchmark for a fund's cash component. Daily index values have been recalculated to December 31, 1985.

BASE DATE

December 31, 1987=100.00

COMPUTATION METHODOLOGY

(1) A present value index formula that measures the total return from rolling over a euro-currency deposit every business day. The calculation assumes that interest rates are calculated for non-standard periods using linear interpolation between the quoted rates. Daily cash returns are chain-linked. The index has a relatively constant maturity within each market as it is assumed that the maturity or duration of each euro-currency deposit is always equal to the term of the deposit. The actual number of days to maturity can vary due to local settlement rules, i.e., the one-month index can vary from 28- to 33-days. (2) From September 1, 1990 forward, the euro-deposit rates for all countries except The Netherlands and Belgium are the composite rates from the British Bankers Association. These are the average of four offered rates at 11 AM London Time from eight designated banks, after the elimination of the two lowest and two highest rates. For The Netherlands and Belgium, composite domestic rates are used. (3) Historical rates have been obtained from either Data Resources, Inc., Datastream International or J.P. Morgan's trading desks.

DERIVATIVE INSTRUMENTS

None

SUBINDICES

Country subindices (local currency): Australia, Belgium, Canada, France, Germany, Italy, Japan, The Netherlands, Spain and the United States.
Maturity subindices: One-, two-, three-, six- and 12-month maturities.
U.S. dollar subindices.

RELATED INDICES

J. P. Morgan Commodity Index
J. P. Morgan ECU Index
J. P. Morgan Emerging Markets Bond Index
J. P. Morgan Global Government Bond Index

REMARKS

(1) Customized indices are available. (2) Returns produced by euro-currency deposits, according to J.P. Morgan, are highly correlated with the returns of domestic money market instruments and are consistent across all markets in terms of liquidity, maturity and credit quality.

PUBLISHER

J.P. Morgan Securities Inc.

MERRILL LYNCH 91-DAY U.S. TREASURY BILL AUCTION RATE AVERAGE

TOTAL RETURN PERFORMANCE

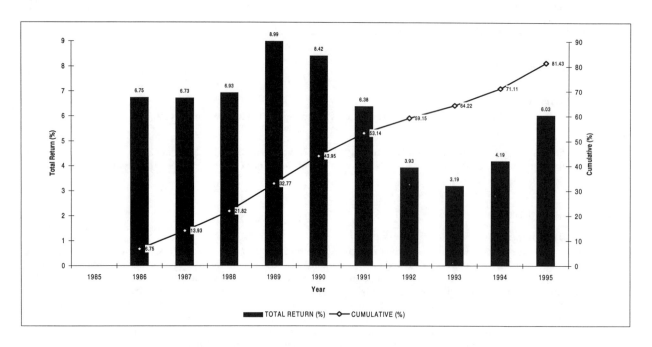

TOTAL RETURN AND PRICE PERFORMANCE

YEAR	VALUE	TOTAL RETURN (%)	CUMULATIVE (%)	PRICE RETURN (%)	MAXIMUM VALUE[1]	DATE	MINIMUM VALUE[1]	DATE
1995	417.98	6.03	81.43	6.03	417.98	31-Dec	396.19	31-Jan
1994	394.21	4.19	71.11	4.19	394.21	31-Dec	379.44	31-Jan
1993	378.35	3.19	64.22	3.19	378.35	31-Dec	367.71	31-Jan
1992	366.66	3.93	59.15	3.93	366.66	31-Dec	354.03	31-Jan
1991	352.80	6.38	53.14	6.38	352.80	31-Dec	333.70	31-Jan
1990	331.64	8.42	43.95	8.42	331.64	31-Dec	308.04	31-Jan
1989	305.89	8.99	32.77	8.99	305.89	31-Dec	282.71	31-Jan
1988	280.66	6.93	21.82	6.93	280.66	31-Dec	263.78	31-Jan
1987	262.47	6.73	13.93	6.73	262.47	31-Dec	247.21	31-Jan
1986	245.93	6.75	6.75	6.75	245.93	31-Dec	231.86	31-Jan
1985	230.39							
Average Annual (%)		6.15		6.15				
Compound Annual (%)		6.14		6.14				
Standard Deviation (%)		1.89		1.89				

[1]Maximum/minimum index values are as of month-end.

SYNOPSIS
The Merrill Lynch 91-Day U.S. Treasury Bill Auction Rate Average tracks the monthly price only and total return performance of a three-month Treasury bill, based on monthly average auction rates.

NUMBER OF ISSUES—DECEMBER 31, 1995
1

MARKET VALUE—DECEMBER 31, 1995
Not Applicable

SELECTION CRITERIA
The index consists of a hypothetical Treasury bill with a discount equal to the average rate established at each of the weekly auctions during a given month.

BACKGROUND
The index represents a component of the Merrill Lynch U.S. Domestic Master Bond Index, which, in turn, forms part of the Merrill Lynch Global Bond Index.

For additional information, refer to the Merrill Lynch Global Bond Index.

BASE DATE
December 31, 1977=100.00

COMPUTATION METHODOLOGY
Total return is computed using a discount-to-par method based on monthly auction averages. Discount-to-par is derived from the average yield on 91-day Treasury Bills that are auctioned on a weekly basis during the month. The result is de-compounded by a factor of one-third to derive a monthly return based on the assumption that the T-bill is held to maturity.

DERIVATIVE INSTRUMENTS
13-week U.S. Treasury Bill options trade on the Chicago Board Options Exchange (CBOE).
13-week Treasury Bill Leaps trade on the Chicago Board Options Exchange (CBOE).
13-week U.S. Treasury bill futures trade on the MidAmerica Stock Exchange (MidAM).
90-day T-bill options trade on the Chicago Mercantile Exchange (CME).

SUBINDICES
None

RELATED INDICES
Merrill Lynch Capital Markets Index
Merrill Lynch Convertible Securities Index
Merrill Lynch Currency Indices
Merrill Lynch Energy & Metals Index
Merrill Lynch Global Bond Index
Merrill Lynch Institutional Municipal Index
Refer to Appendix 5 for additional indices.

REMARKS
(1) The total return on the 91-day auction average Treasury bill represents a proxy for a risk-free return. (2) U.S. Treasury bill options are unrelated to the Merrill Lynch U.S. 91-day Treasury Bill Index. Rather, they are based on the current rate of the most recently auctioned 13-week U.S. Treasury Bill. (3) New money market rate indices that track the total rate of return performance of overnight, one-month and three-month rates for major currencies were introduced starting April 30, 1996.

PUBLISHER
Merrill Lynch & Co.

MERRILL LYNCH 182-DAY U.S. TREASURY BILL INDEX (ACTUAL)

TOTAL RETURN PERFORMANCE

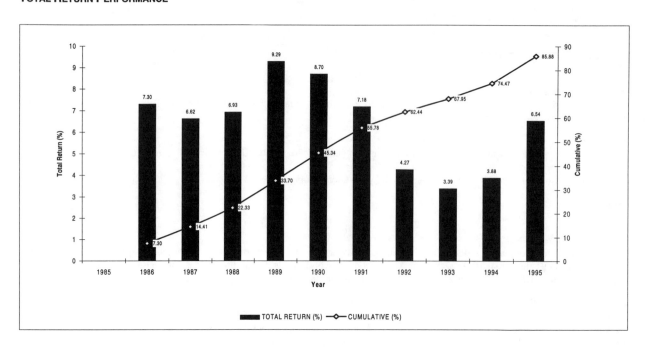

TOTAL RETURN AND PRICE PERFORMANCE

YEAR	VALUE	TOTAL RETURN (%)	CUMULATIVE (%)	PRICE RETURN (%)	MAXIMUM VALUE[1]	DATE	MINIMUM VALUE[1]	DATE
1995	435.05	6.54	85.88	6.54	435.05	31-Dec	410.99	31-Jan
1994	408.33	3.88	74.47	3.88	408.33	31-Dec	394.37	31-Jan
1993	393.07	3.39	67.95	3.39	393.07	31-Dec	381.58	31-Jan
1992	380.17	4.27	62.44	4.27	380.17	31-Dec	365.83	31-Jan
1991	364.59	7.18	55.78	7.18	364.59	31-Dec	342.55	31-Jan
1990	340.16	8.70	45.34	8.70	340.16	31-Dec	314.99	31-Jan
1989	312.93	9.29	33.70	9.29	312.93	31-Dec	288.40	31-Jan
1988	286.32	6.93	22.33	6.93	286.32	31-Dec	269.57	31-Jan
1987	267.77	6.62	14.41	6.62	267.77	31-Dec	252.51	31-Jan
1986	251.14	7.30	7.30	7.30	251.14	31-Dec	235.66	31-Jan
1985	234.04							
Average Annual (%)		6.41		6.41				
Compound Annual (%)		6.40		6.40				
Standard Deviation (%)		1.98		1.98				

[1]Maximum/minimum index values are as of month-end.

SYNOPSIS
The Merrill Lynch 182-Day U.S. Treasury Bill Index tracks the daily total return performance of six-month Treasury bills, based on actual prices.

NUMBER OF ISSUES—DECEMBER 31, 1995
1

MARKET VALUE—DECEMBER 31, 1995
Not Applicable

SELECTION CRITERIA
The index consists of a single Treasury bill that matures closest to, but not beyond 182-days from the last day of the previous month.

BACKGROUND
Monthly data is available to October 31, 1986 and daily values are available thereafter.

    The index represents a component of the Merrill Lynch U.S. Domestic Master Bond Index, which, in turn, forms part of the Merrill Lynch Global Bond Index.

    For additional information, refer to the Merrill Lynch Global Bond Index.

BASE DATE
December 31, 1977=100.00

COMPUTATION METHODOLOGY
(1) Total return is calculated by dividing the Treasury bill's ending price by the beginning price and then subtracting one. (2) Prices are obtained from Merrill Lynch's trading floor.

DERIVATIVE INSTRUMENTS
None

SUBINDICES
None

RELATED INDICES
Merrill Lynch Capital Markets Index
Merrill Lynch Convertible Securities Index
Merrill Lynch Currency Indices
Merrill Lynch Energy & Metals Index
Merrill Lynch Global Bond Index
Merrill Lynch Institutional Municipal Index
Refer to Appendix 5 for additional indices.

REMARKS
New money market rate indices that track the total rate of return performance of overnight, one-month and three-month rates for major currencies were introduced starting April 30, 1996.

PUBLISHER
Merrill Lynch & Co.

MERRILL LYNCH 364-DAYS U.S. TREASURY BILL INDEX (ACTUAL)

TOTAL RETURN PERFORMANCE

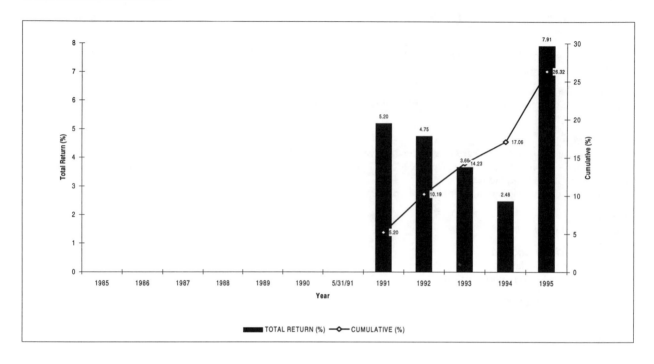

TOTAL RETURN AND PRICE PERFORMANCE

YEAR	VALUE	TOTAL RETURN (%)	CUMULATIVE (%)	PRICE RETURN (%)	MAXIMUM VALUE[1]	DATE	MINIMUM VALUE[1]	DATE
1995	126.32	7.91	26.32	7.91	126.32	31-Dec	118.23	31-Jan
1994	117.06	2.48	17.06	2.48	117.06	31-Dec	114.68	31-Jan
1993	114.23	3.66	14.23	3.67	114.23	31-Dec	110.76	31-Jan
1992	110.19	4.75	10.19	4.75	110.19	31-Dec	105.48	31-Jan
1991	105.20	5.20	5.20	NA	105.20	31-Dec	100.00	31-May
5/31/91	100.00							
1990								
1989								
1988								
1987								
1986								
1985								
Average Annual (%)		5.24		4.70				
Compound Annual (%)		5.23		4.49				
Standard Deviation (%)[2]		2.33		2.33				

[1]Maximum/minimum index values are as of month-end.
[2]Standard deviation applicable to the 4-year period 1992-1995.

SYNOPSIS
The Merrill Lynch 364-Day U.S. Treasury Bill Index tracks the daily price only and total return performance of one-year U.S. Treasury bills, based on actual prices.

NUMBER OF ISSUES—DECEMBER 31, 1995
1

MARKET VALUE—DECEMBER 31, 1995
Not Applicable

SELECTION CRITERIA
The index consists of a single Treasury bill that matures closest to, but not beyond 364-days from the last day of the previous month.

BACKGROUND
Inception date of the index is May 31, 1991. Daily index values are available as of March 31, 1992.

The index represents a component of the Merrill Lynch U.S. Domestic Master Bond Index, which, in turn, forms part of the Merrill Lynch Global Bond Index.

For additional information, refer to the Merrill Lynch Global Bond Index.

BASE DATE
September 30, 1991=100.00

COMPUTATION METHODOLOGY
(1) Total return is calculated by dividing the Treasury bill's ending price by the beginning price and then subtracting one. (2) Prices are obtained from Merrill Lynch's trading floor.

DERIVATIVE INSTRUMENTS
None

SUBINDICES
None

RELATED INDICES
Merrill Lynch Capital Markets Index
Merrill Lynch Convertible Securities Index
Merrill Lynch Currency Indices
Merrill Lynch Energy & Metals Index
Merrill Lynch Global Bond Index
Merrill Lynch Institutional Municipal Index
Refer to Appendix 5 for additional indices.

REMARKS
New money market rate indices that track the total rate of return performance of overnight, one-month and three-month rates for major currencies were introduced starting April 30, 1996.

PUBLISHER
Merrill Lynch & Co.

MERRILL LYNCH DOMESTIC 3-MONTH CERTIFICATE OF DEPOSIT (CD) INDEX

TOTAL RETURN PERFORMANCE

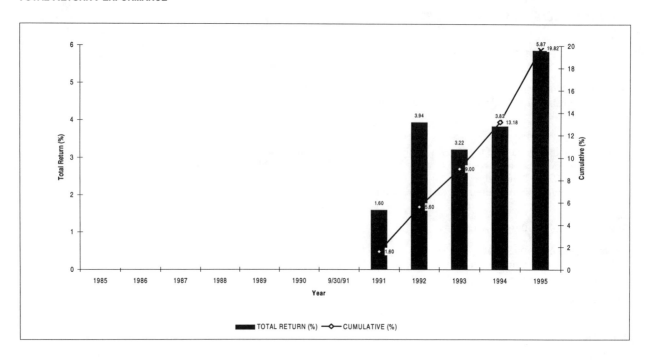

TOTAL RETURN AND PRICE PERFORMANCE

YEAR	VALUE	TOTAL RETURN (%)	CUMULATIVE (%)	PRICE RETURN (%)	MAXIMUM VALUE[1]	DATE	MINIMUM VALUE[1]	DATE
1995	119.82	5.87	19.82	0.14	119.82	31-Dec	113.56	31-Jan
1994	113.18	3.83	13.18	-0.79	113.18	31-Dec	109.32	31-Jan
1993	109.00	3.22	9.00	-0.03	109.00	31-Dec	105.92	31-Jan
1992	105.60	3.94	5.60	0.17	105.60	31-Dec	101.91	31-Jan
1991	101.60	1.60	1.60	NA	101.60	31-Dec	100.00	30-Sep
9/30/91	100.00							
1990								
1989								
1988								
1987								
1986								
1985								
Average Annual (%)		4.34		-0.13				
Compound Annual (%)		4.35		-0.13				
Standard Deviation (%)[2]		1.15		0.45				

[1]Maximum/minimum index values are as of month-end.
[2]Standard deviation applicable to the 4-year period 1992-1995.

SYNOPSIS

The Merrill Lynch Domestic 3-Month Certificate of Deposit (CD) Index tracks the price only and total return performance of nationally-traded three-month Certificates of Deposit (CDs).

NUMBER OF ISSUES—DECEMBER 31, 1995

1

MARKET VALUE—DECEMBER 31, 1995

US$100.0 million

SELECTION CRITERIA

The index consists of a single Certificate of Deposit with a maturity that most closely matches the stated maturity of the index, but not beyond the index, at the beginning of a selected month.

BACKGROUND

The index represents a component of the Merrill Lynch U.S. Domestic Master Bond Index, which, in turn, forms part of the Merrill Lynch Global Bond Index.

For additional information, refer to the Merrill Lynch Global Bond Index.

BASE DATE

September 30, 1991=100.00

COMPUTATION METHODOLOGY

(1) Total return is based on actual prices, calculated by dividing the CD's price at the end of the month by the CD's price at the beginning of the month and subtracting one from the result. (2) Prices obtained from Merrill Lynch's trading floors.

DERIVATIVE INSTRUMENTS

None

SUBINDICES

None

RELATED INDICES

Merrill Lynch Capital Markets Index
Merrill Lynch Convertible Securities Index
Merrill Lynch Currency Indices
Merrill Lynch Energy & Metals Index
Merrill Lynch Global Bond Index
Merrill Lynch Institutional Municipal Index
Refer to Appendix 5 for additional indices.

REMARKS

New money market rate indices that track the total rate of return performance of overnight, one-month and three-month rates for major currencies were introduced starting April 30, 1996.

PUBLISHER

Merrill Lynch & Co.

MERRILL LYNCH U.S. 91-DAY TREASURY BILL INDEX (ACTUAL)

TOTAL RETURN PERFORMANCE

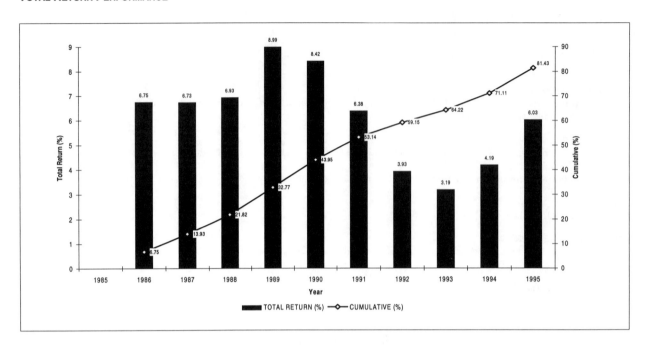

TOTAL RETURN AND PRICE PERFORMANCE

YEAR	VALUE	TOTAL RETURN (%)	CUMULATIVE (%)	PRICE RETURN (%)	MAXIMUM VALUE[1]	DATE	MINIMUM VALUE[1]	DATE
1995	417.98	6.03	81.43	6.03	417.98	31-Dec	396.19	31-Jan
1994	394.21	4.19	71.11	4.19	394.21	31-Dec	379.44	31-Jan
1993	378.35	3.19	64.22	3.19	378.35	31-Dec	367.71	31-Jan
1992	366.66	3.93	59.15	3.93	366.66	31-Dec	354.03	31-Jan
1991	352.80	6.38	53.14	6.38	352.80	31-Dec	333.70	31-Jan
1990	331.64	8.42	43.95	8.42	331.64	31-Dec	308.04	31-Jan
1989	305.89	8.99	32.77	8.99	305.89	31-Dec	282.71	31-Jan
1988	280.66	6.93	21.82	6.93	280.66	31-Dec	263.78	31-Jan
1987	262.47	6.73	13.93	6.73	262.47	31-Dec	247.21	31-Jan
1986	245.93	6.75	6.75	6.75	245.93	31-Dec	230.39	31-Jan
1985	230.39							
Average Annual (%)		6.15		6.15				
Compound Annual (%)		6.14		6.14				
Standard Deviation (%)		1.89		1.89				

[1]Maximum/minimum index values are as of month-end.

SYNOPSIS
The Merrill Lynch U.S. 91-Day Treasury Bill Index tracks the daily total return performance of three-month Treasury bills, based on actual prices.

NUMBER OF ISSUES—DECEMBER 31, 1995
1

MARKET VALUE—DECEMBER 31, 1995
Not Applicable

SELECTION CRITERIA
The index consists of a single Treasury bill that matures closest to, but not beyond 91-days from the last day of the previous month.

BACKGROUND
Monthly data is available to October 31, 1986 and daily values are available thereafter.

    The index represents a component of the Merrill-Lynch U.S. Domestic Master Bond Index, which, in turn, forms part of the Merrill Lynch Global Bond Index.

    For additional information, refer to the Merrill Lynch Global Bond Index.

BASE DATE
December 31, 1977=100.00

COMPUTATION METHODOLOGY
(1) Total return is calculated by dividing the Treasury bill's ending price by the beginning price and then subtracting one. (2) Prices are obtained from Merrill Lynch's trading floor.

DERIVATIVE INSTRUMENTS
13-week U.S. Treasury Bill options trade on the Chicago Board Options Exchange (CBOE).
13-week Treasury Bill Leaps trade on the Chicago Board Options Exchange (CBOE).
13-week U.S. Treasury bill futures trade on the MidAmerica Stock Exchange (MidAM).
90-day T-bill options trade on the Chicago Mercantile Exchange (CME).

SUBINDICES
None

RELATED INDICES
Merrill Lynch Capital Markets Index
Merrill Lynch Convertible Securities Index
Merrill Lynch Currency Indices
Merrill Lynch Energy & Metals Index
Merrill Lynch Global Bond Index
Merrill Lynch Institutional Municipal Index
Refer to Appendix 5 for additional indices.

REMARKS
(1) U.S. Treasury bill options are unrelated to the Merrill Lynch U.S. 91-day Treasury Bill Index. Rather, they are based on the current rate of the most recently auctioned 13-week U.S. Treasury Bill. (2) New money market rate indices that track the total rate of return performance of overnight, one-month and three-month rates for major currencies were introduced starting April 30, 1996.

PUBLISHER
Merrill Lynch & Co.

WORLD

MERRILL LYNCH EURODOLLAR 3-MONTH CERTIFICATE OF DEPOSIT (CD) INDEX

TOTAL RETURN PERFORMANCE

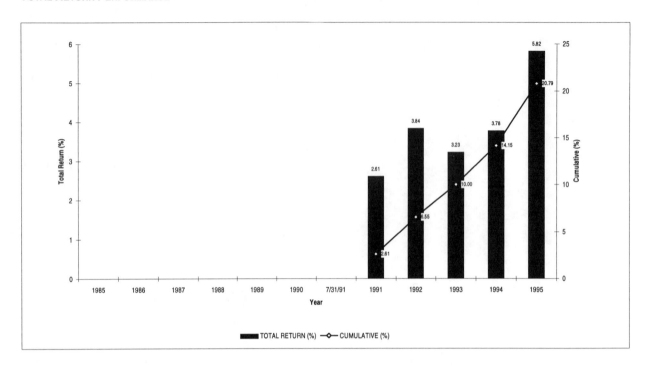

TOTAL RETURN AND PRICE PERFORMANCE

YEAR	VALUE	TOTAL RETURN (%)	CUMULATIVE (%)	PRICE RETURN (%)	MAXIMUM VALUE[1]	DATE	MINIMUM VALUE[1]	DATE
1995	120.79	5.82	20.79	0.13	120.79	31-Dec	114.54	31-Jan
1994	114.15	3.78	14.15	-0.82	114.15	31-Dec	110.30	31-Jan
1993	110.00	3.23	10.00	-0.02	110.00	31-Dec	106.86	31-Jan
1992	106.55	3.84	6.55	0.14	106.55	31-Dec	102.93	31-Jan
1991	102.61	2.61	2.61	NA	102.61	31-Dec	100.00	31-Jul
7/31/91	100.00							
1990								
1989								
1988								
1987								
1986								
1985								
Average Annual (%)		4.36		-0.14				
Compound Annual (%)		4.37		-0.14				
Standard Deviation (%)[2]		1.13		0.46				

[1]Maximum/minimum index values are as of month-end.
[2]Standard deviation applicable to the 4-year period 1992-1995.

SYNOPSIS

The Merrill Lynch 3-Month Eurodollar Certificate of Deposit (CD) Index tracks the price only and total return performance of three-month Eurodollar Certificates of Deposit, based on actual prices.

NUMBER OF ISSUES—DECEMBER 31, 1995

1

MARKET VALUE—DECEMBER 31, 1995

US$100.0 million

SELECTION CRITERIA

The index consists of a single Eurodollar Certificate of Deposit with a maturity that most closely matches the stated maturity of the index, but not beyond the index, at the beginning of a selected month.

BACKGROUND

The index represents a component of the Merrill Lynch U.S. Domestic Master Bond Index, which, in turn, forms part of the Merrill Lynch Global Bond Index.

For additional information, refer to the Merrill Lynch Global Bond Index.

BASE DATE

July 31, 1991=100.00

COMPUTATION METHODOLOGY

(1) Total return is based on actual prices, calculated by dividing the CD's price at the end of the month by the CD's price at the beginning of the month and subtracting one from the result. (2) Prices obtained from Merrill Lynch's trading floors.

DERIVATIVE INSTRUMENTS

None

SUBINDICES

None

RELATED INDICES

Merrill Lynch Capital Markets Index
Merrill Lynch Convertible Securities Index
Merrill Lynch Currency Indices
Merrill Lynch Energy & Metals Index
Merrill Lynch Global Bond Index
Merrill Lynch Institutional Municipal Index
Refer to Appendix 5 for additional indices.

REMARKS

None

PUBLISHER

Merrill Lynch & Co.

SALOMON BROTHERS WORLD MONEY MARKET INDEX

TOTAL RETURN PERFORMANCE

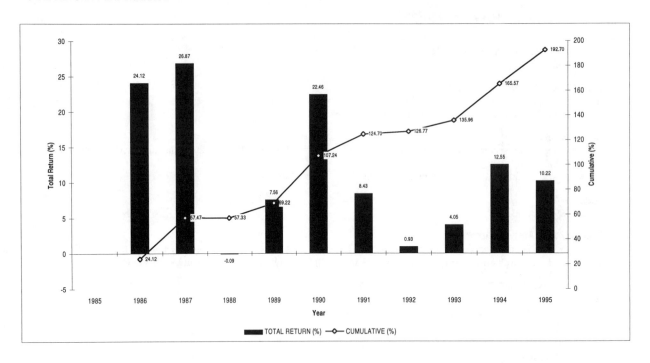

TOTAL RETURN PERFORMANCE

YEAR	VALUE	TOTAL RETURN (%)	CUMULATIVE (%)	MAXIMUM VALUE	DATE	MINIMUM VALUE	DATE
1995	536.43	10.22	192.70	544.40	31-Jul	494.88	31-Jan
1994	486.71	12.55	165.57	496.93	31-Oct	436.05	31-Jan
1993	432.45	4.05	135.96	443.39	31-May	416.62	28-Feb
1992	415.61	0.93	126.77	455.56	31-Aug	395.10	31-Mar
1991	411.80	8.43	124.70	411.80	31-Dec	357.53	31-Mar
1990	379.80	22.46	107.24	379.80	31-Dec	315.41	28-Feb
1989	310.13	7.56	69.22	310.13	31-Dec	272.14	31-May
1988	288.34	-0.09	57.33	292.34	30-Nov	268.40	31-Jul
1987	288.60	26.87	57.47	288.60	31-Dec	236.27	31-Jan
1986	227.47	24.12	24.12	227.47	31-Dec	186.14	31-Jan
1985	183.27						
Average Annual (%)		11.71					
Compound Annual (%)		11.34					
Standard Deviation (%)		9.69					

SYNOPSIS

The Salomon Brothers World Money Market Index is an equally-weighted index that measures the monthly total return performance, in local currency and U.S. dollar terms, of 20 money market instruments with three-month maturities in eight global currency markets.

NUMBER OF ISSUES—DECEMBER 31, 1995

Not Applicable

MARKET VALUE—DECEMBER 31, 1995

Not Applicable

SELECTION CRITERIA

Twenty money market instruments with three-month maturities in eight global currency markets have been selected for measurement. These include U.S. Treasury bills, U.S. Certificates of Deposit, Euro CDs and Eurodeposits, Canadian Treasury bills, Canadian Eurodeposits, German domestic bank deposits and Eurodeposits, Japanese CDs, Gensaki and Japanese Eurodeposits, UK Treasury bills, UK CDs and UK Eurodeposits, Swiss domestic bank deposits and Swiss Eurodeposits, Dutch domestic bank deposits and Dutch Eurodeposits, and French domestic bank deposits and French Eurodeposits. Currencies include the U.S. dollar, Canadian dollar, Deutschemark, Japanese Yen, UK Sterling, Swiss Franc, Dutch Guilder, and French Franc.

BACKGROUND

The index is designed to be relatively stable and easily replicable. Monthly index values for each currency and money market instrument is recomputed back to January 1978, except for Japanese domestic CDs and Japanese Eurodeposits which were established with base dates as of July 31, 1979 and March 31, 1978, respectively.

COMPUTATION METHODOLOGY

(1) Average of the monthly yields for the preceding three months is calculated and converted to an annualized rate of return, using a monthly compounding frequency formula. The monthly return is adjusted with local market-day count conventions and for currency movements to arrive at a local market return. (2) The index invests only in deposits or securities maturing in three months. (3) All deposits and securities are held to maturity. (4) At the beginning of each month, one-third of the index matures and is rolled over into new three-month instruments. (5) Currency exchange rates are bid-side quotes taken at 12:30 PM (EST) on the last business day of each month.

DERIVATIVE INSTRUMENTS

None

SUBINDICES

Separate indexes are computed for each instrument on a local currency and U.S. dollar-basis.

RELATED INDICES

Salomon Brothers Broad Investment-Grade Bond Index
Salomon Brothers Convertible Securities Index
Salomon Brothers High Yield Market Index
Salomon Brothers World Equity Index
Salomon Brothers World Government Bond Index
Refer to Appendix 5 for additional indices.

REMARKS

None

PUBLISHER

Salomon Brothers Inc.

11

INDEX PROFILES — COMMODITIES
NORTH AMERICA

BANKERS TRUST COMMODITY INDEX (BTCI)

PRICE PERFORMANCE

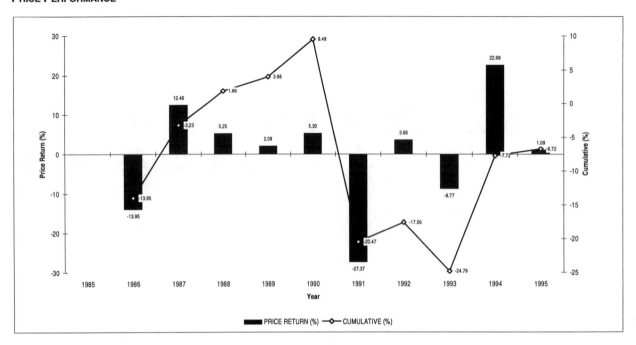

PRICE AND TOTAL RETURN PERFORMANCE

YEAR	VALUE	PRICE RETURN (%)	CUMULATIVE (%)	TOTAL RETURN (%)	MAXIMUM VALUE	DATE	MINIMUM VALUE	DATE
1995	78.31	1.09	-6.72	8.63	81.73	19-Apr	73.32	19-Oct
1994	77.46	22.69	-7.72	29.00	78.89	3-Nov	63.50	9-Mar
1993	63.14	-8.77	-24.79	-13.87	71.87	31-May	61.82	6-Dec
1992	69.20	3.66	-17.56	1.52	76.35	27-Jul	65.80	8-Jan
1991	66.76	-27.37	-20.47	-18.77	98.72	16-Jan	66.65	30-Dec
1990	91.91	5.30	9.49	13.81	119.56	9-Oct	67.36	20-Jun
1989	87.29	2.09	3.98	22.13	87.46	27-Dec	74.60	7-Aug
1988	85.50	5.25	1.86	21.70	88.10	18-Apr	75.76	3-Oct
1987	81.24	12.46	-3.23	31.95	89.40	3-Aug	69.75	2-Mar
1986	72.24	-13.95	-13.95	0.10	83.95	1-Jan	57.11	1-Apr
1985	83.95							
Average Annual (%)		0.25		9.62				
Compound Annual (%)		-0.69		8.32				
Standard Deviation (%)		14.00		17.35				

SYNOPSIS
The Bankers Trust Commodity Index (BTCI) is an optimization-weighted arithmetic average index that tracks the daily spot return, roll yield and collateral yield of five industrial commodities, consisting of a basket of highly liquid real assets including West Texas Intermediate (WTI) Light Sweet Crude Oil, Gold, Aluminum, Heating Oil and Silver.

NUMBER OF COMMODITIES—DECEMBER 31, 1995
5

MARKET VALUE—DECEMBER 31, 1995
Not Applicable

SELECTION CRITERIA
A variety of hard commodities using existing liquidity in spot and forward markets were optimized using quarterly return data over a 10-year period from 1984-1993 for positive correlations to the Consumer Price Index (CPI), Producer Price Index (PPI) for finished goods, Producer Price Index (PPI) for crude materials, Organization for Economic Co-operation and Development (OECD) growth, Gross Domestic Product (GDP) growth and negative correlations to the S&P 500 and benchmark 10- and 30-year Treasury bond prices.

BACKGROUND
The index, introduced in 1995, is designed to serve as a vehicle for capturing commodity market movements.

BASE DATE
January 3, 1994=100.00

COMPUTATION METHODOLOGY
(1) A weighted arithmetic-average index formula that takes into account spot return, roll yield and collateral yield, with base prices computed as the average of the daily prices of each component commodity over the first quarter of 1984. (2) Price or spot yield reflects the return attributable to changes in the prices of the underlying commodities or first nearby futures contract. Current price for crude oil is the official settlement price per barrel made public by New York Mercantile Exchange (NYMEX) for the first WTI futures contract which expires on or after such day; price for gold is the U.S. dollar price per troy ounce of unallocated gold bullion suitable for delivery in the London Gold Market; price for aluminum is the official U.S. dollar cash settlement price per metric ton of high-grade primary aluminum made public on London Metals Exchange (LME) on such day; price for heating oil is the official settlement price per gallon made public on such day by the New York Mercantile Exchange (NYMEX) for the first NYMEX #2 Heating Oil futures contract which expires on or after such day; and the price for silver is the U.S. dollar price per troy ounce of unallocated silver bullion suitable for delivery in the London Silver Market. (3) Roll yield is the component of return that arises from rolling a long position through time in a sloping forward price curve environment. (4) Collateral yield, gained from the return on T-bills use as collateral for futures investments in commodities, is calculated using the return on T-bills. (5) The index weights are not rebalanced.

DERIVATIVE INSTRUMENTS
None

SUBINDICES
Five individual commodity subindices: WTI Crude Oil, Gold, Aluminum, Heating Oil and Silver.

RELATED INDICES
Bankers Trust Bankers Acceptance Index
Bankers Trust Libor Index
Bankers Trust Repo Index

REMARKS
BTCI base weights are, as follows: WTI Crude Oil 45%, Gold 18%, Aluminum 17%, Heating Oil 10% and Silver 10%.

PUBLISHER
Bankers Trust New York Corp.

GOLDMAN SACHS COMMODITY INDEX (GSCI)

PRICE PERFORMANCE

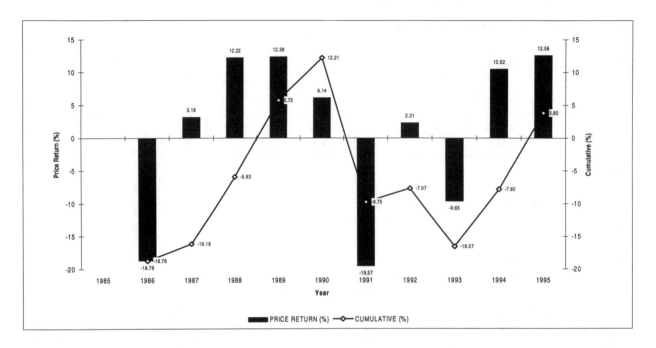

PRICE AND TOTAL RETURN PERFORMANCE

YEAR	VALUE	PRICE RETURN (%)	CUMULATIVE (%)	TOTAL RETURN (%)	MAXIMUM VALUE	DATE	MINIMUM VALUE	DATE
1995	203.50	12.58	3.80	20.33	206.79	27-Dec	171.85	7-Jul
1994	180.76	10.52	-7.80	5.29	184.37	17-Jun	164.53	3-Jan
1993	163.55	-9.65	-16.57	-12.33	190.17	31-Mar	163.55	31-Dec
1992	181.01	2.31	-7.67	4.42	193.02	29-May	180.01	30-Nov
1991	176.92	-19.57	-9.75	-6.13	198.55	31-Oct	176.92	31-Dec
1990	219.97	6.14	12.21	29.08	270.19	28-Sep	184.18	29-Jun
1989	207.25	12.39	5.72	38.28	207.25	31-Dec	179.55	31-Jul
1988	184.41	12.22	-5.93	27.93	184.41	30-Dec	163.79	29-Feb
1987	164.33	3.18	-16.18	23.77	177.81	31-Jul	154.38	27-Feb
1986	159.27	-18.76	-18.76	2.04	173.94	31-Jan	150.35	31-Jul
1985	196.04							
Average Annual (%)		1.14		13.27				
Compound Annual (%)		0.37		12.12				
Standard Deviation (%)		12.65		16.83				

SYNOPSIS

The Goldman Sachs Commodity Index (GSCI), a broad production-weighted index, tracks the daily price and total return of commodity investments consisting of liquid, investable futures contracts on physical commodities bought or sold on exchanges in an OECD country and denominated in U.S. dollars. It is composed of six market segments, including energy, precious metals, base metals, grains, livestock and soft commodities, and 22 commodities traded in the form of 25 commodity contracts.

NUMBER OF COMMODITIES—DECEMBER 31, 1995
22 (25 contracts)

MARKET VALUE—DECEMBER 31, 1995
Not Applicable

SELECTION CRITERIA

The index consists of the following commodity contracts: Crude oil, heating oil, unleaded gasoline, trade on the New York Mercantile Exchange (NYMEX); natural gas/NYMEX, live cattle, pork bellies, and live hogs, trade on the Chicago Mercantile Exchange (CME); wheat, corn, and soybeans, trade on the Chicago Board of Trade (CBT); coffee, sugar, and cocoa, trade on the Coffee Sugar Cocoa Exchange (CSCE); cotton trades on the New York Cotton Exchange (NYCE); copper and high grade copper, trade on the Commodity Exchange, Inc. (COMEX); and copper, aluminum, zinc, nickel, lead and tin, trade on the London Metals Exchange (LME), and gold, silver and platinum which trade on the COMEX. Constituents are limited to physical commodity contracts which are selected on the basis of the following criteria: (1) Futures contracts must be denominated in U.S. dollars and traded on an exchange in an OECD Country. (2) A fixed date price at least one month forward must be available in the event the commodity exchange operates on the basis of perpetual forward prices. (3) Contract prices in U.S dollars must be published daily and be available to Goldman, Sachs & Co. from the exchange via a third party vendor. (4) A commodity's futures contract volume on its most active exchange must be equal to at least 750,000 contracts during the calculation period. A commodity is removed in the event its contract volume falls below 375,000 contracts during the calculation period. (5) A commodity must satisfy contract liquidity requirements, measured in terms of an equivalent physical traded ratio (EPTR), or be removed. EPTR is the product of the annual U.S. dollar-denominated contract volume on the exchange with the largest annual U.S. dollar-denominated volume and the contract size on the exchange, divided by the world production quantity average. (6) Derivative commodities are excluded if they are largely or entirely a derivative of another commodity eligible for inclusion. An exception is made when a single commodity comprises more than 33% of the dollar weight of the index on a particular date each year. To the extent the derivative commodity is included, the weight of the primary commodity is adjusted to avoid double counting.

BACKGROUND
The GSCI was introduced in 1994 and index values have been recalculated to 1970.

BASE DATE
January 2, 1970=100.00

COMPUTATION METHODOLOGY
(1) A world production-weighted arithmetic average index formula that takes into account the daily change in each commodity's settlement price of the futures contract held as well as roll return. A normalizing factor is used to reflect yearly adjustments to world production weights in order to maintain the continuity. (2) Total return combines the daily percentage change in the value of the index and an interest rate component attributable to 100% collateral posted as margin by adding to the basic return the daily interest on the last available weekly 3-month Treasury Bill Auction Rate on the previous business day. (3) The CSCI employs a five business day roll period in which a contract, deliverable in the next month, is rolled forward on the fifth business day of the month. Under this approach, 20% of the contract is rolled each day. The next business day, next non-limit move day or next trading day in which the closing price is not a roll day applies in the event the exchange is closed on any roll day, or a limit price move occurs in either the contract held or the contract being rolled into or the closing price on each of the days of the roll period is a limit price. (4) The index is calculated using daily prices published by the most active exchange applicable to each commodity. All prices used to calculate the index are truncated after the 0.0001 dollar decimal place. (5) The period for contract volume calculations is from May of the previous year to April of the current year. (6) The GSCI uses only the most active contract months for each commodity, based on an analysis of volume and open interest statistics from 1970 to 1994. Excluded are "switching months" and other minor months as they are typically illiquid and may exhibit unusual price behavior, data gaps, etc. Included contract months may change over time due to liquidity considerations. Such changes, effective for the following year's index calculation, are announced in June of each year. (7) Changes in contract specifications involving contract months or the replacement of an entire contract modify the computation of the index, as follows: First, in the event an exchange deletes a contract month, the index is calculated using the next available, previously announced contract month. Second, the addition of a contract month during the year in which the index did not contemplate its inclusion does not effect the computation of the index. Third, the replacement of an entire contract with another essentially similar contract results in a switch to the new contract on the day after the traded daily volume of the nearest contract month of the new contract exceeds the old contract. On the crossover day, all positions in the old contract are liquidated and positions in the new contract are established. (8) A commodity's weight is its production on a worldwide basis, calculated on a five year moving average, with a three year lag, based on the most recently published and available world production statistics obtained from the United Nation's *Statistical Yearbook* and *Industrial Statistics Yearbook*. Other sources are used as required. World Production Weights are updated annually, on the fifth business day of January.

DERIVATIVE INSTRUMENTS
GSCI index futures are traded on the Chicago Mercantile Exchange (CME).

SUBINDICES
Six market sector subindices: Energy, precious metals, base metals, grains, livestock and soft commodities.
Individual commodities.

RELATED INDICES
Financial Times/Standard & Poor's Actuaries World Index   Goldman Sachs International Government Bond Index
Goldman Sachs Convertible 100 Index   Goldman Sachs Liquid Asset-Backed Securities Index

REMARKS
(1)World Production Weights for 1995 were, as follows: Copper-COMEX 0.0000 LBS, Copper-LME 10.36844 MTons, Aluminum 21.9492 MTons, Zinc 6.8231 MTons, Lead 5.4107 MTons, Tin 0.2243 MTons, Gold 56.7108 Troy Oz., Silver 4.4651 Troy Oz., Platinum 8.8955 Troy Oz., Pork Bellies 0.0000 LBS, Live Hogs 793.7565 LBS, Live Cattle 1116.6970 LBS, Wheat 198.3264 Bushels, Corn 179.7255, Bushels, Soybeans 36.9868 Bushels, Sugar 2299.9330 LBS, Coffee 132.1200 LBS, Cocoa 2.2125 MTons, Cotton 377.6960 LBS., Crude Oil 9004.4630 BBL, Heating Oil 1823.917 Gallons, Unleaded Gasoline 1941.9600 Gallons, and Natural Gas 65640.2800 MMBtu. (2) LME-traded commodities were excluded until 1991, at which time the introduction of published Intermediate Closing Prices for delivery on the third Wednesday of each month up to the 15th month established a pricing arrangement that more closely resemble the fixed date futures contracts used by most American commodity exchanges. Previously, pricing was restricted to a perpetual forward pricing scheme. (3) Active exchanges include: NYMEX for crude oil, heating oil, unleaded gasoline and natural gas; CME for live cattle and live hogs; CBOT for wheat, corn and soybeans, CSCE for coffee, sugar and cocoa; NYCE for cotton; LME for copper, aluminum, zinc, nickel, lead and tin; and the Commodity Exchange (a division of NYMEX) for gold, silver and platinum.

PUBLISHER
Goldman, Sachs & Co.

INVESTABLE COMMODITY INDEX (ICI)

PRICE PERFORMANCE

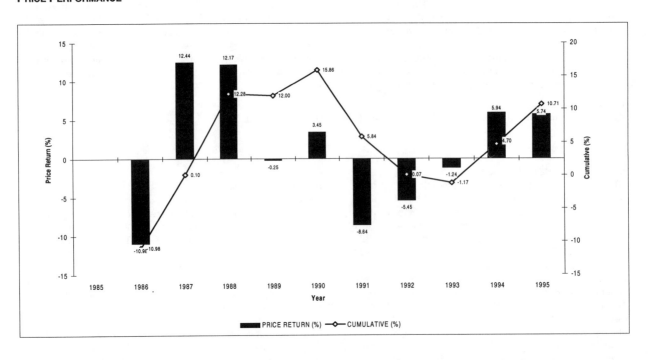

PRICE AND TOTAL RETURN PERFORMANCE

YEAR	VALUE	PRICE RETURN (%)	CUMULATIVE (%)	TOTAL RETURN (%)	MAXIMUM VALUE[1]	DATE	MINIMUM VALUE[1]	DATE
1995	2,416.98	5.74	10.71	11.86	2,416.98	31-Dec	2,224.66	31-Jan
1994	2,285.69	5.94	4.70	10.63	2,380.58	31-Jul	2,189.54	24-Feb
1993	2,157.57	-1.24	-1.17	1.85	2,226.12	30-Apr	2,134.05	30-Nov
1992	2,184.59	-5.45	0.07	-2.06	2,326.50	31-Jan	2,170.29	31-Oct
1991	2,310.61	-8.64	5.84	-3.44	2,462.58	31-Oct	2,310.61	31-Dec
1990	2,529.26	3.45	15.86	11.77	2,771.92	30-Sep	2,434.33	31-Jan
1989	2,444.98	-0.25	12.00	8.38	2,475.57	31-Mar	2,382.28	31-Oct
1988	2,451.12	12.17	12.28	20.06	2,451.12	31-Dec	2,115.33	28-Feb
1987	2,185.21	12.44	0.10	19.33	2,215.80	30-Nov	1,929.59	28-Feb
1986	1,943.40	-10.98	-10.98	-5.37	2,052.86	31-Jan	1,788.23	31-Jul
1985	2,183.10							
Average Annual (%)		1.32		7.30				
Compound Annual (%)		1.02		6.95				
Standard Deviation (%)		8.11		9.15				

[1]Maximum/minimum index values are as of month-end.

Synopsis

The Investable Commodity Index (ICI) is an equally-weighted geometrically averaged index that tracks the daily price only and total return performance of 16 liquid commodities futures contracts spanning five major industry groups, including grains, metals, energy, meats and food fibers that are traded on recognized commodities exchanges in the United States.

Number of Commodities—December 31, 1995

16

Market Value—December 31, 1995

Not Meaningful

Selection Criteria

Commodities are selected on the basis of their importance in world trade and the availability of liquid, exchange-traded futures contracts, and include the following commodities: Wheat, corn, soybeans, gold, silver, copper, crude oil, heating oil, gasoline, natural gas, live cattle, live hogs, cocoa, coffee, sugar and cotton.

At its inception, the following criteria was used to select index constituents:

(1) Availability of exchange-traded futures contracts listed on a U.S. regulated futures exchange. (2) Sufficient level of liquidity, as defined by contract volume and open interest applicable to the most liquid or actively traded contract. Total annual contract volume in excess of one million contracts and average monthly open interest for all contract months equal to or in excess of 20,000 contracts a year. (3) A desire to achieve broad and balanced exposure to five major commodity groups, namely grains, metals, energy, livestock, food and fiber, provided the inclusion of a commodity did not increase the commodity's respective industry group's exposure in the index above 26.7% relative to an optimal balanced weighting of 20%. Unless an industry group's weighting fell below 13.3%, by-products or derivatives of primary markets were excluded from the index at its inception. In this case, by-products of a primary commodity could be added up to 20% of the index.

Background

The index was created in October 1991 by Intermarket Management, Inc. to provide a liquid and investable portfolio benchmark. It was launched with 15 constituent commodities, and expanded as of the close on January 31, 1994 by the addition of natural gas as an index component.

Base Date

January 1, 1972=1000.00

Computation Methodology

(1) An equally-weighted geometric mean index formula is used. (2) The continuous price for an individual commodity market represents the arithmetic mean of the three near delivery month futures contracts. These price series are periodically adjusted when a nearby futures contract approaches expiration. (3) Collateral return is calculated on the full value of the index, using the daily compound yield of the average discount rate for the weekly auction of the 13-week Treasury bill. (4) The index calculation is based on actively traded contract delivery months. Non-cycle months are excluded from consideration. In the event an active contract is eliminated by an exchange, the next available contract will be used to calculate the index. (5) Index constituents, active contracts, and all other U.S. exchange-traded commodities, including volume and open interest, are reviewed annually to validate compliance with ICI's liquidity standards. To the extent a contract delivery month is added or eliminated from the index, such action is announced after January 15th of each year and implemented on the last day of trading in the same month. An Index Committee oversees the implementation of index related policies and procedures. (6) Adjustments to the composition of the index will also be made due to contract delistings, eligibility of non-constituent contracts, a contract's inability to satisfy the minimum liquidity and investability guidelines, and in the event a commodity or a commodity by-product is eclipsed by another commodity or commodity by-product in terms of volume and open interest.

Derivative Instruments

None

Subindices

Sixteen commodity subindices: Wheat, corn, soybeans, gold, silver, copper, crude oil, heating oil, gasoline, natural gas, live cattle, live hogs, cocoa, coffee, sugar and cotton.

Related Indices

Jefferies & Company Convertible Securities Index

Remarks

The following exchanges and contract months are used in the calculation of the index: Wheat and corn traded on CBOT-March, May, July, September and December; Soybeans traded on CBOT-January, March, May, July, August, September and December; Gold traded on COMEX-February, April, June, August, October and December; Silver and copper traded on COMEX-March, May, July, September and December; Crude oil (Sweet Light), Heating Oil #2, Unleaded gasoline and natural gas traded on NYMEX-All months; Live cattle and hogs traded on CME-March, May, July, September and December; Sugar (World #1) traded on CSCE-March, May, July and October; and Cotton #2 traded on NYCE-March May, July. October and December.

Publisher

Jefferies & Company, Inc./Intermarket Management Inc.

J.P. Morgan Commodity Index (JPMCI)

Price Performance

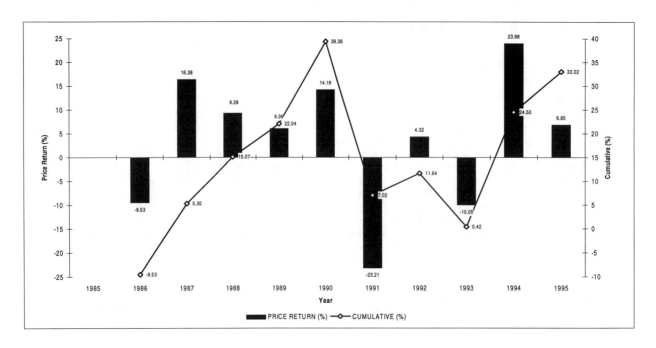

Price and Total Return Performance

YEAR	VALUE	PRICE RETURN (%)	CUMULATIVE (%)	TOTAL RETURN (%)	MAXIMUM VALUE[1]	DATE	MINIMUM VALUE[1]	DATE
1995	135.81	6.85	33.02	14.39	137.66	27-Dec	122.37	19-Oct
1994	127.11	23.98	24.50	24.06	127.50	31-Oct	106.93	28-Feb
1993	102.52	-10.05	0.42	-12.87	119.08	30-Apr	102.52	31-Dec
1992	113.98	4.32	11.64	7.40	125.09	30-Sep	110.53	31-Jan
1991	109.26	-23.21	7.02	-15.80	125.65	31-Oct	109.26	31-Dec
1990	142.28	14.19	39.36	15.27	170.82	30-Sep	109.83	31-May
1989	124.60	6.06	22.04	30.36	124.60	31-Dec	111.64	31-Jul
1988	117.48	9.28	15.07	27.05	117.48	31-Dec	97.07	30-Sep
1987	107.50	16.38	5.30	28.54	111.23	31-Jul	90.25	28-Feb
1986	92.37	-9.53	-9.53	-4.11	92.37	31-Dec	69.94	31-Mar
1985	102.09							
Average Annual (%)		3.83		11.43				
Compound Annual (%)		2.89		10.16				
Standard Deviation (%)		14.21		17.22				

[1]Maximum/minimum index values for the period 1986-1994 are as of month-end.

Synopsis

The J.P. Morgan Commodity Index (JPMCI) is a dollar optimization-weighted arithmetic average index that tracks the daily price or "spot" return, roll return, collateral return and total return performance of the 11 most liquid industrial commodity investments, consisting of futures contracts on base metals, energy and precious metals traded in U.S. dollars on recognized commodities exchanges in the United States or the United Kingdom.

Number of Commodities—December 31, 1995
11

Market Value—December 31, 1995
Not Applicable

SELECTION CRITERIA

Commodities are restricted to the most liquid industrial commodity futures contracts in which an investor can deal in reasonable volumes without expecting to influence price levels significantly. Soft commodities are excluded from the index due to their diminished liquidity and reduction in the correlation of the index to economic indicators and in the exposure of the index to non-macroeconomic weather factors.

The index is composed of the following 11 commodities: Aluminum, copper, nickel, zinc, heating oil #2, natural gas, NY Harbor unleaded gasoline, WTI light sweet crude, gold, silver and platinum.

BACKGROUND

The JPMCI, launched on September 21, 1994, was created to serve as a diversified, liquid, investable vehicle and an effective benchmark for institutional investors.

BASE DATE

January 1, 1985=100.00

COMPUTATION METHODOLOGY

(1) An arithmetic averaging index formula that aggregates spot return, roll return and collateral return to arrive at the total rate of return, based on a strategy that holds forward positions in each of the 11 commodities for a one-month period and then rebalances the volume of commodities held for the following month based on a constant dollar weighting scheme. (2) Price return or spot return represents the change in the nearby prices. Spot prices for energy and base metals are calculated by generating a constant one-month maturity forward price, using the first and second nearby futures contacts and three-month forward and cash contracts, respectively. For precious metals, spot prices are used rather than constant one-month maturity forward prices. (3) Roll return is the component of return that arises from rolling a long position through time in a sloping forward price curve environment. (4) Collateral return, which is the risk-free interest rate component attributable to full collateral posted as margin, is calculated on the full value of the index, using a floating 13-week Treasury bill yield, compounded daily at the decompounded discount rate of the most recent weekly U.S. Treasury Bill auction as found in the H.15 (519) report published by the Board of Governors of the Federal Reserve System. (5) Commodity weights are determined by an optimization process designed to maximize an objective function that includes a high index Sharpe Ratio, or ratio of excess return to standard deviation of return, a positive correlation with unanticipated inflation, positive tracking with industrial growth and negative correlation with stock and bond returns. The optimization is subject to liquidity constraints that serve to establish maximum allowable allocations and diversity constraints that serve to establish minimum allowable allocations. (6) While certain market developments may necessitate future changes, index weights stay constant in proportional dollar terms but units of each commodity vary on a monthly basis. The index is rebalanced at the end of trading on the 4th business day of every month, in either London or New York, on which all relevant exchanges are open. The futures contract used for monthly rebalancing of each commodity is the nearest designated futures contract used in the index, with a termination of trading date not earlier than 10 business days into the following month. To arrive at the number of new units, the index is rebalanced according to a formula in which the product of the current index value multiplied by the weight of the commodity in the index's new units is divided by the current price of the new contract per unit. A neutral business committee has been established for the purpose of evaluating possible changes to the index with regard to its weighting, composition or calculation methodology. (7) Following the rebalancing procedure, contract rolls, are executed. This mechanism, by which the old contracts are sold and the new contracts are purchased, is transacted over a period of five business days immediately following the rebalancing date. Twenty percent of the roll volume is transacted on each business day. (8) Calculations use official exchange settlement prices for the energy and precious metals futures contracts and the London Metals Exchange (LME) closing prices for the base metals.

DERIVATIVE INSTRUMENTS

None

SUBINDICES

J.P. Morgan Commodity Index: Spot.
J.P. Morgan Excess Return, comprised of price and roll return.
Three subindices by commodity type: Energy, base metals and precious metals.
Eleven subindices covering individual commodities.

RELATED INDICES

J. P. Morgan Ecu Index
J. P. Morgan Cash Index
J. P. Morgan Emerging Markets Bond Index
J. P. Morgan Government Bond Index

REMARKS

JPMCI commodity weights are, as follows: Base Metals 22%–Aluminum 9%, Copper 8%, Nickel 2% and Zinc 3%; Energy 55%–WTI Crude Oil 33%, Heating Oil 10%, Unleaded Gasoline 5%, and Natural Gas 7%; Precious metals 23%–Gold 15%, Silver 5% and Platinum 3%.

PUBLISHER

J.P. Morgan Securities Inc.

KNIGHT-RIDDER COMMODITY RESEARCH BUREAU'S FUTURES PRICE INDEX
(KR-CRB)

PRICE PERFORMANCE

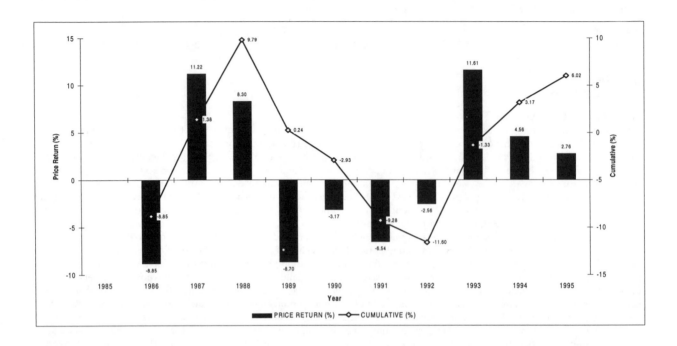

PRICE PERFORMANCE

YEAR	VALUE	PRICE RETURN (%)	CUMULATIVE (%)	MAXIMUM VALUE	DATE	MINIMUM VALUE	DATE
1995	243.18	2.76	6.02	246.02	21-Dec	229.63	13-Jul
1994	236.64	4.56	3.17	239.38	17-Jun	220.21	19-Apr
1993	226.31	11.61	-1.33	226.56	29-Dec	198.46	8-Feb
1992	202.76	-2.56	-11.60	214.98	10-Feb	198.38	12-Aug
1991	208.08	-6.54	-9.28	222.84	16-Jan	204.68	20-Aug
1990	222.64	-3.17	-2.93	247.79	9-May	220.21	18-Dec
1989	229.93	-8.70	0.24	251.59	5-Jan	221.15	31-Jul
1988	251.83	8.30	9.79	270.52	27-Jun	224.24	26-Feb
1987	232.53	11.22	1.38	237.08	27-Nov	204.24	25-Feb
1986	209.07	-8.85	-8.85	230.68	7-Jan	196.87	11-Jul
1985	229.37						
Average Annual (%)		0.87					
Compound Annual (%)		0.59					
Standard Deviation (%)		7.92					

SYNOPSIS
The Knight-Ridder Commodity Research Bureau's Futures Price Index (KR-CRB) Index is an unweighted geometric index that tracks the continuous price only performance of 17 commodities, consisting of futures contracts on metals, energy, precious metals, grains and other soft commodities that are traded in recognized commodities exchanges in the United States.

NUMBER OF COMMODITIES—DECEMBER 31, 1995
17

MARKET VALUE—DECEMBER 31, 1995
Not Applicable

SELECTION CRITERIA
The composition of the index reflects its design consideration which is to provide a dynamic and accurate representation of broad trends in overall commodity prices. It is modified from time to time to reflect changes in market structure and activity.

    The index is now composed of the following 17 commodities: Cocoa, coffee, copper, corn, cotton, crude oil, gold, heating oil, live cattle, live hogs, orange juice, platinum, silver and sugar.

BACKGROUND
The KR-CRB Index was developed in 1957 with 28 components. Since that time, it has been modified nine times. The latest revision took place on December 6, 1995. At that time, four commodities were deleted, including lumber, pork bellies, soybean meal and oil, and unleaded gasoline. Moreover, the calculation of the index was also revised by lowering the number of forward delivery contracts to include those within six months from the calculation versus futures contracts which expire on or before the end of the ninth calendar month. At the same time, a minimum of two delivery months must now be used to calculate the current price, even in the event that the second contract falls outside of the six month time period.

COMPUTATION METHODOLOGY
(1) A geometric average mathematical technique is used in which the prices of each component commodities are averaged. (2) Prices represent those of all the futures contracts which expire on or before the end of the sixth calendar month measured from the current month excluding non-cycle months. (3) Contracts in delivery are excluded from consideration. (4) A minimum of two prices must be used and a maximum of five contract months for each commodity. In the event of an excess number of contracts, the most deferred contracts are dropped. (5) Only settlement and last-sale prices are used in the calculation of the index. In the absence of a last-sale price, typically in the more deferred contract months, the previous day's settlement price is used. (6) The resulting value is divided by a factor of 30.7766 which is the 1967 base year average, which is, in turn, multiplied by 0.8486. This adjustment factor is required in order to maintain the continuity of the index due to prior period constituent changes.

DERIVATIVE INSTRUMENTS
KR-CRB index futures are traded on the New York Futures Exchange (NYFE).

SUBINDICES
Various subindices by commodity type: Imported, industrials, grains, oil seeds, livestock, energy, precious metals and miscellaneous.

RELATED INDICES
Interest Rate Index: 3-month T-bill, 10-year T-note and T-bond.
Currencies Index: DeutscheMark, Canadian Dollar, Swiss Franc, Japanese Yen, and British Pound.

REMARKS
The following exchanges and contract months are eligible for inclusion in the index: Crude oil, heating oil and natural gas traded on NYMEX-All 12 calendar months; Corn, wheat, copper, silver, cocoa, and coffee traded on CBOT, COMEX and CSCE-March, May, July, September and December; Soybeans on CBOT–January, March, May, July, August and November; Cotton on COMEX–March, may, July and December; Live cattle on CME–February, April, June, August, October and December; Live hogs on CME–February, April, June, July, August, October and December; Platinum on COMEX–January, April, July and October; Orange juice on CSCE–January, March, May, July, September and November; Sugar on CSCE–March, May, July and October

PUBLISHER
Knight-Ridder Financial.

LEHMAN BROTHERS COMMODITY INDEX (LBCI)

PRICE PERFORMANCE

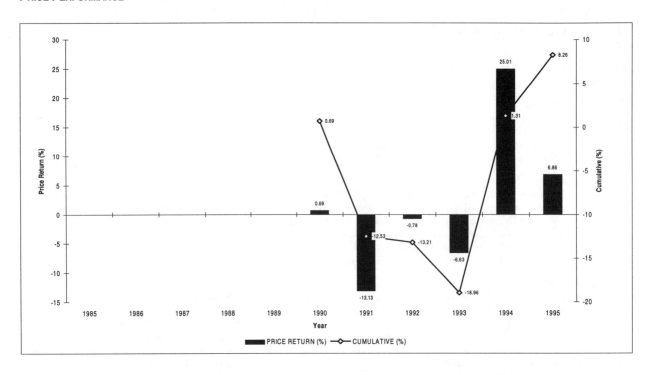

PRICE AND TOTAL RETURN PERFORMANCE

YEAR	VALUE	PRICE RETURN (%)	CUMULATIVE (%)	TOTAL RETURN (%)	MAXIMUM VALUE	DATE	MINIMUM VALUE	DATE
1995	108.26	6.86	8.26	13.47	108.31	26-Dec	98.51	8-Feb
1994	101.31	25.01	1.31	30.45	103.08	12-Jul	80.99	10-Jan
1993	81.04	-6.63	-18.96	-3.73	87.13	7-Jul	77.89	30-Nov
1992	86.79	-0.78	-13.21	2.75	94.67	29-Jun	84.82	4-Dec
1991	87.47	-13.13	-12.53	-8.20	102.10	16-Jan	87.00	30-Dec
1990	100.69	0.69	0.69	8.73	NA	NA	NA	NA
1989	100.00							
1988								
1987								
1986								
1985								
Average Annual (%)		2.01		7.25				
Compound Annual (%)		1.33		6.53				
Standard Deviation (%)		13.16		13.85				

SYNOPSIS

The Lehman Brothers Commodity Index (LBCI) is a trade value-weighted index that tracks the monthly price and total return performance of commodity investments, consisting of a weighted array of forward or futures contracts on products or goods that are bought or sold on recognized commodities exchanges in the United States or the United Kingdom and traded in U.S. dollars. The index is composed of six market sectors, including energy, precious metals, base metals, grains, livestock and soft commodities, and 10 commodities

NUMBER OF COMMODITIES—DECEMBER 31, 1995
10

MARKET VALUE—DECEMBER 31, 1995
Not Applicable

SELECTION CRITERIA

Commodities, which are classified into six markets, are selected as index constituents on the basis of the following guidelines:
(1) Average daily dollar open interest and average daily dollar volume are calculated for all eligible commodities based on activity in the 12-month period from November to December each year, for a period of three years. Average daily open interest is expressed by the number of contracts multiplied by the number of units per contract and by the average daily price per unit. (2) The resulting two numbers are added to arrive at each commodity's index capitalization. Index capitalization refers to the relative size of the

markets for individual commodities. (3) Each commodity's index capitalization is weighted for the last three years using the ratio 1:2:3. Thus, a commodity's index capitalization for the latest year is weighted by three, while the index capitalization of the second year is weighted by two and the index capitalization for the earliest year is weighted by one. (4) The resulting three numbers are added to get the weighted index capitalization. (5) Each weighted index capitalization is ranked, and the lower ranking of similar commodities contracts are excluded from consideration. (6) The highest ranking commodity is selected for each of the six sectors. (7) The second highest ranking commodity is selected for each of four sectors, such that four sectors end up with two commodities each while two sectors are established with one commodity each, for a total of 10 constituent commodities. Commodities currently include: Copper, West Texas Intermediate crude oil, soybeans, gold, aluminum, corn, heating oil, silver, cotton and live cattle.

BACKGROUND
Introduced in May 1995, the LBCI was created to serve as a liquid, transparent and replicable performance benchmark for a market-weighted array of individual commodities.

BASE DATE
December 31, 1989=100.00

COMPUTATION METHODOLOGY
(1) Aggregate of prices times quantities index formula, in which quantities represent commodity weights. (2) Total return combines the monthly percentage change in the value of the index and an interest rate component attributable to collateral posted as margin, by adding to the basic return the one month yield calculated on three month constant maturity U.S. Treasury Bills with a value equal to the beginning of the month index value. (3) The LBCI index employs a constant dollar method along with a three day roll period, beginning five business days before the first notice date. Under this approach, a constant dollar value is maintained for each commodity on each roll day while the number of units of the commodity is subject to upward or downward fluctuation. (4) Commodity weights are determined by dividing each commodity's weighted index capitalization by the sum of the index capitalizations for all the selected commodities. If the weight for any commodity is less than 5%, a 5% weight is applied while other weights are reduced on a proportionate basis. On the other hand, sector weights can not exceed 30%. Sectors with sector weights in excess of 30% are reduced to 30% while other sector weights are increased on a proportionate basis. (5) Index capitalization is the sum of the average daily dollar open interest and average daily dollar volume for each commodity. (6) The average daily open interest, or the amount of the commodity in the market, is expressed in number of contracts multiplied by the number of units per contract and by the average daily price per unit. The average daily price calculation relies on the near-month contract prices, which are added and divided by 12. (7) The average daily dollar volume is the contract volume multiplied by the price per contract. Price per contract is the near-month contract prices. (8) Index components and their respective weights are analyzed once a year, on or about December 15th and modifications, if any, are implemented on the first business day in January. (9) The average daily dollar volume is the contract volume multiplied by the price per contract. Price per contract is the near-month contract prices. (10) A commodity's price is the closing price of the relevant futures contract in the leading exchange for the commodity, either in the U.S. or the UK.

DERIVATIVE INSTRUMENTS
None

SUBINDICES
Six market sector subindices: Energy, precious metals, base metals, grains, livestock and soft commodities.
Ten individual commodity subindices: Copper, West Texas intermediate crude oil, soybeans, gold, aluminum, corn, heating oil, silver, coffee, and live cattle.
Fourteen individual commodity indices, in addition to the 10 commodities tracked in the LBCI: Base metals-aluminum, zinc, and nickel; grains-corn, soy meal and wheat; energy-heating oil, unleaded gasoline and natural gas; precious metals-silver, platinum, and palladium; livestock-live hogs, feeder cattle and pork bellies; soft commodities-cotton, sugar and cocoa.

RELATED INDICES
Lehman Aggregate Bond Index
Lehman Corporate High Yield Bond Index
Lehman Global Index
Lehman Adjustable Rate Mortgage Index
Lehman Emerging Market Bond Index
Lehman Municipal Index
Lehman Mutual Fund Indices
Refer to Appendix 5 for additional indices.

REMARKS
(1) Leading commodity exchanges include London Metals Exchange (LME) for base metals, Chicago Board of Trade (CBOT) for grains, New York Mercantile Exchange (NYMEX) for energy, Commodity Exchange (a division of NYMEX) for gold and silver precious metals, Chicago Mercantile Exchange for livestock and Coffee, Sugar, Cocoa Exchange for sugar. (2) Sector weights for 1996, are as follows: Base metals 29.99%, grains 21.94%, energy 19.98%, precious metals 17.81%, soft commodities 5.14% and livestock 5.14%. (3) Commodity weights for 1996, are as follows: Copper 18.60%, West Texas intermediate crude oil 14.01%, soybeans 12.61%, gold 12.24%, aluminum 11.39%, corn 9.33%, heating oil 5.97%, silver 5.57%, cotton 5.14% and live cattle 5.14%.

PUBLISHER
Lehman Brothers Inc.

12

INDEX PROFILES —
CONVERTIBLE SECURITIES
NORTH AMERICA

CS First Boston Convertible Securities Index

Total Return Performance

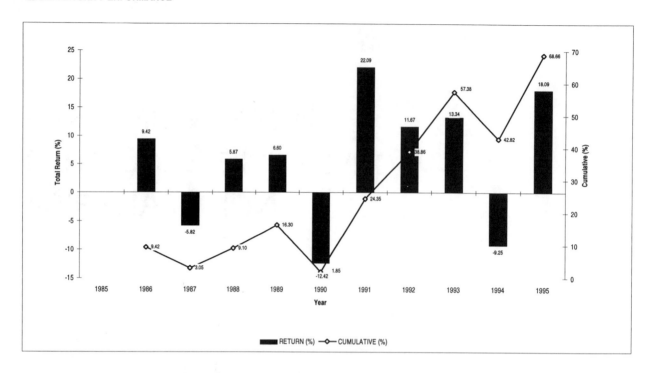

Total Return and Price Performance

YEAR	VALUE	TOTAL RETURN (%)	CUMULATIVE (%)	PRICE RETURN (%)	MAXIMUM VALUE[1]	DATE	MINIMUM VALUE[1]	DATE
1995	2,342.78	23.72	68.66	18.09	2,348.58	29-Sep	1,972.97	31-Jan
1994	1,983.84	-4.72	42.82	-9.25	2,239.72	31-Jan	1,978.48	30-Nov
1993	2,186.00	18.57	57.38	13.34	2,199.13	29-Oct	1,981.96	26-Feb
1992	1,928.78	17.60	38.86	11.67	1,928.78	31-Dec	1,769.41	31-Jan
1991	1,727.25	29.12	24.35	22.09	1,727.25	31-Dec	1,471.54	31-Jan
1990	1,414.69	-6.87	1.85	-12.42	1,596.35	31-May	1,335.74	31-Oct
1989	1,615.38	13.75	16.30	6.60	1,689.46	31-Aug	1,565.81	28-Feb
1988	1,515.39	13.42	9.10	5.87	1,530.24	30-Apr	1,462.58	31-Jan
1987	1,431.42	-0.22	3.05	-5.82	1,798.07	31-Aug	1,370.34	30-Nov
1986	1,519.89	16.94	9.42	9.42	1,554.23	30-Jun	1,398.56	31-Jan
1985	1,389.02							
Average Annual (%)		12.13		5.96				
Compound Annual (%)		11.52		5.37				
Standard Deviation (%)		12.11		11.62				

[1]Maximum/minimum index values apply to price returns.

SYNOPSIS

The CS First Boston Convertible Securities Index is a market value-weighted index that tracks the monthly price only and total return performance of corporate convertible securities, including U.S. domestic convertible bonds, Eurobonds and convertible preferred stocks.

NUMBER OF ISSUES—DECEMBER 31, 1995

331

MARKET VALUE—DECEMBER 31, 1995

US$75,869.0 million

SELECTION CRITERIA

Eligible securities include all corporate convertible securities, including U.S. domestic convertible bonds, Eurobonds and convertible preferred stocks, including 144A securities, with par amounts outstanding equal to or greater than US$50.0 million that are rated B- or better. Non-rated issues that are deemed to be of comparable credit quality are acceptable for inclusion in the index.

Preferred Equity Redemption Cumulative Stock (PERCS) and Equity-Linked Securities (ELKS) are excluded from consideration in the index.

BACKGROUND

None

BASE DATE

January 1, 1982=1000.00

COMPUTATION METHODOLOGY

(1) An aggregate of prices times quantities index formula. (2) Rolling annual coupon is prorated over 12-monthly periods and reinvested at month-end while quarterly dividends applicable to preferred stocks reinvested as of the ex-dividend date for the computation of total rates of return. (3) New issues enter the index on the first business day following one full month past initial settlement. Securities that no longer satisfy the size, rating or maturity criterion are generally removed from the index at the end of the calendar year. Called or defaulted securities are removed following such a determination.

DERIVATIVE INSTRUMENTS

None

SUBINDICES

Subindices by security type: Convertible bonds and convertible preferred stocks.
Subindices by credit quality and industry groupings.

RELATED INDICES

CS First Boston High Yield Index
CS First Boston ROS 30

REMARKS

None

PUBLISHER

CS First Boston.

GOLDMAN SACHS CONVERTIBLE 100 INDEX

TOTAL RETURN PERFORMANCE

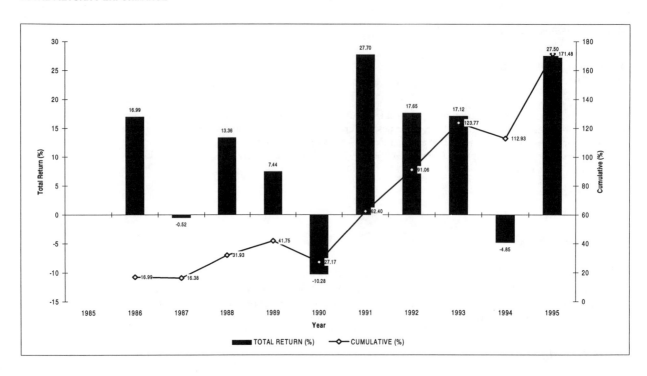

TOTAL RETURN AND PRICE PERFORMANCE

YEAR	VALUE	TOTAL RETURN (%)	CUMULATIVE (%)	PRICE RETURN (%)	MAXIMUM VALUE	DATE	MINIMUM VALUE	DATE
1995	345.572	27.50	171.48	20.74	345.57	31-Dec	276.40	31-Jan
1994	271.037	-4.85	112.93	-10.07	291.85	31-Jan	271.04	31-Dec
1993	284.841	17.12	123.77	10.87	284.84	31-Dec	248.72	29-Jan
1992	243.198	17.65	91.06	10.88	243.20	31-Dec	216.70	31-Jan
1991	206.716	27.70	62.40	19.49	206.72	31-Dec	170.71	31-Jan
1990	161.881	-10.28	27.17	-16.89	179.43	31-May	149.33	31-Oct
1989	180.431	7.44	41.75	0.10	189.53	31-Aug	176.20	31-Jan
1988	167.939	13.36	31.93	5.01	170.59	30-Jun	155.69	29-Jan
1987	148.144	-0.52	16.38	-6.90	182.39	31-Aug	141.95	30-Nov
1986	148.913	16.99	16.99	9.22	149.49	29-Aug	129.15	31-Jan
1985	127.291							
Average Annual (%)		11.21		4.25				
Compound Annual (%)		10.50		3.55				
Standard Deviation (%)		13.01		12.52				

SYNOPSIS
The Goldman Sachs Convertible 100 Index is an equally-weighted index that tracks the monthly price and total return performance of large, highly liquid, convertible issues in which Goldman Sachs makes a market.

NUMBER OF ISSUES—DECEMBER 31, 1995
100

MARKET VALUE—DECEMBER 31, 1995
US$31,827.0 million

SELECTION CRITERIA
Index members consist of publicly-placed corporate, fixed-rate, coupon-bearing, convertible securities with a high level of liquidity, including U.S. domestic bonds, Eurobonds, preferred stocks and Liquid Yield Option Notes (LYONs), with par amounts equal to or greater than $100.0 million, in which Goldman Sachs makes a market.

144A issues as well as Mandatory Conversion issues are excluded from consideration as index constituents.

BACKGROUND
None

BASE DATE
December 31, 1984=100.00

COMPUTATION METHODOLOGY
(1) An equally-weighted, arithmetically averaged index formula is used in which monthly price changes are adjusted for interest income and dividends. The result is aggregated and divided by 100 to arrive at the closing index value. (2) The index is reconstituted on a monthly basis.

DERIVATIVE INSTRUMENTS
None

SUBINDICES
None

RELATED INDICES
Financial Times/Standard & Poor's Actuaries World Index
Goldman Sachs Commodity Index
Goldman Sachs International Government Bond Index
Goldman Sachs Liquid Asset-Backed Securities Index

REMARKS
None

PUBLISHER
Goldman, Sachs & Co.

MERRILL LYNCH CONVERTIBLE SECURITIES INDEX

TOTAL RETURN PERFORMANCE

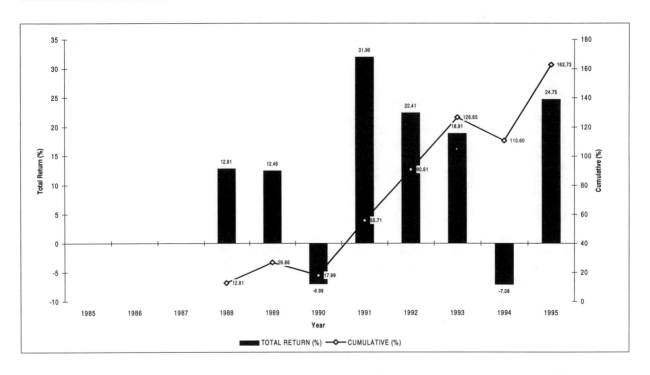

TOTAL RETURN AND PRICE PERFORMANCE

YEAR	VALUE	TOTAL RETURN (%)	CUMULATIVE (%)	PRICE RETURN (%)	MAXIMUM VALUE[1]	DATE	MINIMUM VALUE[1]	DATE
1995	262.73	24.75	162.73	18.54	262.73	31-Dec	211.90	31-Jan
1994	210.60	-7.08	110.60	-11.60	158.43	31-Jan	137.31	31-Dec
1993	226.65	18.91	126.65	13.51	157.03	31-Oct	141.16	31-Jan
1992	190.61	22.41	90.61	15.84	136.84	31-Dec	123.48	31-Jan
1991	155.71	31.96	55.71	24.14	118.13	31-Dec	99.54	31-Jan
1990	117.99	-6.99	17.99	-13.44	109.23	31-May	89.00	31-Oct
1989	126.86	12.46	26.86	4.99	115.97	31-Aug	108.42	31-Jan
1988	112.81	12.81	12.81	4.70	108.18	30-Jun	101.92	31-Jan
1987	100.00							
1986								
1985								
Average Annual (%)		13.65		7.09				
Compound Annual (%)		12.83		6.28				
Standard Deviation (%)		14.25		13.73				

[1]Maximum/minimum index values are as of month-end.

SYNOPSIS

The Merrill Lynch Convertible Securities Index is a market value-weighted index that tracks the daily price only, income and total return performance of corporate convertible securities, including U.S. domestic bonds, Eurobonds, preferred stocks and Liquid Yield Option Notes (LYONs).

NUMBER OF ISSUES—DECEMBER 31, 1995

462

MARKET VALUE—DECEMBER 31, 1995

US$83,896.8 million

SELECTION CRITERIA

Eligible securities include all corporate convertible securities, including U.S. domestic bonds, Eurobonds, preferred stocks and Liquid Yield Option Notes (LYONs), with par amounts outstanding equal to or greater than US$50.0 million and a term to maturity greater than or equal to one year. There are no quality restrictions and index constituents may include non-rated issues, 144A issues and non-coupon bearing securities.

Preferred equity redemption stocks are excluded from consideration in the index.

BACKGROUND

The index is a component of the Merrill Lynch Global Bond Index. It was established with a base value of 100.00 as of January 31, 1987 and daily data is available from January 18, 1988.

For additional information, refer to the Merrill Lynch Global Bond Index.

BASE DATE

January 31, 1987=100.00

COMPUTATION METHODOLOGY

(1) An aggregate of prices times quantities index formula, including gain/loss on repayments of principal and currency conversions, where applicable, as well as coupon received or accrued for total rate of return calculations. (2) Daily price and total return calculations are based on the theory that the portfolio of securities that make up the index is purchased in its entirety at approximately 3 PM (EST) on the initial day and held until the same time on the following day, when it is sold. Price and total returns for a one day period represent the sum of the weighted average price return, weighted average accrued interest return, and weighted average coupon return, weighted by the market value of the outstanding amount of each bond in the index. Total return for extended intervals are calculated by "chain-linking" the periodic rates of return. Transaction costs are not included in the calculations of price and total returns. (3) Except for mortgage and asset backed principal paydowns which are assumed to occur on the 30th of the month, accrued interest and cash flows are assumed to be reinvested on a daily basis in the market. (4) Bonds are generally priced on the basis of bid-side prices obtained from Merrill Lynch's trading floors. These are either hand priced or matrix priced, using price quotes taken at approximately 3 PM (EST). (5) Market values, for total return calculation purposes, are based on the outstanding amounts of each bond, which are reviewed regularly to account for full and partial retirement of debt, calls, sinking-fund requirements, tenders or re-opening of issues. (6) New issues enter the index on the first business day following settlement while bonds that no longer meet the index or subindex criterion are removed from the index one day, or two days, respectively, following such a determination. Bonds are removed from the index when they no longer satisfy the size, rating or maturity criteria.

DERIVATIVE INSTRUMENTS

None

SUBINDICES

Various subindices by security type, quality and maturity.

RELATED INDICES

Merrill Lynch Capital Markets Index
Merrill Lynch Currency Indices
Merrill Lynch Energy & Metals Index
Merrill Lynch Global Bond Index
Merrill Lynch Institutional Municipal Index
Merrill Lynch Money Market Instrument Indices
Refer to Appendix 5 for additional indices.

REMARKS

None

PUBLISHER

Merrill Lynch & Co.

SALOMON BROTHERS CONVERTIBLE SECURITIES INDEX

TOTAL RETURN PERFORMANCE

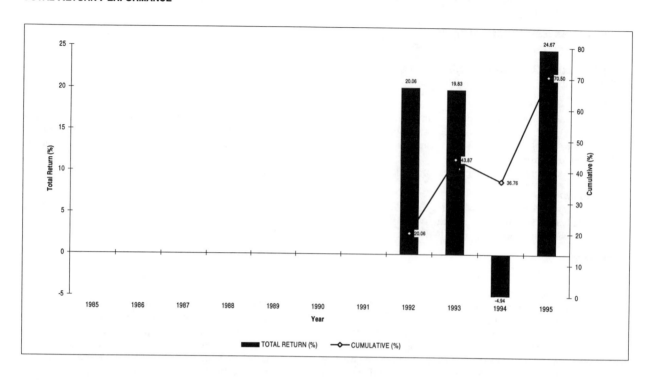

TOTAL RETURN AND PRICE PERFORMANCE

YEAR	VALUE	TOTAL RETURN (%)	CUMULATIVE (%)	PRICE RETURN (%)	MAXIMUM VALUE	DATE	MINIMUM VALUE	DATE
1995	170.50	24.67	70.50	19.10	170.50	29-Dec	137.01	31-Jan
1994	136.76	-4.94	36.76	-9.71	148.15	31-Jan	135.88	30-Jun
1993	143.87	19.83	43.87	14.18	143.87	31-Dec	124.04	31-Jan
1992	120.06	20.06	20.06	13.54	120.06	31-Dec	104.28	31-Jan
1991	100.00							
1990								
1989								
1988								
1987								
1986								
1985								
Average Annual (%)		14.91		9.28				
Compound Annual (%)		14.27		8.66				
Standard Deviation (%)		13.42		12.90				

SYNOPSIS

The Salomon Brothers Convertible Securities Index is a market value-weighted index that tracks the monthly price only and total return performance of an investable universe of convertible securities that includes cash coupon convertible bonds, zero coupon convertible bonds and convertible preferred stocks.

NUMBER OF ISSUES—DECEMBER 31, 1995

493

MARKET VALUE—DECEMBER 31, 1995

US$101,549.2 million

SELECTION CRITERIA

The index consists of all U.S. dollar-denominated convertible securities, mandatory or otherwise, including Eurodollar convertibles, Yankees if company has ADRs listed on the NYSE and 144A securities, with a minimum amount outstanding of US$50.0 million. A security is excluded from the index if its market value falls below US$50.0 million for a period of six months or in the event that a minimum of three pricing sources are not available.

BACKGROUND

The index was introduced in 1993.

BASE DATE

December 31, 1991=100.00

CALCULATION METHODOLOGY

(1) An aggregate of prices times quantities index formula, including gain/loss on repayments of principal and currency conversions, where applicable, as well as coupon received or accrued for total rate of return calculations. (2) Price only and total returns are calculated based on the assumption that each security is purchased at the beginning of the period and sold at the end of the measurement period. Cumulative index results are chain-linked. (3) Pricing sources include Salomon Brothers traders, stock exchange or independent third parties. (4) New issues are monitored on a daily basis and eligible issues are included at the beginning of the month following their first settlement date. Bonds that no longer satisfy maturity, amount outstanding or credit rating criteria are removed from the index at the end of each month. The index is also adjusted monthly for changes in the amount outstanding due to calls, tenders, sinking funds or principal paydowns. (5) Intramonth cash flow payments are reinvested continuously at the daily average of the one-month Treasury bill for the calculation period.

SUBINDICES

Various security type subindices: Cash coupon convertible bonds, zero coupon convertible bonds, convertible preferred stocks, Preferred Equity Redemption Cumulative Stock (PERCS) and Equity-Linked Securities (ELKS).
Subindices by investment grade ratings and industry classifications.

RELATED INDICES

Salomon Brothers Broad Investment-Grade (BIG) Index
Salomon Brothers High Yield Market Index
Salomon Brothers World Equity Index
Salomon Brothers World Government Bond Index
Salomon World Money Market Index
Refer to Appendix 5 for additional indices.

REMARKS

(1) The SB Broad Convertible Index includes PERCS and ELKS. (2) An equal-weighted index and an underlying equity index are planned for introduction at a later date. (3) Customized indices on the basis of issue type, sector or quality are available.

PUBLISHER

Salomon Brothers Inc.

SMITH BARNEY 400 CONVERTIBLE SECURITIES INDEX

TOTAL RETURN PERFORMANCE

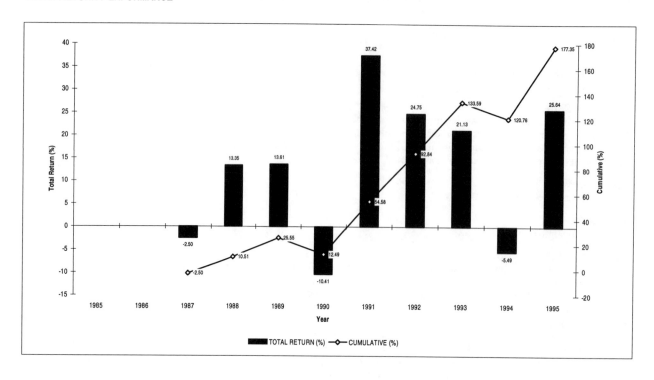

TOTAL RETURN AND PRICE PERFORMANCE[1]

YEAR	VALUE	TOTAL RETURN (%)	CUMULATIVE (%)	PRICE RETURN (%)	MAXIMUM VALUE[2]	DATE	MINIMUM VALUE[2]	DATE
1995	277.35	25.64	177.35	18.69	277.354	31-Dec	234.049	31-Mar
1994	220.76	-5.49	120.76	-10.91	227.963	30-Sep	220.759	31-Dec
1993	233.59	21.13	133.59	14.60	233.591	31-Dec	210.365	31-Mar
1992	192.84	24.75	92.84	16.87	192.836	31-Dec	167.430	31-Mar
1991	154.58	37.42	54.58	27.50	154.584	31-Dec	133.635	31-Mar
1990	112.49	-10.41	12.49	-17.69	126.865	30-Jun	110.271	30-Sep
1989	125.55	13.61	25.55	5.49	128.694	30-Sep	117.973	31-Mar
1988	110.51	13.35	10.51	4.87	111.267	30-Jun	105.807	31-Mar
1987	97.50	-2.50	-2.50	-9.30	NA	NA	NA	NA
1986	100.00							
1985								
Average Annual (%)		13.06		5.57				
Compound Annual (%)		12.00		4.08				
Standard Deviation (%)		16.17		15.40				

[1]Index rebased to 100.00 as of 12/31/86.
[2]Maximum/minimum index values are as of quarter-end.

SYNOPSIS
The Smith Barney 400 Convertible Securities Index is a market value-weighted index that tracks the monthly principal only and total return performance of the 400 largest domestic, coupon paying, convertible bonds and convertible preferred stocks.

NUMBER OF ISSUES—DECEMBER 31, 1995
400

MARKET VALUE—DECEMBER 31, 1995
US$73,900.0 million

SELECTION CRITERIA
Constituents, which include domestic, coupon paying, domestic, convertible bonds and convertible preferred stocks, are selected strictly on the basis of market capitalization regardless of credit rating, price, yield or any other factor. Bonds issued under Rule 144A are also eligible.

Zero coupon issues, issues which are solely or primarily issued as Eurobonds, and Mandatory Conversion issues, are not eligible for inclusion in the index.

BACKGROUND
The index was initiated as of December 31, 1987.

BASE DATE
Not applicable

COMPUTATION METHODOLOGY
(1) Monthly performance of each issue is weighted by its market value at the beginning of the month and the results are aggregated and divided by the number of constituents, to arrive at the month-end index value. (2) For total rate of return calculations, the monthly price changes are adjusted for accrued interest earned and preferred dividends that go ex-dividend during the month. (3) Market capitalizations are based on data as of the beginning of each month. (4) Large convertible bonds are added to the index as of the issue date while at the same time, the smallest issue is simultaneously removed from the index. Redemptions are also immediately removed from the index and replaced with the next largest convertible security. (5) The index is recalculated and rebalanced monthly.

DERIVATIVE INSTRUMENTS
None

SUBINDICES
Equal-weighted index

RELATED INDICES
None

REMARKS
(1) Indices that track the performance of the common stocks underlying the convertible securities, on a capitalization as well as equal-weighted basis, are also published. (2) Base date is not applicable since performance data is not linked into an index series.

PUBLISHER
Smith Barney, Inc.

VALUE LINE CONVERTIBLE SECURITIES INDEX

TOTAL RETURN PERFORMANCE

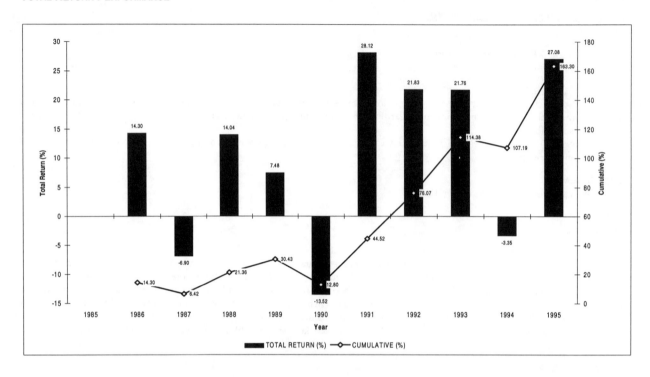

TOTAL RETURN AND PRICE PERFORMANCE

YEAR	VALUE	TOTAL RETURN (%)	CUMULATIVE (%)	PRICE RETURN (%)	MAXIMUM VALUE	DATE	MINIMUM VALUE	DATE
1995	552.02	27.08	163.30	19.10	553.90	18-Dec	437.73	9-Jan
1994	434.39	-3.35	107.19	-9.38	468.28	21-Mar	427.26	12-Dec
1993	449.46	21.76	114.38	14.69	449.46	27-Dec	371.43	4-Jan
1992	369.14	21.83	76.07	14.19	369.14	28-Dec	314.42	6-Jan
1991	302.99	28.12	44.52	19.01	309.74	11-Nov	238.89	7-Jan
1990	236.50	-13.52	12.80	-24.29	277.72	8-Jan	226.03	29-Oct
1989	273.45	7.48	30.43	-1.39	292.69	11-Sep	258.63	9-Jan
1988	254.43	14.04	21.36	4.52	260.40	11-Jul	226.72	4-Jan
1987	223.10	-6.90	6.42	-13.72	282.47	31-Aug	214.17	7-Dec
1986	239.64	14.30	14.30	6.23	244.82	7-Jul	212.31	13-Jan
1985	209.65							
Average Annual (%)		11.08		2.90				
Compound Annual (%)		10.17		1.87				
Standard Deviation (%)		14.70		14.86				

SYNOPSIS

The Value Line Convertible Securities Index is an equally-weighted geometrically averaged index that tracks the weekly principal only and total return performance of publicly placed, corporate, fixed-rate, coupon-bearing, convertible securities, including U.S. domestic bonds, Eurobonds, preferred stocks and Liquid Yield Option Notes (LYONs).

NUMBER OF ISSUES—DECEMBER 31, 1995

585

MARKET VALUE—DECEMBER 31, 1995

US$106,200.0 million

SELECTION CRITERIA

Index constituents are limited to convertible securities and preferred stock that are covered in the *Value Line Convertible Survey* which is constrained by space limitations to the current number of issues. These consist of publicly placed corporate, fixed-rate, coupon-bearing, convertible securities, including U.S. domestic bonds, Eurobonds, preferred stocks and LYONs, with par amounts equal to or greater than $25.0 million and a term-to-maturity greater than or equal to one year at the time of issue. The eligible universe includes Monthly Income Preferred Shares (MIPS) but excludes Mandatory Conversion issues.

There are no quality restrictions and index constituents may include non-rated issues as well as defaulted securities. Preferred equity redemption stocks are excluded from consideration in the index. While 144A issues are generally excluded, convertible securities issued with a companion Eurodollar tranch are eligible for inclusion in the index.

BACKGROUND

None

BASE DATE

March 1, 1982=100.00

COMPUTATION METHODOLOGY

(1) A geometric mean index formula is used in which the closing prices of each convertible bond and preferred stock is divided by the preceding week's close. The price changes for all securities in the group are geometrically averaged and the final average change for the week is then multiplied by the prior week's closing value. Total rates of return are calculated by accruing interest and dividends on a straight line accrual basis. (2) The index is adjusted to reflect stock dividends as well as stock splits by adjusting the prior day's stock price. (3) Pricing sources include closing exchange-listed prices as well as market maker quotations, which are obtained weekly on about 180 issues. (4) The index is usually published on Monday of each week or as of Friday, as well as at month-end on the basis of estimated prices.

DERIVATIVE INSTRUMENTS

None

SUBINDICES

Convertibles Ranked 1
Warrants Index

RELATED INDICES

Value Line Arithmetic Index
Value Line Composite Index

REMARKS

None

PUBLISHER

Value Line Publishing, Inc.

WORLD

ING Barings Asian Convertible Bond (CB) Index

PRICE PERFORMANCE

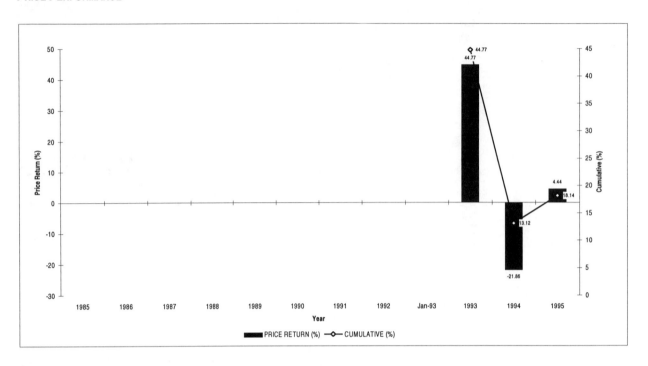

PRICE PERFORMANCE (US$)

YEAR	VALUE	PRICE RETURN (%)	CUMULATIVE (%)	MAXIMUM VALUE[1]	DATE	MINIMUM VALUE[1]	DATE
1995	104.44	4.44	18.14	104.44	29-Dec	92.74	31-Jan
1994	100.00	-21.86	13.12	130.79	31-Jan	100.00	31-Dec
1993	127.98	44.77	44.77	127.98	31-Dec	88.40	31-Jan
Jan-93	88.40						
1992							
1991							
1990							
1989							
1988							
1987							
1986							
1985							
Average Annual (%)		9.37					
Compound Annual (%)		5.88					
Standard Deviation (%)[2]		18.60					

[1]Maximum/minimum index values are as of month-end.
[2]Standard deviation applicable to the 2-year period 1994-1995.

SYNOPSIS

The ING Barings Asian Convertible Bond (CB) Index is a weighted index that tracks the daily price performance of a universe of large, liquid, convertible bonds of eight countries in Asia. These include Hong Kong, India, Indonesia, Korea, Malaysia, Pakistan, Philippines, Taiwan and Thailand.

NUMBER OF ISSUES—DECEMBER 31, 1995

108

MARKET VALUE—DECEMBER 31, 1995

US$11,231.8 million

SELECTION CRITERIA

Index members consist of Asian U.S. dollar and Swiss Franc issues with an initial issue value of not less than US$30.0 million and with no issue more than 75% converted. A minimum number of five market makers per issue are required for inclusion in the index. New issues of more than US$100.0 million, however, only require three market makers during their first two weeks of trading.

A convertible bond is removed from the index in the event that less than 25% of the issue is outstanding, the number of market makers drops below five or the company becomes insolvent.

BACKGROUND

The index, which was introduced in June 1995, has been backdated to January 1993.

BASE DATE

December 31, 1994=100.00

COMPUTATION METHODOLOGY

(1) An aggregate of prices times quantities index formula, including gain/loss on repayments of principal and currency conversions, where applicable, as well as coupon received or accrued for total rate of return calculations. Maintenance adjustments to the divisor are made for capitalization changes, new listings and delistings. The index is calculated in U.S. dollars. (2) Index weighting is based upon the amount of the convertible bond issue outstanding, which is reviewed and updated continuously. (3) Securities prices are derived from market makers' posted closing bid-offer spreads. In establishing a price, the spread with the highest offer and the spread with the lowest bid are discarded and the remaining prices are averaged to create the index issue for the day. In cases where there are only spreads from four market makers on any given day, the spread with the mid-price most different from the others will be excluded from consideration and the final price is determined by averaging the remaining three spreads. (4) Called issues are withdrawn from the index on the call date. Otherwise, issues are included and excluded from the index when appropriate information becomes available. Changes are implemented on the close of each Friday with the benefit of advance notification. Otherwise, the composition of the index is reviewed on a quarterly basis. (5) WM/Reuters Closing Spot Rates as of 4 PM London Time are used for currency conversions.

DERIVATIVE INSTRUMENTS

None

SUBINDICES

CB Underlying Index
CB Premium Index
CB Country indices: Hong Kong, India, Indonesia, Korea, Malaysia, Pakistan, Philippines, Taiwan and Thailand.

RELATED INDICES

ING Barings Emerging Market World Index
ING Barings Pan Asia Index
ING Barings Special Eastern Europe Index

REMARKS

Country weightings are, as follows: Hong Kong 31.73%, Taiwan 17.92%, Thailand 14.09%, Malaysia 12.39%, Korea 11.31%, India 7.98%, Philippines 3.55% and Indonesia 1.03%.

PUBLISHER

ING Baring Securities Limited.

JEFFERIES GLOBAL CONVERTIBLE (JEFFCO) BOND INDEX

TOTAL RETURN PERFORMANCE

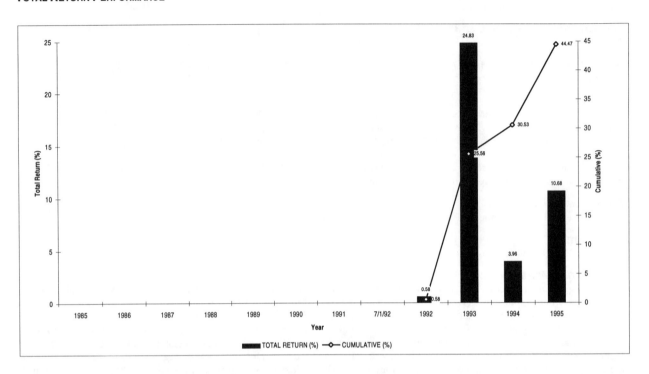

TOTAL RETURN AND PRICE PERFORMANCE (US$)[1]

YEAR	VALUE	TOTAL RETURN (%)	CUMULATIVE (%)	PRICE RETURN (%)	MAXIMUM VALUE[2]	DATE	MINIMUM VALUE[2]	DATE
1995	144.47	10.68	44.47	6.07	144.42	29-Dec	126.26	31-Jan
1994	130.53	3.96	30.53	0.15	136.28	31-Aug	130.41	29-Apr
1993	125.56	24.83	25.56	19.96	127.45	29-Oct	101.79	29-Jan
1992	100.59	0.58	0.58	-1.33	100.59	31-Dec	99.87	30-Nov
7/1/92	100.00							
1991								
1990								
1989								
1988								
1987								
1986								
1985								
Average Annual (%)		13.16		8.73				
Compound Annual (%)		12.83		8.42				
Standard Deviation (%)		10.66		10.17				

[1]Statistical measures applicable to the 3-year period 1993-1995.
[2]Maximum/minimum index values are as of month end.

SYNOPSIS

The Jefferies Global Convertible (JeffCo) Index is a market value-weighted index that tracks the daily price only and total return performance of outstanding convertible Eurobonds, calculated in U.S. dollars and in local currency.

NUMBER OF ISSUES—DECEMBER 31, 1995

335

MARKET VALUE—DECEMBER 31, 1995

US$59,917.52 million

SELECTION CRITERIA

All outstanding convertible Eurobonds are eligible for inclusion in the index provided at least one daily price from an independent source, including Extel, Reuters and Datastream, is available.

The following securities are excluded from consideration: (1) Preference shares, convertible preferred shares, perpetual bonds and private placements. (2) Convertible bonds that limit conversion to common stock to less than 50%. (3) Securities of issuers that are either bankrupt or have defaulted on interest payments. (4) Convertible securities that have publicly confirmed less than 50% of the issue outstanding.

BACKGROUND

The index was launched at the beginning of 1995 to serve as a benchmark for performance assessment.

BASE DATE

July 31, 1992=100.00

COMPUTATION METHODOLOGY

(1) An aggregate of prices times quantities index formula, including gain/loss on repayments of principal and currency conversions, where applicable, as well as coupon received or accrued for total rate of return calculations. Maintenance adjustments to the divisor are made for capitalization changes, new listings and delistings. (2) The index is calculated in U.S. dollars, using Reuters exchange rates as of 10 AM London Time. (3) New issues enter the index within one month of issue at prevailing market prices and issues are removed from the index at the last recorded price. (4) Interest is reinvested as of the ex-dividend date for total rate of return calculations.

DERIVATIVE INSTRUMENTS

None

SUBINDICES

Various subindices by region, country and currency.
Jefferies Active Convertible Index

RELATED INDICES

The Investable Commodity Index

REMARKS

JeffCo market weightings as of December 31, 1995 are, as follows: Americas 17.9%, Europe 45.5% and Far East 36.6%.

PUBLISHER

Jefferies & Company Inc.

MERRILL LYNCH GLOBAL 300 (ML G300) CONVERTIBLE INDEX

TOTAL RETURN PERFORMANCE

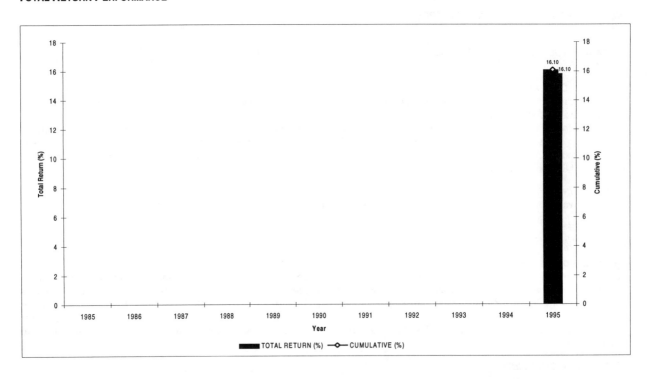

TOTAL RETURN PERFORMANCE (US$)

YEAR	VALUE	TOTAL RETURN (%)	CUMULATIVE (%)	MAXIMUM VALUE	DATE	MINIMUM VALUE	DATE
1995	116.10	16.10	16.10	NA	NA	NA	NA
1994	100.00						
1993							
1992							
1991							
1990							
1989							
1988							
1987							
1986							
1985							
Average Annual (%)		16.10					
Compound Annual (%)		NM					
Standard Deviation (%)		NM					

SYNOPSIS

The Merrill Lynch Global 300 (ML-G300) Convertible Index is a market value-weighted index that tracks the monthly total rate of return performance of the largest, publicly traded convertible securities in Africa, Asia/Pacific, Europe, Latin America and the United States.

NUMBER OF ISSUES—DECEMBER 31, 1995

300

MARKET VALUE—DECEMBER 31, 1995

US$134,000.0 million

SELECTION CRITERIA

Eligible securities include publicly traded convertible securities with a minimum market value of US$50.0 million for which daily pricing is available from independent sources. These consist of domestic bonds, Eurobonds, convertible preferred stocks and Liquid Yield Option Notes (LYONs). There are no quality restrictions and index constituents may include non-rated issues, 144A issues, and non-coupon bearing securities.

The largest issues are selected within each significant market with a view toward reflecting the composition of the global convertible market.

The index is limited to one issue from the same company. Preferred equity redemption stocks are excluded from consideration in the index.

BACKGROUND

The index, which was introduced on August 8, 1995, expands upon the domestic convertible securities index which was introduced in 1988.

BASE DATE

December 31, 1994=100.00

COMPUTATION METHODOLOGY

(1) An aggregate of prices times quantities index formula, including gain/loss on repayments of principal and currency conversions, where applicable, as well as coupon received or accrued for total rate of return calculations. (2) While the index is rebalanced quarterly, new issues enter the index and issues that no longer meet the index criterion are removed from the index, following such a determination. Bonds are removed from the index when they no longer satisfy the size, rating or maturity criteria.

DERIVATIVE INSTRUMENTS

None

SUBINDICES

Subindices by country, region, industry sector and major currencies.

RELATED INDICES

Merrill Lynch Capital Markets Index
Merrill Lynch Currency Indices
Merrill Lynch Energy & Metals Index
Merrill Lynch Global Bond Index
Merrill Lynch Institutional Municipal Index
Merrill Lynch Money Market Instrument Indices
Refer to Appendix 5 for additional indices.

REMARKS

Market values by region as of December 31, 1995 are, as follows: Japan 42.5%, United States 32.8%, Europe 17.0%, Asia 6.3% and Latin America 1.4%.

PUBLISHER

Merrill Lynch & Co.

13

INDEX PROFILES —
GUARANTEED INVESTMENT CONTRACTS
NORTH AMERICA

MORLEY CAPITAL MANAGEMENT 1-YEAR GIC INDEX

TOTAL RETURN PERFORMANCE

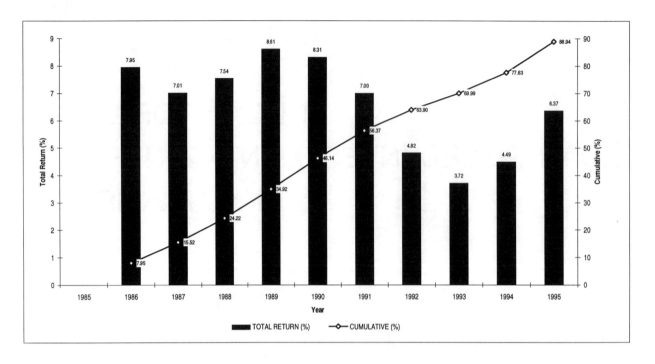

TOTAL RETURN PERFORMANCE

YEAR	VALUE	TOTAL RETURN (%)	CUMULATIVE (%)	MAXIMUM VALUE	DATE	MINIMUM VALUE	DATE
1995	719.36	6.37	88.94	719.36	31-Dec	679.56	31-Jan
1994	676.28	4.49	77.63	676.28	31-Dec	649.12	31-Jan
1993	647.20	3.72	69.99	647.20	31-Dec	626.07	31-Jan
1992	624.00	4.82	63.90	624.00	31-Dec	598.10	31-Jan
1991	595.33	7.00	56.37	595.33	31-Dec	559.96	31-Jan
1990	556.40	8.31	46.14	556.40	31-Dec	517.25	31-Jan
1989	513.69	8.61	34.92	513.69	31-Dec	475.99	31-Jan
1988	472.96	7.54	24.22	472.96	31-Dec	442.42	31-Jan
1987	439.81	7.01	15.52	439.81	31-Dec	413.34	31-Jan
1986	411.00	7.95	7.95	411.00	31-Dec	383.44	31-Jan
1985	380.73						
Average Annual (%)		6.58					
Compound Annual (%)		6.57					
Standard Deviation (%)		1.70					

SYNOPSIS
The Morley Capital 1-Year GIC Index tracks the monthly total return performance of one year compound interest bullet contracts in US$1.0 million denominations.

NUMBER OF CONTRACTS—DECEMBER 31, 1995
Number of contracts offering quotations can vary from month-to-month.

MARKET VALUE—DECEMBER 31, 1995
US$1.0 million

SELECTION CRITERIA
The index consists of 12 contracts with laddered maturities so that one contract matures each month. Contracts are issued by insurance carriers rated Aa1 by Moody's Investors or Aa+ by Standard & Poor's or comparable credit rating as determined by Morley Capital.

Rates are received on a monthly basis from several companies and a single rate, but not the best rate, is selected for use in the index.

BACKGROUND
The index along with its companion indices was introduced on or about 1980, and backdated to 1969 on the basis of certain assumptions.

BASE DATE
December 31, 1969=100.00

COMPUTATION METHODOLOGY
(1) Each month a single contract corresponding to the final maturity of the index is theoretically purchased. The one year index consists of 12 contracts that are laddered so that one contract is purchased each month as another contract matures. The three year contract consists of 36 contracts while the five-year contract consists of 60 contracts. (2) Returns are compounded on a monthly basis. (3) Quotes are net of all expenses and exclude brokers' commissions.

DERIVATIVE INSTRUMENTS
None

SUBINDICES
None

RELATED INDICES
Morley 3-year GIC Index
Morley 5-year GIC Index
Morley Capital Management GIC Index

REMARKS
Market value represents the GIC denomination.

PUBLISHER
Morley Capital Management, Inc.

RYAN LABS 3-YEAR MASTER GIC INDEX

TOTAL RETURN PERFORMANCE

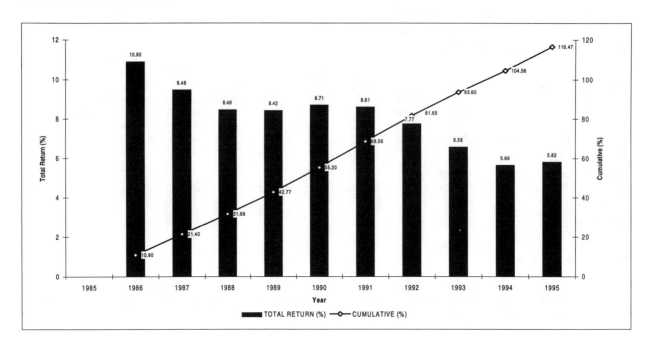

TOTAL RETURN PERFORMANCE

YEAR	VALUE	TOTAL RETURN (%)	CUMULATIVE (%)	MAXIMUM VALUE	DATE	MINIMUM VALUE	DATE
1995	242.53	5.82	116.47	242.53	31-Dec	230.24	31-Jan
1994	229.18	5.66	104.56	229.18	31-Dec	217.95	31-Jan
1993	216.91	6.58	93.60	216.91	31-Dec	204.70	31-Jan
1992	203.51	7.77	81.65	203.51	31-Dec	190.10	31-Jan
1991	188.85	8.61	68.56	188.85	31-Dec	175.10	31-Jan
1990	173.88	8.71	55.20	173.88	31-Dec	161.06	31-Jan
1989	159.96	8.42	42.77	159.96	31-Dec	148.51	31-Jan
1988	147.53	8.46	31.68	147.53	31-Dec	136.98	31-Jan
1987	136.02	9.48	21.40	136.02	31-Dec	125.25	31-Jan
1986	124.24	10.90	10.90	124.24	31-Dec	113.05	31-Jan
1985	112.04						
Average Annual (%)		8.04					
Compound Annual (%)		8.03					
Standard Deviation (%)		1.64					

SYNOPSIS
The Ryan Labs 3-Year Master GIC Index is an equal-weighted index that tracks the monthly representative rates for a diversified investment grade portfolio of 3-year compounded bullet contracts of US$1.0 million deposits.

NUMBER OF CONTRACTS—DECEMBER 31, 1995
10

MARKET VALUE—DECEMBER 31, 1995
US$1.0 million

SELECTION CRITERIA
Inclusion in the index is based on the following five quality considerations that are applied to GIC issuers:
(1) Assets of more than US$1.0 billion, excluding separate accounts. (2) Profitable in three of the last five years. (3) Bond portfolio at least 85% investment grade. (4) Capital and surplus of at least 3%, provided total assets are more than US$4.0 billion, 5% if total assets are between US$2.0 to US$4.0 billion and 8% if total assets are between US$1.0 billion to US$2.0 billion. (5) A credit quality rating of at least AA/Aa by Standard & Poor's, Moody's Investors or Duff & Phelps.

BASE DATE
December 31, 1984=100.00

COMPUTATION METHODOLOGY
(1) The index represents the arithmetic average of market rates, as of the end of every month. Contracts are held for their full term, such that the index series is a moving average of the monthly rates. (2) GIC rates are those quoted prior to 3 PM (EST) on the last business day of each month. The 10 highest quality filtered rates are used to calculate the index. (3) Quotes are net of all expenses and exclude brokers commissions. (4) Each contract must have a complete history of rates for the maturity segment before commencement of the index calculation.

DERIVATIVE INSTRUMENTS
None

SUBINDICES
None

RELATED INDICES
Ryan Labs 5-Year GIC Master Index
Ryan Cash Index
Ryan Treasury Index: 1-year, 2-year, 3-year, 5-year, 10-year and 30-year
Ryan Labs Liability Index

REMARKS
Custom indices over any period of time are available.

PUBLISHER
Ryan Labs Inc.

RYAN LABS 5-YEAR MASTER GIC INDEX

TOTAL RETURN PERFORMANCE

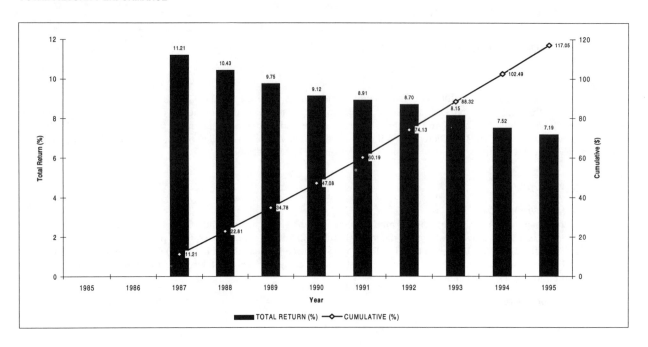

TOTAL RETURN PERFORMANCE

YEAR	VALUE	TOTAL RETURN (%)	CUMULATIVE (%)	MAXIMUM VALUE	DATE	MINIMUM VALUE	DATE
1995	217.05	7.19	117.05	217.05	31-Dec	203.69	31-Jan
1994	202.49	7.52	102.49	202.49	31-Dec	189.50	31-Jan
1993	188.32	8.15	88.32	188.32	31-Dec	175.31	31-Jan
1992	174.13	8.70	74.13	174.13	31-Dec	161.32	31-Jan
1991	160.19	8.91	60.19	160.19	31-Dec	148.13	31-Jan
1990	147.08	9.12	47.08	147.08	31-Dec	135.79	31-Jan
1989	134.78	9.75	34.78	134.78	31-Dec	123.80	31-Jan
1988	122.81	10.43	22.81	122.81	31-Dec	112.15	31-Jan
1987	111.21	11.21	11.21	111.21	31-Dec	100.94	31-Jan
1986	100.00						
1985							
Average Annual (%)		10.12					
Compound Annual (%)		10.17					
Standard Deviation (%)		1.31					

SYNOPSIS
The Ryan Labs 5-Year Master GIC Index is an equal-weighted index that tracks the monthly representative rates for a diversified investment grade portfolio of 5-year compounded bullet contracts of US$1.0 million deposits.

NUMBER OF CONTRACTS—DECEMBER 31, 1995
10

MARKET VALUE—DECEMBER 31, 1995
US$1.0 million

SELECTION CRITERIA
Inclusion in the index is based on the following five quality considerations that are applied to GIC issuers:
(1) Assets of more than US$1.0 billion, excluding separate accounts. (2) Profitable in three of the last five years. (3) Bond portfolio at least 85% investment grade. (4) Capital and surplus of at least 3%, provided total assets are more than US$4.0 billion, 5% if total assets are between US$2.0 to US$4.0 billion and 8% if total assets are between US$1.0 billion to US$2.0 billion. (5) A credit quality rating of at least AA/Aa by Standard & Poor's, Moody's Investors or Duff & Phelps.

BASE DATE
December 31, 1986=100.00

COMPUTATION METHODOLOGY
(1) The index represents the arithmetic average of market rates, as of the end of every month. Contracts are held for their full term, such that the index series is a moving average of the monthly rates. (2) GIC rates are those quoted prior to 3 PM (EST) on the last business day of each month. The 10 highest quality filtered rates are used to calculate the index. (3) Quotes are net of all expenses and exclude brokers commissions. (4) Each contract must have a complete history of rates for the maturity segment before commencement of the index calculation.

DERIVATIVE INSTRUMENTS
None

SUBINDICES
None

RELATED INDICES
Ryan Labs 3-Year GIC Master Index
Ryan Cash Index
Ryan Treasury Index: 1-year, 2-year, 3-year, 5-year, 10-year and 30-year

REMARKS
Custom indices over any period of time are available.

PUBLISHER
Ryan Labs Inc.

SCHMIDT COMPOSITE GIC INDEX

TOTAL RETURN PERFORMANCE

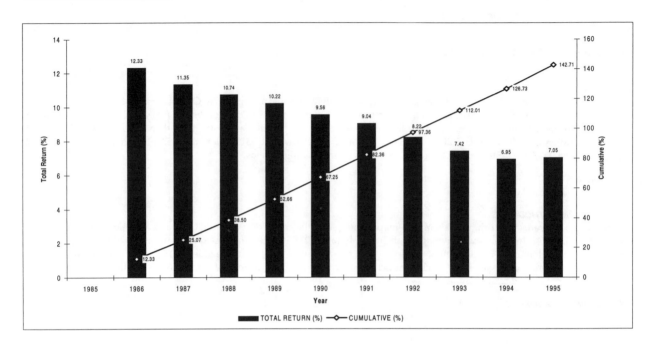

TOTAL RETURN PERFORMANCE

YEAR	VALUE	TOTAL RETURN (%)	CUMULATIVE (%)	MAXIMUM VALUE	DATE	MINIMUM VALUE	DATE
1995	2.55	7.05	142.71	2.55	31-Dec	2.39	31-Jan
1994	2.38	6.95	126.73	2.38	31-Dec	2.24	31-Jan
1993	2.22	7.42	112.01	2.22	31-Dec	2.08	31-Jan
1992	2.07	8.22	97.36	2.07	31-Dec	1.93	31-Jan
1991	1.91	9.04	82.36	1.91	31-Dec	1.77	31-Jan
1990	1.75	9.56	67.25	1.75	31-Dec	1.61	31-Jan
1989	1.60	10.22	52.66	1.60	31-Dec	1.47	31-Jan
1988	1.45	10.74	38.50	1.45	31-Dec	1.32	31-Jan
1987	1.31	11.35	25.07	1.31	31-Dec	1.19	31-Jan
1986	1.18	12.33	12.33	1.18	31-Dec	1.06	31-Jan
1985	1.05						
Average Annual (%)		9.29					
Compound Annual (%)		9.27					
Standard Deviation (%)		1.88					

SYNOPSIS
The Schmidt Composite GIC Index is an equally-weighted index that tracks the monthly total return performance of simple interest contracts in US$1.0 million denominations with maturities of one- to 10 years.

NUMBER OF CONTRACTS—DECEMBER 31, 1995
Number of contracts offering quotations vary from month-to-month and by maturity.

MARKET VALUE—DECEMBER 31, 1995
US$1.0 million

SELECTION CRITERIA
Quotations based on all carriers offering simple interest contracts through NYGIC Capital in Cincinnati, Ohio.

BACKGROUND
The index was introduced in 1986.

BASE DATE
July 31, 1985=1.00

COMPUTATION METHODOLOGY
(1) The index represents the arithmetic average of market rates, as of the end of every month. Contracts are held for their full term, such that the index series is a moving average of the monthly rates. (2) Quotes are net of all expenses and brokers' commissions.

DERIVATIVE INSTRUMENTS
None

SUBINDICES
Book value index and market value index.

RELATED INDICES
Schmidt Short-term GIC Index
Schmidt Long-term GIC Index
Schmidt Common Fund Index

REMARKS
(1) Market value represents the GIC denomination. (2) Book value and market value indices are available for all the short-term and long-term indices, as well as custom indices.

PUBLISHER
Schmidt Management Company.

INDEX PROFILES — MUTUAL FUNDS NORTH AMERICA

LEHMAN BROTHERS MUTUAL FUND CORPORATE DEBT A RATED INDEX

TOTAL RETURN PERFORMANCE

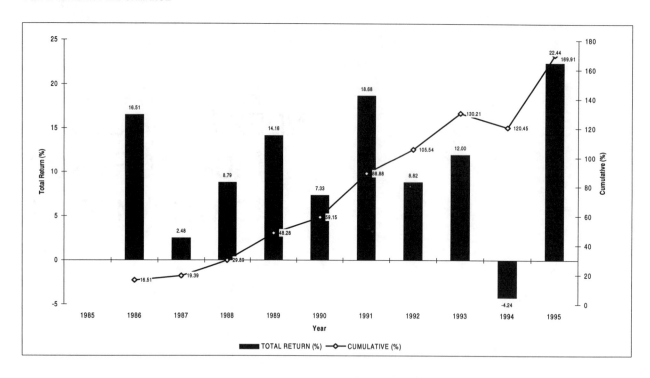

TOTAL RETURN AND PRICE PERFORMANCE

YEAR	VALUE	TOTAL RETURN (%)	CUMULATIVE (%)	PRICE RETURN (%)	MAXIMUM VALUE[1]	DATE	MINIMUM VALUE[1]	DATE
1995	822.51	22.44	169.91	13.69	822.51	31-Dec	685.75	31-Jan
1994	671.79	-4.24	120.45	-11.32	714.26	31-Jan	665.35	30-Jun
1993	701.52	12.00	130.21	4.08	706.47	31-Oct	641.04	31-Jan
1992	626.34	8.82	105.54	0.31	626.34	31-Dec	568.80	31-Jan
1991	575.58	18.68	88.88	8.77	575.58	31-Dec	492.17	31-Jan
1990	484.98	7.33	59.15	-2.06	484.98	31-Dec	443.32	30-Apr
1989	451.84	14.16	48.28	4.22	451.84	31-Dec	398.99	28-Feb
1988	395.81	8.79	29.89	0.90	398.27	31-Oct	374.74	31-May
1987	363.83	2.48	19.39	-6.75	364.81	28-Feb	349.72	31-May
1986	355.03	16.51	16.51	5.87	355.03	31-Dec	307.12	31-Jan
1985	304.73							
Average Annual (%)		10.70		1.77				
Compound Annual (%)		10.44		1.53				
Standard Deviation (%)		7.87		7.31				

[1]Maximum/minimum index values are as of month-end.

SYNOPSIS

The Lehman Brothers Mutual Fund Corporate Debt A Rated Index is a market value-weighted index that tracks the daily price only, coupon, total return performance of fixed-rate, publicly placed Securities and Exchange Commission (SEC)-registered, dollar-denominated and nonconvertible, corporate debt issues with at least $100.0 million par amount outstanding and one year to final maturity rated A or higher.

NUMBER OF BONDS—DECEMBER 31, 1995
1,808

MARKET VALUE—DECEMBER 31, 1995
US$416,000.0 million

SELECTION CRITERIA

The index is identical to the Lehman Brothers A Rated Corporate Index and constituents include fixed rate corporate debt issues that are publicly placed and registered with the Securities and Exchange Commission, including securities that carry a coupon that steps up or changes according to a predetermined schedule and zero coupon bonds, dollar-denominated and nonconvertible issues rated A or better, with at least $100.0 million par amount outstanding, and at least one year to maturity without any restrictions as to final maturity, as follows: Corporate debt issued by companies in the industrial, financial and utility sectors as well as Yankees and Yankee securities that are issued or guaranteed by foreign sovereign governments, municipalities, or government agencies or international agencies.

Non-fixed-rate securities or stripped securities or securities with esoteric or one of a kind features such as structured notes or range notes with coupons that depend on market indices and private placement securities, including 144A securities, are not eligible for inclusion in the index.

BACKGROUND
The Lehman Brothers mutual fund indices were introduced in November 1992. Using methodologies that are identical to the ones employed in the construction of the Lehman bond indices, this and the related mutual fund benchmarks consist of individual securities that correspond directly to the various mutual fund sectors. Initially, the mutual fund index categories corresponded to investment objectives established by Lipper Analytical Services, Inc. These have since been expanded to reflect a full range of available fixed income mutual funds.

BASE DATE
December 31, 1972=100.00

COMPUTATION METHODOLOGY
(1) Index formula is an aggregate value-weighted arithmetic average of the price ratios, coupon received or accrued (for total rate of return calculations), gain/loss on repayments of principal and, where applicable, currency value fluctuations. (2) Returns are based on a universe of securities established at the beginning of each month and held constant until the beginning of the next month. Securities that become ineligible for inclusion in the index during the month due to downgrades, redemptions or calls, securities falling below one year in maturity or newly eligible securities are maintained in a second, statistical universe. The statistical universe drives the production of portfolio statistics during the course of the month, i.e., coupon, duration, maturity, yield and price, and is also used to update the returns universe at the end of each month. (3) Intramonth cash flows are reinvested at month-end. If a security is no longer outstanding at the end of the month, the ending price is the level at which it exited the market. (4) Bonds are priced on the bid side at 3 PM (EST) each day, except that corporate bonds new to the index are initially priced on the offer side. Bonds are predominantly trader priced, with about 99% of the market value of the index priced by traders. Remaining issues, which consist of smaller, less liquid securities, are priced using matrix pricing algorithms that take into account sector, quality, duration, option features as well as issuer specific factors. (5) The final maturity requirement of at least one year is determined regardless of call features and mortgage and asset-backed securities must have a remaining average life of at least one year.

DERIVATIVE INSTRUMENTS
None

SUBINDICES
Sector subindices: Industrial, utility, finance and Yankee bonds.

RELATED INDICES
Lehman Adjustable Rate Mortgage Index
Lehman Aggregate Bond Index
Lehman Commodity Index
Lehman Corporate High Yield Bond Index
Lehman Emerging Americas Bond Index
Lehman Municipal Bond Index
Lehman Mutual Fund Indices
Refer to Appendix 5 for additional indices.

REMARKS
(1) Mutual funds classified as Corporate Debt A Rated bond funds are required to invest a substantial portion, but not necessarily 100%, of assets in A or better rated corporate debt securities. In some cases, funds may invest as much as 35% of assets in various other types of securities, including lower rated issues, while still eligible for classification in the named category. The index, on the other hand, is 100% invested in the named securities. (2) Investment grade debt ratings are based on determinations by Moody's Investors Service. A Standard & Poor's rating is used in the event a Moody's rating is not available, followed by a Fitch Investor's Service rating in the absence of both a Moody's and S&P rating. The Moody's rating prevails in the event of split-rated issues. (3) In addition to the major subindices noted above, each of Lehman's subindices include intermediate and long-term components, comprised of maturities of one- to 10-years and maturities greater than 10 years, respectively, as well as additional maturity, quality and sector breakdowns. To supplement commonly used indices, Lehman offers the flexibility to create customized indices that meet specific investor requirements. (4) The performance of Lehman's mutual fund indices correspond directly to the results achieved by the Lehman's Bond Indices in cases where the investment objectives of the mutual fund and the indices are identical. For example, the Lehman High Yield Index serves as the benchmark for the Lehman Mutual Fund High Yield Composite Index. Otherwise, the Lehman mutual fund index is calculated by market value-weighting the Bond index results at the end of each month.

PUBLISHER
Lehman Brothers.

LEHMAN BROTHERS MUTUAL FUND GNMA INDEX

TOTAL RETURN PERFORMANCE

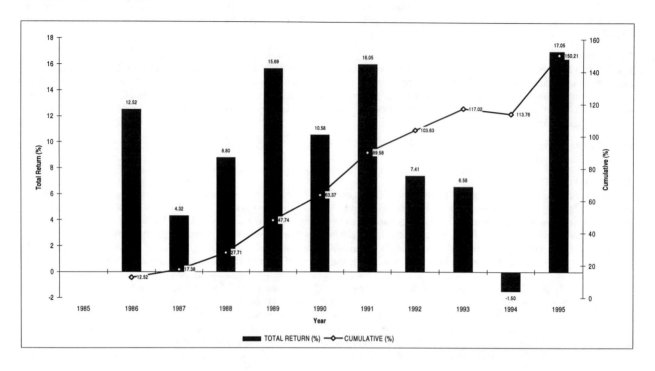

TOTAL RETURN AND PRICE PERFORMANCE

YEAR	VALUE	TOTAL RETURN (%)	CUMULATIVE (%)	PRICE RETURN (%)	MAXIMUM VALUE[1]	DATE	MINIMUM VALUE[1]	DATE
1995	690.70	17.05	150.21	8.62	690.70	31-Dec	602.30	31-Jan
1994	590.08	-1.50	113.76	-8.31	603.80	31-Jan	581.39	30-Jun
1993	599.09	6.58	117.02	0.85	599.09	31-Dec	569.18	31-Jan
1992	562.11	7.41	103.63	0.10	562.11	31-Dec	516.85	31-Jan
1991	523.33	16.05	89.58	6.52	523.33	31-Dec	457.71	31-Jan
1990	450.97	10.58	63.37	0.65	450.97	31-Dec	404.10	30-Apr
1989	407.84	15.69	47.74	5.21	407.84	31-Dec	356.12	28-Feb
1988	352.53	8.80	27.71	-0.97	359.46	31-Oct	334.01	31-May
1987	324.02	4.32	17.38	-4.58	324.02	31-Dec	305.69	30-Sep
1986	310.60	12.52	12.52	3.17	310.60	31-Dec	277.04	31-Jan
1985	276.05							
Average Annual (%)		9.75		1.13				
Compound Annual (%)		9.60		1.01				
Standard Deviation (%)		5.86		5.09				

[1]Maximum/minimum index values are as of month-end.

SYNOPSIS

The Lehman Brothers Mutual Fund GNMA Index is a market value-weighted index that tracks the daily price only, coupon, paydown and total return performance of publicly placed, fixed-rate, securities backed by mortgage pools of the Government National Association (GNMA).

NUMBER OF BONDS—DECEMBER 31, 1995
202

MARKET VALUE—DECEMBER 31, 1995
US$383,787.0 million

SELECTION CRITERIA

The index is identical to the Lehman Brothers GNMA Index and constituents include publicly placed, fixed-rate, securities backed by mortgage pools of the Government National Association (GNMA) with at least one year to maturity and an outstanding par value of at least $100.0 million.

The index includes graduated payment mortgages (GPM's) but excludes Graduated Equity Mortgages (GEMs).

BACKGROUND

The Lehman Brothers mutual fund indices were introduced in November 1992. Using methodologies that are identical to the ones employed in the construction of the Lehman bond indices, this and the related mutual fund benchmarks consist of individual securities that correspond directly to the various mutual fund sectors. Initially, the mutual fund index categories corresponded to investment objectives established by Lipper Analytical Services, Inc. These have since been expanded to reflect a full range of available fixed income mutual funds.

BASE DATE

December 31, 1975=100.00

COMPUTATION METHODOLOGY

(1) Index formula is an aggregate value-weighted arithmetic average of the price ratios, coupon received or accrued (for total rate of return calculations), and gain/loss on repayments of principal. (2) Returns are based on a universe of securities established at the beginning of each month and held constant until the beginning of the next month. Securities that become ineligible for inclusion in the index during the month due to downgrades, redemptions or calls, securities falling below one year in maturity or newly eligible securities are maintained in a second, statistical universe. The statistical universe drives the production of portfolio statistics during the course of the month, i.e., coupon, duration, maturity, yield and price, and is also used to update the returns universe at the end of each month. (3) Intramonth cash flows are reinvested at month-end. If a security is no longer outstanding at the end of the month, the ending price is the level at which it exited the market. (4) Bonds are priced on the bid side at 3 PM (EST) each day, except that corporate bonds new to the index are initially priced on the offer side. Bonds are predominantly trader priced, with about 99% of the market value of the index priced by traders. Remaining issues, which consist of smaller, less liquid securities, are priced using matrix pricing algorithms that take into account sector, quality, duration, option features as well as issuer specific factors. (5) The final maturity requirement of at least one year is determined regardless of call features and mortgage and asset-backed securities must have a remaining average life of at least one year.

DERIVATIVE INSTRUMENTS

None

SUBINDICES

None

RELATED INDICES

Lehman Adjustable Rate Mortgage Index
Lehman Aggregate Bond Index
Lehman Commodity Index
Lehman Corporate High Yield Bond Index
Lehman Emerging Americas Bond Index
Lehman Municipal Bond Index
Lehman Mutual Fund Indices
Refer to Appendix 5 for additional indices.

REMARKS

(1) Mutual funds classified as GNMA funds are required to invest a substantial portion, but not necessarily 100%, of assets in GNMA securities. In some cases, funds may invest as much as 35% of assets in various other types of securities and still be eligible for classification in the named category. The index, on the other hand, is 100% invested in the named securities. (2) The performance of Lehman's mutual fund indices correspond directly to the results achieved by the Lehman's Bond Indices in cases where the investment objectives of the mutual fund and the indices are identical, which is the case with the GNMA index. While no specific GNMA mutual fund subindices are offered, various Lehman price and coupon sector subindices are available for GNMA 30-year and 15-year mortgages. To supplement commonly used indices, Lehman offers the flexibility to create customized indices that meet specific investor requirements.

PUBLISHER

Lehman Brothers.

LIPPER BALANCED FUNDS INDEX

TOTAL RETURN PERFORMANCE

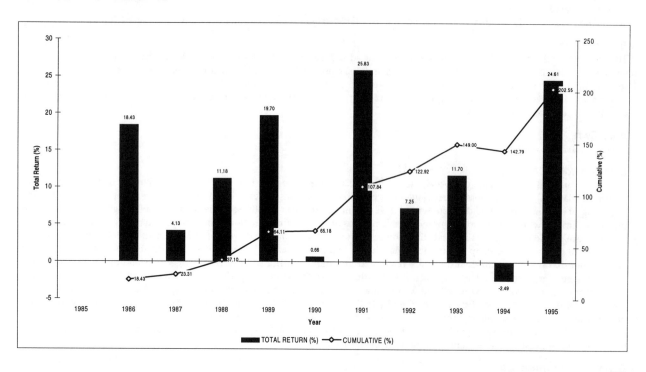

TOTAL RETURN PERFORMANCE

YEAR	VALUE	TOTAL RETURN (%)	CUMULATIVE (%)	MAXIMUM VALUE[1]	DATE	MINIMUM VALUE[1]	DATE
1995	2,682.20	24.61	202.55	2,682.20	29-Dec	2,148.47	3-Jan
1994	2,152.47	-2.49	142.79	2,265.43	31-Jan	2,152.47	31-Dec
1993	2,207.52	11.70	149.00	2,207.52	31-Dec	2,002.59	31-Jan
1992	1,976.27	7.25	122.92	1,976.27	31-Dec	1,820.89	31-Mar
1991	1,842.60	25.83	107.84	1,842.60	31-Dec	1,515.81	31-Jan
1990	1,464.39	0.66	65.18	1,486.36	30-Jun	1,366.15	30-Sep
1989	1,454.86	19.70	64.11	1,454.86	31-Dec	1,249.05	28-Feb
1988	1,215.45	11.18	37.10	1,215.45	31-Dec	1,125.87	31-Jan
1987	1,093.23	4.13	23.31	1,286.68	31-Aug	1,034.59	30-Nov
1986	1,049.89	18.43	18.43	1,071.16	31-Aug	901.74	31-Jan
1985	886.54						
Average Annual (%)		12.10					
Compound Annual (%)		11.71					
Standard Deviation (%)		9.86					

[1]Maximum/minimum index values for the period 1987-1994 are as of month-end.

SYNOPSIS

The Lipper Balanced Funds Index is an equal-weighted index that tracks the daily total return performance of the 30 largest balanced mutual funds. These funds represent about 77% of total net assets in balanced mutual funds.

NUMBER OF FUNDS—DECEMBER 31, 1995

30

MARKET VALUE—DECEMBER 31, 1995

US$51,538.8 million

SELECTION CRITERIA

Constituent funds are selected from the universe of mutual funds that are classified by Lipper Analytical as balanced funds, generally on the basis of the fund's investment objective characterization in its prospectus. A balanced fund's primary investment objective is to conserve principal by maintaining, at all times, a balanced portfolio of both stocks and bonds. Typically, the stock/bond ratio ranges around 60%/40%. The largest 30 funds, on the basis of their total net assets as of December 31st of each year, are selected. Funds established under a master-feeder structure or multiple share classes are limited to a single representation, i.e, the largest fund. Also, funds closed to new investors as well as non-Nasdaq-listed funds are generally excluded from participation as an index constituent.

BACKGROUND

The index was calculated on a net asset value-weighted basis until December 31, 1994.

BASE DATE

December 31, 1959=100.00

COMPUTATION METHODOLOGY

(1) An equal-weighted index, calculated by taking the arithmetic average of the daily total rates of return of constituent funds. Cumulative returns are calculated by chain-linking the daily rates of return. (2) Income dividends and capital gains distributions, if any, are reinvested in each fund as of the ex-dividend date, regardless of actual distribution dates. (3) The index value is computed provided up to 80% of constituent funds are priced. (4) The index is reconstituted annually. Additions to or deletions from the index occur during the month of January of each year, unless circumstances dictate otherwise. For example, substitutions may be made during the course of the year due to fund liquidations or a change in a fund's investment objective. (5) Indices are recomputed annually to reflect all currently available revisions to funds that may have been reported during the course of the calendar year.

DERIVATIVE INSTRUMENTS

None

SUBINDICES

None

RELATED INDICES

Lipper Convertible Securities Funds Index
Lipper Equity Income Funds Index
Lipper GNMA Funds Index
Lipper Growth & Income funds Index
Lipper Growth Funds Index
Lipper High Current Yield Funds Index
Lipper International Funds Index
Lipper Money Market Funds Index
Lipper Small Company Growth Funds Index
Refer to Appendix 5 for additional indices.

REMARKS

None

PUBLISHER

Lipper Analytical Services, Inc.

LIPPER CONVERTIBLE SECURITIES FUNDS INDEX

TOTAL RETURN PERFORMANCE

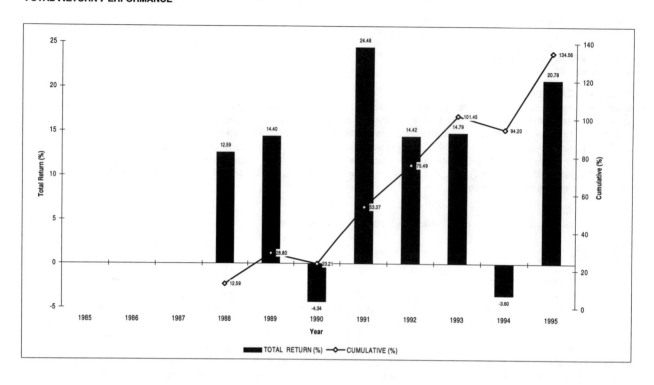

TOTAL RETURN PERFORMANCE

YEAR	VALUE	TOTAL RETURN (%)	CUMULATIVE (%)	MAXIMUM VALUE[1]	DATE	MINIMUM VALUE[1]	DATE
1995	234.56	20.78	134.56	234.56	29-Dec	193.94	3-Jan
1994	194.20	-3.60	94.20	206.53	31-Jan	193.12	30-Jun
1993	201.45	14.79	101.45	201.45	31-Dec	179.42	31-Jan
1992	175.49	14.42	75.49	175.49	31-Dec	157.32	31-Jan
1991	153.37	24.48	53.37	153.37	31-Dec	128.05	31-Jan
1990	123.21	-4.34	23.21	131.27	30-Jun	115.00	31-Oct
1989	128.80	14.40	28.80	130.56	31-Aug	116.62	28-Feb
1988	112.59	12.59	12.59	112.59	31-Dec	102.35	31-Jan
1987	100.00						
1986							
1985							
Average Annual (%)		11.69					
Compound Annual (%)		11.25					
Standard Deviation (%)		10.43					

[1]Maximum/minimum index values for the period 1986-1994 are as of month-end.

SYNOPSIS

The Lipper Convertible Securities Funds Index is an equal-weighted index that tracks the daily total return performance of the 10 largest convertible securities mutual funds. These funds account for 82% of total net assets invested in high current yield mutual funds.

NUMBER OF FUNDS—DECEMBER 31, 1995

10

MARKET VALUE—DECEMBER 31, 1995

US$3,813.9 million

SELECTION CRITERIA

Constituent funds are selected from the universe of bond mutual funds that are classified as convertible securities funds by Lipper Analytical, generally on the basis of the fund's investment objective characterization in its prospectus. A convertible securities fund invests primarily in convertible bonds and convertible preferred stocks. The 10 largest funds, on the basis of their total net assets as of December 31st of each year, are selected. Funds established under a master-feeder structure or multiple share classes are limited to a single representation, i.e., the largest fund. Also, funds closed to new investors as well as non-Nasdaq-listed funds are generally excluded from participation as an index constituent.

BACKGROUND

The index was calculated on a net asset value-weighted basis until December 31, 1994.

BASE DATE

December 31, 1987=100.00

COMPUTATION METHODOLOGY

(1) An equal-weighted index, calculated by taking the arithmetic average of the daily total rates of return of constituent funds. Cumulative returns are calculated by chain-linking the daily rates of return. (2) Income dividends and capital gains distributions, if any, are reinvested in each fund as of the ex-dividend date, regardless of actual distribution dates. (3) The index value is computed provided up to 80% of constituent funds are priced. (4) The index is reconstituted annually. Additions to or deletions from the index occur during the month of January of each year, unless circumstances dictate otherwise. For example, substitutions may be made during the course of the year due to fund liquidations or a change in a fund's investment objective. (5) Indices are recomputed annually to reflect all currently available revisions to funds that may have been reported during the course of the calendar year.

DERIVATIVE INSTRUMENTS

None

SUBINDICES

None

RELATED INDICES

Lipper Balanced Funds Index
Lipper Equity Income Funds Index
Lipper GNMA Funds Index
Lipper Growth & Income Funds Index
Lipper Growth Funds Index
Lipper High Current Yield Funds Index
Lipper International Funds Index
Lipper Money Market Funds Index
Lipper Small Company Growth Funds Index
Refer to Appendix 5 for additional indices.

REMARKS

None

PUBLISHER

Lipper Analytical Services, Inc.

LIPPER EQUITY INCOME FUNDS INDEX

TOTAL RETURN PERFORMANCE

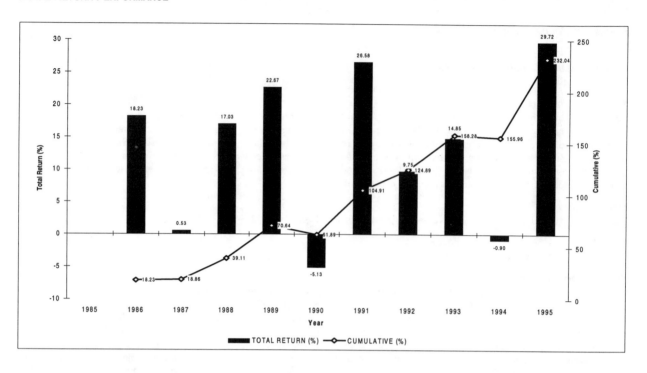

TOTAL RETURN PERFORMANCE

YEAR	VALUE	TOTAL RETURN (%)	CUMULATIVE (%)	MAXIMUM VALUE[1]	DATE	MINIMUM VALUE[1]	DATE
1995	2,163.15	29.72	232.04	2,163.15	29-Dec	1,668.99	3-Jan
1994	1,667.49	-0.90	155.96	1,735.18	31-Jan	1,624.56	31-Mar
1993	1,682.63	14.85	158.28	1,682.63	31-Dec	1,488.80	31-Jan
1992	1,465.12	9.75	124.89	1,465.12	31-Dec	1,329.91	31-Mar
1991	1,334.95	26.58	104.91	1,334.95	31-Dec	1,090.49	31-Jan
1990	1,054.66	-5.13	61.89	1,111.42	31-May	979.38	31-Oct
1989	1,111.68	22.67	70.64	1,111.68	30-Sep	940.66	28-Feb
1988	906.24	17.03	39.11	906.62	31-Oct	815.04	31-Jan
1987	774.34	0.53	18.86	901.59	30-Sep	742.81	30-Nov
1986	770.22	18.23	18.23	780.29	30-Nov	663.62	31-Jan
1985	651.47						
Average Annual (%)		13.33					
Compound Annual (%)		12.75					
Standard Deviation (%)		11.98					

[1]Maximum/minimum index values for the period 1986-1994 are as of month-end.

SYNOPSIS
The Lipper Equity Income Funds Index is an equal-weighted index that tracks the daily total return performance of the 30 largest equity income oriented mutual funds. These funds account for 78% of the total net assets in equity income oriented mutual funds.

NUMBER OF FUNDS—DECEMBER 31, 1995
30

MARKET VALUE—DECEMBER 31, 1995
US$86,603.4 million

SELECTION CRITERIA
Constituent funds are selected from the universe of equity mutual funds that are classified as equity income funds by Lipper Analytical, generally on the basis of the fund's investment objective characterization in its prospectus. An equity income fund seeks relatively high current income and growth of income through investing 60% or more of its portfolio in equities. The largest 30 funds, on the basis of their total net assets as of December 31st of each year, are selected. Funds established under a master-feeder structure or multiple share classes are limited to a single representation, i.e., the largest fund. Also, funds closed to new investors as well as non-Nasdaq-listed funds are generally excluded from participation as an index constituent.

BACKGROUND
The index was calculated on a net asset value-weighted basis until December 31, 1994.

BASE DATE
December 31, 1959=100.00

COMPUTATION METHODOLOGY
(1) An equal-weighted index, calculated by taking the arithmetic average of the daily total rates of return of constituent funds. Cumulative returns are calculated by chain-linking the daily rates of return. (2) Income dividends and capital gains distributions, if any, are reinvested in each fund as of the ex-dividend date, regardless of actual distribution dates. (3) The index value is computed provided up to 80% of constituent funds are priced. (4) The index is reconstituted annually. Additions to or deletions from the index occur during the month of January of each year, unless circumstances dictate otherwise. For example, substitutions may be made during the course of the year due to fund liquidations or a change in a fund's investment objective. (5) Indices are recomputed annually to reflect all currently available revisions to funds that may have been reported during the course of the calendar year.

DERIVATIVE INSTRUMENTS
None

SUBINDICES
None

RELATED INDICES
Lipper Balanced Funds Index
Lipper Convertible Securities Funds Index
Lipper GNMA Funds Index
Lipper Growth & Income funds Index
Lipper Growth Funds Index
Lipper High Current Yield Funds Index
Lipper International Funds Index
Lipper Money Market Funds Index
Lipper Small Company Growth Funds Index
Refer to Appendix 5 for additional indices.

REMARKS
None

PUBLISHER
Lipper Analytical Services, Inc.

LIPPER GOVERNMENT NATIONAL MORTGAGE ASSOCIATION (GNMA) FUNDS INDEX

TOTAL RETURN PERFORMANCE

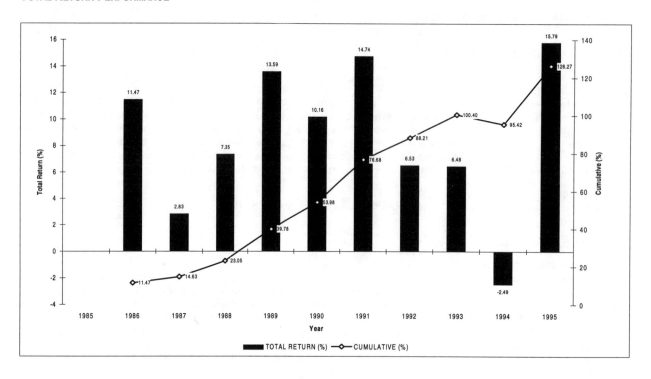

TOTAL RETURN PERFORMANCE

YEAR	VALUE	TOTAL RETURN (%)	CUMULATIVE (%)	MAXIMUM VALUE[1]	DATE	MINIMUM VALUE[1]	DATE
1995	268.72	15.79	126.27	268.72	31-Dec	231.63	3-Jan
1994	232.08	-2.49	95.42	240.29	31-Jan	229.94	30-Nov
1993	238.00	6.48	100.40	238.00	31-Dec	226.89	31-Jan
1992	223.52	6.53	88.21	223.52	31-Dec	206.79	31-Jan
1991	209.82	14.74	76.68	209.82	31-Dec	185.24	31-Jan
1990	182.87	10.16	53.98	182.87	31-Dec	164.28	30-Apr
1989	166.00	13.59	39.78	166.00	31-Dec	147.35	28-Feb
1988	146.14	7.35	23.05	148.50	31-Oct	140.69	31-Jan
1987	136.13	2.83	14.63	136.13	31-Dec	129.05	30-Sep
1986	132.38	11.47	11.47	132.38	31-Dec	119.38	31-Jan
1985	118.76						
Average Annual (%)		8.65					
Compound Annual (%)		8.51					
Standard Deviation (%)		5.69					

[1]Maximum/minimum index values for the period 1986-1994 are as of month-end.

SYNOPSIS

The Lipper Government National Mortgage Association (GNMA) Funds Index is an equal-weighted index that tracks the daily total return performance of the 30 largest GNMA oriented mutual funds. These funds account for 94% of the total net assets in GNMA oriented funds.

NUMBER OF FUNDS—DECEMBER 31, 1995

30

MARKET VALUE—DECEMBER 31, 1995

US$40,763.9 million

SELECTION CRITERIA

Constituent funds are selected from the universe of taxable fixed income mutual funds that are classified as GNMA funds by Lipper Analytical, generally on the basis of the fund's investment objective characterization in its prospectus. A GNMA fund invests at least 65% of total assets in securities issued by the Government National Mortgage Association. The largest 30 funds, on the basis of their total net assets as of December 31st of each year, are selected. Funds established under a master-feeder structure or multiple share classes are limited to a single representation, i.e., the largest fund. Also, funds closed to new investors as well as non-Nasdaq-listed funds are generally excluded from participation as an index constituent.

BACKGROUND

The index was calculated on a net asset value-weighted basis until December 31, 1994.

BASE DATE

December 31, 1983=100.00

COMPUTATION METHODOLOGY

(1) An equal-weighted index, calculated by taking the arithmetic average of the daily total rates of return of constituent funds. Cumulative returns are calculated by chain-linking the daily rates of return. (2) Income dividends applicable to fixed income mutual funds generally go ex-dividend on a daily basis and are distributed monthly. For total return calculation purposes, income dividends are estimated and reinvested on a daily basis regardless of the fund's distribution policy. Capital gains distributions, if any, are reinvested in each fund as of the ex-dividend date, regardless of actual distribution dates. (3) The index value is computed provided up to 80% of constituent funds are priced. (4) The index is reconstituted annually. Additions to or deletions from the index occur during the month of January of each year, unless circumstances dictate otherwise. For example, substitutions may be made during the course of the year due to fund liquidations or a change in a fund's investment objective. (5) Indices are recomputed annually to reflect all currently available revisions to funds that may have been reported during the course of the calendar year.

DERIVATIVE INSTRUMENTS

None

SUBINDICES

None

RELATED INDICES

Lipper Balanced Funds Index
Lipper Convertible Securities Funds Index
Lipper Equity Income Funds Index
Lipper Growth Funds Index
Lipper Growth & Income Funds Index
Lipper High Current Yield Funds Index
Lipper International Funds Index
Lipper Money Market Funds Index
Lipper Small Company Growth Funds Index
Refer to Appendix 5 for additional indices.

REMARKS

None

PUBLISHER

Lipper Analytical Services, Inc.

LIPPER GROWTH FUNDS INDEX

TOTAL RETURN PERFORMANCE

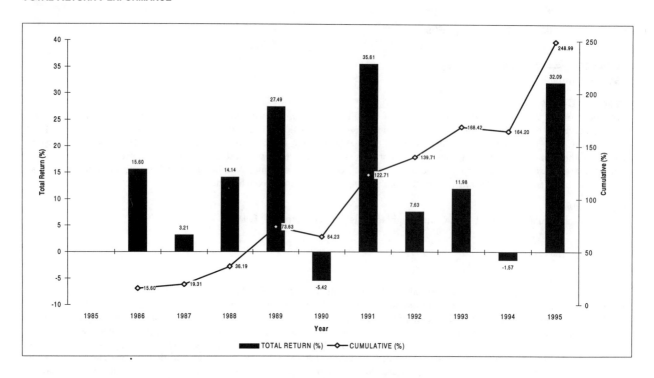

TOTAL RETURN PERFORMANCE

YEAR	VALUE	TOTAL RETURN (%)	CUMULATIVE (%)	MAXIMUM VALUE[1]	DATE	MINIMUM VALUE[1]	DATE
1995	4,147.05	32.09	248.99	4,180.00	5-Dec	3,118.41	3-Jan
1994	3,139.48	-1.57	164.20	3,300.04	31-Jan	3,026.53	30-Jun
1993	3,189.59	11.98	168.42	3,189.59	31-Dec	2,851.31	28-Feb
1992	2,848.46	7.63	139.71	2,848.46	31-Dec	2,553.41	30-Jun
1991	2,646.47	35.61	122.71	2,646.47	31-Dec	2,082.73	31-Jan
1990	1,951.52	-5.42	64.23	2,143.63	30-Jun	1,756.80	31-Oct
1989	2,063.26	27.49	73.63	2,080.43	30-Sep	1,703.17	28-Feb
1988	1,618.32	14.14	36.19	1,618.32	31-Dec	1,452.23	31-Jan
1987	1,417.78	3.21	19.31	1,820.33	31-Aug	1,304.33	30-Nov
1986	1,373.70	15.60	15.60	1,442.93	30-Jun	1,212.82	31-Jan
1985	1,188.29						
Average Annual (%)		14.08					
Compound Annual (%)		13.31					
Standard Deviation (%)		13.98					

[1]Maximum/minimum index values for the period 1986-1994 are as of month-end.

SYNOPSIS

The Lipper Growth Funds Index is an equal-weighted index that tracks the daily total return performance of the 30 largest growth oriented mutual funds. These funds account for 58% of total net assets in growth oriented mutual funds.

NUMBER OF FUNDS—DECEMBER 31, 1995

30

MARKET VALUE—DECEMBER 31, 1995

US$ 175,943.6 million

SELECTION CRITERIA

Constituent funds are selected from the universe of equity mutual funds that are classified as growth funds by Lipper Analytical, generally on the basis of the fund's investment objective characterization in its prospectus. A growth fund is one that invests in companies whose long-term earnings are expected to grow faster than those of the stocks in the major market indices. The largest 30 funds, on the basis of their total net assets as of December 31st of each year, are selected. Funds established under a master-feeder structure or multiple share classes are limited to a single representation, i.e., the largest fund. Also, funds closed to new investors as well as non-Nasdaq-listed funds are generally excluded from participation as an index constituent.

BACKGROUND

The index was calculated on a net asset value-weighted basis until December 31, 1994.

BASE DATE

December 31, 1968=100.00

COMPUTATION METHODOLOGY

(1) An equal-weighted index, calculated by taking the arithmetic average of the daily total rates of return of constituent funds. Cumulative returns are calculated by chain-linking the daily rates of return. (2) Income dividends and capital gains distributions, if any, are reinvested in each fund as of the ex-dividend date, regardless of actual distribution dates. (3) The index value is computed provided up to 80% of constituent funds are priced. (4) The index is reconstituted annually. Additions to or deletions from the index occur during the month of January of each year, unless circumstances dictate otherwise. For example, substitutions may be made during the course of the year due to fund liquidations or a change in a fund's investment objective. (5) Indices are recomputed annually to reflect all currently available revisions to funds that may have been reported during the course of the calendar year.

DERIVATIVE INSTRUMENTS

None

SUBINDICES

None

RELATED INDICES

Lipper Balanced Funds Index
Lipper Convertible Securities Funds Index
Lipper Equity Income Funds Index
Lipper GNMA Funds Index
Lipper Growth & Income Funds Index
Lipper High Current Yield Funds Index
Lipper International Funds Index
Lipper Money Market Funds Index
Lipper Small Company Growth Funds Index
Refer to Appendix 5 for additional indices.

REMARKS

None

PUBLISHER

Lipper Analytical Services, Inc.

LIPPER GROWTH & INCOME FUNDS INDEX

TOTAL RETURN PERFORMANCE

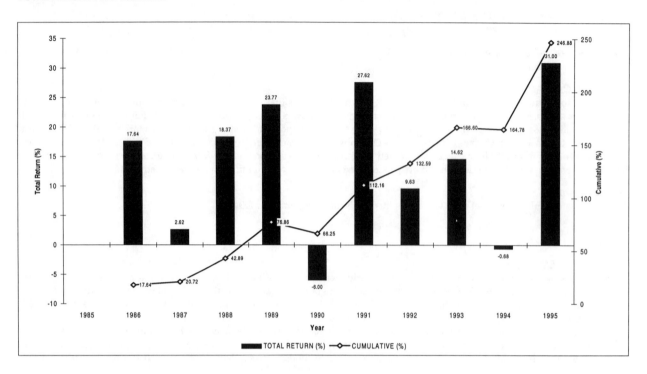

TOTAL RETURN PERFORMANCE

YEAR	VALUE	TOTAL RETURN (%)	CUMULATIVE (%)	MAXIMUM VALUE[1]	DATE	MINIMUM VALUE[1]	DATE
1995	3,926.05	31.00	246.88	3,927.70	6-Dec	2,996.02	3-Jan
1994	2,996.88	-0.68	164.78	3,120.92	31-Jan	2,919.71	31-Mar
1993	3,017.40	14.62	166.60	3,071.40	31-Dec	2,673.38	31-Jan
1992	2,632.52	9.63	132.59	2,632.52	31-Dec	2,398.59	31-Jan
1991	2,401.25	27.62	112.16	2,401.25	31-Dec	1,978.82	31-Jan
1990	1,881.61	-6.00	66.25	2,036.84	31-May	1,723.83	31-Oct
1989	2,001.70	23.77	76.86	2,021.09	31-Aug	1,693.63	28-Feb
1988	1,617.28	18.37	42.89	1,617.28	31-Dec	1,432.13	31-Jan
1987	1,366.29	2.62	20.72	1,734.94	31-Aug	1,281.64	30-Nov
1986	1,331.42	17.64	17.64	1,363.46	31-Aug	1,151.15	31-Jan
1985	1,131.82						
Average Annual (%)		13.86					
Compound Annual (%)		13.24					
Standard Deviation (%)		12.32					

[1]Maximum/minimum index values for the period 1986-1994 are as of month-end.

SYNOPSIS
The Lipper Growth & Income Funds Index is an equal-weighted index that tracks the daily total return performance of the 30 largest growth and income oriented mutual funds. These funds account for 66% of the total net assets in growth and income oriented mutual funds.

NUMBER OF FUNDS—DECEMBER 31, 1995
30

MARKET VALUE—DECEMBER 31, 1995
US$182,155.8 million

SELECTION CRITERIA
Constituent funds are selected from the universe of equity mutual funds that are classified as growth and income funds by Lipper Analytical, generally on the basis of the fund's investment objective characterization in its prospectus. A growth and income fund combines a growth of earnings orientation and an income requirement for level and/or rising dividends. The largest 30 funds, on the basis of their total net assets as of December 31st of each year, are selected. Funds established under a master-feeder structure or multiple share classes are limited to a single representation, i.e., the largest fund. Also, funds closed to new investors as well as non-Nasdaq-listed funds are generally excluded from participation as an index constituent.

BACKGROUND
The index was calculated on a net asset value-weighted basis until December 31, 1994.

BASE DATE
December 31,1959=100.00

COMPUTATION METHODOLOGY
(1) An equal-weighted index, calculated by taking the arithmetic average of the daily total rates of return of constituent funds. Cumulative returns are calculated by chain-linking the daily rates of return. (2) Income dividends and capital gains distributions, if any, are reinvested in each fund as of the ex-dividend date, regardless of actual distribution dates. (3) The index value is computed provided up to 80% of constituent funds are priced. (4) The index is reconstituted annually. Additions to or deletions from the index occur during the month of January of each year, unless circumstances dictate otherwise. For example, substitutions may be made during the course of the year due to fund liquidations or a change in a fund's investment objective. (5) Indices are recomputed annually to reflect all currently available revisions to funds that may have been reported during the course of the calendar year.

DERIVATIVE INSTRUMENTS
None

SUBINDICES
None

RELATED INDICES
Lipper Balanced Funds Index
Lipper Convertible Securities Funds Index
Lipper Equity Income Funds Index
Lipper GNMA Funds Index
Lipper Growth Funds Index
Lipper High Current Yield Funds Index
Lipper International Funds Index
Lipper Money Market Funds Index
Lipper Small Company Growth Funds Index
Refer to Appendix 5 for additional indices.

REMARKS
None

PUBLISHER
Lipper Analytical Services, Inc.

LIPPER HIGH CURRENT YIELD FUNDS INDEX

TOTAL RETURN PERFORMANCE

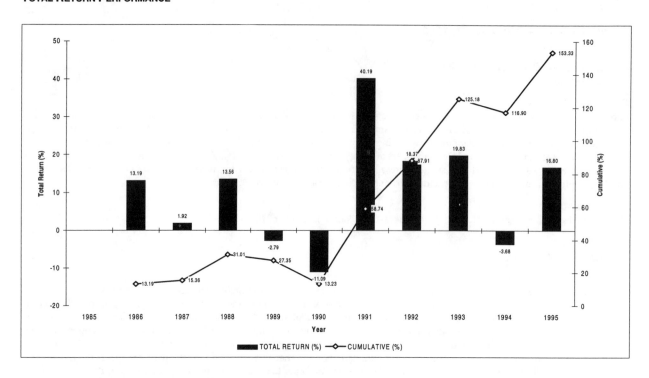

TOTAL RETURN PERFORMANCE

YEAR	VALUE	TOTAL RETURN (%)	CUMULATIVE (%)	MAXIMUM VALUE[1]	DATE	MINIMUM VALUE[1]	DATE
1995	597.21	16.80	153.33	597.21	29-Dec	511.57	3-Jan
1994	511.31	-3.68	116.90	544.20	31-Jan	510.00	30-Nov
1993	530.83	19.83	125.18	530.83	31-Dec	455.72	31-Jan
1992	442.97	18.37	87.91	442.97	31-Dec	390.75	31-Jan
1991	374.21	40.19	58.74	374.21	31-Dec	270.89	31-Jan
1990	266.93	-11.09	13.23	306.42	31-Jul	266.12	30-Nov
1989	300.22	-2.79	27.35	323.08	30-Jun	314.27	31-Jan
1988	308.84	13.56	31.01	308.84	31-Dec	281.12	31-Jan
1987	271.96	1.92	15.36	284.79	31-Aug	263.14	31-Oct
1986	266.84	13.19	13.19	266.84	31-Dec	237.24	31-Jan
1985	235.74						
Average Annual (%)		10.63					
Compound Annual (%)		9.74					
Standard Deviation (%)		14.92					

[1]Maximum/minimum index values for the period 1986-1994 are as of month-end.

SYNOPSIS
The Lipper High Current Yield Funds Index is an equal-weighted index that tracks the daily total return performance of the 30 largest high current yield mutual funds. These funds account for 72% of total net assets invested in high current yield mutual funds.

NUMBER OF FUNDS—DECEMBER 31, 1995
30

MARKET VALUE—DECEMBER 31, 1995
US$39,798.7 million

SELECTION CRITERIA
Constituent funds are selected from the universe of bond mutual funds that are classified as high current yield funds by Lipper Analytical, generally on the basis of the fund's investment objective characterization in its prospectus. A high current yield fund tends to invest in lower grade debt issues and aims at high (relative) current yield by investing in fixed income securities without any restrictions as to quality or maturity. The largest 30 funds, on the basis of their total net assets as of December 31st of each year, are selected. Funds established under a master-feeder structure or multiple share classes are limited to a single representation, i.e., the largest fund. Also, funds closed to new investors as well as non-Nasdaq-listed funds are generally excluded from participation as an index constituent.

BACKGROUND
The index was calculated on a net asset value-weighted basis until December 31, 1994.

BASE DATE
December 31, 1976=100.00

COMPUTATION METHODOLOGY
(1) An equal-weighted index, calculated by taking the arithmetic average of the daily total rates of return of constituent funds. Cumulative returns are calculated by chain-linking the daily rates of return. (2) Income dividends applicable to high current yield mutual funds go ex-dividend on a daily or monthly basis and are distributed monthly. For total return calculation purposes, income dividends are estimated and reinvested on a daily basis regardless of the fund's distribution policy. Capital gains distributions, if any, are reinvested in each fund as of the ex-dividend date, regardless of actual distribution dates. (3) The index value is computed provided up to 80% of constituent funds are priced. (4) The index is reconstituted annually. Additions to or deletions from the index occur during the month of January of each year, unless circumstances dictate otherwise. For example, substitutions may be made during the course of the year due to fund liquidations or a change in a fund's investment objective. (5) Indices are recomputed annually to reflect all currently available revisions to funds that may have been reported during the course of the calendar year.

DERIVATIVE INSTRUMENTS
None

SUBINDICES
None

RELATED INDICES
Lipper Balanced Funds Index
Lipper Convertible Securities Funds Index
Lipper Equity Income Funds Index
Lipper GNMA Funds Index
Lipper Growth Funds Index
Lipper Growth & Income Funds Index
Lipper International Funds Index
Lipper Money Market Funds Index
Lipper Small Company Growth Funds Index
Refer to Appendix 5 for additional indices.

REMARKS
None

PUBLISHER
Lipper Analytical Services, Inc.

LIPPER INTERNATIONAL FUNDS INDEX

TOTAL RETURN PERFORMANCE

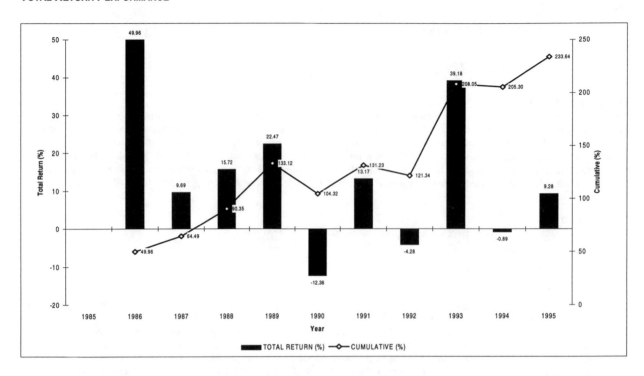

TOTAL RETURN PERFORMANCE

YEAR	VALUE	TOTAL RETURN (%)	CUMULATIVE (%)	MAXIMUM VALUE[1]	DATE	MINIMUM VALUE[1]	DATE
1995	490.18	9.28	233.64	490.48	27-Dec	421.80	10-Mar
1994	448.55	-0.89	205.30	480.82	31-Jan	447.82	31-Mar
1993	452.59	39.18	208.05	452.59	31-Dec	326.38	31-Jan
1992	325.19	-4.28	121.34	358.74	31-May	319.52	31-Oct
1991	339.72	13.17	131.23	339.72	31-Dec	307.45	31-Jan
1990	300.18	-12.36	104.32	365.42	31-Jul	287.20	30-Sep
1989	342.50	22.47	133.12	325.66	30-Sep	288.83	31-Mar
1988	279.66	15.72	90.35	279.96	˙˙-Dec	238.00	31-Jan
1987	241.67	9.69	64.49	296.13	˙˙-Sep	224.35	30-Nov
1986	220.32	49.96	49.96	212.02	30-Nov	150.92	31-Jan
1985	146.92						
Average Annual (%)		14.19					
Compound Annual (%)		12.80					
Standard Deviation (%)		19.13					

[1]Maximum/minimum index values for the period 1986-1994 are as of month-end.

SYNOPSIS
The Lipper International Funds Index is an equal-weighted index that tracks the daily total return performance of the 30 largest international mutual funds. These funds account for 71% of the total net assets in international mutual funds.

NUMBER OF FUNDS—DECEMBER 31, 1995
30

MARKET VALUE—DECEMBER 31, 1995
US$60,723.2 million

SELECTION CRITERIA
Constituent funds are selected from the universe of equity mutual funds that are classified as international funds, generally on the basis of the fund's investment objective characterization in its prospectus. An international fund invests in securities whose primary trading markets are outside the United States, excluding single country funds and small company funds. The largest 30 funds, on the basis of their total net assets as of December 31st of each year, are selected. Funds established under a master-feeder structure or multiple share classes are limited to a single representation, i.e., the largest fund. Also, funds closed to new investors as well as non-Nasdaq-listed funds are generally excluded from participation as an index constituent.

BACKGROUND
The index was calculated on a net asset value-weighted basis until December 31, 1994.

BASE DATE
December 31, 1984=100.00.

COMPUTATION METHODOLOGY
(1) An equal-weighted index, calculated by taking the arithmetic average of the daily total rates of return of constituent funds. Cumulative returns are calculated by chain-linking the daily rates of return. (2) Income dividends and capital gains distributions, if any, are reinvested in each fund as of the ex-dividend date, regardless of actual distribution dates. (3) The index value is computed provided up to 80% of constituent funds are priced. (4) The index is reconstituted annually. Additions to or deletions from the index occur during the month of January of each year, unless circumstances dictate otherwise. For example, substitutions may be made during the course of the year due to fund liquidations or a change in a fund's investment objective. (5) Indices are recomputed annually to reflect all currently available revisions to funds that may have been reported during the course of the calendar year.

DERIVATIVE INSTRUMENTS
None

SUBINDICES
None

RELATED INDICES
Lipper Balanced Funds Index
Lipper Convertible Securities Funds Index
Lipper Equity Income Funds Index
Lipper GNMA Funds Index
Lipper Growth Funds Index
Lipper Growth & Income Funds Index
Lipper High Current Yield Funds Index
Lipper Money Market Funds Index
Lipper Small Company Growth Funds Index
Refer to Appendix 5 for additional indices.

REMARKS
None

PUBLISHER
Lipper Analytical Services, Inc.

LIPPER MONEY MARKET FUNDS INDEX

TOTAL RETURN PERFORMANCE

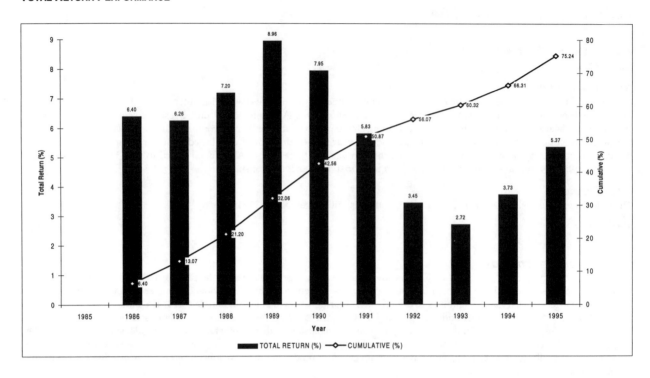

TOTAL RETURN PERFORMANCE

YEAR	VALUE	TOTAL RETURN (%)	CUMULATIVE (%)	MAXIMUM VALUE[1]	DATE	MINIMUM VALUE[1]	DATE
1995	474.10	5.37	75.24	474.10	31-Dec	451.95	31-Jan
1994	449.94	3.73	66.31	449.94	31-Dec	434.73	31-Jan
1993	433.74	2.72	60.32	433.74	31-Dec	423.28	31-Jan
1992	422.26	3.45	56.07	422.26	31-Dec	409.66	31-Jan
1991	408.17	5.83	50.87	408.17	31-Dec	388.05	31-Jan
1990	385.70	7.95	42.56	385.70	31-Dec	359.71	31-Jan
1989	357.28	8.96	32.06	357.28	31-Dec	330.27	31-Jan
1988	327.91	7.20	21.20	327.91	31-Dec	307.61	31-Jan
1987	305.90	6.26	13.07	305.90	31-Dec	289.23	31-Jan
1986	287.87	6.40	6.40	287.87	31-Dec	272.24	31-Jan
1985	270.55						
Average Annual (%)		5.79					
Compound Annual (%)		5.77					
Standard Deviation (%)		2.02					

[1]Maximum/minimum index values are as of month-end.

SYNOPSIS

The Lipper Money Market Funds Index is an equal-weighted index that tracks the monthly total return performance of the 30 largest prime obligations money market mutual funds. These funds account for 71% of prime obligation money market fund total net assets.

NUMBER OF FUNDS—DECEMBER 31, 1995

30

MARKET VALUE—DECEMBER 31, 1995

US$229,732.2 million

SELECTION CRITERIA

Constituent funds are selected from the universe of mutual funds that are classified by Lipper Analytical as prime obligation money market funds, generally on the basis of the fund's investment objective characterization in its prospectus. Prime obligations money market mutual funds maintain an average weighted maturity of 90 days or less and invest in highly-rated commercial paper, U.S. government securities asset-backed securities and repurchase agreements.

The largest 30 funds, on the basis of their total net assets as of December 31st of each year, are selected. Funds established under a master-feeder structure or multiple share classes are limited to a single representation, i.e., the largest fund.

BACKGROUND

The index was calculated on a net asset value-weighted basis until December 31, 1994.

BASE DATE

December 31, 1976=100.00

COMPUTATION METHODOLOGY

(1) An equal-weighted index, calculated by taking the arithmetic average of the monthly total rates of return of constituent funds. Cumulative returns are calculated by chain-linking monthly rates of return. (2) Income dividends and capital gains distributions, if any, are reinvested in each fund as of the first day of the month, regardless of actual distribution dates. (3) The index is reconstituted annually. Additions to or deletions from the index occur during the month of January of each year, unless circumstances dictate otherwise. For example, substitutions may be made during the course of the year due to fund liquidations or a change in a fund's investment objective. (4) Indices are recomputed annually to reflect all currently available revisions to funds that may have been reported during the course of the calendar year.

DERIVATIVE INSTRUMENTS

None

SUBINDICES

None

RELATED INDICES

Lipper Balanced Funds Index
Lipper Convertible Securities Funds Index
Lipper Equity Income Funds Index
Lipper GNMA Funds Index
Lipper Growth & Income Funds Index
Lipper Growth Funds Index
Lipper High Current Yield Funds Index
Lipper International Funds Index
Lipper Small Company Growth Funds Index
Refer to Appendix 5 for additional indices.

REMARKS

None

PUBLISHER

Lipper Analytical Services, Inc.

LIPPER SMALL COMPANY GROWTH FUNDS INDEX

TOTAL RETURN PERFORMANCE

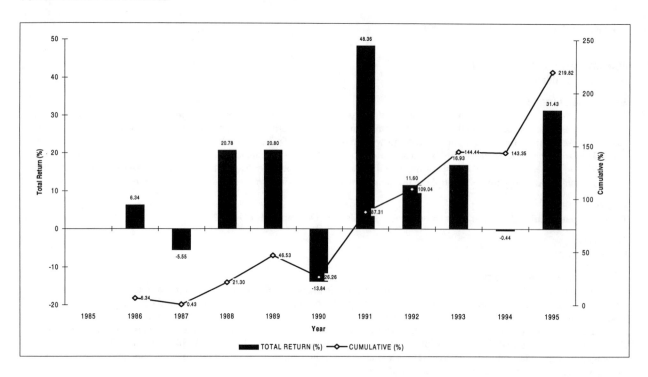

TOTAL RETURN PERFORMANCE

YEAR	VALUE	TOTAL RETURN (%)	CUMULATIVE (%)	MAXIMUM VALUE[1]	DATE	MINIMUM VALUE[1]	DATE
1995	480.28	31.43	219.82	480.83	20-Sep	359.76	5-Jan
1994	365.44	-0.44	143.35	376.65	31-Jan	334.70	30-Jun
1993	367.07	16.93	144.44	367.07	31-Dec	307.78	30-Apr
1992	313.92	11.60	109.04	313.92	31-Dec	261.92	30-Jun
1991	281.29	48.36	87.31	281.29	31-Dec	204.41	31-Jan
1990	189.60	-13.84	26.26	227.97	30-Jun	168.53	31-Oct
1989	220.05	20.80	46.53	226.92	30-Sep	191.31	31-Jan
1988	182.16	20.78	21.30	185.30	30-Jun	154.69	31-Jan
1987	150.82	-5.55	0.43	200.58	31-Aug	138.93	30-Nov
1986	159.69	6.34	6.34	177.63	31-May	153.39	31-Jan
1985	150.17						
Average Annual (%)		13.64					
Compound Annual (%)		12.33					
Standard Deviation (%)		18.30					

[1]Maximum/minimum index values for the period 1986-1994 are as of month-end.

SYNOPSIS
The Lipper Small Company Growth Funds Index is an equal-weighted index that tracks the daily total return performance of the 30 largest small company growth oriented mutual funds. These funds account for 54% of total net assets in small company growth oriented mutual funds.

NUMBER OF FUNDS—DECEMBER 31, 1995
30

MARKET VALUE—DECEMBER 31, 1995
US$35,491.2 million

SELECTION CRITERIA
Constituent funds are selected from the universe of equity mutual funds that are classified as small company growth funds by Lipper Analytical, generally on the basis of the fund's investment objective characterization in its prospectus. A small company growth fund is one that limits its investments to companies on the basis of their market capitalization. The largest 30 funds, on the basis of their total net assets as of December 31st of each year, are selected. Funds established under a master-feeder structure or multiple share classes are limited to a single representation, i.e., the largest fund. Also, funds closed to new investors as well as non-Nasdaq-listed funds are generally excluded from participation as an index constituent.

BACKGROUND
The index was calculated on a net asset value-weighted basis until December 31, 1994.

BASE DATE
December 31, 1982=100.00

COMPUTATION METHODOLOGY
(1) An equal-weighted index, calculated by taking the arithmetic average of the daily total rates of return of constituent funds. Cumulative returns are calculated by chain-linking the daily rates of return. (2) Income dividends and capital gains distributions, if any, are reinvested in each fund as of the ex-dividend date, regardless of actual distribution dates. (3) The index value is computed provided up to 80% of constituent funds are priced. (4) The index is reconstituted annually. Additions to or deletions from the index occur during the month of January of each year, unless circumstances dictate otherwise. For example, substitutions may be made during the course of the year due to fund liquidations or a change in a fund's investment objective. (5) Indices are recomputed annually to reflect all currently available revisions to funds that may have been reported during the course of the calendar year.

DERIVATIVE INSTRUMENTS
None

SUBINDICES
None

RELATED INDICES
Lipper Balanced Funds Index
Lipper Convertible Securities Funds Index
Lipper Equity Income Funds Index
Lipper GNMA Funds Index
Lipper Growth Funds Index
Lipper Growth & Income Funds Index
Lipper High Current Yield Funds Index
Lipper International Funds Index
Lipper Money Market Funds Index
Refer to Appendix 5 for additional indices.

REMARKS
None

PUBLISHER
Lipper Analytical Services, Inc.

MERRILL LYNCH CALIFORNIA MUNICIPAL MUTUAL FUND INDEX

TOTAL RETURN PERFORMANCE

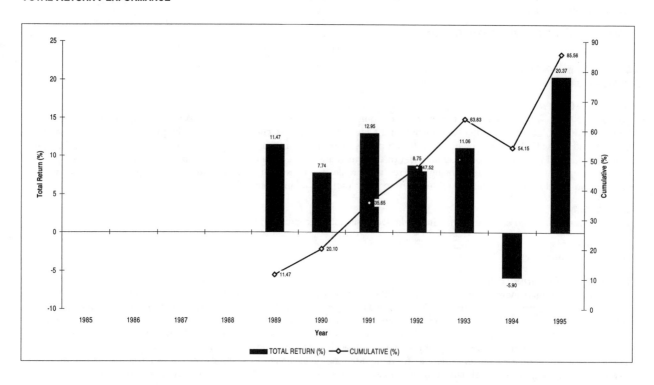

TOTAL RETURN AND PRICE PERFORMANCE

YEAR	VALUE	TOTAL RETURN (%)	CUMULATIVE (%)	PRICE RETURN (%)	MAXIMUM VALUE[1]	DATE	MINIMUM VALUE[1]	DATE
1995	185.56	20.37	85.56	13.31	185.56	31-Dec	159.80	31-Jan
1994	154.15	-5.90	54.15	-11.58	165.60	31-Jan	151.16	30-Nov
1993	163.83	11.06	63.83	4.35	163.83	31-Dec	149.95	31-Jan
1992	147.52	8.75	47.52	1.85	147.52	31-Dec	135.51	31-Jan
1991	135.65	12.95	35.65	5.46	135.65	31-Dec	121.51	31-Jan
1990	120.10	7.74	20.10	0.37	120.10	31-Dec	108.97	31-Jan
1989	111.47	11.47	11.47	3.88	111.47	31-Dec	100.40	31-Mar
1988	100.00							
1987								
1986								
1985								
Average Annual (%)		6.64		2.52				
Compound Annual (%)		6.38		2.28				
Standard Deviation (%)		7.93		7.46				

[1]Maximum/minimum index values are as of month-end.

SYNOPSIS

The Merrill Lynch California Mutual Fund Index is a matrix-weighted index that tracks the daily price only and total return performance of California tax-exempt securities that correspond to holdings in California municipal bond funds, as classified by Lipper Analytical Services, Inc.

NUMBER OF BONDS—DECEMBER 31, 1995

42

MARKET VALUE—DECEMBER 31, 1995

US$100.9 million

SELECTION CRITERIA

Eligible constituents consist of over 300 municipal securities which are selected and priced by Merrill Lynch traders to create a matrix that replicates the performance and characteristics of the municipal market with a reduced number of securities. In this instance, the market is the California municipal bond fund universe, which consists of funds that limit assets to those securities which are exempt from the State of California income taxes.

Constituent municipal bonds include California tax-exempt fixed-rate, coupon bearing securities, without maturity descriptions, that are rated BBB or better by Standard & Poor's Corp. and Baa3 and above by Moody's Investors Service. All issues must be publicly placed and, in addition, eligible issues must fit into one of the established matrix blocks that are defined on the basis of municipal sector, maturity and quality. Each matrix block has a specific weight and set of characteristics assigned to it, and securities are placed in these blocs based on their fit to the block criteria.

BACKGROUND

The index has been calculated monthly to December 31, 1992 and daily thereafter. Refer to the Merrill Lynch Global Bond Index for additional information.

BASE DATE

December 31, 1988=100.00

COMPUTATION METHODOLOGY

(1) Index formula is an aggregate value-weighted arithmetic average of the price ratios, coupon received or accrued (for total rate of return calculations), gain/loss on repayments of principal and, where applicable, currency value fluctuations. (2) Daily total return calculations are based on the theory that the portfolio of securities that make up the index is purchased in its entirety at approximately 3 PM (EST) on the initial day and held until the same time on the following day, when it is sold. Accrued interest and cash flows are assumed to be reinvested on a daily basis in the market. Total return for extended intervals are calculated by "chain-linking" the periodic rates of return. (3) Index weights are derived from a matrix created by Merrill Lynch's Municipal Bond Research Group. Each matrix block has a specific weight and set of sector, maturity and quality characteristics assigned to it, and securities are placed in these blocks based on their fit to the block criteria. For performance calculation purposes, the individual securities within the matrix blocks have equal weighting. (4) Securities prices are obtained from Merrill Lynch's trading floors. The securities are hand priced at least twice a each week, at approximately 3 PM (EST). Spreads calculated for each security on pricing dates are used to create a yield curve pricing matrix which is, in turn, the basis for market pricing on all other days. (5) Bonds are reviewed regularly to account for full and partial retirement of debt, calls, sinking-fund requirements, tenders or re-opening of issues. (6) New issues enter the index on the first business day following settlement while bonds that no longer meet the index or subindex criterion, including quality criteria, are removed from the index one day, or two days, respectively, following such a determination.

DERIVATIVE INSTRUMENTS

None

SUBINDICES

Various subindices by issuer type, maturity and credit ratings.

RELATED INDICES

Merrill Lynch Capital Markets Index
Merrill Lynch Convertible Securities Index
Merrill Lynch Currency Indices
Merrill Lynch Energy & Metals Index
Merrill Lynch Global Bond Index
Merrill Lynch Institutional Municipal Index
Merrill Lynch Money Market Instruments Index
Refer to Appendix 5 for additional indices.

REMARKS

None

PUBLISHER

Merrill Lynch & Co.

MERRILL LYNCH MUNICIPAL MUTUAL FUND INDEX

TOTAL RETURN PERFORMANCE

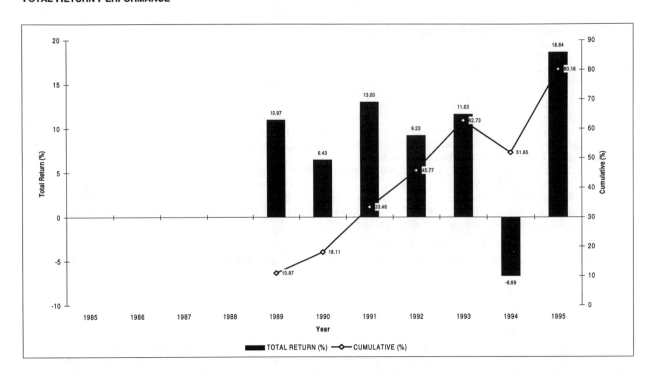

TOTAL RETURN AND PRICE PERFORMANCE

YEAR	VALUE	TOTAL RETURN (%)	CUMULATIVE (%)	PRICE RETURN (%)	MAXIMUM VALUE[1]	DATE	MINIMUM VALUE[1]	DATE
1995	180.16	18.64	80.16	11.80	180.16	31-Dec	156.88	31-Jan
1994	151.85	-6.69	51.85	-12.62	164.39	31-Jan	149.08	30-Nov
1993	162.73	11.63	62.73	4.91	162.73	31-Dec	147.73	31-Jan
1992	145.77	9.23	45.77	2.29	145.77	31-Dec	133.38	31-Jan
1991	133.46	13.00	33.46	5.44	133.46	31-Dec	119.67	31-Jan
1990	118.11	6.43	18.11	-1.04	118.11	31-Dec	108.57	30-Apr
1989	110.97	10.97	10.97	3.32	110.97	31-Dec	100.04	28-Feb
1988	100.00							
1987								
1986								
1985								
Average Annual (%)		6.32		2.01				
Compound Annual (%)		6.06		1.76				
Standard Deviation (%)		7.88		7.54				

[1]Maximum/minimum index values are as of month-end.

SYNOPSIS

The Merrill Lynch Municipal Mutual Fund Index is a matrix-weighted index that tracks the daily price only and total return performance of long-term general tax exempt securities that correspond to holdings in general municipal bond funds, as classified by Lipper Analytical Services, Inc.

NUMBER OF BONDS—DECEMBER 31, 1995

375

MARKET VALUE—DECEMBER 31, 1995

US$99.98 million

SELECTION CRITERIA

Eligible constituents consist of over 300 municipal securities which are selected and priced by Merrill Lynch traders to create a matrix that replicates the performance and characteristics of the municipal market with a reduced number of securities. In this instance, the market is the general municipal bond fund universe, which consists of funds that invest at least 65% of assets in municipal debt issues in the top four investment grade credit categories.

Constituent municipal bonds include fixed-rate, coupon bearing securities, without maturity descriptions, that are rated BBB or better by Standard & Poor's Corp. and Baa3 and above by Moody's Investors Service. All issues must be publicly placed and, in addition, eligible issues must fit into one of the established matrix blocks that are defined on the basis of municipal sector, maturity and quality. Each matrix block has a specific weight and set of characteristics assigned to it, and securities are placed in these blocks based on their fit to the block criteria.

BACKGROUND

The index was calculated monthly to December 31, 1992 and daily thereafter. Refer to the Merrill Lynch Global Bond Index for additional information.

BASE DATE

December 31, 1988=100.00

COMPUTATION METHODOLOGY

(1) Index formula is an aggregate value-weighted arithmetic average of the price ratios, coupon received or accrued (for total rate of return calculations), gain/loss on repayments of principal and, where applicable, currency value fluctuations. (2) Daily total return calculations are based on the theory that the portfolio of securities that make up the index is purchased in its entirety at approximately 3 PM (EST) on the initial day and held until the same time on the following day, when it is sold. Accrued interest and cash flows are assumed to be reinvested on a daily basis in the market. Total return for extended intervals are calculated by chain-linking the periodic rates of return. (3) Index weights are derived from a matrix created by Merrill Lynch's Municipal Bond Research Group. Each matrix block has a specific weight and set of sector, maturity and quality characteristics assigned to it, and securities are placed in these blocks based on their fit to the block criteria. For performance calculation purposes, the individual securities within the matrix blocks have equal weighting. (4) Securities prices are obtained from Merrill Lynch's trading floors. The securities are hand priced at least twice a each week, at approximately 3 PM (EST). Spreads calculated for each security on pricing dates are used to create a yield curve pricing matrix which is, in turn, the basis for market pricing on all other days. (5) Bonds are reviewed regularly to account for full and partial retirement of debt, calls, sinking-fund requirements, tenders or re-opening of issues. (6) New issues enter the index on the first business day following settlement while bonds that no longer meet the index or subindex criterion, including quality criteria, are removed from the index one day, or two days, respectively, following such a determination.

DERIVATIVE INSTRUMENTS

None

SUBINDICES

Various subindices by issuer type, maturity and credit ratings.

RELATED INDICES

Merrill Lynch Capital Markets Index
Merrill Lynch Convertible Securities Index
Merrill Lynch Currency Indices
Merrill Lynch Energy & Metals Index
Merrill Lynch Global Bond Index
Merrill Lynch Institutional Municipal Index
Merrill Lynch Money Market Instruments Index
Refer to Appendix 5 for additional indices.

REMARKS

None

PUBLISHER

Merrill Lynch & Co.

MERRILL LYNCH NEW YORK MUTUAL FUND INDEX

TOTAL RETURN PERFORMANCE

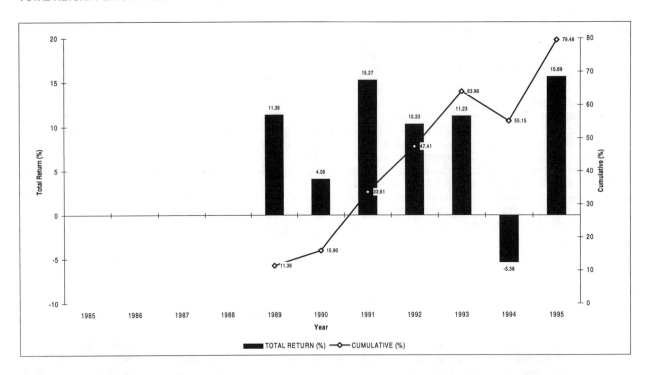

TOTAL RETURN AND PRICE PERFORMANCE

YEAR	VALUE	TOTAL RETURN (%)	CUMULATIVE (%)	PRICE RETURN (%)	MAXIMUM VALUE[1]	DATE	MINIMUM VALUE[1]	DATE
1995	179.48	15.69	79.48	8.68	179.48	31-Dec	158.62	31-Jan
1994	155.15	-5.38	55.15	-11.40	165.16	31-Jan	152.93	30-Nov
1993	163.96	11.23	63.96	4.41	163.96	31-Dec	148.76	31-Jan
1992	147.41	10.33	47.41	3.22	147.41	31-Dec	132.62	31-Jan
1991	133.61	15.27	33.61	7.72	133.61	31-Dec	117.75	31-Jan
1990	115.90	4.08	15.90	-3.44	115.90	31-Dec	108.88	30-Apr
1989	111.36	11.36	11.36	3.46	111.36	31-Dec	100.10	31-Jan
1988	100.00							
1987								
1986								
1985								
Average Annual (%)		6.26		1.81				
Compound Annual (%)		6.02		1.59				
Standard Deviation (%)		7.38		7.02				

[1]Maximum/minimum index values are as of month-end.

SYNOPSIS

The Merrill Lynch New York Mutual Fund Index is a matrix-weighted index that tracks the daily price only and total return performance of New York tax-exempt securities that correspond to holdings in New York State municipal bond funds, as classified by Lipper Analytical Services, Inc.

NUMBER OF BONDS—DECEMBER 31, 1995

89

MARKET VALUE—DECEMBER 31, 1995

US$100.0 million

SELECTION CRITERIA

Eligible constituents consist of over 300 municipal securities which are selected and priced by Merrill Lynch traders to create a matrix that replicates the performance and characteristics of the municipal market with a reduced number of securities. In this instance, the market is the New York municipal bond fund universe, which consists of funds that limit assets to those securities which are exempt from New York State taxes.

Constituent municipal bonds include New York State tax-exempt fixed-rate, coupon bearing securities, without maturity descriptions, that are rated BBB or better by Standard & Poor's Corp. and Baa3 and above by Moody's Investors Service. All issues must be publicly placed and, in addition, eligible issues must fit into one of the established matrix blocks that are defined on the basis of municipal sector, maturity and quality. Each matrix block has a specific weight and set of characteristics assigned to it, and securities are placed in these blocks based on their fit to the block criteria.

BACKGROUND

The Index was calculated monthly to December 31, 1992 and daily thereafter. Refer to the Merrill Lynch Global Bond Index for additional information.

BASE DATE

December 31, 1988=100.00

COMPUTATION METHODOLOGY

(1) Index formula is an aggregate value-weighted arithmetic average of the price ratios, coupon received or accrued (for total rate of return calculations), gain/loss on repayments of principal and, where applicable, currency value fluctuations. (2) Daily total return calculations are based on the theory that the portfolio of securities that make up the index is purchased in its entirety at approximately 3 PM (EST) on the initial day and held until the same time on the following day, when it is sold. Accrued interest and cash flows are assumed to be reinvested on a daily basis in the market. Total return for extended intervals are calculated by chain-linking the periodic rates of return. (3) Index weights are derived from a matrix created by Merrill Lynch's Municipal Bond Research Group. Each matrix block has a specific weight and set of sector, maturity and quality characteristics assigned to it, and securities are placed in these blocks based on their fit to the block criteria. For performance calculation purposes, the individual securities within the matrix blocks have equal weighting. (4) Securities prices are obtained from Merrill Lynch's trading floors. The securities are hand priced at least twice a each week, at approximately 3 PM (EST). Spreads calculated for each security on pricing dates are used to create a yield curve pricing matrix which is, in turn, the basis for market pricing on all other days. (5) Bonds are reviewed regularly to account for full and partial retirement of debt, calls, sinking-fund requirements, tenders or re-opening of issues. (6) New issues enter the index on the first business day following settlement while bonds that no longer meet the index or subindex criterion, including quality criteria, are removed from the index one day, or two days, respectively, following such a determination.

DERIVATIVE INSTRUMENTS

None

SUBINDICES

Various subindices by issuer type, maturity and credit ratings.

RELATED INDICES

Merrill Lynch Capital Markets Index
Merrill Lynch Convertible Securities Index
Merrill Lynch Currency Indices
Merrill Lynch Energy & Metals Index
Merrill Lynch Global Bond Index
Merrill Lynch Institutional Municipal Index
Merrill Lynch Money Market Instruments Index
Refer to Appendix 5 for additional indices.

REMARKS

None

PUBLISHER

Merrill Lynch & Co.

15

INDEX PROFILES — CLOSED-END FUNDS NORTH AMERICA

HERTZFELD CLOSED-END AVERAGE (THCEA)

TOTAL RETURN PERFORMANCE

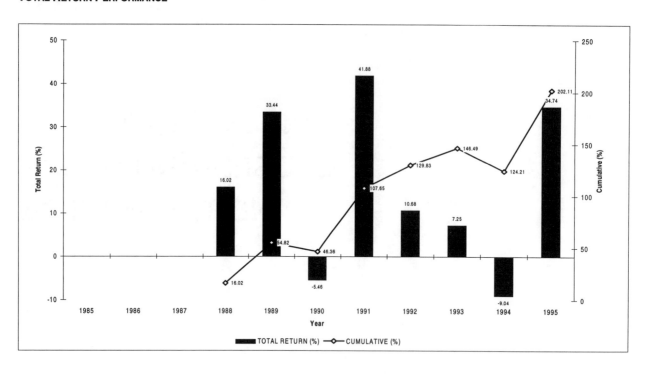

TOTAL RETURN PERFORMANCE

YEAR	VALUE	TOTAL RETURN (%)	CUMULATIVE (%)	MAXIMUM VALUE[1]	DATE	MINIMUM VALUE[1]	DATE
1995	5,856.00	34.74	202.11	5,856.00	31-Dec	4,515.00	31-Jan
1994	4,346.00	-9.04	124.21	4,662.00	31-Aug	4,346.00	31-Dec
1993	4,778.00	7.25	146.49	4,851.00	31-Oct	4,479.00	30-Apr
1992	4,455.00	10.68	129.83	4,455.00	31-Dec	3,981.00	30-Jun
1991	4,025.00	41.88	107.65	4,025.00	31-Dec	3,287.00	28-Feb
1990	2,837.00	-5.46	46.36	3,071.00	30-Jun	2,618.00	31-Oct
1989	3,001.00	33.44	54.82	3,001.00	31-Dec	2,366.00	28-Feb
1988	2,249.00	16.02	16.02	2,249.00	31-Dec	2,019.00	31-Jan
1987	1,938.38						
1986							
1985							
Average Annual (%)		16.19					
Compound Annual (%)		14.82					
Standard Deviation (%)		18.96					

[1]Maximum/minimum index values are as of month-end.

SYNOPSIS

The Hertzfeld Closed-End Average (THCEA) tracks the daily total return performance of 17 closed-end funds traded on the New York Stock Exchange and the American Stock Exchange that invest principally in United States (U.S.) equities.

NUMBER OF FUNDS—DECEMBER 31, 1995

17

MARKET VALUE—DECEMBER 31, 1995

US$9,693.4 million

SELECTION CRITERIA

Constituents include closed-end funds that invest principally in U.S. equities. The following funds are included in the index: The Adams Express, Baker, Fentress and Company, Bergstrom Capital Corp., Blue Chip Value Fund, Inc., Central Securities Corp., Liberty All Star Growth Fund, Engex, Inc., The Gabelli Equity Trust, General American Investors Company, Inc., The Inefficient - Market Fund, Inc., Liberty All Star Equity Fund, Morgan Grenfell SMALLCAP Fund, Inc., Royce Value Trust, The Salomon Brothers Fund, Inc., Source Capital Inc., Tri-Continental Corp. and the Zweig Fund, Inc.

BACKGROUND

The index was established with a universe of 20 funds that were approximately equally-weighted, and had a base value of 1,938.38 as of December 31, 1987 corresponding to the value of the Dow Jones Industrial Average on that day. This was intended to facilitate comparisons between these two benchmarks.

The funds form a portfolio that is modified in response to liquidations, changes in investment objectives, if any, and conversions to open-end fund status.

BASE DATE

December 31, 1988=1,938.38

COMPUTATION METHODOLOGY

Index values are based on portfolio results, calculated daily on the basis of closing prices. Income dividends and capital gains distributions are reinvested in additional fund shares or may be held in cash/cash equivalents pending reinvestment.

DERIVATIVE INSTRUMENTS

None

SUBINDICES

None

RELATED INDICES

THCEA Average is computed on a net asset value basis, along with weekly premiums and discounts.
The Hertzfeld Single Country Average

REMARKS

Market value refers to the combined total net assets of the 17 funds that make up the portfolio.

PUBLISHER

Thomas J. Hertzfeld Advisors, Inc.

16

INDEX PROFILES — REAL ESTATE
NORTH AMERICA

THE CHICAGO BOARD OPTIONS EXCHANGE REIT (RIX) INDEX

PRICE PERFORMANCE

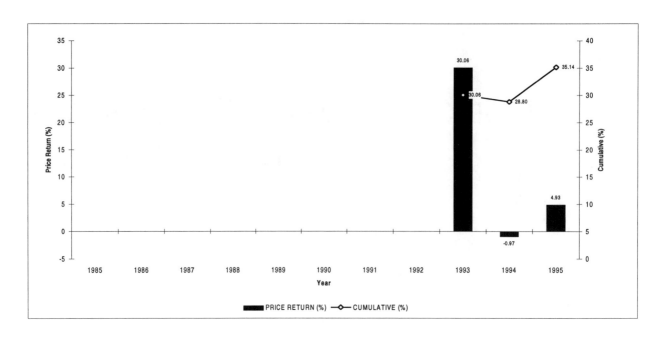

PRICE PERFORMANCE

YEAR	VALUE	PRICE RETURN (%)	CUMULATIVE (%)	MAXIMUM VALUE	DATE	MINIMUM VALUE	DATE
1995	209.85	4.93	35.14	209.85	29-Dec	188.26	20-Apr
1994	200.00	-0.97	28.80	219.18	23-Mar	180.79	22-Nov
1993	201.96	30.06	30.06	221.72	15-Oct	154.95	5-Jan
1992	155.28						
1991							
1990							
1989							
1988							
1987							
1986							
1985							
Average Annual (%)		11.34					
Compound Annual (%)		10.56					
Standard Deviation (%)		16.48					

SYNOPSIS
The Chicago Board Options Exchange REIT (RIX) Index is a price-weighted index that tracks the stock price performance of equity securities of large Real Estate Investment Trusts (REITs) that trade on the New York Stock Exchange (NYSE) or American Stock Exchange (AMEX).

NUMBER OF ISSUES—DECEMBER 31, 1995
25

MARKET VALUE—DECEMBER 31, 1995
Not Available

SELECTION CRITERIA
Constituent REITs invest a preponderance of their assets, usually at least 75%, in properties and the property portfolios owned by these companies constitute a diverse pool of income earning real estate investments.

BACKGROUND
The RIX was created to serve as an underlying vehicle for index options traded on The Chicago Board Options Exchange (CBOE).

BASE DATE
January 4, 1994=200.00

COMPUTATION METHODOLOGY
A simple aggregative of actual prices index formula, with adjustments to reflect stock splits and other capital changes by reducing the value of the divisor accordingly.

DERIVATIVE INSTRUMENTS
RIX index options trade on The Chicago Board Options Exchange.

SUBINDICES
None

RELATED INDICES
CBOE BioTechnology Index
CBOE Computer Software Index
CBOE Environmental Index
CBOE Gaming Index
CBOE Global Telecommunications Index
CBOE Israel Index
CBOE Latin 15 Index
CBOE Mexico Index
CBOE Technology Index
CBOE U.S. Telecommunications Index
Refer to Appendix 5 for additional indices.

REMARKS
None

PUBLISHER
The Chicago Board Options Exchange (CBOE).

NATIONAL COUNCIL OF REAL ESTATE INVESTMENT FIDUCIARIES (NCREIF) PROPERTY INDEX

TOTAL RETURN PERFORMANCE

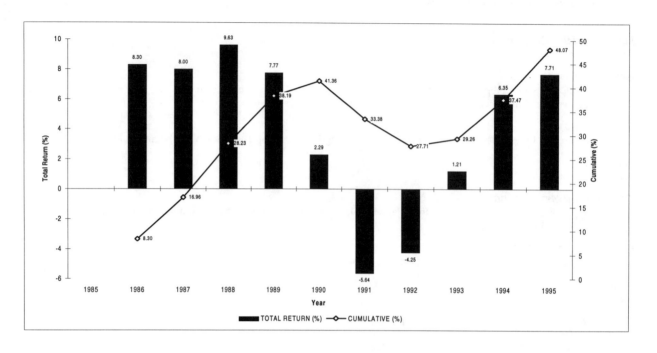

TOTAL RETURN PERFORMANCE

YEAR	VALUE	TOTAL RETURN (%)	CUMULATIVE (%)	MAXIMUM VALUE[1]	DATE	MINIMUM VALUE[1]	DATE
1995	447.07	7.71	48.07	447.07	31-Dec	423.81	31-Mar
1994	415.07	6.35	37.47	415.92	30-Dec	395.37	31-Mar
1993	390.27	1.21	29.26	391.26	30-Sep	387.71	30-Jun
1992	385.59	-4.25	27.71	402.62	31-Mar	385.59	31-Dec
1991	402.72	-5.64	33.38	427.05	30-Jun	402.72	31-Dec
1990	426.80	2.29	41.36	433.00	30-Sep	422.97	31-Mar
1989	417.23	7.77	38.19	417.23	31-Dec	393.94	31-Mar
1988	387.15	9.63	28.23	387.15	31-Dec	359.65	31-Mar
1987	353.14	8.00	16.96	353.14	31-Dec	332.97	31-Mar
1986	326.99	8.30	8.30	326.99	31-Dec	308.07	31-Mar
1985	301.93						
Average Annual (%)		4.14					
Compound Annual (%)		4.00					
Standard Deviation (%)		5.49					

[1]Maximum/minimum index values are as of quarter-end.

SYNOPSIS

The National Council of Real Estate Investment Fiduciaries (NCREIF) Property Index is a market value-weighted index that tracks the quarterly price only, and total return performance of investment grade, non-agricultural, income producing property acquired on behalf of tax exempt institutions and held in a fiduciary capacity.

NUMBER OF PROPERTIES—DECEMBER 31, 1995

2,322

MARKET VALUE—DECEMBER 31, 1995

US$47,850.0 million

SELECTION CRITERIA

The index consists of existing property (no developments) acquired on an-all cash basis by NCREIF members on behalf of tax exempt institutions and held in a fiduciary capacity.

Properties include investment grade, non-agricultural, income producing, wholly owned and joint venture investments, including apartments, hotels, office, retail, office showroom/research and development and warehouses.

Properties are added on a quarterly basis as new properties are acquired and as new member join NCREIF.

BACKGROUND

The index had been published in conjunction with Frank Russell & Co. NCREIF assumed sole responsibility for the index as of March 1995.

BASE DATE

December 31, 1977=100.00

COMPUTATION METHODOLOGY

(1) Total return combines capital appreciation (depreciation), realized gain (loss) and net operating income. (2) Income return, or net operating income (NOI) for the quarter is computed by dividing NOI by the average daily investment for the quarter. Average daily investment for the quarter is in turn computed by adding to the beginning market value one-half the value of capital improvements and subtracting the product of one half of partial sales less one third of net operating income. (3) Capital appreciation for the quarter is computed as the change in market value adjusted for any capital improvements or partial sales. (4) Consistent real estate appraisal methodology is used to determine the market value for each property. (5) Sold properties are removed from the index in the quarter in which the sales take place.

DERIVATIVE INSTRUMENTS

None

SUBINDICES

Five subindices by property types: Apartment, office, research and development/office and retail.
Four subindices by geographic region: East, West, Midwest and South.

RELATED INDICES

None

REMARKS

None

PUBLISHER

National Council of Real Estate Fiduciaries (NCREIF).

NATIONAL ASSOCIATION OF REAL ESTATE INVESTMENT TRUSTS (NAREIT)
COMPOSITE INDEX

TOTAL RETURN PERFORMANCE

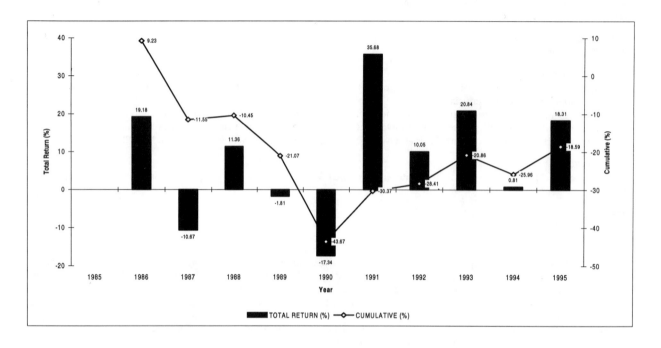

TOTAL RETURN AND PRICE PERFORMANCE

YEAR	VALUE	TOTAL RETURN (%)	CUMULATIVE (%)	PRICE RETURN (%)	MAXIMUM VALUE[1]	DATE	MINIMUM VALUE[1]	DATE
1995	84.57	18.31	-18.59	9.96	84.57	31-Dec	75.08	31-Jan
1994	76.91	0.81	-25.96	-6.45	86.67	28-Feb	72.88	30-Nov
1993	82.21	20.84	-20.86	10.54	89.21	30-Sep	78.68	31-Jan
1992	74.37	10.05	-28.41	2.82	75.43	31-Jan	71.12	30-Apr
1991	72.33	35.68	-30.37	23.60	72.69	31-May	63.16	31-Jan
1990	58.52	-17.34	-43.67	-28.63	79.30	31-Jan	56.20	31-Oct
1989	81.99	-1.81	-21.07	-11.86	93.53	31-Jul	81.99	31-Dec
1988	93.02	11.36	-10.45	1.24	100.39	28-Feb	93.86	30-Nov
1987	91.88	-10.67	-11.55	-19.03	117.88	28-Feb	89.86	31-Oct
1986	113.47	19.18	9.23	9.23	117.24	31-Aug	107.01	31-Jan
1985	103.88							
Average Annual (%)		8.64		-0.86				
Compound Annual (%)		7.55		-2.04				
Standard Deviation (%)		16.03		15.70				

[1]Maximum/Minimum index values apply to price returns.

SYNOPSIS

The National Association of Real Estate Investment Trusts (NAREIT) Composite Index is a market capitalization-weighted index that tracks the monthly stock price and total return performance of the common stock of all tax-qualified Real Estate Investment Trusts (REITs) listed on the New York Stock Exchange (NYSE), American Stock Exchange (AMEX) and Nasdaq National Market System (Nasdaq/NMS). The index includes equity REITs, mortgage REITs as well as hybrid REITs.

NUMBER OF ISSUES—DECEMBER 31, 1995

219

MARKET VALUE—DECEMBER 31, 1995

US$57,541.0 million

SELECTION CRITERIA

Index constituents include the common stock of all tax-qualified equity, mortgage, health care and hybrid Real Estate Investment Trusts listed on the New York Stock Exchange, American Stock Exchange and Nasdaq National Market System.

BACKGROUND

Prior to 1987, REITs were added to the index in January of each year following their listing. Starting in 1987, newly formed or listed REITs have been added in the month in which they became public.

BASE DATE

December 31, 1971=100.00

COMPUTATION METHODOLOGY

(1) An aggregative of prices times quantities index formula. Maintenance adjustments are made for capitalization changes, new listings and delistings. (2) The total return calculation is based upon the weighting of the constituent REITs at the beginning of the period. Also, only REITs that have been listed for the entire calendar month are included in the total return calculation. (3) Prices are the last closing prices of the month. (4) Newly issued shares on the part of existing REITs are added to the total number of shares outstanding in the month in which the new shares are issued. (5) Dividends are included in the month based upon their payment date. Liquidating dividends, whether full or partial, are treated as income.

DERIVATIVE INSTRUMENTS

None

SUBINDICES

Three subindices: Equity, mortgage and hybrid REITs.

RELATED INDICES

None

REMARKS

(1) Equity REITs are REITs with 75% or greater of their gross invested book assets invested directly or indirectly in the equity ownership of real estate. (2) Mortgage REITs are REITs with 75% or more of their gross invested book assets invested directly or indirectly in mortgages. (3) Hybrid REITs are REITs that don't satisfy either of the above definitions.

PUBLISHER

National Association of Real Estate Investment Trusts (NAREIT).

WILSHIRE REAL ESTATE SECURITIES INDEX

TOTAL RETURN PERFORMANCE

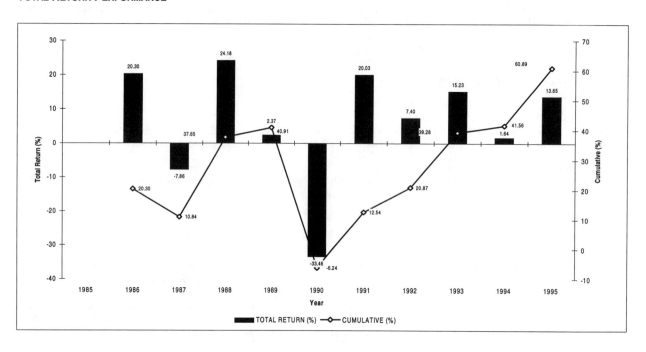

TOTAL RETURN AND PRICE PERFORMANCE[1]

YEAR	VALUE	TOTAL RETURN (%)	CUMULATIVE (%)	PRICE RETURN (%)	MAXIMUM VALUE	DATE	MINIMUM VALUE	DATE
1995	160.89	13.65	60.89	6.23	NA	NA	NA	NA
1994	141.56	1.64	41.56	-4.49	NA	NA	NA	NA
1993	139.28	15.23	39.28	9.39	NA	NA	NA	NA
1992	120.87	7.40	20.87	0.96	NA	NA	NA	NA
1991	112.54	20.03	12.54	12.33	NA	NA	NA	NA
1990	93.76	-33.46	-6.24	-38.62	NA	NA	NA	NA
1989	140.91	2.37	40.91	-4.45	NA	NA	NA	NA
1988	137.65	24.18	37.65	16.00	NA	NA	NA	NA
1987	110.84	-7.86	10.84	-13.47	NA	NA	NA	NA
1986	120.30	20.30	20.30	13.40	NA	NA	NA	NA
1985	100.00							
Average Annual (%)		6.35		-0.27				
Compound Annual (%)		4.87		-1.73				
Standard Deviation (%)		17.18		16.42				

[1]Index rebased to 12/31/85=100.00 and values computed based on annual rates of return.

SYNOPSIS

The Wilshire Real Estate Securities Index is a market value-weighted index that tracks the daily price only and total return performance of the larger and more liquid, publicly traded real estate securities whose charter is the equity ownership and operation of commercial real estate.

NUMBER OF ISSUES—DECEMBER 31, 1995

151

MARKET VALUE—DECEMBER 31, 1995

US$48,782.0 million

SELECTION CRITERIA

The index is comprised of publicly traded real estate securities, including Real Estate Investment Trusts (REITs), Real Estate Operation Companies (REOCs) and master limited partnerships trading on the New York Stock Exchange, American Stock Exchange and Nasdaq whose charter is the equity ownership and operation of commercial real estate, including apartments, factory outlets, industrial, hotels, manufactured housing, office space, local retail, regional retail, storage facilities as well as miscellaneous properties, with real estate of at least US$50.0 million (book value).

On an annual basis, index members are reviewed and eliminated due to any one of the following changes:

(1) A change in basic charter, i.e., the security is no longer an owner operator of equity real estate. (2) A change in type of real estate investment. (3) The level of minimum capitalization falls below US$25.0. (4) Failure to qualify for stock exchange continuous listing.

BACKGROUND

The index was launched in September 1991 and is intended to serve as a broad measure of the performance of publicly traded real estate equity for use by the institutional investment community. The initial date of January 1, 1978 was selected to coincide with the base date of the Russell/NCREIF Property Index.

The initial universe of securities was established by screening listed real estate securities during the period 1978 to 1991. Only securities with real estate assets of at least US$30.0 million (book value) in 1978 were eligible. Mortgage REITs, health care REITs, real estate finance companies, home builders, large land owners and sub-divers (primary land business) and Hybrid REITs, or those with more than 25% of assets in direct mortgage investment did not qualify for inclusion in the index as they were not deemed to be consistent with institutional investor real estate portfolio profiles.

In 1985, the minimum size requirement was lifted to US$40.0 million and increased again in 1990 to US$50.0 million. Effective March 31, 1994, additional annual review procedures outlined above were implemented. At the close of trading in 1995, several securities with market capitalizations of less US$100.0 million and relatively poor liquidity were eliminated from the index while five securities in the Storage sector were added to the index.

BASE DATE

December 31, 1986=100.00

COMPUTATION METHODOLOGY

(1) An aggregative of prices times quantities index formula. Maintenance adjustments to the divisor are made for capitalization changes, new listings and delistings. (2) New issues are added to the index on the first day of the quarter following the new offering. The issue remains in the index regardless of future minimum size guidelines. (3) New companies formed as a result of the consolidation of various private partnerships are not automatically added to the index, but are subject to a suitability review by Wilshire Associates.

DERIVATIVE INSTRUMENTS

None

SUBINDICES

Ten subindices by property classification: Apartments, diversified, factory outlet, industrial, hotel, manufactured housing, office, local retail, regional retail and storage.

RELATED INDICES

Wilshire 5000 Equity Index

REMARKS

None

PUBLISHER

Wilshire Associates.

17

INDEX PROFILES — REAL ESTATE WORLD

SALOMON BROTHERS WORLD EQUITY INDEX (SBWEI)—PROPERTY INDUSTRY INDEX

TOTAL RETURN PERFORMANCE

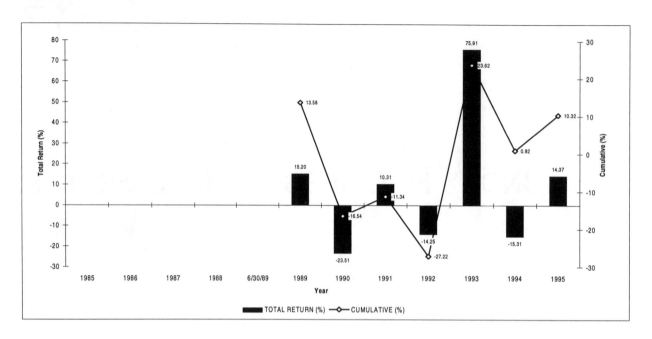

TOTAL RETURN AND PRICE PERFORMANCE

YEAR	VALUE	TOTAL RETURN (%)	CUMULATIVE (%)	PRICE RETURN (%)	MAXIMUM VALUE	DATE	MINIMUM VALUE	DATE
1995	151.58	14.37	10.32	9.31	151.58	29-Dec	125.16	23-Jan
1994	138.67	-15.31	0.92	-18.36	179.99	4-Feb	131.68	12-Dec
1993	169.85	75/91	23.62	69.85	169.85	31-Dec	99.33	4-Jan
1992	100.00	-14.25	-27.22	-17.91	122.95	6-Jan	97.16	3-Dec
1991	121.82	10.31	-11.34	6.24	131.03	18-Feb	109.11	16-Jan
1990	114.67	-23.51	-16.54	-26.52	157.00	4-Jan	106.54	28-Sep
1989	156.06	15.20	13.58	13.58	160.39	18-Dec	137.40	30-Jun
6/30/89	137.40							
1988								
1987								
1986								
1985								
Average Annual (%)		7.92		5.57				
Compound Annual (%)		2.11		-0.48				
Standard Deviation (%)		36.58		35.44				

SYNOPSIS

The Salomon Brothers World Equity Index (SBWEI)—Property Industry Index is a liquid, market value-weighted component of the Salomon Brothers World Equity Index that tracks the daily stock price and monthly total return performance of companies that are primarily involved in the property and real estate markets throughout 22 countries around the world, including Australia, Austria, Belgium, Canada, Denmark, Finland, France, Germany, Hong Kong, Ireland, Italy, Japan, Malaysia, The Netherlands, New Zealand, Norway, Singapore, Spain, Sweden, Switzerland, United Kingdom and the United States.

NUMBER OF STOCKS—DECEMBER 31, 1995
316

MARKET VALUE—DECEMBER 31, 1995
US$172,817.75 million

SELECTION CRITERIA

Index constituents are selected from the universe of stocks that make up the Salomon Brothers World Equity Broad Market Index.

Country selections are based on the size of the country's equity market, the freedom of capital movement and the ability to repatriate dividends.

For stock selection, the index employs a top-down selection approach in which constituents are limited to stock issues that a non-domiciled investor may purchase, with available market capitalization, or float, in excess of US$100.0 million. Companies involved in the property and real estate markets include real estate operators, developers and agents and companies engaged in property management, rental and/or investment. Also included in this sector are closed-end property funds investing in physical assets and having fixed, non-redeemable shares such as Real Estate Investment Trusts or Property Trusts. With few exceptions, issues are included in the index of their country of incorporation.

For additional information, refer to the Salomon Brothers World Equity Index—BMI.

BACKGROUND

Originally jointly compiled by Salomon Brothers and Frank Russell Company, the SBEI has been recalculated back to June 30, 1989.

BASE DATE

December 31, 1992=100.00

COMPUTATION METHODOLOGY

(1) An aggregative of prices times quantities index formula. Maintenance adjustments are made for capitalization changes, new listings and delistings. The index is calculated in local currency and U.S. dollar terms. (2) Available market capitalization, or float capitalization, is calculated once a year on the basis of price multiplied by total shares outstanding multiplied by the share availability factor, which is determined as of the last business day each May. (3) Shares outstanding due to ordinary changes in share capital are updated monthly. Otherwise, the ex-dividend date applies. (4) Changes to the constituent list are effective July 1 each year and are preannounced. Delisted issues are not replaced prior to the annual reconstitution. Large, newly formed companies, spin-offs from index constituents and privatizations falling within the top quartile of their country's capitalization range enter the index at the next month-end following their official listing. (5) Deletions due to mergers, acquisitions and restructurings are deleted from the index on the last trading day of the month in which the event takes place. Until such time, the issue is carried at its last available price. (6) Pricing sources include Ausstock for Australia, Nikkei for Japan, Toronto Stock Exchange for Canada, Interactive Data Services, Inc. for the United States and Extel for all other securities. If trading in a stock is halted, the last bid price or suspension price is used. (7) Gross dividends are tabulated daily, accumulated and reinvested at month-end. (8) WM/Reuters Closing Spot Rates as of 4 PM London Time are used for currency conversions.

DERIVATIVE INSTRUMENTS
None

SUBINDICES
Various individual country, currency and regional indices.

RELATED INDICES
Salomon Brothers Broad Investment Grade Bond Index
Salomon Brothers Convertible Securities Index
Salomon Brothers High Yield Index
Salomon Brothers World Government Bond Index
Salomon Brothers World Money Market Index
Refer to Appendix 5 for additional indices.

REMARKS

(1) SBWEI—Property Industry market weights on the basis of available capitalization as of December 31, 1995 are, as follows: Europe-Belgium 0.26%, Denmark 0.29%, France 2.91%, Germany 0.62%, Italy 0.05%, The Netherlands 3.58%, Spain 0.86%, Sweden 0.36%, Switzerland 0.41%, UK 8.66%; Asia/Pacific-Australia 6.06%, Hong Kong 27.17%, Japan 14.43%, Malaysia 4.15%, Singapore 6.26%, North America-Canada 0.29%, U.S. 23.87%. (2) Customized subindices by country and regions are available.

PUBLISHER
Salomon Brothers Inc.

18

Index Profiles — Miscellaneous North America

MERRILL LYNCH CAPITAL MARKET INDEX (CMI)

PRICE PERFORMANCE

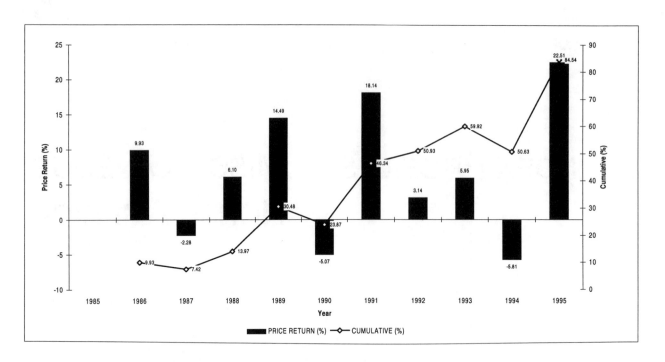

PRICE AND TOTAL RETURN PERFORMANCE

YEAR	VALUE	PRICE RETURN (%)	CUMULATIVE (%)	TOTAL RETURN (%)	MAXIMUM VALUE	DATE	MINIMUM VALUE	DATE
1995	2,633.71	22.51	84.54	28.10	2,633.71	31-Dec	2,185.43	31-Jan
1994	2,149.71	-5.81	50.63	-1.32	2,327.72	31-Jan	2,135.84	30-Nov
1993	2,282.35	5.95	59.92	10.78	2,283.38	30-Sep	2,180.04	31-Jan
1992	2,154.08	3.14	50.93	8.43	2,154.08	31-Dec	2,036.79	31-Mar
1991	2,088.50	18.14	46.34	25.01	2,088.50	31-Dec	1,811.73	31-Jan
1990	1,767.82	-5.07	23.87	1.02	1,845.98	30-Jun	1,681.67	30-Sep
1989	1,862.24	14.49	30.48	21.60	1,862.68	31-Jul	1,657.15	28-Feb
1988	1,626.56	6.10	13.97	13.23	1,649.90	31-Oct	1,584.33	31-May
1987	1,533.07	-2.28	7.42	3.37	1,803.78	31-Aug	1,477.02	30-Nov
1986	1,568.88	9.93	9.93	16.54	1,619.85	31-Aug	1,432.27	31-Jan
1985	1,427.17							
Average Annual (%)		6.71		12.68				
Compound Annual (%)		6.32		12.27				
Standard Deviation (%)		9.67		10.14				

SYNOPSIS
The Merrill Lynch Capital Market Index (CMI) is a market-value weighted index that tracks the monthly price only, income and total return performance of the combined results achieved by the Merrill Lynch Domestic Master Bond Index, the Merrill Lynch High Yield Master Bond Index and the Wilshire 5000 Stock Index.

NUMBER OF ISSUES—DECEMBER 31, 1995
14,662

MARKET VALUE—DECEMBER 31, 1995
US$11,241,793.7 million

SELECTION CRITERIA
Constituent bonds and stocks include all investment grade corporate, government and mortgage bonds, for a total of 6,886 bonds, 849 high-yield bonds and 6,927 U.S.-headquartered, actively traded common stocks listed on the New York Stock Exchange (NYSE), American Stock Exchange (AMEX) and Nasdaq that make up the Merrill Lynch Master Bond and Master High Yield indices along with the Wilshire 5000 Equity Index.

BACKGROUND
Total returns are calculated monthly to that date and price only returns are available on a monthly basis as of December 31, 1980.

BASE DATE
December 31, 1995=1000.00

COMPUTATION METHODOLOGY
Actual month-end price only returns, income and total returns, including reinvestment of income and dividends, produced by each of the three indices are combined by weighting the results of each index by its market value at each month-end.

DERIVATIVE INSTRUMENTS
None

SUBINDICES
None

RELATED INDICES
Merrill Lynch Convertible Securities Index
Merrill Lynch Currency Indices
Merrill Lynch Energy and Metals Index
Merril Lynch Global Bond Index
Merrill Lynch Institutional Municipal Index
Merrill Lynch Money Market Instrument Indices
Refer to Appendix 5 for additional indices.

REMARKS
(1) The index is weighted, as follows: 41.8% corporate, government and mortgage bonds, 1.4% high-yield bonds and 56.8% common stocks, based on data as of December 31, 1995. (2) The Wilshire 5000 Equity Index is a broad based market capitalization-weighted benchmark that measures the daily price only and total return performance of all U.S.-headquartered, actively traded common stocks with readily available price data. The index is comprised of approximately 6,927 issues traded on the New York Stock Exchange, American Stock Exchange and Nasdaq, with a market capitalization of US$6,383,599.0 million as of December 31, 1995.

PUBLISHER
Merrill Lynch & Co.

APPENDIX 1

ILLUSTRATIONS OF INDEX CALCULATIONS

STOCK INDICES

The index calculation illustrations are initially based on a universe of three securities, Company A, Company B and Company C. The following company scenarious are assumed in the illustration:

1.   On February 1, 1996, Company B undergoes a 2:1 stock split.

2.   On February 2, 1996, Company A is replaced by Company D.

3.   Company A declares a cash dividend of US$0.15 per share, which goes "ex-dividend" on February 2, 1996 and is payable on February 15, 1996.

   The number of shares outstanding and corresponding prices used in the next three illustrations are shown in Table A-1.

TABLE A-1: COMPANIES A, B, C AND D—SHARES OUTSTANDING AND CLOSING PRICES

Stock	Number of Shares Outstanding	1/31/96 Closing Price (US$)	2/1/96 Closing Price (US$)	2/2/96 Closing Price (US$)
Company A	1,562,000	15.125	15.375	16.00
Company B	51,016,030[1]	108.500	109.00[2]	53.00
Company C	6,420,100	20.750	20.125	22.00
Company D	5,250,100			12.00

[1] Number of shares outstanding increase to 102,032,060 due to a 2:1 stock split as of February 1, 1996.
[2] Share price is pre 2:1 split, which falls to US$54.50 after the split.

ARITHMETIC AVERAGE

The formula for computing a simple arithmetic index, such as the Dow Jones Industrial Average, is:
$\Sigma p_1 / n$ = Index value

1. The closing price of each security as of January 31, 1996 is aggregated, for a total of 144.38.

2. The result is divided by the number of stocks in the index, to arrive at the closing index value: $144.38 / 3 = 48.13$

3. The operation is repeated on February 1, 1996, to arrive at a closing index value of 48.17 $(144.50/3)$.

4. The index climbs 0.04 (48.17 - 48.13), for a gain of 0.9%.

To preserve its continuity for comparative purposes, adjustments are made to the index in connection with corporate actions and changes to index constituents. This is accomplished by the following equation that serves to reduce the index divisor:
Index value$_0$ / d$_0$ = Index value^1 / d$_1$ or d$_1$ = Index value$_1$ / Index value$_0$

where   Index value$_0$ = the previous day's index value
Index value$_1$ = the current day's index value
d$_0$ = the previous divisor
d$_1$ = the revised or updated divisor

5. The divisor is revised after the close of business on February 1, 1996 to reflect the 2:1 stock split applicable to Company B. Table A-2 reflects companies A - C and share prices before and after the 2:1 stock split.

$144.50 / 3 = 90.00 / d_1$
$d_1 = 1.86851$

TABLE A-2: COMPANY CLOSING PRICES BEFORE AND AFTER THE 2:1 STOCK SPLIT

Stock	Closing Prices Prior to the 2:1 Stock Split (US$)	Closing Prices Following the 2:1 Stock Split (US$)
Company A	15.375	15.375
Company B	109.000	54.500
Company C	20.125	20.125
Total	144.500	90.000

---

6. The index value on February 2, 1996, calculated using the revised divisor, registers a gain of 0.54 to 48.70, or an increase of 1.11%. The same formula is used to adjust the divisor in connection with stock replacements, such as when Company D replaces Company A following the market's close on February 2, 1996. The new divisor is 1.7864.

GEOMETRIC AVERAGE

To illustrate an index calculated on the basis of the geometric average, it is assumed that the index, like the Value Line Composite Index, is equally weighted. The following formula is used:

$$\sqrt{\sum (p_1 / p_0)} = \text{Index value}$$

1. The ratio of each security's closing price as of February 1, 1996 to the previous day's close is computed, as follows:

Company A	15.375 / 15.125 = 1.0165
Company B	109.00 / 108.50 = 1.0046
Company C	20.125 / 20.75 = 0.9699

2. The geometric average of the three prices is the square root of their product:

    $$\sqrt{1.0165 \times 1.004608 \times 0.96988} = 0.996808$$

3. The index declines by 0.32, for a loss of 0.0032% on February 1, 1996.

4. Capital changes, such as stock splits and stock dividends, require an adjustment to the prior day's price, while additions and deletions are ignored to the extent that an index consists of a sufficiently large number of constituent stocks.

5. After adjusting the prior day's price in connection with Company's B stock split, the index value on February 2, 1996 is calculated to be 103.09, for a one day gain of 3.4%.

PRICES TIMES QUANTITIES INDEX FORMULA
(WEIGHTED AGGREGATIVE COMPOSITE)

The following illustration is based on the Paasche index formula, using prices and the number of shares outstanding as of January 31, 1996 to establish the current value of the market portfolio:

$$\Sigma p_1 q_1 / \Sigma p_0 q_0 = \text{Index value}$$

1. The index base date is January 31, 1996 and its initial value is set at 100.00.

2. The base date market value (the divisor) is calculated by aggregating the price times quantity of each constituent company's shares outstanding as of January 31, 1996, for a total of 5,692,081,580.

	Shares Outstanding Price
Company A	1,562,000 x 15.125 = 23,625,250
Company B	51,016,030 x 108.50 = 5,535,239,255
Company C	6,420,100 x 20.75 = 133,217,075
	Market Value = 5,692,081,580

3. The current date market value (the numerator) is calculated in the same fashion, by multiplying each constituent company's number of shares outstanding as of January 31, 1996 by its share price as of the market's close on February 1, 1996, and aggregating the results. The current date market value is 5,591,183,120.

4. The numerator is divided by the index divisor, and the result is multiplied by 100. The index value on February 1, 1996 is 100.38 versus 100.00 on January 31, 1996. The index registers a gain of 0.38%.

5. The index value on February 2, 1996 is calculated in a similar fashion. The 2:1 stock split affecting Company B is self adjusting and does not require a divisor operation. The index value closes at 97.55, and registers a loss of 2.82%.

6. Unlike a stock split, company replacements require an adjustment to the index divisor. On February 2, 1996, Company D replaces Company A as an index constituent. The closing market value of Company D on February 2, 1996 is 63,001,200 (5,250,100 × US$12.00) (see Table A-3).

TABLE A-3: CLOSING AGGREGATE MARKET VALUE BEFORE AND AFTER COMPANY SUBSTITUTION

Stock	Closing Aggregate Market Value Before Substitution (US$)	Closing Aggregate Market Value After Substitution (US$)
Company A	24,992,000	
Company B	5,407,699,180	5,407,699,180
Company C	141,242,200	141,242,200
Company D		63,001,200
Total	5,573,933,380	5,611,942,580

---

7. The divisor adjustment at the close on February 2, 1996 is accomplished by means of the following equation:

$$\text{Index value} = (\text{Aggregate market value after substitution} / d_1) \times 100$$

where d_1 = the revised or updated divisor (base market value)

$$97.549 = (5,611,942,580 / d_1) \times 100$$
$$d_1 = 5,752, 931,639$$

8. The new divisor base market value will be used in the calculation of the index value as of February 3, 1996.

CHAIN LINKING

Daily returns produced in the foregoing illustration may be chain linked, or combined to arrive at the cumulative rate of return for the entire period, by applying the following formula:
$$R = (1 + r_1) (1 + r_2)...(1 + r_n) - 1$$

$$R = (1 + 0.0038) (1 - 0.0282) - 1$$
$$R = -0.9755 - 1$$
$$R = -2.45\%$$

In the same way, calendar year returns for indices in *The Guide* can be chain linked to achieve cumulative performance results. For example, the calendar year total rates of return produced by the S&P 500 during the period 1993-1995 achieved a cumulative return of 53.5%, which is calculated, as follows:

$R = (1 + 0.1008)(1 + 0.0132)(1 + 0.3762) - 1$

$R = 1.53492 - 1$

$R = 53.5\%$

TOTAL RETURN CALCULATION

The computation of an index on a total rate of return basis recognizes the payment of stock dividends as of the ex-dividend date. One approach is to add an indexed dividend, the formula for which is:

Indexed dividend = Total market value of dividends / Latest index divisor

The market value of dividends is shown in Table A-4.

TABLE A-4 MARKET VALUE OF DIVIDENDS

Stock	Number of Shares Outstanding	Dividend Per Share ("ex-dividend" date 2/1/96)	Market Value
Company A	1,562,000	0.15	234,300
Company B	51,016,030		
Company D	5,250,100		
Total			234,300

1. Indexed dividend = 234,300 / 55,433,900.24 = 0.00423

2. The indexed dividend is added to the closing index value as of February 2, 1996 to arrive at the total rate of return index value of 97.90 (97.889 + 0.0042).

MONEY MARKET INSTRUMENTS

TREASURY BILL INDEX (ACTUAL PRICES)

Total returns based on actual prices are calculated as follows using bills that mature closest to, but not beyond the desired maturity, from the last day of the previous month:

$TR = (Price_1 / Price_0) - 1$

where Price = $(1 - rd/360)$

r = the decimal yield (the average between the bid and asked quotes) on the bill on the last trading day of the current month and previous month

d = the number of days to maturity

MERRILLL LYNCH TREASURY BILL INDEX (AUCTION PRICES)

The total return formula based on auction averages uses a discount to par based on the average yield for the month's auction, adjusted to account for slightly more than four bill auctions per month, as follows:

$TR = \{100 / (100-d)\}^{1/3} - 1$

$$d = ay \times (91 \: / \: 360) \times (365.25 \: / \: 364)$$

where   ay = the number of weekly auction averages for the month / # of auctions during the month

d = the discount to par

SALOMON BROTHERS WORLD MONEY MARKET INDEX—3 MONTH MATURITIES

The average of the monthly yields for the preceding three months is calculated and converted to an annualized rate of return, using a monthly compounding frequency formula. The monthly return is adjusted with local market-day count conventions and for currency movements to arrive at a local market return.

OTHER MONEY MARKET INSTRUMENTS

In many money markets, it is normal for interest rates to be quoted only for specific periods, such as overnight, seven days, one-month, three-months, etc. The calculations for non-standard periods use linear interpolations between the quoted rates for the desired time period.

APPENDIX 2

SUPPLEMENTAL SECURITIES MARKET INDICES

Supplemental securities market indices consist of secondary and related benchmarks, along with indices in which there is likely to be special interest, indices launched during the first six months of 1996 as well as indices for which limited descriptive information is available. These supplemental indices are described in an abbreviated format which includes a synopsis of the index, the availability of derivative instruments, if any, and the index publisher. In some cases, computation methodologies are also described.

STOCKS—NORTH AMERICA

UNITED STATES

AMERICAN BANKER BANK INDICES

Various weighted indices that track the price only performance of larger, publicly traded, commercial banking firms and thrifts. These include a composite index of the largest 225 banking firms and the 25 largest thrifts by market value of all common shares outstanding, Top 50 Banks Index, as well as regional indices covering the midwest, south/southeast, west, middle Atlantic and northwest.

PUBLISHER
American Banker.

BARRA ALL U.S. PRICE INDEX

A broad market value-weighted index that tracks the price only and total return performance of all domestic and foreign stocks listed on the New York Stock Exchange (NYSE), American Stock Exchange (AMEX), Nasdaq and regional stock exchanges for which price quotations are available. The index includes all listed shares of beneficial interest, limited partnerships, Master Limited Partnerships (MLPs), initial public offerings listed for a period of 12-months, when issued stocks as well as directly listed foreign stocks. The index excludes the following securities: American Depositary Receipts (ADRs), Real Estate Investment Trusts (REITs), mutual funds, closed-end funds, suspended stocks and preferred stocks. Leveraged buyouts (LBOs) and stocks of companies that have entered into bankruptcy or have been taken over are tracked in the index as long as they trade on one of the exchanges or the OTC market. The index tracked 6,404 issues with a market capitalization of US$6,727,300.0 million as of December 26, 1995.

COMPUTATION METHODOLOGY
An aggregative of prices times quantities index formula. Maintenance adjustments to the divisor are made for capitalization changes, new listings and delistings.

PUBLISHER
BARRA, Inc.

BARRON'S LOW-PRICED STOCK INDEX

An equally-weighted stock price index that tracks the weekly composite price (as of Thursday) only performance of 20 low-priced diversified industrial (railroads and utility stocks are excluded) stocks traded on the New York Stock Exchange (NYSE)) and American Stock Exchange (AMEX). The index, which was originally introduced in April 1938 with 30 stocks, has been revised on several occasions. It was last revised in June 1983 and the current selections were made on the basis of the following factors: (1) A price of $15 or less. (2) A current ratio of at least 2 to 2. (3) A satisfactory earnings record. (4) A substantial drop in price between the 1981 market high and the 1982 market low.

PUBLISHER
Barron's.

BARRON'S 50 STOCK AVERAGE

An equally-weighted stock price index that tracks the weekly price only performance of 50 stocks using closing composite prices on Thursday of each week.

PUBLISHER
Barron's.

BENHAM NORTH AMERICAN GOLD EQUITIES INDEX

A market value-weighted index that tracks the performance of 30 sufficiently large companies engaged directly or indirectly in mining, fabricating, processing or otherwise dealing in gold located in North America.

PUBLISHER
Benham Management Corp.

BLOOMBERG STATE/REGIONAL COMMON STOCK INDICES

Various price-weighted indices that tracks the daily performance of common stocks that are headquartered in the following states or metropolitan areas: Albany, Carolinas, Colorado, Georgia, Illinois, Indiana, Maryland, Michigan, Minnesota, Nebraska, New Jersey/New York Metro, Northeast Ohio, Northwest Ohio, Oregon, Tampa Bay, Tennessee, Texas, Utah and Wisconsin.

PUBLISHER
Bloomberg Financial.

CENTER FOR RESEARCH IN SECURITY PRICES

Various returns on equally-weighted and value-weighted market indices covering common stocks traded on the New York Stock Exchange (NYSE), American Stock Exchange (AMEX) and Nasdaq National Market System (Nasdaq/NMS). In addition to return and index levels for the Standard & Poor's 500, high-grade corporate bonds, long-term U.S. Treasury bonds and Treasury bills are available.

PUBLISHER
The Center for Research in Security Prices.

DALBAR
INVESTMENT COMPANY STOCK INDEX (DICSA)

An index that tracks the performance of 12 publicly traded investment management companies.

DALBAR 30 INDEX

An index that tracks the performance of 30 publicly traded companies involved in the management of mutual funds and service providers to the mutual fund industry, including the 12 money management companies in the DICSA Index, national and regional broker-dealers, financial printers, systems and operations support providers and custodian banks.

PUBLISHER
DALBAR.

DOMINI SOCIAL INDEX

An index consisting of 400 companies that are selected on the basis of various social criteria, including environmental considerations, products, employee relations, and corporate citizenship.

PUBLISHER
Kinder Lydenberg Domini & Co.

FRANKLIN CALIFORNIA 250 GROWTH INDEX

An equally-weighted index that tracks the total return performance of 250 of the largest corporations headquartered in California.

PUBLISHER
Franklin Resources, Inc.

HAMBRECHT & QUIST (H&Q) GROWTH INDEX

The Hambrecht & Quist (H&Q) Growth Index is a market value-weighted subindex of the H&Q Technology Index that measures the daily price only and monthly total return performance of publicly traded stocks in the technology sector, including companies in the electronics, medical and related technology industries, with annual revenue of less than US$300 million. The Growth Index was developed in February 1985. To provide a historical perspective, the index was back-dated to 1970 using the original 100 component companies that made up the index at the time of its inception in 1985. Its initial value was set at 100.00 as of December 31, 1977.

COMPUTATION METHODOLOGY
(1) An aggregative of prices times quantities index formula. Maintenance adjustments to the divisor are made for capitalization changes, new listings and delistings. (2) The market capitalization of individual companies is limited to a maximum value of US$10 billion. (3) While index substitutions are made only once a year, companies that cease to trade due to mergers, acquisitions, and other developments, are removed from the index without being replaced. (4) Total rates of return are calculated at the end of each month.

PUBLISHER
Hembrecht & Quist.

HUBBLE ENVIRONMENTAL INDEX

An index that tracks the performance of stocks on the basis of screening for environmental responsibility.

PUBLISHER
Progressive Asset Management and David L. Hubble.

INVESTORS BUSINESS DAILY 6000

A market value-weighted index that tracks the daily price only performance of common stocks listed on the New York Stock Exchange (NYSE), American Stock Exchange (AMEX) and Nasdaq National Market System (Nasdaq/NMS). The index was initiated with a base date of January 1, 1984=100.00.

PUBLISHER
Investor's Business Daily.

KEEFE BANK INDEX (KBI)

An unweighted index that tracks the price only performance of 24 major banking companies in the U.S. The index has been calculated since the early 1960s.

PUBLISHER
Keefe, Bruyette & Woods, Inc.

KBW 50 INDEX

A market value-weighted index that tracks the price only and total rate of return performance of 50 of the most important banking companies in the U.S., including all money-center and most major regional banks. Six subindices are also calculated for money-center banks, eastern regional banks, midwestern regional banks, southern regional banks and western regional banks. The index, which was established with a base date of December 31, 1987 and an initial value of 100.00, was introduced in January 1993.

CALCULATION METHODOLOGY
(1) Dividends are reinvested on a quarterly basis. (2) Substitutions are kept to a minimum and are occasioned by bank failures or mergers.

PUBLISHER
Keefe, Bruyette & Woods, Inc.

MERRILL LYNCH ADR INDICES

A series of equal-weighted indices that track the monthly price only performance of exchange-listed American Depositary Receipts that trade on the New York Stock Exchange (NYSE), American Stock Exchange (AMEX) and Nasdaq National Market System (Nasdaq/NMS). In addition to a composite and regional indices, country indices include: Argentina, Australia, Brazil, Chile, China, Colombia, Denmark, Finland, France, Germany, Hong Kong, Indonesia, Ireland, Israel, Italy, Japan, Korea, Mexico, Norway, Netherlands, New Zealand, Peru, Philippines, Portugal, Singapore, South Africa, Spain, Sweden, Switzerland, UK and Venezuela.

PUBLISHER
Merrill Lynch.

RUSSELL INDICES
RUSSELL 2500 INDEX

A market value-weighted index that tracks the daily price only and total return performance of 2,500 investable common stocks belonging to small- to medium-small U.S.-domiciled corporations whose shares are publicly traded. These securities consist of the bottom 500 companies in the Russell 1000 Equity Index and all 2,000 companies in the Russell 2000 Index.

RUSSELL TOP 200 INDEX

A market value-weighted index that tracks the daily price only and total return performance of 200 investable common stocks belonging to large "Blue Chip" U.S.-domiciled corporations whose shares are publicly traded. These securities consist of the largest 200 companies in the Russell 1000 Equity Index. When combined with the Russell Midcap Index, these companies make up the Russell 1000 Equity Index.

RUSSELL TOP 200 VALUE INDEX

A market value-weighted index that tracks the daily price only and total return performance of value oriented investable common stocks belonging to large "Blue Chip" U.S.-domiciled corporations whose shares are publicly traded. These securities represent a subset of the stocks that make up the Russell Top 200 Index with a less-than-average growth orientation.

RUSSELL TOP 200 GROWTH INDEX

A market value-weighted index that tracks the daily price only and total return performance of growth oriented investable common stocks belonging to large "Blue Chip" U.S.-domiciled corporations whose shares are publicly traded. These securities represent a subset of the stocks that make up the Russell Top 200 Index with a greater-than-average growth orientation.

COMPUTATION METHODOLOGY
(1) An aggregative of prices times quantities index formula. Maintenance adjustments to the divisor are made daily, after the close on the day that the stock starts trading with prices reflecting the change, for capitalization changes, new listings and delistings. (2) Market capitalization is computed by adjusting, on a continuous basis, shares outstanding for cross ownership so as not to overstate the overall market value of constituent companies. This is accomplished by reducing the total shares outstanding by the number of shares owned by other companies (including companies outside the index), and stocks owned by foreign companies and other non-corporate entities. (3) The indices are reconstituted annually, every June 30th based on May 31st market capitalizations.

PUBLISHER
Frank Russell Co.

SCHWAB 1000 INDEX

A market value-weighted index that tracks the performance of the 1,000 largest U.S.-based operating companies whose shares trade on the New York Stock Exchange (NYSE), American Stock Exchange (AMEX) and Nasdaq National Market System (Nasdaq/NMS).

PUBLISHER
Charles Schwab.& Co.

SNL FINANCIAL SERVICES INDICES

BROKER/DEALERS INDEX

A market value-weighted stock price index that tracks the price only performance of 42 publicly traded companies (as of September 30, 1995) who offer services such as securities brokerage, investment banking, merger and acquisition, advisory services and asset management. The index was established with a base value of 100.00 as of December 31, 1988.

FINANCIAL SERVICES COMPANIES INDEX

A market value-weighted stock price index that tracks the price only performance of publicly traded broker/dealers, finance companies, mortgage banks and related service providers, U.S. Government-Sponsored Enterprises (GSEs), Real Estate Investment Trusts (REITs) and investment advisers. The index was established with a base value of 100.00 as of December 31, 1988.

FINANCE COMPANIES INDEX

A market value-weighted stock price index that tracks the price only performance of 70 publicly traded finance companies (as of September 30, 1995), including consumer finance companies, credit card companies, sales finance companies and commercial finance companies, that make loans to manufacturers and wholesalers securities by accounts receivables, inventories and equipment. The index was established with a base value of 100.00 as of December 31, 1988.

GSE INDEX

A market value-weighted stock price index that tracks the price only performance of 42 publicly traded companies (as of September 30, 1995) who offer services such as securities brokerage, investment banking, merger and acquisition, advisory services and asset management. The index was established with a base value of 100.00 as of December 31, 1988.

MORTGAGE BANKS AND RELATED SERVICES INDEX

A market value-weighted stock price index that tracks the price only performance of 27 publicly traded mortgage banking companies (as of September 30, 1995) that specialize in the origination, sale, and servicing of residential and commercial mortgages. The index was established with a base value of 100.00 as of December 31, 1988.

Financial Services Investment Advisors Index

A market value-weighted index that tracks the daily price only performance of 14 publicly traded money management companies. The index was established with a base value of 100.00 as of December 31, 1988.

PUBLISHER
SNL Securities, L.P.

Value Line
Industrial Average

An equally-weighted, geometrically averaged, measure of the daily price change of the approximately 1,500 industrial stocks reviewed in Value Line's Ratings & Reports. Established at a value of 100.00 as of June 30, 1961, the index has been published daily since that date.

Utility Average

An equally-weighted, geometrically averaged, measure of the daily price change of the approximately 177 utility stocks reviewed in Value Line's Ratings & Reports. Established at a value of 100.00 as of June 30, 1961, the index has been published daily since that date.

Railroad Average

An equally-weighted, geometrically averaged, measure of the daily price change of the approximately 20 rail stocks reviewed in Value Line's Ratings & Reports. Established at a value of 100.00 as of June 30, 1961, the index has been published daily since that date.

PUBLISHER
Value Line, Inc.

Wilshire 2500 Equity Index

A market value-weighted index that tracks the performance of the largest 2,500 companies derived from the Wilshire 5000 Equity index.

PUBLISHER
Wilshire Associates Inc.

Stocks—Asia/Pacific

Australia
ASX 50 Leaders Price and Accumulation Indices

A market value-weighted index that tracks the continuous stock price and total return performance of the 50 largest equity shares on the Australian Stock Exchange (ASX). Constituent stocks include the top 50 companies which are selected on the basis of market capitalization, although relatively inactive stocks have been excluded. Eligible securities include listed and ordinary shares, both fully and partly paid shares, rights and delivery shares as well as listed trust units, which are selected on the basis of market capitalization and trading volume. The 50 Leaders Price Index was established with a base value of 500.00 as of December 31, 1979. The 50 Leaders Accumulation Index was established with a base value of 1000.00 as of the same date.

COMPUTATION METHODOLOGY

(1) An aggregative of prices times quantities index formula. Maintenance adjustments to the divisor are made daily to reflect all types of capitalization changes, new listings and delistings. (2) The value of each security is the last sale price recorded by the Australian Stock Exchange Automated Trading System (SEATS), modified by any subsequent higher bids or lower offers made before trading ends at 1600 hours (EST). (3) The composition of the index is reviewed on a monthly basis. Mergers, takeovers and other delistings are withdrawn from the index universe between monthly reviews. Suspended companies are retained unless the suspension seems likely to be long-term or terminal in nature. (4) Market capitalization is determined on the basis of listed shares. No adjustments are made for cross holdings, controlling, strategic and other long term holdings. (5) Total returns are calculated by reinvesting 100% of dividends at the 1600 hours (EST) market price on the ex-dividend date.

PUBLISHER

The Australian Stock Exchange Limited.

THE WARDLEY INDEX

A market value-weighted index that tracks the continuous stock price and total return performance of 267 equity shares on the Australian Stock Exchange (ASX). Constituent stocks correspond to the shares tracked by the Australian All Ordinaries Stock Exchange Index (ASX) less the 50 stocks that make up the 50 Leaders Index. Eligible securities include listed and ordinary shares, both fully and partly paid shares, rights and delivery shares as well as listed trust units, which are selected on the basis of market capitalization and trading volume. The index was established with a base value of 500.00 for the price only index and a value of 1,000.00 for the accumulation index as of December 31, 1990.

COMPUTATION METHODOLOGY

(1) An aggregative of prices times quantities index formula. Maintenance adjustments to the divisor are made daily to reflect all types of capitalization changes, new listings and delistings to keep the current index numbers comparable to the base period. (2) The value of each security is the last sale price recorded by the Australian Stock Exchange Automated Trading System (SEATS), modified by any subsequent higher bids or lower offers made before trading ends at 1600 hours (EST). (3) The composition of the index is reviewed on a monthly basis. Mergers, takeovers and other delistings are withdrawn from the index universe between monthly reviews. Suspended companies are retained unless the suspension seems likely to be long-term or terminal in nature. (4) Market capitalization is determined on the basis of listed shares. No adjustments are made for cross holdings, controlling, strategic and other long term holdings. (5) Total returns are calculated by reinvesting 100% of dividends at the 1600 hours (EST) market price on the ex-dividend date.

PUBLISHER

The Australian Stock Exchange Limited.

CHINA

CREDIT LYONNAIS SECURITIES ASIA (CLSA) CHINA WORLD INDEX

A free float-weighted index that tracks the performance of 30 Chinese stocks, including B-shares and H-shares, listed on equity exchanges throughout the world. The index was established with a base value of 1,000.00 as of January 3, 1995. It consists of stocks traded on The Stock Exchange of Hong Kong Limited (SEHK), New York Stock Exchange (NYSE), Shanghai Stock Exchange (SSE) and Shenzen Stock Exchange (SSE) that are selected on the basis of market capitalization and free float, liquidity, and sectoral representation.

PUBLISHER
Credit Lyonnais Securities Asia.

SHENZEN STOCK EXCHANGE INDICES
SHENZEN SHARE STOCK PRICE INDEX

A market value-weighted index that tracks the daily price only performance of all A-shares and B-shares listed on the Shenzen Stock Exchange (SSE). An aggregative of prices times quantities index formula is used.

SHENZEN A-SHARE STOCK PRICE INDEX

A market value-weighted index that tracks the daily price only performance of all shares listed on the Shenzen Stock Exchange (SSE) which are restricted to local investors. An aggregative of prices times quantities index formula is used.

SHENZEN B-SHARE STOCK PRICE INDEX

A market value-weighted index that tracks the daily price only performance of shares listed on the Shenzen Stock Exchange (SSE) which are available for investment by foreign investors. An aggregative of prices times quantities index formula is used.

PUBLISHER
Shenzen Stock Exchange.

HONG KONG
AMERICAN STOCK EXCHANGE (AMEX)/HONG KONG OPTION INDEX (HKO)

A market value-weighted index that tracks the daily price only performance of 30 highly capitalized stocks listed on the The Stock Exchange of Hong Kong Limited (SEHK). The constituent stocks represent integral components of the Hong Kong economy and have been selected on the basis of trading activity and market capitalization. These stocks represent approximately 67% of the total capitalization of the SEHK. The index was designed by the American Stock Exchange (AMEX) as a vehicle for stock index options. It was established with a base value of 350.00 as of June 25, 1993. HKO has 21 shares in common with the Hang Seng Index, which consists of 33 constituents.

COMPUTATION METHODOLOGY
(1) An aggregative of prices times quantities index formula. Maintenance adjustments are made to the divisor for new listings, delistings, mergers, changes to share capital, such as rights offerings, capital restructuring, conversion of loan stock and exercise of warrants. (2) The index is denominated in U.S. dollars. It is calculated once a day and disseminated at approximately 8 AM each New York business day based on the most recent official closing prices of the component stocks on The Stock Exchange of Hong Kong. (3) In calculating the index, one Hong Kong Index unit is assigned a fixed value of one U.S. dollar.

DERIVATIVE INSTRUMENTS
HKO stock index options are traded on the American Stock Exchange (AMEX).

PUBLISHER
The American Stock Exchange (AMEX).

HANG SENG LONDON REFERENCE INDEX

A market value-weighted index that tracks the continuous price only performance of actively traded large capitalization shares that make up the Hang Seng Index and are traded on The Stock Exchange of Hong Kong Limited (SEHK) as well as SEAQ International of the London Stock Exchange. Twenty-eight constituent stocks were included in the index as of March 23, 1995. These shares cover about 75% of the total market value of the Hang Seng Index and about 50% of the market value of the Hong Kong stock market. It was introduced December 1, 1994 and established with a base value of 1000.00 on or about September 1, 1994.

COMPUTATION METHODOLOGY
An aggregative of prices times quantities index formula. Maintenance adjustments are made daily to reflect all types of capitalization changes, new listings and delistings.

PUBLISHER
HSI Services Limited, a subsidiary of Hang Seng Bank.

MERRILL LYNCH (FORMERLY THE SMITH NEW COURT) SMALL COMPANY INDEX OF HONG KONG

A market value-weighted index that tracks the daily price only performance of the bottom 10% of all stocks listed on The Stock Exchange of Hong Kong Limited (SEHK). It tracks 360 stocks. The largest stock had a market capitalization of HK$2.5 billion as of January 1, 1996. The index was introduced in May 1995 and was initiated with a base date of January 1, 1986=1000.00.

COMPUTATION METHODOLOGY
(1) The universe is updated once a year as of January 1st. (2) Illiquid companies, or stocks that have traded less than 5% of the total number of shares outstanding during the previous year, are excluded from consideration.

PUBLISHER
Merrill Lynch.

INDIA

AHMEDABAD STOCK EXCHANGE SENSITIVE INDEX OF EQUITY PRICES

The index tracks the daily price performance of 30 shares selected from the specified and non-specified group. It was initiated with a value of 100.00, using 1987 as the base year.

PUBLISHER
The Stock Exchange of Ahmedabad.

BSE DOLLEX INDEX

A dollar-linked version of the BSE 200 Index in which the formula for calculating the BSE 200 Index is modified to express the index results in U.S. dollar terms by dividing the current rupee market value by the current rupee-dollar conversion rate and the base value by a constant average rupee-dollar conversion rate in the base year.

PUBLISHER
Bombay Stock Exchange (BSE) .

ECONOMIC TIMES SHARE ORDINARY PRICE INDEX

An equally-weighted index that tracks the daily stock price only performance of 72 larger, actively traded, shares listed on the largest of India's securities exchanges. These include shares traded on the Bombay, Calcutta, Madras, Delhi, Ahmedabad, Pune, Bangalore and Kanput stock exchanges. Constituent stocks were selected on the basis of market capitalization and trading activity, with an aim to achieve proper representation among the larger stock exchanges and industry groups. The market capitalization of Indias' stock exchanges and relative size of various industry groups as of December 31, 1985 were used for this purpose. To a lesser extent, the number of listed common stocks on each exchange, the number of shares in each industry group and paid-up capital were also taken into consideration in the selection process. The current index, along with subindices by exchange and 13 industry groups, supersedes two previous versions of the ET Ordinary Share Index. The first was introduced on May 18, 1961 with a base period of 1959-1960. The second, introduced on October 20, 1972, consisted of 61shares with a base period 1969-1970.

COMPUTATION METHODOLOGY
(1) A simple aggregative of actual prices index formula. The index is adjusted to reflect stock dividends, bonus issues, as well as rights issues. (2) The average base year prices have been compiled by taking the simple arithmetic average of the daily quotations of the selected stocks for the year.

PUBLISHER
The Economic Times (ET).

ING BARINGS INDIAN GDR INDEX

A market value-weighted index, based on available capital, that tracks the total return performance of Global Depositary Receipts attributable to 24 Indian companies with an available market capitalization of US$2,240.02 million as of December 31, 1995. The index was established with a base value of 100.00 as of December 30, 1994. It is quoted in U.S. dollars.

PUBLISHER
ING Barings Securities Limited.

KLEINWORT BENSON INDIA GDR INDEX

PUBLISHER
Kleinwort Benson.

OTC EXCHANGE OF INDIA COMPOSITE INDEX

The index tracks the daily price performance of all ordinary shares listed on the OTC Exchange of India.

COMPUTATION METHODOLOGY
An equally-weighted price calculation method, using a base date of July 23, 1993. The base value is adjusted for bonus rights and new listings.

PUBLISHER
The OTC Exchange of India.

PEREGRINE INDIA ADR INDEX

PUBLISHER
Peregrine Brokerage Limited.

SSKI INDEX

The index tracks the daily price performance of the largest 200 companies, selected on the basis of market capitalization, that are listed on the Bombay Stock Exchange (BSE).

PUBLISHER
SSKI Securities Ltd.

INDONESIA

SURABAYA STOCK EXCHANGE COMPOSITE PRICE INDEX

The index tracks the daily price performance of all stocks listed on the Surabaya Stock Exchange (SSE). It was established with a base value of 100.00 as of June 16, 1989.

PUBLISHER
Surabaya Stock Exchange.

JAPAN

AMERICAN STOCK EXCHANGE (AMEX)/JAPAN INDEX (JPN)

A modified price-weighted index that measures the daily price only performance of most actively traded large capitalization stocks traded on the Tokyo Stock Exchange (TSE). The 210 component stocks that make up the index represent a broad cross section of Japanese industries. Developed to closely mirror the Nikkei Stock Average, the index was designed by the American Stock Exchange (AMEX) as a vehicle for stock index options. It was established with a base value of 280.00 as of April 2, 1990.

COMPUTATION METHODOLOGY
(1) Simple aggregative of actual prices index formula. (2) The index is denominated in U.S. dollars. It is calculated once a day and disseminated before the opening of trading in New York based on closing prices of the component stocks on the Tokyo Stock Exchange. (3) In calculating the index, 100 yen is assigned to equal one U.S. dollar. This ensures that the index value will correspond directly to changes in the aggregate yen prices of the component stocks and will not be affected by fluctuating yen/dollar exchange rates.

Derivative Instruments
Japan stock index options are traded on the American Stock Exchange (AMEX).

Publisher
The American Stock Exchange (AMEX).

INTERNATIONAL STOCK EXCHANGE/NIKKEI 50 STOCK INDEX (ISE/NIKKEI 50)

A price-weighted index that tracks the continuous price only performance of 50 Japanese international stocks that are traded on the SEAQ International Stock Exchange in London. Constituent shares are selected using rankings that are based on trading volume, trading value as well as year-end market value, and must satisfy the following criteria: (1) The issue must be a component of the Nikkei 225 Stock Average. (2) It must be internationally traded. (3) It must contribute to the achievement of a 0.9 correlation coefficient maintained between the ISE/Nikkei 50 and the Nikkei 225 Stock Average. The index was initiated on July 4, 1988.

Computation Methodology
(1) Simple aggregative of actual prices index formula. (2) The composition of the index is reviewed annually, on April 1, with more frequent changes due to bankruptcy or delisting.

Publisher
Nihon Keizai Shimbun, Inc.

NIKKEI ALL STOCK INDEX

The Nikkei All Stock Index is a market value-weighted index that tracks the daily total return performance of all shares listed on Japan's eight stock exchanges. Constituents include all shares listed on the First and Second Sections of the Tokyo, Osaka, and Nagoya Stock Exchanges as well as shares listed on the Kyoto, Hiroshima, Fukuoka, Nigata and Sapporo regional stock exchanges, without duplication. Stocks listed on two or more exchanges are prioritized as to the Tokyo Stock Exchange, Osaka Stock Exchange and Nagoya Stock Exchange. The Nikkei All Stock Index was introduced on September 1, 1991. It was established with a base value of 100.00 as of January 4, 1980.

Computation Methodology
(1) An aggregative of prices times quantities index formula. (2) For stocks listed on two or more exchanges, the Tokyo Stock Exchange, followed by the Osaka Stock Exchange and Nagoya Stock Exchange have pricing priority in the calculation of market value. Otherwise, regional market prices prevail.

Publisher
Nihon Keizai Shimbun, Inc.

NIKKEI OTC STOCK AVERAGE

A price-weighted benchmark that tracks the twice-daily price only performance of all shares traded on the Japanese Over-The-Counter (OTC) market, except for the Bank of Japan. Constituent shares include all companies traded on the OTC market for which prices are available. The index consisted of 580 stocks as of January 31, 1995 with a market value of US$89,300 million. It was introduced on April 1, 1985 with a base date of November 11, 1983.

COMPUTATION METHODOLOGY

(1) Simple aggregative of actual prices index formula. (2) Prices are the average of the day's lowest and highest traded price. (3) New stocks are added to the index as prices become available.

PUBLISHER

Nihon Keizai Shimbun, Inc.

TOKYO STOCK EXCHANGE ARITHMETIC STOCK PRICE INDEX

An arithmetic index that tracks the performance of all domestic common stocks listed on the First Section of the Tokyo Stock Exchange (TSE)–the same stocks that make up the Tokyo Stock Exchange Price Index (TOPIX) .

PUBLISHER

The Tokyo Stock Exchange (TSE).

OSAKA 250 ADJUSTED STOCK PRICE AVERAGE

A price-weighted index that tracks the price only performance of 250 leading stocks listed on the First Section of the Osaka Securities Exchange (OSE), based on annual trading volume and pricing frequency. Deleted issues, due to bankruptcy, merger, delisting from the First Section due to insolvency or other reasons and reassignments to the Second Section, are replaced with high trading volume and frequently priced constituents that maintain the industrial weighting scheme of the Osaka market. The index was established as of May 16, 1949 with a base value of 1.00. At the same time, the Osaka Securities Exchange introduced the 250 Simple Arithmetic Stock Average (Simple Average). Also computed using an arithmetic average formula, this index, however, was not adjusted to reflect stock substitutions, stock splits and other capital changes.

COMPUTATION METHODOLOGY

A simple aggregative of actual prices index formula.

PUBLISHER

Osaka Securities Exchange (OSE).

OSAKA 40 ADJUSTED STOCK PRICE AVERAGE

A price-weighted index that tracks the price only performance of 40 leading stocks listed on the Second Section of the Osaka Securities Exchange (OSE), based on annual trading volume and pricing frequency. Deleted issues, due to bankruptcy, merger, delisting from the Second Section due to insolvency or other reasons and reassignments to the Second Section, are replaced with high trading volume and frequently priced constituents that maintain the industrial weighting scheme of the Osaka market. The index was initiated on October 2, 1961 at a value of 235.40.

COMPUTATION METHODOLOGY

A simple aggregative of actual prices index formula.

PUBLISHER

Osaka Securities Exchange (OSE).

RUSSELL/NRI JAPANESE TOTAL MARKET INDEX

An adjusted market value-weighted index that tracks the daily price only and total return performance of the top 98% of stocks, or about 1,800 issues on the basis of adjusted market capitalization as of the beginning of January 1995, listed on the Tokyo Stock Exchange First Section, stocks listed on all other Japanese exchanges as well as OTC stocks. The index, along with a series of style indices, was unveiled in December 1995 and released in early 1996. Historical data is expected to be available to 1980.

COMPUTATION METHODOLOGY
(1) An aggregative of prices times quantities index formula. Maintenance adjustments are made for capitalization changes, new listings and delistings. (2) Market capitalization is adjusted for major shareholders. (3) The index is rebalanced once a year.

PUBLISHER
Frank Russell Co./Nomura Research Institute.

RUSSELL/NRI JAPANESE EQUITY STYLE INDEX SERIES

An adjusted market value-weighted index that tracks the daily price only and total return performance of the combined market, top capitalization stocks, large capitalization stocks, mid capitalization stocks and small capitalization stocks listed on the Tokyo Stock Exchange First Section, stocks listed on all other Japanese exchanges as well as OTC stocks, that are further delineated by growth and value orientation on the basis of price-to-book ratio above or below the universe average. The segment definitions are, as follows: (1) Top capitalization stocks cover the top 50% of the total market index in terms of market capitalization. (2) Large capitalization stocks cover the top 85% of the total market index in terms of market capitalization. (3) Mid capitalization stocks includes all the stocks in the large capitalization index minus the issues that make up the top capitalization index. (4) Small capitalization stocks cover the bottom 15% of the total market index in terms of market capitalization.

The index, along with a series of style indices, was unveiled in December 1995 and released in early 1996. Historical data is expected to be available to 1980.

COMPUTATION METHODOLOGY
(1) An aggregative of prices times quantities index formula. Maintenance adjustments are made for capitalization changes, new listings and delistings. (2) Market capitalization is adjusted for major shareholders. (3) The index is rebalanced once a year.

PUBLISHER
Frank Russell Co./Nomura Research Institute.

KOREA

ADJUSTED STOCK PRICE AVERAGE

A price-weighted index that tracks the continuous price only performance of all companies listed on the Korea Stock Exchange (KSE), including First and Second Sections. The index was introduced in 1992.

COMPUTATION METHODOLOGY
A simple aggregative of actual prices index formula. Adjustments are made over the years to reflect stock splits and other capital changes.

PUBLISHER
Korea Stock Exchange (KSE).

MANUFACTURING INDUSTRY INDEX

A market value-weighted index that tracks the continuous price only performance of all manufacturing companies listed on the Korea Stock Exchange (KSE), including First and Second Sections. The index was introduced in 1988.

COMPUTATION METHODOLOGY
An aggregative of prices times quantities index formula. Modifications are made for capitalization changes, new listings, delistings or other non-price related factors.

PUBLISHER
Korea Stock Exchange (KSE).

MALAYSIA
THE NEW STRAITS TIMES INDUSTRIAL INDEX

A simple average of daily closing prices of component stocks listed on the Kuala Lumpur Stock Exchange.

PUBLISHER
The New Straits Times.

NEPAL
NEPAL STOCK EXCHANGE INDEX (NEPSE)

A market value-weighted index that tracks the daily price only performance of equity shares and preference shares listed on the Nepal Stock Exchange (NEPSE). The index accompanied the opening of the NEPSE trading floor on January 13, 1994, and was established with a base date of January 13,1994 and an initial value of 100.00.

COMPUTATION METHODOLOGY
An aggregative of prices times quantities index formula. Maintenance adjustments are made for capitalization changes, new listings and delistings.

PUBLISHER
Nepal Stock Exchange Limited (NEPSE).

MAMPS INDEX

An index that tracks a selected number of companies listed on the Nepal Stock Exchange.

PUBLISHER
MAMPS Group.

GFIL 30 INDEX

The index, introduced on May 16, 1995, tracks a selected number of companies that are listed on the Nepal Stock Exchange.

PUBLISHER
Goodwill Finance and Investment Company.

NEW ZEALAND

THE NEW ZEALAND ALL ORDINARIES INDEX

A market value-weighted index that tracks the continuous stock price (Capital Index) and total return (Gross Index) performance of all domestic New Zealand Stock Exchange (NZSE) listed and quoted ordinary shares and those securities which can be converted into ordinary shares, excepting for listed power companies.

COMPUTATION METHODOLOGY

(1) An aggregative of prices times quantities index formula. Maintenance adjustments are made daily to eliminate the effect of all types of capitalization changes, such as share issuances, share repurchases, special cash dividends, rights offerings and spin-offs, new listings and delistings. Adjustments are made after the close of trading and after the calculation of the closing index value. (2) The total rate of return is calculated using gross dividends that are reinvested as of the ex-dividend date. (3) Market capitalization is determined on the basis of shares outstanding. Equity securities other than ordinary shares that are included in the index, in their own right, are included on the basis of their ordinary share equivalent and thereby increasing the weighting of the ordinary shares in the index. In the case of a convertible or exchangeable security, the equivalent number will be the maximum number of ordinary shares that would be issued on its conversion exchange. In the cases of warrants and partly-paid shares, ordinary share equivalents will be determined by the NZSE at each index revision. Revisions, if any, are communicated to the market at least two weeks before they take effect. (4) New listings are generally eligible for inclusion in the index immediately upon listing.

PUBLISHER
The New Zealand Stock Exchange (NZSE).

THE NEW ZEALAND STOCK EXCHANGE TOP 10 INDEX

A market value-weighted index that tracks the continuous stock price and total return performance of the 10 most actively traded and largest capitalization stocks listed on the New Zealand Stock Exchange (NZSE). The top 10 securities are selected on the basis of market capitalization within the top 20 highest trading domestic or foreign based companies whose shares trade on the NZSE. Constituents stocks are reviewed monthly, and changes, if any, are implemented on the last Friday of each month. If a company is ranked 11th or below on the basis of trading volume and then rises above the 8th position, it will be selected for inclusion in the index while at the same time, the bottom company is removed. If a constituent company drops in rank to below 15th, it is removed from the index. The index was established with a base value of 1,000.00 as of July 1, 1988.

COMPUTATION METHODOLOGY

(1) An aggregative of prices times quantities index formula. Maintenance adjustments are made daily to eliminate the effect of all types of capitalization changes, such as share issuances, share repurchases, special cash dividends, rights offerings and spin-offs, new listings and delistings. Adjustments are made after the close of trading and after the calculation of the closing index value. (2) The total rate of return is calculated using gross dividends that are reinvested as of the ex-dividend date. (3) Market capitalization is determined on the basis of shares outstanding.

DERIVATIVE INSTRUMENTS
Top 10 stock index futures and options are traded on the New Zealand Futures and Options Exchange (NZFOE), a subsidiary of the Sydney Futures Exchange.

PUBLISHER
The New Zealand Stock Exchange (NZSE).

PAKISTAN

KARACHI STOCK EXCHANGE–ALL SHARE INDEX

A market value-weighted index that tracks the stock price performance of all shares listed on the Karachi Stock Exchange.

PUBLISHER
Karachi Stock Exchange.

SINGAPORE

DBS 50 INDEX

A market value-weighted index that tracks the daily price performance of 50 larger, more actively traded stocks that are listed on the Stock Exchange of Singapore (SES). Constituent shares were selected from five different sectors, including commercial, bank and finance, hotels, commercial properties and residential property sectors. Investment companies are excluded from the index while subsidiaries of listed companies have been minimized. The index was established with a base value of 100.00 as of January 2, 1975.

COMPUTATION METHODOLOGY
An aggregative of prices times quantities index formula. Maintenance adjustments to the divisor are made for capitalization changes, new listings and delistings. The base value represents the daily aggregate market value of the index constituents during calendar year 1975.

PUBLISHER
DBS Investment Research.

OVERSEA CHINESE BANKING CORPORATION LIMITED (OCBC) COMPOSITE INDEX

A market value-weighted index that tracks the daily price performance of fifty-five Singapore and Malaysian stocks that are traded on the stock exchanges of both Singapore and Malaysia. These include 27 Singapore stocks and 28 Malaysian stocks that are selected on the basis of market capitalization and liquidity. Subsidiaries of listed companies, however, are excluded from the index. The OCBC Composite Index was constructed in 1972 and published in 1973. It was the first market value-weighted index to monitor the share price movements of stocks traded on the Singapore and Malaysian stock markets. At that time, most Singapore and Malaysian companies were listed on the stock exchanges of both countries. Initially comprised of 40 companies, the index was structured to capture at least 60% of the total market capitalization of the stock market. In addition, the sectoral breakdown of the market capitalization of the index closely corresponds to that of the market as a whole. In April 1982, the number of constituent companies was expanded from 40 to the present number. The index was established with a base value of 98.47 as of January 1, 1970.

COMPUTATION METHODOLOGY

An aggregative of prices times quantities index formula. Maintenance adjustments are made for capitalization changes due to new listings, delistings, mergers, changes to share capital, such as rights offerings, capital restructuring, conversion of loan stock and exercise of warrants.

PUBLISHER

The Oversea-Chinese Banking Corporation Limited/OCBC Investment Research Limited.

OVERSEA CHINESE BANKING CORPORATION LIMITED (OCBC) OTC INDEX

A market value-weighted index that tracks the daily price performance of 30 over-the-counter Malaysian, Hong Kong and Philippine stocks traded on the Central Limit Order Book (CLOB) of the Stock Exchange of Singapore (SES). The 30 stocks are selected on the basis of market capitalization and liquidity. Subsidiaries of listed companies, however, are excluded from the index. The index was launched in 1990 following the separation of the Stock Exchange of Singapore and the Kuala Lumpur Stock Exchange (KLSE) pursuant to which Malaysian companies were delisted from SES and Singapore companies were delisted from KLSE as of January 1, 1990. The SES established an over-the-counter market for Malaysian, Hong Kong and Philippine stocks which are traded on the Central Limit Order Book (CLOB) of the SES. The index was established with a base value of 1000.00 as of January 2, 1990.

COMPUTATION METHODOLOGY

An aggregative of prices times quantities index formula. Maintenance adjustments are made for capitalization changes due to new listings, delistings, mergers, changes to share capital, such as rights offerings, capital restructuring, conversion of loan stock and exercise of warrants.

PUBLISHER

The Oversea-Chinese Banking Corporation Limited/OCBC Investment Research Limited.

THE STRAITS TIMES INDEX

An equal-weighted index that tracks the daily price performance of 30 stocks traded on the Stock Exchange of Singapore (SES).

PUBLISHER

The Straits Times.

UNITED OVERSEAS BANK (UOB) BLUE CHIP INDEX

An equally-weighted, geometrically averaged, measure of the daily price change of 30 large capitalization, actively traded stocks listed on the Singapore Stock Exchange (SES). Component stocks are selected from all sectors of the SES, including industrials, finance, hotels and property sectors. Formerly the UOB Composite Index which covered 100 Singapore and Malaysian stocks since 1981, the Blue Chip Index was introduced on December 29, 1989. Its launch was timed to coincide with the delisting of Malaysian stocks from the SES as of year-end 1989. The index was established with a base value of 100.00 as of January 2, 1975.

COMPUTATION METHODOLOGY

A geometric mean index formula. Adjustments are made to reflect delistings as well as other significant changes in market composition.

PUBLISHER
United Overseas Bank.

UNITED OVERSEAS BANK (UOB) OTC INDEX

An equally-weighted, geometrically averaged, measure of the daily price change of 30 larger capitalization, actively traded Malaysian, Hong Kong and Philippine stocks listed on the Central Limit Order Book (CLOB) of the Stock Exchange of Singapore (SES). The OTC Index was launched on January 4, 1990, following the separation of the Stock Exchange of Singapore and the Kuala Lumpur Stock Exchange (KLSE) pursuant to which Malaysian companies were delisted from SES and Singapore companies were delisted from KLSE as of January 1, 1990, to monitor stocks on the Singapore over-the-counter market. The OTC market was established by the SES for Malaysian, Hong Kong and Philippine stocks which are traded on the Central Limit Order Book (CLOB) of the SES. The index was established with a base value of 1000.00 as of January 2, 1990.

COMPUTATION METHODOLOGY
A geometric mean index formula is used to compute the index. The index is adjusted to reflect delistings as well as other significant changes in market composition.

PUBLISHER
United Overseas Bank.

SRI LANKA

THE CSE SENSITIVE INDEX

A market value-weighted index that tracks the daily price only performance of the largest and most actively traded equity shares listed on the Colombo Stock Exchange (CSE) in Sri Lanka. Constituent shares are selected on the basis of company size, trading volume and earnings per share during the past three years, current market price in relation to the price at the time of issuance and the company's dividend policy. The CSE Sensitive Index was introduced in March 1987 and established with a base value of 100.00 as of December 31, 1984.

COMPUTATION METHODOLOGY
(1) An aggregative of prices times quantities index formula. Maintenance adjustments are made for capitalization changes, new listings and delistings. The market capitalization for the divisor was computed on the basis of the average market capitalization for the entire calendar year 1985, based on listed companies as of January 2, 1985. (2) Last transaction prices on the CSE are used, regardless of when the share was traded.

PUBLISHER
Sri Lanka Stock Exchange.

TAIWAN

OTC INDEX

A market value-weighted index that tracks the price only performance of OTC listed stocks. Beneficiary certificates, convertible bonds and equity issues with volatile performance are excluded from the index. The index was established with a base date of October 30, 1995 with an initial value of 100.00.

Computation Methodology

An aggregative of prices times quantities index formula. Maintenance adjustments to the divisor are made on the ex-date for capitalization changes, new listings and delistings.

Publisher

R.O.C. Over-the-Counter Securities Exchange.

Taiwan Industrial Stock Price Average

A price-weighted index that tracks the continuous price only performance of 20 common stocks listed on the Taiwan Stock Exchange (TSE). Constituent shares are selected from the universe of Category A, Category B and Category C common stocks (TSE classifications made according to levels of capital, profitability, capital structure and distribution of shares) that are tracked in the Taiwan Stock Exchange Weighted Stock Index, excluding stocks from the 15 transportation, tourism, finance/insurance and department/trade industries. The 20 stocks are selected to represent their respective industry by taking into account each company's operating income, trading volume, trading value and turnover ratio. The index was established with a base value of 100.00 as of December 31, 1988.

Computation Methodology

A simple aggregative of actual prices index formula. Adjustments are made over the years to reflect stock splits and other capital changes.

Publisher

Taiwan Stock Exchange Corporation.

THAILAND

Book Club Index

A price-weighted index that tracks the price only performance of all authorized shares listed on the Stock Exchange of Thailand (SET). The index was established with a base value of 100.00 as of April 30, 1975, coinciding with the commencement of operations on the SET.

Computation Methodology

An aggregative of prices times quantities index formula. Adjustments are made for capitalization changes, new listings and delistings. Base market value adjustments for capital changes do not take market price into consideration.

Publisher

The Book Club Finance & Securities Co. Ltd.

SET 50 Index

A market value-weighted index that tracks the daily stock price performance of 50 liquid, large capitalization stocks, traded on the Stock Exchange of Thailand (SET). Constituent shares are selected from a universe consisting of companies whose shares rank within the top 150 by daily market capitalization over the previous 12 months. They must also rank in the top 150 on the basis of average daily turnover during the previous 12-month period, and selected securities must also experience monthly turnover that is higher than 50% of the average monthly turnover in the same month for at least nine out of 12 months or 75% of the trading period.

The index, which is intended to serve as an underlying vehicle for derivative products, is still undergoing testing and has not been formally introduced. It is expected to be launched in 1996, with stock index futures and options to follow.

COMPUTATION METHODOLOGY
(1) An aggregative of prices times quantities index formula. Maintenance adjustments to the divisor are made daily for capitalization changes, new listings and delistings. (2) Constituents will be reviewed every six months, and index revisions will be made in January and June of each year.

DERIVATIVE INSTRUMENTS
SET 50 Index futures and options expected in the future.

PUBLISHER
Stock Exchange of Thailand (SET).

THAI INVESTMENT AND SECURITIES COMPANY LTD. (TISCO) PRICE INDEX

A price-weighted stock price index that tracks the daily price only performance of all securities listed on the Stock Exchange of Thailand (SET).

PUBLISHER
Thai Investment and Securities Company Ltd.

REGIONAL

NOMURA RESEARCH INSTITUTE (NRI) ASIA/PACIFIC-200 INDEX

A market value-weighted index that tracks the daily stock price performance of liquid, large capitalization stocks, available to foreign institutional investors in 10 Asia/Pacific markets. These markets include Indonesia, Malaysia, Philippines, Singapore, Thailand, Hong Kong, Korea, Taiwan, Australia and New Zealand. The index is composed of 200 stocks that are selected on the basis of the following guidelines: (1) Large capitalization stocks with high liquidity which are collectively representative of local markets and are not subject to foreign ownership restrictions. (2) NRI's analytical views with regard to the stability and credibility of the underlying companies. (3) The sector capitalization of the underlying countries is incorporated so as to accurately reflect the special characteristics of each market.

The index, which was established with a base value of 100.00 as of December 31, 1989, includes various subindices by region, country, currency, and economic sectors.

COMPUTATION METHODOLOGY
(1) An aggregative of prices times quantities index formula. Maintenance adjustments are made periodically for capitalization changes, new listings and delistings. Adjustments are usually implemented on ex-date, the effective date of the capital action, or the date on which the relevant information becomes available and is confirmed. (2) Market capitalization is calculated on the basis of each company's shares which are not subject to foreign ownership restrictions. Such restrictions apply in Malaysia, Philippines, Singapore, Thailand, Korea and Taiwan. (3) Constituents are reviewed on a quarterly basis for compliance with guidelines, and proposed changes to the index are announced at least two weeks in advance of the effective date. Index modifications may be made more frequently in the event of newly listed shares with large capitalizations or in cases where an issue drastically fails to meet the index selection guidelines. (4) Newly listed issues are monitored for a period of at least two months before being considered eligible for inclusion in the index.

PUBLISHER
Nomura International plc/Nomura Research Institute, Ltd.

PEREGRINE

ASIA SMALL CAP INDEX

PEREGRINE ASIA INDEX (PAI) (COMBINED + DOMESTIC INVESTORS)

A market value-weighted index that tracks the stock price performance of 292 Asia-Pacific companies available to foreign investors and domestic investors which are listed in nine markets, with a market capitalization of US$428,300 million as of December 31, 1995. The index is intended to be representative of foreign institutional interest in the following nine markets: Hong Kong, India, Indonesia, Korea, Singapore, Malaysia, Thailand, Philippines, and Taiwan. Originally known as the Peregrine 100 Index, the PAI was substantially revised to include new markets and a substantial number of new companies so as to reflect the rapid changes resulting from privatizations and other IPO issues. The index was established as of May 18,1990 at a base value of 100.00. Constituent stocks are selected on the basis of the following criteria: (1) Market capitalization and turnover are utilized to make the initial selections which are ultimately designed to be representative of each market. (2) Subsidiaries of other index constituents are eligible for inclusion in the index. (3) New issues with a market capitalization in excess of 1% of the local market's capitalization may be included, if approved, from the second day of trading.

COMPUTATION METHODOLOGY

(1) An aggregative of prices times quantities index formula (Laspeyres index formula). Maintenance adjustments to the divisor are made daily for capitalization changes, new listings and delistings. (2) Market capitalization is determined on the basis of foreign ownership limits or by the number of designated foreign shares. (3) Changes in foreign ownership restrictions are reflected immediately following implementation or as soon as sufficient data is made available to adjust for the changes in ownership restrictions. (4) Constituent stocks are reviewed and revised on a quarterly basis.

PUBLISHER
Peregrine Brokerage Limited.

TRANS TASMAN 100 INDEX

A market value-weighted index that tracks the continuous stock price performance (capital) and daily total return performance (gross) of the top 100 companies of the combined Australian Stock Exchange and New Zealand Stock Exchange. These companies are selected on the basis of market capitalization and liquidity, from a universe representing the top 150 companies with ordinary shares listed on both markets. The index was introduced in January 1996, having been established with a base value of 1000.00 as of December 31, 1990.

COMPUTATION METHODOLOGY

(1) An aggregative of prices times quantities index formula. Maintenance adjustments to the divisor are made daily for capitalization changes, new listings and delistings. (2) The index is calculated in Australian dollars. The Australian/New Zealand exchange rate, taken at approximately 3:30 PM local time, is applied to the calculation of the index.

PUBLISHER
Australian Stock Exchange Ltd./ and the New Zealand Stock Exchange.

STOCKS—EUROPE

AUSTRIA

ATX 50 INDEX

A market value-weighted index that tracks the price only performance of the 50 largest, most liquid, actively traded, domestic stocks on the Vienna Stock Exchange (VSE). Constituent shares include continuously traded stocks on the so called "Fließhandel," or main market. The index was introduced in November 1995.

PUBLISHER
Austrian Futures & Options Exchange (OTOB).

ATX MIDCAP INDEX

A market value-weighted index that tracks the price only performance of the most liquid, actively traded, middle capitalization domestic stocks on the Vienna Stock Exchange (VSE). Constituent shares include continuously traded stocks on the so called "Fließ-handel," or main market. The index was introduced in November 1995.

PUBLISHER
Austrian Futures & Options Exchange (OTOB).

CREDITANSTALT SHARE INDEX (CA SHARE INDEX)

A share capital-weighted price only index, often referred to as the Credit Aktien Index, that tracks the performance of 32 companies whose shares are traded on the Vienna Stock Exchange (VSE). Calculated daily on the basis of the official closing prices on the VSE, this is the oldest continuously calculated stock index in Austria. The index was reconstituted at the end of 1984 with a base value of 100.00 as of that date. When combined with its predecessor index, the old CA Index, daily values are available to January 2, 1962. The constitution of the index was last modified in July 1989. At that time, nine companies were added, including Vebund A shares with a weighting of one half its share capital value, so as not to dominate the index by its performance results.

COMPUTATION METHODOLOGY
(1) An aggregative of prices times quantities index formula. (2) The permanent index weighting is based on issued share capital as of the end of 1984.

PUBLISHER
The Vienna Stock Exchange (VSE).

PARTICIPATION CERTIFICATE INDEX

An index that tracks the price only performance of participation certificates (Partizipationsscheine) listed on the Vienna Stock Exchange (VSE). Participation certificates have been issued by Austrian banks and insurance companies since 1986. These trade in the same manner as common stock, but entitle the holder to participate in dividend distributions, but not to vote. The index was established with a base value of 100.00 as of December 31, 1987.

PUBLISHER
The Vienna Stock Exchange (VSE).

BELGIUM
BEL 20 RETURN INDEX PRIVATE AND INSTITUTIONAL

These are market value-weighted indices, identical to the BEL 20 Index, that track the continuous price only performance of 20 large, actively traded Belgian companies listed on the liquid, institutionally oriented, Forward Market segment of the Brussels Stock Exchange (BSE), except that the BEL 20 Return Private Index is a total return index that is calculated based on net dividends and the BEL 20 Return Institutional Index is a total return index that is calculated based on gross dividends. Both indices are computed once a day on the basis of closing prices on the Forward Market. The indices were established with a base value of 1000.00 as of January 1, 1991.

COMPUTATION METHODOLOGY
(1) An aggregative of prices times quantities index formula. The index is adjusted periodically to eliminate the effect of all types of capitalization and constituent changes. (2) Unless circumstances dictate otherwise, the composition of the index is updated once a year, as may be required, on the 3rd Friday of the month of December. (3) Component stocks may not exceed 10% of the global value of the index during a continuous six-month period, otherwise, their weighting factor is limited to 10%. (4) Capital events that affect the value of the index by more than 1% are reflected after the close of trading on the Forward Market.

DERIVATIVE INSTRUMENTS
Bel 20 stock index futures and options trade on the Belgian Futures and Options Exchange.

PUBLISHER
Brussels Stock Exchange (BSE).

B-GOLD INDEX

A market value-weighted index that tracks the price only performance of South African gold mining companies whose shares are listed on the Brussels Stock Exchange (BSE). The index consists of five issues which, on a combined basis, represent no less than 65% of the capitalization of the Johannesburg Gold Mining Index. Launched at the end of 1994, the index is designed to enable investors interested in South African gold mining shares to trade in a preestablished portfolio of securities selected on the basis of their market value. Moreover, plans call for the introduction of derivative instruments to be traded on the Belgian Futures and Options Exchange (BELFOX). The index was established with a value of 1000.00 as of December 30, 1993.

DERIVATIVE INSTRUMENTS
None at this time; planned for introduction in the future.

PUBLISHER
Brussels Stock Exchange (BSE).

BELGIAN FOREIGN FORWARD MARKET (CATS) RETURN INDEX

A market value-weighted price only index that tracks the continuous stock performance of the large, actively traded and highly liquid foreign stocks traded largely by institutional investors on the Forward Market of the Brussels Stock Exchange (BSE). The index was established with a base value of 1000.00 as of January 1, 1985.

COMPUTATION METHODOLOGY
An aggregative of prices times quantities (Paasche) index formula.

PUBLISHER
Brussels Stock Exchange (BSE).

CYPRUS

CYPRUS INVESTMENT AND SECURITIES CORP. (CISCO) LTD ALL-SHARE INDEX

A market value-weighted index that tracks the daily price only performance of all ordinary shares, including partly paid shares, listed on the Cyprus OTC list. The index consists of 41 issues with a market capitalization of US$2,275.45 million as of December 31, 1995. Partly paid shares are included in the index, however, preference shares and warrants are not eligible. The index was established in 1984, using a base value of 100.00 as of December 31, 1983, with the participation of the International Finance Corp in an effort to promote the development of the local capital market. At the time of its introduction, 26 companies were listed on the OTC market. Due to low volume and price quotations that were updated weekly, the index was computed on a monthly basis since its inception to August 1989. From September 15, 1989 to December 2, 1993, the index was computed on a weekly basis and daily thereafter.

COMPUTATION METHODOLOGY
(1) An aggregative of prices times quantities index formula. The index is adjusted periodically to eliminate the effect of all types of capitalization and constituent changes. (2) Market capitalization is determined on the basis of total capitalization, updated as information becomes available. (3) Closing mid-market prices are used. These represent the median between buying and selling as quoted by the Cyprus Chamber of Commerce and Industry after the closing of the broker's daily meetings.

PUBLISHER
Cyprus Investment and Securities Corp. Ltd. (CISCO).

HELLENIC BANK INVESTMENTS INDEX (HBI)

A market value-weighted index that tracks the weekly price only and total return performance (with gross dividends reinvested) of all stocks listed on the Cyprus Stock Exchange (CSE). The index was established with a base value of 100.00 as of December 31, 1983. It was calculated on a monthly basis to December 1990. Initially calculated along with three sectoral subindices, the index was expanded to include six sectoral subindices: These are banking, insurance, finance and investment, manufacturing, as well as tourism, trade property and other.

COMPUTATION METHODOLOGY
(1) An aggregative of prices times quantities index formula. Maintenance adjustments to the divisor are made daily for capitalization changes, new listings and delistings. Such adjustments take place after trading hours. (2) Market capitalization is determined on the basis of fully paid shares and partly-paid shares.

PUBLISHER
Hellenic Bank Limited.

CYPRUS STOCK EXCHANGE INSTITUTION INDEX

A comprehensive market value-weighted index that tracks the daily price only performance of all ordinary shares, including partly paid shares, listed on the Cyprus OTC list. The index consists of 38 issues (as of June 1995).

PUBLISHER
Cyprus Stock Exchange (CSE).

CZECH REPUBLIC
THE CZECH NATIONAL BANK CNB-120 INDEX

A market value-weighted index that tracks the price only performance of 120 stocks listed on the Prague Stock Exchange. It was rebased to 1000.00 as of March 1, 1995, following the second tranche of privatization in the Czech Republic, but index values were not recalculated to its inception. Eight sectoral indices are also published: Food, construction, machinery, energy, service/retail, finance, banking and investment funds.

PUBLISHER
Czech National Bank.

HN-WOOD INDEX

A market value-weighted index that tracks the stock price performance of the 60 largest stocks, by market capitalization, listed on the Prague Stock Exchange. The index, which was established with a base value of 1000.00 as of September 7, 1993, had been calculated on a weekly basis to September 10, 1994. Due to market closure, index values are not available for the period December 19, 1994 to January 9, 1995.

COMPUTATION METHODOLOGY
An aggregative of prices times quantities index formula. Maintenance adjustments are made for capitalization changes, new listings and delistings.

PUBLISHER
Wood & Company in conjunction with Hospodarsky Noviny.

FINLAND

HEX-20 INDEX

A market value-weighted subindex of the HEX All-Share Index that tracks the continuous price only and total return performance of 20 stocks with the highest turnover on Finland's Helsinki Stock Exchange. Constituents are updated twice a year, in January and July, based on turnover during the preceding 12 months as calculated in Finnish Markka. Only one share series of a company is included in the index. Like the HEX All-Share Index, the HEX-20 Index was introduced on June 1, 1990, with price only index values that have been recalculated on a daily basis to January 1, 1987. The base year is December 28, 1990=1000.00.

COMPUTATION METHODOLOGY
(1) An aggregative of prices times quantities index formula. Maintenance adjustments are made for capitalization changes, new listings and delistings. New issues are generally added to the index on

the second day of trading. (2) Share prices on the Helsinki Stock Exchange at the time of calculation are used. In the absence of a stock price, the most recently available quotation is used for index computation purposes. (3) Dividends are reinvested as of the ex-dividend date.

PUBLISHER
Helsinki Stock Exchange (HSE).

PORTFOLIO HEX INDEX

A restricted market value-weighted index that tracks the hourly price only performance (a total return index is planned for introduction at a future date) of all equities traded on the Helsinki Stock Exchange. The index was introduced on December 1, 1995, with price only index values that have been recalculated on a daily basis to the beginning of 1991. The base year is December 28, 1990=1000.00.

COMPUTATION METHODOLOGY
(1) An aggregative of prices times quantities index formula. Maintenance adjustments are made to the divisor for capitalization changes, new listings and delistings. (2) A market capitalization limit of 10% per company is applicable. In the event that a company's weight exceeds 10%, the value in excess of 10% is distributed among the other listed companies in proportion to the share of the total market value. (3) New issues are generally added to the index on the second day of trading. (4) Share prices on the Helsinki Stock Exchange at the time of calculation are used. In the absence of a stock price, the most recently available quotation is used for index computation purposes.

PUBLISHER
Helsinki Stock Exchange (HSE).

THE KOP INDEX

A weighted index that tracks the total return performance of all stocks listed on the Helsinki Stock Exchange. Unlike the capitalization weighted HEX Index, the KOP Index weights constituent shares on the basis of nominal assets of share series and uses the arithmetic mean of the highest and lowest trading prices. The index was initiated with a base value of 100.00 on or about 1970.

PUBLISHER
Kansallis-Osake-Pankki.

THE UNITAS INDEX

An index that tracks the total return performance of all stocks listed on the Helsinki Stock Exchange. Shares are weighted on the basis of the geometrical means of the shares in total stock exchange turnover and market values. It was initiated with a base value of 100.00 on or about 1975.

PUBLISHER
Bank of Finland.

GERMANY

DAX 100 SUBINDICES

Ten market value-weighted subindices that track the continuous price and total return performance of the 100 most actively traded, large market capitalization German companies traded on the Frankfurt Stock Exchange that make up the DAX 100 Index. Launched on May 15, 1996, these sector indices are intended to serve as underlying vehicles for derivative products. They include: automobiles and transportation, banking, construction, chemicals and pharmaceuticals, steel, electricity, retailers, machinery companies, insurance and utilities.

PUBLISHER
Deutsche Borse AG.

FRANKFURT STOCK EXCHANGE INDEX

An index that tracks the performance of all stocks listed for trading on the Frankfurt Stock Exchange. Sixteen industrial subindices are also published.

PUBLISHER
Frankfurt Stock Exchange.

FRANKFURTER ALLGEMEINEN ZEITUNG (FAZ) AKTIENINDEX

A market value-weighted index that tracks the price only performance of 100 large capitalization, actively traded, shares listed on the official segment of the Frankfurt Stock Exchange. Component shares are selected to incorporate a sufficiently large segment of the equity market with an emphasis on large capitalization, high turnover stocks that are continuously quoted on the Frankfurt Stock Exchange. Twelve industry subindices are also published. These include: Banks and other finance, insurance companies, electric industry, construction, large chemical plants, other chemical plants, utilities, automobile and parts producers, machinery, raw materials, and consumer goods. The index was established with a base value of 100.00 as of December 31, 1961. The make up of the index is modified periodically, as was the case at the end of 1993, at which time 22 new companies were added. In addition, the industrial classification scheme was changed. Previously, changes in the composition of the index were made in 1988-1989, 1982 and 1970.

COMPUTATION METHODOLOGY
(1) An aggregative of prices times quantities index formula. Maintenance adjustments are made daily for all types of capitalization changes, new listings and delistings. (2) Market capitalization is calculated on the basis of shares registered for trading on the Frankfurt Stock Exchange.

PUBLISHER
Frankfurter Allgemeine Zeitung.

DRESDNER INTERNATIONAL RESEARCH INSTITUTE SMALL CAP DEUTCSCHLAND INDEX

An index that tracks the price performance of a universe of small- and medium-sized German companies.

PUBLISHER
Dresdner International Research Institute.

IRELAND

DAVY IRISH MARKET INDICES

A market value-weighted index that tracks the price only performance of all but the smallest stocks listed on the Irish Stock Exchange. Launched with a base value of 100.00 as of December 31, 1976, the index is calculated once a day along with eight subindices which include the Top Ten Companies Index, Banks Index, Other Financials Index, Total Financials Index, Smaller Capitalization Index, Total Industrials Index, and Food Sector Index. A companion Resource Sector Index is also available.

PUBLISHER
Davy Stockbrokers.

ITALY

BCI 30 INDEX

A market value-weighted index that tracks the continuous stock price only performance of 30 actively traded large capitalization shares traded on the Milan Stock Exchange of Italy and is identical to the MIB 30 Index. The index, which is still calculated by Banca Commerciale Italiana, was modified as of October 17, 1994 so as to directly correspond to the MIB 30 Index. Thus, the two indices are now identical. Its base of 100.00, also established as of December 31, 1992, has been maintained to provide continuity to current users of the index. Thus, the index value is derived by dividing the MIB 30 Index value by 100.

COMPUTATION METHODOLOGY
(1) An aggregative of prices times quantities index formula. Maintenance adjustments are made daily for all types of capitalization changes, new listings and delistings. (2) The index is normally revised once a year. More frequent revisions may be made in cases of a suspension or other events that have a series affect on the liquidity of a constituent share.

DERIVATIVE INSTRUMENTS
MIB 30 stock index options are traded on the IDEM, the Italian Derivatives Market.

PUBLISHER
Banca Commerciale Italiana (BCI).

IMR INDEX-CURRENT

An index that tracks the performance of all shares traded on the Mercato Ristretto, using official prices. The index was established as of January 3, 1979 with a base value of 1.000.

PUBLISHER
Italian Stock Exchange Council.

MILAN INDICE DI BORSA (MIB) INDEX-CURRENT

A market value-weighted historical index that tracks the daily stock price only performance of all ordinary, preference or savings shares listed on the Milan Stock Exchange of Italy, including sector subindices. This index is identical to the MIB Index-Historical, except that it is rebased every year to 1000.00.

PUBLISHER
Italian Stock Exchange Council.

Milan Indice di Borsa (MIB) RNC Index

The index tracks the price only performance of all non-convertible saving shares, using official prices. The index was established as of January 2, 1989 with a base value of 1.000.

Publisher
Italian Stock Exchange Council.

Milan Indice di Borsa (MIB) Telematico Index

A market value-weighted index that tracks the price only performance of all stocks traded electronically on the Milan Stock Exchange. The index was established with a base date of July 16, 1993.

Publisher
Italian Stock Exchange Council.

POLAND

WIG 20

An adjusted market value and volume-weighted index that tracks the daily price only performance of the 20 largest companies listed on the main market of the Warsaw Stock Exchange, in terms of turnover. The index was introduced as of April 16, 1994 with a base value of 1000.00.

Computation Methodology
(1) The index formula takes into account monthly turnover and market capitalization, for both constituent companies and the main market, with modifications that are designed to avoid domination of the biggest and most actively traded companies. (2) The 20 constituent companies are selected on the basis of turnover value which, for two of the previous three months, must register in the top 20. (3) Periodic changes are introduced after the 15th day of the first month of a new quarter.

Publisher
Warsaw Stock Exchange (WSE).

RUSSIA

Moscow Times Dollar Adjusted Index

A market value-weighted index that tracks the daily price only performance of 50 large, actively traded Russian Federation stocks. These are the same shares that make up the Moscow Times Index and the same constituent selection criteria and index calculation methodology apply. The Russian ruble-based index is converted into U.S. dollars.

Publisher
The Moscow Times/Skate-Press.

Skate-Press Consulting Agency MT 100 Index

A market value-weighted price index that tracks the daily price only performance of 100 companies traded on the OTC market, using an average of the daily bid and/or offer quotations received from at least three OTC brokers, and whenever possible, more than three brokers for the more actively traded stocks. Average prices are determined by using the highest and lowest offer prices. If a bid or offer price is not available, the best offer price is used.

PUBLISHER
Skate-Press Consulting Agency.

SKATE-PRESS CONSULTING AGENCY MT 50 INDEX

A market value-weighted price index that tracks the daily price only performance of the most liquid 50 stocks selected from the constituents of the MT 100 Index. The average of the daily bid and/or offer quotations received from at least three OTC brokers, and whenever possible, more than three brokers for the more actively traded stocks, are used. Average prices are determined by using the highest and lowest offer prices. If a bid or offer price is not available, the best offer price is used.

PUBLISHER
Skate-Press Consulting Agency.

SLOVENIA

SBI INDEX

An unweighted arithmetic index that tracks the performance of stocks listed on the Ljubljanska Stock Exchange. The index was initiated with a base date of January 3, 1994 at a value of 1000.00.

PUBLISHER
Ljubljanska Stock Exchange (LSE).

SPAIN

BARCELONA STOCK EXCHANGE INDICE GENERAL

A volume-weighted index that tracks the continuous price only performance of 69 domestic stocks that trade on the Barcelona Stock Exchange. Shares are selected on the basis of liquidity, both frequency and volume of trading, during the previous year. In addition to a historical index with a base date of January 1, 1963, a General Index with a base date of January 1, 1986, and an annual index which is rebased each year, there are nine sectoral indices.

COMPUTATION METHODOLOGY
(1) A trading volume-weighted index formula, in which prices are weighted by each stock's nominal trade volume in the previous year. (2) Stocks are added and deleted from the index at the beginning of each year.

PUBLISHER
Barcelona Stock Exchange (BSE).

BARCELONA STOCK EXCHANGE MID 50 INDEX

A volume-weighted index that tracks the continuous price only performance of medium sized domestic stocks traded on the Barcelona Stock Exchange. The index was established with a base value of 4000.00 as of January 1, 1994.

PUBLISHER
Barcelona Stock Exchange (BSE).

Barcelona Stock Exchange Return Index

A weekly index that tracks the total return performance of stocks listed on the Barcelona Stock Exchange. The index, which is calculated according to the standards of the Federation of International Bourses de Valores (FIBV), was established with a base value of 1000.00 as of January 1, 1985.

Publisher
Barcelona Stock Exchange (BSE).

Madrid General CPI Adjusted Indices

A series of four indices which deflate by the CPI each year the results achieved by the following indices: Madrid General Price Index, Madrid General Long Price Index, Madrid General Total Return Index, and Madrid General Long Total Return Index.

Publisher
The Madrid Stock Exchange (MSE).

SWEDEN

Affarsvarlden All-Share Index

A market value-weighted index that tracks the stock price performance of 128 stocks listed on the Stockholm Stock Exchange. Constituent stocks cover 10 industry groups: Mechanical engineering, forestry, retail/wholesale, real estate and construction, miscellaneous, mixed investment companies, pure investment companies, banking, shipping and insurance. The index was established at a value of 100.00 as of February 1, 1937.

Publisher
Affarsvarlden.

OMSX Indices

Five market value-weighted subindices that track the stock price performance of five sectors that make up the most liquid issues traded on the Stockholm Stock Exchange (SSE), including the bank sector, chemicals and pharmaceuticals sector, engineering sector, forestry sector and metals and steel sector. The subindices, which were introduced on April 19, 1996, will serve as underlying vehicles for derivative products traded on the London Securities and Derivatives Exchange (OMLX) and OM Stockholm AB, a wholly-owned subsidiary of OM Gruppen AB.

Derivative Instruments
OMX index futures and options trade on OM Stockholm AB, a wholly-owned subsidiary of OM Gruppen AB.
OMX index futures and options trade on the London Securities and Derivatives Exchange (OMLX).

Publisher
OM Stockholm AB.

The Stockholm Stock Exchange SX-16 Index

A market value-weighted index that tracks the continuous stock price performance of the 16 most actively traded stocks that are listed on the A-list of the Stockholm Stock Exchange (SSE).

Constituent stocks are selected on the basis of trading volume on the A-list of the Stockholm Stock Exchange. Trading volume is calculated for the 12-month period ending one-month prior to the reconstitution of the index, which takes effect on January 1 and July 1 of each year. The index was initiated with a base value of 100.00 as of December 31, 1979.

COMPUTATION METHODOLOGY
An aggregative of prices times quantities index formula, with the divisor market capitalization adjusted daily to eliminate the effect of all types of capitalization changes, new listings and delistings. Market capitalization is calculated on the basis of a company's principle series or class of stock.

PUBLISHER
Stockholm Stock Exchange (SSE).

THE STOCKHOLM STOCK EXCHANGE SX-70 INDEX

A market value-weighted index that tracks the continuous stock price performance of the 70 least actively traded stocks that are listed on the A-list of the Stockholm Stock Exchange (SSE). Constituent stocks are selected on the basis of trading volume. Trading volume is calculated for the 12-month period ending one-month prior to the reconstitution of the index, which takes effect on January 1 and July 1 of each year. The index was initiated with a base value of 100.00 as of December 31, 1979.

COMPUTATION METHODOLOGY
An aggregative of prices times quantities index formula, with the divisor market capitalization adjusted daily to eliminate the effect of all types of capitalization changes, new listings and delistings. Market capitalization is calculated on the basis of a company's principle series or class of stock.

PUBLISHER
Stockholm Stock Exchange (SSE).

SWITZERLAND

CS INDEX

An index that tracks the performance of Swiss companies.

PUBLISHER
Credit Suisse.

PICTET LPP INDEX

A performance universe for managed portfolios in Switzerland.

PUBLISHER
Pictet & Co.

SBC INDEX OF SWISS SHARES

A market value-weighted index that tracks the price and total return performance of all types of Swiss equity shares, including stocks, participation certificates and dividend right certificates which are traded on the Swiss exchanges. Various subindices are also published. Price data extends back to December 1958 while total rate of return calculations commenced at a value of 100.00 as of April 1, 1987.

COMPUTATION METHODOLOGY
An aggregative of prices times quantities (Laspeyres) index formula.

PUBLISHER
Swiss Bank Corp.

SWISS BID/ASK INDEX (SBAI)

A market value-weighted, double index, that tracks the continuous stock price only and daily total return performance of the largest permanent and most actively traded Swiss securities on the Zurich, Geneva and Basle Stock Exchanges of Switzerland. The index consists of 24 stocks issued by 20 companies, but unlike the Swiss Market Index (SMI) which is based on the last prices paid for constituent shares, the Swiss Bid and Swiss Ask indices are based on the bid or ask prices on the index securities. As such, the indices reflect the actual market conditions as closely as possible and can be used as indicators of the liquidity of the market. The indices have been calculated since August 31, 1990.

COMPUTATION METHODOLOGY
An aggregative of prices times quantities index formula, with the divisor market capitalization adjusted periodically to eliminate the effect of all types of capitalization changes, additions and withdrawals.

PUBLISHER
Association Tripartite Bourses (ATB).

SWISS PERFORMANCE INDEX
SWISS LARGE COMPANY PERFORMANCE INDEX (SLCI)

A market value-weighted subindex of the Swiss Performance Index that tracks the continuous stock price and daily total return performance of large sized companies whose shares are quoted on the main and official parallel markets of the Zurich, Geneva and Basle Stock Exchanges of Switzerland. The index consists of 30 stocks with a market value of US$319,641.4 million as of December 31, 1995. These shares account for 79% of the Swiss market capitalization. All bearer stocks, registered stocks and certificates of participation listed in Zurich, Geneva and Basle and on the official parallel markets in Zurich and Geneva (marche annexe) are ranked according to their market capitalization. Index constituents represent the top one third of all companies by market capitalization. The classification of companies for this as well as the SMCI and SMSC indices are reviewed four times a year and adjusted annually as of July 1, based on the total number of companies included in the Swiss Performance Index as of June 1st. The quarterly reviews are designed to assess the long term capitalization trends of constituent companies. However, more weighting is given to the most recent capitalization rankings such that companies with a strong change in market capitalization over a short period of time are also eligible for reclassification. The subindex was established with a base date of December 30, 1992.

SWISS MEDIUM COMPANY PERFORMANCE INDEX (SMCI)

A market value-weighted subindex of the Swiss Performance Index that tracks the continuous stock price and daily total return performance of medium sized companies whose shares are quoted on the main and official parallel markets of the Zurich, Geneva and Basle Stock Exchanges of Switzerland. The index consists of 114 stocks with a market value of US$63,994.6 million as of December 31, 1995. These shares account for 14% of the Swiss market capitalization. All bearer stocks, registered stocks and certificates of participation listed in Zurich, Geneva and Basle and on the official parallel markets in Zurich and Geneva (marche annexe) are ranked according to their market capitalization. Index constituents represent the middle one third of all companies by market capitalization.

SWISS SMALL COMPANY PERFORMANCE INDEX (SSCI)

A market value-weighted subindex of the Swiss Performance Index that tracks the continuous stock price and daily total return performance of small capitalization securities quoted on the main and official parallel markets of the Zurich, Geneva and Basle Stock Exchanges of Switzerland. The index consists of 194 stocks with a market value of US$13,224.7 million as of December 31, 1995. These shares account for almost 3% of the Swiss market capitalization. All bearer stocks, registered stocks and certificates of participation listed in Zurich, Geneva and Basle and on the official parallel markets in Zurich and Geneva (marche annexe) are ranked according to their market capitalization. Index constituents represent the smallest one third of all companies by market capitalization.

COMPUTATION METHODOLOGY
An aggregative of prices times quantities (Laspeyres) index formula. Maintenance adjustments to the divisor are made daily after the close of trading for capitalization changes, new listings and delistings.

PUBLISHER
Association Tripartite Bourses (ATB).

VONTOBEL SMALL COMPANIES INDEX

An index that tracks the performance of small Swiss capitalization companies.

PUBLISHER
Bank Vontobel.

UNITED KINGDOM
FINANCIAL TIMES GOLD MINES INDEX

An unweighted index that tracks the daily performance of gold mining companies in South Africa, Australia, Asia and North America. At present, 34 constituent companies make up the index. These account for 53% of the western world's gold output. The index was established at a value of 100.00 as of September 12, 1955. Originally limited to South African gold mining stocks, the index was broadened and rebased to a value of 1000.00 as of December 31, 1992.

COMPUTATION METHODOLOGY
A geometric mean index formula. There is no set number of constituents and the eligibility of each company is reviewed four times a year.

PUBLISHER
Financial Times.

HOARE GOVETT 1000 INDEX (HG 1000)

A market value-weighted index that tracks the daily stock price and total return performance of the smallest 1,000 companies in the UK equity market. The index, with its market capitalization of 18 billion pounds as of January 1, 1995, covers the bottom two percent of the market capitalization of the UK equity market, excluding investment trusts.

The index was introduced in 1995 with a base value of 1000.00 as of December 31, 1992 and backdated to 1955 using monthly data from the London Share Price Database (LSPD), which includes a comprehensive record of prices, capital changes and dividends for all UK-registered Sterling-denominated shares traded on the London Stock Exchange since 1975. The companion Extended Market Index, which tracks the daily stock price and total return performance of the companies that make up the Hoare Govett Smaller Companies Index, namely the smallest tenth by market value of the UK equity market, along with all companies listed on the Unlisted Securities Market, is being eliminated due to the demise of the Unlisted Securities Market.

COMPUTATION METHODOLOGY
(1) An aggregative of prices times quantities index formula, with the divisor market capitalization adjusted to eliminate the effect of capitalization changes, including mergers and delistings. (2) The index is rebalanced only once a year. This process takes place at the beginning of the year with additions and deletions, as may be required, to maintain the index's lowest one tenth composition.

PUBLISHER
Hoare Govett Securities Ltd./ABN-AMRO.

HSBC JAMES CAPEL INDICES
GLOBAL MINING INDICES

A base metals index that includes various subindices, such as gold mining.

GREEN INDICES
TOOTSIE INDEX

A market value-weighted index that tracks the daily price only performance of the second 100 stocks that make up the FT-SE All Share Index.

TRIXIE INDEX

A market value-weighted index that tracks the daily price only performance of the shares that make up the FT-SE All Share Index, excepting the second 100 shares of the index (Tootsie) and Investment Trusts.

WARRANT INDEX
TIGER INDEX

A market value-weighted index that tracks the daily price only performance of stocks from seven South East Asia markets.

COMPUTATION METHODOLOGY
An aggregative of prices times quantities index formula.

PUBLISHER
HSBC James Capel.

LONDON AND BISHOPSGATE 100 INDEX

An index that tracks the performance of the 100 largest stocks in the Morgan Stanley EAFE Index.

PUBLISHER
London and Bishopsgate.

REGIONAL

CENTRAL EUROPEAN STOCK INDEX

An index that tracks the performance of 27 stocks listed on the Budapest Stock Exchange, Praha Stock Exchange and Warsaw Stock Exchange. The index was launched in early 1996.

PUBLISHER
Budapest Stock Exchange.

DRESDNER INTERNATIONAL RESEARCH INSTITUTE EUROPA SMALL CAP INDEX

A price performance index that tracks a universe of small- and medium-sized European companies.

PUBLISHER
Dresdner International Research Institute.

EUROPEAN 100 INDEX

A weighted arithmetic index that tracks the daily stock prices of Europe's 100 most valuable companies. Companies are selected on the basis of market capitalization. The index was established with a base date of January 1, 1988.

PUBLISHER
The European, as calculated by Morgan Stanley Capital International.

NOMURA RESEARCH INSTITUTE (NRI) EUROPEAN MULTIMEDIA INDEX

A market value-weighted index that tracks the daily stock price performance of shares attributable to European companies that are engaged in multimedia activities. Constituents are limited to companies with market capitalizations in excess of US$100.0 million, which are subject to exclusion at a level below US$80.0 million. The index consists of 49 companies, including 23 UK-based firms, that are either directly involved in driving developments in multimedia or indirectly gaining from multimedia developments, with a market capitalization of US$270.0 billion as of August 1994. The index was established with a based value of 100.00 as of December 31, 1989. Sector and regional subindices are also published.

COMPUTATION METHODOLOGY
(1) An aggregative of prices times quantities index formula with the divisor market capitalization adjusted to eliminate the effect of all types of capitalization changes, new listings and delistings. (2) Constituents are reviewed on a quarterly basis.

PUBLISHER
Nomura International plc/Nomura Research Institute, Ltd.

STOCKS—AFRICA/MIDDLE EAST

ABU DHABI

THE NATIONAL BANK OF ABU DHABI INDEX

An unofficial stock index that tracks the performance of 27 stocks.

PUBLISHER
The National Bank of Abu Dahbi.

BAHRAIN

BAHRAIN STOCK EXCHANGE (BSE) OFFICIAL SHARE INDEX

An index that tracks the performance of 37 listed stocks, with a market capitalization of about US$4, 500 million as of December 31, 1995.

PUBLISHER
Bahrain Stock Exchange.

EGYPT

EGYPT CAPITAL MARKET AUTHORITY INDEX (ECM)

A price-weighted index that tracks the price only performance of shares listed on the Cairo Stock Exchange and Alexandria Stock Exchange.

PUBLISHER
Capital Market Authority.

EGYPTIAN FINANCIAL GROUP INDEX

PUBLISHER
Egyptian Financial Group.

HERMES FINANCIAL INDEX

A stock price index that tracks the price performance of a universe of 32 liquid stocks that are of interest to an independent investor. Stocks represent 10 industry sectors. To be eligible for inclusion in the index, a stock must be liquid, have a trading history in excess of three months, and be denominated in Egyptian pounds. Liquidity is established on the basis of number of transactions.

PUBLISHER
Hermes Financial.

GHANA

DATABANK BROKERAGE LTD. INDEX

PUBLISHER
Databank Brokerage.

GOLD COAST SECURITIES LIQUIDITY INDEX

A stock index that tracks the price performance of all shares listed on the Ghana Stock Exchange.

PUBLISHER
Gold Coast Securities Ltd.

ISRAEL

COMPUTERIZED CALL MARKET SYSTEM (CCM) INDEX

An index that tracks the price performance of securities, other than the 100 most liquid securities traded in the Semi-Continuous Auction System which are tracked in the TA-100 Index, that are traded via the Computerized Call Market System (CCM).

PUBLISHER
Tel Aviv Stock Exchange (TSE).

TA-100 INDEX

An index that tracks the price performance of the 100 most liquid securities traded in the Semi-Continuous Auction System in Israel.

PUBLISHER
Tel Aviv Stock Exchange (TSE).

JORDAN

AMMAN FINANCIAL MARKET PRICE INDEX

An unweighted index that tracks the price only performance of the 60 most liquid stocks traded on the Amman Stock Exchange.

PUBLISHER
Amman Financial Market.

MOROCCO

UPLINE USI INDEX

A stock index that tracks the 10 most liquid stocks traded on the stock exchange.

PUBLISHER
Upline Securities.

QATAR

COMMERCIAL BANK OF QATAR (CBC) SHARE INDEX

A stock index that tracks the performance of seven stocks. It was launched as of June 1995 with a base value of 100.00.

PUBLISHER
Commercial Bank of Qatar.

SOUTH AFRICA

FINANCIAL/INDUSTRIAL 30 INDEX (FNDI 30)

A market value-weighted index that tracks the stock price only performance of the 30 largest and most liquid South African traded financial/industrial company shares listed on the Johannesburg Stock Exchange (JSE). Financial/industrial companies must be eligible for inclusion in the JSE-Actuaries All Share Index, i.e. they must be ordinary shares of operating companies that are listed on the Johannesburg Stock Exchange (JSE). Companies are selected on the basis of market capitalization and liquidity, each of which is assigned equal weighting in the selection process. Market capitalization and liquidity are determined using average weekly market capitalization and trading activity for the previous twelve month period, calculated on the last business day of each week. Market capitalization and liquidity for newly listed shares are calculated over the time for which the new shares have been listed. Companies are arranged in rank order, by market capitalization and liquidity, and those that rank in the top ten are selected for inclusion in the index.

The index, along with several companion indices, was developed in conjunction with the Actuarial Society, the Johannesburg Stock Exchange and the South African Futures Exchange and was introduced on June 16, 1995 to supplement the JSE Actuaries equity indices and more properly serve as an underlying vehicle for derivative products.

COMPUTATION METHODOLOGY
(1) An aggregative of prices times quantities index formula. Maintenance adjustments are made for capitalization changes, new listings and delistings. (2) The index constituents are reviewed every six months, on June 1 and December 1 of each year and revisions take effect on the first business day following the mid-month expiration of Safex stock index futures contracts. (3) Index constituents are removed due to takeovers, mergers and suspensions and replaced by the next most eligible shares. (4) Latest available ordinary share prices are used or, in the absence of a share price, bid or asked prices. (5) Market capitalization is determined on the basis of the total number of ordinary shares of all classes that the company has issued and listed on the JSE. Only fully paid shares are taken into account. Partly paid shares held by employees and directors are excluded. In the event share capital consists of both "S" and ordinary shares, the combined number of shares is used to compute market capitalization. The effective date of changes in the number of eligible shares for index computation purposes is determined by the JSE Committee.

DERIVATIVE INSTRUMENTS
FNDI 30 futures and options on futures trade on the South African Futures Exchange.

PUBLISHER
The Johannesburg Stock Exchange (JSE).

TUNESIA

INDICE GENERAL BVM

An index that tracks 16 stocks listed on the Permanent Quotation System.

PUBLISHER
Bourse de Valeurs Mobilieres de Tunis.

ZIMBABWE

58 COUNTER INDUSTRIAL INDEX

An index that tracks the performance of industrial companies listed on the Zimbabwe Stock Exchange.

PUBLISHER
The Zimbabwe Stock Exchange (ZSE).

STOCKS—LATIN AMERICA/CENTRAL AMERICA

ARGENTINA

BURCAP INDEX

A theoretical par value-weighted index that tracks the continuous stock price performance of Buenos Aires Stock Exchange listed common shares that make up the Merval Index.

COMPUTATION METHODOLOGY
(1) The index value is the summation of each security's price quotation multiplied by each security's theoretical par value. The theoretical par value is computed in two steps. First, the contribution of each constituent stock is computed by dividing the market capitalization of each stock by the sum of the market capitalizations of all constituent stocks. Second, the contribution of each stock is multiplied by the closing value of the index as of the preceding date. The product is divided by the price quotation of each stock, to arrive at the theoretical par value. (2) The index is reconstituted on a quarterly basis along with the Merval Index.

PUBLISHER
The Buenos Aires Stock Exchange (BASE).

CHILE

INTER-10 INDEX

A market value-weighted price only index that tracks the performance of the most representative stocks listed on Santiago Stock Exchange with American Depositary Receipts. Constituent shares, which numbered ten as of December 31, 1995, are selected from members of the Indice de Precios Selectivo de Acciones (IPSA) Index, which consists of 40 companies selected on the basis of market capitalization. From this universe, ten of the most representative companies with American Depositary Receipts are selected for inclusion in the index. The index, which was introduced on June 1, 1995, is reviewed every three months. It was established with a base value of 100.00 as of December 31, 1994.

COMPUTATION METHODOLOGY
(1) An aggregative of prices times quantities index formula. Maintenance adjustments to the divisor are made for capitalization changes, new listings and delistings. (2) Constituent shares are reviewed on a quarterly basis and the index is reconstituted accordingly.

PUBLISHER
Bolsa de Comercio de Santiago.

COLOMBIA

BOLSA DE MEDELIN
IBOMED INDEX

A general price index of stocks traded on the Medelin Stock Exchange. The index, with a base date of December 31, 1987 at a value of 100.00, also includes sector subindices for industrial, financial, commercial and other companies.

IBOMED SELECTIVO

A price index of selected stocks traded on the Medelin Stock Exchange. The index was established with a base date of December 31, 1987.

PUBLISHER
Bolsa de Medellin S.A.

VALLEJO SELECTED STOCK PRICE INDEX

A volume-weighted index.

PUBLISHER
Corredores Associates.

ECUADOR

INDICE DE RENDIMIENTO (RBQ)

A total return index established in 1993 that tracks the performance of stocks listed on the Quito Stock Exchange. It is computed by multiplying the return of reference securities by total daily volume.

PUBLISHER
Bolsa de Valores de Quito.

INDICE DIARIO DE VOLUMEN (IVQ)

A volume index based on stocks traded on the Quito Stock Exchange.

PUBLISHER
Bolsa de Valores de Quito.

PERU

BANCO INTERANDINO BLUE CHIP INDEX

PUBLISHER
Banco Interandino.

VENEZUELA

VENEZUELA MARINEVEST STOCK COMPOSITE INDEX

PUBLISHER
Marinevest.

STOCKS—WORLD

SCHWAB INTERNATIONAL INDEX

A market-value weighted index that tracks the daily price only and monthly total return performance of common stocks and other equity securities, including preferred stocks, rights and warrants issued by large, publicly traded companies from countries around the world with major developed securities markets, excluding the United States. To be included in the index, a company must satisfy the following selection criteria: (1) It must be an "operating company" whose principal trading market is in a country with a major developed securities market. (2) A liquid market for its shares must exist. (3) Its market value must place it among the top 350 such companies as measured by market value, provided that the total of all companies from any one country may not exceed 35% of the indexed on a rebalancing date.

As of January 31, 1996, the aggregate market value of component stocks stood at US$3,800.0 million.

PUBLISHER
Charles Schwab & Co.

BONDS—NORTH AMERICA

CANADA

NESBIT BURNS GIFFORD FONG ASSOCIATES CANADIAN BOND INDICES

A weighted bond index that tracks the price only, coupon and total return performance of domestic Canadian bonds denominated in Canadian dollars with BBB or better credit ratings. Various subindices, for example, by maturity, issuer, etc., are available.

PUBLISHER
Nesbitt Burns Inc.

THE SCOTIA MCLEOD DEBT MARKET INDICES

A series of market value-weighted indices that track the daily yield, price only and total return performance of marketable Canadian bonds with terms to maturity greater than one year. In addition to short, medium-term and long bond subindices, bond categories for each index include

Canada, Provincials, Municipals and AA through BBB-rated corporate issues. Indices covering the Canadian mortgage and money markets are also published. The index was initiated with a base value of 100.00 as of December 31, 1985, with data to 1979 and, in some, cases to 1976.

PUBLISHER
Scotia McLeod.

UNITED STATES

ALTMAN DEFAULTED DEBT SECURITIES INDEX

An index that gauges the performance of bonds after default or bankruptcy. Bonds enter the index at the end of the month in which they default and are dropped after they resume bond payments.

PUBLISHER
Edward I. Altman/New York University.

BARRON'S BEST GRADE BONDS

The index reflects the average daily closing bond prices of 10 bonds.

COMPUTATION METHODOLOGY
The index is calculated by averaging the closing prices on the New York Stock Exchange (NYSE).

PUBLISHER
Barron's.

BARRON'S INTERMEDIATE GRADE BONDS

The index reflects the average daily closing bond prices of 10 bonds.

COMPUTATION METHODOLOGY
The index is calculated by averaging the closing prices on the New York Stock Exchange (NYSE).

PUBLISHER
Barron's.

BOND BUYER 20 BOND INDEX

The index reflects the theoretical or estimated average yield on 20 general obligation bonds that mature in 20 years. Bonds have a minimum rating of Baa or better by Moody's Investors Service, with an equivalent composite rating of A1. The index has been compiled on a monthly basis since 1917 and continuing to 1944. Since 1944, the index has been calculated on a weekly basis.

COMPUTATION METHODOLOGY
The index is calculated every Thursday, or on Wednesday in the event of a legal holiday that falls on a Thursday or Friday. Municipal bond dealers and banks are asked to estimate what a current coupon bond for each issuer would yield if the bond was sold at par value. The index is computed by averaging the estimated yields on the bonds.

PUBLISHER
Bond Buyer.

Bond Buyer 11 Bond Index

The index reflects the theoretical or estimated average yield on 11 highly rated general obligation bonds that mature in 20 years and which have been selected from the universe of 20 bonds tracked in the Bond Buyer 20 Bond Index. Bonds have a minimum rating of Aa3 or better by Moody's Investors Service, with an equivalent composite rating of Aa. The index has been compiled on a monthly basis since 1917 and continuing to 1944. Since 1944, the index has been calculated on a weekly basis.

Publisher
Bond Buyer.

Bond Buyer Revenue Bond Index

The index reflects the theoretical or estimated average yield on 25 general obligation bonds that mature in 30 years. Bonds have a minimum rating of Baa1 or better by Moody's Investors Service. The index has been compiled on a monthly basis since 1917 and continuing to 1944. Since 1944, the index has been calculated on a weekly basis.

Computation Methodology
The index is calculated every Thursday, or on Wednesday in the event of a legal holiday that falls on a Thursday or Friday. Municipal bond dealers and banks are asked to estimate what a current coupon bond for each issuer would yield if the bond was sold at par value. The index is computed by averaging the estimated yields on the bonds.

Publisher
Bond Buyer.

Chemical Bank Emerging Market Debt Index

Publisher
Chase Bank (formerly Chemical Bank).

Chicago Board of Trade (CBOT) Argentina Brady Bond Index

A weighted index consisting of the following three U.S. dollar-denominated Argentina Brady bonds: Par bonds series L, due March 31, 2023; Discount bonds series L, due March 31, 2023; and Floating Rate Bonds, due March 31, 2005. The bonds are weighted by the face value amount of each bond relative to the other bonds, and revised twice a year to reflect changes in the outstanding value of the bonds as a result of buy backs and amortization payments. The index, which was created to serve as an underlying vehicle for derivative instruments and launched on March 22, 1996, is valued on a continuous basis using transaction prices provided by brokers.

Derivative Instruments
Argentina Brady Bond Index futures trade on the Chicago Board of Trade.

Publisher
Chicago Board of Trade (CBOT).

Chicago Board of Trade (CBOT) Brazil Brady Bond Index

A weighted index consisting of the following three U.S. dollar-denominated Brazil Brady bonds: Par bonds series Z-L (series A or B), due April 15, 2024; Discount bonds series Z (Series A or B), due April 15, 2024; Capitalization bonds (C-bonds) series L, due April 15, 2014; Eligible Interest Bonds ("Els"), due April 15, 2006; and Interest Due and Unpaid Bonds ("IDUs"), due January 1, 2001. The bonds are weighted by the face value amount of each bond relative to the other bonds, and revised twice a year to reflect changes in the outstanding value of the bonds as a result of buy backs and amortization payments. The index, which was created to serve as an underlying vehicle for derivative instruments and launched on March 22, 1996, is valued on a continuous basis using transaction prices provided by brokers.

Derivative Instruments
Brazil Brady Bond Index futures trade on the Chicago Board of Trade.

Publisher
Chicago Board of Trade (CBOT).

Chicago Board of Trade (CBOT) Mexico Brady Bond Index

A weighted index consisting of the following two U.S. dollar-denominated par and discount Brady bonds: Par bonds series A or B, due December 31, 2019, with all unexpired value recovery rights attached and Discount bonds series A,B,C, or D due December 31, 2019, with all unexpired value recovery rights attached. The bonds are weighted by the face value amount of each bond relative to the other bonds, and revised twice a year to reflect changes in the outstanding value of the bonds as a result of buy backs and amortization payments. The index, which was created to serve as an underlying vehicle for derivative instruments and launched on March 1, 1996, is valued on a continuous basis using transaction prices provided by brokers.

Derivative Instruments
Mexico Brady Bond Index futures trade on the Chicago Board of Trade.

Publisher
Chicago Board of Trade (CBOT).

Dow Jones 20 Bond Average

The index reflects the average daily closing bond prices of 20 industrial and public utility bonds. The index has been compiled on a daily basis since about 1976.

Computation Methodology
The index is calculated every day by averaging the closing prices on the New York Stock Exchange (NYSE).

Publisher
Dow Jones & Co.

Goldman Sachs Liquid Asset-Backed Securities Index (LABS)

A market value-weighted index that tracks the performance of a liquid universe of fixed rate asset backed securities, including securities backed by credit card receivables, automobile loans or home equity loans/lines of credit, that are registered with the SEC. Issue size must be equal to or in excess of US$500 million at the time of issue, with a stated maturity or maturity guarantee of less than 10 years and rated triple A by at least two rating agencies at issuance. The index was introduced in June 1991 and recalculated to October 1989.

COMPUTATION METHODOLOGY

COMPUTATION METHODOLOGY

(1) Returns are calculated for individual issues and then aggregated on a market value-weighted basis, which are recalculated daily. (2) Qualifying issues are incorporated in the index for one year. Issues enter the index at their offered price as of the original settlement date and are removed from the index on first anniversary of that date, or earlier due to a downgrade or default. (3) Issues are priced on the bid side.

PUBLISHER
Goldman Sachs & Co.

KNIGHT RIDDER-CRB INTEREST RATES INDEX

An unweighted geometric index that tracks the continuous price only performance of three interest rates, consisting of futures contracts on the 3-month Treasury bill, 10-year Treasury note and Treasury bond that are traded on the International Monetary Market (IMM) of the Chicago Mercantile Exchange and Chicago Board of Trade (CBOT).

PUBLISHER
Knight Ridder.

MOODY'S YIELD AVERAGES

LONG-TERM CORPORATE BOND YIELD AVERAGES

An unweighted average of the yields-to-maturity derived from pricing data on a regularly replenished population of nearly 100 seasoned long-term investment grade, liquid, callable and non-callable industrial and public utility bonds issued in the U.S. Corporate bond market. Corporate yield averages are calculated for Aaa, Aa, A, Baa rating categories. Constituents are larger issues of big, well-capitalized companies with amounts outstanding of at least $100 million, with minimum maturities as close as possible to 30 years. Index constituents can change in response to rating changes, susceptibility to early redemption and a drop by a bond's remaining lifetime below 20 years. Callable bonds are excluded from the yield average whenever a bond's yield-to-call is less than its yield-to-maturity and it is therefore subject to early redemption. Issues that are priced at deep discounts or steep premiums are excluded from consideration. Moody's long-term yield averages have been published since 1929.

INTERMEDIATE-TERM CORPORATE BOND YIELD AVERAGES

An unweighted average of the yields-to-maturity derived from pricing data on a regularly replenished population of nearly 80 fixed-rate corporate bonds in the U.S. market with amounts outstanding of at least US$100 million and remaining maturities between 5 and 9.5 years. Index constituents can change in response to rating changes, susceptibility to early redemption and a drop by a bond's remaining lifetime below 20 years. Callable bonds are excluded from the yield average whenever a bond's yield to call is less than its yield-to-maturity and it is therefore subject to early redemption. Issues that are priced at deep discounts or steep premiums are excluded from consideration. Moody's intermediate-term corporate bond yield averages have been published weekly since July 1994.

COMPUTATION METHODOLOGY
Simple arithmetic average of the yield-to-maturity, without any allowance for the fact that amounts outstanding vary across rating categories and across corporate sectors.

PUBLISHER
Moody's Investors Service.

MOODY'S MUNICIPAL BOND YIELD AVERAGES

An unweighted average of the yields-to-maturity offered weekly by investment grade, non-insured new issues, as reported in the *Bond Buyer*, with 10- and 20-year final maturities. A composite index as well as subindices by maturity and ratings have been calculated since 1936.

COMPUTATION METHODOLOGY
Arithmetic average of the yields-to-maturity.

PUBLISHER
Moody's Investors Service.

PAYDEN & RYGEL TOTAL RETURN INDICES

Indices that track the monthly total rates of return applicable to 1- and 2-year U.S. Treasury notes.

PUBLISHER
Payden & Rygel.

RYAN LABS TREASURY INDICES
TREASURY COMPOSITE INDEX

Equal- and market-weighted price, income and total return indices consisting of U.S. Treasury notes and bonds with initial maturities longer than one year. Bid prices are used based on the U.S. Treasury Bulletin and Federal Reserve Bank of New York data. A composite index along with subindices are calculated, with monthly data to 1949 and daily data starting in 1988.

TREASURY YIELD CURVE INDICES

Equal-weighted indices that track the daily principal only, income and total return performance of 2-, 3-, 4-, 5-, 7-, 10-, 15-, 20- and 30-year U.S. Treasury notes and bonds. The index consists of Treasury auction issues with initial maturities corresponding to the maturity of the index, including flower bonds. New auction issues enter the index and replace the previous auction issue on the weekly auction date. Daily and monthly index values have been computed since 1967.

PUBLISHER
Ryan Labs, Inc.

SALOMON BROTHERS EUROBOND INDICES

A market value-weighted series of indices, each of which measures the daily and monthly principal only and total return performance of tradable investment grade, fixed rate, Eurodollar, Eurosterling, Euroyen, and Euro-Deutschemark bonds with minimum maturities of one year or longer. Eligible securities for each index include Eurobonds, global bonds, Dragon bonds and certain Euro Medium-Term notes and asset-backed bonds with minimum par amounts outstanding and minimum denominations, as follows: Eurodollar-US$150 million and US$100,000; Eurosterling-100 million Pounds and 100,000 Pounds; Euroyen-40 billion Yen and 10 million Yen; and Euro-Deutschemark-1 billion DM and 250,000 DM. In addition, a minimum Standard & Poor's or Moody's Investors Service investment grade rating of BBB/Baa3 or better is required for eligibility.

Bullet bonds, securities with sinking fund features, puttable, extendable or callable bonds are eligible for inclusion in each of the indices. Zero-coupon bonds are excluded from all but the Eurodollar Index.

The indices were reconstituted in January 1994, in terms of index design and calculation methodology, as part of a redefinition of the Eurobond and Foreign bond sectors of the Salomon World Bond Index that is in the process of being phased out. Initiated with a base value of 100.00, the inception date for the Eurodollar Index is June 30, 1993 while for the Eurosterling, Euroyen and Euro-Deutschemark indices the inception date is December 31, 1994. Historical data based on the design and calculation methodology applicable to the World Bond Index is available to December 31, 1977.

Beginning in January 1995, the indices that make up the Eurobond Index will replace the old Eurodollar, Eurosterling, Euroyen and Euro-Deutschemark sectors of the World Bond Index.

COMPUTATION METHODOLOGY
An aggregate of prices times quantities index formula, including gain/loss on repayments of principal and currency conversions, where applicable, as well as coupon received or accrued for total rate of return calculations.

PUBLISHER
Salomon Brothers.

SALOMON BROTHERS WORLD BOND INDEX

A nominal value-weighted measure of the monthly total return performance of high-quality securities in 10 currency sectors of the bond market. Securities include government bonds, Eurobonds, and foreign bonds denominated in 10 different currencies, including the U.S. dollar, Canadian dollar, Deutschemark, Japanese Yen, UK Sterling, Swiss Franc, Dutch Guilder, French Franc, Australian Dollar and the European Currency Unit. The index is comprised of fixed-rate government bonds with remaining maturities of at least five years along with representative samples of Eurobonds and foreign bonds which carry ratings equivalent to AA or better. Salomon intends to eliminate this index as few investors use it, but has elected to extend its life to accommodate a continuing interest on the part of investors in the Euro and Foreign bond sectors. Eventually, the index will be replaced with a market capitalization-weighted all inclusive benchmark, that satisfies all aspects of Salomon's philosophy of index design. The index along with its subindices were, for the most part, introduced in September 1981. The index was initiated with a value of 100.00 as of December 31, 1977. Separate indexes for local currency and U.S. dollar-based returns are updated monthly.

COMPUTATION METHODOLOGY
(1) The index is reweighted annually based on nominal value outstanding in each of the sectors covered as of the previous year-end, using December 1977 spot exchange rates to eliminate the effect of currency on these weights. (2) A mix of individual trader pricing and outside sources are used to price the components of the index.

PUBLISHER
Salomon Brothers.

SALOMON BROTHERS
NEW LARGE PENSION FUND BASELINE BOND INDEX (NEW LPF)

The index tracks the total return performance of Treasury, Government-sponsored and corporate securities from the BIG Index with a minimum maturity of seven years as well as mortgage pass-through securities that are identical to the BIG Index, but using fixed-weights of 40% Treasury/Government sponsored, 30% mortgages and 30% corporate. The New LPF was introduced in May 1994 to replace the Large Pension Fund Base Line Bond Index. This index, as well as its counterpart, are designed to serve as a benchmark and/or tracking vehicle for pension funds seeking to establish long-term core portfolios that more closely match the longer durations of their nominal dollar liabilities. While pension funds would normally use the BIG Index as a benchmark, the New LPF improves on the structure of BIG by using fixed sector weights and a minimum maturity of seven years for non-mortgage issues–design characteristics that more closely satisfy the longer duration goals of pension fund portfolios which, at the same time, emphasize the traditionally higher yielding long-term securities. The index was initiated with a value of 100.00 as of December 31, 1979.

CORE 5 INDEX

The index corresponds to the BIG Index, excluding Treasury and Government-sponsored securities with less than five years to maturity.

CORE 3 INDEX

The index corresponds to the BIG Index, excluding Treasury and Government-sponsored securities with less than three years to maturity.

U.S. TREASURY BENCHMARK (ON-THE-RUN) INDEX

This index tracks the total returns for the current 1-year, 2-year, 3-year, 5-year, 10-year and 30-year on-the-run Treasury security that has been in existence for the entire month.

U.S. TREASURY BENCHMARK YIELD CURVE AVERAGE INDEX

This index tracks the total returns for the current 2-year, 3-year, 5-year, 10-year and 30-year on-the-run Treasury security that has been in existence for the entire month and the two shorter and two longer issues in the Treasury Index nearest each respective benchmark maturity.

PUBLISHER
Salomon Brothers.

STANDARD & POOR'S CORPORATION
CORPORATE BOND INDICES

A weekly index of yields-to-maturity on corporate, industrial and utility bonds of varying credit qualities.

MUNICIPAL BOND INDICES

An arithmetic average of the yields-to-maturity of 15 high-grade series issue municipal bonds with a regional distribution, and a period to maturity of 20 years.

Long-Term U.S. Government Bonds

The average price, expressed in terms of dollars per US$100, of long-term U.S. Government bonds with 20 or more years-to-maturity, based on the median yield-to-maturity of a varying number of bonds, depending upon the issues available.

Intermediate-Term U.S. Government Bonds

The average price, expressed in terms of dollars per US$100, of intermediate-term U.S. Government bonds with more than six but less than nine years-to-maturity, based on the median yield-to-maturity of a varying number of bonds, depending upon the issues available.

Short-Term U.S. Government Bonds

The average price, expressed in terms of dollars per US$100, of U.S. Government bonds with more than two but less than four years-to-maturity, based on the median yield-to-maturity of a varying number of bonds, depending upon the issues available.

PUBLISHER
Standard & Poor's Corporation.

Bonds—Asia/Pacific

AUSTRALIA
BZW Australia Liquid Government Securities Bond Index

A series of indices and subindices that track the price and total return performance of Australia Government Securities.

PUBLISHER
BZW Australia.

Commonwealth Bank Bond Indices

Weekly and month-end price and yield performance for commonwealth bonds in three maturity ranges, including up to five years, five- to 10-years and over 10-years. The indices are calculated by the Commonwealth Bank, CBA Group Treasury Department.

PUBLISHER
Australian Stock Exchange Ltd.

SBC Warburg Australia Bond Index

Daily and monthly price performance for government and corporate bonds in various maturity categories.

PUBLISHER
SBC Warburg Australia.

JAPAN

NIKKEI BOND INDEX

A mean yield benchmark that tracks the daily yields-to-maturity of a small but representative number of bonds traded in Japan, based on over-the-counter price quotations published by the Securities Dealers Association of Japan. The index, which consists of about 20-25 national government bonds, local government bonds, government guaranteed bonds, bank and industrial bonds and yen denominated bonds, consists of short, intermediate and long maturities.

COMPUTATION METHODOLOGY
The yield-to-maturity for each bond is calculated and averaged by maturity segment.

PUBLISHER
Nihon Keizai Shimbun, Inc.

KOREA

KOREA BOND INDEX

A measure of the daily performance, including capital gains and interest accrued, of selected public and corporate bonds, including 15 subindices that group bonds by issuer, terms of issuance and maturity. Both public and corporate bonds are included in the index which was initiated in 1986 at a base value of 100.00 as of December 31, 1985.

PUBLISHER
Korea Stock Exchange (KSE).

SINGAPORE

UNITED OVERSEAS BANK SINGAPORE GOVERNMENT BOND INDEX

A market value-weighted index that tracks the daily price only performance of all Singapore government bonds outstanding, regardless of maturity. Constituents, which numbered 16 issues as of December 31, 1995, include all outstanding and traded government bonds, including four issues with two-year final maturities, nine issues with five-year final maturities and three issues with seven-year final maturities. The index was introduced with a base value of 100.00 as of May 13, 1987, the first day of trading on the reactivated Singapore Government Securities Market (SGSM).

COMPUTATION METHODOLOGY
(1) An aggregative of prices times quantities index formula. (2) Bid prices are used. (3) Market capitalization weights are based on the size of the bond issue.

PUBLISHER
United Overseas Bank.

THAILAND

S-ONE BOND INDEX

A daily value-weighted index that tracks the total return performance of all fixed coupon securities traded on the over-the-counter market in Thailand.

PUBLISHER
Securities One Public Company Limited.

BONDS—EUROPE

AUSTRIA

CA BOND INDEX

A price only index that tracks the performance of Austrian bonds.

PUBLISHER
Creditanstalt Investment Bank AG.

CZECH REPUBLIC

CZECH KOMERCNI BANK BOND PRICE INDEX

PUBLISHER
Komercni Bank.

PATRIABIX INDEX

A weekly index launched in May 1995 that tracks the performance of government bonds and leading corporate issues.
PUBLISHER
Patria Finance.

DENMARK

COPENHAGEN STOCK EXCHANGE TRUE YIELD INDEX

A weighted index of the average interest on bonds, calculated before and after tax on interest. In addition, average interest on bonds issued by the government, standard mortgage credit, specialized institutions and first and second mortgage credit, are also published.

PUBLISHER
Copenhagen Stock Exchange.

GERMANY

GERMAN BOND INDEX (REX)

A market share-weighted bond index, using the "notional bond" concept, that tracks the daily price only and total return performance of German government bonds with identical ratings, through a portfolio consisting of 30 synthetic issues with fixed interest and with a life-to-maturity between 0.5 and 10.5 years. Issues include German Federal bonds (Bunds) and Federal treasury bonds.

Unlike a portfolio consisting of actual securities, the REX synthetic bonds do not change over time. In addition to a price only index (REX), a total return index (REXP) and separate subindices by maturity and coupon classes are also calculated. The index was launched in 1991 with a base value of 100.00 as of December 31, 1967.

COMPUTATION METHODOLOGY
(1) Current yields are calculated on the basis of closing prices. (2) Yield structure is calculated for various life-to-maturity and coupons. From this, the yield on the 30 bonds is derived and transformed into corresponding prices. (3) Weights are determined for each bond according to its market share. Market

share is calculated on the basis of the number of issues in each of the 30 maturity/coupon classes during the previous 25-year period. The weights are reviewed annually. (4) Bond prices are multiplied by their weights and added to arrive at the overall index value.

PUBLISHER
Deutsche Borse AG.

PFANDBRIEF INDEX

A weighted bond index, using the "notional bond" concept, that tracks the daily price only and total return performance of the Pfandbrief market through a portfolio consisting of 30 synthetic Pfandbrief issues with maturities from one- to ten-years and three different coupon classes, including 6%, 7.5% and 9%. Unlike a portfolio consisting of actual securities, the Pfandbrief synthetic bonds do not change over time. In addition to a price only index (PEX), a total return index (PEXP) and separate subindices by maturity and coupon classes are also calculated. The index was launched in April 1995 with a base value of 100.00 as of December 30, 1987.

PUBLISHER
The Association of German Mortgage Banks/The Association of German Public Sector Banks.

PORTUGAL

BVL ORF INDEX

A daily index that tracks the performance of fixed-rate treasury bonds and similar securities listed on the Markets with Official Quotations. Bonds that mature within 90 days or have not been traded in the course of the last six sessions are excluded from consideration.

PUBLISHER
Bolsa de Valores de Lisboa.

SWITZERLAND

THE SWISS BOND INDEX (SBI)

A market value-weighted index that tracks the daily price only and total return performance of liquid baskets of bonds selected on the basis of type, minimum size, quality, and maturity. The index baskets are limited to bonds with minimum nominal amounts outstanding of SFr 100 million. The remaining life must be between 3.5 and 15 years and the bonds must not be subject to premature redemption within a period earlier than 3.5 years. The index consists of a Swiss Domestic Bonds subindex, with domestic federal bonds, and a Swiss Foreign Bond Index with Swiss franc-denominated bond issues of foreign borrowers with AAA/Aaa ratings from Standard & Poor's or Moody's Investors Service, including subindices for public bonds, bonds of supranational organizations, as well as other bonds. The index, which has been calculated on a real time basis since August 3, 1992, was established with a base value of 100.00 as of December 31, 1991.

COMPUTATION METHODOLOGY
(1) An aggregative of prices times quantities index formula, based on nominal amount of bonds outstanding. Total return includes coupon received or accrued. (2) The index is reconstituted once a month by adding and deleting issues.

PUBLISHER
Association of Tripartite Bourses (ATB).

United Kingdom
FT-Actuaries Fixed Interest Indices

A series of indices that track the daily price only performance of all conventional British Government bonds and index-linked securities. Accompanying figures include interest received on a year-to-date basis, which allows computations of total rates of return.

UK Gilts Index

Performance by maturity sectors and coupon ranges. As redefined as of January 1, 1989, low coupon UK Gilts consist of issues with nominal interest rates up to 7.750% while medium coupon yields range from 8% to 10.750% and the high coupon category starts at 12%. Base date is April 30, 1972.

Index-Linked Index

Performance by maturity sector and inflation levels.

PUBLISHER
Financial Times.

Regional
Lombard Odier & Cie (LOC) European Government Bond Index

A GDP-weighted index that tracks the daily unhedged price only and total return performance of 12 central government straight-fixed coupon bearing bonds with maturities in excess of one year, expressed in ECU terms: Switzerland, Germany, Holland, France, Belgium, Italy, Spain, UK, Denmark, Sweden, Norway and Finland.

PUBLISHER
Lombard Odier & Cie.

Bonds—Africa/Middle East

South Africa
Johannesburg Stock Exchange (JSE) Actuaries Bond Performance Index

A weighted, marketable, price yield and total return index that tracks the daily performance of fixed-rate, interest bearing debt of the Government of the Republic of South Africa (RSA), Eskom, Transnet and SA Posts and Telecommunications, or other debt that is guaranteed by the Government of RSA. Eligible debt instruments must have a final maturity date. A full spectrum of maturity dates is established using a universe of sufficiently liquid bonds that range in number from 15 to 35. The index, which replaced the old Fixed Interest Index, was launched along with a JSE-Actuaries Yield Curve, in October 1988. A composite index along with various maturity subindices are calculated from January 1, 1986.

(1) An aggregative of prices times quantities index formula. Total return includes coupon received or accrued. (2) Bonds are weighted by the amount available for trade, established on the basis of the nominal amount in issue held in public hands. (3) The index is reviewed on a quarterly basis.

PUBLISHER
Johannesburg Stock Exchange.

BONDS—LATIN AMERICA/CENTRAL AMERICA

COLOMBIA

IRBB INDEX

The index tracks the performance of fixed-rate instruments of varying maturities up to three years. The index was launched as of July 1992.

PUBLISHER
Bolsa de Bogota S.A.

BONDS—WORLD

CITICORP/IFR IMPAIRED LOAN INDEX

An equally-weighted index that measures the weekly total return performance of a theoretical portfolio of impaired European loans. The index consists of 11 equally-weighted loans, considered to be among the most prominent and liquid loans on the market. These include the following issues as of November 1995: Brent Walker 3rd Pref., Cordiant (Saatchi), Eurodisney, Eurotunnel, GPA CCF, Isosceles, Maxwell, QMH, DNR Term, Rosenhaugh, Signet and Somerfield (Gateway). At inception, the index purchased STG 10 million face amount each of the 11 loans for a total of STG 71.1 million. In the event that a component loan is repaired or otherwise loses its subjective "impaired" status, it may be replaced by another loan. The index was established as of January 1, 1995. Indicative bids are provided by Citicorp.

PUBLISHER
Citicorp/International Financial Review.

GOLDMAN SACHS INTERNATIONAL GOVERNMENT BOND INDEX

The index tracks the performance of government bonds in the following markets: Austria, Canada, France, Germany, Italy, Japan, Spain, UK. and the U.S.

PUBLISHER
Goldman Sachs.

Lombard Odier & Cie (LOC) Individual Bond Market Indices

An unweighted index that tracks the daily unhedged price only and total return performance of 17 central government and Euro-bonds issued in seven currencies, straight fixed coupon bearing bonds with maturities in excess of one year, expressed in local currency terms.

PUBLISHER
Lombard Odier & Cie.

Money Market Instruments—North America

United States

Bankers Trust Indices
Bankers Acceptances

Indices that track the Bankers Acceptances in the 1-6 month maturity range.

LIBOR

Indices that track various London Inter-Bank Offered Rate (LIBOR) rates, from overnight to one year in maturity.

Repurchase Agreements

Indices that track Repurchase Agreement rates, based on maturity of collateral.

PUBLISHER
Bankers Trust New York Corp.

Banxquote Retail and Institutional CD Indices

Various daily indices that track the performance of retail and institutional CDs, U.S. dollar and international time deposits, and Euro markets.

PUBLISHER
Banxquote.

Bond Buyer Short-Term Indices
Commercial Paper Rate

The daily average rate for 30-day tax-exempt commercial paper, based on estimates provided by major note traders and dealers.

Money Market Municipal Index

The daily average rate of all money market municipal securities, with maturities ranging from 25 to 36 days, that are remarketed during the week by Lehman Brothers. The index covers about 50 different issues.

ONE-YEAR NOTE INDEX

The weekly average rate for one-year tax-exempt notes, based on estimates for theoretical new sales from 10 issuers: California, Colorado, Idaho, New York State, Pennsylvania, Texas, Wisconsin, Los Angeles County, New York City and New Jersey.

PUBLISHER
Bond Buyer.

PAYDEN & RYGEL SHORT-TERM TOTAL RETURN INDICES

Indices that track the monthly total rates of return applicable to various short-term instruments, including 90-day Treasury bills, 90-day domestic CDs, 90-day Eurodollar CDs, 180-day U.S. Treasury bills, 180-day domestic CDs, 180-day Eurodollar CDs, 1-year U.S. Treasury notes and 2-year U.S. Treasury notes.

PUBLISHER
Payden & Rygel.

RYAN LABS CASH INDEX

An equally-weighted index that tracks the total return performance of U.S. Treasury bills with three-, six- and 12-month maturities. Composite and individual maturity indices are calculated monthly to 1979 and daily since 1988.

PUBLISHER
Ryan Labs, Inc.

SALOMON BROTHERS CERTIFICATE-OF-DEPOSIT INDEX

This index measures the monthly return equivalents of CD yield averages which are not marked-to-market. The CD rate is a rotating sample of five banks and dealers surveyed on a daily basis on secondary market dealer offer rates for jumbo certificates of deposit, collected by the New York Federal Reserve Bank.

PUBLISHER
Salomon Brothers.

SALOMON BROTHERS U.S. TREASURY BILL INDEX

The index tracks the monthly return equivalents of yield averages for one-month, three-months and six-month Treasury bills which are not marked-to-market.

COMPUTATION METHODOLOGY
Treasury bill monthly return equivalents are computed by taking the average of the last six-, three- or one-month yields, respectively.

PUBLISHER
Salomon Brothers.

COMMODITIES—NORTH AMERICA

UNITED STATES

DOW JONES
DOW JONES FUTURES INDEX

Reconstituted in 1982, the index is an equally-weighted measure that tracks the performance of active commodities with futures contracts, using prices five months in the future based on two contract months. One contract month expires in fewer than 150 days and the other expires in more than 150 days.

DOW JONES SPOT INDEX

Reconstituted in 1982, the index is an equally-weighted measure that tracks the performance of active commodities with futures contracts, using prices for immediate delivery of the same commodities that comprise the futures index.

PUBLISHER
Dow Jones, Inc.

JOURNAL OF COMMERCE INDUSTRIAL PRICE INDEX

A cyclical indicator, sensitive to the cycles in U.S. economic activity and inflation, the index tracks the daily price performance of 17 commodities which are weighted on the basis of economic importance and each commodity's performance as a cyclical economic indicator. The 17 commodities which are classified into three groups are, as follows: (1) Textiles-cotton, burlap, polyester, and printcloth. (2) Metals-steel scrap, copper scrap, aluminum, zinc, lead and tin. (3) Miscellaneous-hides, rubber, tallow, plywood, red oak, benzene and crude petroleum.
      The index was reconstituted in 1994, at which time old corrugated boxes was deleted from the index and the base value and date were reset to 100.00 as of 1990.

PUBLISHER
Journal of Commerce.

MERRILL LYNCH ENERGY AND METALS INDEX (ENMET)

A weighted geometric index that tracks the daily price only performance of six energy and metal commodity investments, consisting of futures contracts. The index is composed of the following six commodities: WTI crude oil, natural gas, gold, silver, aluminum, and copper. The constituent commodities were selected and their weights established to produce optimal historical correlation against two inflation indices, the Consumer Price Index and the Producer Price Index. Also, these commodities have liquid underlying futures contracts, thereby permitting the efficient structuring of swap contracts, forwards and options on the ENMET Index. The ENMET was established with a base value of 86.165 as of January 1, 1984.

COMPUTATION METHODOLOGY
(1) A geometric average formula is used. (2) The following weights are applied: Oil 40.0%, natural gas 15%, gold 20.0%, silver 5.0%, copper 15.0%, and aluminum 5.0%.

PUBLISHER
Merrill Lynch &Co., Inc.

MOODY'S INVESTORS COMMODITY PRICE INDICES
SPOT COMMODITY PRICE INDEX

An unweighted average of the percentage change of the following industrial and soft commodity prices, excluding energy commodities: Corn, soybean, wheat, cocoa, coffee, hogs, steers, sugar, cotton, wool, aluminum, copper scrap, lead, steel scrap, zinc, rubber, hides and silver.

SCRAP COMMODITY PRICE INDEX

An unweighted average of the percentage change of the following industrial metals commodity prices: Aluminum, copper scrap, lead, steel scrap, nickel and zinc.

PUBLISHER
Moody's Investors Service.

COMMODITIES—ASIA/PACIFIC

JAPAN
DAIWA PHYSICAL COMMODITIES INDEX

A value-weighted arithmetically averaged index of commodities.

PUBLISHER
Daiwa.

NIKKEI COMMODITY INDEX

A geometric mean index that tracks the daily, weekly and month-end price only performance of marketable commodities. Coverage on a daily basis includes 17 commodities and this number is expanded to include 42 commodities on a weekly and month-end basis. The index was established with a base value of 100.00 as of 1970.

PUBLISHER
Nihon Keizai Shimbun, Inc.

COMMODITIES—EUROPE

UNITED KINGDOM

REUTERS COMMODITY INDEX

A geometric average of 17 primary commodities, weighted by their relative importance in international trade.

PUBLISHER
Reuters.

CONVERTIBLE SECURITIES—ASIA/PACIFIC

JAPAN

D.E. SHAW JAPANESE CONVERTIBLE BOND INDEX (DESCBI)

PUBLISHER
D.E. Shaw.

ASIA

KLEINWORT BENSON ASIA CONVERTIBLE BOND INDEX

PUBLISHER
Kleinwort Benson.

CONVERTIBLE SECURITIES—EUROPE

FRANCE

EXANE FRENCH CONVERTIBLE INDEX

A market value-weighted index that tracks the daily performance of the 25 most highly capitalized convertible bonds traded on the French market.

PUBLISHER
Exane.

CURRENCIES—WORLD

KNIGHT RIDDER-CRB CURRENCIES INDEX

An unweighted geometric index that tracks the continuous price only performance of five currencies, consisting of futures contracts on the Deutschemark, Canadian Dollar, Swiss Franc, Japanese Yen and British Pound that are traded on the International Monetary Market (IMM) of the Chicago Mercantile Exchange.

PUBLISHER
Knight Ridder.

MERRILL LYNCH CURRENCY INDICES

This index measures the total return of selected currencies based solely on fluctuations in its exchange rates. Index values are quoted in terms U.S. dollars per unit of foreign currency. Total returns of the currency are denominated in U.S. dollars. The total returns of a bond or currency index can be converted from one currency to another. The following currencies are tracked: Austrian Shilling, Australian Dollar, Belgian Franc, British Pound, Canadian Dollar, Dutch Guilder, Danish Krone, Deutschemark, Finnish Markka, French Franc, Hong Kong Dollar, Irish Punt, Italian Lira, Japanese Yen, New Zealand Dollar, Norwegian Krone, Portuguese Escudo, Spanish Peseta, Swedish Krona, Swiss Franc and Euro Currency.

PUBLISHER
Merrill Lynch.

NIKKEI CURRENCY INDEX

A weighted average index that tracks the daily exchange rates for 30 different currencies. The index was established with a base value of 100.00 as of 1990.

PUBLISHER
Nihon Keizai Shimbun, Inc.

GUARANTEED INVESTMENT CONTRACTS—NORTH AMERICA

UNITED STATES
FIDUCIARY CAPITAL MANAGEMENT GIC INDEX

A series of indices tracking rates applicable to nonbenefit responsive, investment only contracts, in denominations of US$1 million, US$5 million, US$10 million and US$25 million, net of expenses and commissions.

PUBLISHER
Fiduciary Capital Management Inc.

MORLEY CAPITAL MANAGEMENT
3 YEAR GIC INDEX

An index that tracks the monthly total return performance of three-year compound interest bullet contracts in US$1 million denominations.

5 YEAR GIC INDEX

An index that tracks the monthly total return performance of five-year compound interest bullet contracts in US$1 million denominations.

GIC INDEX

A blended index that is designed as a benchmark for pooled funds. The index maintains a 50% weighting in the 5-year index, 30% weighting in the 3-year index and 20% weighting in cash equivalents. Cash equivalents are represented by 30-day Prime CPs.

PUBLISHER
Morley Capital Management.

T. ROWE PRICE GIC INDEX

An equal-weighted index that tracks the daily best rate quotes for a US$2-US$5 million immediate lump sum deposit contract with annual interest payments which are issued by investment grade insurance carriers. Rates are received on a daily basis from 15 to 20 companies, but participating company names are not divulged. Contracts are issued by carriers rated BBB or better by Standard & Poor's or equivalent internal ratings. High/medium/low rates are published.

COMPUTATION METHODOLOGY
(1) The index represents the arithmetic average of all rates that are received prior to 10:30 AM (EST).
(2) Quotes are net of all expenses and exclude broker's commissions.

PUBLISHER
T. Rowe Price.

SCHMIDT GIC/COMMON FUND INDICES
SCHMIDT SHORT-TERM GIC INDEX

An equally-weighted index that tracks the monthly total return performance of simple interest contracts in US$1 million denominations with maturities of one-, two- and three-years.

SCHMIDT LONG-TERM GIC INDEX

An equally-weighted index that tracks the monthly total return performance of simple interest contracts in US$1 million denominations with maturities of eight-, nine- and 10-years.

SCHMIDT GIC COMMON FUND INDEX

An equally-weighted index that tracks the monthly total return performance of a portfolio consisting of 50% Treasury bills and 50% simple interest contracts in US$1 million denominations with maturities of one- to five-years.

PUBLISHER
Schmidt Management Company.

MUTUAL FUNDS—NORTH AMERICA

UNITED STATES

BABSON COLLEGE EMERGING MARKET INCOME INDEX

A market value-weighted index that tracks the daily performance of a universe of emerging market closed-end funds.

PUBLISHER
Babson College.

CDA/WEISENBERGER MUTUAL FUND AVERAGES

Equally-weighted average total rate of return performance of U.S. mutual funds by investment objective categories as classified by CDA/Weisenberger.

PUBLISHER
CDA/Weisenberger.

HERTZFELD SINGLE COUNTRY AVERAGE

An equal-weighted index that tracks the daily price only and total return performance of 25 U.S.-traded closed-end funds that invest principally in equity securities of foreign countries. The index was established with a base value of 2000.00 as of December 31, 1989. Initially established with 20 funds, five funds were added as of December 31, 1992.

PUBLISHER
Thomas J. Hertzfeld Advisors, Inc.

IBC MUTUAL FUND AVERAGES

Equally-weighted average yields and total rate of return performance of U.S.-taxable and tax-exempt money market mutual funds and bond funds, by investment objective categories as classified by IBC.

PUBLISHER
IBC/Donoghue Inc.

INVESTORS DAILY MUTUAL FUND INDEX

An equally-weighted index that tracks the Net Asset Value performance of 20 equity mutual funds, including capital appreciation funds, growth funds and small company funds. Additional indices track the average Net Asset Value performance of gold oriented, growth, international, income, balanced, technology and bond mutual funds.

PUBLISHER
Investor's Business Daily.

LEHMAN BROTHERS MUTUAL FUND INDICES

Market value-weighted indices that track the daily price only, coupon, paydown and total return performance of publicly placed, fixed-rate, dollar-denominated and nonconvertible debt issues with at least $100 million par amount outstanding and at least one year to final maturity, which are drawn from the Lehman Brothers Aggregate Bond Index to more precisely reflect the type, quality and maturity characteristics that correspond to the taxable fixed income mutual fund categories established by Lipper Analytical Services, Inc. These have since been expanded to reflect a full range of available fixed income mutual funds.

The Lehman Brothers mutual fund indices were introduced in November 1992, with a base date of December 31, 1975=100.00, using methodologies that are identical to the ones employed in the construction of the Lehman bond indices. In some cases, the indices are identical to or subsets of other Lehman Brothers indices

The following mutual fund indices are offered: Adjustable Rate Mortgage, Short (1-2) U.S. Government, Short (1-3) U.S. Government, Short (1-5) U.S. Government, Short (1-5) U.S. Treasury, Short (1-3) Investment Grade Debt, Short (1-5) Investment Grade Debt, Short (1-3) Government/Corporate Debt, Short (1-5) Government/Corporate Debt, Short World Multimarket Debt, Intermediate (5-10) U.S. Government Debt, Intermediate (5-10) U.S. Treasury Debt, Intermediate (5-10) Investment Grade Debt, Intermediate (1-10) Government/Corporate Debt, Intermediate (5-10) Government/Corporate Debt, General U.S. Government, General U.S. Treasury, GNMA funds, U.S. Mortgage, Corporate A Rated, Corporate BBB rated, High Yield Composite, General Bonds, Government Mortgage, Corporate/Mortgage, Corporate High Yield, and Long Government Corporate.

PUBLISHER
Lehman Brothers.

LIPPER MUTUAL FUND INDICES

Equally-weighted indices that track the daily total return performance of the largest mutual funds within their respective investment objectives, including open-end funds (mutual funds), closed-end investment companies and variable annuities. Constituent funds are selected from their respective universe, generally on the basis of each fund's investment objective characterization in its prospectus.

The number of constituent funds, investment objective, inception date, total net assets and percentage of total net assets attributable to constituent funds are each displayed.

Constituent funds are selected from the universe of bond mutual funds that are classified by Lipper Analytical, generally on the basis of the fund's investment objective characterization in its prospectus. The largest 30 funds, on the basis of their total net assets as of December 31st of each year, are selected. Funds established under a master-feeder structure or multiple share classes are limited to a single representation, i.e., the largest fund. Also, funds closed to new investors as well as non-NASDAQ-listed funds are generally excluded from participation as an index constituent.

Open-end fund indices include: Capital Appreciation Funds, Emerging Markets Funds, European Region Funds, Financial Services Funds, Flexible Portfolio Funds, Global Flexible Portfolio Funds, Global Funds, Gold Oriented Funds, Health/Biotechnology Funds, Income Funds, MidCap Funds, Pacific Region Funds, S&P 500 Index Funds, Science & Technology Funds, Utility Funds, Adjustable Rate Mortgage Funds, Corporate Funds A Rated, Corporate Debt Funds BBB Rated, Flexible Income Funds, General Bond Funds, General U.S. Government Funds, General U.S. Treasury Funds, General World Income, GNMA Funds, High Current Yield Funds, Intermediate Investment Grade Debt Funds, Intermediate U.S. Government Funds, Money Market Funds, Short Intermediate Investment Grade Debt Funds, Short Intermediate U.S. Government Funds, Short Investment Grade Debt Funds, Short U.S. Government Funds, U.S. Mortgage Funds, California

Intermediate Municipal Debt Funds, Various State Specific Municipal Debt Funds, including Californai, Florida, Maryland, Massachussetts, Michigan, Minnesota, New Jersey, New York State, Ohio, Pennsylvania, and Virginia, General Municipal Debt Funds, High Yield Municipal Debt Funds, Insured Municipal Debt Funds, Intermediate Municipal Debt Funds, Short Intermediate Municipal Debt Funds, Short Municipal Debt Funds and Tax-exempt Money Market Funds.

Closed-end fund indices include: Equity Income Funds, European Equity Funds, Global and Internaltional Equity Funds, Latin American Equity Funds, Pacific Equity Funds, Flexible Bond Funds, General Bond Funds, Investment Grade Bond Funds, Levaraged High-Yield Bond Funds, U.S. Mortgage Bond Non-Term Trusts, U.S. Mortgage Bond Term Trusts.

World Income fund indices include: Developed Nations Bond Funds, World Income Emerging Nations Bond Funds, California, Florida, New York and Pennsylvania Municipal Bond Funds, National Muncipal Leverage and Unleveraged Bond Funds.

Variable Annuity fund indices include: Balanced Funds, Capital Appreciation Funds, Flexible Portfolio Funds, Global Funds, Growth & Income Funds, Growth Funds, International Funds, Small Company Growth Funds, Corporate A-Rated Funds, Corporate BBB-Rated Funds, High Yield Funds and U.S. Government Funds.

Offshore fund indices include: Equity and bond funds.

PUBLISHER
Lipper Analytical.

MERRILL LYNCH
INSURED BOND INDEX

A matrix-weighted index that tracks the daily price only and total return performance of insured tax-exempt securities that correspond to holdings in Insured Municipal Bond Funds, as defined by Lipper Analytical Services, Inc. Insured Municipal Bond Funds are defined as funds that invest at least 65% of assets in municipal debt issues insured as to timely payments. Constituent municipal bonds include insured, fixed-rate, coupon bearing securities, without maturity descriptions, that are rated AAA by Standard & Poor's Corp. and/or Aaa by Moody's Investors Service.

INTERMEDIATE MUTUAL FUND INDEX

A matrix-weighted index that tracks the daily price only and total return performance of intermediate tax-exempt securities that correspond to holdings in Intermediate Municipal Bond Funds, as defined by Lipper Analytical Services, Inc. Intermediate Municipal Bond Funds are defined as funds that invest in municipal debt issues with dollar-weighted average maturities of 5 to 10 years. Constituent municipal bonds include fixed rate, coupon bearing securities, with maturities in the 0 to 22 years range, that are rated BBB or better by Standard & Poor's Corp. and/or Baa3 and above by Moody's Investors Service.

PUBLISHER
Merrill Lynch.

MORNINGSTAR MUTUAL FUND PERFORMANCE AVERAGES

Equally-weighted average total rate of return performance of U.S. open-end mutual funds, closed-end mutual funds and variable annuitites, by investment objective categories as classified by Morningstar.

PUBLISHER
Morningstar.

STANDARD & POOR'S RATED MONEY MARKET FUND INDICES

Indices that track the trailing seven-day, 30-day and 12-month yields produced by rated money market mutual funds.

PUBLISHER
Standard & Poor's.

SALOMON EMERGING MARKET MUTUAL FUND (EMMF) DEBT INDEX

A weighted index that tracks the daily price only and monthly total return performance of emerging market debt in proportions that conform with U.S. investment company diversification regulations. Index constituents correspond to the fixed and floating rate U.S. dollar-denominated Brady bonds with minimum par amounts outstanding of $500 million that have been issued by Mexico, Philippines, Venezuela, Nigeria, Brazil, Philippines, Argentina, Bulgaria, and Poland, that make up the Salomon Brady Bond Index. Investment company diversification guidelines limit one half of the portfolio to individual issuers in amounts of less than 5% each. The remaining half may be invested in positions not greater than 25%. Argentina, Brazil and Mexico debt are assigned weightings of 15%, 20% and 15%, respectively. The remaining half of the index is invested in Brady bonds issued by Bulgaria, Nigeria, Philippines, Poland and Venezuela, in 5% positions, as well as the most actively traded, screen quoted, non-Brady assets of Ecuador, Morocco, Panama, Peru and Russia.

COMPUTATION METHODOLOGY
Each sector return is that of the country's portion of the Brady Bond Index. For additional information, refer to the Salomon Brothers Broad-Investment Grade Index.

PUBLISHER
Salomon Brothers.

VALUE LINE MUTUAL FUND PERFORMANCE AVERAGES

Equally-weighted average total rate of return performance of U.S. open-end mutual funds, by investment objective categories as classified by Value Line.

PUBLISHER
Value Line.

MUTUAL FUNDS—WORLD

MICROPAL MUTUAL FUND/UNIT INVESTMENT TRUST PERFORMANCE AVERAGES

Equally-weighted average total rate of return performance of mutual funds on a worldwide basis, including developed and emerging markets, by investment objective categories as classified by Micropal.

PUBLISHER
Micropal.

Real Estate—North America

United States

Bloomberg Real Estate Investment Trust Indices

Market value-weighted indices of Real Estate Investment Trusts (REITs) with a market capitalization of US$10 million or more. These include a composite index, excluding Healthcare and Mortgage REITS, a Healthcare REIT Index, a Mortgage REIT Index and Whole Loan REIT Index.

Publisher
Bloomberg.

Institutional Property Consultants (IPC) Portfolio Index

An equally-weighted index that tracks the income, capital value and total returns of tax-exempt real estate pooled funds, including group trusts, limited partnerships, private real estate investment trust, insurance company separate accounts and collective investment trusts, based on time-weighted rates of return.

Publisher
Institutional Property Consultants (IPC).

Lehman REIT Index

An equal-weighted geometric average index that tracks the daily stock price performance of equity securities of non-healthcare Real Estate Investment Trusts (REITs) with market capitalizations in excess of US$100 million. The index was established with a base value of 100.00 as of December 31, 1991.

Computation Methodology
(1) A geometric average mathematical technique is used in which the closing prices of each REIT is divided by the preceding day's close. The changes for all REIT stocks in the group are geometrically averaged and the final average change for the day is then multiplied by the prior day's closing value. (2) Constituent stocks are updated monthly, at the beginning of the month. (3) The index does not reflect any adjustments for cash dividends.

Publisher
Lehman Brothers Inc.

Morgan Stanley REIT Index

An market value-weighted index that tracks the daily stock price performance of equity securities of the most actively traded Real Estate Investment Trusts (REITs). The index consists of 90 REITs. The index was established with a base value of 200.00 as of December 31, 1994.

Computation Methodology
An aggregate of prices times quantities index formula. Maintenance adjustments are made for capitalization changes, new listings and delistings.

PUBLISHER
Morgan Stanley.

SNL REIT INDEX

A market value-weighted stock price index that tracks the price only performance of 42 publicly traded real estate investment companies (as of September 30, 1995). The index, which is published by SNL Securities, L.P., was established with a base value of 100.00 as of December 31, 1988.

PUBLISHER
SNL Securities.

REAL ESTATE—WORLD

LIFE GLOBAL REAL ESTATE SECURITIES INDEX

An index that tracks the performance of 350 real estate companies as of January 1, 1996.

PUBLISHER
Limburg Institute of Financial Economics (LIFE).

MISCELLANEOUS

UNITED STATES

BARCLAY CTA INDEX

An equal-weighted index that tracks the monthly performance of commodity trading advisors, with a minimum of four years of actual performance history prior to inclusion in the index, that spans various trading methodologies and market concentrations. Subindices focusing on a particular market emphasis, such as agricultural, currencies, diversified, energy, financials and metals, as well as trading styles, are published.

PUBLISHER
Barclay Trading Group.

MAR FUND/POOL QUALIFIED UNIVERSE INDEX

An index that tracks the monthly performance of commodity trading advisers.

PUBLISHER
Managed Account Reports.

MLM MANAGED FUTURES INDEX

An index that tracks the performance of a portfolio consisting of 25 of the most active nearby futures contracts covering the following sectors: Currencies, financials, metals, energy, softs, agricultural products and meats.

PUBLISHER
Mount Lucas Group.

VARIABLE ANNUITY RESEARCH DATA SERVICE

Equally-weighted average total rate of return performance of variable annuity and variable life products.

PUBLISHER
Financial Planning Resources, Inc.

JAPAN

D.E. SHAW JAPANESE WARRANT INDEX

PUBLISHER
D.E. Shaw.

APPENDIX 3

ADDITIONAL PERFORMANCE DATA

STOCKS

NORTH AMERICA

S&P 500 INDUSTRY GROUP PRICE PERFORMANCE (%): CALENDAR YEARS 1986-1995

Industry Group	1986	1987	1988	1989	1990	1991	1992	1993	1994	1995
Industrials										
Aerospace/Defense	5.92	-19.89	21.37	14.7	1.08	16.10	1.98	26.68	0.56	70.09
Aluminum	-7.22	48.37	21.31	14.81	-13.99	4.48	-0.18	0.27	20.52	24.23
Auto Parts (After Mkt.)	15.55	6.76	-2.19	3.67	29.60	78.91	23.57	14.07	-14.80	20.77
Automobile	11.75	7.04	40.32	-13.16	-27.39	-8.43	41.59	62.17	-16.55	14.38
Beverages (Alcoholic)	21.75	25.46	2.70	33.67	2.07	34.44	-6.81	-7.55	7.16	24.79
Beverages (Soft Drinks)	22.32	8.43	19.94	64.55	21.21	56.58	9.48	3.66	5.78	47.18
Broadcast Media	21.79	36.04	16.98	43.16	-17.47	7.54	21.52	40.07	-7.38	30.64
Building Materials	39.02	-11.60	37.90	-0.37	-26.82	40.44	25.82	22.05	-27.85	33.39
Chemicals	35.84	13.59	2.83	24.71	-18.76	25.37	5.59	7.91	12.21	26.83
Chemicals (Diversified)	30.55	6.99	7.86	13.43	1.67	28.02	14.94	4.91	4.19	29.12
Chemicals (Specialty)	11.75	1.32	6.68	18.78	-6.88	43.55	-0.58	11.90	-14.27	29.36
Communications Equipment/Mfrs.	-10.29	9.43	-1.34	42.54	10.23	53.65	7.00	-4.56	13.55	49.21
Computer Software Services	19.82	7.78	-13.03	21.20	-22.58	51.31	17.89	27.14	17.91	40.30
Computer Systems	-10.30	6.48	-3.64	-19.49	8.49	-13.94	-29.48	1.96	27.83	31.94
Conglomerates	13.31	-0.55	12.34	21.21	-19.27	4.34	19.67	29.34	-7.53	27.28
Containers (Metal & Glass)	50.42	7.32	16.55	16.85	-2.37	53.98	22.28	3.38	-7.15	5.53
Containers (Paper)	44.24	20.45	13.31	12.39	-24.54	71.44	-6.55	-12.09	6.72	-4.63
Cosmetics	28.71	4.10	8.30	52.57	14.58	57.49	4.82	1.14	24.07	30.12
Distributors (Consumer Products)	11.42	-19.85	36.86	28.89	-0.97	19.72	11.17	8.69	2.85	22.32
Electrical Equipment	-2.91	5.11	-2.16	36.51	-10.99	28.65	6.40	17.53	-1.66	36.73

Industry Group	1986	1987	1988	1989	1990	1991	1992	1993	1994	1995
Industrials, Cont'd										
Electronics (Defense)	2.06	1.96	3.94	25.25	5.52	36.85	0.89	27.95	-5.12	93.69
Electronics (Semiconductors)	-11.89	37.89	-15.75	20.17	-2.04	32.70	51.95	53.31	16.32	35.21
Engineering & Construction	-11.43	6.98	26.13	52.76	1.04	19.32	-2.96	3.09	-5.62	40.15
Entertainment	12.25	18.39	20.66	64.80	-7.71	7.65	41.90	14.74	-5.28	19.45
Foods	30.17	2.82	33.07	33.29	5.10	42.67	-2.40	-10.41	8.80	24.72
Gold Mining	-1.88	58.18	-14.99	42.89	-12.87	-20.10	-8.14	81.14	-19.88	11.60
Hardware & Tools	2.26	17.59	10.13	3.41	-25.37	31.73	0.97	10.52	-4.83	43.25
Health Care (Drugs)	34.67	8.46	13.17	45.99	11.34	61.19	-21.78	-11.48	12.36	67.12
Health Care (Miscellaneous)	36.91	-16.12	-49.72	25.35	61.62	65.72	-1.10	-26.95	-14.27	57.88
Heavy Duty Trucks & Parts	-8.06	-7.08	24.07	-8.20	-21.19	26.17	30.60	21.31	-16.04	3.78
Homebuilding	21.27	-26.15	18.61	11.20	-19.55	85.16	21.55	30.92	-42.82	41.25
Hospital Management	NA	NA	NA	NA	NA	NA	NA	NA	NA	NA
Hotel-Motel	20.62	3.30	17.54	30.27	-62.74	29.54	38.33	84.54	-11.86	17.25
Household Furniture & Appliances	33.58	-13.53	8.95	12.07	-35.87	42.65	9.42	40.55	-20.25	18.76
Household Products	23.29	12.31	4.22	52.07	15.71	13.48	9.51	8.50	5.82	36.60
Housewares	NA	5.48	22.42	34.65	1.65	87.75	-13.61	17.89	-4.77	5.71
Leisure Time	26.51	-20.90	32.06	-5.79	-45.80	43.78	15.14	6.22	-4.85	23.97
Machine Tools	-5.57	0.57	5.22	-25.03	-40.84	21.02	23.34	12.57	-19.86	11.34
Machinery (Diversified)	-3.70	36.11	7.88	16.21	-16.00	15.80	-0.33	45.31	-4.40	20.68
Manufactured Housing	-1.61	-27.78	40.11	-4.18	-5.76	43.70	38.78	-2.85	-17.94	31.85
Manufacturing (Diversified Industrials)	29.12	23.13	2.35	9.34	-3.05	20.18	6.23	19.15	1.67	38.58
Medical Products and Supplies	30.64	5.07	-7.53	34.34	15.20	61.27	-15.57	-25.26	16.08	66.86
Metals (Misc.)	-5.20	74.90	29.35	11.32	-8.87	8.48	3.89	8.85	13.99	7.99
Miscellaneous	13.27	-3.35	8.54	34.05	-5.78	21.93	8.50	12.20	1.09	17.30
Office Equipment & Supplies	10.46	-2.42	9.65	5.30	-27.10	54.96	14.18	10.38	-0.54	38.22
Oil & Gas Drilling	-55.50	30.03	9.94	78.80	-12.27	-39.02	31.72	14.43	-20.57	36.36
Oil (Domestic Integrated)	-0.39	6.81	12.15	37.75	-8.91	-10.32	-2.44	1.28	0.68	9.52
Oil Exploration & Production	NA	NA	NA	NA	-18.78	-29.74	-8.52	-4.15	-21.23	16.20
Oil (International Integrated)	31.11	5.61	13.44	28.37	1.77	9.92	-2.34	14.77	1.50	28.85
Oil Well Equipment & Services	-9.93	-1.72	11.92	54.96	9.43	-7.89	-4.06	6.18	-10.34	35.43
Paper & Forest Products	25.18	6.30	6.52	17.54	-12.99	22.96	11.29	7.39	1.63	7.39
Photography/Imaging	NA	NA	NA	NA	NA	15.76	-13.48	35.25	6.03	40.75
Pollution Control	52.36	28.23	4.89	59.11	-11.63	15.97	-1.39	-28.45	1.28	11.79
Publishing	17.40	0.00	28.40	-5.16	-18.29	19.40	13.73	23.63	-7.52	23.83
Publishing (Newspapers)	18.14	1.89	-5.47	16.18	-22.35	17.60	9.00	12.95	-9.99	23.14
Restaurants	3.91	-2.04	10.40	41.09	-13.93	33.34	26.91	15.75	-1.18	48.86
Retail (Department Stores)	24.51	-21.08	59.76	35.22	-11.38	27.11	15.87	8.54	-11.94	12.08
Retail (Drug Stores)	18.47	4.86	-1.58	31.32	5.50	32.90	8.31	-10.98	13.75	40.16

Industry Group	1986	1987	1988	1989	1990	1991	1992	1993	1994	1995
Industrials, Cont'd										
Retail (Food Chains)	16.28	14.73	61.11	33.36	3.73	3.78	28.37	-4.68	5.03	25.90
Retail (General Merchandise)	21.24	0.88	20.59	20.69	-0.53	73.32	12.15	-9.38	-15.91	10.46
Retail (Specialty)	20.98	-24.36	38.63	24.55	-2.40	50.65	32.58	-1.28	-6.30	-3.43
Retail (Specialty-Apparel)	40.09	-44.19	63.81	10.82	4.26	99.11	-10.24	-17.38	-16.09	9.74
Shoes	5.43	-8.30	54.53	52.53	-0.24	103.28	6.60	-30.79	33.63	33.82
Specialized Services	19.28	22.46	-6.14	6.03	-18.51	6.11	-3.62	-6.04	-10.68	32.35
Specialty Printing	NA	NA	NA	NA	NA	20.22	23.14	-12.69	-13.06	23.86
Steel	-20.84	56.39	20.99	-5.14	-18.33	20.89	29.22	30.33	-3.58	-8.37
Telecommunications (Long-Distance)	-4.03	9.51	22.50	63.76	-37.86	29.52	28.59	10.76	-10.99	31.99
Textiles	41.27	-20.64	10.80	29.23	-14.89	57.78	4.86	-25.89	-4.28	9.99
Tobacco	56.04	6.71	47.44	54.33	22.65	48.36	-3.34	-25.56	3.93	49.53
Toys	-9.38	-33.04	17.78	48.01	-12.57	131.14	17.99	9.69	-1.65	35.82
Transportation										
Airlines	12.83	-13.11	33.89	35.54	-28.14	26.80	-11.13	4.92	-30.31	45.86
Railroads	-3.61	8.23	16.70	24.61	-7.60	58.27	9.43	21.16	-15.75	42.85
Transportation (Misc.)	NA	NA	NA	-10.57	-26.08	22.21	38.37	28.54	-14.47	19.03
Truckers	24.62	-12.88	8.55	2.35	-20.00	38.92	9.29	-4.22	-4.95	-12.49
Utilities										
Electric Companies	19.44	-14.63	8.22	23.54	-4.63	21.71	-0.61	6.42	-18.86	23.11
Natural Gas (Dist. & Pipelines)	-0.12	-5.36	4.46	48.21	-16.44	-17.09	6.29	15.26	-7.79	36.98
Telephone	25.48	-4.65	12.87	49.88	-9.26	1.95	4.03	10.19	-8.92	43.91
Financial										
Misc. Financial	NA	NA	NA	36.41	-22.00	54.26	14.54	16.68	-6.06	56.61
Insurance Brokers	25.45	-20.54	16.08	35.05	-3.68	2.13	14.39	-13.23	-2.62	10.75
Life Insurance	0.83	-18.38	15.16	53.01	-21.36	39.06	30.00	-1.29	-19.66	39.50
Major Regional Banks	-0.55	-22.23	21.09	17.19	-32.65	71.77	23.46	2.81	-8.83	51.66
Money Center Banks	11.21	-30.48	24.47	16.39	-37.48	39.27	31.99	19.86	-5.86	57.68
Multi-Line Insurance	0.23	-11.39	6.06	34.10	-20.49	30.26	11.69	9.83	3.45	44.99
Personal Loans	13.35	-24.98	31.99	10.37	-27.14	53.24	9.29	11.91	9.13	44.82
Property-Casualty Insurance	2.80	-8.31	-1.75	40.42	-6.09	21.60	13.98	-3.91	2.25	32.88
Savings & Loan Companies	26.95	-24.58	1.37	29.26	-23.58	50.37	1.70	1.48	-15.91	60.01

ASIA/PACIFIC

INDIA

CALCUTTA STOCK EXCHANGE-CSE INDEX   1987=100.00

Year	Value	Price Return (%)	Cumulative (%)
1995	438.70	-10.89	-10.89
1994	492.30		
Average Annual (%)		NM	
Compound Annual (%)		NM	
Standard Deviation (%)		NM	

Madras Stock Exchange-MSE Index 1983=100.00

Year	Value	Price Return (%)	Cumulative (%)
1995	3,114.30	-8.22	1,288.45
1994	3,393.30	30.92	1,412.84
1993	2,591.80	92.00	1,055.51
1992	1,349.90	41.04	501.83
1991	957.10	40.48	326.71
1990	681.30	39.93	203.74
1989	486.90	44.31	117.08
1988	337.40	50.42	50.42
1987	224.30		
Average Annual (%)		41.36	
Compound Annual (%)		38.94	
Standard Deviation (%)		27.32	

EUROPE

BULGARIA
FBSE Index — SEPTEMBER 7, 1993=100.00

Year	Value	Price Return (%)	Cumulative (%)
1995	104.30	-8.19	-11.86
1994	113.60	-4.00	
Average Annual (%)		-6.09	
Compound Annual (%)		-6.12	
Standard Deviation (%)		NM	

AFRICA/MIDDLE EAST

EGYPT
Egyptian Capital Market Authority Index — JANUARY 2, 1992=100.0

Year	Value	Price Return (%)	Cumulative (%)
1995	213.20	-10.57	113.20
1994	238.40	75.68	138.40
1993	135.70	24.61	35.70
1992	108.90	8.90	8.90
1991	100.00		
Average Annual (%)		24.66	
Compound Annual (%)		20.84	
Standard Deviation (%)		36.94	

IRAN
Tepix Index — MARCH 21, 1990=100.00

Year	Value	Price Return (%)	Cumulative (%)
1995	1,288.10	125.78	172.84
1994	570.50	49.03	20.84
1993	382.80	-14.00	-18.92
1992	445.10	-5.72	-5.72
1991	472.10		
Average Annual (%)		38.78	
Compound Annual (%)		28.52	
Standard Deviation (%)		64.40	

COMMERCIAL BANK OF QATAR SHARE INDEX · JUNE 30, 1995=100.00

Year	Value	Price Return (%)	Cumulative (%)
1995	113.43	13.43	13.43
June 30, 1995	100.00		
Average Annual (%)		NM	
Compound Annual (%)		NM	
Standard Deviation (%)		NM	

SAUDI ARABIA
NCFEI INDEX · FEBRUARY 1985=100.00

Year	Value	Price Return (%)	Cumulative (%)
1995	136.80	6.63	6.63
1994	128.30		
Average Annual (%)		NM	
Compound Annual (%)		NM	
Standard Deviation (%)		NM	

TUNISIA
BVM GENERAL INDEX · SEPTEMBER 30, 1990=100.00

Year	Value	Price Return (%)	Cumulative (%)
1995	534.70	5.42	434.70
1994	507.20	102.07	407.20
1993	251.00	25.88	151.00
1992	199.40	16.88	99.40
1991	170.60	33.49	70.60
1990	127.80	27.80	27.80
9/1990	100.00		
Average Annual (%)		40.29	
Compound Annual (%)[1]		33.14	
Standard Deviation (%)[1]		37.99	

[1] Compound annual and standard deviation applicable to the 5-year period 1991-1995.

CENTRAL/LATIN AMERICA

URUGUAY
INDICE DE PRECIOS · 1990=100.00

Year	Value	Price Return (%)	Cumulative (%)
1995	860.30	35.44	760.30
1994	635.20	44.10	535.20
1993	440.80	52.90	340.80
1992	288.30	58.84	188.30
1991	181.50	81.50	81.50
1990	100.00		
Average Annual (%)		54.56	
Compound Annual (%)		53.79	
Standard Deviation (%)		17.48	

IFC GLOBAL INDEX—ARGENTINA

Year	Value	Total Return (%)	Cumulative (%)	Price Return (%)
1995	1,872.13	12.68	854.19	8.70
1994	1,661.44	-23.03	746.81	-25.10
1993	2,158.68	62.55	1,000.24	67.30
1992	1,328.05	-22.10	576.89	-27.50
1991	1,704.77	396.92	768.89	393.90
1990	343.07	-36.54	74.86	-37.30
1989	540.60	175.54	175.54	138.00
1988	196.20			30.70
1987				7.10
1986				-26.60
Average Annual (%)		80.86		59.92
Compound Annual (%)		38.02		22.29
Standard Deviation (%)		157.59		131.35

IFC GLOBAL INDEX—BRAZIL

Year	Value	Total Return (%)	Cumulative (%)	Price Return (%)
1995	429.30	-20.24	251.91	-22.20
1994	538.26	69.84	341.23	67.60
1993	316.92	117.10	159.79	91.30
1992	145.98	-7.85	19.67	-1.50
1991	158.42	170.39	29.86	148.40
1990	58.59	-65.68	-51.97	-67.30
1989	170.72	39.95	39.95	34.40
1988	121.99			105.20
1987				-65.80
1986				-26.70
Average Annual (%)		43.36		26.34
Compound Annual (%)		19.69		3.27
Standard Deviation (%)		82.51		74.76

IFC GLOBAL INDEX—CHILE

Year	Value	Total Return (%)	Cumulative (%)	Price Return (%)
1995	6,508.02	0.50	859.14	-2.90
1994	6,475.78	45.10	854.38	41.20
1993	4,462.93	33.60	557.74	29.50
1992	2,340.48	17.05	392.31	12.30
1991	2,853.87	98.06	320.60	90.00
1990	1,440.88	40.44	112.35	31.30
1989	1,025.95	51.20	51.20	35.40
1988	678.53			22.10
1987				21.50
1986				134.40
Average Annual (%)		40.85		41.48
Compound Annual (%)		38.12		37.08
Standard Deviation (%)		30.68		40.65

IFC GLOBAL INDEX—COLOMBIA

Year	Value	Total Return (%)	Cumulative (%)	Price Return (%)
1995	2,874.52	-23.77	725.35	-25.50
1994	3,770.73	28.90	982.67	26.80
1993	2,925.38	42.53	739.95	31.70
1992	2,052.40	31.47	489.30	36.10
1991	1,561.14	191.32	348.24	173.90
1990	535.89	37.56	53.87	26.40
1989	389.56	11.85	11.85	3.80
1988	348.28			-17.80
1987				65.70
1986				124.00
Average Annual (%)		45.69		44.51
Compound Annual (%)		35.19		33.93
Standard Deviation (%)		67.99		62.21

IFC GLOBAL INDEX—MEXICO

Year	Value	Total Return (%)	Cumulative (%)	Price Return (%)
1995	1,717.89	-25.84	270.99	-27.00
1994	2,316.32	-40.47	400.23	-41.60
1993	3,890.84	49.11	740.26	46.90
1992	2,609.42	21.23	463.53	20.00
1991	2,152.37	106.76	364.82	102.40
1990	1,041.00	29.56	124.81	24.90
1989	803.50	73.52	73.52	67.80
1988	463.05			99.20
1987				-6.40
1986				80.90
Average Annual (%)		30.55		36.71
Compound Annual (%)		20.60		26.81
Standard Deviation (%)		52.14		51.33

IFC GLOBAL INDEX—PERU

Year	Value	Total Return (%)	Cumulative (%)	Price Return (%)
1995	233.80	11.04	133.80	9.30
1994	210.55	53.47	110.55	52.10
1993	137.19	37.19	37.19	34.90
1992	100.00			
Average Annual (%)		33.90		32.10
Compound Annual (%)		32.72		30.89
Standard Deviation (%)		21.41		21.54

BONDS

WORLD

BLOOMBERG/EFFAS GOVERNMENT BOND INDEX—AUSTRALIA

Year	Value	Total Return (%)	Cumulative (%)
1995	147.238	20.05	47.24
1994	122.643	-6.49	22.64
1993	131.148	18.17	31.15
1992	110.983	10.98	10.98
1991	100.000		
Average Annual (%)		10.68	
Compound Annual (%)		10.16	
Standard Deviation (%)		12.09	

BLOOMBERG/EFFAS GOVERNMENT BOND INDEX—AUSTRIA

Year	Value	Total Return (%)	Cumulative (%)
1995	150.390	15.41	50.39
1994	130.306	0.31	30.31
1993	129.897	13.75	29.90
1992	114.193	14.19	14.19
1991	100.000		
Average Annual (%)		10.92	
Compound Annual (%)		10.74	
Standard Deviation (%)		7.10	

BLOOMBERG/EFFAS GOVERNMENT BOND INDEX—BELGIUM

Year	Value	Total Return (%)	Cumulative (%)
1995	153.343	17.24	53.34
1994	130.791	-0.54	30.79
1993	131.500	14.66	31.50
1992	114.685	14.69	14.69
1991	100.000		
Average Annual (%)		11.51	
Compound Annual (%)		11.28	
Standard Deviation (%)		8.13	

BLOOMBERG/EFFAS GOVERNMENT BOND INDEX—CANADA

Year	Value	Total Return (%)	Cumulative (%)
1995	146.954	20.48	46.95
1994	121.978	-4.53	21.98
1993	127.765	16.43	27.77
1992	109.736	9.74	9.74
1991	100.000		
Average Annual (%)		10.53	
Compound Annual (%)		10.10	
Standard Deviation (%)		10.97	

BLOOMBERG/EFFAS GOVERNMENT BOND INDEX—DENMARK

Year	Value	Total Return (%)	Cumulative (%)
1995	148.891	19.13	48.89
1994	124.986	-4.07	24.99
1993	130.286	21.68	30.29
1992	107.075	7.08	7.08
1991	100.000		
Average Annual (%)		10.95	
Compound Annual (%)		10.46	
Standard Deviation (%)		11.87	

BLOOMBERG/EFFAS GOVERNMENT BOND INDEX—FINLAND

Year	Value	Total Return (%)	Cumulative (%)
1995	164.706	19.70	64.71
1994	137.598	-5.29	37.60
1993	145.285	25.49	45.29
1992	115.773	15.77	15.77
1991	100.000		
Average Annual (%)		13.92	
Compound Annual (%)		13.29	
Standard Deviation (%)		13.41	

BLOOMBERG/EFFAS GOVERNMENT BOND INDEX—FRANCE

Year	Value	Total Return (%)	Cumulative (%)
1995	149.724	17.02	49.72
1994	127.948	-5.35	27.95
1993	135.179	21.34	35.18
1992	111.408	11.41	11.41
1991	100.00		
Average Annual (%)		11.10	
Compound Annual (%)		10.62	
Standard Deviation (%)		11.70	

BLOOMBERG/EFFAS GOVERNMENT BOND INDEX—GERMANY

Year	Value	Total Return (%)	Cumulative (%)
1995	147.161	16.31	47.16
1994	126.526	-1.56	26.53
1993	128.531	13.78	28.53
1992	112.961	12.96	12.96
1991	100.000		
Average Annual (%)		10.37	
Compound Annual (%)		10.14	
Standard Deviation (%)		8.08	

BLOOMBERG/EFFAS GOVERNMENT BOND INDEX—IRELAND

Year	Value	Total Return (%)	Cumulative (%)
1995	153.501	17.37	53.50
1994	130.787	-3.35	30.79
1993	135.322	31.48	35.32
1992	102.920	2.92	2.92
1991	100.000		
Average Annual (%)		12.10	
Compound Annual (%)		11.31	
Standard Deviation (%)		15.56	

BLOOMBERG/EFFAS GOVERNMENT BOND INDEX—JAPAN

Year	Value	Total Return (%)	Cumulative (%)
1995	138.124	12.77	38.12
1994	122.483	-3.12	22.48
1993	126.432	13.76	26.43
1992	111.139	11.14	11.14
1991	100.000		
Average Annual (%)		8.64	
Compound Annual (%)		8.41	
Standard Deviation (%)		7.91	

BLOOMBERG/EFFAS GOVERNMENT BOND INDEX—ITALY

Year	Value	Total Return (%)	Cumulative (%)
1995	165.422	16.88	65.42
1994	141.533	-0.87	41.53
1993	142.772	29.68	42.77
1992	110.092	10.09	10.09
1991	100.000		
Average Annual (%)		13.95	
Compound Annual (%)		13.41	
Standard Deviation (%)		12.79	

BLOOMBERG/EFFAS GOVERNMENT BOND INDEX—NETHERLANDS

Year	Value	Total Return (%)	Cumulative (%)
1995	152.578	18.35	52.58
1994	128.925	-4.30	28.93
1993	134.718	16.24	34.72
1992	115.892	15.89	15.89
1991	100.000		
Average Annual (%)		11.55	
Compound Annual (%)		11.14	
Standard Deviation (%)		10.62	

BLOOMBERG/EFFAS GOVERNMENT BOND INDEX—NEW ZEALAND

Year	Value	Total Return (%)	Cumulative (%)
1995	141.166	14.22	41.17
1994	123.591	-3.32	23.59
1993	127.831	14.24	27.83
1992	111.892	11.89	11.89
1991	100.000		
Average Annual (%)		9.26	
Compound Annual (%)		9.00	
Standard Deviation (%)		8.46	

BLOOMBERG/EFFAS GOVERNMENT BOND INDEX—NORWAY

Year	Value	Total Return (%)	Cumulative (%)
1995	146.575	16.04	46.58
1994	126.311	-3.72	26.31
1993	131.189	20.19	31.19
1992	109.152	9.15	9.15
1991	100.000		
Average Annual (%)		10.42	
Compound Annual (%)		10.03	
Standard Deviation (%)		10.47	

Bloomberg/EFFAS Government Bond Index—Portugal

Year	Value	Total Return (%)	Cumulative (%)
1995	128.361	19.47	28.36
1994	107.443	2.94	7.44
1993	104.374	4.37	4.37
1992	100.000		
Average Annual (%)		8.93	
Compound Annual (%)		8.68	
Standard Deviation (%)		9.16	

Bloomberg/EFFAS Government Bond Index—Spain

Year	Value	Total Return (%)	Cumulative (%)
1995	163.207	19.14	63.21
1994	136.982	-3.56	36.98
1993	142.045	31.19	42.05
1992	108.278	8.28	8.28
1991	100.000		
Average Annual (%)		13.76	
Compound Annual (%)		13.03	
Standard Deviation (%)		14.86	

Bloomberg/EFFAS Government Bond Index—Sweden

Year	Value	Total Return (%)	Cumulative (%)
1995	151.377	20.12	51.38
1994	126.023	-6.79	26.02
1993	135.200	21.07	35.20
1992	111.674	11.67	11.67
1991	100.000		
Average Annual (%)		11.52	
Compound Annual (%)		10.92	
Standard Deviation (%)		12.91	

Bloomberg/EFFAS Government Bond Index—Switzerland

Year	Value	Total Return (%)	Cumulative (%)
1995	119.194	14.04	19.19
1994	104.515	-0.71	4.52
1993	105.266	5.27	5.27
1992	100.000		
Average Annual (%)		6.20	
Compound Annual (%)		6.03	
Standard Deviation (%)		7.42	

Bloomberg/EFFAS Government Bond Index—United Kingdom

Year	Value	Total Return (%)	Cumulative (%)
1995	164.275	16.63	64.28
1994	140.852	-5.29	40.85
1993	148.715	23.03	48.72
1992	120.879	20.88	20.88
1991	100.000		
Average Annual (%)		13.81	
Compound Annual (%)		13.21	
Standard Deviation (%)		13.01	

CURRENCY

MERRILL LYNCH CURRENCY INDEX—AUSTRALIAN DOLLAR

Year	Value	Price Return (%)	Cumulative (%)
1995	0.744	-4.10	9.03
1994	0.775	14.22	13.69
1993	0.679	-1.82	-0.47
1992	0.691	-9.29	1.37
1991	0.762	-1.21	11.76
1990	0.772	-2.22	13.12
1989	0.789	-7.50	15.69
1988	0.853	18.14	25.07
1987	0.722	8.57	5.86
1986	0.655	-2.49	-2.49
1985	0.682		
Average Annual (%)		1.23	
Compound Annual (%)		0.87	
Standard Deviation (%)		9.22	

Note: Price returns may not compute due to rounding of currency values.

MERRILL LYNCH CURRENCY INDEX—AUSTRIAN SHILLING

Year	Value	Price Return (%)	Cumulative (%)
1995	0.099	8.26	70.54
1994	0.092	12.20	57.53
1993	0.082	-6.60	40.40
1992	0.088	-6.15	50.32
1991	0.093	-1.35	60.17
1990	0.095	12.04	62.37
1989	0.084	4.99	44.92
1988	0.080	-10.79	38.04
1987	0.090	21.98	54.73
1986	0.074	26.85	26.85
1985	0.058		
Average Annual (%)		6.14	
Compound Annual (%)		5.48	
Standard Deviation (%)		12.53	

Note: Price returns may not compute due to rounding of currency values.

MERRILL LYNCH CURRENCY INDEX—BELGIAN FRANC

Year	Value	Price Return (%)	Cumulative (%)
1995	0.034	8.21	70.01
1994	0.031	13.84	57.11
1993	0.028	-8.17	38.01
1992	0.030	-5.82	50.29
1991	0.032	-1.28	59.58
1990	0.032	14.64	61.64
1989	0.028	4.44	41.00
1988	0.027	-11.18	35.00
1987	0.030	21.60	52.00
1986	0.025	25.00	25.00
1985	0.020		
Average Annual (%)		6.13	
Compound Annual (%)		5.45	
Standard Deviation (%)		12.63	

Note: Price returns may not compute due to rounding of currency values.

MERRILL LYNCH CURRENCY INDEX—BRITISH POUND

Year	Value	Price Return (%)	Cumulative (%)
1995	1.552	-0.80	7.37
1994	1.565	5.85	8.23
1993	1.478	-2.67	2.25
1992	1.519	-18.81	6.06
1991	1.871	-3.07	29.40
1990	1.930	19.73	33.50
1989	1.612	-10.84	11.50
1988	1.808	-3.73	25.06
1987	1.878	26.72	29.90
1986	1.482	2.56	2.51
1985	1.445		
Average Annual (%)		1.49	
Compound Annual (%)		0.71	
Standard Deviation (%)		13.43	

Note: Price returns may not compute due to rounding of currency values.

MERRILL LYNCH CURRENCY INDEX—CANADIAN DOLLAR

Year	Value	Price Return (%)	Cumulative (%)
1995	0.733	2.81	14.88
1994	0.713	5.69	11.74
1993	0.756	-3.93	5.73
1992	0.787	-9.00	10.05
1991	0.865	0.34	20.93
1990	0.862	-0.10	20.52
1989	0.863	2.94	20.63
1988	0.838	8.89	17.18
1987	0.770	6.31	7.62
1986	0.724	1.23	1.23
1985	0.715		
Average Annual (%)		1.52	
Compound Annual (%)		1.40	
Standard Deviation (%)		5.19	

Note: Price returns may not compute due to rounding of currency values.

MERRILL LYNCH CURRENCY INDEX—EUROPEAN CURRENCY UNIT (ECU)

Year	Value	Price Return (%)	Cumulative (%)
1995	1.280	4.42	43.84
1994	1.226	10.15	37.75
1993	1.113	-7.94	25.06
1992	1.209	-9.44	35.84
1991	1.335	-2.38	50.00
1990	1.368	14.69	53.65
1989	1.192	1.73	33.97
1988	1.172	-10.47	31.69
1987	1.309	21.65	47.08
1986	1.076	20.90	20.90
1985	0.890		
Average Annual (%)		4.33	
Compound Annual (%)		3.70	
Standard Deviation (%)		12.14	

Note: Price returns may not compute due to rounding of currency values.

MERRILL LYNCH CURRENCY INDEX—DUTCH GUILDER

Year	Value	Price Return (%)	Cumulative (%)
1995	0.624	8.21	71.83
1994	0.577	12.22	58.79
1993	0.514	-6.57	41.50
1992	0.550	-5.76	51.45
1991	0.583	-1.43	60.70
1990	0.592	13.01	63.03
1989	0.524	4.87	44.27
1988	0.500	-11.54	37.56
1987	0.565	22.64	55.51
1986	0.460	26.80	26.80
1985	0.363		
Average Annual (%)		6.25	
Compound Annual (%)		5.56	
Standard Deviation (%)		12.74	

Note: Price returns may not compute due to rounding of currency values.

MERRILL LYNCH CURRENCY INDEX—DANISH KRONE

Year	Value	Price Return (%)	Cumulative (%)
1995	0.180	9.78	61.01
1994	0.164	11.65	46.66
1993	0.147	-7.67	31.36
1992	0.159	-5.26	42.27
1991	0.168	-2.53	50.18
1990	0.173	13.63	54.07
1989	0.152	4.25	35.59
1988	0.146	-11.37	30.06
1987	0.164	19.99	46.74
1986	0.137	22.30	22.30
1985	0.112		
Average Annual (%)		5.48	
Compound Annual (%)		4.88	
Standard Deviation (%)		11.80	

Note: Price returns may not compute due to rounding of currency values.

MERRILL LYNCH CURRENCY INDEX—DEUTSCHE MARK

Year	Value	Price Return (%)	Cumulative (%)
1995	0.699	8.28	71.00
1994	0.645	12.26	57.92
1993	0.575	-6.73	40.67
1992	0.616	-6.28	50.82
1991	0.658	-1.57	60.93
1990	0.668	12.94	63.50
1989	0.592	4.90	44.77
1988	0.564	-11.17	38.01
1987	0.635	22.10	55.36
1986	0.520	27.25	27.25
1985	0.409		
Average Annual (%)		6.20	
Compound Annual (%)		5.51	
Standard Deviation (%)		12.78	

Note: Price returns may not compute due to rounding of currency values.

MERRILL LYNCH CURRENCY INDEX—FINNISH MARKKA

Year	Value	Price Return (%)	Cumulative (%)
1995	0.230	9.22	24.18
1994	0.211	22.57	13.70
1993	0.172	-9.35	-7.23
1992	0.190	-20.99	2.34
1991	0.240	-12.80	29.52
1990	0.276	11.34	48.53
1989	0.248	2.87	33.41
1988	0.241	-5.27	29.69
1987	0.254	21.06	36.91
1986	0.210	13.09	13.09
1985	0.186		
Average Annual (%)		3.17	
Compound Annual (%)		2.19	
Standard Deviation (%)		14.78	

Note: Price returns may not compute due to rounding of currency values.

MERRILL LYNCH CURRENCY INDEX—FRENCH FRANC

Year	Value	Price Return (%)	Cumulative (%)
1995	0.205	9.15	53.55
1994	0.187	10.94	40.68
1993	0.169	-6.63	26.81
1992	0.181	-6.01	35.82
1991	0.192	-1.97	44.50
1990	0.196	13.50	47.40
1989	0.173	4.83	29.87
1988	0.165	-11.90	23.89
1987	0.187	19.46	40.63
1986	0.157	17.72	17.72
1985	0.133		
Average Annual (%)		4.91	
Compound Annual (%)		4.38	
Standard Deviation (%)		10.99	

Note: Price returns may not compute due to rounding of currency values.

MERRILL LYNCH CURRENCY INDEX—HONG KONG DOLLAR

Year	Value	Price Return (%)	Cumulative (%)
1995	0.129	0.08	0.97
1994	0.129	-0.19	0.89
1993	0.129	0.27	1.08
1992	0.129	0.47	0.81
1991	0.129	0.25	0.34
1990	0.128	0.09	0.09
1989	0.128	-0.08	0.00
1988	0.128	-0.39	0.08
1987	0.129	0.23	0.47
1986	0.128	0.23	0.23
1985	0.128		
Average Annual (%)		0.10	
Compound Annual (%)		0.10	
Standard Deviation (%)		0.25	

Note: Price returns may not compute due to rounding of currency values.

MERRILL LYNCH CURRENCY INDEX—IRISH PUNT

Year	Value	Price Return (%)	Cumulative (%)
1995	1.602	3.41	28.40
1994	1.549	9.90	24.16
1993	1.410	-13.94	12.97
1992	1.638	-6.27	31.28
1991	1.748	-1.58	40.06
1990	1.776	14.08	42.30
1989	1.556	3.37	24.74
1988	1.506	-10.24	20.67
1987	1.677	18.86	34.43
1986	1.411	13.10	13.10
1985	1.248		
Average Annual (%)		3.07	
Compound Annual (%)		2.53	
Standard Deviation (%)		11.02	

Note: Price returns may not compute due to rounding of currency values.

MERRILL LYNCH CURRENCY INDEX—ITALIAN LIRA

Year	Value	Price Return (%)	Cumulative (%)
1995	0.000631	2.26	5.24
1994	0.000617	5.95	2.92
1993	0.000582	-14.03	-2.86
1992	0.000677	-22.82	12.99
1991	0.000877	-0.98	46.39
1990	0.000885	12.23	47.83
1989	0.000789	2.96	31.72
1988	0.000766	-10.79	27.94
1987	0.000859	14.96	43.42
1986	0.000747	24.76	24.76
1985	0.000599		
Average Annual (%)		1.45	
Compound Annual (%)		0.51	
Standard Deviation (%)		14.34	

Note: Price returns may not compute due to rounding of currency values.

MERRILL LYNCH CURRENCY INDEX—JAPANESE YEN

Year	Value	Price Return (%)	Cumulative (%)
1995	0.009697	3.43	94.18
1994	0.010000	12.19	101.08
1993	0.008951	11.79	79.23
1992	0.008007	-0.09	60.32
1991	0.008014	8.97	60.47
1990	0.007354	5.86	47.26
1989	0.006947	-13.13	39.10
1988	0.007997	-3.00	60.13
1987	0.008244	30.51	65.08
1986	0.006317	26.49	26.49
1985	0.004994		
Average Annual (%)		7.62	
Compound Annual (%)		6.86	
Standard Deviation (%)		13.53	

Note: Price returns may not compute due to rounding of currency values.

Year	Value	Price Return (%)	Cumulative (%)
1995	0.653	2.28	30.68
1994	0.639	14.18	27.77
1993	0.560	8.58	11.90
1992	0.515	-4.62	3.06
1991	0.540	-8.05	8.06
1990	0.588	-1.33	17.52
1989	0.596	-5.33	19.10
1988	0.629	-4.41	25.80
1987	0.658	24.15	31.60
1986	0.530	6.00	6.00
1985	0.500		
Average Annual (%)		3.15	
Compound Annual (%)		2.71	
Standard Deviation (%)		10.20	

Note: Price returns may not compute due to rounding of currency values.

MERRILL LYNCH CURRENCY INDEX—NORWEGIAN KRONE

Year	Value	Price Return (%)	Cumulative (%)
1995	0.158	7.12	20.16
1994	0.148	11.39	12.17
1993	0.133	-7.79	0.70
1992	0.144	-13.71	9.21
1991	0.167	-1.84	26.56
1990	0.170	12.09	28.92
1989	0.152	-0.46	15.02
1988	0.152	-5.17	15.55
1987	0.161	18.35	21.85
1986	0.136	2.96	2.96
1985	0.132		
Average Annual (%)		2.29	
Compound Annual (%)		1.85	
Standard Deviation (%)		9.99	

Note: Price returns may not compute due to rounding of currency values.

MERRILL LYNCH CURRENCY INDEX—PORTUGUESE ESCUDO

Year	Value	Price Return (%)	Cumulative (%)
1995	0.006696	6.47	18.64
1994	0.006289	11.43	11.43
1993	0.005644		
1992			
1991			
1990			
1989			
1988			
1987			
1986			
1985			
Average Annual (%)		8.95	
Compound Annual (%)		8.92	
Standard Deviation (%)		3.51	

Note: Price returns may not compute due to rounding of currency values.

MERRILL LYNCH CURRENCY INDEX—SPANISH PESETA

Year	Value	Price Return (%)	Cumulative (%)
1995	0.008248	8.53	-11.75
1994	0.007600	8.80	-18.68
1993	0.006985	-19.57	-25.26
1992	0.008684	-16.02	-7.08
1991	0.010000	-1.34	10.65
1990	0.010000	15.46	12.16
1989	0.009079	1.77	-2.86
1988	0.008921	-4.55	-4.55
1987	0.009346		
1986			
1985			
Average Annual (%)		-0.87	
Compound Annual (%)		-1.55	
Standard Deviation (%)		12.24	

Note: Price returns may not compute due to rounding of currency values.

MERRILL LYNCH CURRENCY INDEX—SWEDISH KRONA

Year	Value	Price Return (%)	Cumulative (%)
1995	0.151	12.10	14.37
1994	0.135	12.48	2.03
1993	0.120	-15.36	-9.29
1992	0.141	-21.26	7.17
1991	0.180	1.21	36.11
1990	0.177	9.84	34.48
1989	0.161	-1.10	22.44
1988	0.163	-5.55	23.81
1987	0.173	16.82	31.08
1986	0.148	12.21	12.21
1985	0.132		
Average Annual (%)		2.14	
Compound Annual (%)		1.35	
Standard Deviation (%)		12.94	

Note: Price returns may not compute due to rounding of currency values.

MERRILL LYNCH CURRENCY INDEX—SWISS FRANC

Year	Value	Price Return (%)	Cumulative (%)
1995	0.869	13.77	79.10
1994	0.764	13.25	57.43
1993	0.675	-1.03	39.01
1992	0.682	-7.59	40.45
1991	0.738	-5.78	51.99
1990	0.783	20.71	61.32
1989	0.649	-2.56	33.64
1988	0.666	-15.11	37.15
1987	0.784	26.59	61.57
1986	0.620	27.63	27.63
1985	0.485		
Average Annual (%)		6.99	
Compound Annual (%)		6.00	
Standard Deviation (%)		15.29	

Note: Price returns may not compute due to rounding of currency values.

APPENDIX 4

GLOSSARY

AMERICAN DEPOSITARY RECEIPT (ADR)

A receipt, held in the vault of a United States (U.S.) bank, representing shares of a foreign corporation. ADRs, which are traded on a the New York Stock Exchange, American Stock Exchange and Nasdaq, entitle holders to all payments of income and capital gains. Also called American Depositary Shares (ADSs).

AVERAGE ANNUAL RATE OF RETURN

A simple average of the annual rates of return earned or produced over a period in excess of a year. The annual rates of return for the period are summed and the result is divided by the number of calendar years to arrive at the average annual rate of return. The formula for the average annual rate of return R, where n is the number of years, is:

$$R = \Sigma r/n$$

BACKDATING/BACKTESTING

The process by which historical index performance results are created for time periods that actually precede the introduction of the index and, in some cases, its base date. This is usually accomplished by applying current selection criteria, maintenance rules and calculation methodologies, combined with historical pricing to previously existing securities, so as to simulate the composition of the index and recreate a series of historical index values.

CAPITAL MARKET ASSET PRICING MODEL (CAPM)

A description of the relationship between the return on a security or a portfolio of securities and the overall market. In theory, the overall market is a market portfolio consisting of all securities, each in proportion to their market value (prices times quantities of shares). In practice, a market value-weighted index, such as the Standard & Poor's 500 Composite Stock Price Index, is used as a proxy for the overall market.

The concept can be summarized graphically by means of a capital market line, which represents the relationship between risk and expected return underlying the CAPM (see Chart). The horizontal axis measures risk, defined as the standard deviation of returns, while the vertical axis measures expected return. Point F represents the risk free rate of return, or the rate of return earned from 90-day U.S. Treasury bills (auction rate average). Point M represents the expected return from the market, or the S&P 500 Index. The line joining the two points is known as the security market line, the slope of which shows the trade-off between risk and expected returns. Higher risk should be rewarded by higher returns while low risk should produce commensurably lower returns.

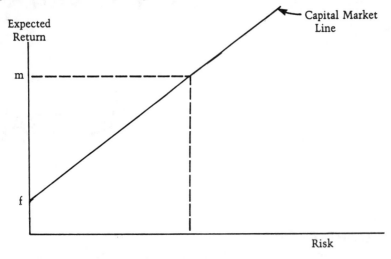

CAPS

A Flex stock index option listed at a strike price close to the current index value, but with a capped value that is higher (calls) or lower (puts) by a specified number of points. The option is automatically exercised on any given day that the index exceeds or falls below the capped value.

CLOSED-END INVESTMENT COMPANY

An investment company with a fixed number of shares of common stock that are traded on a securities exchange. Unlike mutual funds whose shares may be redeemed at their fair market value, or net asset value (NAV), the prices of closed-end fund shares are determined by investors and their expectations. They normally trade at a discount or premium to the NAV.

COMPOUND ANNUAL RATE OF RETURN

The annual rate of return which, when compounded (reinvested) for a time t, will result in the cumulative rate of return R. It is computed by taking the "n^{th}" root of the cumulative rate of return, where n is the number of years, and then subtracting one, as follows:

$$r = \sqrt[n]{(1 + R)} - 1$$

CUMULATIVE RATE OF RETURN

The final percentage earned or produced over a period of time, calculated by compounding or linking periodic rates of return together, thereby creating an accelerated rate of growth over time. The cumulative rate of return formula for n years is:

$$R = (1 + r_1)(1 + r_2)...(1 + r_n) - 1$$

COMPUSTAT

A database maintained by the Standard & Poor's Corp. that contains income statement, balance sheet, sources and application of funds, line of business, and market information for publicly held U.S. and non-U.S. corporations.

CountryBaskets (CB) Index Fund, Inc.

A management investment company organized as a series fund each consisting of a country-specific index fund which holds a portfolio of securities that are intended to replicate the price and yield performance of a particular Financial Times/Standard & Poor's Actuaries World Index country index. Countries represented include Australia, France, Germany, Hong Kong, Italy, Japan, South Africa, the United Kingdom (UK) and the United States. Developed by Deutsche Morgan Grenfell/C.J. Lawrence Inc., Country Basket shares trade exactly like other stocks on the New York Stock Exchange.

Derivative Instrument

A security or asset whose value is derived in part or in whole from the value and characteristics of another security or asset. Derivative instruments include forwards, stock index options and futures, swaps, index notes and index-linked bonds, to mention just a few. Such instruments may be traded on an organized stock exchange anywhere in the world or Over-the-Counter (OTC) through a dealer, commercial bank, investment bank or other financial institution, which offer a variety of non-exchange listed customized financial products.

Dividend Payout

A company's earnings that are paid out in the form of dividends, expressed as a ratio of dividends per share divided by earnings per share.

Efficient Market Hypothesis (EMH)

The assertion, which has been developed in various forms, that security prices fully reflect all available information. New information is discounted as it arrives and the prices of all stocks quickly adjust to a new and correct level. Security analysis does not result in judgments different from the market's prices with enough consistency to produce incremental returns, such that profit opportunities for active portfolio managers are severely restricted, if not entirely eliminated. On the basis of this theory, investors should use low-cost market index portfolios rather than actively managed investment vehicles.

European Currency Unit (ECU)

The monetary unit used in the European Monetary System (EMS). The ECU is composed of the currencies of the following EMS member states (excepting UK): Belgian francs 3.66, Luxembourg francs 0.14, German marks 0.828, Dutch guilders 0.286, UK pounds 0.0885, Italian Lira, 109.00, French Francs 1.15, Danish krone 0.217 and Irish pounds 0.00759.

Ex-Dividend Date

The date that determines a shareholder's entitlement to a recently declared cash or stock dividend, prior to actual payment date. A stock quoted ex-dividend no longer entitles purchasers on or following the ex-dividend date to receive the dividend at payment date. Share prices theoretically reflect the dividend up to the ex-dividend date, at which time the value of the dividend is deducted from the share price. For this reason, total rate of return calculations normally reflect the reinvestment of stock dividends as of this date.

Federation Internationale des Bourses Valeurs (FIBV) Standards

Common standards applicable to the calculation of a stock return index that was adopted for use by member stock exchanges on a voluntary basis by the FIBV at the 1983 General Assembly meeting in Toronto, Canada. The common standard involves a weighted total rate of return index, with dividends reinvested on the ex-dividend date, composed of all domestic shares listed on the individual stock exchange, using a computation derived from the Paasche index formula. Also, the base market capitalization must be adjusted whenever the current market capitalization undergoes a variation which is not due to normal market mechanism of supply and demand. Such events include the issuance of additional equity, new listings and delistings.

FLEX OPTIONS

Exchange traded, institutionally oriented options, that permit investors to set the strike price of the put or call, to establish any expiration date up to five years from the trade date, and to choose a European, American or capped exercise style.

FLOAT CAPITALIZATION (AVAILABLE EQUITY CAPITAL)

A company's share price multiplied by the number of outstanding shares, which are adjusted for the percentage of a company's shares that are freely tradable. Share availability may be restricted due to government holdings, large private holdings and corporate cross-holdings. Overseas, legal restrictions against foreign ownership may apply, including restrictions due to any corporate by-law, corporate charter, industry limitations on foreign ownership, the amount of company capital a single foreign investor may hold and separate limits on the amount that such an investor may hold collectively. Float capitalization is not a fixed value. It will vary from one index to the next on the basis of the variables that index publishers deem relevant, and the availability as well as timeliness of good information sources which varies somewhat.

INSTITUTIONAL BROKERS ESTIMATE SYSTEM (I/B/E/S)

A service that provides earnings estimates on listed equity securities based on estimates that are supplied on a regular basis by security analysts who follow specific stocks.

INDEX

A securities market index is a statistical indicator, benchmark or measure of movements in the general level and direction of prices of financial instruments or securities, such as stocks, bonds, money market instruments, commodities, convertible securities, currencies, Guaranteed Investment Contracts (GICs), mutual funds and real estate.

INVESTABLE STOCKS

Stocks which are available for purchase either in the United States or overseas by individual or institutional investors. Domestic stocks may not be available for purchase due to ownership by other companies, including stocks owned by foreign companies and other non-corporate entities, while foreign stocks may be restricted to foreign investors by class of shares, percentage limitations, market sectors, investor type, company statutes and certain national limits.

ETIENNE LASPEYRES (1834-1913)

German economist who in 1864 proposed the use of a weighted index formula for measuring current prices or quantities of commodities in relation to those of a selected base period. When applied to a securities market, a Laspaeyres price index is computed by taking the ratio between the current market value and the market value of the constituent securities at the base date, using current prices, and the number of shares outstanding as of the base period. The result is multiplied by 100.00 to arrive at the initial index value.

Long-Term Equity Anticipation Securities (LEAPS)

Long-term put and call options on underlying securities market indices, with expirations of up to three years. There are two types of LEAPS—Equity LEAPS and Index LEAPS. Index LEAPS are based either on the full value of the underlying index or on a fractional value of one-tenth of the value of the underlying index. Index LEAPS settle on a cash basis, which is determined on the difference between the exercise settlement value of the index on the settlement date and the exercise price of the option. Index leaps may be exercised on any business day prior to expiration. (American style) or during a specified period of time immediately prior to expiration (European Style).

Modern Portfolio Theory (MPT)

A framework that enables investment managers to classify, estimate and control the sources of risk and return. In its most basic form, MPT represents an approach to managing the combined holdings of securities that emphasizes the relationship between risk and return and the assumptions that, given two portfolios with the same risk, investors prefer the portfolio with the highest rate of return. Also, given two portfolios with the same total rate of return, investors prefer the portfolio with the lowest risk.

Muller Data Services

A subsidiary of Thomson Financial Services, Muller is a supplier of securities markets data, including securities pricing to banks, brokerage firms, insurance companies and mutual funds.

Organization for Economic Cooperation and Development (OECD)

An organization founded in 1961 to stimulate economic progress and world trade. Members in 1995 include Australia, Austria, Belgium, Canada, Denmark, Finland, France, Germany, Greece, Iceland, Ireland, Italy, Japan, Luxembourg, Mexico, The Netherlands, New Zealand, Norway, Portugal, Spain, Sweden, Switzerland, Turkey, United Kingdom (UK) and the United States (U.S.).

Over-The-Counter (OTC) trade

A security that is bought or sold directly through a dealer, commercial bank, investment bank or other financial institution, rather than an organized exchange, such as the New York Stock Exchange or Chicago Board Options Exchange. Instruments and transaction terms can be tailored to meet a client's particular needs.

Hermann Paasche

A German economist who in 1874 proposed the use of a weighted index formula for measuring current prices or quantities of commodities in relation to those of a selected base period. Unlike the Laspayeres formula, the Paasche index formula, when a applied to a securities market, establishes a ratio between the current market value and the market value of the constituent securities at the base date, using current prices and the number of shares outstanding in the current period. The result is multiplied by 100.00 to arrive at the initial index value.

Price/Book ratio (P/B)

A ratio showing the relationship between the price of a stock and its book value per common share.

PRICE/EARNINGS RATIO (P/E)

A ratio showing the relationship between the price of a stock and its earnings per share, using either reported earnings for the latest year or an analyst's forecast for the next year's earnings.

RATE OF RETURN

The percentage earned or produced over a specified time period. The rate of return derived from index values is the change in index value (ending index value minus the beginning index value) divided by the index value at the beginning of the period. Index values and rates of return are calculated on the basis of price only results (price only rate of return) as well as price plus income earned during the period, including interest paid, accrued interest or dividends (total rate of return). The annual rate of return is the percentage earned or produced over a 12-month period, usually a calendar year. The formula for rates of return derived from index values, where V_1 is the ending value and V_0 is the beginning value, is:

$$R = (V_1 - V_0) / V_0$$

RETURN ON EQUITY

A key measure of profitability, it is the ratio of net income earned by a company to shareholders equity.

STANDARD & POOR'S DEPOSITARY RECEIPTS (SPDRs)

A unit investment trust which holds a portfolio of common stocks intended to closely track the price and dividend yield performance of a particular securities market index, such as the S&P 500 Index and S&P MidCap Index. SPDRs are exchange-listed. They trade and are priced like a stock and pay dividends.

STANDARD DEVIATION

A statistical measure that describes the range or variability in a series of numbers or observations around an average or mean. Widely accepted as a proxy for risk, standard deviation is calculated for sample or entire populations using available annual data. The formula for the standard deviation for a sample population, where the annual rate of return, r is the average annual rate of return and n is the number of observations, is:

$$S = \sqrt{\sum f(r - \bar{r})^2 / n - 1}$$

SUBINDEX

A narrow, strictly constructed segment of securities that constitute a securities market index. Employing the same maintenance and calculation methodologies as are applicable to the index, subindex members are selected on the basis of narrower criteria, such as security type, geographic subdivision, industry segments, economic sectors, quality and maturity, to mention just a few.

TURNOVER

A measure of volume in a security, calculated by dividing the total number of traded shares by the total number of shares listed or outstanding.

VALUE LINE INVESTMENT SURVEY

A weekly stock market information service published by Value Line, Inc. that covers approximately 1,700 companies in 98 industries.

VALUE TRADED

The value of total number of shares traded during the period.

VOLUME TRADED

The total number of shares traded during the period.

"WHEN ISSUED STOCK"

A security that is purchased for delivery beyond the normal settlement date at a stated price. The transaction is made conditionally because the security has not yet been issued.

WM/REUTERS CLOSING SPOT RATES

A single standardized source for foreign exchange closing spot rates that are calculated daily at 4 PM London Time by The WM Company based on data provided by Reuters. Representative rates are selected from each currency based on a number of "snapshots" of the latest contributed quotations taken from the Reuters System at short intervals around 4 PM London Time. Quotes to the U.S. dollar are used and cross-rates are calculated.

WORLD EQUITY BENCHMARK SHARES FOREIGN FUND., INC. (WEBS)

A management investment company organized as a series fund each consisting of a country-specific index fund which holds a portfolio of securities that are intended to replicate the price and yield performance of a particular Morgan Stanley Capital International (MSCI) Index. Countries and/or indices represented include Australia, Austria, Belgium, Canada, France, Germany, Hong Kong, Italy, Japan, Malaysia, Mexico (Free), The Netherlands, Singapore (Free), Spain, Sweden, Switzerland and the United Kingdom (UK). Managed by BZW Barclays Global Fund Advisors, WEBS shares trade exactly like other stocks on the American Stock Exchange.

YIELD

The dividends or interest paid by a company, expressed as a percentage of the current share or bond price.

APPENDIX 5

COMPREHENSIVE DIRECTORY OF INDICES

INDEX	PUBLISHER	ASSET CLASS	REGION	COUNTRY	PAGE
58 Counter Industrial Index	Zimbabwe Stock Exchange (ZSE)	Stock	Africa/Middle East	Zimbabwe	890
Adjusted Stock Price Average	Korea Stock Exchange (KSE)	Stock	Asia/Pacific	Korea	863
Affarsvarlden All-Share Index	Affarsvarlden	Stock	Europe	Sweden	881
Ahmedabad Stock Exchange Sensitive Index of Equity Prices	Stock Exchange of Ahmedabad, The	Stock	Asia/Pacific	India	858
ALSI 40 Index	Johannesburg Stock Exchange (JSE), The	Stock	Africa/Middle East	South Africa	592
Altman Defaulted Debt Securities Index	Edward I. Altman/New York University	Bond	North America	United States	893
American Banker Bank Indices	American Banker	Stock	North America	United States	849
American Stock Exchange (AMEX)/Hong Kong Option Index (HKO)	American Stock Exchange (AMEX), The	Stock	Asia/Pacific	Hong Kong	857
American Stock Exchange (AMEX)/Japan Index (JPN)	American Stock Exchange (AMEX), The	Stock	Asia/Pacific	Japan	860
American Stock Exchange Market Value Index (AMVI)	American Stock Exchange (AMEX), The	Stock	North America	United States	58
AMEX Airline (XAL) Index	American Stock Exchange (AMEX), The	Stock	North America	United States	60
AMEX BioTechnology (BTK) Index	American Stock Exchange (AMEX), The	Stock	North America	United States	62
AMEX Computer Technology (XCI) Index	American Stock Exchange (AMEX), The	Stock	North America	United States	64
AMEX Institutional (XII) Index	American Stock Exchange (AMEX), The	Stock	North America	United States	66
AMEX International Market (IMI) Index	American Stock Exchange (AMEX), The	Stock	North America	United States	68
AMEX Major Market (XMI) Index	American Stock Exchange (AMEX), The	Stock	North America	United States	70
AMEX Mexico (MXY) Index	American Stock Exchange (AMEX), The	Stock	North America	United States	72
AMEX Natural Gas (XNG) Index	American Stock Exchange (AMEX), The	Stock	North America	United States	74
AMEX North American Telecommunications (XTC) Index	American Stock Exchange (AMEX), The	Stock	North America	United States	76
AMEX Oil (XOI) Index	American Stock Exchange (AMEX), The	Stock	North America	United States	78
AMEX/Oscar Gruss Israel (XIS) Index	American Stock Exchange (AMEX), The	Stock	North America	United States	80
AMEX Pharmaceutical (DRG) Index	American Stock Exchange (AMEX), The	Stock	North America	United States	82
AMEX Retail Index	American Stock Exchange (AMEX), The	Stock	North America	United States	84
AMEX Securities Broker/Dealer (XBD) Index	American Stock Exchange (AMEX), The	Stock	North America	United States	86

INDEX	PUBLISHER	ASSET CLASS	REGION	COUNTRY	PAGE
Amman Financial Market (AFM) Price Index, The	Amman Financial Market (AFM)	Stock	Africa/Middle East	Jordan	576
Amman Financial Market Price Index	Amman Financial Market	Stock	Africa/Middle East	Jordan	888
Amsterdam EOE (EOE) Index	Amsterdam EOE-Optiebeurs	Stock	Europe	Netherlands	442
Amsterdam Midkap-Index	Amsterdam EOE-Optiebeurs	Stock	Europe	Netherlands	444
ASX 50 Leaders Price and Accumulation Indices	Australian Stock Exchange Limited, The	Stock	Asia/Pacific	Australia	855
Athens Stock Exchange (ASE) Composite Share Index	Athens Stock Exchange (ASE), The	Stock	Europe	Greece	426
ATX 50 Index	Austrian Futures & Options Exchange	Stock	Europe	Austria	872
ATX Midcap Index	Austrian Futures & Options Exchange	Stock	Europe	Austria	872
Australian All Ordinaries Stock Exchange Index (ASX)	Australian Stock Exchange Limited, The	Stock	Asia/Pacific	Australia	262
Australian Stock Exchange 100 Index (ASX 100)	Australian Stock Exchange Limited, The	Stock	Asia/Pacific	Australia	264
Australian Stock Exchange Mid Cap Index	Australian Stock Exchange Limited, The	Stock	Asia/Pacific	Australia	266
Australian Stock Exchange Small Cap Index	Australian Stock Exchange Limited, The	Stock	Asia/Pacific	Australia	268
Australian Stock Exchange Twenty Leaders Index	Australian Stock Exchange Limited, The	Stock	Asia/Pacific	Australia	270
Austrian Traded Index (ATX)	Osterreichische Termin-Und Optionenborse (OTOB)	Stock	Europe	Austria	380
B-Gold Index	Brussels Stock Exchange	Stock	Europe	Belgium	873
Babson College Emerging Market Income Indes	Babson College	Mutual Funds	North America	United States	913
Bahrain Stock Exchange (BSE) Official Share Index	Bahrain Stock Exchange	Stock	Africa/Middle East	Bahrain	887
Banca Commerciale Italiana All-Share (BCI) Index	Banca Commerciale Italiana (BCI)	Stock	Europe	Italy	434
Banco Interandino Blue Chip Index	Banco Interandino	Stock	Latin/Central America	Peru	892
Banco Totta & Acores (BT&A) Shares Index	Banco Totta & Acores (BT&A)	Stock	Europe	Portugal	458
Bankers Trust Bankers Acceptances	Bankers Trust New York Corp.	Money Market Instruments	North America	United States	906
Bankers Trust Banxquote Retail and Institutional CD Indices	Bankers Trust New York Corp.	Money Market Instruments	North America	United States	906
Bankers Trust Commodity Index (BTCI)	Bankers Trust New York Corp.	Commodities	North America	United States	744
Bankers Trust LIBOR	Bankers Trust New York Corp.	Money Market Instruments	North America	United States	906
Bankers Trust Repurchase Agreements	Bankers Trust New York Corp.	Money Market Instruments	North America	United States	906
Barcelona Stock Exchange Indice General	Barcelona Stock Exchange	Stock	Europe	Spain	880
Barcelona Stock Exchange MID 50 Index	Barcelona Stock Exchange	Stock	Europe	Spain	880
Barcelona Stock Exchange Return Index	Barcelona Stock Exchange	Stock	Europe	Spain	881
Barclay CTA Index	Barclay Trading Group	Miscellaneous	North America	United States	918
Barra All U.S. Price Index	BARRA, Inc.	Stock	North America	United States	849
Barron's 50 Stock Average	Barron's	Stock	North America	United States	850
Barron's Best Grade Bonds	Barron's	Bond	North America	United States	893
Barron's Intermediate Grade Bonds	Barron's	Bond	North America	United States	893
Barron's Low-Priced Stock Index	Barron's	Stock	North America	United States	850
BCI 30 Index	Banca Commerciale Italiana (BCI)	Stock	Europe	Italy	878
BEL 20 Return Index Private and Industrial	Brussels Stock Exchange	Stock	Europe	Belgium	873
Belgian (Bel) 20 Index	Brussels Stock Exchange	Stock	Europe	Belgium	386
Belgian Computer Assisted Trading System (CATS) Market Return Index	Brussels Stock Exchange	Stock	Europe	Belgium	388

INDEX	PUBLISHER	ASSET CLASS	REGION	COUNTRY	PAGE
Belgian Foreign Forward Market (CATS) Return Index	Brussels Stock Exchange	Stock	Europe	Belgium	873
Belgian Medium Capitalization Return Index	Brussels Stock Exchange	Stock	Europe	Belgium	390
Belgian Small Capitalization Return Index	Brussels Stock Exchange	Stock	Europe	Belgium	392
Belgian Spot Market Index	Brussels Stock Exchange	Stock	Europe	Belgium	394
Benham North American Gold Equities Index	Benham Management Corp.	Stock	North America	United States	850
Bermuda Stock Exchange Index	Bermuda Stock Exchange	Stock	North America	Bermuda	40
Bloomberg Real Estate Investment Trust Indices	Bloomberg Financial Services	Real Estate	North America	United States	917
Bloomberg State/Regional Common Stock Indices	Bloomberg Financial Services Financial	Stock	North America	United States	850
Bloomberg/European Federation of Financial Analyst Societies (EFFAS) All Government Bond Index—U.S. Government	Bloomberg Financial Services	Bond	World	NA	690
Bolsa de Medelin-IBOMED Index	Corredores Associates	Stock	Latin/Central America	Colombia	891
Bolsa de Medelin-IBOMED Selectivo	Corredores Associates	Stock	Latin/Central America	Colombia	891
Bolsa de Valores de Caracas Indice de Capitalization	Bolsa de Valores de Caracas	Stock	Central/Latin America	Venezuela	558
Bolsa de Valores de Lisboa (BVL) 30 Index	Bolsa de Valores de Lisboa (BVL)	Stock	Europe	Portugal	462
Bolsa de Valores de Lisboa (BVL) General Index	Bolsa de Valores de Lisboa (BVL)	Stock	Europe	Portugal	460
Bolsa Mexicana de Valores Indice de Precios y Cotizaciones (IPC) Index	Bolsa Mexicana de Valores	Stock	North America	Mexico	54
Bolsa Nacional de Valores Indice Accionario (BNV)	Bolsa National de Valores	Stock	Central/Latin America	Costa Rica	544
Bombay Stock Exchange (BSE) 200 Index	Bombay Stock Exchange (BSE), The	Stock	Asia/Pacific	India	290
Bombay Stock Exchange (BSE) National Index of Equity Prices	Bombay Stock Exchange (BSE), The	Stock	Asia/Pacific	India	292
Bombay Stock Exchange (BSE) Sensitive Index of Equity Prices	Bombay Stock Exchange (BSE), The	Stock	Asia/Pacific	India	294
Bond Buyer 11 Bond Index	Bond Buyer, The	Bond	North America	United States	894
Bond Buyer 20 Bond Index	Bond Buyer, The	Bond	North America	United States	893
Bond Buyer Municipal Bond Index (BBI)	Bond Buyer, The	Bond	North America	United States	644
Bond Buyer Revenue Bond Index	Bond Buyer, The	Bond	North America	United States	894
Bond Buyer Short-Term Commercial Paper Rate	Bond Buyer, The	Money Market Instruments	North America	United States	906
Bond Buyer Short-Term Money Market Municipal Index	Bond Buyer, The	Money Market Instruments	North America	United States	906
Bond Buyer Short-Term One-Year Note Index	Bond Buyer, The	Money Market Instruments	North America	United States	907
Book Club Index	Book Club Finance & Securities Co. Ltd., The	Stock	Asia/Pacific	Thailand	869
Botswana Share Market Index	Stockbrokers Botswana Ltd.	Stock	Africa/Middle East	Botswana	566
BSE DOLLEX Index	Bombay Stock Exchange	Stock	Asia/Pacific	India	859
Budapest Stock Index (BUX)	Budapest Stock Exchange, The	Stock	Europe	Hungary	428
Buenos Aires Stock Exchange Value Index-Composite	Buenos Aires Stock Exchange (BASE), The	Stock	Central/Latin America	Argentina	526
Burcap Index	Buenos Aires Stock Exchange (BASE), The	Stock	Latin/Central America	Argentina	890
BVA General Index	Abidjan Stock Exchange	Stock	Africa/Middle East	Cote d'Iviore	568
BVL ORF Index	Bolsa de Valores de Lisboa	Bond	Europe	Portugal	903
BZW Australia Liquid Government Securities Bond Index	BZW Australia	Bond	Asia/Pacific	Australia	900
CA Bond Index	Creditanstalt Investment Bank AG	Bond	Europe	Austria	902

INDEX	PUBLISHER	ASSET CLASS	REGION	COUNTRY	PAGE
CAC-40 (Cotation Automatique Continue) Index	SBF-Bourse de Paris, The	Stock	Europe	France	408
Canadian Market Porfolio Index (XXM), The	Montreal Stock Exchange (MSE), The	Stock	North America	Canada	42
CDA/Weisenberger Mutual Fund Averages	CDA/Weisenberger	Mutual Funds	North America	United States	913
Center for Research in Security Prices	Center for Research in Security Prices, The	Stock	North America	United States	851
Central Bureau of Statistics (CBS) All Share Index	Amsterdam Stock Exchange (ASE)	Stock	Europe	Netherlands	446
Central European Stock Index	Budapest Stock Exchange	Stock	Europe	Regional	886
Chemical Bank Emerging Market Debt Index	Chase Bank	Bond	North America	United States	894
Chicago Board of Trade (CBOT) Argentina Brady Bond Index	Chicago Board of Trade	Bond	North America	United States	894
Chicago Board of Trade (CBOT) Brazil Brady Bond Index	Chicago Board of Trade	Bond	North America	United States	895
Chicago Board of Trade (CBOT) Mexico Brady Bond Index	Chicago Board of Trade	Bond	North America	United States	895
Chicago Board Options Exchange Automotive (CAUX) Index	Chicago Board Options Exchange (CBOE), The	Stock	North America	United States	88
Chicago Board Options Exchange BioTechnology (BGX) Index	Chicago Board Options Exchange (CBOE), The	Stock	North America	United States	90
Chicago Board Options Exchange Computer Software (CWX) Index	Chicago Board Options Exchange (CBOE), The	Stock	North America	United States	92
Chicago Board Options Exchange Environmental (EVX) Index	Chicago Board Options Exchange (CBOE), The	Stock	North America	United States	94
Chicago Board Options Exchange Gaming (GAX) Index	Chicago Board Options Exchange (CBOE), The	Stock	North America	United States	96
Chicago Board Options Exchange Global Telecommunications (GTX) Index	Chicago Board Options Exchange (CBOE), The	Stock	North America	United States	98
Chicago Board Options Exchange Internet (CINX) Index	Chicago Board Options Exchange (CBOE), The	Stock	North America	United States	100
Chicago Board Options Exchange Israel (ISX) Index	Chicago Board Options Exchange (CBOE), The	Stock	North America	United States	102
Chicago Board Options Exchange Latin 15 (LTX) Index	Chicago Board Options Exchange (CBOE), The	Stock	North America	United States	104
Chicago Board Options Exchange Mexico (MEX) Index	Chicago Board Options Exchange (CBOE), The	Stock	North America	United States	106
Chicago Board Options Exchange REIT (RIX) Index	Chicago Board Options Exchange (CBOE), The	Real Estate	North America	United States	826
Chicago Board Options Exchange Technology (TXX) Index	Chicago Board Options Exchange (CBOE), The	Stock	North America	United States	108
Chicago Board Options Exchange U.S. Telecommunications (TCX) Index	Chicago Board Options Exchange (CBOE), The	Stock	North America	United States	110
Citicorp/IFR Impaired Loan Index	Citicorp/International Financial Review	Bond	World	NA	905
Colombo Stock Exchange (CSE) All Share Price Index	Sri Lanka Stock Exchange	Stock	Asia/Pacific	Sri Lanka	360
Commercial Bank of Qatar (CBC) Share Index	Commercial Bank of Qatar	Stock	Africa/Middle East	Qatar	889
Commerzbank Share Index	Commerzbank AG	Stock	Europe	Germany	416
Commonwealth Bank Bond Indices	Australian Stock Exchange Limited, The	Bond	Asia/Pacific	Australia	900
Composite DAX Performance Index	Deutsche Borse AG	Stock	Europe	Germany	418
Computerized Call Market System (CCM) Index	Tel Aviv Stock Exchange (TSE)	Stock	Africa/Middle East	Israel	888
Copenhagen Stock Exchange (KFX) Index	Copenhagen Stock Exchange (CSE)	Stock	Europe	Denmark	400
Copenhagen Stock Exchange True Yield Index	Copenhagen Stock Exchange	Bond	Europe	Denmark	902
Credit Lyonnais Securities Asia (CLSA) China World Index	Credit Lyonnais Securities Asia	Stock	Asia/Pacific	China	856
Creditanstalt Share Index (CA Share Index)	Vienna Stock Exchange (Weiner Borse), The	Stock	Europe	Austria	872
CS First Boston Convertible Securities Index	CS First Boston	Convertible Securities	North America	United States	758
CS First Boston High Yield Index	Cs First Boston	Bond	North America	United States	646

INDEX	PUBLISHER	ASSET CLASS	REGION	COUNTRY	PAGE
CS First Boston ROS 30 Index	CS First Boston	Stock	Europe	Russia	466
CS Index	Credit Suisse	Stock	Europe	Switzerland	882
CSE Sensitive Index, The	Sri Lanka Stock Exchange	Stock	Asia/Pacific	Sri Lanka	868
Cyprus Investment and Securities Corp. (CISCO) Ltd All-Share Index	Cyprus Investment and Securities Corp. Ltd.	Stock	Europe	Cyprus	874
Cyprus Stock Exchange (CYSE) All-Share Index	Cyprus Stock Exchange (CYSE)	Stock	Europe	Cyprus	396
Cyprus Stock Exchange Institution Index	Cyprus Stock Exchange (CYSE)	Stock	Europe	Cyprus	875
Czech Komercni Bank Bond Price Index	Komercni Bank	Bond	Europe	Czech Republic	902
Czech National Bank CNB-120 Index	Czech National Bank	Stock	Europe	Czech Republic	875
D.E. Shaw Japanese Convertible Bond Index (DESCBI)	D.E. Shaw	Convertible Securities	Asia/Pacific	Japan	910
D.E. Shaw Japanese Warrant Index	D.E. Shaw	Miscellaneous	Asia/Pacific	Japan	919
Daiwa Physical Commodities Index	Daiwa	Commodities	Asia/Pacific	Japan	909
DALBAR 30 Index	DALBAR	Stock	North America	United States	851
DALBAR Investment Company Stock Index (DICSA)	DALBAR	Stock	North America	United States	851
Databank Brokerage Ltd. Index	Databank Brokerage	Stock	Africa/Middle East	Ghana	888
Davy Irish Market Indices	Davy Stockbrokers	Stock	Europe	Ireland	877
DAX 100 Performance Index	Deutsche Borse AG	Stock	Europe	Germany	420
DAX 100 Subindices	Deutsche Borse AG	Stock	Europe	Germany	876
DAX Performance Index (Deutcher Aktienindex)	Deutsche Borse AG	Stock	Europe	Germany	422
DBS 50 Index	DBS Investment Research	Stock	Asia/Pacific	Pakistan	866
Delhi Stock Exchange (DSE) Sensitive Index of Equity Prices	Delhi Stock Exchange (DSE), The	Stock	Asia/Pacific	India	296
Dhaka Stock Exchange (DSE) All Share Price Index	Dhaka Stock Exchange (DSE), The	Stock	Asia/Pacific	Bangladesh	272
Domini Social Index	Kinder Lydenberg Domini & Co.	Stock	North America	United States	851
Dow Jones 20 Bond Average	Dow Jones & Company, Inc.	Bond	North America	United States	895
Dow Jones Composite Average	Dow Jones & Company, Inc.	Stock	North America	United States	112
Dow Jones Equity Market Index	Dow Jones & Company, Inc.	Stock	North America	United States	114
Dow Jones Futures Index	Dow Jones & Company, Inc., Inc.	Commodities	North America	United States	908
Dow Jones Global Stock Index	Dow Jones & Company, Inc.	Stock	World	NA	608
Dow Jones Industrial Average (DJIA)	Dow Jones & Company, Inc.	Stock	North America	United States	116
Dow Jones Spot Index	Dow Jones & Company, Inc., Inc.	Commodities	North America	United States	908
Dow Jones Transportation Average	Dow Jones & Company, Inc.	Stock	North America	United States	118
Dow Jones Utilities Average	Dow Jones & Company, Inc.	Stock	North America	United States	120
Dresdner International Research Institute Europa Small Cap Index	Dresdner International Research Institute	Stock	Europe	Regional	886
Dresdner International Research Institute Small Cap Deutcshland Index	Dresdner International Research Institute	Stock	Europe	Germany	877
Dutch Top 5 Index (TOPS)	Amsterdam EOE-Optiebeurs	Stock	Europe	Netherlands	448
Economic Daily News Index	Economic Daily News	Stock	Asia/Pacific	Taiwan	362
Economic Times Share Ordinary Price Index	Economic Times, The	Stock	Asia/Pacific	India	859
Egypt Capital Market Authority Index (ECM)	Capital Market Authority	Stock	Africa/Middle East	Egypt	887
Egyptian Financial Group Index	Egyptian Financial Group	Stock	Africa/Middle East	Egypt	887
Emerging Markets Bond Index Plus (EMBI+)	J.P. Morgan Securities Inc.	Bond	World	NA	692

INDEX	Publisher	Asset Class	Region	Country	Page
European 100 Index	Morgan Stanley Capital International, The European, as calculated by	Stock	Europe	Regional	886
Eurotop 100 (E100) Index	Amsterdam EOE-Optiebeurs	Stock	Europe	Regional	510
Exane French Convertible Index	Exane	Convertible Securities	Europe	France	910
Fiduciary Capital Management GIC Index	Fiduciary Capital Management Inc.	Guaranteed Investment Contracts	North America	United States	911
Financial Times Gold Mines Index	Financial Times	Stock	Europe	United Kingdom	884
Financial Times Ordinary Share Index (30 Share Index)	Financial Times Ltd., The	Stock	Europe	United Kingdom	490
Financial Times-Stock Exchange 100 (FT-SE 100) Index	FT-SE International Ltd.	Stock	Europe	United Kingdom	492
Financial Times-Stock Exchange Actuaries 350 (FT-SE Actuaries 350) Index	FT-SE International Ltd.	Stock	Europe	United Kingdom	494
Financial Times-Stock Exchange Alternative Investment Market (FT-SE AIM) Index	FT-SE International Ltd.	Stock	Europe	United Kingdom	500
Financial Times-Stock Exchange Mid 250 (FT-SE Mid 250) Index	FT-SE International Ltd.	Stock	Europe	United Kingdom	502
Financial Times/Standard & Poor's (FT/S&P) Actuaries World Index	Financial Times Ltd., Goldman Sachs & Co. and Standard & Poor's	Stock	World	NA	610
Financial/Industrial 30 Index (FNDI 30)	Johannesburg Stock Exchange (JSE), The	Stock	Africa/Middle East	South Africa	889
Finnish Traded Stock (FOX) Index	Finnish Securities and Derivatives Exchange (SOM)	Stock	Europe	Finland	404
Frankfurt Stock Exchange Index	Frankfurt Stock Exchange	Stock	Europe	Germany	877
Frankfurter Allgemeinen Zeitung (FAZ) Aktienindex	Frankfurter Allgemeine Zeitung	Stock	Europe	Germany	877
Franklin California 250 Growth Index	Franklin Resources, Inc.	Stock	North America	United States	851
FT-Actuaries Fixed Interest Indices	Financial Times	Bond	Europe	United Kingdom	904
FT-SE Actuaries All-Share Index	FT-SE International Ltd.	Stock	Europe	United Kingdom	496
FT-SE Actuaries Fledgling Index	FT-SE International Ltd.	Stock	Europe	United Kingdom	498
FT-SE Eurotrack 100 Index	FT-SE International Ltd.	Stock	Europe	Regional	512
FT-SE Eurotrack 200 Index	FT-SE International Ltd.	Stock	Europe	Regional	514
FT-SE SmallCap Index	FT-SE International Ltd.	Stock	Europe	United Kingdom	504
German Bond Index (REX)	Deutsche Borse AG	Bond	Europe	Germany	902
GFIL 30 Index	Goodwill Finance and Investment Company	Stock	Asia/Pacific	Nepal	864
Ghana Stock Exchange (GSE) All-Share Index	Ghana Stock Exchange (GSE)	Stock	Africa/Middle East	Ghana	570
GLDI 10 Index	Johannesburg Stock Exchange (JSE), The	Stock	Africa/Middle East	South Africa	594
Global Mining Indices	HSBC James Capel & Co. Limited	Stock	Europe	United Kingdom	885
Gold Coast Securities Liquidity Index	Gold Coast Securities Ltd.	Stock	Africa/Middle East	Ghana	888
Goldman Sachs Commodity Index (GSCI)	Goldman, Sachs & Co.	Commodities	North America	United States	746
Goldman Sachs Convertible 100 Index	Goldman, Sachs & Co.	Convertible Securities	North America	United States	760
Goldman Sachs International Government Bond Index	Goldman Sachs & Co.	Bond	World	NA	905
Goldman Sachs Liquid Asset-Backed Securities Index (LABS)	Goldman Sachs & Co.	Bond	North America	United States	895
Green Indices	HSBC James Capel & Co. Limited	Stock	Europe	United Kingdom	885
Hambrecht & Quist (H&Q) Growth Index	Hambrecht & Quist	Stock	North America	United States	851
Hambrecht & Quist (H&Q) Technology Index	Hambrecht & Quist LLC	Stock	North America	United States	122

INDEX	PUBLISHER	ASSET CLASS	REGION	COUNTRY	PAGE
Hang Seng China Enterprises Index (HSCEI)	HSI Services Limited, a subsidiary of Hang Seng Bank	Stock	Asia/Pacific	Hong Kong	282
Hang Seng Index (HSI)	HSI Services Limited, a subsidiary of Hang Seng Bank	Stock	Asia/Pacific	Hong Kong	284
Hang Seng London Reference Index	HSI Services Limited, a subsidiary of Hang Seng Bank	Stock	Asia/Pacific	Hong Kong	858
Hang Seng Midcap Index	HSI Services Limited, a subsidiary of Hang Seng Bank	Stock	Asia/Pacific	Hong Kong	286
Hellenic Bank Investments Index (HBI)	Hellenic Bank Limited	Stock	Europe	Cyprus	874
Hermes Financial Index	Hermes Financial	Stock	Africa/Middle East	Egypt	887
Hertzfeld Closed-End Average (THCEA)	Thomas J. Hertzfeld Advisors, Inc.	Closed-End Funds	North America	United States	822
Hertzfeld Single Country Average	Thomas J. Hertzfeld Advisors, Inc.	Mutual Funds	North America	United States	913
HEX All-Share Price Index	Helsinki Stock Exchange	Stock	Europe	Finland	406
HEX-20 Index	Helsinki Stock Exchange	Stock	Europe	Finland	875
HN-Wood Index	Wood & Company in conjunction with Hospodarsky Noviny	Stock	Europe	Czech Republic	875
Hoare Govett 1000 Index (HG 1000)	Hoare Govett Securities Ltd./ABN-AMRO	Stock	Europe	United Kingdom	885
Hoare Govett Smaller Companies (HGSC) Index	Hoare Govett Securities Ltd./ABN-AMRO	Stock	Europe	United Kingdom	506
Hong Kong All Ordinaries Index (AOI)	Stock Exchange of Hong Kong Limited (SEHK), The	Stock	Asia/Pacific	Hong Kong	288
HSBC James Capel Dragon 300 Index	HSBC James Capel & Co. Limited	Stock	Asia/Pacific	Regional	376
HSBC James Capel Latin America 100 Index	HSBC James Capel & Co. Limited	Stock	Central/Latin America	Regional	562
HSBC James Capel Small Japanese Companies Index	HSBC James Capel & Co. Limited	Stock	Asia/Pacific	Japan	300
HSBC James Capel Smaller European Companies Index	HSBC James Capel & Co. Limited	Stock	Europe	Regional	516
Hubble Environmental Index	Progressive Asset Management and David L. Hubble	Stock	North America	United States	852
I-SENN Index	Rio de Janeiro Stock Exchange, The	Stock	Central/Latin America	Brazil	534
IBC Mutual Fund Averages	IBC/Donoghue Inc.	Mutual Funds	North America	United States	913
IBEX-35 Index	Sociedad de Bolsas S.A.	Stock	Europe	Spain	472
IBV Profitability Index of Rio de Janeiro Stock Exchange (IBV)	Rio de Janeiro Stock Exchange, The	Stock	Central/Latin America	Brazil	532
Iceland Stock Exchange Index (ICEX)	Iceland Stock Exchange	Stock	Europe	Iceland	430
IMR Index-Current	Italian Stock Exchange Council	Stock	Europe	Italy	878
Index of Bolsa de Bogota (IBB)	Bolsa de Bogota, S.A.	Stock	Central/Latin America	Colombia	542
Index-Linked Index	Financial Times	Bond	Europe	United Kingdom	904
INDI 25 Index	Johannesburg Stock Exchange (JSE), The	Stock	Africa/Middle East	South Africa	596
Indice Accionario de la Bolsa de Valores de Quito 8 (I.A.Q. 8)	Bolsa de Valores de Quito	Stock	Central/Latin America	Ecuador	546
Indice de Precios Selectivo de Acciones (IPSA)	Bolsa de Comercio de Santiago (Santiago Stock Exchange)	Stock	Central/Latin America	Chile	538
Indice de Rendimiento (RBQ)	Bolsa de Valores de Quito	Stock	Latin/Central America	Ecuador	891
Indice Diario de Volumen (IVQ)	Bolsa de Valores de Quito	Stock	Latin/Central America	Ecuador	891
Indice General (IGBVL)	Bolsa de Valores de Lima	Stock	Central/Latin America	Peru	552
Indice General BVM	Bourse de Valeurs Mobilieres de Tunis	Stock	Africa/Middle East	Tunesia	890

INDEX	PUBLISHER	ASSET CLASS	REGION	COUNTRY	PAGE
Indice General de Precios de Acciones (IGPA)	Bolsa de Comercio de Santiago (Santiago Stock Exchange)	Stock	Central/Latin America	Chile	540
Indice Moyen General Annual	Casablanca Stock Exchange	Stock	Africa/Middle East	Morocco	584
Indices Selectivo (ISBVL)	Bolsa de Valores de Lima	Stock	Central/Latin America	Peru	554
ING Barings Asian Convertible Bond (CB) Index	ING Baring Securities Limited	Convertible Securities	North America	United States	772
ING Barings Emerging Market World Index (BEMI)	ING Baring Securities Limited	Stock	World	NA	614
ING Barings Indian GDR Index	ING Baring Securities Limited	Stock	Asia/Pacific	India	859
ING Barings Pan-Asia Index	ING Barings Securities Limited	Stock	Asia/Pacific	Regional	374
ING Barings Special Eastern Europe Index	ING Baring Securities Limited	Stock	Europe	Regional	518
INMEX Index	Bolsa Mexicana de Valores	Stock	North America	Mexico	56
Institutional Property Consultants (IPC) Portfolio ndex	Institutional Property Consultants	Real Estate	North America	United States	917
INTER-10 Index	Bolsa de Comercio de Santiago	Stock	Latin/Central America	Chile	890
International Finance Corporation (IFC) Global Index	International Finance Corporation	Stock	World	NA	616
International Finance Corporation (IFC) Investable Index	International Finance Corporation	Stock	World	NA	618
International Finance Corporation (IFC) Tradeable Asia50 Index	International Finance Corporation	Stock	World	NA	620
International Finance Corporation (IFC) Tradeable Latin50 Index	International Finance Corporation	Stock	World	NA	622
International Finance Corporation (IFC) Tradeable100 Index	International Finance Corporation	Stock	World	NA	624
International Stock Exchange/Nikkei 50 Stock Index (ISE/Nikkei 50)	Nihon Keizai Shimbun, Inc.	Stock	Asia/Pacific	Japan	861
Investable Commodity Index (ICI)	Jefferies & Company, Inc./Intermarket Management Inc.	Commodities	North America	United States	748
Investors Business Daily 6000	Investor's Business Daily	Stock	North America	United States	852
Investors Daily Mutual Fund Index	Investor's Business Daily	Mutual Funds	North America	United States	913
IRBB Index	Bolsa de Bogota S.A.	Bond	Latin/Central America	Colombia	905
Irish Stock Exchange Equity Price (ISEQ) Index	Irish Stock Exchange (ISE)	Stock	Europe	Ireland	432
Istanbul Stock Exchange (ISE) Composite Index	Istanbul Stock Exchange (ISE)	Stock	Europe	Turkey	488
J.P. Morgan Cash Index	J.P. Morgan Securities Inc.	Money Market Instruments	North America	United States	724
J.P. Morgan Commodity Index (JPMCI)	J.P. Morgan Securities Inc.	Commodities	North America	United States	750
J.P. Morgan ECU Bond Index	J.P. Morgan Securities Inc.	Bond	World	NA	694
J.P. Morgan Global Government Bond Index	J.P. Morgan Securities Inc.	Bond	World	NA	696
Jakarta Stock Exchange (JSX) Composite Stock Price Index	Jakarta Stock Exchange (JSX), The	Stock	Asia/Pacific	Indonesia	298
Jamaica Stock Exchange (JSE) Market Index	Jamaica Stock Exchange, The	Stock	Central/Latin America	Jamaica	548
Jefferies Global Convertible (JeffCo) Bond Index	Jefferies & Company Inc.	Convertible Securities	World	NA	774
Johannesburg Stock Exchange (JSE) Actuaries Bond Performance Index	Johannesburg Stock Exchange (JSE)	Bond	Africa/Middle East	South Africa	904
Johannesburg Stock Exchange (JSE)-Actuaries (JSE Actuaries) All Share Index	Johannesburg Stock Exchange (JSE), The	Stock	Africa/Middle East	South Africa	600
Johannesburg Stock Exchange (JSE)-Actuaries All Gold Subindex	Johannesburg Stock Exchange (JSE), The	Stock	Africa/Middle East	South Africa	598
Journal of Commerce Industrial Price Index	Journal of Commerce	Commodities	North America	United States	908
Karachi Stock Exchange (KSE)—100 Index	Karachi Stock Exchange (KSE)	Stock	Asia/Pacific	Pakistan	348
Karachi Stock Exchange-All Share Index	Karachi Stock Exchange	Stock	Asia/Pacific	Pakistan	866

INDEX	PUBLISHER	ASSET CLASS	REGION	COUNTRY	PAGE
KBW 50 Index	Keefe, Bruyette & Woods, Inc.	Stock	North America	United States	852
Keefe Bank Index (KBI)	Keefe, Bruyette & Woods, Inc.	Stock	North America	United States	852
Kleinwort Benson Asia Convertible Bond Index	Kleinwort Benson	Convertible Securities	Asia/Pacific	Asia	910
Kleinwort Benson India GDR Index	Kleinwort Benson	Stock	Asia/Pacific	India	859
Knight Ridder-CRB Interest Rates Index	Knight Ridder Financial	Bond	North America	United States	896
Knight-Ridder Commodity Research Bureau's Futures Price Index (KR-CRB)	Knight-Ridder Financial	Commodities	North America	United States	752
Knight-Ridder-CRB Currencies Index	Knight Ridder Financial	Currencies	World	NA	911
KOP Index, The	Kansallis-Osake-Pankki	Stock	Europe	Finland	876
Korea Bond Index	Korea Stock Exchange (KSE)	Bond	Asia/Pacific	Korea	901
Korea Composite Stock Price Index (KOSPI)	Korea Stock Exchange (KSE)	Stock	Asia/Pacific	Korea	322
Korea Composite Stock Price Index (KOSPI)—Large-Sized Companies Subindex	Korea Stock Exchange (KSE)	Stock	Asia/Pacific	Korea	324
INDEX	PUBLISHER	ASSET CLASS	REGION	COUNTRY	PAGE
Korea Composite Stock Price Index (KOSPI)—Medium-Sized Companies Subindex	Korea Stock Exchange (KSE)	Stock	Asia/Pacific	Korea	326
Korea Composite Stock Price Index (KOSPI)—Small-Sized Companies Subindex	Korea Stock Exchange (KSE)	Stock	Asia/Pacific	Korea	328
Korea Stock Price Index 200 (KOSPI 200)	Korea Stock Exchange (KSE)	Stock	Asia/Pacific	Korea	330
Kuala Lumpur Composite Index	Kuala Lumpur Stock Exchange (KLSE)	Stock	Asia/Pacific	Malaysia	332
Kuala Lumpur EMAS Index	Kuala Lumpur Stock Exchange (KLSE)	Stock	Asia/Pacific	Malaysia	334
Kuala Lumpur Second Board Index	Kuala Lumpur Stock Exchange (KLSE)	Stock	Asia/Pacific	Malaysia	336
Kuwait Stock Exchange (KSE) Index	Kuwait Stock Exchange (KSE)	Stock	Africa/Middle East	Kuwait	580
Lehman Brothers Adjustable Rate Mortgage (ARM) Index	Lehman Brothers	Bond	North America	United States	648
Lehman Brothers Aggregate Bond Index	Lehman Brothers	Bond	North America	United States	650
Lehman Brothers Commodity Index (LBCI)	Lehman Brothers Inc.	Commodities	North America	United States	754
Lehman Brothers Corporate Bond Index	Lehman Brothers	Bond	North America	United States	652
Lehman Brothers Emerging Americas Bond Index	Lehman Brothers	Bond	World	NA	698
Lehman Brothers Eurobond Index	Lehman Brothers	Bond	World	NA	700
Lehman Brothers Global Bond Index	Lehman Brothers	Bond	World	NA	702
Lehman Brothers Government/Corporate Bond Index	Lehman Brothers	Bond	North America	United States	554
Lehman Brothers High Yield Composite Bond Index	Lehman Brothers	Bond	North America	United States	556
Lehman Brothers Mortgage-Backed Securities Index	Lehman Brothers	Bond	North America	United States	558
Lehman Brothers Municipal Bond Index	Lehman Brothers	Bond	North America	United States	560
Lehman Brothers Mutual Fund Corporate Debt A Rated Index	Lehman Brothers	Mutual Funds	North America	United States	790
Lehman Brothers Mutual Fund GNMA Index	Lehman Brothers	Mutual Funds	North America	United States	792
Lehman Brothers Mutual Fund Indices	Lehman Brothers	Mutual Funds	North America	United States	914
Lehman Brothers U.S. Government Bond Index	Lehman Brothers	Bond	North America	United States	562
Lehman REIT Index	Lehman Brothers	Real Estate	North America	United States	917
Life Global Real Estate Securities Index	Limburg Institute of Financial Economics	Real Estate	World	NA	918
Lipper Balanced Funds Index	Lipper Analytical Services, Inc.	Mutual Funds	North America	United States	794
Lipper Convertible Securities Funds Index	Lipper Analytical Services, Inc.	Mutual Funds	North America	United States	796

INDEX	PUBLISHER	ASSET CLASS	REGION	COUNTRY	PAGE
Lipper Equity Income Funds Index	Lipper Analytical Services, Inc.	Mutual Funds	North America	United States	798
Lipper Government National Mortgage Association (GNMA) Funds Index	Lipper Analytical Services, Inc.	Mutual Funds	North America	United States	800
Lipper Growth & Income Funds Index	Lipper Analytical Services, Inc.	Mutual Funds	North America	United States	804
Lipper Growth Funds Index	Lipper Analytical Services, Inc.	Mutual Funds	North America	United States	802
Lipper High Current Yield Funds Index	Lipper Analytical Services, Inc.	Mutual Funds	North America	United States	806
Lipper International Funds Index	Lipper Analytical Services, Inc.	Mutual Funds	North America	United States	808
Lipper Money Market Funds Index	Lipper Analytical Services, Inc.	Mutual Funds	North America	United States	810
Lipper Mutual Fund Indices	Lipper Analytical Services, Inc.	Mutual Funds	North America	United States	914
Lipper Small Company Growth Funds Index	Lipper Analytical Services, Inc.	Mutual Funds	North America	United States	812
Lombard Odier & Cie (LOC) European Government Bond Index	Lombard Odier & Cie	Bond	Europe	Regional	904
Lombard Odier & Cie (LOC) Global World Government Bond Index	Lombard Odier & Cie	Bond	World	NA	704
Lombard Odier & Cie (LOC) Individual Bond Market Indices	Lombard Odier & Cie	Bond	World	NA	906
London and Bishopsgate 100 Index	London and Bishopsgate	Stock	Europe	United Kingdom	886
Luxembourg Stock Exchange Index	Luxembourg Stock Exchange	Stock	Europe	Luxembourg	440
Madrid General CPI Adjusted Indices	Madrid Stock Exchange, The European, as calculated by	Stock	Europe	Spain	881
Madrid General Index	Madrid Stock Exchange, The	Stock	Europe	Spain	474
MAMPS Index	MAMPS Group	Stock	Asia/Pacific	Nepal	864
Manufacturing Industry Index	Korea Stock Exchange (KSE)	Stock	Asia/Pacific	Korea	864
MAR Fund/Pool Qualified Universe Index	Managed Account Reports	Miscellaneous	North America	United States	918
Merrill Lynch (Formerly Smith New Court) Small Company Index of Hong Kong	Merrill Lynch & Co.	Stock	Asia/Pacific	Hong Kong	858
Merrill Lynch 182-Day U.S. Treasury Bill Index (Actual)	Merrill Lynch & Co.	Money Market Instruments	North America	United States	728
Merrill Lynch 364-Day U.S. Treasury Bill Index (Actual)	Merrill Lynch & Co.	Money Market Instruments	North America	United States	730
Merrill Lynch 91-Day U.S. Treasury Bill Auction Rate Average	Merrill Lynch & Co.	Money Market Instruments	North America	United States	726
Merrill Lynch ADR Indices	Merrill Lynch & Co.	Stock	North America	United States	853
Merrill Lynch Brady Bond Index	Merrill Lynch & Co.	Bond	World	NA	706
Merrill Lynch California Municipal Mutual Fund Index	Merrill Lynch & Co.	Mutual Funds	North America	United States	814
Merrill Lynch Canadian Bond Master Index	Merrill Lynch & Co.	Bond	World	NA	708
Merrill Lynch Capital Market Index	Merrill Lynch & Co.	Miscellaneous	NA	NA	840
Merrill Lynch Capital Market Index	Merrill Lynch & Co.	Miscellaneous	North America	United States	918
Merrill Lynch Convertible Securities Index	Merrill Lynch & Co.	Convertible Securities	North America	United States	762
Merrill Lynch Currency Indices	Merrill Lynch & Co.	Currencies	World	NA	911
Merrill Lynch Domestic 3-Month Certificate of Deposit (CD) Index	Merrill Lynch & Co.	Money Market Instruments	North America	United States	732
Merrill Lynch Energy and Metals Index (ENMET)	Merrill Lynch & Co.	Commodities	North America	United States	908
Merrill Lynch Eurodollar 3-Month Certificate of Deposit (CD) Index	Merrill Lynch & Co.	Money Market Instruments	World	NA	738
Merrill Lynch Eurodollar Bond Index	Merrill Lynch & Co.	Bond	World	NA	710
Merrill Lynch Global 300 (ML G300) Convertible Index	Merrill Lynch & Co.	Convertible Securities	World	NA	776
Merrill Lynch Global Bond Index	Merrill Lynch & Co.	Bond	World	NA	712
Merrill Lynch Global Government Bond Index	Merrill Lynch & Co.	Bond	World	NA	714

INDEX	PUBLISHER	ASSET CLASS	REGION	COUNTRY	PAGE
Merrill Lynch High Yield Master Index	Merrill Lynch & Co.	Bond	North America	United States	664
Merrill Lynch Institutional Municipal Index	Merrill Lynch & Co.	Bond	North America	United States	666
Merrill Lynch Insured Bond Index	Merrill Lynch & Co.	Mutual Funds	North America	United States	915
Merrill Lynch Intermediate Mutual Fund Index	Merrill Lynch & Co.	Mutual Funds	North America	United States	915
Merrill Lynch Mortgage Master Bond Index	Merrill Lynch & Co.	Bond	North America	United States	668
Merrill Lynch Municipal Mutual Fund Index	Merrill Lynch & Co.	Mutual Funds	North America	United States	816
Merrill Lynch New York Mutual Fund Index	Merrill Lynch & Co.	Mutual Funds	North America	United States	818
Merrill Lynch U.S. 91-Day Treasury Bill Index (Actual)	Merrill Lynch & Co.	Money Market Instruments	North America	United States	734
Merrill Lynch U.S. Corporate and Government Master Bond Index	Merrill Lynch & Co.	Bond	North America	United States	670
Merrill Lynch U.S. Domestic Corporate Bond Index	Merrill Lynch & Co.	Bond	North America	United States	672
Merrill Lynch U.S. Domestic Master Bond Index	Merrill Lynch & Co.	Bond	North America	United States	674
Merrill Lynch U.S. Government Master Bond Index	Merrill Lynch & Co.	Bond	North America	United States	676
Merval Index	Buenos Aires Stock Exchange (BASE), The	Stock	Central/Latin America	Argentina	528
Micropal Mutual Fund/Unit Investment Trust Performance Averages	Micropal	Mutual Funds	World	NA	916
Mid Cap DAX (MDAX) Performance Index	Deutsche Borse AG	Stock	Europe	Germany	424
MIDCAC Index	SBF-Bourse de Paris, The	Stock	Europe	France	410
Milan Indice di Borsa (MIB) Index- Historical	Italian Stock Exchange Council	Stock	Europe	Italy	438
Milan Indice di Borsa (MIB) Index-Current	Italian Stock Exchange Council	Stock	Europe	Italy	878
Milan Indice di Borsa (MIB) RNC Index	Italian Stock Exchange Council	Stock	Europe	Italy	879
Milan Indice di Borsa (MIB) Telematico Index	Italian Stock Exchange Council	Stock	Europe	Italy	879
Milan Indice di Borsa (MIB30) Index	Italian Stock Exchange Council	Stock	Europe	Italy	436
MLM Managed Futures Index	Mount Lucas Group	Miscellaneous	North America	United States	918
Moody's Intermediate-Term Corporate Bond Yield Averages	Moody's Investors Service	Bond	North America	United States	896
Moody's Investors Scrap Commodity Price Index	Moody's Investors Service	Commodities	North America	United States	909
Moody's Investors Spot Commodity Price Index	Moody's Investors Service	Commodities	North America	United States	909
Moody's Long-Term Corporate Bond Yield Averages	Moody's Investors Service	Bond	North America	United States	896
Moody's Municipal Bond Yield Averages	Moody's Investors Service	Bond	North America	United States	897
Morgan Stanley Capital International (MSCI) Emerging Markets Free Global Index	Morgan Stanley Capital International (MSCI)	Stock	World	NA	626
Morgan Stanley Capital International (MSCI) Emerging Markets Global Index	Morgan Stanley Capital International (MSCI)	Stock	World	NA	628
Morgan Stanley Capital International (MSCI) Europe Australia and Far East (EAFE) Index	Morgan Stanley Capital International (MSCI)	Stock	World	NA	630
Morgan Stanley Capital International (MSCI) World Index	Morgan Stanley Capital International (MSCI)	Stock	World	NA	632
Morgan Stanley Consumer (CMR) Index	Morgan Stanley & Co.	Stock	North America	United States	124
Morgan Stanley Cyclical (CYC) Index	Morgan Stanley & Co.	Stock	North America	United States	126
Morgan Stanley High-Technology 35 (Tech 35) Index	Morgan Stanley & Co.	Stock	North America	United States	128
Morgan Stanley REIT Index	Morgan Stanley & Co.	Real Estate	North America	United States	917
Morley Capital Management 1-Year GIC Index	Morley Capital Management, Inc.	Guaranteed Investment Contracts	North America	United States	780
Morley Capital Management 3 Year GIC Index	Morley Capital Management, Inc.	Guaranteed Investment Contracts	North America	United States	912
Morley Capital Management 5 Year GIC Index	Morley Capital Management, Inc.	Guaranteed Investment Contracts	North America	United States	912

INDEX	PUBLISHER	ASSET CLASS	REGION	COUNTRY	PAGE
Morley Capital Management GIC Index	Morley Capital Management, Inc.	Guaranteed Investment Contracts	North America	United States	912
Morningstar Mutual Fund Performance Averages	Morningstar	Mutual Funds	North America	United States	915
Moscow Times Dollar Adjusted Index	Moscow Times, The/Skate-Press	Stock	Europe	Russia	879
Moscow Times Stock Index	Moscow Times, The/Skate-Press	Stock	Europe	Russia	468
Muscat Securities Market (MSM) Price Index	Muscat Securities Market (MSM), The	Stock	Africa/Middle East	Oman	590
Nagoya 25 Index	Nagoya Stock Exchange	Stock	Asia/Pacific	Japan	302
Nairobi Stock Exchange 20 Index	Nairobi Stock Exchange	Stock	Africa/Middle East	Kenya	578
Namibia Stock Exchange (NSE) Index	Namibian Stock Exchange	Stock	Africa/Middle East	Namibia	586
Nasdaq 100 Index	National Association of Securities Dealers, Inc. (NASD), The/Nasdaq Stock Market Inc., The	Stock	North America	United States	130
Nasdaq American Depositary Receipts (ADRs) Index	National Association of Securities Dealers, Inc. (NASD), The/Nasdaq Stock Market Inc., The	Stock	North America	United States	132
Nasdaq Bank Index	National Association of Securities Dealers, Inc. (NASD), The/Nasdaq Stock Market Inc., The	Stock	North America	United States	134
Nasdaq Biotechnology Index	National Association of Securities Dealers, Inc. (NASD), The/Nasdaq Stock Market Inc., The	Stock	North America	United States	136
Nasdaq Composite Index	National Association of Securities Dealers, Inc. (NASD), The/Nasdaq Stock Market Inc., The	Stock	North America	United States	138
Nasdaq Computer Index	National Association of Securities Dealers, Inc. (NASD), The/Nasdaq Stock Market Inc., The	Stock	North America	United States	140
Nasdaq Financial Index 100	National Association of Securities Dealers, Inc. (NASD), The/Nasdaq Stock Market Inc., The	Stock	North America	United States	142
Nasdaq Industrial Index	National Association of Securities Dealers, Inc. (NASD), The/Nasdaq Stock Market Inc., The	Stock	North America	United States	144
Nasdaq Insurance Index	National Association of Securities Dealers, Inc. (NASD), The/Nasdaq Stock Market Inc., The	Stock	North America	United States	146
Nasdaq Other Finance Index	National Association of Securities Dealers, Inc. (NASD), The/Nasdaq Stock Market Inc., The	Stock	North America	United States	152
Nasdaq Telecommunications Index	National Association of Securities Dealers, Inc. (NASD), The/Nasdaq Stock Market Inc., The	Stock	North America	United States	154
Nasdaq Transportation Index	National Association of Securities Dealers, Inc. (NASD), The/Nasdaq Stock Market Inc., The	Stock	North America	United States	156
Nasdaq/National Market System (NMS) Composite Index	National Association of Securities Dealers, Inc. (NASD), The/Nasdaq Stock Market Inc., The	Stock	North America	United States	148

INDEX	PUBLISHER	ASSET CLASS	REGION	COUNTRY	PAGE
Nasdaq/National Market System (NMS) Industrial Index	National Association of Securities Dealers, Inc. (NASD), The/Nasdaq Stock Market Inc., The	Stock	North America	United States	150
National Association of Real Estate Investment Trusts (NAREIT) Composite Index	National Association of Real Estate Investment Trusts (NAREIT)	Real Estate	North America	United States	830
National Bank of Abu Dhabi Index, The	National Bank of Abu Dahbi, The	Stock	Africa/Middle East	Abu Dhabi	887
National Council of Real Estate Investment Fiduciaries (NCREIF) Property Index	National Council of Real Estate Fiduciaries (NCREIF)	Real Estate	North America	United States	828
Nepal Index	Capital Nepal	Stock	Asia/Pacific	Nepal	338
Nepal Stock Exchange Index (NEPSE)	Nepal Stock Exchange Limited	Stock	Asia/Pacific	Nepal	864
Nesbit Burns Gifford Fong Associates Canadian Bond Indices	Nesbitt Burns Inc.	Bond	North America	Canada	892
New Straits Times Industrial Index	New Straits Times, The	Stock	Asia/Pacific	Malaysia	864
New York Stock Exchange (NYSE) Composite Index, The	New York Stock Exchange (NYSE)	Stock	North America	United States	158
New York Stock Exchange (NYSE) Finance Sub-Group Index, The	New York Stock Exchange (NYSE)	Stock	North America	United States	160
New York Stock Exchange (NYSE) Industrial Sub-Group Index, The	New York Stock Exchange (NYSE)	Stock	North America	United States	162
New York Stock Exchange (NYSE) Transportation Sub-Group Index, The	New York Stock Exchange (NYSE)	Stock	North America	United States	164
New York Stock Exchange (NYSE) Utilities Sub-Group Index, The	New York Stock Exchange (NYSE)	Stock	North America	United States	166
New Zealand All Ordinaries Index	New Zealand Stock Exchange (NZSE), The	Stock	Asia/Pacific	New Zealand	865
New Zealand Stock Exchange (NZSE), Market Index, The	New Zealand Stock Exchange (NZSE), The	Stock	Asia/Pacific	Nepal	340
New Zealand Stock Exchange Top 10 Index	New Zealand Stock Exchange (NZSE), The	Stock	Asia/Pacific	New Zealand	865
New Zealand Stock Exchange—30 Selection (NZSE-30) Index, The	New Zealand Stock Exchange (NZSE), The	Stock	Asia/Pacific	New Zealand	344
New Zealand Stock Exchange—40 (NZSE-40) Index, The	New Zealand Stock Exchange (NZSE), The	Stock	Asia/Pacific	New Zealand	346
New Zealand Stock Exchange—Smaller Companies Index (NZSE-SCI), The	New Zealand Stock Exchange (NZSE), The	Stock	Asia/Pacific	Nepal	342
Nigeria Stock Exchange (NSE) All-Share Index	Nigerian Stock Exchange (NSE), The	Stock	Africa/Middle East	Nigeria	588
Nikkei 225 Stock Average	Nihon Keizai Shimbun, Inc.	Stock	Asia/Pacific	Japan	304
Nikkei 500 Stock Average	Nihon Keizai Shimbun, Inc.	Stock	Asia/Pacific	Japan	308
Nikkei All Stock Index	Nihon Keizai Shimbun, Inc.	Stock	Asia/Pacific	Japan	861
Nikkei Bond Index	Nihon Keizai Shimbun, Inc.	Bond	Asia/Pacific	Japan	901
Nikkei Commodity Index	Nihon Keizai Shimbun, Inc.	Commodities	Asia/Pacific	Japan	909
Nikkei Currency Index	Nihon Keizai Shimbun, Inc.	Currencies	World	NA	911
Nikkei OTC Stock Average	Nihon Keizai Shimbun, Inc.	Stock	Asia/Pacific	Japan	861
Nikkei Stock Index 300 (NIK 300)	Nihon Keizai Shimbun, Inc.	Stock	Asia/Pacific	Japan	306
Nomura Research Institute (NRI) Asia/Pacific-200 Index	Nomura International plc/Nomura Research Institute, Ltd.	Stock	Asia/Pacific	Regional	870
Nomura Research Institute (NRI) East European Index	Nomura International plc/Nomura Research Institute, Ltd.	Stock	Europe	Regional	520
Nomura Research Institute (NRI) European Multimedia Index	Nomura International plc/Nomura Research Institute, Ltd.	Stock	Europe	Regional	886
Nordic Securities Market Index	Nordic Stock Exchanges, The	Stock	Europe	Regional	522
OBX Index	Oslo Stock Exchange (Oslo Bors), The	Stock	Europe	Norway	450

INDEX	PUBLISHER	ASSET CLASS	REGION	COUNTRY	PAGE
OMSX Indices	OM Stockholm AB	Stock	Europe	Sweden	881
OMX Index	OM Stockholm AB	Stock	Europe	Sweden	476
Osaka 250 Adjusted Stock Price Average	Osaka Securities Exchange (OSE)	Stock	Asia/Pacific	Japan	862
Osaka 300 Stock Price Index	Osaka Securities Exchange (OSE)	Stock	Asia/Pacific	Japan	310
Osaka 40 Adjusted Stock Price Average	Osaka Securities Exchange (OSE)	Stock	Asia/Pacific	Japan	862
Oslo Stock Exchange All-Share Index	Oslo Stock Exchange (Oslo Bors), The	Stock	Europe	Norway	452
OTC Exchange of India Composite Index	OTC Exchange of India, The	Stock	Asia/Pacific	India	860
OTC Index	R.O.C. Over-the-Counter Securities Exchange	Stock	Asia/Pacific	Taiwan	868
Oversea Chinese Banking Corporation Limited (OCBC) Composite Index	Oversea-Chinese Banking Corporation Limited, The/OCBC Investment Research Limited	Stock	Asia/Pacific	Singapore	866
Oversea Chinese Banking Corporation Limited (OCBC) OTC Index	Oversea-Chinese Banking Corporation Limited, The/OCBC Investment Research Limited	Stock	Asia/Pacific	Singapore	867
Oversea-Chinese Banking Corp., Ltd. (OCBC) 30-Share Index	Oversea-Chinese Banking Corp. Limited/OCBC Investment Research Limited	Stock	Asia/Pacific	Singapore	352
Pacific Stock Exchange Tech 100 (PSE Tech 100) Index	Pacific Stock Exchange (PSE)	Stock	North America	United States	168
Panama Stock Exchange General Index (PSE)	Bolsa de Valores de Panama, S.A., The	Stock	Central/Latin America	Panama	550
Participation Certificate Index	Vienna Stock Exchange (Weiner Borse), The	Stock	Europe	Austria	872
PatriaBIX Index	Patria Finance	Bond	Europe	Czech Republic	902
Payden & Rygel Short-Term Total Return Indices	Payden & Rygel	Money Market Instruments	North America	United States	897
Payden & Rygel Total Return Indices	Payden & Rygel	Bond	North America	United States	897
Peregrine Asia Index (PAI) (Combined + Domestic Investors)	Peregrine Brokerage LImited	Stock	Asia/Pacific	Regional	871
Peregrine Asia Index (PAI)-Foreign	Peregrine Brokerage Limited	Stock	Asia/Pacific	Regional	372
Peregrine Asia Small Cap Index	Peregrine Brokerage LImited	Stock	Asia/Pacific	Regional	871
Peregrine Greater China Index	Peregrine Brokerage Limited	Stock	Asia/Pacific	China	274
Peregrine India ADR Index	Peregrine Brokerage Limited	Stock	Asia/Pacific	India	860
Pfandbrief Index	Association of German Mortgage Banks, The/Association of German Public Sector Banks, The	Bond	Europe	Germany	903
Philadelphia Stock Exchange Airline Sector (PLN) Index	Philadelphia Stock Exchange (PHLX), The	Stock	North America	United States	170
Philadelphia Stock Exchange Forest & Paper Products Sector (FPP) Index	Philadelphia Stock Exchange (PHLX), The	Stock	North America	United States	172
Philadelphia Stock Exchange Gold/Silver Sector (XAU) Index	Philadelphia Stock Exchange (PHLX), The	Stock	North America	United States	174
Philadelphia Stock Exchange Keefe, Bruyette & Woods, Inc. Bank Sector (BKK)	Philadelphia Stock Exchange (PHLX), The	Stock	North America	United States	176
Philadelphia Stock Exchange National Over-the-Counter (XOC) Index	Philadelphia Stock Exchange (PHLX), The	Stock	North America	United States	178
Philadelphia Stock Exchange Phone Sector (PNX) Index	Philadelphia Stock Exchange (PHLX), The	Stock	North America	United States	180
Philadelphia Stock Exchange Semiconductor Sector (SOX) Index	Philadelphia Stock Exchange (PHLX), The	Stock	North America	United States	182
Philadelphia Stock Exchange Supercap (HFX) Index	Philadelphia Stock Exchange (PHLX), The	Stock	North America	United States	184
Philadelphia Stock Exchange U.S. Top 100 (TPX) Index	Philadelphia Stock Exchange (PHLX), The	Stock	North America	United States	186

INDEX	PUBLISHER	ASSET CLASS	REGION	COUNTRY	PAGE
Philadelphia Stock Exchange Utility Sector (UTY) Index	Philadelphia Stock Exchange (PHLX), The	Stock	North America	United States	188
Philippine Stock Exchange (PSE) Composite Index	Philippine Stock Exchange (PSE), The	Stock	Asia/Pacific	Philippines	350
Pictet LPP Index	Pictet & Co.	Stock	Europe	Switzerland	882
Portfolio HEX Index	Helsinki Stock Exchange	Stock	Europe	Finland	876
Portugal Stock Market PSI-20 Index	Oporto Stock Exchange	Stock	Europe	Portugal	464
Prague Stock Exchange 50 (PX 50) Index	Prague Stock Exchange, The	Stock	Europe	Czech Republic	398
Reuters Commodity Index	Reuters	Commodities	Europe	United Kingdom	910
Russell 1000 Growth Index	Frank Russell Company	Stock	North America	United States	192
Russell 1000 Index	Frank Russell Company	Stock	North America	United States	190
Russell 1000 Value Index	Frank Russell Company	Stock	North America	United States	194
Russell 2000 Growth Index	Frank Russell Company	Stock	North America	United States	198
Russell 2000 Index	Frank Russell Company	Stock	North America	United States	196
Russell 2000 Value Index	Frank Russell Company	Stock	North America	United States	200
Russell 2500 Index	Frank Russell Company	Stock	North America	United States	853
Russell 3000 Index	Frank Russell Company	Stock	North America	United States	202
Russell Midcap Growth Index	Frank Russell Company	Stock	North America	United States	206
Russell Midcap Index	Frank Russell Company	Stock	North America	United States	204
Russell Midcap Value Index	Frank Russell Company	Stock	North America	United States	208
Russell Top 200 Growth Index	Frank Russell Company	Stock	North America	United States	853
Russell Top 200 Index	Frank Russell Company	Stock	North America	United States	853
Russell Top 200 Value Index	Frank Russell Company	Stock	North America	United States	853
Russell/NRI Japanese Equity Style Index Series	Frank Russell Company/Nomura Research Institute	Stock	Asia/Pacific	Japan	863
Russell/NRI Japanese Total Market Index	Frank Russell Company/Nomura Research Institute	Stock	Asia/Pacific	Japan	863
Ryan Labs 3-Year Master GIC Index	Ryan Labs Inc.	Guaranteed Investment Contracts	North America	United States	782
Ryan Labs 5-Year Master GIC Index	Ryan Labs Inc.	Guaranteed Investment Contracts	North America	United States	784
Ryan Labs Cash Index	Ryan Labs, Inc.	Money Market Instruments	North America	United States	907
Ryan Labs Treasury Composite Index	Ryan Labs, Inc.	Bond	North America	United States	897
Ryan Labs Treasury Yield Curve Indices	Ryan Labs, Inc.	Bond	North America	United States	897
S-One Bond Index	Securities One Public Company Limited	Bond	Asia/Pacific	Thailand	901
Salomon Brothers Brady Bond Index	Salomon Brothers Inc.	Bond	World	NA	716
Salomon Brothers Broad Investment-Grade (BIG) Bond Index	Salomon Brothers Inc.	Bond	North America	United States	678
Salomon Brothers Broad Investment-Grade (BIG) Corporate Bond Index	Salomon Brothers Inc.	Bond	North America	United States	680
Salomon Brothers Broad Investment-Grade (BIG) Mortgage Index	Salomon Brothers Inc.	Bond	North America	United States	682
Salomon Brothers Broad Investment-Grade (BIG) Treasury/Government Sponsored Bond Index	Salomon Brothers Inc.	Bond	North America	United States	684
Salomon Brothers Certificate-of Deposit Index	Salomon Brothers Inc.	Money Market Instruments	North America	United States	907
Salomon Brothers Convertible Securities Index	Salomon Brothers Inc.	Convertible Securities	North America	United States	764

INDEX	PUBLISHER	ASSET CLASS	REGION	COUNTRY	PAGE
Salomon Brothers Core 3 Index	Salomon Brothers Inc.	Bond	North America	United States	899
Salomon Brothers Core 5 Index	Salomon Brothers Inc.	Bond	North America	United States	899
Salomon Brothers Eurobond Indices	Salomon Brothers Inc.	Bond	North America	United States	897
Salomon Brothers Eurodollar Bond Index	Salomon Brothers Inc.	Bond	World	NA	718
Salomon Brothers High-Yield Market Index	Salomon Brothers Inc.	Bond	North America	United States	686
Salomon Brothers New Large Pension Fund Baseline Bond Index (New LPF)	Salomon Brothers Inc.	Bond	North America	United States	899
Salomon Brothers U.S. Treasury Benchmark (On-The-Run) Index	Salomon Brothers Inc.	Bond	North America	United States	899
Salomon Brothers U.S. Treasury Benchmark Yield Curve Average	Salomon Brothers Inc.	Bond	North America	United States	899
Salomon Brothers U.S. Treasury Bill Index	Salomon Brothers Inc.	Money Market Instruments	North America	United States	907
Salomon Brothers World Bond Index	Salomon Brothers Inc.	Bond	North America	United States	898
Salomon Brothers World Equity Index (SBWEI)-Property Industry Index	Salomon Brothers Inc.	Real Estate	World	NA	836
Salomon Brothers World Equity Index-Broad Market Index (SBWEI-BMI)	Salomon Brothers Inc.	Stock	World	NA	636
Salomon Brothers World Equity Index-Extended Market Index (SBWEI-EMI)	Salomon Brothers Inc.	Stock	World	NA	638
Salomon Brothers World Equity Index-Primary Market Index (SBWEI-PMI)	Salomon Brothers Inc.	Stock	World	NA	640
Salomon Brothers World Government Bond Index (WGBI)	Salomon Brothers Inc.	Bond	World	NA	720
Salomon Brothers World Money Market Index	Salomon Brothers Inc.	Money Market Instruments	World	NA	740
Salomon Emerging Market Mutual Fund (EMMF) Debt Index	Salomon Brothers Inc.	Mutual Funds	North America	United States	916
Sao Paulo Stock Exchange Index (BOVESPA)	The Sao Paulo Stock Exchange	Stock	Central/Latin America	Brazil	536
SBC Index of Swiss Shares	Swiss Bank Corp.	Stock	Europe	Switzerland	882
SBC Warburg Australia Bond Index	SBC Warburg Australia	Bond	Asia/Pacific	Australia	900
SBF-120 Index	SBF-Bourse de Paris, The	Stock	Europe	France	412
SBF-250 Index	SBF-Bourse de Paris, The	Stock	Europe	France	414
SBI Index	Ljubljanska Stock Exchange	Stock	Europe	Slovenia	880
Schmidt Composite GIC Index	Schmidt Management Company	Guaranteed Investment Contracts	North America	United States	786
Schmidt GIC Common Fund Index	Schmidt Management Company	Guaranteed Investment Contracts	North America	United States	912
Schmidt Long-Term GIC Index	Schmidt Management Company	Guaranteed Investment Contracts	North America	United States	912
Schmidt Short-Term GIC Index	Schmidt Management Company	Guaranteed Investment Contracts	North America	United States	912
Schwab 1000 Index	Charles Schwab & Co.	Stock	North America	United States	854
Schwab International Index	Charles Schwab & Co.	Stock	World	NA	892
Scotia McLeod Debt Market Indices, The	Scotia McLeod	Bond	North America	Canada	892
Securities Exchange of Barbados Share Index	Securities Exchange of Barbados	Stock	Central/Latin America	Barbados	530
Securities Exchange of Thailand (SET) Index, The	Stock Exchange of Thailand (SET), The	Stock	Asia/Pacific	Thailand	368
SET 50 Index	Stock Exchange of Thailand (SET), The	Stock	Asia/Pacific	Thailand	869
Shanghai A-Share Stock Price Index (SSE)	Shanghai Stock Exchange, The (SSE)	Stock	Asia/Pacific	China	276
Shanghai B-Share Stock Price Index (SSE)	Shanghai Stock Exchange, The (SSE)	Stock	Asia/Pacific	China	278
Shanghai Share Stock Price Index (SSE)	Shanghai Stock Exchange, The (SSE)	Stock	Asia/Pacific	China	280
Shenzen A-Share Stock Price Index	Shenzen Stock Exchange	Stock	Asia/Pacific	China	857

INDEX	PUBLISHER	ASSET CLASS	REGION	COUNTRY	PAGE
Shenzen B-Share Stock Price Index	Shenzen Stock Exchange	Stock	Asia/Pacific	China	857
Shenzen Share Stock Price Index	Shenzen Stock Exchange	Stock	Asia/Pacific	China	857
Skate-Press Consulting Agency MT 100 Index	Skate-Press Consulting Agency	Stock	Europe	Russia	879
Skate-Press Consulting Agency MT 50 Index	Skate-Press Consulting Agency	Stock	Europe	Russia	880
Slovak Share Index (SAX)	Bratislava Stock Exchange (BSE), The	Stock	Europe	Slovakia	470
Smith Barney 400 Convertible Securities Index	Smith Barney, Inc.	Convertible Securities	North America	United States	766
SNL Broker/ Dealers Index	SNL Securities, L.P.	Stock	North America	United States	854
SNL Finance Companies Index	SNL Securities, L.P.	Stock	North America	United States	854
SNL Financial Services Companies Index	SNL Securities, L.P.	Stock	North America	United States	854
SNL Financial Services Investment Advisors Index	SNL Securities, L.P.	Stock	North America	United States	855
SNL GSE Index	SNL Securities, L.P.	Stock	North America	United States	854
SNL Mortgage Banks and Related Services Index	SNL Securities, L.P.	Stock	North America	United States	854
SNL REIT Index	SNL Securities	Real Estate	North America	United States	918
SSKI Index	SSKI Securities Ltd.	Stock	Asia/Pacific	India	860
Standard & Poor's (S&P) Financial Price Index	Standard & Poor's Corporation (S&P Corp.)	Stock	North America	United States	216
Standard & Poor's (S&P) Industrial Price Index	Standard & Poor's Corporation (S&P Corp.)	Stock	North America	United States	218
Standard & Poor's (S&P) MidCap 400 Index	Standard & Poor's Corporation (S&P Corp.)	Stock	North America	United States	220
Standard & Poor's (S&P) Supercomposite Stock Price Index	Standard & Poor's Corporation (S&P Corp.)	Stock	North America	United States	224
Standard & Poor's (S&P) Transportation Price Index (TRX)	Standard & Poor's Corporation (S&P Corp.)	Stock	North America	United States	226
Standard & Poor's (S&P) Utilities Price Index	Standard & Poor's Corporation (S&P Corp.)	Stock	North America	United States	228
Standard & Poor's (S&P)/BARRA Growth Index	Standard & Poor's Corporation (S&P Corp.)/BARRA, Inc.	Stock	North America	United States	230
Standard & Poor's (S&P)/BARRA Value Index	Standard & Poor's Corporation (S&P Corp.)/BARRA, Inc.	Stock	North America	United States	232
Standard & Poor's 100 (S&P 100) Index (OEX)	Standard & Poor's Corporation (S&P Corp.)	Stock	North America	United States	210
Standard & Poor's 500 (S&P 500) Composite Stock Price Index	Standard & Poor's Corporation (S&P Corp.)	Stock	North America	United States	212
Standard & Poor's Corporate Bond Indices	Standard & Poor's Corporation (S&P Corp.)	Bond	North America	United States	899
Standard & Poor's Intermediate-Term U.S. Government Bonds	Standard & Poor's Corporation (S&P Corp.)	Bond	North America	United States	900
Standard & Poor's Long-Term U.S. Government Bonds	Standard & Poor's Corporation (S&P Corp.)	Bond	North America	United States	900
Standard & Poor's Municipal Bond Indices	Standard & Poor's Corporation (S&P Corp.)	Bond	North America	United States	899
Standard & Poor's Rated Money Market Fund Indices	Standard & Poor's Corporation (S&P Corp.)	Mutual Funds	North America	United States	916
Standard & Poor's Short-Term U.S. Government Bonds	Standard & Poor's Corporation (S&P Corp.)	Bond	North America	United States	900
Standard & Poor's SmallCap 600 Index	Standard & Poor's Corporation (S&P Corp.)	Stock	North America	United States	222
Stock Exchange of Mauritius Index (SEMDEX)	Stock Exchange of Mauritius Ltd., The	Stock	Africa/Middle East	Mauritius	582
Stock Exchange of Singapore (SES) All-Singapore Index	Stock Exchange of Singapore Ltd.	Stock	Asia/Pacific	Singapore	354
Stockholm Stock Exchange General (SX-General) Index	Stockholm Fondbors AB, The	Stock	Europe	Sweden	478
Stockholm Stock Exchange O-list Index, The	Stockholm Fondbors AB, The	Stock	Europe	Sweden	480
Stockholm Stock Exchange OTC Index, The	Stockholm Fondbors AB, The	Stock	Europe	Sweden	482

INDEX	PUBLISHER	ASSET CLASS	REGION	COUNTRY	PAGE
Stockholm Stock Exchange SX-16 Index, The	Stockholm Stock Exchange	Stock	Europe	Sweden	881
Stockholm Stock Exchange SX-70 Index	Stockholm Stock Exchange	Stock	Europe	Sweden	882
Straits Times Index, The	Straits Times, The	Stock	Asia/Pacific	Singapore	867
Straits Times Industrial (STI) Index, The	Business Times, The/Times Business Publications Limited	Stock	Asia/Pacific	Singapore	356
Surabaya Stock Exchange Composite Price Index	Surabaya Stock Exchange	Stock	Asia/Pacific	Indonesia	860
Swaziland Stock Market (SSM) Index	Swaziland Stockbrokers Ltd.	Stock	Africa/Middle East	Swaziland	602
Swiss Bid/Ask Index (SBAI)	Association Tripartite Bourses (ATB)	Stock	Europe	Switzerland	883
Swiss Bond Index (SBI)	Association of Tripartite Bourses	Bond	Europe	Switzerland	903
Swiss Large Company Performance Index (SLCI)	Association Tripartite Bourses (ATB)	Stock	Europe	Switzerland	883
Swiss Market Index (SMI)	Association Tripartite Bourses (ATB)	Stock	Europe	Switzerland	484
Swiss Medium Company Performance Index (SMCI)	Association Tripartite Bourses (ATB)	Stock	Europe	Switzerland	883
Swiss Performance Index		Stock	Europe	Switzerland	883
Swiss Performance Index (SPI)	Association Tripartite Bourses (ATB)	Stock	Europe	Switzerland	486
Swiss Small Company Performance Index (SSCI)	Association Tripartite Bourses (ATB)	Stock	Europe	Switzerland	884
T. Rowe Price GIC Index	T. Rowe Price	Guaranteed Investment Contracts	North America	United States	912
TA-100 Index	Tel Aviv Stock Exchange (TSE), The	Stock	Africa/Middle East	Israel	888
Taiwan Industrial Stock Price Average	Taiwan Stock Exchange Corporation	Stock	Asia/Pacific	Taiwan	869
Taiwan Stock Exchange Capitalization-Weighted Stock Index (TAIEX)	Taiwan Stock Exchange Corporation	Stock	Asia/Pacific	Taiwan	364
Taiwan Stock Exchange Composite Stock Price Average	Taiwan Stock Exchange Corporation	Stock	Asia/Pacific	Taiwan	366
Tel Aviv Stock Exchange General Share Index	Tel Aviv Stock Exchange (TSE), The	Stock	Africa/Middle East	Israel	572
Tel Aviv Stock Exchange MAOF-25 Index	Tel Aviv Stock Exchange (TSE), The	Stock	Africa/Middle East	Israel	574
Thai Investment and Securities Company Ltd. (TISCO) Price Index	Thai Investment and Securities Company Ltd.	Stock	Asia/Pacific	Thailand	870
Tiger Index	HSBC James Capel & Co. Limited	Stock	Europe	United Kingdom	885
Tokyo Stock Exchange (TSE) Second Section Stock Price Index	Tokyo Stock Exchange (TSE), The	Stock	Asia/Pacific	Japan	320
Tokyo Stock Exchange Arithmetic Stock Price Index	Tokyo Stock Exchange (TSE), The	Stock	Asia/Pacific	Japan	862
Tokyo Stock Exchange Price Index (TOPIX)	Tokyo Stock Exchange (TSE), The	Stock	Asia/Pacific	Japan	312
Tokyo Stock Exchange Price Index (TOPIX)—Large-Sized Companies Subindex	Tokyo Stock Exchange (TSE), The	Stock	Asia/Pacific	Japan	314
Tokyo Stock Exchange Price Index (TOPIX)—Medium-Sized Companies Subindex	Tokyo Stock Exchange (TSE), The	Stock	Asia/Pacific	Japan	316
Tokyo Stock Exchange Price Index (TOPIX)—Small-Sized Companies Subindex	Tokyo Stock Exchange (TSE), The	Stock	Asia/Pacific	Japan	318
Tootsie Index	HSBC James Capel & Co. Limited	Stock	Europe	United Kingdom	885
Toronto Stock Exchange 100 (TSE 100) Composite Index	Toronto Stock Exchange (TSE), The	Stock	North America	Canada	46
Toronto Stock Exchange 200 (TSE 200) Composite Index	Toronto Stock Exchange (TSE), The	Stock	North America	Canada	48
Toronto Stock Exchange 300 (TSE 300) Composite Index	Toronto Stock Exchange (TSE), The	Stock	North America	Canada	50
Toronto Stock Exchange 35 (TSE 35) Index	Toronto Stock Exchange (TSE), The	Stock	North America	Canada	44
Total Share Index of Copenhagen Stock Exchange (CSE)	Copenhagen Stock Exchange (CSE)	Stock	Europe	Denmark	402

INDEX	PUBLISHER	ASSET CLASS	REGION	COUNTRY	PAGE
Trans Tasman 100 Index	Australian Stock Exchange Ltd./and the New Zealand Stock Exchange	Stock	Asia/Pacific	Regional	871
Trinidad & Tobago Stock Exchange Daily Index of Stock Market Values	Trinidad & Tobago Stock Exchange	Stock	Central/Latin America	Trinidad & Tobago	556
Trixie Indes	HSBC James Capel & Co. Limited	Stock	Europe	United Kingdom	885
UK Gilts Index	Financial Times	Bond	Europe	United Kingdom	904
Unitas Index, The	Bank of Finland	Stock	Europe	Finland	876
United Overseas Bank (UOB) Blue Chip Index	United Overseas Bank (UOB)	Stock	Asia/Pacific	Singapore	867
United Overseas Bank (UOB) Dealing and Automated Quotation System (SESDAQ) Index	United Overseas Bank (UOB)	Stock	Asia/Pacific	Singapore	358
United Overseas Bank (UOB) OTC Index	United Overseas Bank (UOB)	Stock	Asia/Pacific	Singapore	868
United Overseas Bank Singapore Government Bond Index	United Overseas Bank (UOB)	Bond	Asia/Pacific	Singapore	901
Upline USI Index	Upline Securities	Stock	Africa/Middle East	Morocco	888
Vallejo Selected Stock Price Index	Corredores Associates	Stock	Latin/Central America	Colombia	891
Value Line Arithmetic (VLA) Index	Value Line, Inc.	Stock	North America	United States	234
Value Line Composite Index (XVL)	Value Line, Inc.	Stock	North America	United States	236
Value Line Convertible Securities Index	Value Line Publishing, Inc.	Convertible Securities	North America	United States	768
Value Line Industrial Average	Value Line, Inc.	Stock	North America	United States	855
Value Line Mutual Fund Performance Averages	Value Line, Inc.	Mutual Funds	North America	United States	916
Value Line Railroad Average	Value Line, Inc.	Stock	North America	United States	855
Value Line Utility Average	Value Line, Inc.	Stock	North America	United States	855
Vancouver Stock Exchange (VSE) Index	Vancouver Stock Exchange (VSE), The	Stock	North America	Canada	52
Variable Annuity Research Data Service	Financial Planning Resources, Inc.	Miscellaneous	North America	United States	919
Venezuela Marinevest Stock Composite Index	Marinevest	Stock	Latin/Central America	Venezuela	892
Vienna Stock Exchange Share (Weiner Borse) Index (WBI)	Vienna Stock Exchange (Weiner Borse), The	Stock	Europe	Austria	382
Vontobel Small Companies Index	Bank Vontobel	Stock	Europe	Switzerland	884
Wardley Index, The	Australian Stock Exchange Limited, The	Stock	Asia/Pacific	Australia	856
Warrant Index	HSBC James Capel & Co. Limited	Stock	Europe	United Kingdom	885
Warsaw Stock Exchange (WIG) Index	Warsaw Stock Exchange (WSE)	Stock	Europe	Poland	454
Warsaw Stock Exchange WIRR Index	Warsaw Stock Exchange (WSE)	Stock	Europe	Poland	456
Wiener Borse Index 30 (WBI 30) Index	Osterreichische Termin-Und Optionenborse (OTOB)	Stock	Europe	Austria	384
WIG 20	Warsaw Stock Exchange	Stock	Europe	Poland	879
Wilshire 2500 Equity Index	Wilshire Associates Inc.	Stock	North America	United States	855
Wilshire 5000 Equity Index	Wilshire Associates Inc.	Stock	North America	United States	238
Wilshire Associates Small Cap (WSX) Index	Wilshire Associates Inc.	Stock	North America	United States	240
Wilshire Large Company (Top 750) Equity Index	Wilshire Associates Inc.	Stock	North America	United States	242
Wilshire Large Company Growth Equity Style Index	Wilshire Associates Inc.	Stock	North America	United States	244
Wilshire Large Company Value Equity Style Index	Wilshire Associates Inc.	Stock	North America	United States	246
Wilshire Middle Capitalization Company (MidCap 750) Equity Index	Wilshire Associates Inc.	Stock	North America	United States	248

INDEX	PUBLISHER	ASSET CLASS	REGION	COUNTRY	PAGE
Wilshire Middle Capitalization Company Growth Equity Style Index	Wilshire Associates Inc.	Stock	North America	United States	250
Wilshire Middle Capitalization Company Value Equity Style Index	Wilshire Associates Inc.	Stock	North America	United States	252
Wilshire Real Estate Securities Index	Wilshire Associates	Real Estate	North America	United States	832
Wilshire Small Company (Next 1750) Equity Index	Wilshire Associates Inc.	Stock	North America	United States	254
Wilshire Small Company Growth Equity Style Index	Wilshire Associates Inc.	Stock	North America	United States	256
Wilshire Small Company Value Equity Style Index	Wilshire Associates Inc.	Stock	North America	United States	258
Zimbabwe Stock Exchange (ZSE) Industrial and Mining Index	Zimbabwe Stock Exchange (ZSE)	Stock	Africa/Middle East	Zimbabwe	604

APPENDIX 6

INDICES BY ASSET CLASS AND COUNTRY

BONDS

COUNTRY	INDEX	PUBLISHER	PAGE
Australia	BZW Australia Liquid Government Securities Bond Index	BZW Australia	900
	Commonwealth Bank Bond Indices	Australian Stock Exchange Limited, The	900
	SBC Warburg Australia Bond Index	SBC Warburg Australia	900
Austria	CA Bond Index	Creditanstalt Investment Bank AG	902
Canada	Nesbit Burns Gifford Fong Associates Canadian Bond Indices	Nesbitt Burns Inc.	892
	Scotia McLeod Debt Market Indices, The	Scotia McLeod	892
Colombia	IRBB Index	Bolsa de Bogota S.A.	905
Czech Republic	Czech Komercni Bank Bond Price Index	Komercni Bank	902
	PatriaBIX Index	Patria Finance	902
Denmark	Copenhagen Stock Exchange True Yield Index	Copenhagen Stock Exchange	902
Germany	German Bond Index (REX)	Deutsche Borse AG	902
	Pfandbrief Index	Association of German Mortgage Banks, The/Association of German Public Sector Banks, The	903
Japan	Nikkei Bond Index	Nihon Keizai Shimbun, Inc.	901
Korea	Korea Bond Index	Korea Stock Exchange (KSE)	901
Portugal	BVL ORF Index	Bolsa de Valores de Lisboa	903
Regional--	Lombard Odier & Cie (LOC) European Government Bond Index	Lombard Odier & Cie	904
Singapore	United Overseas Bank Singapore Government Bond Index	United Overseas Bank (UOB)	901
South Africa	Johannesburg Stock Exchange (JSE) Actuaries Bond Performance Index	Johannesburg Stock Exchange (JSE)	904
Switzerland	Swiss Bond Index (SBI)	Association of Tripartite Bourses	903
Thailand	S-One Bond Index	Securities One Public Company Limited	901
United Kingdom	FT-Actuaries Fixed Interest Indices	Financial Times	904
	Index-Linked Index	Financial Times	904
	UK Gilts Index	Financial Times	904
United States	Altman Defaulted Debt Securities Index	Edward I. Altman/New York University	893
	Barron's Best Grade Bonds	Barron's	893
	Barron's Intermediate Grade Bonds	Barron's	893
	Bond Buyer 11 Bond Index	Bond Buyer, The	894
	Bond Buyer 20 Bond Index	Bond Buyer, The	893
	Bond Buyer Municipal Bond Index (BBI)	Bond Buyer, The	644
	Bond Buyer Revenue Bond Index	Bond Buyer, The	894
	Chemical Bank Emerging Market Debt Index	Chase Bank	894

COUNTRY	INDEX	PUBLISHER	PAGE
United States, *Cont'd*	Chicago Board of Trade (CBOT) Argentina Brady Bond Index	Chicago Board of Trade	894
	Chicago Board of Trade (CBOT) Brazil Brady Bond Index	Chicago Board of Trade	895
	Chicago Board of Trade (CBOT) Mexico Brady Bond Index	Chicago Board of Trade	895
	CS First Boston High Yield Index	Cs First Boston	646
	Dow Jones 20 Bond Average	Dow Jones & Company, Inc.	895
	Goldman Sachs Liquid Asset-Backed Securities Index (LABS)	Goldman Sachs & Co.	895
	Knight Ridder-CRB Interest Rates Index	Knight Ridder Financial	896
	Lehman Brothers Adjustable Rate Mortgage (ARM) Index	Lehman Brothers	648
	Lehman Brothers Aggregate Bond Index	Lehman Brothers	650
	Lehman Brothers Corporate Bond Index	Lehman Brothers	652
	Lehman Brothers Government/Corporate Bond Index	Lehman Brothers	554
	Lehman Brothers High Yield Composite Bond Index	Lehman Brothers	556
	Lehman Brothers Mortgage-Backed Securities Index	Lehman Brothers	558
	Lehman Brothers Municipal Bond Index	Lehman Brothers	560
	Lehman Brothers U.S. Government Bond Index	Lehman Brothers	562
	Merrill Lynch High Yield Master Index	Merrill Lynch & Co.	664
	Merrill Lynch Institutional Municipal Index	Merrill Lynch & Co.	666
	Merrill Lynch Mortgage Master Bond Index	Merrill Lynch & Co.	668
	Merrill Lynch U.S. Corporate and Government Master Bond Index	Merrill Lynch & Co.	670
	Merrill Lynch U.S. Domestic Corporate Bond Index	Merrill Lynch & Co.	672
	Merrill Lynch U.S. Domestic Master Bond Index	Merrill Lynch & Co.	674
	Merrill Lynch U.S. Government Master Bond Index	Merrill Lynch & Co.	676
	Moody's Intermediate-Term Corporate Bond Yield Averages	Moody's Investors Service	896
	Moody's Long-Term Corporate Bond Yield Averages	Moody's Investors Service	896
	Moody's Municipal Bond Yield Averages	Moody's Investors Service	897
	Payden & Rygel Total Return Indices	Payden & Rygel	897
	Ryan Labs Treasury Composite Index	Ryan Labs, Inc.	897
	Ryan Labs Treasury Yield Curve Indices	Ryan Labs, Inc.	897
	Salomon Brothers Broad Investment-Grade (BIG) Bond Index	Salomon Brothers Inc.	678
	Salomon Brothers Broad Investment-Grade (BIG) Corporate Bond Index	Salomon Brothers Inc.	680
	Salomon Brothers Broad Investment-Grade (BIG) Mortgage Index	Salomon Brothers Inc.	682
	Salomon Brothers Broad Investment-Grade (BIG) Treasury/Government Sponsored Bond Index	Salomon Brothers Inc.	684
	Salomon Brothers Core 3 Index	Salomon Brothers Inc.	899
	Salomon Brothers Core 5 Index	Salomon Brothers Inc.	899
	Salomon Brothers Eurobond Indices	Salomon Brothers Inc.	897
	Salomon Brothers High-Yield Market Index	Salomon Brothers Inc.	686
	Salomon Brothers New Large Pension Fund Baseline Bond Index (New LPF)	Salomon Brothers Inc.	899
	Salomon Brothers U.S. Treasury Benchmark (On-The-Run) Index	Salomon Brothers Inc.	899

COUNTRY	INDEX	PUBLISHER	PAGE
United States, Cont'd	Standard & Poor's Corporate Bond Indices	Standard & Poor's Corporation (S&P Corp.)	899
	Standard & Poor's Intermediate-Term U.S. Government Bonds	Standard & Poor's Corporation (S&P Corp.)	900
	Standard & Poor's Long-Term U.S. Government Bonds	Standard & Poor's Corporation (S&P Corp.)	900
	Standard & Poor's Municipal Bond Indices	Standard & Poor's Corporation (S&P Corp.)	899
	Standard & Poor's Short-Term U.S. Government Bonds	Standard & Poor's Corporation (S&P Corp.)	900
World	Bloomberg/European Federation of Financial Analyst Societies (EFFAS) All Government Bond Index--U.S. Government	Bloomberg Financial Services	690
	Citicorp/IFR Impaired Loan Index	Citicorp/International Financial Review	905
	Emerging Markets Bond Index Plus (EMBI+)	J.P. Morgan Securities Inc.	692
	Goldman Sachs International Government Bond Index	Goldman Sachs & Co.	905
	J.P. Morgan ECU Bond Index	J.P. Morgan Securities Inc.	694
	J.P. Morgan Global Government Bond Index	J.P. Morgan Securities Inc.	696
	Lehman Brothers Emerging Americas Bond Index	Lehman Brothers	698
	Lehman Brothers Eurobond Index	Lehman Brothers	700
	Lehman Brothers Global Bond Index	Lehman Brothers	702
	Lombard Odier & Cie (LOC) Individual Bond Market Indices	Lombard Odier & Cie	906
	Lombard Odier & Cie Global World Government Bond Index	Lombard Odier & Cie	704
	Merrill Lynch Brady Bond Index	Merrill Lynch & Co.	706
	Merrill Lynch Canadian Bond Master Index	Merrill Lynch & Co.	708
	Merrill Lynch Eurodollar Bond Index	Merrill Lynch & Co.	710
	Merrill Lynch Global Bond Index	Merrill Lynch & Co.	712
	Merrill Lynch Global Government Bond Index	Merrill Lynch & Co.	714
	Salomon Brothers Brady Bond Index	Salomon Brothers Inc.	716
	Salomon Brothers Eurobond Index	Salomon Brothers Inc.	718
	Salomon Brothers World Government Bond Index (WGBI)	Salomon Brothers Inc.	720

CLOSED-END FUNDS

COUNTRY	INDEX	PUBLISHER	PAGE
United States	Hertzfeld Closed-End Average (THCEA)	Thomas J. Hertzfeld Advisors, Inc.	822

COMMODITIES

COUNTRY	INDEX	PUBLISHER	PAGE
Japan	Daiwa Physical Commodities Index	Daiwa	909
	Nikkei Commodity Index	Nihon Keizai Shimbun, Inc.	909
United Kingdom	Reuters Commodity Index	Reuters	910
United States	Bankers Trust Commodity Index (BTCI)	Bankers Trust New York Corp.	744
	Dow Jones Futures Index	Dow Jones & Company, Inc., Inc.	908
	Dow Jones Spot Index	Dow Jones & Company, Inc., Inc.	908
	Goldman Sachs Commodity Index (GSCI)	Goldman, Sachs & Co.	746
	Investable Commodity Index (ICI)	Jefferies & Company, Inc./Intermarket Management Inc.	748
	J.P. Morgan Commodity Index (JPMCI)	J.P. Morgan Securities Inc.	750
	Journal of Commerce Industrial Price Index	Journal of Commerce	908
	Knight-Ridder Commodity Research Bureau's Futures Price Index (KR-CRB)	Knight-Ridder Financial	752
	Lehman Brothers Commodity Index (LBCI)	Lehman Brothers Inc.	754
	Merrill Lynch Energy and Metals Index (ENMET)	Merrill Lynch & Co.	908

COMMODITIES

COUNTRY	INDEX	PUBLISHER	PAGE
United States, *Cont'd*	Moody's Investors Scrap Commodity Price Index	Moody's Investors Service	909
	Moody's Investors Spot Commodity Price Index	Moody's Investors Service	909

CONVERTIBLE SECURITIES

COUNTRY	INDEX	PUBLISHER	PAGE
Asia	Kleinwort Benson Asia Convertible Bond Index	Kleinwort Benson	910
France	Exane French Convertible Index	Exane	910
Japan	D.E. Shaw Japanese Convertible Bond Index (DESCBI)	D.E. Shaw	910
United States	CS First Boston Convertible Securities Index	CS First Boston	758
	Goldman Sachs Convertible 100 Index	Goldman, Sachs & Co.	760
	ING Barings Asian Convertible Bond (CB) Index	ING Baring Securities Limited	772
	Merrill Lynch Convertible Securities Index	Merrill Lynch & Co.	762
	Salomon Brothers Convertible Securities Index	Salomon Brothers Inc.	764
	Smith Barney 400 Convertible Securities Index	Smith Barney, Inc.	766
	Value Line Convertible Securities Index	Value Line Publishing, Inc.	768
World	Jefferies Global Convertible (JeffCo) Bond Index	Jefferies & Company Inc.	774
	Merrill Lynch Global 300 (ML G300) Convertible Index	Merrill Lynch & Co.	776

CURRENCIES

COUNTRY	INDEX	PUBLISHER	PAGE
World	Knight-Ridder-CRB Currencies Index	Knight Ridder Financial	911
	Merrill Lynch Currency Indices	Merrill Lynch & Co.	911
	Nikkei Currency Index	Nihon Keizai Shimbun, Inc.	911

GUARANTEED INVESTMENT CONTRACTS

COUNTRY	INDEX	PUBLISHER	PAGE
United States	Fiduciary Capital Management GIC Index	Fiduciary Capital Management Inc.	911
	Morley Capital Management 3 Year GIC Index	Morley Capital Management, Inc.	912
	Morley Capital Management 5 Year GIC Index	Morley Capital Management, Inc.	912
	Morley Capital Management GIC Index	Morley Capital Management, Inc.	912
	Schmidt GIC Common Fund Index	Schmidt Management Company	912
	Schmidt Long-Term GIC Index	Schmidt Management Company	912
	Schmidt Short-Term GIC Index	Schmidt Management Company	912
	T. Rowe Price GIC Index	T. Rowe Price	912
	Morley Capital Management 1-Year GIC Index	Morley Capital Management, Inc.	780
	Ryan Labs 3-Year Master GIC Index	Ryan Labs Inc.	782
	Ryan Labs 5-Year Master GIC Index	Ryan Labs Inc.	784
	Schmidt Composite GIC Index	Schmidt Management Company	786

MISCELLANEOUS

COUNTRY	INDEX	PUBLISHER	PAGE
Japan	D.E. Shaw Japanese Warrant Index	D.E. Shaw	919
Miscellaneous	Merrill Lynch Capital Market Index	Merrill Lynch & Co.	840
United States	Barclay CTA Index	Barclay Trading Group	918
	MAR Fund/Pool Qualified Universe Index	Managed Account Reports	918
	Merrill Lynch Capital Market Index	Merrill Lynch & Co.	918
	MLM Managed Futures Index	Mount Lucas Group	918
	Variable Annuity Research Data Service	Financial Planning Resources, Inc.	919

MONEY MARKET INSTRUMENTS

COUNTRY	INDEX	PUBLISHER	PAGE
United States, Cont'd	Bankers Trust Bankers Acceptances		906
	Bankers Trust Banxquote Retail and Institutional CD Indices	Bankers Trust New York Corp.	906
	Bankers Trust LIBOR	Bankers Trust New York Corp.	906
	Bankers Trust Repurchase Agreements	Bankers Trust New York Corp.	906
	Bond Buyer Short-Term Commercial Paper Rate		906
	Bond Buyer Short-Term Money Market Municipal Index	Bond Buyer, The	906
	Bond Buyer Short-Term One-Year Note Index	Bond Buyer, The	907
	Payden & Rygel Short-Term Total Return Indices	Payden & Rygel	897
	Ryan Labs Cash Index	Ryan Labs, Inc.	907
	Salomon Brothers Certificate-of Deposit Index	Salomon Brothers Inc.	907
	Salomon Brothers U.S. Treasury Bill Index	Salomon Brothers Inc.	907
	J.P. Morgan Cash Index	J.P. Morgan Securities Inc.	724
	Merrill Lynch 182-Day U.S. Treasury Bill Index (Actual)	Merrill Lynch & Co.	728
	Merrill Lynch 364-Day U.S. Treasury Bill Index (Actual)	Merrill Lynch & Co.	730
	Merrill Lynch 91-Day U.S. Treasury Bill Auction Rate Average	Merrill Lynch & Co.	726
	Merrill Lynch Domestic 3-Month Certificate of Deposit (CD) Index	Merrill Lynch & Co.	732
	Merrill Lynch U.S. 91-Day Treasury Bill Index (Actual)	Merrill Lynch & Co.	734
World	Merrill Lynch Eurodollar 3-Month Certificate of Deposit (CD) Index	Merrill Lynch & Co.	738
	Salomon Brothers World Money Market Index	Salomon Brothers Inc.	740

MUTUAL FUNDS

COUNTRY	INDEX	PUBLISHER	PAGE
United States	Babson College Emerging Market Income Indes	Babson College	913
	CDA/Weisenberger Mutual Fund Averages	CDA/Weisenberger	913
	Hertzfeld Single Country Average	Thomas J. Hertzfeld Advisors, Inc.	913
	IBC Mutual Fund Averages	IBC/Donoghue Inc.	913
	Investors Daily Mutual Fund Index	Investor's Business Daily	913
	Lehman Brothers Mutual Fund Corporate Debt A Rated Index	Lehman Brothers	790
	Lehman Brothers Mutual Fund GNMA Index	Lehman Brothers	792
	Lehman Brothers Mutual Fund Indices	Lehman Brothers	914
	Lipper Balanced Funds Index	Lipper Analytical Services, Inc.	794
	Lipper Convertible Securities Funds Index	Lipper Analytical Services, Inc.	796
	Lipper Equity Income Funds Index	Lipper Analytical Services, Inc.	798
	Lipper Government National Mortgage Association (GNMA) Funds Index	Lipper Analytical Services, Inc.	800
	Lipper Growth & Income Funds Index	Lipper Analytical Services, Inc.	804
	Lipper Growth Funds Index	Lipper Analytical Services, Inc.	802
	Lipper High Current Yield Funds Index	Lipper Analytical Services, Inc.	806
	Lipper International Funds Index	Lipper Analytical Services, Inc.	808
	Lipper Money Market Funds Index	Lipper Analytical Services, Inc.	810
	Lipper Mutual Fund Indices	Lipper Analytical Services, Inc.	914
	Lipper Small Company Growth Funds Index	Lipper Analytical Services, Inc.	812
	Merrill Lynch California Municipal Mutual Fund Index	Merrill Lynch & Co.	814
	Merrill Lynch Insured Bond Index	Merrill Lynch & Co.	915
	Merrill Lynch Intermediate Mutual Fund Index	Merrill Lynch & Co.	915

MUTUAL FUNDS, *CONT'D*

COUNTRY	INDEX	PUBLISHER	PAGE
United States, *Cont'd*	Merrill Lynch Municipal Mutual Fund Index	Merrill Lynch & Co.	816
	Merrill Lynch New York Mutual Fund Index	Merrill Lynch & Co.	818
	Morningstar Mutual Fund Performance Averages	Morningstar	915
	Salomon Emerging Market Mutual Fund (EMMF) Debt Index	Salomon Brothers Inc.	916
	Standard & Poor's Rated Money Market Fund Indices	Standard & Poor's Corporation (S&P Corp.)	916
	Value Line Mutual Fund Performance Averages	Value Line, Inc.	916
World	Micropal Mutual Fund/Unit Investment Trust Performance Averages	Micropal	916

REAL ESTATE

COUNTRY	INDEX	PUBLISHER	PAGE
United States	Bloomberg Real Estate Investment Trust Indices	Bloomberg Financial Services	917
	Chicago Board Options Exchange REIT (RIX) Index	Chicago Board Options Exchange (CBOE), The	826
	Institutional Property Consultants (IPC) Portfolio Index	Institutional Property Consultants	917
	Lehman REIT Index	Lehman Brothers	917
	Morgan Stanley REIT Index	Morgan Stanley & Co.	917
	National Association of Real Estate Investment Trusts (NAREIT) Composite Index	National Association of Real Estate Investment Trusts (NAREIT)	830
	National Council of Real Estate Investment Fiduciaries (NCREIF) Property Index	National Council of Real Estate Fiduciaries (NCREIF)	828
	SNL REIT Index	SNL Securities	918
	Wilshire Real Estate Securities Index	Wilshire Associates	832
World	Life Global Real Estate Securities Index	Limburg Institute of Financial Economics	918
	Salomon Brothers World Equity Index (SBWEI)-Property Industry Index	Salomon Brothers Inc.	836

STOCKS

COUNTRY	INDEX	PUBLISHER	PAGE
Abu Dhabi	National Bank of Abu Dhabi Index, The	National Bank of Abu Dahbi, The	887
Argentina	Buenos Aires Stock Exchange Value Index-Composite	Buenos Aires Stock Exchange (BASE), The	526
Argentina	Burcap Index	Buenos Aires Stock Exchange (BASE), The	890
	Merval Index	Buenos Aires Stock Exchange (BASE), The	528
Australia	ASX 50 Leaders Price and Accumulation Indices	Australian Stock Exchange Limited, The	855
	Australian All Ordinaries Stock Exchange Index (ASX)	Australian Stock Exchange Limited, The	262
	Australian Stock Exchange 100 Index (ASX 100)	Australian Stock Exchange Limited, The	264
	Australian Stock Exchange Mid Cap Index	Australian Stock Exchange Limited, The	266
	Australian Stock Exchange Small Cap Index	Australian Stock Exchange Limited, The	268
	Australian Stock Exchange Twenty Leaders Index	Australian Stock Exchange Limited, The	270
	Wardley Index, The	Australian Stock Exchange Limited, The	856
Austria	ATX 50 Index	Austrian Futures & Options Exchange	872
	ATX Midcap Index	Austrian Futures & Options Exchange	872
	Austrian Traded Index (ATX)	Osterreichische Termin-Und Optionenborse (OTOB)	380

COUNTRY	INDEX	PUBLISHER	PAGE
Austria, *Cont'd*	Creditanstalt Share Index (CA Share Index)	Vienna Stock Exchange (Weiner Borse), The	872
	Participation Certificate Index	Vienna Stock Exchange (Weiner Borse), The	872
	Vienna Stock Exchange Share (Weiner Borse) Index (WBI)	Vienna Stock Exchange (Weiner Borse), The	382
	Wiener Borse Index 30 (WBI 30) Index	Osterreichische Termin-Und Optionenborse (OTOB)	384
Bahrain	Bahrain Stock Exchange (BSE) Official Share Index	Bahrain Stock Exchange	887
Bangladesh	Dhaka Stock Exchange (DSE) All Share Price Index	Dhaka Stock Exchange (DSE), The	272
Barbados	Securities Exchange of Barbados Share Index	Securities Exchange of Barbados	530
Belgium	B-Gold Index	Brussels Stock Exchange	873
	BEL 20 Return Index Private and Industrial	Brussels Stock Exchange	873
	Belgian (Bel) 20 Index	Brussels Stock Exchange	386
	Belgian Computer Assisted Trading System (CATS) Market Return Index	Brussels Stock Exchange	388
	Belgian Foreign Forward Market (CATS) Return Index	Brussels Stock Exchange	873
	Belgian Medium Capitalization Return Index	Brussels Stock Exchange	390
	Belgian Small Capitalization Return Index	Brussels Stock Exchange	392
	Belgian Spot Market Index	Brussels Stock Exchange	394
Bermuda	Bermuda Stock Exchange Index	Bermuda Stock Exchange	40
Botswana	Botswana Share Market Index	Stockbrokers Botswana Ltd.	566
Brazil	I-SENN Index	Rio de Janeiro Stock Exchange, The	534
	IBV Profitability Index of Rio de Janeiro Stock Exchange (IBV)	Rio de Janeiro Stock Exchange, The	532
	Sao Paulo Stock Exchange Index (BOVESPA)	The Sao Paulo Stock Exchange	536
Canada	Canadian Market Porfolio Index (XXM), The	Montreal Stock Exchange (MSE), The	42
	Toronto Stock Exchange 100 (TSE 100) Composite Index	Toronto Stock Exchange (TSE), The	46
	Toronto Stock Exchange 200 (TSE 200) Composite Index	Toronto Stock Exchange (TSE), The	48
	Toronto Stock Exchange 300 (TSE 300) Composite Index	Toronto Stock Exchange (TSE), The	50
	Toronto Stock Exchange 35 (TSE 35) Index	Toronto Stock Exchange (TSE), The	44
	Vancouver Stock Exchange (VSE) Index	Vancouver Stock Exchange (VSE), The	52
Chile	Indice de Precios Selectivo de Acciones (IPSA)	Bolsa de Comercio de Santiago (Santiago Stock Exchange)	538
	Indice General de Precios de Acciones (IGPA)	Bolsa de Comercio de Santiago (Santiago Stock Exchange)	540
	INTER-10 Index	Bolsa de Comercio de Santiago	890
China	Credit Lyonnais Securities Asia (CLSA) China World Index	Credit Lyonnais Securities Asia	856
	Peregrine Greater China Index	Peregrine Brokerage Limited	274
	Shanghai A-Share Stock Price Index (SSE)	Shanghai Stock Exchange, The (SSE)	276
	Shanghai B-Share Stock Price Index (SSE)	Shanghai Stock Exchange, The (SSE)	278
	Shanghai Share Stock Price Index (SSE)	Shanghai Stock Exchange, The (SSE)	280
	Shenzen A-Share Stock Price Index	Shenzen Stock Exchange	857
	Shenzen B-Share Stock Price Index	Shenzen Stock Exchange	857
	Shenzen Share Stock Price Index	Shenzen Stock Exchange	857
Colombia	Bolsa de Medelin-IBOMED Index	Corredores Associates	891
	Bolsa de Medelin-IBOMED Selectivo	Corredores Associates	891
	Index of Bolsa de Bogota (IBB)	Bolsa de Bogota, S.A.	542
	Vallejo Selected Stock Price Index	Corredores Associates	891
Costa Rica	Bolsa Nacional de Valores Indice Accionario (BNV)	Bolsa National de Valores	544

COUNTRY	INDEX	PUBLISHER	PAGE
Cote d'Iviore	BVA General Index	Abidjan Stock Exchange	568
Cyprus	Cyprus Investment and Securities Corp. (CISCO) Ltd All-Share Index	Cyprus Investment and Securities Corp. Ltd.	874
	Cyprus Stock Exchange (CYSE) All-Share Index	Cyprus Stock Exchange (CYSE)	396
	Cyprus Stock Exchange Institution Index	Cyprus Stock Exchange (CYSE)	875
	Hellenic Bank Investments Index (HBI)	Hellenic Bank Limited	874
Czech Republic	Czech National Bank CNB-120 Index	Czech National Bank	875
	HN-Wood Index	Wood & Company in conjunction with Hospodarsky Noviny	875
	Prague Stock Exchange 50 (PX 50) Index	Prague Stock Exchange, The	398
Denmark	Copenhagen Stock Exchange (KFX) Index	Copenhagen Stock Exchange (CSE)	400
	Total Share Index of Copenhagen Stock Exchange (CSE)	Copenhagen Stock Exchange (CSE)	402
Ecuador	Indice Accionario de la Bolsa de Valores de Quito 8 (I.A.Q. 8)	Bolsa de Valores de Quito	546
	Indice de Rendimiento (RBQ)	Bolsa de Valores de Quito	891
	Indice Diario de Volumen (IVQ)	Bolsa de Valores de Quito	891
Egypt	Egypt Capital Market Authority Index (ECM)	Capital Market Authority	887
	Egyptian Financial Group Index	Egyptian Financial Group	887
	Hermes Financial Index	Hermes Financial	887
Finland	Finnish Traded Stock (FOX) Index	Finnish Securities and Derivatives Exchange	404
	HEX All-Share Price Index	Helsinki Stock Exchange	406
	HEX-20 Index	Helsinki Stock Exchange	875
	KOP Index, The	Kansallis-Osake-Pankki	876
	Portfolio HEX Index	Helsinki Stock Exchange	876
	Unitas Index, The	Bank of Finland	876
France	CAC-40 (Cotation Automatique Continue) Index	SBF-Bourse de Paris, The	408
	MIDCAC Index	SBF-Bourse de Paris, The	410
	SBF-120 Index	SBF-Bourse de Paris, The	412
	SBF-250 Index	SBF-Bourse de Paris, The	414
Germany	Commerzbank Share Index	Commerzbank AG	416
	Composite DAX Performance Index	Deutsche Borse AG	418
	DAX 100 Performance Index	Deutsche Borse AG	420
	DAX 100 Subindices	Deutsche Borse AG	876
	DAX Performance Index (Deutcher Aktienindex)	Deutsche Borse AG	422
	Dresdner International Research Institute Small Cap Deutcshland Index	Dresdner International Research Institute	877
	Frankfurt Stock Exchange Index	Frankfurt Stock Exchange	877
	Frankfurter Allgemeinen Zeitung (FAZ) Aktienindex	Frankfurter Allgemeine Zeitung	877
	Mid Cap DAX (MDAX) Performance Index	Deutsche Borse AG	424
Ghana	Databank Brokerage Ltd. Index	Databank Brokerage	888
	Ghana Stock Exchange (GSE) All-Share Index	Ghana Stock Exchange (GSE)	570
	Gold Coast Securities Liquidity Index	Gold Coast Securities Ltd.	888
Greece	Athens Stock Exchange (ASE) Composite Share Index	Athens Stock Exchange (ASE), The	426
Hong Kong	American Stock Exchange (AMEX)/Hong Kong Option Index (HKO)	American Stock Exchange (AMEX), The	857
	Hang Seng China Enterprises Index (HSCEI)	HSI Services Limited, a subsidiary of Hang Seng Bank	282
	Hang Seng Index (HSI)	HSI Services Limited, a subsidiary of Hang Seng Bank	284
	Hang Seng London Reference Index	HSI Services Limited, a subsidiary of Hang Seng Bank	858

COUNTRY	INDEX	PUBLISHER	PAGE
Hong Kong, *Cont'd*	Hang Seng Midcap Index	HSI Services Limited, a subsidiary of Hang Seng Bank	286
	Hong Kong All Ordinaries Index (AOI)	Stock Exchange of Hong Kong Limited (SEHK), The	288
	Merrill Lynch (Formerly Smith New Court) Small Company Index of Hong Kong	Merrill Lynch & Co.	858
Hungary	Budapest Stock Index (BUX)	Budapest Stock Exchange, The	428
Iceland	Iceland Stock Exchange Index (ICEX)	Iceland Stock Exchange	430
India	Ahmedabad Stock Exchange Sensitive Index of Equity Prices	Stock Exchange of Ahmedabad, The	858
	Bombay Stock Exchange (BSE) 200 Index	Bombay Stock Exchange (BSE), The	290
	Bombay Stock Exchange (BSE) National Index of Equity Prices	Bombay Stock Exchange (BSE), The	292
	Bombay Stock Exchange (BSE) Sensitive Index of Equity Prices	Bombay Stock Exchange (BSE), The	294
	BSE DOLLEX Index	Bombay Stock Exchange	859
	Delhi Stock Exchange (DSE) Sensitive Index of Equity Prices	Delhi Stock Exchange (DSE), The	296
	Economic Times Share Ordinary Price Index	Economic Times, The	859
	ING Barings Indian GDR Index	ING Baring Securities Limited	859
	Kleinwort Benson India GDR Index	Kleinwort Benson	859
	OTC Exchange of India Composite Index	OTC Exchange of India, The	860
	Peregrine India ADR Index	Peregrine Brokerage Limited	860
	SSKI Index	SSKI Securities Ltd.	860
Indonesia	Jakarta Stock Exchange (JSX) Composite Stock Price Index	Jakarta Stock Exchange (JSX), The	298
	Surabaya Stock Exchange Composite Price Index	Surabaya Stock Exchange	860
Ireland	Davy Irish Market Indices	Davy Stockbrokers	877
	Irish Stock Exchange Equity Price (ISEQ) Index	Irish Stock Exchange (ISE)	432
Israel	Computerized Call Market System (CCM) Index	Tel Aviv Stock Exchange (TSE)	888
	TA-100 Index	Tel Aviv Stock Exchange (TSE), The	888
	Tel Aviv Stock Exchange General Share Index	Tel Aviv Stock Exchange (TSE), The	572
	Tel Aviv Stock Exchange MAOF-25 Index	Tel Aviv Stock Exchange (TSE), The	574
Italy	Banca Commerciale Italiana All-Share (BCI) Index	Banca Commerciale Italiana (BCI)	434
	BCI 30 Index	Banca Commerciale Italiana (BCI)	878
	IMR Index-Current	Italian Stock Exchange Council	878
	Milan Indice di Borsa (MIB) Index- Historical	Italian Stock Exchange Council	438
	Milan Indice di Borsa (MIB) Index-Current	Italian Stock Exchange Council	878
	Milan Indice di Borsa (MIB) RNC Index	Italian Stock Exchange Council	879
	Milan Indice di Borsa (MIB) Telematico Index	Italian Stock Exchange Council	879
	Milan Indice di Borsa (MIB30) Index	Italian Stock Exchange Council	436
Jamaica	Jamaica Stock Exchange (JSE) Market Index	Jamaica Stock Exchange, The	548
Japan	American Stock Exchange (AMEX)/Japan Index (JPN)	American Stock Exchange (AMEX), The	860
	HSBC James Capel Small Japanese Companies Index	HSBC James Capel & Co. Limited	300
	International Stock Exchange/Nikkei 50 Stock Index (ISE/Nikkei 50)	Nihon Keizai Shimbun, Inc.	861
	Nagoya 25 Index	Nagoya Stock Exchange	302
	Nikkei 225 Stock Average	Nihon Keizai Shimbun, Inc.	304
	Nikkei 500 Stock Average	Nihon Keizai Shimbun, Inc.	308
	Nikkei All Stock Index	Nihon Keizai Shimbun, Inc.	861
	Nikkei OTC Stock Average	Nihon Keizai Shimbun, Inc.	861
	Nikkei Stock Index 300 (NIK 300)	Nihon Keizai Shimbun, Inc.	306

COUNTRY	INDEX	PUBLISHER	PAGE
Japan, *Cont'd*	Osaka 250 Adjusted Stock Price Average	Osaka Securities Exchange (OSE)	862
	Osaka 300 Stock Price Index	Osaka Securities Exchange (OSE)	310
	Osaka 40 Adjusted Stock Price Average	Osaka Securities Exchange (OSE)	862
	Russell/NRI Japanese Equity Style Index Series	Frank Russell Company/Nomura Research Institute	863
	Russell/NRI Japanese Total Market Index	Frank Russell Company/Nomura Research Institute	863
	Tokyo Stock Exchange (TSE) Second Section Stock Price Index	Tokyo Stock Exchange (TSE), The	320
	Tokyo Stock Exchange Arithmetic Stock Price Index	Tokyo Stock Exchange (TSE), The	862
	Tokyo Stock Exchange Price Index (TOPIX)	Tokyo Stock Exchange (TSE), The	312
	Tokyo Stock Exchange Price Index (TOPIX)--Large-Sized Companies Subindex	Tokyo Stock Exchange (TSE), The	314
	Tokyo Stock Exchange Price Index (TOPIX)--Medium-Sized Companies Subindex	Tokyo Stock Exchange (TSE), The	316
	Tokyo Stock Exchange Price Index (TOPIX)--Small-Sized Companies Subindex	Tokyo Stock Exchange (TSE), The	318
Jordan	Amman Financial Market (AFM) Price Index	Amman Financial Market (AFM)	576
	Amman Financial Market Price Index	Amman Financial Market	888
Kenya	Nairobi Stock Exchange 20 Index	Nairobi Stock Exchange	578
Korea	Adjusted Stock Price Average	Korea Stock Exchange (KSE)	863
	Korea Composite Stock Price Index (KOSPI)	Korea Stock Exchange (KSE)	322
	Korea Composite Stock Price Index (KOSPI)--Large-Sized Companies Subindex	Korea Stock Exchange (KSE)	324
	Korea Composite Stock Price Index (KOSPI)--Medium-Sized Companies Subindex	Korea Stock Exchange (KSE)	326
	Korea Composite Stock Price Index (KOSPI)--Small-Sized Companies Subindex	Korea Stock Exchange (KSE)	328
	Korea Stock Price Index 200 (KOSPI 200)	Korea Stock Exchange (KSE)	330
	Manufacturing Industry Index	Korea Stock Exchange (KSE)	864
Kuwait	Kuwait Stock Exchange (KSE) Index	Kuwait Stock Exchange (KSE)	580
Luxembourg	Luxembourg Stock Exchange Index	Luxembourg Stock Exchange	440
Malaysia	Kuala Lumpur Composite Index	Kuala Lumpur Stock Exchange (KLSE)	332
	Kuala Lumpur EMAS Index	Kuala Lumpur Stock Exchange (KLSE)	334
	Kuala Lumpur Second Board Index	Kuala Lumpur Stock Exchange (KLSE)	336
	New Straits Times Industrial Index	New Straits Times, The	864
Mauritius	Stock Exchange of Mauritius Index (SEMDEX)	Stock Exchange of Mauritius Ltd., The	582
Mexico	Bolsa Mexicana de Valores Indice de Precios y Cotizaciones (IPC) Index	Bolsa Mexicana de Valores	54
	INMEX Index	Bolsa Mexicana de Valores	56
Morocco	Indice Moyen General Annual	Casablanca Stock Exchange	584
	Upline USI Index	Upline Securities	888
Namibia	Namibia Stock Exchange (NSE) Index	Namibian Stock Exchange	586
Nepal	GFIL 30 Index	Goodwill Finance and Investment Company	864
	MAMPS Index	MAMPS Group	864
	Nepal Index	Capital Nepal	338
	Nepal Stock Exchange Index (NEPSE)	Nepal Stock Exchange Limited	864
Netherlands	Amsterdam EOE (EOE) Index	Amsterdam EOE-Optiebeurs	442
	Amsterdam Midkap-Index	Amsterdam EOE-Optiebeurs	444
	Central Bureau of Statistics (CBS) All Share Index	Amsterdam Stock Exchange (ASE)	446
	Dutch Top 5 Index (TOPS)	Amsterdam EOE-Optiebeurs	448
New Zealand	New Zealand All Ordinaries Index	New Zealand Stock Exchange (NZSE), The	865
	New Zealand Stock Exchange (NZSE), Market Index	New Zealand Stock Exchange (NZSE), The	340

COUNTRY	INDEX	PUBLISHER	PAGE
New Zealand, Cont'd	New Zealand Stock Exchange--Smaller Companies Index (NZSE-SCI)	New Zealand Stock Exchange (NZSE), The	342
	New Zealand Stock Exchange Top 10 Index	New Zealand Stock Exchange (NZSE), The	865
	New Zealand Stock Exchange--30 Selection (NZSE-30) Index	New Zealand Stock Exchange (NZSE), The	344
	New Zealand Stock Exchange--40 (NZSE-40) Index	New Zealand Stock Exchange (NZSE), The	346
Nigeria	Nigeria Stock Exchange (NSE) All-Share Index	Nigerian Stock Exchange (NSE), The	588
Norway	OBX Index	Oslo Stock Exchange (Oslo Bors), The	450
	Oslo Stock Exchange All-Share Index	Oslo Stock Exchange (Oslo Bors), The	452
Oman	Muscat Securities Market (MSM) Price Index	Muscat Securities Market (MSM), The	590
Pakistan	DBS 50 Index	DBS Investment Research	866
	Karachi Stock Exchange (KSE)--100 Index	Karachi Stock Exchange (KSE)	348
	Karachi Stock Exchange-All Share Index	Karachi Stock Exchange	866
Panama	Panama Stock Exchange General Index (PSE)	Bolsa de Valores de Panama, S.A., The	550
Peru	Banco Interandino Blue Chip Index	Banco Interandino	892
	Indice General (IGBVL)	Bolsa de Valores de Lima	552
	Indices Selectivo (ISBVL)	Bolsa de Valores de Lima	554
Philippines	Philippine Stock Exchange (PSE) Composite Index	Philippine Stock Exchange (PSE), The	350
Poland	Warsaw Stock Exchange (WIG) Index	Warsaw Stock Exchange (WSE)	454
	Warsaw Stock Exchange WIRR Index	Warsaw Stock Exchange (WSE)	456
	WIG 20	Warsaw Stock Exchange	879
Portugal	Banco Totta & Acores (BT&A) Shares Index	Banco Totta & Acores (BT&A)	458
	Bolsa de Valores de Lisboa (BVL) 30 Index	Bolsa de Valores de Lisboa (BVL)	462
	Bolsa de Valores de Lisboa (BVL) General Index	Bolsa de Valores de Lisboa (BVL)	460
	Portugal Stock Market PSI-20 Index	Oporto Stock Exchange	464
Qatar	Commercial Bank of Qatar (CBC) Share Index	Commercial Bank of Qatar	889
Regional-- Asia/Pacific	HSBC James Capel Dragon 300 Index	HSBC James Capel & Co. Limited	376
Asia/Pacific	ING Barings Pan-Asia Index	ING Baring Securities Limited	374
Asia/Pacific	Nomura Research Institute (NRI) Asia/Pacific-200 Index	Nomura International plc/Nomura Research Institute, Ltd.	870
Asia/Pacific	Peregrine Asia Index (PAI) (Combined + Domestic Investors)	Peregrine Brokerage LImited	871
Asia/Pacific	Peregrine Asia Index (PAI)-Foreign	Peregrine Brokerage Limited	372
Aia/Pacific	Peregrine Asia Small Cap Index	Peregrine Brokerage LImited	871
Asia/Pacific	Trans Tasman 100 Index	Australian Stock Exchange Ltd./and the New Zealand Stock Exchange	871
Central/Latin America	HSBC James Capel Latin America 100 Index	HSBC James Capel & Co. Limited	562
Europe	Central European Stock Index	Budapest Stock Exchange	886
Europe	Dresdner International Research Institute Europa Small Cap Index	Dresdner International Research Institute	886
Europe	European 100 Index	Morgan Stanley Capital International, The European, as calculated by	886
Europe	Eurotop 100 (E100) Index	Amsterdam EOE-Optiebeurs	510
Europe	FT-SE Eurotrack 100 Index	FT-SE International Ltd.	512
Europe	FT-SE Eurotrack 200 Index	FT-SE International Ltd.	514
Europe	HSBC James Capel Smaller European Companies Index	HSBC James Capel & Co. Limited	516
Europe	ING Barings Special Eastern Europe Index	ING Baring Securities Limited	518
Europe	Nomura Research Institute (NRI) East European Index	Nomura International plc/Nomura Research Institute, Ltd.	520

COUNTRY	INDEX	PUBLISHER	PAGE
Regional, *Cont'd* Europe	Nomura Research Institute (NRI) European Multimedia Index	Nomura International plc/Nomura Research Institute, Ltd.	886
Europe	Nordic Securities Market Index	Nordic Stock Exchanges, The	522
Russia	CS First Boston ROS 30 Index	CS First Boston	466
	Moscow Times Dollar Adjusted Index	Moscow Times, The/Skate-Press	879
	Moscow Times Stock Index	Moscow Times, The/Skate-Press	468
	Skate-Press Consulting Agency MT 100 Index	Skate-Press Consulting Agency	879
	Skate-Press Consulting Agency MT 50 Index	Skate-Press Consulting Agency	880
Singapore	Oversea Chinese Banking Corporation Limited (OCBC) Composite Index	Oversea-Chinese Banking Corporation Limited, The/OCBC Investment Research Limited	866
	Oversea Chinese Banking Corporation Limited (OCBC) OTC Index	Oversea-Chinese Banking Corporation Limited, The/OCBC Investment Research Limited	867
	Oversea-Chinese Banking Corp., Ltd. (OCBC) 30-Share Index	Oversea-Chinese Banking Corp. Limited/OCBC Investment Research Limited	352
	Stock Exchange of Singapore (SES) All-Singapore Index	Stock Exchange of Singapore Ltd.	354
	Straits Times Index, The	Straits Times, The	867
	Straits Times Industrial (STI) Index	Business Times, The/Times Business Publications Limited	356
	United Overseas Bank (UOB) Blue Chip Index	United Overseas Bank (UOB)	867
	United Overseas Bank (UOB) Dealing and Automated Quotation System (SESDAQ) Index	United Overseas Bank (UOB)	858
	United Overseas Bank (UOB) OTC Index	United Overseas Bank (UOB)	868
Slovakia	Slovak Share Index (SAX)	Bratislava Stock Exchange (BSE), The	470
Slovenia	SBI Index	Ljubljanska Stock Exchange	880
South Africa	ALSI 40 Index	Johannesburg Stock Exchange (JSE), The	592
	Financial/Industrial 30 Index (FNDI 30)	Johannesburg Stock Exchange (JSE), The	889
	GLDI 10 Index	Johannesburg Stock Exchange (JSE), The	594
	INDI 25 Index	Johannesburg Stock Exchange (JSE), The	596
	Johannesburg Stock Exchange (JSE)-Actuaries (JSE Actuaries) All Share Index	Johannesburg Stock Exchange (JSE), The	600
	Johannesburg Stock Exchange (JSE)-Actuaries All Gold Subindex	Johannesburg Stock Exchange (JSE), The	598
Spain	Barcelona Stock Exchange Indice General	Barcelona Stock Exchange	880
	Barcelona Stock Exchange MID 50 Index	Barcelona Stock Exchange	880
	Barcelona Stock Exchange Return Index	Barcelona Stock Exchange	881
	IBEX-35 Index	Sociedad de Bolsas S.A.	472
	Madrid General CPI Adjusted Indices	Madrid Stock Exchange, The European, as calculated by	881
	Madrid General Index	Madrid Stock Exchange, The	474
Sri Lanka	Colombo Stock Exchange (CSE) All Share Price Index	Sri Lanka Stock Exchange	360
	CSE Sensitive Index, The	Sri Lanka Stock Exchange	868
Swaziland	Swaziland Stock Market (SSM) Index	Swaziland Stockbrokers Ltd.	602
Sweden	Affarsvarlden All-Share Index	Affarsvarlden	881
	OMSX Indices	OM Stockholm AB	881
	OMX Index	OM Stockholm AB	476
	Stockholm Stock Exchange General (SX-General) Index	Stockholm Fondbors AB, The	478
	Stockholm Stock Exchange O-list Index	Stockholm Fondbors AB, The	480
	Stockholm Stock Exchange OTC Index	Stockholm Fondbors AB, The	482
	Stockholm Stock Exchange SX-16 Index, The	Stockholm Stock Exchange	881
	Stockholm Stock Exchange SX-70 Index	Stockholm Stock Exchange	882

COUNTRY	INDEX	PUBLISHER	PAGE
Switzerland	CS Index	Credit Suisse	882
	Pictet LPP Index	Pictet & Co.	882
	SBC Index of Swiss Shares	Swiss Bank Corp.	882
	Swiss Bid/Ask Index (SBAI)	Association Tripartite Bourses (ATB)	883
	Swiss Large Company Performance Index (SLCI)	Association Tripartite Bourses (ATB)	883
	Swiss Market Index (SMI)	Association Tripartite Bourses (ATB)	484
	Swiss Medium Company Performance Index (SMCI)	Association Tripartite Bourses (ATB)	883
	Swiss Performance Index		883
	Swiss Performance Index (SPI)	Association Tripartite Bourses (ATB)	486
	Swiss Small Company Performance Index (SSCI)	Association Tripartite Bourses (ATB)	884
	Vontobel Small Companies Index	Bank Vontobel	884
Taiwan	Economic Daily News Index	Economic Daily News	362
	OTC Index	R.O.C. Over-the-Counter Securities Exchange	868
	Taiwan Industrial Stock Price Average	Taiwan Stock Exchange Corporation	869
	Taiwan Stock Exchange Capitalization Weighted Stock Index (TAIEX)	Taiwan Stock Exchange Corporation	364
	Taiwan Stock Exchange Composite Stock Price Average	Taiwan Stock Exchange Corporation	366
Thailand	Book Club Index	Book Club Finance & Securities Co. Ltd., The	869
	Securities Exchange of Thailand (SET) Index	Stock Exchange of Thailand (SET), The	368
	SET 50 Index	Stock Exchange of Thailand (SET), The	869
	Thai Investment and Securities Company Ltd. (TISCO) Price Index	Thai Investment and Securities Company Ltd.	870
Trinidad & Tobago	Trinidad & Tobago Stock Exchange Daily Index of Stock Market Values	Trinidad & Tobago Stock Exchange	556
Tunesia	Indice General BVM	Bourse de Valeurs Mobilieres de Tunis	890
Turkey	Istanbul Stock Exchange (ISE) Composite Index	Istanbul Stock Exchange (ISE)	488
United Kingdom	Financial Times Gold Mines Index	Financial Times	884
	Financial Times Ordinary Share Index (30 Share Index)	Financial Times Ltd., The	490
	Financial Times-Stock Exchange 100 (FT-SE 100) Index	FT-SE International Ltd.	492
	Financial Times-Stock Exchange Actuaries 350 (FT-SE Actuaries 350) Index	FT-SE International Ltd.	494
	Financial Times-Stock Exchange Alternative Investment Market (FT-SE AIM) Index	FT-SE International Ltd.	500
	Financial Times-Stock Exchange Mid 250 (FT-SE Mid 250) Index	FT-SE International Ltd.	502
	FT-SE Actuaries All-Share Index	FT-SE International Ltd.	496
	FT-SE Actuaries Fledgling Index	FT-SE International Ltd.	498
	FT-SE SmallCap Index	FT-SE International Ltd.	504
	Global Mining Indices	HSBC James Capel & Co. Limited	885
	Green Indices	HSBC James Capel & Co. Limited	885
	Hoare Govett 1000 Index (HG 1000)	Hoare Govett Securities Ltd./ABN-AMRO	885
	Hoare Govett Smaller Companies (HGSC) Index	Hoare Govett Securities Ltd./ABN-AMRO	506
	London and Bishopsgate 100 Index	London and Bishopsgate	886
	Tiger Index	HSBC James Capel & Co. Limited	885
	Tootsie Index	HSBC James Capel & Co. Limited	885
	Trixie Indes	HSBC James Capel & Co. Limited	885
	Warrant Index	HSBC James Capel & Co. Limited	885

COUNTRY	INDEX	PUBLISHER	PAGE
United States	American Banker Bank Indices	American Banker	849
	American Stock Exchange Market Value Index (AMVI)	American Stock Exchange (AMEX), The	58
	AMEX Airline (XAL) Index	American Stock Exchange (AMEX), The	60
	AMEX Biotechnology (BTK) Index	American Stock Exchange (AMEX), The	62
	AMEX Computer Technology (XCI) Index	American Stock Exchange (AMEX), The	64
	AMEX Institutional (XII) Index	American Stock Exchange (AMEX), The	66
	AMEX International Market (IMI) Index	American Stock Exchange (AMEX), The	68
	AMEX Major Market (XMI) Index	American Stock Exchange (AMEX), The	70
	AMEX Mexico (MXY) Index	American Stock Exchange (AMEX), The	72
	AMEX Natural Gas (XNG) Index	American Stock Exchange (AMEX), The	74
	AMEX North American Telecommunications (XTC) Index	American Stock Exchange (AMEX), The	76
	AMEX Oil (XOI) Index	American Stock Exchange (AMEX), The	78
	AMEX Pharmaceutical (DRG) Index	American Stock Exchange (AMEX), The	82
	AMEX Retail Index	American Stock Exchange (AMEX), The	84
	AMEX Securities Broker/Dealer (XBD) Index	American Stock Exchange (AMEX), The	86
	AMEX/Oscar Gruss Israel (XIS) Index	American Stock Exchange (AMEX), The	80
	Barra All U.S. Price Index	BARRA, Inc.	849
	Barron's 50 Stock Average	Barron's	850
	Barron's Low-Priced Stock Index	Barron's	850
	Benham North American Gold Equities Index	Benham Management Corp.	850
	Bloomberg State/Regional Common Stock Indices	Bloomberg Financial Services Financial	850
	Center for Research in Security Prices	Center for Research in Security Prices, The	851
	Chicago Board Options Exchange Automotive (CAUX) Index	Chicago Board Options Exchange (CBOE), The	88
	Chicago Board Options Exchange Biotechnology (BGX) Index	Chicago Board Options Exchange (CBOE), The	90
	Chicago Board Options Exchange Computer Software (CWX) Index	Chicago Board Options Exchange (CBOE), The	92
	Chicago Board Options Exchange Environmental (EVX) Index	Chicago Board Options Exchange (CBOE), The	94
	Chicago Board Options Exchange Gaming (GAX) Index	Chicago Board Options Exchange (CBOE), The	96
	Chicago Board Options Exchange Global Telecommunications (GTX) Index	Chicago Board Options Exchange (CBOE), The	98
	Chicago Board Options Exchange Internet (CINX) Index	Chicago Board Options Exchange (CBOE), The	100
	Chicago Board Options Exchange Israel (ISX) Index	Chicago Board Options Exchange (CBOE), The	102
	Chicago Board Options Exchange Latin 15 (LTX) Index	Chicago Board Options Exchange (CBOE), The	104
	Chicago Board Options Exchange Mexico (MEX) Index	Chicago Board Options Exchange (CBOE), The	106
	Chicago Board Options Exchange Technology (TXX) Index	Chicago Board Options Exchange (CBOE), The	108
	Chicago Board Options Exchange U.S. Telecommunications (TCX) Index	Chicago Board Options Exchange (CBOE), The	110
	DALBAR 30 Index	DALBAR	851
	DALBAR Investment Company Stock Index (DICSA)	DALBAR	851
	Domini Social Index	Kinder Lydenberg Domini & Co.	851
	Dow Jones Composite Average	Dow Jones & Company, Inc.	112
	Dow Jones Equity Market Index	Dow Jones & Company, Inc.	114
	Dow Jones Industrial Average (DJIA)	Dow Jones & Company, Inc.	116
	Dow Jones Transportation Average	Dow Jones & Company, Inc.	118
	Dow Jones Utilities Average	Dow Jones & Company, Inc.	120

COUNTRY	INDEX	PUBLISHER	PAGE
United States, Cont'd	Franklin California 250 Growth Index	Franklin Resources, Inc.	851
	Hambrecht & Quist (H&Q) Growth Index	Hambrecht & Quist	851
	Hambrecht & Quist (H&Q) Technology Index	Hambrecht & Quist LLC	122
	Hubble Environmental Index	Progressive Asset Management and David L. Hubble	852
	Investors Business Daily 6000	Investor's Business Daily	852
	KBW 50 Index	Keefe, Bruyette & Woods, Inc.	852
	Keefe Bank Index (KBI)	Keefe, Bruyette & Woods, Inc.	852
	Merrill Lynch ADR Indices	Merrill Lynch & Co.	853
	Morgan Stanley Consumer (CMR) Index	Morgan Stanley & Co.	124
	Morgan Stanley Cyclical (CYC) Index	Morgan Stanley & Co.	126
	Morgan Stanley High-Technology 35 (Tech 35) Index	Morgan Stanley & Co.	128
	Nasdaq 100 Index	National Association of Securities Dealers, Inc. (NASD), The/Nasdaq Stock Market Inc., The	130
	Nasdaq American Depositary Receipts (ADRs) Index	National Association of Securities Dealers, Inc. (NASD), The/Nasdaq Stock Market Inc., The	132
	Nasdaq Bank Index	National Association of Securities Dealers, Inc. (NASD), The/Nasdaq Stock Market Inc., The	134
	Nasdaq Biotechnology Index	National Association of Securities Dealers, Inc. (NASD), The/Nasdaq Stock Market Inc., The	136
	Nasdaq Composite Index	National Association of Securities Dealers, Inc. (NASD), The/Nasdaq Stock Market Inc., The	138
	Nasdaq Computer Index	National Association of Securities Dealers, Inc. (NASD), The/Nasdaq Stock Market Inc., The	140
	Nasdaq Financial Index 100	National Association of Securities Dealers, Inc. (NASD), The/Nasdaq Stock Market Inc., The	142
	Nasdaq Industrial Index	National Association of Securities Dealers, Inc. (NASD), The/Nasdaq Stock Market Inc., The	144
	Nasdaq Insurance Index	National Association of Securities Dealers, Inc. (NASD), The/Nasdaq Stock Market Inc., The	146
	Nasdaq Other Finance Index	National Association of Securities Dealers, Inc. (NASD), The/Nasdaq Stock Market Inc., The	152
	Nasdaq Telecommunications Index	National Association of Securities Dealers, Inc. (NASD), The/Nasdaq Stock Market Inc., The	154
	Nasdaq Transportation Index	National Association of Securities Dealers, Inc. (NASD), The/Nasdaq Stock Market Inc., The	156
	Nasdaq/National Market System (NMS) Composite Index	National Association of Securities Dealers, Inc. (NASD), The/Nasdaq Stock Market Inc., The	148
	Nasdaq/National Market System (NMS) Industrial Index	National Association of Securities Dealers, Inc. (NASD), The/Nasdaq Stock Market Inc., The	150
	New York Stock Exchange (NYSE) Composite Index	New York Stock Exchange (NYSE)	158
	New York Stock Exchange (NYSE) Finance Sub-Group Index	New York Stock Exchange (NYSE)	160

COUNTRY	INDEX	PUBLISHER	PAGE
United States, *Cont'd*	New York Stock Exchange (NYSE) Industrial Sub-Group Index	New York Stock Exchange (NYSE)	162
	New York Stock Exchange (NYSE) Transportation Sub-Group Index	New York Stock Exchange (NYSE)	164
	New York Stock Exchange (NYSE) Utilities Sub-Group Index	New York Stock Exchange (NYSE)	166
	Pacific Stock Exchange Tech 100 (PSE Tech 100) Index	Pacific Stock Exchange (PSE)	168
	Philadelphia Stock Exchange Airline Sector (PLN) Index	Philadelphia Stock Exchange (PHLX), The	170
	Philadelphia Stock Exchange Forest & Paper Products Sector (FPP) Index	Philadelphia Stock Exchange (PHLX), The	172
	Philadelphia Stock Exchange Gold/Silver Sector (XAU) Index	Philadelphia Stock Exchange (PHLX), The	174
	Philadelphia Stock Exchange Keefe, Bruyette & Woods, Inc. Bank Sector (BKK)	Philadelphia Stock Exchange (PHLX), The	176
	Philadelphia Stock Exchange National Over-the-Counter (XOC) Index	Philadelphia Stock Exchange (PHLX), The	178
	Philadelphia Stock Exchange Phone Sector (PNX) Index	Philadelphia Stock Exchange (PHLX), The	180
	Philadelphia Stock Exchange Semiconductor Sector (SOX) Index	Philadelphia Stock Exchange (PHLX), The	182
	Philadelphia Stock Exchange Supercap (HFX) Index	Philadelphia Stock Exchange (PHLX), The	184
	Philadelphia Stock Exchange U.S. Top 100 (TPX) Index	Philadelphia Stock Exchange (PHLX), The	186
	Philadelphia Stock Exchange Utility Sector (UTY) Index	Philadelphia Stock Exchange (PHLX), The	188
	Russell 1000 Growth Index	Frank Russell Company	192
	Russell 1000 Index	Frank Russell Company	190
	Russell 1000 Value Index	Frank Russell Company	194
	Russell 2000 Growth Index	Frank Russell Company	198
	Russell 2000 Index	Frank Russell Company	196
	Russell 2000 Value Index	Frank Russell Company	200
	Russell 2500 Index	Frank Russell Company	853
	Russell 3000 Index	Frank Russell Company	202
	Russell Midcap Growth Index	Frank Russell Company	206
	Russell Midcap Index	Frank Russell Company	204
	Russell Midcap Value Index	Frank Russell Company	208
	Russell Top 200 Growth Index	Frank Russell Company	853
	Russell Top 200 Index	Frank Russell Company	853
	Russell Top 200 Value Index	Frank Russell Company	853
	Schwab 1000 Index	Charles Schwab & Co.	854
	SNL Broker/ Dealers Index	SNL Securities, L.P.	854
	SNL Finance Companies Index	SNL Securities, L.P.	854
	SNL Financial Services Companies Index	SNL Securities, L.P.	854
	SNL Financial Services Investment Advisors Index	SNL Securities, L.P.	855
	SNL GSE Index	SNL Securities, L.P.	854
	SNL Mortgage Banks and Related Services Index	SNL Securities, L.P.	854
	Standard & Poor's (S&P) Financial Price Index	Standard & Poor's Corporation (S&P Corp.)	216
	Standard & Poor's (S&P) Industrial Price Index	Standard & Poor's Corporation (S&P Corp.)	218
	Standard & Poor's (S&P) MidCap 400 Index	Standard & Poor's Corporation (S&P Corp.)	220
	Standard & Poor's (S&P) Supercomposite Stock Price Index	Standard & Poor's Corporation (S&P Corp.)	224

COUNTRY	INDEX	PUBLISHER	PAGE
United States, *Cont'd*	Standard & Poor's (S&P) Transportation Price Index (TRX)	Standard & Poor's Corporation (S&P Corp.)	226
	Standard & Poor's (S&P) Utilities Price Index	Standard & Poor's Corporation (S&P Corp.)	228
	Standard & Poor's (S&P)/BARRA Growth Index	Standard & Poor's Corporation (S&P Corp.)/BARRA, Inc.	230
	Standard & Poor's (S&P)/BARRA Value Index	Standard & Poor's Corporation (S&P Corp.)/BARRA, Inc.	232
	Standard & Poor's 100 (S&P 100) Index (OEX)	Standard & Poor's Corporation (S&P Corp.)	210
	Standard & Poor's 500 (S&P 500) Composite Stock Price Index	Standard & Poor's Corporation (S&P Corp.)	212
	Standard & Poor's SmallCap 600 Index	Standard & Poor's Corporation (S&P Corp.)	222
	Value Line Arithmetic (VLA) Index	Value Line, Inc.	234
	Value Line Composite Index (XVL)	Value Line, Inc.	236
	Value Line Industrial Average	Value Line, Inc.	855
	Value Line Railroad Average	Value Line, Inc.	855
	Value Line Utility Average	Value Line, Inc.	855
	Wilshire 2500 Equity Index	Wilshire Associates Inc.	855
	Wilshire 5000 Equity Index	Wilshire Associates Inc.	238
	Wilshire Associates Small Cap (WSX) Index	Wilshire Associates Inc.	240
	Wilshire Large Company (Top 750) Equity Index	Wilshire Associates Inc.	242
	Wilshire Large Company Growth Equity Index	Wilshire Associates Inc.	244
	Wilshire Large Company Value Equity Style Index	Wilshire Associates Inc.	246
	Wilshire Middle Capitalization Company (Mid Cap 750) Equity Index	Wilshire Associates Inc.	248
	Wilshire Middle Capitalization Company Growth Equity Style Index	Wilshire Associates Inc.	250
	Wilshire Middle Capitalization Company Value Equity Style Index	Wilshire Associates Inc.	252
	Wilshire Small Capitalization Company Growth Equity Style Index	Wilshire Associates Inc.	256
	Wilshire Small Capitalization Company Value Equity Style Index	Wilshire Associates Inc.	258
	Wilshire Small Company (Next 1750) Equity Index	Wilshire Associates Inc.	254
Venezuela	Bolsa de Valores de Caracas Indice de Capitalization	Bolsa de Valores de Caracas	558
	Venezuela Marinevest Stock Composite Index	Marinevest	892
World	Dow Jones Global Stock Index	Dow Jones & Company, Inc.	608
	Financial Times/Standard & Poor's (FT/S&P) Actuaries World Index	Financial Times Ltd., Goldman Sachs & Co. and Standard & Poor's	610
	ING Barings Emerging Market World Index (BEMI)	ING Baring Securities Limited	614
	International Finance Corporation (IFC) Global Index	International Finance Corporation	616
	International Finance Corporation (IFC) Investable Index	International Finance Corporation	618
	International Finance Corporation (IFC) Tradeable 100 Index	International Finance Corporation	624
	International Finance Corporation (IFC) Tradeable Asia 50 Index	International Finance Corporation	620
	International Finance Corporation (IFC) Tradeable Latin 50 Index	International Finance Corporation	622

STOCKS, *CONT'D*

COUNTRY	INDEX	PUBLISHER	PAGE
World, *Cont'd*	Morgan Stanley Capital International (MSCI) Emerging Markets Free Global Index	Morgan Stanley Capital International (MSCI)	626
	Morgan Stanley Capital International (MSCI) Emerging Markets Global Index	Morgan Stanley Capital International (MSCI)	628
	Morgan Stanley Capital International (MSCI) Europe Australia and Far East (EAFE) Index	Morgan Stanley Capital International (MSCI)	630
	Morgan Stanley Capital International (MSCI) World Index	Morgan Stanley Capital International (MSCI)	632
	Salomon Brothers World Equity Index-Broad Market Index (SBWEI-BMI)	Salomon Brothers Inc.	636
	Salomon Brothers World Equity Index-Extended Market Index (SBWEI-EMI)	Salomon Brothers Inc.	638
	Salomon Brothers World Equity Index-Primary Market Index (SBWEI-PMI)	Salomon Brothers Inc.	640
	Schwab International Index	Charles Schwab & Co.	892
Zimbabwe	58 Counter Industrial Index	Zimbabwe Stock Exchange (ZSE)	890
	Zimbabwe Stock Exchange (ZSE) Industrial and Mining Index	Zimbabwe Stock Exchange (ZSE)	604

APPENDIX 7

DIRECTORY OF INDEX PUBLISHERS

PUBLISHER	INDEX	PAGE
Abidjan Stock Exchange	BVA General Index	568
Affarsvarlden	Affarsvarlden All-Share Index	881
American Banker	American Banker Bank Indices	849
American Stock Exchange (AMEX), The	American Stock Exchange (AMEX)/Hong Kong Option Index (HKO)	857
	American Stock Exchange (AMEX)/Japan Index (JPN)	860
	American Stock Exchange Market Value Index (AMVI)	58
	AMEX Airline (XAL) Index	60
	AMEX BioTechnology (BTK) Index	62
	AMEX Computer Technology (XCI) Index	64
	AMEX Institutional (XII) Index	66
	AMEX International Market (IMI) Index	68
	AMEX Major Market (XMI) Index	70
	AMEX Mexico (MXY) Index	72
	AMEX Natural Gas (XNG) Index	74
	AMEX North American Telecommunications (XTC) Index	76
	AMEX Oil (XOI) Index	78
	AMEX Pharmaceutical (DRG) Index	82
	AMEX Retail Index	84
	AMEX Securities Broker/Dealer (XBD) Index	86
	AMEX/Oscar Gruss Israel (XIS) Index	80
Amman Financial Market (AFM)	Amman Financial Market Price Index	888
	Amman Financial Market (AFM) Price Index, The	576
Amsterdam EOE-Optiebeurs	Amsterdam EOE (EOE) Index	442
	Amsterdam Midkap-Index	444
	Dutch Top 5 Index (TOPS)	448
	Eurotop 100 (E100) Index	510
	Central Bureau of Statistics (CBS) All Share Index	446
Association of German Mortgage Banks, The/Association of German Public Sector Banks, The	Pfandbrief Index	903

PUBLISHER	INDEX	PAGE
Association of Tripartite Bourses	Swiss Bond Index (SBI)	903
	Swiss Bid/Ask Index (SBAI)	883
	Swiss Large Company Performance Index (SLCI)	883
	Swiss Market Index (SMI)	484
	Swiss Medium Company Performance Index (SMCI)	883
	Swiss Performance Index (SPI)	486
	Swiss Small Company Performance Index (SSCI)	884
Athens Stock Exchange (ASE), The	Athens Stock Exchange (ASE) Composite Share Index	426
Australian Stock Exchange Limited, The	ASX 50 Leaders Price and Accumulation Indices	855
	Australian All Ordinaries Stock Exchange Index (ASX)	262
	Australian Stock Exchange 100 Index (ASX 100)	264
	Australian Stock Exchange Mid Cap Index	266
	Australian Stock Exchange Small Cap Index	268
	Australian Stock Exchange Twenty Leaders Index	270
	Commonwealth Bank Bond Indices	900
	Wardley Index, The	856
Australian Stock Exchange Ltd./and the New Zealand Stock Exchange	Trans Tasman 100 Index	871
Austrian Futures & Options Exchange	ATX 50 Index	872
	ATX Midcap Index	872
Babson College	Babson College Emerging Market Income Indes	913
Bahrain Stock Exchange	Bahrain Stock Exchange (BSE) Official Share Index	887
Banca Commerciale Italiana (BCI)	Banca Commerciale Italiana All-Share (BCI) Index	434
	BCI 30 Index	878
Banco Interandino	Banco Interandino Blue Chip Index	892
Banco Totta & Acores (BT&A)	Banco Totta & Acores (BT&A) Shares Index	458
Bank of Finland	Unitas Index, The	876
Bank Vontobel	Vontobel Small Companies Index	884
Bankers Trust New York Corp.	Bankers Trust Bankers Acceptances	906
	Bankers Trust Banxquote Retail and Institutional CD Indices	906
	Bankers Trust Commodity Index (BTCI)	744
	Bankers Trust LIBOR	906
	Bankers Trust Repurchase Agreements	906
Barcelona Stock Exchange	Barcelona Stock Exchange Indice General	880
	Barcelona Stock Exchange MID 50 Index	880
	Barcelona Stock Exchange Return Index	881
Barclay Trading Group	Barclay CTA Index	918
BARRA, Inc.	Barra All U.S. Price Index	849
Barron's	Barron's 50 Stock Average	850
	Barron's Best Grade Bonds	893
	Barron's Intermediate Grade Bonds	893
	Barron's Low-Priced Stock Index	850
Benham Management Corp.	Benham North American Gold Equities Index	850

PUBLISHER	INDEX	PAGE
Bermuda Stock Exchange	Bermuda Stock Exchange Index	40
Bloomberg Financial Services	Bloomberg Real Estate Investment Trust Indices	917
	Bloomberg/European Federation of Financial Analyst Societies (EFFAS) All Government Bond Index--U.S. Government	690
	Bloomberg State/Regional Common Stock Indices	850
Bolsa de Bogota S.A.	IRBB Index	905
	Index of Bolsa de Bogota (IBB)	542
Bolsa de Comercio de Santiago	INTER-10 Index	890
(Santiago Stock Exchange)	Indice de Precios Selectivo de Acciones (IPSA)	538
	Indice General de Precios de Acciones (IGPA)	540
Bolsa de Valores de Caracas	Bolsa de Valores de Caracas Indice de Capitalization	558
Bolsa de Valores de Lima	Indice General (IGBVL)	552
	Indices Selectivo (ISBVL)	554
Bolsa de Valores de Lisboa (BVL)	BVL ORF Index	903
	Bolsa de Valores de Lisboa (BVL) 30 Index	462
	Bolsa de Valores de Lisboa (BVL) General Index	460
Bolsa de Valores de Panama, S.A., The	Panama Stock Exchange General Index (PSE)	550
Bolsa de Valores de Quito	Indice Accionario de la Bolsa de Valores de Quito 8 (I.A.Q. 8)	546
	Indice de Rendimiento (RBQ)	891
	Indice Diario de Volumen (IVQ)	891
Bolsa Mexicana de Valores	Bolsa Mexicana de Valores Indice de Precios y Cotizaciones (IPC) Index	54
	INMEX Index	56
	Bolsa Nacional de Valores Indice Accionario (BNV)	544
Bombay Stock Exchange	BSE DOLLEX Index	859
	Bombay Stock Exchange (BSE) 200 Index	290
	Bombay Stock Exchange (BSE) National Index of Equity Prices	292
	Bombay Stock Exchange (BSE) Sensitive Index of Equity Prices	294
Bond Buyer, The	Bond Buyer 11 Bond Index	894
	Bond Buyer 20 Bond Index	893
	Bond Buyer Municipal Bond Index (BBI)	644
	Bond Buyer Revenue Bond Index	894
	Bond Buyer Short-Term Commercial Paper Rate	906
	Bond Buyer Short-Term Money Market Municipal Index	906
	Bond Buyer Short-Term One-Year Note Index	907
	Book Club Index	869
Bourse de Valeurs Mobilieres de Tunis	Indice General BVM	890
Bratislava Stock Exchange (BSE), The	Slovak Share Index (SAX)	470
Brussels Stock Exchange	B-Gold Index	873
	BEL 20 Return Index Private and Industrial	873
	Belgian (Bel) 20 Index	386
	Belgian Computer Assisted Trading System (CATS) Market Return Index	388

PUBLISHER	INDEX	PAGE
Brussels Stock Exchange, *Cont'd*	Belgian Foreign Forward Market (CATS) Return Index	873
	Belgian Medium Capitalization Return Index	390
	Belgian Small Capitalization Return Index	392
	Belgian Spot Market Index	394
Budapest Stock Exchange	Central European Stock Index	886
	Budapest Stock Index (BUX)	428
Buenos Aires Stock Exchange (BASE), The	Buenos Aires Stock Exchange Value Index-Composite	526
	Burcap Index	890
	Merval Index	528
Business Times, The/Times Business Publications Limited	Straits Times Industrial (STI) Index, The	356
BZW Australia	BZW Australia Liquid Government Securities Bond Index	900
Capital Market Authority	Egypt Capital Market Authority Index (ECM)	887
Capital Nepal	Nepal Index	338
Casablanca Stock Exchange	Indice Moyen General Annual	584
CDA/Weisenberger	CDA/Weisenberger Mutual Fund Averages	913
Center for Research in Security Prices, The	Center for Research in Security Prices	851
Charles Schwab & Co.	Schwab 1000 Index	854
	Schwab International Index	892
Chase Bank	Chemical Bank Emerging Market Debt Index	894
Chicago Board of Trade	Chicago Board of Trade (CBOT) Argentina Brady Bond Index	894
	Chicago Board of Trade (CBOT) Brazil Brady Bond Index	895
	Chicago Board of Trade (CBOT) Mexico Brady Bond Index	895
Chicago Board Options Exchange (CBOE), The	Chicago Board Options Exchange Automotive (CAUX) Index	88
	Chicago Board Options Exchange BioTechnology (BGX) Index	90
	Chicago Board Options Exchange Computer Software (CWX) Index	92
	Chicago Board Options Exchange Environmental (EVX) Index	94
	Chicago Board Options Exchange Gaming (GAX) Index	96
	Chicago Board Options Exchange Global Telecommunications (GTX) Index	98
	Chicago Board Options Exchange Internet (CINX) Index	100
	Chicago Board Options Exchange Israel (ISX) Index	102
	Chicago Board Options Exchange Latin 15 (LTX) Index	104
	Chicago Board Options Exchange Mexico (MEX) Index	106
	Chicago Board Options Exchange Technology (TXX) Index	108
	Chicago Board Options Exchange U.S. Telecommunications (TCX) Index	110
	Chicago Board Options Exchange REIT (RIX) Index	826
Citicorp/International Financial Review	Citicorp/IFR Impaired Loan Index	905
Commercial Bank of Qatar	Commercial Bank of Qatar (CBC) Share Index	889
Commerzbank AG	Commerzbank Share Index	416
Copenhagen Stock Exchange	Copenhagen Stock Exchange True Yield Index	902
	Copenhagen Stock Exchange (KFX) Index	400
	Total Share Index of Copenhagen Stock Exchange (CSE)	402

PUBLISHER	INDEX	PAGE
Corredores Associates	Bolsa de Medelin-IBOMED Index	891
	Bolsa de Medelin-IBOMED Selectivo	891
	Vallejo Selected Stock Price Index	891
Credit Lyonnais Securities Asia	Credit Lyonnais Securities Asia (CLSA) China World Index	856
Credit Suisse	CS Index	882
Creditanstalt Investment Bank AG	CA Bond Index	902
CS First Boston	CS First Boston Convertible Securities Index	758
	CS First Boston High Yield Index	646
	CS First Boston ROS 30 Index	466
Cyprus Investment and Securities Corp. Ltd.	Cyprus Investment and Securities Corp. (CISCO) Ltd All-Share Index	874
	Cyprus Stock Exchange (CYSE) All-Share Index	396
	Cyprus Stock Exchange Institution Index	875
Czech National Bank	Czech National Bank CNB-120 Index	875
D.E. Shaw	D.E. Shaw Japanese Convertible Bond Index (DESCBI)	910
	D.E. Shaw Japanese Warrant Index	919
Daiwa	Daiwa Physical Commodities Index	909
DALBAR	DALBAR 30 Index	851
	DALBAR Investment Company Stock Index (DICSA)	851
Databank Brokerage	Databank Brokerage Ltd. Index	888
Davy Stockbrokers	Davy Irish Market Indices	877
DBS Investment Research	DBS 50 Index	866
Delhi Stock Exchange (DSE), The	Delhi Stock Exchange (DSE) Sensitive Index of Equity Prices	296
Deutsche Borse AG	Composite DAX Performance Index	418
	DAX 100 Performance Index	420
	DAX 100 Subindices	876
	DAX Performance Index (Deutcher Aktienindex)	422
	German Bond Index (REX)	902
	Mid Cap DAX (MDAX) Performance Index	424
Dhaka Stock Exchange (DSE), The	Dhaka Stock Exchange (DSE) All Share Price Index	272
Dow Jones & Company, Inc.	Dow Jones 20 Bond Average	895
	Dow Jones Composite Average	112
	Dow Jones Equity Market Index	114
	Dow Jones Global Stock Index	608
	Dow Jones Industrial Average (DJIA)	116
	Dow Jones Transportation Average	118
	Dow Jones Utilities Average	120
	Dow Jones Futures Index	908
	Dow Jones Spot Index	908
Dresdner International Research Institute	Dresdner International Research Institute Europa Small Cap Index	886
	Dresdner International Research Institute Small Cap Deutcshland Index	877
Economic Daily News	Economic Daily News Index	362
Economic Times, The	Economic Times Share Ordinary Price Index	859

Publisher	Index	Page
Edward I. Altman/New York University	Altman Defaulted Debt Securities Index	893
Egyptian Financial Group	Egyptian Financial Group Index	887
Exane	Exane French Convertible Index	910
Fiduciary Capital Management Inc.	Fiduciary Capital Management GIC Index	911
Financial Planning Resources, Inc.	Variable Annuity Research Data Service	919
Financial Times	Financial Times Gold Mines Index	884
	FT-Actuaries Fixed Interest Indices	904
	Index-Linked Index	904
	UK Gilts Index	904
Financial Times Ltd., Goldman Sachs & Co. and Standard & Poor's	Financial Times/Standard & Poor's (FT/S&P) Actuaries World Index	610
Financial Times Ltd., The	Financial Times Ordinary Share Index (30 Share Index)	490
Finnish Securities and Derivatives Exchange (SOM)	Finnish Traded Stock (FOX) Index	404
Frank Russell Company	Russell 1000 Growth Index	192
	Russell 1000 Index	190
	Russell 1000 Value Index	194
	Russell 2000 Growth Index	198
	Russell 2000 Index	196
	Russell 2000 Value Index	200
	Russell 2500 Index	853
	Russell 3000 Index	202
	Russell Midcap Growth Index	206
	Russell Midcap Index	204
	Russell Midcap Value Index	208
	Russell Top 200 Growth Index	853
	Russell Top 200 Index	853
	Russell Top 200 Value Index	853
Frank Russell Company/Nomura Research Institute	Russell/NRI Japanese Equity Style Index Series	863
	Russell/NRI Japanese Total Market Index	863
Frankfurt Stock Exchange	Frankfurt Stock Exchange Index	877
Frankfurter Allgemeine Zeitung	Frankfurter Allgemeinen Zeitung (FAZ) Aktienindex	877
Franklin Resources, Inc.	Franklin California 250 Growth Index	851
FT-SE International Ltd.	Financial Times-Stock Exchange 100 (FT-SE 100) Index	492
	Financial Times-Stock Exchange Actuaries 350 (FT-SE Actuaries 350) Index	494
	Financial Times-Stock Exchange Alternative Investment Market (FT-SE AIM) Index	500
	Financial Times-Stock Exchange Mid 250 (FT-SE Mid 250) Index	502
	FT-SE Actuaries All-Share Index	496
	FT-SE Actuaries Fledgling Index	498
	FT-SE Eurotrack 100 Index	512
	FT-SE Eurotrack 200 Index	514
	FT-SE SmallCap Index	504

PUBLISHER	INDEX	PAGE
Ghana Stock Exchange (GSE)	Ghana Stock Exchange (GSE) All-Share Index	570
Gold Coast Securities Ltd.	Gold Coast Securities Liquidity Index	888
Goldman Sachs & Co.	Goldman Sachs International Government Bond Index	905
	Goldman Sachs Liquid Asset-Backed Securities Index (LABS)	895
	Goldman Sachs Commodity Index (GSCI)	746
	Goldman Sachs Convertible 100 Index	760
Goodwill Finance and Investment Company	GFIL 30 Index	864
Hambrecht & Quist	Hambrecht & Quist (H&Q) Growth Index	851
	Hambrecht & Quist (H&Q) Technology Index	122
Hellenic Bank Limited	Hellenic Bank Investments Index (HBI)	874
Helsinki Stock Exchange	HEX All-Share Price Index	406
	HEX-20 Index	875
	Portfolio HEX Index	876
Hermes Financial	Hermes Financial Index	887
Hoare Govett Securities Ltd./ABN-AMRO	Hoare Govett 1000 Index (HG 1000)	885
	Hoare Govett Smaller Companies (HGSC) Index	506
HSBC James Capel & Co. Limited	HSBC James Capel Small Japanese Companies Index	300
	HSBC James Capel Smaller European Companies Index	516
	Global Mining Indices	885
	Green Indices	885
	HSBC James Capel Dragon 300 Index	376
	HSBC James Capel Latin America 100 Index	562
	Tiger Index	885
	Tootsie Index	885
	Trixie Indes	885
	Warrant Index	885
HSI Services Limited, a subsidiary of Hang Seng Bank	Hang Seng China Enterprises Index (HSCEI)	282
	Hang Seng Index (HSI)	284
	Hang Seng London Reference Index	858
	Hang Seng Midcap Index	286
IBC/Donoghue Inc.	IBC Mutual Fund Averages	913
Iceland Stock Exchange	Iceland Stock Exchange Index (ICEX)	430
ING Baring Securities Limited	ING Barings Asian Convertible Bond (CB) Index	772
	ING Barings Emerging Market World Index (BEMI)	614
	ING Barings Indian GDR Index	859
	ING Barings Special Eastern Europe Index	518
	ING Barings Pan-Asia Index	374
Institutional Property Consultants	Institutional Property Consultants (IPC) Portfolio Index	917
International Finance Corporation	International Finance Corporation (IFC) Global Index	616
	International Finance Corporation (IFC) Investable Index	618
	International Finance Corporation (IFC) Tradeable Asia50 Index	620

PUBLISHER	INDEX	PAGE
International Finance Corporation, *Cont'd*	International Finance Corporation (IFC) Tradeable Latin50 Index	622
	International Finance Corporation (IFC) Tradeable100 Index	624
Investor's Business Daily	Investors Business Daily 6000	852
	Investors Daily Mutual Fund Index	913
Irish Stock Exchange (ISE)	Irish Stock Exchange Equity Price (ISEQ) Index	432
Istanbul Stock Exchange (ISE)	Istanbul Stock Exchange (ISE) Composite Index	488
Italian Stock Exchange Council	IMR Index-Current	878
	Milan Indice di Borsa (MIB) Index- Historical	438
	Milan Indice di Borsa (MIB) Index-Current	878
	Milan Indice di Borsa (MIB) RNC Index	879
	Milan Indice di Borsa (MIB) Telematico Index	879
	Milan Indice di Borsa (MIB30) Index	436
J.P. Morgan Securities Inc.	Emerging Markets Bond Index Plus (EMBI+)	692
	J.P. Morgan Cash Index	724
	J.P. Morgan Commodity Index (JPMCI)	750
	J.P. Morgan ECU Bond Index	694
	J.P. Morgan Global Government Bond Index	696
Jakarta Stock Exchange (JSX), The	Jakarta Stock Exchange (JSX) Composite Stock Price Index	298
Jamaica Stock Exchange, The	Jamaica Stock Exchange (JSE) Market Index	548
Jefferies & Company Inc.	Jefferies Global Convertible (JeffCo) Bond Index	774
Jefferies & Company, Inc./Intermarket Management Inc.	Investable Commodity Index (ICI)	748
Johannesburg Stock Exchange (JSE)	Johannesburg Stock Exchange (JSE) Actuaries Bond Performance Index	904
	ALSI 40 Index	592
	Financial/Industrial 30 Index (FNDI 30)	889
	GLDI 10 Index	594
	INDI 25 Index	596
	Johannesburg Stock Exchange (JSE)-Actuaries (JSE Actuaries) All Share Index	600
	Johannesburg Stock Exchange (JSE)-Actuaries All Gold Subindex	598
Journal of Commerce	Journal of Commerce Industrial Price Index	908
Kansallis-Osake-Pankki	KOP Index, The	876
Karachi Stock Exchange	Karachi Stock Exchange-All Share Index	866
	Karachi Stock Exchange (KSE)--100 Index	348
Keefe, Bruyette & Woods, Inc.	KBW 50 Index	852
	Keefe Bank Index (KBI)	852
Kinder Lydenberg Domini & Co.	Domini Social Index	851
Kleinwort Benson	Kleinwort Benson Asia Convertible Bond Index	910
	Kleinwort Benson India GDR Index	859
Knight Ridder Financial	Knight Ridder-CRB Interest Rates Index	896
	Knight-Ridder-CRB Currencies Index	911
	Knight-Ridder Commodity Research Bureau's Futures Price Index (KR-CRB)	752
Komercni Bank	Czech Komercni Bank Bond Price Index	902

PUBLISHER	INDEX	PAGE
Korea Stock Exchange (KSE)	Adjusted Stock Price Average	863
	Korea Bond Index	901
	Korea Composite Stock Price Index (KOSPI)	322
	Korea Composite Stock Price Index (KOSPI)--Large-Sized Companies Subindex	324
	Korea Composite Stock Price Index (KOSPI)--Medium-Sized Companies Subindex	326
	Korea Composite Stock Price Index (KOSPI)--Small-Sized Companies Subindex	328
	Korea Stock Price Index 200 (KOSPI 200)	330
	Manufacturing Industry Index	864
Kuala Lumpur Stock Exchange (KLSE)	Kuala Lumpur Composite Index	332
	Kuala Lumpur EMAS Index	334
	Kuala Lumpur Second Board Index	336
Kuwait Stock Exchange (KSE)	Kuwait Stock Exchange (KSE) Index	580
Lehman Brothers	Lehman Brothers Adjustable Rate Mortgage (ARM) Index	648
	Lehman Brothers Aggregate Bond Index	650
	Lehman Brothers Corporate Bond Index	652
	Lehman Brothers Emerging Americas Bond Index	698
	Lehman Brothers Eurobond Index	700
	Lehman Brothers Global Bond Index	702
	Lehman Brothers Government/Corporate Bond Index	554
	Lehman Brothers High Yield Composite Bond Index	556
	Lehman Brothers Mortgage-Backed Securities Index	558
	Lehman Brothers Municipal Bond Index	560
	Lehman Brothers Mutual Fund Corporate Debt A Rated Index	790
	Lehman Brothers Mutual Fund GNMA Index	792
	Lehman Brothers Mutual Fund Indices	914
	Lehman Brothers U.S. Government Bond Index	562
	Lehman REIT Index	917
	Lehman Brothers Commodity Index (LBCI)	754
Limburg Institute of Financial Economics	Life Global Real Estate Securities Index	918
Lipper Analytical Services, Inc.	Lipper Balanced Funds Index	794
	Lipper Convertible Securities Funds Index	796
	Lipper Equity Income Funds Index	798
	Lipper Government National Mortgage Association (GNMA) Funds Index	800
	Lipper Growth & Income Funds Index	804
	Lipper Growth Funds Index	802
	Lipper High Current Yield Funds Index	806
	Lipper International Funds Index	808
	Lipper Money Market Funds Index	810
	Lipper Mutual Fund Indices	914
	Lipper Small Company Growth Funds Index	812
Ljubljanska Stock Exchange	SBI Index	880

PUBLISHER	INDEX	PAGE
Lombard Odier & Cie	Lombard Odier & Cie (LOC) European Government Bond Index	904
	Lombard Odier & Cie (LOC) Global World Government Bond Index	704
	Lombard Odier & Cie (LOC) Individual Bond Market Indices	906
London and Bishopsgate	London and Bishopsgate 100 Index	886
Luxembourg Stock Exchange	Luxembourg Stock Exchange Index	440
Madrid Stock Exchange, The	Madrid General Index	474
Madrid Stock Exchange, The European, as calculated by	Madrid General CPI Adjusted Indices	881
MAMPS Group	MAMPS Index	864
Managed Account Reports	MAR Fund/Pool Qualified Universe Index	918
Marinevest	Venezuela Marinevest Stock Composite Index	892
Merrill Lynch & Co.	Merrill Lynch (Formerly Smith New Court) Small Company Index of Hong Kong	858
	Merrill Lynch 182-Day U.S. Treasury Bill Index (Actual)	728
	Merrill Lynch 364-Day U.S. Treasury Bill Index (Actual)	730
	Merrill Lynch 91-Day U.S. Treasury Bill Auction Rate Average	726
	Merrill Lynch ADR Indices	853
	Merrill Lynch Brady Bond Index	706
	Merrill Lynch California Municipal Mutual Fund Index	814
	Merrill Lynch Canadian Bond Master Index	708
	Merrill Lynch Capital Market Index	840
	Merrill Lynch Capital Market Index	918
	Merrill Lynch Convertible Securities Index	762
	Merrill Lynch Currency Indices	911
	Merrill Lynch Domestic 3-Month Certificate of Deposit (CD) Index	732
	Merrill Lynch Energy and Metals Index (ENMET)	908
	Merrill Lynch Eurodollar 3-Month Certificate of Deposit (CD) Index	738
	Merrill Lynch Eurodollar Bond Index	710
	Merrill Lynch Global 300 (ML G300) Convertible Index	776
	Merrill Lynch Global Bond Index	712
	Merrill Lynch Global Government Bond Index	714
	Merrill Lynch High Yield Master Index	664
	Merrill Lynch Institutional Municipal Index	666
	Merrill Lynch Insured Bond Index	915
	Merrill Lynch Intermediate Mutual Fund Index	915
	Merrill Lynch Mortgage Master Bond Index	668
	Merrill Lynch Municipal Mutual Fund Index	816
	Merrill Lynch New York Mutual Fund Index	818
	Merrill Lynch U.S. 91-Day Treasury Bill Index (Actual)	734
	Merrill Lynch U.S. Corporate and Government Master Bond Index	670
	Merrill Lynch U.S. Domestic Corporate Bond Index	672
	Merrill Lynch U.S. Domestic Master Bond Index	674
	Merrill Lynch U.S. Government Master Bond Index	676
Micropal	Micropal Mutual Fund/Unit Investment Trust Performance Averages	916

PUBLISHER	INDEX	PAGE
Montreal Stock Exchange (MSE), The	Canadian Market Porfolio Index (XXM), The	42
Moody's Investors Service	Moody's Intermediate-Term Corporate Bond Yield Averages	896
	Moody's Investors Scrap Commodity Price Index	909
	Moody's Investors Spot Commodity Price Index	909
	Moody's Long-Term Corporate Bond Yield Averages	896
	Moody's Municipal Bond Yield Averages	897
Morgan Stanley & Co.	Morgan Stanley Consumer (CMR) Index	124
	Morgan Stanley Cyclical (CYC) Index	126
	Morgan Stanley High-Technology 35 (Tech 35) Index	128
	Morgan Stanley REIT Index	917
Morgan Stanley Capital International (MSCI)	Morgan Stanley Capital International (MSCI) Emerging Markets Free Global Index	626
	Morgan Stanley Capital International (MSCI) Emerging Markets Global Index	628
	Morgan Stanley Capital International (MSCI) Europe Australia and Far East (EAFE) Index	630
	Morgan Stanley Capital International (MSCI) World Index	632
Morgan Stanley Capital International, The European, as calculated by	European 100 Index	886
Morley Capital Management, Inc.	Morley Capital Management 1-Year GIC Index	780
	Morley Capital Management 3 Year GIC Index	912
	Morley Capital Management 5 Year GIC Index	912
	Morley Capital Management GIC Index	912
Morningstar	Morningstar Mutual Fund Performance Averages	915
Moscow Times, The/Skate-Press	Moscow Times Dollar Adjusted Index	879
	Moscow Times Stock Index	468
Mount Lucas Group	MLM Managed Futures Index	918
Muscat Securities Market (MSM), The	Muscat Securities Market (MSM) Price Index	590
Nagoya Stock Exchange	Nagoya 25 Index	302
Nairobi Stock Exchange	Nairobi Stock Exchange 20 Index	578
Namibian Stock Exchange	Namibia Stock Exchange (NSE) Index	586
National Association of Real Estate Investment Trusts (NAREIT)	National Association of Real Estate Investment Trusts (NAREIT) Composite Index	830
National Association of Securities Dealers, Inc. (NASD), The/Nasdaq Stock Market Inc., The	Nasdaq 100 Index	130
	Nasdaq American Depositary Receipts (ADRs) Index	132
	Nasdaq Bank Index	134
	Nasdaq Biotechnology Index	136
	Nasdaq Composite Index	138
	Nasdaq Computer Index	140
	Nasdaq Financial Index 100	142
	Nasdaq Industrial Index	144
	Nasdaq Insurance Index	146

PUBLISHER	INDEX	PAGE
National Association of Securities Dealers, Inc. (NASD), The/Nasdaq Stock Market Inc., The, *Cont'd*	Nasdaq Other Finance Index	152
	Nasdaq Telecommunications Index	154
	Nasdaq Transportation Index	156
	Nasdaq/National Market System (NMS) Composite Index	148
	Nasdaq/National Market System (NMS) Industrial Index	150
National Bank of Abu Dahbi, The	National Bank of Abu Dhabi Index, The	887
National Council of Real Estate Fiduciaries (NCREIF)	National Council of Real Estate Investment Fiduciaries (NCREIF) Property Index	828
Nepal Stock Exchange Limited	Nepal Stock Exchange Index (NEPSE)	864
Nesbitt Burns Inc.	Nesbit Burns Gifford Fong Associates Canadian Bond Indices	892
New Straits Times, The	New Straits Times Industrial Index	864
New York Stock Exchange (NYSE)	New York Stock Exchange (NYSE) Composite Index, The	158
	New York Stock Exchange (NYSE) Finance Sub-Group Index, The	160
	New York Stock Exchange (NYSE) Industrial Sub-Group Index, The	162
	New York Stock Exchange (NYSE) Transportation Sub-Group Index, The	164
	New York Stock Exchange (NYSE) Utilities Sub-Group Index, The	166
New Zealand Stock Exchange (NZSE), The	New Zealand All Ordinaries Index	865
	New Zealand Stock Exchange (NZSE), Market Index, The	340
	New Zealand Stock Exchange Top 10 Index	865
	New Zealand Stock Exchange--30 Selection (NZSE-30) Index, The	344
	New Zealand Stock Exchange--40 (NZSE-40) Index, The	346
	New Zealand Stock Exchange--Smaller Companies Index (NZSE-SCI), The	342
Nigerian Stock Exchange (NSE), The	Nigeria Stock Exchange (NSE) All-Share Index	588
Nihon Keizai Shimbun, Inc.	International Stock Exchange/Nikkei 50 Stock Index (ISE/Nikkei 50)	861
	Nikkei 225 Stock Average	304
	Nikkei 500 Stock Average	308
	Nikkei All Stock Index	861
	Nikkei Bond Index	901
	Nikkei Commodity Index	909
	Nikkei Currency Index	911
	Nikkei OTC Stock Average	861
	Nikkei Stock Index 300 (NIK 300)	306
Nomura International plc/Nomura Research Institute, Ltd.	Nomura Research Institute (NRI) Asia/Pacific-200 Index	870
	Nomura Research Institute (NRI) East European Index	520
	Nomura Research Institute (NRI) European Multimedia Index	886
Nordic Stock Exchanges, The	Nordic Securities Market Index	522
OM Stockholm AB	OMSX Indices	881
	OMX Index	476
Oporto Stock Exchange	Portugal Stock Market PSI-20 Index	464

PUBLISHER	INDEX	PAGE
Osaka Securities Exchange (OSE)	Osaka 250 Adjusted Stock Price Average	862
	Osaka 300 Stock Price Index	310
	Osaka 40 Adjusted Stock Price Average	862
Oslo Stock Exchange (Oslo Bors), The	OBX Index	450
	Oslo Stock Exchange All-Share Index	452
Osterreichische Termin-Und Optionenborse (OTOB)	Austrian Traded Index (ATX)	380
	Wiener Borse Index 30 (WBI 30) Index	384
OTC Exchange of India, The	OTC Exchange of India Composite Index	860
Oversea-Chinese Banking Corp. Limited/OCBC Investment Research Limited	Oversea-Chinese Banking Corp., Ltd. (OCBC) 30-Share Index	352
	Oversea Chinese Banking Corporation Limited (OCBC) Composite Index	866
	Oversea Chinese Banking Corporation Limited (OCBC) OTC Index	867
Pacific Stock Exchange (PSE)	Pacific Stock Exchange Tech 100 (PSE Tech 100) Index	168
Patria Finance	PatriaBIX Index	902
Payden & Rygel	Payden & Rygel Short-Term Total Return Indices	897
	Payden & Rygel Total Return Indices	897
Peregrine Brokerage LImited	Peregrine Asia Index (PAI) (Combined + Domestic Investors)	871
	Peregrine Asia Index (PAI)-Foreign	372
	Peregrine Asia Small Cap Index	871
	Peregrine Greater China Index	274
	Peregrine India ADR Index	860
Philadelphia Stock Exchange (PHLX), The	Philadelphia Stock Exchange Airline Sector (PLN) Index	170
	Philadelphia Stock Exchange Forest & Paper Products Sector (FPP) Index	172
	Philadelphia Stock Exchange Gold/Silver Sector (XAU) Index	174
	Philadelphia Stock Exchange Keefe, Bruyette & Woods, Inc. Bank Sector (BKK)	176
	Philadelphia Stock Exchange National Over-the-Counter (XOC) Index	178
	Philadelphia Stock Exchange Phone Sector (PNX) Index	180
	Philadelphia Stock Exchange Semiconductor Sector (SOX) Index	182
	Philadelphia Stock Exchange Supercap (HFX) Index	184
	Philadelphia Stock Exchange U.S. Top 100 (TPX) Index	186
	Philadelphia Stock Exchange Utility Sector (UTY) Index	188
	Philippine Stock Exchange (PSE) Composite Index	350
Pictet & Co.	Pictet LPP Index	882
Prague Stock Exchange, The	Prague Stock Exchange 50 (PX 50) Index	398
Progressive Asset Management and David L. Hubble	Hubble Environmental Index	852
R.O.C. Over-the-Counter Securities Exchange	OTC Index	868
Reuters	Reuters Commodity Index	910
Rio de Janeiro Stock Exchange, The	I-SENN Index	534
	IBV Profitability Index of Rio de Janeiro Stock Exchange (IBV)	532

PUBLISHER	INDEX	PAGE
Ryan Labs Inc.	Ryan Labs 3-Year Master GIC Index	782
	Ryan Labs 5-Year Master GIC Index	784
	Ryan Labs Cash Index	907
	Ryan Labs Treasury Composite Index	897
	Ryan Labs Treasury Yield Curve Indices	897
Salomon Brothers Inc.	Salomon Brothers Brady Bond Index	716
	Salomon Brothers Broad Investment-Grade (BIG) Bond Index	678
	Salomon Brothers Broad Investment-Grade (BIG) Corporate Bond Index	680
	Salomon Brothers Broad Investment-Grade (BIG) Mortgage Index	682
	Salomon Brothers Broad Investment-Grade (BIG) Treasury/Governent Sponsored Bond Index	684
	Salomon Brothers Certificate-of Deposit Index	907
	Salomon Brothers Convertible Securities Index	764
	Salomon Brothers Core 3 Index	899
	Salomon Brothers Core 5 Index	899
	Salomon Brothers Eurobond Indices	897
	Salomon Brothers Eurodollar Bond Index	718
	Salomon Brothers High-Yield Market Index	686
	Salomon Brothers New Large Pension Fund Baseline Bond Index (New LPF)	899
	Salomon Brothers U.S. Treasury Benchmark (On-The-Run) Index	899
	Salomon Brothers U.S. Treasury Benchmark Yield Curve Average	899
	Salomon Brothers U.S. Treasury Bill Index	907
	Salomon Brothers World Bond Index	898
	Salomon Brothers World Equity Index (SBWEI)-Property Industry Index	836
	Salomon Brothers World Equity Index-Broad Market Index (SBWEI-BMI)	636
	Salomon Brothers World Equity Index-Extended Market Index (SBWEI-EMI)	638
	Salomon Brothers World Equity Index-Primary Market Index (SBWEI-PMI)	640
	Salomon Brothers World Government Bond Index (WGBI)	720
	Salomon Brothers World Money Market Index	740
	Salomon Emerging Market Mutual Fund (EMMF) Debt Index	916
SBC Warburg Australia	SBC Warburg Australia Bond Index	900
SBF-Bourse de Paris, The	CAC-40 (Cotation Automatique Continue) Index	408
	MIDCAC Index	410
	SBF-120 Index	412
	SBF-250 Index	414
Schmidt Management Company	Schmidt Composite GIC Index	786
	Schmidt GIC Common Fund Index	912
	Schmidt Long-Term GIC Index	912
	Schmidt Short-Term GIC Index	912
Scotia McLeod	Scotia McLeod Debt Market Indices, The	892

PUBLISHER	INDEX	PAGE
Securities Exchange of Barbados	Securities Exchange of Barbados Share Index	530
Securities One Public Company Limited	S-One Bond Index	901
Shanghai Stock Exchange, The (SSE)	Shanghai A-Share Stock Price Index (SSE)	276
	Shanghai B-Share Stock Price Index (SSE)	278
	Shanghai Share Stock Price Index (SSE)	280
Shenzen Stock Exchange	Shenzen A-Share Stock Price Index	857
	Shenzen B-Share Stock Price Index	857
	Shenzen Share Stock Price Index	857
Skate-Press Consulting Agency	Skate-Press Consulting Agency MT 100 Index	879
	Skate-Press Consulting Agency MT 50 Index	880
Smith Barney, Inc.	Smith Barney 400 Convertible Securities Index	766
SNL Securities, L.P.	SNL REIT Index	918
	SNL Broker/ Dealers Index	854
	SNL Finance Companies Index	854
	SNL Financial Services Companies Index	854
	SNL Financial Services Investment Advisors Index	855
	SNL GSE Index	854
	SNL Mortgage Banks and Related Services Index	854
Sociedad de Bolsas S.A.	IBEX-35 Index	472
Sri Lanka Stock Exchange	Colombo Stock Exchange (CSE) All Share Price Index	360
	CSE Sensitive Index, The	868
SSKI Securities Ltd.	SSKI Index	860
Standard & Poor's Corporation (S&P Corp.)	Standard & Poor's (S&P) Financial Price Index	216
	Standard & Poor's (S&P) Industrial Price Index	218
	Standard & Poor's (S&P) MidCap 400 Index	220
	Standard & Poor's (S&P) Supercomposite Stock Price Index	224
	Standard & Poor's (S&P) Transportation Price Index (TRX)	226
	Standard & Poor's (S&P) Utilities Price Index	228
	Standard & Poor's 100 (S&P 100) Index (OEX)	210
	Standard & Poor's 500 (S&P 500) Composite Stock Price Index	212
	Standard & Poor's Corporate Bond Indices	899
	Standard & Poor's Intermediate-Term U.S. Government Bonds	900
	Standard & Poor's Long-Term U.S. Government Bonds	900
	Standard & Poor's Municipal Bond Indices	899
	Standard & Poor's Rated Money Market Fund Indices	916
	Standard & Poor's Short-Term U.S. Government Bonds	900
	Standard & Poor's SmallCap 600 Index	222
Standard & Poor's Corporation (S&P Corp.)/BARRA, Inc.	Standard & Poor's (S&P)/BARRA Growth Index	230
	Standard & Poor's (S&P)/BARRA Value Index	232
Stock Exchange of Ahmedabad, The	Ahmedabad Stock Exchange Sensitive Index of Equity Prices	858
Stock Exchange of Hong Kong Limited (SEHK), The	Hong Kong All Ordinaries Index (AOI)	288

PUBLISHER	INDEX	PAGE
Stock Exchange of Mauritius Ltd., The	Stock Exchange of Mauritius Index (SEMDEX)	582
Stock Exchange of Singapore Ltd.	Stock Exchange of Singapore (SES) All-Singapore Index	354
Stock Exchange of Thailand (SET), The	Securities Exchange of Thailand (SET) Index, The	368
	SET 50 Index	869
Stockbrokers Botswana Ltd.	Botswana Share Market Index	566
Stockholm Fondbors AB, The	Stockholm Stock Exchange General (SX-General) Index	478
	Stockholm Stock Exchange O-list Index, The	480
	Stockholm Stock Exchange OTC Index, The	482
Stockholm Stock Exchange	Stockholm Stock Exchange SX-16 Index, The	881
	Stockholm Stock Exchange SX-70 Index	882
Straits Times, The	Straits Times Index, The	867
Surabaya Stock Exchange	Surabaya Stock Exchange Composite Price Index	860
Swaziland Stockbrokers Ltd.	Swaziland Stock Market (SSM) Index	602
Swiss Bank Corp.	SBC Index of Swiss Shares	882
T. Rowe Price	T. Rowe Price GIC Index	912
Taiwan Stock Exchange Corporation	Taiwan Industrial Stock Price Average	869
	Taiwan Stock Exchange Capitalization-Weighted Stock Index (TAIEX)	364
	Taiwan Stock Exchange Composite Stock Price Average	366
Tel Aviv Stock Exchange (TSE)	Computerized Call Market System (CCM) Index	888
	TA-100 Index	888
	Tel Aviv Stock Exchange General Share Index	572
	Tel Aviv Stock Exchange MAOF-25 Index	574
Thai Investment and Securities Company Ltd.	Thai Investment and Securities Company Ltd. (TISCO) Price Index	870
The Sao Paulo Stock Exchange	Sao Paulo Stock Exchange Index (BOVESPA)	536
Thomas J. Hertzfeld Advisors, Inc.	Hertzfeld Closed-End Average (THCEA)	822
	Hertzfeld Single Country Average	913
Tokyo Stock Exchange (TSE), The	Tokyo Stock Exchange (TSE) Second Section Stock Price Index	320
	Tokyo Stock Exchange Arithmetic Stock Price Index	862
	Tokyo Stock Exchange Price Index (TOPIX)	312
	Tokyo Stock Exchange Price Index (TOPIX)--Large-Sized Companies Subindex	314
	Tokyo Stock Exchange Price Index (TOPIX)--Medium-Sized Companies Subindex	316
	Tokyo Stock Exchange Price Index (TOPIX)--Small-Sized Companies Subindex	318
Toronto Stock Exchange (TSE), The	Toronto Stock Exchange 100 (TSE 100) Composite Index	46
	Toronto Stock Exchange 200 (TSE 200) Composite Index	48
	Toronto Stock Exchange 300 (TSE 300) Composite Index	50
	Toronto Stock Exchange 35 (TSE 35) Index	44
Trinidad & Tobago Stock Exchange	Trinidad & Tobago Stock Exchange Daily Index of Stock Market Values	556
United Overseas Bank (UOB)	United Overseas Bank (UOB) Blue Chip Index	867
	United Overseas Bank (UOB) Dealing and Automated Quotation System (SESDAQ) Index	358
	United Overseas Bank (UOB) OTC Index	868
	United Overseas Bank Singapore Government Bond Index	901

PUBLISHER	INDEX	PAGE
Upline Securities	Upline USI Index	888
Value Line Publishing, Inc.	Value Line Convertible Securities Index	768
Value Line, Inc.	Value Line Arithmetic (VLA) Index	234
	Value Line Composite Index (XVL)	236
	Value Line Industrial Average	855
	Value Line Mutual Fund Performance Averages	916
	Value Line Railroad Average	855
	Value Line Utility Average	855
Vancouver Stock Exchange (VSE), The	Vancouver Stock Exchange (VSE) Index	52
Vienna Stock Exchange (Weiner Borse), The	Creditanstalt Share Index (CA Share Index)	872
	Participation Certificate Index	872
	Vienna Stock Exchange Share (Weiner Borse) Index (WBI)	382
Warsaw Stock Exchange	WIG 20	879
	Warsaw Stock Exchange (WIG) Index	454
	Warsaw Stock Exchange WIRR Index	456
Wilshire Associates	Wilshire Real Estate Securities Index	832
	Wilshire 2500 Equity Index	855
	Wilshire 5000 Equity Index	238
	Wilshire Associates Small Cap (WSX) Index	240
	Wilshire Large Company (Top 750) Equity Index	242
	Wilshire Large Company Growth Equity Style Index	244
	Wilshire Large Company Value Equity Style Index	246
	Wilshire Middle Capitalization Company (MidCap 750) Equity Index	248
	Wilshire Middle Capitalization Company Growth Equity Style Index	250
	Wilshire Middle Capitalization Company Value Equity Style Index	252
	Wilshire Small Company (Next 1750) Equity Index	254
	Wilshire Small Company Growth Equity Style Index	256
	Wilshire Small Company Value Equity Style Index	258
Wood & Company in conjunction with Hospodarsky Noviny	HN-Wood Index	875
Zimbabwe Stock Exchange (ZSE)	58 Counter Industrial Index	890
	Zimbabwe Stock Exchange (ZSE) Industrial and Mining Index	604

APPENDIX 8

GLOBAL MARKET CAPITALIZATIONS

STOCKS: 1995

COUNTRY	GEOGRAPHIC AREA	ISSUES/ COMPANIES	MARKET VALUE (US$ MILLIONS)
Botswana	Africa	12	397.7
Cote d'Ivoire	Africa	118	867.0
Egypt	Africa	718	8,088.0
Ghana	Africa	18	1,650.0
Kenya	Africa	22	2,017.5
Malawi	Africa	NA	NA
Mauritius	Africa	40	1,381.0
Morocco	Africa	44	6,018.8
Namibia	Africa	26	191.0
Nairobi	Africa	22	6,017.9
Nigeria	Africa	181	1,952.5
South Africa	Africa	614	261,866.9
Sudan	Africa	NA	233.0
Swaziland	Africa	4	338.9
Tunisia	Africa	26	4,006.0
Zambia	Africa	NA	NA
Zimbabwe	Africa	65	2,038.0
Australia	Asia/Pacific	1,130	244,861.8
Bangladesh	Asia/Pacific	176	1,319.9
China	Asia/Pacific	323	42,055.0
Hong Kong	Asia/Pacific	526	303,666.7
India	Asia/Pacific	14,087	139,177.8
Indonesia	Asia/Pacific	238	66,580.4
Japan	Asia/Pacific	2,263	3,654,542.8
Korea	Asia/Pacific	714	183,265.9
Malaysia	Asia/Pacific	529	221,260.4
Nepal	Asia/Pacific	82	244.7
New Zealand	Asia/Pacific	132	32,050.8
Pakistan	Asia/Pacific	764	9,570.3

Stocks: 1995, Cont'd

Country	Geographic Area	Issues/ Companies	Market Value (US$ millions)
Singapore	Asia/Pacific	212	148,025.2
Sri Lanka	Asia/Pacific	226	2,884.0
Taiwan	Asia/Pacific	328	187,212.9
Thailand	Asia/Pacific	416	141,507.3
Barbados	Central America	18	490.5
Costa Rica	Central America	27	92.5
Honduras	Central America	99	338.0
Jamaica	Central America	48	1,390.6
Panama	Central America	18	831.0
Trinidad & Tobago	Central America	31	1,154.0
Armenia	Europe	1	3.0
Austria	Europe	128	31,104.5
Belgium	Europe	205	101,162.4
Bulgaria	Europe	26	62.0
Croatia	Europe	61	581.0
Cyprus	Europe	70	2,857.8
Czech Republic	Europe	1,635	15,664.0
Denmark	Europe	384	59,946.2
Finland	Europe	92	43,927.1
France	Europe	904	497,861.1
Germany	Europe	802	574,754.7
Greece	Europe	212	17,060.0
Hungary	Europe	45	2,350.2
Iceland	Europe	27	721.0
Ireland	Europe	80	25,777.7
Italy	Europe	221	205,080.0
Lithuania	Europe	351	158.0
Luxembourg	Europe	61	30,328.5
Malta	Europe	54	1,251.1
Netherlands	Europe	433	285,690.0
Norway	Europe	167	44,393.0
Poland	Europe	56	4,566.5
Portugal	Europe	169	18,299.3
Russian Federation	Europe	170	15,863.0
Slovakia	Europe	18	1,237.5
Slovenia	Europe	17	302.0
Spain	Europe	365	189,700.4
Sweden	Europe	223	177,240.0
Switzerland	Europe	338	396,860.7
Turkey	Europe	205	21,030.7
United Kingdom	Europe	2,255	1,329,935.9
Argentina	Latin America	149	37,783.0
Brazil	Latin America	543	147,679.3
Chile	Latin America	284	73,047.9
Colombia	Latin America	190	10,267.3
Ecuador	Latin America	37	2,571.8
Peru	Latin America	246	10,820.0
Uruguay	Latin America	20	183.0

STOCKS: 1995, CONT'D

COUNTRY	GEOGRAPHIC AREA	ISSUES/ COMPANIES	MARKET VALUE (US$ MILLIONS)
Venezuela	Latin America	90	3,655.0
Bolivia	Latin America	7	97.0
Iran	Middle East	169	6,561.0
Israel	Middle East	1,012	36,459.3
Jordan	Middle East	97	4,676.3
Abu Dhabi	Middle East	27	NA
Qatar	Middle East	17	1,600.0
Kuwait	Middle East	51	13,623.0
Oman	Middle East	80	1,980.0
Saudi Arabia	Middle East	69	40,961.0
Bermuda	North America	44	2,000.0
Canada	North America	2,483	371,552.6
Mexico	North America	185	90,811.8
U.S.	North America	7,614	6,964,392.0
TOTALS		47,687	17,655,119.35

BONDS: 1994

MAJOR BOND MARKETS (NOMINAL VALUE OUTSTANDING; IN US$ MILLIONS)

BOND MARKET	TOTAL PUBLICLY ISSUED	%	CENTRAL GVT.	%	GVT. AGENCY	%	STATE & LOCAL GVT.	%	CORP.	%	OTHER DOMESTIC	%	INTERNATIONAL BONDS(A) FOREIGN	EURO	%	PRIVATE PLACEMENTS (UNCLASSIFIED)	%
US Dollar	8,023.1	43.4	2,422.1	30.2	2,195.1	27.4	904.2	11.3	1,509.0	18.8	235.6	2.9	137.5	619.6	9.4	0.0	0.0
Japanese Yen	3,669.3	19.9	1,906.6	52.0	197.5	5.4	90.3	2.5	382.8	10.4	784.5	21.4	81.0	226.6	8.4	689.4	18.8
Deutsche Mark	1,963.5	10.6	656.4	33.4	65.8	3.4	72.8	3.7	2.0	0.1	925.0	47.1		241.5	12.3	433.9	22.1
Italian Lira	955.7	5.2	752.4	78.7	21.1	2.2		0.0	3.7	0.4	131.9	13.8	1.4	45.1	4.9	0.0	0.0
French Franc	891.4	4.8	402.6	45.2	215.5	24.2	3.8	0.4	144.3	16.2		0.0	6.2	119.1	14.1	0.0	0.0
U.K. Sterling	501.8	2.7	331.0	66.0		0.0	0.1	0.0	28.6	5.7		0.0	6.2	135.9	28.3	0.0	0.0
Canadian Dollar	404.4	2.2	162.9	40.3		0.0	111.0	27.4	51.5	12.7	0.8	0.2	0.6	77.6	19.3	0.0	0.0
Beglian Franc	347.1	1.9	179.2	51.6	7.7	2.2		0.0	13.2	3.8	119.9	34.5	26.6	0.5	7.8	0.0	0.0
Dutch Guilder	280.5	1.5	162.0	57.8		0.0	2.7	1.0	68.4	24.4		0.0	5.6	41.7	16.9	90.0	32.1
Danish Krone	251.0	1.4	90.9	36.2		0.0		0.0		0.0	156.7	62.4		3.4	1.4	0.0	0.0
Swiss Franc	231.0	1.2	23.0	10.0		0.0	17.6	7.6	32.3	14.0	63.6	27.5	94.6		41.0	0.0	0.0
Swedish Krona	210.3	1.1	77.3	36.8		0.0	1.0	0.5	8.2	3.9	120.2	57.2		3.7	1.8	0.0	0.0
Spanish Paseta	171.0	0.9	119.4	69.8		0.0	8.7	5.1	19.8	11.6	12.5	7.3	10.5		6.1	0.0	0.0
European Currency Unite (EUC)	154.6	0.8	61.8	40.0		0.0		0.0		0.0		0.0		92.8	60.0	0.0	0.0
Australian Dollar	123.6	0.7	59.9	48.5	24.9	20.1		0.0	15.5	12.5		0.0		23.3	18.9	0.0	0.0
Austrian Shilling	108.3	0.6	42.7	39.4	2.5	2.3	0.4	0.4	3.8	3.5	56.6	52.3	2.4		2.2	6.7	6.2
Norwegian Krone	45.8	0.2	16.5	36.0	2.6	5.7	6.5	14.2	3.2	7.0	16.2	35.4	0.8	0.0	1.7	0.0	0.0
Finnish Markka	43.9	0.2	20.0	45.6		0.0	1.5	3.4	6.3	14.4	14.5	33.0		1.5	3.4	0.0	0.0
Portuguese Escudo	34.1	0.2	22.7	66.6		0.0	0.6	1.8	3.6	10.6	4.5	13.2	2.8		8.2	0.0	0.0
Greek Drachma	30.0	0.2	29.7	99.0		0.0		0.0		0.0		0.0	0.2	0.1	1.0	0.0	0.0
Irish Pound	23.8	0.1	22.3	93.7	0.4	1.7		0.0	0.5	2.1		0.0	0.2	0.5	2.9	0.0	0.0
New Zealand Dollar	17.7	0.0	12.9	72.9	1.3	7.3		0.0	2.4	13.6		0.0	0.2	0.9	6.2	0.0	0.0
Total	18,481.9	100.0	7,574.3	41.0	2,734.4	14.8	1,221.2	6.6	2,299.1	12.4	2,642.5	14.3	376.8	241.5 1,392.3	10.9	1,220.0	6.6

(a) Includes straight, convertible and floating-rate debt.
(b) The German bond market does not distinguish between Euro and foreign international issues.
(c) Includes foreign and Eurobond totals.
(d) In addition, an uspecified amount of privately placed issues of the private sectors exists.

TABLE NOTES

STOCK MARKET CAPITALIZATION

Stock market capitalization figures and the number of listed issues were collected directly by surveying the local stock exchanges listed below. In most cases, the number of stocks listed along with combined market capitalizations were reported in local currency and converted into US dollars on the basis of exchange rates prevailing at year-end 1995. See Appendix 9 for exchange rates.

The table displays the number of domestic common and preferred issues listed on local exchanges. In some cases, however, it is evident on the basis of additional research and analysis that: (1) the number of issues listed may actually represents the number of companies; (2) a limited number of foreign companies are included along with domestic companies; and (3) responses are not limited to common and preferred stocks, but may also include unit trusts, convertible securities or equity-linked derivative products, to mention just a few. Every effort has been made to validate the data and minimize the influence of these factors on the quality of the figures contained in the table.

JAPAN
Figures reflect the number of domestic companies listed and stock market capitalization applicable to all stock exchanges in Japan, without overlap. Source: Tokyo Stock Exchange Fact Book 1996.

UNITED STATES
Figures applicable to domestic common and preferred shares listed on the New York Stock Exchange, American Stock Exchange and Nasdaq, excluding ADRs.

CANADA
Figures include Toronto Stock Exchange and Vancouver Stock Exchange.

INDIA
Figures, which consist of listings on the Bombay Stock Exchange, Calcutta Stock Exchange, Delhi Stock Exchange and Madras Stock Exchange, may include duplicate listings and foreign companies. Sources for figures applicable to the Calcutta and Delhi Stock Exchanges: International Finance Corp.

CHINA
Figures include Shenzen Stock Exchange and Shanghai Stock Exchange. Source for Shenzen figures: International Finance Corp.

SRI LANKA
Figures are as of December 31, 1994.

ABU DHABI, QATAR, MALTA, AND NAIROBI
Source for figures: Reuters.

ARGENTINA, BULGARIA, BOLIVIA, COTE D'IVOIRE, CROATIA, EGYPT, HONDURAS, IRAN, IRAN, KUWAIT, LITHUANIA, MAURITIUS, OMAN, RUSSIAN FEDERATION, QATAR, SAUDI ARABIA, SLOVENIA, TUNISIA, URUGUAY, VENEZUELA AND ZIMBABWE
Source for market capitalization and listed companies figures as of December 31, 1995: International Finance Corp.

The following is a list of stock exchanges that furnished the figures referred to in the table:

Argentina	Buenos Aires Stock Exchange
Australia	Australian Stock Exchange
Austria	Vienna Stock Exchange
Bangladesh	Dhaka Stock Exchange
Barbados	Securities Exchange of Barbados
Belgium	Brussels Stock Exchange
Bahrain	Bahrain Stock Exchange
Brazil	Sao Paulo Stock Exchange
Bulgaria	First Bulgarian Stock Exchange
Canada	Toronto Stock Exchange
	Vancouver Stock Exchange
Chile	Santiago Stock Exchange
Columbia	Bogota Stock Exchange
Costa Rica	Costa Rica Stock Exchange
Cyprus	Cyprus Stock Exchange
Czech Republic	Prague Stock Exchange
Denmark	Copenhagen Stock Exchange
Ecuador	Quito Stock Exchange
Finland	Helsinki Stock Exchange
France	Paris Stock Exchange
Germany	German Stock Exchange
Ghana	Ghana Stock Exchange
Greece	Athens Stock Exchange
Hong Kong	Hong Kong Stock Exchange
Hungary	Budapest Stock Exchange
Iceland	Iceland Stock Exchange
Indonesia	Jakarta Stock Exchange
Ireland	Irish Stock Exchange
Israel	Tel Aviv Stock Exchange
Italy	Italian Stock Exchange Council
Jamaica	Jamaica Stock Exchange
Jordan	Amman Financial Market
Kenya	Nairobi Stock Exchange
Korea	Korea Stock Exchange
Kuwait	Kuwait Stock Exchange
Luxembourg	Luxembourg Stock Exchange
Malaysia	Kuala Lampur Stock Exchange
Mauritius	Mauritius Stock Exchange
Mexico	Mexican Stock Exchange
Morocco	Casablanca Stock Exchange
Namibia	Namibia Stock Exchange
Nepal	Nepal Stock Exchange
Netherlands	Amsterdam Stock Exchange
New Zealand	New Zealand Stock Exchange
Nigeria	Nigeria Stock Exchange
Norway	Oslo Stock Exchange
Oman	Muscat Securities Market
Pakistan	Karachi Stock Exchange
Panama	Panama Stock Exchange

Peru	Lima Stock Exchange
Philippines	Manila and Makati Stock Exchanges
Poland	Warsaw Stock Exchange
Portugal	Lisbon Stock Exchange
Singapore	Singapore Stock Exchange
Slovak Republic	Bratislava Stock Exchange
South Africa	Johannesburg Stock Exchange
Spain	Madrid Stock Exchange
Sri Lanka	Colombia Stock Exchange
Swaziland	Swaziland Stock Exchange
Sweden	Stockholm Stock Exchange
Switzerland	Swiss Stock Exchange
Taiwan	Taiwan Stock Exchange
Thailand	Securities Exchange of Thailand
Trinidad & Tobago	Trinidad & Tobago Stock Exchange
Turkey	Istanbul Stock Exchange
United Kingdom	London Stock Exchange
United States	American Stock Exchange
	Nasdaq
	New York Stock Exchange
Zimbabwe	Zimbabwe Stock Exchange

BOND MARKET CAPITALIZATION

SOURCE
Salomon Brothers

EXCHANGE RATES
The following exchange rates versus the US$ apply as of December 31, 1994:

Australian Dollar	1.2873/US$
Belgian Franc	31.838/US$
Canadian Dollar	1.3884/US$
Danish Krone	6.083/US$
Deutsche Mark	1.5488/US$
Dutch Guilder	1.7351/US$
European Currency Unit (ECU)	0.8129/US$
Finnish Markka	4.7432/US$
French Franc	5.346/US$
Greek Drachma	240.1/US$
Irish Pound	0.6464/US$
Italian Lira	1,629.7/US$
Japanese Yen	99.74/US$
New Zealand Dollar	1.5564/US$
Norwegian Dollar	6.762/US$
Portuguese Escudo	159.09/US$
Spanish Peseta	131.74/US$
Swedish Krona	7.4615/US$
Swiss Franc	1.3115/US$
United Kingdom Sterling	0.64/US$

APPENDIX 9

YEAR-END 1995 CURRENCY EXCHANGE RATES

COUNTRY	MONETARY UNIT	EXCHANGE RATE PER US$
Argentina	Peso	1.0005
Australia	Dollar	0.7428
Austria	Schilling	10.1075
Bahamas	Dollar	1.00
Bahrain	Dinar	0.3774
Bangladesh	Taka	40.34
Barbados	Dollar	2.0113
Belgium	Franc	29.525
Bermuda	Dollar	0.999
Bolivia	Boliviano	4.91
Botswana	Pula	0.355
Brazil	Real	0.9717
Bulgaria	Lev	70.704
Canada	Dollar	1.3645
Chile	Peso	407.13
China	Renminbi	8.3174
Colombia	Peso	988.16
Costa Rica	Colon	194.00
Cypress	Pound	0.4549
Czech Republic	Koruna	26.58
Denmark	Krone	5.5664
Ecuador	Sucre	2912
Egypt	Pound	3.3959
European Currency Unit	ECU	1.226
Finland	Markka	4.363
France	Franc	4.909
Germany	Mark	1.4378
Ghana	Cedi	1455
Greece	Drachma	237.675
Hong Kong	Dollar	7.7325
Hungary	Forint	139.47
Iceland	Krona	65.14

COUNTRY	MONETARY UNIT	EXCHANGE RATE PER US$
India	Rupee	35.1785
Indonesia	Ruplah	2287
Iran	Rial	1745
Iraq	Dinar	0.3109
Ireland	Punt	1.6005
Israel	Shekel	3.135
Italy	Lira	1587.5
Ivory Coast	Franc	489.82
Jamaica	Dollar	36.5
Japan	Yen	103.515
Jordan	Dinar	0.708
Kenya	Shilling	55.95
Kuwait	Dinar	0.29875
Lebanon	Pound	1595.5
Luxembourg	Franc	29.525
Malaysia	Ringgit	2.5397
Malta	Lira	0.3517
Mauritius	Rupee	18.18
Mexico	Peso	7.695
Morocco	Dirham	8.4415
Namibia	Rand	3.6455
Nepal	Rupee	55.92
Netherlands	Guilder	1.6085
New Zealand	Dollar	0.6538
Nigeria	Naira	85
Norway	Krone	6.3457
Pakistan	Rupee	34.25
Panama	Balboa	1
Paraguay	Guarani	1966
Peru	New Sol	2.322
Philippines	Peso	26.18
Poland	Zloty	2.4655
Portugal	Escudo	149.9

Country	Monetary Unit	Exchange Rate Per US$	Country	Monetary Unit	Exchange Rate Per US$
Russia	Ruble	4645	Switzerland	Franc	1.1543
Saudi Arabia	Riyal	3.7505	Taiwan	Dollar	27.286
Singapore	Dollar	1.4143	Thailand	Baht	25.19
Slovak Republic	Koruna	29.569	Trinidad/ Tobago	Dollar	5.85
South Africa- Commercial	Rand	3.6455	Tunesia	Dinar	0.9448
South Africa- Financial	Rand	3.6455	Turkey	Lira	60150
South Korea	Won	770.2	United Kingdom	Pound	1.54955
Spain	Peseta	121.67	United Arab Emirates	Dirham	3.67
Sri Lanka	Rupee	53.5	Uruguay	New Peso	7.03
Swaziland	Lilangeni	3.6453	Venezuela	Bolivar	286
Sweden	Krona	6.65775	Zambia	Kwacha	930
			Zimbabwe	Dollar	9.305

Sources:
Nepal exchange rate as of 1/1/96=average between buying and selling rate per Nepal Inc.
Bloomberg Financial.

APPENDIX 10

INDEX-BASED DERIVATIVE INSTRUMENTS[1]

STOCK INDICES

NORTH AMERICA

COUNTRY/INDEX	EXCHANGE	MARKET COVERAGE	CALCULATION	FU	OP	OTHER
Canada TSE 35 Index	Toronto Futures Exchange	35 largest and most actively traded stocks	Market value weight			
Mexico IPC Index	Chicago Board Options Exchange Chicago Mercantile Exchange	35 largest and most actively traded stocks	Market value weight	√	√	
United States Airline Index	American Stock Exchange	10 large companies in U.S. and overseas	Equal weight		√	
Airline Index	Philadelphia Stock Exchange	12 major domestic airline companies	Equal weight		√	
Automotive Index	Chicago Board Options Exchange	10 design and manufacturing companies in the sector	Modified equal weight		√	
Big Cap Sector	Philadelphia Stock Exchange	50 most highly capitalized and widely held U.S. companies	Market value weight		√	
BioTechnology Index	Chicago Board Options Exchange	19 small and medium sized companies in the sector	Price weight		√	LEAPS
Biotechnology Index	American Stock Exchange	15 companies in the biotechnology industry	Equal weight		√	Long-Term Options
Computer Software Index	Chicago Board Options Exchange	15 domestic companies in the computer software sector	Price weight		√	
Computer Technology Index	American Stock Exchange	26 large U.S. corporations	Market value weight		√	
Environmental Index	Chicago Board Options Exchange	15 domestic companies involved in environmental control	Price weight		√	
Forest and Paper Products	Philadelphia Stock Exchange	14 forest and paper industry companies	Price weight		√	
Gaming Index	Chicago Board Options Exchange	15 domestic companies involved in the sector	Price weight		√	
Global Telecom-munications Index	Chicago Board Options Exchange	20 domestic companies involved in the sector	Price weight		√	

COUNTRY/INDEX	EXCHANGE	MARKET COVERAGE	CALCULATION	FU	OP	OTHER
United States, *Cont'd* Gold/Silver Sector Index	Philadelphia Stock Exchange	9 global gold and silver companies	Market value weight		√	LEAPS
Institutional Index	American Stock Exchange	75 most widely held stocks in institutional portfolios	Market value weight		√	FLEX Options LEAPS
Inter@ctive Week Internet Index	American Stock Exchange	38 companies representing an industry cross-section	Market value weight		√	
Internet Index	Chicago Board Options Exchange	15 internet related software and hardware companies	Equal weight		√	LEAPS
Israel Index	Chicago Board Options Exchange	15 U.S. traded Israeli stocks	Price weight		√	
KBW Bank Index	Philadelphia Stock Exchange	20 major U.S. banking companies	Market value weight		√	
Latin America Index	Chicago Board Options Exchange	15 U.S. traded stocks representing Argentina, Brazil, Chile and Mexico	Modified equal weight		√	
Major Market Index	American Stock Exchange European Options Exchange	20 U.S. blue chip companies/designed to follow Dow Jones Industrial Average movements	Price weight	√	√	LEAPS Long-Term Options FLEX Options
Mexico Index	American Stock Exchange	10 large companies with major business interests in Mexico	Modified equal weight		√	LEAPS
Mexico Index	Chicago Board Options Exchange	10 U.S. traded Mexican ADRs, ADSs and a closed-end investment company	Price weight		√	LEAPS
Morgan Stanley Consumer Index	American Stock Exchange	30 large capitalization consumer oriented, stable growth companies	Equal weight		√	
Morgan Stanley Cyclical Index	American Stock Exchange	30 large capitalization, economically sensitive companies	Equal weight		√	
Morgan Stanley Technology Index	American Stock Exchange	35 highly capitalized stocks from nine technology subsectors	Equal weight		√	
NASDAQ 100	Chicago Board Options Exchange Chicago Mercantile Exchange	100 largest NADAQ listed domestic, non-financial companies	Market value weight	√	√	FLEX Options
National OTC Index	Philadelphia Stock Exchange	100 largest over-the-counter traded stocks	Market value weight		√	Long-Term Options
Natural Gas Index	American Stock Exchange	15 large capitalization natural gas companies	Equal weight		√	
New York Stock Exchange Utility Subindex	New York Stock Exchange New York Futures Exchange	246 utility companies that are traded on the New York Stock Exchange	Market value weight	√	√	
North American Telecommunica-tions Index	American Stock Exchange	15 large capitalization companies	Equal weight		√	
NYSE Composite Index	New York Stock Exchange New York Futures Exchange	2,637 common stocks traded on the New York Stock Exchange	Market value weight	√	√	
Oil Index	American Stock Exchange	16 leading oil companies	Equal weight		√	
Oscar Grus Israel Index	American Stock Exchange	11 large companies with major business interests in Israel	Modified equal weight		√	
Pharmaceutical Index	American Stock Exchange	15 large companies in the U.S. and Europe	Market value weight		√	Long-Term Options

COUNTRY/INDEX	EXCHANGE	MARKET COVERAGE	CALCULATION	FU	OP	OTHER
United States, *Cont'd* Phone Sector Index	Philadelphia Stock Exchange	8 companies that made up AT&T prior to divestiture	Market value weight		√	
PSE Tech 100 Index	Pacific Stock Exchange	100 broad based stocks representing fifteen industries within the technology sector	Price weight	√	√	
Russell 2000 Index	Chicago Board Options Exchange Chicago Mercantile Exchange	2000 smallest investable U.S. companies within the Russell universe of the large 3000 companies	Market value weight	√	√	FLEX Options LEAPS
S&P 100 Index	Chicago Board Options Exchange	100 largest capitalization companies within the S&P 500 Index	Market value weight		√	CAPS, SPX CAPS, FLEX Op-tions and LEAPS
S&P 500 Index	American Stock Exchange Chicago Board Options Exchange Chicago Mercantile Exchange New York Stock Exchange Philadelphia Stock Exchange	500 large capitalization stocks in leading companies	Market value weight	√	√	CAPS, Indexed Debt and CD Options, End Quarter Options, ESPs, FLEX, LEAPS, Long-Term Options, Cash & Index Participation products, SPDRs
S&P Banks Index	Chicago Board Options Exchange	30 companies that make up the bank sector of the S&P 500 Index	Market value weight		√	
S&P Chemicals Index	Chicago Board Options Exchange	19 companies that make up the chemicals sector of the S&P 500 Index	Market value weight		√	
S&P Healthcare Index	Chicago Board Options Exchange	31 companies that make up the healthcare sector of the S&P 500 Index	Market value weight		√	
S&P Insurance Index	Chicago Board Options Exchange	17 companies that make up the insurance sector of the S&P 500 Index	Market value weight		√	
S&P MidCap 400 Index	American Stock Exchange Chicago Board Options Exchange Chicago Mercantile Exchange	400 investable domestic middle capitalization companies	Market value weight	√	√	FLEX Options
S&P Retail Index	Chicago Board Options Exchange	32 companies that make up the retail sector of the S&P 500 Index	Market value weight		√	
S&P SmallCap 600 Index	Chicago Board Options Exchange	600 investable domestic small capitalization companies	Market value weight		√	
S&P Transporta-tion Index	Chicago Board Options Exchange	15 companies that make up the transportation sector of the S&P 500 Index	Market value weight		√	
S&P/BARRA Growth Index	Chicago Board Options Exchange Chicago Mercantile Exchange	184 growth oriented large capitalization stocks that make up the S&P 500 Index	Market value weight	√	√	
S&P/BARRA Value Index	Chicago Board Options Exchange Chicago Mercantile Exchange	316 value oriented large capitalization stocks that make up the S&P 500 Index	Market value weight	√	√	
Securities Broker/ Dealer Index	American Stock Exchange	11 large U.S. securities firms and broker/dealers	Equal weight		√	
Semiconductor Sector Index	Philadelphia Stock Exchange	16 largest and most widely held companies in sector	Price weight		√	

COUNTRY/INDEX	EXCHANGE	MARKET COVERAGE	CALCULATION	FU	OP	OTHER
United States, *Cont'd* Supercap Sector	Philadelphia Stock Exchange	5 largest U.S. companies, based on market capitalization	Market value weight		√	
Technology Index	Chicago Board Options Exchange	30 high technology companies	Price weight		√	LEAPS
U.S. Telecommuni-cations Index	Chicago Board Options Exchange	24 U.S. telecommunications companies	Price weight		√	
U.S. Top 100 Index	Philadelphia Stock Exchange	100 most highly capitalized and widely held U.S. companies	Market value weight		√	LEAPS
Utility Sector Index	Philadelphia Stock Exchange	20 utility companies/designed to track Dow Jones Utility Average	Market value weight		√	
Value Line Index	Philadelphia Stock Exchange	About 1,632 common stocks covered in the Value Line Investment Survey	Equal weight/ Geometric average		√	LEAPS Long-Term Options
Wilshire Small Cap Index	Pacific Stock Exchange	250 small capitalization companies selected from Wilshire's Small Company Equity Index	Market value weight		√	

ASIA/PACIFIC

COUNTRY/INDEX	EXCHANGE	MARKET COVERAGE	CALCULATION	FU	OP	OTHER
Australia ASX 20 Leaders	Australian Stock Exchange	20 largest and most actively traded stocks	Market value weight	√	√+	
ASX Gold Subindex	Australian Stock Exchange	46 gold sector stocks	Market value weight	√	√+	
ASX All Ordinaries	Australian Stock Exchange/ Sydney Futures Exchange	All 347 listed and ordinary shares traded on the ASE	Market value weight	√	√+	Overnight Options
Hong Kong AMEX Hong Kong 30 Index	American Stock Exchange	30 large actively traded stocks, twenty-one of which are in common with the Hang Seng Index	Market value weight		√	LEAPS, Morgan Stanley Call Warrants
Hang Seng Index (HSI)	Hong Kong Futures Exchange	33 large, actively traded stocks	Market value weight	√		
HSI Commerce and Industry Subindex	Hong Kong Futures Exchange	16 large, actively traded HSI Index member stocks in the commerce and industry sector	Market value weight	√		
HSI Finance Subindex	Hong Kong Futures Exchange	3 large, actively traded HSI Index member stocks in the finance sector	Market value weight	√		
HSI Properties Subindex	Hong Kong Futures Exchange	10 large, actively traded HSI Index members stocks in the properties sector	Market value weight	√		
HSI Utilities Subindex	Hong Kong Futures Exchange	4 large, actively traded HSI Index member stocks in the utilities sector	Market value weight	√		
Japan AMEX Japan Index	American Stock Exchange	210 actively traded large capitalization stocks. The index is intended to mirror the Nikkei 225 Index	Price weight		√	LEAPS, Long-Term Options
Nagoya 25 Index	Nagoya Stock Exchange	25 leading, diversified stocks	Price weight		√	

COUNTRY/INDEX	EXCHANGE	MARKET COVERAGE	CALCULATION	FU	OP	OTHER
Japan, *Cont'd* Nikkei 225 Index	Osaka Securities Exchange	225 actively traded stocks	Price weight	√	√	
Nikkei 225 Index	Singapore International Monetary Exchange Ltd.	225 actively traded stocks	Price weight	√	√	
Nikkei 225 Index	American Stock Exchange Chicago Mercantile Exchange	225 actively traded stocks. Intended to closely mirror the Nikkei 225 Index	Price weight	√	√+	Morgan Stanley Call Warrants, Bear Stearns Strike Reset Call Warrants, Goldman Sachs Indexed Notes
Nikkei 300 Index	American Stock Exchange Chicago Board Options Exchange Singapore International Monetary Exchange Ltd. Osaka Securities Exchange	300 large capitalization, liquid stocks	Market value weight	√	√	Merrill Lynch Call Warrants, LEAPS
TOPIX Index	Tokyo Stock Exchange	1,255 larger, established companies	Market value weight	√	√	
New Zealand NZSE 40 Index	New Zealand Futures & Options Exchange	40 largest and most liquid stocks	Market value weight	√	√	
NZSE Top 10 Index	New Zealand Futures & Options Exchange	10 largest and most actively traded stocks	Market value weight	√	√	

AFRICA/MIDDLE EAST

COUNTRY/INDEX	EXCHANGE	MARKET COVERAGE	CALCULATION	FU	OP	OTHER
Israel MAOF-25 Index	Tel Aviv Stock Exchange	25 largest stocks	Market value weight		√	
South Africa ALSI 40 Index[2]	South African Futures Exchange	40 largest and most liquid stocks	Market value weight	√	√	
GLDI 10 Index[2]	South African Futures Exchange	10 largest and most liquid gold mining stocks	Market value weight	√	√	
INDI 25 Index	South African Futures Exchange	25 largest and most liquid industrial stocks	Market value weight	√	√	
FNDI 30 Index	South African Futures Exchange	30 largest and most liquid financial/industrial stocks	Market value weight	√	√	

CENTRAL/LATIN AMERICA

COUNTRY/INDEX	EXCHANGE	MARKET COVERAGE	CALCULATION	FU	OP	OTHER
Brazil I-SENN Index	Rio de Janeiro Stock Exchange Bolsa de Mercadorias & Futuros (BM&F)	50 most actively traded stocks	Trading volume weight	√	√	
BOVESPA Index	Bolsa Brasileira de Futuros Bolsa de Mercadorias & Futuros (BM&F)	Most actively traded stocks, accounting for about 80% of the Sao Paulo Stock Exchange trading volume	Market value weight	√		

EUROPE

Country/Index	Exchange	Market Coverage	Calculation	Fu	Op	Other
Austria Austrian Traded Index (ATX)	(Osterreichische Termin-Und Optionenborse-OTOB)	20 largest, actively traded and most liquid domestic stocks	Market value weight	√		Long-Term Options
Belgium BEL 20 Index	Belgian Futures and Options Ex-change (BELFOX)	20 large, actively traded domestic companies listed in Forward Market	Market value weight	√	√	
Denmark KFX Index	FUTOP Clearing Centre/ Copenhagen Stock Exchange (CSE)	20 large, actively traded domestic companies	Market value weight	√	√	
Finland FOX Index	Finnish Options Exchanges	25 most actively traded domestic stocks	Market value weight	√	√	
France CAC 40 Index	Marche a Terme International de France Marche des Options Negociable de Paris	40 largest, actively traded domestic stocks listed on the Monthly Settlement Market (RM)	Market value weight	√	√	Long-Term Options
Germany DAX Index	Deutsche Borse AG-DTB Deutsche Terminborse	30 largest, actively traded domestic stocks	Market value weight	√	√	
Italy MIB 30 Index	Milan Stock Exchange	30 large, actively traded domestic stocks	Market value weight	√		
Netherlands Amsterdam EOE Index	Amsterdam EOE-Optiebeurs	25 largest and most actively traded domestic stocks	Market value weight	√	√	
Amsterdam Midkap-Index	Amsterdam EOE-Optiebeurs	25 middle market capitalization companies with high turnover	Market value weight			Rabobank call and put warrants
Dutch Top 5 Index	Amsterdam EOE-Optiebeurs	5 Dutch leading international stocks listed on the ASE as well as leading European exchanges	Modified equal weight	√	√	Citibank call and put warrants
Norway OBX 25 Index	Oslo Stock Exchange	25 most actively traded investable domestic stocks	Market value weight	√	√	
Portugal PSI-20 Index	Oporto Stock Exchange	20 largest, most actively traded stocks listed on the Lisbon Stock Exchange	Market value weight	√		
Spain IBEX 35 Index	MEFF Sociedad Rectora De Productos Financieros Derivados De Renta Variable SA	35 most actively traded stocks	Market value weight	√	√	
Sweden OMX Index	OM Stockholm AB (OM Gruppen AB) London Securi-ties and Deriva-tives Exchange	30 most actively traded stocks	Market value weight	√	√	FLEX contracts
Switzerland Swiss Market Index (SMI)	Swiss Options and Financial Futures Exchange AG	21 largest and most actively traded stocks	Market value weight	√	√	Long-Term Options
United Kingdom FT-SE 100 Index	London International Financial Futures and Options Exchange London Securities and Derivatives Exchange Chicago Board Options Exchange Chicago Mercantile Exchange	100 most highly capitalized stocks	Market value weight	√	√	FLEX contracts

COUNTRY/INDEX	EXCHANGE	MARKET COVERAGE	CALCULATION	FU	OP	OTHER
United Kingdom, *Cont'd* FT-SE Mid 250 Index	London International Financial Futures and Options Exchange London Securities and Derivatives Exchange	250 middle capitalization stocks, based on market value following the largest 100 stocks	Market value weight	√	√	FLEX contracts
FT-SE Actuaries 350	London International Financial Futures and Options Exchange London Securities and Derivatives Exchange	350 most highly capitalized stocks (combines FT-SE 100 and FT-SE 250 indices)	Market value weight			FLEX contracts, FLEX Baskets contracts, covering various sector subindices
Europe Eurotop 100 Index	American Stock Exchange Amsterdam OEO-Optiebeurs New York Mercantile Exchange	100 most actively traded stocks listed on leading European exchanges	Turnover weight	√	√	

WORLD

COUNTRY/INDEX	EXCHANGE	MARKET COVERAGE	CALCULATION	FU	OP	OTHER
World Financial Times/Standard & Poor's Actuaries World Index	New York Stock Exchange	2,396 large capitalization, broad based, investable stocks in twenty-six countries[3]	Market value weight			Country Baskets Index Fund, Inc.
World Morgan Stanley Capital International World Index	New York Stock Exchange	1,579 large capitalization stocks in twenty-two developed markets[4]	Market value weight			World Equity Benchmark Shares Foreign Fund, Inc. (WEBS)

BONDS, COMMODITIES AND REAL ESTATE

NORTH AMERICA

COUNTRY/INDEX	EXCHANGE	MARKET COVERAGE	CALCULATION	FU	OP	OTHER
United States Argentina Brady Bond Index	Chicago Board of Trade	3 U.S. dollar-denominated Argentina Brady bonds	Modified market value weight	√	√	
Bond Buyer Municipal Index	Chicago Board of Trade	40 long-term, high quality, actively traded general obligation bonds	Modified price weight	√	√	
Brazil Brady Bond Index	Chicago Board of Trade	3 U.S. dollar denominated Brazil Brady bonds	Modified market value weight	√	√	
Emerging Markets Debt Index	New York Cotton Exchange/FINEX	U.S. dollar denominated Brady bonds of Argentina, Brazil, Mexico and Venezuela	Modified market value weight	√	√	
Mexico Brady Bond Index	Chicago Board of Trade	3 U.S. dollar denominated Mexico Brady bonds	Modified market value weight	√	√	
Goldman Sachs Commodity Index	Chicago Mercantile Exchange	22 commodities consisting of liquid, investable contracts on physical commodities	World production weight	√		
Knight-Ridder Commodity Research Bureau's Futures Price Index	New York Futures Exchange	17 commodities consisting of futures contracts	Equal weight/ geometric average	√		
REIT Index	Chicago Board Options Exchange	25 REITS investing in properties	Price weight		√	

Various Other Derivative Instruments: Currency[5] and Selected Money Market (U.S. Only)

COUNTRY/INSTRUMENT	EXCHANGE	MARKET COVERAGE	CALCULATION	FU	OP	OTHER
United States 13 Week U.S. Treasury Bill	Chicago Board Options Exchange MidAmerica Stock Exchange	NA	NA	√	√	LEAPS
90 day Treasury Bill	Chicago Mercantile Exchange	NA	NA	√		
Australian Dollar	Chicago Mercantile Exchange Philadelphia Stock Exchange	NA	NA	√	√	Month-End Options
Brazilian Real	Chicago Mercantile Exchange	NA	NA	√	√+	
British Pound	Chicago Mercantile Exchange Philadelphia Stock Exchange	NA	NA	√	√++	Month-End Options, Long-Term Options
Canadian Dollar	Chicago Mercantile Exchange Philadelphia Stock Exchange	NA	NA	√	√++	Month-End Options
Deutsche Mark	Chicago Mercantile Exchange Philadelphia Stock Exchange	NA	NA	√	√++	Month-End Options, Long-Term Options
European Currency Unit (ECU)	Philadelphia Stock Exchange	NA	NA		√	Month-End Options
French Franc	Chicago Mercantile Exchange Philadelphia Stock Exchange	NA	NA	√	√	Month-End Options, Long-Term Options
Japanese Yen	Chicago Mercantile Exchange Philadelphia Stock Exchange	NA	NA	√	√++	Month-End Options, Long-Term Options
Mexican Peso	Chicago Mercantile Exchange	NA	NA	√		
Swiss Franc	Chicago Mercantile Exchange Philadelphia Stock Exchange	NA	NA	√	√++	Month-End Options
U.S. Dollar Index	New York Cotton Exchange/FINEX	10 currencies versus U.S. dollar	Trade weight/ geometric average	√	√	

[1] Table covers exchange-traded index-based derivative instruments.

[2] Futures and options on these new indices replaced equity index products based on the old JSE Indices subsequent to March 31, 1996.

[3] Shares offered on nine country indices.

[4] Shares offered on 17 country indices.

[5] Currency contracts are versus US$.

Notes:

1. Options include American and/or European style options.
2. Options may consist of options, futures contracts on options, or both.
3. √+ refers to futures contracts on options.
4. √++ refers to options *and* futures contracts on options.
5. NA = Not applicable.

APPENDIX 11

1994 – 1995 PERFORMANCE TABLES

1995 PRICE PERFORMANCE RESULTS: NORTH AMERICA STOCKS

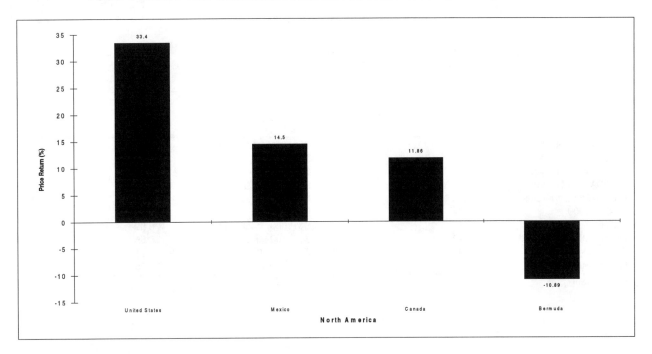

PRICE PERFORMANCE (%)	
U.S.[1]	33.40
Mexico[2]	14.50
Canada[3]	11.86
Bermuda[4]	-10.89

[1] Wilshire 5000 Equity Index.
[2] INMEX Index.
[3] TSE 300 Index.
[4] Bermuda SE Index.

1995 PRICE PERFORMANCE RESULTS: UNITED STATES STOCKS

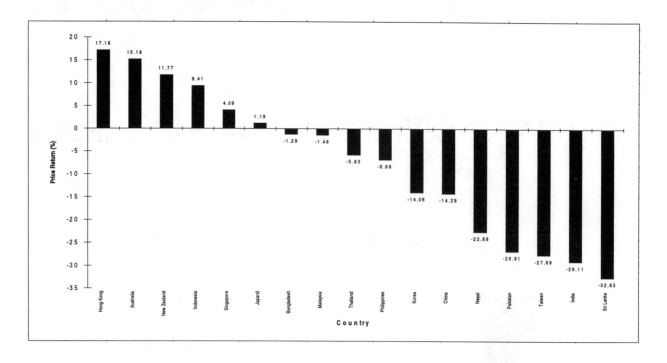

PRICE PERFORMANCE (%)

NASDAQ Composite	39.92	Wilshire 5000 Index	33.40
Russell 1000 Value	38.36	DJIA	33.14
Russell 1000 Growth	37.18	S&P/BARRA Value	32.53
S&P/BARRA Growth	35.64	Russell Mid Cap	31.67
Russell Mid Cap Value	34.93	NYSE Composite	31.31
Russell 1000	34.44	Russell 2000 Growth	31.04
S&P 500	34.11	S&P 600 Small Cap	28.60
Russell Mid Cap Growth	33.98	S&P 400 Midcap	28.56
AMVI[1]	33.92	Russell 2000	26.21
Russell 3000	33.58	Russell 2000 Value	25.75

[1] Total Return

1995 PRICE PERFORMANCE RESULTS: ASIA/PACIFIC STOCKS[1]

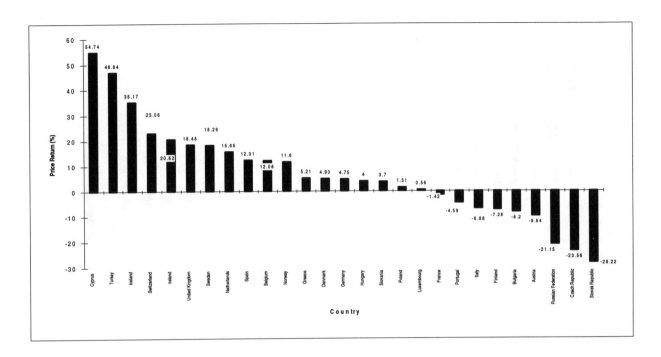

PRICE PERFORMANCE (%)

Hong Kong	17.18	Philippines	-6.88
Australia	15.18	Korea	-14.06
New Zealand	11.77	China	-14.29
Indonesia	9.41	Nepal	-22.68
Singapore	4.09	Pakistan	-26.91
Japan[2]	1.19	Taiwan	-27.69
Bangladesh	-1.29	India	-29.11
Malaysia	-1.48	Sri Lanka	-32.63
Thailand	-5.83		

[1] Performance results attributable to the broadest available local securities market indices.
[2] Tokyo Stock Exchange Price Index.

1995 PRICE PERFORMANCE RESULTS: EUROPE STOCKS[1]

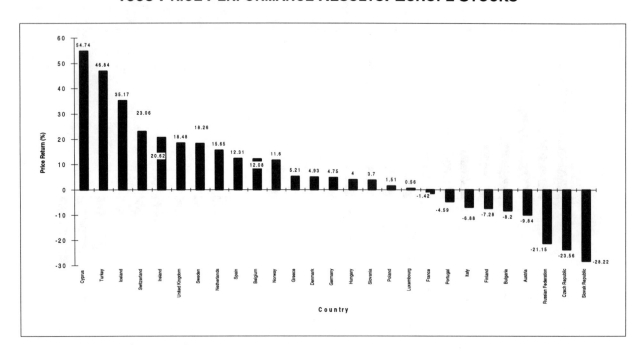

PRICE PERFORMANCE (%)

Cyprus SE Index	54.74	Hungary	4.00
Turkey	46.84	Slovania	3.70
Iceland	35.17	Poland	1.51
Switzerland	23.06	Luxembourg	0.56
Ireland	20.62	France	-1.42
UK-FT All-Share Index	18.48	Portugal[2]	-4.59
Sweden	18.26	Italy	-6.88
Netherlands	15.65	Finland	-7.28
Spain	12.31	Bulgaria	-8.20
Belgium Spot Market Index	12.08	Austria-Vienna SE Share Index	-9.84
Norway	11.60	Russian Federation[3]	-21.15
Greece	5.21	Czech Republic	-23.56
Denmark	4.93	Slovak Republic-Slovak Share	-28.22
Germany	4.75	Index	

[1] Unless otherwise indicated, performance results attributable to the broadest available local securities market indices.

[2] Total rate of return.

[3] CS First Boston ROS 30 Index.

1995 PRICE PERFORMANCE RESULTS: AFRICA/MIDDLE EAST STOCKS

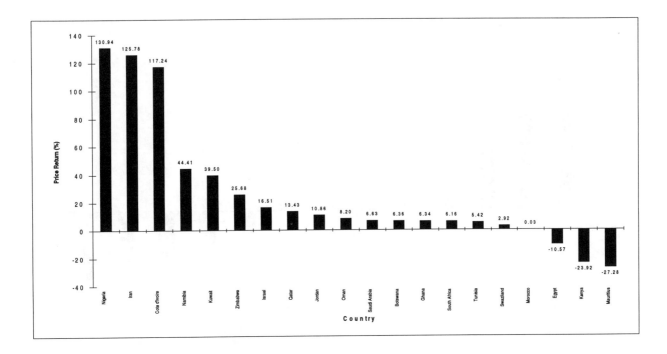

PRICE PERFORMANCE[1] (%)

Nigeria	130.94	Saudi Arabia	6.63
Iran	125.78	Botswana	6.36
Cote d'Ivoire	117.24	Ghana	6.34
Namibia	44.41	South Africa	6.16
Kuwait	39.50	Tunisia	5.42
Zimbabwe	25.68	Swaziland	2.92
Israel	16.51	Morocco	0.03
Qatar	13.43	Egypt	-10.57
Jordan	10.86	Kenya	-23.92
Oman	8.20	Mauritius	-27.28

[1] Performance results attributable to the broadest available local securities market indices.

1995 PRICE PERFORMANCE RESULTS: CENTRAL/SOUTH AMERICA STOCKS

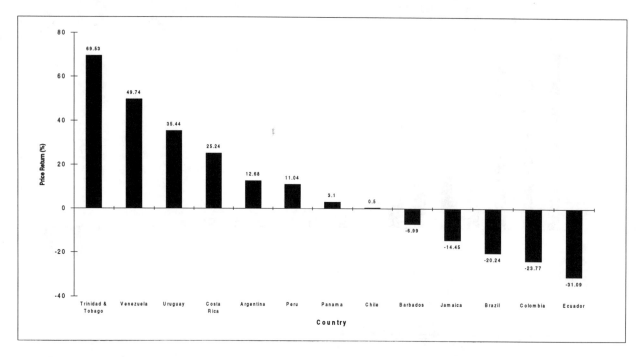

PRICE PERFORMANCE[1] (%)

Trinidad & Tobago	69.53	Chile[2]	0.50
Venezuela	49.74	Barbados	-6.99
Uruguay[2]	35.44	Jamaica	-14.45
Costa Rica	25.24	Brazil[2]	-20.24
Argentina[2]	12.68	Colombia[2]	-23.77
Peru[2]	11.04	Ecuador	-31.09
Panama	3.10		

[1] Unless otherwise indicated, performance results attributable to the broadest available local securities market indices.
[2] IFC Global Index.

1995 PRICE PERFORMANCE RESULTS: WORLD STOCKS[1]

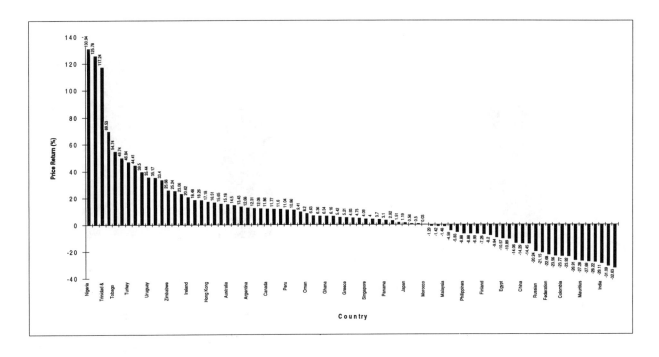

PRICE PERFORMANCE (%)[1]

Nigeria	130.94	Canada	11.86	Malaysia	-1.48
Iran	125.78	New Zealand	11.77	Portugal[5]	-4.59
Cote d'Ivoire	117.24	Norway	11.60	Thailand	-5.83
Trinidad & Tobago	69.53	Peru[2]	11.04	Philippines	-6.88
Cyprus	54.74	Jordan	10.86	Italy	-6.88
Venezuela	49.74	Indonesia	9.41	Barbados	-6.99
Turkey	46.84	Oman	8.20	Finland	-7.28
Namibia	44.41	Saudi Arabia	6.63	Bulgaria	-8.20
Kuwait	39.50	Botswana	6.36	Austria	-9.84
Uruguay[2]	35.44	Ghana	6.34	Egypt	-10.57
Iceland	35.17	South Africa	6.16	Bermuda	-10.89
U.S.3	33.40	Tunisia	5.42	Korea	-14.06
Zimbabwe	25.68	Greece	5.21	China	-14.29
Costa Rica	25.24	Denmark	4.93	Jamaica	-14.45
Switzerland	23.06	Germany	4.75	Brazil[2]	-20.24
Ireland	20.62	Singapore	4.09	Russian Federation6	-21.15
UK	18.48	Hungary	4.00	Nepal	-22.68
Sweden	18.26	Slovania	3.70	Czech Republic	-23.56
Hong Kong	17.18	Panama	3.10	Colombia[2]	-23.77
Israel	16.51	Swaziland	2.92	Kenya	-23.92
Netherlands	15.65	Poland	1.51	Pakistan	-26.91
Australia	15.18	Japan[4]	1.19	Mauritius	-27.28
Mexico	14.50	Luxembourg	0.56	Taiwan	-27.69
Qatar	13.43	Chile[2]	0.50	Slovak Republic	-28.22
Argentina[2]	12.68	Morocco	0.03	India	-29.11
Spain	12.31	Bangladesh	-1.29	Ecuador	-31.09
Belgium	12.08	France	-1.42	Sri Lanka	-32.63

[1] Unless otherwise indicated, performance results attributable to the broadest available local securities market indices.
[2] IFC Global Index.
[3] Wilshire 5000 Equity Index.
[4] Tokyo Stock Exchange Price Index.
[5] Total return.
[6] CS First Boston ROS Index.

1995 TOTAL RETURN PERFORMANCE RESULTS: GLOBAL STOCKS AND BONDS

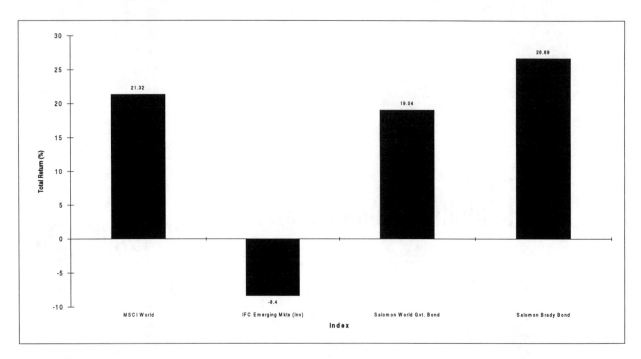

TOTAL RETURN PERFORMANCE (%)	
MSCI World	21.32
IFC Emerging Mkts (Inv)	-8.40
Salomon World Gvt. Bond	19.04
Salomon Brady Bond	26.69

1995 TOTAL RETURN PERFORMANCE RESULTS U.S. BONDS, CONVERTIBLE SECURITIES AND MONEY MARKET INSTRUMENTS

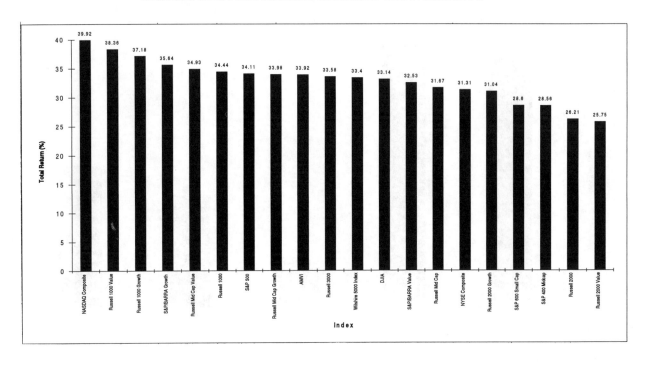

TOTAL RETURN PERFORMANCE (%)

CS FB High Yield	17.38	LB Govt/Corp.	19.24
LB Aggregate Bond	18.47	LB Mtge.	16.80
LB Adj Rate Mtge	11.72	LB Muni Bond	17.46
LB Corporate	22.25	Salomon Convertibles	24.67
LB Govt	18.34	Merrill Lynch U.S. T bill	6.14

1995 TOTAL RETURN PERFORMANCE RESULTS: VARIOUS OTHER ASSET CLASSES

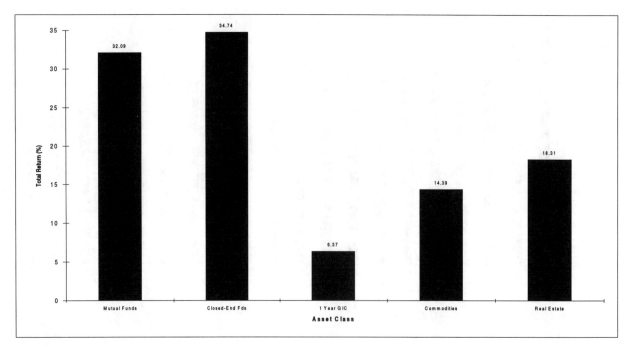

TOTAL RETURN PERFORMANCE (%)

Mutual Funds[1]	32.09
Closed-End Fds[2]	34.74
1 Year GIC[3]	6.37
Commodities[4]	14.39
Real Estate[5]	18.31

[1] Lipper Growth Funds Index.
[2] Hertzfeld Closed-End Funds Average.
[3] Morley Capital Mgt. 1 Year GIC Index.
[4] J P Morgan Commodity Index.
[5] NAREIT Composite Index.